WileyPLUS is available with this book.

WileyPLUS helps today's students succeed in the classroom using resources relevant to their everyday lives and to the workplace that will help make them globally competitive. With the complete e-book plus a variety of interactive tools, *WileyPLUS* makes teaching, learning, and retaining the material easier, more relevant, and more exciting than ever.

"I wish all my classes had WileyPLUS linked to their textbooks so I could study better in all my classes"
- Student David Delgado

Instructors using *WileyPLUS* easily choose all of the resources they need to effectively design and deliver their courses with maximum impact and minimum preparation time. Conveniently organized and highly integrated resources include the Instructor's Manual, PowerPoint slides, Cases, Videos, and more!

WileyPLUS links students directly from homework assignments to specific portions of the online text for the contextual help they need - when they need it.

WILEY
HIGHER EDUCATION

• See and try *WileyPLUS* in action! •
• **www.wileyplus.com** •

The book makes particularly good use of up to date examples using well known international firms to demonstrate some of the key concepts of firm finance, including debt financing and issues around ethics and market efficiency.

Jim Hanly, Dublin Institute of Technology, Republic of Ireland

This text offers a comprehensive and topical introduction to the key areas of corporate financial management with a wealth of illustrative examples and case studies and is suitable for both undergraduate accounting students and students from other disciplines undertaking professional or postgraduate programmes.

Jim Rankin, University of the West of Scotland, UK

An excellent text with a practical and easy to follow approach. Full of relevant examples and case studies, the book is ideal for European students wishing to understand the fundamentals of corporate finance.'

Arif Khurshed, Manchester Business School, UK

This book provides a truly global perspective thanks to the numerous examples and detailed documentation drew from the international markets. Every chapter opens with a real life example of a non-US company (or market). Throughout the text there are several tables that compare corporate finance practices around the world. Explanations are very clear and intuitive to maintain high the reader's interest. In particular, the "Capital budgeting decisions" part is well structured and detailed, rich of examples and common practices.

Maria-Teresa Marchica, Manchester Business School, UK

Throughout this new edition the author shows concretely how managers can use financial theory to solve practical problems and respond to environmental changes. The new case studies are particularly appropriate to highlight the European specificities and the ramifications between concepts. This text is an essential reference!

Laurent Bodson, HEC-ULg Management School, Belgium

Corporate Finance

Corporate Finance

European Edition

Peter Moles,
Robert Parrino and
David Kidwell

A John Wiley and Sons, Ltd, Publication

Library of Congress Cataloging-in-Publication Data

Moles, Peter.
Fundamentals of corporate finance/Peter Moles, Robert Parrino and David Kidwell. – European ed.
    p. cm.
Includes bibliographical references and index.
ISBN 978-0-470-68370-5 (pbk.)
  1. Corporations–Finance. I. Parrino, Robert, 1957- II. Kidwell, David S. III. Title.
HG4026.M65 2011
658.15–dc22   2010041870

A catalogue record for this book is available from the British Library.

Set in 10/13pt Sabon-Roman by Thomson Digital, India

Printed in Great Britain by Bell and Bain, Glasgow

BRIEF CONTENTS

FULL CONTENTS

PART 2 FOUNDATIONS   37

PART 7   CORPORATE RISK MANAGEMENT AND INTERNATIONAL DECISIONS   777

PREFACE

We have written *Corporate Finance* for use in an introductory course in corporate finance. It is suitable for undergraduate courses and for executive and MBA courses when supplemented with cases and outside readings. Given the careful way finance topics are introduced, it is particularly suitable for students who are not specialising in finance but who need to have a working knowledge of the key ideas. The main chapters of the book make few assumptions about the prior knowledge of students, although some familiarity with algebra and financial accounting is helpful. Optional chapters covering important economic and accounting concepts are included for students and instructors seeking such coverage.

BALANCE BETWEEN CONCEPTUAL UNDERSTANDING AND COMPUTATIONAL SKILLS

We decided to write an introductory corporate finance text for one very important reason. We want to provide students and instructors with a book that strikes the best possible balance between helping students develop an intuitive understanding of key financial concepts and providing them with problem-solving and decision-making skills. In our experience, teaching students at all levels and across a range of business schools, we have found that students who understand the intuition underlying the basic concepts of finance are better able to develop the critical judgement necessary to apply tools of finance to a broad range of real-world situations. An introductory corporate finance course should provide students with a strong understanding of both the concepts and tools that will help them in their subsequent business studies and personal and professional lives.

Finance instructors support our view. Many faculty members who teach introductory corporate finance courses express a desire for a book that bridges the gap between conceptually focused and computationally focused books. The text is designed to bridge this gap. Specifically, the text develops the fundamental concepts underlying corporate finance in an intuitive manner while maintaining a strong emphasis on developing computational skills. It also takes the students one step further by emphasising the use of intuition and analytical skills in decision making.

Our ultimate goal has been to write a book and develop associated learning tools that help our colleagues succeed in the classroom – materials that are genuinely helpful in the learning process. Our book offers a level of rigour that is appropriate for students of finance and yet presents content in a manner that both finance and non-finance students find accessible and want to read. Writing a book that is both *rigorous* and *accessible* has been one of our key objectives, and student reviews of the preliminary edition suggest we have achieved this objective.

We have also tried to provide solutions to many of the challenges facing finance faculty in the current environment, who are asked to teach ever-increasing numbers of students with limited resources. Faculty members need a book and associated learning tools that help them effectively leverage their time. The organisation of this book and the supplementary materials provide such leverage to an extent not found with other textbooks.

A FOCUS ON VALUE CREATION

This book is more than a collection of ideas, equations and chapters. It has an important integrating theme – that of value creation. This theme, which is carried throughout the book, provides a framework that helps students understand the relations between the various concepts covered in the book and makes it easier for them to learn these concepts.

The concept of value creation is one of the most fundamental ideas in corporate finance. It is in shareholders' best interests for value maximisation to be at the heart of the financial decisions made within the firm. Thus it is critical that students be able to analyse and make business decisions with a focus on value creation. The concept of value creation is introduced in the first chapter of the book and is further developed and applied throughout the remaining chapters.

The theme of value creation is operationalised through the net present value (NPV) concept. Once students grasp the fundamental idea that financial decision makers should only choose courses of action whose benefits exceed their costs, analysis and decision making using NPV becomes common sense. By helping students better understand the economic rationale for a decision from the outset, rather than initially focusing on computational skills, our text helps students remain focused on the true purpose of the calculations and the decision to hand.

INTEGRATED APPROACH: INTUITION, ANALYSIS AND DECISION MAKING

To support the focus on value creation, we have emphasised three approaches: (1) providing an intuitive framework for understanding fundamental financial concepts, (2) teaching students how to analyse and solve finance problems, and (3) helping students develop the ability to use the results from their analyses to make good financial decisions.

1. **An Intuitive Approach.** We believe that explaining finance concepts in an intuitive context helps students to develop a richer understanding of those concepts and gain better insights into how finance problems can be approached. It is our experience that students who have a strong conceptual understanding of finance theory better understand how things really work and are better problem solvers and decision makers than students who focus primarily on computational skills.

2. **Analysis and Problem Solving.** With a strong understanding of the basic principles of finance, students are equipped to tackle a wide range of financial problems. In addition to the many numerical examples that are solved in the text for each chapter, this book has more than 1000 end-of-chapter homework and review problems that have been written with Bloom's Taxonomy in mind. Solutions for these problems and charts showing how they relate to the levels of Bloom's Taxonomy are provided in the Instructor's Manual. We strive to help students acquire the ability to analyse and solve finance problems.

3. **Decision Making.** In the end, we want to prepare students to make sound financial decisions. To help students develop these skills, throughout the text we illustrate how the results from financial analyses are used in decision making.

ORGANISATION AND COVERAGE

In order to help students develop the necessary skills to tackle investment and financing decisions, we have arranged the book's 21 chapters into five major building blocks that collectively make up the seven parts of the book, as illustrated in the accompanying exhibit and described below.

arise, and the importance of ethics in financial decision making. These discussions set the stage and provide a framework that students can use to think about key concepts as they work through the subsequent chapters.

INTRODUCTION

Part 1, which consists of Chapter 1, provides an introduction to corporate finance. It describes the role of the financial manager, the types of fundamental decisions that financial managers make, alternative forms of business organisation, the goal of the firm, agency problems and how they

FOUNDATIONS

Part 2 of the text consists of Chapters 2–4. These chapters present the basic institutional, economic and accounting knowledge and tools that students should understand before they begin the study of financial concepts. The material in these chapters is typically taught in other courses. Since students come to corporate finance with varying academic

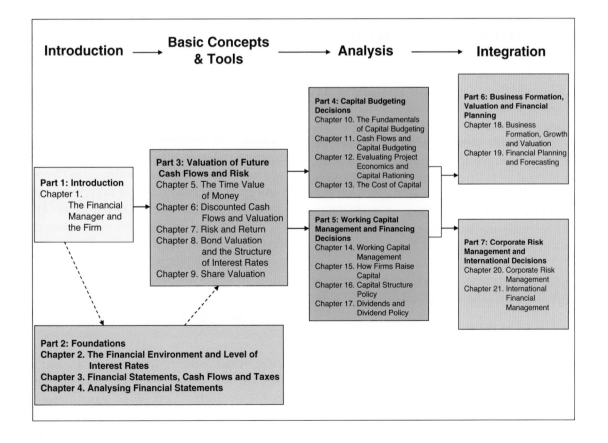

backgrounds and because the time that has elapsed since students have taken courses in these subjects also varies, the chapters in Part 2 can help the instructor ensure that all students have the same base level of knowledge early on in the course. Depending on the educational background of the students, the instructor might not find it necessary to cover all or any of the material in these chapters. The chapters might, instead, be assigned as additional readings.

Chapter 2 describes the services financial institutions provide to new businesses, how domestic and international financial markets work, how firms use financial markets and how the level of interest rates in the economy is determined. Chapter 3 describes the key financial statements and how they are related, while Chapter 4 discusses ratio analysis and other tools used to evaluate financial statements. Throughout Part 2, we emphasise the importance of cash flows to get students thinking about cash flows as a critical component of all valuation calculations and financial decisions.

BASIC TOOLS AND CONCEPTS

Part 3 presents basic financial concepts and tools and illustrates their application. This part of the text, which consists of Chapters 5–9, introduces the time value of money and risk and return concepts and extends them to cover the principles underlying the application of present value concepts to bond and share valuation. These chapters provide students with basic financial intuitions and computational tools that will serve as the building blocks for analysing investment and financing decisions in subsequent chapters.

ANALYSIS

Parts 4 and 5 of the text focus on investment and financing decisions. Part 4 covers capital budgeting. Chapter 10 introduces the concept of net present value and illustrates its application. This discussion provides a framework that will help students in the

rest of Part 4 as they learn the nuances of capital budgeting analysis in realistic settings.

Chapters 11 and 12 follow, with in-depth discussions of how cash flows are calculated and forecast. The cash flow calculations are presented in Chapter 11 using a valuation framework that will help students think about valuation concepts in an intuitive way and will prepare them for an extension of these concepts to business valuation in Chapter 18. Chapter 12 covers analytical tools – such as break-even, sensitivity, scenario and simulation analysis – that will give students a better appreciation of how they can deal with the uncertainties associated with cash flow forecasts. Capital rationing is also covered in Chapter 12.

Chapter 13 explains how the discount rates used in capital budgeting are estimated. This chapter uses an innovative concept – that of the market value balance sheet – to help students develop an intuitive understanding of the relations between the costs of the individual components of capital and the firm's overall weighted average cost of capital. It also provides a detailed discussion of methods used to estimate the cost of the individual components of capital that are used to finance the firm's investments and how these estimates are used in capital budgeting.

Part 5 covers working capital management and financing decisions. It begins in Chapter 14 with a discussion of how firms manage their working capital and the implications of working capital management decisions for financing decisions and firm value. This discussion is followed in Chapters 15 and 16 by discussions of how firms raise capital to fund their real activities and what factors affect how firms choose among the various sources of capital available to them. Chapter 17 rounds out the discussion of financing decisions with a discussion of dividends and dividend policy.

INTEGRATION

Part 6, which consists of Chapters 18 and 19, brings together many of the key concepts introduced in the earlier parts of the text. Chapter 18 covers financial aspects of business formation and growth and introduces students to business valuation concepts for both private and public firms. The discussions in this chapter integrate the investment and financing concepts discussed in Parts 4 and 5 to provide students with a more complete picture of how all the financial concepts fit together. Chapter 19 covers concepts related to financial planning and forecasting.

Part 7 introduces students to some important issues that managers must deal with in applying the concepts covered in the text to real-world problems. Chapter 20 discusses corporate risk management and the way firms use financial instruments, namely derivatives, to manage particular risks in order to create value. The discussion emphasises how the use of derivatives relates to investment and financing decisions. In particular, it explains at an accessible level the idea behind real options and why traditional NPV analysis does not take such options into account. Using the insights from option theory, the chapter also discusses the agency costs of debt and financing decisions.

Chapter 21 considers the additional complications of financial management in an international context and how this affects the application of concepts covered in this book. It first focuses on two key elements of international operations, foreign exchange and country risk, before considering how to evaluate international capital projects. It concludes by considering the complexities of Islamic finance.

UNIQUE CHAPTERS

Chapter on Business Formation, Growth and Valuation

We wrote Chapter 18 in response to students' heightened interest in new business formation (entrepreneurship) and in order to draw together in a comprehensive way the key concepts from capital budgeting, working capital management and financial policy. This integrative chapter provides an overview of practical finance issues associated with forecasting cash flows and capital requirements for a new business, preparing a business plan and business valuation. The discussion of business valuation extends far beyond that found in other corporate finance textbooks.

Chapter on Corporate Risk Management

Many corporate finance textbooks have a chapter that introduces students to derivatives and how they are valued. This chapter goes further. It integrates risk management and derivatives with earlier elements in the book. In particular, it provides a discussion of the different types of non-financial options that are of concern to financial managers, including real options and their effect on project analysis and how option-like payoff functions faced by shareholders, bondholders and managers affect agency relationships.

PROVEN PEDAGOGICAL FRAMEWORK

Distinctive pedagogical features have been included throughout the book to aid student learning. The pedagogical features included in the text are as follows:

Each chapter begins with a **vignette** that describes a real company application. The vignettes illustrate concepts that will be presented in the chapter and are designed to heighten student interest, motivate learning, and demonstra0074e the real-life relevance of the material in the chapter.

The introduction of the euro as a common currency across much of Europe, following the decision by the European Union (EU) to pursue European Monetary Union, also saw the creation of a major new supranational institution, the European Central Bank (ECB). Why did the introduction of the euro require a major change in the way EC countries managed their currencies? With one currency serving many countries, it is necessary to have a central bank that manages liquidity and short-term interest rates across the single-currency eurozone. The Eurosystem that was created through monetary union comprises the national central banks of member countries and the ECB. As the supranational institution tasked with setting monetary policy across the euro area, the ECB has a Governing Council and an Executive Board. The Governing Council is the prime decision-making body that sets monetary policy. In pursuit of this goal, the central bank manages liquidity and short-term interest rates. As its most senior officer, Jean-Claude Trichet, the current President of the ECB since October 2003, is often in the news. The reason is that decisions made by the Governing Council concerning monetary policy affect interest

LEARNING OBJECTIVES

1. Explain why incremental after-tax free cash flows are relevant in evaluating a project and be able to calculate them for a project.
2. Discuss the five general rules for incremental after-tax free cash flow calculations and explain why cash flows stated in nominal (real) money should be discounted using a nominal (real) discount rate.
3. Describe how distinguishing between variable and fixed costs can be useful in forecasting operating expenses.
4. Explain the concept of equivalent annual cost and be able to use it to compare projects with unequal lives, decide when to replace an existing asset and calculate the opportunity cost of using an existing asset.
5. Determine the appropriate time to disinvest an asset.

The opening vignette is accompanied by **learning objectives** that identify the most important material for students to understand while reading the chapter. At the end of the chapter, the Summary of Learning Objectives summarizes the chapter content in the context of the learning objectives.

Along with a generous number of in text examples, most chapters include several **Learning by Doing Applications**. These applications contain quantitative problems with step-by-step solutions to help students better understand how to apply their intuition and analytical skills to solve important problems. By including these exercises, we provide students with additional practice in the application of the concepts, tools, and methods that are discussed in the text.

Learning by Doing Application 11.2

The Investment Decision and Nominal versus Real Values

Problem: You are trying to decide how to invest €25 000, which you just inherited from a distant relative. You do not want to take any risks with this money because you want to use it as a down payment on a home when you graduate in three years' time. Therefore, you have decided to invest the money in securities that are guaranteed by the government. You are considering two alternatives: a three-year government bond and an inflation-indexed government security. If you invest in the three-year bond, you will be paid 3% per year in interest and will get your €25 000 back at the end of three years. If you invest in the inflation-indexed security, you will be paid 1% per year plus an amount that reflects actual inflation in each of the next three years. For example, if inflation equals 2% per year for each of the next three years, you will receive 3% each year in total interest. This interest on the inflation-indexed security will compound, and you will receive a single payment at the end of three years. If you expect inflation to average 2.5% per year over the next three years,

should you invest in the three-year government bond or in the inflation-indexed security?

Approach: Compare the 3% return on the three-year government bond, which is a nominal rate of return, with the nominal rate of return that you can expect to receive from the inflation-indexed security and invest in the security with the highest rate. The nominal rate on the inflation-indexed security in each year equals the real rate of 1% plus the rate of inflation.

Solution: Without doing any detailed calculations, it is apparent that you should invest in the inflation-indexed security. The reason is that if the rate of inflation turns out to be 2.5%, the inflation-indexed security will yield 3.5% (1% plus 2.5% inflation adjustment) per year. With this investment, the real purchasing power of your money will increase by 1% per year. This will be true regardless of what inflation turns out to be during the three-year period. Assuming that you can reinvest the annual interest payments from the three-year government bond at 3%, if you buy this security, the real purchasing power of your money will increase by only 0.5% (3% interest rate less 2.5% inflation) per year.

Students must have an intuitive understanding of a number of important rinciples and concepts to successfully master the finance curriculum. Throughout the book, we emphasize these important concepts by presenting them in **Building Intuition** boxes. These boxes provide a tatement of an important finance concept, such as the relation between risk and expected returns, along with an intuitive example or explanation to help the student understand the concept. These boxes help the students develop finance intuition. Collectively the Building Intuition boxes cover the most important concepts in corporate finance.

BUILDING INTUITION

Cash Flows Matter Most to Investors

Cash is what investors ultimately care about when making an investment. The value of any asset – shares, bonds or a business – is determined by the future cash flows it will generate. To understand this concept, just consider how much you would pay for an asset from which you could never expect to obtain any cash flows. Buying such an asset would be like giving your money away. It would have a value of exactly zero. Conversely, as the expected future cash flows from an investment increase, you would be willing to pay more and more for it.

Decision-Making Example 20.2

The Value of Real Options

Situation: You work for a company that manufactures cardboard packaging for consumer product companies under long-term contracts. For example, your company manufactures the boxes for several popular cereal and pharmaceutical products. You have just won a large five-year contract to produce packaging materials for a company that sells furniture on the Internet. Since this contract will require you to produce much larger boxes than you currently can produce, you must purchase some new equipment. You have narrowed your choices to two alternatives. The first is a capital-intensive process that will cost more up-front but will be less expensive to operate. This process requires very specialised equipment that can be used only for the type of packaging that your furniture

client needs. The second alternative is a labour-intensive process that will require a smaller up-front investment but will have higher unit costs. This process involves equipment that can be used to produce a wide range of other packages. If the expected life of both alternatives is 10 years and you estimate the NPV to be the same for both, which should you choose?

Decision: You should choose the labour-intensive alternative. Your contract is only for five years and there is a chance that it will not be renewed before the equipment's useful life is over. If the contract is not renewed, it will be easier to convert the labour-intensive equipment to another use. In other words, the labour-intensive alternative gives you the added value of having the option to abandon producing packaging for furniture.

Throughout the book, the role of the financial manager as a decision maker is emphasized. To that end, nearly every chapter includes **Decision-Making Examples**. These examples, which emphasize the decision-making process rather than computation, provide students with experience in financial decision making. Each Decision-Making Example outlines a scenario and asks the student to make a decision based on the information presented.

SUMMARY OF LEARNING OBJECTIVES

At the end of the chapter, you will find a **summary** of the key chapter content related to each of the learning objectives listed at the beginning of the chapter, as well as an exhibit listing the key equations in the chapter.

1. **Discuss the primary role of the financial system in the economy and describe the two basic ways in which fund transfers take place.**
    The primary role of the financial system is to gather money from people and businesses with surplus funds to invest (lender-savers) and channel money to businesses and consumers who need to borrow money (borrower-spenders). If the financial system works properly, only investment projects with high rates of return and good credit are financed and all other projects are rejected. Money flows through the financial system in two basic ways: (1) directly, through financial markets, or (2) indirectly, through financial institutions.

SUMMARY OF KEY EQUATIONS

Equation	Description	Formula
(2.1)	Fisher equation	$i = r + \Delta P_e + r\Delta P_e$
(2.2)	Fisher equation simplified	$i = r + \Delta P_e$

SELF-STUDY PROBLEMS

1.1. Give an example of a financing decision and a capital budgeting decision.

1.2. What is the decision criterion for financial managers when selecting a capital project?

1.3. What are some ways to manage working capital?

1.4. Which one of the following characteristics does not pertain to companies?

a. can enter into contracts
b. can borrow money
c. are the easiest type of business to form
d. can be sued
e. can own shares in other companies.

1.5. What are typically the main components of an executive compensation package?

SOLUTIONS TO SELF-STUDY PROBLEMS

1.1. Financing decisions determine how a firm will raise capital. Examples of financing decisions would be securing a bank loan or selling debt in the public capital markets. Capital budgeting involves deciding which productive assets the firm invests in, such as buying a new plant or investing in a renovation of an existing facility.

1.2. Financial managers should select a capital project only if the value of the project's future cash flows exceeds the cost of the project. In other words, firms should only take on investments that will increase their value and thus increase the shareholders' wealth.

1.3. Working capital is the day-to-day management of a firm's short-term assets and

liabilities. It can be managed through maintaining the optimal level of inventory, keeping track of all the receivables and payables, deciding to whom the firm should extend credit and making appropriate investments with excess cash.

1.4. The answer that does *not* pertain to companies is (c) are the easiest type of business to form.

1.5. The three main components of an executive compensation package are: base salary, bonus based on accounting performance and some compensation tied to the firm's share price.

Five problems similar to the in-text Learning by Doing Applications follow the summary and provide additional examples with step-by-step solutions to help students further develop their problem-solving and computational skills.

At least ten qualitative questions, called **Critical Thinking Questions**, require students to think through their understanding of key concepts and apply those concepts to a problem.

CRITICAL THINKING QUESTIONS

5.1. Explain the phrase 'money today is worth more than money tomorrow'.

5.2. Explain the importance of a time line.

5.3. Differentiate future value from present value.

5.4. What are the two factors to be considered in the time value of money?

5.5. Differentiate between compounding and discounting.

5.6. Explain how compound interest differs from simple interest.

5.7. If you were given a choice of investing in an account that paid quarterly interest and one

The **Questions and Problems**, numbering 25 to 35 per chapter, are primarily quantitative and are classified as Basic, Intermediate, or Advanced.

QUESTIONS AND PROBLEMS

Basic

5.1. **Future value:** Gunnar Ottenberg is planning to invest SKr 25 000 today in a mutual fund that will provide a return of 8% each year. What will be the value of the investment in 10 years?

5.2. **Future value:** Marcello Esposito is investing €7500 in a bank deposit that pays a 6% annual interest. How much will be in the deposit account at the end of five years?

Intermediate

5.17. **Growth rate:** Your finance textbook sold 53 250 copies in its first year. The publishing company expects the sales to grow at a rate of 20% for the next three years and by 10% in the fourth year. Calculate the total number of copies that the publisher expects to sell in years 3 and 4. Draw a time line to show the sales level for each of the next four years.

Advanced

5.29. You have €2500 you want to invest in your classmate's start-up business. You believe the business idea to be great and hope to get €3700 back at the end of three years. If all goes according to plan, what will be your return on investment?

5.32. EXCEL© When you were born your parents set up a bank account in your name with an initial investment of €5000. You are turning 21 in a few days and will have access to all your funds. The account was earning 7.3% for the first seven years but then the rates went down to 5.5% for six years. The economy was doing well at the end of the 1990s, and your account was earning 8.2% for three years in a row. Unfortunately, the next two years you earned only 4.6%. Finally, as the economy recovered, your return jumped to 7.6% for the last three years.
  a. How much money was in your account before the rates went down drastically (end of year 16)?
  b. How much money is in your account now (end of year 21)?
  c. What would be the balance now if your parents made another deposit of €1200 at the end of year 7?

An icon identifies selected problems that can be solved using Excel templates at the student Web site within WileyPLUS.

SAMPLE TEST PROBLEMS

1.1. Why is value maximisation superior to profit maximisation as a goal for the firm?

1.2. The major advantage of debt financing is:
  a. it allows a firm to use creditors' money
  b. interest payments are more predictable than dividend payments
  c. interest payments are not required when a firm is not doing well
  d. interest payments are tax deductible.

1.3. Identify three fundamental decisions that a financial manager has to make in running a firm.

1.4. What are agency costs? Explain.

1.5. Identify four of the seven mechanisms that align the goals of managers with those of shareholders.

Finally, five **Sample Test Problems** call for straightforward applications of the chapter concepts. These problems are intended to be representative of the kind of problems that may be used in a test, and instructors can encourage students to solve them as if they were taking a quiz. Solutions are provided in the Instructor's Manual.

INSTRUCTOR AND STUDENT RESOURCES

Fundamentals of Corporate Finance features a comprehensive range of teaching and learning resources that have been developed by the author. Driven by the same basic beliefs as the textbook, these supplements provide a consistent and well-integrated learning system. This hands-on package guides instructors through the process of active learning and provides them with the tools to create an interactive learning environment. With its emphasis on activities, exercises, and the internet, the package encourages students to take an active role in the course and prepares them for decision making in a real-world context.

WILEYPLUS – FOR INSTRUCTORS

WileyPLUS is an online suite of resources that contains online homework and practice activities with access to an online version of the text. *WileyPLUS* gives you the technology to create an environment where students reach their full potential and experience academic success. Instructor resources include a wealth of presentation and preparation tools, easy-to navigate assignment and assessment tools, and a complete system to administer and manage your course exactly as you wish.

WileyPLUS is built around the activities you regularly perform:

- **Prepare and present class presentations** using relevant Wiley resources such as PowerPoint slides, image galleries, including all of the exhibits from the book, animations, and other *WileyPLUS* materials. You can also upload your own resources or web pages to use in conjunction with Wiley materials.
- **Create assignments** by choosing from end-of-chapter questions, problems, and test bank

questions organized by chapter, study objective, level of difficulty, and source — or add your own questions. Algorithmic versions are available for some questions and problems, allowing for additional drill and practice. *WileyPLUS* automatically grades students' homework and quizzes and records the results in your gradebook.

- **Offer context-sensitive help to students.** When you assign homework or quizzes, you decide if and when students get access to hints, solutions, or answers where appropriate. Or students can be linked to relevant sections of their complete, online text for additional help whenever and wherever they need it most.
- **Track student progress.** You can analyze students' results and assess their level of understanding on an individual and class level using the *WileyPLUS* gradebook, and you can export data to your own personal gradebook.
- **Compatible with all major learning management systems, including WebCT, Angel and Blackboard.** Seamlessly integrate all of the rich *WileyPLUS* content and resources with the power and convenience of your LMS with a single sign-on.

BOOK COMPANION SITE - FOR INSTRUCTORS

The Book Companion Site can be found at www.wiley.com/college/moles and contains an extensive support package for instructors with varying levels of experience and different instructional circumstances. On the website, instructors will find:

- Instructor's Manual which includes lecture outlines, summary of learning objectives, key equations and alternative approaches to the material. Also included are detailed solutions to the Before You Go On questions, Self-Study problems,

Critical Thinking Questions and all of the Questions and Problems at the end of each chapter.

- Test Bank with over 1000 questions, including algorithmic, true/false, multiple choice and essay questions.
- Computerized Test Bank which allows instructors to create and print multiple versions of the test bank, as well as, allowing users to customize exams by altering or adding new problems.
- PowerPoint Presentations containing a combination of key concepts, problems, examples, figures and tables from the textbook.
- Ethics Cases introduce students to the framework for consideration of ethical issues in corporate finance. Each case includes questions for follow-up discussion in class or as an assignment.

WILEYPLUS — FOR STUDENTS .

The WileyPLUS course for *Fundamentals of Corporate Finance* offers students several tools designed to help them grasp key finance concepts discussed in the text:

- An "Assignment" area helps students stay on task by containing all homework assignments in one location. Many homework problems contain a link to the relevant sections of the e-book, providing students with context-sensitive help

that allows them to conquer problem-solving obstacles.
- A Personal Gradebook for each student will allow students to view their results from past assignments at any time.

BOOK COMPANION SITE - FOR STUDENTS

The *Fundamentals of Corporate Finance* student website provides a wealth of support materials that will help students develop their conceptual understanding of the material and increase their ability to solve problems. The student website includes:

- Self Study Quizzes including multiple choice and true/false questions to aid students' learning and self-study.
- Excel Problems and Solutions provide an online collection of Excel templates allowing students to complete select end-of-chapter questions and problems identified by an Excel icon in the textbook.
- Learning by Doing Animations are selected from the textbook and animated in flash presentations with narrated descriptions, allowing students to see the impact of key finance concepts on real world events.

The Book Companion Site can be accessed at www.wiley.com/college/moles

ACKNOWLEDGEMENTS

Dr Maria-Teresa Marchica, Manchester Business School, UK

Gianluca Mattarocci, University of Rome Tor Vergata, Italy

Dr Arjen Mulder, Rotterdam School of Management, The Netherlands

Jim Rankin, University of the West of Scotland, UK

Dr Jim Hanly, Dublin Institute of Technology, Republic of Ireland

Laurent Bodson, HEC-ULg Management School, University of Liege, Belgium

Dr Arif Khurshed, Manchester Business School, UK

Dr Christos Floros, University of Portsmouth, UK

Professor Aydin Ozkan, Hull University Business School, UK

Dr P.J. Engelen, Utrecht School of Economics, The Netherlands

Conor McKeating, Dublin City University, Republic of Ireland

Dr Irena Jindrichovska, University of Economics and Management in Prague, Czech Republic

Dr Bolli Hédinsson, Reykjavik University, Iceland

Dr Nnamdi Obiosa, Regents College London, UK

PART 1

INTRODUCTION

CHAPTER

1

The Financial Manager and the Firm

In this Chapter:

The Role of the Financial Manager

Forms of Business Organisation

Managing the Financial Function

The Goal of the Firm

Agency Conflicts: Separation of Ownership and Control

The Importance of Ethics in Business

LEARNING OBJECTIVES

1. Identify the key financial decisions facing the financial manager of any business firm.

2. Identify the basic forms of business organisation and review their respective strengths and weaknesses.

3. Describe the typical organisation of the financial function in a large company.

4. Explain why maximising the current value of the firm's shares is the appropriate goal for management.

5. Discuss how agency conflicts affect the goal of maximising shareholder value.

6. Explain why ethics is an appropriate topic in the study of corporate finance.

On 19 March 2010, Arrow Energy Ltd announced a suspension in the trading of its shares pending an update on the takeover approach made earlier in the month by Royal Dutch Shell, the Anglo-Netherlands integrated oil company, and PetroChina. The initial offer by the two companies was for A$4.45 a share, valuing the Brisbane-based Arrow Energy at A$3.3bn (€2.4bn; US$3.1bn). What had attracted the bidders' attention was Arrow's leading position in Australia's fast-expanding coalbed methane gas sector, a new source of clean energy that extracts gas from coal seams. This is subsequently liquefied, making it much easier to transport. Royal Dutch Shell had the technical expertise, financial resources, major project expertise and marketing competence to develop the business. PetroChina would provide distribution in China's fast-expanding clean energy market.

In the month prior to the announcement, the share price had averaged A$3.50. The price offered by Royal Dutch Shell and PetroChina represented a 27.1% premium to this recent average market price. The board of directors of Arrow Energy rejected the offer but both sides entered into negotiations. Less than two weeks later, the board recommended a revised bid at A$4.70 a share (€2.5bn; US$3.2bn) but this excluded Arrow's international operations, which would be retained by Arrow's shareholders as a separate company, which had a book value in excess of A$400 million (€290 million; US$360 million).

How did Royal Dutch Shell and PetroChina arrive at the offering price and how could they justify it? They did not make the offer planning to lose money and yet were prepared to pay a significant premium to the prevailing market price. By integrating Arrow Energy's activities, increasing the efficiency of operations, borrowing money to pay for the purchase and exploiting their position in the global energy market, the new owners planned to increase the value of the cash flows Arrow Energy would generate.

Firms making investments, such as purchasing an existing business or starting a new project from scratch, use many of the concepts covered in this chapter and elsewhere in this book to create the most value possible. They begin by structuring the compensation of firm managers to provide them with incentives to focus on value creation. Managers create value by investing only in projects whose benefits exceed their costs, managing the assets of the company as efficiently as possible, and financing the company with the least expensive combination of debt and equity. This chapter introduces you to the key financial aspects of these activities, and the remainder of the book fills in many of the details.

CHAPTER PREVIEW

This book is an introduction to corporate finance. In it, we focus on the responsibilities of the financial manager, who oversees the accounting and treasury functions and sets the overall financial strategy for the firm, i.e. the business. We pay special attention to the financial manager's role as a decision maker. To that end, we emphasise the mastery of fundamental finance concepts and the use of a set of financial tools, which will result in sound financial decisions that create value for the firm's owners. These financial concepts and tools apply not only to businesses but also to other organisations, such as government and not-for-profit entities, and sometimes even your own personal finances.

We open this chapter by discussing the three major types of decisions that a financial manager makes. We then describe common forms of business organisation. After next discussing the major responsibilities of the financial manager, we explain why maximising the price of the firm's shares is an appropriate goal for a financial manager. We go on to describe the conflicts of interest that can arise between shareholders and managers, and the mechanisms that help align the interests of these two groups. Finally, we discuss the importance of ethical conduct in business.

THE ROLE OF THE FINANCIAL MANAGER

Learning Objective 1

Identify the key financial decisions facing the financial manager of any business firm.

The financial manager is responsible for making decisions that are in the best interests of the firm's owners, whether the firm is a start-up business with a single owner or a large business owned by thousands of shareholders. The decisions made by the financial manager or owner should be the same. In most situations, this means that the financial manager should make decisions that maximise the value of the owners' shares. This helps maximise the owners' **wealth**. Our underlying assumption in this book is that most people who invest in businesses do so because they want to increase their wealth. In the following discussion, we describe the responsibilities of the financial manager in a new business in order to illustrate the types of decisions that such a manager makes.

Wealth

the economic value of the assets someone possesses

Stakeholders

Before we discuss the new business, you may want to look at Exhibit 1.1, which shows the cash flows between a firm and its owners (in a company, the

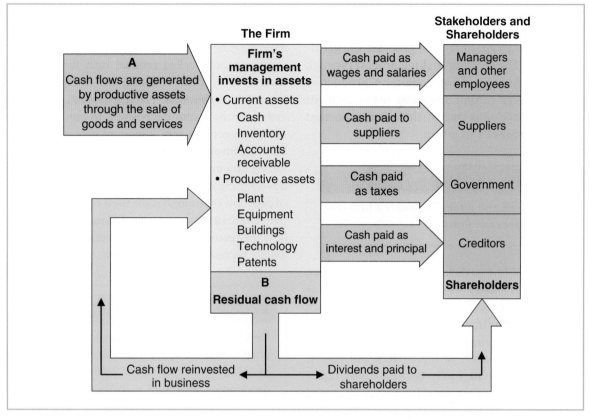

Exhibit 1.1: Cash Flows Between the Firm and its Shareholders and Owners A. Making business decisions is all about cash flows, because only cash can be used to pay bills and buy new assets. Cash initially flows into the firm as a result of the sale of goods or services. The firm uses these cash inflows in a number of ways: to invest in assets, to pay wages and salaries, to buy supplies, to pay taxes, and to repay creditors. B. Any cash that is left over (residual cash flows), can be reinvested in the business or paid as dividends to stockholders.

shareholders) and various stakeholders. A **stakeholder** is someone other than an owner who has a claim on the cash flows of the firm. This includes *managers*, who want to be paid salaries and performance bonuses; *creditors*, who want to be paid interest and principal; *employees*, who want to be paid wages; *suppliers*, who want to be paid for goods or services; and the *government*, which wants the firm to pay taxes. Stakeholders may have interests that differ from those of the owners. When this is the case, they may exert pressure on management to make decisions that benefit them. We will return to these types of conflict of interest later in the book. For now, though, we are primarily concerned with the overall flow of cash between the firm and its shareholders and stakeholders.

> **Stakeholder**
>
> anyone other than an owner (stockholder) with a claim on the cash flows of a firm, including employees, suppliers, creditors and the government

It's All About Cash Flows

To generate its products or services, a new firm needs to acquire a variety of assets. Most will be long-term assets or **productive assets**. Productive assets can be tangible assets, such as equipment, machinery or a manufacturing facility, or intangible assets, such as patents, trademarks, technical expertise or other types of intellectual property. Regardless of the type of asset, the firm tries to select assets that will generate the greatest profits. The decision-making process through which the firm purchases long-term productive assets is called *capital budgeting* (or investment appraisal) and it is one of the most important decision processes in a firm.

> ### Productive assets
>
> the tangible and intangible assets a firm uses to generate cash flows

Once the firm has selected its productive assets, it must raise money to pay for them. *Financing decisions* are concerned with the ways in which firms obtain and manage long-term financing to acquire and support their productive assets. There are two basic sources of funds: debt and equity. Every firm has some equity because equity represents ownership in the firm. It consists of capital contributions by the owners plus earnings that have been reinvested in the firm. In addition, most firms borrow from a bank or issue some type of long-term debt to finance productive assets.

After the productive assets have been purchased and the business is operating, the firm will try to produce products at the lowest possible cost while maintaining quality. This means buying raw materials at the lowest possible cost, holding production and labour costs down, keeping management and administrative costs to a minimum, and seeing that shipping and delivery costs are competitive. In addition, the firm must manage its day-to-day finances so that it will have sufficient cash on hand to pay salaries, purchase supplies, maintain inventories, pay taxes and cover the myriad of other expenses necessary to run a business. The management of current assets, such as money owed by customers who purchase on credit, inventory and current liabilities, such as money owed to suppliers, is called *working capital management*.[1]

A firm generates cash inflows by selling the goods and services it produces. A firm is successful when these cash inflows exceed the cash outflows needed to pay operating expenses, creditors and taxes. After meeting these obligations, the firm can pay the remaining cash, called **residual cash flows**, to the owners as a cash dividend, or it can reinvest the cash in the business. The reinvestment of residual cash flows back into the business to buy more productive assets is a very important concept. If these funds are invested wisely, they provide the foundation for the firm to grow and provide larger residual cash flows for the owners in the future. The reinvestment of cash flows (earnings) is the most fundamental way that businesses grow in size. Exhibit 1.1 illustrates how the revenue generated by productive assets ultimately becomes residual cash flow.

> ### Residual cash flows
>
> the cash remaining after a firm has paid operating expenses and what it owes creditors and in taxes; can be paid to the owners as a cash dividend or reinvested in the business

A firm is unprofitable when it fails to generate sufficient cash inflows to pay operating expenses, creditors and taxes. Firms that are unprofitable over time will be forced into **bankruptcy** by their creditors if the owners do not shut them down first. In bankruptcy, the company will be reorganised or the company's assets will be liquidated, whichever is the more valuable. If the company is liquidated, creditors are paid in a priority order according to the structure of the firm's financial contracts and prevailing bankruptcy law. If anything is left after all creditor and tax claims have been satisfied, which usually does not happen, the remaining cash, or residual value, is distributed to the owners.

> ### Bankruptcy
>
> legally declared inability of an individual or a company to pay its creditors. Also called insolvency in the case of companies

BUILDING INTUITION

Cash Flows Matter Most to Investors

Cash is what investors ultimately care about when making an investment. The value of any asset – shares, bonds or a business – is determined by the future cash flows it will generate. To understand this concept, just consider how much you would pay for an asset from which you could never expect to obtain any cash flows. Buying such an asset would be like giving your money away. It would have a value of exactly zero. Conversely, as the expected future cash flows from an investment increase, you would be willing to pay more and more for it.

Three Fundamental Decisions in Financial Management

Based on our discussion so far, we can see that financial managers are concerned with three fundamental decisions when running a business.

1. *Capital budgeting (investment) decisions:* Identifying the productive assets the firm should buy.
2. *Financing decisions:* Determining how the firm should finance or pay for assets.
3. *Working capital management decisions:* Determining how day-to-day financial matters should be managed so that the firm can pay its bills, and how surplus cash should be invested.

Exhibit 1.2 shows the impact of each decision on the firm's balance sheet. We briefly introduce each decision here and discuss them in greater detail in later chapters.

Capital Budgeting Decisions

A firm's capital budget is simply a list of the productive (capital) assets management wants to purchase over a budget cycle, typically one year. The capital budgeting decision process addresses which productive assets the firm should purchase and how much money the firm can afford to spend. As shown in Exhibit 1.2, capital budgeting decisions affect the asset side of the balance sheet and are concerned with a firm's long-term investments. Capital budgeting decisions, as we mentioned

earlier, are among management's most important decisions. Over the long run, they have a large impact on the firm's success or failure. The reason is twofold. First, capital assets generate most of the cash flows for the firm. Second, capital assets are long term in nature. Once they are purchased, the firm owns them for a long time, and they may be hard to sell without taking a financial loss.

The fundamental question in capital budgeting is this: Which productive assets should the firm purchase? A capital budgeting decision may be as simple as a cinema's decision to buy a coffee machine or as complicated as Airbus' decision to invest more than €8.8 billion to design and build the A380 super jumbo passenger jet. Capital investments may also involve the purchase of an entire business, such as ABB's (the global power and automation group domiciled in Switzerland) purchase of Kuhlman Electric Corporation (KEC), based in Versailles, Kentucky.

Regardless of the project, a good capital budgeting decision is one in which the benefits are worth more to the firm than the cost of the asset. For example, ABB purchased KEC for US$520 million. Presumably, ABB expects that the investment will produce a stream of cash flows worth more than that. Suppose ABB estimates that in terms of the current market value, the future cash flows from the KEC acquisition are worth US$750 million. Is the acquisition a good deal for ABB? The answer is yes, because the value of the cash flow benefits from the acquisition exceeds the cost by US$230 million

BUILDING INTUITION

Sound Investments are Those Where the Value of the Benefits Exceeds Their Costs

Financial managers should invest in a capital project only if the value of its future cash flows exceeds the cost of the project (i.e. benefits > cost). Such investments increase the value of the firm and thus increase shareholders' (that is, owners') wealth. This rule holds whether you are making the decision to purchase new machinery, build a new plant, or buy an entire business.

(US$750 million – US$520 million). If the KEC acquisition works out as planned, the value of ABB will be increased by US$230 million.

Not all investment decisions are successful. Just open the business section of any newspaper on any day, and you will find stories of bad decisions. For example, the Korean automobile manufacturer Daewoo Motors' investment in Central and Eastern Europe in the mid-1990s, after an initially promising start, led to losses in the financial year 2000 of over €400 million and the bankruptcy of its van-making business in Poland in 2001. When, as in this case, the cost exceeds the value of the future cash flows, the project will decrease the value of the firm by that amount.

Financing Decisions

Financing decisions concern how firms raise cash to pay for their investments, as shown in Exhibit 1.2. Productive assets, which are long term in nature, are financed by long-term borrowing, equity investment, or both. Financing decisions involve trade-offs between advantages and disadvantages to the firm.

A major advantage of debt financing is that debt payments are tax deductible for most businesses. However, debt financing increases a firm's risk because it creates a contractual obligation to make periodic interest payments and, at maturity, to repay the amount borrowed. These contractual obligations must be paid regardless of the firm's operating cash flow, even if the firm suffers a financial loss. If the firm fails to make payments as promised, it defaults on its debt obligation and may be forced into bankruptcy and liquidation.

In contrast, equity has no maturity, and there are no guaranteed payments to equity investors. In a company, the board of directors has the right to decide whether dividends should be paid to shareholders. This means that if the board decides to omit or reduce a dividend payment, the firm will not be in default. Unlike interest payments, however, dividend payments to shareholders are not usually tax deductible.

Capital structure

the mix of debt and equity that is used to finance a firm

Capital markets

financial markets where equity and debt instruments with maturities greater than one year are traded

The mix of debt and equity on the balance sheet is known as the firm's **capital structure**. The term *capital structure* is used because long-term funds are considered capital, and these funds are raised in **capital markets** – financial markets where equity and debt instruments with maturities greater than one year are traded.

BUILDING INTUITION

Financing Decisions Affect the Value of the Firm

How a firm is financed with debt and equity affects the value of the firm. The reason is that the mix between debt and equity affects the taxes the firm pays and the probability that the firm will go bankrupt. The financial manager's goal is to determine the combination of debt and equity that minimises the cost of financing the firm.

Working Capital Management Decisions
Management must also decide how to manage the firm's current assets, such as cash, inventory and accounts receivable, and its current liabilities, such as trade credit and accounts payable. The monetary difference between current assets and current liabilities is called **net working capital**, as shown in Exhibit 1.2. As mentioned earlier, working capital

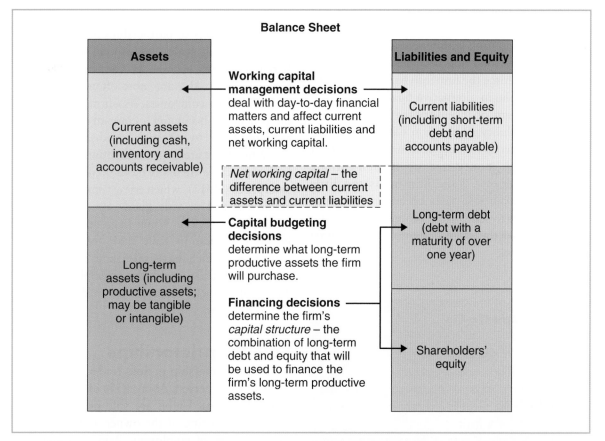

Exhibit 1.2: How the Financial Manager's Decisions Affect the Balance Sheet Financial managers are concerned with three fundamental types of decisions: capital budgeting decisions, financing decisions, and working capital management decisions. Each type of decision has a direct and important effect on the firm's balance sheet—in other words, on the firm's profitability.

management is the day-to-day management of the firm's short-term assets and liabilities. The goals of managing working capital are to ensure that the firm has enough money to pay its bills and to invest any spare cash to earn interest.

> ### Net working capital
>
> the difference between the current assets and current liabilities

The mismanagement of working capital can cause a firm to default on its debt and go into bankruptcy, even though, over the long term, the firm may be profitable. For example, a firm that makes sales to customers on credit but is not diligent about collecting the accounts receivable can quickly find itself without enough cash to pay its bills. If this condition becomes chronic, trade creditors can force the firm into bankruptcy if the firm cannot obtain alternative financing.

The amount of inventory may also affect a firm's profitability. If the firm has more inventory than it needs to meet customer demands, it has too much money tied up in non-earning assets. Conversely, if the firm holds too little inventory, it can lose sales because it does not have products to sell when customers want them. The firm must therefore determine the optimal inventory level.

Before You Go On

1. What are the three most basic types of financial decisions managers must make?
2. Why are capital budgeting decisions among the most important decisions in the life of a firm?
3. Explain why you would accept an investment project if the value of the expected cash flows exceeds the cost of the project.

FORMS OF BUSINESS ORGANISATION

Learning Objective 2

Identify the basic forms of business organisation and review their respective strengths and weaknesses.

In this section, we look at the way firms structure their business activities. The owners of a business usually choose the organisational form that will help management to maximise the value of the firm. Important considerations are the size of the business, the manner in which income from the business is taxed, the legal liability of the owners and the ability to raise cash to finance the business.

Most start-ups and small businesses operate as either sole traders or partnerships because of their small operating scale and capital requirements. Large businesses, such as the German automotive group Daimler AG, are most often organised as limited liability companies. As a firm grows in size, the benefits to becoming a company increase and are more likely to outweigh any disadvantages.

While there are large multinational companies in Europe, there are many more small and medium enterprises (SMEs), which have a small number of employees and provide goods and services to a locality or a region. While their operations may be more modest in scale than those of public companies, which have sales and operations in many parts of the world, the principles and techniques of financial management in this book are just as relevant.

Sole Proprietorships

A **sole proprietorship** or **sole trader** is a business owned by one person. About 85% of all businesses in the European Union are sole proprietorships, typically consisting of the owner and, perhaps, a small number of employees. Being a sole trader offers several advantages. It is the simplest type of business to start, and it is the least regulated. In addition, sole traders keep all the profits from the business and do not have to share decision-making authority. Finally, profits may be subject to lower income taxes than those for the most common type of company.

On the downside, a sole proprietor is responsible for paying all the firm's bills and has unlimited liability for all business debts and other obligations of the firm. This means that creditors can look beyond the assets of the business to the proprietor's personal wealth for payment. Another disadvantage is that the amount of equity capital that can be invested in the business is limited to the owner's personal wealth, which may restrict the possibilities for growth. Finally, it is difficult to transfer ownership of a sole proprietorship because there are no shares or other such interest to sell. The owner must sell the company's assets, which can reduce the price that the owner receives for the business.

> ## Sole proprietorship or sole trader
>
> a business owned by a single individual

Partnerships

A **partnership** consists of two or more owners who have joined together legally to manage a business. Partnerships are typically larger than sole proprietorships, and about 6% of all businesses in the European Union are organised in this manner. To form a partnership, the owners enter into an agreement that details how much capital each partner will contribute to the partnership, what their management roles will be, how key management decisions will be made, how the profits will be divided and how ownership will be transferred in case of specified events, such as the retirement or death of a partner.

> ## Partnership
>
> two or more owners who have joined together legally to manage a business and share its profits

A *general partnership* has the same basic advantages and disadvantages as a sole trader. A key disadvantage of a general partnership is that all partners have unlimited liability for the partnership's debts and actions, regardless of what proportion of the business they own or how the debt or obligations were incurred. The problem of unlimited liability can be avoided in a *limited partnership*, which consists of *general* and *limited* partners. Here, one or more general partners have unlimited liability and actively manage the business, while each limited partner is liable for business obligations only up to the amount of capital he or she contributed to the partnership. In other words, the limited partners have **limited liability**. To qualify for limited partner status, a partner cannot be actively engaged in managing the business.

> ## Limited liability
>
> the legal liability of a limited partner or shareholder in a business which extends only to the capital contributed or the amount invested

Companies

Most large businesses are incorporated as companies. A **company** (also known as a *corporation*) is a legal entity created by law. In a legal sense, it is a 'person' distinct from its owners. Companies can sue and be sued, enter into contracts, issue debt, borrow money and own assets, such as property. They can also be general or limited partners in partnerships, and they can own shares in other companies. The owners of a company are its shareholders.

> ## Company
>
> a legal entity formed and authorised under law; in a legal sense, a company is a 'person' distinct from its owners

Starting a company is more costly than starting a sole proprietorship or partnership. Those starting the company, for example, must create articles of incorporation and bylaws that conform to the laws of the country or state in which it is incorporated. These documents spell out the name of the company, its business purpose, its intended life span (it can be for ever), the amount of shares to be issued and the number of directors and their responsibilities.[2]

A major advantage of the corporate form of business organisation is that shareholders have limited liability for debts and other obligations of the company. The 'corporate veil' of limited liability exists because companies are 'legal persons' that borrow in their own names, not in the names of any individual owners. A major disadvantage of the most common corporate form of organisation, compared with sole proprietorships and partnerships, is the way they are treated for tax purposes. Because the company is a legal 'person', it must pay taxes on the income it earns. If the company then pays a cash dividend, the shareholders pay taxes on that dividend as income. Thus, the owners of companies in most countries are subject to double taxation – first at the corporate level and then at the personal level when they receive dividends.[3]

Companies can be classified as public or private. In many countries, there are two forms of incorporation. For instance in Germany, large limited companies are called Aktiengesellschaft (AG) and private companies are called Gesellschaft mit beschränkter Haftung (GmbH).[4] Most large companies prefer to operate as public companies, which can sell their debt or equity in the public markets, because large amounts of capital can be sold in these markets at a relatively low cost. **Public markets**, such as the Deutsche Börse and London Stock Exchange, are subject to financial regulatory oversight. Although firms whose securities are publicly traded are technically called public companies, they are generally referred to simply as companies. We will follow that convention.

> ### Public markets
> regulated markets in which large amounts of debt and equity are publicly traded

> ### Privately held companies
> companies whose shares are not traded in public markets; also called closely held corporations

In contrast, **privately held** or **closely held** companies are typically owned by a small number of investors and their shares are not traded publicly. When a company is first formed, the shares are often held by just a few investors, typically the founder, a small number of key managers and financial backers. Over time, as the company grows in size and needs larger amounts of capital, management may decide that the company should 'go public' in order to gain access to the public markets. Not all privately held companies go public, however.

A list of the most common terms used for private and public companies you are likely to meet is given below.

Country	Private Company	Public Company
Austria, Germany and Switzerland	Gesellschaft mit beschränkter Haftung (GmbH)	Aktiengesellschaft (AG)
Denmark	Anpartsselskab (ApS)	Aktieselskab (A/S)
European Union	Societas Privata Europaea (SPE)	Societas Europaea (SE)
Finland	osakeyhtiö (OY)	julkinen osakeyhtiö (OYJ)

France, Luxembourg and Switzerland	Société à responsabilité limitée (SARL)	Société anonyme (SA)
Italy and Switzerland	Società a responsabilità limitata (S.r.l)	Società per Azioni (S.p.A.)
Netherlands	Besloten Vennootschap (BV)	Naamloze Vennootschap (NV)
Norway	Aksjeselskap (AS)	Allmennaksjeselskap (ASA)
Poland	spółka z ograniczoną odpowiedzialnością (Spzoo)	spółka akcyjna (SA)
Spain	Sociedad Limitada (SL)	Sociedad Anónima (SA)
Sweden	Aktiebolag (AB)	Publikt aktiebolag (AB (publ))
United Kingdom	Limited (Ltd)	public limited company (plc)
United States	Corporation, Incorporated (Corp., Inc.)	

We address the issues of business formation and organisation in more detail in Chapter 18.

WEB

Visit the websites of the London Stock Exchange, the Deutsche Börse and the pan-European exchange Euronext-NYSE Liffe at: www.londonstockexchange.com, www.deutsche-boerse.com and www.euronext.com.

Hybrid Forms of Business Organisation

Historically, law firms, accounting firms, investment banks and other professional groups were organised as sole proprietorships or partnerships. For partners in these firms, all income was taxed as personal income, and general partners had unlimited liability for all debts and other financial obligations of the firm. It was widely believed that in professional partnerships, such as those of lawyers, accountants or doctors, the partners should be liable individually and collectively for the professional conduct of each partner. This structure gave the partners an incentive to monitor each other's professional conduct and discipline poorly performing partners, resulting in a higher quality of service and greater professional integrity. Financially, however, misconduct by one partner could result in disaster for the entire firm. For example, a doctor found guilty of malpractice exposes every partner in the medical practice to financial liability, even though the others never treated the patient in question.

In response to internationalisation, the increasing size and reach of many professional firms and also as a result of sharp increases in the number of professional malpractice cases and large damages awards in the courts, professional groups have largely converted to a hybrid form of business organisation. These organisations, known as **limited liability partnerships (LLPs)**, are now permitted in most countries. An LLP combines the limited liability of a company with the tax advantage of a partnership – there is no double taxation. In general, income to the partners of an LLP is taxed as personal income, the partners have limited liability for the business, and they are not personally liable for other partners' malpractice or professional misconduct. Other more recent organisational forms that are essentially equivalent to LLPs include limited liability companies (LLCs) and professional corporations (PCs).

Limited liability partnerships (LLPs)

hybrid business organisations that combine some of the advantages of companies and partnerships; in general, income to the partners is taxed as personal income, but the partners have limited liability

Before You Go On

1. Why are many businesses operated as sole proprietorships or partnerships?
2. What are some advantages and disadvantages of operating as a public company?
3. Explain why professional partnerships such as medical practices organise as limited liability partnerships.

MANAGING THE FINANCIAL FUNCTION

Learning Objective 3

Describe the typical organisation of the financial function in a large company.

As we discussed earlier in the chapter, financial managers are concerned with a firm's investment, financing and working capital management decisions. The senior financial manager holds one of the top executive positions in the firm. In a large corporation, the senior financial manager usually has the rank of director (that is, the individual will be an officer of the company and in the USA and elsewhere may be ranked as vice president or senior vice president) and goes by the title of **chief financial officer (CFO)**, or **finance director**. In smaller firms, the job tends to focus more on the accounting function, and the top financial officer may be called the chief accountant or controller. In this section we focus on the financial function in a large company.

Chief financial officer (CFO)

the most senior financial manager in a company

Organisational Structure

Exhibit 1.3 shows a typical organisational structure for a large company, with special attention to the financial function. As shown, the top management position in the firm is the chief executive officer (CEO), who has the final decision-making authority among all the firm's executives. The CEO's most important responsibilities are to set the strategic direction of the firm and see that the management team executes the strategic plan. The CEO reports directly to the board of directors, which is accountable to the company's shareholders. The board's responsibility is to see that the top management makes decisions that are in the best interest of the shareholders.

The CFO reports directly to the CEO and focuses on managing all aspects of the firm's financial side, as well as working closely with the CEO on strategic issues. A number of positions report directly to the CFO. In addition, the CFO often interacts with people in other functional areas on a regular basis because all senior executives are involved in financial decisions that affect the firm and their areas of responsibility.

WEB

Go to www.cfo.com to get a better idea of the responsibilities of the CFO.

Positions Reporting to the CFO

Exhibit 1.3 also shows the positions that typically report to the CFO in a large company and the activities managed in each area.

- The *treasurer* looks after the collection and disbursement of cash, investing excess cash so that it earns interest, raising new capital, handling foreign exchange transactions and overseeing the firm's pension fund managers. The treasurer also assists the CFO in handling important financial market relationships, such as those with investment banks and credit rating agencies.
- The *risk mana*ger monitors and manages the firm's risk exposure in financial and commodity

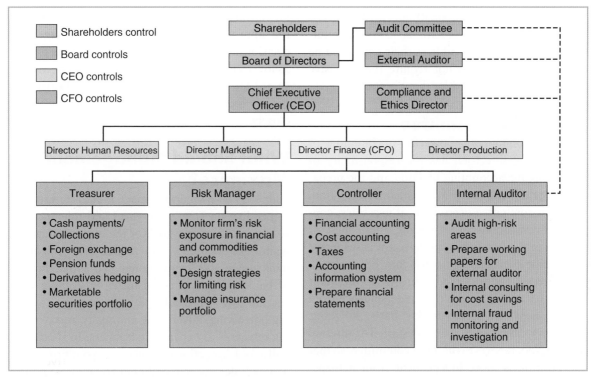

Exhibit 1.3: Simplified Corporate Organisation Chart The firm's top finance and accounting executive is the CFO, who reports directly to the CEO. Positions that report directly to the CFO include the treasurer, risk manager, and controller. The internal auditor reports both to the CFO and to the audit committee of the board of directors. The external auditor and the ethics director also are ultimately responsible to the audit committee.

markets and the firm's relationships with insurance providers.

• The *chief accountant* and associated staff prepare the financial statements, maintain the firm's financial and cost accounting systems, prepare the taxes and work closely with the firm's external auditors.

• The *internal auditor* is responsible for identifying and assessing major risks facing the firm and performing audits in areas where the firm might incur substantial losses. The internal auditor reports to the board of directors as well as the CFO.

External Auditors

Nearly every business hires an external accountancy firm to provide an independent annual audit of the firm's financial statements. Through this audit, the accountant determines whether the firm's financial statement presents fairly, in all material respects, the financial position of the firm and the results of its activities. In other words, whether the financial numbers are reasonably accurate, that accounting principles have been consistently applied year to year and do not significantly distort the firm's performance, and that the accounting principles used conform to those generally accepted by the accounting profession. Creditors and investors require independent audits, and exchanges require publicly traded firms to supply audited financial statements.

There are four major international accounting firms (Deloitte Touche Tohmatsu, Ernst & Young, KPMG and PriceWaterhouseCoopers) which provide accountancy, audit and corporate advisory services to large companies worldwide. The extensive network means that the same firm can audit the accounts of all the various foreign subsidiaries of companies that operate internationally.

On the other hand, small and medium-sized firms may select a local or national firm of accountants, which will better address their needs and be less costly, as they do not require the extensive global services provided by the 'big four'.

The Audit Committee

The audit committee, a powerful subcommittee of the board of directors, has the responsibility of overseeing the accounting function and the preparation of the firm's financial statements. In addition, the audit committee oversees or, if necessary, conducts investigations of significant fraud, theft or malfeasance in the firm, especially if it is suspected that senior managers in the firm may be involved.

External auditors report directly to the audit committee to help ensure their independence from management. On a day-to-day basis, however, they work closely with the CFO staff. The internal auditor, too, reports to the audit committee, so that the position is more independent from management and his or her ultimate responsibility is to the audit committee. On a day-to-day basis, however, the internal auditor, like the external auditors, works closely with the CFO staff.

Before You Go On

1. What are the major responsibilities of the CFO?
2. Identify three financial officers who typically report to the CFO and describe their duties.
3. Why does the internal auditor report to both the CFO and the board of directors?

THE GOAL OF THE FIRM

Learning Objective 4

Explain why maximising the current value of the firm's shares is the appropriate goal for management.

For business owners, it is important to determine the appropriate goal for financial management decisions. Should the goal be to try to keep costs as low as possible? Or to maximise sales or market share? Or to achieve steady growth and earnings? Let us look at this fundamental question more closely.

What Should Management Maximise?

Suppose you own and manage a pizza restaurant. Depending on your preferences and tolerance for risk, you can set any goal for the business that you want. For example, you might have a fear of bankruptcy and losing money. To avoid the risk of bankruptcy, you could focus on keeping your costs as low as possible, paying low wages, avoiding borrowing, advertising minimally and remaining reluctant to expand the business. In short, you will avoid any action that increases your firm's risk. You will sleep well at night but you may eat poorly because of meagre profits.

Conversely, you could focus on maximising market share and becoming the largest pizza business in town. Your strategy might include cutting prices to increase sales, borrowing heavily to open new pizza outlets, spending lavishly on advertising and developing exotic menu items such as *pizza de foie gras*. In the short run, your high-risk, high-growth strategy will have you both eating poorly and sleeping poorly as you push the firm to the edge. In the long run, you will either become very rich or go bankrupt! There must be a better operational goal than either of these extremes.

Why Not Maximise Profits?

One goal for financial decision making that seems reasonable is *profit maximisation*. After all, do not shareholders and business owners want their companies to be profitable? Although profit maximisation seems a logical goal for a business, it has some serious drawbacks.

One problem with profit maximisation is that it is hard to pin down what is 'profit'. To the average businessperson, profits are just revenues minus expenses. To an accountant, however, a

BUILDING INTUITION

The Timing of Cash Flows Affects Their Value

Money today is worth more than money in the future because if you have money today, you can invest it and earn interest. For businesses, cash flows can involve large sums of money and receiving money one day late can cost a great deal. For example, if a bank has €100 billion of consumer loans outstanding and the average annual interest payment is 5%, it would cost the bank €13.7 million if every consumer decided to make an interest payment one day later.

decision that increases profits under one set of accounting rules can reduce it under another. This is the origin of the term *creative accounting*. A second problem is that accounting profits are not necessarily the same as cash flows. For example, many firms recognise revenues at the time a sale is made, which is typically before the cash payment for the sale is received. Ultimately, the owners of a business want cash because only cash can be used to make investments or to buy goods and services.

Yet another problem with profit maximisation as a goal is that it does not distinguish between getting money today and getting the same amount of money at some point in the future. In finance, the timing of cash flows is extremely important. For example, the longer you go without paying your credit card balance, the more interest you must pay the bank for the use of the money. The interest accrues because of the *time value of money*; the longer you have access to money, the more you

have to pay for it. The time value of money is one of the most important concepts in finance and is the focus of Chapters 5 and 6.

Finally, profit maximisation ignores the uncertainty, or risk, associated with future cash flows. A basic principle of finance is that there is a trade-off between expected return and risk. When given a choice between two investments that have the same expected returns but different risk, most people choose the less risky one. This makes sense because most people do not like bearing risk and, as a result, must be compensated for taking it. The profit maximisation goal ignores differences in value caused by differences in risk. We return to the important topics of risk, its measurement and the trade-off between risk and return in Chapter 7. What is important at this time is that you understand that investors do not like risk and must be rewarded for bearing it.

In sum, it appears that profit maximisation is not an appropriate goal for a firm because the

BUILDING INTUITION

The Riskiness of Cash Flows Affects Their Value

A risky sum of money is worth less than a safe sum. The reason is that investors do not like risk and must be compensated for bearing it. For example, if two investments have the same return – say 5% – most people will prefer the investment with the lower risk. Thus, the more risky are an investment's cash flows, the less it is worth.

BUILDING INTUITION

The Financial Manager's Goal is to Maximise the Value of the Firm's Shares

The goal for financial managers is to make decisions that maximise the firm's share price. By maximising the share price, management will help maximise shareholders' wealth. To do this, managers must make investment and financing decisions so that the total value of cash inflows exceeds the total value of cash outflows by the greatest possible amount (benefits > costs). Notice that the focus is on maximising the value of cash flows, not profits.

concept is difficult to define and does not directly account for the firm's cash flows. What we need is a goal that looks at a firm's cash flows and considers both their timing and their riskiness. Fortunately, we have just such a measure: the market value of the firm's shares.

Maximise the Value of the Firm's Shares

The underlying value of any asset is determined by the future cash flows generated by that asset. This principle holds whether we are buying a bank certificate of deposit, a corporate bond or an office building. Furthermore, as we will discuss in Chapter 9, when security analysts and investors in the financial markets determine the value of a firm's shares, they consider (1) the size of the expected cash flows, (2) the timing of the cash flows and (3) the riskiness of the cash flows. Notice that the mechanism for determining share values overcomes all the cash flow objections we raised with regard to profit maximisation as a goal.

Thus, an appropriate goal for financial management is to maximise the current value of the firm's shares. By maximising the current share price, the financial manager will be maximising the value of the shareholders' shares. Notice that maximising share value is an unambiguous objective and it is easy to measure. We simply look at the market value of the shares in the newspaper on a given day to determine the value of the shareholders' shares – and

whether it has gone up or down. Publicly traded securities are ideally suited for this task because public markets are wholesale markets with large numbers of buyers and sellers where securities trade near their true value.

What about those firms, such as private companies and partnerships, whose equity is not publicly traded? The total value of the shares in such a company is equal to the value of the shareholders' equity. *Thus, our goal can be restated for these firms as this: maximise the current value of owner's equity.* The only other restriction is that the entities must be for-profit businesses.

Can Management Decisions Affect Share Prices?

An important question is whether management decisions actually affect the firm's share price. Fortunately, the answer is yes. As noted earlier, a basic principle in finance is that the value of an asset is determined by the future cash flows it is expected to generate. As shown in Exhibit 1.4, a firm's management makes numerous decisions that affect its cash flows. For example, management decides what type of products or services to produce and what productive assets to purchase. Managers also make decisions concerning the mix of debt to equity, debt collection policies and policies for paying suppliers, to mention a few. In addition, cash flows are affected by how efficient management is in making products, the

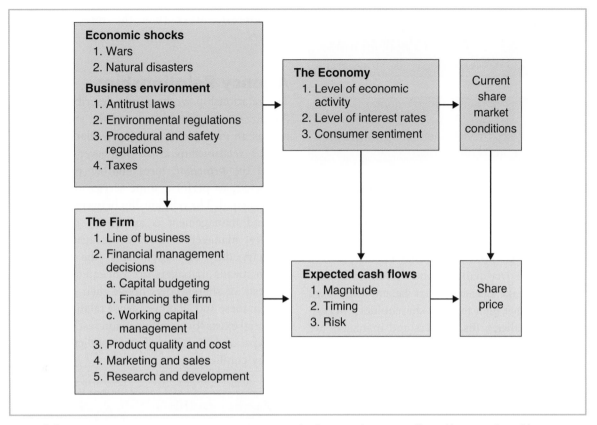

Exhibit 1.4: Major Factors Affecting Stock Prices The firms'stock price is affected by a number of factors, and management can control only some of them. Managers exercise little control over external conditions (blue boxes), such as the general economy, although they can closely observe these conditions and make appropriate changes in strategy. Also, managers make many other decisions that directly affect the firm's expected cash flows (green boxes)—and hence the price of the firms' stock.

quality of the products, management's sales and marketing skills and the firm's investment in research and development for new products. Some of these decisions affect cash flows over the long term, such as the decision to build a new plant, and other decisions have a short-term impact on cash flows, such as launching an advertising campaign.

Of course, the firm must also deal with a number of external factors over which it has little or no control, such as economic conditions (recession or expansion), war or peace, and new government regulations. External factors are constantly changing, and management must weigh the impact of these changes and adjust its strategy and decisions accordingly.

The important point here is that, over time, management makes a series of decisions when executing the firm's strategy that affect the firm's cash flows and, hence, the price of the firm's shares. Firms that have a better business strategy, are more nimble, make better business decisions and can execute their plans well will have a higher share price than similar firms that just cannot get it right.

Before You Go On

1. Why is profit maximisation an unsatisfactory goal for managing a firm?
2. Explain why maximising the current market price of a firm's shares is an appropriate goal for the firm's management.
3. What is the fundamental determinant of an asset's value?

AGENCY CONFLICTS: SEPARATION OF OWNERSHIP AND CONTROL

Learning Objective 5

Discuss how agency conflicts affect the goal of maximising shareholder value.

We turn next to an important issue facing shareholders of large companies: the separation of the ownership and control of the firm. In a large company, ownership is often spread over a large number of shareholders who may effectively have little control over management. Management may therefore make decisions that benefit their own interests rather than those of shareholders. In contrast, in smaller firms, owners and managers are usually the same, and there is no conflict of interest between owners and managers. As you will see, this self-interested behaviour may affect the value of the firm.

Ownership and Control

To illustrate, we will continue with our pizza restaurant example. As the owner of the pizza restaurant, you have decided your goal is to maximise the value of the business, and thereby your ownership interest. There is no conflict of interest in your dual roles as owner and manager because your personal and economic self-interest is tied to the success of the pizza business. The restaurant has succeeded because you have worked hard and have focused on customer satisfaction.

Now suppose you decide to hire a college student to manage the restaurant. Will the new manager always act in your interest? Or could the new manager be tempted to give free pizza to friends now and then or, after an exhausting day, leave early rather than spend time cleaning and preparing for the next day? From this example, you can see that once ownership and management are separated, managers may be tempted to pursue goals that are in their own self-interest rather than the interests of the owners.

Agency Relationships

The relationship we have just described between the pizza restaurant owner and the student manager is an example of an agency relationship. An agency relationship arises whenever one party, called the *principal*, hires another party, called the *agent*, to perform some service on behalf of the principal. The relationship between shareholders and management is an agency relationship. Legally, managers (who are the agents) have a fiduciary duty to shareholders (the principals), which means managers are obligated to put the interests of shareholders above their own. However, in these and all other agency relationships, the potential exists for a conflict of interest between the principal and the agent. These conflicts are called **agency conflicts**.

Agency conflicts

conflicts of interest between a principal and an agent

Do Managers Really Want to Maximise the Share Price?

It is not difficult to see how conflicts of interest between managers and shareholders can arise in the corporate setting. In most large companies, especially those that are publicly traded, there is a significant degree of separation between ownership and management. For example, BP – a British oil company with a global reach that is listed on the London, New York and Frankfurt stock exchanges – has more than 1.2 million shareholders. As a practical matter, it is not possible for all of the shareholders to be active in the management of the firm or to individually bear the high cost of monitoring management. The bottom line is that shareholders own the company, but managers control the money and have the opportunity to use it for their own benefit.

How might management be tempted to indulge itself and pursue its own self-interest? We need not look far for an answer to this question. Corporate excesses are legion, but high on the list are palatial office buildings, corporate hunting and fishing lodges in exotic places, expensive corporate jets, extravagant expense-account dinners kicked off with bottles of Dom Perignon champagne and washed down with 1953 Margaux – and, of course, a king's compensation package. Besides economic nest feathering, corporate managers may focus on maximising market share and their industry prestige, job security and other personal benefits.

Needless to say, these types of activities and spending conflict with the goal of maximising a firm's share price. The costs of these activities are called *agency costs*. **Agency costs** are the costs incurred because of conflicts of interest between a principal and an agent. Examples are the cost of the lavish dinner mentioned earlier and the cost of a corporate jet for executives. However, not all agency costs are frivolous. The cost of hiring an external auditor to certify financial statements is also an agency cost.

> **Agency costs**
>
> the costs arising from conflicts of interest between a principal and an agent; for example, between a firm's owners and its management

Aligning the Interests of Management and Shareholders

If the linkage between shareholder and management goals is weak, a number of mechanisms can help to better align the behaviour of managers with the goals of corporate shareholders. These include (1) management compensation, (2) managerial labour markets, (3) board of directors, (4) other managers, (5) large shareholders, (6) the takeover market and (7) the legal and regulatory environment.

Management Compensation

The most effective means of aligning the interests of managers with those of shareholders is a well-designed compensation (pay) package that rewards managers when they do what shareholders want them to do and penalises them when they do not. This type of plan is effective because a manager will quickly internalise the benefits and costs of making good and bad decisions and, thus, will be more likely to make the decisions that shareholders want. Therefore, there is no need for some outside monitor, such as the board of directors, to try to figure out whether the managers are making the right decisions. The information that outside monitors have is not as good as the managers' information, so these outside monitors are always at a disadvantage in trying to determine whether a manager is acting in the interest of shareholders. Allied to this is the problem of **moral hazard**, where managers are in a position to take unobservable actions that are detrimental to shareholders. For instance, they may be able to use the firm's assets for personal gain. This works against shareholders. Given this, it makes sense to get managers to act like owners and not misuse the firm's resources; that is, to act in the best interests of shareholders.

> **Moral hazard**
>
> any contract or arrangement that provides incentives for one party to take (or not take) unobservable steps which are prejudicial to another party

Most companies have management compensation plans that tie compensation to the performance of the firm. The idea behind these plans is that if compensation is sensitive to the performance of the firm, managers will have greater incentives to make decisions that increase shareholders' wealth. Although these incentive plans vary widely, they usually include (1) a base salary, (2) a bonus based on the accounting performance and (3) some compensation that is tied to the firm's share price.[5] The base salary assures the executive some minimum compensation as long as he or she remains with the firm, and the bonus and share price-based compensations are designed to align the manager's incentives with those of shareholders. The trick in designing such a remuneration package is to choose the right mix of these three components so that the manager has the right incentives and the overall package is sufficiently appealing to attract and retain high-quality managers at the lowest possible cost.

Managerial Labour Market

The managerial labour market also provides managers with incentives to act in the interests of shareholders. Firms that have a history of poor performance or a reputation for 'shady operations' or unethical behaviour have difficulty hiring top managerial talent. Individuals who are top performers have better alternatives than to work for such firms. Therefore, to the extent that managers want to attract high-quality people, the labour market provides incentives to run a good company.

Furthermore, studies show that executives who 'manage' firms into bankruptcy or are convicted of white-collar crimes can rarely secure equivalent positions after being fired for poor performance or convicted for criminal behaviour. Thus, the penalty for extremely poor performance or a criminal conviction is a significant reduction in the manager's lifetime earnings potential. Managers know this, and the fear of such consequences helps keep them working hard and honestly.[6]

Board of Directors

A company's board of directors has a legal responsibility to represent shareholders' interests. The board's duties include hiring and firing the CEO, setting his or her compensation, and monitoring his or her performance. The board also approves major decisions concerning the firm, such as the firm's annual capital budget or the acquisition of another business. These responsibilities make the board a key mechanism for ensuring that managers' decisions are aligned with those of shareholders.

How well boards actually perform in this role has been questioned in recent years. As an example, critics point out that some boards are unwilling to make hard decisions such as firing the CEO when a firm performs poorly. Other people believe that a lack of independence is a reason that boards are not as effective as they might be. For example, in many cases the CEO is also chair of the board of directors. This dual position can give the CEO undue influence over the board, as the chairperson sets the agenda for and chairs board meetings, appoints committees and controls the flow of information to the board. Also inhibiting board independence in the past was the practice that allowed any number of the companies' own executives to serve on the board. These inside directors could actually outnumber outside directors, who were not employees of the firm. Changing attitudes to corporate governance, as encapsulated in the OECD principles of corporate governance discussed below, have encouraged the separation of the role of CEO and chairperson and a predominance of outside directors, to ensure the strategic guidance of the company, the effective monitoring of management by the board, and the board's accountability to the company and its shareholders.[7]

It should be noted that board structures and procedures vary both within and among OECD countries. Some countries – notably Germany – use a system of two-tier boards that separate the supervisory function and the management function into different bodies. Such systems typically have a 'supervisory board' composed of non-executive board members and a 'management board' composed entirely of executives. Other countries have 'unitary' boards, which bring together executive and non-executive board members. In some countries, such as Italy, there is a quasi-two-tier system where the unitary board is supplemented by an additional statutory board for audit purposes.

Other Managers

Competition among managers within firms also helps provide incentives for management to act in the interests of shareholders. Managers compete to attain the CEO position and in doing so try to attract the board of directors' attention by acting in the shareholders' interests. Furthermore, even when a manager becomes CEO, he or she is always looking over his or her shoulder because other managers covet that job.

Large Shareholders

All shareholders obviously have a strong interest in providing managers with incentives to maximise shareholder value. After all, that is what shareholders want, and it is an appropriate goal for management. We single out shareholders who own a large number of shares because they have enough money at stake – and enough power – to make it worthwhile to actively monitor managers and try to influence their decisions.

While large shareholders can be a force for good, the fact that they may control the firm can also lead to conflict with other shareholders who have a minority of the shares in the company. Controlling shareholders, such as the founder of the business and his or her family, may have a lot of their wealth tied up in the firm. This means they can end up behaving more like managers than owners.

The Takeover Market

The market for corporate control provides incentives for managers to act in the interests of shareholders. When a firm performs poorly because management is doing a poor job, an opportunity arises for astute investors, so-called corporate raiders, to make money by buying the company at a price that reflects its poor performance and replacing the current managers with a top-flight management team. If the investors have evaluated the situation correctly, the firm will soon be transformed into a strong performer, its share price will increase and investors can sell their stock for a significant profit. The possibility that corporate raiders might discover such a firm provides incentives for management to perform.

The Legal and Regulatory Environment

Finally, the laws and regulations that firms must adhere to limit the ability of managers to make decisions that harm the interests of shareholders. An example is the law against corporate theft that make it illegal for managers to steal corporate assets. Similarly, regulatory reforms and codes of conduct, discussed next, limit the ability of managers to mislead shareholders.

Corporate Governance Frameworks

Corporate accounting scandals in the USA, such as WorldCom, Enron, Global Crossing and Tyco, and similar cases in Europe, such as the fraud at Parmalat (the largest Italian food company and the fourth largest in Europe, that went bankrupt in December 2003 owing over €8 billion to creditors), the bribery scandals at Volkswagen, MAN and Siemens, and Royal Ahold's misstatement of its 2001/2 earnings, as well as other examples, have raised the attention of regulators concerning best practice in corporate governance. In particular, strengthened control, monitoring and oversight of managers have become an aim of good corporate governance structures. The main proposals put forward require a strong and independent group of outside directors who can vet the firm's corporate strategy, overall direction, mission and vision, hire and fire the CEO and top management, review and approve the use of resources and care for shareholder interests. We first discuss the Organisation of Economic Cooperation and Development's (OECD) principles. We then briefly discuss the corporate governance reforms in the United States made by the Sarbanes-Oxley Act of 2002, which focuses on (1) reducing agency costs in companies, (2) restoring ethical conduct within the business sector and (3) improving the integrity of accounting reporting systems within firms.

WEB

To find out more about current issues of corporate governance in Europe, visit www.ecgi.org.

OECD Principles of Corporate Governance

The OECD's principles of corporate governance aim to provide the right incentives for the board and management to pursue objectives that are in the interests of the company and its shareholders and that facilitate effective monitoring. Although there is no single model for corporate governance and it is recognised that practice differs somewhat from country to country, there are nevertheless common elements that underlie good corporate governance systems and practice. Of particular relevance for corporate finance are principles that address (1) agency costs in companies (see Exhibit 1.5), (2) ethical conduct within the business sector and (3) the quality of reporting by firms.

The principles identify objectives and means to achieve these. (The principles are aimed at the governance of public companies and private companies and partnerships are not required to conform to these principles, although elements in the code may be useful as a tool for improving corporate governance in non-traded companies and state-owned enterprises.) The code proposes the following:

1. Transparent and efficient markets, consistent with the rule of law and arrangements that articulate the division of responsibilities among the different parties involved.
2. Corporate governance should protect and facilitate the exercise of shareholders' rights.
3. Provide for the equitable treatment of all shareholders.
4. Recognise the rights of stakeholders established by law or through mutual agreements and encourage active cooperation between companies and stakeholders.

5. Timely and accurate disclosure of material matters regarding the company, including its financial situation, performance, ownership and governance.
6. The board should ensure the strategic guidance of the company, the effective monitoring of management and be accountable to the company and its shareholders.

As a result of corporate scandals and the development of principles of corporate governance at country level, across Europe boards appear much more serious about monitoring firms' performance and ratifying important decisions by management. For European companies, compliance with local corporate governance standards has become a fact of life, although conformity to the key principles outlined above varies between countries and even within countries. Overall, board structures are in place that allow director independence, define committee membership and modus operandi and provide transparency. Leading countries in this regard are the Netherlands, Switzerland and the United Kingdom. Countries with historically weaker corporate governance arrangements, such as Portugal, Spain and Italy, have seen reforms aimed at addressing deficiencies. Across Europe, corporate governance pressures remain at the forefront of boards' agendas. The major complaint from business has been the cost of compliance.

Sarbanes-Oxley and Other Regulatory Reforms in the United States

The series of accounting scandals and ethical lapses by corporate officers in the early years of the 21st century resulted in a set of far-reaching regulatory reforms passed by Congress in 2002. The Sarbanes-Oxley Act of 2002 lays out comprehensive mandatory regulations that require all public companies to implement five overarching strategies. (Private companies and partnerships are not required to implement these measures.)

EXHIBIT 1.5

ELEMENTS OF THE OECD CORPORATE GOVERNANCE PRINCIPLES THAT REDUCE AGENCY COSTS

Rights of shareholders and key ownership functions
- Ability to obtain relevant and material information on the company on a timely and regular basis.
- Participate and vote in general shareholder meetings.
- Elect and remove members of the board.
- Right to be informed of and participate in decisions concerning fundamental corporate changes (e.g. the authorisation of the issue of additional shares or extraordinary transactions such as the sale of a large part of the company).
- Capital structure arrangements that enable certain shareholders to obtain a disproportionate degree of control should be disclosed.
- The market for corporate control should be allowed to function in an efficient and transparent manner.
- Minority shareholders should be protected from abusive actions.

Disclosure and transparency
- Companies should disclose material information on its financial and operating results, major share ownership and voting rights, remuneration policy for board and key executives, related party transactions, and governance structures and policies.
- Undertake an annual audit by an independent, competent and qualified auditor.
- External auditors should be accountable to shareholders.

The responsibilities of the board of directors
- Should act in the best interest of the company and the shareholders.
- Should apply high ethical standards and take into account the interests of stakeholders.
- Fulfil certain key functions, including reviewing and guiding corporate strategy, monitoring the effectiveness of the company's governance practices, selecting, compensating, monitoring and, when necessary, replacing key executives and overseeing succession planning.
- Align key executive and board remuneration with the longer-term interests of the company and its shareholders.
- Monitor and manage potential conflicts of interest including misuse of corporate assets and abuse in related-party transactions.
- Ensure the integrity of the company's accounting and financial reporting systems and compliance with the law and relevant standards.
- Oversee the process of disclosure and communications.
- Exercise objective independent judgement on corporate affairs, in particular where there is a potential for conflict of interest.

Source: OECD Principles of Corporate Governance, Organisation of Economic Cooperation and Development, 2004.

1. **Ensure greater board independence.** Firms must restructure their boards so that the majority of the members are outside directors. Furthermore, it is recommended that the positions of chair and CEO be separated. Finally, Sarbanes-Oxley makes it clear that board members have a fiduciary responsibility to represent and act in the interest of shareholders, and board members who fail to meet their fiduciary duty can be fined and receive jail sentences.

2. **Establish internal accounting controls.** Firms must establish internal accounting control systems to protect the integrity of the accounting systems and safeguard the firms' assets. The internal controls are intended to improve the reliability of accounting data and the quality of financial reporting and to reduce the likelihood that individuals within the firm engage in accounting fraud.

3. **Establish compliance programmes.** Firms must establish corporate compliance programmes that ensure the firms comply with important US federal and state regulations. For example, a compliance programme would document whether a firm's truck drivers complied with all federal and state truck and driver safety regulations, such as the number of hours one can drive during the day and the gross highway weight of the truck.

4. **Establish an ethics programme.** Firms must establish ethics programmes that monitor the ethical conduct of employees and executives through a compliance hotline, which must include a whistleblower protection provision. The intent is to create an ethical work environment so that employees will know what is expected of them and their relationships with customers, suppliers and other stakeholders. If fraud is detected, the programmes should provide an established procedure to follow.

5. **Expand the audit committee's oversight powers.** The external auditor, the internal auditor and the compliance/ethics officer owe their ultimate legal responsibilities to the audit committee, not to the firm. These reporting lines give the audit committee deep tentacles into the firm to discover financial improprieties. In addition, the audit committee has the unconditional power to probe and question any person in the firm, including the CEO, regarding any matter that might materially impact the firm or its financial statements.

Exhibit 1.6 summarises some of the recent regulatory changes that significantly expand the board of directors' powers. While these regulations only apply to US-domiciled companies, the key role of the United States and the fact that many foreign companies operate in the USA and raise finance from the capital markets there mean the rules have international implications. Also, they are seen as a model for corporate governance and have been adopted in part in other countries.

Before You Go On

1. What are agency conflicts?
2. What are corporate raiders?
3. List the six main objectives of the OECD's principles of corporate governance.

THE IMPORTANCE OF ETHICS IN BUSINESS

Learning Objective 6
Explain why ethics is an appropriate topic in the study of corporate finance.

We have seen that the principles of corporate governance require the application of ethical standards. Why are ethics important to business?

WEB

The websites www.ibe.org.uk and www.web-miner.com/busethics offer a wide range of articles on the role of ethics in business.

Business Ethics

The term *ethics* describes a society's ideas about what actions are right and wrong. Ethical values are not moral absolutes, and they can and do vary across societies. Regardless of cultural differences, however, if we think about it, all of us would probably prefer to live in a world where people behave ethically – where people try to do what is right.

EXHIBIT 1.6

SARBANES-OXLEY CORPORATE AGENCY REGULATIONS THAT EXPAND THE BOARD OF DIRECTORS' POWERS

Board of Directors
- Board has a fiduciary responsibility to represent the best interest of the firm's owners.
- Majority of the board must be outside independent directors.
- Firm is required to have code of ethics, which has to be approved by the board.
- Firm must establish an ethics programme that has a complaint hotline and a whistleblower protection provision which is approved by the board of directors.
- Separation of chairman and CEO positions is recommended.
- Board members can be fined or receive jail sentences if they fail to fulfil their fiduciary responsibilities.

Audit Committee
- External auditor, internal auditor and compliance officer's fiduciary (legal) responsibilities are to the audit committee.
- Audit committee approves the hiring, firing and fees paid to external auditors.
- CEO and CFO must certify financial statements.
- All audit committee members must be outside independent directors.
- One member must be a financial expert.

External Auditors
- Lead partner must change every five years.
- There are limits on consulting (non-audit) services that external auditors can provide.

Source: Sarbanes-Oxley Act, the Public Accounting Reform and Investor Protection Act and NYSE and NASDAQ new listing requirements.

In our society, ethical rules include considering the impact of our actions on others, being willing at times to put the interests of others ahead of our own interests, and realising that we must follow the same rules we expect others to follow. The golden rule – 'Do unto others as you would have done unto you' – is an example of a widely accepted ethical norm.[8]

Are Business Ethics Different from Everyday Ethics?

Perhaps business is a dog-eat-dog world where ethics do not matter. People who take this point of view link business ethics to the 'ethics of the poker game' and not to the ethics of everyday morality. Poker players, they suggest, must practice cunning deception and must conceal their strengths and their intentions. After all, they are playing the game to win. How far does one go to win?

In the opening years of this century, investors learned the hard way about a number of firms that had been behaving according to the ethics of the poker game: cunning deception and concealment of information were the order of the day at Volkswagen, Siemens, Enron, Parmalat and a host of other firms. The market's reaction to their concealment and deception was to wipe out billions of shareholder value.

We believe that those who argue that ethics do not matter in business are mistaken. Indeed, most academic studies on the topic suggest that traditions of morality are very relevant to business and to financial markets in particular. The reasons are practical as well as ethical. Corruption in business creates inefficiencies in an economy, inhibits the growth of capital markets and slows a country's rate of economic growth.

For example, as Russia made the transition to a market economy, it had a difficult time establishing a stock market and attracting foreign investment. The reason was a simple one. Corruption was rampant in local government and in business. Contractual agreements were not enforceable, and there was no reliable financial information about Russian companies. Not until the mid-1990s did some Russian companies begin to display enough honesty and financial transparency to attract investment capital.[9]

Types of Ethical Conflicts in Business

We turn next to a consideration of the ethical problems that arise in business dealings. Most problems involve three related areas: agency costs, conflicts of interest and informational asymmetry.

Agency Costs

As we discussed earlier in this chapter, many relationships in business are agency relationships. Agents can be bound both legally and ethically to act in the interest of the principal. Financial managers have agency obligations to act honestly and to see that subordinates act honestly with respect to financial transactions. Of all the corporate officers, financial managers, when they are guilty of misconduct, present among the most serious danger to shareholder wealth. A product recall or environmental wrongdoing may cause a temporary decline in the share price. However, revelations of dishonesty, deception and fraud in financial matters have a huge impact on the share price. If the dishonesty is flagrant, the firm may go bankrupt, as we saw with the bankruptcies of Parmalat and Enron.

Conflicts of Interest

Conflicts of interest often arise in agency relationships. A conflict of interest in such a situation can arise when the agent's interests are different from those of the principal. For example, suppose you are interested in buying a house and a local estate agent is helping you find the home of your dreams. As it turns out, the dream house is one for which your agent is also the listing agent. Your agent has a conflict of interest because her professional obligation to help you find the right house at a fair price conflicts with her professional obligation to get the highest price possible for the client whose house she has listed.

Organisations can be either principals or agents and, hence, can be parties to conflicts of interest. In the past, for example, many large accounting firms provided both consulting services and company audits. This dual function may compromise the independence and objectivity of the audit opinion, even though the work is done by different parts of the firm. For example, if consulting fees from an audit client become a large source of income, is the auditing firm less likely to render an adverse audit opinion and thereby risk losing the consulting business?

Conflicts of interest are typically resolved in one of two ways. Sometimes complete disclosure is sufficient. Thus, in property transactions, it is not unusual for the same lawyer or estate agent to represent both the buyer and the seller. This practice is not considered unethical as long as both sides are aware of the fact and give their consent. Alternatively, the conflicted party can withdraw from serving the interests of one of the parties. Sometimes the law mandates this solution. For example, in some countries, legislation requires that accounting firms stop providing certain consulting services to their audit clients.

Information Asymmetry

Information asymmetry occurs when one party in a business transaction has information that is unavailable to the other parties in the transaction. The existence of information asymmetry in business relationships is commonplace. For example, suppose you decide to sell your 10-year-old car. You know much more about the real condition of the car than does the prospective buyer. The moral issue is this: How much should you tell the prospective buyer? In other words, to what extent is the party with the information advantage obligated to reduce the amount of information asymmetry?

> ### Information asymmetry
>
> the situation in which one party in a business transaction has information that is unavailable to the other parties in the transaction

Decisions in this area often centre on issues of fairness. Consider the insider trading of shares based on confidential information not available to the public. Using insider information is considered morally wrong and, as a result, has been made illegal. The rationale for the notion is ethical fairness. The central idea is that investment decisions should be made on a 'level playing field'.

What counts as fair and as unfair is somewhat controversial, but there are a few ways to determine fairness. One relates to the golden rule and the notion of impartiality that underlies it. You treat another fairly when you 'do unto others as you want them to do unto you'. Another test of fairness is whether you are willing to publicly advocate the principle behind your decision. Actions based on principles that do not pass the golden rule test or that cannot be publicly advocated are not likely to be fair.

The Importance of an Ethical Business Culture

Some economists have noted that the legal system and market forces impose substantial costs on individuals and institutions that engage in unethical behaviour. As a result, these forces provide important incentives that foster ethical behaviour in the business community. The incentives include financial losses, legal fines, jail time and the destruction of companies (bankruptcy). Ethicists argue, however, that laws and market forces are not enough. For example, the financial sector is one of the most heavily regulated areas. Yet despite heavy regulation, the sector has a long and rich history of financial scandals.

In addition to laws and market forces, then, it is important to create an ethical culture in the firm. Why is this important? An ethical business culture means that people have a set of principles – a moral compass, so to speak – that helps them identify moral issues and make ethical judgements without being told what to do. The culture has a powerful influence on the way people behave and the way they make decisions.

The people at the top of a company determine whether or not the culture of that company is ethical. At Enron, for example, top officers promoted a culture of aggressive risk taking and willingness, at times, to cross over ethical and even legal lines. Once this type of culture is established at the top, people in the organisation think it is acceptable to step over legal and ethical boundaries themselves.

More than likely, you will be confronted with ethical issues during your professional career. Knowing how to identify and deal with ethical issues is thus an important part of your professional 'survival kit'. Exhibit 1.7 presents a framework for making ethical judgements.

Serious Consequences

In recent years the 'rules' have changed, and the cost of ethical mistakes can be extremely high. In the past, the business community and legal authorities often dismissed corporate scandals as a 'few rotten apples' in an otherwise sound barrel. This is no longer true today.

When news of the Royal Ahold accounting scandal broke, Cees van der Hoeven (the chairman and chief executive) and A. Michiel Meurs (the chief financial officer), as well as others, were forced to resign. They subsequently faced fraud proceedings in the Netherlands and were indicted by the Securities and Exchange Commission in the USA. In 2006, at the court in Amsterdam, they were found guilty of fraud and fined €225,000 each, but escaped a prison sentence. Both men reached a settlement with the Securities and

EXHIBIT 1.7
A FRAMEWORK FOR THE ANALYSIS OF ETHICAL CONFLICTS

The first step towards ethical behaviour is to recognise that you face a moral issue. In general, if your actions or decisions will cause harm to others, you are facing a moral issue. When you find yourself in this position, you might ask yourself the following questions:

1. What does the law require? When in doubt, consult the legal department.
2. What do your role-related obligations require? What is your position, and what are its duties? If you are a member of a profession, what does the code of conduct of your profession say you should do in these circumstances?
3. Are you an agent employed on behalf of another in these circumstances? If so, what are the interests and desires of the employing party?
4. Are the interests of the shareholders materially affected? Your obligation is to represent the best interests of the firm's owners.
5. Do you have a conflict of interest? Will full disclosure of the conflict be sufficient? If not, you must determine what interest has priority.
6. Are you abusing information asymmetry? Is your use of the information asymmetry fair? It probably is fair if you would make the same decision if the roles of the parties were reversed, or if you would publicly advocate the principle behind your decision.
7. Would you be willing to have your action and all the reasons that motivated it reported in the press and how would your family feel about it?

Exchange Commission in which they admitted no guilt but accepted a lifetime ban from holding office in a publicly traded company. However, the company was prosecuted for accounting fraud in the Netherlands and paid a corporate fine of €8 million. In addition, a class action lawsuit brought by shareholders in the United States who had lost money as the share price plunged by two-thirds after the scandal came to light eventually led to an out-of-court settlement worth US$1.1 billion. Although the executives involved in the Ahold case escaped relatively lightly, others did not fare so well – for example Bernie J. Ebbers, convicted of fraud and theft at WorldCom, who was sentenced to 25 years in prison.

In the past, sentences for white-collar crimes have been minimal; even for serious crimes, there often was no jail time at all. This is changing. A case in point is Bernard Madoff, who defrauded investors in his firm of US$65 billion. In June 2009,

he was sentenced to 150 years in jail, in effect a life sentence.

Business ethics is a topic of high interest and increasing importance in the business community and it is a topic that will be discussed throughout the book.

Dealing with ethical conflicts is an inescapable part of professional life for most people. An analytical framework can be helpful in understanding and resolving such conflicts.

Before You Go On

1. What is a conflict of interest in a business setting?
2. How would you define an ethical business culture?

SUMMARY OF LEARNING OBJECTIVES

1. **Identify the key financial decisions facing the financial manager of any business firm.**

   In running a business, the financial manager faces three basic decisions: (1) which productive assets the firm should buy (capital budgeting), (2) how the firm should finance the productive assets purchased (financing decision) and (3) how the firm should manage its day-to-day financial activities (working capital decisions). The financial manager should make these decisions in a way that maximises the current value of the firm's shares.

2. **Identify the basic forms of business organisation and review their respective strengths and weaknesses.**

   A business can organise in three basic ways: as a sole proprietorship, a partnership or a company (public or private). The owners of a firm select the form of organisation that they believe will best allow management to maximise the value of the firm. Most large firms elect to organise as public companies because of the ease of raising money; the major disadvantage is double taxation. Smaller companies tend to organise as sole proprietorships or partnerships. The advantages of these forms of organisation include ease of formation and taxation at the personal income tax rate. The major disadvantage is the owners' unlimited personal liability.

3. **Describe the typical organisation of the financial function in a large company.**

   In a large company, the financial manager generally has the rank of director and goes by the title of chief financial officer. The CFO reports directly to the firm's CEO. Positions reporting directly to the CFO generally include the treasurer, the risk manager, the chief accountant and the internal auditor. The audit committee of the board of directors is also important in the financial function. The committee hires the external auditor for the firm, and the internal auditor, external auditor and compliance officer all report to the audit committee.

4. **Explain why maximising the current value of the firm's shares is the appropriate goal for management.**

   The goal of the financial manager is to maximise the current value of the firm's shares. Maximising share value is an appropriate goal because it forces management to focus on decisions that will generate the greatest amount of wealth for shareholders. Since the value of a share (or any asset) is determined by its cash flows, management's decisions must consider the size of the cash flow (larger is better), the timing of the cash flow (sooner is better) and the riskiness of the cash flow (given equal returns, lower risk is better).

5. **Discuss how agency conflicts affect the goal of maximising shareholder value.**

   In most large companies, there is a significant degree of separation between management and ownership. As a result, shareholders have little control over corporate managers, and management may thus be tempted to pursue its own self-interest rather than maximising the wealth of the owners. The resulting conflicts give rise to agency costs. Ways of reducing agency costs include developing compensation agreements that link employee compensation to the firm's performance and having independent boards of directors monitor management.

6. **Explain why ethics is an appropriate topic in the study of managerial finance.**

   If we lived in a world without ethical norms, we would soon discover that it would be difficult to do business. As a practical matter, the law and market forces provide important incentives that foster ethical behaviour in the business community, but they are not enough to ensure ethical behaviour. An ethical culture is also needed. In an ethical culture, people have a set of moral principles – a moral compass – that helps them identify ethical issues and make ethical judgements without being told what to do.

SELF-STUDY PROBLEMS

1.1. Give an example of a financing decision and a capital budgeting decision.

1.2. What is the decision criterion for financial managers when selecting a capital project?

1.3. What are some ways to manage working capital?

1.4. Which one of the following characteristics does not pertain to companies?

a. can enter into contracts

b. can borrow money

c. are the easiest type of business to form

d. can be sued

e. can own shares in other companies.

1.5. What are typically the main components of an executive compensation package?

SOLUTIONS TO SELF-STUDY PROBLEMS

1.1. Financing decisions determine how a firm will raise capital. Examples of financing decisions would be securing a bank loan or selling debt in the public capital markets. Capital budgeting involves deciding which productive assets the firm invests in, such as buying a new plant or investing in a renovation of an existing facility.

1.2. Financial managers should select a capital project only if the value of the project's future cash flows exceeds the cost of the project. In other words, firms should only take on investments that will increase their value and thus increase the shareholders' wealth.

1.3. Working capital is the day-to-day management of a firm's short-term assets and liabilities. It can be managed through maintaining the optimal level of inventory, keeping track of all the receivables and payables, deciding to whom the firm should extend credit and making appropriate investments with excess cash.

1.4. The answer that does *not* pertain to companies is (c) are the easiest type of business to form.

1.5. The three main components of an executive compensation package are: base salary, bonus based on accounting performance and some compensation tied to the firm's share price.

CRITICAL THINKING QUESTIONS

1.1. Describe the cash flows between a firm and its stakeholders.

1.2. What are the three fundamental decisions the financial management team is concerned with, and how do they affect the firm's balance sheet?

1.3. What is the difference between shareholders and stakeholders?

1.4. Suppose that a group of accountants wants to start their own accounting company. What organisational form of business would they choose, and why?

1.5. What does double taxation in the corporate setting mean?

1.6. Explain why profit maximisation is not the best goal for a company. What is an appropriate goal?

1.7. In determining the price of a firm's shares, what are some of the external and internal factors that affect price? What is the difference between these two types of variables?

1.8. Identify the sources of agency costs. What are some ways a company can control these factors?

1.9. What is corporate governance, and what are its main effects on the role of the board of directors?

1.10. Give an example of a conflict of interest in a business setting other than the one involving the estate agent discussed in the text.

QUESTIONS AND PROBLEMS

1.1. Capital: What are the two basic sources of funds for all businesses?

1.2. Management role: What is working capital management?

1.3. Cash flows: Explain the difference between profitable and unprofitable firms.

1.4. Management role: What three major decisions are of most concern to financial managers?

1.5. Cash flows: What is the general decision rule for a firm considering undertaking a project? Give a real-life example.

1.6. Management role: What is capital structure, and why is it important to a company?

1.7. Management role: What are some of the working capital decisions that a financial manager faces?

1.8. Organisational form: What are the three basic forms of business organisation discussed in this chapter?

1.9. Organisational form: What are the advantages and disadvantages of a sole proprietorship (sole trader)?

1.10. Organisational form: What is a partnership, and what is the biggest disadvantage of this form of business organisation? How can this disadvantage be avoided?

1.11. Organisational form: Who are the owners of a company, and how is their ownership represented?

1.12. Organisational form: Explain what is meant by shareholders' limited liability.

1.13. Organisational form: What is double taxation?

1.14. Organisational form: What is the business organisation form preferred by most doctors, lawyers and accountants, and why?

1.15. Finance function: What is the most important governing body within a business organisation? What responsibilities does it have?

1.16. Finance function: Almost all public companies hire a qualified accounting firm to perform an independent audit of the financial statements. What exactly does an audit mean?

1.17. Firm's goal: What are some of the drawbacks to setting profit maximisation as the main goal of a company?

1.18. Firm's goal: What is the appropriate goal of financial managers? Can managers' decisions affect this goal in any way? If so, how?

1.19. Firm's goal: What are the major factors affecting the share price?

1.20. Agency conflicts: What is an agency relationship, and what is an agency conflict? How can agency conflicts be reduced in a company?

1.21. Firm's goal: What can happen if a firm is poorly managed and its share price falls substantially below its maximum?

1.22. Agency conflicts: What are some of the regulations that pertain to boards of directors that have been put in place to reduce agency conflicts?

1.23. Business ethics: How could business dishonesty and low integrity cause an economic downfall? Give an example.

1.24. Agency conflicts: What are some possible ways to resolve a conflict of interest?

1.25. Business ethics: What ethical conflict does insider trading present?

SAMPLE TEST PROBLEMS

1.1. Why is value maximisation superior to profit maximisation as a goal for the firm?

1.2. The major advantage of debt financing is:
   a. it allows a firm to use creditors' money
   b. interest payments are more predictable than dividend payments
   c. interest payments are not required when a firm is not doing well
   d. interest payments are tax deductible.

1.3. Identify three fundamental decisions that a financial manager has to make in running a firm.

1.4. What are agency costs? Explain.

1.5. Identify four of the seven mechanisms that align the goals of managers with those of shareholders.

ENDNOTES

1. From accounting, *current assets* are assets that will be converted into cash within a year and *current liabilities* are liabilities that must be paid within a year.

2. In some countries, such as the United Kingdom, companies are subject to an imputation tax system where dividends include a tax credit that can be set against investors' personal tax liability, thereby reducing in full or in part the effects of the double taxation of dividends from the classical system of corporate taxation.

3. Owners of companies are issued with ownership rights that represent their investment in the capital of the company and which are variously known as ordinary shares or – in the United States – as common stock. We will use the term shares and shareholder for these ownership rights, which are also simply referred to as equity.

4. The distinction between public companies and private companies is a common feature of corporate law throughout Europe. The UK, for instance has public limited company (PLC) and limited company (Ltd), Denmark has Aktieselskab (A/S) for large companies and Anpartsselskab (ApS) for private companies, while France has Société anonyme (SA) for large companies and Société à responsabilité limitée (SàRL) for smaller limited liability companies.

5. This component, which may include executive share options, will increase and decrease with the share price.

6. Non-quantifiable costs of prosecution for crimes are the perpetrators' personal embarrassment and the embarrassment of their families and the effect it may have on their lives. On average, the overall cost of such prosecutions is higher even than that suggested by the labour market argument.

7. The Organisation of Economic Cooperation and Development (OECD) has been at the forefront of developing an internationally accepted set of corporate governance guidelines.

8. The golden rule or ethic of reciprocity appears in a number of contexts. A well-known version in the Gospel of Matthew states: 'In everything do to others as you would have them do to you'. A less noble version you occasionally hear in business is: 'He who has the gold makes the rules'.

9. In economics, *transparency* refers to openness and access to information.

PART 2

FOUNDATIONS

CHAPTER

2

The Financial Environment and the Level of Interest Rates

In this Chapter:

The Financial System

Direct Financing

Types of Financial Markets

The Stock Market

Financial Institutions and Indirect Financing

The Determinants of Interest Rate Levels

LEARNING OBJECTIVES

1. Discuss the primary role of the financial system in the economy and describe the two basic ways in which fund transfers take place.

2. Discuss direct financing and the important role that investment banks play in this process.

3. Describe the primary and secondary markets and explain why secondary markets are so important to businesses.

4. Explain why money markets are important financial markets for large companies.

5. Discuss the most important stock market exchanges and indexes.

6. Explain how financial institutions serve consumers and small businesses that are unable to participate in the direct financial markets and describe how companies use the financial system.

7. Explain how the real rate of interest is determined in the economy, differentiate between the real rate and the nominal rate of interest, and be able to compute the nominal or real rate of interest.

The introduction of the euro as a common currency across much of Europe, following the decision by the European Union (EU) to pursue European Monetary Union, also saw the creation of a major new supranational institution, the European Central Bank (ECB). Why did the introduction of the euro require a major change in the way EC countries managed their currencies? With one currency serving many countries, it is necessary to have a central bank that manages liquidity and short-term interest

rates across the single-currency eurozone. The Eurosystem that was created through monetary union comprises the national central banks of member countries and the ECB. As the supranational institution tasked with setting monetary policy across the euro area, the ECB has a Governing Council and an Executive Board. The Governing Council is the prime decision-making body that sets monetary policy. In pursuit of this goal, the central bank manages liquidity and short-term interest rates. As its most senior officer, Jean-Claude Trichet, the current President of the ECB since October 2003, is often in the news. The reason is that decisions made by the Governing Council concerning monetary policy affect interest rates across Europe and the exchange rate of the euro against other currencies.

The primary objective of the Eurosystem is to maintain price stability and as a second objective to support the general economic policies of the EU. As the coordinating institution for the eurozone the ECB sets a target short-term interest rate at which credit institutions lend to each other by providing or removing money from the system. It does this primarily through refinancing activities that involve buying and selling eligible securities with credit institutions.[1] Buying securities increases the amount of money or liquidity held by credit institutions and puts downward pressure on interest rates. Over time, this can lead to increases in economic activity, along with higher inflation. On the other hand, selling securities drains liquidity from the system and puts upward pressure on short-term interest rates. This can lead to a lower level of economic activity and lower inflation.

Given the power of the ECB to affect short-term interest rates and how this will affect all the economies in the eurozone, it is not surprising that the daily actions to add or drain liquidity from the system are closely watched and any official or unofficial pronouncements by staff carefully scrutinised. The ECB makes a concerted effort to be transparent in its policy. Frequent speeches by the President and other members of the Governing Council lay out their policy stance and views on developments. In addition, the ECB adheres to a stated inflation target of 2%, changing interest rates as necessary to meet this goal. Because of this, decisions to change the level of short-term interest rates are generally well anticipated, but very important nonetheless. The rate decision has an enormous influence on financial markets. The interest rate the ECB sets is essentially the return investors receive while holding euros, and changes in interest rates affect the exchange rate of the euro against other currencies.

As decisions to change the level of short-term interest rates are usually well anticipated, the actual decision does not tend to affect the market. However, if the ECB does change rates it will hold a press conference where some rationale for the decision is offered. Market participants pay close attention to the press conference, hoping to get insights into the likelihood of further changes in interest rates. Often, the language used provides important signals as to how the ECB feels about inflation and the economic outlook for the eurozone. If the ECB President's language is pessimistic about the inflation outlook, this will be taken as a sign for likely future interest rate increases. On the other hand, if the ECB President believes inflation is under control, the market would view a future interest rate increase as unlikely.

All countries have central banks. In Europe, the major ones outside the eurozone are the Bank of England (United Kingdom), the Riksbank (Sweden) and Narodowy Bank Polski (Poland). Outside Europe, the principal ones are the Federal Reserve (United States), the Bank of Japan and the People's Bank of China. Given the importance of the US dollar as an international currency, the chairman of the Federal Reserve, Ben Bernanke, is an important voice on monetary matters.

Furthermore, while the function of central banks is the same everywhere, although there may be some institutional differences, they may have somewhat different policy objectives. For instance, the ECB has price stability as its primary objective and this is defined in precise quantitative terms. On the other hand, the Federal Reserve has multiple objectives – to promote employment, to ensure stable prices and moderate long-term interest rates. Consequently, given the same situation, they may act somewhat differently. Therefore, to understand interest rate formation in different countries, it is important to know how economic developments affect their policy objectives.

CHAPTER PREVIEW

Chapter 1 identified three kinds of decisions that financial managers make: *capital budgeting decisions*, which concern the purchase of capital assets; *financing decisions*, which concern how assets will be paid for; and *working capital management decisions*, which concern day-to-day financial matters. Making sound decisions in any of these areas requires knowledge of financial markets and services.

In making capital budgeting decisions, financial managers should select projects whose cash flows increase the value of the firm. The financial models used to evaluate these projects require an understanding of financial markets and interest rates. In making financing decisions, financial managers naturally want to obtain capital at the lowest possible cost, which means that they need to understand how financial markets work and what financing alternatives are available. Finally, working capital management is concerned with whether a firm has enough money to pay its bills and how it invests its spare cash to earn interest. Making decisions in these areas requires knowledge of money markets and financial services.

Clearly, then, financial managers need a working knowledge of financial markets and financial institutions. This chapter provides a quick overview of the financial sector and the services it provides to businesses. We will revisit many of the topics covered here in later chapters.

We begin the chapter by looking at how the financial system facilitates the transfer of money from those who have it to those who need it. Then we describe direct financing, through which large business firms finance themselves by issuing debt and equity, and the important role that investment banks play in the process. Next we explain why smaller firms and consumers must finance themselves indirectly by borrowing from financial institutions such as commercial banks. We then examine other types of services that financial institutions provide to large and small businesses. Finally, we discuss the factors that determine the general level of interest rates in the economy and explain why interest rates vary over the business cycle.

THE FINANCIAL SYSTEM

Learning Objective 1
Discuss the primary role of the financial system in the economy and describe the two basic ways in which fund transfers take place.

The financial system consists of financial markets and financial institutions. *Financial market* is a general term that includes a number of different types of markets for the creation and exchange of financial assets, such as shares and bonds. *Financial institutions* are firms such as commercial banks, credit unions, insurance companies, pension funds and finance companies that provide financial services to the economy. The distinguishing feature of financial institutions is that they invest their funds in financial assets, such as business loans, shares and bonds, rather than real assets, such as plant and equipment.

The critical role of the financial system in the economy is to gather money from people and businesses with surplus funds to invest and channel money to those who need it. Businesses need money to invest in new productive assets to expand their operations and increase the firm's cash flow, which should increase the value of the firm. Consumers, too, need money, which they use to purchase things such as apartments, cars and boats – or to pay to go to university. Some of the participants in the financial system are well-known brand names, such as the Deutsche Börse (Germany), the London Stock Exchange (United Kingdom), Credit Suisse (Switzerland), Deutsche Bank (Germany), Banco Santander (Spain), Société Generale (France), Banca Monte dei Paschi di Siena (Italy), Handelsbanken (Sweden) and similar institutions in other countries. Others are lesser-known but important financial institutions, such as Eurex, the pan-European stock exchange, and LCH Clearnet, the European clearing house.

A well-developed financial system is critical for the operation of a complex industrial economy. Highly industrialised countries cannot function without a competitive and sound financial system that efficiently gathers money and channels it into the best investment opportunities. Let us look at a simple example to illustrate how the financial system channels money to businesses.

The Financial System at Work

Suppose you are a student attending university. At the beginning of the academic year, you receive a €12 000 student loan to help pay your expenses for the year, but you need only €7000 for the first semester. You wisely decide to invest the remaining €5000 to earn some interest income. After shopping at several banks near the university, you decide that the best deal is a special student deposit that matures in three months and pays 3% interest.

The bank pools your money with funds from other depositors, buyers of its certificates of deposit (CDs), and uses this money to make business and consumer loans.[2] In this case, the bank makes a loan to the pizza restaurant near the university: €130 000 for five years at a 7% interest rate. The bank decides to make the loan because of the pizza restaurant's sound credit rating, and because it expects the restaurant to generate enough cash flows to repay the loan with interest. The pizza restaurant owner wants the money to invest in additional earning assets to earn greater profits (cash flows) and thereby increase the value of the firm. During the same week, the bank makes loans to other businesses and, at the same time, rejects a number of loan requests because the borrowers have poor credit ratings or the proposed projects have low rates of return.

From this example, we can draw some important inferences about financial systems:

- If the financial system is *competitive*, the interest rate the bank pays on deposits will be at or near the highest rate that you can earn on a deposit of similar maturity and risk. At the same time, the pizza restaurant and other businesses will have borrowed at or near the lowest possible interest cost, given their risk class. Competition among banks for deposits will drive deposit rates up and loan rates down.
- The bank gathers money from you and other consumers in small amounts, aggregates it and then makes loans in much larger amounts. Saving by consumers in small amounts is the origin of

much of the money that funds large business loans in the economy.

- An important function of the financial system is to direct money to the best investment opportunities in the economy. If the financial system works properly, only business projects with high rates of return and good credit are financed. Those with low rates of return or poor credit will be rejected. Thus, financial systems contribute to higher production and efficiency in the overall economy.

- Finally, note that the bank has earned a tidy profit from the deal. The bank has borrowed money at 3% by taking deposits from consumers and has lent money to the pizza restaurant and other businesses at 7%. Thus, the bank's gross profit is 4% (7% – 3%), which is the difference between the bank's lending and borrowing rates. Banks earn much of their profits from the spread between the lending and borrowing rates.

How Funds Flow Through the Financial System

We have seen that the financial system plays a critical role in the economy. The system moves money from *lender-savers* (whose income exceeds their spending) to *borrower-spenders* (whose spending exceeds their income), as shown schematically in Exhibit 2.1.[3] The largest lender-savers in the economy are households, but some businesses and many state and local governments at times have excess funds to lend to those who need money. The largest

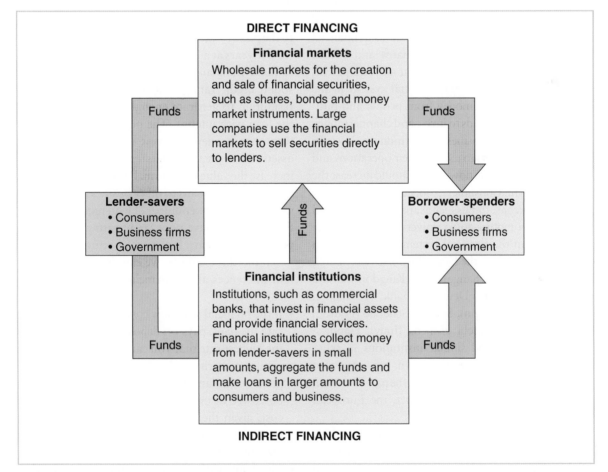

Exhibit 2.1: **The Flow of Funds Through the Financial System** The role of the financial system is to gather money from people and businesses with surplus funds and channel it of those who need it. Money flows through the financial system in two basic ways: *directly*, through wholesale financial markets, as shown in the top route of the diagram, and *indirectly*, through financial institutions, as shown in the bottom route.

borrower-spenders in the economy are businesses, followed by the central government.

The arrows in Exhibit 2.1 show that there are two basic mechanisms by which funds flow through the financial system: (1) funds can flow *directly* through financial markets (the route at the top of the diagram) and (2) funds can flow *indirectly* through financial institutions (the route at the bottom of the diagram). In the following sections, we look more closely at the direct flow of funds and at the financial markets. After that, we discuss financial institutions and the indirect flow of funds.

Before You Go On

1. What essential economic role does the financial system play in the economy?
2. What are the two basic ways in which funds flow through the financial system from lender-savers to borrower-spenders?

DIRECT FINANCING

Learning Objective 2

Discuss direct financing and the important role that investment banks play in this process.

In this section we turn our attention to direct financing, in which funds flow directly through financial markets. In direct transactions, the lender-savers and the borrower-spenders deal 'directly' with one another; borrower-spenders sell securities, such as shares and bonds, to lender-savers in exchange for money. These securities represent claims on the borrowers' future income or assets. A number of different interchangeable terms are used to refer to securities, including *financial instruments* and *financial claims.*

The financial markets where direct transactions take place are wholesale markets with large minimum sizes (the typical minimum transaction size

would be €1 million – or the equivalent in other currencies). For most business firms, these markets provide funds at the lowest possible cost. The major buyers and sellers of securities in the direct financial markets are commercial banks; other financial institutions, such as insurance companies and business finance companies; large companies; the central government; hedge funds; and some wealthy individuals. It is important to note that financial institutions are major buyers of securities in the direct financial markets. For example, insurance companies buy large quantities of corporate bonds and shares for their investment portfolios. In Exhibit 2.1 the arrow leading from financial institutions to financial markets depicts this flow.

Although few individuals participate in direct financial markets, individuals can gain access to many of the financial products produced in these markets through retail channels at investment banking firms or financial institutions such as commercial banks (the lower route in Exhibit 2.1). For example, individuals can buy or sell shares and bonds in small amounts via a stockbroker or a bank that offers a securities dealing service. We discuss indirect financing through financial institutions later in this chapter.

A Direct Market Transaction

Let us look at a typical direct market transaction. When managers decide to engage in a direct market transaction, they often have a specific capital project in mind that needs financing, such as building a new manufacturing facility. Suppose that L'Oreal, the French cosmetics company, needs €200 million to build a new facility and decides to fund it by selling long-term bonds with a 15-year maturity. Say that L'Oreal contacts a group of insurance companies, which express an interest in buying the bonds. The insurance companies will buy L'Oreal's bonds only after determining that they are priced fairly for their level of risk. L'Oreal will sell its bonds to the insurance companies only after checking the market for corporate debt to be sure the investors are offering a competitive price.

If L'Oreal and the insurance companies strike a deal, the flow of funds between them will be as shown below:

L'Oreal sells its bonds to the insurance group for €200 million and gets the use of the money for 15 years. For L'Oreal, the bonds are a liability and it pays the bondholders interest for use of the money. For the insurance companies, the bonds are assets that earn interest.

Investment Banks and Direct Financing

Two important players that deliver critical services to firms transacting in the direct financial markets are investment banks and money centre banks. **Investment banks** specialise in helping companies sell new debt or equity, although they also provide other services, such as the broker and dealer services that are discussed later. **Money centre banks** are large commercial banks located in major financial centres. Investment banks and money centre banks compete against each other to obtain mandates to raise new finance. When investment bankers help firms bring new debt or equity securities to market, they perform three tasks: origination, underwriting and distribution.

> ### Investment banks
>
> firms that underwrite new security issues and provide broker-dealer services

> ### Money centre banks
>
> large commercial banks that transact in both the national and international financial markets

> ### WEB
>
> To get a better idea of all the lines of business in which large investment banking firms engage, go to BNP Paribas' homepage at: www.bnpparibas.com.

Origination

Origination is the process of preparing a security issue for sale. During the origination phase, the investment banker may help the client company determine the feasibility of the project being funded and the amount of capital that needs to be raised. Once this is done, the investment banker helps secure a credit rating, if needed, determines the sale date, obtains legal clearances to sell the securities and gets the securities printed. If securities are to be sold in the public markets, the issuer must also comply with the relevant securities laws. In most countries, securities sold in the private markets are subject to less stringent regulations than those offered in the public markets.

Underwriting

Underwriting is the process by which the investment banker helps the company sell its new security issue. In the most common type of underwriting arrangement, called *firm-commitment underwriting*, the investment banker assumes the risk of buying the new securities from the issuing company and reselling them to investors. Note that the investment banker guarantees to buy the entire security issue from the company at a fixed price and then re-offer it to investors. The guaranteed price is important to the issuing company. The company likely needs a certain amount of money to pay for a particular project or to fund operations, and getting anything less than this amount will pose a serious problem. As you would expect, financial managers almost always prefer to have their new security issues underwritten on a firm-commitment basis.[4]

Once the investment bankers buy the securities from the issuer, they immediately offer to resell individual securities to institutional investors and the public at a specified offering price. The underwriters hope to be able to sell the offering at the market-clearing price, which is the price that will allow the entire security issue to be sold during the offering period. Underwriting involves considerable risk because it is difficult to estimate the price that will clear the market. The risk is that the investment bank may eventually have to sell the securities at a price below the guaranteed price that it paid to the issuing company. If this happens, the investment bank suffers a financial loss.

The investment banker's compensation is known as the *underwriting spread*. It is the difference between the price the investment banker pays for the security issue and the offering price. The underwriting spread is one of the costs to the firm of selling new securities issues. This spread is often formally part of the offer document, where separate fees are indicated for underwriting and selling bonds.

Distribution

Distribution is the process of marketing and reselling the securities to investors. Because security prices can take large, unexpected swings, a quick resale of all the securities is important. To that end, the underwriters often form large sales syndicates, consisting of a number of different investment banking firms, to sell the securities. If the securities are not sold within a few days, the syndicate is disbanded and the individual syndicate members sell the unsold securities at whatever price they can get.

Underwriter's Compensation

Problem: Marqués de Riscal SA, the Spanish wine producer, needs to raise €15 million for expansion and decides to issue long-term bonds. The financial manager hires an investment banking firm to help design the bond issue and underwrite it. The issue consists of 1500 bonds worth €10 000 each and the investment banker agrees to purchase the entire issue for €15 million. The investment banker then resells the bonds to individual investors at the offering price. The sale totals €15.3 million. What is the underwriter's compensation?

Approach: The underwriter's compensation is the underwriting spread, which is the difference between the price at which the bonds were resold to individual investors and the price the underwriter paid for the issue. The underwriting spread per bond is then calculated by dividing the total spread by the number of bonds that are issued.

Solution:

Underwriting spread:
€15 300 000 – €15 000 000 = €300 000
Underwriting spread per bond:
€300 000/1500 = €200

Notice that the issuer gets a cheque from the underwriter for €15.0 million regardless of the price at which the bonds are resold because of the guarantee.

Before You Go On

1. Why is it difficult for individuals to participate in direct financial markets?
2. Why might a firm prefer to have a security issue underwritten by an investment banking firm?

TYPES OF FINANCIAL MARKETS

Learning Objective 3

Describe the primary and secondary markets and explain why secondary markets are so important to businesses.

We have seen that direct flows of funds occur in financial markets. However, as already mentioned, *financial market* is a very general term. A complex industrial economy includes many different types of financial markets and not all of them are involved in direct financing. Next, we examine some of the more important ways to classify financial markets. Note that these classifications overlap to a large extent. Thus, for example, a stock exchange such as Eurex fits into several different categories.

Primary and Secondary Markets

A **primary market** is any market where companies sell new security issues (debt or equity). For example, Fiat, the Italian automotive group, needs to raise €500 million for business expansion and decides to raise the money through the sale of ordinary shares. The company will sell the new equity issue in the primary market for equity – probably with the help of an underwriter, as discussed earlier. The primary markets are not well known to the general public because they are wholesale markets and the sales take place outside public view.

> **Primary market**
>
> a financial market in which new security issues are sold by companies directly to investors

A **secondary market** is any market where owners of outstanding securities can sell them to other investors. Secondary markets are like used-car markets in that they allow investors to buy or sell second-hand, or previously owned, securities for cash. These markets are important because they enable investors to buy and sell securities as frequently as they want. As you might expect, investors are willing to pay higher prices for securities that have active secondary markets. Secondary markets are important to companies as well because investors are willing to pay higher prices for securities in primary markets if the securities have active secondary markets. Thus, companies whose securities have active secondary markets enjoy lower funding costs than similar firms whose securities do not have active secondary markets.

> **Secondary market**
>
> a financial market in which the owners of outstanding securities can sell them to other investors

Marketability Versus Liquidity

An important characteristic of a security to investors is its marketability. **Marketability** is the ease with which a security can be sold and converted into cash. A security's marketability depends in part on the costs of trading and searching for information, so-called *transaction costs*. The lower the transaction costs, the greater a security's marketability. Because secondary markets make it easier to trade securities, their presence increases a security's marketability.

> **Marketability**
>
> the ease with which a security can be sold and converted into cash

A term closely related to marketability is **liquidity**. Liquidity is the ability to convert an asset into cash quickly without loss of value. The terms *marketability* and *liquidity* are often used interchangeably, but they are different. Liquidity implies that when the security is sold, its value will be preserved; marketability does not carry this implication.

> **Liquidity**
>
> the ability to convert an asset into cash quickly without loss of value

Brokers Versus Dealers

Two types of market specialists facilitate transactions in secondary markets. **Brokers** are market specialists who bring buyers and sellers together when a sale takes place. They execute the transaction for their client and are compensated for their services with a commission fee. They bear no risk of ownership of the securities during the transactions; their only service is that of 'matchmaker'.

Dealers, in contrast, 'make markets' for securities and do bear risk. They make a market for a security by buying and selling from an inventory of securities they own. Dealers make their profit, just as retail merchants do, by selling securities at a price above what they paid for it. The risk that dealers bear is *price risk*, which is the risk that they will sell a security for less than what they paid for it.

> **Brokers**
>
> market specialists who bring buyers and sellers together, usually for a commission

> **Dealers**
>
> market specialists who 'make markets' for securities by buying and selling from their own inventories

Exchanges and Over-the-Counter Markets

Financial markets can be classified as either 'organised' markets (more commonly called exchanges) or over-the-counter markets. Traditional exchanges, such as the United Kingdom's London Stock Exchange (LSE), provide a physical meeting place and communication facilities for members to buy and sell securities or other assets (such as commodities) under a specific set of rules and regulations. Members are individuals who represent securities firms as well as people who trade for their own accounts. Only members can use the exchange.

Securities not listed on an exchange are bought and sold in the over-the-counter (OTC) market. The OTC market differs from organised exchanges in that the 'market' has no central trading location. Instead, investors can execute OTC transactions by visiting or telephoning an OTC dealer or by using a computer-based electronic trading system linked to the OTC dealer. Traditionally, shares traded over the counter have been those of small and relatively unknown firms, most of which would not qualify to be listed on a major exchange. However, electronic trading has become much more important in recent years, as you will see later in the chapter, and has increased the opportunities for trading in the securities of smaller firms.

Money and Capital Markets

Money markets are global markets where short-term debt instruments (with maturities of less than one year) are sold. Money markets are wholesale markets in which the minimum transaction is approximately €1 million and transactions of €10 million or €100 million are not uncommon. Money market instruments are lower in risk than other securities because of their high liquidity and low default risk. In fact, the term '*money*' *market* is used because these instruments are close substitutes for cash. The most important and largest money markets are in New York City, London and Tokyo. Exhibit 2.2 provides an indication of the outstanding amounts by type of issuer for the eurozone.

> **Money markets**
>
> markets where short-term financial instruments are traded

This exhibit shows the size of the European market for each of the most important money market and capital market issuers. Notice that governments and then monetary financial institutions, which consist mainly of banks, make up the bulk of the outstanding issuance. Non-financial corporate issues are for large, well-established companies that can access the money markets and capital markets directly. Small and medium-sized

EXHIBIT 2.2

EUROZONE MONEY MARKET AND CAPITAL MARKET OUTSTANDING AMOUNTS BY CATEGORY (€ BILLIONS)

Money markets

Central governments	€681
Other general governments	21
Non-financial corporations	73
Monetary financial institutions	734
Financial corporations (other than MFIs)	94
	€1 603

Capital markets	Total	Of which fixed rate	Fixed rate percentage of total
Central governments	€5 089	4 625	90.9%
Other general governments	397	285	71.8%
Non-financial corporations	789	650	82.4%
Monetary financial institutions[a]	4 731	2 668	56.4%
Financial corporations (other than MFIs)	3 163	1 087	34.4%
	€14 169	€9 315	65.7%

ECB latest issue statistics; June 2010

[a]Monetary Financial Institutions (MFIs) are central banks, resident credit institutions as defined in Community law, and other resident financial institutions whose business is to receive deposits and/or close substitutes for deposits from entities other than MFIs and, for their own account (at least in economic terms), to grant credits and/or make investments in securities.
Source: European Central Bank.

enterprises have no direct access to the public markets.

Large companies use money markets to adjust their liquidity positions. Liquidity, as mentioned, is the ability to convert an asset into cash quickly without loss of value. Liquidity problems arise because companies' cash receipts and expenditures are rarely perfectly synchronised. To manage liquidity, a firm can invest idle cash in money market instruments; then, if the firm has a temporary cash shortfall, it can raise cash overnight by selling money market instruments from its portfolio.

Recall from Chapter 1 that capital markets are global markets where the intermediate-term and long-term debt and the shares of companies are traded. In these markets, large firms finance capital assets such as plant and equipment. The stock exchanges situated in Frankfurt (Deutsche Börse), Stockholm (Stockholmsbörsen), as well as those in London, Paris, Milan, Lisbon, New York, Tokyo and elsewhere, are all capital markets. Compared with money market instruments, capital market instruments are less marketable, carry more default risk and have longer maturities.

Public and Private Markets

Public markets are organised financial markets where the general public buys and sells securities through their stockbrokers. The Madrid Stock Exchange, for example, is a public market. These are regulated markets and are recognised investment exchanges. Each country has a financial regulator, although for European Union countries, there is a common regulatory framework called the Markets in Financial Instruments Directive (MiFID) issued by the European Commission in consultation with European Union countries. This sets common standards for the oversight of the securities industry and regulates all primary and secondary markets in which securities are traded. Most companies want access to the public markets because they are wholesale markets where issuers can sell their securities at the lowest possible funding cost. The downside for companies selling in the public markets is the cost of complying with the listing requirements.

> ### Public markets
>
> financial markets where securities are sold to the general public

In contrast to the public market, the *private market* involves direct transactions between two parties. Transactions in the private market are often called **private placements**. In the private market, a company contacts investors directly and negotiates a deal to sell them all or part of a security issue. Larger firms may be equipped to handle these transactions themselves. Smaller firms are more likely to use the services of an investment bank, which will help locate investors, help negotiate the deal and handle the legal aspects of the transaction. Major advantages of a private placement are the speed at which funds can be raised and low transaction costs. Downsides are that privately placed securities cannot legally be sold in the public markets because they do not comply with listing requirements and the amounts that can be raised tend to be smaller.

> ### Private placement
>
> the sale of a security directly to an investor, such as an insurance company

Futures and Options Markets

Markets also exist for trading in futures and options. There are a number of large pan-European exchanges in Europe, such as Eurex and Euronext-NYSE Liffe, as well as a number of smaller exchanges that specialise in particular products, such as MEFF in Spain, the London Metal Exchange (commodities) or the International Petroleum Exchange (energy products).

Futures and options are often called *derivative securities* because they derive their value from some underlying asset. Futures contracts are contracts for the future delivery of such assets as securities, foreign currencies, interest cash flows or commodities. Companies use these contracts to reduce (hedge) risk exposure caused by fluctuation in things such as foreign exchange rates or commodity prices. We discuss this use of futures contracts further in Chapter 20.

Options contracts call for one party (the option writer) to perform a specific act if called upon to do so by the option buyer or owner. Options contracts, like futures contracts, can be used to hedge risk in situations where the firm faces risk from price fluctuations. Options are discussed in more detail in Chapter 20.

> ### Before You Go On
>
> 1. What is the difference between primary and secondary markets?
> 2. How and why do large business firms use money markets?
> 3. What are capital markets and why are they important to companies?

THE STOCK MARKET

> ### Learning Objective 4
>
> Explain why money markets are important financial markets for large companies.

We noted earlier that secondary markets are important to companies because companies whose securities trade in active secondary markets enjoy lower funding costs than firms whose securities do not. Here, we discuss a particularly important secondary market: the large, public market in which company shares are bought and sold.

Recall that a traditional securities exchange is an organised market that provides a physical meeting place and communication facilities for members to buy and sell securities under a specific set of rules and regulations. Almost every country has a stock exchange and sometimes more than one, but with the increasing internationalisation of finance, there have been a number of cross-country amalgamations. An exchange will list the ordinary shares (common stock) and preference shares (preferred stocks) of major companies, as well as their bonds, and possibly other types of securities as well. It may also trade derivatives on these securities. For example, the OMX (Finland) – which is part of the OM group that includes the Stockholm (Sweden), Tallin (Estonia) and Riga (Latvia) stock exchanges – trades shares in large Finnish companies such as Nokia (the mobile phone maker) and Wartsila (the shipbuilder), as well as derivative instruments.

Securities that are traded on an exchange are said to be *listed* on that exchange. For a firm's shares to be listed on an exchange, the firm must pay a fee and meet the exchange's requirements for membership. Because of the need to protect investors, exchanges set minimum listing requirements that include a minimum firm size, total share value, a minimum number of shares outstanding and a minimum number of shareholders. As a result, listed companies tend to be large, well-established firms.

> **WEB**
>
> Learn more about the major exchanges across the world by visiting: http://www.tdd.lt/slnews/Stock_Exchanges/ Stock.Exchanges.html.

Second Markets and Multilateral Trading Facilities

To service the needs of smaller companies that do not meet the stringent criteria for listing that exchanges demand, there has been a proliferation of second-tier markets. The London Stock Exchange operates a special subsidiary market called the Alternative Investment Market (AIM), which provides lower-cost listings for growth companies that do not meet the criteria for listing on the main market. The Deutsche Börse has a similar facility in its 'Entry Standard', which forms part of its Open Market (regulated unofficial market) section, and there is the Nouveau Marché operated by Euronext-NYSE Liffe.

Multilateral trading facilities (MTFs) provide another means for securities to be traded and allow for order matching between buyers and sellers. A key attraction of MTFs for investors is that they help reduce transaction costs. The third largest share-trading platform in Europe by volume is Chi-X, a pan-European MTF. However, a number of new ventures such as Equiduct, introduced by the Berlin Stock Exchange (Germany), have struggled to establish a pan-European trading platform for smaller companies.

Stock Market Indices

Stock market indices are used to measure the performance of the stock market – whether share prices on average are moving up or down. The indices are watched closely, not only to track economic activity but also to measure the performance of specific types of firms. Exhibit 2.3 shows a selection of indices for a number of countries as well as broader international indices and some specialised ones.

Stock market indices are designed to indicate the performance of a particular market, a sector of the overall market or a particular type of investment. In the table, we have stock indices that reflect the behaviour of the stock market in particular countries, such as the CAC-40 for France, the Dax for Germany, the AEX for the Netherlands, the FTSE 100 for the UK, the S&P 500 for the USA or the Hang Seng for China. Closely followed international indices are the MSCI EAFE index that combines the performance of companies in Europe, Australia and the Far East. The Amex Oil index and the FTSE4Good represent specialised indices,

EXHIBIT 2.3

SELECTED NATIONAL, INTERNATIONAL AND SECTOR INDICES

Americas	Europe	Africa/Asia/Pacific
United States:	ATX (Austria)	All Ordinaries (Australia)
DJIA	Bel-20 (Belgium)	Hang Seng (China)
S&P 500	CAC-40 (France)	CASE 30 (Eqypt)
Wiltshire 5000	DAX (Germany)	BSE Sensex (India)
NYSE Composite	Athex 20 (Greece)	Nikkei 225 (Japan)
Nasdaq Composite	BUX (Hungary)	ASE Weighted (Jordan)
	MIBTEL (Italy)	Straits Times (Singapore)
TSE 300 (Canada)	AEX (Netherlands)	ALSI (South Africa)
Merval (Argentina)	OSE All share (Norway)	
Bovespa (Brazil)	WIG (Poland)	
IPC (Mexico)	MICEX (Russia)	
	Madrid General (Spain)	
	SSMI (Switzerland)	
	FTSE 100 (United Kingdom)	

International	Sector and others
MSCI (World)	Amex Oil Index (international energy companies)
MSCI EAFE (Europe, Australia & Far East)	The Cleantech Index (clean technology companies)
Dow Jones Euro Stoxx 50 (Europe)	FTSE4Good (ethical investing)
Euronext 100 (Europe)	
S&P Europe 350 (Europe)	

respectively tracking the performance of oil companies and companies that are environmentally friendly. Furthermore, many of the indices in the table have sub-indices that are made up of elements of the major index.

WEB

The world stock exchanges website has information on all the major stock indices, at: http://www.world-stock-exchanges.net/indices.html.

Indices vary as to their purpose. The oldest continuously calculated stock index, the Dow Jones Industrial Average (DJIA), dates from 1896 and is a 'price' index in that it measures how the prices of its constituents change between each computation. Most indices are 'value' indices that track how the portfolio of shares that make up the index changes in value over time. Typical examples of such indices are those that cover the French market CAC-40, made up of the leading 40 French listed companies or the United Kingdom's FTSE 100 index of the top 100 companies by market value. Some indices, such as the German market's DAX (*Deutscher Aktien IndeX*) include the effect of dividends paid by companies and are 'total return' indices. Exhibit 2.3 also shows a few specialised indices such as the Amex Oil index that tracks the performance of the major international energy companies or the FTSE4Good set of indices that measure the performance of companies that meet globally recognised corporate responsibility standards.

Before You Go On

1. In what way is a value index different from a return index?
2. Why do you think there are different indices for the same market? (For instance, Exhibit 2.3 lists five for the United States, but there are a lot more that could have been included; a similar situation exists in other countries – Germany has five major ones.)

FINANCIAL INSTITUTIONS AND INDIRECT FINANCING

Learning Objective 5

Discuss the most important stock market exchanges and indexes.

As we mentioned earlier, many business firms are too small to sell their debt or equity directly to investors. They have neither the expert knowledge nor the money to transact in wholesale markets. When these companies need funds for capital investments or for liquidity adjustments, their only choice may be to borrow in the *indirect* market from a financial institution. These financial institutions act as intermediaries, converting financial securities with one set of characteristics into securities with another set of characteristics. This process is called **financial intermediation**. The hallmark of indirect financing is that a financial institution – an intermediary – stands between the lender-saver and the borrower-spender. This route is shown at the bottom of Exhibit 2.1.

Financial intermediation

conversion of securities with one set of characteristics into securities with another set of characteristics

Indirect Market Transactions

We worked through an example of indirect financing at the beginning of the chapter. In that situation, a college student had €5000 to invest for three months. The bank took a three-month deposit from the student for €5000, pooled this €5000 with the proceeds from other deposits and used the money to make small business loans, one of which was a €130 000 loan to our pizza restaurant owner. Below is a schematic diagram of that transaction.

The bank raises money by selling services such as current accounts, savings accounts and consumer certificates of deposit and then uses the money to make loans to businesses or consumers.

On a larger scale, insurance companies provide much of the long-term financing in the economy through the indirect credit market. These companies invest heavily in corporate bonds and equity securities using funds they receive when they sell insurance policies to individuals and businesses. The schematic diagram for intermediation by an insurance company is as follows:

Notice an important difference between the indirect and direct financial markets. In the direct market, as securities flow between lender-savers and borrower-spenders, the form of the securities remains unchanged. In the indirect market, however, as securities flow between lender-savers and borrower-spenders, they are repackaged, and their form is changed. In the example above, money from the sale of insurance policies becomes investments in corporate debt or equity. By repackaging securities, financial intermediaries tailor-make a wide range of financial products and services that meet the needs of consumers, small businesses and large companies. Their products and services are particularly important for smaller businesses that do not have access to direct financial markets.

Somewhat surprisingly, the indirect markets are a much larger and more important source of financing to businesses than the more newsworthy direct financial markets. This is the case even in countries with highly developed direct markets. In those countries with smaller traded capital markets, indirect markets provide most of the sources of finance to the corporate sector.

Financial Institutions and their Services

We have briefly discussed the role of financial institutions as intermediaries in the indirect financial market. Next, we look at various types of financial institutions and the services they provide to small businesses as well as large companies. We discuss only those financial institutions that provide a significant amount of services to businesses.

Commercial Banks

Commercial banks are the most prominent and largest financial intermediaries in the economy and offer the widest range of financial services to businesses. Nearly every business, small or large, has a significant relationship with a commercial bank – usually a clearing or transaction account and some type of credit or loan arrangement.[5] For businesses, the most common type of bank loan is a line of credit (often called revolving credit), which works much like a credit card. A line of credit is a commitment by the bank to lend a firm an amount up to a predetermined limit, which can be used as needed. Banks also make term loans, which are fixed-rate loans with a maturity of one year to ten years. In addition, banks do a significant amount of equipment lease financing. A lease is a contract that gives a business the right to use an asset, such as a truck or a computer mainframe, for a period of time in exchange for payments.

General and Life Insurance Companies

Two types of insurance companies are important in the financial markets: (1) general insurance companies, which sell protection against loss of property from fire, theft, accidents and other predictable causes; and (2) life insurance companies. The cash flows for both types of companies are fairly predictable. As a result, they are able to provide funding to companies through the purchase of bonds and shares in the direct credit markets as well as funding for private companies through private placement financing. Businesses of all sizes purchase life insurance policies as part of their employee benefit packages and purchase general insurance policies to protect physical assets such as automobiles, truck fleets, equipment and entire plants.

Pension Funds

Pension funds invest funds on behalf of businesses or government agencies that provide pension plans for their employees. Pension funds obtain money from employee and employer contributions during the employee's working years and they provide monthly cash payments upon retirement. Because of the predictability of these cash flows, pension fund managers invest in corporate bonds and equity securities purchased in the direct financial markets and participate in the private placement market.

Investment Funds

Collective investment funds, such as open-ended investment companies, sell shares to investors and use the funds to purchase a wide variety of direct and indirect financial instruments. As a result, they are an important source of business funding. For example, such funds may focus on purchasing (1) equity or debt securities; (2) securities of small or medium-sized companies; (3) securities of companies in a particular industry, such as energy, computer or information technology; or (4) foreign investments.

Finance Companies

Finance companies obtain the majority of their funds by selling short-term debt, called commercial paper, to investors in direct credit markets. These funds are used to make a variety of short- and intermediate-term loans and leases to small and large businesses. The loans are often secured by accounts receivable or

inventories. Finance companies are typically more willing than commercial banks to make loans and leases to firms with higher levels of default risk.

Companies and the Financial System

We began this chapter by saying that financial managers need to understand the financial system in order to make sound decisions. We now follow up on that statement by briefly describing how large firms operate within the financial system. The interaction between the financial system and a large public company is shown in Exhibit 2.4. The arrows show the major cash flows for a firm over a typical operating cycle. These cash flows relate to some of the key decisions that the financial manager must make. As you know, those decisions involve three major areas: capital budgeting, financing and working capital management.

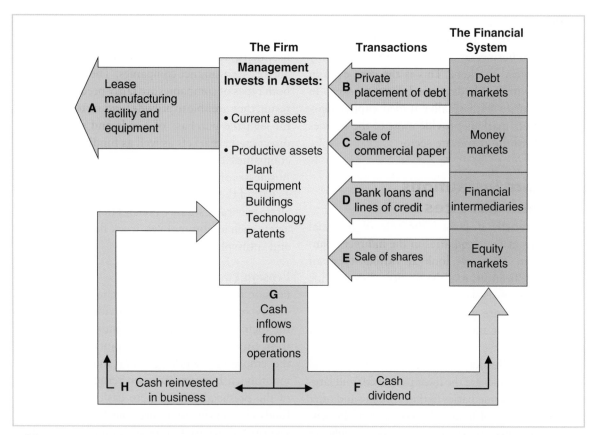

Exhibit 2.4: Cash Flows Between the Firm and the Financial System This exhibit shows how the financial system helps businesses finance their activities. The arrows in the exhibit indicate the major cash flows into and out of a firm over a typical operating cycle. Money obtained from the financial system, combined with reinvested cash from operations, enables a firm to make necessary investments and fund any other requirements.

We will work through an example using Exhibit 2.4 to illustrate how corporate businesses use the financial system. Suppose you are the CFO of a recently established high-tech firm with business ties to EADS, the pan-European aerospace, defence and related services company. The new venture has a well-thought-out business plan, owns some valuable technology and has one manufacturing facility. The company is large enough to have access to public markets. The company plans to use its core technology to develop and sell a number of new products that the marketing department believes will generate a strong market demand.

This exhibit shows how the financial system helps businesses finance their activities. The arrows in the exhibit indicate the major cash flows into and out of a firm over a typical operating cycle. Money obtained from the financial system, combined with reinvested cash from operations, enables a firm to make necessary investments and fund any other requirements.

To start the new company, management's first task is to sell equity and debt to finance the expansion of the firm. EADS and the senior management team will provide 40% of the equity and the balance will come from an **initial public offering (IPO)** of the company's ordinary shares. An IPO is a company's first offering of its shares to the public. For example, management hires Deutsche Bank as its investment bank to underwrite the new securities. After the deal is underwritten, the new venture receives the proceeds from the sale of the shares, less Deutsche Bank's fees (see arrow E in the exhibit).[6]

Initial public offering (IPO)

the first offering of a company's shares to the public. Also called a floatation or listing (on the stock exchange)

In addition to the equity financing, 30% of the firm's total funding will come from the sale of long-term debt through a private placement deal with a large insurance company (see arrow B). Management decided to use a private placement because the lender is willing to commit to lend the firm additional money in the future if the firm meets certain performance goals. Since management has ambitious growth plans, locking in a future source of funds is important.

Once the funds from the debt and equity sales are in hand, they are deposited in the firm's bank account at a commercial bank. Management then decides to lease the existing manufacturing facility and equipment to manufacture the new high-technology products; the cash outflow is represented by arrow A.

To begin manufacturing, the firm needs to raise working capital and does this by (1) selling commercial paper in the money markets (arrow C) and (2) getting a line of credit from a bank (arrow D). As the firm becomes operational, it generates cash inflows from its earning assets (arrow G). Some of this cash inflow is reinvested in the firm (arrow H) and the remainder is used to pay a cash dividend to shareholders (arrow F).

Before You Go On

1. What is financial intermediation and why is it important?
2. What are some services that commercial banks provide to businesses?
3. What is an IPO and what role does an investment banker play in the process?

THE DETERMINANTS OF INTEREST RATE LEVELS

Learning Objective 6

Explain how financial institutions serve consumers and small businesses that are unable to participate in the direct financial markets and describe how companies use the financial system.

We conclude this chapter by examining the factors that determine the general level of interest rates in the economy and describing how interest rates vary over the business cycle. Understanding interest rates is important because the financial instruments and most of the financial services discussed in this chapter are priced in terms of interest rates. We will continue our study of interest rates in Chapter 8, where we discuss the structure of interest rates and explain why different firms have different borrowing costs.

> ### Real rate of interest
>
> the interest rate that would exist in the absence of inflation

> ### Nominal rate of interest
>
> the rate of interest unadjusted for inflation

Learning Objective 7

Explain how the real rate of interest is determined in the economy, differentiate between the real rate and the nominal rate of interest, and be able to compute the nominal or real rate of interest.

The Real Rate of Interest

One of the most important economic variables in the economy is the **real rate of interest** – an interest rate determined in the absence of inflation. *Inflation* is the amount by which aggregate price levels rise over time. The real rate of interest measures the inflation-adjusted return earned by lender-savers and represents the inflation-adjusted cost incurred by borrower-spenders when they borrow to finance capital goods. We focus on capital investments because they are the productive assets that create economic wealth in the economy.

The real rate of interest is rarely observable because most industrial economies operate with some degree of inflation and periods of zero inflation are not common. The rate that we actually observe in the marketplace at a given time is called the **nominal rate of interest**. The factors that determine the real rate of interest, however, are the underlying determinants of all interest rates we observe in the marketplace. For this reason, an understanding of the real interest rate is important.

Determinants of the Real Rate of Interest

The fundamental determinants of interest rates are the return earned on capital investments (productive assets) and individuals' time preference for consumption. Let us examine how these two factors interact to determine the real rate of interest.

Return on Investment   Recall from Chapter 1 that businesses invest in capital projects that are expected to generate positive cash flows by producing additional real output – cars, machinery, computers and video games.[7] The output generated by the capital projects constitutes the return on investment, which is usually measured as a percentage. For example, if a capital investment project with a one-year life costs €1000 and produces €180 in cash flows, the project's return on investment is 18% (€180/€1000). The higher the return on investment, the more likely that a particular project will be undertaken by a firm.

For a capital project to be accepted, its return on investment must exceed the firm's cost of funds (debt and equity); otherwise, the project will be rejected. Intuitively, this decision rule makes sense because if an investment earns a return greater than the firm's cost of funding, it should be profitable and thus should increase the value of the firm. For example, if a firm's average cost of funding – often called the *cost of capital* – is 15%, the one-year capital project mentioned above would be accepted (18% > 15%). If the capital project was expected to earn only 13%, though, the project would be rejected (13% < 15%). The firm's cost of capital is the minimum acceptable rate of return on capital projects.

Decision-Making Example 2.1

Capital Budgeting Preview

Situation: Rotterdam Engineering's capital budget includes six projects that management has identified as having merit. The CFO's staff computed the return on investment for each project. The firm's average cost of funding is 10%. The projects are as follows:

Project	Return on Investment
A	13.0%
B	12.0%
C	10.9%
D	10.5%
E	9.8%
F	8.9%

Which capital projects should the firm undertake?

Decision: The firm should accept all projects with a return on investment greater than the firm's average cost of funding, which is 10%. These projects are A, B, C and D. As noted in the text, this decision-making principle makes intuitive sense because all projects with a return on investment greater than the cost of funds will increase the value of the firm. In Chapters 10–13, we will delve much more deeply into capital budgeting, and you will find out a great deal more about how these decisions are made.

Time Preference for Consumption All other things being equal, most people prefer to consume goods today rather than tomorrow. This is called a positive time preference for consumption. For example, most people who want to buy a new car prefer to have it now rather than wait until they have earned enough cash to make the purchase. When people consume today, however, they realise that their future consumption may be less because they have forgone the opportunity to save and earn interest on their savings.

Given people's positive time preference for consumption, the interest rate offered on financial instruments determines how much people will save. At low rates of interest, it hardly makes sense to save, so most people will continue to spend money on cars and plasma screens rather than put money aside in savings. To coax people to postpone current spending, interest rates must be raised.

Equilibrium Condition We have just seen that people save more and spend less when interest rates are higher. Also, higher interest rates choke off business investment (or spending) because fewer business projects can earn a high enough return on investment to cover the added interest cost. Thus, at higher interest rates, people want to spend less on consumer purchases and businesses want to finance fewer investment projects. At the same time, lender-savers would like to lend more money. The real rate of interest depends on the interaction

between these two opposing factors. Using a supply-and-demand framework, Exhibit 2.5 shows that the equilibrium rate of interest (r) is the point where the desired level of lending (L) by lender-savers equals the desired level of borrowing (B) by people and businesses to finance capital projects.[8]

Fluctuations in the Real Rate

In the supply-and-demand framework discussed above, any economic factor that causes a shift in desired lending or desired borrowing will cause a change in the equilibrium rate of interest. For example, a major breakthrough in technology should cause a shift to the right in the desired level of borrowing schedule, thus increasing the real rate of interest. This makes intuitive sense because the new technology should spawn an increase in investment opportunities, increasing the desired level of borrowing. Similarly, a reduction in the corporate tax rate should provide businesses with more money to spend on investments, which should increase the desired level of borrowing schedule, causing the real rate of interest to increase.

One factor that would shift the desired level of lending to the right, and hence lead to a decrease in the real rate of interest, would be a decrease in the tax rates for individuals. Another would be monetary policy action by the central bank to increase the money supply.

Other forces that could affect the real rate of interest include growth in population, demographic variables such as the age of the population

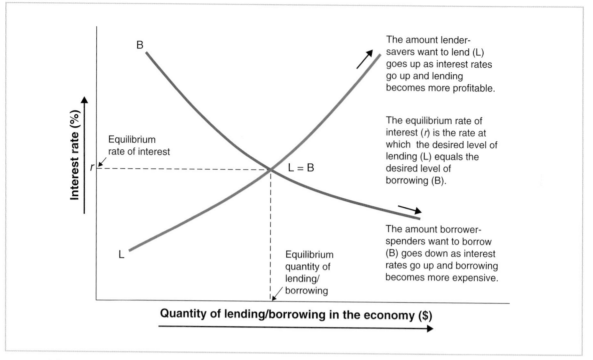

Exhibit 2.5: The Determinants of the Equilibrium Rate of Interest The equilibrium rate of interest is a function of supply and demand. Lender-savers are willing to supply more funds as interest rates go up, but borrower-spenders demand fewer funds at higher interest rates. The interest rate at which the supply of funds equals the demand for those funds is the equilibrium rate.

and cultural differences. In sum, the real rate of interest reflects a complex set of forces that control the desired level of lending and borrowing in the economy. The real rate of interest has historically been around 3% for European Union countries, but has varied between 2% and 4% because of changes in economic conditions.

Loan Contracts and Inflation

The real rate of interest ignores inflation, but in the real world, price-level changes are a fact of life and these changes affect the value of a loan contract or, for that matter, any financial contract. For example, if prices rise (inflation) during the life of a loan contract, the purchasing power of the loaned amount decreases because the borrower repays the lender with inflated money – money that has less buying power.[9]

To see the impact of inflation on a loan, we will look at an example. Suppose that you lend a friend €1000 for one year at a 4% interest rate.

Furthermore, you plan to buy a new mountain bike for €1040 in one year when you graduate from university. With the €40 of interest you earn (€1000 × 0.04), you will have just enough money to buy the mountain bike. At the end of the year, you graduate and your friend pays off the loan, giving you €1040. Unfortunately, the rate of inflation during the year was an unexpected 10% and your mountain bike will now cost 10% more, or €1144 (€1040 × 1.10). You have experienced a 10% decrease in your purchasing power due to the unanticipated inflation. The loss of purchasing power is €104 (€1144 – €1040).

The Fisher Equation and Inflation

How do we write a loan contract that provides protection against loss of purchasing power due to inflation? We have no crystal ball to tell us what the actual rate of inflation will be when the loan contract is written. However, market participants collectively (often called 'the market') have expectations about how prices will change during the contract period.

To incorporate these 'inflationary expectations' into a loan contract, we need to adjust the real rate of interest by the amount of inflation that is expected during the contract period. The mathematical formula used to adjust the real rate of interest for the expected rate of inflation is as follows:

$$1 + i = (1 + r) \times (1 + \Delta P_e)$$
$$1 + i = 1 + r + \Delta P_e + r\Delta P_e \qquad (2.1)$$
$$i = r + \Delta P_e + r\Delta P_e$$

where:

i = nominal (or market) rate of interest
r = real rate of interest
ΔP_e = expected annualised price-level change
$r\Delta P_e$ = adjustment of the interest rate for expected price-level change

Equation (2.1) is called the Fisher equation. It is named after Irving Fisher, who first developed the concept and is considered by many to be one of America's greatest economists.

Applying Equation (2.1) to our earlier example, we can find out what the nominal rate of interest should be if the expected inflation rate is 10% and the real rate of interest is 4%:

$$i = r + \Delta P_e + r\Delta P_e$$
$$= 0.04 + 0.10 + (0.04 \times 0.10)$$
$$= 0.1440, \text{ or } 14.40\%$$

Looking at Equation (2.1), notice that ΔP_e is the *expected* price-level change and not the *realised* (actual) rate of inflation. Thus, to properly determine the nominal rate of interest, it is necessary to predict prices over the life of the loan contract. Also, recall that the nominal rate of interest is the market rate of interest – the rate actually observed in financial markets. The real and nominal rates of interest are equal only when the expected rate of inflation over the contract period is zero $(\Delta P_e = 0)$.[10]

When either r or ΔP_e is a small number, or when both are small, then $r\Delta P_e$ is very small and is approximately equal to zero. In these situations, it is common practice to write the Fisher equation as a simple additive function, where the nominal rate of interest is divided into two parts: (1) the real rate of interest and (2) the anticipated percentage change in the price level over the life of the loan contract. The simplified Fisher equation can be written as follows:

$$i = r + \Delta P_e \qquad (2.2)$$

Thus, for our one-year loan example:

$$i = 0.04 + 0.10 = 0.1400, \text{ or } 14.00\%$$

The difference in the contract loan rates between the two variations of the Fisher equation is 0.40% (14.40 – 14.00), a difference of less than 3% (0.40/14.40 = 0.0278, or 2.78%). Thus, dropping $r\Delta P_e$ from the equation makes the equation easier to understand without creating a significant computational error.

Learning by Doing
Application 2.1

Calculating a New Inflation Premium

Problem: The current one-year interbank rate for the eurozone is 4.5%. On the evening news, several economists at leading investment and commercial banks predict that the annual inflation rate is going to be 0.25% higher than originally expected. The higher inflation forecasts reflect unexpectedly strong employment figures for the European Union released that afternoon. What is the current inflation premium? When the market opens tomorrow, what should happen to the interbank rate? (Assume that the real rate of interest is 3.0%.)

Approach: You must first estimate the current inflation premium using Equation (2.2). You should then adjust this premium to reflect the economists' revised beliefs. Finally, this revised inflation premium can be used in the Fisher equation to estimate what the interbank rate will be tomorrow morning.

Solution: Current inflation premium:

$$i = r + \Delta P_e$$
$$\Delta P_e = i - r$$
$$= 4.5\% - 3.0\%$$
$$= 1.5\%$$

New inflation premium:

$$\Delta P_e = 1.5\% + 0.25\% = 1.75\%$$

The opening interbank rate in the morning:

$$i = r + \Delta P_e = 3.0\% + 1.75\% = 4.75\%$$

Learning by Doing Application 2.2

International Consulting Experience

Problem: You are a financial manager at a manufacturing company that is going to make a one-year loan to a key supplier in another country. The loan will be made in the supplier's local currency. The supplier's government controls the banking system and there is no reliable market data available. For this reason, you have spoken with five economists who have some knowledge about the economy. Their predictions for inflation next year are 30, 40, 45, 50 and 60%.

What rate should your firm charge for the one-year business loan if you are not concerned about the possibility that your supplier will default? You recall from your managerial finance course that the real rate of interest is, on average, 3%.

Approach: Although the sample of economists is small, it should provide a reasonable estimate of the expected rate of inflation (ΔP_e). This value can be used in Equation (2.2) to calculate the nominal rate of interest.

Solution:

$$\Delta P_e = (30\% + 40\% + 45\% + 50\% + 60\%)/5$$
$$= 225\%/5$$
$$= 45\%$$

Nominal rate of interest:

$$i = r + \Delta P_e$$
$$= 3\% + 45\%$$
$$= 48\%$$

This number is a reasonable estimate, given that you have no market data.

Cyclical and Long-Term Trends in Interest Rates

Now let us look at some market data to see how interest rates have actually fluctuated over the past in the European Union. Exhibit 2.6 plots the interest rate yield on the 10-year bond benchmark since 1980 to represent interest rate movements. In addition, the exhibit plots the annual rate of inflation, represented by the annual percentage change in the consumer price index (CPI). The CPI is a price index that measures the change in prices of a market basket of goods and services that a typical

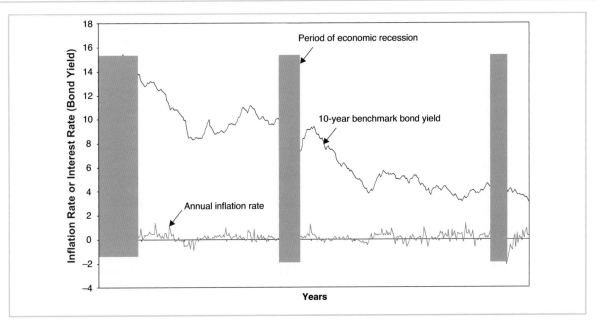

Exhibit 2.6: Relation between Annual Inflation Rate and Long-Term Interest Rates (1980–2009) for the European Union Based on the graphs shown in the exhibit, we can draw two important conclusions about interest rate movements. First, the level of interest rates tends to rise and fall with the actual rate of inflation – a conclusion also supported by the Fisher equation, which suggests that interest rates rise and fall with the expected rate of inflation. Second, the level of interest rates tends to rise during periods of economic expansion and fall during periods of economic contraction.

consumer purchases. Finally, the shaded areas on the chart indicate periods of recession. Recession occurs when real output from the economy is decreasing and unemployment is increasing. Each shaded area begins at the peak of the business cycle and ends at the bottom (or trough) of the recession. From our discussion of interest rates and an examination of Exhibit 2.6, we can draw two general conclusions:

1. *The level of interest rates tends to rise and fall with changes in the actual rate of inflation.* The positive relation between the rate of inflation and the level of interest rates is what we should expect given Equation (2.1). Thus, we feel comfortable concluding that inflationary expectations have a major impact on interest rates.

   Our findings also explain in part why interest rates can vary substantially between countries. For example, during April 2009 the rate of inflation in the United Kingdom was 2.3%; during the same period, the rate of inflation in Russia was 13.2%. If the real rate of interest is 3.0%, the short-term interest rate in the United Kingdom should have been around 5.3% (2.7 + 3.0) and the Russian interest rate should have been around 16.2% (3.0 + 13.2). In fact, during that period the United Kingdom short-term interest rate was 1.5% and the Russian rate was 11.5%. Though hardly scientific, this analysis illustrates the point that countries with higher rates of inflation or expected rates of inflation will have higher interest rates than countries with lower inflation rates.

2. *The level of interest rates tends to rise during periods of economic expansion and decline during periods of economic contraction.*

   It makes sense that interest rates should increase during years of economic expansion. The reasoning is that as the economy expands, businesses begin to borrow money to build up inventories and to invest in more production capacity in anticipation of increased sales. As unemployment begins to decrease, the economic future looks bright and consumers begin to buy more homes, cars and other durable items on credit. As a result, the demand for funds by both businesses and consumers increases, driving interest rates up. Also, near the end of the expansion, the rate of inflation begins to accelerate, which puts upward pressure on interest rates. At some point, the central bank becomes concerned over the increasing inflation in the economy and begins to tighten credit, which further raises interest rates, slowing the economy down. The higher interest rates in the economy choke off spending by both businesses and consumers. In addition, with an inflation target to meet, such as the one discussed at the start of the chapter for the European Central Bank, monetary tightening will take place, which will drive up interest rates.

During a recession, the opposite takes place; businesses and consumers rein in their spending and their use of credit, putting downward pressure on interest rates. To stimulate demand for goods and services, the central bank will typically begin to make more credit available through a looser monetary policy. The result is to lower interest rates in the economy and encourage business and consumer spending.

Also notice in Exhibit 2.6 that periods of business expansion tend to be much longer than periods of contraction (recessions). Looking across economies, it is noticeable that the periods of economic expansion have lasted considerably longer than periods of contraction. An OECD study indicates that the average length of a recession is 3.5 quarters and that for expansions 24.5 quarters.[11]

Planning Ahead by Financial Managers

It is important for a financial manager to understand what factors determine the level of interest rates and what causes interest rates to vary over the business cycle. The financial manager's goal is to obtain funds at the lowest possible cost so that the firm's management can achieve its strategic objectives. The lower the firm's overall cost of funds, the greater the value of the firm.

Before You Go On

1. Explain how the real rate of interest is determined.
2. How are inflationary expectations accounted for in the nominal rate of interest?
3. Explain why interest rates follow the business cycle.

SUMMARY OF LEARNING OBJECTIVES

1. **Discuss the primary role of the financial system in the economy and describe the two basic ways in which fund transfers take place.**

    The primary role of the financial system is to gather money from people and businesses with surplus funds to invest (lender-savers) and channel money to businesses and consumers who need to borrow money (borrower-spenders). If the financial system works properly, only investment projects with high rates of return and good credit are financed and all other projects are rejected. Money flows through the financial system in two basic ways: (1) directly, through financial markets, or (2) indirectly, through financial institutions.

2. **Discuss direct financing and the important role that investment banks play in this process.**

    Direct markets are wholesale markets where large public companies transact. These companies sell securities, such as shares and bonds, directly to investors in exchange for money, which they use to invest in their businesses. Investment banks are important in the direct markets because they help firms sell their new security issues. The services provided by investment bankers include origination, underwriting and distribution.

3. **Describe the primary and secondary markets, and explain why secondary markets are so important to businesses.**

    Primary markets are markets in which new securities are sold for the first time. Secondary markets provide the aftermarket for securities previously issued. Not all securities have secondary markets. Secondary markets are important because they enable investors to convert securities easily to cash. Business firms whose securities are traded in secondary markets are able to issue new securities at a lower cost than they otherwise could because investors are willing to pay a premium price for securities that have secondary markets.

4. **Explain why money markets are important financial markets for large companies.**

    Large companies use money markets to adjust their liquidity because cash inflows and outflows are rarely perfectly synchronised. Thus, on the one hand, if cash expenditures exceed cash receipts, a firm can borrow short term in the money markets or, if the firm holds a portfolio of money market instruments, it can sell some of these securities for cash. On the other hand, if cash receipts exceed expenditures, the firm can temporarily invest the funds in short-term money market instruments. Businesses are willing to invest large amounts of idle cash in money market instruments because of their high liquidity and their low default risk.

5. **Discuss the most important stock market exchanges and indexes.**

    A traditional stock exchange is an organised market that provides a physical meeting place and communication facilities for members to buy and sell securities under a specific set of rules and regulations. Securities that are traded on the exchange are said to be listed on the exchange. Countries with market economies will have a stock exchange in which larger companies have their shares traded. Indices are used to measure the performance of a particular stock market, some aspect of the market or provide an international benchmark for global investment.

6. **Explain how financial institutions serve consumers and small businesses that are unable to participate in the direct financial markets and describe how companies use the financial system.**

    One problem with direct financing is that it takes place in a wholesale market. Most small businesses and consumers do not have the expert skills or the money to transact in this market. In contrast, a large portion of the indirect market focuses on providing financial services to consumers and small businesses. For example, commercial banks collect money from consumers in small sums by selling them current accounts, savings accounts and consumer certificates of deposit. They then aggregate the funds and make loans in larger amounts to consumers and businesses. The financial services bought or sold by financial institutions are tailor-made to fit the needs of the market they serve. Exhibit 2.4 illustrates how companies use the financial system.

7. **Explain how the real rate of interest is determined in the economy, differentiate between the real rate and the nominal rate of interest and be able to compute the nominal or real rate of interest.**

    The real rate of interest is the interest rate in the economy in the absence of inflation. It is determined by the interaction of (1) the rate of return that businesses can expect to earn on capital goods and (2) individuals' time preference for consumption. The interest rate we observe in the marketplace is called the nominal rate of interest. The nominal rate of interest is composed of two parts: (1) the real rate of interest and (2) the expected rate of inflation. Equations (2.1) and (2.2) are used to compute the nominal (real) rate of interest when you have the real (nominal) rate and the inflation rate.

SUMMARY OF KEY EQUATIONS

Equation	Description	Formula
(2.1)	Fisher equation	$i = r + \Delta P_e + r\Delta P_e$
(2.2)	Fisher equation simplified	$i = r + \Delta P_e$

SELF-STUDY PROBLEMS

2.1. Economic units that need to borrow money are said to be:
   a. lender-savers
   b. borrower-spenders
   c. balanced budget keepers
   d. none of the above

2.2. Explain what marketability of a security means and how it is determined.

2.3. What are over-the-counter markets (OTCs) and how do they differ from organised exchanges?

2.4. What effect does an increase in demand for business goods and services have on the real interest rate? What other factors can affect the real interest rate?

2.5. How does the business cycle affect the interest rate and inflation rate?

SOLUTIONS TO SELF-STUDY PROBLEMS

2.1. Such units are said to be (b) borrower-spenders.

2.2. Marketability refers to the ease with which a security can be sold and converted into cash. The level of marketability depends on the cost of trading the security and the cost of searching for information. The lower these costs are, the greater the security's marketability.

2.3. Securities that are not listed on an organised exchange are sold OTC. An OTC market differs from an organised exchange in that there is no central trading location. Security transactions are made via phone or computer as opposed to on the floor of an exchange.

2.4. An increase in the demand for business goods and services will cause the borrowing schedule to shift to the right, thus increasing the real rate of interest. Other factors that can affect the real interest rate are increases in productivity, changes in technology or changes in the corporate tax rate. Demographic factors, such as growth or age of the population and cultural differences, can also affect the real rate of interest.

2.5. Both the nominal interest and inflation rates follow the business cycle; that is, they rise with economic expansion and fall during a recession.

CRITICAL THINKING QUESTIONS

2.1. Explain why total financial assets in the economy must equal total financial liabilities.

2.2. Why do small businesses not make greater use of the direct credit markets since these markets enable firms to finance their activities at a very low cost?

2.3. Explain the economic role of brokers and dealers. How does each make a profit?

2.4. What distinguishes commercial banking from investment banking?

2.5. What are the two basic services that investment banks provide in the economy?

2.6. Many large companies sell commercial paper as a source of funds. From time to time, some of these firms find that they are unable to issue commercial paper. Why is this true?

2.7. How do large companies adjust their liquidity in the money markets?

2.8. Should not the nominal rate of interest [Equation (2.1)] be determined by the actual rate of inflation (ΔP_a), which can easily be measured, rather than by the expected rate of inflation (ΔP_e)?

2.9. How does Exhibit 2.6 help explain why interest rates were so high during the early 1980s as compared to the relatively low interest rates in the early 1990s?

2.10. When determining the real interest rate, what happens to businesses that find themselves with unfunded capital projects whose rate of return exceeds the firms' cost of capital?

QUESTIONS AND PROBLEMS

2.1. **Financial system:** What is the role of the financial system and what are the two major components of the financial system?

2.2. **Financial system:** What does a competitive financial system imply about interest rates?

2.3. **Financial system:** What is the difference between saver-lenders and borrower-spenders and who are the major representatives of each group?

2.4. **Financial markets:** List the two ways in which a transfer of funds takes place in an economy. What is the main difference between these two?

2.5. **Financial markets:** Suppose you own a security that you know can be sold easily in the secondary market, but the security will sell at a lower price than you paid for it. What would this mean for the security's marketability and liquidity?

2.6. **Financial markets:** Why are direct financial markets also called wholesale markets?

2.7. **Financial markets:** Le Vaux SA is a €300 million company, as measured by asset value, and Horstelle AG is a €35 million company. Both are privately held companies. Explain which firm is more likely to go public and why.

2.8. **Primary markets:** What is a primary market? What does IPO stand for?

2.9. **Primary markets:** Identify whether the following transactions are primary market or secondary market transactions.

   a. Jean Bart bought 300 shares of BASF through his broker account.

b. Martina Padrul bought €5000 of Fiat bonds from the firm.

c. Swiss Re bought 500 000 shares of the Roche Group when the company issued shares.

2.10. Investment banking: What does it mean to 'underwrite' a new security issue? What compensation does an investment banker get from underwriting a security issue?

2.11. Investment banking: SASA Group is issuing 10 000 bonds and its investment banker has guaranteed a price of €985 per bond. The investment banker sells the entire issue to investors for €10 150 000.

a. What is the underwriting spread for this issue?

b. What is the percentage underwriting cost?

c. How much did the SASA Group raise?

2.12. Financial institutions: What are some of the ways in which a financial institution or intermediary can raise money?

2.13. Financial institutions: How do financial institutions act as 'intermediaries' to provide services to small businesses?

2.14. Financial institutions: Which financial institution is usually the most important to businesses?

2.15. Financial markets: What is the main difference between money markets and capital markets?

2.16. Stock market index: What is a stock market index? List three stock market indices.

2.17. Stock market index: What is a price index?

2.18. Stock market index: What aspect of performance does a capitalisation-weighted index measure?

2.19. Money markets: What are Treasury bills?

2.20. Money markets: Besides Treasury bills, what are other money market instruments?

2.21. Money markets: What is the primary role of money markets? Explain how money markets work.

2.22. Capital markets: How do capital market instruments differ from money market instruments?

2.23. Interest rates: What are the major differences between public and private markets?

2.24. Financial instruments: What are the two risk-hedging instruments discussed in the chapter?

2.25. Interest rates: What is the real rate of interest and how is it determined?

2.26. Interest rates: How does the nominal rate of interest vary over time?

2.27. Interest rates: What is the Fisher equation, and how is it used?

2.28. Interest rates: Imagine you borrow €500 from one of your friends, agreeing to pay her back €500 plus 7% nominal interest in one year. Assume inflation over the life of the contract is expected to be 4.25%. What is the total amount you will have to pay her back in a year? What percentage of the interest payment is the result of the real rate of interest?

2.29. Interest rates: Your parents have given you €1000 a year before your graduation so that you can take a trip when you graduate. You wisely decide to invest the money in a bank deposit that pays 6.75% interest. You know that the trip costs €1025 right now and that inflation for the year is predicted to be 4%. Will you have enough money in a year to purchase the trip?

2.30. Interest rates: When are the nominal and real interest rates equal?

SAMPLE TEST PROBLEMS

2.1. How are brokers different from dealers?

2.2. What is a total return index?

2.3. Identify what type of transactions (direct or indirect) the following are:

    a. You buy 200 shares of Invesco Pan European Equity Fund.

    b. Renaldo buys a bank CD for €5000.

    c. Bank Przemyslowo-Handlowy makes a Zloty 250 000 loan to Wałęsa's Coffee Shop in Krakow, Poland.

    d. Nadine buys €3000 of bonds from a new issue.

2.4. If the nominal rate of interest is 7.5% and the real rate is 4%, what is the expected inflation premium?

2.5. What is the relationship between business cycles and the general level of interest rates?

ENDNOTES

1. The ECB has three monetary policy instruments to influence interest rates: open market operations (the purchase and sale of eligible securities), standing facilities (which aim to set boundaries for overnight market interest rates) and reserve requirements (which relate to the minimum reserves in accounts at national central banks). While open-market operations are the normal way to influence interest rates, changes in minimum reserve requirements will also add or drain liquidity from the Eurosystem. Modifying reserve requirements aims to stabilise money market interest rates and create a structural liquidity deficit in the banking system.

2. A certificate of deposit (CD) is a negotiable security evidencing a short-term interest-bearing deposit held by a bank and is functionally equivalent to opening an account and placing money with the bank for a set period of time.

3. Lender-savers are also called surplus spending units (SSU), and borrower-spenders are also called deficit spending units (DSU).

4. If the risk of underwriting a new security issue is high, investment bankers may refuse to underwrite the securities for a guaranteed price. Instead, they will underwrite the new issue on a best-efforts basis, which means that they will sell the securities for the highest price that investors are willing to pay. These issues are discussed in more detail in Chapter 15.

5. For an example of the range of services provided by commercial banks to businesses, visit the small-business section of www.pncbank.com.

6. Chapter 15 contains a detailed discussion of the IPO process.

7. Note that business investment is just a formal name that economists give to business spending.

8. The model presented here is based on the loanable funds theory of market equilibrium. Saving (or giving up current consumption) is the source of loanable funds, and business spending (or investment) is the use of funds.

9. Recall from economics two important relationships: (1) the value of money is its purchasing power – what you can buy with it and (2) there is a negative relation between changes in price level and the

value of money. As the price level increases (inflation), the value of money decreases and as the price level decreases (deflation), the value of money increases. This makes sense because when we have rising prices (inflation), our money will buy less.

10. In economics the terms nominal and real are frequently used as modifiers, as in nominal GNP and real GNP. Nominal means that the data are from the marketplace; thus, the values may contain price-level changes due to inflation. Real means the data are corrected for changes in purchasing power.

11. Jean-Philippe Cotis and Jonathan Coppel, 2005. Business Cycle Dynamics in OECD Countries: Evidence, Causes and Policy Implications. Conference Paper, OECD, Paris.

CHAPTER

3

Financial Statements, Cash Flows and Taxes

In this Chapter:

Financial Statements and Accounting Principles
The Balance Sheet
Market Value versus Book Value
The Income Statement and the Statement of Retained Earnings
Cash Flows
Tying the Financial Statements Together
International Accounting Issues
Corporate Income Tax

LEARNING OBJECTIVES

1. Discuss generally accepted accounting principles (GAAP) and their importance to an understanding of financial statements.
2. Know the balance sheet identity and explain why a balance sheet must balance.
3. Describe how market-value balance sheets differ from book-value balance sheets.
4. Identify the basic equation for the income statement and the information it provides.
5. Explain the difference between cash flows and accounting income.
6. Explain how the four major financial statements discussed in this chapter are related.
7. Understand that differences exist in the quality and way financial statements are reported between countries.
8. Discuss the difference between average and marginal tax rates.

With the integration of financial markets across the world and the increased internationalisation of business, global cooperation in developing a common set of standards for financial reporting has become a priority. Before the formation of the International Accounting Standards Board (IASB), countries allowed companies and other entities to produce accounting statements using a variety of different local standards that made comparison difficult and often lacked transparency. In 2002, the development of a global standard for financial reporting received a boost when the European Union (EU) made it mandatory that from 2005 onwards listed companies report using the International Financial Reporting Standards (IFRS) issued by the IASB. In addition, in 2006, the United States standard-setting body, the Financial Accounting Standards Board (FASB) and the IASB agreed a roadmap for the convergence between IFRS and US reporting standards. These two developments provided the momentum for the establishment of IFRS as the global standard for financial reporting, and over 100 countries have now required or permitted the use of IFRS for reporting purposes.

The advantages of a common standard worldwide are that they provide additional information and disclosure, facilitate comparability within and across countries, increase the transparency of financial statements and the efficiency and quality of audited accounts. The disadvantages are that it is difficult to remove cultural influences in accounting practices, adherence to the standards is costly and it is hard to regulate all countries. In addition, the standards remove many hitherto accepted accounting practices and hence change the nature of reported profits for many firms.

Clearly, the correct preparation of financial statements is crucial. In this chapter and the next, we focus on the preparation, interpretation and limitations of financial statements. As you will see, the preparation of financial statements is not a cut-and-dried affair but involves considerable professional judgement, which can and does lead to variations in financial statements.

CHAPTER PREVIEW

In Chapter 1 we noted that all businesses have stakeholders – managers, creditors, suppliers and the government, among others – who have some claim on the firms' cash flows. The stakeholders in a firm, along with the shareholders, need to monitor the firm's progress and evaluate its performance. Financial statements enable them to do these things. The accounting system is the framework that gathers information about the firm's business activities and translates the information into objective numerical financial reports.

Most firms prepare financial statements on a regular basis and have independent auditors certify that the financial statements have been prepared in accordance with generally accepted accounting principles and contain no material misstatements. The audit increases the confidence of the stakeholders that the financial statements prepared by management present a 'fair and accurate' picture of the firm's financial condition at a particular point in time. In fact, it is difficult to get any type of legitimate business loan without audited financial statements.

This chapter reviews the basic structure of a firm's financial statements and explains how the various statements fit together. We examine the preparation of the balance sheet, the income statement (also called the profit and loss statement), the statement of retained earnings and the statement of cash flows. As you read this part of the chapter, pay particular attention to the differences between (1) cash flows and accounting income and (2) book value and market value. Understanding the differences between these two sets of concepts is necessary to avoid serious analytical and decision-making errors. The last part of the chapter discusses how companies are taxed. In finance, we make most decisions on an after-tax basis, so understanding the way firms are taxed is very important.

FINANCIAL STATEMENTS AND ACCOUNTING PRINCIPLES

Learning Objective 1

Discuss generally accepted accounting principles (GAAP) and their importance to an understanding of financial statements.

Before we can meaningfully interpret and analyse financial statements, we need to understand some accounting principles that guide their preparation. Thus, we begin the chapter with a discussion of generally accepted accounting principles (GAAP), which guide firms in the preparation of financial statements. First, however, we briefly discuss the annual report.

Annual Reports

The *annual report* is the most important report that firms issue to their shareholders and make available to the general public. Historically, annual reports were dull, black-and-white publications that presented the firm's audited financial statements. Today some annual reports, especially those of large public companies, are slick, picture-laden, glossy 'magazines' in full colour with orchestrated media messages exalting the deeds of top management.

WEB

To see samples of annual reports from a variety of companies, visit: www.order annualreports.com or www.carol.co.uk.

Annual reports typically are divided into three distinct sections. First are the financial tables, which contain financial information about the firm and its operations for the year and an accompanying summary explaining the firm's performance over the past year. For example, the summary might explain that sales and profits were down because of lost sales that arose from a major plant shutdown. Often, there is a letter from the chairman or CEO that provides some insights into the reasons for the firm's performance, a discussion of new developments, and a high-level view of the firm's strategy and future direction. It is important to note that the financial tables are historical records reflecting past performance of the firm and do not necessarily indicate what the firm will do in the future.

The second part of the report is often a corporate public relations piece discussing the firm's product lines, its services to its customers and its contributions to the communities in which it operates.

The third part of the annual report presents the audited financial statements: the balance sheet, the income statement (or profit and loss account), the statement of retained earnings and the statement of cash flows. Overall, the annual report provides a good overview of the firm's operating and financial performance and states why, in management's judgement, things turned out the way they did.

Generally Accepted Accounting Principles

Accounting statements are prepared in accordance with generally accepted accounting principles (GAAP), a set of widely agreed-upon rules and procedures that define how companies are to maintain financial records and prepare financial reports. These principles are important because without them, financial statements would be less standardised. Accounting standards such as GAAP make it easier for analysts and management to make meaningful comparisons of a company's performance against that of other companies. GAAP and reporting practices are published in the form of reporting standards and accountants are required to follow these statements in their auditing and accounting practices.

Generally accepted accounting principles (GAAP)

a set of rules that defines how companies are to prepare financial statements

WEB

You can find more information about the International Accounting Standards Board (IASB) at: www.iasb.org.

Accounting is often called the language of business. Just as there are different dialects within languages, there are different international 'dialects' in accounting. For example, the set of generally accepted accounting principles in the United Kingdom is called UK GAAP. With the emergence of the EU, member countries are moving towards a 'European GAAP'. In other parts of the world, the accounting system used often depends on a country's history. For example, Hong Kong and India, which were once colonies of England, use a variant of the British accounting system.

The good news is that it is not difficult for accountants to adjust financial statements, so that meaningful comparisons can be made between statements based on differing accounting principles. At the same time, these adjustments represent an economic inefficiency that adds a cost to international business transactions.

As more businesses operate internationally and world economies become more integrated, maintaining and translating between different accounting systems makes less and less economic sense. Economic and political pressures are thus building in both the United States, Europe and elsewhere to develop a unified accounting system. As the opening account of the introduction of International Financial Reporting Standards (IFRS) by the IASB indicates, a global standard is beginning to emerge. However, the adoption of a common accounting standard is still not around the corner. In particular, while many countries have embraced IFRS and it has been made mandatory throughout the European Union, the United States as the world's leading economy retains its own accounting standards. How soon a single global standard is established depends on the political climate between the major OECD countries and the continued globalisation of commerce.

WEB

A good source of information on international accounting standards can be found at: http://www.iasplus.com/index.htm.

Fundamental Accounting Principles

To better understand financial statements, it is helpful to look at some fundamental accounting principles embodied in GAAP. These principles determine the manner of recording, measuring and reporting company transactions. As you will see, the practical application of these principles requires professional judgement, which can result in considerable differences in financial statements.

The Assumption of Arm's-Length Transactions

Accounting is based on the recording of economic transactions that can be quantified in monetary amounts. It assumes that the parties to a transaction are economically rational and are free to act *independently* of each other. To illustrate, let us assume that you are preparing a personal balance sheet for a bank loan on which you must list all your assets. You are including your BMW 325 as an asset. You bought the car a few months ago from your father for €3000 when the retail price of the car was €15 000. You got a good deal. However, the price you paid, which would be the number recorded on your balance sheet, was not the market price. Since you did not purchase the BMW in an arm's-length transaction, your balance sheet would not reflect the true value of the asset.

The Cost Principle

Generally, the value of an asset that is recorded on a company's 'books' reflects its historical cost. The historical cost is assumed to represent the fair market value of the item at the time it was acquired

and is recorded as the book value. Over time, it is unlikely that an asset's book value will be equal to its market value because market values tend to change over time. The major exception to this principle is marketable securities, such as the shares of another company, which are recorded at their current market value.

It is important to note that accounting statements are records of past performance; they are based on historical costs, not on current market prices or values. Accounting statements translate the business' past performance into monetary values, which helps management and investors better understand how the business has performed in the past.

Book value

the net value of an asset or liability recorded on the financial statements – normally reflects historical cost

The Realisation Principle

Under the realisation principle, revenue is recognised only when the sale is virtually complete and the exchange value for the goods or services can be reliably determined. As a practical matter, this means that most revenues are recognised at the time of sale whether or not cash is actually received. At this time, if a firm sells to its customers on credit, an account receivable is recorded. The firm receives the cash only when the customer actually makes the payment. Although the realisation principle concept seems straightforward, there can be considerable ambiguity in its interpretation. For example, should revenues be recognised when goods are ordered, when they are shipped or when payment is received from the customer?

The Matching Principle

Accounting tries to match revenue on the income statement with the expenses used to generate the revenue. In practice, this principle means that revenue is first recognised (according to the realisation principle) and then is matched with the costs associated with producing the revenue. For example, if we manufacture a product and sell it on credit (accounts receivable), the revenue is recognised at the time of sale. The expenses associated with manufacturing the product – expenditures for raw materials, labour, equipment and facilities – will be recognised at the same time. Notice that the actual cash outflows for expenses may not occur at the same time the expenses are recognised. It should be clear that the figures on the income statement more than likely will not correspond to the actual cash inflows and outflows during the period.

The Going Concern Assumption

The going concern assumption is the assumption that a business will remain in operation for the foreseeable future. This assumption underlies much of what is done in accounting. For example, suppose that Carrefour SA, the French supermarket chain, has €4.6 billion of inventories on its balance sheet, representing what the firm actually paid for the inventory in arm's-length transactions. If we assume that Carrefour is a going concern, the balance sheet figure is a reasonable number because in the normal course of business we expect Carrefour to be able to sell the goods for its cost plus some reasonable mark-up.

However, suppose Carrefour declares bankruptcy and is forced by its creditors to liquidate its assets. If this happens, Carrefour is no longer a going concern. What will the inventory be worth then? We cannot be certain, but 50 cents on the euro might be a high figure. The going concern assumption allows the accountant to record assets at cost rather than at their value in a liquidation sale, which is usually much less.

You can see that the fundamental accounting principles just discussed leave considerable professional discretion to accountants in the preparation of financial statements. As a result, financial statements can and do differ because of honest differences in professional judgements. Of course, there are limits on 'honest professional differences' and, at some point, an accountant's choices can cross a line and result in 'cooking the books'.

Before You Go On

1. What kind of information does a firm's annual report contain?
2. What is the realisation principle, and why may it lead to a difference in the timing of when revenues are recognised and cash is collected?

Illustrative Company: Fabrique Aérospatiale SE

In the next part of the chapter, we turn to a discussion of four fundamental financial statements: the balance sheet, the income statement (or profit and loss account), the statement of retained earnings and the statement of cash flows. To more clearly illustrate these financial statements, we use data from Fabrique Aérospatiale SE, a fictional Belgian manufacturer of components for the aerospace industry.[1] Fabrique Aérospatiale was formed in 2001 as a result of the consolidation of several smaller Belgian and Netherlands aerospace firms. The firm specialises in the design and manufacture of control systems used in small and large commercial aircraft and has two divisions: (1) FA Control Systems, which manufactures aircraft control systems, and (2) FA Espace, which makes spacecraft components.

In 2010 Fabrique Aérospatiale's sales increased to €1.32 billion, an increase of 87.8% from the previous year. This increase arose partly from a recovery in new aircraft orders, but also as a result of acquisitions made in the past year. A letter to shareholders in the 2010 annual report stated that management did not expect net profit (also called net income, net earnings or simply earnings) in 2011 to exceed the net profit for 2010. The reason for caution was that Fabrique Aérospatiale's profits are very susceptible to changes in the global demand for commercial aircraft and in 2010 predictions for future demand were at best stable. Management reassured investors, however, that Fabrique Aérospatiale had the financial strength and the management team needed to weather a downturn in the demand for commercial jets.

THE BALANCE SHEET

Learning Objective 2
Know the balance sheet identity and explain why a balance sheet must balance.

The balance sheet reports the firm's financial position at a particular point in time. Exhibit 3.1 shows the balance sheets for Fabrique Aérospatiale SE as of 31 December 2010 and for comparison purposes as of the previous year (31 December 2009). The left-hand side of the balance sheet identifies the firm's assets, most of which are listed at book value. These assets are owned by the firm and are used to generate income. The right-hand side of the balance sheet includes shareholders' equity and liabilities, which tell us how the firm has financed its assets. Liabilities are obligations of the firm that represent claims against its assets. These claims arise from debts and other obligations to pay creditors, employees or the government. In contrast, shareholders' equity represents the residual claim of the owners on the remaining assets of the firm after all liabilities have been paid.[2] The basic balance sheet identity can thus be stated as follows:[3]

$$\text{Total assets} = \text{Total liabilities} + \text{Total shareholders' equity} \quad (3.1)$$

Since shareholders' equity is the residual claim, shareholders would receive the residual value if the firm decided to sell off all of its assets and use the money to pay back its creditors. That is why the balance sheet always balances. Simply put, if you total what the firm owns and what it owes then the difference between the two is the total shareholders' equity:

$$\text{Total shareholders' equity} = \text{Total assets} - \text{Total liabilities}$$

Notice that total shareholders' equity can be positive, negative or equal to zero.

Next, we examine some important balance sheet accounts of Fabrique Aérospatiale as of 31 December 2010 (see Exhibit 3.1). As a matter of convention, accountants divide assets and liabilities into short-term (or current) and long-term parts. We will start by looking at current assets and liabilities.

Balance sheet
financial statement that shows a firm's financial position (assets, liabilities and equity) at a point in time

Current Assets and Liabilities

Current assets are assets that can reasonably be expected to be converted into cash within one year. Besides cash, other current assets are available-for-sale financial instruments, trade and other receivables, which are typically payable within 30 to 45 days and inventories, which are money invested in raw materials, work-in-process and finished goods. Fabrique Aérospatiale's current assets total €483 million.

Current liabilities are obligations payable within one year. Typical current liabilities are trade and other accounts payable, which arise in the purchases of goods and services from vendors and are normally paid within 30 to 60 days; borrowings, which are formal borrowing agreements with a bank or some other lender that have a stated maturity; and taxes due to central and local government, which are taxes Fabrique Aérospatiale owes but has not yet paid. Fabrique Aérospatiale's total current liabilities equal €210 million.

Net Working Capital
Recall from Chapter 1 that the monetary difference between total current assets and total current liabilities is the firm's net working capital:

$$\text{Net working capital} = \text{Total current assets} - \text{Total current liabilities} \quad (3.2)$$

Net working capital is a measure of a firm's liquidity, which is the ability of the firm to meet its

EXHIBIT 3.1

FABRIQUE AÉROSPATIALE SE CONSOLIDATED
BALANCE SHEET AS OF 31 DECEMBER (€ MILLIONS)

Assets	2010	2009
Non-current assets		
Property plant and equipment (net)	€971	€626
Intangible assets	164	129
Investments in associates	84	83
Deferred income tax assets	21	21
Available-for-sale financial assets	109	93
Derivative financial assets	2	2
Trade and other receivables	15	8
	1366	962
Current assets		
Inventories	154	114
Trade and other receivables	124	115
Available-for-sale financial assets	12	0
Derivative financial instruments	7	6
Financial assets at fair value through profit and loss	74	50
Cash and cash equivalents	112	213
	483	498
Assets of disposal group as held-for-sale	21	
	504	497
Total assets	€1870	€1459

Equity	2010	2009
Capital and reserves attributable to equity holders of the company		
Ordinary shares[a,b]	€158	€131
Share premium	107	66
Other reserves	97	44
Retained earnings	416	304
	779	545
Minority interest in equity	45	11
Total equity	824	556
Liabilities		
Non-current liabilities		
Borrowings[c]	720	602
Derivative financial instruments	1	1
Deferred income tax liabilities	77	57
Retirement benefit obligations	29	14
Provisions for other liabilities and charges	8	2
	835	675
Current liabilities		
Trade and other payables	104	78
Current income tax liabilities	16	17
Borrowings	73	114
Derivative financial instruments	3	4
Provisions for other liabilities and charges	14	15
	210	228
Liabilities of disposal group classified as held-for-sale	1	
Total liabilities	211	228
	1046	903
Total equity and liabilities	€1870	€1459

[a]The company has 20 million ordinary shares authorised.
[b]The company has in issue 15.8 million (2010) and 12.5 million (2009) ordinary shares.
[c]The company has issued 1.88 million redeemable preference shares with a value of €188 million in 2010 and a convertible bond with a value of €268 million.
The left-hand side of the balance sheet lists the assets that the firm has at a particular point in time, while the right-hand side shows how the firm has financed those assets.

obligations as they come due. One way that firms maintain their liquidity is by holding assets that are highly liquid. Recall that the liquidity of an asset is how quickly it can be converted into cash without loss of value. Thus, an asset's liquidity has two dimensions: (1) the speed and ease with which the asset can be sold and (2) whether the asset can be sold without loss of value. Of course, any asset can be sold easily and quickly if the price is low enough.

For Fabrique Aérospatiale, total current assets are €483 million, and total current liabilities are €210 million. The firm's net working capital is thus:

$$
\begin{aligned}
\text{Net working capital} &= \text{Total current assets} \\
&\quad - \text{Total current liabilities} \\
&= \text{€483 million} \\
&\quad - \text{€210 million} \\
&= \text{€273 million}
\end{aligned}
$$

To interpret this number, if Fabrique Aérospatiale took its current cash and cash equivalents, liquidated its financial assets, trade and other accounts receivable and inventories at book value, it would have €483 million with which to pay off its short-term liabilities of €210 million, leaving €273 million of 'cushion'. As a short-term creditor, such as a bank, you would view the net working capital position as positive because Fabrique Aérospatiale's current assets exceed current liabilities by over two times (€483m/€210m = 2.3).

Accounting for Inventories

Inventories, as noted earlier, are a current asset on the balance sheet, but it is usually the least liquid of the current assets. The reason is that it can take a long time for a firm to convert inventories into cash. For a manufacturing firm, the inventory cycle begins with raw materials, continues with goods in process, proceeds with finished goods and finally concludes with selling the asset for cash or an account receivable. For a firm such as Airbus, the pan-European aircraft manufacturer, the inventory cycle in manufacturing an aircraft can be a year or longer.

An important decision for management is the selection of an inventory valuation method. Under IFRS rules FIFO (first in, first out) and a weighted-average method are allowed. LIFO (last in, first out), which is permitted under US GAAP, is not allowed under IFRS. While this may seem a trivial distinction, the accounting method can have a major effect on reported results. During periods of changing price levels, how a firm values its inventories affects both its balance sheet and its income statement. For example, suppose that prices have been rising (inflation). If a company values its inventory using the FIFO method, when the firm makes a sale, it assumes the sale is from the oldest, lowest-cost inventory – first in, first out. Thus, during rising prices, firms using FIFO will have the lowest cost of goods sold, the highest net income and the highest inventory value. In contrast, a company using the LIFO method assumes the sale is from the newest, highest-cost inventory – last in, first out. During a period of inflation, firms using LIFO will have the highest cost of goods sold, the lowest net income and the lowest inventory value. Firms using the weighted-average method will have a cost of good sold, a net income and value for inventories somewhere between the FIFO and LIFO values.

When financial analysts compare companies, they adjust the financial statements if the companies use different methods for valuing inventories. Although firms can switch from one inventory valuation method to another, this type of change is an extraordinary event and cannot be done frequently.

Fabrique Aérospatiale reports inventory values for its operations within the European Union using the FIFO method as required by IFRS standards. The remaining inventories, which are located in Brazil, are calculated using the LIFO method. Fabrique Aérospatiale's total inventory is €154 million.

Non-Current Assets and Liabilities

The remaining assets on the balance sheet are classified as non-current (long-term) assets. Typically, these assets are financed by long-term liabilities and shareholders' equity.

Long-Term Assets

Long-term or productive assets are the assets that the firm uses to generate most of its income.

Long-term assets may be tangible or intangible. Tangible assets are balance sheet items such as land, mineral resources, buildings, equipment, machinery and vehicles that are used over an extended period of time. In addition, tangible assets can include other businesses that a firm wholly or partially owns, such as foreign subsidiaries. Intangible assets are items such as patents, copyrights, licensing agreements, technology and other intellectual capital the firm owns, and goodwill.

Goodwill is an intangible asset that arises only when a firm purchases another firm. Conceptually, goodwill is a measure of how much the value of the acquired firm exceeds the sum of the values of its individual assets. This additional value is created by the way in which those assets are being used. For example, if Fabrique Aérospatiale paid €2.0 million for a company that had individual assets with a total fair market value of €1.9 million, the goodwill premium paid would be €100 000 (€2.0 million – €1.9 million). For Fabrique Aérospatiale, the goodwill on its balance sheet is €76 million and is part of the total intangible assets of €164 million.

Fabrique Aérospatiale's long-term assets comprise net property, plant and equipment of €971 million. The term *net property, plant and equipment* indicates that accumulated depreciation has been subtracted to arrive at the net value. That is, net property, plant and equipment equals total property, plant and equipment less accumulated depreciation; accumulated depreciation is the total amount of depreciation expense taken on property, plant and equipment up to the balance sheet date.

Accumulated Depreciation

When a firm acquires a tangible asset that deteriorates with use and wears out, accountants try to allocate the asset's cost over its useful life. The matching principle requires that the cost be expensed against the period in which the firm benefited from the use of the asset. Thus, depreciation allocates the cost of a limited-life asset to the periods in which the firm is assumed to benefit from the asset. Tangible assets with an unlimited life, such as land, are not depreciated. Depreciation affects the balance sheet through the accumulated depreciation account; we discuss its effect on the income statement later in this chapter.

A company can elect whether to depreciate its assets using straight-line depreciation over the economic life of the asset or use one of the approved accelerated depreciation methods. Accelerated depreciation methods allow for more depreciation expense in the early years of an asset's life than straight-line depreciation.

Fabrique Aérospatiale uses the straight-line method of depreciation. Had Fabrique Aérospatiale elected to use accelerated depreciation, the value of its depreciable assets would have been written off to the income statement more quickly (through higher depreciation expense), resulting in a lower 'net property, plant and equipment' account on its balance sheet and a lower net income (net profit) for the period.

> ## Depreciation
>
> allocation of the cost of an asset over its estimated life to reflect the wear and tear on the asset as it is used to produce the firm's goods and services

Non-Current Liabilities

Non-current liabilities include debt instruments due and payable beyond one year as well as other long-term obligations of the firm. They include bonds, bank term loans, mortgages, finance leases and other types of liabilities, such as pension obligations and deferred compensation. Typically, firms finance long-term assets with long-term liabilities. Fabrique Aérospatiale has long-term liabilities of €835 million, which is mostly long-term borrowings (€720 million), consisting of a mixture of bank borrowings, a convertible bond issued in 2010, debentures and other loans, finance leases and redeemable preference shares.

Equity

We have summarised the types of assets and liabilities that appear on the balance sheet. Now we look at the equity accounts. Fabrique Aérospatiale's total shareholders' equity at the end of 2010 is €824 million and is made up of four accounts – ordinary shares, share premium, other reserves and retained earnings – which we discuss next. We conclude with a discussion of preference shares, which are included under borrowings, but which represent a hybrid security that has some debt and some equity features.[4]

Ordinary Share Accounts

The most important equity accounts are those related to ordinary shares, which represent the true ownership of the firm. Certain basic rights of ownership typically come with ordinary shares; those rights are as follows:

1. The right to vote on corporate matters such as the election of the board of directors or important actions such as the purchase of another company.
2. The pre-emptive right, which allows shareholders to purchase any additional shares issued by the company in proportion to the number of shares they currently own. This allows ordinary shareholders to retain the same percentage of ownership in the firm, if they choose to do so, when the company issues more shares.
3. The right to receive cash dividends, if they are paid.
4. If the firm is liquidated, the right to all remaining corporate assets after all creditors and preference shareholders have been paid.

A common source of confusion is the number of different ordinary share accounts, each of which identifies a source of the firm's equity. The *ordinary shares account* identifies the initial funding from investors that was used to start the business and is priced at a par value. The par value is an arbitrary number set by management, usually a nominal amount such as €1.

Clearly, par value has little to do with the market value of the shares. The *share premium account* is the amount of capital received for the ordinary shares in excess of par value. Thus, if the

new business is started with €40 000 in cash and the firm decides to issue 1000 ordinary shares with a par value of €1, the owners' equity account looks as follows:

Ordinary shares	€1 000
(1000 shares @ €1 par value)	
Share premium	39 000
Total paid-in capital	€40 000

Note the money put up by the initial investors: €1000 in total par value (1000 ordinary shares with a par value of €1) and €39 000 premium for the shares, for a total of €40 000.

As you can see in Exhibit 3.1, Fabrique Aérospatiale has 15.8 million ordinary shares in issue with a par value of €10, for a total value of €158 million (15.8 million shares × €10). The additional paid-in capital is €107 million. Thus, Fabrique Aérospatiale's total paid-in capital is €265 million (€158m + €107m).

Other Reserves

This is a catch-all category that includes a range of changes to values of assets and liabilities that affect the net position of the equity element. Recall from Equation (3.1) that total assets is equal to total liabilities plus shareholders' equity. A change in the value of assets while the liabilities remain unaltered will change the value of the equity account. This can arise through changes in the recorded value of certain assets – and is most common for assets which have a long life such as land and buildings. In order to show a fair view of the company's fixed assets it is not uncommon to revalue items such as land and buildings on a periodic basis (every three years is normal). For instance, if the land and buildings owned by Fabrique Aérospatiale were previously reported on the balance sheet as €100 million and are subsequently revalued such that they are then recorded in the accounts at their new value of €120 million, the balance sheet will no longer balance. A new item on the liabilities side for €20 million needs to be added to compensate. Since this amount is not a liability item, nor is it new money being invested, it is added to the shareholders' equity account as an increase in *other reserves*. Note that with impairments, where the value of assets is reduced, this would lead to a decrease in the other reserves account such that, as a result, this may have a negative value.

Retained Earnings

The retained earnings account represents earnings that have been retained and reinvested in the business over time rather than being paid out as cash dividends. Fabrique Aérospatiale's retained earnings account is €416 million, compared with the total paid-in capital of €266 million.

Note that retained earnings are not the same as cash. In fact, a company can have a very large retained earnings account and no cash. Conversely, it can have lots of cash and a very small retained earnings account. Because retained earnings appear on the liability side of the balance sheet, they do not represent an asset, as cash and marketable securities do.

Treasury Shares

Treasury shares represent ordinary shares that the firm has purchased back from investors. Publicly traded companies can simply buy shares from shareholders on the market at the prevailing price. Typically, repurchased shares are held as 'treasury shares' and the firm can reissue these in the future if it desires. While not shown in the retained earnings account, Fabrique Aérospatiale has spent €7 million to repurchase its ordinary shares. You may wonder why a firm's management would repurchase its own shares. This is a classic finance question and it has no simple answer. The conventional wisdom is that when a company has excess cash and management believes its share price is undervalued, it makes sense to purchase shares with the cash. However, it is not obvious that management can beat the market over the long term when buying and selling its own shares.

> **Treasury shares**
>
> ordinary shares that the firm has repurchased from investors

Preference Shares

Preference shares are a cross between ordinary shares and long-term debt. Preference shares pay dividends at a specified fixed rate, which means that the firm cannot increase or decrease the dividend rate, regardless of whether the firm's earnings increase or decrease. However, like the dividends for ordinary shares, preference share dividends are declared by the board of directors and, in the event of financial distress, the board can elect not to pay a preference share dividend. If preference share dividends are missed, the firm is typically required to pay dividends that have been skipped in the past before they can pay dividends to ordinary shareholders. In the event of bankruptcy, preference shareholders are paid before ordinary shareholders but after bondholders and other creditors. As shown in Exhibit 3.1, Fabrique Aérospatiale has 1.88 million preference shares outstanding for which it received €188 million.

Minority Interests

The Fabrique Aérospatiale group consists of a number of different companies. In the case of a number of these subsidiaries, the parent does not own 100% of the ordinary shares of these companies. Outside investors hold some shares and hence have an economic interest in these subsidiaries. When the financial statements of the group are consolidated, the outside shareholdings are included, but are separately reported as *minority interest in equity* to reflect the fact that these other shareholders also have a part claim on some of the group's assets. At 31 December 2010, Fabrique Aérospatiale had shareholder minority interests of €45 million.

Held For Sale

One of the principles in drawing up financial statements discussed earlier related to going concern. Under IFRS reporting, companies separate the assets, liabilities and profits of activities and businesses which they expect to maintain over the coming 12-month reporting period from those that either will be wound up or sold within this period. These are separately reported from the assets and liabilities of continuing operations. As of 31

December 2010, Fabrique Aérospatiale has indicated it plans to dispose of assets worth €21 million that have matched liabilities of €1 million.

Before You Go On

1. What is net working capital? Why might a low value for this number be considered undesirable?
2. Explain the accounting concept behind depreciation.
3. What are treasury shares?

MARKET VALUE VERSUS BOOK VALUE

Learning Objective 3
Describe how market-value balance sheets differ from book-value balance sheets.

Although accounting statements are helpful to analysts and managers, they have a number of limitations. One of these limitations, mentioned earlier, is that accounting statements are historical – they are based on data such as the cost of a building that was built years ago and have possibly not been revalued since. Thus, the value of many assets on the balance sheet is what the firm paid for them and not their current market value – the amount they are worth today.

Investors and management, however, care about how the company will do in the future. The best information concerning how much a company's assets can earn in the future, as well as how much of a burden its liabilities are, comes from the current market value of those assets and liabilities. Accounting statements would therefore be more valuable if they measured current value. In theory, everyone agrees that it is better to base financial statements on current information.

The process of recording assets at their current market value is often called *marking to market*.

Under IFRS certain categories of assets and liabilities are mandated to be recorded at their current market value. Marking to market provides decision makers with financial statements that more closely reflect a company's true financial condition; thus, they have a better chance of making the correct economic decision, given the information available. For example, providing current market values means that managers can no longer conceal a failing business or hide unrealised gains on assets.

On the downside, the current value of some assets can be hard to estimate and accountants are reluctant to make estimates. Critics also point out that some of the valuation models used to estimate market values are complicated to apply and the resulting numbers are potentially open to abuse.

Market price
the price at which an item can be sold

WEB
http://www.pwc.com/us/en/point-of-view/fair-value-accounting-finance-proposal.jhtml

---

A More Informative Balance Sheet
To illustrate why market value provides better economic information than book value, let us revisit the balance sheet components discussed earlier. Our discussion will also help you understand why there can be such large differences between some book-value and market-value balance sheet accounts.[5]

Assets
For current assets, market value and book value may be reasonably close. The reason is that current assets have a short life cycle and typically are converted into cash quickly. Then, as new current assets are

added to the balance sheet, they are entered at their current market price. Also IFRS requires certain types of current assets such as financial assets to be stated at a 'fair value' that approximates their realisable value at the balance sheet date.

Fair value

the amount for which an asset could be exchanged, or a liability settled, between knowledgeable, willing parties in an arm's-length transaction

In contrast, fixed assets have a long life cycle and their market value and book value are not likely to be equal. In addition, if an asset is depreciable, the amount of depreciation shown on the balance sheet does not necessarily reflect actual loss of economic value. As a general rule, the longer the time that has passed since an asset was acquired, the more likely it is that the current market value will differ from the book value.[6]

For example, suppose a firm purchased land for a warehouse near Vienna, Austria, 30 years ago for €100 000. Today the land is nestled in an expanding suburb and is worth around €5.5 million. The difference between the book value of €100 000 and the market value is €5.4 million. In another example, say an airline company decided to replace its aging fleet of aircraft with new fuel-efficient jets in the late 1990s. Following the 11 September 2001 terrorist attack, airline travel declined dramatically; and during 2003 nearly one-third of all commercial jets were 'mothballed'. In 2003 the current market value of the replacement commercial jets was about two-thirds their original cost. Why the decline? Because the expected cash flows from owning a commercial aircraft had declined a great deal.

Liabilities

The market value of liabilities can also differ from their book value, though typically by smaller amounts than is the case with assets. For liabilities, the balance sheet shows the amount of money that the company has promised to pay. This figure is generally close to the actual market value for short-term liabilities.

For long-term debt, however, book value and market value can differ substantially. The market value of debt with fixed interest payments is affected by the level of interest rates in the economy. More specifically, after long-term debt is issued, if the market rate of interest increases, the market price of the debt will decline. Conversely, if interest rates decline, the value of the debt will increase. For example, assume that a firm has €1 million of 20-year bonds outstanding. If the market rate of interest increases from 5% to 8%, the price of the bonds will decline to around €700 000.[7] Thus, changes in interest rates can have an important effect on the market values of long-term liabilities, such as corporate bonds. Even if interest rates do not change, the market value of long-term liabilities can change if the performance of the firm declines and the probability of default increases.

Shareholders' Equity

The book value of the firm's equity is one of the least informative items on the balance sheet. The book value of equity, as suggested earlier, is simply a historical record. As a result, it says very little about the market value of the shareholders' stake in the firm.

In contrast, on a balance sheet where both assets and liabilities are marked to market, the firm's equity is more informative to management and investors. *The difference between the market values of the assets and liabilities provides a better estimate of the market value of shareholders' equity than the difference in the book values.* Intuitively, this makes sense because if you know the 'true' market value of the firm's assets and liabilities, the difference must equal the market value of the shareholders' equity.

You should be aware, however, that the difference between the sum of the market values of the individual assets and total liabilities will not give us an exact estimate of the market value of shareholders' equity. The reason is that the true total value of a firm's assets depends on how these assets are used. By utilising the assets efficiently, management can make the total value greater than the simple sum of parts. We will discuss this concept in more detail in Chapter 18.

Finally, if you know the market value of the shareholders' equity and the number of ordinary shares outstanding, it is easy to compute the share price. Specifically, the price of an ordinary share is the market value of the company's shareholders' equity divided by the number of shares outstanding.

A Market-Value Balance Sheet

Let us now look at an example of how a market-value balance sheet can differ from a book-value balance sheet. PanEurope Airline is a small regional carrier that has been serving Eastern Europe for five years. The airline has a fleet of short-haul jets, most of which were purchased over the past two years. The fleet has a book value of €600 million. Recently, the airline industry has suffered substantial losses in revenue due to price competition coupled to high jet fuel prices and most carriers are projecting operating losses for the near future. As a result, the market value of PanEurope's fleet of aircraft is only €400 million. The book value of PanEurope's long-term debt is €300 million, which is near its current market value. The firm has 100 million shares outstanding. Using these data, we can construct two balance sheets, one based on historical book values and the other based on market values:

PanEurope Airlines
Market-Value versus Book-Value Balance Sheets (€ millions)

Assets			Liabilities and shareholders' equity		
	Book	Market		Book	Market
Aircraft	€600	€400	Long-term debt	€300	€300
			Shareholders' equity	€300	€100
Total	€600	€400		€600	€400

Based on the book-value balance sheet, the firm's financial condition looks fine; the book value of PanEurope's aircraft at €600 million is near what the firm paid and the shareholders' equity account is €300 million. But when we look at the market-value balance sheet, a different story emerges. We immediately see that the value of the aircraft has declined by €200 million and the shareholders' equity has declined by €200 million!

Why the decline in shareholders' equity? Recall that in Chapter 1 we argued that the value of any asset – stocks, bonds or a firm – is determined by the future cash flows the asset will generate. At the time the aircraft were purchased, it was expected that they would generate a certain amount of cash flows over time. Now that hard times plague the industry, the cash flow expectations have been lowered and hence the decline in the value of shareholders' equity.

Learning by
Doing
Application
3.1

The Market-Value Balance Sheet

Problem: De Buren NV, a small Netherlands-based engineering firm, have developed a revolutionary new continuous screening system that can monitor high-risk areas within a production process and identify abnormalities so that corrective actions can be taken. The firm has spent about €300 000 developing the technology. The firm's bookkeeper carries the research and development costs as an asset valued at cost, which is €300 000. To launch the product, shareholders recently invested an additional €1 million and the money is currently in the firm's bank account. At a recent trade show, a number of engineering firms tried to buy the new technology – the highest offer being €15 million. Assuming these are De Buren's only assets and liabilities, prepare the firm's book-value and market-value balance sheets and explain the difference between the two.

Approach: The main differences between the two balance sheets will be the treatment of the €300 000 already spent to develop the screening system and the €15 million offer. The book-value balance sheet is a historical document, which means all assets are valued at what it cost to put them in service, while the market-value balance sheet reflects the value of the assets if they were sold under current market conditions. The differences between the two approaches can be considerable.

The book-value balance sheet provides little useful information. The book value of the firm's total assets is €1.3 million, which consists of cash in the bank and the cost of developing the monitoring system. Since the firm has no debt, total assets must equal the book value of shareholders' equity. The market value tells a dramatically different story. The market value of the monitoring technology is estimated to be €15.0 million; thus, the market value of shareholders' equity is €16.0 million and not €1.3 million as reported in the book-value balance sheet.

Solution: The two balance sheets are as follows:

De Buren NV
Market-Value versus Book-Value Balance Sheets (€ thousands)

Assets				Liabilities and shareholders' equity		
	Book	Market			Book	Market
Cash in bank	€1 000	€1 000	Long-term debt			
Intangible assets	300	15 000	Shareholders' equity		€1 300	€16 000
Total	€1 300	€16 000			€1 300	€16 000

Before You Go On

1. What is the difference between book value and market value?
2. What are some of the objections to the preparation of market-based balance sheets?

THE INCOME STATEMENT AND THE STATEMENT OF RETAINED EARNINGS

Learning Objective 4

Identify the basic equation for the income statement and the information it provides.

In the previous sections, we examined a firm's balance sheet, which is like a financial snapshot of the firm at a point in time. In contrast, the income statement (also called a profit and loss account) is like a video clip showing how profitable a firm is between two points in time.

The Income Statement

The income statement (or profit and loss account) summarises the revenues, expenses and profitability (or losses) of the firm over some period, usually a month, a quarter or a year. The basic equation for the income statement can be expressed as follows:

$$\text{Net income or Net profit} = \text{Revenues} - \text{Expenses}$$
$$(3.3)$$

Let us look more closely at each element in this equation.

Income statement

a financial statement that reports a firm's revenues, expenses and profits or losses over a given period. Also called the profit and loss account or statement

Revenues

A firm's revenues arise from the products and services it creates through its business operations. For industrial and retailing companies, revenues come from the sale of products. Service companies, such as consulting firms, generate fees for the services they perform. Other kinds of businesses earn revenues by charging interest or collecting rent. Regardless of how they earn revenues, most firms either receive cash or create an account receivable for each transaction, which increases their total assets.

Expenses

Expenses are the various costs that the firm incurs to generate revenues. Broadly speaking, expenses are (1) the value of long-term assets consumed through business operations, such as depreciation expense, and (2) the costs incurred in conducting business, such as labour, utilities, materials and taxes.

Net Income

Net income is often referred to as net profit or simply as income, profits, earnings or the 'bottom line', since it is the last item on the income statement. The firm's net income (net profit) reflects its accomplishments (revenues) relative to its efforts (expenses) over a particular period. If revenues exceed expenses, the firm generates net income for the period. If expenses exceed revenues, the firm has a net loss. Net income or net profit is often reported on a per-share basis and is then called earnings per share (EPS), where EPS equals net income divided by the number of ordinary shares outstanding. A firm's earnings per share tell a shareholder how much the firm has earned (or lost) for each ordinary share issued.

> ### Earnings per share (EPS)
>
> net income (net earnings) divided by the number of ordinary shares outstanding

Income statements for Fabrique Aérospatiale for 2009 and 2010 are shown in Exhibit 3.2. You can see that in 2010 total revenues from continuing operations were €1 319 million. The cost of goods sold was €484 million. Total expenses for producing and selling those goods were €1 117 million – the total of the amounts for cost of goods sold, selling and administrative expenses, depreciation, interest expense and taxes.[8]

Using Equation (3.3), we can use these numbers to calculate Fabrique Aérospatiale's net income for the year:

$$
\begin{aligned}
&\text{Net income or Net profit} \\
&= \text{Revenues} - \text{Expenses} \\
&= \text{€1319 million} - \text{€1117 million} \\
&= \text{€202 million}
\end{aligned}
$$

Since Fabrique Aérospatiale had 15.8 million ordinary shares outstanding at year's end, its earnings per share (EPS) was €11.77 per share (€186 million/15.8 million).

A Closer Look at Some Expense Categories

Next, we take a closer look at some of the expense items that form part of the income statement. We discussed depreciation earlier in relation to the balance sheet and we now look at the role of depreciation in the income statement.

Depreciation Expense An interesting feature of financial reporting is that companies are allowed to prepare two sets of financial statements: one for tax purposes and one for managing the company and for financial reporting to investors and regulators. For tax purposes, most firms elect to accelerate depreciation as quickly as is permitted under the tax rules. The reason is that accelerated depreciation results in a higher depreciation expense to the income statement, which in turn results in a lower pre-tax income and a lower tax liability in the first few years after the asset is acquired. The good news about accelerating depreciation for tax purposes is that the firm pays lower taxes but does not actually write a bigger cheque for depreciation expense. The depreciation method does not affect the cost of the asset. In contrast, straight-line depreciation results in lower depreciation expenses to the income statement, which results in higher pre-tax income and higher tax payments. Firms generally use straight-line depreciation in the financial statements they report to investors and regulators because it makes their earnings look better.

It is important to understand that the company does not take more total depreciation under accelerated depreciation methods than under the straight-line method; the total amount of depreciation expensed to the income statement over the life of an asset is the same. Total depreciation cannot exceed the price paid for the asset. Accelerating depreciation only alters the timing of when the depreciation is expensed.

Amortisation Expense   Amortisation is the process of writing off expenses for intangible assets – such as patents, licenses, copyrights and trademarks – over their useful life. Since depreciation and amortisation are very similar, they are often lumped together on the income statement. Both are non-cash expenses, which mean that an expense is recorded on the income statement, but the associated cash does not necessarily leave the firm in that period. For Fabrique Aérospatiale, the depreciation and amortisation expense for 2010 was €116 million.[9]

At one time, goodwill was one of the intangible assets subject to amortisation. Under IFRS standards goodwill is not amortised. The value of the goodwill on a firm's balance sheet is subject to an annual *impairment test*. This test requires that the company annually value the businesses that were acquired in the past to see if the value of the goodwill associated with those businesses has declined below the value at which it is being carried on the balance sheet. If the value of the goodwill has declined (been impaired), management must write off the amount of the impairment. This write-off reduces the firm's reported net income.

Extraordinary Items   Extraordinary items are unusual and infrequent occurrences, such as gains or losses from floods, fires or earthquakes. It used to be the case that these could be reported separately in the income statement as extraordinary items, which are reserved for non-operating gains or losses. Under US GAAP companies can separate out such items. For example, in 1980 the volcano Mount St. Helens erupted in Washington State, and the Weyerhaeuser Company reported an extraordinary loss of $67 million to cover the damage to its standing timber, buildings and equipment. IFRS prohibits reporting items as extraordinary and all such items must be expensed through the income statement.

Step by Step to the Bottom Line

You probably noticed in Exhibit 3.2 that Fabrique Aérospatiale's income statement showed income at a number of intermediate steps before reaching profit for the year (net income), the so-called bottom line. These intermediate income figures, which are typically included on a firm's income statement, provide important information about the firm's performance and help identify what factors are driving the firm's income or losses.

Operating Profit   The profit earned from ongoing operations including the direct cost of sales and the establishment and other costs of being in business such as administrative expense. Operating profit is also called earnings before interest and taxes (EBIT). The operating profit for Fabrique Aérospatiale in 2010 was €334 million.

Profit before Tax   When net interest expense is subtracted from operating profit, the result is profit or earnings before taxes (EBT). Profit before tax for Fabrique Aérospatiale was €292 million in 2010.

Profit for the Year   Finally, taxes are subtracted from profit before tax or EBT to arrive at profit for the year, which is also known as net income, net earnings or net profit. For Fabrique Aérospatiale, as we have already seen, net income in 2010 was €202 million.

As discussed earlier, financial analysts often want to compare the performance of different companies. It is clear that depreciation and amortisation policies and the amount of debt and hence net interest paid by a particular company will affect the amount of the reported profit. In order to get a clean estimate of performance analysts often use a

EXHIBIT 3.2

FABRIQUE AÉROSPATIALE SE INCOME STATEMENTS FOR YEAR ENDING 31 DECEMBER (€ MILLIONS)

Continuing operations	Year ended 31 December	
	2010	2009
Revenue	€1319	€702
Cost of sales[a]	(484)	(292)
Gross profit	835	410
Service and distribution costs[a]	(326)	(133)
Administration expenses[b]	(180)	(65)
Other income	12	8
Other (losses)/gains – net	(1)	—
Loss on sale of land	(6)	—
Operating profit	334	221
Finance income	11	10
Finance costs	(51)	(76)
Finance costs – net	(40)	(66)
Share of (loss)/profit of associates	(2)	1
Profit before income tax	292	156
Income tax expense	(91)	(54)
Profit for the year from continuing operations	201	102
Discontinued operations		
Profit for the year from discontinued operations	1	1
Profit for the year (net income)	€202	€102
Attributable to:		
Equity holders of the company	186	97
Minority interest	16	5
	€202	€102
Per share data:	In euros	
Share price	—	—
Earnings per share (EPS)	€11.77	€7.76
Dividends per share (DPS)	3.99	7.87
Book value per share (BVPS)	52.08	44.47
Cash flow per share (CFPS)	13.47	8.24

[a]Includes depreciation expense for goods sold and distribution of €111 million in 2010 (2009: €60 million).
[b]Includes amortisation expense of €5 million for 2010 (2009: €4 million).
The income statement shows the sales, expenses and profits earned by the firm over a specific period.

measure called EBITDA, *earnings before interest, tax, depreciation and amortisation*. This is not reported on the income statement, but can easily be calculated by adding back interest expense, tax, depreciation and amortisation. For Fabrique Aérospatiale, EBITDA is €449 million in 2010.[10]

In Chapter 4 you will see how to use these intermediate income figures to evaluate the firm's financial condition. Next, we look at the statement of retained earnings, which provides detailed information about how management allocated the €202 million of net income earned during the period.

The Statement of Retained Earnings

Companies often prepare a statement of retained earnings, which identifies the changes in the retained earnings account from one accounting period to the next. During any accounting period, two events can affect the retained earnings account balance:

1. When the firm reports net income or loss.
2. When the board of directors declares and pays a cash dividend.

Exhibit 3.3 shows the activity in the retained earnings account for 2010 for Fabrique Aérospatiale. The beginning balance of €304 million is as reported for retained earnings on the 2009 balance sheet. As reported in the 2010 income statement (Exhibit 3.2), the firm earned €202 million that year and the board of directors elected to declare dividends for the ordinary shares and preference shares for 2009 worth €90 million. Retained earnings consequently went from €304 million to €416 million, an increase of €112 million.

Before You Go On

1. How do you compute net income?
2. What is EBITDA and what does it measure?
3. What accounting events trigger changes to the retained earnings account?

CASH FLOWS

Learning Objective 5

Explain the difference between cash flows and accounting income.

As we discussed in Chapter 1, the concept of cash flows is an important one in financial management. Financial managers are concerned with maximising the value of shareholders' shares, which means making decisions that will maximise the value of the firm's future cash flows. It is important to recognise that the revenues, expenses and net income reported in a firm's income statement do not necessarily reflect cash flows. We must therefore distinguish between a company's net income and the cash flows it generates.

Net Income versus Cash Flows

As we explained earlier, net income is equal to revenues minus expenses. Net cash flow is the cash that a firm generates in a given period (cash receipts less cash payments). Why is net income different from net cash flow? The reason is that when accountants prepare financial statements, they do not count the cash coming in and the cash going out. Under GAAP, they recognise revenues at the time a sale is substantially completed, not when the customer pays. In addition, because of

EXHIBIT 3.3

FABRIQUE AÉROSPATIALE SE STATEMENT OF RETAINED EARNINGS FOR THE YEAR ENDING 31 DECEMBER 2010 (€ MILLIONS)

Retained earnings at 31 December 2009	€304
Profit for the year	202
Dividends (relating to 2009)	(90)
Retained earnings at 31 December 2010	€416

the matching principle, accountants match revenues with the costs of producing the revenues. Finally, capital expenditures are paid for at the time of purchase, but the expense for the use of the capital asset is spread out over the asset's useful life through depreciation and amortisation. As a result of these accounting rules, typically a significant lag in time exists between when revenues and expenses are recorded and when the cash is actually collected (in the case of revenue) or paid (in the case of expenses).[11]

> **Net cash flow**
>
> a firm's actual cash receipts less cash payments in a given period

Though neither method is precise, two 'rough and ready' ways can be used to convert accounting profits into net cash flows from operating activities. The first method adjusts the firm's net income for all non-cash revenue and non-cash expenses. Net cash flow from operating activities (NCFOA) is

$$\text{NCFOA} = \text{Net income} - \text{Non-cash revenues} + \text{Non-cash expenses} \qquad (3.4)$$

For most businesses, the largest non-cash expenses are depreciation and amortisation. These two items are deducted from revenues on the income statement, but no cash is paid out. The cash outflows took place when the assets were purchased. Other non-cash items include the following:

- Depletion charges, which are like depreciation but which apply to extractive natural resources, such as crude oil, natural gas, timber and mineral deposits (non-cash expense).
- Deferred taxes, which are the portion of a firm's income tax expense that is postponed because of differences in the accounting policies adopted for management financial reporting and for tax reporting (non-cash expense).
- Prepaid expenses that are paid in advance, such as for rent and insurance (non-cash expense).

- Deferred revenues, which are revenues received as cash but not yet earned. An example of deferred revenue would be prepaid magazine subscriptions to a publishing company (non-cash revenue).

The second method simply recognises the fact that depreciation and amortisation are usually the largest non-cash charges and assumes that the remaining non-cash revenues or charges cancel one another. The result is a simplified version of Equation (3.4):

$$\text{NCFOA} = \text{Net income} - \text{Depreciation and amortisation} \qquad (3.5)$$

Equation (3.5) provides satisfactory estimates of NCFOA for many finance problems, unless there are significant non-cash items beyond depreciation and amortisation. To illustrate, we can use the data from Fabrique Aérospatiale's 2010 income statement (Exhibit 3.2):

$$\text{NCFOA} = \text{€}202 + \text{€}116 = \text{€}318\,\text{million}$$

Fabrique Aérospatiale's net cash flow is much larger than its net income, illustrating the point that profits and net cash flow are not the same. However, as a cautionary warning, note that neither Equation (3.4) nor Equation (3.5) adjusts for changes in the working capital accounts, such as inventory levels and accounts payable, and if changes in these accounts are significant, the equations cannot be used. We consider these adjustments next.

The Statement of Cash Flows

There are times when the financial manager wants to know in detail all the cash flows that have taken place during the year and reconcile the beginning-of-year and end-of-year cash balances. The reason for the focus on cash flows is very practical. There is ample evidence from practice that business firms can post significant earnings (net income) but still have inadequate cash to pay wages, suppliers and other creditors. On occasion, these firms have had to file for bankruptcy. The problem, of course, lies in the fact that profits (net income) are not the same as cash flows.

Statement of cash flows

a financial statement that shows a firm's cash receipts and cash payments for a period of time

Sources and Uses of Cash

The statement of cash flows shows the company's cash inflows (receipts) and cash outflows (payments) for a period of time. We derive these cash flows by looking at changes in balance sheet accounts from the end of one accounting period to the end of the next, and at the firm's net income for the period. In analysing the cash flow statement, it is important to understand that changes in the balance sheet accounts reflect cash flows. More specifically, increases in assets or decreases in liabilities and equity are uses of cash, while decreases in assets or increases in liabilities and equity are sources of cash, as explained in the following.

- *Working capital.* An increase in current assets (such as trade accounts receivable and inventories) is a use of cash. For example, if a firm increases its inventories, it must use cash to purchase the additional inventory. Conversely, the sale of inventory increases a firm's cash position. An increase in current liabilities (such as trade accounts and notes payable) is a source of cash. For example, if during the year a firm increases its accounts payable, it has effectively 'borrowed' money from suppliers and increased its cash position.
- *Fixed assets.* An increase in fixed assets is a use of cash. If a company purchases fixed assets during the year, it decreases cash because it must use cash to pay for the purchase. If the firm sells a fixed asset during the year, the firm's cash position will increase.
- *Equity and long-term liabilities.* An increase in equity (ordinary shares) or in long-term borrowings (bonds, preference shares or bank loans) is a source of cash. The retirement of borrowings or the purchase of treasury shares requires the firm to pay out cash, reducing cash balances.

- *Dividends.* Any cash dividend payment decreases a firm's cash balance.

Organisation of the Statement of Cash Flows

The statement of cash flows is organised around three business activities – operating activities, investing activities and financing activities – and the reconciliation of the cash account. We discuss each of these elements next and illustrate them with reference to the statement of cash flows for Fabrique Aérospatiale, which is shown in Exhibit 3.4.

Operating Activities   Cash flows from operations are the net cash flows that are related to a firm's principal business activities. The most important items are the firm's operating profit, tax, depreciation expense and working capital accounts (other than cash and short-term debt obligations, which are classified elsewhere).

In Exhibit 3.4, the first section of the statement of cash flows for Fabrique Aérospatiale shows the cash flow from operations. The section starts with the firm's operating profit of €334 million for the year ending 31 December 2010. Depreciation and amortisation expenses (€116 million) are added back because they are a non-cash expense on the income statement.

Next come changes in the firm's working capital accounts that affect operating activities. Note that working capital accounts that involve financing (bank loans and debt issues) and cash reconciliation (cash and marketable securities) will be classified separately. For Fabrique Aérospatiale, the working capital accounts show that there is only one *source* of cash: an increase in trade and other accounts payable of €26 million (€104 – €78). Changes in working capital items that are *uses* of cash are: (1) increase in inventories of €41 million (€154 – €114) and (2) an increase in trade and other accounts receivable of €15 million (€124 + €15 – €115 + €9). The total cash provided to the firm from operations is €420 million.

To clarify why changes in working capital accounts affect the statement of cash flows, let us look at some of the changes. Fabrique Aérospatiale had a €15 million increase in trade accounts receivable, which is subtracted from operating profit as a

EXHIBIT 3.4

FABRIQUE AÉROSPATIALE STATEMENT OF CASH FLOWS FOR THE YEAR ENDING 31 DECEMBER 2010 (€ MILLION)

Cash flows from operating activities	(€ millions)
Operating profit	334
Depreciation & amortisation	116
Increase in trade accounts payable	26
Increase in inventories	(41)
Increase in trade accounts receivable	(15)
Operating cash flows before finance charges and taxes	420
Net change in provisions	6
Net finance charges	(40)
Dividends paid	(90)
Income tax	(91)
Operating cash flows after finance charges and taxes	204
Cash flows from investing activities	
Property plant and equipment	(344)
Intangible assets & investments in associates	(36)
Available for sale financial assets	(51)
Assets of disposal group as held for sale	(19)
Net cash used in investing activities	(450)
Cash flows from financing activities	
Net new equity	68
Net new borrowings	76
Net cash provided by financing activities	145
	(€101)
Net change in cash position	
Cash reconciliation	
Net decrease in cash and cash equivalents	(€101)
Cash and cash equivalents at beginning of year	213
Cash and cash equivalents at end of year	€112

use of cash. The increase in trade accounts receivable is a use of cash because the number represents sales that were included in the income statement but for which no cash has been collected. Fabrique Aérospatiale provided financing for these sales to its customers. The €26 million increase in trade accounts payable represents a source of cash because goods and services the company purchased were received but no cash was paid out.

Moving down the cash flow statement, there is a net change in provisions of €5 million. The company paid net interest expenses of €40 million and this needs to be subtracted, as does the dividend payment of €90 million. The company paid taxes, so €91 million of income tax needs to be deducted from operating profit to give the after-tax and financing charges operating cash flow of €204 million.

Investing Activities Cash flows from investing activities primarily relate to the buying and selling of long-term assets. The primary investment activities for manufacturing and service firms are the purchase or sale of land, buildings and plant and equipment. It also includes a range of financial transactions. In Exhibit 3.4, the second section shows the cash flows from investing activities. Fabrique Aérospatiale invested in a number of areas, which resulted in a cash outflow of €450 million. They were as follows: (1) the purchase of plant and equipment, totalling €344 million (€971 − €626) and (2) an increase in intangible assets and investments in associates of €36 million (€164 + €84 − (€129 + €83)), and (3) an increase in available-for-sale financial assets and derivatives of €51 million (€121 − €93 + €12 + €74 − €50 + €3 − €4) and a new item of assets of disposal group held for sale of €19 million, which represents the net between the assets held for sale and related liabilities (€21 − €1; note the difference of €1 here, due to rounding of the numbers in the accounts to the nearest €1 million).

Financing Activities Cash flows from financing come from activities in which cash is obtained from or repaid to creditors or owners (shareholders). Typical financing activities involve cash received from owners as they invest in the firm by buying ordinary shares, as well as cash from debt issues – such as preference shares – and bank loans. Cash purchases of treasury shares reduce a company's cash position and repayment of debt is a *use* of cash.

Fabrique Aérospatiale's financing activities include net new equity of €68 million (€158 + €107 − €131 − €66), net new borrowings of €76 million (€720 + €73 − €602 − €114), which together provide a source of cash. Overall, Fabrique Aérospatiale had a net cash inflow from financing activities of €145 million.

Cash Reconciliation The final part of the statement of cash flows is a reconciliation of the firm's beginning and ending year cash and cash equivalents positions. For Fabrique Aérospatiale, these cash positions are as shown on the 2009 and 2010 balance sheets. The first step to reconciling the company's beginning and ending cash positions is to add together the amounts from the first three sections of the statement of cash flows: (1) the net cash inflows from operations of €204 million, (2) the net cash outflow from long-term investment activities of €450 million, and (3) the net cash inflow from financing activities of €145 million. Together, these three items represent a total net decrease in cash to the firm of €101 million (€204 − €450 + €145). Finally, we subtract this amount (€101 million) from the beginning cash balance of €213 million to obtain the ending cash balance for 2010 of €112 million.

Additional Cash Flow Calculations

This section has introduced cash flow calculations. We will return to the topic of cash flows in Chapters 11 and 18. In those chapters we will develop more precise measures of cash flows that will allow us to determine (1) the incremental cash flows necessary to estimate the value of a capital project and (2) the free cash flows needed to estimate the value of a firm.

Before You Go On

1. What is the difference between accounting profits and net cash flows?
2. Should a firm consider only depreciation and amortisation expenses when calculating the net cash flow? Explain.

TYING THE FINANCIAL STATEMENTS TOGETHER

Learning Objective 6

Explain how the four major financial statements discussed in this chapter are related.

Up to this point, we have treated a firm's financial statements as if they were independent of one another. As you might suspect, though, the four financial statements presented in this chapter are related. Let us see how.

Recall that the balance sheet summarises what assets the firm has at a particular point in time and how the firm has financed those assets with debt and equity. From one year to the next, the firm's balance sheet will change because the firm will buy or sell assets and the value of the debt and equity financing will change. These changes are exactly the ones presented in the statement of cash flows. In other words, the statement of cash flows presents a summary of the changes in a firm's balance sheet from the beginning of a period to the end of that period.

This concept is illustrated in Exhibit 3.5, which presents summaries of the four financial statements for Fabrique Aérospatiale for the year 2010. The exhibit also presents the balance sheet for the beginning of that year, which is dated 31 December 2009. If you compare the changes in the balance sheet numbers from the beginning of the year to the end of the year, you can see that these changes are in fact summarised in the statement of cash flows. For example, the change in the cash balance of €101 million (€112 − €213) appears at the bottom of the statement of cash flows. Similarly, excluding cash, the change in current assets from the beginning to the end of 2010 is €89 million, which is calculated as follows: [(€292 + €114 − (€104 + €34)) − (€237 + €56 − (€78 + €36))] = (€268 − €179) = €89. The net working capital investment reflected in the statement of cash flows (€24) is less than this since it excludes the net position in financial instruments and in derivatives reported on the balance sheet.[12] Note, too, that the net working capital investment in Fabrique Aérospatiale's statement of cash flows is just the total change in the firm's investment in the working capital accounts – trade and other accounts payable and trade and other accounts receivable and inventories. You can also see in Exhibit 3.5 that the change in non-current assets – which includes net property, plant and equipment, goodwill and other assets – is €398 million (€1352 −

€954). This number is equal to the cash flows from investing activities less the change in assets held for sale given in the statement of cash flows (€450 − €51 = €399).[13]

Turning to the liability and equity side of the balance sheet, notice the change in the amount of debt plus equity that the firm has sold in 2010, which is represented by the sum of the long-term liabilities and borrowings and invested capital in the balance sheet. The change in the balance sheet values is calculated as follows: (€908 − €789) + (€310 − €208) = (€119 + €102) = €221.[14] However, part of the increase is not shown as a cash flow item since it was contributed to by minority shareholders and an increase in non-current liabilities.[15] Finally, we can reconcile the figures to the statement of retained earnings. As Fabrique Aérospatiale paid dividends in 2010 on its ordinary and preference shares, the change in retained earnings of €112 million equals the profit for the year less the dividends paid (€202 − €90).

Again, the important point here is that the statement of cash flows summarises the changes in the balance sheet. How do the other financial statements fit into the picture? Well, the income statement calculates the firm's net income, which is used to calculate the retained earnings at the end of the year and is included as part of statement of cash flows. The income statement provides an input that is used in the balance sheet and the statement of cash flows. The statement of retained earnings just summarises the changes to the retained earnings account a little differently than the statement of cash flows. This different format makes it simpler for managers and investors to see why retained earnings changed as it did.

Before You Go On

1. Explain how the four financial statements are related.

EXHIBIT 3.5

THE INTERRELATION BETWEEN THE FINANCIAL STATEMENTS: ILLUSTRATED USING FABRIQUE AÉROSPATIALE'S FINANCIAL RESULTS

Balance sheet at 31/12/09

Non-current assets	€954
Working capital assets, excluding cash	237
Other short-term assets, excluding cash	56
Cash and cash equivalents	213
Total assets	**€1459**
Invested capital	€208
Retained earnings	304
Other reserves	44
Long-term liabilities and borrowings	789
Working capital liabilities	78
Other short-term liabilities excluding borrowings	36
Total liabilities and equity	**€1459**

Income statement for year ended 31/12/2010

Revenues	€1319
Expenses	1117
Profit for the year	€202

Statement of cash flows 31/12/2010

Profit for the year after tax	€202
Depreciation and amortisation	116
Net working capital investment including provisions	(24)
Operating activities	294
Dividends	(90)
	204
Investing activities	(450)
Financing activities	145
Net decrease in cash	(101)

Statement of retained earnings 31/12/2010

Retained earnings at 31/12/2009	€304
Net income	202
Dividends	(90)
Retained earnings at 31/12/2010	€416

Balance sheet at 31/12/10

Non-current assets	€1352
Working capital assets, excluding cash	292
Other short-term assets, excluding cash	114
Cash and cash equivalents	112
Total assets	**€1870**
Invested capital	€310
Retained earnings	416
Other reserves	97
Long-term liabilities and borrowings	908
Working capital liabilities	104
Other short-term liabilities excluding borrowings	34
Total liabilities and equity	**€1870**

The statement of cash flows ties together the income statement with the balance sheets from the beginning and the end of the period. The statement of retained earnings shows how the retained earnings account has changed from the beginning to the end of the period.

INTERNATIONAL ACCOUNTING ISSUES

Learning Objective 7

Understand that differences exist in the quality and way financial statements are reported between countries.

Our opening discussion highlighted the fact that there is a growing use of common accounting standards by countries that either adhere to, or to some extent comply with, IFRS standards. However, there are a number of issues with financial statements due to differences in the way they are presented and what information is disclosed. As a whole, large international companies provide a good degree of disclosure and may present accounts in accordance with IFRS even though they are not required to do so in their country of domicile. For small and medium-sized enterprises that operate locally, this may not be the case. While a complete treatment of the potential problems with financial statements is beyond the scope of this chapter, anyone who analyses companies in different countries should be aware of the potential pitfalls.

We can identify a range of issues when looking at the disclosure and information provided by financial statements across countries. Some are not a major problem, but others will complicate any analysis and understanding of financial statements. The problems can be classified as: (1) information, timeliness and language; (2) foreign currency issues; (3) differences in presentation of financial statements, accounting principles and disclosures; and (4) differences in the business environment, in particular countries that experience high rates of inflation.

Information, Timeliness and Language

Information on companies may be difficult to obtain in many countries since the company in question may not be included in any database of company accounts. In addition, the differences in presentation may mean that any foreign companies in a database may contain errors and present the information in a variety of formats. In addition, while it is possible to obtain an annual report for a foreign company, this may only be available in the local language and, given the varying degree of enforcement, may well be significantly out of date. For many companies, only annual reports will be available as it is not a requirement to file quarterly or semi-annual statements.

Foreign Currency Issues

Outside of the eurozone, companies will produce their financial statements in the local currency. A number of members of the European Union still use their national currencies (for instance Denmark, Sweden and the United Kingdom). This creates a comparability issue between companies reporting in different currencies. Because one currency may have a significantly different value from another, just viewing the financials in the local currency can lead to misinterpretation. This can be overcome by notionally converting the financial statements into the desired currency using the exchange rate that prevailed at the end of the year and using financial ratios, a topic that will be discussed in the next chapter.

Differences in Presentation and Accounting Standards

The presentation of the balance sheet and income statement formats varies from country to country. For instance, IFRS standards give the long-dated assets and liabilities at the top of the balance sheet statement. US companies, in contrast, show these at the bottom of the balance sheet. In the USA companies report assets gross of depreciation and net of accumulated depreciation. In Germany, for instance, depreciable assets are usually reported net of accumulated depreciation.

Countries will all have their own standards for GAAP and this will affect the presentation of financial statements. The major problem areas are consolidation, the valuation of fixed assets and goodwill. For instance, while IFRS allows for goodwill to be treated as an intangible asset subject to an impairment test, it is possible that goodwill is written off rather than carried. This will affect the presentation of the balance sheet. Take the following two companies, Leuven Software and PAT, which are the same except that PAT is required to write off the goodwill from acquisitions.

Leuven Software NV			
Assets		Liabilities	
Fixed assets	€50	Invested capital	€100
Goodwill	200	Reserves	150
Intangible assets	50	Long-term borrowings	100
Current assets	100	Current liabilities	50
Total assets	€400	Liabilities and equity	€400

PAT			
Assets		Liabilities	
Fixed assets	€50	Invested capital	€100
Intangible assets	50	Reserves	(50)
Current assets	100	Long-term borrowings	100
		Current liabilities	50
Total assets	€200	Liabilities and equity	€200

It would appear that Leuven is twice the size of PAT, but the difference is due to the latter writing off its goodwill against its reserves.

In addition, there may be elements of financial statements that are missing or are inadequately reported. For instance, there may be a lack of segmentation information, disclosure as to the method of asset valuation, details on foreign operations, description of capital expenditures, the use of hidden reserves and inadequate disclosure of off-balance sheet items.

Differences in the Business Environment

The differences in business environment can be related to culture and the economic environment. For instance, Japanese and Korean companies borrow more than most Western companies – hence they will have lower amounts of equity on the balance sheet as a proportion of all liabilities.

Countries with high inflation will also present problems. For instance, Turkey had over 10% inflation in 2010. This affects the value of assets and liabilities and the ability of the company to maintain its purchasing power. If inflation is ignored, the results can be seriously distorted. The following example will illustrate the effect, and how inflation accounting for countries with rapid changes in price levels aims to show an undistorted view of the underlying economic activity. First using historical accounting, the results for Ramero and Zultan Enterprises are:

	Ramero Enterprises			
	2009	2010	2011	Total
Revenue	60 000	69 500	78 250	207 750
Depreciation	55 000	55 000	55 000	165 000
Operating income	5 000	14 500	23 250	42 750

	Zultan Enterprises			
	2009	2010	2011	Total
Revenue	60 000	72 800	84 600	217 400
Depreciation	55 000	55 000	55 000	165 000
Operating income	5 000	17 800	29 600	52 400

The two companies are identical in their assets and hence depreciation. Under historical accounting, the performance of the two companies does not appear to be that different. However, when we account for the change in the price level as a result of inflation, we get a very different result:

Price level index	100	110	124.3
Inflation		10%	13%

Ramero Enterprises

	2009	2010	2011	Total
Revenue	60 000	69 500	78 250	207 750
Depreciation	55 000	60 500	68 365	183 865
Operating income	5 000	9 000	9 885	23 885
Purchasing power loss	0	500	7 150	7 650
Profit for the year	5 000	8 500	2 735	16 235

Zultan Enterprises

	2009	2010	2011	Total
Revenue	60 000	72 800	84 600	217 400
Depreciation	55 000	60 500	68 365	183 865
Operating income	5 000	12 300	16 235	33 535
Purchasing power loss	0	500	7 150	7 650
Profit for the year	5 000	11 800	9 085	25 885

Using an inflation accounting approach, depreciation is adjusted each year for the change in the price level. The difference in the two companies' performance is now clear in that Zultan Enterprises has been able to increase its sales over and above the change in the price level. On the other hand, Ramero Enterprises' sales are not keeping pace with inflation. If sales are 60 000 in 2009, then they need to be 60 000 × 124.3/100 = 74 580 in 2011 just to maintain purchasing power. If depreciation had not been adjusted for the change in price levels and the loss of purchasing power, Ramero Enterprises would have reported net income for 2011 of 23 250 – which would have masked the reality that it is failing to maintain its real profitability and ability to replace previously purchased assets at inflated prices.

There are a number of different methods that accountants have developed to account for inflation, including current cost accounting, replacement value accounting and current exit price accounting. Note that **inflation accounting**, also called price level accounting, is not fair value accounting as required under IFRS. As a process, inflation accounting is similar to converting financial statements into another currency using an exchange rate. Under some (not all) inflation accounting models, historical costs are converted to price-level-adjusted costs using general or specific price indices.

> ### Inflation accounting
>
> adjustments made to historical accounting to deal with the problem of the impact of changing price levels on financial statements. Also called price level accounting

Other factors that need to be taken into account are variations in depreciation methods, taxes on dividends and tax shields from expenses, such as interest payments.

CORPORATE INCOME TAX

Learning Objective 8

Discuss the difference between average and marginal tax rates.

We conclude the chapter with a discussion of corporate income taxes. Taxes take a big bite out of the income of most businesses and represent one of their largest cash outflows. For example, as shown in the income statement (Exhibit 3.2) for Fabrique Aérospatiale, the firm's earnings before taxes (EBT) in 2010 amounted to €293 million, and its tax bill was €91 million, or 31% of EBT (€91/€293) – not a trivial amount by any standard. Because of their magnitude, taxes play a critical role in most business financial decisions.

As you might suspect, companies spend a considerable amount of effort and money deploying tax specialists to find legal ways to minimise their tax burdens. The tax laws are complicated, continually changing and at times seemingly bizarre – in part because the tax system is not an economically rational document but reflects the political and social values of the country.

If you work in the finance or accounting area, a tax specialist will advise you on the tax implications of most decisions in which you will be involved as a businessperson. Consequently, we will not try to make you a tax expert but we will present a high-level view of the major portions of corporate income tax that have a significant impact on the operations of companies and their business decision making.

Corporate Income Taxes

Fabrique Aérospatiale is domiciled in Belgium and can expect to pay income tax to the Belgian tax authorities as a result. But it also has business units in the Netherlands and elsewhere, including Brazil, and these will also pay taxes locally. How companies are taxed is a complex issue, but generally firms pay a percentage of their profits after allowable deductions such as depreciation, certain losses and interest. In Belgium, as Exhibit 3.6 indicates, the standard corporate income tax rate is 33%, although various additional levies and special taxes increase this to a higher effective rate for larger businesses of 36%. Belgium, as do a number of other countries, allows small and medium-sized enterprises (SMEs) to pay a lower rate of income tax as a way of helping smaller businesses. The exact schedule is:

Profits	Effective Tax Rate (%)
Less than €25 000	24.25
€25 001 – €90 000	31
€90 001 – €322 500	34.5
More than €322 500	36

The lower tax rate thresholds are quite small in terms of earned profit before tax, so Fabrique Aérospatiale, as a large company, will pay tax on its profits at, or close to, the top rate. However, being an international company with operations in several countries, the actual amount of tax it pays will depend on very complex factors. Namely, where its profits are generated, whether tax paid in one country can be offset against taxes due elsewhere (principally Belgium, as its country of domicile) and the rates at which corporate income tax is levied in the different countries. An examination of Exhibit 3.6 shows a wide range of corporate income tax rates.

In addition, there are complex local rules and treaty agreements between countries about the way profits earned in one country are included in the tax payable by a company domiciled in another country. Just to illustrate the complexities, Brazil – where Fabrique Aérospatiale has a majority-owned subsidiary – has a complex system of corporate taxation that includes among its possible components a corporate income tax, a financial transactions tax, an exercise tax and a social security tax. Also, the profits earned by the subsidiary in Brazil and any dividends remitted to the parent are governed by the taxation treaty agreements between the two countries. It is clear that in this situation Fabrique Aérospatiale will engage the services of an international tax specialist firm to help it manage its tax liabilities in the most efficient way possible.

WEB

Information on international corporate income tax rates can be found at: www.dits.deloitte.com.

Average versus Marginal Tax Rates

The difference between the average tax rate and the marginal tax rate is an important consideration in financial decision making. The average tax rate is simply the total taxes paid divided by taxable income. In contrast, the marginal tax rate is the tax rate that is levied on the last unit of profit earned.

Average tax rate

total taxes paid divided by taxable income

Marginal tax rate

the tax rate paid on the last unit of profit earned

EXHIBIT 3.6

CORPORATE INCOME TAX RATES IN SELECTED COUNTRIES WORLDWIDE IN 2010

European Union[a]	Headline	Effective	SME	Other Europe	Headline	Effective	SME
Austria	25	25		Belarus	24	26.28	
Belgium	33	36	✓	Norway	28	28	
Bulgaria	10	10		Russia	20	20	
Czech Republic	19	19		Switzerland	8.5	13–22	
Denmark	25	25		Turkey	20	20	
Estonia	21	21		Ukraine	25	25	
Finland	26	26					
France	33.33	34.43	✓				
Germany	15	30–33		**Africa & Middle East**	**Headline**	**Effective**	**SME**
				Egypt	20	20–40.55	
Greece	24	24		Kazakhstan	20	20–30	
Hungary	19	19		Mauritius	15	15	
Ireland	12.5	12.5		Morocco	30	30	
Italy	27.5	30.4–32.4		South Africa	28	28	
Netherlands	25.5	25.5	✓	Tunisia	30	30–35	
Poland	19	19					
Portugal	25	26.5	✓				
Romania	16	16					
Spain	30	30	✓	**Asia/Pacific**	**Headline**	**Effective**	**SME**
Sweden	26.3	26.3		Australia	30	30	
United Kingdom	28	28	✓	China	25	25	✓
				Hong Kong	16.5	16.5	
Americas	**Headline**	**Effective**	**SME**	India	30–40	33.2175–42.23	✓
Argentina	35	35		Indonesia	25	25	
Brazil	15	34	✓	Japan	30	41–42	
Canada	18	28–34		Korea (R.O.K.)	22	22	
Chile	17	35		Malaysia	25	25	✓
Colombia	33	33		New Zealand	30	30	
Ecuador	25	25		Pakistan	35	35	
Mexico	30	30		Philippines	30	30	
Peru	30	30		Singapore	17	17	
United States	35	35	✓	Taiwan	17	17	
Uruguay	25	25		Thailand	30	30	✓
Venezuela	34	34–50		Vietnam	25	25	

[a]Excludes some smaller member countries of the European Union.

Source: Tax guides. 2010 edition of the Worldwide Corporate Tax Guide, Ernst & Young. Reprinted with permission.

Note: Differences between headline rate and effective rate reflects various country-specific tax elements, such as a local corporate income tax and surtax, and so forth.

The table provides the headline rate and the effective rate after including a range of additional taxes on companies and indicates whether a country allows small and medium-sized enterprises (SMEs) to benefit from lower rates of corporate income tax.

A simple example will clarify the difference between the average and marginal tax rates. In Belgium, there are concessionary tax rates for companies which earn profits of less than €322 500. The schedule is given below:

	Taxable Profit	Tax Rate (%)
On first	€25 000	24.25
On profit between	€25 001 – €90 000	31
On profit between	€90 001 – €322 500	34.5
Profits over	€322 501	36

Now suppose a small Belgian company has a taxable income of €100 000. This puts the company well below the standard threshold rate of 36% that is applied to profits over €322 500. As shown below on the left-hand side of the table, the amount of tax the company pays will be €29 663 – an average of the different tax bands for SMEs which starts at 24.25% for profits below €25 000, then rises to 31% for that part of the taxable profit made between €25 001 and €90 000, to 34.5% for any profits over €90 001 and up to €322 500, leading to an effective rate of 29.7% (€29 633/€100 000).

	Income tax before new investment		Income tax after new investment	
Tax Rate (%)	Profits	Income Tax	Profits	Income Tax
24.25	€25 000	€6 063	€25 000	€6 063
31	65 000	20 150	65 000	20 150
34.5	10 000	3 450	232 500	80 213
36			47 500	17 100
	€100 000	€29 663	€370 000	€123 525

Now let us assume that the company makes a new investment and this generates an additional €270 000 of profit while it still makes the same profit on its existing activities. The tax the company now pays as a result of the additional profit it generates is given on the right of the table above. The effective rate is 33.4% of its profits (€123 525/€370 000). However, the marginal rate on the last €17 100 of profit is 36% (€17 100/€47 500 = 36%).

When you are making investment decisions for a firm, the relevant tax rate to use is usually the marginal tax rate. The reason, as shown above, is that new investments (projects) are expected to generate new cash flows, which will be taxed at the firm's marginal tax rate. Thus, the marginal tax rate is used to compute the project's tax bill.

To simplify calculations throughout the book, we will generally specify a single tax rate for a company, such as 40%. The rate may include some payment for state and local taxes, which will add an upward adjustment to the total tax rate firms pay. We use different corporate tax rates to emphasise that taxes change over time and may differ from one location to another.

Unequal Treatment of Dividends and Interest Payments

An anomaly of corporate income tax in many countries is the unequal treatment of interest expense and dividend payments. For most companies, interest paid on debt obligations is a tax-deductible business expense. However, dividends paid to ordinary and preference shareholders may not be deductible. Because of this difference, a firm must generate more earnings to support a €100 payment of dividends than a €100 payment of interest. For example, if a firm pays €100 in interest, it must generate €100 of earnings before interest and taxes (EBIT) to support this payment. However, for the €100 of dividends, the firm will need more than €100 of EBIT because the dividends are not tax deductible. More specifically, if the average tax rate is 30%, the firm will need to generate €142.86 to cover the cash dividend.[16] Investors who receive the dividend may also be liable to further income tax on this income.

The unequal treatment of interest expense and dividend payments is not without consequences. In effect, it lowers the cost of debt financing compared with the cost of an equal amount of equity financing (ordinary shares or preference shares). Thus, there is a tax-induced bias towards the use of debt financing, which we discuss more thoroughly in later chapters.

EXHIBIT 3.7

EFFECT OF THE CLASSICAL AND IMPUTATION SYSTEMS OF DIVIDEND TAXATION ON THE TAX ON DIVIDENDS

	Classical system	Imputation system
Company level:		
Pre-tax income	A$142.86	A$142.86
Company tax (30%)	42.86	42.86
Net profit after tax paid as a dividend	A$100.00	A$100.00
Shareholder level:		
Dividend	A$100.00	A$100.00
Imputation credit		42.86
Taxable dividend income	100.00	142.86
Tax payable (45%)	45.00	64.29
Less imputation credit		42.86
Tax paid by shareholder	45.00	21.43
Net after-tax dividend to shareholder	A$55.00	A$78.57
Tax rate on profits paid as dividends	62%	45%

Note that in order to address this bias some countries, such as Australia, Greece, Norway and the United Kingdom, have switched to a more neutral method of taxing cash dividends, called an imputation system. Under the imputation system, investors receive the same cash dividend, but will also receive a tax credit equal to the amount of corporate income tax paid. The difference between the classical double taxation of dividends and the imputation system is shown in Exhibit 3.7. The corporate tax rate in Australia is 30%, so a recipient of a dividend of A$100 would have been deemed to have received A$142.86 in dividends, of which A$42.86 is in the form of a certificate of tax paid. This tax paid at the corporate level is used to offset the tax liability of the investor. So if the investor is taxed at the same rate of 30%, there is no subsequent tax liability due on the dividend income received. If the investor has a higher tax rate, then the tax payment that is due is offset by the amount of the certificate of tax paid.

Under both systems, a company pays tax on its taxable income at the corporate tax rate, which in this example is 30% – leaving a net profit of A$100 on pre-tax income of A$142.86. At this point, the company pays all its after-tax profit as a dividend (A$100). Under the classical system, the dividend is now taxed at the recipient's income tax rate, which is 45%, so the shareholder has to pay tax of A$45 on the A$100 dividend. As a result, the shareholder is being taxed twice – once at the company level (at 30%) and again as personal income (at 45%). The combined effect is to raise the tax on the pre-tax income of the company's dividends from 30% to 62%.

With the imputation system, the tax paid at the company level (A$42.86) is treated as a certificate of tax paid on the dividend. In effect, the shareholder has received A$142.86 in dividends, made up of A$100 in cash and the tax certificate of A$42.86. This is now taxed at the shareholder's personal tax rate, which is 45%. The total tax due is A$64.29 (A$142.86 × 0.45). As the company has already paid A$42.86, the amount the shareholder has to pay is A$21.43 (A$64.29 – A$42.86). The tax rate paid by the shareholder on the dividends is 45% – the shareholder's personal tax rate. The difference in the tax rate on the dividends imputation system does not discriminate against the payment of dividends.

Learning by Doing Application 3.2

The Difference between Average and Marginal Tax Rates

Problem: The Belgian Dentist Company has taxable corporate income of €125 000. What is the firm's income tax liability? What are the firm's average and marginal tax rates?

Approach: Use the information in the text to calculate the firm's tax bill. To calculate the average tax rate, divide the total amount of taxes paid by the €125 000 of taxable income. The

marginal tax rate is the tax rate paid on the last unit of taxable income.

Solution:

$$
\begin{aligned}
\text{Tax payment} &= (0.2425 \times €25\,000) \\
&\quad + (0.31 \times €90\,000 - €25\,000) \\
&\quad + (0.345 \times €125\,000 - €90\,000) \\
&= €6\,063 + €20\,150 + €12\,075 \\
&= €38\,288
\end{aligned}
$$

$$
\begin{aligned}
\text{Average tax rate} &= €38\,288/€125\,000 \\
&= 0.306, \text{ or } 30.6\%
\end{aligned}
$$

$$
\text{Marginal tax rate} = 34.5\%
$$

Before You Go On

1. Why is it important to consider the consequences of taxes when financing a new project?
2. Which type of tax rate, marginal or average, should be used in analysing the expansion of a product line, and why?
3. What are the tax implications of a decision to finance a project using debt rather than new equity?

SUMMARY OF LEARNING OBJECTIVES

1. **Discuss generally accepted accounting principles (GAAP) and their importance.**

    IFRS are a set of authoritative standards that define accounting practices at a particular point in time and are used by many countries. The principles determine the rules for how a company maintains its accounting system and how it prepares financial statements. Accounting standards are important because without them, each firm could develop its own unique accounting practices, which would make it difficult for anyone to monitor the firm's true performance or compare the performance of different firms. The result would be a loss of confidence in the accounting system and the financial reports it produces. Fundamental accounting principles include that transactions are arm's-length, the cost principle, the realisation principle, the matching principle and the going concern assumption.

2. **Know the balance sheet identity and explain why a balance sheet must balance.**

   A balance sheet provides a summary of a firm's financial position at a particular point in time. The balance sheet identifies the productive resources (assets) that a firm uses to generate income, as well as the sources of funding from creditors (liabilities) and owners (shareholders' equity) that were used to buy the assets. The balance sheet identity is: Total assets = Total liabilities + Total shareholders' equity. Shareholders' equity represents ownership in the firm and is the residual claim of the owners after all other obligations to creditors, employees and vendors have been paid. The balance sheet must always balance because the owners get what is left over after all creditors have been paid – that is Total shareholders' equity = Total assets – Total liabilities.

3. **Describe how market-value balance sheets differ from book-value balance sheets.**

   Book value is the amount a firm paid for its assets at the time of purchase. The current market value of an asset is the amount that a firm would receive for the asset if it were sold on the open market (not in a forced liquidation). Most managers and investors are more concerned about what a firm's assets can earn in the future than what the assets cost in the past. Thus, balance sheets marked-to-market are more helpful in showing a company's true financial condition than balance sheets based on historical costs. Of course, the problem with marked-to-market balance sheets is that it is difficult to estimate market values for some assets and liabilities.

4. **Identify the basic equation for the income statement and the information it provides.**

   An income statement is a video clip of the firm's profit or loss for a period of time, usually a month, quarter or year. The income statement identifies the major sources of revenues generated by the firm and the corresponding expenses needed to generate those revenues. The equation for the income statement is Net income = Revenues – Expenses. If revenues exceed expenses, the firm generates a net profit for the period. If expenses exceed revenues, the firm generates a net loss. Net profit or income is the most comprehensive accounting measure of a firm's performance.

5. **Explain the difference between cash flows and accounting income.**

   Cash flows represent the movement of cash within the firm. Cash flows are important in finance because the value of any asset – shares, bonds or a business – is determined by the future cash flows generated by the asset. Accounting profits, in contrast, are calculated according to GAAP to determine taxes and to report to stakeholders in a consistent manner. Accounting profits include non-cash revenues (such as revenue booked by a manufacturer when products are shipped on credit) and non-cash expenses (such as depreciation); whereas cash flows do not include these items.

6. **Explain how the four major financial statements discussed in this chapter are related.**

   The four financial statements discussed in the chapter are the balance sheet, the income statement, the statement of cash flows and the statement of retained earnings. The key financial statement that ties the other three statements together is the statement of cash flows, which summarises changes in the balance sheet from the beginning of the year to the end. These changes reflect the information in the income statement and in the statement of retained earnings.

7. **Know that there are international differences in financial statements.**

   The move to IFRS as a global standard has reduced many difficulties of analysing financial statements in different countries, but differences and difficulties remain. These mainly relate to what is disclosed, differences in presentation, reports presented in foreign currencies and differences in the business environment. In particular, high rates of inflation in a particular country require a different approach to the presentation of financial statements to reflect the loss of purchasing power over time.

8. Discuss the difference between average and marginal tax rates.

The average tax rate is computed by dividing the total taxes by taxable income. It takes into account the taxes paid at all levels of income and will normally be lower than the marginal tax rate, which is the rate that is paid on the last unit of income earned. However, for very high income earners, these two rates can be equal. When companies are making financial investment decisions, they use the marginal tax rate because new projects are expected to generate additional cash flows, which will be taxed at the firm's marginal tax rate.

SUMMARY OF KEY EQUATIONS

Equation	Description	Formula
(3.1)	Balance sheet identity	Total assets = Total liabilities + Total shareholders' equity
(3.2)	Net working capital	Net working capital = Total current assets – Total current liabilities
(3.3)	Income statement identity	Net income = Revenues – Expenses
(3.4)	Net cash flow from operating activities	NCFOA = Net income + Non-cash revenues – Non-cash expenses
(3.5)	Net cash flow from operating activities	NCFOA = Net income + Depreciation and amortisation

SELF-STUDY PROBLEMS

3.1. The *going concern assumption* of GAAP implies that the firm:
  a. Is going under and needs to be liquidated at historical cost.
  b. Will continue to operate and its assets should be recorded at historical cost.
  c. Will continue to operate and all assets should be recorded at their cost rather than at their liquidation value.
  d. Is going under and needs to be liquidated at liquidation value.

3.2. The Krakow Ice Cream Company management has just completed an assessment of its assets and liabilities and has come up with the following information. It has total current assets worth Zł 625 000 at book value and Zł 519 000 at market value. In addition, its long-term assets

include plant and equipment valued at market for Zł 695 000, while their book value is Zł 940 000. The company's total current liabilities are valued at market for Zł 543 000, while their book value is Zł 495 000. Both the book value and the market value of its long-term debt is Zł 350 000. If the company's total assets are equal to a market value of Zł 1 214 000 (book value of Zł 1 565 000), what are the book value and market value of its shareholders' equity?

3.3. Depreciation and amortisation expenses are:
  a. Part of current assets on the balance sheet.
  b. After-tax expenses that reduce a firm's cash flows.

c. Long-term liabilities that reduce a firm's net worth.
d. Non-cash expenses that cause a firm's after-tax cash flows to exceed its net income.

3.4. You are given the following information about the Copenhagen Plumbing Company. The company's annual report on 31 December 2010 showed that during the year its revenues totalled DKr 896, current assets DKr 121,

current liabilities DKr 107, depreciation expenses DKr 75, cost of goods sold DKr 365 and interest expenses DKr 54. The company is in the 25% tax bracket. Calculate its net income by setting up an income statement.

3.5. The Brugge Tour Company had €633 125 in taxable income in the year ending 30 September 2010. Calculate the company's tax using the tax schedule given for Belgian companies in the text. What is its effective tax rate?

SOLUTIONS TO SELF-STUDY PROBLEMS

3.1. One of the key assumptions under GAAP is the *going concern assumption*, which states that the firm (c) will continue to operate and all assets should be recorded at their cost rather than at their liquidation value.

3.2. The book value and market value are as follows (in thousands of Polish zloty (Zł)):

Assets	Book value	Market value	Liabilities	Book value	Market value
Fixed assets	Zł 940	Zł 695	Shareholders' equity	Zł 720	Zł 321
Total current assets	625	519	Long-term debt	350	350
			Total current liabilities	495	543
Total assets	Zł 1565	Zł 1214	Total liabilities and equity	Zł 1565	Zł 1214

3.3. Depreciation and amortisation expenses are (d) non-cash expenses that cause a firm's after-tax cash flows to exceed its net income.

3.4. The Copenhagen Plumbing Company's income statement and net income are as follows:

Copenhagen Plumbing Company Income Statement for the Year Ending 31 December 2010

Amount	DKr
Revenues	896.00
Costs	365.00
Depreciation	75.00
EBIT	456.00
Interest	54.00
EBT	402.00
Income taxes (25%)	100.50
Net income	301.50

3.5. The Brugge Tour Company's income tax is calculated as follows:

Profits	Tax Rate	Income Tax
€25 000	24.25	€6 063
90 000	31	27 900
232 500	34.5	80 213
285 625	36	102 825
€633 125		€217 000

The total tax payable is €217 000 on profit of €633 125, so the effective tax rate is €217 000/€633 125 = 34.3%.

CRITICAL THINKING QUESTIONS

3.1. What is a major reason for the development of internationally agreed standards for financial statements?

3.2. Why are taxes and tax laws important for managerial decision making?

3.3. Identify the five fundamental principles of GAAP and explain briefly their importance.

3.4. Explain why firms prefer to use accelerated depreciation methods over the straight-line method for tax purposes.

3.5. What are treasury shares? Why do firms have treasury shares?

3.6. Define book-value accounting and market-value accounting.

3.7. Compare and contrast depreciation expense and amortisation expense.

3.8. Why are retained earnings not considered an asset of the firm?

3.9. How does net cash flow differ from net income and why?

3.10. What is the statement of cash flows and what is its role?

QUESTIONS AND PROBLEMS

Basic

3.1. Balance sheet: Given the following information about the Davos Sports AG, construct a balance sheet for the period ending 30 June 2010. The firm had cash and marketable securities of SFr 25 135, accounts receivable of SFr 43 758, inventories of SFr 167 112, net fixed assets of SFr 325 422 and other assets of SFr 13 125. It had trade and other accounts payables of SFr 67 855, short-term borrowings of SFr 36 454, long-term borrowings of SFr 223 125 and ordinary shares of SFr 150 000. How much retained earnings does the firm have?

3.2. Inventory accounting: Differentiate between FIFO and LIFO.

3.3. Inventory accounting: Explain how the choice of FIFO versus LIFO can affect a firm's balance sheet and income statement.

3.4. Market-value accounting: How does the use of market-value accounting help managers?

3.5. Working capital: Athens Electronics reported the following information at its annual meetings: the company had cash and marketable securities worth €1 235 455, trade and other accounts payables worth €4 159 357, inventories of €7 121 599, trade and other accounts receivables of €3 488 121, short-term borrowings of €1 151 663 and other current assets of €121 455. What is the company's net working capital?

3.6. Working capital: The financial information for Athens Electronics referred to in Problem 3.5 is all book value. Suppose marking to market reveals that the market value of the firm's inventories is 20% below its book value and its trade and other account receivables are 25% below its book value. The market value of its current liabilities is identical to the book value. What is the firm's net working capital using market values? What is the percentage change in net working capital?

3.7. Income statement: The Pyrenees Sawmill Company has disclosed the following financial information in its annual reports for the period ending 31 March 2010: sales of €1.45 million, costs of goods sold to the tune of €812 500, depreciation expenses of €175 000 and interest expenses of €89 575. Assume that the firm has a tax rate of 35%. What is the company's net income? Set up an income statement to answer the question.

3.8. Cash flows: Describe the organisation of the statement of cash flows.

3.9. Cash flows: During 2010 Turin Music increased its investment in available-for-sale financial assets by €36 845, funded fixed-assets acquisitions of €109 455 and had available for sale financial assets of €14 215 mature. What is the net cash used in investing activities?

3.10. Cash flows: Innsbruck Chemicals GmbH identified the following cash flows as significant in its meeting with analysts: during the year it had repaid existing debt of €312 080 and raised additional debt capital of €650 000. It also repurchased ordinary shares in the open market for a total of €645 250. What is the net cash provided by financing activities?

3.11. Cash flows: Identify and explain the non-cash expenses that a firm may incur.

3.12. Tax: Define average tax rate and marginal tax rate.

3.13. Tax: What is the relevant tax rate to use when making financial decisions? Explain why.

3.14. Tax: Oostende Dokken NV in the year ended 30 June 2010 had profits before taxes of €1 478 936. Calculate its taxes using the information on Belgian tax rates supplied in the chapter.

Intermediate

3.15. EXCEL® **Balance sheet:** Daan Van Raalte, the CFO of Schiphol Airport Services NV, is putting together this year's financial statements. He has gathered the following information: the firm had a cash balance of €23 015, trade and other accounts payable of €163 257, ordinary shares of €313 299, retained earnings of €512 159, inventories of €212 444, goodwill and other intangible assets equal to €78 656, net plant and equipment of €711 256 and short-term borrowings of €21 115. It also had trade and other accounts receivables of €141 258 and other current assets of €11 223. What amount of long-term debt does Schiphol Airport Services have?

3.16. Balance sheet: Refer to the information for Schiphol Airport Services in Problem 3.15. What level of net working capital does Schiphol Airport Services have?

3.17. Working capital: Oslo Network Associates has a current ratio of 1.60, where the current ratio is defined as follows: Current ratio =

Current assets/Current liabilities. The firm's current assets are equal to NKr 1 233 265, its accounts payables are NKr 419 357 and its short-term borrowings are NKr 351 663. Its inventories are currently at NKr 721 599. The company plans to raise funds in the short-term debt market and invest the entire amount in additional inventories. How much can their short-term borrowings increase without lowering their current ratio below 1.50?

3.18. **Market value:** Eau Vive SA reported to shareholders the following information: total current assets worth €237 513 at book value and €219 344 at market value. In addition, its long-term assets include plant and equipment valued at market for €343 222, while their book value is €362 145. The company's total current liabilities are valued at market for €134 889, while their book value is €129 175. Both the book value and the market value of its long-term debt is €144 000. If the company's total assets are equal to a market value of €562 566 (book value of €599 658), what is the difference in the book value and market value of the company's shareholders' equity?

3.19. **Income statement:** L'Alqueria Vinedo SL provided the following information to its auditors: for the year ended 31 March 2010, the company had revenues of €878 412, general and administrative expenses of €352 666, depreciation expenses of €131 455, leasing expenses of €108 195 and interest expenses equal to €78 122. If the company's tax rate is 34%, what is its profit for the year after taxes (net income)?

3.20. **Income statement:** Sosa Corporation recently reported an EBITDA of $31.3 million and net income of $9.7 million. The company has $6.8 million interest expense and the corporate tax rate is 35%. What was its depreciation and amortisation expense?

3.21. **Income statement:** Modena Leather announced that its profit for the year ended 30 June 2010 is €1 353 412. The company had an EBITDA of €4 967 855, and its depreciation and amortisation expense was equal to €1 112 685. The company's tax rate is 34%. What is the amount of interest expense for Modena Leather?

3.22. EXCEL® **Income statement:** Berlin Tours AG has an EBITDA of €512 725.20, EBIT of €362 450.20 and a cash flow of €348 461.25. What is this firm's profit for the year after taxes?

3.23. **Retained earnings:** Cordoba Construcción SL earned €451 888 during the year ending 31 December 2010. After paying out €225 794 in dividends, the balance went into retained earnings. If the firm's total retained earnings were €846 972, what was the level of retained earnings on its balance sheet on 1 January 2010?

3.24. **Cash flows:** Refer to the information given in Problem 3.19. What is the cash flow for L'Alqueria Vinedo?

3.25. **Tax:** The financial statements for Liège Electrique SA, a company that is based in and generates all its revenues in Belgium, indicated that the company had earnings before interest and taxes of €718 323. Its interest rate on debt of €850 000 was 8.95%. Calculate the amount of taxes the company is likely to owe. What are the marginal and average tax rates for this company?

Advanced

3.26. EXCEL® La Tour Eiffel SA announced that for the period ending 31 December 2010, it had earned income after taxes worth €5 330 275 on revenues of €13 144 680. The company's costs (excluding depreciation and amortisation) amounted to 61% of sales and it had interest expenses of €392 168. What is the firm's depreciation and amortisation expense if its tax rate is 34%?

3.27. Claire Paper Mill plc had, at the beginning of the fiscal year 1 January 2010, retained earnings of £323 325. During the year ended 31 December 2010, the company produced net income after taxes of £713 445 and paid out 45% of its net income as dividends.

Construct a statement of retained earnings and compute the year-end balance of retained earnings.

3.28. Lariat NV, a Belgian-domiciled company, earned €458 933 before interest and taxes for the fiscal year ending 31 December 2010. If Lariat had interest expenses of €165 123, calculate its tax burden using information on Belgian tax rates given in the chapter. What are the marginal tax rate and the average tax rate for this company?

3.29. EXCEL© Vanderheiden Varken NV provided the following financial information for the quarter ending 30 June 2010:

Net income: €189 425

Depreciation and amortisation: €63 114

Increase in trade and other accounts receivable: €62 154

Increase in inventories: €57 338

Increase in trade and other accounts payable: €37 655

Decrease in other current assets: €27 450

What is this firm's cash flow from operating activities during this quarter?

3.30. Analysts following the Oporto Madeira Serrada SA were given the following information for the year ended 31 December 2010:

Assets:	2010	2009
Non-current assets		
Plant and equipment (net)	€1 512 675	€1 403 220
Goodwill and other intangible assets	382 145	412 565
Total non-current assets	€1 894 820	€1 815 785
Current assets		
Inventories	423 819	352 740
Trade and other accounts receivable	260 205	318 768
Other current assets	41 251	29 912
Cash and marketable securities	33 411	16 566
Total current assets	€758 686	€717 986
Total assets	€2 653 506	€2 533 771
Shareholders' equity		
Ordinary shares (10 000 shares)	€10 000	€10 000
Additional paid-in capital	975 465	975 465
Retained earnings	587 546	398 110
Treasury shares	(13 334)	—
	€1 559 677	€1 383 575
Liabilities		
Non-current liabilities		
Borrowings	€679 981	€793 515
Current liabilities		
Accrued income taxes	21 125	16 815
Borrowings	14 487	7 862
Trade accounts payable and accruals	378 236	332 004
Total current liabilities	€413 848	€356 681
Total liabilities	1 093 829	1 150 196
Total liabilities and shareholders' equity	€2 653 506	€2 533 771

EXCEL® In addition, it was reported that the company had a net income of €3 155 848 and that depreciation expenses were equal to €212 366.

a. Construct a cash flow statement for this firm.

b. Calculate the net cash provided by operating activities.
c. What is the net cash used in investing activities?
d. Compute the net cash provided by financing activities.

SAMPLE TEST PROBLEMS

3.1. Drayton, Inc. has current assets of US$256 312 and total assets of US$861 889. It also has current liabilities of US$141 097, ordinary shares (common stock) of US$200 000 and retained earnings of US$133 667. How much non-current (long-term) debt does the firm have?

3.2. Transporto Trieste SA produced revenues of €745 000 in 2010. It has expenses (excluding depreciation) of €312 640, depreciation of €65 000 and interest expenses of €41 823. It pays a marginal tax rate of 34%. What is the firm's net income after taxes?

3.3. Marrakech Enterprises reported an EBITDA of Dirham 7 300 125 and Dirham 3 328 950 of profit for the fiscal year ended 30 September 2010. The company has Dirham 1 155 378 interest expenses and the company's effective corporate tax rate is 35%. What was the company's depreciation and amortisation expense?

3.4. In the year ended 30 June 2010, The Ontario Engineering Company, Inc. increased its investment in marketable securities by C$234 375, funded fixed-assets acquisition by C$1 324 766 and sold C$77 215 of long-term debt. In addition, the firm had a net inflow of C$365 778 from selling certain assets. What is the net cash used in investing activities?

3.5. The Trionfo Soccer Club has the following cash flows during this year: it repaid existing debt of €875 430, while raising additional debt capital of €1 213 455. It also repurchased ordinary shares in the open markets for a total of €71 112. What is the net cash provided by financing activities?

ENDNOTES

1. SE stands for Societas Europaea, a pan-European company organisational form established by the European Union. If the company had been incorporated locally, it would either be SA (Société Anonyme), if established in the French-speaking part of Belgium, or NV (Naamloze Vennootschap), if in the Flemish-speaking part, and indicates it is a limited liability company.
2. The terms *owners' equity*, *shareholders' equity*, *net worth* and *equity* are used interchangeably to refer to the ownership of a company's ordinary shares.
3. An *identity* is an equation that is true by definition; thus, a balance sheet must balance.
4. Preference shares are called preferred stock in the United States.
5. Note that one of the objectives of the IFRS standards is to present accounts that help users make economic decisions and hence require, whenever possible, assets and liabilities to be as current as

possible in their valuation, as laid down by the standards.

6. IFRS allows a company regularly to revalue property, plant and equipment to fair market value. However, the company cannot pick and choose under IFRS and if it revalues one item within a class of assets, it must revalue all items within the same class.

7. We will discuss precisely how changes in interest rates affect the market price of debt in Chapter 8, so for now, do not worry about the numerical calculation.

8. Looking at Exhibit 3.2, we find the total expenses as follows: €484 + €326 + €180 − €12 + €1 + €7 + €40 + €1 + €91 = €1118.

9. Under IFRS reporting, depreciation is not reported as a separate item on the income statement, but can be found in the detailed tables that accompany the main statements. For instance, the depreciation for fixed assets for Fabrique Aérospatiale is found in the detailed notes relating to the balance sheet item for property, plant and equipment and intangible assets.

10. Starting with profit for year (€202 million), we add back tax (€91 million), net interest (€40 million) and the depreciation and amortisation charge (€116 million).

11. From the balance sheet, we need to separate out those current assets and liabilities that are related to working capital. For 2009 we have inventories (€114) and trade and other receivables (€115 + €8), so investment in the production process is €237 million and other current assets €56 million. For current liabilities, there is only trade and other payables with a value of €78 million and other short-term liabilities, excluding borrowings of €36 million. Hence, the net short-term capital requirement for 2009 is €178 million (€293 − €114). For 2010 the net figure is €268 million, an increase of €89 million. The difference from the cash flow statement of net working capital investment of €84 million is that we classified the increase in financial instruments available for sale as an investing activity, rather than an operating activity.

12. Other possible sources might include a decrease in current assets and an increase in deferred taxes. As it is, current assets increased in 2010 and deferred taxes fell, rather than increased in the year to 2010.

13. The difference of €1 is due to rounding the values on the balance sheet to the nearest €1 million.

14. The difference is new equity (€102), plus an increase in the minority interest in equity (€34) plus net debt (€77) and an increase in deferred income tax liabilities (€21).

15. The accounting practice of recognising revenues and expenses as they are earned and incurred and not when cash is received or paid is called 'accrual accounting'.

16. To find the amount of EBIT necessary to support the cash dividend, simply divide the amount by 1 minus the average tax rate $(1 - t)$. If the average tax rate is 30%, the necessary EBIT to support €100 of cash dividends is as follows: EBIT necessary = €100/(1 − 0.30) = €100/0.70 = €142.86.

CHAPTER
4

Analysing Financial Statements

In this Chapter:

LEARNING OBJECTIVES

1. Explain the three perspectives from which financial statements can be viewed.
2. Describe common-size financial statements, explain why they are used and be able to prepare and use them to analyse the historical performance of a firm.
3. Discuss how financial ratios facilitate financial analysis and be able to compute and use them to analyse a firm's performance.
4. Describe the DuPont system of analysis and be able to use it to evaluate a firm's performance and identify corrective actions that may be necessary.
5. Explain what benchmarks are, describe how they are prepared and discuss why they are important in financial statement analysis.
6. Identify the major limitations in using financial statement analysis.

T oday, established national airlines across the world are struggling to compete against smaller, more nimble carriers that feature low-cost fares with no-frills service. As a result, several large airlines have been forced into significant restructuring, alliances or bankruptcy, while a number of smaller carriers, such as Ryanair or EasyJet, have achieved rapid growth and profitability.

Just how do analysts compare the performance of companies like those named above? One approach is to compare the accounting data from the financial statements that the companies publish every year. Below are selected accounting data for Lufthansa, the German airline, and Ryanair, the successful Ireland-based pan-European low-cost carrier, for the year ending in 2008:

	Lufthansa (€ millions)	Ryanair (€ millions)
Net revenues	€24 842	€2 714
Profits for the year (net income)	€542	€391

The accounting numbers by themselves do not provide much insight, and they are difficult to analyse because of the size difference between the two firms. Lufthansa is about 10 times the size of Ryanair in terms of net revenues. However, if we compute one of the profitability ratios discussed in this chapter, the net profit margin, we see a dramatic difference in performance between the two airlines. The net profit margins (Profit for the year/Total revenues) for Lufthansa and Ryanair are 2.18% and 14.40%, respectively. This means that for every €100 in revenues, Ryanair is able to generate €14.40 of profit, whereas Lufthansa can only obtain €2.18. As this example illustrates, one advantage of using ratios is that they make direct comparisons possible by adjusting for size differences. In terms of revenues, Ryanair is only 11% the size of Lufthansa but earns about 70% of the profit of the larger airline (€391/€542 = 0.72).

This chapter focuses on financial ratio analysis (or financial statement analysis), which involves the calculation and comparison of ratios derived from financial statements. These ratios can be used to draw useful conclusions about a company's financial condition, its operating efficiency and the attractiveness of its securities as investments.

CHAPTER PREVIEW

In Chapter 3 we reviewed the basic structure of financial statements. This chapter explains how financial statements are used to evaluate a company's overall performance and assess its strengths and shortcomings. The basic tool used to do this is financial ratio analysis. Financial ratios are computed by dividing one number from a firm's financial statements by another such number in order to allow for meaningful comparisons between firms or areas within a firm.

Management can use the information from this type of analysis to help maximise the firm's value by identifying areas where performance improvements are needed. For example, the analysis of data from financial statements can help determine why a firm's cash flows are increasing or decreasing, why a firm's profitability is changing and whether a firm will be able to pay its bills next month.

We begin the chapter by discussing some general guidelines for financial statement analysis, along with three different perspectives on financial analysis: those of the shareholder, manager and creditor. Next, we describe how to prepare common-size financial statements, which allow us to compare firms that differ in size and to analyse a firm's financial performance over time. We then explain how to calculate and interpret key financial ratios and discuss the DuPont system, a diagnostic tool that uses financial ratios. After a discussion of benchmarks, we conclude with a description of the limitations of financial statement analysis.

BACKGROUND FOR FINANCIAL STATEMENT ANALYSIS

Learning Objective 1

Explain the three perspectives from which financial statements can be viewed.

This chapter will guide you through a typical **financial statement analysis**, which involves the use of financial ratios to analyse a firm's performance. We start with some general background. First, we look at the different perspectives we can take when analysing financial statements; then we present some helpful guidelines for financial statement analysis.

Financial statement analysis

the use of financial statements to evaluate a company's overall performance and assess its strengths and shortcomings

Perspectives on Financial Statement Analysis

Shareholders and stakeholders may differ in the information they want to gain when analysing financial statements. In this section, we discuss three perspectives from which we can view financial statement analysis: those of (1) shareholders, (2) managers and (3) creditors. Although members of each of these groups view financial statements from their own point of view, the perspectives are not mutually exclusive.

Shareholders' Perspective

Shareholders are primarily concerned with the value of their shares and with how much cash they can expect to receive from dividends and/or capital appreciation. Therefore, shareholders want financial statements to tell them how profitable the firm is, what the return on their investment is, whether the firm can pay a dividend and, if so, how much, and how much cash is available for shareholders, both in total and on a per-share basis. Ultimately, shareholders are interested in how much their ordinary shares are worth in the market and whether the market is pricing the shares correctly. We address pricing issues in detail in Chapter 9, but financial analysis is a key step in valuing a company's shares.

Managers' Perspective

Broadly speaking, management's perspective of financial statement analysis is similar to that of shareholders. The reason is that shareholders own the firm and managers have a fiduciary responsibility to make decisions that are in the owners' best interests. Thus, managers are interested in the same performance measures as shareholders: profitability, dividends, capital appreciation, return on investment, and the like.

Managers, however, are also responsible for running the business on a daily basis and must make decisions that will maximise shareholder wealth in the long run. Maximising shareholder wealth is not a single 'big decision', but a series of day-to-day decisions. Thus, managers need feedback on the short-term impact these decisions have on the firm's financial statements and the current share price. For example, managers can track trends in sales and can determine how well they are controlling expenses and how much of each sale goes to profits or the bottom line. In addition, managers can see the impact of their investment, financing and working capital decisions reflected in the financial statements. Keep in mind that managers, as insiders, have access to much more detailed financial information than those outside the firm. Generally, outsiders have access to only published financial statements for publicly traded firms.

Creditors' Perspective

The primary concern of creditors is whether and when they will receive the interest payments they are entitled to and when they will be repaid the money they loaned to the firm. Thus, a firm's creditors, including long-term bondholders, closely monitor how much debt the firm is currently using, whether the firm is generating enough cash to pay its day-to-day bills, and whether the firm will have sufficient cash in the future to make interest and principal payments on long-term debt *after* satisfying obligations that have a higher legal priority, such as paying employees' wages. Of course, the firm's ability to pay ultimately depends on cash flows and profitability; hence, creditors – like shareholders and managers – are interested in those aspects of the firm's financial performance. When millions or billions are at stake, you can bet that banks, insurance companies and other creditors will examine the financial statements closely to uncover potential future problems.

Guidelines for Financial Statement Analysis

We turn now to some general guidelines that will help you when analysing a firm's financial statements. First, make sure you understand which perspective you are adopting to conduct your analysis: shareholder, manager or creditor. The perspective will dictate the type of information you need for the analysis and may affect the actions you take based on the results.

Second, always use audited financial statements, if they are available. As we discussed in Chapter 1, an audit means that an independent accountant has attested that the financial statements were correctly prepared and fairly represent the firm's financial condition at a point in time. If the statements are unaudited, you may need to make an extra effort. For example, if you are a creditor considering making a loan, you will need to make an especially diligent examination of the company's books before closing the deal. It would also be a good idea to make sure you know the company's management team and accountant very well. This will provide additional insight into the credit-worthiness of the firm.

Third, use financial statements that cover three to five years, or more, to conduct your analysis. This enables you to perform a **trend analysis,** which involves looking at historical financial statements to see how various ratios are increasing, decreasing or staying constant over time.

Trend analysis

analysis of trends in financial data

Fourth, when possible, it is always best to compare a firm's financial statements with those of competitors that are roughly the same size and that offer similar products and services. If you compare firms of disparate size, the results may be meaningless because the two firms may have very different infrastructures, sources of financing, production capabilities, product mixes and distribution channels. For example, comparing the financial statements of EADS, the pan-European aeronautic and space company with those of Piaggio Aero Industries S.p.A., a firm that manufactures small aircraft, makes no sense whatsoever, although both firms manufacture aircraft. You will have to use your judgement as to whether relevant comparisons can be made between firms with large size differences. In general, the greater the size disparity, the less likely the comparisons between firms in the same business will be relevant.

In business it is common to **benchmark** a firm's performance, as discussed in the previous paragraph. The most common type of benchmarking involves comparing a firm's performance with the performance of similar firms that are relevant competitors. For example, Volkswagen may want to benchmark itself against Renault, Fiat and Toyota. These are major competitors in the European market with similar product lines. Firms can also benchmark against themselves – comparing this year's performance with last year's, for example – or compare against a goal, such as a 10% growth in sales. We discuss benchmarking in more detail later in the chapter.

Benchmark

a standard against which performance is measured

Before You Go On

1. Why is it important to look at a firm's historical financial statements?
2. What is the primary concern of a firm's creditors?

COMMON-SIZE FINANCIAL STATEMENTS

Learning Objective 2

Describe common-size financial statements, explain why they are used and be able to prepare and use them to analyse the historical performance of a firm.

Common-size financial statement analysis is one of the most basic forms of financial statement analysis. A **common-size financial statement** is one in which each number is expressed as a percentage of some base number, such as total assets or total revenues. For example, each number on a balance sheet may be divided by total assets. Dividing numbers by a common base to form a ratio is called *scaling*. It is an important concept, and you will read more about it later in the chapter, in the discussion of financial ratios. Financial statements scaled in this manner are also called *standardised financial statements*.

Common-size financial statement

a financial statement in which each number is expressed as a percentage of a base number, such as total assets or total revenues

Common-size financial statements allow you to make meaningful comparisons between the financial statements of two firms that are different in size. For example, in the aerospace market,

Bombardier, Inc. is the major competitor of Fabrique Aérospatiale, the illustrative firm introduced in Chapter 3. However, Bombardier has US$21.3 billion in total assets while Fabrique Aérospatiale's assets are only €1.9 billion. Without common-size financial statements, comparisons of these two firms would be difficult to interpret. Common-size financial statements are also useful for analysing trends within a single firm over time, as you will see.

Common-Size Balance Sheets

To create a *common-size balance sheet*, we divide each of the asset accounts by total assets. We also divide each of the liability and equity accounts by

total assets since Total assets = Total equity + Total liabilities. You can see the common-size balance sheet for Fabrique Aérospatiale SE in Exhibit 4.1. Assets are shown in the top half of the exhibit and liabilities and equity in the lower half. The calculations are simple. For example, on the asset side in 2010, cash and marketable securities were 6.0% of total assets (€112/€1870), and inventories were 8.3% of total assets (€154/€1870). Notice that the percentages of total assets add up to 100%. On the liability side, trade and other accounts payable are 5.6% of total assets (€104/€1870) and long-term borrowings are 38.5% (€720/€1870). To test yourself, see if you can recreate the percentages in Exhibit 4.1.

EXHIBIT 4.1

COMMON-SIZE BALANCE SHEET FOR FABRIQUE AÉROSPATIALE SE ON 31 DECEMBER (€ MILLIONS)

Assets	2010	% of total	2009	% of total	2008	% of total
Non-current assets						
Property plant and equipment	€ 971	51.9	€ 626	42.9	€ 592	42.1
Intangible assets	164	8.8	129	8.9	124	8.8
Investments in associates	84	4.5	83	5.7	82	5.8
Deferred income tax assets	21	1.2	21	1.4	20	1.4
Available-for-sale financial assets	109	5.8	93	6.4	89	6.3
Derivative financial assets	2	0.1	2	0.1	2	0.1
Trade and other receivables	15	0.8	8	0.6	7	0.5
Total non-current assets	€1 366	73.1	€ 963	66.0	€ 916	65.2
Current assets						
Inventories	154	8.3	114	7.8	107	7.6
Trade and other receivables	124	6.6	115	7.9	112	8.0
Available-for-sale financial assets	12	0.7				
Derivative financial instruments	7	0.4	6	0.4	2	0.1
Financial assets at fair value through profit and loss	74	4.0	50	3.4	41	2.9
Cash and cash equivalents	112	6.0	213	14.6	228	16.2
	483	25.8	497	34.0	490	34.8
Assets of disposal group as held-for-sale	21	1.1	—	—	—	—
Total current assets	€ 504	26.9	€ 497	34.0	€ 490	34.8
Total assets	€1 870	100.0	€1 459	100.0	€1 406	100.0

Equity
Capital and reserves attributable to equity holders of the company

Ordinary shares	€ 158	8.5	€ 131	9.0	€ 131	9.3
Share premium	107	5.7	66	4.5	66	4.7
Other reserves	97	5.2	44	3.0	36	2.6
Retained earnings	416	22.3	304	20.8	261	18.6
	779	41.6	545	37.3	494	35.1
Minority interest in equity	45	2.4	11	0.8	11	0.8
Total equity	€ 824	44.0	€ 556	38.1	€ 505	36.9
Liabilities						
Non-current liabilities						
Borrowings	720	38.5	602	41.3	578	41.1
Derivative financial instruments	1	0.0	1	0.1		
Deferred income tax liabilities	77	4.1	57	3.9	47	3.3
Retirement benefit obligations	29	1.5	14	1.0	12	0.9
Provisions for other liabilities and charges	8	0.4	2	0.1	1	0.1
Total non-current liabilities	€835	44.6	€ 675	46.3	€ 638	45.4
Current liabilities						
Trade and other payables	104	5.6	78	5.3	73	5.2
Current income tax liabilities	16	0.9	17	1.2	71	5.1
Borrowings	73	3.9	114	7.8	103	7.3
Derivative financial instruments	3	0.2	4	0.3	1	0.1
Provisions for other liabilities and charges	14	0.7	15	1.0	15	1.1
	€ 210	11.2	€ 228	15.6	€ 263	18.7
Liabilities of disposal group classified as held-for-sale	1	0.1	—	—	—	—
Total current liabilities	€ 211	11.3	€ 228	15.6	€ 263	18.7
Total liabilities	€1 046	56.0	€ 903	61.9	€ 901	64.1
Total equity and liabilities	€1 870	100.0	€1 459	100.0	€1 406	100.0

In common-size balance sheets, such as those in this exhibit, each asset account and each liability and equity account is expressed as a percentage of total assets. Common-size statements allow financial analysts to compare firms that are different in size and to identify trends within a single firm over time.

Make sure the percentages add up to 100, but realise that you may obtain slight variations from 100 because of rounding.

What kind of information can Exhibit 4.1 tell us about Fabrique Aérospatiale's operations? Here are some examples. Notice that in 2010, inventories accounted for 8.3% of total assets, up from 7.8% in 2009 and 7.6% in 2008. In other words, Fabrique Aérospatiale has been increasing the proportion of its money tied up in inventories. This is probably not good news because it may be a sign of inefficient inventory management.[1]

WEB

A good source for financial statements is www.carol.co.uk.
You can get summary financial information on a wide range of companies from Google finance at: http://www.google.co.uk/finance.

Now look at the equity and liabilities, and notice that in 2010 total liabilities represent 56% of Fabrique Aérospatiale's total liabilities and equity. This means that ordinary shareholders have provided 44% of the firm's total financing and that creditors have provided 56% of the financing. In addition, you can see that from 2008 to 2010, Fabrique Aérospatiale reduced the proportion of financing from creditors. Long-term borrowings provided 41.1% (€578/ €1406) of the financing in 2008 and 38.5% (€720/€1870) in 2010.

Overall, we can identify the following trends in Fabrique Aérospatiale's common-size balance sheet. First, Fabrique Aérospatiale is a growing company. Its assets increased from €1406 million in 2008 to €1870 million in 2010. Second, the percentage of total assets held in current assets fell from 2008 to 2010, a sign of decreasing liquidity. Recall from Chapter 2 that assets are liquid if they can be sold easily and quickly for cash without a loss of value. Third, the percentage of total assets in plant and equipment rose from 2008 to 2010, a sign that Fabrique Aérospatiale is becoming less efficient because it is using more long-term assets in producing sales (below you will see that sales have increased over the same period). Finally, as mentioned, Fabrique Aérospatiale has reduced the percentage of its financing from long-term borrowings. Generally, there may be concerns with these trends, but we have a long way to go before we can confidently reach that conclusion. We will now turn to Fabrique Aérospatiale's common-size income statement.

Common-Size Income Statements

The most useful way to prepare a *common-size income statement* is to express each account as a percentage of revenues, as shown for Fabrique Aérospatiale in Exhibit 4.2. *Revenues* are defined as total sales less all sales discounts and sales returns and allowances. You should note that when looking

at accounting information and 'revenue' numbers as reported, they almost always mean net revenues or net sales, unless otherwise stated. We will follow this convention in the book. Again, the per cent calculations are simple. For example, in 2010 administrative expenses are 13.6% of sales (€180/€1319) and profit for the year is 15.3% of revenues (€202/€1319). Before proceeding, make sure that you can calculate each percentage in Exhibit 4.2.

Interpreting the common-size income statement is also straightforward. As you move down the income statement, you will find out exactly what happens to the revenue that the firm generates. For example, in 2010 it cost Fabrique Aérospatiale 36.7 cents in cost of goods sold to generate one euro of revenue. Similarly, it cost 13.6 cents in administrative expenses to generate one euro of revenue. The government takes 6.9% of revenue in the form of taxes.

The common-size income statement can tell us a lot about a firm's efficiency and profitability. For example, in 2008, Fabrique Aérospatiale's cost of goods sold and distribution and administrative expenses totalled 72.3% of revenues (42.2 + 20.5 + 9.6). By 2010, these expenses had increased to 75% of sales (36.7 + 24.7 + 13.6). This might mean that Fabrique Aérospatiale is facing higher prices from its suppliers or is becoming less efficient in its use of materials and labour. Or it could mean that the company is getting lower net prices for its products since it may have to provide bigger discounts or rebates. The important point, however, is that it is costing the company more in expenses to generate each euro of profit.

Examination of the trends in the income statement and balance sheet suggests that Fabrique Aérospatiale's performance has deteriorated in a number of areas. The real question, however, is whether Fabrique Aérospatiale is performing well, as compared with other firms in the same industry. For example, the fact that 15.3 cents of every euro of revenue reaches the bottom line may not be a good sign if we find out that Fabrique

EXHIBIT 4.2

COMMON-SIZE INCOME STATEMENTS FOR FABRIQUE AÉROSPATIALE FOR FISCAL YEARS ENDING DECEMBER 31 (€ MILLIONS)

Continuing operations	2010	% of revenues	2009	% of revenues	2008	% of revenues
Revenue	€1 319	100.0	€702	100.0	€689	100.0
Cost of sales	(484)	36.7	(292)	41.5	(291)	42.2
Gross profit	€835	63.3	€410	58.5	€398	57.8
Distribution costs	(326)	24.7	(133)	18.9	(141)	20.5
Administration expenses	(180)	13.6	(65)	9.3	(66)	9.6
Other income	12	0.9	8	1.1	7	1.0
Other (losses)/gains – net	(1)	0.0			(6)	0.9
Loss on sale of land	(7)	0.5				
Operating profit	€ 334	25.3	€221	31.5	€192	27.9
Finance income	11	0.8	10	1.4	7	1.0
Finance costs	(51)	–3.9	(76)	10.9	(71)	10.3
Finance costs – net	(40)	–3.1	(66)	9.4	(64)	9.3
Share of (loss)/profit of associates	(1)	–0.1	1	0.1	1	0.1
Profit before income tax	€ 293	22.2	€156	22.2	€129	18.7
Income tax expense	(91)	6.9	(54)	7.7	(40)	5.8
	201	15.3	102	14.5	89	12.9
Discontinued operations						
Profit for the year from discontinued operations	1		1	0.1		
Profit for the year	€ 202	15.3	€102	14.6	€89	12.9
Dividends	(90)		(59)		(52)	
Retained earnings	112		43		37	

Common-size income statements express each account as a percentage of revenues. These statements better allow financial analysts to compare firms of different sizes and to analyse trends in a single firm's income statement accounts over time.

Aérospatiale's competitors average 20 cents of profit for every euro of revenue.

WEB

The Yahoo Finance website offers lots of financial information, including ratios of firms of your choice: http://finance.yahoo.com/.

Before You Go On

1. Why does it make sense to standardise financial statements?
2. What are common-size, or standardised, financial statements and how are they prepared?

FINANCIAL STATEMENT ANALYSIS

Learning Objective 3

Discuss how financial ratios facilitate financial analysis and be able to compute and use them to analyse a firm's performance.

In addition to the common-size ratios we have just discussed, other specialised financial ratios help analysts interpret the myriad of numbers in financial statements. In this section we examine financial ratios that measure a firm's liquidity, efficiency, leverage, profitability and market value, using Fabrique Aérospatiale as an example. Keep in mind that for ratio analysis to be most useful, it should also include trend and benchmark analysis, which we discuss in more detail later in the chapter.

Why Ratios are Better Measures

A **financial ratio** is simply one number from a financial statement that has been divided by another financial number. Like the percentages in common-size financial statements, ratios eliminate problems arising from differences in size because size is effectively 'divided out'; more precisely, the denominator of the ratio adjusts, or scales, the numerator to a common base.

Financial ratio

a number from a financial statement that has been scaled by dividing by another financial number

WEB

Another source of annual reports and financial statements for listed companies worldwide is at: http://londonstockexchange.ar.wilink.com

Here is an example. Suppose you want to assess the profitability of two firms. Firm A's profit for the year is €5, and firm B's is €50. Which firm had the best performance? You really cannot tell because you have no idea what asset base was used to generate the net income. In this case, a relevant measure of financial performance might be net income scaled by the firm's shareholders' equity – that is, the return on equity (ROE):

$$ROE = \frac{\text{Profit for the year (net income)}}{\text{Shareholders' equity}}$$

If firm A's total shareholders' equity is €25 and firm B's shareholders' equity is €5000, the ROE for each firm is as follows:

Company	ROE Calculation	ROE Ratio	ROE
Firm A	€5/€25	0.20	20%
Firm B	€50/€5000	0.01	1%

As you can see, the ROE for firm A is 20% – much larger than the ROE for firm B at 1%. Even though firm B had the higher profit in absolute terms (€50 versus €5), its shareholders had invested more money in the firm (€5000 versus €25) and it generated less income per unit of invested equity than firm A did. Clearly, firm A's performance is better than firm B's, given its smaller equity investment.

This shows that accounting numbers are more easily compared and interpreted when they are scaled. This is why, for example, consumer groups pressured grocery stores to provide unit pricing. When comparing a bottle of pasta sauce from four other brands, all in different-sized bottles, you need to know the cost per gram, not the cost per bottle. The same is true in business. Common-size financial statements, for example, allow us to compare the financial data of large and small firms with the effect of size held constant.

Choice of Scale is Important

An important decision is your choice of the 'size factor' for scaling. The size factor you select must be relevant and make economic sense. For example, suppose you want a measure that will enable you to compare the productivity of employees at a particular plant with the productivity of employees at other plants that make similar products. Your assistant makes a suggestion: divide revenue by the number of parking spaces available at the plant. Will this ratio tell you how productive labour is at a plant? Clearly, the answer is no.

Your assistant comes up with another idea: divide revenue by the number of employees. This ratio makes sense as a measure of employee productivity. A higher ratio indicates that employees are more productive because, on average, each employee is generating more revenue. In business, the type of variable most commonly used for scaling is a measure of size, such as total assets or total net revenue. Other scaling variables are used in specific industries where they are especially informative. For example, in the airline industry, a key measure of performance is revenue per available seat kilometre; in the steel industry, it is sales or cost per tonne; and in the automotive industry, it is cost per car.

Other Comments on Ratios

The ratios we present in this chapter are widely accepted and are almost always included in any financial analysis. However, you will find that different analysts will compute many of these standard ratios slightly differently. Modest variations in how ratios are calculated are not a problem as long as the analyst carefully documents the work done and discloses the ratio formula. These differences are particularly important when you are comparing data from different sources.

Short-Term Liquidity Ratios

Liquid assets have active secondary markets and can be sold quickly for cash without a loss of value. Some assets are more liquid than others. For example, short-term marketable securities are very liquid because they can easily be sold in the secondary market at or near the original purchase price. In

contrast, plant and equipment can take months or years to sell and often must be sold substantially below the cost of building or acquiring them.

When we examine a company's *liquidity position*, we want to know whether the firm can pay its bills when cash from operations is insufficient to pay short-term obligations, such as payroll, invoices from vendors and maturing bank loans. As the name implies, *short-term liquidity ratios* focus on whether the firm has the ability to convert current assets into cash quickly without loss of value. As we have noted before, even a profitable business can fail if it cannot pay its current bills on time. The inability to pay debts when they are due is known as **insolvency**. Thus, liquidity ratios are also known as *short-term solvency ratios*. The two most important liquidity ratios are the current ratio and the quick ratio.

> **Insolvency**
>
> the inability to pay debts when they are due

The Current Ratio

To calculate the current ratio, we divide current assets by current liabilities.[2] The formula appears in the following, along with a calculation of the current ratio for Fabrique Aérospatiale for 2010 based on balance sheet account data from Exhibit 4.1:

$$\text{Current ratio} = \frac{\text{Current assets}}{\text{Current liabilities}} \qquad (4.1)$$
$$= \frac{€504}{€212} = 2.38$$

Fabrique Aérospatiale's current ratio is 2.39, which should be read as '2.39 times'. What does this number mean? If Fabrique Aérospatiale were to take its current supply of cash and add to it the proceeds of liquidating its other current assets – such as marketable securities, trade accounts receivable and inventories – it would have €504 million. This €504 million would cover the firm's short-term liabilities of €212 million approximately

2.39 times, leaving a 'cushion' of €293 million (€504 – €211).

Now turn to Exhibit 4.3, which shows the ratios discussed in this chapter for Fabrique Aérospatiale for the three-year period 2008–2010. The exhibit will allow us to identify important trends in the company's financial statements. Note that Fabrique Aérospatiale's current ratio has been steadily increasing over time. What does this trend mean? From the perspective of a potential creditor, it is a positive sign. To a potential creditor, more liquidity is better because it means that the firm will have the ability, at least in the short term, to make payments. From a shareholder's perspective, however, too much liquidity is not necessarily a good thing. If we were to discover that Fabrique Aérospatiale has a much higher current ratio than its competitors, it could mean that management is being too conservative by keeping too much money tied up in low-risk and low-yielding assets, such as available-for-sale financial instruments. Generally, more liquidity is better and is a sign of a healthy firm. Only a benchmark analysis can tell us the complete story, however.

The Quick Ratio

The quick ratio is similar to the current ratio except that inventories are subtracted from current assets in the numerator. This change reflects the fact that inventories are often much less liquid than other current assets. Inventories are the most difficult current asset to convert into cash without loss of value. Of course, the liquidity of inventories varies with the industry. For example, inventories of a raw material commodity, such as gold or crude oil,

are more likely to be sold with little loss in value than inventories consisting of perishables, such as fruit or fashion items (e.g. trainers). Another reason for excluding inventories in the quick ratio calculation is that the book value of inventories may be significantly more than their market value because they may be obsolete, partially completed, spoiled, out of fashion or out of season.

To calculate the quick ratio – or *acid-test ratio*, as it is sometimes called – we divide current assets, less inventories, by current liabilities. The calculation for Fabrique Aérospatiale for 2010 is as follows, based on balance sheet data from Exhibit 4.1:

$$\text{Quick ratio} = \frac{\text{Current assets} - \text{Inventories}}{\text{Current liabilities}}$$
$$= \frac{€504 - €154}{€212} = 1.65 \tag{4.2}$$

The quick ratio of 1.65 times means that if we exclude inventories, Fabrique Aérospatiale had €1.65 of current assets for each euro of current liabilities. You can see from Exhibit 4.3 that Fabrique Aérospatiale's liquidity position, as measured by its quick ratio, has improved since 2008; this is generally a sign of good financial health.

Note that the quick ratio is almost always less than the current ratio, as it was for Fabrique Aérospatiale in 2010.[3] The quick ratio is a very conservative measure of liquidity because the calculation assumes that the inventories have zero value, which in most cases is not a realistic assumption.[4] Even in a bankruptcy 'fire sale', inventories can be sold for some small percentage of their book value, generating at least some cash.

Decision-Making Example 4.1

The Liquidity Paradox

Situation: Your manager asks you whether the French supermarket chain Carrefour SA or De La Rue plc, the UK commercial security printer, is the more liquid. You have the following information:

	Carrefour SA	De La Rue plc
Current ratio	0.70	1.07
Quick ratio	0.46	0.93

You also know that Carrefour carries large inventories and that De La Rue, as a security printer, has very small amounts of trade and other accounts receivable. Which firm is the most liquid? Your manager asks you to explain the reasons for your answers.

Decision: De La Rue is more liquid than Carrefour. Looking at the difference between the quick ratios – 0.46 versus 0.93 – pretty much tells the story. Inventories are the least liquid of all the current assets. Because De La Rue receives payment when it delivers its product, the current and quick ratios are not that different. Carrefour has a lot of inventories relative to the rest of its current assets and that explains the near halving in value between the current and quick ratios.

EXHIBIT 4.3

RATIOS FOR TIME-TREND ANALYSIS FOR FABRIQUE AÉROSPATIALE FOR FINANCIAL YEARS ENDING 31 DECEMBER

	2010	2009	2008
Liquidity ratios			
Current ratio	2.39	2.18	1.86
Quick ratio	1.66	1.68	1.46
Efficiency ratios			
Inventory turnover	3.13	2.57	2.72
Days' sales in inventories	116.53	142.16	134.18
Accounts receivable turnover	10.68	6.13	6.15
Days' sales outstanding	34.19	59.54	59.32
Total asset turnover	0.71	0.48	0.49
Fixed asset turnover	1.36	1.12	1.16
Leverage ratios			
Total debt ratio	0.56	0.62	0.64
Debt-to-equity ratio	1.27	1.63	1.78
Equity multiplier	2.27	2.63	2.78
Times interest earned	8.29	3.34	3.00
Cash coverage	11.17	4.31	3.94
Profitability ratios			
Gross profit margin	63.34%	58.45%	57.76%
Operating profit margin	25.32%	31.47%	27.87%
Net profit margin	15.31%	14.57%	12.92%
EBIT return on assets	17.86%	15.14%	13.66%
Return on assets	10.80%	7.01%	6.33%
Return on equity	24.52%	18.40%	17.64%
Market-value indicators			
Price-to-earnings ratio	12.39	12.79	12.43
Earnings per share	€12.77	€7.79	€6.78

Note: Numbers may not add up because of rounding.

Comparing how financial ratios, such as these ratios for Fabrique Aérospatiale, change over time enables financial analysts to identify trends in company performance.

Efficiency Ratios

Now we turn to a group of ratios called *efficiency ratios* or *asset turnover ratios*, which measure how efficiently a firm uses its assets to generate sales. These ratios are most useful to managers, who use them to identify inefficiencies in operations, and to creditors, who use them to find out how quickly inventory can be turned into receivables and ultimately into cash that can be used to satisfy debt obligations.

Inventory Turnover and Days' Sales in Inventory

We measure inventory turnover by dividing the cost of goods sold from the income statement by inventories from the balance sheet (see Exhibits 4.1 and 4.2). The formula for inventory turnover and its value for Fabrique Aérospatiale in 2010 are:

$$\text{Inventory turnover} = \frac{\text{Cost of goods sold}}{\text{Inventories}} \quad (4.3)$$
$$= \frac{€484}{€154} = 3.14$$

The firm 'turned over' its inventories 3.14 times during the year. Looking back at Exhibit 4.3, you can see that this ratio has increased in 2010 but was reasonably constant for 2008 and 2009.

What exactly does 'turning over' inventories mean? Consider a simple example. Assume that a firm starts the year with inventories worth €100 and replaces the inventories when all sold; that is, the inventory goes to zero. Over the course of the year, the firm sells the inventory and replaces it three times. For the year, the firm has an inventory turnover of three times.

As a general rule, turning over inventories faster is a good thing because it means that the firm is doing a good job of minimising its investment in inventories. Nevertheless, like all ratios, inventory turnover can be either too high or too low. Too high an inventory turnover ratio may signal that the firm has too little inventory and could be losing sales as a result. If the firm's inventory turnover level is too low, it could mean that management is not managing the firm's inventories efficiently or that an unusually large portion of the inventories are obsolete or out of date and have not yet been written off. In sum, inventory turnover that is significantly lower or significantly higher than that of competitors calls for further investigation.[5]

Based on the inventory turnover figure, and using a 365-day year, we can also calculate the *days' sales in inventory*, which tells us how long it takes a firm on average to turn over its inventories. The formula for days' sales in inventories, along with a calculation for Fabrique Aérospatiale, is as follows:

$$\text{Days' sales in inventories} = \frac{365 \text{ days}}{\text{Inventory turnover}}$$
$$= \frac{365}{3.14} = 116.24$$
$$(4.4)$$

Note that inventory turnover in the formula is computed from Equation (4.3). On average, Fabrique Aérospatiale takes about 116 days to turn over its inventories. Generally speaking, the smaller the number, the more efficient the firm is at moving its inventories.

Alternative Calculation for Inventory Turnover

Normally, we determine inventory turnover by dividing cost of goods sold by the inventory level at the end of the period. However, if a firm's inventories fluctuate widely or are growing (or decreasing) over time, some analysts prefer to compute inventory turnover using the average inventory value for the time period. In this case, the inventory turnover is calculated in two steps:

1. First calculate average inventories by adding beginning and ending inventories and dividing by 2:

   Average inventories
   $$= \frac{\text{Beginning inventories} + \text{Ending inventories}}{2}$$

2. Then divide the cost of goods sold by average inventory to find inventory turnover:

   $$\text{Inventory turnover} = \frac{\text{Cost of goods sold}}{\text{Average inventories}}$$

Alternative Calculations for Efficiency Ratios

Problem: For Fabrique Aérospatiale, compute the inventory turnover based on the average inventories. Then compare that value with 3.14, the turnover ratio based on Equation (4.3). Why do you think the two values differ?

Approach: Use the alternative calculation described above. In comparing the two values, you want to consider fluctuations in inventory over time.

Solution:

1. $\text{Average inventories} = \dfrac{\text{Beginning inventories} + \text{Ending inventories}}{2}$

$$= \dfrac{\text{€}154 + \text{€}114}{2} = \text{€}134$$

2. $\text{Inventory turnover} = \dfrac{\text{Cost of goods sold}}{\text{Average inventories}}$

$$= \dfrac{\text{€}484}{\text{€}134} = 3.61$$

The inventory turnover computed with average inventory, 3.61 times, is higher than 3.14 because inventories increased during the year (from €114 million at the end of 2009 to €154 million at the end of 2010).

Note that all six efficiency ratios presented in the chapter [Equations (4.3)–(4.8)] can be computed using an average asset value. For much work that financial analysts do, the adjustment will have little effect on either the analysis or the decision reached. For simplicity, we will generally use the ending of the period asset value in our calculations.

Accounts Receivable Turnover and Days' Sales Outstanding

Many firms make sales to their customers on credit, which creates a trade receivable account on the balance sheet. It does not do the firm much good to ship products or provide the services on credit if it cannot ultimately collect the cash from its customers. A firm that collects its receivables faster is generating cash faster. We can measure the speed at which a firm converts its receivables into cash with a ratio called accounts receivable turnover; the formula and calculated values for Fabrique Aérospatiale in 2010 are as follows:

$$\begin{array}{l} \text{Accounts receivable} \\ \text{turnover} \end{array} = \dfrac{\text{Net revenues}}{\text{Trade accounts receivable}}$$

$$= \dfrac{\text{€}1319}{\text{€}124} = 10.68$$

(4.5)

The data to compute this ratio is from Fabrique Aérospatiale's balance sheet and income statement (Exhibits 4.1 and 4.2). Roughly, this ratio means that Fabrique Aérospatiale loans out and collects an amount equal to its outstanding accounts receivable 10.68 times over the course of a year.

In most circumstances, higher accounts receivable turnover is a good thing – it means that the firm is collecting cash payments from its credit customers faster. As shown in Exhibit 4.3, Fabrique Aérospatiale's collection speed rose significantly from 2009 to 2010. There may be a number of explanations for this. First, Fabrique Aérospatiale's system for collecting accounts receivable may have improved in efficiency. Second, the firm has made new acquisitions and for these new businesses, customers may be paying on a different basis than existing customers. Finally, Fabrique Aérospatiale may have tightened the conditions under which it offered trade credit to avoid taking on poor credit risks. Making a determination of the cause would require us to compare Fabrique Aérospatiale's accounts receivable turnover with corresponding figures from its competitors.

You may find it easier to evaluate a firm's credit and collection policies by using days' sales outstanding, often referred to as DSO, which is calculated as follows:

Days' sales outstanding

$$= \frac{365 \text{ days}}{\text{Accounts receivable turnover}} \quad (4.6)$$
$$= \frac{365}{10.68} = 34.19$$

Note that accounts receivable turnover is computed from Equation (4.5). The DSO for Fabrique Aérospatiale means that, on average for 2010, the company converts its credit sales into cash in 34.19 days – a significant improvement on the performance for 2009 of 59.54 days. DSO is commonly called the *average collection period*.

Generally, faster collection is better. Whether 31.19 days is fast enough really depends on industry norms and on the credit terms Fabrique Aérospatiale extends to its customers. For example, if the industry average DSO is 30 days and Fabrique Aérospatiale gives customers 45 days to pay, then a DSO of 31.19 days is an indication of good management. If, in contrast, Fabrique Aérospatiale gives customers 28 days to pay, the

company has a problem and management needs to determine why customers are not paying on time.

Asset Turnover Ratios

We turn next to a discussion of some broader efficiency ratios. In this section, we discuss two ratios that measure how efficiently management is using the firm's assets to generate sales or revenues.

Total asset turnover measures the monetary value of revenues generated with each monetary unit of total assets. Generally, the higher the total asset turnover, the more efficiently management is using total assets. Thus, if a firm increases its asset turnover, management is squeezing more sales out of a constant asset base. When a firm's asset turnover ratio is high for its industry, the firm may be approaching full capacity. In such a situation, if management wants to increase sales, it will need to make an investment in additional fixed assets.

The formula for total asset turnover and the calculation for Fabrique Aérospatiale's turnover value in 2008 (based on data from Exhibits 4.1 and 4.2) are as follows:

$$\text{Total asset turnover} = \frac{\text{Net revenues or net sales}}{\text{Total assets}}$$
$$= \frac{€1319}{€1870} = 0.71 \quad (4.7)$$

Total asset turnover for Fabrique Aérospatiale is 0.71 times. In other words, in 2010, Fabrique Aérospatiale generated €0.71 in revenue or sales for every euro in assets. In Exhibit 4.3 you can see that Fabrique Aérospatiale's total asset turnover has increased significantly between 2009 and 2010.[6] This does not necessarily mean that the company's management team is performing well. The increase could be part of a typical industry sales cycle or it could be due to a pick-up in the business of Fabrique Aérospatiale's customers. Also, the figures for 2009 and 2010 may not be entirely comparable due to the acquisitions made in 2010. As always, getting a better fix on how the company is performing requires comparing Fabrique Aérospatiale's total asset turnover with comparable figures for its close competitors.

The turnover of total assets is a 'big picture' measure. In addition, management may want to see how particular types of assets are being put to use. A common asset turnover ratio measures sales in relation to fixed assets (plant and equipment). The fixed asset turnover formula and the 2010 calculation for Fabrique Aérospatiale are:

$$\text{Fixed asset turnover} = \frac{\text{Net revenues}}{\text{Net fixed assets}} \quad (4.8)$$
$$= \frac{€1319}{€971} = 1.36$$

Fabrique Aérospatiale generates €1.36 of sales for each euro of tangible fixed assets in 2010, which is an increase over the 2009 value of €1.12. This means that the firm is generating more sales for every euro in fixed assets. In a manufacturing firm that relies heavily on plant and equipment to generate output, the fixed asset turnover number is an important ratio. In contrast, in a service-industry firm with little plant and equipment, *total* asset turnover is more relevant.

Decision-Making Example 4.2

Ranking Firms by Fixed Asset Turnover

Situation: Different industries use different amounts of fixed assets to generate their revenues. For example, the airline industry is capital intensive, with large investments in airplanes, whereas firms in service industries use more human capital (people) and have very little invested in fixed assets. As a financial analyst, you are given the following fixed-asset turnover ratios: 2.19, 3.39 and 5.87. You must decide which ratios match up with three firms: Lufthansa, Carrefour and De La Rue. Make this decision, and explain your reasoning.

Decision: Lufthansa is the most capital-intensive firm, and Carrefour the least capital intensive. We would expect firms with large investments in fixed assets (Lufthansa) to have lower asset turnover than firms that have fewer fixed assets. De La Rue is in the middle, with fixed asset holdings primarily in relatively small amounts of very specialised plant and equipment. Thus, the firms and their respective fixed-asset turnovers are: Lufthansa 2.19, De La Rue 3.39 and Carrefour 5.87, whose fixed assets are primarily land and buildings.

Leverage Ratios

Leverage ratios measure the extent to which a firm uses debt rather than equity financing and indicate the firm's ability to meet its long-term financial obligations, such as interest payments on debt and lease payments. The ratios are also called *long-term solvency ratios*. They are of interest to the firm's creditors, shareholders and managers. Many different leverage ratios are used in industry; in this chapter we present some of the most widely used.

Financial Leverage

The term **financial leverage** refers to the use of debt in a firm's capital structure. When a firm uses debt financing, rather than only equity financing, the returns to shareholders may be magnified. This so-called leveraging effect occurs because the interest payments associated with debt are fixed, regardless of the level of the firm's operating profits. On the one hand, if the firm's operating profits increase from one year to the next, debtholders continue to receive only their fixed-interest payments and all of the increase goes to the shareholders. On the other hand, if the firm falls on hard times and suffers an operating loss, debtholders receive the same fixed-interest payment (assuming that the firm does not go bankrupt) and the loss is charged against the shareholders' equity. Thus, debt increases the returns to shareholders during good times and reduces the returns during bad times. In Chapter 16 we discuss financial leverage in greater depth and present a detailed example of how debt financing creates the leveraging effect.

> ### Financial leverage
>
> the use of debt in a firm's capital structure; the more debt, the higher the financial leverage. Also called *gearing*

The use of debt in a company's capital structure increases the firm's **default risk** – the risk that it will not be able to pay its debt as it comes due. The explanation is, of course, that debt payments are a fixed obligation and debtholders must be paid the interest and principal payments they are owed, regardless of whether the company earns a profit or suffers a loss. If a company fails to make an interest payment on the prescribed date, the company defaults on its debt and could be forced into bankruptcy by creditors.

> ### Default risk
>
> the risk that a firm will not be able to pay its debt obligations as they come due

Debt Ratios

We next look at three leverage ratios that focus on how much debt, rather than equity, the firm employs in its capital structure. The more debt a firm uses, the higher its financial leverage, the more volatile its earnings and the greater its risk of default.

Total Debt Ratio The total debt ratio measures the extent to which the firm finances its assets from sources other than the shareholders. The higher the total debt ratio, the more debt the firm has in its capital structure. The total debt ratio and a calculation for Fabrique Aérospatiale for 2010 based on data from Exhibit 4.1 appear as follows:

$$\text{Total debt ratio} = \frac{\text{Total debt}}{\text{Total assets}}$$
$$= \frac{€1046}{€1870} = 0.56 \qquad (4.9)$$

How do we determine the figure to use for total debt? Many variations are used, but perhaps the easiest is to subtract total equity from total assets. In other words, total debt is equal to total liabilities. Using Exhibit 4.1, we can calculate total debt for Fabrique Aérospatiale in 2010 as follows:

$$\text{Total debt} = €1870 - €824 = €1046$$

As you can see from Equation (4.9), the total debt ratio for Fabrique Aérospatiale is 0.56, which means that 56% of the company's assets are financed with debt. Looking back at Exhibit 4.3, we find that Fabrique Aérospatiale decreased its use of debt from 2008 to 2010. The current total debt ratio of 56% appears relatively high, raising possible questions about the company's financing strategy. Whether a high or low value for the total debt ratio is good or bad, however, depends on how the firm's capital structure affects the value of the firm. We explore this topic in greater detail in Chapter 16.

We turn next to two common variations of the total debt ratio: the debt-to-equity ratio and the equity multiplier.

Debt-to-Equity Ratio The *total debt ratio* tells us the amount of debt that makes up total assets. The *debt-to-equity ratio* tells us the amount of debt for each euro of equity. Based on data from Exhibit 4.1, Fabrique Aérospatiale's debt-to-equity ratio for 2010 is 1.27:

$$\text{Debt-to-equity ratio} = \frac{\text{Total debt}}{\text{Total equity}}$$

$$= \frac{€1046}{€824} = 1.27 \qquad (4.10)$$

The total debt ratio and the debt-to-equity ratio are directly related by the following formula, shown with a calculation for Fabrique Aérospatiale:

$$\text{Total debt ratio} = \frac{\text{Debt-to-equity ratio}}{1 + \text{Debt-to-equity ratio}}$$

$$= \frac{1.27}{1 + 1.27} = 0.56$$

As you can see, once you know one of these ratios, you can compute the other. Which of the two ratios you use is really a matter of personal preference.

Equity Multiplier   The equity multiplier tells us the amount of assets that the firm has for every euro of equity. Fabrique Aérospatiale's equity multiplier ratio is 2.27, as shown here:

$$\text{Equity multiplier} = \frac{\text{Total assets}}{\text{Total equity}}$$

$$= \frac{€1870}{€824} = 2.27 \qquad (4.11)$$

Notice that the equity multiplier is directly related to the debt-to-equity ratio:

$$\text{Equity multiplier} = 1 + \text{Debt-to-equity ratio}$$

This is no accident. Recall the balance sheet identity: Total assets = Total liabilities (debt) + Total shareholders' equity. This identity can be substituted into the numerator of the equity multiplier formula [Equation (4.11)]:

$$
\begin{aligned}
\text{Equity multiplier} &= \frac{\text{Total assets}}{\text{Total equity}} \\
&= \frac{\text{Total equity} + \text{Total debt}}{\text{Total equity}} \\
&= \frac{\text{Total equity}}{\text{Total equity}} + \frac{\text{Total debt}}{\text{Total equity}} \\
&= 1 + \frac{\text{Total debt}}{\text{Total equity}} \\
&= 1 + \frac{€1046}{€824} \\
&= 1 + 1.27 = 2.27
\end{aligned}
$$

Therefore, all three of these leverage ratios [Equations (4.9)–(4.11)] are related by the balance sheet identity, and once you know one of the three ratios, you can compute the other two ratios. All three ratios provide the same information.

Learning by Doing Application 4.2

Finding a Leverage Ratio

Problem: A firm's debt-to-equity ratio is 0.5. What is the firm's total debt ratio?

Approach: Use the equation that relates the total debt ratio to the debt-to-equity ratio.

Solution:

$$
\begin{aligned}
\text{Total debt ratio} &= \frac{\text{Debt-to-equity ratio}}{1 + \text{Debt-to-equity ratio}} \\
&= \frac{0.5}{1 + 0.5} = 0.33
\end{aligned}
$$

Learning by
Doing
Application
4.3

Solving for an Unknown Using the Debt-to-Equity Ratio

Problem: You are given the follow information about De La Rue plc's year-end balance sheet. The firm's debt-to-equity ratio is 2.89 and its total equity is €160.50 million. Determine the book (accounting) values for De La Rue's total debt and total assets.

Approach: We know that the debt-to-equity ratio is 2.89 and that total equity is £160.50 million. We also know that the debt-to-equity ratio [Equation (4.10)] is equal to total debt

divided by total equity, and we can use this information to solve for total debt. Once we have a figure for total debt, we can use the basic accounting identity to solve for total assets.

Solution:

$$\text{Total debt} = \text{Debt-to-equity ratio} \times \text{Total equity}$$
$$= 2.89 \times £160.50$$
$$= £463.85$$

$$\text{Total assets} = \text{Total debt} + \text{Total equity}$$
$$= £463.85 + £160.50$$
$$= £624.35 \text{ million}$$

Coverage Ratios

A second type of leverage ratio measures the firm's ability to service its debts, or how easily the firm can 'cover' debt payments out of earnings or cash flow. What does 'coverage' mean? If your monthly take-home pay from your part-time job is €400 and the rent on your apartment is €450, you are going to be in some financial distress because your income does not 'cover' your €450 fixed obligation to pay the rent. If, on the other hand, your take-home pay is €900, your monthly coverage ratio with respect to rent is €900/€450 = 2 times. This means that for every euro of rent you must pay, you earn two euros of income. The higher your coverage ratio, the less likely you will default on your rent payments.

Times Interest Earned   Our first coverage ratio is times interest earned, which measures the extent to which operating profits (earnings before interest and taxes, or EBIT) cover the firm's interest expenses. Creditors prefer to lend to firms whose EBIT is far in excess of their interest payments. The equation for the times-interest-earned ratio and a

calculation for Fabrique Aérospatiale from its income statement (Exhibit 4.2) for 2010 are:

$$\text{Times interest earned} = \frac{\text{EBIT}}{\text{Interest expense}} \quad (4.12)$$
$$= \frac{€334}{€40} = 8.35$$

Fabrique Aérospatiale can cover its interest charges about 8.35 times with its operating income. This is a good degree of cover that appears to point to a good margin of safety for creditors. In general, the larger the times-interest-earned figure, the more likely the firm is to meet its interest payments.

Cash Coverage   As we have discussed before, depreciation is a non-cash expense and as a result, no cash goes out the door when depreciation is deducted on the income statement. Thus, rather than asking whether operating profits (EBIT) are sufficient to cover interest payments, we might ask how much cash is available to cover interest payments. The cash a firm has available from operations to meet interest payments is better measured by EBIT plus depreciation and amortisation (EBITDA).[7] Thus, the cash coverage ratio for Fabrique Aérospatiale in 2010 is:

$$\text{Cash coverage} = \frac{\text{EBITDA}}{\text{Interest expense}}$$
$$= \frac{€450}{€40} = 11.25 \qquad (4.13)$$

For a firm with depreciation or amortisation expenses, which includes virtually all firms, EBITDA coverage will be larger than times interest earned coverage.

Profitability Ratios

Profitability ratios measure management's ability to make efficient use of the firm's assets to generate sales and manage the firm's operations. These measurements are of interest to shareholders, creditors and managers because they focus on the firm's earnings. The profitability ratios presented in this chapter are among a handful of ratios used by virtually all stakeholders when analysing a firm's performance. In general, the higher the profitability ratios, the better the firm is performing.

Gross Profit Margin

The gross profit margin measures the percentage of net sales remaining after the cost of goods sold is paid. It captures the firm's ability to manage the expenses directly associated with producing the firm's products or services. Next, we show the gross profit margin formula, along with a calculation for Fabrique Aérospatiale in 2010, using data from Exhibit 4.2:

Gross profit margin
$$= \frac{\text{Net sales} - \text{Cost of goods sold}}{\text{Net sales}}$$
$$= \frac{€1319 - €484}{€1319} = 63.31\% \qquad (4.14)$$

Thus, after paying the cost of goods sold, Fabrique Aérospatiale has 63.31% of the sales amount remaining to pay other expenses. From Exhibit 4.3, you can see that Fabrique Aérospatiale's gross profit margin has been increasing over the past several years, which is good news.

Operating Profit Margin and EBITDA Margin

Moving farther down the income statement, you can measure the percentage of sales that remains after payment of cost of goods sold and all other expenses, except for interest and taxes. Operating profit is typically measured as EBIT. The operating profit margin, therefore, gives an indication of the profitability of the firm's operations, independent of its financing policies or tax management strategies. The operating profit margin formula, along with Fabrique Aérospatiale's 2010 operating profit margin calculated from Exhibit 4.2, is as follows:

$$\text{Operating profit margin} = \frac{\text{EBIT}}{\text{Net sales}}$$
$$= \frac{€334}{€1319} = 25.32\% \qquad (4.15)$$

Many share analysts are concerned with cash flows generated by operations rather than operating earnings and will use EBITDA in the numerator instead of EBIT.[8] Calculated in this way, the operating profit margin is known as the EBITDA margin.

Net Profit Margin

The net profit margin indicates the percentage of sales remaining after all of the firm's expenses, including interest and taxes, have been paid. The net profit margin formula is shown here, along with the calculated value for Fabrique Aérospatiale in 2010, using data from the firm's income statement (Exhibit 4.2):

Net profit margin
$$= \frac{\text{Net income (Profit for the year)}}{\text{Net sales}} \qquad (4.16)$$
$$= \frac{€202}{€1319} = 15.31\%$$

As you can see from Exhibit 4.3, Fabrique Aérospatiale's net profit margin has declined from that for 2009. This decline is potentially a concern, although the 2010 net profit margin is close to that reported for 2008. The question remains, however, whether 15.31% is a good profit margin in an absolute sense. Answering this question requires us to compare Fabrique Aérospatiale's performance to the performance of its competitors, which we will do later in this chapter. What qualifies as a good profit margin varies significantly across industries; generally speaking, the higher a company's profit margin, the better the company's performance.

Return on Assets

So far, we have examined profitability as a percentage of sales. It is also important that we analyse profitability as a percentage of investment, either in assets or in equity. First, we will look at return on assets. In practice, return on assets is calculated in two different ways.

One approach provides a measure of operating profit (EBIT) in relation to assets. This is a powerful measure of return because it tells us how efficiently management utilised the assets under their command, independent of financing decisions and taxes. It can be thought of as a measure of the pre-tax return on the total net investment in the firm from operations. The formula for this version of return on assets, which we call EBIT return on assets (EROA), is shown next, together with the calculated value for Fabrique Aérospatiale in 2010, using data from Exhibits 4.1 and 4.2:

$$EROA = \frac{EBIT}{Total\ assets} \qquad (4.17)$$
$$= \frac{€334}{€1870} = 17.86\%$$

Exhibit 4.3 shows us that, in line with the other profitability ratios, Fabrique Aérospatiale's EROA did improve from 2008 to 2010.

Some analysts calculate return on assets (ROA) as:

$$Return\ on\ assets = \frac{Net\ income}{Total\ assets} \qquad (4.18)$$
$$= \frac{€202}{€1870} = 10.80\%$$

Although it is a common calculation, we advise against using the calculation in Equation (4.18) unless you are using the DuPont system, which we discuss shortly. The ROA calculation divides a measure of earnings available to shareholders (net income) by total assets (debt plus equity), which is a measure of the investment in the firm by both shareholders and creditors. Constructing a ratio of those two numbers is like mixing apples and oranges. The information that this ratio provides about the efficiency of asset utilisation is obscured by the financing decisions the firm has made and the taxes it pays.

The key point is that EROA is a better measure than ROA of how efficiently assets are utilised in operations. Dividing a measure of earnings to both debtholders and shareholders by a measure of how much both debtholders and shareholders have invested gives us a clearer view of what we are trying to measure.

In general, when you calculate a financial ratio, if you have a measure of income to shareholders in the numerator, you want to make sure that you have only investments by shareholders in the denominator. Similarly, if you have a measure of total profits from operations in the numerator, you want to divide it by a measure of total investments by both debtholders and shareholders.

Return on Equity

Return on equity (ROE) measures net income as a percentage of the shareholders' investment in the firm. The return on equity formula and the calculation for Fabrique Aérospatiale in 2010 based on data from Exhibits 4.1 and 4.2 are as follows:

$$Return\ on\ equity = \frac{Net\ income}{Total\ equity} \qquad (4.19)$$
$$= \frac{€202}{€824} = 24.52\%$$

Alternative Calculation of ROA and ROE

As with efficiency ratios, the calculation of ROA and ROE involves dividing an income statement value, which relates to a period of time, by a balance sheet value from the end of the time period. Some analysts prefer to calculate ROA and ROE using the average asset value or equity value, where the average value is determined as follows:

Average asset or equity value

$$= \frac{\text{Beginning value} + \text{Ending value}}{2}$$

Learning by Doing
Application 4.4

Alternative Calculations for EROA and ROE Ratios

Problem: Calculate the EROA and ROE for Fabrique Aérospatiale using average balance sheet values, compare the results with the calculations based on Equations (4.17) and (4.19) and explain why some analysts might prefer the alternative calculation.

Approach: To make the calculations, first find average values for the asset and equity accounts using data in Exhibit 4.1. Then use these values to calculate the EROA and ROE. In explaining why some analysts might prefer the alternative calculation, consider possible fluctuations of assets or equity over time.

Solution:

Average asset or equity value

$$= \frac{\text{Beginning value} + \text{Ending value}}{2}$$

$$\text{Average asset value} = \frac{€1870 + €1459}{2}$$

$$= €1664.5$$

$$\text{Average equity value} = \frac{€824 + €556}{2}$$

$$= €690$$

$$\text{EROA} = \frac{€334}{€1664.5}$$

$$= 20.07\%$$

$$\text{ROE} = \frac{€202}{€690}$$

$$= 29.28\%$$

Both EROA (20.07% versus 17.86%) and ROE (29.28% versus 24.52%) are higher when the average values are used. The reason is that Fabrique Aérospatiale's total assets grew significantly from €1459 million in 2009 to €1870 million in 2010 and its equity grew from €556 million to €824 million during the same period. We could argue in favour of using the average asset or equity value by pointing out that the profits for the one-year period are earned with the average value of assets or equity over the period.

Market-Value Indicators

The ratios we have discussed so far rely solely on the firm's financial statements and we know that much of the data in those statements are historical and do not represent current market value. Also, as we discussed in Chapter 1, the appropriate objective for the firm's management is to maximise shareholder value and the market value of the shareholders' claims is the value of the *cash flows* that they are entitled to receive, which is not necessarily the same as accounting income. To find out how the stock market evaluates a firm's liquidity, efficiency, leverage and profitability, we need ratios based on market values.

Over the years, financial analysts have developed a number of ratios, called *market-value ratios*, which combine market-value data with data from a firm's financial statements. Here we examine the most commonly used market-value ratios: earnings per share and the price-to-earnings ratio.

Earnings per Share

Dividing a firm's net income by the number of shares outstanding yields earnings per share (EPS). At the end of 2010, Fabrique Aérospatiale had 15.8 million shares outstanding (see Exhibit 3.1 in Chapter 3) and net income of €202 million (Exhibit 4.2). Its EPS at that point is thus calculated as follows:

$$\text{Earnings per share} = \frac{\text{Net income}}{\text{Shares outstanding}}$$

$$= \frac{€202}{15.8} = €12.77 \text{ per share}$$

$$(4.20)$$

Price-to-Earnings Ratio

The price-to-earnings (P/E) ratio relates earnings per share to price per share. The formula, with a calculation for Fabrique Aérospatiale for the end of 2010, is as follows:

$$\text{Price-to-earnings ratio} = \frac{\text{Price per share}}{\text{Earnings per share}}$$

$$= \frac{€158.3}{€12.77} = 12.39$$

$$(4.21)$$

The current share price on a given date can be obtained from listings in a good financial paper or from an online source, such as Reuters Yahoo! Finance.

WEB

You can get current share prices for a large number of listed companies from: http://uk. reuters.com/business/quotes.

What does it mean for a firm to have a price-to-earnings ratio of 12.39? It means that the stock market places a value of €12.39 on every €1 of net income. Why are investors willing to pay €12.39 for a claim on €1 of earnings? The answer is that the share price not only reflects the earnings this year. It also reflects all future cash flows from earnings and a high P/E ratio can indicate that investors expect the firm's earnings to grow in the future. Alternatively, a high P/E ratio might be due to unusually low earnings in a particular year and investors might expect earnings to recover to a normal level soon. We will discuss how expected growth affects P/E ratios in detail in later chapters. As with other measures, to understand whether the P/E ratio is too high or too low, we must compare the firm's P/E ratio with those of competitors and, at the same time, look at movements in the firm's P/E ratio relative to market trends.

Concluding Comments on Ratios

We could have covered many more ratios, but that is enough for now; we will introduce additional ratios as we need them in future chapters. However, the group of ratios presented in this chapter is a fair representation of the ratios needed to analyse the performance of a business. When using ratios, it is important that you consider each ratio and ask yourself 'What does this ratio mean, or what is it measuring?', rather than trying to memorise a definition. Good ratios make good economic sense when you look at them.

Before You Go On

1. What are the efficiency ratios, and what do they measure? Why, for some firms, is the total asset turnover more important than the fixed asset turnover?
2. List the leverage ratios discussed in this section and explain how they are related.
3. List the profitability ratios discussed in this section and explain how they differ from each other.

THE DuPont SYSTEM: A DIAGNOSTIC TOOL

Learning Objective 4

Describe the DuPont system of analysis and be able to use it to evaluate a firm's performance and identify corrective actions that may be necessary.

By now, your mind may be swimming with ratios. Fortunately, some enterprising financial managers at the DuPont Company developed a system in the 1960s that ties together some of the most important financial ratios and provides a systematic approach to financial ratio analysis.

An Overview of the DuPont System

The DuPont system of analysis is a diagnostic tool that uses financial ratios to evaluate a company's financial health. The process has three steps. First, management assesses the company's financial health using the DuPont ratios. Second, if any problems are identified, management corrects them. Finally, management monitors the firm's financial performance over time, looking for differences from ratios established as benchmarks by management.

Under the DuPont system, management is charged with making decisions that maximise the firm's ROE as opposed to maximising the value of the shareholders' equity. The system is primarily designed to be used by management as a diagnostic and corrective tool, though investors and other stakeholders have found its diagnostic powers of interest.

The DuPont system is derived from two equations that link the firm's ROA and ROE. The system identifies three areas where management should focus its efforts in order to maximise the firm's ROE: (1) how much profit management can earn on sales, (2) how efficient management is in using the firm's assets and (3) how much financial leverage management is using. Each of these areas is monitored by a single ratio and together the ratios comprise the *DuPont equation*. We now develop the DuPont equation and discuss its managerial implications. We start by looking at the equation for ROA.

The ROA Equation

The ROA equation links the firm's return on assets with its total asset turnover and net profit margin. We derive this relationship from the ROA equation as follows:

$$
\begin{aligned}
\text{ROA} &= \frac{\text{Net income}}{\text{Total assets}} \\
&= \frac{\text{Net income}}{\text{Total assets}} \times \frac{\text{Net sales}}{\text{Net sales}} \\
&= \frac{\text{Net income}}{\text{Net sales}} \times \frac{\text{Net sales}}{\text{Total assets}} \\
&= \text{Net profit margin} \times \text{Total asset turnover}
\end{aligned}
$$

As you can see, we start with the ROA formula presented earlier as Equation (4.18). Then we multiply ROA by net sales divided by net sales. In the third line, we rearrange the terms, coming up with the expression ROA = (Net income/Net sales) × (Net sales/Total assets). You may recognise the first ratio in the third line as the firm's net profit margin [Equation (4.16)] and the second ratio as the firm's total asset turnover [Equation (4.7)].

Thus, we end up with the final equation for ROA, which is restated as:

$$\text{ROA} = \text{Net profit margin} \times \text{Total asset turnover} \tag{4.22}$$

Equation (4.22) says that a firm's ROA is determined by two factors: (1) the firm's net profit margin and (2) the firm's total asset turnover. Let us look at the managerial implications of each of these terms.

Net Profit Margin   The net profit margin ratio can be written as follows:

$$\text{Net profit margin} = \frac{\text{Net income}}{\text{Net sales}}$$

$$= \frac{\text{EBIT}}{\text{Net sales}} \times \frac{\text{EBT}}{\text{EBIT}} \times \frac{\text{Net income}}{\text{EBT}}$$

As you can see, the net profit margin can be viewed as the product of three ratios: (1) the operating profit margin (EBIT/Net sales), which is Equation (4.15); (2) a ratio that measures the impact of interest expenses on profits (EBT/EBIT); and (3) a ratio that measures the impact of taxes on profits (Net income/EBT). Thus, the profit margin focuses on management's ability to generate profits from sales by efficiently managing the firm's (1) operating expenses, (2) interest expenses and (3) tax expenses.

Total Asset Turnover   Total asset turnover, which is defined as Net sales/Total assets, measures how efficiently management uses the assets under its command – that is, how much output management can generate with a given asset base. Thus, total asset turnover is a measure of *asset use efficiency*.

Profit Margins Versus Asset Turnover

The ROA equation provides some very interesting managerial insights. It says that if management wants to increase the firm's ROA, it can increase the net profit margin, total asset turnover, or both. Of course, every firm would like to make both terms as large as possible in order to earn the highest possible ROA. While every industry is different, competition, marketing considerations, technology and manufacturing capabilities, to name a few, place upper limits on asset turnover and net profit margins and, thus, ROA. However, Equation (4.22) suggests that management can follow two distinct strategies to maximise ROA. Deciding between the strategies involves a trade-off between asset turnover and profit margin.

The first management strategy emphasises high profit margin and low asset turnover. Examples of companies that use this strategy are luxury stores, such as jewellery shops, high-end department stores and upscale specialty boutiques. Such stores carry expensive merchandise that has a high profit margin but tends to sell slowly. The second management strategy depends on low profit margins and high turnover. Typical examples of firms that use this strategy are discount stores and grocery stores, which have very low profit margins but make up for it by very rapidly turning over their inventories. A typical supermarket chain, for example, turns over its inventories more than 12 times per year.

Exhibit 4.4 illustrates both strategies. The exhibit shows asset turnover, profit margin and ROA for four retailing firms in 2009. Christian Dior is a fashion chain that sells expensive merchandise and Polo Ralph Lauren stores are upscale boutiques that carry expensive casual wear for men and women. At the other end of the spectrum, Carrefour is a volume-based supermarket that uses a low-price, high-volume strategy and Metro is a successful discount chain based in Germany.

Notice that the luxury-item stores (Christian Dior and Polo Ralph Lauren) have lower asset turnover and higher profit margins, while the discount and grocery stores have lower profit margins and much higher asset turnover. Carrefour and Metro are strong financial performers in their industry sectors. Carrefour's ROA of 2.44% is very acceptable for a supermarket business. Polo Ralph Lauren is a top performer in its sector and its high ROA of 9.55% corroborates this fact, as well as reflecting the strength of the company given the weakness of the US economy during 2008/9.

EXHIBIT 4.4

TWO BASIC STRATEGIES TO EARN A HIGHER ROA[a]

Company	Asset turnover	x	Profit margin (%)	=	ROA (%)
High profit margins:					
Christian Dior (France)	0.514		4.44		2.28
Polo Ralph Lauren (USA)	1.180		8.09		9.55
High turnover:					
Carrefour SA (France)	1.692		1.44		2.44
Metro AG (Germany)	2.073		0.67		1.34

[a]Ratios are calculated using financial ratios for 2009.
To maximise a firm's ROA, management can focus more on achieving high profit margins or on achieving high asset turnover. High-end retailers like Christian Dior and Polo Ralph Lauren focus more on achieving high profit margins, while supermarkets and discount stores such as Carrefour and Metro tend to focus more on achieving high asset turnover because competition limits their ability to achieve very high profit margins.

The ROE Equation

To derive the ROE equation, we start with the formula from Equation (4.19):

$$\text{ROE} = \frac{\text{Net income}}{\text{Total equity}}$$

$$= \frac{\text{Net income}}{\text{Total equity}} \times \frac{\text{Total assets}}{\text{Total assets}}$$

$$= \frac{\text{Net income}}{\text{Total assets}} \times \frac{\text{Total assets}}{\text{Total equity}}$$

$$= \text{ROA} \times \text{Equity multiplier}$$

Next, we multiply by total assets divided by total assets, and then we rearrange the terms so that ROE = (Net income/Total assets) × (Total assets/Total equity), as shown in the third line. By this definition, ROE is the product of two ratios already familiar to us: ROA [Equation (4.18)] and the equity multiplier [Equation (4.11)]. The equation for ROE is shown as:

$$\text{ROE} = \text{ROA} \times \text{Equity multiplier} \quad (4.23)$$

Interesting here is the fact that ROE is determined by the firm's ROA and its use of leverage. The greater the use of debt in the firm's capital structure, the greater the ROE. Thus, increasing the use of leverage is one way management can increase the firm's ROE

– but at a price. That is, the greater the use of financial leverage, the more risky the firm. How aggressively a company uses this strategy depends on management's preferences for risk and the willingness of creditors to lend money and bear the risk.

The DuPont System

Now we can combine our two equations into a single equation. From Equation (4.23), we know that ROE = ROA × Equity multiplier; and from Equation (4.22), we know that ROA = Net profit margin × Total asset turnover. Substituting Equation (4.22) into Equation (4.23) yields an expression formally called the DuPont equation, as follows:

$$\text{ROE} = \text{Net profit margin} \times \text{Total asset turnover} \times \text{Equity multiplier}$$

$$(4.24)$$

We can also express the DuPont equation in ratio form:

$$\text{ROE} = \frac{\text{Net income}}{\text{Net sales}} \times \frac{\text{Net sales}}{\text{Total assets}} \times \frac{\text{Total assets}}{\text{Total equity}}$$

$$(4.25)$$

To check the DuPont relationship, we will use some values from Exhibit 4.3, which lists financial ratios for Fabrique Aérospatiale. For 2010, Fabrique Aérospatiale's net profit margin is 15.31%, total asset turnover is 0.71 and the equity multiplier is 2.27. Substituting these values into Equation (4.24) yields:

$$\text{ROE} = \text{Net profit margin} \times \text{Total asset turnover}$$
$$\times \text{Equity multiplier}$$
$$= 15.31 \times 0.71 \times 2.27$$
$$= 24.68\%$$

With rounding error, this agrees with the value computed for ROE in Exhibit 4.3.

Applying the DuPont System

In summary, the DuPont equation tells us that a firm's ROE is determined by three factors: (1) net profit margin, which measures the firm's operating efficiency and how it manages its interest expense and taxes; (2) total asset turnover, which measures the efficiency with which the firm's assets are utilised; and (3) the equity multiplier, which measures the firm's use of financial leverage. The ROA is the product of the firm's net profit margin and total asset turnover. The schematic diagram in Exhibit 4.5 shows how the three key DuPont ratios are linked together and how they relate to the

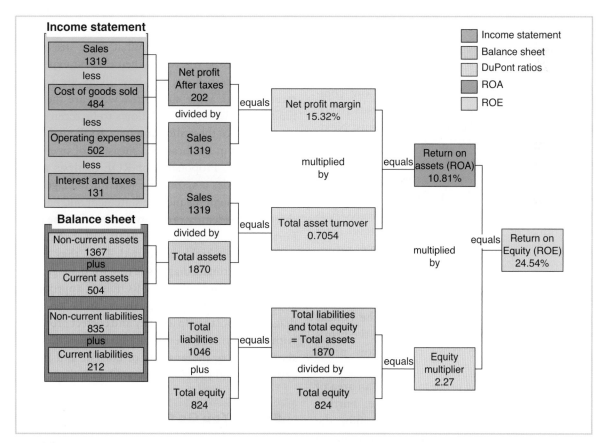

Exhibit 4.5: Relations in the DuPont System of Analysis for Fabrique Aérospatiale in 2010 (€ millions)
The diagram shows how the three key DuPont ratios are linked together and to the firm's balance sheet and income statement. Numbers in the exhibit are in millions of euros and represent 2010 data from Fabrique Aérospatiale. The ROE is 24.54% and differs from the 24.53% in Exhibit 4.3 due to rounding.

balance sheet and income statement for Fabrique Aérospatiale.

The DuPont system of analysis is a useful tool to help identify problem areas within a firm. For example, suppose that Baltic Yachting Group, a sailing boat manufacturer located in Värmdö, Sweden, is in financial difficulty. The firm hires you to help apply the DuPont system of analysis to find out why the ship is sinking financially. The firm's CFO has you calculate the DuPont ratio values for the firm and obtain some industry averages to use as benchmarks, as shown.

DuPont Ratios	Firm	Industry
ROE	8%	16%
ROA	4%	8%
Equity multiplier	2	2
Net profit margin	8%	16%
Asset turnover	0.5	0.5

Clearly, the firm's ROE is quite low compared with the benchmark data (8% versus 16%), so without question the firm has problems. Next, you examine the values for the firm's ROA and equity multiplier and find that the firm's use of financial leverage is equal to the industry standard of 2 times but that its ROA is half that of the industry (4% versus 8%). Because ROA is the product of net profit margin and total asset turnover, you next examine these two ratios. Asset turnover does not appear to be a problem because the firm's ratio is equal to the industry standard of 0.5 times. However, the firm's net profit margin is substantially below the benchmark standard (8% versus 16%). Thus, the firm's performance problem stems from a low profit margin.

Identifying the low profit margin as an area of concern is only a first step, of course. Further investigation will be necessary to determine the underlying problem and its causes. The point to remember is that financial analysis identifies areas of concern within the firm, but rarely does such analysis tell us all we need to know.

Is Maximising ROE an Appropriate Goal?

Throughout the book we have stressed the notion that management should make decisions that maximise the current value of the company's shares. An important question is whether maximising the value of ROE, as suggested by the DuPont system, is equivalent to wealth maximisation. The short answer is that the two goals are not equivalent, but this warrants some discussion.

A major shortcoming of ROE is that it does not directly consider cash flow. ROE considers earnings, but earnings are not the same as future cash flows. Second, ROE does not consider risk. As discussed in Chapter 1, management and shareholders are very concerned about the degree of risk they face. Third, ROE does not consider the size of the initial investment or the size of future cash payments. As we stressed in Chapter 1, the essence of any business or investment decision is this: What is the size of the cash flows to be received, when do you expect to receive the cash flows and how likely are you to receive them? More succinctly, what are the size, timing and risk of the cash flows to be received?

In spite of these shortcomings, ROE analysis is widely used in business as a measure of operating performance. Proponents of ROE analysis argue that it provides a systematic way for management to work through the income statement and balance sheet and to identify problem areas within the firm. Furthermore, they note that ROE and shareholder value are often highly correlated. Thus, they argue, ROE is a legitimate diagnostic tool for management and focusing on maximising ROE is an appropriate goal. We agree that ROE analysis can be a helpful diagnostic tool to help identify and correct problems within the firm. However, any investment decision should involve the analysis of current and future cash flows and the risk associated with them.

Before You Go On

1. What is the purpose of the DuPont system of analysis?

2. What is the equation for ROA in the DuPont system, and how do the factors in that equation influence the ratio?

3. What are the three major shortcomings of ROE?

SELECTING A BENCHMARK

Learning Objective 5

Explain what benchmarks are, describe how they are prepared and discuss why they are important in financial statement analysis.

How do you judge whether a ratio value is too high or too low? Is the value good or bad? We touched on these questions several times earlier in the chapter. As we suggested, the starting point for making these judgements is selecting an appropriate benchmark – a standard that will be the basis for meaningful comparisons. Financial managers can gather appropriate benchmark data in three ways: through trend, industry and peer group analysis.

Trend Analysis

Trend analysis uses history as its standard by evaluating a single firm's performance over time. This sort of analysis allows management to determine whether a given ratio value has increased or decreased over time and whether there has been an abrupt shift in the value of a ratio. An increase or decrease in a ratio value is in itself neither good nor bad. However, a ratio value that is changing typically prompts the financial manager to sort out the issues surrounding the change and to take any action that is warranted. Exhibit 4.3 shows the trends in Fabrique Aérospatiale's ratios. For example, the exhibit shows that Fabrique Aérospatiale's current ratio has improved, suggesting that at the present time the company is not having a problem with liquidity.

Industry Analysis

A second way to establish a benchmark is to conduct an industry group analysis. To do that, we identify a group of firms that have the same product line, compete in the same market and are about the same size. The average ratio values for these firms will be our benchmarks. Obviously, no two firms are identical and deciding which firms to include in the analysis is always a judgement call. If we can construct a sample of reasonable size, however, the average values provide defensible benchmarks.

International Standard Industrial Classification (ISIC) System

a numerical system developed under the auspices of the United Nations to classify industrial activity by type

Financial ratios and other financial data for industry groups are published by a number of sources – Dun & Bradstreet, Fitch IBCA, Moody's Investors Service and Standard & Poor's (S&P), to name a few. There is a common international system developed by the United Nations for identifying industry groups, the **International Standard Industrial Classification (ISIC) System**. The ISIC codes use an alphanumeric system for classifying industry activity. The first level is characterised by the use of the letters of the alphabet from A to U, level 2 covers 62 divisions identified by two-digit numerical codes and level 3 is defined by 161 groups identified by three-digit numerical codes. The letter of the alphabet identifies the sector. Manufacturing has been allocated the letter C and the following list gives the two-digit ISIC codes for manufacturing. Fabrique Aérospatiale's two-digit code is 30, 'Manufacture of other transport equipment': The manufacturing group C is given below:

- **C - Manufacturing**
  - **10** - Manufacture of food products
  - **11** - Manufacture of beverages

- 12 - Manufacture of tobacco products
- 13 - Manufacture of textiles
- 14 - Manufacture of wearing apparel
- 15 - Manufacture of leather and related products
- 16 - Manufacture of wood and of products of wood and cork, except furniture; manufacture of articles of straw and plaiting materials
- 17 - Manufacture of paper and paper products
- 18 - Printing and reproduction of recorded media
- 19 - Manufacture of coke and refined petroleum products
- 20 - Manufacture of chemicals and chemical products
- 21 - Manufacture of basic pharmaceutical products and pharmaceutical preparations
- 22 - Manufacture of rubber and plastics products
- 23 - Manufacture of other non-metallic mineral products
- 24 - Manufacture of basic metals
- 25 - Manufacture of fabricated metal products, except machinery and equipment
- 26 - Manufacture of computer, electronic and optical products
- 27 - Manufacture of electrical equipment
- 28 - Manufacture of machinery and equipment n.e.c.
- 29 - Manufacture of motor vehicles, trailers and semi-trailers
- 30 - Manufacture of other transport equipment
  - 301 - Building of ships and boats
  - 302 - Manufacture of railway locomotives and rolling stock
  - 303 - Manufacture of air and spacecraft and related machinery
  - 304 - Manufacture of military fighting vehicles
  - 309 - Manufacture of transport equipment n.e.c.

- 31 - Manufacture of furniture
- 32 - Other manufacturing
- 33 - Repair and installation of machinery and equipment

> **WEB**
>
> You can find information about ISIC at: http://unstats.un.org/unsd/cr/registry.

To narrow the group, we use more digits. Fabrique Aérospatiale's four-digit code is C303 ('Manufacture of air and spacecraft and related machinery'). For firms within a given ISIC code, financial ratio data can be further categorised by asset size or by sales, which allows for more meaningful comparisons. There are no further subdivisions, so the company's full ISIC code is C3030.

Although industry databases are readily available and easy to use, they are far from perfect. When trying to find a sample of firms that are 'similar' to your company, you may find the classifications too broad. For example, Carrefour and Metro have the same ISIC code, but operate in different countries and face different operating conditions and competitors. Another problem is that different industrial databases may compute ratios differently. Thus, when making benchmark comparisons, you must be careful that your calculations match those in the database or there could be some distortions in your findings.

Peer Group Analysis

The third way to establish benchmark information is to identify a group of firms that compete with the company we are analysing. Ideally, the firms are in similar lines of business, are about the same size and are direct competitors of the target firm. These firms form a *peer group*. Once a peer group has been identified, management can obtain their annual reports and compute average ratio values against which the firm can compare its performance.

EXHIBIT 4.6

PEER GROUP RATINGS FOR FABRIQUE AÉROSPATIALE

	2010	2009	2008
Liquidity Ratios:			
Current ratio	0.95	0.94	0.99
Quick ratio	0.68	0.68	0.81
Efficiency Ratios:			
Inventory turnover	18.00	20.41	31.22
Days' sales in inventory	20.27	17.88	11.69
Accounts receivable turnover	4.65	5.21	5.96
Days' sales outstanding	78.43	70.07	61.26
Total asset turnover	0.68	0.73	0.72
Fixed asset turnover	1.01	1.13	1.15
Leverage Ratios:			
Total debt ratio	11.28	12.67	15.98
Debt-to-equity ratio	2.40	2.29	3.16
Equity multiplier	3.41	3.30	4.22
Times interest earned	9.58	5.42	5.42
Cash coverage	11.65	7.07	7.12
Profitability Ratios:			
Gross profit margin	29.62	29.94	30.88
Operating profit margin	18.18	12.19	11.40
Net profit margin	10.47	6.14	5.21
Return on assets	7.08	4.46	3.77
Return on equity	24.12	14.73	15.91
Market-Value Indicators:			
Price-to-earnings ratio	19.14	21.41	20.87
Earnings per share	0.50	0.26	0.20

Peer group analysis is one way to establish benchmarks for a firm. Ideally, a firm's peer group is made up of firms that are direct competitors and are about the same size. Fabrique Aérospatiale's peer group is made up of Augusta/Westland (UK), Bombardier (Canada), Dassault (France), Finnemeccanica (Italy) and Embraer (Brazil). The exhibit shows the average financial ratios for 2008, 2009 and 2010.

How do we determine which firms should be in the peer group? The senior management team within a company will know its competitors. If you are working outside the firm, you can look at the firm's annual report and at financial analysts' reports. Both of these sources usually identify key competitors. Exhibit 4.6 shows ratios for a five-firm peer group constructed for Fabrique Aérospatiale for 2008–2010.

We consider the peer group methodology the best way to establish a benchmark if financial data for peer firms are publicly available. We should note, however, that comparison against a single firm is acceptable when there is a clear market leader and we want to compare a firm's performance and other characteristics against those of a firm considered the best. For example, Volkswagen may want to compare itself directly against Toyota, which is the 'best in breed' in manufacturing productivity and quality. It is worthwhile to compare a firm with the market leader to identify areas of weakness as well as of possible strength.

Before You Go On

1. In what three ways can a financial manager choose a benchmark?
2. Explain what the ISIC codes are, and discuss the pros and cons of using them in financial analysis.

USING FINANCIAL RATIOS

Learning Objective 6

Identify the major limitations in using financial statement analysis.

So far, our focus has been on the calculation of financial ratios. As you may already have concluded, however, the most important tasks are to *correctly interpret* the ratio values and to *make appropriate decisions* based on this interpretation. In this section we discuss using financial ratios in performance analysis.

Performance Analysis of Fabrique Aérospatiale

Let us examine Fabrique Aérospatiale's performance during 2010 using the DuPont system of analysis as our diagnostic tool and the peer group sample in Exhibit 4.6 as our benchmark. For ease of discussion, Fabrique Aérospatiale's financial ratios and the benchmark data are assembled in Exhibit 4.7.

We start our analysis by looking at the big picture – the three key DuPont ratios for the firm and a peer group of firms (see Exhibit 4.7). We see that Fabrique Aérospatiale's ROE of 24.52% is

EXHIBIT 4.7

PEER GROUP ANALYSIS FOR FABRIQUE AÉROSPATIALE

	(1) Fabrique Aérospatiale	(2) Peer Group Ratio	(3) Difference (Column 1 – Column 2)
DuPont Ratios:			
Return on equity (%)	24.52	24.12	0.10
Return on assets (%)	10.80	7.08	3.72
Equity multiplier (%)	2.27	3.41	(1.14)
Net profit margin (%)	15.31	10.47	4.84
Total asset turnover	0.71	0.68	0.03
Profit Margins:			
Gross profit margin (%)	63.34	29.62	33.72
Operating margin (%)	25.32	18.18	7.14
Net profit margin (%)	15.31	10.47	4.84
Asset Ratios:			
Current ratio	2.38	0.75	1.63
Fixed asset turnover	1.36	1.01	0.35
Inventory turnover	3.13	18.00	(14.87)
Accounts receivable turnover	10.68	4.65	6.02

Examining the differences between the ratios of a firm and its peer group is a good way to spot areas that require further analysis.

just above the benchmark value of 24.12%, a difference of just 0.10%. More dramatically, Fabrique Aérospatiale's ROA is 10.78% – above the peer group benchmark – and is a major difference. Clearly, Fabrique Aérospatiale's performance is very good based on the peer group performance, but we want to know why it is only average in terms of ROE.

To determine the problems, we examine the firm's equity multiplier and ROA results in more detail. The equity multiplier value of 2.27, versus the benchmark value of 3.41, suggests that Fabrique Aérospatiale is using much less leverage than the average firm in the benchmark sample. Management is comfortable with the lower-than-average leverage. By having less debt and hence the potential to borrow more, the company takes the view that it is well placed to take advantage of acquisition opportunities if they should arise without unduly leveraging its balance sheet in the future.

As a result of the lower equity multiplier and management's unwillingness to substitute debt for equity in the balance sheet, Fabrique Aérospatiale's ROE is in line with the peer group average of 24.12%. To illustrate this point, suppose management sought to increase its ROE significantly; it would need to increase leverage. The best performer in the group has a ROE of 28.79% in 2010. To match this, Fabrique Aérospatiale would need to leverage the balance sheet 2.68. With an equity multiplier of 2.68, the firm's ROE would be 28.94% (0.1080 × 2.68); this is 18.03% above the firm's current ROE of 24.52% and 19.98% above the peer group benchmark. Thus, the use of lower leverage has, to some extent, masked the firm's better-than-average performance on ROA.

Recall that ROA equals the product of the net profit margin and total asset turnover. Fabrique Aérospatiale's net profit margin is 4.85% above the benchmark value (15.31 – 10.47 = 4.85), and its total asset turnover ratio is slightly above the benchmark value (0.71 versus 0.68). Thus, both ratios that comprise ROA are above the peer group benchmark standard and contribute to its above-average net profit margin.

Turning to the detailed asset turnover ratios shown in Exhibit 4.7, we find that the ratios for Fabrique Aérospatiale are generally similar to the corresponding peer group ratios. An exception is inventory turnover ratio, which is substantially below the benchmark: 3.13 for Fabrique Aérospatiale versus 18.00 for the benchmark. Fabrique Aérospatiale's management needs to investigate why the inventory turnover ratio is so far off the mark.

We next look at the various profit margins shown in Exhibit 4.7 to gain insight into Fabrique Aérospatiale's exceptional performance. The gross profit margin is 33.72 percentage points above the benchmark value (63.34 – 29.62 = 33.72), which is good news. Since gross profit margin is a factor of sales and the cost of goods sold, we can conclude that there is no problem with the price the firm is charging for its products or with its cost of goods sold.

Fabrique Aérospatiale's operating margin of 25.32%, which is 7.15 percentage points above the peer group benchmark of 18.18% (25.32 – 18.18), indicates that it is good at managing its controllable expenses such as selling and administrative costs.

In sum, the DuPont analysis of Fabrique Aérospatiale has identified one area that warrants detailed investigation by management: the larger-than-average inventories (slow inventory turnover). Management must now investigate and come up with a course of action. Management may want to give careful consideration to the firm's lower-than-average financial leverage and whether it represents an appropriate degree of risk.

Financial ratio analysis is an excellent diagnostic tool. It helps management identify the problem areas in the firm – the symptoms. However, it does not tell management what the causes of the problems are or what course of action should be taken. Management must drill down into the accounting data, talk with managers in the field and, if appropriate, talk with people outside the firm, such as suppliers, to understand what is causing the problems.

Learning by Doing Application 4.5

Roget's Jewellers and the Missing Data

Problem: Jean Roget has owned and managed a profitable jewellers at Charles De Gaulle airport outside Paris for the past five years. He believes his jewellers is one of the best managed in the country and he is considering opening several new stores.

When Jean opened the store, he supplied all the equity financing himself and financed the rest with personal loans from friends and family members. To open more stores at other airports, Jean needs a bank loan. The bank will want to examine his financial statements and know something about the competition he faces.

Jean has asked his brother-in-law, Sébastien Fournier, a practicing accountant, to analyse the financials. Jean has also gathered some financial information about a company he considers the chief competition at Charles de Gaulle. The company has been in business for 25 years, has a number of outlets both at airports and in a number of major cities in France, and is widely admired for its owners' management skills. Jean has partial information on its operations at its Charles de Gaulle boutique.

Sébastien organises the available information in the following table:

Financial Ratio Data	Roget's Jewellers	Competitor
Sales	€240	€300
Net income	€6	—
ROE	13.13%	—
Net profit margin	—	5.84%
Asset turnover	1.5	1.5
Equity multiplier	—	1.5
Debt-to-equity ratio	2.5	—

Calculate the missing values for the financial data above.

Approach: Use the ratio equations discussed in the text to calculate the missing financial ratios for both Roget's store and the competitor.

Solution: Roget's jewellers:

1. Net profit margin $= \dfrac{\text{Net income}}{\text{Sales}}$

$= \dfrac{€6}{€240} = 0.025$, or 2.5%

2. Equity multiplier $=$
$1 + \text{Debt-to-equity ratio} = 1 + 2.5 = 3.5$

Competitor:

1. ROE $=$ Net profit margin
$\times$ Asset turnover $\times$ Equity multiplier
$= 0.0584 \times 1.5 \times 1.5$
$= 0.1314$, or 13.14%

2. Net profit $=$ Net profit margin $\times$ Net sales
$= 0.0584 \times €300 = €17.52$

Debt-to-equity ratio

$= \dfrac{\text{Debt}}{\text{Equity}} = \dfrac{€66.82}{€133.1} = 0.50$

(a) Equity $= \dfrac{\text{Net income}}{\text{ROE}} = \dfrac{€17.50}{0.1314} = €133.18$

(b) Assets $= \dfrac{\text{Net sales}}{\text{Asset turnover}} = \dfrac{€300}{1.5} = €200.0$

(c) Debt $=$ Assets $-$ Equity
$= €200.0 - €133.18 = €66.82$

Decision-Making Example 4.3

Roget's Jewellers and the DuPont Analysis

Situation: Let us continue with our analysis of Roget's jewellers, introduced in Learning by Doing Application 4.5. Brother-in-law Sébastien has been asked to analyse the company's financials. He decides to use the DuPont system of analysis as a framework. He arranges the critical information as follows:

Financial Ratios	Roget's jewellers	Competitor
ROE	13.13%	13.14%
ROA	3.75%	8.76%
Net profit margin	2.50%	5.84%
Asset turnover	1.5	1.5
Equity multiplier	3.5	1.5
Debt-to-equity ratio	2.5	0.5
Net sales	€240	€300
Net income	€6.0	€17.5

Given the above financial ratios, what recommendations should Sébastien make regarding Roget's jewellers and its management?

Decision: The good news is that Roget is able to earn about the same ROE as his major on-site competitor. Unfortunately for Roget, the rest of the analysis is less favourable. Turning to the first two DuPont system ratios, we can see that Roget's ROA of 3.75% is much lower than his major competitor's ROA of 8.76%. Roget's business is also very highly leveraged, with an equity multiplier of 3.5 times, compared with 1.5 times for the competitor. In fact, the only reason Roget's ROE is comparable to the competitor's is the high leverage.

Breaking the ROA into its components, we find that Roget's asset turnover ratio is the same as the competitor's, 1.5. However, the profitability of Roget's store is extremely poor as measured by the firm's net profit margin of 2.50%, compared with the competitor's margin of 5.84%. One possible explanation is that to stimulate sales and maintain asset turnover, Roget has been selling his merchandise at too low a price.

As mentioned, Roget is employing a very high degree of financial leverage. Roget's debt-to-equity ratio is 2.5, while the competitor's is only 0.5. To illustrate how big the difference is, suppose both firms have €100 in equity financing. For €100 of equity, the competitor would hold €50 in debt, and Roget would hold €250.

In summary, Roget's jewellers is not well managed. Roget needs to either increase his net profit margin or increase his inventory turnover to bring his ROA into line with that of his major competitor. Roget also needs to reduce his dependence on financial leverage. If Charles de Gaulle airport were to suffer a significant downturn in traffic, Roget's business would be a likely candidate for failure.

Limitations of Financial Statement Analysis

Financial statement and ratio analysis as discussed in this chapter presents two major problems. First, it depends on accounting data based on historical costs. As we discussed in Chapter 3, knowledgeable financial managers would prefer to use financial statements in which all of the firm's assets and liabilities are valued at market. Financial statements based on current market values more closely reflect a firm's true economic conditions than do statements based on historical cost.

Second, there is little theory to guide us in making judgements based on financial statement and ratio analysis. That is why it is difficult to say a current ratio of 2.0 is good or bad or to say whether

ROE or ROA is a more important ratio. The lack of theory explains, in part, why rules of thumb are often used as decision rules in financial statement analysis. The problem with decision rules based on experience and 'common sense' rather than theory is that they may work fine in a stable economic environment but may fail when a significant shift takes place. For example, if you were in an economic environment with low inflation, you could develop a set of decision rules to help manage your business. However, if the economy became inflationary, more than likely many of your decision rules would fail.

Despite the limitations, we know that financial managers and analysts routinely use financial statements and ratio analysis to evaluate a firm's performance and to make a variety of decisions about the firm. These financial statements and the resulting analysis are the primary means by which financial information is communicated both inside and outside firms. At this time, the availability of market value data is limited for public companies and not available for privately held firms and other entities such as government units.

Thus, we conclude that, practically speaking, historical accounting information represents the best available information. However, times are changing. As the accounting profession becomes more comfortable with the use of market data and as technology increases its availability and reliability and lowers its cost, we expect to see an increase in the use of market-based financial statements.

Before You Go On

1. Explain how the DuPont identity allows us to evaluate a firm's performance.
2. What are the limitations on traditional financial statement analysis?
3. List some of the problems that financial analysts confront when analysing financial statements.

SUMMARY OF LEARNING OBJECTIVES

1. **Explain the three perspectives from which financial statements can be viewed.**

   Financial statements can be viewed from the owners', managers' or creditors' perspective. All three groups are ultimately interested in a firm's profitability, but each group takes a different view. Shareholders want to know how much cash they can expect to receive for their shares, what their return on investment will be and/or how much their shares are worth in the market. Managers are concerned with maximising the firm's long-term value through a series of day-to-day management decisions; thus, they need to see the impact of their decisions on the financial statements to confirm that things are going as planned. Creditors monitor the firm's use of debt and are concerned with how much debt the firm is using and whether the firm will have enough cash to meet its obligations.

2. **Describe common-size financial statements, explain why they are used and be able to prepare and use them to analyse the historical performance of a firm.**

   Common-size financial statements are financial statements in which each number has been scaled by a common measure of firm size: balance sheets are expressed as a percentage of total assets and income statements are expressed as a percentage of net sales. Common-size financial statements are necessary when comparing firms that are significantly different in size. The preparation of common-size financial statements and their use are illustrated for Fabrique Aérospatiale.

3. **Discuss how financial ratios facilitate financial analysis and be able to compute and use them to analyse a firm's performance.**

Financial ratios are used in financial analysis because they eliminate problems caused by comparing two or more companies of different size or when looking at the same company over time as the size changes. Financial ratios can be divided into five categories: (1) Liquidity ratios measure the ability of a company to cover its current bills; (2) efficiency ratios tell how efficiently the firm uses its assets; (3) leverage ratios tell how much debt a firm has in its capital structure and whether the firm can meet its long-term financial obligations; (4) profitability ratios focus on the firm's earnings. Finally, (5) market value indicators look at a company based on market data as opposed to historical data used in financial statements. The computation and analysis of major financial ratios are presented (see also the Summary of Key Equations that follows).

4. **Describe the DuPont system of analysis and be able to use it to evaluate a firm's performance and identify corrective actions that may be necessary.**

The DuPont system of analysis is a diagnostic tool that uses financial ratios to assess a firm's financial strength. Once the financial ratios are calculated and the assessment is complete, management focuses on correcting the problems within the context of maximising the firm's ROE. For analysis, the DuPont system breaks ROE into three components: net profit margin, which measures operating efficiency; total asset turnover, which measures how efficiently the firm deploys its assets; and the equity multiplier, which measures financial leverage. A diagnostic analysis of a firm's performance using the DuPont system is illustrated.

5. **Explain what benchmarks are, describe how they are prepared and discuss why they are important in financial statement analysis.**

Once we have calculated financial ratios, we need some way to evaluate them. A benchmark provides a standard for comparison. In financial statement analysis, a number of benchmarks are used. Most often, benchmark comparisons involve competitors that are roughly the same size and that offer a similar range of products. Another form of benchmarking is time-trend analysis, which compares a firm's current financial ratios against the same ratios from past years. Time-trend analysis tells us whether a ratio is increasing or decreasing over time. The preparation and use of peer group benchmark data are illustrated.

6. **Identify the major limitations in using financial statement analysis.**

The major limitations to financial statement and ratio analysis are the use of historical accounting data and the lack of theory to guide the decision maker. The lack of theory explains, in part, why there are so many rules of thumb. Though rules of thumb are useful, and might work under certain conditions, they may lead to poor decisions if circumstances or the economic environment have changed.

SUMMARY OF KEY EQUATIONS

Equation	Description	Formula
(4.1)		$\text{Current ratio} = \dfrac{\text{Current assets}}{\text{Current liabilities}}$
(4.2)	Liquidity ratios	$\text{Quick ratio} = \dfrac{\text{Current assets} - \text{Inventories}}{\text{Current liabilities}}$

(4.3)		$\text{Inventory turnover} = \dfrac{\text{Cost of goods sold}}{\text{Inventories}}$
(4.4)		$\text{Days' sales in inventories} = \dfrac{365 \text{ days}}{\text{Inventory turnover}}$
(4.5)		$\text{Accounts receivable turnover} = \dfrac{\text{Net revenues}}{\text{Trade accounts receivable}}$
(4.6)	Efficiency ratios	$\text{Days' sales outstanding} = \dfrac{365 \text{ days}}{\text{Accounts receivable turnover}}$
(4.7)		$\text{Total asset turnover} = \dfrac{\text{Net revenues or net sales}}{\text{Total assets}}$
(4.8)		$\text{Fixed asset turnover} = \dfrac{\text{Net revenues}}{\text{Net fixed assets}}$
(4.9)		$\text{Total debt ratio} = \dfrac{\text{Total debt}}{\text{Total assets}}$
(4.10)		$\text{Debt-to-equity ratio} = \dfrac{\text{Total debt}}{\text{Total equity}}$
(4.11)	Leverage ratios	$\text{Equity multiplier} = \dfrac{\text{Total assets}}{\text{Total equity}}$
(4.12)		$\text{Times interest earned} = \dfrac{\text{EBIT}}{\text{Interest expense}}$
(4.13)		$\text{Cash coverage} = \dfrac{\text{EBITDA}}{\text{Interest expense}}$
(4.14)		$\text{Gross profit margin} = \dfrac{\text{Net sales} - \text{Cost of goods sold}}{\text{Net sales}}$
(4.15)		$\text{Operating profit margin} = \dfrac{\text{EBIT}}{\text{Net sales}}$
(4.16)		$\text{Net profit margin} = \dfrac{\text{Net income (Profit for the year)}}{\text{Net sales}}$
(4.17)	Profitability ratios	$\text{EBIT return on assets (EROA)} = \dfrac{\text{EBIT}}{\text{Total assets}}$
(4.18)		$\text{Return on assets} = \dfrac{\text{Net income}}{\text{Total assets}}$
(4.19)		$\text{Return on equity} = \dfrac{\text{Net income}}{\text{Total equity}}$
(4.20)		$\text{Earnings per share} = \dfrac{\text{Net income}}{\text{Shares outstanding}}$
(4.21)	Market value indicators	$\text{Price-to-earnings ratio} = \dfrac{\text{Price per share}}{\text{Earnings per share}}$
(4.22)		$\text{ROA} = \text{Net profit margin} \times \text{Total asset turnover}$
(4.23)	DuPont equation	$\text{ROE} = \text{ROA} \times \text{Equity multiplier}$
(4.24)		$\text{ROE} = \text{Net profit margin} \times \text{Total asset turnover} \times \text{Equity multiplier}$
(4.25)		$\text{ROE} = \dfrac{\text{Net income}}{\text{Net sales}} \times \dfrac{\text{Net sales}}{\text{Total assets}} \times \dfrac{\text{Total assets}}{\text{Total equity}}$

SELF-STUDY PROBLEMS

4.1. Industriale Bologna SpA reported the following information for the year ended 31 December 2010. Prepare a common-size income statement for the year ended 31 December 2010.

Industriale Bologna SpA

Income Statement (€ thousands)

2008

Net sales	€2 110 965
Cost of goods sold	1 459 455
Selling and administrative expenses	312 044
Non-recurring expenses	27 215
Earnings before interest, taxes, depreciation and amortisation (EBITDA)	€ 312 251
Depreciation	112 178
Earnings before interest and taxes (EBIT)	€ 200 073
Interest expense	117 587
Earnings before taxes (EBT)	€ 82 486
Taxes (35%)	28 870
Net income	€ 53 616

4.2. Prepare a common-size balance sheet from the following information for Industriale Bologna SpA.

Industriale Bologna SpA

Balance Sheet as of 31 December 2010 (€ thousands)

Assets:		Liabilities and Equity:	
Non-current assets		Equity	
Net plant and equipment	€1 978 455	Ordinary shares	€1 312 137
Total non-current assets	1 978 455	Retained earnings	855 684
Current assets		Total common equity	2 167 821
Inventories	1 152 398	Non-current liabilities	
Accounts receivable	708 275	Long-term borrowings	1 149 520
Other current assets	42 115	Current liabilities	
Cash and marketable securities	396 494	Borrowings payable	101 229
Total current assets	2 299 282	Accrued income taxes	41 322
		Accounts payable	817 845
		Total current liabilities	960 396
		Total liabilities	2 109 916
Total assets	€4 277 737	Total liabilities and equity	€4 277 737

4.3. Using the 2010 data for Industriale Bologna SpA, calculate the following liquidity ratios:
  a. Current ratio.
  b. Quick ratio.

4.4. Refer to the balance sheet and income statement for Industriale Bologna SpA for the year ended 31 December 2010. Calculate the following ratios:
  a. Inventory turnover ratio.
  b. Days' sales outstanding.
  c. Total asset turnover.
  d. Fixed asset turnover.
  e. Total debt ratio.
  f. Debt-to-equity ratio.
  g. Times-interest-earned ratio.
  h. Cash coverage ratio.

4.5. Refer to the balance sheet and income statement for Industriale Bologna SpA for the year ended 31 December 2010. Use the DuPont equation to calculate the return on equity (ROE). In the process, calculate the following ratios: profit margin, total asset turnover, equity multiplier, EBIT return on assets and return on assets.

SOLUTIONS TO SELF-STUDY PROBLEMS

4.1. The standardised income statement for Industriale Bologna SpA should look like the following:

Industriale Bologna SpA

Income Statement (€ thousands)

	2008	Percentage of Sales
Net sales	€2 110 965	100.0%
Cost of goods sold	1 459 455	69.1
Selling and administrative expenses	312 044	14.8
Non-recurring expenses	27 215	1.3
Earnings before interest, taxes, depreciation and amortisation (EBITDA)	312 251	14.8%
Depreciation	112 178	5.3
Earnings before interest and taxes (EBIT)	200 073	9.5%
Interest expense	117 587	5.6
Earnings before taxes (EBT)	82 486	3.9%
Taxes (35%)	28 870	1.4
Net income	€ 53 616	2.5%

4.2. Industriale Bologna SpA's common-size balance sheet is as follows:

Balance Sheet as of 31 December 2010 (€ thousands)

Assets:	2010	Percentage of total	Liabilities and Equity:	2010	Percentage of total
Non-current assets			Equity		
Net plant and equipment	€1 978 455	46.25%	Ordinary shares	€1 312 137	30.67%
Total non-current assets	1978455		Retained earnings	855 684	20.00%
Current assets			Total common equity	2 167 821	50.68%
Inventories	1 152 398	26.94%	Non-current liabilities		
Accounts receivable	708 275	16.56%	Long-term borrowings	1 149 520	26.87%
Other current assets	42 115	0.98%	Current liabilities		
Cash and marketable securities	396 494	9.27%	Borrowings payable	101 229	2.37%
Total current assets	2 299 282		Accrued income taxes	41 322	0.97%
			Accounts payable	817 845	19.12%
			Total current liabilities	960 396	22.45%
			Total liabilities	2 109 916	49.32%
Total assets	€4 277 737	100.00%	Total liabilities and equity	€4 277 737	100.00%

4.3. Industriale Bologna SpA's current ratio and quick ratio are calculated as follows:

a. Current ratio = €2 299 282/€960 396 = 2.39

b. Quick ratio = (€2 299 282 – €1 152 375)/ €960 396 = 1.19

4.4. The ratios are calculated as shown in the following table:

Ratio	Calculation	Value
Inventory turnover ratio	€1 459 455/€1 152 398	1.27
Days' sales outstanding	€708 275/(€2 110 965/365)	122.5 days
Total asset turnover	€2 110 965/€4 277 737	0.49
Fixed asset turnover	€2 110 965/€1 978 455	1.07
Total debt ratio	€2 109 916/€4 277 737	0.493
Debt-to-equity ratio	€2 109 916/€2 167 821	0.974
Times-interest-earned ratio	€200 073/€117 587	1.7
Cash coverage ratio	€312 251/€117 587	2.66

4.5. Following are the calculations for the ROE and associated ratios:

$$\text{Profit margin} = \text{Net income}/\text{Net sales} = €53\ 616/€2\ 110\ 965 = 2.54\%.$$
$$\text{EBIT ROA} = \text{EBIT}/\text{Total assets} = €200\ 073/€4\ 277\ 737 = 4.68\%$$
$$\text{Return on assets} = \text{Net income}/\text{Total assets} = €53\ 616/€4\ 277\ 737 = 1.25\%$$
$$\text{Equity multiplier} = \text{Total assets}/\text{Total equity} = €4\ 277\ 737/€2\ 167\ 821 = 1.97$$
$$\text{Total asset turnover} = \text{Net sales}/\text{Total assets} = €2\ 110\ 965/€4\ 277\ 737 = 0.49$$

DuPont identity:

$$
\begin{aligned}
\text{ROE} &= \text{ROA*EM} \\
&= \text{Profit margin} \times \text{Total assets turnover ratio} \times \text{EM} \\
&= \text{Net income}/\text{Net sales} \times \text{Net sales}/\text{Total assets} \times \text{Total assets}/\text{Total equity} \\
&= 0.0254 \times 0.49 \times 1.97 \\
&= 2.45\%
\end{aligned}
$$

CRITICAL THINKING QUESTIONS

4.1. What does it mean when a company's return on assets (ROA) is equal to its return on equity (ROE)?

4.2. Why is too much liquidity not a good thing?

4.3. Inventories are excluded when the quick ratio or acid-test ratio is calculated because inventories are the most difficult current asset to convert to cash without loss of value. What types of inventories are likely to be most easily converted to cash?

4.4. What does a very high inventory turnover ratio signify?

4.5. How would one explain a low receivables turnover ratio?

4.6. What additional information does the fixed assets turnover ratio provide over the total assets turnover ratio? For which industries does it carry greater significance?

4.7. How does financial leverage help shareholders?

4.8. Why do banks have a low ROA (relative to other industries) but a high ROE?

4.9. Why is the ROE a more appropriate proxy of wealth maximisation for smaller firms rather than for larger ones?

4.10. Why is it not enough for an analyst to look at just the short-term and long-term debt on a firm's balance sheet?

QUESTIONS AND PROBLEMS

Basic

4.1. Liquidity ratios: Explain why the quick ratio or acid-test ratio is a better measure of a firm's liquidity than the current ratio.

4.2. Liquidity ratios: Danusab AG has total current assets of €11 845 175, current liabilities of €5 311 020 and a quick ratio of 0.89. What are its inventories?

4.3. Efficiency ratio: If Newton Manufacturers has an accounts receivable turnover of 4.8 times and net sales of £7 812 379, what is its level of receivables?

4.4. Efficiency ratio: Brunner und Grabben AG has a gross profit margin of 33.7%, sales of €47 112 365 and inventories of €14 595 435. What is its inventory turnover ratio?

4.5. Efficiency ratio: Sorenson AB has sales of DKr 3 112 489, a gross profit margin of 23.1% and inventory of DKr 833 145. What are the company's inventory turnover ratio and days' sales in inventories?

4.6. Leverage ratios: Verbier Ski SA has total assets of SFr 422 235 811 and a debt ratio of 29.5%. Calculate the company's debt-to-equity ratio and the equity multiplier.

4.7. Leverage ratios: Productos de Cuero de Córdoba SA has a debt-to-equity ratio of 1.65, ROA of 11.3% and total equity of €1 322 796. What are the company's equity multiplier, debt ratio and ROE?

4.8. DuPont equation: The Rangoon Timber Company has the following relationships:

Sales/Total assets = 2.23; ROA = 9.69%; ROE = 16.4%

What are Rangoon's profit margin and debt ratio?

4.9. Benchmark analysis: List the ways a company's financial manager can benchmark the company's own performance.

4.10. Benchmark analysis: Védjegy zrt's financial manager collected the following information for its peer group so that it can compare its own performance against that of its peers:

Ratios	Védjegy	Peer Group
DSO	33.5 days	27.9 days
Total assets turnover	2.3	3.7
Inventory turnover	1.8	2.8
Quick ratio	0.6	1.3

a. Explain how Védjegy is doing relative to its peers.

b. How do the industry ratios help Védjegy's management?

4.11. Market-value ratios: Salzburg Juweliere AG has announced net earnings of €6 481 778 for this year. The company has 2 543 800 shares outstanding, and the year-end stock price is €54.21. What are the company's earnings per share and P/E ratio?

Intermediate

4.12. Liquidity ratios: Poznań Elektronika SA has a quick ratio of 1.15, current liabilities of Zł 5 311 020 and inventories of Zł 7 121 599. What is the firm's current ratio?

4.13. Efficiency ratio: Lisboa Logística SA has total sales of €31 115 964, inventories of €4 412 933, cash and equivalents of €2 469 050 and days' sales outstanding of 39 days. If the firm's management wanted its DSO to be 30 days, by how much will the accounts receivable have to change?

4.14. Efficiency ratio: Norske Skogbruk Produkter AS currently has accounts receivable of NKr 1 223 675 on net sales of NKr 6 216 900. What are its accounts receivable turnover ratio and days' sales outstanding?

4.15. Efficiency ratio: If Norske Skogbruk Produkter's management wants to reduce the DSO from that calculated in the above problem to an industry average of 56.3 days and its net sales are expected to decline by about 12%, what would be the new level of receivables?

4.16. Coverage ratios: Location Le Bourget SA had depreciation expenses of €108 905, interest expenses of €78 112 and an EBIT of €1 254 338 for the year ended 31 December 2009. What are the times-interest-earned and cash coverage ratios for this company?

4.17. Leverage ratios: Conseco AAT has a debt ratio of 0.56. What are the company's debt-to-equity ratio and equity multiplier?

4.18. Profitability ratios: Relay TV SpA has total assets of €35.594 million, total debt of €9.678 million and net sales of €22.045 million. Their net profit margin for the year is 20%, while the operating profit margin was 30%. What are Relay TV's net income, EBIT ROA, ROA and ROE?

4.19. Profitability ratios: Dolce Vita A.E. reported the following information for year-end 2010: On net sales of €51.407 million, the company earned a net income after taxes of €6.481 million. It had a cost of goods sold of €25.076 million and an EBIT of

€9.827 million. What is the company's (a) gross profit margin, (b) operating profit margin and (c) net profit margin?

4.20. Profitability ratios: Maxi Supermarkt AG has net income of €9 054 000 on net sales of €256 329 812. The company has total assets of €104 912 112 and shareholders' equity of €43 623 445. Use the extended DuPont identity to find the return on assets and return on equity for the firm.

4.21. Profitability ratios: Xtreme Sports de Val-d'Isère has disclosed the following information:

1. EBIT = €25 664 300
2. Net income = €13 054 000
3. Net sales = €83 125 336
4. Total debt = €20 885 753
5. Total assets = €71 244 863

Compute the following ratios for this firm using the DuPont identity: debt-to-equity ratio, EBIT ROA, ROA and ROE.

4.22. Market-value ratios: InterSystèmes SA had net income of €4.401 million and, at year-end, 6.735 million shares outstanding. Calculate the earnings per share for the company.

4.23. Market-value ratios: Use the information for InterSystèmes SA in the last problem. In addition, the company's EBITDA was €6.834 million and its share price was €22.36. Compute the firm's price-to-earnings ratio and the price-to-EBITDA ratio.

4.24. DuPont equation: Integrierte Elektrosysteme AG, a manufacturer of electrical supplies, has an ROE of 23.1%, a profit margin of 4.9% and a total asset turnover ratio of 2.6 times. Its peer group also has an ROE of 23.1% but has outperformed Integrierte Elektrosysteme with a profit margin of 5.3% and a total assets turnover ratio of 3.0 times. Explain how Integrierte Elektrosysteme managed to achieve the same level of profitability as reflected by the ROE.

4.25. DuPont equation: Grossman Enterprises has an equity multiplier of 2.6 times, total assets of £2 312 000, an ROE of 14.8% and a total assets turnover of 2.8 times. Calculate the firm's sales and ROA.

Advanced

4.26. Complete the balance sheet of Trasporto Rapido SpA, given the information below.

4.27. For the year ended 31 December 2010, Norge Beklædning AB has total assets of DKr 87 631 181, ROA of 11.67%, ROE of 21.19% and a profit margin of 11.59%. What are the company's net income and net sales? Calculate the firm's debt-to-equity ratio.

Trasporto Rapido SpA Balance Sheet as of 31/12/2010

Assets:		Liabilities and Equity:	
Net plant and equipment		Ordinary shares	
		Retained earnings	€1 250 000
Inventories			
Accounts receivable		Long-term borrowings	€2 000 000
Cash and marketable securities		Accounts payable and accruals	
Total current assets		Current borrowings	€ 300 000
Total assets	€8 000 000	Total liabilities and equity	

You are also given the following information:

Debt ratio = 40%	DSO = 39 days
Current ratio = 1.5	Inventory turnover ratio = 3.375
Sales = €2.25 million	Cost of goods sold = €1.6875 million

4.28. Antwerpen Autohantering NV's balance sheet at year-end 2010 shows the following information:

Antwerpen Autohantering NV Balance Sheet as of 31/12/2010

Assets:	€	Liabilities and Equity:	€
Net plant and equipment	711 256	Ordinary shares	313 299
Goodwill and other assets	89 899	Retained earnings	512 159
Total non-current assets	801 155	Total shareholders' equity	825 458
		Non-current borrowings	168 022
Inventories	212 444	Current borrowings	21 115
Accounts receivable	141 258	Accounts payable and accruals	163 257
Cash and marketable sec.	23 015	Total current liabilities	184 372
Total current assets	376 717	Total liabilities	352 394
Total assets	€1 177 852	Total liabilities and equity	€1 177 852

In addition, it was reported that the firm had a net income of €156 042 on sales of €4 063 589.

a. What are the firm's current ratio and quick ratio?

b. Calculate the firm's days' sales outstanding, total asset turnover ratio and fixed asset turnover ratio.

4.29. The following are the financial statements for Nederland Consument Producten NV for the fiscal year ended 31 December 2010.

As Reported on Annual Income Statement	31/12/10
Net sales	€51 407
Cost of products sold	25 076
Gross margin	26 331
Marketing, research, administrative exp.	15 746
Depreciation	758
Operating income (loss)	€ 9 827
Interest expense	477
Earnings (loss) before income taxes	€ 9 350
Income taxes	2 869
Net earnings (loss)	€ 6 481

Balance Sheet as of 31/12/10

Assets:	€	Liabilities and Equity:	€
Net property, plant and equipment	14 108	Ordinary shares	2 141
Net goodwill and other intangible assets	23 900	Retained earnings	13 611
		Total shareholders' equity	15 752
Other non-current assets	1 925		
Total non-current assets	39 933	Convertible preference shares	1 526
		Long-term borrowings	12 554
		Deferred income taxes	2 261
Prepaid expenses and other receivables	1 803	Other non-current liabilities	2 808
Deferred income taxes	958	Total non-current liabilities	19 149
Total inventories	4 400		
Accounts receivable	4 062		
Investment securities	423	Debt due within one year	8 287
Cash and marketable securities	5 469	Taxes payable	2 554
Total current assets	17 115	Accrued and other liabilities	7 689
		Accounts payable	3 617
		Total current liabilities	22 147
		Total liabilities	41 296
Total assets	57 048	Total liabilities and equity	57 048

Calculate all the ratios (for which industry figures are available) for Nederland Consument Producten and compare the firm's ratios with the industry ratios.

Industry Ratio	Average
Current ratio	2.05
Quick ratio	0.78
Gross margin	23.9%
Net profit margin	12.3%
Debt ratio	0.23
Long-term debt to equity	0.98
Interest coverage	5.62
ROA	5.3%
ROE	18.8%

4.30. Refer to the preceding information for Nederland Consument Producten NV. Compute the firm's ratios for the following categories and briefly evaluate the company's performance from these numbers.
  a. Efficiency ratios
  b. Asset turnover ratios
  c. Leverage ratios
  d. Coverage ratios

4.31. Refer to the earlier information for Nederland Consument Producten NV. Using the DuPont identity, calculate the return on equity for Nederland Consument Producten, after calculating the ratios that make up the DuPont identity.

4.32. Nugent plc has a gross profit margin of 31.7% on sales of £9 865 214 and total assets of £7 125 852. The company has a current ratio of 2.7 times, accounts receivable of £1 715 363, cash and marketable securities of £315 488 and current liabilities of £870 938.
  a. What is Nugent's level of current assets?
  b. How much in inventories does the firm have? What is the inventory turnover ratio?
  c. What is Nugent's days' sales outstanding?

  d. If management wants to set a target DSO of 30 days, what should Nugent's accounts receivable be?

4.33. Sports Loisirs SA has net sales of €11 655 000, an ROE of 17.64% and a total asset turnover of 2.89 times. If the firm has a debt-to-equity ratio of 1.43, what is the company's net income?

4.34. Haushalts-Gewürze AG has an operating profit margin of 10.3% on revenues of €24 547 125 and total assets of €8 652 352.
  a. Find the company's total asset turnover ratio and its operating profit (EBIT).
  b. If the company's management has set a target for the total asset turnover ratio to be 3.25 next year without any change in the total assets of the company, what will have to be the new sales level for the next year? Calculate change in sales necessary and the percentage sales necessary.
  c. If the operating profit margin now shrinks to 10%, what will be the EBIT at the new level of sales?

4.35. Strumento Moderna SpA has reported its financial results for the year ended 31 December 2010.

**Income Statement for the Fiscal
Year Ended 31 December 2010**

Net sales	€5 398 412.00
Cost of goods sold	3 432 925.25
Gross profit	€1 965 486.75
Selling, general and administrative expenses	1 036 311.23
Depreciation	299 928.16
Operating income	€ 629 247.36
Interest expense	35 826.00
EBT	€ 593 421.36
Income taxes	163 104.55
Net earnings	€ 430 316.81

Consolidated Balance Sheet Strumento Moderna SpA 31 December 2010

Assets:	€	Liabilities and Equity:	€
Non-current assets		Ordinary shares	3 974 073.52
Net fixed assets	7 546 602.75	Retained earnings	12 182 075.88
Goodwill	1 184 077.10	Total equity	16 156 149.40
Other assets	6 650 587.61	Non-current liabilities	
	15 381 267.46	Non-current borrowings	12 006 915.65
		Current liabilities	
Inventories	9 818 709.90	Trade accounts payable	4 669 379.85
Accounts receivables	10 466 122.33	Other current liabilities	9 942 893.83
Other current assets	3 136 216.10	Short-term borrowings	1 171 098.65
Cash and cash equivalents	5 144 121.59	Total current liabilities	15 783 372.33
Total current assets	28 565 169.92		
		Total liabilities	27 790 287.98
Total assets	€43 946 437.38	Total liabilities & equity	€43 946 437.38

Using the information from the financial statements, complete a comprehensive ratio analysis for Strumento Moderna SpA.

a. Calculate these liquidity ratios: current and quick ratios.

b. Calculate these efficiency ratios: inventory turnover, accounts receivable turnover, DSO.

c. Calculate these asset turnover ratios: total asset turnover, fixed asset turnover.

d. Calculate these leverage ratios: total debt ratio, debt-to-equity ratio, equity multiplier.

e. Calculate these coverage ratios: times interest earned, cash coverage.

f. Calculate these profitability ratios: gross profit margin, net profit margin, ROA, ROE.

g. Use the DuPont identity, and after calculating the component ratios, compute the ROE for this firm.

4.36. Common-size analysis is used in financial analysis to:

a. evaluate changes in a company's operating cycle over time;

b. predict changes in a company's capital structure using regression analysis;

c. compare companies of different sizes or compare a company with itself over time;

d. restate each element in a company's financial statement as a proportion of the similar account for another company in the same industry.

4.37. The Compagnie TBI SA has a number of days of inventory of 50. Therefore, Compagnie TBI's inventory turnover is closest to

a. 4.8 times

b. 7.3 times

c. 8.4 times

d. 9.6 times.

4.38. DuPont analysis involves breaking return-on-assets ratios into their

a. profit components

b. marginal and average components

c. operating and financing components

d. profit margin and turnover components.

4.39. If a company's net profit margin is 25%, its total asset turnover is 1.5 times and its financial leverage ratio is 1.2 times, its return on equity is closest to

a. 29.0%

b. 27.5%

c. 23.2%

d. 1.8%.

SAMPLE TEST PROBLEMS

4.1. Montana Sports D'Hiver SA has accounts payable of SFr 1 221 669, cash of SFr 677 423, inventories of SFr 2 312 478, accounts receivable of SFr 845 113 and net working capital of SFr 2 297 945. What are the company's current ratio and quick ratio?

4.2. Sardinia Air SpA has total operating revenues of €6.53 million on total assets of €11.337 million. Their property, plant and equipment, including their ground equipment and other assets, are listed on the balance sheet at €8.723 million. What are the airline's total asset turnover and fixed asset turnover ratios?

4.3. Haugen NV has an equity multiplier of 2.5. What is the firm's debt ratio?

4.4. Zagreb Kemijski d.d. has a gross profit margin of 31.4% on revenues of kn 13 144 680 and EBIT of kn 2 586 150. What are the company's cost of goods sold and operating profit margin?

4.5. Banque Internationale de Bruxelles has 646 749 650 ordinary shares outstanding, and they are currently priced at €37.55. If its net income is €2 780 955 000, what are its earnings per share and price-to-earnings ratio?

ENDNOTES

1. As mentioned, one must be cautious in any interpretation. Fabrique Aérospatiale grew significantly in size between 2009 and 2010 and the increase in inventories may reflect a more complex business and hence the ratios may not be entirely comparable across time. We discuss this later in the chapter.
2. This calculation involves dividing total current assets by total current liabilities. We drop the word 'total' in the interest of brevity.
3. The quick ratio will always be less than the current ratio for any firm that holds inventories.
4. Note we included assets and liabilities for the disposal group as held-for-sale (that is, parts of the business or assets owned by the business) in our calculation. We mentioned earlier the need for judgement on what is appropriate. A financial analyst might take the view that these are illiquid, like inventories, and not include them in the quick ratio. If we take this line, the quick ratio for 2010 is lower still at 1.56 times.
5. Some financial analysts compute inventory using sales rather than cost of goods sold in the numerator. On the other hand, this alternative calculation (Inventory turnover = Sales/Inventories) makes sense if the analyst wants to know the value of sales generated per unit of inventories. On the other hand, the calculation can be misleading if the firm generates a significant amount of revenues from activities that are not associated with inventories, such as providing services.
6. That the asset turnover ratio has risen more between 2009 and 2010 than the fixed asset turnover ratio suggests that Fabrique Aérospatiale has changed its business mix somewhat as a result of its acquisitions.
7. We have used an estimate that includes earned interest – if we used the gross interest figure and ignored the interest income, the times interest earned is 5.55 (€334/€51), somewhat lower, but still an acceptable level of cover.
8. EBITDA can differ from actual cash flows because of the accounting accruals discussed in Chapter 3.

PART 3

VALUATION OF FUTURE CASH FLOWS AND RISK

CHAPTER
5

The Time Value of Money

In this Chapter:

The Time Value of Money

Future Value and Compounding

Present Value and Discounting

Additional Concepts and Applications

LEARNING OBJECTIVES

1. Explain what the time value of money is and why it is so important in the field of finance.

2. Explain the concept of future value, including the meaning of *principal amount, simple interest and compound interest*, and be able to use the future value formula to make business decisions.

3. Explain the concept of present value and how it relates to future value, and be able to use the present value formula to make business decisions.

4. Discuss why the concept of compounding is not restricted to money, and be able to use the future value formula to calculate growth rates.

When you purchase a car from a dealer, the decision of whether to pay cash or use a loan to finance your purchase can affect the price you pay. For example, when market conditions are tough, automobile manufacturers often offer customers a choice between a cash discount and low-cost financing. Both of these alternatives affect the cost of purchasing a car, but one alternative can be worth more than the other.

To see why, consider the following. In September 2010, the automobile manufacturer Peugeot wanted to increase sales of its 308CC model. The company offered consumers a choice between (1) receiving €1500 off the base price of €25 840 if they paid cash and (2) receiving 0% financing on a three-year loan if they paid the base price. For someone who had enough cash to buy the car outright and did not need the cash for some other use, the decision of whether to pay cash or finance the purchase of the 308 depended on the rate of return that they could earn by investing the cash. On the one hand, if it was possible to earn only a 3% interest rate by investing in a bank deposit, the buyer was better off paying cash. On the other hand, if it was possible to earn 5%, the buyer was better off taking the financing. With a 4% rate of return, the buyer would have been largely indifferent between the two alternatives.

As with most business transactions, a crucial element in the analysis of the alternatives offered by Peugeot is the value of the expected cash flows. Because the cash flows for the two alternatives take place in different time periods, they must be adjusted to account for the time value of money before they can be compared. A car buyer wants to select the alternative with the cash flows that have the lowest value (price). This chapter and the next provide the knowledge and tools you need to make the correct decision. You will learn that at the bank, in the boardroom or in the showroom, money has a time value – money today is worth more than money in the future – and you must account for this when making financial decisions.

CHAPTER PREVIEW

Business firms routinely make decisions to invest in productive assets to earn income. Some assets, such as plant and equipment, are tangible and other assets, such as patents and trademarks, are intangible. Regardless of the type of investment, a firm pays out money now in the hope that the value of the future benefits (cash inflows) will exceed the cost of the asset. This process is what *value creation* is all about – buying capital assets that are worth more than they cost.

The valuation models presented in this book will require you to compute the present and future values of cash flows. This chapter and the next provide the fundamental tools for making these calculations. This chapter explains how to value a single cash flow in different time periods, while Chapter 6 covers valuation of multiple cash flows. These two chapters are critical for your understanding of corporate finance.

We begin this chapter with a discussion of the time value of money. We then look at future value, which tells us how funds will grow if they are invested at a particular interest rate. Next, we discuss present value, which answers the question 'What is the value today of cash payments received in the future?' We conclude the chapter with a discussion of several additional topics related to time value calculations.

THE TIME VALUE OF MONEY

Learning Objective 1

Explain what the time value of money is and why it is so important in the field of finance.

In financial decision making, one basic problem managers face is determining the value of (or price to pay for) cash flows expected in the future. Why is this a problem? Consider as an example the popular Mega Millions™ lottery game, which is played in 12 states across the United States. In Mega Millions, the jackpot continues to build up until some lucky person buys a winning ticket – the payouts for a number of jackpot-winning tickets have exceeded $100 million.[1]

If you won $100 million, headlines would read 'Lucky Student Wins $100 Million Jackpot!' Does this mean that your ticket is worth $100 million on the day you win? The answer is no. A Mega Millions jackpot is paid either as a series of 26 payments over 25 years or as a cash lump sum. If you win '$100 million' and choose to receive the series of payments, the 26 payments will total $100 million. If you choose the lump sum option, Mega Millions will pay you less than the stated value of US$100 million. This amount was about $60 million in February 2010. Thus, the value, or market price, of a '$100 million' winning Mega Millions ticket is really about $60 million because of the time value of money and the timing of the 26 cash payments. This would not be the case if you had won €100 million in the EuroMillions lottery in Europe – if you are the lucky winner, you get all the cash immediately!

An appropriate question to ask now is, 'What is the time value of money?'

WEB

Take an online lesson on the time value of money from TeachMeFinance.com at: www.teachmefinance.com/timevalueofmoney.html.

Consuming Today or Tomorrow

The **time value of money** is based on the belief that people have a positive time preference for consumption. That is, people prefer to consume goods

BUILDING INTUITION

The Value of Money Changes with Time

The term *time value of money* reflects the notion that people prefer to consume things today rather than at some time in the future. For this reason, people require compensation for deferring consumption. The effect is to make a unit of currency in the future worth less than a unit today.

today rather than wait to consume similar goods in the future. Most people would prefer to have a large-screen TV today than to have one a year from now, for example. Money has a time value because money in hand today is worth more than money to be received in the future. This makes sense because if you had the money today, you could buy something with it – or, instead, you could invest it and earn interest. For example, if you had €100 000, you could make a one-year bank deposit paying 5% interest and earn €5000 interest for the year. At the end of the year, you would have €105 000 (€100 000 + €5000). The €100 000 today is worth €105 000 a year from today. If the interest rate was higher, you would have even more money at the end of the year.

Time value of money

the difference in value between money in hand today and money promised in the future; money today is worth more than money in the future

Based on this example, we can make several generalisations. First, the value of money invested at a positive interest rate grows over time. Thus, the further in the future you receive the money, the less it is worth today. Second, the trade-off between money today and money at some future date depends in part on the rate of interest you can earn by investing. The higher the rate of interest, the more likely you will elect to invest your funds and forgo current consumption. Why? At the higher interest rate, your investment will earn more money.

In the remainder of this section, we look at two views of time value – future value and present value. First, however, we describe time lines, which are pictorial aids to help solve future and present value problems.

Time Lines as Aids to Problem Solving

Time lines are an important tool for analysing problems that involve cash flows over time. They provide an easy way to visualise the cash flows associated with investment decisions. A time line is a horizontal line that starts at time zero (today) and shows cash flows as they occur over time. For example, Exhibit 5.1 shows the time line for a five-year investment opportunity and its cash flows. Here, as in most finance problems, cash flows are assumed to occur at the end of the period. The project involves a €10 000 initial investment (cash outflow), such as the purchase of a new machine, that is expected to generate cash inflows over a five-year period: €5000 at the end of year 1, €4000 at the end of year 2, €3000 at the end of year 3, €2000 at the end of year 4, €1000 at the end of year 5. Because of the time value of money, it is critical that you identify not only the size of the cash flows, but also the timing.

If it is appropriate, the time line will also show the relevant interest rate for the problem. In Exhibit 5.1 this is shown as 5%. Also, note in Exhibit 5.1 that the initial cash flow of €10 000 is represented

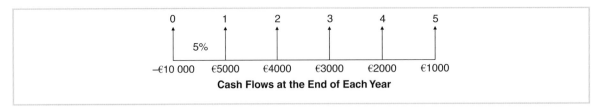

Exhibit 5.1: **Five-Year Time Line for a €10 000 Investment** Time lines help us to correctly identify the size and timing of cash flows – critical tasks in solving time value problems. This time line shows the cash flows generated over five years by a €10 000 investment in a situation where the relevant interest rate is 5%.

by a negative number. It is conventional that cash outflows from the firm, such as for the purchase of a new machine, are treated as negative values on a time line and that cash inflows to the firm, such as revenues earned, are treated as positive values. The −€10 000 therefore means that there is a cash outflow of €10 000 at time zero. As you will see, it makes no difference how you label cash inflows and outflows as long as you are consistent. That is, if *all* cash outflows are given a negative value, then *all* cash inflows must have a positive value. If the signs get 'mixed up' – if some cash inflows are negative and some positive – you will get the wrong answer to any problem you are trying to solve.

Future Value versus Present Value

We can analyse financial decisions using either future value or present value techniques. Although the two techniques approach the decision differently, both yield the same result. Both techniques focus on the valuation of cash flows received over time. In corporate finance, future value problems typically measure the value of cash flows at the end of a project, whereas present value problems measure the value of cash flows at the start of a project (time zero).

Exhibit 5.2 compares the €10 000 investment decision shown in Exhibit 5.1 in terms of future value and present value. When managers are making

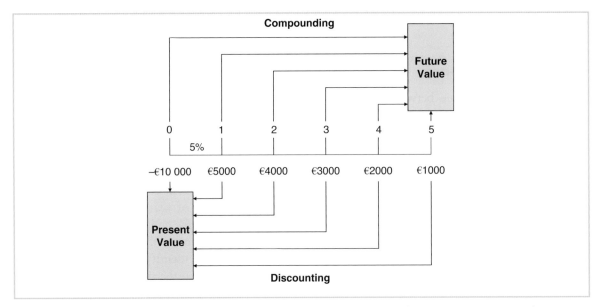

Exhibit 5.2: **Future Value and Present Value Compared** Compounding converts a present value into its future value, taking into account the time value of money. Discounting is just the reverse – it converts future cash flows into their present value.

a decision about whether to accept a project, they must look at all of the cash flows associated with that project with reference to the same point in time. As Exhibit 5.2 shows, for most business decisions, that point is either the start (time zero) or the end of the project (in this example, year 5). The present value technique uses *discounting* to find the present value of each cash flow at the beginning of the project. Alternatively, the future value technique uses *compounding* to find the future value of each cash flow at the end of the project's life. We will look more closely at compounding and discounting later in the chapter.

WEB

For a discussion of simple versus compound interest, go to:
http://www.financeprofessor.com/introcorp finnotes/smplevscompound.htm.

Before You Go On

1. Why is money today worth more than money one year from now?
2. What is a time line and why is it important in financial analysis?

FUTURE VALUE AND COMPOUNDING

Learning Objective 2

Explain the concept of future value, including the meaning of *principal amount, simple interest and compound interest*, and be able to use the future value formula to make business decisions.

The **future value** (FV) of an investment is what the investment will be worth after earning interest for

one or more time periods. The process of converting the initial amount into future value is called *compounding*. We will define this term more precisely later. First, though, we illustrate the concepts of future value and compounding with a simple example.

Future value (FV)

the value of an investment after it earns interest for one or more periods

---

Single-Period Investment

Suppose you place €100 in a bank savings account that pays interest at 10% a year. How much money will you have in one year? Go ahead and make the calculation. Most people can intuitively arrive at the correct answer, €110, without the aid of a formula. Your calculation could have looked something like this:

Future value at the

$$\text{end of year } 1 = \text{Principal} + \text{Interest earned}$$
$$= €100 + (100 \times 0.10)$$
$$= €100 \times (1 + 0.10)$$
$$= €100 \times (1.10)$$
$$= €110$$

This approach computes the amount of interest earned (€100 × 0.10) and then adds it to the initial, or *principal*, amount (€100). Notice that when we solve the equation, we factor out the €100. Recall from algebra that if you have the equation $y = c + (c \times x)$, you can factor out the common term c as follows:

$$y = c + (c \times x)$$
$$= c \times (1 + x)$$

By doing this in our future value calculation, we arrived at the term (1 + 0.10). This term can be stated more generally as $(1 + i)$, where i is the interest rate. As you will see, this is a pivotal term in both future value and present value calculations.

Let us use our intuitive calculation to generate a more general formula. First, we need to define the variables used to calculate the answer. In our example €100 is the principal amount (P_0), which is the amount of money at the beginning of the transaction (time zero); the 10% is the simple interest rate (i); and the €110 is the future value (FV_1) of the deposit after one year, which is one year in the future. We can write the formula for a single-period investment as follows:

$$FV_1 = P_0 + (P_0 \times i)$$
$$= P_0 \times (1 + i)$$

Looking at the formula, we more easily see mathematically what is happening in our intuitive calculation. P_0 is the principal amount invested at time zero. If you invest for one period at an interest rate of i, your investment, or principal, will grow by $(1 + i)$ per unit invested. The term $(1 + i)$ is the *future value interest factor* – often called simply the *future value factor* – for a single period, such as one year. To test the equation, we plug in our values:

$$FV_1 = €100 + (€100 \times 0.10)$$
$$= €100 \times 1.10$$
$$= €110$$

Good, it works!

Two-Period Investment

We have determined that at the end of one year (one period), your €100 investment has grown to €110. Now let's say you decide to leave this new principal amount (FV_1) of €110 in the bank for another year earning 10% interest. How much money would you have at the end of the second year (FV_2)? To arrive at the value for FV_2, we multiply the new principal amount by the future value factor $(1 + i)$. That is, $FV_2 = FV_1 \times (1 + i)$. We then substitute the value of FV_1 (the single-period investment value) into the equation and algebraically rearrange terms, which yields $FV_2 = P_0 \times (1 + i)^2$. The mathematical steps to arrive at the equation for FV_2 are shown in the following; recall that $FV_1 = P_0 \times (1 + i)$:

$$FV_2 = FV_1 \times (1 + i)$$
$$= [P_0 \times (1 + i)] \times (1 + i)$$
$$= P_0 \times (1 + i)^2$$

The future value of your $110 at the end of the second year (FV_2) is as follows:

$$FV_2 = P_0 \times (1 + i)^2$$
$$= €100 \times (1 + 0.10)^2$$
$$= €100 \times (1.10)^2$$
$$= €100 \times 1.21$$
$$= €121$$

Another way of thinking of a two-period investment is that it is two single-period investments back to back. From that perspective, based on the preceding equations, we can represent the future value of the deposit held in the bank for two years as follows:

$$FV_2 = P_0 \times (1 + i)^2$$

Turning to Exhibit 5.3, we can see what is happening to your €100 investment over the two years we have already discussed and beyond. The future value of €121 at year 2 consists of three parts. First is the initial *principal* of €100 (column 2). Second is the €20 (€10 + €10) of *simple interest* earned at 10% for the first and second years (column 3). Third is the €1 interest earned during the second year (column 4) on the €10 of interest from the first year (€10 × 0.10 = €1.00). This is called *interest on interest*. The total amount of interest earned is €21 (€10 + €11), which is shown in column 5 and is called *compound interest*.

We are now in a position to formally define some important terms already mentioned in our discussion. The **principal** is the amount of money on which interest is paid. In our example, the principal amount is €100. **Simple interest** is the amount of interest paid on the original principal amount. With simple interest, the interest earned each period is paid only on the original principal. In our example, the simple interest is €10 per year or €20 for the two years. **Interest on interest** is the interest earned on the reinvestment of previous

EXHIBIT 5.3

FUTURE VALUE OF $100 AT 10%

(1)	(2)	(3)		(4) Interest Earned		(5)	(6)
Year	Value at Beginning of Year	Simple Interest		Interest on Interest		Total (Compound) Interest	Value at End of Year
1	€100.00	€10.00	+	€ 0.00	=	€10.00	€110.00
2	110.00	10.00	+	1.00	=	11.00	121.00
3	121.00	10.00	+	2.10	=	12.10	133.10
4	133.10	10.00	+	3.31	=	13.31	146.41
5	146.41	10.00	+	4.64	=	14.64	161.05
Five-year total	€100.00	€50.00	+	€11.05	=	€61.05	€161.05

With compounding, interest earned on an investment is reinvested so that in future periods, interest is earned on interest as well as on the principal amount. Here, interest on interest begins accruing in year 2.

interest payments. In our example, the interest on interest is €1. **Compounding** is the process by which interest earned on an investment is reinvested so that in future periods, interest is earned on the interest previously earned as well as the principal. In other words, with compounding, you are able to earn **compound interest**, which consists of both simple interest and interest on interest. In our example, the compound interest is €21.

Interest on interest

interest earned on interest that is earned in previous periods

Compounding

the process by which interest earned on an investment is reinvested, so in future periods interest is earned on the interest as well as the principal

Principal

the amount of money on which interest is paid

Simple interest

interest earned on the original principal amount only

Compound interest

interest earned both on the original principal amount and on interest previously earned

The Future Value Equation

Let us continue our bank example. Suppose you decide to leave your money in the bank for three years. Looking back at equations for a single-period and two-period investment, you can probably guess that the equation for the future value of money invested for three years would be:

$$FV_3 = P_0 \times (1 + i)^3$$

With this pattern clearly established, we can see that the general equation to find the future value after any number of periods is as follows:

$$FV_n = PV \times (1 + i)^n \qquad (5.1)$$

where:

> FV_n = future value of investment at the end of period n
>
> PV = original principal (P_0) or the present value
>
> I = the rate of interest per period, which is often a year
>
> n = the number of periods; a period is typically a year but can be a quarter, month, day or some other unit of time
>
> $(1 + i)^n$ = the future value factor

Let us test our general equation. Say you leave your €100 invested in the bank savings account at 10% interest for five years. How much would you have in the bank at the end of five years? Applying Equation (5.1) yields the following:

$$
\begin{aligned}
FV_5 &= €100 \times (1 + 0.10)^5 \\
&= €100 \times (1.10)^5 \\
&= €100 \times (1.6105) \\
&= €161.05
\end{aligned}
$$

Exhibit 5.3 shows how the interest is earned on a year-by-year basis. Notice that the total compound interest earned over the five-year period is €61.05 (column 5) and that it is made up of two parts: (1) €50.00 of simple interest (column 3) and (2) €11.05 of interest on interest (column 4). Thus, the total interest can be expressed as follows :

Total compound interest
= Total simple interest+Total interest on interest
= €50 + €11.05
= €61.05

The simple interest earned is (€100 × 0.10) = €10.00 per year and, thus, the total simple interest for the five-year period is €50.00 (5 years × €10.00). The remaining balance of €11.05 (€61.05 − €50.00) comes from earning interest on interest.

A helpful equation for calculating the simple interest can be derived by using the equation for a single-period investment and solving for the term $FV_1 - P_0$, which is equal to the simple interest.[2] The equation for the simple interest earned (SI) is:

$$SI = P_0 \times i$$

where:

> i = the simple interest rate for the period, usually one year
>
> P_0 = the initial or beginning principal amount

Thus, the calculation for simple interest is:[3]

$$SI = P_0 \times i = €100 \times 0.10 = €10.00$$

Exhibit 5.4 shows graphically how the compound interest in Exhibit 5.3 grows. Notice that the simple interest earned each year remains constant at €10 per year but that the amount of interest on interest increases every year. The reason, of course, is that interest on interest begins to build every time you compound. As more and more interest builds, the effect of compounding accelerates the growth of the total interest earned.

An interesting observation about Equation (5.1) is that the higher the interest rate, the faster the investment will grow. This fact can be seen in Exhibit 5.5, which shows the growth in the future

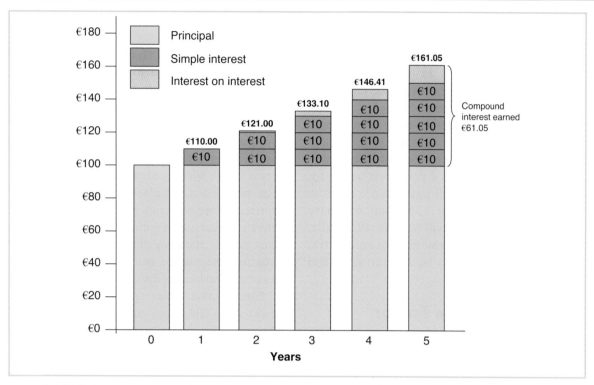

Exhibit 5.4: How Compound Interest Grows on €100 at 10% The amount of simple interest earned on €100 invested at 10% remains constant at €10 per year, but the amount of interest earned on interest increases each year. As more and more interest builds, the effect of compounding accelerates the growth of the total interest earned.

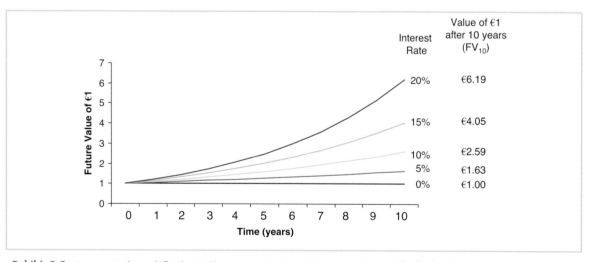

Exhibit 5.5: Future Value of €1 for Different Periods and Interest Rates The higher the interest rate, the faster the value of an investment will grow and the larger the amount of money that will accumulate over time. Because of compounding, the growth over time is not linear but exponential – the monetary increase in the future value is greater with each period.

value of €1.00 at different interest rates and for different time periods into the future. First, notice that the growth in the future value over time is not linear, but exponential. In other words, the growth of the invested funds is accelerated by the compounding of interest. Second, the higher the interest rate, the more money is accumulated for any time period. Looking at the right-hand side of the exhibit, you can see the difference in total money accumulated if you invest a euro for 10 years: at 5%, you will have €1.63; at 10%, you will have €2.59; at 15%, you will have €4.05; and at 20%, you will have €6.19. Finally, as you should expect, if you invest a euro at 0% for 10 years, you will only have a euro at the end of the period.

The Future Value Factor

To solve a future value problem, we need to know the future value factor, $(1 + i)^n$. Fortunately, almost any calculator has a power key (the y^x key) that we can use to make this computation. For example, to compute $(1.08)^{10}$, we enter 1.08, press the y^x key and enter 10 and press the '=' key. The number

2.159 should emerge.[4] Give it a try with your calculator.

Alternatively, we can use future value tables to find the future value factor at different interest rates and maturity periods. Exhibit 5.6 is an example of a future value table. For example, to find the future value factor $(1.08)^{10}$, we first go to the row corresponding to 10 years and then move along the row until we reach the 8% interest column. The entry is 2.159, which is identical to what we found when we used a calculator. This comes as no surprise, but we sometimes find small differences between calculator solutions and future value tables due to rounding differences. Exhibit A.1 in the Appendix at the end of this book provides a more comprehensive version of Exhibit 5.6.

Future value tables (and the corresponding present value tables) are rarely used today, partly because they are tedious to work with. In addition, the tables show values for only a limited number of interest rates and time periods. For example, what if the interest rate on your €100 investment was not a nice round number such as 10% but was 10.236%? You would not find that number in the

EXHIBIT 5.6

FUTURE VALUE FACTORS

Number of Years	Interest Rate per Year						
	1%	5%	6%	7%	8%	9%	10%
1	1.010	1.050	1.060	1.070	1.080	1.090	1.100
2	1.020	1.103	1.124	1.145	1.166	1.188	1.210
3	1.030	1.158	1.191	1.225	1.260	1.295	1.331
4	1.041	1.216	1.262	1.311	1.360	1.412	1.464
5	1.051	1.276	1.338	1.403	1.469	1.539	1.611
10	1.105	1.629	1.791	1.967	2.159	2.367	2.594
20	1.220	2.653	3.207	3.870	4.661	5.604	6.727
30	1.348	4.322	5.743	7.612	10.063	13.268	17.449

To find a future value factor, simply locate the row with the appropriate number of periods and the column with the desired interest rate. The future value factor for 10 years at 8% is 2.159.

future value table. In spite of their shortcomings, tables were very commonly used in the days before financial calculators and spreadsheet programs were readily available. You can still use them – for example, to check the answers from your computations of future value factors.

Applying the Future Value Formula

Next, we will review a number of examples of future value problems to illustrate the typical types of problems you will encounter in business and in your personal life.

The Power of Compounding

Our first example illustrates the effects of compounding. Suppose you have an opportunity to make a €5000 investment that pays 15% per year. How much money will you have at the end of 10 years? The time line for the investment opportunity is:

We can apply Equation (5.1) to find the future value of €5000 invested for 10 years at 15% interest. We want to multiply the principal amount

(PV) times the appropriate future value factor for 10 years at 15%, which is $(1 + 0.15)^{10}$; thus:

$$
\begin{aligned}
FV_n &= PV \times (1 + i)^n \\
&= €5000 \times (1 + 0.15)^{10} \\
&= €5000 \times 4.045558 \\
&= €20227.79
\end{aligned}
$$

Now we determine how much of the interest is from simple interest and how much is from interest on interest. The total compound interest earned is €15 227.79 (€20 227.79 – €5000.00). The simple interest is the amount of interest paid on the original principal amount: $SI = P_0 \times i = €5000 \times 0.15 = €750$ per year, which over 10 years is €750 × 10 = €7500. The interest on interest must be the difference between the total compound interest earned and the simple interest: €15 227.79 – €7500 = €7727.79. Notice how quickly the value of an investment increases and how the reinvestment of interest earned – interest on interest – impacts that total compound interest when the interest rates are high.

WEB

You can find a compound interest calculator at: SmartMoney.com: www.smartmoney.com/compoundcalc.

Learning by Doing Application 5.1

The Power of Compounding

Problem: Your wealthy uncle passed away, and one of the assets he left to you was a savings account that your great-grandfather had set up 100 years ago. The account had a single deposit of £1000 and paid 10% interest. How much

money have you inherited, what is the total compound interest and how much of the interest earned came from interest on interest?

Approach: We first need to determine the value of the inheritance, which is the future value of £1000 retained in a savings account for

100 years at 10% interest. Our time line for the problem is:

To calculate FV_{100}, we begin by computing the future value factor. We then plug this number into the future value formula [Equation (5.1)] and solve for the total inheritance. Finally, we calculate the total compound interest and the total simple interest and find the difference between these two numbers, which will give us the interest earned on interest.

Solution: First, we find the future value factor:

$$(1+i)^n = (1+0.10)^{100} = (1.10)^{100}$$
$$= 13780.612$$

Then we find the future value:

$$FV_n = PV \times (1+i)^n$$
$$= £1000 \times (1.10)^{100}$$

$$= £1000 \times 13780.612$$
$$= £13780612$$

Your total inheritance is £13 780 612. The total compound interest earned is this amount less the original £1000 investment, or £13 779 612:

$$£13780612 - £1000 = £13779612$$

The total simple interest earned is calculated as follows:

$$P_0 \times i = £1000 \times 0.10 = £100 \text{ per year}$$
$$£100 \times 100 \text{ years} = £10000$$

The interest earned on interest is the difference between the total compound interest earned and the simple interest:

$$£13779612 - £10000 = £13769612$$

That is quite a difference!

The following table shows the exponential growth of interest on interest in the savings account described in Learning by Doing Application 5.1. In the first year, simple interest equals compound interest. By year 10, total interest on interest, at €594, is still less than total simple interest, at €1000. But after 20 years, interest on interest is €3727 – almost double the simple interest of €2000. After 60 years, interest on interest is nearly 50 times the size of the simple interest – €297 482 versus €6000. After 80 years, the difference is 255 times (€2 039 400 versus €8000); and after 100 years, the difference is staggering (€13.78 million versus a mere €10 000). This example illustrates the power of compounding and explains why the future value curves in Exhibit 5.5 increase so sharply for longer time periods at higher interest rates.

Investment Period (years)	Total Compound Interest	Total Simple Interest	Total Interest on Interest
1	€100	€100	€0
10	€1 594	€1 000	€594
20	€5 727	€2 000	€3 727
40	€44 259	€4 000	€40 259
60	€303 482	€6 000	€297 482
80	€2 047 400	€8 000	€2 039 400
100	€13 779 612	€10 000	€13 769 612

Compounding More Frequently than Once a Year

Interest can, of course, be compounded more frequently than once a year. In Equation (5.1), the term n represents the number of periods and can describe annual, semi-annual, quarterly, monthly

BUILDING INTUITION

Compounding Drives Much of the Earnings on Long-Term Investments

The earnings from compounding drive much of the return earned on a long-term investment. The reason is that the longer the investment period, the greater the proportion of total earnings from interest earned on interest. Interest earned on interest grows exponentially as the investment period increases.

or daily payments. The more frequently interest payments are compounded, the larger the future value of one unit of currency for a given time period. Equation (5.1) can be rewritten to explicitly recognise different compounding periods:

$$FV_n = PV \times (1 + i/m)^{m \times n} \qquad (5.2)$$

where m is the number of times per year that interest is compounded and n is the number of periods specified in years.

Let us say you invest €100 in a bank account that pays a 5% interest rate semi-annually (2.5% twice a year) for two years. In that case, the amount of interest you would have at the end of the period would be:

$$FV_2 = €100 \times (1 + 0.05/2)^{2 \times 2}$$
$$= €100 \times (1.025)^4$$
$$= €100 \times 1.1038$$
$$= €110.38$$

It is not necessary to 'memorise' Equation (5.2); using Equation (5.1) will do fine. All you have to do is determine the interest paid per compounding period (i/m) and calculate the total number of compounding periods $(m \times n)$ as the exponent for the future value factor. For example, if the bank compounds interest quarterly, then both the interest rate and compounding periods must be expressed in quarterly terms: $(i/4)$ and $(4 \times n)$. You can see the difference between quarterly and daily compounding in Learning by Doing Application 5.2.

WEB

Moneychimp.com provides a compound interest calculator at:
www.moneychimp.com/calculator/compound_interest_calculator.htm.

Learning by Doing Application 5.2

Changing the Compounding Period

Problem: Your grandmother has €10 000 she wants to put into a bank savings account for five years. The bank she is considering is within walking distance, pays 5% annual interest compounded quarterly (5/4 = 1.25% each quarter) and provides free coffee and cakes in the morning. Another bank in town pays 5% interest compounded daily. Getting to this bank requires a bus trip, but your grandmother can ride free as a senior citizen. More important, though, this bank does not serve coffee and cake. Which bank should your grandmother select?

Approach: We need to calculate the difference between the two banks' interest payments. Bank A, which compounds quarterly, will pay one-fourth of the annual interest per quarter $(0.05/4) = 0.0125$ and there will be 20 compounding periods over the five-year investment horizon (5 years × 4). The time line for quarterly compounding is as follows:

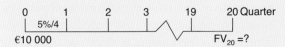

Bank B, which compounds daily, has 365 compounding periods per year. Thus, the daily interest rate is 0.000137 (0.05/365) and there are 1825 (5 years × 365) compounding periods. The time line for daily compounding is:

0   1   2   3   1 824   1 825 Day
| 5%/365 | | | |
€10 000 FV_{1825} =?

We use Equation (5.2) to solve for the future values the investment would generate at each bank. We then compare the two.

Solution:
Bank A:

$$FV_n = PV \times (1 + i/m)^{m \times n}$$
$$= €10\,000 \times (1 + 0.05/4)^{4 \times 5}$$
$$= €10\,000 \times (1 + 0.0125)^{20}$$
$$= €12\,820.37$$

Bank B:

$$FV_n = PV \times (1 + i/m)^{m \times n}$$
$$= €10\,000 \times (1 + 0.05/365)^{365 \times 5}$$
$$= €10\,000 \times (1 + 0.000137)^{1825}$$
$$= €12\,840.03$$

With daily compounding, the additional interest earned by your grandmother is €19.66:

$$€12\,840.03 - €12\,820.37 = €19.66$$

Given that the interest gained by daily compounding is less than €20, your grandmother should probably select her local bank and enjoy the daily coffee and cake. (If she is on a diet, of course, she should take the higher interest payment and walk to the other bank.)

Continuous Compounding

We can continue to divide the compounding interval into smaller and smaller time periods, such as minutes and seconds, until, at the extreme, we would compound continuously. In this case, m in Equation (5.2) would approach infinity (∞). The formula to compute the future value for continuous compounding (FV_∞) is stated as follows:

$$FV_\infty = PV \times e^{i \times n} \qquad (5.3)$$

where e is the exponential function, which has a known mathematical value of about 2.71828, n is the number of periods specified in years and i is the annual interest rate. Although the formula may look a little intimidating, it is really quite easy to apply.

Let us go back to the example in Learning by Doing Application 5.2, in which your grandmother wants to put €10 000 in a savings account at a bank. How much money would she have at the end of five years if the bank paid 5% annual interest compounded continuously? To find out, we enter these values into Equation (5.3):

$$FV_\infty = PV \times e^{i \times n}$$
$$= €10\,000 \times e^{0.05 \times 5}$$
$$= €10\,000 \times e^{0.25}$$
$$= €10\,000 \times 2.71828^{0.25}$$
$$= €10\,000 \times 1.284025$$
$$= €12\,840.25$$

Let us look at your grandmother's €10 000 bank balance at the end of five years with several different compounding periods: yearly, quarterly, daily and continuous:[5]

Notice that your grandmother's total earnings get larger as the frequency of compounding increases, as shown in column 2, but the earnings increase at a decreasing rate, as shown in column 4. The biggest gain comes when the compounding period goes from an annual interest payment to quarterly interest payments. The gain from daily compounding to continuous compounding is small on a modest savings balance such as your grandmother's. Twenty-two cents over five years will not buy your grandmother a cup of coffee, let alone a cake to go with it. However, for businesses and governments with large balances at financial institutions, the difference in compounding periods can be substantial.

(1) Compounding Period	(2) Total Earnings	(3) Compound Interest	(4) Additional Interest
Yearly	€12 762.82	€2762.82	—
Quarterly	€12 820.37	€2820.37	€57.55 more than yearly compounding
Daily	€12 840.03	€2840.03	€19.66 more than quarterly compounding
Continuous	€12 840.25	€2840.25	€0.22 more than daily compounding

Decision-Making Example 5.1

Which Bank Offers Depositors the Best Deal?

Situation: You have just received a bonus of €10 000 and are looking to deposit the money in a bank account for five years. You investigate the annual deposit rates of several banks and collect the following information:

Bank	Compounding Frequency	Annual Rate
A	Annually	5.00%
B	Quarterly	5.00%
C	Monthly	4.80%
D	Daily	4.85%

You understand that the more frequently interest is earned in each year, the more you will have at the end of your investment horizon. To determine in which bank you should deposit your money, you calculate how much money you will earn at the end of five years at each bank. You apply Equation (5.2) and come up with these results. Which bank should you choose?

Bank	Investment Amount	Compounding Frequency	Rate	Value after 5 Years
A	€10 000	Annually	5.00%	€12 762.82
B	€10 000	Quarterly	5.00%	€12 820.37
C	€10 000	Monthly	4.80%	€12 706.41
D	€10 000	Daily	4.85%	€12 744.11

Decision: Even though you might expect Bank D's daily compounding to result in the highest value, the calculations reveal that Bank B provides the highest value at the end of five years.

Thus, you should deposit the amount in Bank B because its higher rate offsets the more frequent compounding at Banks C and D.

USING EXCEL

Time Value of Money

Spreadsheet computer programs are a popular method for setting up and solving finance and accounting problems. Throughout this book, we will show you how to structure and calculate some problems using Microsoft Excel, a widely used spreadsheet program. Spreadsheet programs are like a calculator but are especially efficient at doing repetitive calculations. For example, once the spreadsheet program is set up, it will allow you to make computations using pre-programmed formulas. Thus, you can simply change any of the input cells, and the preset formula will automatically recalculate the answer based on the new input values. For this reason, we recommend that you use formulas whenever possible.

We begin our spreadsheet applications with time value of money calculations. As with the financial calculator approach, there are five variables used in these calculations, and knowing any four of them will let you calculate the fifth one. Excel has already preset formulas for you to use. These are as follows:

Solving for	Formula
PV	= PV(RATE, NPER, PMT, FV)
FV	= FV(RATE, NPER, PMT, PV)
Discount Rate	= RATE(NPER, PMT, PV, FV)
Payment	= PMT(RATE, NPER, PV, FV)
Number of Periods	= NPER(RATE, PMT, PV, FV)

To enter a formula, all you have to do is type in the equal sign, the abbreviated name of the variable you want to compute and an open parenthesis, and Excel will automatically prompt you to enter the rest of the variables. Here is an example of what you would type to compute the future value:

1. 5
2. FV
3. (

Here are a few important things to note when entering the formulas: (1) be consistent with signs for cash inflows and outflows; (2) enter the rate of return as a decimal number, not a percentage; (3) enter the amount of an unknown payment as zero.

	A	B	C	D	E	F
1						
2			Time Value of Money Calculations			
3						
4	Your grandmother wants to put €10 000 into a bank savings account for five years. Bank A pays 5 per					
5	cent interest compounded quarterly, while bank B offers 5 per cent compounded daily. Which bank					
6	should your grandmother choose?					
7						
8						
9	To answer the question., we need to solve for the future value					
10						
11	Problem set up and solution:					
12						
13		Bank A	Bank B			
14	Present value	-€ 10,000	-€ 10,000		Value given	
15	Interest rate	0.0125	0.00014		Interest rate/# compounding periods per year	
16	Number of periods	20	1825		# years × # compounding periods per year	
17	Future value	€ 12,820.37	€ 12,840.03		See note below	
18						
19						
20	The formula entered to calculate the future value for Bank A in cell B17 is =FV(B15, B16, 0, B14).					
21	Similarly, the formula to calculate the future value for Bank B in cell C17 is =FV(C15, C16, 0, C14).					
22	Since there are no payments, we enter PMT as zero. Also, notice that to be consistent with what we					
23	have said about cash inflows and outflows so far, the present value is entered as a negative number.					
24						

To see how a problem is set up and how the calculations are made using a spreadsheet, return to Learning by Doing Application 5.2.

Before You Go On

1. What is compounding, and how does it affect the future value of an investment?
2. What is the difference between simple interest and compound interest?
3. How does changing the compounding period affect the amount of interest earned on an investment?

PRESENT VALUE AND DISCOUNTING

Explain the concept of present value and how it relates to future value, and be able to use the present value formula to make business decisions.

In our discussion of future value, we asked the question 'If you put €100 in a bank savings account that paid 10% annual interest, how much money would accumulate in one year?' Another type of question that arises frequently in finance concerns present value. This question asks, 'What is the value today of a cash flow promised in the future?' We'll illustrate the present value concept with a simple example.

Single-Period Investment

Suppose that a rich uncle gives you a bank certificate of deposit (CD) that matures in one year and pays €110. The CD pays 10% interest annually and cannot be redeemed until maturity. Being a student, you need the money and would like to sell the asset. What would be a fair price if you sold the CD today?

From our earlier discussion, we know that if we invest €100 in a bank at 10% for one year, it will grow to a future value of €110 = €100 × (1 + 0.10). It seems reasonable to conclude that if a CD has an interest rate of 10% and will have a value of €110 a year from now; it is worth €100 today.

More formally, to find the present value of a future cash flow, or its value today, we 'reverse' the compounding process and divide the future value (€110) by the future value factor (1 + 0.10). The result is €100 = $110/(1 + 0.10), which is the same answer we derived from our intuitive calculation. If we write the calculations above as a formula, we have a one-period model for calculating the present value of a future cash flow:

$$PV = \frac{FV_1}{1+i}$$

The numerical calculation for the present value (PV) from our one-period model follows:

$$PV = \frac{FV_1}{1+i}$$
$$= \frac{€110}{1+0.10}$$
$$= \frac{€110}{1.10} = €100$$

We have noted that while future value calculations involve *compounding* an amount forward into the future, *present value* calculations involve the reverse. That is, present value calculations involve determining the current value (or present value) of a future cash flow. The process of calculating the present value is called **discounting**, and the interest rate i is known as the **discount rate**. Accordingly, the **present value** (**PV**) can be thought of as the *discounted value of a future amount*. The present value is simply the current value of a future cash flow that has been discounted at the appropriate discount rate.

Just as we have a future value factor, (1 + *i*), we also have a *present value factor*, which is more commonly called the *discount factor*. The discount factor, which is 1/(1 + *i*), is the reciprocal of the future value factor. This expression may not be obvious in the equation above, but note that we can write that equation in two ways:

1. $PV = \dfrac{FV_1}{1+i}$

2. $PV = FV_1 \times \dfrac{1}{1+i}$

These equations amount to the same thing; the discount factor is explicit in the second one.

> **Discounting**
>
> the process by which the present value of future cash flows is obtained

> **Discount rate**
>
> the interest rate used in the discounting process to find the present value of future cash flows

> **Present value (PV)**
>
> the current value of future cash flows discounted at the appropriate discount rate

Multiple-Period Investment

Now suppose your uncle gives you another 10% bank certificate of deposit (CD), but this CD matures in two years and pays €121 at maturity. Like the other CD, it cannot be redeemed until maturity. From the previous section, we know that if we invest €100 in a bank at 10% for two years, it will grow to a future value of €121 = $100 × (1 + 0.10)². To calculate the present value, or today's price, we divide the future value (€121) by the future value factor (1 + 0.10)². The result is €100 = €121/(1 + 0.10)².

If we capture the calculations we made as an equation, the result is a two-period model for computing the present value of a future cash flow:

$$PV = \frac{FV_2}{(1+i)^2}$$

Plugging the data from our example into the equation yields no surprises:

$$PV = \frac{FV_2}{(1+i)^2}$$
$$= \frac{€121}{(1+0.10)^2}$$
$$= \frac{€121}{1.21} = €100$$

By now, you know the drill. We can extend the equation to a third year, a fourth year and so on until we reach n years:

Year	Equation
1	$PV = \dfrac{FV_1}{1 + i}$
2	$PV = \dfrac{FV_2}{(1 + i)^2}$
3	$PV = \dfrac{FV_3}{(1 + i)^3}$
4	$PV = \dfrac{FV_4}{(1 + i)^4}$
. . .	
n	$PV = \dfrac{FV_n}{(1 + i)^n}$

The Present Value Equation

Given the pattern shown in the foregoing, we can see that the general formula for the present value is:[6]

$$PV = \frac{FV_n}{(1 + i)^n} \qquad (5.4)$$

where:

PV = the value today ($t = 0$) of a cash flow or series of cash flows
FV_n = the future value at the end of period n
i = the discount rate, which is the interest rate per period
n = the number of periods, which could be years, months, days or some other unit of time

Note that Equation (5.4) is sometimes written in a slightly different way, which we will use sometimes in the book. The first form, introduced earlier, separates out the discount factor, $1/(1 + i)$:

$$PV = FV_n \times \frac{1}{(1 + i)^n}$$

In the second form, DF_n is the discount factor for the nth period: $DF_n = 1/(1 + i)^n$:

$$PV = FV_n \times DF_n$$

Future and Present Value Equations are the Same

By now, you may have recognised that the present value equation, Equation (5.4), is just a restatement of the future value equation, Equation (5.1). That is, to get the future value (FV_n) of funds invested for n years, we multiply the original investment by $(1 + i)^n$. To find the present value of a future payment (FV_n), we divide FV_n by $(1 + i)^n$. Stated another way, we can start with the future value equation [Equation (5.1)], $FV_n = PV \times (1 + i)^n$ and then solve it for PV; the resulting equation is the present value equation [Equation (5.4)], $PV = FV_n/(1 + i)^n$.

Exhibit 5.7 illustrates the relationship between the future value and present value calculations for €100 invested at 10% interest. You can see from the exhibit that present value and future value are just two sides of the same coin. The formula used to calculate the present value is really the same as the formula for future value, just rearranged.

Applying the Present Value Formula

Let us work through some examples to see how the present value equation is used. Suppose you are interested in buying a new BMW 330 Sports Coupe a year from now. You estimate that the car will cost €40 000. If your local bank pays 5% interest on savings deposits, how much money will you need to save in order to buy the car as planned? The time line for the car purchase problem is as follows:

```
0                                          1 Year
| 5%                                          |
  PV = ?                                    €40 000
```

The problem is a direct application of Equation (5.4). What we want to know is how much money you have to put in the bank today to have €40 000 a year from now to buy your BMW. To find out, we

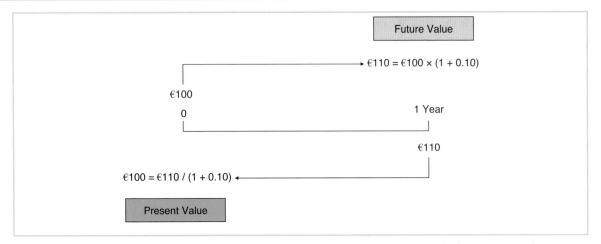

Exhibit 5.7: **Comparing Future Value and Present Value Calculations** The future value and present value formulas are one and the same; the present value factor $1/(1 + i)^n$ is just the reciprocal of the future value factor $(1 + i)^n$:

compute the present value of €40 000 using a 5% discount rate:

$$PV = \frac{FV_1}{1 + i}$$
$$= \frac{€40\,000}{1 + 0.05}$$
$$= \frac{€40\,000}{1.05} = €38\,095.24$$

If you put €38 095.24 in a bank savings account at 5% today, you will have the €40 000 to buy the car in one year.

Since that is a lot of money to come up with, your mother suggests that you leave the money in the bank for two years instead of one year. If you follow her advice, how much money do you need to invest? The time line is as follows:

```
0              1          2 Years
| 5%           |              |
  PV = ?                    €40 000
```

For a two-year waiting period, assuming the car price will stay the same, the calculation is:

$$PV = \frac{FV_2}{(1 + i)^2}$$
$$= \frac{€40\,000}{(1 + 0.05)^2}$$
$$= \frac{€40\,000}{1.1025} = €36\,281.18$$

Given the time value of money, the result is exactly what we would expect. The present value of €40 000 two years out is lower than the present value of €40 000 one year out – €36 281.18 compared with €38 095.24. Thus, if you are willing to leave your money in the bank for two years instead of one, you can make a smaller initial investment to reach your goal.

Now suppose your rich neighbour says that if you invest your money with him for one year, he will pay you 15% interest. The time line is:

```
0                          1 Year
| 15%                          |
  PV = ?                    €40 000
```

The calculation for the initial investment at this new rate is as follows:

$$PV = \frac{FV_1}{1 + i}$$
$$= \frac{€40\,000}{1 + 0.15}$$
$$= \frac{€40\,000}{1.15} = €34\,782.61$$

Thus, when the interest rate, or discount rate, is 15%, the present value of €40 000 to be received in a year's time is €34 782.61, compared with €38 095.24 at a rate of 5% and a time of one year.

Holding maturity constant, an increase in the discount rate decreases the present value of the future cash flow. This makes sense because when interest rates are higher, it is more valuable to have dollars in hand today to invest; thus, money in the future is worth less.

Learning by Doing Application 5.3

Asian Graduation Fling

Problem: Suppose you plan to take a 'graduation vacation' to Asia when you finish university in two years. If your savings account at the bank pays 6%, how much money do you need to set aside today to have €8000 when you leave for Asia?

Approach: The money you need today is the present value of the amount you will need for your trip in two years. Thus, the value of FV_2 is €8000. The interest rate is 6%. Using these values and the present value equation, we can calculate how much money you need to put in the bank at 6% to generate €8000. The time line is:

```
0              1            2 Years
|  6%          |            |
PV = ?                      €8 000
```

Solution:

$$PV = FV_n \times \frac{1}{(1+i)^n}$$

$$= FV_2 \times \frac{1}{(1+i)^2}$$

$$= €8\,000 \times \frac{1}{(1.06)^2}$$

$$= €8\,000 \times 0.889996 = €7\,119.97$$

Thus, if you invest €7119.97 in your savings account today, at the end of two years you will have exactly €8000.

The Relations among Time, the Discount Rate and Present Value

From our discussion so far, we can see that (1) the farther in the future money will be received, the less it is worth today and (2) the higher the discount rate, the lower the present value of one unit of currency. Let us look a bit more closely at these relations.

Recall from Exhibit 5.5 that future value factors grow exponentially over time because of compounding. Similarly, present value factors become smaller the longer the time horizon. The reason is that the present value factor $1/(1 + i)^n$ is the reciprocal of the future value factor $(1 + i)^n$. Thus, the present value of €1 must become smaller as the time to payment becomes longer. You can see this relation in Exhibit 5.8, which shows the present value of €1 for various interest rates and time periods. For example, at 10%, the present value of €1 one year in the future is 90.9 cents (€1/1.10); at two years in the future, 82.6 cents [€1/(1.10)^2]; at five years in the future, 62.1 cents [€1/(1.10)^5]; and at 30 years in the future, 5.7 cents [€1/(1.10)^{30}]. The relation is consistent with our view of the time value of money. That is, the longer you have to wait for money, the

EXHIBIT 5.8

PRESENT VALUE FACTORS

Number of Years	Interest Rate per Year						
	1%	5%	6%	7%	8%	9%	10%
1	0.990	0.952	0.943	0.935	0.926	0.917	0.909
2	0.980	0.907	0.890	0.873	0.857	0.842	0.826
3	0.971	0.864	0.840	0.816	0.794	0.772	0.751
4	0.961	0.823	0.792	0.763	0.735	0.708	0.683
5	0.951	0.784	0.747	0.713	0.681	0.650	0.621
10	0.905	0.614	0.558	0.508	0.463	0.422	0.386
20	0.820	0.377	0.312	0.258	0.215	0.178	0.149
30	0.742	0.231	0.174	0.131	0.099	0.075	0.057

To locate a present value factor, find the row for the number of periods and the column for the proper discount rate. Notice that whereas future value factors grow larger over time and with increasing interest rates, present value factors become smaller. This pattern reflects the fact that the present value factor is the reciprocal of the future value factor.

less it is worth today. Exhibit A.2, in the Appendix at the end of this book, provides present value factors for a wider range of years and interest rates.

Exhibit 5.9 shows the present values of €1 for different time periods and discount rates. For example, at 10 years, the present value of €1 discounted at 5% is 61 cents, at 10% it is 39 cents and at 20%, 16 cents. Thus, the higher the discount rate, the lower the present value of €1 for a given time period. Exhibit 5.9 also shows that, just as

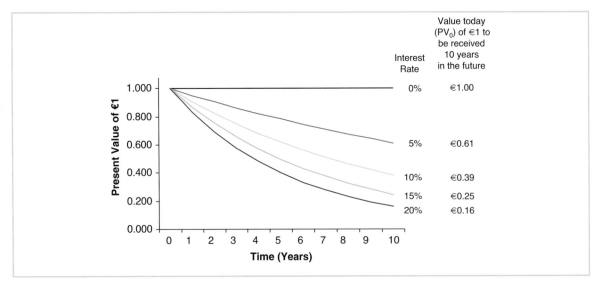

Exhibit 5.9: **Present Value of €1 for Different Time Periods and Discount Rates** The higher the discount rate, the lower the present value of €1 for a given time period. Just as with future value, the relation between the present value and time is not linear but exponential.

with future value, the relation between the present value of €1 and time is not linear but exponential. Finally, it is interesting to note that if interest rates are zero, the present value of €1 is €1; that is, there is no time value of money. In this situation, €1000 today has the same value as €1000 a year from now or, for that matter, 10 years from now.

Decision-Making Example 5.2

Picking the Best Lottery Payoff Option

Situation: Congratulations! You have won the €100 million lottery grand prize. You have been presented with several payout alternatives and you have to decide which one to accept. The alternatives are as follows:

- €10 million today
- €12 million lump sum in two years
- €15 million lump sum in five years
- €20 million lump sum in eight years

You are intrigued by the choice of collecting the prize money today or receiving double the amount of money in the future. Which payout option should you choose?

Your cousin, a stockbroker, advises you that over the long term you should be able to earn 10% on an investment portfolio. Based on that rate of return, you make the following calculations:

Alternative	Nominal Value	Present Value
Today	€10 million	€10 million
2 years	€12 million	€9 917 36
5 years	€15 million	€9 313 82
8 years	€20 million	€9 330 15

Decision: As appealing as the higher amounts may sound, waiting for the big payout is not worthwhile in this case. Applying the present value formula has enabled you to convert future money into present, or current, money. Now the decision is simple – you can directly compare the present values. Given the above choices, you should take the €10 million today.

Before You Go On

1. What is the present value and when is it used?
2. What is the discount rate? How does the discount rate differ from the interest rate in the future value equation?
3. What is the relation between the present value factor and the future value factor?
4. Explain why you would expect the discount factor to become smaller the longer the time to payment.

ADDITIONAL CONCEPTS AND APPLICATIONS

Learning Objective 4

Discuss why the concept of compounding is not restricted to money, and be able to use the future value formula to calculate growth rates.

In this final section, we discuss several additional issues concerning present and future value, including how to find an unknown discount rate, how to estimate the length of time it will take to 'double your money' and how to find the growth rates of various kinds of investments.

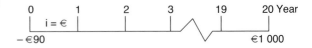

Finding the Interest Rate

In finance, some situations require you to determine the interest rate (or discount rate) for a given future cash flow. These situations typically arise when you want to determine the return on an investment. For example, an interesting innovation is the *zero-coupon bond*. These bonds pay no periodic interest; instead, at maturity the issuer (the firm that borrows the money) makes a payment that includes repayment of the amount borrowed plus interest. Needless to say, the issuer must prepare in advance to have the cash to pay off bondholders.

Suppose a firm is planning to issue €100 million worth of zero-coupon bonds with 20 years to maturity. The bonds are issued in denominations of €1000 and are sold for €90 each. In other words, you buy the bond today for €90 and 20 years from now the firm pays you €1000. If you bought one of these bonds, what would be your return on investment?

To find the return, we need to solve Equation (5.4), the present value equation, for i, the interest, or discount, rate. The €90 you pay today is the PV (present value), the €1000 you get in 20 years is the FV (future value) and 20 years is n (the compounding period). The resulting calculation is as follows:

$$PV = \frac{FV_n}{(1+i)^n}$$

$$€90 = \frac{€1000}{(1+i)^{20}}$$

$$(1+i)^{20} = \frac{€1000}{€90}$$

$$1+i = \left(\frac{€1000}{€90}\right)^{1/20}$$

$$i = (11.1111)^{1/20} - 1$$

$$= 1.1279 - 1$$

$$= 0.1279, \text{ or } 12.79\%$$

The rate of return on your investment, compounded annually, is 12.79%.

Learning by Doing Application 5.4

Interest Rate on a Loan

Problem: Claude and Pauline Desmarais are getting ready to buy their first house. To help make the down payment, Claude's aunt offers to loan them €15 000, which can be repaid in 10 years. If Claude and Pauline borrow the money, they will have to repay Claude's aunt the amount of €23 750. What rate of interest would Claude and Pauline be paying on the 10-year loan?

Approach: In this case, the present value is the value of the loan (€15 000) and the future value is the amount due at the end of 10 years (€23 750). To solve for the rate of interest on the loan, we can use the present value equation, Equation (5.4). The time line for the loan is as follows:

Solution:

Using Equation (5.4):

$$PV = \frac{FV_n}{(1+i)^n}$$

$$€15\,000 = \frac{€23\,750}{(1+i)^{10}}$$

$$(1+i)^{10} = \frac{€23\,750}{€15\,000}$$

$$1+i = \left(\frac{€23\,750}{€15\,000}\right)^{1/10}$$

$$i = (1.58333)^{1/10} - 1$$

$$= 1.04703 - 1$$

$$= 0.04703, \text{ or } 4.703\%$$

The Rule of 72

People are fascinated by the possibility of doubling their money. Infomercials on television tout speculative land investments, claiming that 'some investors have doubled their money in four years'. Before there were financial calculators, people used rules of thumb to approximate difficult present value calculations. One such rule is the Rule of 72, which was used to determine the amount of time it takes to double an investment. The **Rule of 72** says that the time to double your money (TDM) approximately equals $72/i$, where i is expressed as a percentage. Thus,

$$\text{TDM} = \frac{72}{i}$$

Applying the Rule of 72 to our land investment example suggests that if you double your money in four years, your annual rate of return will be 18% ($i = 72/4 = 18$).

> **Rule of 72**
>
> a rule proposing that the time required to double money invested (TDM) approximately equals $72/i$, where i is expressed as a percentage

Let us check the rule's accuracy by applying the present value formula to the land example. We are assuming that you will double your money in four years, so $n = 4$. We did not specify a present value or future value amount; however, doubling your money means that you will get back €2 (FV)

for every €1 invested (PV). Using Equation (5.4) and solving for the interest rate (i), we find that $i = 0.1892$, or 18.92%.[7]

That is not bad for a simple rule of thumb: 18.92% versus 18%. Within limits, the Rule of 72 provides a quick 'back of the envelope' method for determining the amount of time it will take to double an investment for a particular rate of return. The Rule of 72 is a linear approximation of a nonlinear function and, as such, the rule is fairly accurate for interest rates between 5% and 20%. Outside these limits, the rule is not very accurate.

Compound Growth Rates

The concept of compounding is not restricted to money. Any number that changes over time, such as the population of a city, changes at some compound growth rate. Compound growth occurs when the initial value of a number increases or decreases each period by the factor (1 + growth rate). As we go through the course, we will discuss many different types of interest rates, such as the discount rate on capital budgeting projects, the yield on a bond and the internal rate of return on an investment. All of these 'interest rates' can be thought of as growth rates (g) that relate future values to present values.

When we refer to the compounding effect, we are really talking about what happens when the value of a number increases or decreases by (1 + growth rate)^n. That is, the future value of a number after n periods will equal the initial value times (1 + growth rate)^n. Does this sound familiar?

If we want, we can rewrite Equation (5.1) in a more general form as a compound growth rate formula, substituting g, the growth rate, for i, the interest rate:

$$FV_n = PV \times (1+g)^n \qquad (5.6)$$

where:

FV_n = future value of the economic factor, such as sales or population, at the end of period n

PV = original amount or present value of economic factor

g = growth rate per period

n = number of periods: a period may be a year but can also be a quarter, month, week, day, minute or any other length of time

Suppose, for example, that because of an advertising campaign, a firm's sales increased from €20 million in 2009 to more than €35 million three years later. What has been the average annual growth rate in sales? Here, the future value is €35 million, the present value is €20 million and n is 3 since we are interested in the annual growth rate over three years.

Applying Equation (5.6) and solving for the growth factor (g) yields:

$$FV_3 = PV \times (1+g)^3$$
$$€35m = €20m \times (1+g)^3$$
$$g = (1.75)^{1/3} - 1$$
$$= 1.2051 - 1$$
$$= 0.2051, \text{ or } 20.51\%$$

Thus, sales grew nearly 21% per year. More precisely, we could say that sales grew at a **compound annual growth rate (CAGR)** of nearly 21%.

> **Compound annual growth rate (CAGR)**
>
> the average annual growth rate over a specified period of time

---

Learning by Doing Application 5.5

The Growth Rate in L'Oreal's Dividends

Problem: Hannah, who is studying finance, is writing an essay paper and needs an estimate of how fast L'Oreal's dividend payments are growing. In 2004, L'Oreal paid a dividend of €0.82 per share and in 2009 it paid a dividend of €1.50 per share. Calculate the annual growth rate implied by these numbers. If L'Oreal maintains its historical growth rate in dividends, what will be the dividend it would pay in 2015?

Approach: We first find the annual rate of growth from 2004 to 2009 by applying Equation (5.6) for the five-year period 2004–2009. For the purpose of this calculation, we can use the 2004 value as the present value, the 2009 dividend payment as the future value and 5 as the number of compounding periods (n). We want to solve for g, which is the annual compound growth rate over the five-year period. We can then plug the five-year dividend growth rate into Equation (5.6) and solve for L'Oreal's dividend in 2015 (FV_6).

Solution:
Using Equation (5.6), we find the growth rate as follows:

$$FV_n = PV \times (1 + g)^n$$
$$€1.50 = €0.82 \times (1 + g)^5$$
$$(1.82927)^{1/5} = 1 + g$$
$$g = (1.82927)^{1/5} - 1$$
$$= 1.12838 - 1$$
$$= 0.12838, \text{ or } 12.84\%$$

L'Oreal's dividends grew at 12.84% per year for the period 2004–2009.

Using the growth estimate for 2004–2009, L'Oreal's dividend in 2015 is therefore estimated to be:

$$FV_6 = €1.50 \times (1 + 0.12838)^6$$
$$= €1.50 \times 2.06411$$
$$= €3.10$$

Learning by Doing Application 5.6

Calculating Projected Earnings

Problem: SAP AG current revenues are €11 575 million. Securities analysts expect revenues to increase by 10.65% per year over the next three years. Determine what SAP's revenues should be in three years.

Approach: This problem involves the growth rate (g) of SAP's revenues. We already know the value of g, which is 10.65%, and we need to find the future value. Since the general

compound growth rate formula, Equation (5.6), is the same as Equation (5.1), the future value formula, we can use the same procedure we used earlier to find the future value.

Solution:

$$FV_n = PV \times (1 + g)^n$$
$$= €11\,575 \times (1 + 0.1065)^3$$
$$= €11\,575 \times 1.3547347$$
$$= €15\,681.05 \text{ million}$$

Concluding Comments

This chapter has introduced the basic principles of present value and future value. The table at the end of the chapter summarises the key equations developed in the chapter. The basic equations for present value [Equation (5.4)] and future value [Equation (5.1)] are two of the most fundamental relations in finance and will be applied throughout the balance of the textbook.

Before You Go On

1. What is the difference between the interest rate (i) and the growth rate (g) in the future value equation?

SUMMARY OF LEARNING OBJECTIVES

1. **Explain what the time value of money is and why it is so important in the field of finance.**

   The idea that money has a time value is one of the most fundamental concepts in the field of finance. The concept is based on the idea that most people prefer to have goods today rather than wait to have similar goods in the future. Since money buys goods, they would rather have money today than in the future. Thus, *money today is worth more than money received in the future*. Another way of viewing the time value of money is that your money is worth more today than at some point in the future because, if you had the money now, you could invest it and earn interest. Thus, the time value of money is the opportunity cost of forgoing consumption today.

   Applications of the time value of money focus on the trade-off between current money and money received at some future date. This is an important element in financial decisions because most investment decisions require the comparison of cash invested today with the value of expected future cash inflows. Investment opportunities are undertaken only when the value of future cash inflows exceeds the cost of the investment (the initial cash outflow).

2. **Explain the concept of future value, including the meaning of *principal amount, simple interest* and *compound interest*, and be able to use the future value formula to make business decisions.**

   The future value is the sum to which an investment will grow after earning interest. The principal amount is the amount of the investment. Simple interest is the interest paid on the original investment; the amount of money earned on simple interest remains constant from period to period. Compound interest includes not only simple interest, but also interest earned on the reinvestment of previously earned interest, the so-called interest on interest. For future value calculations, the higher the interest rate, the faster the investment will grow. The application of the future value formula in business decisions is presented.

3. **Explain the concept of present value and how it relates to future value, and be able to use the present value formula to make business decisions.**

   The present value is the value today of a future cash flow. Computing the present value involves discounting future cash flows back to the present at an appropriate discount rate. The process of discounting cash flows adjusts the cash flows for the time value of money. Computationally, the present value factor is the reciprocal of the future value factor, or $1/(1 + i)$. The computation and application of the present value formula in business decisions is presented.

4. **Discuss why the concept of compounding is not restricted to money, and be able to use the future value formula to calculate growth rates.**

   Any number of changes that are observed over time in the physical and social sciences follow a compound growth rate pattern. The future value formula can be used in calculating these growth rates.

SUMMARY OF KEY EQUATIONS

Equation	Description	Formula
(5.1)	Future value of an n-period investment with annual compounding	$FV_n = P_0 \times (1 + i)^n$
(5.2)	Future value with compounding more than annually	$FV_n = P_0 \times (1 + i/m)^{m \times n}$
(5.3)	Future value with continuous compounding	$FV_\infty = P_0 \times e^{i \times n}$
(5.4)	Present value	$PV = \dfrac{FV_n}{(1 + i)^n}$
(5.5)	Rule of 72	$TDM = \dfrac{72}{i}$
(5.6)	Future value with general growth rate	$FV_n = PV \times (1 + g)^n$

SELF-STUDY PROBLEMS

5.1. Amit Patel is planning to invest €10 000 in a bank deposit for five years. The deposit will pay interest of 9%. What is the future value of Amit's investment?

5.2. Martine Gautier expects to need €50 000 as a down payment on a house in six years. How much does she need to invest today in an account paying 7.25%?

5.3. Raul Martinez has €10 000 that she can deposit into a savings account for five years. Bank A pays compounds interest annually, Bank B twice a year and Bank C quarterly. Each bank has a stated interest rate of 4%. What amount would Raul have at the end of the fifth year if she left all the interest paid on the deposit in each bank?

5.4. You have an opportunity to invest Dkr 25 000 today and receive Dkr 30 000 in three years. What will be the return on your investment?

5.5. Arianna De Luca deposits €1200 in her bank today. If the bank pays 4% simple interest, how much money will she have at the end of five years? What if the bank pays compound interest? How much of the earnings will be interest on interest?

SOLUTIONS TO SELF-STUDY PROBLEMS

5.1. Present value of Amit's investment = PV = €10 000
Interest rate on bank deposit = i = 9%
Number of years = n = 5

$$FV_n = PV \times (1 + i)^n = €10\,000 \times (1 + 0.09)^5 = €15\,386.24$$

5.2. Amount Martine will need in six years $= FV_6 = €50\,000$
Number of years $= n = 6$
Interest rate on investment $= i = 7.25\%$
Amount needed to be invested now $= PV = ?$

$$PV = \frac{FV_n}{(1+i)^n} = \frac{€50\,000}{(1+0.0725)^6} = €32\,853.84$$

5.3. Present value of Raul's deposit $= PV = €10\,000$
Number of years $= n = 5$
Interest rate $= i = 4\%$
Compound period (m):
$\qquad A = 1$
$\qquad B = 2$
$\qquad C = 4$
Amount at the end of five years $= FV_5 = ?$
$\qquad FV_n = PV \times (1 + i/m)^{m \times n}$
Bank A: $FV_5 = €10\,000 \times (1 + 0.04/1)^{1 \times 5}$
$\qquad FV_5 = €12\,166.53$
Bank B: $FV_5 = €10\,000 \times (1 + 0.04/2)^{2 \times 5}$
$\qquad FV_5 = €12\,189.94$
Bank C: $FV_5 = €10\,000 \times (1 + 0.04/4)^{4 \times 5}$
$\qquad FV_5 = €12\,201.90$

5.4. Your investment today $= PV = Dkr\,25\,000$
Amount to be received $= FV_3 = Dkr\,30\,000$
Time of investment $= n = 3$
Return on the investment $= i = ?$
$FV_n = PV \times (1 + i)^n$
$Dkr\,30\,000 = Dkr\,25\,000 \times (1 + i)^3$
$Dkr\,30\,000/Dkr\,25\,000 = (1 + i)^3$
$i = 6.27\%$

5.5. Arianna's deposit today $= PV = €1200$
Interest rate $= i = 4\%$
Number of years $= n = 5$
Amount to be received back $= FV_5 = ?$
a. Future value with simple interest
Simple interest per year $= €1200 \times 0.04 = €48.00$
Simple interest for 5 years $= €48 \times 5 = €240.00$
$FV_5 = €1200 + €240 = €1440.00$
b. Future value with compound interest
$FV_5 = €1200 \times (1 + 0.04)^5$
$FV_5 = €1459.98$
Simple interest $= (€1440 - €1200) = €240$
Interest on interest $= €1459.98 - €1200 - €240 = €19.98$

CRITICAL THINKING QUESTIONS

5.1. Explain the phrase 'money today is worth more than money tomorrow'.

5.2. Explain the importance of a time line.

5.3. Differentiate future value from present value.

5.4. What are the two factors to be considered in the time value of money?

5.5. Differentiate between compounding and discounting.

5.6. Explain how compound interest differs from simple interest.

5.7. If you were given a choice of investing in an account that paid quarterly interest and one that paid monthly interest, which one should you choose and why?

5.8. Growth rates are exponential over time. Explain.

5.9. What is the Rule of 72?

5.10. You are planning to take a spring break trip to Barcelona in your last year at university. The trip is exactly two years away, but you want to be prepared and have enough money when the time comes. Explain how you would determine the amount of money you will have to save in order to pay for the trip.

QUESTIONS AND PROBLEMS

Basic

5.1. **Future value:** Gunnar Ottenberg is planning to invest SKr 25 000 today in a mutual fund that will provide a return of 8% each year. What will be the value of the investment in 10 years?

5.2. **Future value:** Marcello Esposito is investing €7500 in a bank deposit that pays a 6% annual interest. How much will be in the deposit account at the end of five years?

5.3. **Future value:** Your aunt is planning to invest in a bank deposit that will pay 7.5% interest semi-annually. If she has €5000 to invest, how much will she have at the end of four years?

5.4. **Future value:** Anna Kaufman received a graduation present of €2000 that she is planning on investing in a mutual fund that earns 8.5% each year. How much money can she collect in three years?

5.5. **Future value:** Your bank pays 5% interest semi-annually on your savings account. You do not expect the current balance of €2700

to change over the next four years. How much money can you expect to have at the end of this period?

5.6. **Future value:** Your birthday is coming up and instead of any presents, your parents promised to give you €1000 in cash. Since you have a part-time job and, thus, do not need the cash immediately, you decide to invest the money in a bank deposit that pays 5.2% quarterly for the next two years. How much money can you expect to gain in this period of time?

5.7. **Multiple compounding periods:** Find the future value of an investment of €100 000 made today for five years and paying 8.75% for the following compounding periods:
a. Quarterly
b. Monthly
c. Daily
d. Continuous

5.8. **Growth rates:** Julio Lopez, a footballer for Real Madrid, is expected to score 25 goals in 2010. If his goal-scoring ability is expected to grow by 12% every year for the next five years, how many goals is he expected to hit in 2015?

5.9. Present value: Gunter Weber is considering an investment that pays 7.6%. How much will he have to invest today so that the investment will be worth €25 000 in six years?

5.10. Present value: Maria Addai has been offered a future payment of €750 two years from now. If her opportunity cost is 6.5% compounded annually, what should she pay for this investment today?

5.11. Present value: You brother has asked you for a loan and has promised to pay back €7750 at the end of three years. If you normally invest to earn 6%, how much will you be willing to lend to your brother?

5.12. Present value: Tracy Chapman is saving to buy a house in five years. She plans to put 20% down at that time, and she believes that she will need £35 000 for the down payment. If Tracy can invest in a fund that pays 9.25% annually, how much will she need to invest today?

5.13. Present value: You want to buy some deep-discount zero-coupon bonds that have a value of €1000 at the end of seven years. You hear that similar bonds are said to pay 4.5% interest. How much should you pay for the zero-coupon bonds today?

5.14. Present value: Eira Svenning wants to accumulate €12 000 by the end of 12 years. If the interest rate is 7%, how much will she have to invest today to achieve her goal?

5.15. Interest rate: You are in desperate need of cash and turn to your uncle, who has offered to lend you some money. You decide to borrow €1300 and agree to pay back €1500 in two years. Alternatively, you could borrow from your bank that is charging 6.5% interest. Should you go with your uncle or the bank?

5.16. Time to attain goal: You invest €150 in a mutual fund today that pays 9% interest. How long will it take to double your money?

Intermediate

5.17. Growth rate: Your finance textbook sold 53 250 copies in its first year. The publishing company expects the sales to grow at a rate of 20% for the next three years and by 10% in the fourth year. Calculate the total number of copies that the publisher expects to sell in years 3 and 4. Draw a time line to show the sales level for each of the next four years.

5.18. Growth rate: Palermo Elettronica SpA had sales last year of €700 000 and the analysts are predicting a good year for the start-up, with sales growing 20% a year for the next three years. After that, the sales should grow 11% per year for two years, at which time the owners are planning to sell the company. What are the projected sales for the last year of the company's operation?

5.19. Growth rate: You decide to take advantage of the current online dating craze and start your own website. You know that you have 450 people who will sign up immediately and, through a careful marketing research and analysis, determine that membership can grow by 27% in the first two years, 22% in year 3 and 18% in year 4. How many members do you expect to have at the end of four years?

5.20. Multiple compounding periods: Find the future value of an investment of €2500 made today for the following rates and periods:
  a. 6.25% compounded semi-annually for 12 years
  b. 7.63% compounded quarterly for 6 years
  c. 8.9% compounded monthly for 10 years
  d. 10% compounded daily for 3 years
  e. 8% compounded continuously for 2 years

5.21. Growth rates: Cork Business Systems Ltd had sales of €353 866 in 2008. If it expects its sales to be at €476 450 in three years, what is the rate at which the company's sales are expected to grow?

5.22. Growth rates: Infosys Technologies Inc., an Indian technology company, reported a net income of $419 million this year. Analysts expect the company's earnings to be $1.468 billion in five years. What is the company's earnings expected growth rate?

5.23. **Time to attain goal:** Oporto Vendas SA has currently reported sales of €1.125 million. If the company expects its sales to grow at 6.5% annually, how long will it be before the company can double its sales?

5.24. **Time to attain goal:** You are able to deposit €850 in a bank deposit today, and you will withdraw the money only once the balance is €1000. If the bank pays 5% interest, how long will it take you to attain your goal?

5.25. **Time to attain goal:** La Lumière Magique SARL is a private company with sales of €13 million a year. They want to go public but have to wait until the sales reach €20 million. Providing that they are expected to grow at a steady 12% annually, when is the earliest that La Lumière Magique can start selling their shares?

5.26. **Present value:** Cabrina de Silva needs to decide whether to accept a bonus of €1900 today or wait two years and receive €2100 then. She can invest at 6%. What should she do?

5.27. **Multiple compounding periods:** Find the present value of €3500 under each of the following rates and periods:
   a. 8.9% compounded monthly for 5 years
   b. 6.6% compounded quarterly for 8 years
   c. 4.3% compounded daily for 4 years
   d. 5.7% compounded continuously for 3 years

5.28. **Multiple compounding periods:** Sabine is looking to invest some money, so she can collect €5500 at the end of three years. Which investment should she make given the following choices:
   a. 4.2% compounded daily
   b. 4.9% compounded monthly
   c. 5.2% compounded quarterly
   d. 5.4% compounded annually

Advanced

5.29. You have €2500 you want to invest in your classmate's start-up business. You believe the business idea to be great and hope to get €3700 back at the end of three years. If all goes according to plan, what will be your return on investment?

5.30. Patrick Murphy has €2400 that he is looking to invest. His brother approached him with an investment opportunity that could double his money in four years. What interest rate would the investment have to yield in order for Patrick's brother to deliver on his promise?

5.31. [EXCEL®] You have €12 000 in cash. You can deposit it today in a mutual fund earning 8.2% semi-annually, or you can wait, enjoy some of it, and invest €11 000 in your brother's business in two years. Your brother is promising you a return of at least 10% on your investment. Whichever alternative you choose, you will need to cash in at the end of 10 years. Assume your brother is trustworthy and both investments carry the same risk. Which one will you choose?

5.32. [EXCEL®] When you were born your parents set up a bank account in your name with an initial investment of €5000. You are turning 21 in a few days and will have access to all your funds. The account was earning 7.3% for the first seven years but then the rates went down to 5.5% for six years. The economy was doing well at the end of the 1990s, and your account was earning 8.2% for three years in a row. Unfortunately, the next two years you earned only 4.6%. Finally, as the economy recovered, your return jumped to 7.6% for the last three years.
   a. How much money was in your account before the rates went down drastically (end of year 16)?
   b. How much money is in your account now (end of year 21)?
   c. What would be the balance now if your parents made another deposit of €1200 at the end of year 7?

5.33. EXCEL® Gunter Koch, a top-five draft pick of FC Bayern Munich, and his agent are evaluating three contract options. Each option offers a signing bonus and a series of payments over the life of the contract. Koch uses a 10.25% rate of return to evaluate the contracts. Given the cash flows for each option, which one should he choose?

Year	Cash Flow Type	Option A	Option B	Option C
0	Signing Bonus	€3 100 000	€4 000 000	€4 250 000
1	Annual Salary	650 000	825 000	550 000
2	Annual Salary	715 000	850 000	625 000
3	Annual Salary	822 250	925 000	800 000
4	Annual Salary	975 000	1 250 000	900 000
5	Annual Salary	1 100 000		1 000 000
6	Annual Salary	1 250 000		

5.34. EXCEL® Surmec AG reported earnings (sales or net income) of €2.1 million last year. The company's primary business line is manufacturing of nuts and bolts. Since this is a mature industry, the analysts are certain that the sales will grow at a steady rate of 7% a year for as far as they can tell. The company reports net income that represents 23% of sales. The management would like to buy a new fleet of trucks but can only do so once the profit reaches €620 000 a year. At the end of what year will Surmec be able to buy the new fleet of trucks? What will the sales and profit be that year?

5.35. EXCEL® You are graduating in two years, and you start thinking about your future. You know that you will want to buy a house five years after you graduate and that you will want to put down €60 000. As of right now, you have €8000 in your savings account. You are also fairly certain that once you graduate, you can work in the family business and earn €32 000 a year, with a 5% raise every year. You plan to live with your parents for the first two years after graduation, which will enable you to minimise your expenses and put away €10 000 each year. The next three years, you will have to live on your own as your younger sister will be graduating from college and has already announced her plan to move back into the family house. Thus, you will be able to save only 13% of your annual salary. Assume that you will be able to invest savings from your salary at 7.2%. At what interest rate will you need to invest the current savings account balance in order to achieve your goal? *Hint:* Draw a time line that shows all the cash flows for years 0–7. Remember, you want to buy a house seven years from now and your first salary will be in year 3.

SAMPLE TEST PROBLEMS

5.1. Santiago Hernandez is planning to invest €25 000 in a money market account for two years. The account pays interest of 5.75% compounded on a monthly basis. How much will Santiago Hernandez have at the end of two years?

5.2. Jean-Luc Cartier is expecting an inheritance of €1.25 million in four years. If he had the money today, he could earn interest at an annual rate of 7.35%. What is the present value of his inheritance?

5.3. What is the future value of an investment of €3000 for three years compounded at the following rates and frequencies?

a. 8.75% compounded monthly

b. 8.625% compounded daily

c. 8.5% compounded continuously

5.4. Twenty-five years ago, Amanda Cortez invested €10 000 in an account paying an annual interest rate of 5.75%. What is the value of the investment today? What is the interest on interest earned on this investment?

5.5. You just bought a corporate bond at £863.75 today. In five years the bond will mature and you will receive £1000. What is the rate of return on this bond?

ENDNOTES

1. As of June 2010, the largest Mega Million jackpot was $370 million, won in March 2007. Mega Millions is operated by a consortium of the state lottery commissions in California, Georgia, Illinois, Maryland, Massachusetts, Michigan, New Jersey, New York, Ohio, Texas, Virginia and Washington. To play the game, a player pays one dollar and picks five numbers from 1 to 56 and one additional number from 1 to 46 (the Mega Ball number). Twice a week, a machine mixes numbered balls and randomly selects six balls (five white balls and one Mega Ball), which determines the winning combination for that drawing. There are various winning combinations, but a ticket that matches all six numbers, including the Mega Ball number, is the jackpot winner.

2. The formula for a single-period investment is $FV_1 = P_0 + (P_0 \times i)$. Solving the equation for $FV_1 = P_0$ yields the simple interest, SI.

3. Another helpful equation is the one which computes the total simple interest over several periods (TSI): $TSI = $ Number of periods $ \times SI = $ Number of periods $ \times (P_0 \times i)$.

4. An alternative way to perform the calculation is to multiply 1.08 by itself 10 times. However, we do not recommend this procedure.

5. The future value calculation for annual compounding is: $FV_{yearly} = €10\ 000 \times (1.05)^5 = €12\ 762.82$.

6. Equation (5.4) can also be written as $PV = FV_n \times (1 + i)^{-n}$.

7. Solve Equation (5.4) for i: $PV = FV_n/(1 + i)^n$, where $PV = €1$, $FV = €2$ and $n = 4$.

CHAPTER

6

Discounted Cash Flows and Valuation

In this Chapter:

LEARNING OBJECTIVES

1. Explain why cash flows occurring at different times must be adjusted to reflect their value as of a common date, before they can be compared, and be able to compute the present value and future value for multiple cash flows.

2. Describe how to calculate the present value of an ordinary annuity and how an ordinary annuity differs from an annuity due.

3. Explain what a perpetuity is and how it is used in business and be able to calculate the value of a perpetuity.

4. Discuss growing annuities and perpetuities, as well as their application in business, and be able to calculate their value.

5. Discuss why the effective annual interest rate (EAR) is the appropriate way to annualise interest rates and be able to calculate EAR.

In September 2009, as a result of rising foreign interest in Brazil's fast-growing telecoms market, Vivendi, the French media conglomerate, put forward a deal to acquire control of GVT, a small but fast growing local fixed-line provider. GVT had a 5% share of the market but its revenues had risen by 40% in 2008. However, in a surprise move that caught Vivendi off guard, the Madrid-based telecoms company Telefónica launched a higher bid for control of GVT. The offer was 14% above that proposed by Vivendi.

Telefónica, the third largest telecoms company by market capitalisation, already had a presence in Brazil with its mobile joint venture, Vivo, and a fixed-line provider, Telesp. Vivo was experiencing very significant increases in revenues but as the fragmented Brazilian market evolved from a series of regional monopolies into a single national market, Telesp faced increasing competition. By buying GVT, Telefónica would be able to link Telesp's operations, which centred on the São Paulo province, with GVT's operations in the North and West. Size would allow the new group to compete more effectively with Oi, Brazil's largest fixed-line telecoms provider.

Telefónica offered 10 times forecast 2009 earnings that valued the company at R$6.5 billion or R48 per share versus Vivendi's R$42 per share. Faced with this outcome, Vivendi had to decide whether to raise its bid to top its rival's price.

In the excitement of an acquisition like this one, it is important not to lose sight of the central question: What is the firm really worth? A company invests in an asset – a business or a capital project – because it expects the asset to be worth more than it costs. That is how value is created. The value of a business is the sum of its discounted future cash flows. Thus, the task for both Vivendi and Telefónica was to estimate the value of the future cash flows that GVT could generate under their ownership. This chapter, which discusses the discounting of future cash flows, provides the tools that help answer the key question in the GVT bidding war: What is the firm worth?

CHAPTER PREVIEW

In the previous chapter, we introduced the concept of the time value of money: money today is more valuable than money to be received in the future. Starting with that concept, we developed the basics of simple interest, compound interest and future value calculations. We then went on to discuss present value and discounted cash flow analysis. This was all done in the context of a single cash flow.

In this chapter, we consider the value of multiple cash flows. Most business decisions, after all, involve cash flows over time. For example, if Henry Lambertz GmbH, the German biscuit maker, wants to consider adding a production line, the decision will require an analysis of the project's expected cash flows over a number of periods. Initially, there will be large cash outlays to build and get the new line operational. Thereafter, the project should produce cash inflows for many years. Because the cash flows occur over time, the analysis must consider the time value of money, discounting each of the cash flows by using the present value formula.

We begin the chapter by describing calculations of future and present values for multiple cash flows. We then examine some situations in which future cash flows are level over time: these involve annuities, in which the cash flow stream goes on for a finite period, and perpetuities, in which the stream goes on forever. Next, we examine annuities and perpetuities in which the cash flows grow at a constant rate over time. These cash flows resemble common cash flow patterns encountered in business. Finally, we describe the effective annual interest rate and compare it with the annual percentage rate (APR), which is a rate that is used to describe the interest rate in consumer loans.

MULTIPLE CASH FLOWS

Learning Objective 1

Explain why cash flows occurring at different times must be adjusted to reflect their value as of a common date, before they can be compared, and be able to compute the present value and future value for multiple cash flows.

We begin our discussion of the time value of multiple cash flows by calculating the future value and then the present value of multiple cash flows. These calculations, as you will see, are nothing more than applications of the techniques you learned in Chapter 5.

Future Value of Multiple Cash Flows

In Chapter 5, we worked through several examples that involved the future value of a lump sum

of money invested in a savings account that paid 10% interest per year. But suppose you are investing more than one lump sum. For instance, you put €1000 in your bank savings account today and another €1000 a year from now. If the bank continues to pay 10% interest per year, how much money will you have at the end of two years?

To solve this future value problem, we can use Equation (5.1): $FV_n = PV \times (1 + i)^n$. First, however, we construct a time line so that we can see the magnitude and timing of the cash flows. As Exhibit 6.1 shows, there are two cash flows into the savings plan. The first cash flow is invested for two years and compounds to a value that is computed as follows:

$$
\begin{aligned}
FV_2 &= PV \times (1 + i)^2 \\
&= €1000 \times (1 + 0.10)^2 \\
&= €1000 \times 1.21 \\
&= €1210
\end{aligned}
$$

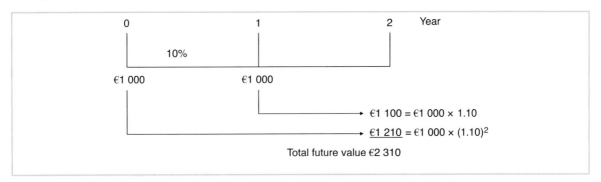

Exhibit 6.1: **Future Value of Two Cash Flows** This exhibit shows a time line for two cash flows invested in a savings account that pays 10% interest annually. The total amount in the savings account after two years is €2310, which is the sum of the future values of the cash flows.

The second cash flow earns simple interest for a single period only and grows to:

$$FV_2 = PV \times (1 + i)$$
$$= €1000 \times (1 + 0.10)$$
$$= €1000 \times 1.10$$
$$= €1100$$

As Exhibit 6.1 shows, the total amount of money in the savings account after two years is the sum of these two amounts, which is €2310 (€1100 + €1210).

Now suppose that you expand your investment horizon to three years and invest €1000 today, €1000 a year from now and €1000 at the end of two years. How much money will you have at the end of three years? First, we draw a time line to be sure that we have correctly identified the time period for each cash flow. This is shown in Exhibit 6.2. Then we compute the future value of each of the individual cash flows using Equation (5.1). Finally, we add up the future values. The total future value is €3641. The calculations are as follows:

$$FV_1 = PV \times (1 + i) = €1000 \times (1 + 0.10)$$
$$= €1000 \times 1.100 = €1100$$
$$FV_2 = PV \times (1 + i)^2 = €1000 \times (1 + 0.10)^2$$
$$= €1000 \times 1.210 = €1210$$
$$FV_3 = PV \times (1 + i)^3 = €1000 \times (1 + 0.10)^3$$
$$= €1000 \times 1.331 = \underline{€1331}$$
$$\text{Total future value} \quad €3641$$

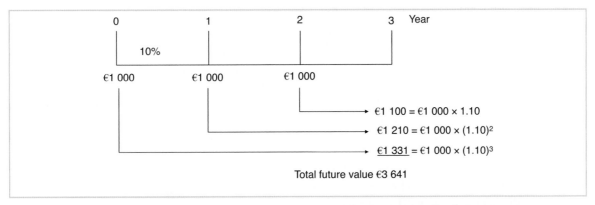

Exhibit 6.2: **Future Value of Three Cash Flows** This exhibit shows a time line for an investment programme with a three-year horizon. The value of the investment at the end of three years is €3641, the sum of the future values of the three separate cash flows.

To summarise, solving future value problems with multiple cash flows involves a simple process. First, draw a time line to make sure that each cash flow is placed in the correct time period. Second, calculate the future value of each cash flow for its time period. Third, add up the future values. It is that simple!

Let us use this process to solve a practical problem. Suppose you want to buy an apartment in three years and estimate that you will need €20 000 for a down payment. If the interest rate you can earn at the bank is 8% and you can save €3000 now, €4000 at the end of the first year and €5000 at the end of the second year, how much money will you have to come up with at the end of the third year to have a €20 000 down payment?

The time line for the future value calculation in this problem looks like this:

To solve the problem, we need to calculate the future value for each of the expected cash flows, add up these values, and find the difference between this amount and the €20 000 needed for the down payment. Using Equation (5.1), we find that the future values of the cash flows at the end of the third year are:

$$FV_1 = PV \times (1 + i) = €5000 \times 1.08$$
$$= €5000 \times 1.0800 = €5400.00$$
$$FV_2 = PV \times (1 + i)^2 = €4000 \times (1.08)^2$$
$$= €4000 \times 1.1664 = €4665.40$$
$$FV_3 = PV \times (1 + i)^3 = €3000 \times (1.08)^3$$
$$= €3000 \times 1.2597 = \underline{€3779.14}$$
$$\text{Total future value} \quad €13\,844.74$$

At the end of the third year, you will have €13 844.74, so you will need an additional €6155.26 (€20 000 − €13 844.74).

Learning by Doing Application 6.1

Government Contract in L'Aquila

Problem: The firm you work for is considering bidding on a government contract to rebuild a power station in L'Aquila, Italy, that was damaged during the April 2009 earthquake. The two-year contract will pay the firm €9000 at the end of the second year. The firm's estimator believes that the project will require an initial expenditure of €5000 for equipment. The expenses for years 1 and 2 are estimated at €1000 per year. Because the cash inflow of €9000 at the end of the contract exceeds the total cash outflows of €7000 (€5000 + €1000 + €1000), the estimator believes that the firm should accept the job. Drawing on your

knowledge of finance from your university course, you point out that the estimator's decision process ignores the time value of money. Not fully understanding what you mean, the estimator asks you how the time value of money should be incorporated into the decision process. Assume that the appropriate interest rate is 18%.

Approach: First, construct the time line for the costs in this problem, as shown here:

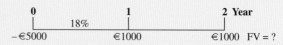

Second, use Equation (5.1) to convert all of the cash outflows into period-two money. This will make all the cash flows comparable because they will represent the same amount of purchasing power – period-two money. Finally, compare the sum of the cash outflows, stated in period-two money, to the €9000 that you would receive under the contract.

Solution:

$$FV_2 = PV \times (1 + i)^2 = -€5000 \times (1.18)^2$$
$$= -€5000 \times 1.3924 = -€6962$$
$$FV_1 = PV \times (1 + i)^1 = -€1000 \times (1.18)^1$$
$$= -€1000 \times 1.1800 = -€1180$$

$$FV0 = PV \times (1 + i)^0 = -€1000 \times (1.18)^0$$
$$= -€1000 \times 1.0000 = \underline{-€1000}$$

Total net future value   – €9141

Once the future value calculations have been made, the decision is self-evident. With all the euros stated as period-two money, the cash inflow (benefits) is €9000 and the cash outflow (costs) is €9141. Thus, the costs exceed the benefits and the firm's management should reject the contract. If management accepts the contract, the value of the firm will be reduced.

Present Value of Multiple Cash Flows

In business situations, we often need to compute the present value of a series of future cash flows. We do this, for example, to determine the market price of a bond, to decide whether to purchase a new machine, or to determine the value of a business. Solving present value problems involving multiple cash flows is similar to solving future value problems involving multiple cash flows. First, we prepare a time line to identify the magnitude and timing of the cash flows. Second, we calculate the present value of each individual cash flow using Equation (5.4): $PV = FV_n/(1 + i)^n$. Finally, we add up the present values. The sum of the present values of a stream of future cash flows is their current market price, or value. There is nothing new here!

Using the Present Value Equation

Next, we will work through some examples to see how we can use Equation (5.4) to find the present value of multiple cash flows. Suppose that your best friend needs cash and offers to pay you €1000 at the end of each of the next three years if you will give him €3000 cash today. You realise, of course, that because of the time value of money, the cash flows he has promised to pay are worth less than €3000. If the interest rate on similar loans is 7%, how much should you pay for the cash flows your friend is offering?

To solve the problem, we first construct a time line, as shown in Exhibit 6.3. Then, using Equation (5.4), we calculate the present value for each of the three cash flows, as follows:

$$PV = FV_1 \times 1/(1 + i) = FV_1 \times 1/1.07$$
$$= €1000 \times 0.9346 = €934.58$$
$$PV = FV_2 \times 1/(1 + i)^2 = FV_2 \times 1/(1.07)^2$$
$$= €1000 \times 0.8734 = €873.44$$
$$PV = FV_3 \times 1/(1 + i)^3 = FV_3 \times 1/(1.07)^3$$
$$= €1000 \times 0.8163 = \underline{€816.30}$$

Total present value   €2624.32

If you view this transaction from a purely business perspective, you should not give your friend more than €2624.32, which is the sum of the individual discounted cash flows.

WEB

You can find plenty of problems to work out at StudyFinance.com:
www.studyfinance.com/lectures/time-value/index.mv.

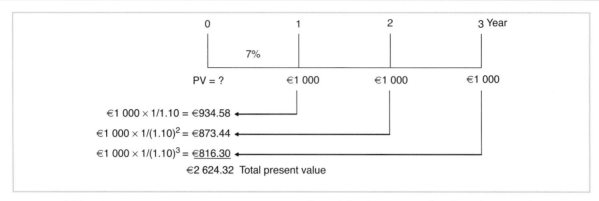

Exhibit 6.3: **Present Value of Three Cash Flows** This exhibit shows a time line for a three-year loan with a payment of €1000 at the end of each year and an annual interest rate of 7%. To calculate the value of the loan today, we compute the present value of each of the three cash flows and then add them up. The present value of the loan is €2624.32.

Learning by Doing Application 6.2

The Value of a Gift to the University

Problem: Suppose that you made a gift to your university, pledging €1000 per year for four years and €3000 for the fifth year, for a total of €7000. After making the first three payments, you decide to pay off the final two payments of your pledge because your financial situation has improved. How much should you pay to the university if the interest rate is 6%?

Approach: The key to understanding this problem, of course, is to recognise the need for a present value calculation. Because your pledge to the university is for future cash payments, the value of the amount you will pay for the remaining two years is worth less than the €4000 (€1000 + €3000) you promised. If the appropriate discount rate is 6%, the time line for the cash payments for the remaining two years of the pledge is as follows:

We now need only calculate the present value of the last two payments.

Solution: The present value calculation for the last two payments is:

$$PV = FV_1 \times 1/(1+i) = €1000 \times 1.06$$
$$= €943.40$$
$$PV = FV_2 \times 1/(1+i)^2 = €3000 \times (1.06)^2$$
$$= €2669.99$$

Total present value   €3613.39

The payment of €3613.39 to the university today (the end of year 3) is a fair payment because at a 6% interest rate, it has precisely the same value as paying the university €1000 at the end of year 4 and €3000 at the end of year 5.

We will now consider another example. Suppose you have the opportunity to buy a small business while you are at university. The business involves selling sandwiches, soft drinks and snack foods to students from a van that you drive around campus. The annual cash flows from the business have been predictable. You believe you can expand the business, and you estimate that cash flows will be as follows: €2000 the first year, €3000 the second and third years, and €4000 the fourth year. At the end of the fourth year, the business will be closed down because the van and other equipment will need to be replaced. The total of the estimated cash flows is €12 000. You did some research at university and found that a 10% discount rate would be appropriate. How much should you pay for the business?

To value the business, we compute the present value of the expected cash flows, discounted at 10%. The time line for the investment is:

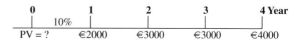

We compute the present value of each cash flow and then add them up:

$$PV = FV_1 \times 1/(1+i) = €2000 \times 1/1.10$$
$$= €2000 \times 0.9091 = €1818.18$$
$$PV = FV_1 \times 1/(1+i)^2 = €2000 \times 1/(1.10)^2$$
$$= €3000 \times 0.8264 = €2479.34$$
$$PV = FV_1 \times 1/(1+i)^3 = €2000 \times 1/(1.10)^3$$
$$= €3000 \times 0.7513 = €2253.94$$
$$PV = FV_1 \times 1/(1+i)^4 = €2000 \times 1/(1.10)^4$$
$$= €4000 \times 0.6830 = \underline{€2732.05}$$
$$\text{Total present value}\quad €9283.51$$

This computation tells us that the value of the business is €9283.51. Of course, you should buy the business for the lowest price possible. If the price goes above €9283.51, however, you should walk away from the deal. You should never pay more for an investment than it is worth.

Learning by Doing Application 6.3

Buying a Used Car – Help!

Problem: For a student – or anyone else – buying a used car can be a harrowing experience. Once you find the car you want, the next difficult decision is how to pay for it – cash or a loan. Suppose the cash price you have negotiated for the car is €5600, but that amount will stretch your budget for the year. The dealer says, 'No problem. The car is yours for €4000 down and payments of €1000 per year for the next two years. Or you can put €2000 down and pay €2000 per year for two years. The choice is yours.' Which offer is the best deal? The interest rate you can earn on your money is 8%.

Approach: In this problem, we have three alternative cash flows. We need to convert all of the cash flows (CF_n) into today's money (present value) and select the alternative with the lowest present value or price.[1] The time line for the three alternatives, along with the cash flows for each alternative, is as follows. (The cash flows at time zero represent the cash price of the car in the case of alternative A and the down payment in the case of alternatives B and C.)

	Cash Price or Down Payment	CF_1	CF_2	Total
Alternative A	€5600	—	—	€5600
Alternative B	€4000	€1000	€1000	€6000
Alternative C	€2000	€2000	€2000	€6000

Now we use Equation (5.4) to find the present value of each alternative.

Solution:

Alternative A:

$$€5600 \times (1.08)^0 = €5600.00$$

Alternative B:

$$
\begin{aligned}
€4000 \times (1.08)^0 &= €4000.00 \\
€4000 \times 1.08 &= €\ 925.93 \\
€4000 \times (1.08)^0 &= €\ 857.34 \\
\textit{Total} &\quad €5783.27
\end{aligned}
$$

Alternative C:

$$
\begin{aligned}
€2000 \times (1.08)^0 &= €2000.00 \\
€2000 \times 1.08 &= €1851.85 \\
€2000 \times (1.08)^2 &= €1714.68 \\
\textit{Total} &\quad €5566.53
\end{aligned}
$$

Once we have converted the three cash flow streams into present money, the answer is clear. Alternative C has the lowest present value, so it has the lowest price and is the alternative you should choose.

Decision-Making Example 6.1

The Investment Decision

Problem: You are thinking of buying a business and your investment adviser presents you with two possibilities. Both businesses are priced at €60 000 and you have only €60 000 to invest. She has provided you with the cash flows for each business, along with the present value of the cash flows discounted at 10%, as follows:

Cash flow per year (€ thousands)

Business	1	2	3	Total	PV at 10%
A	€50	€30	€ 20	€100	€85.27
B	€ 5	€ 5	€100	€110	€83.81

Which business should you acquire?

Decision: At first glance, business B may look to be the best choice because its undiscounted cash flows for the three years total €110 000, versus €100 000 for A. However, to make the decision on the basis of the undiscounted cash flows ignores the time value of money. By discounting the cash flows, we eliminate the time value of money effect by converting all cash flows to current money. The present value of business A is €85 270 and that of B is €83 810. Thus, you should acquire business A.

Before You Go On

1. Explain how to calculate the future value of a stream of cash flows.
2. Explain how to calculate the present value of a stream of cash flows.
3. Why is it important to adjust all cash flows to a common date?

LEVEL CASH FLOWS: ANNUITIES AND PERPETUITIES

Learning Objective 2

Describe how to calculate the present value of an ordinary annuity and how an ordinary annuity differs from an annuity due.

In finance we commonly encounter contracts that call for the payment of equal amounts of cash over several time periods. For example, most business term loans and insurance policies require the holder to make a series of equal payments, usually monthly. Similarly, nearly all consumer finance, such as motor, personal and home mortgage loans, call for equal monthly payments. Any financial contract that calls for equally spaced and level cash flows over a finite number of periods is called an **annuity**. If the cash flow payments continue forever, the contract is called a **perpetuity**. Most annuities are structured so that cash payments are received at the end of each period. Because this is the most common structure, these annuities are often called **ordinary annuities**.

> ### Annuity
>
> a series of equally spaced and level cash flows extending over a finite number of periods

> ### Perpetuity
>
> a series of level cash flows that continue forever

> ### Ordinary annuity
>
> an annuity in which payments are made at the ends of the periods

> ### WEB
>
> Visit the following webform that provides an online annuity calculator: http://www.feike.biz/annuity.php.

Present Value of an Annuity

We frequently need to find the **present value of an annuity (PVA)**. Suppose, for example, that a financial contract pays €2000 at the end of each year for three years and the appropriate discount rate is 8%. The time line for the situation is:

> ### Present value of an annuity (PVA)
>
> the present value of the cash flows from an annuity, discounted at the appropriate discount rate

What is the most we should pay for this annuity? Of course, we have worked problems like this one before. All we need to do is calculate the present value of each individual cash flow (CF_n) and add them up. Using Equation (5.4), we find that the present value of the three-year annuity (PVA_3) at 8% interest is:

$$PVA_3 = CF_1 \times \frac{1}{1+i} + CF_2 \times \frac{1}{(1+i)^2}$$
$$+ CF_3 \times \frac{1}{(1+i)^3}$$
$$= €2000 \times \frac{1}{1.08} + €2000 \times \frac{1}{(1.08)^2}$$
$$+ €2000 \times \frac{1}{(1.08)^3}$$
$$= €1851.85 + €1714.68 + €1587.66$$
$$= €5154.19$$

This approach to computing the present value of an annuity works as long as the number of cash flows is relatively small. In many situations that involve annuities, however, the number of cash flows is large, and doing the calculations by hand would be tedious. For example, a typical 30-year home mortgage has 360 (12 months × 30 years) monthly payments.

Fortunately, our problem can be simplified because the cash flows (CF) for an annuity are all the same $(CF_1 = CF_2 = \cdots = CF_n = CF)$. Thus, the present value of an annuity (PVA_n)

with n equal cash flows (CF) at interest rate i is the sum of the individual present value calculations:

$$PVA_n = CF \times \frac{1}{1+i} + CF \times \frac{1}{(1+i)^2} + \cdots$$
$$+ CF \times \frac{1}{(1+i)^n}$$

With some mathematical manipulations that are beyond the scope of this discussion, we can simplify this equation to yield a useful formula for the present value of an annuity:

$$PVA_n = \frac{CF}{i} \times \left[1 - \frac{1}{(1+i)^n} \right]$$
$$= CF \times \frac{1 - 1/(1+i)^n}{i} \qquad (6.1)$$

where:

PVA_n = present value of an n-period annuity
CF = level and equally spaced cash flow
i = discount rate, or interest rate
n = number of periods (often called the annuity's maturity)

Notice in Equation (6.1) that $1/(1 + i)^n$ is a term you have already encountered: it is the present value factor. Thus, we can also write Equation (6.1) as follows:

$$PVA_n = CF \times \frac{1 - Present\ value\ factor}{i}$$

where the term on the right is what we call the PV annuity factor:

$$PV\ annuity\ factor = \frac{1 - Present\ value\ factor}{i}$$

It follows that yet another way to state Equation (6.1) is:

$$PVA_n = CF \times PV\ annuity\ factor$$

Let us apply Equation (6.1) to the example involving the three-year annuity with a €2000 annual cash flow. To solve for PVA_n, we first compute the PV annuity factor for three years at 8%. The calculation is made in two steps.

1. Calculate the present value factor for three years at 8%:

$$Present\ value\ factor = \frac{1}{(1+i)^n}$$
$$= \frac{1}{(1+0.08)^3}$$
$$= \frac{1}{(1.08)^3}$$
$$= \frac{1}{1.2597} = 0.7938$$

2. Calculate the PV annuity factor for three years at 8%, using the present value factor calculated in step 1:

$$PV\ annuity\ factor = \frac{1 - Present\ value\ factor}{i}$$
$$= \frac{1 - 0.7938}{0.08}$$
$$= \frac{0.2062}{0.08} = 2.577$$

We can now calculate PVA_3 by plugging our values into the equation:

$$PVA_3 = CF \times PV\ annuity\ factor$$
$$= €2000 \times 2.577$$
$$= €5154.00$$

The calculation nearly agrees with our earlier hand calculation. The difference is due to rounding.

WEB

Investopedia is a great website for a variety of finance topics. For example, you can find a discussion of annuities at: www.investopedia.com/articles/03/101503.asp.

Annuity Tables: Present Value Factors

Instead of calculating the PV annuity factor by hand, we can use tables that list selected annuity

EXHIBIT 6.4

PRESENT VALUE ANNUITY FACTORS

Number of Years	Interest Rate per Year						
	1%	5%	6%	7%	8%	9%	10%
1	€0.990	€0.952	€0.943	€0.935	€0.926	€0.917	€0.909
2	1.970	1.859	1.833	1.808	1.783	1.759	1.736
3	2.941	2.723	2.673	2.624	2.577	2.531	2.487
4	3.902	3.546	3.465	3.387	3.312	3.240	3.170
5	4.853	4.329	4.212	4.100	3.993	3.890	3.791
10	9.471	7.722	7.360	7.024	6.710	6.418	6.145
20	18.046	12.462	11.470	10.594	9.818	9.129	8.514
30	25.808	15.372	13.765	12.409	11.258	10.274	9.427

The table of present value annuity factors shows the present value of €1 for different numbers of years and different interest rates. To locate the desired PV annuity factor, find the row for the appropriate number of years and the column for the proper interest rate.

factors. Exhibit 6.4 contains some entries from such a table, and a more complete set of tables can be found in Appendix A. The annuity table shows the present value of a stream of cash flows that equals €1 a year for n years at different interest rates. Looking at the exhibit, we find that the value for a three-year annuity factor at 8% is 2.577, which agrees with our previous calculations.

Learning by Doing Application 6.4

Computing a PV Annuity Factor

Problem: Compute the PV annuity factor for 30 years at a 10% interest rate.

Approach: First, we calculate the present value factor at 10% for 30 years. Then, using this value, we calculate the PV annuity factor.

Solution:

$$\text{Present value factor} = \frac{1}{(1+i)^n}$$

$$= \frac{1}{(1.10)^{30}}$$

$$= \frac{1}{17.44941} = 0.0573$$

Then, using this value, we calculate the PV annuity factor:

$$PV \text{ annuity factor} = \frac{1 - \text{Present value factor}}{i}$$

$$= \frac{1 - 0.0573}{0.10}$$

$$= \frac{0.9427}{0.10} = 9.427$$

The answer matches the number in Exhibit 6.4.

Fortunately, no one in business today calculates the present value of an annuity by hand or uses annuity tables. We worked through the tedious calculations to show where the numbers come from and how the calculations are made. Generally, analysts use financial calculators or spreadsheet programs.[2]

Finding Monthly or Yearly Payments

A very common problem in finance is determining the payment schedule for a loan on a consumer asset, such as a car or a home that was purchased on credit. Nearly all consumer credit loans call for equal monthly payments. Suppose, for example, that you have just purchased a €450 000 apartment in Stuttgart. You were able to put €50 000 down and obtain a 30-year fixed-rate mortgage at 6.125% for the balance. What are your monthly payments?

In this problem we know the present value of the annuity. It is €400 000, the price of the apartment less the down payment (€450 000 – €50 000). We also know the number of payments; since the payments will be made monthly for 30 years, you will make 360 payments (12 months × 30 years). Because the payments are monthly, both the interest rate and maturity must be expressed in monthly terms. For consumer loans, to get the monthly interest rate, we divide the annual interest rate by 12. Thus, the monthly interest rate equals 0.51042% (6.125%/12 months). What we need to calculate is the monthly cash payments (CF) over the loan period. The time line looks as follows:

```
0        1        2        3              360 month
|  0.51042%  |        |        |    /\       |
€400 000   CF_1     CF_2     CF_3    \/    CF_360
```

To find CF (remember that $CF_1 = CF_2 = \cdots = CF_{360} = CF$), we use Equation (6.1). We need to make two preliminary calculations.

1. First, we calculate the present value factor for 360 months at 0.51042% per month (or, in decimal form, 0.0051042):

$$\text{Present value factor} = \frac{1}{(1+i)^n}$$

$$= \frac{1}{(1.0051042)^{360}}$$

$$= \frac{1}{6.25160595}$$

$$= 0.1599589$$

2. Next, we solve for the PV annuity factor:

$$PV \text{ annuity factor} = \frac{1 - \text{Present value factor}}{i}$$

$$= \frac{1 - 0.1599589}{0.0051042}$$

$$= \frac{0.8400411}{0.0051042} = 164.578406$$

We can now plug all the data into Equation (6.1) and solve it for CF:

$$PVA_n = CF \times PV \text{ annuity factor}$$

$$€400\,000 = CF \times 164.578406$$

$$CF = \frac{€400\,000}{164.578406}$$

$$CF = €2430.45$$

Your mortgage payments will be about €2430.45 per month.

Learning by Doing Application 6.5

What are your Monthly Car Payments?

Problem: You have decided to buy a new car and the dealer's best price is €16 000. The dealer agrees to provide financing with a five-year auto loan at 12% interest.

Approach: All the problem data must be converted to monthly terms. The number of periods is 60 months (5 years × 12 months per year), and the monthly interest charge is 1% (12%/12 months). The time line for the car purchase is as follows:

First, we calculate the present value factor at 1% for 60 months. Then, using this value, we calculate the PV annuity factor.

Solution:: Step 1. Calculate the present value factor:

$$\text{Present value factor} = \frac{1}{(1+i)^n}$$
$$= \frac{1}{(1.01)^{60}}$$
$$= \frac{1}{1.8166967} = 0.55045$$

Step 2. Calculate the present value annuity factor:

$$\text{PV annuity factor} = \frac{1 - \text{Present value factor}}{i}$$
$$= \frac{1 - 0.55045}{0.0051042}$$
$$= \frac{0.44955}{0.01} = 44.955$$

Step 3. Calculate the payment on the car loan:

$$\text{PVA}_n = \text{CF} \times \text{PV annuity factor}$$
$$€16\,000 = \text{CF} \times 44.955$$
$$\text{CF} = \frac{€16\,000}{44.955} = €355.91$$

Preparing a Loan Amortisation Schedule

Once you understand how to calculate a monthly or yearly loan payment, you have all of the tools that you need to prepare a loan amortisation schedule. The term *amortisation* describes the way in which the principal (the amount borrowed) is repaid over the life of a loan. With an amortising loan, some portion of each month's loan payment goes to paying down the principal. When the final loan payment is made, the unpaid principal is reduced to zero and the loan is paid off. The other portion of each loan payment is interest, which is payment for the use of outstanding principal (the amount of money still owed). Thus, with an **amortising loan,** each loan payment contains some repayment of principal and an interest payment. Nearly all loans to consumers are amortising loans.

Amortising loan

a loan for which each loan payment contains repayment of some principal and a payment of interest that is based on the remaining principal to be repaid

Amortisation schedule

with regard to a loan, a table that shows the loan balance at the beginning and end of each period, the payment made during that period and how much of that payment represents interest and how much represents repayment of principal

A loan **amortisation schedule** is just a table that shows the loan balance at the beginning and end of each period, the payment made during that period, and how much of that payment represents interest and how much represents repayment of principal. To see how an amortisation schedule is prepared, consider an example. Suppose that you have just borrowed €10 000 at a 5% interest rate from a bank to purchase a car. Typically, you would make monthly payments on such a loan. For simplicity, however, we will assume that the bank allows you to make annual payments and that the loan will be repaid over five years. Exhibit 6.5 shows the amortisation schedule for this loan.

EXHIBIT 6.5

AMORTISATION TABLE FOR A 5-YEAR LOAN AT 5% INTEREST

Year	(1) Beginning Balance	(2) Total Annual Payment[a]	(3) Interest Paid[b]	(4) Principal Paid (2) – (3)	(5) Ending Balance (1) – (4)
1	€10 000.00	€2 309.75	€500.00	€1 809.75	€8 190.25
2	8 190.25	2 309.75	409.51	1 900.24	6 290.02
3	6 290.02	2 309.75	314.50	1 995.25	4 294.77
4	4 294.77	2 309.75	214.74	2 095.01	2 199.76
5	2 199.76	2 309.75	109.99	2 199.76	0.00

[a]The total annual payment is calculated using the formula for the present value of an annuity, Equation (6.1). The total annual payment is CF in $PVA_n = CF \times PV$ annuity factor.
[b]Interest paid equals the beginning balance times the interest rate.

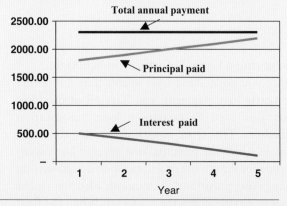

A loan amortisation table shows how regular payments of principal and interest are applied to repay a loan. The exhibit is an amortisation table for a five-year €10 000 loan with an interest rate of 5% and annual payments of €2309.75. Notice that the interest paid declines with each payment while the principal paid increases. These relations are illustrated in the pullout graphic in the exhibit.

To prepare a loan amortisation schedule, we must first compute the loan payment. Since for consumer loans, the amount of the loan payment is fixed, all the payments are identical in amount. Applying Equation (6.1) and noting from Exhibit 6.4 that the PV annuity factor for five years at 5% is 4.329, we calculate as follows:

$$PVA_n = CF \times \text{Annuity factor}$$
$$€10\,000 = CF \times 4.329$$
$$CF = \frac{€10\,000}{4.329} = €2310.00 \text{ per year}$$

Turning to Exhibit 6.5, we can work through the amortisation schedule to see how the table is prepared. For the first year, the values are determined as follows:

1. The amount borrowed, or the beginning principal balance, is €10 000.
2. The annual loan payment, as calculated earlier, is €2309.75.
3. The interest payment for the first year is €500 and is calculated as follows:

$$\text{Interest payment} = i \times P_0$$
$$= 0.05 \times €10\,000$$
$$= €500$$

4. The principal paid for the year is €1809.75, calculated as follows:

$$\text{Principal paid}$$
$$= \text{Loan payment} - \text{Interest payment}$$
$$= €2309.75 - €500$$
$$= €1809.75$$

5. The ending principal balance is €8190.25, computed as follows:

$$\text{Ending principal balance}$$
$$= \text{Beginning principal balance} - \text{Principal paid}$$
$$= €10\,000 - €1809.75$$
$$= €8190.25$$

Note that the ending principal balance for the first year (€8190.25) becomes the beginning principal balance for the second year (€8190.25), which in turn is used in calculating the interest payment for the second year:

$$\text{Interest payment} = i \times P_0$$
$$= 0.05 \times €8190.25$$
$$= €409.51$$

This calculation makes sense because each loan payment includes some principal repayment. This is why the interest in column 3 declines each year. We repeat the calculations until the loan is fully amortised, at which point the principal balance goes to zero and the loan is paid off.

If you are preparing an amortisation table for monthly payments, of course, all of your principal balances, loan payments and interest rates must be adjusted to a monthly basis. For example, to calculate monthly payments for our car loan, we would make the following adjustments: $n = 60$ payments (12 months per year × 5 years), $i = 0.4167\%$ (5%/12 months per year) and monthly payment = €188.71.

An interesting characteristic of amortised loans is the breakdown between the payment of interest and the repayment of principal in each loan payment. In the early years of a loan, interest payments are at their peak because very little principal has been repaid (see column 1). Near the end of the loan contract, when most of the principal has been paid off, payments to principal are at their peak, and interest payments have become smaller. Thus, as a loan is gradually paid off, the proportion of a monthly payment devoted to interest steadily declines, while the proportion used to reduce the principal steadily increases. The final loan payment repays just enough principal to pay off the loan in full.

Finally, the separation between interest and principal payments is also important for tax purposes. In some countries, individuals can deduct interest on a home mortgage for their principal residence against their income before paying tax. For corporations, interest expense is tax deductible.

USING EXCEL

Loan Amortisation Table

Loan amortisation tables are most easily constructed using a spreadsheet program. Here, we have reconstructed the loan amortisation table shown in Exhibit 6.5 using Excel.

	A	B	C	D	E	F	G	H	I	J	K	L	M
1													
2						Loan Amortisation Table							
3													
4		Loan amount		€ 10,000									
5		Interest rate		0.05									
6		Loan period		5									
7		PMT		€ 2,309.75									
8													
9		Year		Beginning Balance		Total Annual Payment		Simple Interest Paid		Principal Paid		Ending Balance	
10		1		€ 10,000.00		€ 2,309.75		€ 500.00		€ 1,809.75		€ 8,190.25	
11		2		8,190.25		2,309.75		409.51		1,900.24		6,290.02	
12		3		6,290.02		2,309.75		314.50		1,995.25		4,294.77	
13		4		4,294.77		2,309.75		214.74		2,095.01		2,199.76	
14		5		2,199.76		2,309.75		109.99		2,199.76		0.00	
15													
16	Corresponding formulas:												
17													
18		Payment:		=PMT(D5, D6, -D4)									
19													
20		Year		Beginning Balance		Total Annual Payment		Simple Interest Paid		Principal Paid		Ending Balance	
21		1		=D4		=$D$7		=D10*$D$5		=F10-H10		=D10-J10	
22		2		=L10		=$D$7		=D11*$D$5		=F11-H11		=D11-J11	
23		3		=L11		=$D$7		=D12*$D$5		=F12-H12		=D12-J12	
24		4		=L12		=$D$7		=D13*$D$5		=F13-H13		=D13-J13	
25		5		=L13		=$D$7		=D14*$D$5		=F14-H14		=D14-J14	
26													
27													

Notice that all the values in the amortisation table are obtained by using formulas. Once you have built an amortisation table like this one, you can change any of the input variables, such as the loan amount, and all of the other numbers will be updated automatically.

Finding the Interest Rate

Another important calculation in finance is determining the interest, or discount, rate for an annuity. The interest rate tells us the rate of return on an annuity contract. For example, suppose your parents are getting ready to retire and decide to convert some of their retirement portfolio, which is invested in the stock market, into an annuity that guarantees them a fixed annual income. Their insurance agent asks for €350 000 for an annuity that guarantees to pay them €50 000 a year for 10 years. What is the rate of return on the annuity?

As we did when we found the payment amount, we can insert these values into Equation (6.1):

$$PVA_n = CF \times \frac{1 - 1/(1+i)^n}{i}$$

$$€350\,000 = €50\,000 \times \frac{1 - 1/(1+i)^{10}}{i}$$

To determine the rate of return for the annuity, we need to solve the equation for the unknown value i. Unfortunately, it is not possible to solve the resulting equation for i algebraically. The only way to solve the problem is by trial and error. We can also get a close approximation by the intelligent use of interpolation. However, we normally solve this kind of problem using a financial calculator or computer spreadsheet program that finds the solution for us. However, it is important to understand how the solution is arrived at by trial and error, so we will work this problem without such aids.

To start the process, we must select an initial value for i, plug it into the right-hand side of the equation, and solve the equation to see if the present value of the annuity stream equals €350 000, which is the left-hand side of the equation. If the present value of the annuity is too large (PVA > €350 000), we need to select a higher value for i. If the present value of the annuity stream is too small (PVA < €350 000), we need to select a smaller value. We continue the trial-and-error process until we find the value for i at which PVA = €350 000.

The key to getting started is to make the best guess we can as to the possible value of the interest rate given the information and data available to us. We will assume that the current bank savings rate is 4%. Since the annuity rate of return should exceed the bank rate, we will start our calculations with a 5% discount rate. The present value of the annuity is:

$$PVA_{5\%} = €50\,000 \times \frac{1 - 1/(1 + 0.05)^{10}}{0.05}$$
$$= €50\,000 \times 7.222$$
$$= €386\,100$$

That is a pretty good first guess, but our present value is greater than €350 000, so we need to try a higher discount rate.[3] We will try 7%:

$$PVA_{7\%} = €50\,000 \times \frac{1 - 1/(1 + 0.07)^{10}}{0.07}$$
$$= €50\,000 \times 7.024$$
$$= €351\,200$$

The present value of the annuity is still slightly higher than €350 000, so we still need a larger value of i. How about 7.10%:

$$PVA_{7.10\%} = €50\,000 \times \frac{1 - 1/(1 + 0.071)^{10}}{0.071}$$
$$= €50\,000 \times 6.991$$
$$= €349\,550$$

The value is too small, but we now know that i is between 7.00% and 7.10%. On the next try, we need to use a slightly smaller value of i – say, 7.07%:

$$PVA_{7.07\%} = €50\,000 \times \frac{1 - 1/(1 + 0.0707)^{10}}{0.0707}$$
$$= €50\,000 \times 7.001$$
$$= €350\,050$$

Since this value is slightly too high, we should try a number for i that is only slightly greater than 7.07%. We will try 7.073%:

$$PVA_{7.073\%} = €50\,000 \times \frac{1 - 1/(1 + 0.07073)^{10}}{0.07073}$$
$$= €50\,000 \times 7.000$$
$$= €350\,000$$

The cost of the annuity, €350 000, is now exactly the same as the present value of the annuity stream (€350 000); thus, 7.073% is the rate of return earned by the annuity.

It typically takes many more guesses to solve for the interest rate than it did in this example. Our 'guesses' were good because we knew the answer before we started guessing! Clearly, solving for i by trial and error can be a long and tedious process. Fortunately, as mentioned, these types of problems are easily solved with a financial calculator or computer spreadsheet program.

We can get a close approximation to the correct interest rate by interpolation of the values if we assume there is a linear relationship between value and the discount rate. From our earlier calculations, we have the following values for the trials:

Interest Rate	Value
7.10%	€349 550
?	€350 000
7.00%	€351 200
5.00%	€386 100

A simple linear interpolation indicates that the correct discount rate lies somewhere between 7.00% and 7.10% as shown in the following diagram:

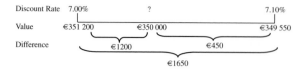

The value difference for the annuity between the interest rates of 7.00% and 7.10% is €1650 (€351 200 – €349 550). At 7.00%, the value of the annuity is €351 200, which is €1200 too much. So using linear interpolation, we want to adjust the value difference by €1200/€1650 to get the correct value of €350 000. To do this we need to raise the interest rate somewhat – to somewhere between 7.00% and 7.10% (that is, by less than 0.10%). We can apply a formula for estimating the discount rate or interest rate via interpolation:

$$i_{unknown} = i_{low} + \frac{(Value_{low\,i} - Value_{unknown\,i})}{(Value_{low\,i} - Value_{high\,i})}$$
$$\times (i_{high} - i_{low}) \qquad (6.2)$$

where:

$Value_{low\,i}$ = value for the annuity at the low discount rate or interest rate

$Value_{high\,i}$ = value for the annuity at the high discount rate or interest rate

i_{low} = lower discount rate or interest rate used for the interpolation

i_{high} = higher discount rate or interest rate used for the interpolation

$i_{unknown}$ = discount rate or interest rate derived from the interpolation

Using the above, we can calculate the proportions between the two estimated values for the present value of the annuity and the actual present value of the annuity, using the following formula:

$$i = 7.00\% + \frac{(€351\,200 - €350\,000)}{(€351\,200 - €349\,550)}$$
$$\times (7.10\% - 7.00\%)$$
$$= 7.00\% + \frac{€1200}{€1650} \times 0.10\%$$
$$= 7.00\% + 0.7273 \times 0.10\%$$
$$= 7.00\% + 0.0727\% = 7.073\%$$

To two decimal places, this is the same as the solution we derived earlier. Note the accuracy of the method relies on having values close to the target value since, as is shown in Chapter 5, the relationship between the interest rate and present value is curved and not linear. We ignore this curvature when we interpolate the interest rate. For instance, if we had used the value for 5.0%, we would have got a less accurate interpolation of the interest rate:

$$i = 5.00\% + \frac{(€386\,100 - €350\,000)}{(€386\,100 - €349\,550)}$$
$$\times (7.10\% - 5.00\%)$$
$$= 5.00\% + \frac{€36\,100}{€36\,550} \times 2.10\%$$
$$= 5.00\% + 0.9877 \times 2.10\%$$
$$= 5.00\% + 2.074\% = 7.074\%$$

Return on Investments: Good Deal or Bad?

Problem: With some business opportunities you know the price of a financial contract and the promised cash flows and you want to calculate the interest rate or rate of return on the investment. For example, suppose you have a chance to invest in a small business. The owner wants to borrow €200 000 from you for five years and will make yearly payments of €60 000 at the end of each year. Similar types of investment opportunities will pay 5%. Is this a good investment opportunity?

Approach: First, we draw a time line for this situation:

```
 0        1        2        3        4      5 Year
 |   i=?  |        |        |        |        |
-€200 000 €60 000  €60 000  €60 000  €60 000  €60 000
```

To compute the rate of return on the investment, we need to compute the interest rate that equates the initial investment of €200 000 to the present value of the promised cash flows of €60 000 per year. We can use the trial-and-error approach with Equation (6.1), a financial calculator or a spreadsheet program to solve this problem. Here we will use trial and error.

Solution: The value we want for the annuity factor will be 3.333 (that is, €200 000/ €60 000 = annuity factor). This implies an interest rate well above 5%, where the annuity factor would be 4.329 as shown in Exhibit 6.4. A value of 3.333 is above 10% and close to 15%. We will start with this interest rate:

$$PVA_{15\%} = €200\,000 \times \frac{1 - 1/(1 + 0.15)^5}{0.15}$$
$$= €60\,000 \times 3.352$$
$$= €201\,129$$

Not a bad first try. As the value is too high, we need to raise the interest rate. At 15.5%, we have:

$$PVA_{15.5\%} = €200\,000 \times \frac{1 - 1/(1 + 0.155)^5}{0.155}$$
$$= €60\,000 \times 3.313$$
$$= €198\,771$$

Now we are too low. If we split the difference and choose 15.25%, we get:

$$PVA_{15.25\%} = €200\,000 \times \frac{1 - 1/(1 + 0.155)^5}{0.155}$$
$$= €60\,000 \times 3.332$$
$$= €199\,945$$

We are nearly there. The interest rate is still slightly too high. If we reduce it slightly to 15.23%:

$$PVA_{15.23\%} = €200\,000 \times \frac{1 - 1/(1 + 0.153)^5}{0.153}$$
$$= €60\,000 \times 3.334$$
$$= €200\,039$$

The return on this investment is 15.23%, well above the market interest rate of 5%. It is a good investment opportunity.

Decision-Making Example 6.2

The Pizza Dough Machine

Problem: As the owner of the pizza restaurant, you are considering whether to buy a fully automated pizza dough preparation machine. Your staff are wildly supportive of the purchase because it would eliminate a tedious part of their work. Your accountant provides you with the following information:

- The cost, including shipping, for the Italian Pizza Dough Machine is €25 000.
- Cash savings, including labour, raw materials and tax savings due to depreciation, are €3500 per year for 10 years.
- The present value of cash savings is €21 506 at a 10% discount rate.[4]

Given the above data, what should you do?

Decision: As you arrive at the pizza restaurant in the morning, the staff is in a festive mood because word has leaked out that the new machine will save the shop €35 000 and only cost €25 000.

With a heavy heart, you explain that the analysis done by some of the staff is incorrect. To make economic decisions involving cash flows, even for a small business such as your pizza restaurant, you cannot compare cash values from different time periods unless they are adjusted for the time value of money. The present value formula takes into account the time value of money and converts the future cash flows into current money present values. The cost of the machine is already in current money.

The correct analysis is as follows: the machine costs €25 000 and the present value of the cost savings is €21 506. Thus, the cost of the machine exceeds the benefits; the correct decision is not to buy the new dough preparation machine.

Future Value of an Annuity

Generally, when we are working with annuities, we are interested in computing their present value. On occasion, though, we need to compute the **future value of an annuity** (FVA). Such computations typically involve some type of saving activity, such as a monthly savings plan. Another application is computing terminal values for retirement or pension plans with constant contributions.

> ### Future value of an annuity (FVA)
>
> the value of an annuity at some point in the future

We will start with a simple example. Suppose that you plan to save €1000 at the end of every year for four years with the goal of buying a racing bicycle. The bicycle you want is an Orbea Orca, a top-of-the-line Spanish racing bicycle that costs around €4500. The bicycle has a carbon frame and forks, is fitted with Shimano Dura Ace components and weighs 7.2 kilos. If your bank pays 8% interest a year, will you have enough money to buy the bicycle at the end of four years?

To solve this problem, we can first lay out the cash flows on a time line, as we discussed earlier in this chapter. We can then calculate the future value for each cash flow using Equation (5.1), which is $FV_n = PV \times (1 + i)^n$. Finally, we can add up all the cash flows. The time line and calculations are shown in Exhibit 6.6. Given that the total future value of the four payments is €4506.11, as shown in the exhibit, you should have enough money to buy the bike.

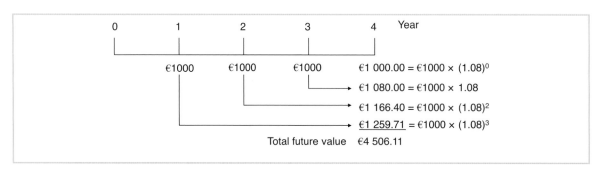

Exhibit 6.6: Future Value of a Four-Year Annuity: Orbea Orca Bicycle The exhibit shows a time line for a savings plan to buy an Orbea bicycle. Under the savings plan, €1000 is invested at the end of each year for four years at an annual interest rate of 8%. We find the value at the end of the four-year period by adding the future values of the separate cash flows, just as in Exhibits 6.1 and 6.2

Future Value of Annuity Equations

Of course, most business applications involve longer periods of time than the Orbea bicycle example. One way to solve more complex problems involving the future value of an annuity is first to calculate the present value of the annuity, PVA, using Equation (6.1) and then to use Equation (5.1) to calculate the future value of the PVA. In practice, many analyses condense this calculation into a single step by using the future value of annuity (FVA) formula, which we obtain by substituting PVA for PV in Equation (5.1).

$$FVA_n = PVA_n \times (1+i)^n$$

$$= \frac{CF}{i} \times \left[1 - \frac{1}{(1+i)^n}\right] \times (1+i)^n \qquad (6.3)$$

$$= CF \times \frac{(1+i)^n - 1}{i}$$

where:

FVA_n = future value of an annuity at the end of n periods

PVA_n = present value of an n-period annuity

CF = level and equally spaced cash flow

i = discount rate, or interest rate

n = number of periods

We can rearrange Equation (6.3) to write it in terms of the future value factor and the FV annuity factor:

$$FVA_n = CF \times \frac{(1+i)^n - 1}{i}$$

$$= CF \times \frac{\text{Future value factor} - 1}{i}$$

$$= CF \times \text{FV annuity factor}$$

As you would expect, there are tables listing FV annuity factors. Appendix A includes a table that shows the value of a €1 annuity for various interest rates and maturities.

Using Equation (6.3) to compute FVA for the Orbea bicycle problem is straightforward. The calculation and process are similar to those we developed for PVA problems. That is, we first calculate the FV annuity factor for four

years at 8%:

$$\text{Future value factor} = (1+i)^n = 1.36049$$

$$\text{FV annuity factor} = \frac{\text{Future value factor} - 1}{i}$$

$$= \frac{1.36049 - 1}{0.08} = 4.5061$$

Now we can compute the future value of the annuity by multiplying the constant cash flow (CF) by the FV annuity factor. We plug our computed values into the equation:

$$FVA_n = CF \times \text{FV annuity factor}$$
$$= €1000 \times 4.5061 = €4506.10$$

This value differs slightly from the one we calculated in Exhibit 6.6 because of rounding.

Perpetuities

A perpetuity is a constant stream of cash flows that goes on forever. Perpetuities in the form of bonds were used by the British Government to pay off the debt incurred by the government to finance the Napoleonic wars. These perpetual bonds, called *consols*, have no maturity date and are still traded in the international bond markets today.

The most important perpetuities in the securities markets today are preference share issues. The issuer of preference shares promises to pay investors a fixed dividend forever unless a retirement date for the preference shares has been set. If preference share dividends are not paid, all previous unpaid dividends must be repaid before any dividends are paid to ordinary shareholders. This preferential treatment is one source of the term *preference* shares.

From Equation (6.1), we can calculate the present value of a perpetuity by setting n, which is the number of periods, equal to infinity.[5] When that is done, the value of the term approaches 0, and thus:

$$PVA_\infty = \frac{CF}{i} \times \left[1 - \frac{1}{(1+i)^\infty}\right]$$

$$= \frac{CF}{i} \times [1 - 0] \qquad (6.4)$$

$$= \frac{CF}{i}$$

As you can see, the present value of a perpetuity is the promised constant cash payment (CF) divided by the interest rate (*i*). A nice feature of the final equation is that it is algebraically very simple to work with, since it allows us to solve for *i* directly rather than by trial and error, as is required with Equations (6.1) and (6.3).

For example, suppose you had a great experience during university at the business school and decided to endow a chair in finance. Endowed chairs provide salary and research support for top faculty.[6] The goal of the chair is to provide the chair holder with €100 000 of additional financial support per year forever. If the rate of interest is 8%, how much money will you have to give the university foundation to provide the desired level of support? Using Equation (6.4), we find that the present value of the perpetuity is:

$$PVA_\infty = \frac{CF}{i} = \frac{€100\,000}{0.08} = €1\,250\,000$$

Thus, a gift of €1.25 million will provide a constant annual payment of €100 000 to the chair holder forever.

There are two subtleties here that you should note. First, as mentioned earlier, the present value formula assumes that cash flows are paid at the end of the year. If our worthy chair holder needs to be paid when the chair is awarded, the donor would have to provide the university with an additional €100 000. Thus, the total gift would be €1.35 million. Note that the €100 000 is already in present value terms, so it can be added to the €1.25 million, which has been converted into present value terms. Second, in our problem, no adjustment was made for inflation. If the economy is expected to experience inflation, which is generally the case, the chair holder's purchasing power will decline each year.

Learning by Doing Application 6.7

Preference Share Dividends

Problem: Suppose that you are the CEO of a public company and your investment banker recommends that you issue some preference shares at €50 per share. Similar preference share issues are yielding 6%. What annual cash dividend does the firm need to offer to be competitive in the marketplace? In other words, what cash dividend paid annually forever would be worth €50 with a 6% discount rate?

Approach: As we have already mentioned, preference shares are a type of perpetuity; thus, we can solve this problem by applying Equation (6.3). As usual, we begin by laying out the time line for the cash flows:

For preference shares, the value is €50 per share. The discount rate is 6%. CF is the fixed-rate cash dividend, which is the unknown value. Knowing all this information, we can use Equation (6.4) and solve for CF.

Solution:

$$PVA_\infty = \frac{CF}{i}$$
$$CF = PVA_\infty \times i$$
$$= €50 \times 0.06$$
$$= €3$$

The annual dividend on the preference shares would be €3 per share.

Annuities Due

So far we have discussed only annuities whose cash flow payments occur at the end of the period, so-called ordinary annuities. Another type of annuity that is fairly common in business is known as an **annuity due**. Here, cash payments start immediately, at the beginning of the first period. For example, when you rent an apartment, the first rent payment is typically due immediately. The second rent payment is due the first of the second month, and so on. In this kind of payment pattern, you are effectively prepaying for the service.

> **Annuity due**
>
> an annuity in which payments are made at the beginning of each period

> **WEB**
>
> More examples concerning topics discussed in this chapter can be found at Modlin.org: www.modlin.org/L1ModVidDemo.htm.

Exhibit 6.7 compares the cash flows for an ordinary annuity and an annuity due. Note that both annuities are made up of four €1000 cash flows and carry an 8% interest rate. Part A shows an ordinary annuity, in which the cash flows take place at the end of the period, and part B shows an annuity due, in which the cash flows take place at the beginning of the period. There are several ways to calculate the present and future values of an annuity due, and we discuss them next.

Present Value Method

One way to compute the present value of an annuity due is to discount each individual cash flow to the present, as shown in Exhibit 6.7B. Note that since the first €1000 cash flow takes place at the current time ($t = 0$), the cash flow is already in present value terms. The present value of the cash flows is €3577.

Compare this present value with the present value of the ordinary annuity, €3312, as calculated in Exhibit 6.7A. It should be no surprise that the present value of the annuity due is larger than the present value of the ordinary annuity (€3577 > €3312), even though both annuities have four €1000 cash flows. The reason is that the cash flows of the annuity due are shifted forward one year and, thus, are discounted less.

Annuity Transformation Method

An easier way to work annuity due problems is to transform our formula for the present value of an annuity [Equation (6.1)] so that it will work for annuity due problems. To do this, we pretend that each cash flow occurs at the end of the period (although it actually occurs at the beginning of the period) and use Equation (6.1). Since Equation (6.1) discounts each cash flow by one period too many, we then correct for the extra discounting by multiplying our answer by $(1 + i)$, where i is the discount rate or interest rate.

The relation between an ordinary annuity and an annuity due can be formally expressed as:

$$\text{Annuity due value} = \text{Ordinary annuity value} \times (1 + i) \qquad (6.5)$$

This relation is especially helpful because it works for both present value and future value calculations. Calculating the value of an annuity due using Equation (6.5) involves three steps:

1. Adjust the problem time line as if the cash flows were an ordinary annuity.
2. Calculate the present or future value as though the cash flows were an ordinary annuity.
3. Finally, multiply the answer by $(1 + i)$.

Let us calculate the value of the annuity due shown in Exhibit 6.7B using Equation (6.5), the transformation technique. First, we restate the time line as if the problem were an ordinary annuity; the revised time line looks like the one in Exhibit 6.7A. Second, we calculate the present value of the annuity as if the problem involved an ordinary

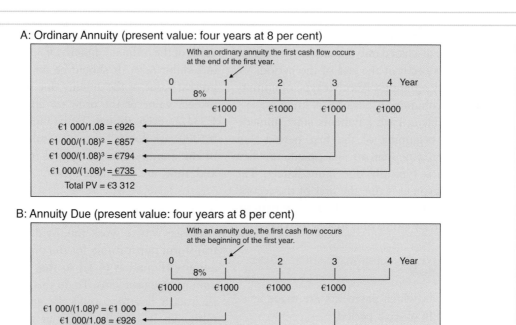

Exhibit 6.7: Ordinary Annuity versus Annuity Due The difference between an ordinary annuity (part A) and an annuity due (part B) is that with an ordinary annuity, the cash flows take place at the end of the period, while with an annuity due, the cash flows take place at the beginning of each period. As you can see in this example, the PV of the annuity due is larger than the PV of the ordinary annuity. The reason is that the cash flows of the annuity due are shifted by one year and thus are discounted less.

annuity. The value of the ordinary annuity is €3312, as shown in part A of the exhibit. Finally, we use Equation (6.5) to make the adjustment to an annuity due:

$$\begin{aligned}\text{Annuity due value} &= \text{Ordinary annuity value} \\ &\quad \times (1+i) \\ &= €3312 \times 1.08 \\ &= €3577\end{aligned}$$

As they should, the answers for the two methods of calculation agree.

Before You Go On

1. How do an ordinary annuity, an annuity due and a perpetuity differ?
2. Give two examples of perpetuities.

3. What is the annuity transformation method?

CASH FLOWS THAT GROW AT A CONSTANT RATE

Learning Objective 3

Explain what a perpetuity is and how it is used in business and be able to calculate the value of a perpetuity.

So far, we have been examining level cash flow streams. Often, though, management needs to value a cash flow stream that increases at a constant rate over time. These cash flow streams are called growing annuities or growing perpetuities.

Growing Annuity

Financial managers often need to compute the value of multiyear product or service contracts with cash flows that increase each year at a constant rate. These are called **growing annuities**. For example, you may want to value the cost of a 25-year lease that adjusts annually for the expected rate of inflation over the life of the contract. Equation (6.5) can be used to compute the present value of an annuity growing at a constant rate for a finite time period:

$$PVA_n = \frac{CF_1}{i - g} \times \left[1 - \left(\frac{1+g}{1+i} \right)^n \right] \qquad (6.6)$$

where:

PVA_n = present value of a growing annuity with n periods

CF_1 = cash flow one period in the future $(t = 1)$

i = interest rate, or discount rate

g = constant growth rate per period

> ### Growing annuity
>
> an annuity in which the cash flows increase at a constant rate

You should be aware of several important points when applying Equation (6.6). First, the cash flow (CF_1) used is not the cash flow for the current period (CF_0), but is the cash flow to be received in the next period $(t = 1)$. The relation between these two cash flows is $CF_1 = CF_0 \times (1 + g)$. Second, a necessary condition for using Equation (6.6) is that $i > g$. If this condition is not met, the calculations from the equation will be meaningless, as you will get a negative value for positive cash flows. A negative value essentially says that someone would have to pay you money to get you to accept a positive cash flow.

As an example of how Equation (6.6) is applied, suppose you work for a company that owns a number of coffee shops in the city and areas around Berlin. One coffee shop is located in the Tiergaten and your boss wants to know how much it is worth. The coffee shop has a 50-year lease, so we will assume that it will be in business for 50 years. It produced cash flows of €300 000 after all expenses this year, and the discount rate used by similar businesses is 15%. You estimate that, over the long term, cash flows will grow at 2.5% per year because of inflation. Thus, you calculate that the coffee shop's cash flow next year (CF_1) will be €307 500, or €300 000 × (1 + 0.025).

Plugging the values from the coffee shop example into Equation (6.6) yields the following result:

$$PVA_n = \frac{€307\,500}{0.15 - 0.025} \times \left[1 - \left(\frac{1.025}{1.15} \right)^{50} \right]$$

$$= €2\,460\,000 \times 0.9968$$

$$= €2\,452\,128$$

The estimated value of the coffee shop is €2 452 128.

Growing Perpetuity

Sometimes cash flows are expected to grow at a constant rate indefinitely. In this case the cash flow stream is called a **growing perpetuity**. The formula to compute the present value for a growing perpetuity is as follows:

$$PVA_\infty = \frac{CF_1}{i - g} \qquad (6.7)$$

As before, CF_1 is the cash flow occurring at the end of the first period, i is the discount rate and g is the constant rate of growth of the cash flow (CF). Equation (6.7) is an easy equation to work with and it is used widely in the valuation of ordinary shares for firms that have a policy and history of paying dividends that grow at a constant rate. It is also widely used in the valuation of entire companies, as we will discuss in Chapter 18.

> ### Growing perpetuity
>
> a cash flow stream that grows at a constant rate forever

Notice that we can easily derive Equation (6.7) from Equation (6.6) by setting n equal to ∞. If i is greater than g, as we said it must be, the term $[(1 + g)/(1 + i)]^{\infty}$ is equal to 0, leading to the following result:

$$PVA_{\infty} = \frac{CF_1}{i - g} \times \left[1 - \left(\frac{1 + g}{1 + i}\right)^{\infty}\right]$$

$$= \frac{CF_1}{i - g} \times [1 - 0]$$

$$= \frac{CF_1}{i - g}$$

This makes sense, of course, since Equation (6.6) describes a growing annuity and Equation (6.7) describes a growing cash flow stream that goes on forever. Notice that Equations (6.6) and (6.7) are exactly the same as Equations (6.1) and (6.4) when g equals zero.

To illustrate a growing perpetuity, we will consider an example. Suppose that you and a partner, after graduating from university, started a health and athletic club. Your concept included not only providing workout facilities, such as weights, treadmills and elliptical trainers, but also promoting a healthy lifestyle through a focus on cooking and nutrition. The concept has proved popular and after only five years you have seven clubs in operation. Your accountant reports that the firm's cash flow last year was €450 000 and the appropriate discount rate for the club is 18%. You expect the firm's cash flows to increase by 5% per year, which includes 2% for expected inflation. The business has no fixed life, so you can assume it will continue operating indefinitely into the future. What is the value of the firm?

We can use Equation (6.7) to solve this problem. Although the equation is very easy to use, a common mistake is using the current period's cash flow (CF_0) and not the *next* period's cash flow (CF_1). Since the cash flow is growing at a constant growth rate, g, we simply multiply CF_0 by $(1 + g)$ to get the value of CF_1. Thus,

$$CF_1 = CF_0 \times (1 + g)$$

We can then substitute the result into Equation (6.7), which yields a helpful variant of this equation:

$$PVA_{\infty} = \frac{CF_1}{i - g} = \frac{CF_0 \times (1 + g)}{i - g}$$

Now we can insert the values for the health club into the equation and solve for PVA_{∞}:

$$PVA_{\infty} = \frac{CF_0 \times (1 + g)}{i - g}$$

$$= \frac{€450\,000 \times (1 + 0.05)}{0.18 - 0.05}$$

$$= €3\,634\,615$$

The business is worth €3 634 615.

The growing annuity and perpetuity formulas are useful and we will be applying them later on in the book.

> ### Before You Go On
>
> 1. What is the difference between a growing annuity and a growing perpetuity?

THE EFFECTIVE ANNUAL INTEREST RATE

> ### Learning Objective 4
>
> Discuss growing annuities and perpetuities, as well as their application in business, and be able to calculate their value.

In this chapter and the preceding one, there has been little question about which interest rate to use in a particular computation. In most cases, a single interest rate was supplied. When working with real market data, however, the situation is not so clear-cut. We often encounter interest rates that can be computed in different ways. In this final section, we try to untangle some of the issues that can cause problems.

Why the Confusion?

To better understand why interest rates can be so confusing, consider a familiar situation. Suppose you borrow €100 on your bank credit card and plan to keep the balance outstanding for one year. The credit card's stated interest rate is 1% per month. In most countries, consumer protection laws mandate that lenders disclose the **annual percentage rate (APR)** charged on a loan. The APR is the annualised interest rate using *simple interest*. Thus, the APR is defined as the simple interest charged per period multiplied by the number of periods per year. For the bank credit card loan, the APR is 12% (1% per month × 12 months).

> ### Annual percentage rate (APR)
>
> the simple interest rate charged per period multiplied by the number of periods per year

At the end of the year, you go to pay off the credit card balance as planned. It seems reasonable to assume that with an APR of 12%, your credit card balance at the end of one year would be €112 (1.12 × €100). Wrong! The bank's *actual* interest rate is 1% per month, meaning that the bank will compound your credit card balance monthly, 12 times over the year. The bank's calculation for the balance due is €112.68 [€100 × $(1.01)^{12}$].[7] The bank is actually charging you 12.68% per year and the total interest paid for the one-year loan is €12.68 rather than €12.00. This example raises a question: What is the correct way to annualise an interest rate?

Calculating the Effective Annual Interest Rate

In making financial decisions, the correct way to annualise an interest rate is to compute the effective annual interest rate. The **effective annual interest rate (EAR)** is defined as the annual growth rate that takes compounding into account. Mathematically, the EAR can be stated as follows:

$$1 + \text{EAR} = \left(1 + \frac{\text{Quoted interest rate}}{m}\right)^{m}$$
$$\text{EAR} = \left(1 + \frac{\text{Quoted interest rate}}{m}\right)^{m} - 1$$

(6.8)

where m is the number of compounding periods during a year. The **quoted interest rate** is by definition a *simple* annual interest rate, like the APR. That means the quoted interest rate has been annualised by multiplying the rate per period by the number of periods per year. The EAR conversion formula accounts for the number of compounding periods and, thus, effectively adjusts the annualised quoted interest rate for the time value of money. Because the EAR is the true cost of borrowing and lending, it is the rate that should be used for making all finance decisions.

> ### Effective annual interest rate (EAR)
>
> the annual interest rate that reflects compounding within a year

> ### Quoted interest rate
>
> a simple annual interest rate, such as the APR

> ### WEB
>
> Many useful financial calculators, including an APR calculator, can be found at Efunda. com. Go to www.efunda.com/formulae/finance/apr_calculator.cfm.

We will use our bank credit card example to illustrate the use of Equation (6.8). Recall that the credit card has an APR of 12% (1% per month). The APR is the quoted interest rate, and the number of compounding periods (m) is 12. Applying Equation (6.8), we find that the effective annual interest rate is:

$$\text{EAR} = \left(1 + \frac{\text{Quoted interest rate}}{m}\right)^m - 1$$

$$= \left(1 + \frac{0.12}{12}\right)^{12} - 1$$

$$= (1.01)^{12} - 1$$

$$= 1.1268 - 1$$

$$= 0.1268, \text{ or } 12.68\%$$

The EAR value of 12.68% is the true cost of borrowing the €100 on the bank credit card for one year. The EAR calculation adjusts for the effects of compounding and, hence, the time value of money.

Finally, notice that interest rates are quoted in the marketplace in three ways:

1. *The quoted interest rate.* This is an interest rate that has been annualised by multiplying the rate per period by the number of compounding periods. The APR is an example. All consumer borrowing and lending rates are annualised in this manner.
2. *The interest rate per period.* The bank credit card rate of 1% per month is an example of this kind of rate. You can find the interest rate per period by dividing the quoted interest rate by the number of compounding periods.
3. *The effective annual interest rate (EAR).* This is the interest rate actually paid (or earned), which takes compounding into account. Sometimes it is difficult to distinguish a quoted rate from an EAR. Generally, however, an annualised consumer rate is an APR rather than an EAR.

Comparing Interest Rates

Sometimes when borrowing or lending money, it is necessary to compare and select among interest rate alternatives. Quoted interest rates are comparable when they cover the same overall time period, such as one year, and have the same number of compounding periods. If quoted interest rates are *not* comparable, we must adjust them to a common time period. The easiest way, and the correct way, to make interest rates comparable for making finance decisions is to convert them to effective annual interest rates. Consider an example.

Suppose you are the chief financial officer of a manufacturing company. The company is planning a €1 billion plant expansion and will finance it by borrowing money for five years. Three financial institutions have submitted interest rate quotes – all are APRs:

> Lender A: 10.40% compounded monthly
> Lender B: 10.90% compounded annually
> Lender C: 10.50% compounded quarterly

Although all the loans have the same maturity, the loans are not comparable because the APRs have different compounding periods. To make the adjustments for the different time periods, we apply Equation (6.8) to convert each of the APR quotes into an EAR:

$$\text{Lender A}: \text{EAR} = \left(1 + \frac{0.1040}{12}\right)^{12} - 1$$

$$= (1.0087)^{12} - 1$$

$$= 1.1091 - 1$$

$$= 0.1091, \text{ or } 10.91\%$$

$$\text{Lender B}: \text{EAR} = \left(1 + \frac{0.1090}{1}\right)^{1} - 1$$

$$= 1.1090 - 1$$

$$= 0.1090, \text{ or } 10.90\%$$

$$\text{Lender C}: \text{EAR} = \left(1 + \frac{0.1050}{4}\right)^{4} - 1$$

$$= (1.0087)^{4} - 1$$

$$= 1.1092 - 1$$

$$= 0.1092, \text{ or } 10.92\%$$

As shown, Lender B offers the lowest interest cost at 10.90%.

Notice the shift in rankings that takes place as a result of the EAR calculations. When we initially looked at the APR quotes, it appeared that Lender A offered the lowest rate and Lender B had the highest. After computing the EAR, we find that when we account for the effect of compounding, Lender B actually offers the lowest interest rate.

Another important point is that if all the interest rates are quoted as APRs with the same annualising period, such as monthly, the interest rates are comparable and you can select the correct rate by simply comparing the quotes. That is, the lowest APR corresponds to the lowest cost of funds. Thus, it is correct for borrowers or lenders to make economic decisions with APR data as long as interest rates have the same maturity and the same compounding period. To find the true cost of the loan, however, it is still necessary to compute the EAR.

What is the True Cost of a Loan?

Problem: During a period of economic expansion, Felipe Garcia became financially overextended and was forced to consolidate his debt with a loan from a consumer finance company. The consolidated debt provided Felipe with a single loan and lower monthly payments than he had previously been making. The loan agreement quotes an APR of 20% and Felipe must make monthly payments. What is the true cost of the loan?

Approach: The true cost of the loan is the EAR, not the APR. Thus, we must convert the quoted rate into the EAR, using Equation (6.8), to get the true cost of the loan.

Solution:

$$\text{EAR} = \left(1 + \frac{\text{Quoted interest rate}}{m}\right)^m - 1$$
$$= \left(1 + \frac{0.20}{12}\right)^{12} - 1$$
$$= (1 + 0.0167)^{12} - 1$$
$$= (1.0167)^{12} - 1$$
$$= 1.2194 - 1$$
$$= 0.2194, \text{ or } 21.94\%$$

The true cost of the loan is 21.94%, not the 20% APR.

Consumer Protection and Interest Rate Disclosure

For firms and consumers operating in member states of the European Union, the regulation of credit lending standards is governed by the Consumer Credit Directive 2008 that came into force in mid-2010. The directive represents an acknowledgement that consumer credit is still largely governed by national legislation and that the information provided to consumers varied considerably across countries. It harmonises existing practices and is designed to ensure that all borrowers receive meaningful information about the cost of credit so that they can make intelligent economic decisions on consumer loans, although secured loans such as home mortgage loans are not covered by the directive. The directive covers all unsecured credit agreements between €200 and €75 000 and prescribes the pre-contractual information and contractual information that must be given to consumers. In particular, it details the requirement for lenders to provide an EU-wide standardised APR.

From our earlier discussions, we know that the EAR, not the APR, represents the true economic interest rate. So why did the Consumer Credit Directive require that a standardised APR must be the disclosed rate? The APR was selected because it is easy to calculate and easy to understand. Down at the car showroom, salespeople need an easy way to explain and annualise the monthly interest charge and the APR provides just such a method. And most important, if all the auto lenders quoted a monthly APR, consumers could select the loan with the lowest economic interest cost.

Today, although lenders and borrowers are legally required to quote the APR, they run their businesses using interest rate calculations based on the present value and future value formulas. In some countries, consumers are bombarded with both APR and EAR rates – and confusion reigns. At the car dealership, for example, you may find that your auto loan's APR is 5% but the 'actual borrowing rate' is 5.12%. Because of confusion arising from conflicting interest rates in the marketplace, some observers believe that the APR calculation has outlived its usefulness and should be abandoned by regulators and replaced by the EAR.

The Appropriate Interest Rate Factor

Here is a final question to consider: What is the appropriate interest rate to use when making future or present value calculations? The answer is simple: use the EAR. Under no circumstance should the APR or any other quoted rate be used

as the interest rate in present or future value calculations. Consider an example of using the EAR in such a calculation.

Petra, an MBA student at Genoa University, has purchased a €100 savings note with a two-year maturity from a small consumer finance company. The contract states that the note has a 20% APR and pays interest quarterly. The quarterly interest rate is thus 5% (20%/4). Petra has several questions about the note: (1) What is the note's actual interest rate (EAR)? (2) How much money will she have at the end of two years? (3) When making the future value calculation, should she use the quarterly interest rate or the annual EAR?

To answer Petra's questions, we first compute the EAR, which is the actual interest earned on the note:

$$
\begin{aligned}
\text{EAR} &= \left(1 + \frac{\text{APR}}{m}\right)^m - 1 \\
&= \left(1 + \frac{0.20}{4}\right)^4 - 1 \\
&= (1 + 0.05)^4 - 1 \\
&= 1.21551 - 1 \\
&= 0.21551, \text{ or } 21.551\%
\end{aligned}
$$

Next, we calculate the future value of the note using the EAR. Because the EAR is an annual rate, for this problem we use a total of two compounding periods. The calculation is as follows:

$$
\begin{aligned}
\text{FV}_2 &= \text{PV} \times (1 + i)^n \\
&= €100 \times (1 + 0.21551)^2 \\
&= €100 \times 1.4775 \\
&= €147.75
\end{aligned}
$$

We can also calculate the future value using the quarterly rate of interest of 5% with a total of eight compounding periods. In this case, the calculation is as follows:

$$
\begin{aligned}
\text{FV}_2 &= €100 \times (1 + 0.050)^8 \\
&= €100 \times 1.4775 \\
&= €147.75
\end{aligned}
$$

The two calculation methods yield the same answer, €147.75.

In sum, any time you do a future value or present value calculation, you must use either the interest rate per period (quoted rate/*m*) or the EAR as the interest rate factor. It does not matter which of these you use. Both will properly account for the impact of compounding on the value of cash flows. Interest rate proxies such as the APR should never be used as interest rate factors for calculating future or present values. Because they do not properly account for the number of compounding periods, their use can lead to answers that are economically incorrect.

Before You Go On

1. What is the APR and why are lending institutions required to disclose this rate?
2. What is the correct way to annualise an interest rate in financial decision making?
3. Distinguish between quoted interest rate, interest rate per period and effective annual interest rate.

SUMMARY OF LEARNING OBJECTIVES

1. **Explain why cash flows occurring at different times must be adjusted to reflect their value as of a common date before they can be compared and be able to compute the present value and future value for multiple cash flows.**

   When making decisions involving cash flows over time, we should first identify the magnitude and timing of the cash flows and then adjust each individual cash flow to reflect its value as of a common date. For example, the process of discounting (compounding) the cash flows adjusts them for the time value of money because today's money is not equal in value to money in the future. Once all of the cash flows are in present (future) value terms, they can be compared to make decisions. We discuss the computation of present values and future values of multiple cash flows.

2. **Describe how to calculate the present value of an ordinary annuity and how an ordinary annuity differs from an annuity due.**

   An ordinary annuity is a series of equally spaced, level cash flows over time. The cash flows for an ordinary annuity are assumed to take place at the end of each period. To find the present value of an ordinary annuity, we multiply the present value of an annuity factor, which is equal to (1 − Present value factor)/*i*, by the amount of the constant cash flow. An annuity due is an annuity in which the cash flows occur at the beginning of each period. A lease is an example of an annuity due. In this case, we are effectively prepaying for the service. To calculate the value of an annuity due, we calculate the present value (or future value) as though the cash flows were an ordinary annuity. We then multiply the ordinary annuity value times (1 + *i*). We discuss the calculation of the present value of an ordinary annuity and annuity due.

3. **Explain what a perpetuity is and how it is used in business and be able to calculate the value of a perpetuity.**

   A perpetuity is like an annuity except that the cash flows are perpetual – they never end. British Government bonds, called consols, were the first widely available securities of this kind. The most common example of a perpetuity today are preference shares. The issuer of preference shares promises to pay fixed-rate dividends forever. To calculate the present value of a perpetuity, we simply divide the promised constant payment (CF) by the interest rate (*i*).

4. **Discuss growing annuities and perpetuities, as well as their application in business and be able to calculate their value.**

   Financial managers often need to value cash flow streams that increase at a constant rate over time. These cash flow streams are called growing annuities or growing perpetuities. An example of a growing annuity is a 10-year lease contract with an annual adjustment for the expected rate of inflation over the life of the contract. If the cash flows continue to grow at a constant rate indefinitely, this cash flow stream is called a growing perpetuity. We discuss the application and calculation of cash flows that grow at a constant rate.

5. **Discuss why the effective annual interest rate (EAR) is the appropriate way to annualise interest rates, and be able to calculate EAR.**

The EAR is the annual growth rate that takes compounding into account. Thus, the EAR is the true cost of borrowing or lending money. When we need to compare interest rates, we must make sure that the rates to be compared have the same time and compounding periods. If interest rates are not comparable, they must be converted into common terms. The easiest way to convert rates to common terms is to calculate the EAR for each interest rate. The use and calculations of EAR are discussed.

SUMMARY OF KEY EQUATIONS

Equation	Description	Formula
(6.1)	Present value of an ordinary annuity	$PVA_n = \dfrac{CF}{i} \times \left[1 - \dfrac{1}{(1+i)^n} \right]$
		$= CF \times \dfrac{1 - 1/(1+i)^n}{i}$
		$= CF \times \dfrac{1 - \text{Present value factor}}{i}$
		$= CF \times \text{PV annuity factor}$
(6.2)	Interpolation of an interest rate	$i_{unknown} = i_{low} + \dfrac{(Value_{low\,i} - Value_{unknown\,i})}{\left(Value_{low\,i} - Value_{high\,i}\right)} \times \left(i_{high} - i_{low}\right)$
(6.3)	Future value of an ordinary annuity	$FVA_n = PVA_n \times (1+i)^n$
		$= \dfrac{CF}{i} \times \left[1 - \dfrac{1}{(1+i)^n} \right] \times (1+i)^n$
		$= CF \times \dfrac{(1+i)^n - 1}{i}$
		$= CF \times \dfrac{\text{Future value factor} - 1}{i}$
		$= CF \times \text{FV annuity factor}$
(6.4)	Present value of a perpetuity	$PVA_\infty = \dfrac{CF}{i}$

(6.5)	Value of an annuity due	Annuity due $=$ Ordinary annuity $\times (1+i)$
(6.6)	Present value of a growing annuity	$PVA_n = \dfrac{CF_1}{i-g} \times \left[1 - \left(\dfrac{1+g}{1+i}\right)^n\right]$
(6.7)	Present value of a growing perpetuity	$PVA_\infty = \dfrac{CF_1}{i-g}$
(6.8)	Effective annual interest rate	$EAR = \left(1 + \dfrac{\text{Quoted interest rate}}{m}\right)^m - 1$

SELF-STUDY PROBLEMS

6.1. Kronika GmbH is expecting cash flows of €13 000, €11 500, €12 750 and €9635 over the next four years. What is the present value of these cash flows if the appropriate discount rate is 8%?

6.2. Your grandfather has agreed to deposit a certain amount of money each year into an account paying 7.25% annually to help you do a postgraduate course. Starting next year, and for the following four years, he plans to deposit €2250, €8150, €7675, €6125 and €12 345 into the account. How much will you have at the end of the five years?

6.3. Markus Winkler is planning to save up for a trip to America in three years. He will need €7500 when he is ready to make the trip. He plans to invest the same amount at the end of each of the next three years in an account paying 6%. What is the amount that he will have to save every year to reach his goal of €7500 in three years?

6.4. Birgitte Olsen has €150 000 to invest. She wants to be able to withdraw €12 500 every year forever without using up any of her principal. What interest rate would her investment have to earn in order for her to be able to so?

6.5. Maersk Handlung is expecting annual payments of €34 225 for the next seven years from a customer. What is the present value of this annuity if the discount rate is 8.5%?

SOLUTIONS TO SELF-STUDY PROBLEMS

6.1. The time line for Kronika's cash flows and their present value is as follows:

$$PV_4 = \frac{€13\,000}{1.08} + \frac{€11\,500}{(1.08)^2} + \frac{€12\,750}{(1.08)^3} + \frac{€9635}{(1.08)^4}$$
$$= €12\,037.03 + €9859.40 + €10\,121.36 + €7082.01 = €39\,099.80$$

6.2. The time line for your cash flows and their future value is as follows:

6.3. Amount Markus Winkler will need in three years $= \text{FVA}_3 = €7500$
Number of years $= n = 3$
Interest rate on investment $= i = 6.0\%$
Amount that Markus needs to invest every year $= \text{PMT} = ?$

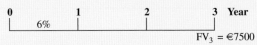

$$\text{FV}_n = \text{CF} \times \frac{(1+i)^n - 1}{i} \quad €7500 = \text{CF} \times \frac{(1+0.06)^3 - 1}{0.06} = \text{CF} \times 3.1836 \quad \text{CF} = \frac{€7500}{3.1836} = €2355.82$$

Markus will have to invest €2355.82 every year for the next three years.

6.4. Present value of Birgitte Olsen's investment $= €150\,000$
Amount needed annually $= €12\,500$
This is a perpetuity!

$$\text{PVA}_\infty = \frac{\text{CF}}{i} \quad i = \frac{\text{CF}}{\text{PVA}_\infty} = \frac{€12\,500}{€150\,000} = 8.33\%$$

6.5. The time line for Maersk Handlung's cash flows and their present value is as follows:

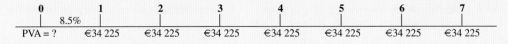

$$\text{PVA}_7 = \text{CF} \times \frac{1 - 1/(1+i)^n}{i} = €34\,225 \times \frac{1 - 1/(1+0.085)^7}{0.085} = €34\,225 \times 5.118514 = €175\,181.14$$

CRITICAL THINKING QUESTIONS

6.1. Identify the steps involved in computing the future value when you have multiple cash flows.

6.2. What is the key economic principle involved in calculating the present value and future value of multiple cash flows?

6.3. What is the difference between a perpetuity and an annuity?

6.4. Define *annuity due*. Would an investment be worth more if it were an ordinary annuity or an annuity due? Explain.

6.5. Raymond Bartz is trying to choose between two equally risky annuities, each paying €5000 per year for five years. One is an ordinary annuity, the other is an annuity due. Which of the following statements is most correct?

a. The present value of the ordinary annuity must exceed the present value of the annuity due, but the future value of an ordinary annuity may be less than the future value of the annuity due.

b. The present value of the annuity due exceeds the present value of the ordinary annuity, while the future value of the annuity due is less than the future value of the ordinary annuity.

c. The present value of the annuity due exceeds the present value of the ordinary annuity and the future value of the annuity due also exceeds the future value of the ordinary annuity.

d. If interest rates increase, the difference between the present value of the ordinary annuity and the present value of the annuity due remains the same.

6.6. Which of the following investments will have the highest future value at the end of three years? Assume that the effective annual rate for all investments is the same.

a. You earn €3000 at the end of three years (a total of one payment).

b. You earn €1000 at the end of every year for the next three years (a total of three payments).

c. You earn €1000 at the beginning of every year for the next three years (a total of three payments).

6.7. Explain whether or not each of the following statements is correct.

a. A 15-year mortgage will have larger monthly payments than a 30-year mortgage of the same amount and same interest rate.

b. If an investment pays 10% interest compounded annually, its effective rate will also be 10%.

6.8. When will the annual percentage rate (APR) be the same as the effective annual rate (EAR)?

6.9. Why is the EAR superior to the APR in measuring the true economic cost or return?

6.10. Suppose two investments have equal lives and multiple cash flows. A high discount rate tends to favour

a. the investment with large cash flows early

b. the investment with large cash flows late

c. the investment with even cash flows

d. neither investment since they have equal lives.

QUESTIONS AND PROBLEMS

Basic

6.1. **Future value with multiple cash flows:** Konerko AB expects to earn cash flows of €13 227, €15 611, €18 970 and €19 114 over the next four years. If the company uses an 8% discount rate, what is the future value of these cash flows at the end of year 4?

6.2. **Future value with multiple cash flows:** Bjorn Sorenson has an investment that will pay him the following cash flows over the next five years: NKr 2350, NKr 2725, NKr 3128, NKr 3366 and NKr 3695. If his investments typically earn 7.65%, what is the future value of the investment's cash flows at the end of five years?

6.3. **Future value with multiple cash flows:** You are a freshman at university and are planning a trip to India when you graduate at the end of four years. You plan to save the following amounts annually, starting today: €625, €700, €700 and €750. If the account pays 5.75% annually, how much will you have at the end of four years?

6.4. **Present value with multiple cash flows:** Pablo Cervantes has just purchased some equipment for his landscaping business. He plans to pay the following amounts at the end of each of the next five years: €10 450, €8500, €9675, €12 500 and €11 635. If he uses a discount rate of 10.875%, what is the cost of the equipment he purchased today?

6.5. **Present value with multiple cash flows:** Jeremy Fenloch borrowed a certain amount from his friend and promised to repay him the amounts of £1225, £1350, £1500, £1600 and £1600 over the next five years. If the friend normally discounts investments at 8% annually, how much did Jeremy borrow?

6.6. **Present value with multiple cash flows:** Biogenesis SA expects the following cash flow stream over the next five years. The company discounts all cash flows at a 23% discount rate. What is the present value of this cash flow stream?

6.7. **Present value of an ordinary annuity:** An investment opportunity requires a payment of €750 for 12 years, starting a year from today. If your required rate of return is 8%, what is the value of the investment today?

6.8. **Present value of an ordinary annuity:** Grupa Piwo Sprzedaży has made an investment in another company that will guarantee it a cash flow of €22 500 each year for the next five years. If the company uses a discount rate of 15% on its investments, what is the present value of this investment?

6.9. **Future value of an ordinary annuity:** Georgiou Therakis plans to invest €25 000 a year at the end of each year for the next seven years in an investment that will pay him a rate of return of 11.4%. How much money will Therakis have at the end of seven years?

6.10. **Future value of an ordinary annuity:** Celine Thomas is a sales executive at a firm based in Lyon, France. She is 25 years old and plans to invest €3000 every year in a retirement account, beginning at the end of this year until she turns 65 years old. If the retirement investment will earn 9.75% annually, how much will she have in 40 years, when she turns 65 years old?

6.11. **Future value of an annuity due:** Refer to Problem 6.10. If Celine Thomas invests at the beginning of each year, how much will she have at age 65?

6.12. **Computing annuity payment:** Kevin Winthrop is saving for an Australian vacation in three years. He estimates that he will need €5000 to cover his airfare and all other expenses for a week-long holiday in Australia. If he can invest his money in an equity index fund that is expected to earn an average return of 10.3% over the next three years, how much will he have to save every year if he starts saving at the end of this year?

6.13. **Computing annuity payment:** Cervecería Matador has a seven-year loan of €23 500 with Banco Santander. It plans to repay the loan in seven equal instalments starting today. If the rate of interest is 8.4%, how much will each payment be worth?

6.14. **Perpetuity:** Your grandfather is retiring at the end of next year. He would like to ensure that he, and after he dies, his heirs receive payments of €10 000 a year forever, starting when he retires. If he can invest at 6.5%, how much does your grandfather need to invest to receive the desired cash flow?

6.15. **Perpetuity:** Calculate the perpetuity payments for each of the following cases:
   a. €250 000 invested at 6%.
   b. €50 000 invested at 12%.
   c. €100 000 invested at 10%.

6.16. **Effective annual interest rate:** Raj Krishnan bought a Honda Accord for a price of €17 345. He put down €6000 and financed the rest through the dealer at an APR of 4.9% for four years. What is the effective annual interest rate (EAR) if payments are made monthly?

6.17. **Effective annual interest rate:** Location Velo Cyclone borrowed €15 550 from a bank for three years. If the quoted rate (APR) is 6.75%, and the compounding is daily, what is the effective annual interest rate (EAR)?

6.18. Growing perpetuity: You are evaluating a growing perpetuity product from a large financial services firm. The product promises an initial payment of €20 000 at the end of this year and subsequent payments will thereafter grow at a rate of 3.4% annually. If you use a 9% discount rate for investment products, what is the present value of this growing perpetuity?

Intermediate

6.19. Future value with multiple cash flows: Genoa Electro Transporte SpA is expecting to invest cash flows of €331 000, €616 450, €212 775, €818 400, €1 239 644 and €1 617 848 in research and development over the next six years. If the appropriate interest rate is 6.75%, what is the future value of these investment cash flows?

6.20. Future value with multiple cash flows: Stephanie Becker plans to adopt the following investment pattern beginning next year. She will invest €3125 in each of the next three years and will then make investments of €3650, €3725, €3875 and €4000 over the following four years. If the investments are expected to earn 11.5% annually, how much will she have at the end of the seven years?

6.21. Present value with multiple cash flows: Carol Jenkins, a lottery winner, will receive the following payments over the next seven years. If she can invest her cash flows in a fund that will earn 10.5% annually, what is the present value of her winnings?

6.22. Computing annuity payment: Francois Depardieu currently has €7500 in a savings account that pays 5.65% annually. Francois plans to use his current savings plus what he can save over the next four years to buy a car. He estimates that the car will cost €12 000 in four years. How much money should Francois save each year if he wants to buy the car?

6.23. Growing annuity: Petrofina owns several petrol stations. Management is looking to open a new station in the western suburbs of Milan. One possibility they are evaluating is to take over a station located at a site that has been leased from the city. The lease, originally for 99 years, currently has 73 years before expiration. The petrol station generated a net cash flow of €92 500 last year and the current owners expect an annual growth rate of 6.3%. If Petrofina uses a discount rate of 14.5% to evaluate such businesses, what is the present value of this growing annuity?

6.24. Future value of annuity due: Jakob Kovács plans to save €5000 every year for the next eight years, starting today. At the end of eight years, Jakob will turn 30 years old and plans to use his savings toward the down payment on a house. If his investment in a mutual fund will earn him 10.3% annually, how much will he have saved in eight years when he will need the money to buy a house?

6.25. Present value of an annuity due: Stavanger Oil Services has borrowed a huge sum from the Norwegian Finance Company at a rate of 17.5% for a seven-year period. The loan calls for a payment of NKr 1 540 862.19 each year beginning today. What is the amount borrowed by this company? Round to the nearest kroner.

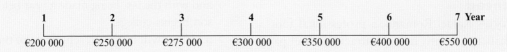

1	2	3	4	5	6	7 Year
€200 000	€250 000	€275 000	€300 000	€350 000	€400 000	€550 000

6.26. Present value of an annuity due: Sabine Kabana has won a state lottery and will receive a payment of €89 729.45 every year, starting today, for the next 20 years. If she invests the proceeds at a rate of 7.25%, what is the present value of the cash flows that she will receive? Round to the nearest euro.

6.27. Perpetuity: Calculate the present value of the following perpetuities:
a. €1250 discounted to the present at 7%.
b. €7250 discounted to the present at 6.33%.
c. €850 discounted to the present at 20%.

6.28. Effective annual interest rate: Find the effective annual interest rate (EAR) on each of the following:
a. 6% compounded quarterly.
b. 4.99% compounded monthly.
c. 7.25% compounded semi-annually.
d. 5.6% compounded daily.

6.29. Effective annual interest rate: Which of the following investments has the highest effective annual interest rate (EAR)?
a. A bank deposit that pays 8.25% compounded quarterly.
b. A bank deposit that pays 8.25% compounded monthly.
c. A bank deposit that pays 8.45% compounded annually.
d. A bank deposit that pays 8.25% compounded semi-annually.
e. A bank deposit that pays 8% compounded daily (on a 365-day basis).

6.30. Effective annual interest rate: You are considering three alternative investments: (1) a three-year bank deposit paying 7.5% compounded quarterly; (2) a three-year bank deposit paying 7.3% compounded monthly; and (3) a three-year bank deposit paying 7.75% compounded annually. Which investment has the highest effective annual interest rate?

Advanced

6.31. EXCEL® Rafael Romano, a professional footballer, currently has a contract that will pay him a large amount in the first year of his contract and smaller amounts thereafter. He and his agent have asked the football club to restructure the contract. The club, though reluctant, obliged. Romano and his agent came up with a counter offer. What are the present values of each of the contracts using a 14% discount rate? Which of the three contracts has the highest present value?

Year	Current Contract	Team's Offer	Counter Offer
1	€8 125 000	€4 000 000	€5 250 000
2	€3 650 000	€3 825 000	€7 550 000
3	€2 715 000	€3 850 000	€3 625 000
4	€1 822 250	€3 925 000	€2 800 000

6.32. EXCEL® Gerhard Kornig will be 30 years old next year and wants to retire when he is 65. So far he has saved (1) €6950 in a savings account in which his money is earning 8.3% annually and (2) €5000 in a money market fund in which he is earning 5.25% annually. Gerhard wants to have €1 million when he retires. Starting next year, he plans to invest a fixed amount of money every year until he retires in a mutual fund in which he expects to earn 9% annually. How much will Gerhard have to invest every year to achieve his savings goal?

6.33. EXCEL® Babu Baradwaj is saving for his son's university tuition. His son is currently 11 years old and will begin university in seven years. Babu has an index fund investment worth €7500 that is earning 9.5% annually. Total expenses at the university where his son says he plans to go currently total €15 000 per year, but are expected to grow at roughly 6% each year. Babu plans to invest in a mutual fund that will earn 11% annually to make up the difference between the university expenses and his current savings. In total, Babu will make seven equal investments with the first starting today and with the last being made a year before his son begins college.
a. What will be the present value of the four years of university expenses at the time

that Babu's son starts college? Assume a discount rate of 5.5%.

b. What will be the value of the index mutual fund when his son just starts university?

c. What is the amount that Babu will have to have saved when his son turns 18 if Babu plans to cover all of his son's university expenses?

d. How much will Babu have to invest every year in order to have enough funds to cover all his son's expenses?

6.34. EXCEL® You are now 50 years old and plan to retire at age 65. You currently have an equity portfolio worth €150 000, a pension plan worth €250 000 and a money market account worth €50 000. Your equity portfolio is expected to provide you with annual returns of 12%, your pension plan will earn you 9.5% annually and the money market account earns 5.25%, compounded monthly.

a. If you do not save another cent, what will be the total value of your investments when you retire at age 65?

b. Assume you plan to invest €12 000 every year in your pension plan for the next 15 years (starting one year from now). How much will your investments be worth when you retire at 65?

c. Assume that you expect to live 25 years after you retire (until age 90). Today, at age 50, you take all of your investments and place them in an account that pays 8% (use the scenario from part b in which you continue saving). If you start withdrawing funds starting at age 66, how much can you withdraw every year (e.g., an ordinary annuity) and leave nothing in your account after a 25th and final withdrawal at age 90?

d. You want your current investments, which are described in the problem statement, to support a perpetuity that starts a year from now. How much can you withdraw each year without touching your principal?

6.35. EXCEL® Teodoro Diaz is looking to purchase a Mercedes Benz SL600, which has an invoice price of €121 737 and a total cost of €129 482. Teodoro plans to put down €20 000 and will pay the rest by taking on a 5.75% five-year bank loan. What is the monthly payment on this car loan? Prepare an amortisation table using Excel.

6.36. EXCEL® The Sundarams are buying a new house and will borrow €237 000 from a bank at a rate of 6.375% for 15 years. What is their monthly loan payment? Prepare an amortisation schedule using Excel.

6.37. EXCEL® Assume you will start on a job as soon as you graduate. You plan to start saving for your retirement when you turn 25 years old. Assume you are 21 years of age at the time of graduation. Everybody needs a break! Currently, you plan to retire when you turn 65 years old. After retirement, you expect to live at least until you are 85. You wish to be able to withdraw €40 000 (in today's money) every year from the time of your retirement until you are 85 years old (i.e., for 20 years). You can invest, starting when you turn 25 years old, in a portfolio fund. The average inflation rate is likely to be 5%.

a. Calculate the lump sum you need to have accumulated at age 65 to be able to draw the desired income. Assume that your return on the portfolio investment is likely to be 10%.

b. What is the amount you need to invest every year, starting at age 26 and ending at age 65 (i.e., for 40 years) to reach the target lump sum at age 65?

c. Now answer questions a and b assuming your rate of return to be 8% per year, then again at 15% per year.

d. Now assume you start investing for your retirement when you turn 30 years old and analyse the situation under rate of return assumptions of (i) 8%, (ii) 10% and (iii) 15%.

e. Repeat the analysis by assuming that you start investing when you are 35 years old.

SAMPLE TEST PROBLEMS

6.1. Groves Services plc is expecting annual cash flows of £225 000, £278 000, £312 500 and £410 000 over the next four years. If it uses a discount rate of 6.25%, what will be the present value of this cash flow stream?

6.2. Freisinger AG is expecting a new project to start paying off, beginning at the end of next year. It expects cash flows to be as follows:

If Freisinger AG can reinvest these cash flows to earn a return of 7.8%, what is the future value of this cash flow stream at the end of five years?

6.3. London, England, is the site of the next Olympics in 2012. City officials plan to build a new multipurpose stadium. The projected cost of the stadium in 2012 money is £750 million. Assume that it is 2009 and city officials intend to put away a certain amount at the end of each of the next three years in an account that will pay 8.75%. What is the annual payment necessary to meet the projected cost of the stadium?

6.4. You have just won a lottery that promises an annual payment of €118 312 beginning immediately. You will receive a total of 10 payments. If you can invest the cash flows in an investment paying 7.65% annually, what is the present value of this annuity?

6.5. Which of the following investments has the highest effective annual interest rate (EAR)?

a. A bank deposit that pays 5.50% compounded quarterly.

b. A bank deposit that pays 5.45% compounded monthly.

c. A bank deposit that pays 5.65% compounded annually.

d. A bank deposit that pays 5.55% compounded semi-annually.

e. A bank deposit that pays 5.35% compounded daily (on a 365-day basis).

APPENDIX: DERIVING THE FORMULA FOR THE PRESENT VALUE OF AN ORDINARY ANNUITY

In this chapter we showed that the formula for a perpetuity can be obtained from the formula for the present value of an ordinary annuity if n is set equal to ∞. It is also possible to go the other way. In other words, the present value of an ordinary annuity formula can be derived from the formula for a perpetuity. In fact, this is how the annuity formula was originally obtained. To see how this was done, assume that someone has offered to pay you €1 per year forever, beginning next year, but that, in return, you will have to pay that person €1 per year forever, beginning in year $n + 1$.

The cash flows you will receive and the cash flows you will pay are represented in the following time line:

The first row of values shows the cash flows for the perpetuity that you will receive. This perpetuity is worth:

$$PVA_{\infty,\ Receive} = \frac{€1}{i} = \frac{CF}{i}p$$

	0	1	2	3		n − 1	n	n + 1	n + 2
Difference		€1	€1	€1		€1	€1	€0	€0

The second row shows the cash flows for the perpetuity that you will pay. The present value of what you owe is the value of a €1 perpetuity that is discounted for n years.

$$PVA_{\infty,\ Pay} = \frac{€1/i}{(1+i)^n} = \frac{CF/i}{(1+i)^n}$$

Notice that if you subtract, year by year, the cash flows you would pay from the cash flows you would receive, you get the cash flows for an n-year annuity.

Therefore, the value of the offer equals the value of an n-year annuity. Solving for the difference between $PVA_{\infty,\ Receive}$ and $PVA_{\infty,\ Pay}$ we see that this is the same as Equation (6.1):

$$
\begin{aligned}
PVA_n &= PVA_{\infty,\ Receive} - PVA_{\infty,\ Pay} \\
&= \frac{CF}{i} - \frac{CF/i}{(1+i)^n} \\
&= \frac{CF}{i} \times \left[1 - \frac{1}{(1+i)^n}\right]
\end{aligned}
$$

PROBLEM

6.1. In the chapter text, you saw that the formula for a growing perpetuity can be obtained from the formula for the present value of a growing annuity if n is set equal to ∞. It is also possible to go the other way. In other words, the present value of a growing annuity formula can be derived from the formula for a growing perpetuity. In fact, this is how Equation (6.5) was actually derived. Show how Equation (6.5) can be derived from Equation (6.6).

ENDNOTES

1. Up to this point, we have used the notation FV_n to represent a cash flow in period n. We have done this to stress that, for $n > 0$, we were referring to a future value. From this point on, we will use the notation CF_n, instead of FV_n, because the CF_n notation is more commonly used by financial analysts.
2. Recall that, when using a financial calculator, it is common practice to enter cash outflows as negative numbers and cash inflows as positive numbers. See Chapter 5 for a complete discussion of the importance of assigning the proper sign (+ or −) to cash flows when using a financial calculator.

3. Notice that we have rounded the PV annuity factor to three decimal places (7.722). If we use a financial calculator and do not round, we get a more precise answer of €386 086.75.

4. The annuity present value factor for 10 years at 10% is 6.1446. Thus, $PV_{10} = CF \times$ Annuity factor = €3500 × 6.1446 = €21 506.10. Using a financial calculator, PV_{10} = €21 505.98. The difference is due to rounding errors.

5. Conversely, we can derive the formula for the present value of an ordinary annuity, Equation (6.1), from the formula for a perpetuity, as explained in the appendix at the end of this chapter.

6. The market for top research and teaching faculty is very competitive. Endowed chairs are a means that universities use to attract and retain their best faculty. The typical chair is endowed for €1 million or more and is usually named after the donor.

7. If you have any doubt about the total credit card debt at the end of one year, make the calculation 12 times on your calculator: the first month is €100 × 1.01 = €101.00; the second month is €101.00 × 1.01 = €102.01; the third month is €102.01 × 1.01 = €103.03; and so on for 12 months.

CHAPTER
7

Risk and Return

In this Chapter:

LEARNING OBJECTIVES

1. Explain the relation between risk and return.
2. Describe the two components of a total holding period return and calculate this return for an asset.
3. Explain what an expected return is and calculate the expected return for an asset.
4. Explain what the standard deviation of returns is, explain why it is especially useful in finance and be able to calculate it.
5. Explain the concept of diversification.
6. Discuss which type of risk matters to investors and why.
7. Describe what the Capital Asset Pricing Model (CAPM) tells us and how to use it to evaluate whether the expected return of an asset is sufficient to compensate an investor for the risks associated with that asset.

'I can't stop partying' may be the title to a great song and the motto of ardent clubbers but for Luminar, the London Stock Exchange-listed nightclub operator of Liquid and Oceana, all the glitz has failed to hide the company's poor fortunes from 2005 onwards. With its extensive range of clubs, the company dominated the late-night entertainment industry during the 1990s and into the early 2000s. But from about 2005, changes in the UK's licensing laws increased competition as many high street bars were allowed to stay open late, cutting into Luminar's profitable drink

sales. Furthermore, the effects of the recession, which badly affected its core clientele of 18–24-year-olds as unemployment for the under 25s increased rapidly, led to increasing problems at the company.

From the mid-1990s, when the share price had been around 250 pence, to the early 2000s, when the share price rose to nearly 900 pence, shareholders did very well. The shares had comfortably outperformed the London benchmark index, the FTSE 100 index, as well as paying shareholders a dividend. Undiversified shareholders in Luminar, such as Stephen Thomas, the founder and chief executive, took a lot of risk in anticipation of earning high returns. They did well when the business did well and the share price was rising and paid a steep price when it was not. However, all that changed as the company's problems increased and the shares fell from a high of 825 pence to a low of just 8.75 pence – a fall of nearly 100%.

The continued stream of bad news, failure to meet targets and poor prospects, combined with increasing problems at Luminar, which culminated in the departure of Stephen Thomas in February 2010, greatly disappointed shareholders, who reacted accordingly – selling the shares and driving down the price.

The precipitous decline in the value of Luminar shares since 2007 can be contrasted with the performance of the stock market as a whole. Luminar shareholders who did not hold diversified investment portfolios were much worse off after 2007 than they would have been if they had held diversified portfolios. They suffered large losses because they had not diversified their risk by investing in a range of shares and other types of assets. They bet on one company and when that company share price collapsed, so did the value of their investment portfolios.

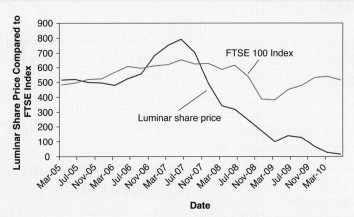

Luminar's share price outperformed the FTSE 100 index from 2006 to mid-2007, thereafter, the stock price has fallen from over 800 pence to around 15 pence in June 2010, a drop of 99.9%!

CHAPTER PREVIEW

Up to this point, we have often mentioned the rate of return that we use to discount cash flows, but we have not explained how that rate is determined. We have now reached the point where it is time to examine key concepts underlying the discount rate. This chapter introduces a quantitative framework for measuring risk and return. This framework will help you develop an intuitive understanding of how risk and return are related and what risks matter to investors. The relation between risk and return has implications for the rate we use to discount cash flows because the time value of money that we discussed in Chapters 5 and 6 is directly related to the returns that investors require. We must understand these concepts in order to determine the correct present value for a series of cash flows and be able to make investment decisions that create value for shareholders.

We begin this chapter with a discussion of the general relation between risk and return to introduce the idea that investors require a higher rate of return from riskier assets. This is one of the most fundamental relations in finance. We next develop the statistical concepts required to quantify holding period returns, expected returns and risk. We then apply these concepts to portfolios with a single asset, two assets and more than two assets to illustrate the benefit of diversification. From this discussion, you will see how investing in more than one asset enables an investor to reduce the total risk associated with his or her investment portfolio, and you will learn how to quantify this benefit.

Once we have discussed the concept of diversification, we examine what it means for the relation between risk and return. We find that the total risk associated with an investment consists of two components: (1) unsystematic risk and (2) systematic risk. Diversification enables investors to eliminate the *unsystematic risk*, or unique risk, associated with an individual asset. Investors do not require higher returns for the *unsystematic risk*, which they can eliminate through diversification. Only *systematic risk* – risk that cannot be diversified away – affects expected returns on an investment. The distinction between unsystematic and systematic risk, and the recognition that unsystematic risk can be diversified away, are extremely important in finance. After reading this chapter, you will understand precisely what the term *risk* means in finance and how it is related to the rates of return that investors require.

RISK AND RETURN

Learning Objective 1

Explain the relation between risk and return.

The rate of return that investors require for an investment depends on the risk associated with that investment. The greater the risk, the larger the return investors require as compensation for bearing that risk. This is one of the most fundamental relations in finance. The *rate of return* is what you earn on an investment, stated in percentage terms. We will be more specific later, but for now you might think of *risk* as a measure of how certain you are that you will receive a particular return. Higher risk means you are less certain.

To get a better understanding of how risk and return are related, consider an example. You are trying to select the best investment from among the following three shares:

Shares	Expected Return (%)	Risk Level (%)
A	12	12
B	12	16
C	16	16

Which would you choose? If you were comparing only Shares A and B, you should choose Share A. Both shares have the same expected return, but Share A has less risk. It does not make sense to invest in the riskier share if the expected return is the same. Similarly, you can see that Share C is clearly

superior to Share B. Shares B and C have the same level of risk but Share C has a higher expected return. It would not make sense to accept a lower return for taking on the same level of risk.

However, what about the choice between Shares A and C? This choice is less obvious. Making it requires understanding the concepts that we discuss in the rest of this chapter.

QUANTITATIVE MEASURES OF RETURN

Learning Objective 2

Describe the two components of a total holding period return and calculate this return for an asset.

Before we begin a detailed discussion of the relation between risk and return, we should define more precisely what these terms mean. We begin with measures of return.

Holding Period Returns

When people refer to the return from an investment, they are generally referring to the total return over some *investment period*, or *holding period*. The **total holding period return** consists of two components: (1) capital appreciation and (2) income. The capital appreciation component of a return, R_{CA}, arises from a change in the price of the asset over the investment or holding period and

BUILDING INTUITION

More Risk Means a Higher Expected Return

The greater the risk associated with an investment, the greater the return investors expect from it. A corollary to this idea is that investors want the highest return for a given level of risk or the lowest risk for a given level of return. When choosing between two investments that have the same level of risk, investors prefer the investment with the higher return. Alternatively, if two investments have the same expected return, investors prefer the less risky alternative.

is calculated as follows:

$$R_{CA} = \frac{\text{Capital appreciation}}{\text{Initial price}} = \frac{P_1 - P_0}{P_0} = \frac{\Delta P}{P_0}$$

where P_0 is the price paid for the asset at time zero and P_1 is the price at a later point in time.

The income component of a return arises from income that an investor receives from the asset while he or she owns it. For example, when a firm pays a cash dividend on its shares, the income component of the return on the shares, R_I, is calculated as follows:

$$R_I = \frac{\text{Cash flow}}{\text{Initial price}} = \frac{CF_1}{P_0}$$

where CF_1 is the cash flow from the dividend.

The total holding period return is simply the sum of the capital appreciation and income components of return:

$$R_T = R_{CA} + R_I = \frac{\Delta P}{P_0} + \frac{CF_1}{P_0} = \frac{\Delta P + CF_1}{P_0} \quad (7.1)$$

> ### Total holding period return
>
> the total return on an asset over a specific period of time or holding period

Let us consider an example of calculating the total holding period return on an investment. One year ago today, you purchased a share of Nokia for €26.50. Today it is worth €29.00. Nokia paid no dividend on its shares. What total return did you earn on this share over the past year?

If Nokia paid no dividend and you received no other income from holding the shares, the total return for the year equals the return from the capital appreciation, calculated as follows:

$$R_T = R_{CA} + R_I = \frac{P_1 - P_0 + CF_1}{P_0}$$

$$= \frac{€29.00 - €26.50 + €0.00}{€26.50}$$

$$= 0.0943, \text{ or } 9.43\%$$

What return would you have earned if Nokia had paid a €1 dividend and today's price was €28.00? With the €1 dividend and a correspondingly lower price, the total return is the same:

$$R_T = R_{CA} + R_I = \frac{P_1 - P_0 + CF_1}{P_0}$$

$$= \frac{€28.00 - €26.50 + €1.00}{€26.50}$$

$$= 0.0943, \text{ or } 9.43\%$$

You can see from this example that a euro of capital appreciation is worth the same as a euro of income.

> **WEB**
>
> You can download actual realised investment returns for a large number of shares market indexes at the Callan Associates website: www.callan.com/resource/periodic_table/pertbl.pdf.

Learning by Doing Application 7.1

Calculating the Return on an Investment

Problem: You purchased a beat-up 1974 Datsun 240Z sports car a year ago for €1500. Datsun is what Nissan, the Japanese car company, was called in the 1970s. The 240Z was the first in a series of cars that led to the Nissan 350Z that is being sold today. Recognising that a mint-condition 240Z is a much sought-after car, you invested €7000 and a lot of your time fixing up the car. Last week, you sold it to a collector for €18 000. Not counting the value of the time you spent restoring the car, what is the total return you earned on this investment over the one-year holding period?

Approach: Use Equation (7.1) to calculate the total holding period return. To calculate R_T using Equation (7.1), you must know P_0, P_1 and CF_1. In this problem, you can assume that the €7000 was spent at the time you bought the car to purchase parts and materials. Therefore, your

initial investment, P_0, was €1500 + €7000 = €8500. Since there were no other cash inflows or outflows between the time that you bought the car and the time that you sold it, CF_1 equals €0.

Solution: The total holding period return is:

$$R_T = R_{CA} + R_I = \frac{P_1 - P_0 + CF_1}{P_0}$$

$$= \frac{€18\,000 - €8500 + €0}{€8500}$$

$$= 1.118, \text{ or } 111.8\%$$

Expected Returns

Suppose that you are in your last year at university and play football for the university, and that your team is in the European Universities Football Championship. Furthermore, suppose that you have been asked to turn professional and you are playing your last game as a striker for the university team. The fact that you expect this to be your last game is important because you just signed a very unusual contract with the football club. Your signing bonus will be determined solely by whether you score in your final game for the university. If you score, then your signing bonus will be €800 000. Otherwise, it will be €400 000. This past season, you scored 32.5% of the times you played (you did not score 67.5% of the time), and you believe this reflects the likelihood that you will score in your last game for the university.[1]

What is the expected value of your bonus? If you have taken a statistics course, you might recall that an expected value represents the sum of the products of the possible outcomes and the probabilities that those outcomes will be realised. In our example, the expected value of the bonus can be calculated using the following formula:

$$E(\text{Bonus}) = (p_S \times B_S) + (p_{NS} \times B_{NS})$$

where $E(\text{Bonus})$ is your expected bonus, p_S is the probability of scoring a goal, p_{NS} is the probability

of not scoring, B_S is the bonus you receive if you score and B_{NS} is the bonus you receive if you do not score a goal. Since p_S equals 0.325, p_{NS} equals 0.675, B_S equals €800 000 and B_{NS} equals €400 000, the expected value of your bonus is:

$$E(\text{Bonus}) = (P_S \times B_S) + (P_{NS} \times B_{NS})$$

$$= (0.325 \times €800\,000) + (0.675 \times €400\,000)$$

$$= €530\,000$$

Notice that the expected bonus of €530 000 is not equal to either of the two possible payoffs. Neither is it equal to the simple average of the two possible payoffs. This is because the expected bonus takes into account the probability of each event occurring. If the probability of each event had been 50%, then the expected bonus would have equalled the simple average of the two payoffs:

$$E(\text{Bonus}) = (0.5 \times €800\,000)$$
$$+ (0.5 \times €400\,000)$$
$$= €600\,000$$

However, since it is more likely that you will not score (a 67.5% chance) than that you will score a goal (a 32.5% chance), and the payoff is lower if you do not score a goal, the expected bonus is less than the simple average.

What would your expected payoff be if you scored 99% of the time? We intuitively know that the expected bonus should be much closer to €800 000 in this case. In fact, it is:

$$E(\text{Bonus}) = (0.99 \times €800\,000)$$
$$+ (0.01 \times €400\,000)$$
$$= €796\,000$$

The key point here is that the expected value reflects the relative likelihoods of the possible outcomes.

We calculate an **expected return** in finance in the same way that we calculate any expected value. The expected return is a weighted average of the possible returns from an investment, where each of these returns is weighted by the probability that it will occur. In general terms, the expected return on an asset, $E(R_{\text{Asset}})$, is calculated as follows:

$$E(R_{\text{Asset}}) = \sum_{i=1}^{n} (p_i \times R_i)$$
$$= (p_1 \times R_1) + (p_2 \times R_2) + \cdots$$
$$+ (p_n \times R_n) \qquad (7.2)$$

where R_i is the possible return i and p_i is the probability that you will actually earn return R_i. The summation symbol in this equation

$$\sum_{i=1}^{n}$$

is mathematical shorthand indicating that n values are added together. In Equation (7.2), each of the n possible returns is multiplied by the probability that it will be realised and these products are then added together to calculate the expected return.

> ### Expected return
>
> an average of the possible returns from an investment, where each return is weighted by the probability that it will occur

It is important to make sure that the sum of the n individual probabilities, the p_i's, always equals 1, or 100%, when you calculate an expected value. The sum of the probabilities cannot be less than 100% because you must account for all possible outcomes in the calculation. On the other hand, as you may recall from statistics, the sum of the probabilities of all possible outcomes cannot exceed 100%. For example, notice that the sum of the p_i's equals 1 in each of the expected bonus calculations that we discussed earlier ($0.325 + 0.625$ in the first calculation, $0.5 + 0.5$ in the second and $0.99 + 0.01$ in the third).

The expected return on an asset reflects the return that you can expect to receive from investing in that asset over the period that you plan to own it. It is your best estimate of this return, given the possible outcomes and their associated probabilities.

Note that if each of the possible outcomes is equally likely (that is, $p_1 = p_2 = p_3 = \cdots = p_n = p = 1/n$), this formula reduces to the formula for a simple (equally weighted) average of the possible returns:

$$E(R_{\text{Asset}}) = \frac{\sum_{i=1}^{n} (R_i)}{n} = \frac{R_1 + R_2 + \cdots + R_n}{n}$$

To see how we calculate the expected return on an asset, suppose you are considering purchasing Nokia shares for €29.00 per share. You plan to sell the shares in one year. You estimate that there is a 30% chance that Nokia shares will sell for €28.00 at the end of one year, a 30% chance that they will sell for €30.50, a 30% chance that they will sell for €32.50 and a 10% chance that they will sell for €36.00. If Nokia pays no dividends on its shares, what is the return that you expect from the shares in the next year?

Since Nokia pays no dividends, the total return on its shares equals the return from capital appreciation:

$$R_{\text{T}} = R_{\text{CA}} = \frac{P_1 - P_0}{P_0}$$

Therefore, we can calculate the return from owning Nokia shares under each of the four possible outcomes using the approach we used for the similar Nokia problem we solved earlier in the chapter. These returns are calculated as follows:

Nokia Shares Price in One Year

One Year	Total Return
(1) €28.00	$\dfrac{€28.00 - €29.00}{€29.00} = -0.0345$
(2) €30.50	$\dfrac{€30.50 - €29.00}{€29.00} = 0.0517$
(3) €32.50	$\dfrac{€32.50 - €29.00}{€29.00} = 0.1207$
(4) €36.00	$\dfrac{€36.00 - €29.00}{€29.00} = 0.2414$

Applying Equation (7.2), the expected return on Nokia shares over the next year is therefore

6.55%, calculated as follows:

$$E(R_{\text{Nokia}}) = \sum_{i=1}^{n}(p_i \times R_1) = (p_1 \times R_1)$$
$$+(p_2 \times R_2) + \cdots + (p_n \times R_n)$$
$$= (0.3 \times -0.0345) + (0.3 \times 0.0517)$$
$$+(0.3 \times 0.1207) + (0.1 \times 0.2414)$$
$$= -0.01035 + 0.01551 + 0.03621$$
$$+0.02414$$
$$= 0.0655, \text{ or } 6.55\%$$

Notice that the negative return is entered into the formula just like any other. Also notice that the sum of the p_i's equals 1.

Learning by Doing Application 7.2

Calculating Expected Returns

Problem: You have just purchased 100 containers that you plan to lease to carry freight by rail. Demand for shipping goods by rail has recently increased dramatically due to the rising price of oil. You expect oil prices, which are currently at US$115.00 per barrel, to reach US$130.00 per barrel in the next year. If this happens, demand for containers for use for transporting goods by rail will increase, thereby driving up the value of your containers as increases in demand outpace the rate at which new containers are being produced.

Given your oil price prediction, you estimate that there is a 30% chance that the value of your containers will increase by 15%, a 40% chance that their value will increase by 25% and a 30% chance that their value will increase by 30% in the next year. In addition to appreciation in the value of your containers, you expect to earn 10%

on your investment over the next year (after expenses) from leasing the containers. What total return do you expect to earn on your container investment over the next year?

Approach: Use Equation (7.1) first to calculate the total return that you would earn under each of the three possible outcomes. Next use these total return values, along with the associated probabilities, in Equation (7.2) to calculate the expected total return.

Solution: To calculate the total returns using Equation (7.1),

$$R_T = R_{CA} + R_I = \frac{\Delta P}{P_0} + \frac{CF_1}{P_0}$$

you must recognise that $\Delta P/P_0$ is the capital appreciation under each outcome and that CF_1/P_0 equals the 10% that you expect to receive from leasing the containers. The expected returns for the three outcomes are:

Increase in Value of Containers in One Year	Return from Renting Containers	Total Return
15%	10%	$R_T = \dfrac{\Delta P}{P_0} + \dfrac{R_1}{P_0} = 0.15 + 0.10 = 0.25$, or 25%
25%	10%	$R_T = \dfrac{\Delta P}{P_0} + \dfrac{R_1}{P_0} = 0.25 + 0.10 = 0.35$, or 35%
30%	10%	$R_T = \dfrac{\Delta P}{P_0} + \dfrac{R_1}{P_0} = 0.30 + 0.10 = 0.40$, or 40%

You can then use Equation (7.2) to calculate the expected return for your container investment:

$$E(R_{Containers}) = \sum_{i=1}^{3}(p_i \times R_i) = (p_1 \times R_1)$$
$$+ (p_2 \times R_2) + (p_3 \times R_3)$$
$$= (0.3 \times 0.25) + (0.4 \times 0.35)$$
$$+ (0.3 \times 0.40)$$
$$= 0.335, \text{ or } 33.5\%$$

Alternatively, since there is a 100% probability that the return from leasing the containers is 10%, you could have simply calculated the expected increase in value of the railroad cars:

$$E\left(\frac{\Delta P}{P_0}\right) = (0.3 \times 0.15) + (0.4 \times 0.25)$$
$$+ (0.3 \times 0.30)$$
$$= 0.235, \text{ or } 23.5\%$$

and added the 10% to arrive at the answer of 33.5%. Of course, this simpler approach only works if the return from leasing is known with certainty.

Decision-Making Example 7.1

Using Expected Values in Decision Making

Situation: You are deciding whether you should advertise your pizza business on the radio or use posters on local taxis. For €1000 per month, you can either buy 20 one-minute commercials on the radio or place your advertisement on 40 taxis that operate in your locality.

There is some uncertainty regarding how many new customers will visit your restaurant after hearing one of your radio commercials. You estimate that there is a 30% chance that 35 people will visit, a 45% chance that 50 people will visit and a 25% chance that 60 people will visit. Therefore, you expect the following number of new customers to visit your restaurant in a month in response to each radio commercial:

$E(\text{New customers per commercial}_{Radio})$
$= (0.30 \times 35) + (0.45 \times 50) + (0.25 \times 60)$
$= 48$

This means that you expect 20 one-minute commercials to bring in $20 \times 48 = 960$ new customers.

Similarly, you estimate that there is a 20% chance you will get 20 new customers in response to a poster placed on a taxi, a 30% chance you will get 30 new customers, a 30% chance you will get 40 new customers and a 20% chance you will get 50 new customers.

Therefore, you expect the following number of new customers in response to each poster that you place on a taxi:

$$E(\text{New customers per commercial}_{\text{Taxi}})$$
$$= (0.2 \times 20) + (0.3 \times 30) + (0.3 \times 40)$$
$$+ (0.2 \times 50)$$
$$= 35$$

Placing posters on 40 taxis is therefore expected to bring in $40 \times 35 = 1400$ new customers.

Which of these two advertising options is more attractive? Is it cost effective?

Decision: You should advertise on taxis. For a monthly cost of €1000, you expect to attract 1400 new customers with taxi advertisements but only 960 new customers if you advertise on the radio.

The answer to the question of whether advertising on taxicabs is cost effective depends on how much gross profits (profits after variable costs) are increased by those 1400 customers. Gross profits will have to increase by €1000, or average 72 cents per new customer (€1000/1400), to cover the cost of the advertising campaign.

Before You Go On

1. What are the two components of a total holding period return?
2. How is the expected return on an investment calculated?

THE VARIANCE AND STANDARD DEVIATION AS MEASURES OF RISK

Learning Objective 3

Explain what an expected return is and calculate the expected return for an asset.

We turn next to a discussion of the two most basic measures of risk used in finance – the variance and the standard deviation. These are the same variance and standard deviation measures that you have studied if you have taken a course in statistics.

Calculating the Variance and Standard Deviation

Let us begin by returning to our European Universities Football Championship example. Recall

that you will receive a bonus of €800 000 if you score in your final game and a bonus of €400 000 if you do not. The expected value of your bonus is €530 000. Suppose you want to measure the risk, or uncertainty, associated with the payoff. How can you do this? One approach would be to compute a measure of how much, on average, the bonus payoffs deviate from the expected value. The underlying intuition here is that the greater the difference between the actual payoff and the expected value, the greater the risk. For example, you might calculate the difference between each individual bonus payment and the expected value and sum these differences. If you do this, you will get the following result:

$$\begin{aligned}
\text{Risk} &= (\text{€}800\,000 - \text{€}530\,000) \\
&+ (\text{€}400\,000 - \text{€}530\,000) \\
&= \text{€}270\,000 + (-\text{€}130\,000) \\
&= \text{€}140\,000
\end{aligned}$$

Unfortunately, using this calculation to obtain a measure of risk presents two problems. First, since one difference is positive and the other difference is negative, one difference partially cancels the other. As a result, you are not getting an accurate measure of total risk. Second, this calculation does not take into account the number of potential outcomes or the probability of each outcome.

A better approach would be to square the differences (squaring the differences makes all the numbers positive) and multiply each difference by its associated probability before summing them up. This calculation yields the **variance (σ^2)** of the possible outcomes. The variance does not suffer from the two problems mentioned earlier, and provides a measure of risk that has a consistent interpretation across different situations or assets. For the original bonus arrangement, the variance is:

$$
\begin{aligned}
\text{Var(Bonus)} = \sigma^2_{(\text{Bonus})} &= \left\{ p_S \times [B_S - E(\text{Bonus})]^2 \right\} \\
&+ \left\{ p_{NS} \times [B_{NS} - E(\text{Bonus})]^2 \right\} \\
&= \left[0.325 \times (\text{€}800\,000 - \text{€}530\,000)^2 \right] \\
&+ \left[0.675 \times (\text{€}400\,000 - \text{€}530\,000)^2 \right] \\
&= 35\,100\,000\,000 \text{ euros}^2
\end{aligned}
$$

Note that the square of the Greek symbol sigma, σ^2, is generally used to represent the variance.

Because it is somewhat awkward to work with units of squared euros or other currencies, in a calculation such as this we would typically take the square root of the variance. The square root gives us the **standard deviation (σ)** of the possible outcomes. For our example, the standard deviation is:

$$
\begin{aligned}
\sigma_{(\text{Bonus})} &= \left(\sigma^2_{(\text{Bonus})} \right)^{1/2} \\
&= (35\,100\,000\,000 \text{ euros}^2)^{1/2} \\
&= \text{€}187\,349.94
\end{aligned}
$$

As you will see when we discuss the normal distribution, the standard deviation has a natural interpretation that is very useful for assessing investment risks.

The general formula for calculating the variance of returns can be written as follows:

$$
\text{Var}(R) = \sigma^2_R = \sum_{i=1}^{n} \left\{ p_i \times [R_i - E(R)]^2 \right\} \quad (7.3)
$$

Equation (7.3) simply extends the calculation illustrated above to the situation where there are n possible outcomes. Like the expected return

calculation [Equation (7.2)], Equation (7.3) can be simplified if all of the possible outcomes are equally likely. In this case it becomes:

$$
\sigma^2_R = \frac{\sum\limits_{i=1}^{n} \left\{ p_i \times [R_i - E(R)]^2 \right\}}{n}
$$

In both the general case and the case where all possible outcomes are equally likely, the standard deviation is simply the square root of the variance $\sigma_R = \left(\sigma^2_R \right)^{1/2}$.

> **Variance (σ^2)**
>
> a measure of the uncertainty surrounding an outcome

> **Standard deviation (σ)**
>
> the square root of the variance

> **Normal distribution**
>
> a symmetric frequency distribution that is completely described by its mean and standard deviation; also known as a bell curve due to its shape

Interpreting the Variance and Standard Deviation

The variance and standard deviation are especially useful measures of risk for variables that are normally distributed – those that can be represented by a normal distribution. The **normal distribution** is a symmetric frequency distribution that is completely described by its mean (average) and standard deviation. Exhibit 7.1 illustrates what this distribution looks like. Many natural phenomena follow a normal distribution or 'bell curve'. For instance, the height of adult men and intelligence

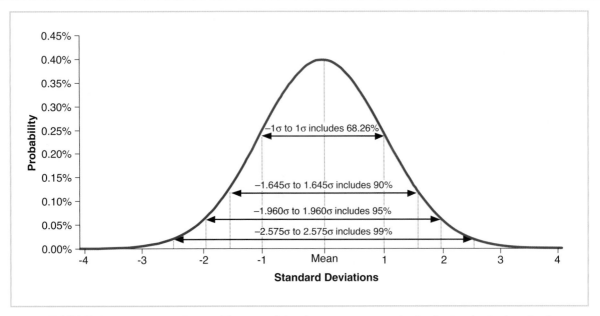

Exhibit 7.1: Normal Distribution The normal distribution is a symmetric distribution that is described by its mean and standard deviation. The mean is the value that defines the centre of the distribution, and the standard deviation, σ, describes the dispersion of the values centered around the mean.

quotient (IQ) scores are based on normal distributions.

This distribution is very useful in finance because the returns for many assets tend to be approximately normally distributed. This makes the variance and standard deviation practical measures of the uncertainty associated with investment returns. Since the standard deviation is more easily interpreted than the variance, we will focus on the standard deviation as we discuss the normal distribution and its application in finance.

In Exhibit 7.1, you can see that the normal distribution is symmetric: the left and right sides are mirror images of each other. The mean falls directly in the centre of the distribution and the probability that an outcome is less than or greater than a particular distance from the mean is the same, whether the outcome is on the left or the right side of the distribution. For example, if the mean is 0, the probability that a particular outcome is −3 or less is the same as the probability that it is +3 or more (both are 3 or more units from the mean). This enables us to use a single measure of risk for the normal distribution. That measure is the standard deviation.

The standard deviation tells us everything we need to know about the width of the normal distribution or, in other words, the variation in the individual values. This variation is what we mean when we talk about risk in finance. In general terms, risk is a measure of the range of potential outcomes. The standard deviation is an especially useful measure of risk because it tells us the probability that an outcome will fall a particular distance from the mean or within a particular range. You can see this in the following table, which shows the fraction of all observations in a normal distribution that are within the indicated number of standard deviations from the mean.

Number of Standard Deviations from the Mean	Fraction of Total Observations
1.000	68.26%
1.645	90%
1.960	95%
2.575	99%

Since the returns on many assets are approximately normally distributed, the standard deviation provides a convenient way of computing the probability that the return on an asset will fall within a particular range. In these applications, the expected return on an asset equals the mean of the distribution and the standard deviation is a measure of the uncertainty associated with the return.

For example, if the expected return for a property investment in the Algarve, Portugal, is 10% with a standard deviation of 2%, there is a 90% chance that the actual return will be within 3.29% of 10%. How do we know this? As shown in the table, 90% of all outcomes in a normal distribution have a value that is within 1.645 standard deviations of the mean value and 1.645 × 2% = 3.29%. This tells us that there is a 90% chance that the realised return on the investment in the Algarve will be between 6.71% (10% − 3.29%) and 13.29% (10% + 3.29%), a range of 6.58% (13.29% − 6.71%).

You may be wondering what is *standard* about the standard deviation. The answer is that this statistic is standard in the sense that it can be used to directly compare the uncertainties (risks) associated with the returns on different investments. For instance, suppose you are comparing the property investment in the Algarve with a property investment on the Costa Del Sol in the Spanish region of Andalusia. Assume that the expected return on the Costa Del Sol investment is also 10%. If the standard deviation for the returns on the Costa Del Sol investment is 3%, there is a 90% chance that the actual return is within 4.935% (1.645 × 3% = 4.935%) of 10%. In other words, 90% of the time, the return will be between 5.065% (10% − 4.935%) and 14.935% (10% + 4.935%), a range of 9.87% (14.935% − 5.065%).

This range is exactly 9.87%/6.58% = 1.5 times as large as the range for the Algarve investment opportunity. Notice that the ratio of the two standard deviations also equals 1.5 (3%/2% = 1.5). This is not a coincidence. We could have used the standard deviations to directly compute the relative uncertainty associated with the Costa Del Sol and Algarve investment returns. The relation between the standard deviation of returns and the width of a normal distribution (the uncertainty) is illustrated in Exhibit 7.2.

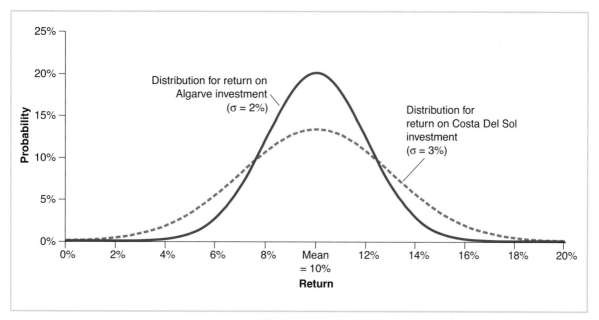

Exhibit 7.2: **Standard Deviation and Width of the Normal Distribution** The larger standard deviation for the return on the Costa Del Sol investment means that the Costa Del Sol investment is riskier than the Algarve investment. The actual return for the Costa Del Sol investment is more likely to be further from its expected return.

Let us consider another example of how the standard deviation is interpreted. Suppose customers at your pizza restaurant have complained that there is no consistency in the number of slices of pepperoni that your cooks are putting on large pepperoni pizzas. One night you decide to work in the area where the pizzas are made so that you can count the number of pepperoni slices on the large pizzas to get a better idea of just how much variation there is. After counting the slices of pepperoni on 50 pizzas, you estimate that, on average, your pizzas have 18 slices of pepperoni and that the standard deviation is three slices.

With this information, you estimate that 95% of the large pepperoni pizzas sold in your restaurant have between 12.12 and 23.88 slices. You are able to estimate this range because you know that 95% of the observations in a normal distribution fall within 1.96 standard deviations of the mean. With a standard deviation of three slices, this implies that the number of pepperoni slices on 95% of your pizzas is within 5.88 slices of the mean (3 slices × 1.96). This, in turn, indicates a range of 12.12 (18 − 5.88) to 23.88 (18 + 5.88) slices.

Since you put only whole slices of pepperoni on your pizzas, 95% of the time the number of slices is somewhere between 12 and 24. No wonder your customers are up in arms! In response to this information, you decide to implement a standard policy regarding the number of pepperoni slices that go on each type of pizza.

Learning by Doing Application 7.3

Understanding the Standard Deviation

Problem: You are considering investing in Nokia shares and want to evaluate how risky this potential investment is. You know that share returns tend to be normally distributed and you have calculated the expected return on Nokia shares to be 4.67%, and the standard deviation of the annual return to be 23%. Based on these statistics, within what range would you expect the return on the shares to fall during the next year? Calculate this range for a 90% level of confidence (that is, 90% of the time, the returns will fall within the specified range).

Approach: Use the values in the previous table or Exhibit 7.1 to compute the range within which Nokia's shares return will fall 90% of the time. First, find the number of standard deviations associated with a 90% level of confidence in the table or Exhibit 7.1, and then multiply this number by the standard deviation of the annual return for Nokia's shares. Then subtract the resulting value from the expected return (mean) to obtain the lower end of the range and add it to the expected return to obtain the upper end.

Solution: From the table, you can see that we would expect the return over the next year to be within 1.645 standard deviations of the mean 90% of the time. Multiplying this value by the standard deviation of Nokia's shares (23%) yields 23% × 1.645 = 37.835%. This means that there is a 90% chance that the return will be between −33.165% (4.67% − 37.835%) and 42.505% (4.67% + 37.835%).

While the expected return of 4.67% is relatively low, the returns on Nokia shares can vary considerably and there is a reasonable chance that the return in the next year could be quite high or quite low (even negative). As you will see shortly, this wide range of possible returns is similar to the range we observe for typical shares.

Other Measures of Risk

While the standard deviation is the most commonly used measure of risk and one which, as we will see later, is very useful, there are other ways of measuring risk. We could, for instance, measure risk in relative terms – as we did when we compared the Portuguese and Andalusia property investments. Or we can conceive of risk as being the chance of getting an outcome above or below a given value. These different concepts of risk all have a place and, while it is beyond the scope of this book to go into details, you will encounter them since many businesspeople often think of risk this way.

Historical Market Performance

Now that we have discussed how returns and risks can be measured, we are ready to examine the characteristics of the historical returns earned by securities such as shares and bonds. Exhibit 7.3 illustrates the distributions of historical returns for some securities in the United Kingdom and shows the average and standard deviations of these annual returns for the period from 1900 to 2009.

Note that the statistics reported in Exhibit 7.3 are for indices that represent total *average* returns for the indicated types of securities, not total returns on individual securities. We generally use indices to represent the performance of the shares or bond markets. For instance, when news services report on the performance of the shares market, they often report that the CAC-40 (France), the DAX (Germany) or the FTSE 100 (UK) index went up or down on a particular day. These and other indices were discussed in Chapter 2.

The plots in Exhibit 7.3 are arranged in order of decreasing risk, which is indicated by the decreasing standard deviation of the annual returns. The top plot shows returns for the equity index that represents the performance of the London market. The middle plot shows the performance for UK government bonds while the bottom plot shows the performance for treasury bills. Treasury bills are short-term debt of the British Government with maturities ranging from 30 days to one year.

The key point to note in Exhibit 7.3 is that, on average, annual returns have been higher for riskier securities. Ordinary shares or equities, which have the largest standard deviation of total returns, at 21.8%, also have the largest average return, 11.3%. At the other end of the spectrum, treasury bills have the smallest standard deviation, 3.8%, and the smallest average annual return, 5.1%. Returns for shares in any particular year may have been higher or lower than returns for the other types of securities, but on average, they were higher. This is evidence that investors require higher returns for investments with greater risks.

The statistics in Exhibit 7.3 describe actual investment returns, as opposed to expected returns. In other words, they represent what has happened in the past. Financial analysts often use historical numbers such as these to estimate the returns that might be expected in the future. That is exactly what we did in the football example earlier in this chapter. We used the percentage of goal shots in which you scored in the past season to estimate the likelihood that you would score in your last game for the university. We assumed that your past performance was a reasonable indicator of your future performance.

To see how historical numbers are used in finance, let us suppose that you are considering investing in a fund that mimics the London stock market (this is what we call an *index fund*) and that you want to estimate what the returns are likely to be in the future. If you believe that the 1900 to 2009 period provides a reasonable indication of what we can expect in the future, then the average historical return on equities in the London market of 11.30% provides a perfectly reasonable estimate of the return you can expect from your investment in UK equities. In Chapter 13 we will explore in detail how historical data can be used in this way to estimate the discount rate used to evaluate projects in the capital budgeting process.

Comparing the historical returns for an individual share with the historical returns for an index

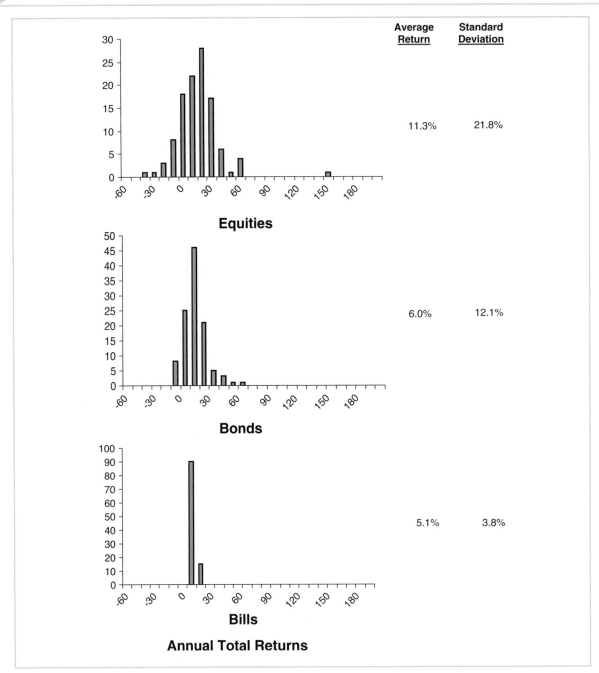

Exhibit 7.3: Distributions of Annual Total Returns for United Kingdom Equities, Bonds and Bills from 1900 to 2009 Higher standard deviations of returns have historically been associated with higher returns. For example, between 1900 and 2009, the standard deviation of annual returns for equities in the UK was higher than the standard deviations of the returns earned by other types of securities and the average return that investors earned from equities was also higher. At the other end of the spectrum, the return on treasury bills had the smallest standard deviation and earned the smallest average return.

Source: Elroy Dimson, Paul Marsh and Mike Staunton, *Triumph of the Optimists: 101 Years of Global Investment Returns*, Princeton University Press, 2002; Credit Suisse Global Investment Returns Sourcebook 2010. Copyright © 2010 Elroy Dimson, Paul Marsh and Mike Staunton. Used by permission.

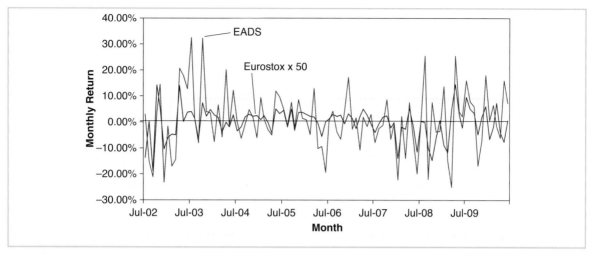

Exhibit 7.4: Monthly Returns for EADS and the Dow Jones Euro Stoxx 50 Index from June 2002 to June 2010 The returns on individual shares tend to be much more volatile than the returns on portfolios of shares, such as the Euro Stoxx 50 index. The Euro Stoxx 50 index is a free-float market capitalisation-weighted index of 50 leaders drawn from the eurozone stock markets and provides a representation of the leading shares in the Eurozone. EADS is the pan-European aerospace, defence and related services company, best known for its commercial airlines division that makes the Airbus series of commercial jets.

can also be instructive. Exhibit 7.4 shows such a comparison for EADS (the European Aeronautic Defence and Space Company) and the Dow Jones Euro Stoxx 50 index, that consists of 50 leading companies in Europe, using monthly returns for the period from June 2002 to June 2010. Notice in the exhibit that the returns on EADS shares are much more volatile than the average returns on the firms represented in the Euro Stoxx 50 index. In other words, the standard deviation of returns for EADS shares is higher than that for the Euro Stoxx 50 index. This is not a coincidence; we will discuss shortly why returns on individual shares tend to be riskier than returns on indices.

One last point is worth noting while we are examining historical returns: the value of a unit investment in 1900 would have varied greatly by 2009, depending on where the money had been invested. Exhibit 7.5 shows what money invested in treasury bills, bonds or equities in 1900 would have been worth by 2009. The star performer for the group is the United States, where one dollar invested in treasury bills would have increased by 2.8 times, for bonds that would be 8.2 times and for equities a massive 727 times. For the UK, also

a good performer over the same period, the corresponding figures are 3.1, 4.3 and 287 times.[2] Other countries have had a more chequered history with, for instance, Germany returning 0.07 for bills, 0.11 for bonds and 25 times for equities.

Over a long period of time, earning higher rates of return can have a dramatic impact on the value of an investment. This huge difference reflects the impact of compounding of returns (returns earned on returns), much like the compounding of interest we discussed in Chapter 5.

WEB

To get an idea of long-term rates of return for different countries, you can download the Credit Suisse Global Investment Yearbook at: http://emagazine.credit-suisse.com/app/shop/index.cfm.

So what return can investors get over the long term? The following table summarises the nominal

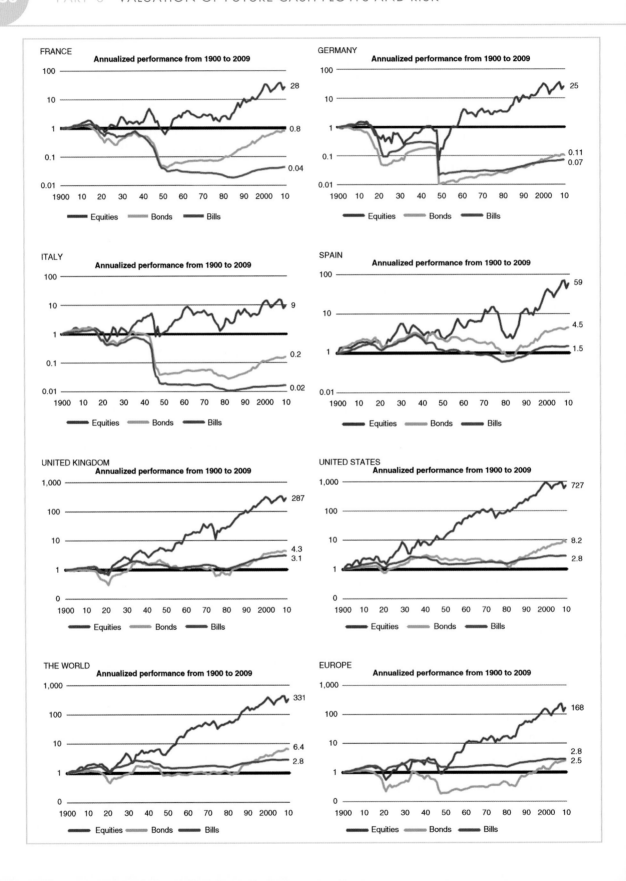

Exhibit 7.5: Cumulative Value of One Unit of Currency Invested in 1900 for Selected Countries The value of one unit of currency invested in equities grew much more rapidly than one unit invested in bonds or treasury bills over the period 1900 to the end of 2009. The graphs illustrate how earning a higher rate of return over a long period can affect the value of an investment portfolio. Although annual equity returns were less certain over the period 1900 to 2009, the returns on equity investments were much greater. Note too, that different countries have had a different experience over this period, with countries such as France, Germany and Italy experiencing periods of significant negative returns for bonds and bills. The best performer overall is the United States. For comparison purposes, the combined world and European performances are also shown.

Source: Elroy Dimson, Paul Marsh and Mike Staunton, *Triumph of the Optimists: 101 Years of Global Investment Returns*, Princeton University Press, 2002; Credit Suisse Global Investment Returns Sourcebook 2010. Copyright © 2010 Elroy Dimson, Paul Marsh and Mike Staunton. Used by permission.

return, real return and the standard deviation of returns for the period 1900 to 2009 based on the Credit Suisse Global Investment Returns Sourcebook 2010:

Returns and Risk of Major Asset Classes 1900–2009

	The World			Europe			United States		
	Bills	Bonds	Equities	Bills	Bonds	Equities	Bills	Bonds	Equities
Nominal return (%)	3.9	4.7	8.6	3.9	3.8	7.9	3.9	5.0	9.3
Nominal return (%)	0.9	1.7	5.4	0.9	0.8	4.8	0.9	1.9	6.2
Standard deviation	4.7	10.4	17.8	4.7	15.4	21.6	4.7	10.2	20.4

Source: Elroy Dimson, Paul Marsh and Mike Staunton, *Triumph of the Optimists: 101 Years of Global Investment Returns*, Princeton University Press, 2002; Credit Suisse Global Investment Returns Sourcebook 2010. Copyright © 2010 Elroy Dimson, Paul Marsh and Mike Staunton. Used by permission.

While there are differences between the results, they all show a clear link between the average return and the standard deviation of return: the higher the return that was earned, the greater the variability of that return over the period, as measured by the standard deviation.

Before You Go On

1. What is the relation between the variance and the standard deviation?
2. What relation do we generally observe between risk and return when we examine historical returns?
3. How would we expect the standard deviation of the return on an individual share to compare with the standard deviation of the return on a share index?

RISK AND DIVERSIFICATION

Learning Objective 4

Explain what the standard deviation of returns is, explain why it is especially useful in finance and be able to calculate it.

It does not generally make sense to invest all of your money in a single asset. The reason is directly related to the fact that returns on individual shares tend to be riskier than returns on indices. By investing in two or more assets whose values do not always move in the same direction at the same time, an investor can reduce the risk of his or her collection of investments, or **portfolio**. This is the idea behind the concept of **diversification**.

Portfolio

the collection of assets an investor owns

Diversification

a strategy of reducing risk by investing in two or more assets whose values do not always move in the same direction at the same time

This section develops the tools necessary to evaluate the benefits of diversification. We begin with a discussion of how to quantify risk and return for a single-asset portfolio and then we discuss more realistic and complicated portfolios that have two or more assets. Although our discussion focuses on equity portfolios, it is important to recognise that the concepts discussed apply equally well to portfolios that include a range of assets, including shares, bonds and property, among others.

Single-Asset Portfolios

Returns for individual shares from one day to the next have been found to be largely independent of each other and approximately normally distributed. In other words, the return for a share on one day is largely independent of the return on that same share the next day, two days later and three days later, and so on. Each daily return can be viewed as having been randomly drawn from a normal distribution where the probability associated with the return depends on how far it is from the expected value. If we know what the expected value and standard deviation are for the distribution of returns for a share, it is possible to quantify the risks and expected returns that an investment in the shares might yield in the future.

To see how we might do this, assume that you are considering investing in one of two shares for the next year: Air France-KLM or Deutsche Lufthansa. Also, to keep things simple, assume that there are only three possible economic conditions (outcomes) a year from now and that the

returns on Air France-KLM and Deutsche Lufthansa under each of these outcomes are as follows:

Economic Outcome	Probability	Air France-KLM Return	Deutsche Lufthansa Return
Poor	0.2	−0.13	−0.10
Neutral	0.5	0.10	0.07
Good	0.3	0.25	0.22

With this information, we can calculate the expected returns for Air France-KLM and Deutsche Lufthansa by using Equation (7.2):

$$E(R_{\text{Air France-KLM}}) = (p_{\text{Poor}} \times R_{\text{Poor}})$$
$$+ (p_{\text{Neutral}} \times R_{\text{Neutral}})$$
$$+ (p_{\text{Good}} \times R_{\text{Good}})$$
$$= (0.2 \times -0.13) + (0.5 \times 0.10)$$
$$+ (0.3 \times 0.25)$$
$$= 0.099, \text{ or } 9.9\%$$

and

$$E(R_{\text{Deutsche Lufthansa}}) = (p_{\text{Poor}} \times R_{\text{Poor}})$$
$$+ (p_{\text{Neutral}} \times R_{\text{Neutral}})$$
$$+ (p_{\text{Good}} \times R_{\text{Good}})$$
$$= (0.2 \times -0.10) + (0.5 \times 0.07)$$
$$+ (0.3 \times 0.22)$$
$$= 0.081, \text{ or } 8.1\%$$

Similarly, we can calculate the standard deviations of the returns for Air France-KLM and Deutsche Lufthansa in the same way that we calculated the standard deviation for our football bonus example earlier:

$$\sigma^2_{\text{Air France-KLM}} = \left\{ p_{\text{Poor}} \times [R_{\text{Poor}} - E(R_{\text{Air France-KLM}})]^2 \right\}$$
$$+ \left\{ p_{\text{Neutral}} \times [R_{\text{Neutral}} - E(R_{\text{Air France-KLM}})]^2 \right\}$$
$$+ \left\{ p_{\text{Good}} \times [R_{\text{Good}} - E(R_{\text{Air France-KLM}})]^2 \right\}$$
$$= \left[0.2 \times (-0.13 - 0.099)^2 \right]$$
$$+ \left[0.5 \times (0.10 - 0.099)^2 \right]$$
$$+ \left[0.3 \times (0.25 - 0.099)^2 \right]$$
$$= 0.01733$$
$$\sigma_{\text{Air France-KLM}} = (\sigma^2_{\text{Air France-KLM}})^{1/2} = (0.01733)^{1/2}$$
$$= 0.13164, \text{ or } 13.164\%$$

and

$$\sigma^2_{\text{Deutsche Lufthansa}} = \left\{p_{\text{Poor}} \times [R_{\text{Poor}} - E(R_{\text{Deutsche Lufthansa}})]^2\right\}$$
$$+ \left\{p_{\text{Neutral}} \times [R_{\text{Neutral}} - E(R_{\text{Deutsche Lufthansa}})]^2\right\}$$
$$+ \left\{p_{\text{Good}} \times [R_{\text{Good}} - E(R_{\text{Deutsche Lufthansa}})]^2\right\}$$
$$= \left[0.2 \times (-0.10 - 0.081)^2\right]$$
$$+ \left[0.5 \times (0.07 - 0.081)^2\right]$$
$$+ \left[0.3 \times (0.22 - 0.081)^2\right]$$
$$= 0.01241$$

$$\sigma_{\text{Deutsche Lufthansa}} = \left(\sigma^2_{\text{Deutsche Lufthansa}}\right)^{1/2} = (0.01241)^{1/2}$$
$$= 0.11140, \text{ or } 11.140\%$$

Having calculated the expected returns and standard deviations for the expected returns on Air France-KLM and Deutsche Lufthansa shares, the natural question to ask is which provides the highest risk-adjusted return. Before we answer this question, we will return to our earlier example of choosing among three shares: A, B and C. We stated that investors would prefer the investment that provides the highest expected return for a given level of risk or the lowest risk for a given expected return. This made it easy to choose between Shares A and B, which had the same return but different risk levels, and between Shares B and C, which had the same risk but different returns. We were stuck when trying to choose between Shares A and C, however, because they differed in both risk and return. Now, armed with tools for quantifying expected returns and risk, we can at least take a first pass at comparing shares such as these.

The **coefficient of variation (CV)** is a measure that can help us in making comparisons such as that between Shares A and C. The coefficient of variation for share i is calculated as follows:

$$CV_i = \frac{\sigma_{R_i}}{E(R_i)} \qquad (7.4)$$

In this equation, CV is a measure of the risk associated with an investment for each 1% of expected return.

Coefficient of variation (CV)

a measure of the risk associated with an investment for each 1% of expected return

Recall that Share A has an expected return of 12% and a risk level of 12%, while Share C has an expected return of 16% and a risk level of 16%. If we assume that the risk level given for each share is equal to the standard deviation of its return, we can find the coefficients of variation for the shares as follows:

$$CV(R_A) = \frac{0.12}{0.12} = 1.00 \text{ and } CV(R_C) = \frac{0.16}{0.16}$$
$$= 1.00$$

Since these values are equal, the coefficient of variation measure suggests that these two investments are equally attractive on a risk-adjusted basis.

Now returning to our Air France-KLM and Lufthansa example, we find that the coefficients of variation for those shares are:

$$CV_{\text{Air France-KLM}} = \frac{\sigma_{R_{\text{Air France-KLM}}}}{E(R_{\text{Air France-KLM}})} = \frac{0.13164}{0.099}$$
$$= 1.330$$

and

$$CV_{\text{Deutsche Lufthansa}} = \frac{\sigma_{R_{\text{Deutsche Lufthansa}}}}{E(R_{\text{Deutsche Lufthansa}})}$$
$$= \frac{0.11140}{0.081} = 1.375$$

We can see that while Air France-KLM shares have a higher expected return (9.9% versus 8.1%) and a higher standard deviation of returns (13.164% versus 11.140%), they have a lower coefficient of variation than the Lufthansa shares. This tells us that the amount of risk for each 1% of expected return is lower for Air France-KLM shares than for Lufthansa shares. On a risk-adjusted basis, then, the expected returns from Lufthansa shares are more attractive.

Learning by Doing Application 7.4

Calculating and Using the Coefficient of Variation

Problem: You are trying to choose between two investments. The first investment, a painting by Picasso, has an expected return of 14% with a standard deviation of 30% over the next year. The second investment, a pair of blue suede shoes once worn by Elvis Presley, has an expected return of 20% with a standard deviation of return of 40%. What is the coefficient of variation for each of these investments and what do these coefficients tell us?

Approach: Use Equation (7.4) to compute the coefficients of variation for the two investments.

Solution: The coefficients of variation are:

$$CV(R_{Painting}) = \frac{0.30}{0.14} = 2.14 \text{ and } CV(R_{Shoes})$$
$$= \frac{0.40}{0.20} = 2.00$$

The coefficient of variation for the Picasso painting is slightly higher than that for Elvis's blue suede shoes. This indicates that the risk for each 1% of expected return is higher for the painting than for Elvis's shoes.

WEB

You can read about other ratios that are used to measure risk-adjusted returns for investments at the following website: www.andreassteiner.net/performanceanalysis/?external_analysis:risk-adjusted_performance_measures.

Portfolios with More Than One Asset

It may seem like a good idea to evaluate investments by calculating a measure of risk for each 1% of expected return. However, the coefficient of variation has a critical shortcoming that is not quite evident when we are considering only a single asset. In order to explain this shortcoming, we must discuss the more realistic setting in which an investor has constructed a two-asset portfolio.

Expected Return on a Portfolio with more than one Asset

Suppose that you own a portfolio that consists of €500 of Air France-KLM shares and €500 of Lufthansa shares and that over the next year you expect to earn returns on the Air France-KLM and Deutsche Lufthansa shares of 9.9% and 8.1%, respectively. How would you calculate the expected return for the overall portfolio?

Let us try to answer this question using our intuition. If half of your funds are invested in each company's shares, it would seem reasonable that the expected return for this portfolio should be a 50:50 mixture of the expected returns from the two shares, or:

$$E(R_{Portfolio}) = (0.5 \times 0.099) + (0.5 \times 0.081)$$
$$= 0.09, \text{ or } 9.0\%$$

Notice that this formula is just like the expected return formula for an individual share. However, in this case, instead of multiplying outcomes by their associated probabilities, we are multiplying expected returns for individual shares by the fraction of the total portfolio value that each of these shares represents. In other words, the formula for the expected return for a two-share portfolio is:

$$E(R_{Portfolio}) = x_1 E(R_1) + x_2 E(R_2)$$

where x_i represents the fraction of the portfolio invested in asset i. The corresponding equation for a portfolio with n assets is:

$$E(R_{Portfolio}) = \sum_{i=1}^{n} [x_i \times E(R_i)]$$
$$= [x_1 \times E(R_1)] + [x_2 \times E(R_2)] \qquad (7.5)$$
$$+ \ldots + [x_n \times E(R_n)]$$

This equation is just like Equation (7.2), except that (1) the returns are expected returns for individual assets and (2) instead of multiplying by the probability of an outcome we are multiplying by the fraction of the portfolio invested in each asset. Note that this equation can be used only if you have already calculated the expected return for each share.

To see how Equation (7.5) is used to calculate the expected return on a portfolio with more than two assets, consider an example. Suppose that you were recently awarded a €500 000 grant from a national foundation to pursue your interest in advancing the art of trout tickling – a popular pastime in some parts of Europe in which people catch trout by putting their hands into streams and gently stroking the trout before grabbing it and flipping it out of the water.[3] Since your grant is intended to support your activities for five years, you kept €100 000 to cover your expenses for the next year and invested the remaining €400 000 in treasury bills and shares. Specifically, you invested €100 000 in treasury bills (TB) that yield 4.5%; €150 000 in Unilever, which has an expected return of 7.5%; and €150 000 in Royal Dutch Shell (Shell), which has an expected return of 9.0%. What is the expected return on this €400 000 portfolio?

In order to use Equation (7.5), we must first calculate x_i, the fraction of the portfolio invested in asset i, for each investment. These fractions are as follows:

$$x_{TB} = \frac{€100\,000}{€400\,000} = 0.25$$

$$x_{Unilever} = x_{Shell} = \frac{€150\,000}{€400\,000} = 0.375$$

Therefore, the expected return on the portfolio is:

$$E(R_{Portfolio}) = [x_{TB} \times E(R_{TB})]$$
$$+ [x_{Unilever} \times E(R_{Unilever})]$$
$$+ x_{Shell} \times E(R_{Shell})$$
$$= (0.25 \times 0.045) + (0.375 \times 0.075)$$
$$+ (0.375 \times 0.090)$$
$$= 0.0731, \text{ or } 7.31\%$$

Learning by Doing Application 7.5

Calculating the Expected Return on a Portfolio

Problem: You have become concerned that you have too much of your money invested in your pizza restaurant and have decided to diversify your personal portfolio. Right now the pizza restaurant is your only investment. To diversify, you plan to sell 45% of your restaurant and invest the proceeds from the sale, in equal proportions, into an equity index fund and a bond index fund. Over the next year, you expect to earn a return of 15% on your remaining investment in the pizza restaurant, 12% on your investment in the equity index fund and 8% on your investment in the bond index fund. What return will you expect from your diversified portfolio over the next year?

Approach: First, calculate the fraction of your portfolio that will be invested in each type of asset after you have diversified. Then use Equation (7.5) to calculate the expected return on the portfolio.

Solution: After you have diversified, 55% (100% − 45%) of your portfolio will be invested in your restaurant, 22.5% (45% × 0.50) will be invested in the shares market index fund and 22.5% (45% × 0.50) will be invested in the bond market index fund. Therefore, from Equation (7.5), we know that the expected return for

your portfolio is:

$$E(R_{Portfolio}) = [x_{Rest} \times E(R_{Rest})]$$
$$+ [x_{Equities} \times E(R_{Equities})]$$
$$+ [x_{Bonds} \times E(R_{Bonds})]$$
$$= (0.550 \times 0.15) + (0.225 \times 0.12)$$
$$+ (0.225 \times 0.08)$$
$$= 0.1275, \text{ or } 12.75\%$$

At 12.75%, the expected return is an average of the returns on the individual assets in your portfolio, weighted by the fraction of your portfolio that is invested in each.

Risk of a Portfolio with more than one Asset

Now that we have calculated the expected return on a portfolio with more than one asset, the next question is how to quantify the risk of such a portfolio. Before we discuss the mechanics of how to do this, it is important to have some intuitive understanding of how volatility in the returns for different assets interacts to determine the volatility of the overall portfolio.

The prices of two shares in a portfolio will rarely, if ever, change by the same amount and in the same direction at the same time. Normally, the price of one share will change by more than the price of the other. In fact, the prices of two shares will frequently move in different directions. These differences in price movements affect the total volatility in the returns for a portfolio.

Exhibit 7.6 shows monthly returns for the shares of Carrefour SA (France) and Deutsche Bank AG (Germany) over the period from January 2005 to June 2010. Notice that the returns on these shares are generally different and that the prices of

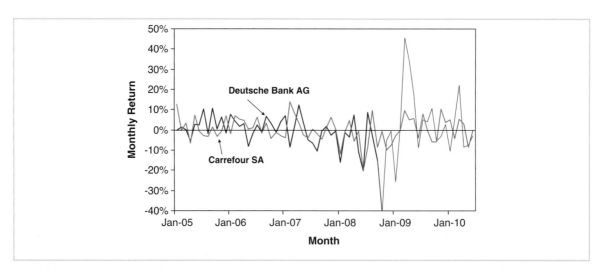

Exhibit 7.6: Monthly Returns for Carrefour SA and Deutsche Bank AG from January 2003 to June 2010
The returns on the two shares are generally different. In some periods, the return on one share is positive while the return on the other is negative. Even when both returns are positive or negative, they are not the same.

the shares can move in different directions in a given month (one share has a positive return when the other has a negative return). When the share prices move in opposite directions, the change in the price of one share offsets at least some of the change in the price of the other share. As a result, the level of risk for a portfolio of the two shares is less than the average of the risks associated with the individual shares.

This means that we *cannot* calculate the variance of a portfolio containing two assets simply by calculating the average of the variances of the individual shares using a formula such as:

$$\sigma^2_{R_{2 \text{ Asset portfolio}}} = x_1^2 \sigma^2_{R_1} + x_2^2 \sigma^2_{R_2}$$

where x_i represents the fraction of the portfolio invested in share i and $\sigma^2_{R_i}$ is the variance of the return on share i. We have to account for the fact that the returns on different shares in a portfolio tend to partially offset each other. We do this by adding a third term to the formula. For a two-asset portfolio, we calculate the variance of the returns using the following formula:

$$\sigma^2_{R_{2 \text{ Asset portfolio}}} = x_1^2 \sigma^2_{R_1} + x_2^2 \sigma^2_{R_2} + 2x_1 x_2 \sigma_{R_{1,2}} \quad (7.6)$$

where $\sigma_{R_{1,2}}$ is the **covariance** between share 1 and 2. The covariance is a measure of how the returns on two assets co-vary, or move together. The third term in Equation (7.6) accounts for the fact that returns from the two assets will offset each other to some extent. The covariance is calculated using the following formula:

$$COV(R_1, R_2) = \sigma_{R_{1,2}} = \sum \{p_i \times [R_{1,i} - E(R_1)]$$

$$\times [R_{2,i} - E(R_2)]\} \quad (7.7)$$

where i represents outcomes rather than assets. Compare this equation with Equation (7.3), reproduced here:

$$Var(R) = \sigma^2_R = \sum_{i=1}^{n} \{p_i \times [R_i - E(R)]^2\}$$

Covariance

a measure of how the returns on two assets co-vary, or move together

You can see that the covariance calculation is very similar to the variance calculation. The difference is that, instead of squaring the difference between the value from each outcome and the expected value for an individual asset, we calculate the product of this difference for two different assets.

Just as it is difficult to directly interpret the variance of the returns for an asset – recall that the variance is in units of squared euros – it is difficult to directly interpret the covariance of returns between two assets (as it is in squared units of return). We get around this problem by dividing the covariance by the product of the standard deviations of the returns for the two assets. This gives us the correlation, ρ, between the returns on those assets:

$$\rho = \frac{\sigma_{R_{1,2}}}{\sigma_{R_1}\sigma_{R_2}} \quad (7.8)$$

The correlation between the returns on two assets will always have a value between -1 and $+1$. This makes the interpretation of this variable straightforward. A *negative correlation* means that the returns tend to have opposite signs. For example, when the return on one asset is positive, the return on the other asset tends to be negative. If the correlation is exactly -1, the returns on the two assets are perfectly negatively correlated. In other words, when the return on one asset is positive, the return on the other asset will always be negative. A *positive correlation* means that when the return on one asset is positive, the return on the other asset also tends to be positive. If the correlation is exactly equal to $+1$, then the returns on the two assets are said to be perfectly positively correlated. The return on one asset will always be positive when the return on the other asset is positive. Finally, a *correlation of 0* means that the returns on the assets are not correlated. In this case, the fact that the return on one asset is positive or negative tells you nothing about how likely it is that the return on the other asset will be positive or negative.

Let us work an example to see how Equation (7.6) is used to calculate the variance of a portfolio that consists of 50% Carrefour SA and 50% Deutsche Bank AG shares. Using the data plotted in Exhibit 7.6, we can calculate the variance of the returns for Carrefour and Deutsche Bank shares, σ_R^2, to be 0.046820 and 0.170791, respectively. The covariance between the returns on these two shares is 0.068893. We do not show the calculations for the variances and the covariance because each of these numbers was calculated using 64 different monthly returns. These calculations are too cumbersome to illustrate. Rest assured, however, that they were calculated using Equations (7.3) and (7.7).[4] With these values, we can calculate the variance of a portfolio that consists of 50% Carrefour shares and 50% Deutsche Bank shares as:

Exhibit 7.7 illustrates the monthly returns for the portfolio of Carrefour and Deutsche Bank shares, along with the monthly returns for the individual shares. You can see in this exhibit that, while the returns on the portfolio vary quite a bit, this variation is less than that for the individual company shares.

Using Equation (7.8), we can calculate the correlation of the returns between Carrefour and Deutsche Bank shares as:

$$\rho = \frac{\sigma_{R_{1,2}}}{\sigma_{R_1}\sigma_{R_2}} = \frac{0.068893}{0.46820 \times 0.170791} = 0.7704$$

The positive correlation tells us that the prices of Carrefour and Deutsche Bank shares tend to move in the same direction. However, the correlation of less than one tells us that they do not always do so. The fact that the prices of these two shares do not always move together is the reason that the

0.170791	0.04682	0.068893	Deutsche	0.170791	0.413268	0.5	0.08540
0.413268	0.21638		Carrefour	0.04682	0.21638	0.5	0.02341
			Covariance	0.068893			0.03445
							0.14325
							0.37849

$$\sigma_{R_{\text{Portfolio of Carrefour and Deutsche Bank}}}^2 = x_{\text{Carrefour}}^2 \sigma_{R_{\text{Carrefour}}}^2$$
$$+ x_{\text{Deutsche Bank}}^2 \sigma_{R_{\text{Deutsche Bank}}}^2$$
$$+ 2x_{\text{Carrefour}} x_{\text{Deutsche Bank}}$$
$$\times \sigma_{R_{\text{Carrefour, Deutsche Bank}}}$$
$$= (0.5)^2 (0.046820)$$
$$+ (0.5)^2 (0.170791)$$
$$+ 2(0.5)(0.5)(0.068893)$$
$$= 0.14325$$

You can see that this portfolio variance is smaller than the variance of Deutsche Bank shares on its own, but somewhat larger than that for Carrefour, which is a low-risk share.

If we calculate the standard deviations by taking the square roots of the variances, we find that the standard deviations for Carrefour, Deutsche Bank and the portfolio consisting of those two shares are 0.21638 (21.638%), 0.413268 (41.3268%) and 0.378486 (37.8486%), respectively.

returns on a portfolio of the two shares have less variation than the returns on the individual company shares. This example illustrates the benefit of *diversification* – how holding more than one asset with different risk characteristics can reduce the risk of a portfolio. Note that if the correlation of the returns between Carrefour and Deutsche Bank shares equalled one, holding these two shares would not reduce risk because their prices would always move up or down together.

As we add more and more shares to a portfolio, calculating the variance using the approach illustrated in Equation (7.6) becomes increasingly complex. The reason for this is that we have to account for the covariance between each pair of assets. These more extensive calculations are beyond the scope of this book, but they are conceptually the same as those for a portfolio with two assets.

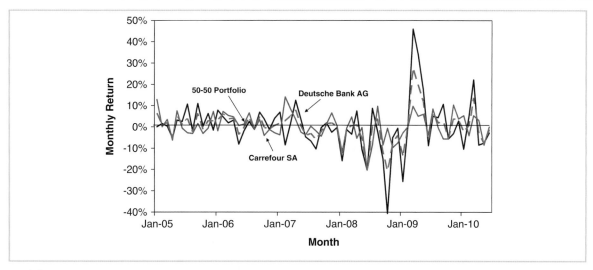

Exhibit 7.7: Monthly Returns for Carrefour SA and Deutsche Bank AG and for a Portfolio with 50% of the Value in Each of These Two Shares from January 2005 to June 2010 The variation in the returns of a portfolio that consists of Carrefour and Deutsche Bank shares in equal proportions is less than the variation in the returns from either of the shares on their own.

Learning by Doing Application 7.6

Calculating the Variance of a Two-Asset Portfolio

Problem: You are still planning to sell 45% of your pizza restaurant in order to diversify your personal portfolio. However, you have now decided to invest all of the proceeds in the equity index fund. After you diversify, you will have 55% of your wealth invested in the restaurant and 45% invested in the equity index fund. You have estimated the variances of the returns for these two investments and the covariance between their returns to be as follows:

$\sigma^2_{R_{Restaurant}}$	0.0625
$\sigma^2_{R_{Stock\ market\ index}}$	0.0400
$\sigma_{R_{Restaurant,\ Stock\ market\ index}}$	0.0250

What will be the variance and standard deviation of your portfolio after you have sold

the ownership interest in your restaurant and invested in the equity index fund?

Approach: Use Equation (7.6) to calculate the variance of the portfolio and then take the square root of this value to obtain the standard deviation.

Solution: The variance of the portfolio is:

$$
\begin{aligned}
\sigma^2_{R_{Portfolio}} &= x^2_{R_{Restaurant}}\, \sigma^2_{R_{Restaurant}} \\
&\quad + x^2_{R_{Stock\ market\ index}}\, \sigma^2_{R_{Stock\ market\ index}} \\
&\quad + 2x_{R_{Restaurant}} x_{R_{Stock\ market\ index}} \\
&\qquad \times\, \sigma_{R_{Restaurant,\ Stock\ market\ index}} \\
&= \left[(0.55)^2 \times 0.0625\right] \\
&\quad + \left[(0.45)^2 \times 0.0400\right] \\
&\quad + (2 \times 0.55 \times 0.45 \times 0.0250) \\
&= 0.0394
\end{aligned}
$$

and the standard deviation is $(0.0394)^{1/2} = 0.1985$, or 19.85%.

Comparing the portfolio variance of 0.0394 with the variances of the restaurant, 0.0625, and the shares market index fund, 0.0400, shows once again that a portfolio with two or more assets can have a smaller variance (and thus a smaller standard deviation) than any of the individual assets in the portfolio.

The Limits of Diversification

In the sample calculations for the portfolio containing Carrefour and Deutsche Bank shares, we saw that the standard deviation of the returns for a portfolio consisting of equal investments in those two shares was 10.926% from January 2005 to June 2010 and that this figure was lower than the standard deviation for Deutsche Bank alone (11.93%). You might wonder how the standard deviation for the portfolio is likely to change if we increase the number of assets in the portfolio. The answer is simple. If the returns on the individual shares added to our portfolio do not all change in the same way, then increasing the number of shares in the portfolio will reduce the standard deviation of the portfolio returns even further.

Let us consider a simple example to illustrate this point. Suppose that all assets have a standard deviation of returns that is equal to 40% and that the covariance between the returns for each pair of assets is 0.048. If we form a portfolio in which we have an equal investment in two assets, the standard deviation of returns for the portfolio will be 32.25%. If we add a third asset, the portfolio standard deviation of returns will decrease to 29.21%. It will be even lower, at 27.57%, for a four-asset portfolio. Exhibit 7.8 illustrates how the standard deviation for the portfolio declines as more shares are added.

In addition to showing how increasing the number of assets decreases the overall risk of a portfolio, Exhibit 7.8 illustrates three other very important points. First, the decrease in the standard deviation for the portfolio gets smaller and smaller as more assets are added. You can see this effect by looking at the distance between the straight horizontal line and the plot of the standard deviation of the portfolio returns.

The second important point is that, as the number of assets becomes very large, the portfolio standard deviation does not approach zero. It decreases only so far. In the example in Exhibit 7.8, it approaches 21.9%. The standard deviation does not approach zero because we are assuming that the variations in the asset returns do not completely cancel each other out. This is a realistic assumption because in practice investors can rarely diversify away all risk. They can diversify away risk that is unique to the individual assets, but they cannot diversify away risk that is common to all

BUILDING INTUITION

Diversified Portfolios are Less Risky

Diversified portfolios generally have less risk for a given level of return than the individual risky assets in the portfolio. This is because the prices of individual assets rarely change by the same amount and in the same direction at the same time. As a result, some of the variation in an asset's price can be diversified away by owning another asset at the same time. This is important because it tells us that investors can eliminate some of the risk associated with individual investments by holding them in a diversified portfolio.

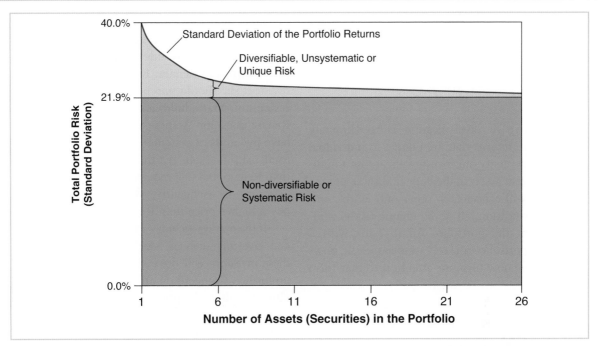

Exhibit 7.8: Unique and Systematic Risk of a Portfolio as the Number of Assets Increases
The total risk of a portfolio decreases as the number of assets increases. This is because the amount of unsystematic or unique risk in the portfolio decreases. The diversification benefit from adding another asset declines as the total number of assets in the portfolio increases and the unsystematic or unique risk approaches zero. Most of the diversification benefit can often be achieved with as few as 15 or 20 assets.

assets. The risk that can be diversified away is called **diversifiable, unsystematic** or **unique risk**, and the risk that cannot be diversified away is called **non-diversifiable** or **systematic risk**. In the next section, we will discuss systematic risk in detail.

> ### Diversifiable, unsystematic or unique risk
>
> risk that can be eliminated through diversification

> ### Non-diversifiable or systematic risk
>
> risk that cannot be eliminated through diversification

The third key point illustrated in Exhibit 7.8 is that most of the risk-reduction benefits from diversification can be achieved in a portfolio with 15 to 20 assets. Of course, the number of assets required to achieve a high level of diversification depends on the covariances between the assets in the portfolio. However, in general, it is not necessary to invest in a very large number of different assets.

> ### Before You Go On
>
> 1. What does the coefficient of variation tell us?
> 2. What are the two components of total risk?
> 3. Why does the total risk of a portfolio not approach zero as the number of assets in a portfolio becomes very large?

SYSTEMATIC RISK

Learning Objective 5
Explain the concept of diversification.

The objective of diversification is to eliminate variations in returns that are unique to individual assets. We diversify our investments across a number of different assets in the hope that these unique variations will cancel each other out. With complete diversification, all of the unique risk is eliminated from the portfolio. An investor with a diversified portfolio still faces systematic risk, however, and we now turn our attention to that form of risk.

Why Systematic Risk is All that Matters

The idea that unique, or unsystematic, risk can be diversified away has direct implications for the relation between risk and return. If the transaction costs associated with constructing a diversified portfolio are relatively low, then rational, informed investors, such as the students who are taking this course, will prefer to hold diversified portfolios.

Diversified investors face only systematic risk, whereas investors whose portfolios are not well diversified face systematic risk plus unsystematic risk. Because they face less risk, the diversified investors will be willing to pay higher prices for individual assets than the other investors. Therefore, expected returns on individual assets will be lower than the total risk (systematic plus unsystematic risk) of those assets suggests they should be.

To illustrate, consider two individual investors, Maria and Renata. Each of them is trying to decide if she should purchase shares in your pizza restaurant. Maria holds a diversified portfolio and Renata does not. Assume your restaurant's shares have five units of systematic risk and nine units of total risk. You can see that Maria faces less risk than Renata and will require a lower expected rate of return. Consequently, Maria will be willing to pay a higher price than Renata.

If the market includes a large number of diversified investors such as Maria, competition among these investors will drive the price of your shares up further. Competition among these investors will ultimately drive the price up to the point where the expected return just compensates all investors for the systematic risk associated with your shares. The bottom line is that because of competition among diversified investors only systematic risk is rewarded in asset markets. For this reason, we are concerned only about systematic risk when we think about the relation between risk and return in finance.

Measuring Systematic Risk

If systematic risk is all that matters when we think about expected returns, then we cannot use the standard deviation as a measure of risk.[5] The standard deviation is a measure of total risk. We need a way of quantifying the systematic risk of individual assets.

A natural starting point for doing this is to recognise that the most diversified portfolio possible

BUILDING INTUITION

Systematic Risk is the Risk that Matters

The required rate of return on an asset depends only on the systematic risk associated with that asset. Because unique (unsystematic) risk can be diversified away, investors can and will eliminate their exposure to this risk. Competition among diversified investors will drive the prices of assets to the point where the expected returns will compensate investors for only the systematic risk that they bear.

will come closest to eliminating all unique risk. Such a portfolio provides a natural benchmark against which we can measure the systematic risk of an individual asset. What is the most diversified portfolio possible? The answer is simple. It is the portfolio that consists of all assets, including shares, bonds, real estate, precious metals, commodities, art, collectibles and so forth from all over the world. In finance, we call this the **market portfolio.**

Unfortunately, we do not have very good data for most of these assets for most of the world, so we use the next best thing: the market in listed shares. A large number of shares from a broad range of industries trade in this market. The companies that issue these shares own a wide range of assets all over the world. These characteristics, combined with the facts that these markets have been operating for a very long time and that we have very reliable and detailed information on prices for traded shares, make the stock market a natural benchmark for estimating systematic risk.

> ## Market portfolio
>
> the portfolio of all assets

> ## Market risk
>
> a term commonly used to refer to non-diversifiable, or systematic, risk

Since systematic risk is, by definition, risk that cannot be diversified away, the systematic risk of an individual asset is really just a measure of the relation between the returns on the individual asset and the returns on the market. In fact, systematic risk is often referred to as **market risk.** To see how we might use data from the public shares market to estimate the systematic risk of an individual asset, look at Exhibit 7.9, which plots 110 historical monthly returns for the European Aeronautic Defence and Space Company EADS NV (EADS) against the corresponding monthly returns for the Deutscher Aktien Index (DAX) (a proxy for the market in listed shares). In this plot, you can see that returns on EADS shares tend to be higher when returns on the DAX tend to be higher. The measure of systematic risk that we use in finance is a statistical measure of this relation.

We quantify the relation between the returns on EADS shares and the general market by finding

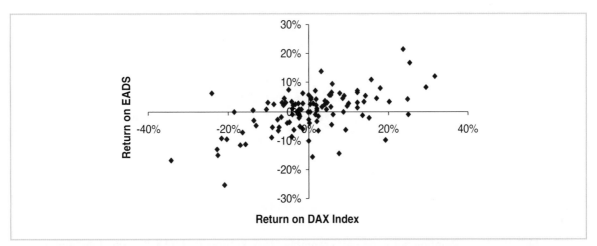

Exhibit 7.9: Plot of Monthly EADS Share and DAX Index Returns: July 2000 to August 2009
The monthly returns on European Aeronautic Defence and Space Company (EADS) shares are positively related to the returns on the Deutscher Aktien Index (DAX). In other words, the return on EADS shares tends to be higher when the return on the DAX index is higher and lower when the return on the DAX index is lower.

the slope of the line that best represents the relation illustrated in Exhibit 7.9. Specifically, we estimate the slope of the *line of best fit*. We do this using the statistical technique called regression analysis. If you are not familiar with regression analysis, do not worry; the details are beyond the scope of this course. All you have to know is that this technique gives us the line that fits the data best.

Exhibit 7.10 illustrates the line that was estimated for the data in Exhibit 7.9 using regression analysis. Note that the slope of this line is 0.98. Recall from your maths classes that the slope of a line equals the ratio of the rise (vertical distance) divided by the corresponding run (horizontal distance). In this case, the slope is the change in the return on EADS shares divided by the change in the return on the shares market. A slope of 0.98 therefore means that, on average, the change in the return on shares was 0.98 times as large as the change in the return on the DAX index. Thus, if the DAX index goes up 1%, the average increase in EADS shares is 0.98%. This is a measure of systematic risk because it tells us that the volatility of

the returns on EADS shares is 0.98 times as large as that for the DAX as a whole.

To explore this idea more completely, we will consider another, simpler example. Suppose that you have data for Nokia shares and for the shares market for Europe for each of the past two years. In the first year, the return on the market was 10%, and the return on Nokia shares was 15%. In the second year, the return on the market was 12%, and the return on Nokia shares was 19%. From this information, we know that the return on Nokia shares increased by 4% while the return on the market increased by 2%. If we plotted the returns for Nokia shares and for the market for each of the last two periods, as we did for EADS shares and the market in Exhibits 7.9 and 7.10 and estimated the line that best fit the data, it would be a line that connected the dots for the two periods. The slope of this line would equal 2, calculated as follows:

$$\text{Slope} = \frac{\text{Rise}}{\text{Run}} = \frac{\text{Change in Nokia return}}{\text{Change in market return}}$$

$$= \frac{19\% - 15\%}{12\% - 10\%} = \frac{4\%}{2\%} = 2$$

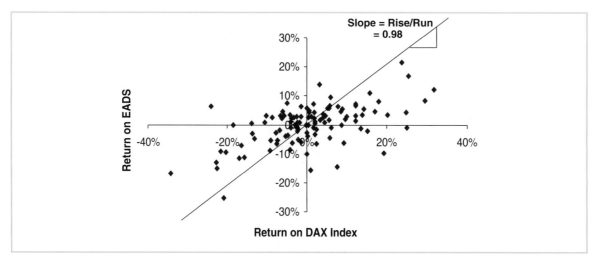

Exhibit 7.10: Slope Relation between EADS Monthly Stock Returns and DAX Returns: July 2000 to August 2009 The line shown in the exhibit best represents the relation between the monthly returns on EADS shares and the returns on the DAX index. The slope of this line, which equals 0.98, indicates that the return on EADS shares tends to equal 0.98 the return on the DAX index. This indicates that over time, the return on EADS closely tracks the return on the market, although as the data shows there will be considerable variations month on month.

Although we have to be careful about drawing conclusions when we have only two data points, we might interpret the slope of 2 to indicate that new information that causes the market return to increase by 1% will tend to cause the return on Nokia shares to increase by 2%. Of course, the reverse might also be true. That is, new information that causes the market return to decrease by 1% may also cause the return on Nokia shares to go down by 2%. To the extent that the same information is driving the changes in returns on Nokia shares and on the market, it would not be possible for an investor in Nokia shares to diversify this risk away. It is non-diversifiable, or systematic, risk.

In finance, we call the slope of the line of best fit **beta**. Often we simply use the corresponding Greek letter, β, to refer to this measure of systematic risk. As shown below, a beta of 1 tells us that an asset has just as much systematic risk as the market. A beta higher than or lower than 1 tells us that the asset has more or less systematic risk than the market, respectively. A beta of 0 indicates a risk-free security, such as a treasury bill.

$\beta = 1$	Same systematic risk as market
$\beta > 1$	More systematic risk than market
$\beta < 1$	Less systematic risk than market
$\beta = 0$	No systematic risk

Now you might ask yourself what happened to the unique risk of EADS or Nokia shares. This is best illustrated by the EADS example, where we have more than two observations. As you can see in Exhibit 7.10, the line of best fit does not go through each data point. That is because some of the change in the EADS shares price each month reflected information that did not affect the market as a whole. That information is the unsystematic, or unique, component of the risk of EADS shares. The distance between each data point and the line of best fit represents variation in EADS shares return that can be attributed to this unique risk.

Beta (β)

a measure of non-diversifiable, systematic or market risk

WEB

A convenient place to find betas for individual companies is euroland.com – the European Investor – at http://www.euroland.com. Just enter the name of the company at the top of the page and hit 'Enter' on your computer (try Royal Dutch Shell, for example). You will get a pop-up that gives you a selection of companies and exchanges. Choose the most appropriate one and you will be provided with a series of tabs giving recent traded prices, an estimate of the beta and other key financial information.

The positive slope (β) of the regression line in Exhibit 7.9 tells us that returns for the DAX and for EADS shares will tend to move in the same direction. The return on the DAX and the return on EADS shares will not always change in the same direction, however, because the unique risk associated with EADS shares can more than offset the effect of the market in any particular period. In the next section, we will discuss the implications of beta for the level (as opposed to the change) in the expected return for a share such as EADS.

Before You Go On

1. Why are returns on the shares market used as a benchmark in measuring systematic risk?
2. How is beta estimated?
3. How would you interpret a beta of 1.5 for an asset? A beta of 0.75?

COMPENSATION FOR BEARING SYSTEMATIC RISK

Learning Objective 6
Discuss which type of risk matters to investors and why.

Now that we have identified the measure of the risk that diversified investors care about – systematic risk – we are in a position to examine how this measure relates to expected returns. Let us begin by thinking about the rate of return that you would require for an investment. First, you would want to make sure that you were compensated for inflation. It would not make sense to invest if you expected the investment to return an amount that did not at least allow you to have the same purchasing power that the money you invested had when you made the investment. Second, you would want some compensation for the fact that you are giving up the use of your money for a period of time. This compensation may be very small if you are forgoing the use of your money for only a short time, such as when you invest in a 30-day treasury bill, but it might be relatively large if you are investing for several years. Finally, you are also going to require compensation for the systematic risk associated with the investment.

When you invest in a government security such as a treasury bill or bond, you are investing in a security that has no risk of default. After all, the government can always increase taxes or print more money to pay you back. Changes in economic conditions and other factors that affect the returns on other assets do not affect the default risk of government securities. As a result, these securities do not have systematic risk and their returns can be viewed as risk-free. In other words, returns on government bonds reflect the compensation required by investors to account for the impact of inflation on purchasing power and for their inability to use the money during the life of the investment.

It follows that the difference between required returns on government securities and required returns for risky investments represents the compensation investors require for taking risk. Recognising this allows us to write the expected return for an asset i as:

$$E(R_i) = R_{rf} + \text{Compensation for taking risk}_i$$

where R_{rf} is the return on a security with a risk-free rate of return, which analysts typically estimate by looking at returns on government securities. The compensation for taking risk, which varies with the risk of the asset, is added to the risk-free rate of return to get an estimate of the expected rate of return for an asset. If we recognise that the compensation for taking risk varies with asset risk and that systematic risk is what matters, we can write the preceding equation as follows:

$$E(R_i) = R_{rf} + (\text{Units of systematic risk}_i \\ \times \text{Compensation per unit of systematic risk})$$

where units of systematic risk$_i$ is the number of units of systematic risk associated with asset i. Finally, if beta, β, is the appropriate measure for the number of units of systematic risk, we can also define compensation for taking risk as follows:

Compensation for taking risk
$$= \beta_i \times \text{Compensation per unit of systematic risk}$$

where β_i is the beta for asset i.

Remember that beta is a measure of systematic risk that is directly related to the risk of the market as a whole. If the beta for an asset is 2, that asset has twice as much systematic risk as the market. If the beta for an asset is 0.5, then the asset has half as much systematic risk as the market. Recognising this natural interpretation of beta suggests that the appropriate 'unit of systematic risk' is the level of risk in the market as a whole and that the appropriate 'compensation per unit of systematic risk' is the expected return required for the level of systematic risk in the market as a whole. The required rate of return on the market, over and above that of the risk-free return, represents compensation required by investors for bearing a market (systematic) risk. This suggests that:

Compensation per unit of systematic risk
$$= E(R_m) - R_{rf}$$

where $E(R_m)$ is the expected return on the market. The term $E(R_m) - R_{rf}$ is called the *market risk premium*. Consequently, we can now write the equation for expected return as:

$$E(R_i) = R_{rf} + \beta_i[E(R_m) - R_{rf}] \qquad (7.9)$$

THE CAPITAL ASSET PRICING MODEL

Learning Objective 7

Describe what the Capital Asset Pricing Model (CAPM) tells us and how to use it to evaluate whether the expected return of an asset is sufficient to compensate an investor for the risks associated with that asset.

In deriving Equation (7.9), we intuitively arrived at the **Capital Asset Pricing Model (CAPM)**. Equation (7.9) is the CAPM, a model that describes the relation between risk and expected return. We will discuss the predictions of the CAPM in more detail shortly, but first we will look more closely at how it works.

Capital asset pricing model (CAPM)

a model that describes the relation between risk and expected return

Suppose that you want to estimate the expected return for a share that has a beta of 1.5 and that the expected returns on the market and risk-free rate are 10% and 4%, respectively. We can use Equation (7.9) (the CAPM) to find the expected return for this share:

$$E(R_i) = R_{rf} + \beta_i[E(R_m) - R_{rf}]$$
$$= 0.04 + [1.5 \times (0.10 - 0.04)]$$
$$= 0.13, \text{ or } 13\%$$

Note that we must have three pieces of information in order to use Equation (7.9): (1) the risk-free rate, (2) the beta and (3) either the market risk premium or the expected return on the market. Recall that the market risk premium is the difference between the expected return on the market and the risk-free rate $[E(R_m) - R_{rf}]$, which is 6% in the above example.

Learning by Doing Application 7.7

Expected Returns and Systematic Risk

Problem: You are considering buying 100 Nokia shares. Bloomberg (a financial reporting service) reports that the beta for Nokia is 0.76. The risk-free rate is 4%, and the market risk premium is 6%. What is the expected rate of return on Nokia shares according to the CAPM?

Approach: Use Equation (7.9) to calculate the expected return on Nokia shares.

Solution: The expected return is:

$$E(R_i) = R_{rf} + \beta_i[E(R_m) - R_{rf}]$$
$$= 0.04 + (0.76 \times 0.06)$$
$$= 0.0856, \text{ or } 8.56\%$$

The Security Market Line

Exhibit 7.11 displays a plot of Equation (7.9) to illustrate how the expected return on an asset varies with systematic risk. This plot shows that the relation between the expected return on an asset and beta is positive and linear. In other words, it is a straight line with a positive slope. The line in Exhibit 7.11 is known as the **Security Market Line (SML)**.

> ### Security market line (SML)
>
> a plot of the relation between expected return and systematic risk

In Exhibit 7.11 you can see that the expected rate of return equals the risk-free rate when beta equals 0. This makes sense because when investors do not face systematic risk, they will only require a return that reflects the expected rate of inflation and the fact that they are giving up the use of their money for a period of time. Exhibit 7.11 also shows that the expected return on an asset equals the expected return on the market when beta equals 1. This is not surprising, given that both the asset and the market would have the same level of systematic risk if this were the case.

It is important to recognise that the SML illustrates what the CAPM predicts the expected total return should be for various values of beta. The actual expected total return depends on the price of the asset. You can see this from Equation (7.1):

$$R_T = \frac{\Delta P + CF_1}{P_0}$$

where P_0 is the price that the asset is currently selling for. If an asset's price implies that the

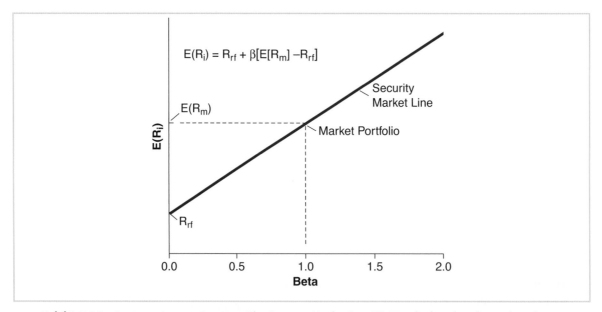

Exhibit 7.11: The Security Market Line The Security Market Line (SML) is the line that shows the relation between expected returns and systematic risk, as measured by beta. When beta equals zero and there is no systematic risk, the expected return equals the risk-free rate. As systematic risk (beta) increases, the expected return increases. This is an illustration of the positive relation between risk and return. The SML shows that it is systematic risk that matters to investors.

expected return is greater than that predicted by the CAPM, that asset will plot above the SML in Exhibit 7.11. This means that the asset's price is lower than the CAPM suggests it should be. Conversely, if the expected return on an asset plots below the SML, this implies that the asset's price is higher than the CAPM suggests it should be. The point at which a particular asset plots relative to the SML, then, tells us something about whether the price of that asset might be low or high. Recognising this fact can be helpful in evaluating the attractiveness of an investment such as the Nokia shares in Learning by Doing Application 7.7.

The Capital Asset Pricing Model and Portfolio Returns

The expected return for a portfolio can also be predicted using the CAPM. The expected return on a portfolio with n assets is calculated using the relation:

$$E\left(R_{n\text{-asset portfolio}}\right) = R_{\text{rf}} + \beta_{n\text{-asset portfolio}}[E(R_{\text{m}}) - R_{\text{rf}}]$$

Of course, this should not be surprising since investing in a portfolio is simply an alternative to investing in a single asset.

The fact that the SML is a straight line turns out to be rather convenient if we want to estimate the beta for a portfolio. Recall that the equation for the expected return for a portfolio with n assets was given by Equation (7.5):

$$E(R_{\text{Portfolio}}) = \sum_{i=1}^{n}[x_i \times E(R_i)]$$
$$= [x_1 \times E(R_1)] + [x_2 \times E(R_2)]$$
$$+ \cdots + [x_n \times E(R_n)]$$

If we substitute Equation (7.9) into Equation (7.5) for each of the n assets and rearrange the equation, we find that the beta for a portfolio is simply a weighted average of the betas for the individual assets in the portfolio. In other words:

$$\beta_{n\text{-asset portfolio}} = \sum_{i=1}^{n} x_i\beta_i$$
$$= x_1\beta_1 + x_2\beta_2 + x_3\beta_3 + \cdots + x_n\beta_n$$
$$(7.10)$$

where x_i is the proportion of the portfolio value that is invested in asset i, β_i is the beta of asset i and n is the number of assets in the portfolio. This formula makes it simple to calculate the beta of any portfolio of assets once you know the betas of the individual assets. As an exercise, you might prove this to yourself by using Equations (7.5) and (7.9) to derive Equation (7.10).

We will consider an example to see how Equation (7.10) is used. Suppose that you invested 25% of your wealth in a fully diversified market fund, 25% in risk-free treasury bills and 50% in a house with twice as much systematic risk as the market. What is the beta of your overall portfolio? What rate of return would you expect to earn from this portfolio if the risk-free rate is 4% and the market risk premium is 6%?

We know that the beta for the market must equal 1 by definition and that the beta for a risk-free asset equals 0. The beta for your home must be 2 since it has twice the systematic risk of the market. Therefore, the beta of your portfolio is:

$$\beta_{\text{Portfolio}} = x_{\text{Fund}}\beta_{\text{Fund}} + x_{\text{TB}}\beta_{\text{TB}} + x_{\text{House}}\beta_{\text{House}}$$
$$= (0.25 \times 1.0) + (0.25 \times 0.0)$$
$$+ (0.50 \times 2.0)$$
$$= 1.25$$

Your portfolio has 1.25 times as much systematic risk as the market. Based on Equation (7.9), therefore, you would expect to earn a return of 11.5%, calculated as follows:

$$E(R_{\text{Portfolio}}) = R_{\text{rf}} + \beta_{\text{Portfolio}}[E(R_{\text{m}}) - R_{\text{rf}}]$$
$$= 0.04 + (1.25 \times 0.06)$$
$$= 0.115, \text{ or } 11.5\%$$

Learning by Doing Application 7.8

Portfolio Risk and Expected Return

Problem: You have recently become very interested in property. To gain some experience as a property investor, you have decided to get together with nine of your friends to buy three small cottages near your university. If you and your friends pool your money, you will have just enough to buy the three properties. Since each investment requires the same amount of money and you will have a 10% interest in each, you will effectively have one-third of your portfolio invested in each cottage.

While the cottages cost the same, they are different distances from the university and in different neighbourhoods. You believe that this causes them to have different levels of systematic risk and you estimate that the betas for the individual cottages are 1.2, 1.3 and 1.5. If the risk-free rate is 4% and the market risk premium is 6%, what will be the expected return on your property portfolio after you make all three investments?

Approach: There are two approaches that you can use to solve this problem. First, you can estimate the expected return for each cottage using Equation (7.9) and then calculate the expected return on the portfolio using Equation (7.5). Alternatively, you can calculate the beta for the portfolio using Equation (7.10) and then use Equation (7.9) to calculate the expected return.

Solution: Using the first approach, we find that Equation (7.9) gives us the following expected returns:

$$E(R_i) = R_{rf} + \beta_i[E(R_m) - R_{rf}]$$
$$= 0.04 + (1.2 \times 0.06) = 0.112,$$
$$\text{or } 11.2\% \text{ for cottage 1}$$
$$= 0.04 + (1.3 \times 0.06)$$
$$= 0.118, \text{ or } 11.8\% \text{ for cottage 2}$$
$$= 0.04 + (1.5 \times 0.06) = 0.130, \text{ or}$$
$$13.0\% \text{ for cottage 3}$$

Therefore, from Equation (7.5), the expected return on the portfolio is:

$$E(R_{Portfolio}) = [x_1 \times E(R_1)] + [x_2 \times E(R_2)]$$
$$+ [x_3 \times E(R_3)]$$
$$= (1/3 \times 0.112) + (1/3 \times 0.118)$$
$$+ (1/3 \times 0.130) = 0.12, \text{ or } 12\%$$

Using the second approach, from Equation (7.10), the beta of the portfolio is:

$$\beta_{Portfolio} = x_1\beta_1 + x_2\beta_2 + x_3\beta_3$$
$$= (1/3)(1.2) + (1/3)(1.3)$$
$$+ (1/3)(1.5)$$
$$= 1.33333$$

and from Equation (7.9), the expected return is:

$$E(R_{Portfolio}) = R_{rf} + \beta_{Portfolio}[E(R_m) - R_{rf}]$$
$$= 0.04 + (1.33333 \times 0.06)$$
$$= 0.12, \text{ or } 12\%$$

Decision-Making Example 7.2

Choosing between Two Investments

Situation: You are trying to decide whether to invest in one or both of two different shares. Share 1 has a beta of 0.8 and an expected return of 7.0%. Share 2 has a beta of 1.2 and an expected return of 9.5%. You remember learning about the CAPM during your finance course and believe that it does a good job of telling you what the appropriate expected return should be for a given level of risk. Since the risk-free rate is 4% and the market risk premium is 6%, the CAPM tells you that the appropriate expected rate of return for an asset with a beta of 0.8 is 8.8%. The corresponding value for an asset with a beta of 1.2 is 11.2%. Should you invest in either or both of these shares?

Decision: You should not invest in either share. The expected returns for both of them are below the values predicted by the CAPM for investments with the same level of risk. In other words, both would plot below the line in Exhibit 7.11. This implies that they are both overpriced.

Up to this point, we have focused on calculating the expected rate of return for an investment in any asset from the perspective of an investor, such as a shareholder. A natural question that might arise is how these concepts relate to the rate of return that should be used within a firm to evaluate a project. The short answer is that they are the same. The rate of return used to discount the cash flows for a project with a particular level of systematic risk is exactly the same as the rate of return that an investor would expect to receive from an investment in any asset having the same level of systematic risk. In Chapter 13 we will explore the relation between the expected return and the rate used to discount project cash flows in much more detail. By the time we finish that discussion, you will understand thoroughly how businesses determine the rate that they use to discount the cash flows from their investments.

Before You Go On

1. How is the expected return on an asset related to its systematic risk?
2. What name is given to the relation between risk and expected return implied by the CAPM?
3. If an asset's expected return does not plot on the line in question 2 above, what does that imply about its price?

SUMMARY OF LEARNING OBJECTIVES

1. **Explain the relation between risk and return.**

   Investors require greater returns for taking greater risk. They prefer the investment with the highest possible return for a given level of risk or the investment with the lowest risk for a given level of return.

2. **Describe the two components of a total holding period return and calculate this return for an asset.**

   The total holding period return on an investment consists of a capital appreciation component and an income component. This return is calculated using Equation (7.1). It is important to recognise that investors do not care whether they receive the return through capital appreciation or as a cash dividend. Investors value both sources of return equally.

3. **Explain what an expected return is and calculate the expected return for an asset.**

   The expected return is a weighted average of the possible returns from an investment, where each of these returns is weighted by the probability that it will occur. It is calculated using Equation (7.2).

4. **Explain what the standard deviation of returns is, explain why it is especially useful in finance and be able to calculate it.**

   The standard deviation of returns is a measure of the total risk associated with the returns from an asset. It is useful in evaluating returns in finance because the returns on many assets tend to be normally distributed. The standard deviation of returns provides a convenient measure of the dispersion of returns. In other words, it tells us about the probability that a return will fall within a particular distance from the expected value or within a particular range. To calculate the standard deviation, the variance is first calculated using Equation (7.3). The standard deviation of returns is then calculated by taking the square root of the variance.

5. **Explain the concept of diversification.**

   Diversification is a strategy of investing in two or more assets whose values do not always move in the same direction at the same time in order to reduce risk. Investing in a portfolio containing assets whose prices do not always move together reduces risk because some of the changes in the prices of individual assets offset each other. This can cause the overall volatility in the value of the portfolio to be lower than if it were invested in a single asset.

6. **Discuss which type of risk matters to investors and why.**

   Investors only care about systematic risk. This is because they can eliminate unique risk by holding a diversified portfolio. Diversified investors will bid up prices for assets to the point at which they are just being compensated for the systematic risks they must bear.

7. **Describe what the Capital Asset Pricing Model (CAPM) tells us and how to use it to evaluate whether the expected return of an asset is sufficient to compensate an investor for the risks associated with that asset.**

   The CAPM tells us that the relation between systematic risk and return is linear and that the risk-free rate of return is the appropriate return for an asset with no systematic risk. From the CAPM we know what rate of return investors will require for an investment with a particular amount of systematic risk (beta). This means that we can use the expected return predicted by the CAPM as a benchmark for evaluating whether expected returns for individual assets are sufficient. If the expected return for an asset is less than that predicted by the CAPM, then the asset is an unattractive investment because its return is lower than the CAPM indicates it should be. By the same token, if the expected return for an asset is greater than that predicted by the CAPM, then the asset is an attractive investment because its return is higher than it should be.

SUMMARY OF KEY EQUATIONS

Equation	Description	Formula
(7.1)	Total holding period return	$R_T = R_{CA} + R_I = \frac{P_1 - P_0}{P_0} + \frac{CF_1}{P_0}$
(7.2)	Expected return on an asset	$E(R_{Asset}) = \sum_{i=1}^{n} (p_i \times R_i)$
(7.3)	Variance of return on an asset	$Var(R) = \sigma_R^2 = \sum_{i=1}^{n} \left\{ p_i \times [R_i - E(R)]^2 \right\}$
(7.4)	Coefficient of variation	$CV_i = \dfrac{\sigma_{R_i}}{E(R_i)}$
(7.5)	Expected return for a portfolio	$E(R_{Portfolio}) = \sum_{i=1}^{n} [x_i \times E(R_i)]$

(7.6)	Variance for a two-asset portfolio	$\sigma^2_{R_{2 \text{ Asset portfolio}}} = x_1^2 \sigma^2_{R_1} + x_2^2 \sigma^2_{R_2} + 2x_1 x_2 \sigma_{R_{1,2}}$
(7.7)	Covariance between two assets	$\sigma_{R_{1,2}} = \sum_{i=1}^{n} \{p_i[R_{1,i} - E(R_1)] \times [R_{2,i} - E(R_2)]\}$
(7.8)	Correlation between two assets	$\rho_{R_{1,2}} = \dfrac{\sigma_{R_{1,2}}}{\sigma_{R_1}\sigma_{R_2}}$
(7.9)	Expected return and systematic risk	$E(R_i) = R_{rf} + \beta_i[E(R_m) - R_{rf}]$
(7.10)	Portfolio beta	$\beta_{n\text{-asset portfolio}} = \sum_{i=1}^{n} x_i \beta_i$

SELF-STUDY PROBLEMS

7.1. Kaaran made a friendly wager with a colleague that involves the result from flipping a coin. If heads comes up, Kaaran must pay her colleague €15; otherwise, her colleague will pay Kaaran €15. What is Kaaran's expected cash flow and what is the variance of that cash flow if the coin has an equal probability of coming up heads or tails? Suppose Kaaran's colleague is willing to handicap the bet by paying her €20 if the coin toss results in tails. If everything else remains the same, what are Kaaran's expected cash flow and the variance of that cash flow?

7.2. You know that the price of DNC NV shares will be €12 exactly one year from today. Today the price of the shares is €11. Describe what must happen to the price of DNC NV today in order for an investor to generate a 20% return over the next year. Assume that DNC does not pay dividends.

7.3. Two men are making a bet according to the outcome of the toss of a coin. You know that the expected outcome of the bet is that one man will lose €20. Suppose you know that if that same man wins the coin toss, he will receive €80. How much will he pay out if he loses the coin toss?

7.4. The expected value of a normal distribution of prices for a share is €50. If you are 90% sure that the price of the shares will be between €40 and €60, then what is the variance of the share price?

7.5. Cairn Energy plc's ordinary shares have an expected return of 25% and a coefficient of variation of 2.0. What is the variance of Cairn Energy's ordinary shares returns?

SOLUTIONS TO SELF-STUDY PROBLEMS

7.1. Part 1: $E(\text{Cash flow}) = (0.5 \times -€15)$
$+ (0.5 \times €15) = 0$

$\sigma^2_{\text{Cash flow}} = \left[0.5 \times (-€15 - €0)^2\right]$
$+ \left[0.5 \times (€15 - €0)^2\right] = €225$

Part 2: $E(\text{Cash flow}) = (0.5 \times -€15)$
$+ (0.5 \times €20) = €2.50$

$\sigma^2_{\text{Cash flow}} = \left[0.5 \times (-€15 - €0)^2\right]$
$+ \left[0.5 \times (€20 - €0)^2\right] = €306.25$

7.2. The expected return for DNC based on today's share price is ($€12 - €11$)/$€11 =$ 9.09%, which is lower than 20%. Since the share price one year from today is fixed, the only way that you will generate a 20% return is if the price of the shares drops today. Consequently, the price of the shares today must drop to $€10$. It is found by solving the following: $0.2 = (€12 - x)/x$, or $x = €10$.

7.3. Since you know that the probability of any coin toss outcome is equal to 0.5, you can solve the problem by setting up the following equation:

$$-20 = (0.5 \times €80) + (0.5 \times x)$$

and solving for x:

$$0.5 \times x = -€20 - (0.5 \times €80)$$
$$x = [-€20 - (0.5 \times €80)]/0.5$$
$$= -€120$$

which means that he pays $€120$ if he loses the bet.

7.4. Since you know that 1.645 standard deviations around the expected return captures 90% of the distribution, you can set up either of the following equations:

$$€40 = €50 - 1.645\sigma \quad \text{or}$$
$$€60 = €50 + 1.645\sigma$$

and solve for σ. Doing this with either equation yields:

$$\sigma = €6.079 \text{ and } \sigma^2 = 36.954$$

7.5. Since the coefficient of variation is $CV_i = \frac{\sigma_{R_i}}{E(R_i)}$, substituting in the coefficient of variation and $E(R_i)$ allows us to solve for σ^2 as follows:

$$2.0 = \frac{\sigma_{R_i}}{E(R_i)}$$
$$\sigma_{R_i} = 0.5$$
$$\sigma_{R_i}^2 = (0.5)^2 = 0.25$$

CRITICAL THINKING QUESTIONS

7.1. Given that you know the risk as well as the expected return for two shares, discuss what process you might utilise to determine which of the two shares is the better buy. You may assume that the two shares will be the only assets held in your portfolio.

7.2. What is the difference between the expected rate of return and the required rate of return? What does it mean if they are different for a particular asset at a particular point in time?

7.3. Suppose that the standard deviation of the returns on the shares of two different companies is exactly the same. Does this mean that the required rate of return will be the same for these two shares? How might the required

rate of return on the shares of a third company be greater than the required rates of return on the shares of the first two companies even if the standard deviation of the returns of the third company's shares is lower?

7.4. The correlation between Share A and B is 0.50, while the correlation between Share A and C is −0.5. You already own Share A and are thinking of buying either Share B or Share C. If you want your portfolio to have the lowest possible risk, would you buy Share B or C? Would you expect the share you choose to affect the return that you earn on your portfolio?

7.5. The idea that we can know the return on a security for each possible outcome is overly simplistic. However, even though we cannot possibly predict all possible outcomes, this fact has little bearing on the risk-free return. Explain why.

7.6. Which investment category has shown the greatest degree of risk in the United Kingdom since 1900? Explain why that makes sense in a world where the price of equities is likely to be more adversely affected by a particular negative event than the price of a bond. Use the same type of explanation to help explain other investment choices since 1900.

7.7. You are concerned about one of the investments in your fully diversified portfolio. You just have an uneasy feeling about the CFO, I.M. Shifty, of that particular firm. You do believe, however, that the firm makes a good product and that it is appropriately priced by the market. Should you be concerned about the effect on your portfolio if Shifty embezzles a portion of the firm's cash?

7.8. The CAPM is used to price the risk in any asset. Our examples have focused on shares, but we could also price the expected rate of return for bonds. Explain how debt securities are also subject to systematic risk.

7.9. In recent years, investors have correctly agreed that the market portfolio consists of more than just a group of shares and bonds. If you are an investor who invests only in shares, describe the effects on the risk in your portfolio.

7.10. You may have heard the statement that you should not include your home as an asset in your investment portfolio. Assume that your house will comprise up to 75% of your assets in the early part of your investment life. Evaluate the implications of omitting it from your portfolio when calculating the risk of your overall investment portfolio.

QUESTIONS AND PROBLEMS

Basic

7.1. Returns: Describe the difference between a total holding period return and an expected return.

7.2. Expected returns: John is watching an old game show rerun on television called *Let's Make a Deal* in which the contestant chooses a prize behind one of two curtains. One of the curtains will yield a gag prize worth $150 and the other will give a car worth $7200. The game show has placed a subliminal message on the curtain containing the gag prize, which makes the probability of choosing the gag prize equal to 75%. What is the expected value of the selection and what is the standard deviation of that selection?

7.3. Expected returns: You have chosen to study biology at university because you would like to be a medical doctor. However, you find that the probability of being accepted to medical school is about 10%. If you are accepted to medical school, then your starting salary when you graduate will be €300 000 per year. However, if you are not accepted, then you would choose to work in a zoo, where you will earn €40 000 per year. Without considering the additional educational years or the time value of money, what is your expected starting salary as well as the standard deviation of that starting salary?

7.4. Historical market: Describe the general relation between risk and return that we observe in the historical bond and equity market data.

7.5. Single-asset portfolios: Shares A, B and C have expected returns of 15%, 15% and 12%, respectively, while their standard deviations are 45%, 30% and 30%, respectively. If you were considering the purchase of each of these shares as the only holding in your portfolio, which share should you choose?

7.6. Diversification: Describe how investing in more than one asset can reduce risk through diversification.

7.7. Systematic risk: Define systematic risk.

7.8. Measuring systematic risk: Sophie is expecting the returns on the market portfolio to be negative in the near term. Since she is managing an equity mutual fund, she must remain invested in a portfolio of shares. However, she is allowed to adjust the beta of her portfolio. What kind of beta would you recommend for Sophie's portfolio?

7.9. Measuring systematic risk: Describe and justify what the value of the beta of a treasury bill should be.

7.10. Measuring systematic risk: If the expected rate of return for the market is not much greater than the risk-free rate of return, what is the general level of compensation for bearing systematic risk?

7.11. CAPM: Describe the Capital Asset Pricing Model (CAPM) and what it tells us.

7.12. The Security Market Line: If the expected return on the market is 10% and the risk-free rate is 4%, what is the expected return for a share with a beta equal to 1.5? What is the market risk premium for the set of circumstances described?

Intermediate

7.13. Expected returns: José is thinking about purchasing a soft drinks machine and placing it in a business office. He knows that there is a 5% probability that someone who walks by the machine will make a purchase from the machine and he knows that the profit on each soft drink sold is €0.10. If Jose expects a thousand people per day to pass by the machine and requires a complete return of his investment in one year, then what is the maximum price that he should be willing to pay for the soft drinks machine? Assume 250 working days in a year and ignore taxes and the time value of money.

7.14. Interpreting the variance and standard deviation: The grades in an introductory finance class are normally distributed, with an expected grade of 75. If the standard deviation of grades is 7, in what range would you expect 95% of the grades to fall?

7.15. Calculating the variance and standard deviation: Corrine recently invested in property with the intention of selling one year from today. She has modelled the returns on that investment based on three economic scenarios. She believes that if the economy stays healthy, then her investment will generate a 30% return. However, if the economy softens, as predicted, the return will be 10%, while the return will be −25% if the economy slips into a recession. If the probabilities of the healthy, soft and recessionary states are 0.4, 0.5 and 0.1, respectively, then what are the expected return and the standard deviation of the return on Corrine's investment?

7.16. Calculating the variance and standard deviation: Adriana is considering investing in a share and is aware that the return on that investment is particularly sensitive to how the economy is performing. Her analysis suggests that four states of the economy can affect the return on the investment. Using the table of returns and probabilities below, find the expected return and the standard deviation of the return on Adriana's investment.

	Probability	Return
Boom	0.1	25.00%
Good	0.4	15.00%
Level	0.3	10.00%
Slump	0.2	−5.00%

7.17. Calculating the variance and standard deviation: Bjorn would like to invest in gold and is aware that the returns on such an investment can be quite volatile. Use the following table of states, probabilities and returns to determine the expected return and the standard deviation of the return on Bjorn's gold investment.

	Probability	Return
Boom	0.1	40.00%
Good	0.2	30.00%
OK	0.3	15.00%
Level	0.2	2.00%
Slump	0.2	−12.00%

7.18. Single-asset portfolios: Using the information from Problems 7.15, 7.16 and 7.17, calculate each coefficient of variation.

7.19. Portfolios with more than one asset: Isabelle is analysing a two-share portfolio that consists of a utility share and a commodity share. She knows that the return on the utility share has a standard deviation of 40% and the return on the commodity share has a standard deviation of 30%. However, she does not know the exact covariance in the returns of the two shares. Isabelle would like to plot the variance of the portfolio for each of three cases – covariance of 0.12, 0 and −0.12 – in order to understand how the variance of such a portfolio would react. Do the calculation for each of the extreme cases (0.12 and −0.12), assuming an equal proportion of each share in the portfolio.

7.20. Portfolios with more than one asset: Given the returns and probabilities for the three possible states listed here, calculate the covariance between the returns of Share A and Share B. For convenience, assume that the expected returns of Share A and Share B are 11.75% and 18%, respectively.

	Probability	Return(A)	Return(B)
Good	0.35	0.30	0.50
OK	0.50	0.10	0.10
Poor	0.15	20.25	−0.30

7.21. Compensation for bearing systematic risk: You have constructed a diversified portfolio of shares such that there is no unsystematic risk. Explain why the expected return of that portfolio should be greater than the expected return of a risk-free security.

7.22. Compensation for bearing systematic risk: Write out the equation for the covariance in the returns of two assets, Asset 1 and Asset 2. Using that equation, explain the easiest way for the two asset returns to have a covariance of zero.

7.23. Compensation for bearing systematic risk: Evaluate the following statement: By fully diversifying a portfolio, such as buying every asset in the market, we can completely eliminate all types of risk, thereby creating a synthetic treasury bill.

7.24. CAPM: Damien knows that the beta of his portfolio is equal to 1, but he does not know the risk-free rate of return or the market risk premium. He also knows that the expected return on the market is 8%. What is the expected return on Damien's portfolio?

Advanced

7.25. David is going to purchase two shares to form the initial holdings in his portfolio. The Iron shares have an expected return of 15%, while the Copper shares have an expected return of 20%. If David plans to invest 30% of his funds in Iron and the remainder in Copper, what will be the expected return from his portfolio? What if David invests 70% of his funds in Iron shares?

7.26. Sumeet knows that the covariance in the return on two assets is −0.0025. Without knowing the expected return of the two assets, explain what that covariance means.

7.27. In order to fund her retirement, Chantal requires a portfolio with an expected return of 12% per year over the next 30 years. She has decided to invest in shares 1, 2 and 3, with 25% in share 1, 50% in share 2 and 25% in share 3. If shares 1 and 2 have expected returns of 9% and 10% per year, respectively, then what is the minimum expected annual return for share 3 that will enable Chantal to achieve her investment requirement?

7.28. Tonalli is putting together a portfolio of 10 shares in equal proportions. What is the relative importance of the variance for each share versus the covariance for the pairs of shares in her portfolio? For this exercise, ignore the actual values of the variance and covariance terms and explain their importance conceptually.

7.29. Explain why investors who have diversified their portfolios will determine the price and, consequently, the expected return on an asset.

7.30. Georg is about to purchase an additional asset for his well-diversified portfolio. He notices that when he plots the historical returns of the asset against those of the market portfolio, the line of best fit tends to have a large amount of prediction error for each data point (the scatter plot is not very tight around the line of best fit). Do you think that this will have a large or a small impact on the beta of the asset? Explain your opinion.

7.31. The beta of an asset is equal to 0. Discuss what the asset must be.

7.32. The expected return on the market portfolio is 15% and the return on the risk-free security is 5%. What is the expected return on a portfolio with a beta equal to 0.5?

7.33. Draw the Security Market Line (SML) for the case where the market risk premium is 5% and the risk-free rate is 7%. Now suppose an asset has a beta of −1.0 and an expected return of 4%. Plot it on your graph. Is the security properly priced? If not, explain what we might expect to happen to the price of this security in the market. Next, suppose another asset has a beta of 3.0 and an expected return of 20%. Plot it on the graph. Is this security properly priced? If not, explain what we might expect to happen to the price of this security in the market.

SAMPLE TEST PROBLEMS

7.1. Lennulinn Estonia shares are selling at a current price of €37.50 per share. If the shares do not pay a dividend and have a 12% expected return, what is the expected price of the shares one year from today?

7.2. Stefan's parents are about to invest their nest egg in a share that he has estimated to have an expected return of 9% over the next year. If the share is normally distributed with a 3% standard deviation, what will be the range of the share's return 95% of the time?

7.3. Elaine has narrowed her investment alternatives to two shares (at this time she is not worried about diversifying): share M, which has a 23% expected return and share Y, which has an 8% expected return. If Elaine requires a 16% return on her total investment, then what proportion of her portfolio will she invest in each share?

7.4. You have just prepared a graph similar to Exhibit 7.9, comparing historical data for Praha Výpočetní Technika A.S. and the general market. When you plot the line of best fit for these data, you find that the slope of that line is 2.5. If you know that the market generated a return of 12% and that the risk-free rate is 5%, then what would your best estimate be for the return of Praha Výpočetní Technika during that same time period?

7.5. The CAPM predicts that the return of MoonBucks Tea Corp. is 23.6%. If the risk-free rate of return is 8% and the expected return on the market is 20%, then what is MoonBucks' beta?

ENDNOTES

1. For simplicity, we will ignore the possibility that you are unable to play or are sent off or injured and other such outcomes.

2. From a practical standpoint, it would not really have been possible to grow £1 to £287 by investing in UK equities because this increase assumes that an investor is able to rebalance the shares portfolio by buying and selling shares as necessary at no cost. Since buying and selling shares is costly, the final wealth would have been lower. Nevertheless, even after transaction costs, it would have been much more profitable to invest in equities than in treasury bills.

3. For more information on trout tickling as an activity, see the entry in Wikipedia at: http://en.wikipedia.org/wiki/Trout_tickling.

4. The only adjustment that we had to make was to account for the fact that our calculations used monthly returns rather than annual returns. This adjustment simply required us to multiply each number we calculated by 12 because there are 12 months in a year.

5. This statement is true in the context of how expected returns are determined. However, the standard deviation is still a very useful measure of the risk faced by an individual investor who does not hold a diversified portfolio. For example, the owners of most small businesses have much of their personal wealth tied up in their businesses. They are certainly concerned about the total risk because it is directly related to the probability that they will go out of business and lose much of their wealth.

CHAPTER

8

Bond Valuation and the Structure of Interest Rates

In this Chapter:

Capital Market Efficiency

Corporate Bonds

Bond Valuation

Bond Yields

Interest Rate Risk

The Structure of Interest Rates

LEARNING OBJECTIVES

1. Explain what an efficient capital market is and why 'market efficiency' is important to financial managers.
2. Describe the market for corporate bonds and three types of corporate bonds.
3. Explain how to calculate the value of a bond and why bond prices vary negatively with interest rate movements.
4. Distinguish between a bond's coupon rate, yield to maturity and effective annual yield and be able to calculate their values.
5. Explain why investors in bonds are subject to interest rate risk and why it is important to understand the bond theorems.
6. Discuss the concept of default risk and know how to compute a default risk premium.
7. Describe the factors that determine the level and shape of the yield curve.

Alarm bells started ringing in the international bond market when on 8 December 2003, the giant Italian dairy and food conglomerate Parmalat defaulted on a €150 million bond issue. The following day, as rumours spread that Parmalat was unable to service its debts, Standard & Poor's (the credit rating agency) downgraded the company's bonds to speculative grade. Such a rating indicated that there was considerable doubt about the firm's ability to service its debt. Up to this point, Parmalat had been a major issuer of corporate bonds, with about €8 billion outstanding, and these bonds had found a place in many fixed-income investors' portfolios in Italy and across Europe – and even further afield. In the following days, evidence of a huge fraud emerged with a massive shortfall in the company's assets estimated to be around €10 billion. On 19 December, Standard & Poor's withdrew its rating, having previously made successive downgrades to finally assign 'D', its lowest possible rating; defined as 'payment default on financial commitments'. At the same time, the spreads on Parmalat's five-year bonds increased to a massive 2400 basis points and the bonds traded at a tiny fraction of their face value.[1] Holders of the bonds faced huge losses on these securities.

On 24 December, Parmalat was placed into administration and shortly afterwards several senior managers, including the founder and chief executive Calisto Tanzi, were arrested. In the subsequent months, as investigators painstakingly worked over the company, the details of the fraud that started as early as the late 1980s were revealed. In 2008 – four years after the collapse – Tanzi was sentenced to 10 years in jail for securities fraud. The process of restructuring the company and settling the numerous claims and lawsuits is still ongoing.

Among investors most hurt by Parmalat's failure were bondholders. One of the major risks faced by bondholders is the risk of default – the risk that a firm which has issued bonds will not meet the terms of the bond contract. In Parmalat's case, the firm failed to make interest payments as promised. When bond defaults occur, bondholders can be lucky to get 50% of their original investment back. Often they recover much less. In this chapter, we explore default risk, along with other topics related to the valuation of bonds.

CHAPTER PREVIEW

This chapter is all about bonds and how they are valued, or priced, in the marketplace. As you might suspect, the bond valuation models presented in this chapter are derived from the present value concepts discussed in Chapters 5 and 6. The market price of a bond is simply the present value of the promised cash flows (coupon and principal payments), discounted at the current market rate of interest for bonds of similar risk.

In the first part of the chapter, we discuss the concept of *efficient capital markets*. A capital market is efficient if current market prices reflect all relevant information about an asset's value. Economists care whether markets are efficient because the more efficient the markets, the more likely securities are to be priced at their true value. Not all financial markets are equally efficient.

Next, we discuss the corporate bond market, bond price information that is available and the types of bonds found in the market. Then we develop the basic equation used to calculate bond prices and show how to compute the following characteristics of a bond: (1) the yield to maturity and (2) the effective annual yield. We next discuss interest rate risk and identify three bond theorems that describe how bond prices respond to changes in interest rates.

Finally, we explain why firms have different borrowing costs. We find that four factors affect a firm's cost of borrowing: (1) the debt's marketability, (2) default risk, (3) call risk and (4) term to maturity.

CAPITAL MARKET EFFICIENCY

Learning Objective 1

Explain what an efficient capital market is and why 'market efficiency' is important to financial managers.

Security markets, such as the bond and stock markets, help bring buyers and sellers of securities together. They reduce the cost of buying and selling securities by providing a physical location or computer trading system where investors can trade securities. The supply and demand for securities is better reflected in organised markets because much of the total supply and demand for securities flows through these centralised locations or trading systems. Any price that balances the overall supply and demand for a security is a market equilibrium price.

Ideally, economists would like financial markets to price securities at their **true (intrinsic) value**. A security's true value is the present value of the cash flows an investor who owns that security can expect to receive in the future. This present value, in turn, reflects all available information about the size, timing and riskiness of the cash flows at the time the price was set. As new information becomes available, investors adjust their cash flow estimates through buying and selling, and the price of a security adjusts to reflect this information.

Markets such as those just described are called 'efficient' capital markets. More formally, in an **efficient capital market**, security prices fully reflect the knowledge and expectations of all investors at a particular point in time. If markets are efficient, investors and financial managers have no reason to believe the securities are not priced at or near their true value. The more efficient a security market, the more likely securities are to be priced at or near their true value.

> ### True (intrinsic) value
> for a security, the value of the cash flows an investor who owns that security can expect to receive in the future

> ### Efficient capital market
> market where prices reflect the knowledge and expectations of all investors

> ### Market operational efficiency
> the degree to which the transaction costs of bringing buyers and sellers together are minimised

> ### Market informational efficiency
> the degree to which current market prices reflect relevant information and, therefore, the true value of the security

The overall efficiency of a capital market depends on its *operational efficiency* and its *informational efficiency*. **Market operational efficiency** focuses on bringing buyers and sellers together at the lowest possible cost. The costs of bringing buyers and sellers together are called *transaction costs* and include such things as broker commissions and other fees and expenses. The lower these costs, the more operationally efficient markets are. Why is operational efficiency important? If transaction costs are high, market prices will be more volatile, fewer financial transactions will take place and prices will not reflect the knowledge and expectations of investors as accurately.

Markets exhibit **informational efficiency** if market prices reflect all relevant information about securities at a particular point in time. As suggested above, informational efficiency is influenced by operational efficiency but it also depends on the availability of information and the ability of investors to buy and sell securities based on that information. In an informationally efficient market, market prices adjust quickly to new information as it becomes available. Prices adjust quickly because many security analysts and investors are gathering and trading on information about securities in a quest to make a profit. Note that competition among investors is an important driver of informational efficiency.

Efficient Market Hypotheses

Public financial markets are efficient in part because regulators require issuers of publicly traded securities to disclose a great deal of information about those securities to investors. Investors are constantly evaluating the prospects for these securities and acting on the conclusions from their analyses by trading them. If the price of a security is out of line with what investors think it should be, then they will buy or sell that security, causing its price to adjust to reflect their assessment of its value. The ability of investors to easily observe transaction prices and trade volumes, and to inexpensively trade securities in public markets, contributes to the efficiency of this process. This buying and selling by investors is the mechanism through which prices adjust to reflect the market's consensus. The theory about how well this mechanism works is known as the **efficient market hypothesis**.

WEB

The concept of market efficiency originated with the PhD dissertation that Eugene Fama wrote at the University of Chicago. You can read an interview with Dr Fama that relates to market efficiency and other concepts discussed in this chapter at: library.dfaus.com/reprints/interview_fama_tanous.

Efficient market hypothesis

a theory concerning the extent to which information is reflected in security prices and how information is incorporated into security prices

Strong form (of the efficient market hypothesis)

the theory that security prices reflect all available information

Private information

information that is not available to all investors

Semi-strong form (of the efficient market hypothesis)

the theory that security prices reflect all public information but not all private information

Public information

information that is available to all investors

Weak form (of the efficient market hypothesis)

the theory that security prices reflect all information in past prices but do not reflect all private or all public information

Strong-Form Efficiency   The market for a security is perfectly informationally efficient if the security's price always reflects all available information. The idea that all information about a security is reflected in its price is known as the **strong form** of the efficient market hypothesis. Few people really believe that market prices of public securities reflect all available information, however. It is widely accepted that insiders have information that is not reflected in the security prices. Thus, the concept of strong-form market efficiency represents the ideal case rather than the real world.

If a security market were strong-form efficient, then it would not be possible to earn abnormally high returns (returns greater than those justified by the risks) by trading on **private information** – information unavailable to other investors – because there would be no such information. In addition, since all available information would already be reflected in security prices, the price of a particular security would change only when new information about its prospects became available.

Semi-Strong-Form Efficiency   A weaker form of the efficient market hypothesis, known as the **semi-strong form**, holds only that all **public information** – information that is available to all investors – is reflected in security prices. Investors who have private information are able to profit by trading on this information before it becomes public. As a result of this trading, prices adjust to reflect the private information. For example, suppose that conversations with the customers of a firm indicate to an investor that the firm's sales, and thereby its cash flows, are increasing more rapidly than other investors expect. To profit from this information, the investor buys the firm's shares. By buying the shares, the investor helps drive up the price to the point where it accurately reflects the higher level of cash flows.

The concept of semi-strong-form efficiency is a reasonable representation of the public stock markets in developed countries, such as those in the major European countries. In a market characterised by this sort of efficiency, as soon as information becomes public, it is quickly reflected in share prices through trading activity. Studies of the speed at which new information is reflected in share prices indicate that by the time you read a hot tip in the *Financial Times* or a business magazine, it is too late to benefit by trading on it.

Weak-Form Efficiency The weakest form of the efficient market hypothesis is known, aptly enough, as the **weak form**. This hypothesis holds that all information contained in past prices of a security is reflected in current prices, but there is both public and private information that is not. In a weak-form efficient market, it would not be possible to earn abnormally high returns by looking for patterns in security prices, but it would be possible to do so by trading on public or private information.

An important conclusion from efficient market theory is that at any point in time, all securities of the same risk class should be priced to offer the same expected return. The more efficient the market, the more likely this is to happen. Since both the bond and stock markets are relatively efficient, this means that securities of similar risk will offer the same expected return. This conclusion is important because it provides the basis for identifying the proper discount rate to use in applying the bond and share valuation models developed in this chapter and Chapter 9.

Before You Go On

1. How does information about a firm's prospects get reflected in its share price?

2. What is strong-form market efficiency? Semi-strong-form market efficiency? Weak-form market efficiency?

CORPORATE BONDS

Learning Objective 2

Describe the market for corporate bonds and three types of corporate bonds.

Now that we have discussed the concept of market efficiency, we are ready to discuss the market for corporate bonds and some of the types of bonds that firms issue.

Market for Corporate Bonds

The market for corporate bonds is enormous. As of March 2010, for example, the value of corporate bonds issued by companies and financial institutions outstanding globally was US$53 622.2 billion, making it the second largest portion of the international capital markets. The largest was the market for corporate equity, with a value of US$20.8 trillion. The state and local government debt market was a distant third at US$36 394.6 billion. The most important investors in corporate bonds are big institutional investors such as life insurance companies, pension funds and mutual funds. Because the primary investors are so big, trades in this market tend to involve very large blocks of securities.

Although the large majority of corporate bonds are listed on an exchange, such at the Luxembourg Stock Exchange, most secondary market transactions for corporate bonds take place through dealers in the over-the-counter (OTC) market. An interesting characteristic of the corporate bond market is that there are a large number of different bond issues that trade in the market. The reason is that while a corporation typically has a single issue of ordinary shares outstanding, it may have a dozen or more different notes and bonds outstanding. Therefore, despite the large overall trading volume of corporate bonds, the bonds in any particular issue will not necessarily trade on a given day. As a result, the market for corporate bonds is thin compared to the market for money market securities or ordinary shares. The term *thin* means that secondary market trades of individual securities are relatively infrequent. Thus, corporate bonds are less marketable than the securities that have higher daily trading volumes.

Prices in the corporate bond market also tend to be more volatile than prices of securities sold in markets with greater trading volumes. This is because a few large trades can have a larger impact on a security's price than numerous trades of various sizes. As a result, information is not reflected in prices as efficiently and the market for corporate bonds is not as efficient as those for highly marketable shares or money market instruments, such as government bonds.

WEB

A primer on bonds can be found at the Yahoo! Finance website at: finance.yahoo.com/bonds/bonds_101.

Bond Price Information

The corporate bond market has little *transparency* because it is almost entirely an OTC market. A financial market is transparent if it is easy to view prices and trading volume. An example of a transparent market is the London Stock Exchange (LSE), where price information on every trade and trade size is available for every transaction during the day. In contrast, corporate bond market transactions are widely dispersed, with dealers located in different countries and there are an enormous number of different securities. Furthermore, many corporate bond transactions are negotiated directly between the buyer and the seller and there is little centralised reporting of these deals. As

a result, information on individual corporate bond transactions is not widely published as the transactions occur, supporting our earlier statement that the corporate bond market is not as efficient as the stock market or money markets.

WEB

Investinginbonds.com is another website providing educational information about bonds and their markets. Go to www.investinginbonds.com/learnmore.asp?catid=5&subcatid=18.

Types of Corporate Bonds

Corporate bonds are long-term obligations that represent claims against a firm's assets. Unlike shareholders' returns, most bondholders' returns are *fixed* – they receive only the interest payments that are promised plus the repayment of the loan amount at the end of the contract. Debt instruments where the interest paid to investors is fixed for the life of the contract are called **fixed-income securities**. We examine three types of fixed-income securities in this section.

Plain Vanilla Bonds

The most common bonds issued by corporations are called plain vanilla bonds or straight bonds. These bonds have coupon payments that are fixed for the life of the bond and, at maturity, the entire original principal is paid and the bonds are redeemed. Vanilla bonds have no special provisions and the provisions they do have follow convention.

This time line shows the cash payments for a three-year vanilla bond with a €1000 face value and an 8% coupon rate. P_B is the price (value) of the bond, which will be discussed in the next section.

The €80 cash payments (€1000 × 8%) made each year are called the coupon payments. **Coupon payments** are the interest payments made to bondholders. These payments are usually made annually, or semi-annually, and the payment amount (or rate) remains fixed for the life of the bond contract, which for our example is three years. The **face value**, or **par value**, for most corporate bonds is €1000, and it is the principal amount owed to the bondholder at maturity. Finally, the bond's **coupon rate** is the annual coupon payment (C) divided by the bond's face value (F). Our vanilla bond pays €80 coupon interest annually, and the face value is €1000. The coupon rate is thus:

$$\text{Coupon rate} = \frac{C}{F}$$
$$= \frac{€80}{€1000}$$
$$= 8\%$$

Fixed-income securities

debt instruments that pay interest in amounts that are fixed for the life of the contract

Coupon payments

the interest payments made to bondholders

Face value, or par value

the amount on which interest is calculated and that is owed to the bondholder when a bond reaches maturity

Coupon rate

the annual coupon payment of a bond divided by the bond's face value

Zero-Coupon Bonds

At times, corporations issue bonds that have no coupon payments but promise a single payment at maturity. The interest paid to a bondholder is the difference between the price paid for the bond and the face amount received at maturity. These bonds are sold at a price well below their face value because all of the interest is 'paid' when the bonds are retired at maturity rather than in semi-annual or yearly coupon payments.

Governments keen to tap investor demand for their securities sometimes issue zero-coupon bonds. For instance, the UK's Debt Management Office has facility for issuing zero-coupon bonds on demand. Companies also issue zero-coupon bonds from time to time. Firms that are expanding operations but have little cash on hand are especially likely to use zero-coupon bonds for funding. In the 1990s, the bond market was 'flooded' with zero-coupon bonds issued by telecommunications firms. These firms were spending huge amounts to build fibre-optic networks, which generated few cash inflows until they were completed.

WEB

You can find more information about zero-coupon bonds at: www.beginnersinvest.about
.com/od/zerocouponbonds.

Convertible Bonds

Corporate convertible bonds can be converted into ordinary shares at some predetermined ratio at the discretion of the bondholder. For example, a €1000 face value bond may be convertible into 100 shares in the issuer. The convertible feature allows the bondholders to share in the good fortunes of the firm if the firm's share price rises above a certain level. Specifically, it is to the bondholders' advantage to exchange their bonds for shares if the market value of the shares they receive exceeds the market value of the bonds.

Clearly, convertibility is an attractive feature for investors. Typically, the conversion ratio is set so that the firm's share price must appreciate at least 15–20% before it is profitable to convert the bonds into equity. As you would expect from our discussion, bondholders pay a premium (a higher price) for bonds with a conversion feature, which means the issuing firm is able to issue the bonds with a lower interest rate.

Callable, Puttable and Perpetual Bonds

Companies sometimes issue bonds with a stated maturity but may include a special provision that allows the issuer to redeem the bonds at a preset price, which is typically the face value of the bonds. These bonds are known as **callable bonds**, since the issuer has the option to redeem the bonds early. There is also the mirror provision that allows the investor who owns the bond to get early repayment before the stated maturity. These are **puttable bonds**, since the investor has the option to redeem the bonds early. The language here is derived from options, discussed in Chapter 20, and refers to the idea that the issuer can 'call' back the bonds or the investor can 'put' or return the bonds to the issuer for cash.

Callable bond

bond which can be redeemed at the option of the issuer prior to its stated maturity

---

Puttable bond

bond which can be redeemed at the option of the investor (holder) prior to its stated maturity

---

A few companies have been able to issue perpetual bonds, that is, bonds without any stated redemption date. Since the bonds are unlikely to be repaid, they are more like equity capital than debt. That is, they are very similar to fixed-dividend preference shares.

Before You Go On

1. What are the main differences between the bond markets and stock markets?
2. A bond has a 7% coupon rate, a face value of €1000 and a maturity of four years. On a time line, lay out the cash flows for the bond.
3. Explain what a convertible bond is.

BOND VALUATION

Learning Objective 3

Explain how to calculate the value of a bond and why bond prices vary negatively with interest rate movements.

We turn now to the topic of bond valuation – how bonds are priced. Throughout the book, we have stressed that the value, or price, of any asset is the present value of its future cash flows. The steps necessary to value an asset are as follows:

1. Estimate the expected future cash flows.
2. Determine the required rate of return, or discount rate. This rate depends on the riskiness of the cash flow stream.
3. Compute the discounted present value of the future cash flows. This present value is what the asset is worth at a particular point in time.

For bonds, the valuation procedure is relatively easy. The cash flows (coupon and principal payments) are contractual obligations of the firm and are known by market participants, since they are stated in the bond contract. Thus, market participants know the magnitude and timing of the expected cash flows as promised by the borrower (the bond issuer). The required rate of return, or discount rate, for a bond is the market interest rate, called the bond's *yield to maturity* (or more commonly, simply its *yield*). This rate is determined from the market prices of bonds that have features similar to those of the bond being valued; by 'similar', we mean bonds that have the same term to maturity, the same bond rating (default risk class) and are similar in other ways.

Notice that the required rate of return is really investors' **opportunity cost**, which is the highest alternative return that is given up if a certain investment is made. For example, if bonds identical to the bond being valued – having the same risk – yield 9%, the threshold yield or required return on the bond being valued is 9%. Why? An investor would not buy a bond with an 8% yield when an identical bond yielding 9% was available.

> **Opportunity cost**
>
> the return from the best alternative investment with similar risk that an investor gives up when he or she makes a certain investment

Given the above information, we can compute the current value, or price, of a bond (P_B) by calculating the present value of the bond's expected cash flows:

$$P_B = \text{PV(Coupon payments)} + \text{PV(Principal payment)}$$

Next, we examine this calculation in detail.

The Bond Valuation Formula

To begin, refer to Exhibit 8.1, which shows the cash flows for a three-year corporate bond with an 8% coupon rate and a €1000 face value. If the market rate of interest on similar bonds is 10% and interest payments are made annually, what is the market price of the bond? In other words, how much should you be willing to pay for the promised cash flow stream?

There are a number of ways to solve this problem. Probably the simplest is to write the bond valuation formula in terms of the individual cash flows. Thus, the price of the bond (P_B) is the sum of

the present value calculations for the coupon payments (C) and the principal amount (F) discounted at the required rate (i). That calculation follows:

$$
\begin{aligned}
P_B &= \text{PV(Each coupon payment)} \\
&\quad + \text{PV(Principal payment)} \\
&= \left(C_1 \times \frac{1}{1+i} \right) + \left(C_2 \times \frac{1}{(1+i)^2} \right) \\
&\quad + \left(C_3 \times \frac{1}{(1+i)^3} \right) + \left(F_3 \times \frac{1}{(1+i)^3} \right) \\
&= \left(\text{€}80 \times \frac{1}{1.10} \right) + \left(\text{€}80 \times \frac{1}{(1.10)^2} \right) \\
&\quad + \left(\text{€}80 \times \frac{1}{(1.10)^3} \right) + \left(\text{€}1000 \times \frac{1}{(1.10)^3} \right) \\
&= (\text{€}80 \times 0.9091) + (\text{€}80 \times 0.8264) \\
&\quad + (\text{€}80 \times 0.7513) + (\text{€}1000 \times 0.7513) \\
&= \text{€}72.73 + \text{€}66.11 + \text{€}60.10 + \text{€}751.30 \\
&= \text{€}950.24
\end{aligned}
$$

Notice that you could have simplified the calculation by combining the final coupon payment and the principal payment ($C_3 + F_3$), since both cash flows occur at time $t = 3$.

To develop the general bond pricing formula, we can write the equations for the price of a four-year, five-year and six-year maturity bond, as follows:

$$
\begin{aligned}
P_B &= \left(C_1 \times \frac{1}{1+i} \right) + \left(C_2 \times \frac{1}{(1+i)^2} \right) \\
&\quad + \cdots + \left(C_4 + F_4 \times \frac{1}{(1+i)^4} \right) \\
&= \left(C_1 \times \frac{1}{1+i} \right) + \left(C_2 \times \frac{1}{(1+i)^2} \right) \\
&\quad + \cdots + \left(C_5 + F_5 \times \frac{1}{(1+i)^5} \right) \\
&= \left(C_1 \times \frac{1}{1+i} \right) + \left(C_2 \times \frac{1}{(1+i)^2} \right) \\
&\quad + \cdots + \left(C_6 + F_6 \times \frac{1}{(1+i)^6} \right)
\end{aligned}
$$

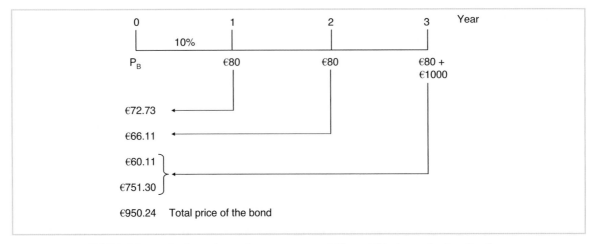

Exhibit 8.1: Cash Flows for a Three-Year Bond The exhibit shows the time line for a three-year bond that pays an 8% coupon rate and has a face value of €1000. How much should one pay for such a bond if the market rate of interest is 10%? To solve this problem, we discount the expected cash flows to the present and add them up.

If we continue the process for n periods, we arrive at the general equation for the price of the bond:

$$P_B = \left(C_1 \times \frac{1}{1+i} \right) + \left(C_2 \times \frac{1}{(1+i)^2} \right)$$
$$+ \cdots + \left(C_n + F_n \times \frac{1}{(1+i)^n} \right)$$

In practice, the bond pricing equation is usually written with the discount factor shown as the denominator rather than being multiplied by $1/(1+i)$. Thus, the general equation for the price of a bond can be written as follows:

$$P_B = \frac{C_1}{1+i} + \frac{C_2}{(1+i)^2} + \cdots + \frac{C_n + F_n}{(1+i)^n} \quad (8.1)$$

where:

P_B = the price of the bond, or present value of the stream of cash payments
C_t = the coupon payment in period t, where $t = 1, 2, 3, \ldots, n$
F_n = the par value or face value (principal amount) to be paid at maturity

i = the market interest rate (discount rate or market yield)
n = the number of periods to maturity

Note that there are five variables in the bond pricing equation. If we know any four of them, we can solve for the fifth.

Par, Premium and Discount Bonds

One of the mathematical properties of the bond formula is that whenever a bond's coupon rate is equal to the market rate of interest on similar bonds (the bond's yield), the bond will sell at par. We call such bonds **par-value bonds**. For example, say that you own a three-year bond with a face value of €1000 and an annual coupon rate of 5%, when the yield or market rate of interest on similar bonds is 5%. The price of the bond, based on Equation (8.1), is:

$$P_B = \frac{€50}{1.05} + \frac{€50}{(1.05)^2} + \frac{€1050}{(1.05)^3}$$
$$= €47.62 + €45.35 + €907.03$$
$$= €1000$$

As predicted, the bond's price equals its par value.

Now assume that the market rate of interest rises overnight to 8%. What happens to the price of the bond? Will the bond's price be below, above, or at par?

$$P_B = \frac{€50}{1.08} + \frac{€50}{(1.08)^2} + \frac{€1050}{(1.08)^3}$$

$$= €46.30 + €42.87 + €833.52$$

$$= €922.69$$

When i is equal to 8%, the price of the bond declines to €922.69. The bond sells below par; such bonds are called **discount bonds**.

Whenever a bond's coupon rate is lower than the market rate of interest on similar bonds, the bond will sell at a discount. This is true because of the fixed nature of a bond's coupon payments. Let us return to our 5% coupon bond. If the market rate of interest is 8% and our bond pays only 5%, no economically rational person would buy the bond at its par value. This would be like choosing a bond with a 5% yield over one with an 8% yield. We cannot change the coupon rate to 8% because it is fixed for the life of the bond. That is why bonds are called fixed-income securities! The only way to increase our bond's yield to 8% is to reduce the price of the bond to €922.69. At this price, the bond's yield will be precisely 8%, which is the current market rate for similar bonds. Through the price reduction of €77.31 (€1000 – €922.69), the seller provides the new owner with additional 'interest' in the form of a capital gain.

What would happen to the price of the bond if interest rates on similar bonds declined to 2% and the coupon rate remained at 5%? The price of our bond would rise to €1086.52. At this price, the bond's yield would be precisely 2%, which is the current market yield. The €86.52 (€1086.52 – €1000) premium that the investor paid adjusts the bond's yield to 2%, which is the current market yield for similar bonds. Bonds

that sell above par are called **premium bonds**. Whenever a bond's coupon rate is higher than the market rate of interest, the bond will sell at a premium.

Par-value bonds

bonds that sell at par value, or face value; whenever a bond's coupon rate is equal to the market rate of interest on similar bonds, the bond will sell at par

---

Discount bonds

bonds that sell at below par (face) value

Premium bonds

bonds that sell at above par (face) value

Our discussion of bond pricing can be summarized as follows, where i is the market rate of interest:

1. $i >$ coupon rate – the bond sells for a discount
2. $i <$ coupon rate – the bond sells for a premium
3. $i =$ coupon rate – the bond sells at par value

This negative relation between changes in the level of interest rates and changes in the price of a bond (or any fixed-income security) is one of the most fundamental relations in corporate finance. The relation exists because the coupon payments on most bonds are fixed and the only way bonds can pay the current market rate of interest to investors is through adjustment of the price of the bond.

Pricing a Bond

Problem: Your stockbroker is trying to sell you a 15-year bond with a 7% coupon and the interest, or yield, on similar bonds is 10%. Is the bond selling at a premium, at par or at a discount? Answer the question without making any calculations and then prove that your answer is correct. The time line is as follows:

Approach: Since the market rate of interest is greater than the coupon rate (i > coupon rate), the bond must sell at a discount.

Solution: To prove the answer is correct (or wrong), we can compute the bond's price using Equation (8.1):

$$P_B = \frac{C_1}{1+i} + \frac{C_2}{(1+i)^2} + \cdots + \frac{C_n + F_n}{(1+i)^n}$$

$$= \frac{€70}{1.10} + \frac{€70}{(1.10)^2} + \cdots + \frac{€70 + €1000}{(1.10)^{15}}$$

$$= €63.64 + €57.85 + €52.59 + €47.81$$
$$+ €43.46 + €39.51 + €35.92 + €32.66$$
$$+ €29.69 + €26.99 + €24.53 + €22.30$$
$$+ €20.28 + €18.43 + €256.15$$

$$= €771.82$$

The bond is selling at a discount, and it should. Why? The market rate of interest is 10% and our bond is paying only 7%. Since the bond's coupon rate is fixed, the only way we can bring the bond's yield up to the current market rate of 10% is to reduce the price of the bond.

USING EXCEL

Bond Prices and Yields

Calculating bond prices and yields using a spreadsheet may seem daunting at first. However, understanding the terminology used in the formulas will make the calculations a matter of common sense.

Settlement date – the date a buyer purchases the bond.

Maturity date – the date the bond expires. If you know only the 'n' (number of years remaining) of the bond, use a date that is n years in the future in this field.

Redemption – the security's redemption value per €10 face value. In other words, if the bond has a par of €1000, you enter 100 in this field.

Frequency – the number of coupon payments per year.

Here is a spreadsheet showing the setup for calculating the price of the discount bond described in Learning by Doing Application 8.1.

We first use the '=PRICE(settlement, maturity, rate, yield, redemption, frequency)' formula in Excel to calculate the bond price as a percentage of par. We then multiply this percentage (77.18 in the above example) by €1000 to obtain the bond price in euros. A bond yield, which is discussed in the next section, is calculated in a similar manner, using the '=YIELD(settlement, maturity, rate, price, redemption, frequency)' formula.

	A	B	C	D
1				
2		Bond Price Calculations		
3		Inputs		
4	Settlement date	01/01/2011		
5	Maturity date	31/12/2025		
6	Rate	0.07		
7	Yield	0.10		
8	Redemption (% of par)	100		
9	Frequency	1		
10				
11		Bond Price		Formulas used
12	Bond price as % of par	77.18		=PRICE(B4,B5,B6,B7,B8,B9)
13	Par value	€ 1,000.00		
14	Bond price	€ 771.83		=B12%*B13
15				

Semi-annual Compounding

In Europe, bonds generally pay coupon interest on an annual basis. In contrast, in Australia, Canada, the United Kingdom, South Africa and the United States, most bonds pay coupon interest semi-annually – that is, twice a year.[2] Thus, if a bond has an 8% coupon rate (paid semi-annually), the bondholder will in one year receive two coupon payments of €40 each, totalling €80 (€40 × 2). We can modify Equation (8.1) as follows to adjust for coupon payments made more than once a year:

$$P_B = \frac{C/m}{1+i/m} + \frac{C/m}{(1+i/m)^2} + \frac{C/m}{(1+i/m)^3}$$
$$+ \cdots + \frac{C/m + F_{mn}}{(1+i/m)^{mn}} \qquad (8.2)$$

where C is the annual coupon payment, m is the number of times coupon payments are made each year, n is the number of years to maturity and i is the annual interest rate. In the case of a bond with semi-annual coupon payments, m equals 2.

Whether we are computing bond prices annually, semi-annually, quarterly or for some other period, the computation is the same. We need only be sure that the bond's yield, coupon payment and maturity are adjusted to be consistent with the bond's stated compounding period. Once that information is converted to the correct compounding period, it can simply be entered into Equation (8.1). Thus, there is really no need to memorise or use Equation (8.2) unless you find it helpful. We will work through an example to demonstrate.

Earlier we determined that a three-year, 5% coupon bond will sell for €922.69 when the market rate of interest is 8%. Our computation assumed that coupon payments were made annually. What is the price of the bond if the coupon payments are made semi-annually? The time line for the semi-annual bond situation follows:

0	1	2	3	4	5	6 Semi-annual period
8%/2						
P_B	€50/2	€50/2	€50/2	€50/2	€50/2	€50/2 + €1000

We convert the bond data to semi-annual compounding as follows: (1) the market yield is 4% semi-annually (8% per year/2), (2) the coupon payment is €25 semi-annually (€50 per year/2), (3) the total number of coupon payments is 6 (2 per year × 3 years). Plug the data into Equation (8.1), and the bond price is:

$$P_B = \frac{€25}{1.04} + \frac{€25}{(1.04)^2} + \frac{€25}{(1.04)^3} + \frac{€25}{(1.04)^4}$$
$$+ \frac{€25}{(1.04)^5} + \frac{€1025}{(1.04)^6}$$
$$= €921.37$$

Notice that the price of the bond is slightly less with semi-annual compounding than with annual compounding (€921.37 < €922.69). The slight difference in price reflects the change in the timing of the cash flows and the interest rate adjustment.[3]

Note that we can consider a bond to be a package of (1) an annuity flow with value C, which is equal to the coupon payment to time m, the

bond's maturity date and (2) a single cash flow for the face amount of the bond, F. Therefore, we can write the bond's value as:

$$P_B = C \times PV \text{ annuity factor}_{i,n} + F \times DF_{i,n}$$

where C is the coupon paid on the bond (for frequencies greater than a year, this will be C/m), i is the interest rate and n is the number of periods to the bond's maturity. So we could have written Equation (8.2) as:

$$P_B = C/2 \times \left[\frac{1 - 1/\left(1 + i/2\right)^{mn}}{i/2} \right] + \frac{F_{mn}}{\left(1 + i/2\right)^{mn}}$$

We discussed annuities in Chapter 6. Here you can see how useful they are. We do not really want to discount a bond's individual cash flows from the coupon payments since this is both tedious and likely to lead to mistakes. The annuity method provides a neat 'shorthand' method to get the answer that saves us a lot of work.

Learning by Doing Application 8.2

Bond Pricing with Semi-annual Coupon Payments

Problem: A corporate treasurer decides to purchase a 20-year UK government bond with a 4% coupon rate. If the current market rate of interest for similar government securities is 4.5%, what is the price of the bond?

Approach: UK government bond securities pay interest semi-annually, so convert the bond data

to semi-annual compounding as follows: (1) the bond's semi-annual yield is 2.25% (4.5% per year/2), (2) the semi-annual coupon payment is £20 [(£1000 × 4%)/2 = £40/2], (3) the total number of compounding periods is 40 (2 per year × 20 years). Note that at maturity, the bond pays its principal, or face value, of £1000 to the investor. Thus, the bond's time line for the cash payments is as follows:

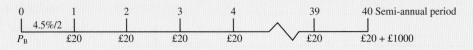

Solution: We can recognise that the cash flows represent two elements: (1) a 40-period annuity of £20 every six months discounted at 4.5%/2 (= 2.25% every six months) and (2) the present value of a single cash flow for the principal amount of £1000. Combining these two elements, we price our bond using the following:

The bond sells for a discount, and its price is £934.52. If the bond sold at a premium, the reverse would be true; that is, the price with semi-annual compounding would be slightly more than the price with annual compounding.

$$P_B = C/2 \times \left[\frac{1 - 1/\left(1 + i/2\right)^{mn}}{i/2} \right] + \frac{F_{mn}}{\left(1 + i/2\right)^{mn}}$$

$$= £40/2 \times \left[\frac{1 - 1/\left(1 + 0.045/2\right)^{(2 \times 20)}}{0.045/2} \right] + \frac{£1000}{\left(1 + 0.045/2\right)^{(2 \times 20)}}$$

$$= £20 \times [26.1935] + £1000 \times 0.41065$$

$$= £523.87 + £410.65$$

$$= £934.52$$

Zero-Coupon Bonds

As previously mentioned, zero-coupon bonds have no coupon payments but promise a single payment at maturity. The price (or yield) of a zero-coupon bond is simply a special case of Equation (8.2) in which all the coupon payments are equal to zero.

Hence, the pricing equation is:

$$P_B = \frac{F_{mn}}{(1 + i/m)^{mn}} \tag{8.3}$$

where:

P_B = the price of the bond
F_{mn} = the amount of the cash payment at maturity (face value)
i = the interest rate (yield) for n periods
n = the number of periods until the payment is due
m = the number of times interest is compounded each year

Notice that if a zero-coupon bond compounds annually, $m = 1$ and Equation (8.3)

becomes:

$$P_B = \frac{F_n}{(1 + i)^n}$$

This is similar to the annual bond pricing equation, Equation (8.1).

Now let us work an example. What is the price of a zero-coupon bond with a £1000 face value, 10-year maturity and semi-annual compounding when the market interest rate is 12%? Since the bond compounds interest semi-annually, the number of compounding periods is 20 ($m \times n = 2 \times 10 = 20$). The semi-annual interest is 6% (12%/2). The time line for the cash flows is as follows:

Plugging the data into Equation (8.3), we find that the price of the bond is £311.80:

$$P_B = \frac{£1000}{(1.06)^{20}}$$

$$= £1000 \times 0.3118 = £311.80$$

Notice that the zero-coupon bond is selling at a deep discount. This should come as no surprise, since the bond has no coupon payment and all the value is paid to investors at maturity. Why are zero-coupon bonds so heavily discounted compared with similar bonds that do have coupon payments? From Chapter 5, we know that because of the time value of money, money to be received in the future has less value than current money. Thus, zero-coupon bonds, for which all the cash payments are made at maturity, must sell for less than similar bonds that make coupon payments before maturity.

Learning by Doing Application 8.3

The Price of a Bond

Problem: An investor is considering buying a South African corporate bond with an eight-year maturity and a coupon rate of 6%. Similar bonds in the marketplace yield 14%. How much should the investor be willing to pay for the bond? Using Equation (8.1) [or (8.2)], set up the equation to be solved and then solve the problem. Note that the discount rate used in the problem is the 14% market yield on similar bonds (i.e. bonds of similar risk), which is the investor's opportunity cost.

Approach: Since South African corporate bonds pay coupon interest semi-annually, we first need to convert all of the bond data to reflect semi-annual compounding: (1) the annual coupon payment is South African Rand (R) 60 per year (6% × R1000) and the semi-annual payment is R30 per period (R60/2); (2) the appropriate semi-annual yield is 7% (14%/2); and (3) the total number of compounding periods is 16 (2 per year × 8 years). The time line for the semi-annual cash flows is as follows:

```
0      1     2     3         15     16 Semi-annual period
|14%/2 |     |     |          |      |
P_B   R30   R30   R30        R30   R30 + R1000
```

Solution: Using Equation (8.1) [or (8.2)], the setup is as follows:

$$P_B = \frac{R30}{1.07} + \frac{R30}{(1.07)^2} + \cdots + \frac{R30 + R1000}{(1.07)^{16}}$$

Using (1) a 16-period annuity at 7% for the coupon payments of R30 due every six months and (2) a single payment present-valued at 7%, we price the bond as follows:

$$P_B = R30 \times \left[\frac{1 - 1/(1.07)^{16}}{0.07}\right] + \frac{R1000}{(1.07)^{16}}$$

$$= R30 \times [9.4466] + R1000 \times 0.3387$$

$$= R622.13$$

The investor should be willing to pay R622.13 because the bond's yield at this price would be exactly 14%, which is the current market yield on similar bonds. If the investor paid more than R622.13, the investment would yield a return of less than 14%. In this situation the investor would be better off buying the similar bonds in the market that yield 14%. Of course, if the investor can buy the bond for less than R622.13, the price is a bargain and the return on investment will be greater than the market yield.

BOND YIELDS

In dealing with bonds, we frequently know the bond's price but not its yield – or, more formally, the bond's yield to maturity. In this section, we discuss how to compute the yield to maturity and some other important bond yields.

Yield to Maturity

The **yield to maturity** of a bond is the discount rate that makes the present value of the coupon and principal payments equal to the price of the bond. The yield to maturity can be viewed as a 'promised yield' because it is the yield that the investor earns if the bond is held to maturity and all the coupon and principal payments are made as promised. A bond's yield to maturity changes daily as interest rates increase or decrease, but its calculation is always based on the issuer's promise to make interest and principal payments as stipulated in the bond contract.

Yield to maturity

for a bond, the discount rate that makes the present value of the coupon and principal payments equal to the price of the bond

---

Let us work through an example to see how a bond's yield to maturity is calculated. Suppose you decide to buy a three-year bond with a 6% coupon rate for €960.99. For simplicity, we will assume that the coupon payments are made annually. The time line for the cash flows is as follows:

To compute the yield to maturity, we apply Equation (8.1) and solve for i. We can set up the problem using Equation (8.1) as follows:

$$\text{€}960.99 = \frac{\text{€}60}{1+i} + \frac{\text{€}60}{(1+i)^2} + \frac{\text{€}1060}{(1+i)^3}$$

As we discussed in Chapter 6, we cannot solve for i mathematically; we must find it by trial and error. We know that the bond is selling for a discount because its price is below par, so the yield must be higher than the 6% coupon rate. We will try 7%:

$$\frac{\text{€}60}{1.07} + \frac{\text{€}60}{(1.07)^2} + \frac{\text{€}1060}{(1.07)^3} = \text{€}973.76$$

The computed price of €973.76 is still greater than our market price of €960.99; thus, we need to use a slightly larger discount rate. We will raise the yield to 7.7%:

$$\frac{\text{€}60}{1.077} + \frac{\text{€}60}{(1.077)^2} + \frac{\text{€}1060}{(1.077)^3} = \text{€}955.95$$

Our computed value of €955.95 is now less than the market price of €960.99, so we need a lower discount rate. We will try 7.5%:[4]

$$\frac{\text{€}60}{1.075} + \frac{\text{€}60}{(1.075)^2} + \frac{\text{€}1060}{(1.075)^3} = \text{€}960.99$$

At a discount rate of 7.5%, the price of the bond is exactly equal to the market price, and thus, the bond's yield to maturity is 7.5%.

We can, of course, also compute the bond's yield to maturity using a financial calculator or a spreadsheet and avoid the need for iteration. You can also use interpolation when using the trial-and-error approach.

Effective Annual Yield

Up to now, when pricing a bond with a semi-annual compounding period, we assumed the bond's annual yield to be twice the semi-annual yield. This is the convention used by bond markets. However, notice that bond yields quoted in this manner are just like the bank credit card APR calculations discussed in Chapter 6. To get a credit card's APR, we multiplied the monthly interest rate of 1% by 12, for an APR of 12%. As you recall, interest rates (or yields) annualised in this manner do not take compounding into account. Hence, the values calculated are not the true cost of funds and their use can lead to decisions that are economically incorrect.

As a result, annualised yields calculated by multiplying a period yield by the number of compounding periods is only acceptable for decision-making purposes when comparing bonds that have the same compounding frequencies. Thus, for example, an investor must be careful when evaluating yields between European and US bonds, since the European bond is compounded annually while the US bond compounds interest twice a year.

The correct way to annualise an interest rate is to compute the effective annual interest rate (EAR). In the bond markets, the EAR is called the **effective annual yield (EAY)**; thus, EAR = EAY. Drawing on Equation (6.7) (see Chapter 6), we find that the correct way to annualise the yield on a bond is as follows:

$$\text{EAY} = \left(1 + \frac{\text{Quoted interest rate}}{m}\right)^m - 1$$

where:

quoted interest rate = simple annual yield (semi-annual yield × 2)

m = the number of compounding periods per year

> ### Effective annual yield (EAY)
>
> the annual yield that takes compounding into account; another name for the *effective annual interest rate* (EAR)

We can work through an example to clarify how the EAY differs from the yield to maturity. Suppose an investor buys a 30-year UK government bond with a £1000 face value for £800. The bond's coupon rate is 8%, and interest payments are made semi-annually. What is the bond's yield to maturity and what is its effective annual yield? To find out, we first need to convert the bond's annual data into semi-annual data: (1) the 30-year bond has 60 compounding periods (30 years × 2 periods per year) and (2) the bond's semi-annual coupon payment is £40 [(£1000 × 0.08)/2 = £80/2]. The time line for this bond is:

We can set up the problem using Equation (8.1) as:

$$£800 = \frac{£40}{1+i/2} + \frac{£40}{(1+i/2)^2} + \frac{£40}{(1+i/2)^3}$$
$$+ \ldots + \frac{£40}{(1+i/2)^{59}} + \frac{£40 + £1000}{(1+i/2)^{60}}$$

However, as shown above, we can solve this as the product of a 60-period annuity paying £40 and a single payment of £1000. The formula will therefore be:

$$£800 = £40 \times \left[\frac{1 - 1/(1+i/2)^{mn}}{i/2}\right] + \frac{£1000}{(1+i/2)^{mn}}$$

From our earlier discussion, we know that since the bond is at a discount, the yield will be higher than the coupon rate ($C > i$). We will try 10%. This gives us:

$$£40 \times \left[\frac{1-1/(1+0.10/2)^{60}}{0.10/2}\right] + \frac{£1000}{(1+0.10/2)^{60}} = P_B$$

$$£40 \times [18.929] + £1000 \times 0.0535 = £810.66$$

The value is too high, but quite close. Let us use 10.20% for our next try:

$$£40 \times \left[\frac{1 - 1/(1.102/2)^{60}}{0.102/2}\right] + \frac{£1000}{(1.102/2)^{60}} = P_B$$

$$£40 \times [18.616] + £1000 \times 0.0506 = £795.24$$

Too low, but now we can interpolate the values using Equation (6.2):

$$i_{\text{unknown}} = i_{\text{low}} + \frac{(\text{Value}_{\text{low }i} - \text{Value}_{\text{unknown }i})}{(\text{Value}_{\text{low }i} - \text{Value}_{\text{high }i})}$$

$$\times (i_{\text{high}} - i_{\text{low}})$$

$$= 5\% + \frac{£810.66 - £800.00}{£810.66 - £795.24}$$

$$\times (5.10\% - 5.00\%)$$

$$= 5\% + \frac{10.66}{15.42} + 0.1\%$$

$$= 5\% + 0.69131 \times 0.1\% = 5.07\%$$

The answer is 5.07%. We then multiply the semi-annual yield by 2 to convert it to an annual yield: $2 \times 5.07 = 10.14\%$. This is the bond's yield to maturity.

Now we will enter the appropriate values into the formula given earlier and calculate the EAY for the bond:

$$\text{EAY} = \left(1 + \frac{\text{Quoted interest rate}}{m}\right)^m - 1$$

$$= \left(1 + \frac{0.1014}{2}\right)^2 - 1$$

$$= (1.0507)^2 - 1 = 0.1040, \text{ or } 10.40\%$$

The EAY is 10.40%, compared with the annual yield to maturity of 10.14%. The EAY is greater because it takes into account the effects of compounding – earning interest on interest. As mentioned earlier, calculating the EAY is the proper way to annualise the bond's yield because it takes compounding into account.

**Learning by Doing
Application
8.4**

A Bond's Yield to Maturity

Problem: You can purchase an Australian corporate bond from your broker for A$1099.50. The bond has a maturity of six years and an annual coupon rate of 5%. Another broker offers you an Australian-dollar-denominated Eurobond (a bond sold internationally to investors) with a yield of 3.175%, which is also denominated in Australian dollars and has the same maturity and credit rating as the domestic corporate bond. Which bond should you buy?

Approach: Solving this problem involves two steps. First, we must compute the domestic

Australian bond's yield to maturity. The bond pays coupon interest semi-annually, so we have to convert the bond data to semi-annual periods: (1) the number of compounding periods is 12 (6 years × 2 periods per year) and (2) the semi-annual coupon payment is A$25 [(A$1000 × 0.05)/2 = A$50/2]. Second, we must annualise the yield for the domestic bond so that we can compare its yield with that of the Eurobond, which pays interest annually.

Solution: We need to solve for the yield to maturity for the domestic bond using the iterative process. Since the bond is trading at a premium to par, the yield will be less than the coupon rate. So we will start with 4% per annum:

$$P_B = A\$25 \times \left[\frac{1 - 1/(1 + 0.04/2)^6}{0.04/2}\right]$$

$$+ \frac{A\$1000}{(1 + 0.04/2)^6}$$

$$= A\$1052.88$$

At a yield of 4%, the bond price is too low. We therefore repeat the exercise at 3%:

$$P_B = A\$25 \times \left[\frac{1 - 1/(1 + 0.03/2)^6}{0.03/2}\right]$$

$$+ \frac{A\$1000}{(1 + 0.03/2)^6}$$

$$= A\$1109.08$$

This is slightly too high but we can now interpolate the yield:

$$i_{unknown} = i_{low} + \frac{(Value_{low\ i} - Value_{unknown\ i})}{\left(Value_{low\ i} - Value_{high\ i}\right)}$$

$$\times \left(i_{high} - i_{low}\right)$$

$$= 1.5\% + \left[\frac{A\$1109.08 - A\$1099.50}{A\$1109.08 - A\$1052.88}\right]$$

$$\times (2\% - 1.5\%)$$

$$= 1.5\% + A\$9.58/A\$56.20 \times 0.5\%$$

$$= 1.5\% + 0.08519\%$$

$$= 1.58519\%$$

The answer, 1.5852%, is the yield every six months. Convention is to use the APR, which is 3.17038% (1.5852% × 2 = 3.17038%). Since the Eurobond's yield, 3.175%, is an annualised yield because the bond compounds interest yearly, we must annualise the yield on the domestic bond in order to compare the two.[5] We annualise the yield on the domestic bond by computing its effective annual yield:

$$EAY = \left(1 + \frac{Quoted\ interest\ rate}{m}\right)^m - 1$$

$$= \left(1 + \frac{0.0317038}{2}\right)^2 - 1$$

$$= (1.015852)^2 - 1$$

$$= 0.031955,\ or\ 3.196\%$$

The domestic corporate bond is a better deal because of its higher EAY (3.196% > 3.175%). Notice that if we had just annualised the yield on the domestic bond by multiplying the semi-annual yield by two (1.5852% × 2 = 3.17038%) and compared the simple yields for the Eurobond and the domestic bond (3.175% > 3.17038%), we would have selected the Eurobond. This would have been the wrong economic decision.

Realised Yield

The yield to maturity tells the investor the return on a bond if the bond is held to maturity and all the coupon and principal payments are made as promised. More than likely, however, the investor will sell the bond before maturity. The **realised yield** is the return earned on a bond given the cash flows *actually received* by the investor. More formally, it is the interest rate at which the present value of the actual cash flows generated by the investment equals the bond's price. The realised yield allows investors to see the return they actually earned on their investment. It is the same as the holding period return discussed in Chapter 7.

Let us return to the situation involving a three-year bond with a 6% coupon that was purchased for €960.99 and had a promised yield of 7.5%. Suppose that interest rates increased sharply and the price of the bond plummeted. Disgruntled, you sold the bond for €750.79 after having owned it for two years. The time line for the realised cash flows looks like this:

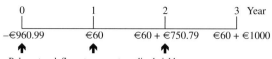

----Relevant cash flows to compute realised yield-----

Substituting the cash flows into Equation (8.1) yields the following:

$$P_B = €960.99 = \frac{€60}{1+i} + \frac{€60}{(1+i)^2} + \frac{€750.79}{(1+i)^2}$$

We have to solve this equation for i either by trial and error or quickly using a spreadsheet, as described earlier. Using trial and error, we need to guess the likely interest rate. Since the bond price when sold is less than the bond price when purchased and we have lost money, it is likely that the interest rate is negative ($€750.79 < €960.99$). As a first try, we will take a negative 2.0%:

$$P_B = \frac{€60}{1-0.02} + \frac{€60}{(1-0.02)^2} + \frac{€750.79}{(1-0.02)^2}$$

$$= €61.22 + €62.47 + €781.75 = €905.46$$

With a negative interest rate of 2.0%, we get too low a price for the bond.[6] So, the negative interest rate must be much higher. We will try a negative rate of 5.0%:

$$P_B = \frac{€60}{1-0.05} + \frac{€60}{(1-0.05)^2} + \frac{€750.79}{(1-0.05)^2}$$

$$= €63.16 + €66.48 + €831.90 = €961.50$$

This is slightly above the purchase price of €960.99. Using interpolation we get a realised negative yield of 4.97%:

$$i_{unknown} = i_{low} + \frac{(Value_{low\ i} - Value_{unknown\ i})}{(Value_{low\ i} - Value_{high\ i})}$$

$$\times (i_{high} - i_{low})$$

$$= -2.0\% + \left(\frac{€960.99 - €905.46}{€961.50 - €905.46}\right)$$

$$\times ((-2\%) - (-5\%))$$

$$= -2\% + (-2.97058) = -4.97\%$$

The difference between the promised yield of 7.50% and the realised yield of negative 4.97% is 12.47% [7.50 – (–4.97)], which can be accounted for by the capital loss of €210.20 (€960.99 – €750.79) from the decline in the bond price.

Before You Go On

1. Explain how bond yields are calculated.

INTEREST RATE RISK

Learning Objective 5

Explain why investors in bonds are subject to interest rate risk and why it is important to understand the bond theorems.

As discussed previously, the prices of bonds fluctuate with changes in interest rates, giving rise to **interest rate risk**. Anyone who owns bonds is subject to interest rate risk because interest rates are always changing in financial markets. A number of relations exist between bond prices and changes in interest rates. These relations are often called the bond theorems, but they apply to all fixed-income securities. It is important that investors and financial managers understand these relations.

Interest rate risk

uncertainty about future bond values that is caused by the unpredictability of interest rates

Bond Theorems

1. **Bond prices are negatively related to interest rate movements.** As interest rates decline, the prices of bonds rise; and as interest rates rise, the prices of bonds decline. As mentioned earlier, this negative relation exists because the coupon

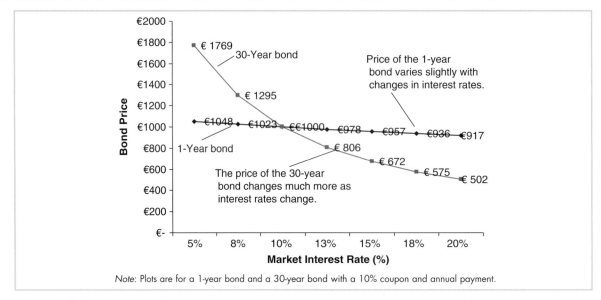

Note: Plots are for a 1-year bond and a 30-year bond with a 10% coupon and annual payment.

Exhibit 8.2: Relation between Bond Price Volatility and Maturity The prices of a 1-year and a 30-year bond respond differently to changes in interest rates. The long-term bond has a much wider price swing than the short-term bond, as predicted by the second bond theorem.

rate on most bonds is fixed at the time the bonds are issued. Note that the negative relation is observed not only for bonds but also for all other financial claims that pay a fixed rate of interest to investors.

2. **For a given change in interest rates, the prices of long-term bonds will change more than the prices of short-term bonds.** In other words, long-term bonds have greater price volatility than short-term bonds. Thus, all other things being equal, long-term bonds are more risky than short-term bonds. Exhibit 8.2 illustrates the fact that bond values are not equally affected by changes in interest rates. The exhibit shows how the prices of a 1-year bond and a 30-year bond change with changing interest rates. As you can see, the long-term bond has much wider price swings than the short-term bond. Why? The answer is that long-term bonds receive much of their cash flows far into the future, and because of the time value of money, these cash flows are heavily discounted.

3. **For a given change in interest rates, the prices of lower-coupon bonds change more than the prices**

of higher-coupon bonds. Exhibit 8.3 illustrates the relation between bond price volatility and coupon rates. The exhibit shows the prices of three 10-year bonds: a zero-coupon bond, a 5% coupon bond and a 10% coupon bond. Initially, the bonds are priced to yield 5% (see column 2). The bonds are then priced at yields of 6% and 4% (see columns 3 and 6). The value changes for each bond given the appropriate interest rate change are recorded in columns 4 and 7, and percentage price changes (price volatilities) are shown in columns 5 and 8.

As shown in column 5, when interest rates increase from 5% to 6%, the zero-coupon bond experiences the greatest percentage price decline and the 10% bond experiences the smallest percentage price decline. Similar results are shown in column 8 for interest rate decreases. In sum, the lower a bond's coupon rate, the greater its price volatility and, hence, lower-coupon bonds have greater interest rate risk.

The reason for the higher interest rate risk for low-coupon bonds is essentially the same as the

EXHIBIT 8.3

RELATIONSHIP BETWEEN BOND PRICE VOLATILITY AND THE COUPON RATE

		Price Change if Yield Increases from 5% to 6%			Price Change if Yield Decreases from 5% to 4%		
(1)	**(2)**	**(3)**	**(4)**	**(5)**	**(6)**	**(7)**	**(8)**
Coupon Rate	**Bond Price at 5% Yield**	**Bond Price at 6% Yield**	**Loss from Increase in Yield**	**% Price Change**	**Bond Price at 4%**	**Gain from Decrease in Yield**	**% Price Change**
0%	€613.91	€588.39	€25.52	−9.04%	€675.56	€61.65	10.04%
5%	€1000.00	€926.40	€73.60	−7.36%	€1081.11	€81.11	8.11%
10%	€1386.09	€1294.40	€91.69	−6.62%	€1486.65	€100.56	7.25%

Note: Calculations are based on a bond with a €1000 face value and a 10-year maturity and assume annual compounding. The exhibit shows the prices of three 10-year bonds: a zero-coupon bond, a 5% coupon bond and a 10% coupon bond. Initially, the bonds are priced at a 5% yield (column 2). The bonds are then priced at yields of 6% and 4% (columns 3 and 6). The price changes shown are consistent with the third bond theorem: the smaller the coupon rate, the greater the percentage price change for a given change in interest rates.

reason for the higher interest rate risk for long-term bonds. The lower the bond's coupon rate, the greater the amount of the bond's cash flow investors will receive at maturity. This is clearly seen with a zero-coupon bond, where all of the bond's cash flows are received at maturity. The further into the future the cash flows will be received, the greater the impact of a change in the discount rate on their present value. Thus, all other things being equal, a given change in interest rates will have a greater impact on the price of a low-coupon bond than a higher-coupon bond with the same maturity.

Bond Theorem Applications

The bond theorems provide important information about bond price behaviour for financial managers. For example, if you are the treasurer of a firm and are investing cash temporarily – say, for a few days – the last security you want to purchase is a long-term zero-coupon bond. In contrast, if you are an investor and you expect interest rates to decline, you may well want to invest in long-term zero-coupon bonds. This is because as interest rates decline, the price of long-term zero-coupon bonds will increase more than that of any other type of bond.

Make no mistake, forecasting interest rate movements and investing in long-term bonds is a very high-risk strategy. In 1994, Glaxo, the UK-based pharmaceutical company, reported a £132 million loss on its corporate and government bond portfolio of about £1.7bn – or about 8% of the portfolio value – as a result of a sudden plunge in bond prices worldwide. The moral of the story is simple. Long-term bonds carry substantially more interest rate risk than short-term bonds and investors in long-term bonds need to fully understand the magnitude of the risk involved. Furthermore, no one can predict interest rate movements consistently, including central banks, such as the Bank of England, the European Central Bank or the Federal Reserve Bank – and they control the money supply.

Decision-Making Example 8.1

Risk Taking

Situation: You work for the treasurer of a large manufacturing company where earnings are down substantially for the year. The treasurer's staff are convinced that interest rates are going to decline over the next three months and they want to invest in fixed-income securities to make as much money as possible for the firm. The staff recommend investing in one of the following securities:

- Three-month T-bills.
- Twenty-year corporate bonds.
- Twenty-year zero-coupon government bonds.

The treasurer asks you to answer the following questions about the staff's plan: (1) What is the underlying strategy of the proposed plan? (2) Which investment should be selected if the plan were to be executed? (3) What should the treasurer do?

Decision: First, the staff's strategy is based on the negative relation between interest rates and bond prices. Thus, if interest rates decline, bond prices will rise, and the firm will earn a capital gain. Second, to maximise earnings, the treasurer should select bonds that will have the largest price swing for a given change in interest rates. Bond theorems 2 and 3 suggest that for a given change in interest rates, low-coupon, long-term bonds will have the largest price swing. Thus, the treasurer should invest in the 20-year zero-coupon government bonds. With respect to the plan's merits, the intentions are good, but the investment plan is pure folly and wild speculation. Generating 'earnings' from risky financial investments is not the firm's line of business or one of its core competencies. As was discussed in Chapter 1, the treasurer's primary investment function is to invest idle cash in safe investments such as money market instruments that have very low default and interest rate risk.

Before You Go On

1. What is interest rate risk?
2. Explain why long-term bonds with zero coupons are riskier than short-term bonds that pay coupon interest.

THE STRUCTURE OF INTEREST RATES

In Chapter 2 we discussed the economic forces that determine the level of interest rates, and so far in this chapter we have discussed how to price various types of debt securities. Armed with this knowledge, we now explore why, on the same day, different companies have different borrowing costs. As you will see, market analysts have identified four risk characteristics of debt instruments that are responsible for most of the differences in corporate borrowing costs: the security's marketability, call provision, default risk and term to maturity.

WEB

You can get international data on government bonds from Bloomberg at: http://noir.bloomberg.com/markets/rates/index.html.

Marketability

The interest rate, or yield, on a security varies with its degree of marketability. Recall from Chapter 2 that marketability refers to the ease with which an investor can sell a security quickly at a low transaction cost. The transaction costs include all fees and the cost of searching for information: the lower the costs, the greater a security's marketability. Because investors prefer marketable securities, they must be paid a premium to purchase similar securities that are less marketable. The difference in interest rates or yields between a marketable security ($i_{\text{high mkt}}$) and a less marketable security ($i_{\text{low mkt}}$) is known as the *marketability risk premium* (MRP):

$$MRP = i_{\text{low mkt}} - i_{\text{high mkt}} > 0$$

Government securities have the largest and most active secondary market and are considered to be the most marketable of all securities. Investors can sell virtually any amount of government securities quickly without disrupting the market. Similarly, the securities of many well-known businesses enjoy a high degree of marketability, especially firms whose securities are traded on the major exchanges. For thousands of other firms whose securities are not traded actively, marketability can pose a problem and can raise borrowing costs substantially.

Call Provision

A number of corporate bonds contain a call provision in their contract. A call provision gives the firm issuing the bonds the option to purchase the bond from an investor at a predetermined price (the call price) and the investor must sell the bond at that price. Bonds with a call provision sell at higher market yields than comparable non-callable bonds. Investors require the higher yield because call provisions work to the benefit of the borrower and to the detriment of the investor. For example, if interest rates decline after the bond is issued, the issuer can call (retire) the bonds at the call price and refinance with a new bond issued at the lower prevailing market rate of interest. The issuing firm is delighted because the refinancing has lowered its interest expense. However, investors lose out. When bonds are called, investors suffer a financial loss because they are forced to surrender their high-yielding bonds and reinvest their funds at the lower prevailing market rate of interest.

The difference in interest rates between a callable bond and a comparable non-callable bond is called the *call interest premium* (CIP) and can be defined as follows:

$$CIP = i_{\text{call}} - i_{\text{ncall}} > 0$$

where CIP is the call interest premium, i_{call} is the yield on a callable bond and i_{ncall} is the yield on a non-callable bond of the same maturity and default risk. Thus, the more likely a bond is to be called, the higher the CIP and the higher the bond's market yield. Bonds issued during periods when interest rates are high are likely to be called when interest rates decline and, as a result, these bonds have a high CIP. Conversely, bonds sold when interest rates are relatively low are less likely to be called and have a smaller CIP.

Default Risk

Recall that any debt, such as a bond or a bank loan, is a formal promise by the borrower to make periodic interest payments and pay the principal as specified in the debt contract. Failure on the borrower's part to meet any condition of the debt or loan contract constitutes default. Recall from Chapter 4 that default risk refers to the possibility that the lender may not receive the payments as promised.

The Default Risk Premium

Because investors are risk averse, they must be paid a premium to purchase a security that exposes them to default risk. The size of the premium has two components: (1) compensation for the expected loss if a default occurs and (2) compensation for bearing the risk that a default could occur. The degree of default risk a security possesses can be measured as the difference between the interest rate on a risky security and the interest rate on a default-free security – all other factors, such as maturity and marketability, held constant. The *default risk premium* (DRP) can thus be defined as follows:

$$DRP = i_{dr} - i_{rf}$$

where i_{dr} is the interest rate (yield) on a security that has default risk and i_{rf} is the interest rate (yield) on a risk-free security. Government debt securities are the best proxy measure for the risk-free rate. The larger the default risk premium, the higher the probability of default, and the higher the security's market yield.

Bond Ratings

Many investors, especially individuals and smaller businesses, do not have the expertise to formulate the probabilities of default themselves, so they must rely on credit rating agencies to provide this information. The most prominent credit rating agencies are Fitch IBCA (Fitch), Moody's Investors Service (Moody's) and Standard & Poor's (S&P). The credit rating services class bonds in order of their expected probability of default and publish the ratings as letter grades. The rating schemes used are shown in Exhibit 8.4. The highest-grade bonds, those with the lowest default risk, are rated Aaa (or AAA). The default risk premium on corporate bonds increases as the bond rating becomes lower.

EXHIBIT 8.4

CORPORATE BOND RATING SYSTEMS

Explanation	Fitch IBCA	Moody's	Standard & Poor's	Default Risk Premium	Regulatory Designation
Best quality, smallest degree of risk	AAA	Aaa	AAA	Lowest	Investment Grade
High quality, slightly more long-term risk than top rating	AA	Aa	AA		
Upper-medium grade, possible impairment in the future	A	A	A		
Medium grade, lacks outstanding investment characteristics	BBB	Baa	BBB		
Speculative, protection may be very moderate	BB	Ba	BB		Non-investment Grade
Very speculative, may have small assurance of interest and principal payments	B	B	B		
Issues in poor standing, may be in default	CCC	Caa	CCC		
Speculative in a high degree, with marked shortcomings	CC	Ca	CC		
Lowest quality, poor prospects of attaining real investment standing	C	C	C		
In bankruptcy, winding up or has otherwise ceased in business	D	D	D	Highest	

Moody's uses a slightly different notation in their ratings of corporate bonds compared to Fitch IBCA and Standard & Poor's, but the interpretation is the same. Bonds with the highest credit standing are rated Aaa (or AAA) and have the lowest default risk. The credit rating declines as the default risk of the bonds increases.

Investment grade bonds

bonds with low risk of default that are rated Baa (BBB) or above

Non-investment grade bonds

bonds rated below Baa (or BBB) by rating agencies; often called *speculative grade bonds, high-yield bonds* or *junk bonds*

Exhibit 8.4 also shows that bonds in the top four rating categories are called **investment grade bonds.** Moody's calls bonds rated below Baa (or BBB) **non-investment grade bonds,** but most financial practitioners refer to them as *speculative grade* bonds, *high-yield bonds* or simply *junk bonds.* The distinction between investment grade and non-investment grade bonds is important because regulations typically require commercial banks, insurance companies, pension funds, other financial institutions and government agencies to purchase securities rated only as investment grade.

Exhibit 8.5 shows default risk premiums associated with selected bonds with investment grade bond ratings in August 2009. The premiums measure the difference between yields on US treasury securities – which, as mentioned, are the proxy for the risk-free rate – and yields on riskier securities of similar maturity.[7] The 82-basis-point (0.82%) default risk premium on Aaa-rated corporate bonds represents the market consensus of the amount investors must be compensated to induce them to purchase typical Aaa-rated bonds instead of a risk-free security. As credit quality declines from Aaa to Baa, the default risk premiums increase from 82 basis points to 302 basis points.

The Term Structure of Interest Rates

The term to maturity of a loan is the length of time until the principal amount is payable. The relation

EXHIBIT 8.5

DEFAULT RISK PREMIUMS FOR SELECTED BOND RATINGS

Security: Moody's Credit Rating	Security Yield (%) (1)	Risk-Free Rate[a] (%) (2)	Default Risk Premium (%) (1) – (2)
Aaa	3.72	2.90	0.82
Aa	4.18	2.90	1.28
A	5.10	2.90	2.20
Baa	5.92	2.90	3.02

[a]Ten-year US treasury bond yield as of 28 August 2009.

Sources: Federal Reserve Statistical Release H.15 (www.federalreserve.gov) and Moody's (www.moodys.com).

The default risk premium (DRP) measures the yield difference between the yield on treasury securities (the risk-free rate) and the yields on riskier securities of the same maturity.

between yield to maturity and term to maturity is known as the **term structure of interest rates**. We can view the term structure visually by plotting the **yield curve**, a graph with term to maturity on the horizontal axis and yield to maturity on the vertical axis. Yield curves show graphically how market yields vary as term to maturity changes.

Term structure of interest rates

the relation between yield and term to maturity

Yield curve

a graph representing the term structure of interest rates, with the term to maturity on the horizontal axis and the yield on the vertical axis

WEB

Smart Money's website gives a good overview of yield curves. Go to: www.smartmoney.com/onebond/index.cfm?story=yieldcurve.

For yield curves to be meaningful, the securities used to plot the curves should be similar in all features (for example, default risk and marketability) except for maturity. We do not want to confound the relation of yield and term to maturity with other factors that also affect interest rates. We can best see the term structure relation by examining yields on government securities because they have similar default risk (none) and marketability.

Exhibit 8.6 shows data and yield curve plots for government securities in the 2000s. As you can see, the shape of the yield curve is not constant over time. As the general level of interest rises and falls, the yield curve shifts up and down and has different slopes. We can observe three basic shapes (slopes)

of yield curves in the marketplace. First is the ascending, or upward-sloping, yield curve (May 2003 and February 2005), which is the yield curve most commonly observed. Descending, or downward-sloping, yield curves (September 2006) appear periodically and are earmarked by short-term rates (for example, six-month yield) exceeding long-term rates (for example, 10- or 20-year rates). Downward-sloping yield curves often appear before the beginning of a recession. Flat yield curves (not shown in the exhibit) are not common but do occur from time to time. Three factors affect the level and the shape (the slope) of the yield curve over time: the real rate of interest, the expected rate of inflation and interest rate risk.

The real rate of interest is the base interest rate in the economy and is determined by individuals' time preference for consumption; that is, it tells us how much individuals must be paid to forgo spending their money today. The real rate of interest varies with the business cycle, with the highest rates seen at the end of a period of business expansion and the lowest at the bottom of a recession. The real rate is not affected by the term to maturity. Thus, the real rate of interest affects the level of interest rates but not the shape of the yield curve.

The expected rate of inflation can influence the shape of the yield curve. If investors believe that inflation will increase in the future, the yield curve will be upward sloping because long-term interest rates will contain a larger inflation premium than short-term interest rates. The inflation premium is the market's best estimate of future inflation. Conversely, if investors believe inflation will fall in the future, the prevailing yield will be downward sloping.

Finally, the presence of interest rate risk affects the shape of the yield curve. As discussed earlier, long-term bonds have greater price volatility than short-term bonds. Because investors are aware of this risk, they demand compensation in the form of an interest rate premium. It follows that the longer the maturity of a security, the greater its interest rate risk, and the higher the interest rate. It is important to note that the interest rate risk premium always adds an upward bias to the slope of the yield curve.

EXHIBIT 8.6

YIELD CURVES FOR EUROZONE AAA GOVERNMENT SECURITIES AT THREE DIFFERENT POINTS IN TIME

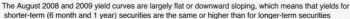

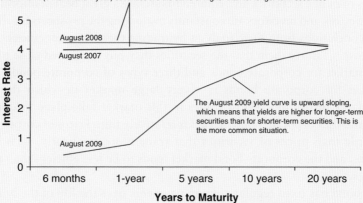

The August 2008 and 2009 yield curves are largely flat or downward sloping, which means that yields for shorter-term (6 month and 1 year) securities are the same or higher than for longer-term securities

The August 2009 yield curve is upward sloping, which means that yields are higher for longer-term securities than for shorter-term securities. This is the more common situation.

Interest Rate (%)

Terms to Maturity	August 2007	August 2008	August 2009
6 months	3.98	4.24	0.41
1 year	4.02	4.23	0.76
5 years	4.10	4.15	2.62
10 years	4.27	4.35	3.51
20 years	4.11	4.15	4.02

Source: European Central Bank (www.ecb.int).

The shape or slope of the yield curve is not constant over time. The exhibit shows two shapes: (1) the curves for August 2007 and August 2008 are largely flat or downward sloping and (2) the curve for August 2009 is upward sloping, which is the shape of the yield curve most commonly observed.

In sum, the cumulative effect of three economic factors determines the level and shape of the yield curve: (1) the cyclical movements of the real rate of interest affect the level of the yield curve, (2) the expected rate of inflation can bias the slope of the yield curve either positively or negatively, depending on market expectations of inflation, and (3) interest rate risk always provides an upward bias to the slope of the yield curve.

Before You Go On

1. What are default risk premiums and what do they measure?
2. Describe the two most prominent bond-rating systems.
3. What are the key factors that most affect the level and shape of the yield curve?

SUMMARY OF LEARNING OBJECTIVES

1. **Explain what an efficient capital market is and why 'market efficiency' is important to financial managers.**

   An efficient capital market is a market where security prices reflect the knowledge and expectations of all investors. Public markets, for example, are more efficient than private markets because issuers of public securities are required to disclose a great deal of information about these securities to investors and investors are constantly evaluating the prospects for these securities and acting on the conclusions from their analyses by trading them. Market efficiency is important to investors because it assures them that the securities they buy are priced close to their true value.

2. **Describe the market for corporate bonds and three types of corporate bonds.**

   The market for corporate bonds is a very large market in which the most important investors are large institutions. Most trades in this market take place through dealers in the OTC market and the corporate bond market is relatively thin. Prices of corporate bonds tend to be more volatile than prices of securities that trade more frequently, such as the stock and money markets, and the corporate bond market tends to be less efficient than markets for these other securities.

   A vanilla bond has fixed regular coupon payments over the life of the bond and the entire principal is repaid at maturity. A zero-coupon bond pays all interest and all principal at maturity. Since there are no payments before maturity, zero-coupon bonds are issued at prices well below their face value. Convertible bonds can be exchanged for ordinary shares at a predetermined ratio.

3. **Explain how to calculate the value of a bond and why bond prices vary negatively with interest rate movements.**

   The value of a bond is equal to the present value of the future cash flows (coupons and principal repayment) discounted at the market rate of interest for bonds with similar characteristics. Bond prices vary negatively with interest rates because the coupon rate on most bonds is fixed at the time the bond is issued. Therefore, as interest rates go up, investors seek other forms of investment that will allow them to take advantage of the higher returns. Because the bond's coupon payments are fixed, the only way the yields can be adjusted to the current market rate of interest is to reduce the bond's price. Similarly, when interest rates are declining, the yield on fixed-income securities will be higher relative to the yield on similar securities priced to market; the favourable yield will increase the demand for these securities, increasing their price and lowering their yield to the market yield.

4. **Distinguish between a bond's coupon rate, yield to maturity and effective annual yield, and be able to calculate their values.**

   A bond's coupon rate is the stated interest rate on the bond when it is issued. Bonds typically pay interest either semi-annually or annually; most European bonds pay coupon interest once a year. The yield to maturity is the expected return on a bond if it is held to its maturity date. The effective annual yield is the yield an investor actually earns in one year, adjusting for the effects of compounding. If the bond pays coupon payments more often than annually, the effective annual yield will be higher than the simple annual yield because of compounding. Work through Learning by Doing Applications 8.2, 8.3 and 8.4 to master these calculations.

5. **Explain why investors in bonds are subject to interest rate risk and why it is important to understand the bond theorems.**

Because interest rates are always changing in the market, all investors who hold bonds are subject to interest rate risk. Interest rate risk is uncertainty about future bond values caused by fluctuations in interest rates. Three of the most important bond theorems can be summarised as follows:

1. Bond prices are negatively related to interest rate movements.
2. For a given change in interest rates, the prices of long-term bonds will change more than the prices of short-term bonds.
3. For a given change in interest rates, the prices of lower-coupon bonds will change more than the prices of higher-coupon bonds.

Understanding these relations is important because it helps investors to better understand why bond prices change and, thus, to make better decisions regarding the purchase or sale of bonds and other fixed-income securities.

6. **Discuss the concept of default risk and know how to compute a default risk premium.**

Default risk is the risk that the issuer will be unable to pay its debt obligation. Since investors are risk averse, they must be paid a premium to purchase a security that exposes them to default risk. The default risk premium has two components: (1) compensation for the expected loss if a default occurs and (2) compensation for bearing the risk that a default could occur. All factors held constant, the degree of default risk a security possesses can be measured as the difference between the interest rate on a risky security and the interest rate on a default-free security. The default risk is also reflected in the company's bond rating. The highest-grade bonds, those with the lowest default risk, are rated Aaa (or AAA). The default risk premium on corporate bonds increases as the rating on bonds is lowered.

7. **Describe the factors that determine the level and shape of the yield curve.**

The level and shape of the yield curve are determined by three factors: (1) the real rate of interest, (2) the expected rate of inflation and (3) the interest rate risk. The real rate of interest is the base interest rate in the economy and varies with the business cycle. The real rate of interest affects only the level of the yield curve and not its shape. The expected rate of inflation does affect the shape of the yield curve. If investors believe inflation will rise in the future, for example, the curve will be upward sloping, as long-term rates will contain a larger inflation premium than short-term rates. Finally, interest rate risk, which increases with a security's maturity, adds an upward bias to the slope of the yield curve.

SUMMARY OF KEY EQUATIONS

Equation	Description	Formula
(8.1)	Price of a bond	$P_B = \dfrac{C_1}{1+i} + \dfrac{C_2}{(1+i)^2} + \cdots + \dfrac{C_n + F_n}{(1+i)^n}$
(8.2)	Price of a bond making multiple payments each year	$P_B = \dfrac{C/m}{1+i/m} + \dfrac{C/m}{(1+i/m)^2} + \cdots + \dfrac{C/m + F_{mn}}{(1+i/m)^{mn}}$
(8.3)	Price of a zero-coupon bond	$P_B = \dfrac{F_{mn}}{(1+i/m)^{mn}}$

SELF-STUDY PROBLEMS

8.1. Calculate the price of a five-year bond that has a coupon of 6.5% and pays annual interest. The current market rate is 5.75%.

8.2. The Bigbie Company issued a five-year bond one year ago with a coupon of 8%. The bond pays interest semi-annually. If the yield to maturity on this bond is 9%, what is the price of the bond?

8.3. La Roche has a three-year bond outstanding that pays a 7.25% coupon and is currently priced at SFr 913.88. What is the yield to maturity of this bond? Assume annual coupon payments.

8.4. Highland Hotels plc has a 10-year bond that is priced at £1100.00. It has a coupon of 8% paid semi-annually. What is the yield to maturity on this bond?

8.5. Herstellungs-Dortmund AG has a five-year bond whose yield to maturity is 6.5%. The bond has no coupon payments. What is the price of this zero-coupon bond?

SOLUTIONS TO SELF-STUDY PROBLEMS

8.1. The time line and calculations for the five-year bond are as follows:

```
0        1         2         3         4       5 Year
| 5.75% |         |         |         |        |
P_B = ?  €65      €65       €65       €65    €1065
```

$$P_B = \frac{C_1}{1+i} + \frac{C_2}{(1+i)^2} + \frac{C_3}{(1+i)^3} + \frac{C_4}{(1+i)^4} + \frac{C_5 + F_5}{(1+i)^5}$$

$$= \frac{€65}{1.075} + \frac{€65}{(1.075)^2} + \frac{€65}{(1.075)^3} + \frac{€65}{(1.075)^4} + \frac{€65 + €1000}{(1.075)^5}$$

$$= €61.47 + €48.12 + €54.96 + €51.95 + €805.28$$

$$= €1031.81$$

8.2. We can find the price of the Bigbie Company's bond as follows:

```
0   1   2   3   4   5   6   7   8 Semi-annual
| 9% |   |   |   |   |   |   |     period
P_B = ? 40  40  40  40  40  40  40  1040
```

$$P_B = \frac{C/m}{1+i/m} + \frac{C/m}{(1+i/m)^2} + \frac{C/m}{(1+i/m)^3} + \ldots + \frac{C/m + F_8}{(1+i/m)^8}$$

$$= \frac{40}{1.045} + \frac{40}{(1.045)^2} + \frac{40}{(1.045)^3} + \ldots + \frac{40+1000}{(1.045)^8}$$

$$= 38.28 + 36.63 + 35.05 + 33.54 + 32.10 + 30.72$$
$$+ 29.39 + 732.31 = 967.02$$

Alternatively, we can use the present value annuity factor from Chapter 6 and the present value equation from Chapter 5 to solve for the price of the bond:

$$P_B = C \times \left[\frac{1 - \frac{1}{(1+i/m)^{mn}}}{1/m} \right] + \frac{F_n}{(1+i/m)^{mn}}$$

$$= 40 \times \left[\frac{1 - \frac{1}{(1+0.045)^8}}{0.045} \right] + \frac{1000}{(1+0.045)^8}$$

$$= 263.84 + 703.19 = 967.03$$

8.3. We start with a time line for La Roche's bond:

```
0              1            2            3 Year
|     i = ?    |            |            |
P_B = - SFr 913.88  SFr 72.50    SFr 72.50   SFr 1072.50
```

Use trial and error to solve for the yield to maturity (YTM). Since the bond is selling at a discount, we know that the yield to maturity is higher than the coupon rate.

Try YTM = 10%:

$$P_B = \frac{C_1}{1+i} + \frac{C_2}{(1+i)^2} + \frac{C_3 + F_3}{(1+i)^3}$$

$$\text{SFr } 913.88 = \frac{\text{SFr } 72.50}{1.10} + \frac{\text{SFr } 72.50}{(1.10)^2} + \frac{\text{SFr } 72.50 + \text{SFr } 1000}{(1.10)^3}$$

$$= \text{SFr } 65.91 + \text{SFr } 59.92 + \text{SFr } 805.79$$

$$= \text{SFr } 931.62$$

Try a higher rate, say YTM = 11%:

$$P_B = \frac{C_1}{1+i} + \frac{C_2}{(1+i)^2} + \frac{C_3 + F_3}{(1+i)^3}$$

$$\text{SFr } 913.88 = \frac{\text{SFr } 72.50}{1.11} + \frac{\text{SFr } 72.50}{(1.11)^2} + \frac{\text{SFr } 72.50 + \text{SFr } 1000}{(1.11)^3}$$

$$= \text{SFr } 65.32 + \text{SFr } 58.84 + \text{SFr } 784.20$$

$$= \text{SFr } 908.36$$

Since this is less than the price of the bond, we know that the YTM is between 10% and 11% and closer to 11%.

We will try YTM = 10.75%:

$$P_B = \frac{C_1}{1+i} + \frac{C_2}{(1+i)^2} + \frac{C_3 + F_3}{(1+i)^3}$$

$$\text{SFr } 913.88 = \frac{\text{SFr } 72.50}{1.1075} + \frac{\text{SFr } 72.50}{(1.1075)^2} + \frac{\text{SFr } 72.50 + \text{SFr } 1000}{(1.1075)^3}$$

$$= \text{SFr } 65.46 + \text{SFr } 59.11 + \text{SFr } 789.53$$

$$= \text{SFr } 914.10$$

Alternatively, we can use Equation (6.1) and the present value equation from Chapter 5 to solve for the price of the bond:

$$P_B = C \times \left[\frac{1 - \frac{1}{(1+i)^n}}{i} \right] + \frac{F_n}{(1+i)^n}$$

$$= \text{SFr } 72.50 \times \left[\frac{1 - \frac{1}{(1+0.1075)^3}}{0.1075} \right] + \frac{\text{SFr } 1000}{(1+0.1075)^3}$$

$$= \text{SFr } 914.09$$

We can now use the interpolation method to determine the YTM:

$$i_{\text{unknown}} = i_{\text{low}} + \frac{(\text{Value}_{\text{low } i} - \text{Value}_{\text{unknown } i})}{(\text{Value}_{\text{low } i} - \text{Value}_{\text{high } i})} \times (i_{\text{high}} - i_{\text{low}})$$

$$\text{YTM} = 10.75\% + \frac{\text{SFr } 914.09 - \text{SFr } 913.88}{\text{SFr } 914.09 - \text{SFr } 908.36} \times (11\% - 10.75\%)$$

$$= 10\% + 0.0366 \times 0.25\%$$

$$= 10.7592\%$$

Using a spreadsheet or financial calculator to calculate the YTM, the exact value is 10.7594%.

8.4. The time line for Highland Hotels' 10-year bond looks like this:

As the bond is standing at a premium, the yield to maturity must be less than the coupon rate. We will start with 7%:

$$P_B = C \times \left[\frac{1 - \frac{1}{(1+i)^n}}{i} \right] + \frac{F_n}{(1+i)^n}$$

$$= £40 \times \left[\frac{1 - \frac{1}{(1+0.07/2)^{20}}}{0.07/2} \right] + \frac{£1000}{(1+0.07/2)^{20}}$$

$$= £40 \times 14.2124 + £1000 \times 0.5026$$

$$= £1071.06$$

This is somewhat less than the market price, so the YTM is too high. We will try 6.50%:

$$P_B = C \times \left[\frac{1 - \frac{1}{(1+i)^n}}{i} \right] + \frac{F_n}{(1+i)^n}$$

$$= £40 \times \left[\frac{1 - \frac{1}{(1+0.065/2)^{20}}}{0.065/2} \right] + \frac{£1000}{(1+0.065/2)^{20}}$$

$$= £40 \times 14.5393 + £1000 \times 0.5275$$

$$= £1109.05$$

Now the price is too high, so the YTM lies between 7% and 6.50%. Interpolating gives us:

$$i_{\text{unknown}} = i_{\text{low}} + \frac{(\text{Value}_{\text{low } i} - \text{Value}_{\text{unknown } i})}{(\text{Value}_{\text{low } i} - \text{Value}_{\text{high } i})} \times (i_{\text{high}} - i_{\text{low}})$$

$$\text{YTM} = 3.25\% + \frac{£1109.05 - £1100}{£1109.05 - £1071.06} \times (3.50\% - 3.25\%)$$

$$= 3.25\% + 0.2321 \times 0.25\%$$

$$= 3.31\%$$

The answer we get is 3.31%, which is the semi-annual interest rate. To obtain an annualised yield to maturity, we multiply this by two:

$$\text{YTM} = 3.31\% \times 2$$

$$\text{YTM} = 6.62\%$$

8.5. You have the following information about Herstellungs-Dortmund's bonds:

YTM = 6.5%; $m = 1$
No coupon payments

Most European corporate bonds pay interest annually. Thus $n = 5$ and $i = 0.065$. Using Equation (8.3), we obtain the following calculation:

$$P_B = \frac{F_n}{(1+i)^n}$$
$$= \frac{€1000}{(1+0.065)^5} = €729.88$$

CRITICAL THINKING QUESTIONS

8.1. You believe that you can make abnormally profitable trades by observing that the CFO of a certain company always wears his green suit on days that the firm is about to release positive information about his company. Describe which form of market efficiency is consistent with your belief.

8.2. Describe the informational differences that separate the three forms of market efficiency.

8.3. What economic conditions would prompt investors to take advantage of a bond's convertibility feature?

8.4. Define *yield to maturity*. Why is it important?

8.5. Define *interest rate risk*. How can CFOs manage this risk?

8.6. Explain why bond prices and interest rates are negatively related. What is the role of the coupon rate and term to maturity in this relation?

8.7. If rates are expected to increase, should investors look to long-term bonds or short-term securities? Explain.

8.8. Explain what you would assume the yield curve to look like during economic expansion and why.

8.9. An investor holds a 10-year bond paying a coupon of 9%. The yield to maturity of the bond is 7.8%. Would you expect the investor to be holding a par-value, premium or discount bond? What if the yield to maturity were 10.2%? Explain.

8.10. a. Investor A holds a 10-year bond, while investor B holds an 8-year bond. If the interest rate increases by 1%, which investor will have the higher interest rate risk? Explain.

b. Investor A holds a 10-year bond paying 8% a year, while investor B also has a 10-year bond that pays a 6% coupon. Which investor will have the higher interest rate risk? Explain.

QUESTIONS AND PROBLEMS

Basic

8.1. Bond price: British Airways is issuing a 10-year bond with a coupon rate of 8%. The interest rate for similar bonds is currently 6%. Assuming annual payments, what is the present value of the bond?

8.2. Bond price: Pierre Dupont just received a gift from his grandfather. He plans to invest in a five-year bond issued by the City of Venice that pays annual coupons of 5.5%. If the current market rate is 7.25%, what is the maximum amount Pierre should be willing to pay for this bond?

8.3. **Bond price:** Knight plc has issued a three-year bond that pays a coupon of 6.10%. Coupon payments are made semi-annually. Given the market rate of interest of 5.80%, what is the market value of the bond?

8.4. **Bond price:** Regata SA has seven-year bonds outstanding that pay a 12% coupon rate. Investors buying the bond today can expect to earn a yield to maturity of 8.875%. What is the current value of these bonds? Assume annual coupon payments.

8.5. **Bond price:** You are interested in investing in a five-year bond that pays 7.8% coupon with interest to be received semi-annually. Your required rate of return is 8.4%. What is the most you would be willing to pay for this bond?

8.6. **Zero-coupon bonds:** Diana Moretti is interested in buying a five-year zero-coupon bond whose face value is €1000. She understands that the market interest rate for similar investments is 9%. Assume annual coupon payments. What is the current price of this bond?

8.7. **Zero-coupon bonds:** Ten-year zero-coupon bonds issued by the US Treasury have a face value of $1000 and interest is compounded semi-annually. If similar bonds in the market yield 10.5%, what is the value of these bonds?

8.8. **Zero-coupon bonds:** The Newcastle Property Company is planning to fund a development project by issuing 10-year zero-coupon bonds with a face value of £1000. Assuming semi-annual compounding, what will be the price of these bonds if the appropriate discount rate is 14%?

8.9. **Yield to maturity:** Ruth Hornsby is looking to invest in a three-year bond that pays semi-annual coupons at a coupon rate of 5.875%. If these bonds have a market price of A$981.13, what yield to maturity and effective annual yield can she expect to earn?

8.10. **Yield to maturity:** Rudy Sandberg wants to invest in four-year bonds that are currently priced at £868.43. These bonds have a coupon rate of 6% and pay semi-annual coupons. What is the current market yield on this bond?

8.11. **Realised yield:** Alfred Kavern bought 10-year Bundesobligationen (German government bonds) with a 12% coupon bond issued three years ago at €913.44. If he sells these bonds, which have a face value of €1000, at the current price of €804.59, what is the realised yield on the bonds? Assume annual coupons on similar coupon-paying bonds.

8.12. **Realised yield:** Four years ago, Inga Sorenson bought six-year, 5.5% coupon bonds issued by AGA AB for SKr 947.68. If she sells these bonds at the current price of SKr 894.52, what will be the realised yield on the bonds? Assume annual coupons on similar coupon-paying bonds.

Intermediate

8.13. **Bond price:** Transport-Antwerpen Internationaal NV is raising €10 million by issuing 15-year bonds with a coupon rate of 8.5%. Coupon payments will be annual. Investors buying the bond currently will earn a yield to maturity of 8.5%. At what price will the bonds sell in the marketplace? Explain.

8.14. **Bond price:** Pullman Railways plc issued 10-year bonds four years ago with a coupon rate of 9.375%. At the time of issue, the bonds sold at par. Today, bonds of similar risk and maturity will pay annual coupons of 6.25%. Assuming semi-annual coupon payments, what will be the current market price of the firm's bonds?

8.15. Bond price: Marshall Outback Services of Australia is issuing eight-year bonds with a coupon rate of 6.5% and semi-annual coupon payments. If the current market rate for similar bonds is 8%, what will be the bond price? If the company wants to raise A$1.25 million, how many bonds does the firm have to sell?

8.16. Bond price: The South African Mining Services Group Ltd has outstanding bonds that will mature in six years and pay an 8% coupon, interest being paid semi-annually. If you paid R1036.65 today and your required rate of return was 6.6%, did you pay the right price for the bond?

8.17. Bond price: Nanotech plc has a bond issue maturing in seven years and paying a coupon rate of 9.5% (semi-annual payments). The company wants to retire a portion of the issue by buying the securities in the open market. If it can refinance at 8%, how much will Nanotech pay to buy back its current outstanding bonds?

8.18. Zero-coupon bonds: Kintel, Inc. wants to raise $1 million by issuing six-year zero-coupon bonds with a face value of $1000. Its investment banker states that investors would use an 11.4% discount rate on such bonds. At what price would these bonds sell in the marketplace? How many bonds would the firm have to issue to raise $1 million? Assume semi-annual coupon payments.

8.19. Zero-coupon bonds: Le Chocolatier de Rouen SA plans to issue seven-year zero-coupon bonds. It has learned that these bonds will sell today at a price of €439.76. Assuming annual coupon payments, what is the yield to maturity on these bonds?

8.20. Yield to maturity: Outback Mines of Queensland plc has four-year bonds outstanding that pay a coupon rate of 6.6% semi-annually. If these bonds are currently selling at A$914.89, what is the yield to maturity that an investor can expect to earn on these bonds? What is the effective annual yield?

8.21. Yield to maturity: Serengeti Ltd, the South African industrial group, has five-year bonds outstanding that pay a coupon of 8.8%. If these bonds are priced at R1064.86, what is the yield to maturity on these bonds? Assume semi-annual coupon payments. What is the effective annual yield?

8.22. Yield to maturity: Adrienne Dawson is planning to buy 10-year zero-coupon bonds issued by the US Treasury. If these bonds with a face value of $1000 are currently selling at $404.59, what is the expected return on these bonds? Assume that interest compounds semi-annually on similar coupon-paying bonds.

8.23. Realised yield: Brown & Co. issued seven-year bonds two years ago that can be called after five years. The bond makes semi-annual coupon payments at a coupon rate of 7.875%. The bond has a market value of £1053.40, and the call price is £1078.75. If the bonds are called by the firm, what is the investor's realised yield?

8.24. Realised yield: Trevor Price bought 10-year bonds issued by Harvest Foods five years ago for $936.05. The bonds make semi-annual coupon payments at a rate of 8.4%. If the current price of the bond is $1048.77, what is the yield that Trevor would earn by selling the bonds today?

8.25. Realised yield: You bought a six-year bond issued by the Sydney Harbour Authority four years ago. At that time, you paid A$974.33 for the bond. The bond pays a coupon rate of 7.375% and interest is paid semi-annually. Currently, the bond is priced at A$1023.56. What yield can you expect to earn on this bond if you sell it today?

Advanced

8.26. [EXCEL®] Lopez Information Systems is planning to issue 10-year bonds. The going market rate for such bonds is 8.125%. Assume that coupon payments will be semi-annual. The firm is trying to decide between issuing an 8% coupon bond or a zero-coupon bond. The company needs to raise $1 million.

a. What will be the price of the 8% coupon bonds?

b. How many coupon bonds would have to be issued?

c. What will be the price of the zero-coupon bonds?

d. How many zero-coupon bonds will have to be issued?

8.27. EXCEL® Media Entertainment plc has issued eight-year bonds with a coupon of 6.375% and semi-annual coupon payments. The market's required rate of return on such bonds is 7.65%.

a. What is the market price of these bonds?

b. Now assume that the above bond is callable after five years at an 8.5% premium on the face value. What is the expected return on this bond?

8.28. EXCEL® Peabody Corp. has seven-year bonds outstanding. The bonds pay a coupon of 8.375% semi-annually and are currently worth $1063.49. The bonds can be called in three years at a price of $1075.

a. What is the yield to maturity on the bond?

b. What is the effective annual yield?

c. What is the realised yield on the bonds if they are called?

d. If you plan to invest in this bond today, what is the expected yield on the investment? Explain.

8.29. EXCEL® The City of Liverpool has issued 25-year bonds that pay semi-annual coupons at a rate of 9.875%. The current market rate for similar securities is 11%.

a. What is the bond's current market value?

b. What will be the bond's price if rates in the market (i) decrease to 9% or (ii) increase to 12%?

c. Refer to your answers in part b. How do the interest rate changes affect premium bonds and discount bonds?

d. Suppose the bond were to mature in 12 years. How do the interest rate changes in part b affect the bond prices?

8.30. EXCEL® Rachette Corp. has 18-year bonds outstanding. These bonds, which pay semi-annual coupons, have a coupon rate of 9.735% and a yield to maturity of 7.95%.

a. Compute the bond's current price.

b. If the bonds can be called after five more years at a premium of 13.5% over par value, what is the investor's realised yield?

c. If you bought the bond today, what is your expected rate of return? Explain.

SAMPLE TEST PROBLEMS

8.1. Alimento Torino S.p.A. issued 10-year bonds three years ago with a coupon of 6%. If the current market rate is 8.5% and the bonds pay annual coupons, what is the current market price of this bond?

8.2. Kim Sundaram recently bought a 20-year zero-coupon bond which compounds interest semi-annually. If the current market rate is 7.75%, what is the maximum price he should have paid for this bond?

8.3. Five-year bonds of Infotech Corporation are currently priced at $1065.23. They pay semi-annual coupons of 8.5%. If you bought these bonds today, what would be the yield to maturity and effective annual yield that you would earn?

8.4. The Gold Company wants to borrow on a five-year term from its bank. The lender determines that the firm should pay a default risk premium of 1.75% over the government bond rate. The five-year government bond rate is currently 5.65%. The firm also faces a marketability risk premium of 0.80%. What is the total borrowing cost to the firm?

8.5. Trojan Corp. has issued seven-year bonds that are paying 7% semi-annual coupons. If the opportunity cost for Brianna Lindner is 8.25%, what is the maximum price that she would be willing to pay for this bond?

ENDNOTES

1. A basis point is 100th of a per cent (or 0.01%).

2. Former British colonies and territories tend to use semi-annual coupon interest since this was the standard in the United Kingdom.

3. If the bond sold at a premium, the reverse would be true; that is, the price with semi-annual compounding would be slightly more than the price with annual compounding.

4. Now we are close to the correct yield, we applied a little mathematics to the problem and interpolated between the values. We want to find the interest rate that equates the price of our bond. The price of the bond is €960.99. At 7%, the price is €973.76, so the price difference is €12.77 (€973.66 – €960.99). The price difference between the bond at the 7% yield and the 7.7% yield is €17.80 (= €973.76 – €955.96). We can therefore interpolate the yield we want by 7% + €12.77 / €17.80 × (7.7% – 7%) = 7.50%. The interpolation approach assumes a straight line between the two discount rates. We know this to be incorrect from the discussion in Chapter 5, but when the difference in yields is small, the error from curvature is not that significant and our approximation works reasonably well. With a wider range of yields (say 5% and 10%), the result would be very inaccurate; we get a yield of 7.61% – when it should be 7.50%!

5. Note that, for annual compounding, the yield to maturity equals the EAY; for the Eurobond, the yield to maturity = 3.175% and the EAY = $(1 + \text{quoted interest rate}/m)^m - 1 = (1 + 0.03175/1)^1 - 1 = (1 + 0.03175) - 1 = 0.03175$, or 3.175%.

6. At first glance the calculation looks wrong; surely the present values should be lower than the future values! However, let us consider what a negative interest rate does. If we start today with €100 and we face a negative interest rate of 3%, the future value in one year will be €100 × (1 – 0.03) = €97.00. Reverse this: how much is €97.00 worth today, if we have a negative interest rate of 3%, and we get €97.00 / (1 – 0.03) = €100. That is a lesser sum in the future is worth more to us today since it is losing value with time and hence its present value is larger. Inflation acts like a negative interest rate in that it reduces the value of money with time. Note that all the calculations and conventions of time money calculations are honoured when using negative interest rates. If you are using tables, you only need to switch the discount table for the compounding table – and vice versa – since future money will now be worth less than present money in order to be able to solve such problems.

7. Default risk premiums are typically quoted in terms of basis points. A basis point is simply 1/100 of a per cent. Therefore, 50 basis points equals 0.5%, 100 basis points equals 1.0%, and so on.

CHAPTER

9

Share Valuation

In this Chapter:

The Market for Shares

Valuing Ordinary Shares

Share Valuation: Some Simplifying Assumptions

Valuing Preference Shares

LEARNING OBJECTIVES

1. List and describe the four types of secondary markets.
2. Explain why many financial analysts treat preference shares as a special type of bond rather than as an equity security.
3. Describe how the general dividend-valuation model values ordinary shares.
4. Discuss the assumptions that are necessary to make the general dividend-valuation model easier to use and be able to use the model to compute the value of a firm's ordinary shares.
5. Explain why g must be less than R in the constant-growth dividend model.
6. Explain how valuing preference shares with a stated maturity differs from valuing preference shares with no maturity date and be able to calculate the price of both types of preference share.

inding the actual market price of a publicly traded share is easy. You can just look it up in the business section of a newspaper. But do not expect the market price to stay the same; share prices change all the time – sometimes dramatically. On Thursday 2 September 2009, for the European stock markets, the following companies' shares had the biggest one-day price change:

Company	Industry	Country	Price Per Share (€)	Change in Price	Percentage Change
KBC Group SA/NV	Financial services	Belgium	26.10	+2.36	+9.94
Fortis SA/NV	Financial services	Belgium	2.97	+0.16	+5.66
Safran Group SA	Defence	France	12.45	+0.39	+3.23
ING Group CVA	Financial services	Netherlands	10.05	+0.30	+3.03
Carrefour SA	Food retailing	France	31.40	−1.01	−3.12
Vienna Insurance AG	Financial services	Austria	34.18	−1.17	−3.31
National Bank of Greece SA	Financial services	Greece	22.20	−0.69	−3.44
Pernod Ricard SA	Drinks	France	51.11	−2.39	−4.47

The table shows that on the same day, some of the companies experienced significant price rises in their shares, while others had equally significant price falls. The Belgian financial services group KBC Group shares rose nearly 10%. At the other end of the spectrum, Pernod Ricard, the French drinks company, saw its shares fall by just under 4.5%. When share prices rise or fall, how do investors or financial managers know when it is time to sell or buy? In other words, how can they tell if the market price of a share reflects its value? One approach is to develop a share-valuation model and compare the estimate from the model with the market price. If the market price is below the estimate, the shares may be undervalued, in which case an investor might buy the shares. (Of course, other factors may also weigh into the final decision to buy.) In this chapter, we develop and apply share-valuation models that enable us to estimate a share's value. The models are very similar to those used by professional investors and analysts.

CHAPTER PREVIEW

This chapter focuses on equity securities and how they are valued. We first examine the fundamental factors that determine the value of ordinary shares then we discuss several valuation models. These models tell us what the share price *should* be. We can compare our estimates from such models with *actual* market prices.

Why are equity-valuation formulas important for you to study in a corporate finance course? First, management may want to know if the firm's shares are undervalued or overvalued. For example, if the shares are undervalued, management may want to repurchase shares to reissue in the future or postpone an equity offering until the share price increases. Second, as we mentioned in Chapter 1, the overarching goal of financial management is to maximise the current value of the firm's shares. To make investment or financing decisions that increase shareholder value, you must understand the fundamental factors that determine the market value of the firm's shares.

We begin this chapter with a discussion of the secondary markets for equity securities and their efficiency, explain how to read stock market price listings in the newspaper and introduce the types of equity securities that firms typically issue. Then we develop a general valuation model and demonstrate that the value of a share is the present value of *all* expected future cash dividends. We use some simplifying assumptions about dividend payments to implement this valuation model. These assumptions correspond to actual practice and allow us to develop several specific valuation models that are theoretically sound.

THE MARKET FOR SHARES

Equity securities are certificates of ownership of a company. Equities are the most visible and talked about securities on the financial landscape. In April 2010, more than $49.2 trillion worth of public equity securities were outstanding globally. Every day investors around the globe eagerly track the ups and downs of the stock market. Most people instinctively believe that the performance of the stock market is an important barometer of a country's economic health. Also fuelling interest is the large number of people who actually own equity securities directly as investors or indirectly through their pension or retirement plans.

Secondary Markets

Learning Objective 1

List and describe the four types of secondary markets.

Recall from Chapter 2 that the stock market consists of primary and secondary markets. In the primary market, firms sell new shares to investors to raise money. In secondary markets, outstanding shares are bought and sold among investors. We will discuss the primary markets for bonds and equity securities further in Chapter 15. Our focus here is on secondary markets.

Any trade of a security after its primary offering is said to be a secondary market transaction. Most secondary market transactions do not directly affect the firm that issues the securities. For example, when an investor buys 100 shares of Nokia on the Helsinki Exchange, Nokia's cash position is not affected since the exchange of money is only between the investors buying and selling the securities.

The presence of a secondary market does, however, affect the issuer indirectly. Simply put, investors will pay a higher price for primary securities that have an active secondary market because of the marketability the secondary market provides. As a result, firms whose securities trade on a secondary market can sell their new debt or equity issues at a lower funding cost than firms selling similar securities that have no secondary market.

Secondary Markets and their Efficiency

In Europe, most secondary market transactions take place on one of the many stock exchanges, the most important ones being given in Exhibit 9.1. Measured in terms of total volume of activity and total equity value of the firms listed, the London Stock Exchange is the largest in Europe and Euronext is the second largest. In addition to the main exchanges, there are second-tier exchanges, either tied to the main exchanges, or operating as separate institutions. These cater for a large number of smaller companies that want to have a listing but do not qualify for the main exchanges. For instance, the London Stock Exchange operates the Alternative Investment Market (AIM) for smaller-growth companies. As a rule, the firms listed on the main European exchanges are larger companies and their shares trade more frequently than firms whose securities trade on second-tier markets.

The role of these and other secondary markets is to bring buyers and sellers together. As we discussed in Chapter 8, ideally we would like security markets to be as efficient as possible. Markets are efficient when current market prices of securities traded reflect all available information relevant to the security. If this is the case, security prices will be near or at their true value. The more efficient the market, the more likely this is to happen.

There are four types of secondary markets, and each type differs according to the amount of price

EXHIBIT 9.1

MAJOR STOCK EXCHANGES IN EUROPE

Exchange	Market Value of Shares Traded on the Exchange (€ billions)	Daily Turnover[a] (€ millions)
Euronext[1]	2 263	742 886
Deutsche Börse	1 132	1 101 065
London Stock Exchange	2 204	1 483 263
Bolsas y Mercados Españoles	1 085	591 217
Borsa Italiana	555	341 421
Nordic Stock Exchange Group[2]	665	319 398
Swiss Exchange	855	272 201

[1] Euronext is a pan-European stock exchange based in Paris and with subsidiaries in Belgium, France, the Netherlands and Portugal, and is part of the Euronext-NYSE Liffe group.

[2] This group includes the Copenhagen, Helsinki, Iceland, Stockholm, Tallinn, Riga and Vilnius stock exchanges.

[a] The list excludes trading platforms such as Chi-X Europe, the largest trading system for European equities by volume, since they are not a primary listing authority.

The market value or total capitalisation and the daily turnover by value of shares listed on the exchanges are given for the end of May 2009.

information available to investors, which in turn affects the efficiency of the market. We discuss the four types of secondary markets – direct search, brokered, dealer and auction – in the order of their increasing market efficiency.

Direct Search The secondary markets furthest from the ideal of complete availability of price information are those in which buyers and sellers must seek each other out directly. In these markets, individuals bear the full cost of locating and negotiating and it is typically too costly for them to conduct a thorough search to locate the best price. Securities that sell in direct search markets are usually bought and sold so infrequently that few third parties, such as brokers or dealers, find it profitable enough to serve the market. In these markets, sellers often rely on word-of-mouth communication to find interested buyers. The ordinary shares of small private companies are a good example of the securities that trade in this manner.

Broker When trading in a security issue becomes sufficiently heavy, brokers find it profitable to offer specialised search services to market participants. Brokers bring buyers and sellers together to earn a fee, called a commission. To provide investors with an incentive to hire them, brokers may charge a commission that is less than the cost of a direct search. Brokers are not passive agents but aggressively seek out buyers or sellers and try to negotiate an acceptable transaction price for their clients. The presence of active brokers increases market efficiency because brokers are in frequent contact with market participants and are likely to know what constitutes a 'fair' price for a security.

Dealer If the trading in a given security has sufficient volume, market efficiency is improved if there is someone in the marketplace to provide continuous bidding (selling or buying) for the security. Dealers provide this service by holding inventories of securities, which they own, and then buying and selling from the inventory to earn a profit. Unlike brokers, dealers have capital at risk. Dealers earn

their profits from the *spread* on the securities they trade – the difference between their **bid price** (the price at which they buy) and their **offer (ask) price** (the price at which they sell).

> **Bid price**
>
> the price a securities dealer will pay for a given security

> **Offer (ask) price**
>
> the price at which a securities dealer seeks to sell a given security

The advantage of a dealer over a brokered market is that brokers cannot guarantee that an order to buy or sell will be executed promptly. This uncertainty about the speed of execution creates price risk. During the time a broker is trying to sell a security, its price may change and the client could suffer a loss. A dealer market eliminates the need for time-consuming searches for a fair deal because buying and selling take place immediately from the dealer's inventory of securities.

Dealers make markets in securities using electronic computer networks to quote prices at which they are willing to buy or sell a particular security and are often called **market makers**. These networks enable dealers to electronically survey the prices quoted by different market makers to help establish their sense of a fair price and to trade. A major development in the 1990s was the opening of the so-called electronic communications network (ECN). ECN is a Web-based system that allows individual investors to trade securities directly with one another, much like dealers. In Europe these are called multilateral trading facilities (MTFs) and they compete with the established exchanges. An example is Chi-X, the pan-European MTF, which has about 19% of trading volume for European equities. Similar systems exist for trading bonds and other securities.

Market maker

dealer in securities at a stock exchange who undertakes to buy or sell at all times accepting the risks involved

Auction   In an auction market, buyers and sellers confront each other directly and bargain over price. The major exchanges operate as auction markets. While exchanges used to have a physical floor where buyers and sellers interacted, now this has been superseded by electronic trading. Nevertheless, these replicate the way transactions occurred when markets communicated orally.

Reading the Stock Market Listings

The *Wall Street Journal Europe*, *The Financial Times* and other newspapers provide share listings for the major stock exchanges, such as Euronext, the London Stock Exchange and other exchanges around the world. Online resources, such as *Google Finance* and *Yahoo Finance*, provide up-to-date information on individual companies as well as stock market indices. Exhibit 9.2 lists the kind of information that is available.

As you can see, the information that is available is quite extensive. This is in order to allow you to understand the share's prospects and the risks involved. The most important piece of data is the current share price. This tells us the actual trading price in the market, and the price at which you can buy or sell the shares. The time at which the trade was recorded may also be given. Other useful market information is the high and low prices at which the shares traded during the day and the price at which the shares started trading at the beginning of the session or finished trading at the previous day's close. The range is simply the difference between the high and low price and this is often expressed as a percentage. So if the share price traded at a high of €35.25 and a low of €33.90, the range is €1.35 (€35.25 − €33.90) or 3.98% (€1.35/€33.90 = 0.0398). The same information for the previous 52 weeks is also usually given. This is useful to see whether the shares are trading close to their highs or lows over the preceding 12 months. The 52-week price range will be much greater than the intra-day price range, reflecting the fact that over longer periods of time share prices tend to change much more substantially than over a single day.

There is also information that changes less frequently but is nevertheless important. Investors want to know what dividend they can expect to receive. We will discuss the importance of dividends in more detail in the next section. The yield is simply the dividend on the shares divided by the share price. For instance, if the share price is €34.50 and the cash dividend is €1.95 per share, the **dividend yield** is €1.95/€34.50 = 0.0565, or 5.65%. Investors are willing to accept low dividend payouts, or none at all, as long as they expect higher cash dividends and/or a higher share price in the future.

Dividend yield

a share's dividend payout divided by its current price

A key measure of the attractiveness of shares is the earnings per share (EPS). We discussed this in Chapter 4 when looking at analysing financial statements. It provides an important link between the reported financial statements of the company and the market's estimate of the value of the shares. By combining the EPS with the current share price, we get the price-to-earnings ratio (*P/E*). This indicates the number of years' earnings that go into the share price. So if the EPS is €3.69 then the *P/E* ratio will be 9.35 (€34.50/€3.69). We can compare different companies by looking at their *P/E* ratios. So if there is a company with a *P/E* of 12.74, the market places a higher value on this company's earnings since it is willing to pay 12.74 times the earnings of this firm rather than only 9.35 for the other company's earnings.

EXHIBIT 9.2
INFORMATION ON LISTED SHARES

Information	Definition
Current price or last trade	The price of the shares as traded in the market
Trade time	The time at which the last trade took place
Bid price	The price at which shares can be sold
Offer or ask price	The price at which shares can be purchased
High	The highest price the shares have traded at during the trading session; this might refer to the previous day's trading
Low	The lowest price the shares have traded at during the trading session; this might refer to the previous day's trading
Open	The price at which the shares initially traded at the start of the session
Close (previous close)	The price of the shares when the trading session ended or were last traded during the session
Net change and percentage change	The net price change from one close to the next or from the opening price to the current price and the percentage change in value
Day's range	The difference between the highest and lowest price that the shares traded during the session
52-week high	The highest price at which the shares traded during the last year
52-week low	The lowest price at which the shares traded during the last year
52-week range	The difference between the highest and lowest price that the shares traded during the last year
Dividend	The amount of the current dividend
Yield	The dividend per share divided by the current share price
Earnings per share	The latest net income (or net profit) divided by the number of outstanding shares[a]
Price-to-earnings ratio (P/E)	Price of shares/Earnings per share[a]
Volume	The number of shares traded on the exchange during the session
Average volume (t)	The average volume of shares traded over a given period, usually 3 months
Market capitalisation	The current or closing price of the shares times the number of shares that are outstanding in the market
Analysts' opinion and estimates	Information on what equity analysts think about the company and whether they are making buy, sell or hold recommendations for the shares
Historical prices	A back history of the share price
Other information and data	This includes a range of information of use to investors. This can include, for instance, the share's beta[b]

[a]How the P/E ratio and earnings per share are calculated and used is discussed in Chapter 4.
[b]The beta is discussed in Chapter 7.

Not all the information above is provided in newspapers. Typically, they will provide end-of-trading session information. Additional information is available via the Web from the following sources:

The Financial Times: www.ft.com
The Wall Street Journal Europe Online: www.wsj.com
Google Finance: www.google.com
Reuters: www.reuters.com
Yahoo Finance: www.yahoo.com

The number of shares traded in a day or over the longer term is important. In Chapter 2, we discussed the concept of marketability. Companies where the volume of shares which are traded is large have greater marketability than those where the volume is low. The market capitalisation is simply the price of the shares times the number of shares that the company has issued. If the above company has 25 million shares outstanding then the market capitalisation will be €862.5 million (€34.50 × 25 million). We would expect large capitalisation companies to have greater marketability than smaller capitalisation companies.

Finally, other useful information on the company is often available. Of particular interest to buyers of shares are the opinions and recommendations of equity analysts. These provide insight into what professional investors think about the share's prospects. Also, historical prices (usually the day's closing price) are now generally available and can be downloaded for further analysis, for instance to create graphs. In addition, for many companies, it is possible to get technical analysis, such as the share's beta. We discussed the importance of beta in Chapter 7 as it is a measure of systematic risk. Investors want to know how much risk they are taking when buying shares.

Ordinary and Preference Shares

Equity securities take several forms. The most prevalent type of equity security, as its name implies, are **ordinary shares**.[1] Ordinary shares represent the basic ownership claim in a company. One of the basic rights of the owners is to vote on all important matters that affect the life of the company, such as the election of the board of directors or a proposed merger or acquisition. Owners of ordinary shares are not guaranteed any dividend payments and have the lowest-priority claim on the firm's assets in the event of bankruptcy. Legally, ordinary shareholders enjoy limited liability; that is, their losses are limited to the original amount of their investment in the firm and their personal assets cannot be taken to satisfy the

obligations of the company. Finally, ordinary shares are perpetuities in the sense that they have no maturity. Ordinary shares can be retired only if management buys them in the open market from investors or if the firm is liquidated, in which case its assets are sold, as described in the next section.

> ### Ordinary shares
>
> an equity share that represents the basic ownership claim in a company; the most common type of equity security

> ### Preference shares
>
> an equity share in a company that entitles the owner to preferred treatment over owners of ordinary shares with respect to dividend payments and claims against the firm's assets in the event of bankruptcy or liquidation but that typically has no voting rights

Like ordinary shares, **preference shares** represent an ownership interest in the company, but as the name implies, preference shares receive preferential treatment over ordinary shares. Specifically, preference shareholders take precedence over ordinary shareholders in the payment of dividends and in the distribution of corporate assets in the event of liquidation. Unlike the interest payments on bonds, which are contractual obligations, preference share dividends are declared by the board of directors and if a dividend is not paid, the lack of payment is not legally viewed as a default.

Preference shares are legally a form of equity. Thus, preference share dividends are paid by the issuer with after-tax income. Even though preference shares are an equity security, the owners have no voting privileges unless the preference shares are convertible into ordinary shares. Preference shares are generally viewed as perpetuities because they have no maturity. However, most preference shares are not true perpetuities because their share contracts often contain call provisions and can even include *sinking fund* provisions, which require management to retire a certain percentage of the preference shares issue annually until the entire amount is retired.

Preference Shares: Debt or Equity?

One of the ongoing debates in finance is whether preference shares are debt or equity. A strong case can be made that preference shares are a special type of bond. The argument behind this case is as follows. First, regular (non-convertible) preference shares confer no voting rights. Second, preference shareholders receive a fixed dividend, regardless of the firm's earnings and if the firm is liquidated they receive a stated value (usually par) and not a residual value. Third, preference shares often have 'credit' ratings that are similar in nature to those issued to bonds. Fourth, preference shares are sometimes convertible into ordinary shares. Finally, most preference share issues are not true perpetuities. For these reasons, many investors consider preference shares to be a special type of debt rather than equity.

Before You Go On

1. How do dealers differ from brokers?
2. What does the price-to-earnings ratio tell us?
3. Why are preference shares often viewed as a special type of bond rather than as shares?

VALUING ORDINARY SHARES

In earlier chapters we emphasised that the value of any asset is the present value of its future cash

flows. The steps in valuing an asset are as follows:

1. Estimate the future cash flows.
2. Determine the required rate of return, or discount rate, which depends on the riskiness of the future cash flows.
3. Compute the present value of the future cash flows to determine what the asset is worth.

It is relatively straightforward to apply these steps in valuing a bond because the cash flows are stated as part of the bond contract and the required rate of return or discount rate is just the yield to maturity on bonds with comparable risk characteristics. However, ordinary share valuation is more difficult for several reasons. First, while the expected cash flows for bonds are well documented and easy to determine, dividends on ordinary shares are much less certain. Dividends are declared by the board of directors and a board may, or may not, decide to pay a cash dividend at a particular time. Thus, the size and the timing of dividend cash flows are less certain. Second, ordinary shares are true perpetuities in that they have no final maturity date. Thus, firms never have to redeem them. In contrast, bonds have a finite maturity. Finally, unlike the rate of return, or yield, on bonds, the rate of return on ordinary shares is not directly observable. Thus, grouping ordinary shares into risk classes is more difficult than grouping bonds. Keeping these complexities in mind, we now turn to a discussion of ordinary share valuation.

WEB

You can read about share (stock)-valuation models at the Motley Fool: www.fool.com/research/2000/features000406.htm.

A One-Period Model

Let us assume that you have a genie that can tell the future with perfect certainty. Suppose you are thinking about buying a share and selling it after a year. The genie volunteers that in one year you will be able to sell the share for €100 (P_1) and it will pay an €8 dividend (D_1) at the end of the year. The time line for the transaction is:

```
0                          1  Year
|_____|
Buy share                  €8 + €100
```

If you and the other investors require a 20% return on investments in securities in this risk class, what price would you be willing to pay for the share today?

The value of the share is the present value of the future cash flows you can expect to receive from it. The cash flows you will receive are as follows: (1) the €8 dividend and (2) the €100 sale price. Using a 20% rate of return, we see that the value of the share equals the present value (PV) of the dividend plus the present value of the cash received from the sale of the share:

$$PV(share) = PV(dividend) + PV(sale\ price)$$
$$= \frac{€8}{1 + 0.2} + \frac{€100}{1 + 0.2}$$
$$= \frac{€8 + €100}{1.2} = \frac{€108}{1.2}$$
$$= €90$$

Thus, the value of the share today is €90. If you pay €90 for the share, you will have a one-year holding period return of exactly 20%. More formally, the time line and the current value of the share for our one-period model can be shown as:

```
0                          1  Year
|_____|
P₀                         D₁ + P₁
```

$$P_0 = \frac{D_1 + P_1}{1 + R}$$

where:

P_0 = the current value, price or present value of the share

D_1 = the dividend paid at the end of the period

P_1 = the price of the share at the end of the period

R = the required return on an ordinary share, or discount rate, in a particular risk class

Note that P_0 denotes time zero, which is today; P_1 is the price one period later; P_2 is two periods in the future; and so on. Note also that when we speak of the price (P) in this context, we mean the value – what we have determined is what the price *should* be, given our model – not the actual market price. Our one-period model provides an estimate of what the market price should be.

Now what if at the beginning of year 2, we are again asked to determine the price of a share with the same dividend pattern and a one-year holding period. As in our first calculation, the current price (P_1) of the share is the present value of the dividend and the share's sale price, both received at the end of the year (P_2). Specifically, our time line and the share pricing formula are as follows:

```
1                          2  Year
|_____|
P₁                         D₂ + P₂
```

$$P_1 = \frac{D_2 + P_2}{1 + R}$$

If we repeat the process again at the beginning of year 3, the result is similar:

$$P_2 = \frac{D_3 + P_3}{1 + R}$$

and at the beginning of year 4:

$$P_3 = \frac{D_4 + P_4}{1 + R}$$

Each single-period model discounts the dividend and sale price at the end of the period by the required return.

A Perpetuity Model

Unfortunately, although our one-period model is correct, it is not very realistic. We need a share-valuation formula for perpetuity, not for one or two periods. However, we can string together a series of one-period share pricing models to arrive at a perpetuity model for shares. Here is how we are going to do it.

First, we will construct a two-period share-valuation model. The time line for the two-period model follows:

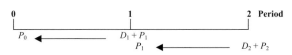

To construct our two-period model, we start with our initial single-period valuation formula:

$$P_0 = \frac{D_1 + P_1}{1 + R}$$

Now we substitute into this equation the expression derived earlier for $P_1 = (D_2 + P_2)/(1 + R)$, which is as follows:

$$P_0 = \frac{D_1 + [(D_2 + P_2)/(1 + R)]}{1 + R}$$

Solving this equation results in a share-valuation model for two periods:

$$P_0 = \frac{D_1}{1 + R} + \frac{D_2}{(1 + R)^2} + \frac{P_2}{(1 + R)^2}$$

Finally, we combine the second-period terms, resulting in this two-period share valuation equation:

$$P_0 = \frac{D_1}{1 + R} + \frac{D_2 + P_2}{(1 + R)^2}$$

This equation shows that the price of the shares for two periods is the present value of the dividend in period 1 (D_1) plus the present value of the dividend and sale price in period 2 (D_2 and P_2).

Now let us construct a three-period model. The time line for the three-period model is:

If we substitute the equation for P_2 into the two-period valuation model shown above, we have a three-period model, which is shown in the following equations. Recall that $P_2 = (D_3 + P_3)/(1 + R)$. This

model was developed in precisely the same way as our two-period model:

$$P_0 = \frac{D_1}{1 + R} + \frac{D_2}{(1 + R)^2} + \frac{P_2}{(1 + R)^2}$$

$$= \frac{D_1}{1 + R} + \frac{D_2}{(1 + R)^2} + \frac{(D_3 + P_3)/(1 + R)}{(1 + R)^2}$$

$$= \frac{D_1}{1 + R} + \frac{D_2}{(1 + R)^2} + \frac{D_3}{(1 + R)^3} + \frac{P_3}{(1 + R)^3}$$

$$= \frac{D_1}{1 + R} + \frac{D_2}{(1 + R)^2} + \frac{D_3 + P_3}{(1 + R)^3}$$

By now, it should be clear that we could go on to develop a four-period model, a five-period model, a six-period model and so on, ad infinitum. The ultimate result is the following equation:

$$P_0 = \frac{D_1}{1 + R} + \frac{D_2}{(1 + R)^2} + \frac{D_3}{(1 + R)^3} + \cdots + \frac{D_t}{(1 + R)^t} + \frac{P_t}{(1 + R)^t}$$

Here, t is the number of time periods, which can be any number from one to infinity (∞).

In summary, we have developed a model showing that the value, or price, of a share today (P_0) is the present value of all future dividends and the share's sale price in the future. Although theoretically sound, this model is not practical to apply because the number of dividends could be infinite. It is unlikely that we can successfully forecast an infinite number of dividend payments or a share's sale price far into the future. What we need are some realistic simplifying assumptions.

The General Dividend Valuation Model

Learning Objective 3

Describe how the general dividend-valuation model values ordinary shares.

In the preceding equation, notice that the final term, as in the earlier valuation models, is always the sale price of the share in period t (P_t) and that t can be any number, including infinity. The model assumes that we can forecast the sale price of the share far into the future, which does not seem very likely in real life. However, as a practical matter, as P_t moves further out in time towards infinity, the value of P_t approaches zero. Why? No matter how large the sale price of the share, the present value of P_t will approach zero because the discount factor approaches zero. Therefore, if we go out to infinity, we can ignore the $P_t/(1+R)^t$ term and write our final equation as:

$$P_0 = \frac{D_1}{1+R} + \frac{D_2}{(1+R)^2} + \frac{D_3}{(1+R)^3} + \frac{D_4}{(1+R)^4}$$

$$+ \frac{D_5}{(1+R)^5} + \cdots + \frac{D_\infty}{(1+R)^\infty} \qquad (9.1)$$

$$= \sum_{t=1}^{\infty} \frac{D_t}{(1+R)^t}$$

where:

P_0 = the current value, or price, of the share
D_t = the dividend received in period t, where t
    $= 1, 2, 3, \ldots, \infty$
R = the required return on an ordinary share
    or discount rate

Equation (9.1) is a general expression for the value of a share. It says that the price of a share is the present value of *all* expected future dividends:

Share price = PV(All future dividends)

The formula does not assume any specific pattern for future dividends, such as a constant growth rate. Nor does it make any assumption about when the share is going to be sold in the future. Furthermore, the model says that to compute a share's current value, we need to forecast an infinite number of dividends, which is a daunting task at best.

Equation (9.1) provides some insights into why share prices are changing all the time and why, at certain times, price changes can be dramatic – as shown in the opening vignette. Equation (9.1) implies that the underlying value of a share is determined by the market's expectations of the future cash flows (from dividends) that the firm can generate. In efficient markets, share prices change constantly as new information becomes available and is incorporated into the firm's market price. For publicly traded companies, the market is inundated with facts and rumours, such as when a firm fails to meet sales projections, the CEO resigns or is fired, or the company gets involved in a legal dispute with one of its customers. Some events may have little or no impact on the firm's cash flows and, hence, its share price. Others can have very large effects on cash flows. Examples include Black Monday (19 October 1987) or the effects of the credit crunch in 2008, which was accompanied by a slowdown in the global economy. On 24 October 2008 alone the indices for the major stock markets fell by nearly 10%.

The Growth Share Pricing Paradox

An interesting issue concerning growth shares arises out of the fact that the share-valuation equation is based on dividend payments. *Growth shares* are typically defined as the shares of companies whose earnings are growing at above-average rates and are expected to continue to do so for some time. A company of this type typically pays little or no dividends on its shares because management believes that the company has a number of high-return investment opportunities and that both the company and its investors will be better off if earnings are reinvested rather than paid out as dividends.

To illustrate the problem with valuing growth shares, let us suppose that the earnings of the Whiz Growth Company are growing at an exceptionally high rate. The company's shares pay no dividends and management states that there are no plans to pay any dividends. Based on our share-valuation equation, what is the value of Whiz Growth's shares?

Obviously, since all the dividend values are zero, the value of our growth share is zero!

$$P_0 = \frac{0}{1+R} + \frac{0}{(1+R)^2} + \frac{0}{(1+R)^3} + \cdots = 0$$

How can the value of a growth share be zero? What is going on here?

The problem is that our definition of growth shares was less than precise. Our application of

Equation (9.1) assumes that Whiz Growth will never pay a dividend. If Whiz Growth had a charter that stated it would *never* pay dividends and would *never* liquidate itself (unless it went bankrupt), the value of its shares would indeed be zero. Equation (9.1) predicts – and common sense says – that if you own shares in a company that will *never* pay you any cash, the market value of those shares is absolutely nothing. As you may recall, this is a point we emphasised in Chapter 1.

What we should have said is that growth shares are shares in a company that *currently* has exceptional investment opportunities and thus is not *currently* paying dividends because it is reinvesting earnings. At some time in the future, growth share companies will pay dividends or will liquidate themselves (for example, by selling out to other companies) and pay a single large 'cash dividend'. People who buy growth shares expect rapid price appreciation because management reinvests the cash flows from earnings internally in investment projects believed to have high rates of return. If the internal investments succeed, the share price should go up significantly and investors can sell their shares at a price that is higher than the price they paid.

Before You Go On

1. What is the general formula used to calculate the price of a share? What does it mean?
2. What are growth shares and why do they typically pay little or no dividends?

SHARE VALUATION: SOME SIMPLIFYING ASSUMPTIONS

Learning Objective 4

Discuss the assumptions that are necessary to make the general dividend-valuation model easier to use and be able to use the model to compute the value of a firm's ordinary shares.

Conceptually, our dividend model [Equation (9.1)] is consistent with the notion that the value of an asset is the discounted value of future cash flows. Unfortunately, at a practical level, the model is not easy to use because of the difficulty of estimating future dividends over a long period of time. We can, however, make some simplifying assumptions about the pattern of dividends that will make the model more manageable. Fortunately, these assumptions closely resemble the way many firms manage their dividend payments. We have a choice among three different assumptions. (1) Dividend payments remain constant over time; that is, they have a growth rate of zero. (2) Dividends have a constant growth rate; for example, they grow at 3% per year. (3) Dividends have a mixed growth rate pattern; that is, dividends have one payment pattern and then switch to another. Next, we discuss each assumption in turn.

Note that we value shares using dividends rather than earnings or profits since dividends represent a distribution of cash that shareholders actually get. Shareholders do not receive profits: earnings are what firms make; dividends are cash flows to shareholders. The value we give to shares is based on their future cash flows, not accounting profits.

Zero-Growth Dividend Model

The simplest assumption is that dividends will have a growth rate of zero. Thus, the dividend payment pattern remains constant over time:

$$D_1 = D_2 = D_3 = \cdots = D_\infty$$

In this case, the dividend-discount model [Equation (9.1)] becomes:

$$P_0 = \frac{D}{1+R} + \frac{D}{(1+R)^2} + \frac{D}{(1+R)^3} + \frac{D}{(1+R)^4} + \frac{D}{(1+R)^5} + \cdots + \frac{D}{(1+R)^\infty}$$

This cash flow pattern essentially describes a perpetuity with a constant cash flow. You may recall that we developed an equation for such a perpetuity in Chapter 6. Equation (6.3) said that the present value of a perpetuity with a constant cash flow is CF/*i*, where CF is the constant cash flow and *i* is the interest rate. In terms of our share-valuation model, we can present the same relationship as follows:

$$P_0 = \frac{D}{R} \qquad (9.2)$$

where:

P_0 = the current value, or price, of the share

D = the constant cash dividend received in each time period

R = the required return on the shares or discount rate

This model fits the dividend pattern for ordinary shares of a company that is not growing and has little growth potential or for preference shares, which we discuss in the next section.

For example, Del Marino SA is a small printing company that serves a rural area near Córdoba in Spain. The area's economic base has remained constant over the years and Del Marino's sales and earnings reflect this trend. The firm pays a €5 dividend per year and the board of directors has no plans to change the dividend. The firm's investors are mostly local business people who expect a 20% return on their investment. What should be the price of the firm's shares?

Since the cash dividend payments are constant, we can use Equation (9.2) to find the price of the shares:

$$P_0 = \frac{D}{R} = \frac{€5}{0.20} = €25 \text{ per share}$$

Learning by Doing Application 9.1

The Value of a Small Business

Problem: For the past 15 years, a family has operated the gift shop in a luxury hotel near the Place Vendôme in Paris. The hotel management wants to sell the gift shop to the family members rather than paying them to operate it. The family's accountant will incorporate the new business and estimates that it will generate an annual cash dividend of €150 000 for the new shareholders. The hotel will provide the family with an infinite guarantee for the space and a generous buyout plan in the event that the hotel closes its doors. The accountant estimates that a 20%

discount rate is appropriate. What is the value of the shares?

Approach: Assuming that the business will operate indefinitely and that its growth is constrained by its circumstances, the zero-growth discount model can be used to value the shares. Thus, we can use Equation (9.2). Since the number of shares outstanding is not known, we can simply interpret P_0 as being the total value of all the outstanding shares.

Solution:

$$P_0 = \frac{D}{R} = \frac{€150\,000}{0.20} = €750\,000$$

Constant-Growth Dividend Model

Under the next dividend assumption, cash dividends do not remain constant but instead grow at some average rate g from one period to the next forever. The rate of

growth can be positive or negative. And, as it turns out, a constant-growth rate is not a bad approximation of the actual dividend pattern for some firms. Constant dividend growth is an appropriate assumption for mature companies with a history of stable growth.

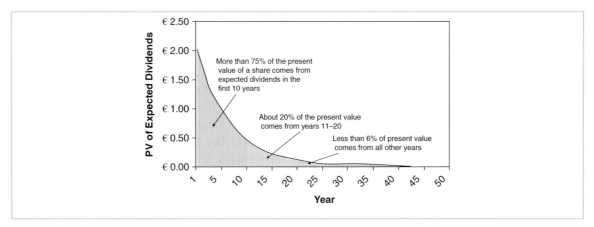

Exhibit 9.3: Impact on Share Prices of Near and Distant Future Dividends Dividends expected far in the future have a smaller present value than dividends expected in the next few years and so have less effect on the price of the share. As you can see in the exhibit, with constant dividends, more than 75% of the current share price comes from expected dividends in the first 10 years.

You may have concerns about the assumption of an infinite time horizon. In practice, though, it does not present a problem. It is true that most companies do not live on forever. We know, however, that the further in the future a cash flow will occur, the smaller its present value. Thus, far-distant dividends have a small present value and contribute very little to the price of the shares. For example, as shown in Exhibit 9.3, with constant dividends and a 15% discount rate, dividends paid during the first 10 years account for more than 75% of the value of a share, while dividends paid after the twentieth year contribute less than 6% of the value.

Identifying and applying the constant-growth dividend model is fairly straightforward. First, we need a model to compute the value of dividend payments for any time period. We will assume that the cash dividends grow at a constant rate g from one period to the next forever. This situation is an application of the compound growth rate formula, Equation (5.6), developed in Chapter 5:

$$FV_n = PV \times (1 + g)^n$$

where g is the compound growth rate and n is the number of compounding periods. We can apply this formula to our dividend payments. We note that D_0 is the current dividend, paid at time $t = 0$, and it grows at a constant growth rate g. The next dividend, paid at time $t = 1$, is D_1, which is just the current dividend (D_0) multiplied by the growth factor, $(1 + g)$. Thus,

$D_1 = D_0 \times (1 + g)$. The general formula for dividend values over time is stated as follows:

$$D_t = D_0 \times (1 + g)^t \qquad (9.3)$$

where:

D_t = dividend payment in period t, where $t = 1, 2, 3, \cdots, \infty$
D_0 = dividend paid in the current period, $t = 0$
g = the constant growth rate for dividends

Equation (9.3) allows us to compute the dividend payment for any time period.

Notice that to compute the dividend for any period, we multiply D_0 by the growth rate factor to some power, but we *always* start with D_0.

We can now develop the constant-growth dividend model, which is easy to do because it is just an application of Equation (6.6) from Chapter 6. Equation (6.6) says that the present value of a growing perpetuity (PVA) is the growing cash flow value (CF$_1$) from period 1, divided by the difference between the discount rate (i) and the rate of growth (g) of the cash flow (CF$_1$):

$$PVA_\infty = \frac{CF_1}{i - g}$$

We can represent this same relationship as follows:

$$P_0 = \frac{D_1}{R - g} \qquad (9.4)$$

where:

P_0 = the current value, or price, of the share
D_1 = the dividend paid in the next period ($t = 1$)
g = the constant growth rate for dividends
R = the required return on ordinary shares or discount rate

In other words, the constant-growth dividend model tells us that the current price of a share is the next period dividend divided by the difference between the discount rate and the dividend growth rate. Note that PVA$_\infty$ is the current value or price of the share (P_0), which is the present value of the dividend cash flows.

As discussed in Chapter 6, the growing-perpetuity model is valid only as long as the growth rate is less than the discount rate, or required rate of return. In terms of Equation (9.4), then, the value of g must be less than the value of R ($g < R$). If the equation is used in situations where R is equal to or less than g ($R \leq g$), the computed results will be meaningless.

Finally, notice that if $g = 0$, there is no dividend growth, the dividend payment pattern becomes a constant no-growth dividend stream and Equation (9.4) becomes $P_0 = D/R$. This equation is precisely the same as Equation (9.2), which is our zero-growth dividend model. Thus, Equation (9.2) is just a special case of Equation (9.4) where $g = 0$.

We will work through an example using the constant-growth dividend model. Bayern Automotive AG is a regional auto parts supplier based in Munich, Germany. At the firm's year-end shareholders' meeting, the CFO announces that this year's dividend will be €4.81. The announcement conforms to Bayern Automotive's dividend policy, which sets dividend growth at a 4% annual rate. Investors who own shares in similar types of firms expect to earn a return of 18%. What is the value of the firm's shares?

First, we need to compute the cash dividend payment for next year (D_1). Applying Equation (9.3) for $t = 1$ yields the following:

$$D_1 = D_0 \times (1 + g) = €4.81 \times (1 + 0.04)$$
$$= €4.81 \times 1.04 = €5.00$$

Next, we apply Equation (9.4) to find the value of the firm's shares, which is €35.71 per share:

$$P_0 = \frac{D_1}{R}$$
$$= \frac{€5.00}{0.18 - 0.04}$$
$$= \frac{€5.00}{0.14} = €35.71$$

Learning by Doing Application 9.2

Bayern Automotive AG Grows Faster

Problem: Using the information given in the text, compute the value of Bayern Automotive AG shares if dividends grow at 12% rather than 4%. Explain why the answer makes sense.

Approach: First compute the cash dividend payment for next year (D_1) using the 12% growth rate. Then apply Equation (9.4) to solve for the firm's share price.

Solution:

$$D_1 = €4.81 \times 1.12 = €5.39$$
$$P_0 = \frac{€5.39}{0.18 - 0.12} = \frac{€5.39}{0.06} = €89.83$$

The higher share value of €89.83 is no surprise because dividends are now growing at a rate of 12% rather than 4%. Hence, value from cash payments to investors (dividends) is expected to be larger.

We should warn you about the danger of overestimating long-run dividend growth rates. Companies in expanding industries can grow rapidly but eventually the growth rate will decline. In the long term, companies will not grow faster than the economy as a whole and, for the most part, at rates that are below this. Long-run growth rates should therefore be modest to reflect this fact.

Computing Future Share Prices

The constant-growth dividend model [Equation (9.4)] can be modified to determine the value, or price, of a share at any point in time. In general, the price of a share, P_t, can be expressed in terms of the dividend in the next period (D_{t+1}), g and R, when the dividends from D_{t+1} forward are expected to grow at a constant rate. Thus, the price of a share of stock at time t is as follows:

$$P_t = \frac{D_{t+1}}{R - g} \qquad (9.5)$$

Notice that Equation (9.4) is just a special case of Equation (9.5) in which $t = 0$. To be sure that you understand this, set up Equation (9.5) to compute a share's current price at $t = 0$. When you are done, the resulting equation should look exactly like Equation (9.4).

An example will illustrate how Equation (9.5) is used. Suppose that a firm has a current dividend (D_0) of €2.50, R is 15% and g is 5%. What is the price of the share today (P_0) and what will it be in five years (P_5)? To help visualise the problem, we will lay out a time line and identify some of the important variables necessary to solve the problem:

	0	1	2	3	4	5	6	Year
Dividend: €2.50		D_1	D_2	D_3	D_4	D_5	D_6	
Share Price: P_0						P_5		

To find the current share price, we can apply Equation (9.4), but we must first compute the dividend for the next period (D_1), which is at $t = 1$. Using Equation (9.3), we compute the firm's dividend for next year:

$$D_1 = D_0 \times (1 + g) = €2.50 \times 1.05 = €2.625$$

Now we can use Equation (9.4) to find the price of the share today:

$$P_0 = \frac{D_1}{R - g} = \frac{€2.625}{0.15 - 0.05} = \frac{€2.625}{0.10} = €26.25$$

Now we will find the value of the share in five years. In this situation Equation (9.5) is expressed as:

$$P_5 = \frac{D_6}{R - g}$$

We need to compute D_6, and we do so by using Equation (9.3):

$$D_6 = D_0 \times (1 + g)^6 = €2.50 \times (1.05)^6 = €2.50 \times 1.34 = €3.35$$

The price of the share in five years is therefore:

$$P_5 = \frac{€3.35}{0.15 - 0.05} = \frac{€3.35}{0.10} = €33.50$$

Finally, note that €33.50/(1.05)^5 = €26.25, which is the value of the share today.

Learning by Doing
Application 9.3

Novartis' Current Share Price

Problem: Suppose that the current cash dividend on Novartis' ordinary shares is SFr 4.72. Financial analysts expect the dividends to grow at a constant rate of 6% per year and investors require a 10% return on this class of shares. What should be the current price of Novartis' shares?

Approach: In this scenario, $D_0 = $ SFr 4.72, $R = 0.10$ and $g = 0.06$. We first find D_1 using Equation (9.3) and we then calculate the value of the shares using Equation (9.4).

Solution:

Dividend: $D_1 = D_0 \times (1 + g) = $ SFr 4.72 $\times 1.06 = $ SFr 5.00

Value of share: $P_0 = \dfrac{D_1}{R - g} = \dfrac{\text{SFr } 5.00}{0.10 - 0.06}$

$$= \frac{\text{SFr } 5.00}{0.04} = \text{SFr } 125.00$$

Learning by Doing Application 9.4

Novartis' Future Share Price

Problem: Continuing the example in Learning by Doing Application 9.3, what should be Novartis' share price seven years from now (P_7)?

Approach: This is an application of Equation (9.5). We first need to calculate Novartis' dividend in period (year) 8 using Equation (9.3). Then we can apply Equation (9.5) to compute the estimated price of the shares seven years in the future.

Solution:

Dividend in period 8: $D_8 = D_0 \times (1 + g)^8$

$= $ SFr 4.72 $\times (1.06)^8$

$= $ SFr 4.72 $\times 1.594$

$= $ SFr 7.52

Price of Novartis' shares in 7 years:

$$P_7 = \frac{D_8}{R - g} = \frac{\text{SFr } 5.72}{1.10 - 0.06} = \frac{\text{SFr } 5.72}{0.04}$$

$= $ SFr 188.00

The Relationship between R and g

We previously mentioned that the divided growth model provides valid solutions only when $g < R$. Students frequently ask what happens to Equation (9.4) or (9.5) if this condition does not hold (if $g \geq R$). Mathematically, as g approaches R, the share price becomes larger and larger and when $g = R$ the value of the share

is infinite, which is, of course, nonsense. When the growth rate (g) is larger than the discount rate (R), the constant-growth dividend model tells us that the value of the share is negative. You will see in Chapter 20 that this is not possible. The value of a share can never be negative.

From a practical perspective, the growth rate in the constant-growth dividend model cannot be greater than the sum of the long-term rate of inflation and the long-term real growth rate of the economy. Since this model assumes that the firm will grow at a constant rate forever, any growth rate that is greater than this sum would imply that the firm will eventually take over the entire economy. Of course, we know this is not possible. Since the sum of the long-term rate of inflation and the long-term real growth rate has historically been less than 6–7%, the growth rate (g) is virtually always less than the discount rate (R) for the shares that we would want to use the constant-growth dividend model to value.

It is possible for firms to grow faster than the long-term rate of inflation plus the real growth rate of the economy – just not forever. A firm that is growing at such a high rate is said to be growing at a supernormal growth rate. We must use a different model to value the shares of a firm like this. We discuss one such model next.

Mixed (Supernormal) Growth Dividend Model

For many firms, it is not appropriate to assume that dividends will grow at a constant rate. Firms typically go through *lifecycles* and, as a result, exhibit different dividend patterns over time.

During the early part of their lives, successful firms experience a supernormal rate of growth in earnings. These firms tend to pay lower dividends or no dividends at all because many good investment projects are available to them and management wants to reinvest earnings in the firm to take

advantage of these opportunities. If a growth firm does not pay regular dividends, investors receive their returns from capital appreciation of the firm's shares (which reflect increases in expected future dividends), from a cash or share payout if the firm is acquired, or possibly from a large special cash dividend. As a firm matures, it will settle into a growth rate at or below the long-term rate of inflation plus the long-term real growth rate of the economy. When a firm reaches this stage, it will typically be paying a fairly predictable regular dividend.

Exhibit 9.4 shows several dividend growth curves. In the top curve, dividends exhibit a supernormal growth rate of 25% for four years, then a more sustainable nominal growth rate of 5% (this might, for example, be made up of 2.5% growth from inflation plus a 2.5% real growth rate). By comparison, the remaining curves show dividends with a constant nominal growth rate of 5%, a zero-growth rate and a negative 10% growth rate.

As mentioned earlier, successful companies often experience supernormal growth early in their lifecycles. During the 1990s, for example, firms such as BHP Billiton, the global mining company, Intel, Statoil and Grupo Ferrovial all experienced periods of supernormal growth. Older companies that

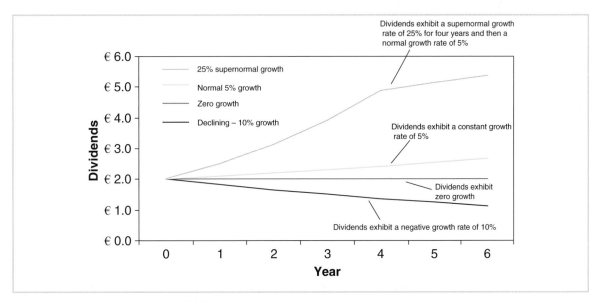

Exhibit 9.4: **Dividend Growth Rate Patterns**

reinvent themselves with new products or strategies may also experience periods of supernormal growth. Tesco plc, the UK supermarket chain established in 1919, during the first decade of the 21st century has strategically repositioned itself from simply offering food to include financial services and broadened its sales base by opening mini stores and diversifying abroad. It achieved sales of £2bn in 1982 and these have grown to £59.4bn by year end 2009 – a compound annual growth rate of 13.4% over the 27-year period.[2] Profits have matched the sales growth, generating huge returns for investors.

To value a share for a firm with supernormal dividend growth patterns, we do not need to develop any new equations. Instead, we can apply Equation (9.1), our general dividend model and Equation (9.5), which gives us the price of a share with constant dividend growth at any point in time.

We will illustrate with an example. Suppose a company's expected dividend pattern for three years is as follows: $D_1 = €1$, $D_2 = €2$, $D_3 = €3$. After three years, the dividends are expected to grow at a constant rate of 6% a year. What should be the current price (P_0) of the firm's shares if the required rate of return demanded by investors is 15%?

We begin by drawing a time line, as shown in Exhibit 9.5. We recommend that you prepare a time line whenever you solve a problem with a complex dividend pattern, so that you can be sure the cash flows are placed in the proper time periods. The critical element in working these problems is to correctly identify when the constant growth starts and to value it properly.

Looking at Exhibit 9.5, it is easy to see that we have two different dividend patterns. (1) D_1–D_3 represent a mixed dividend pattern, which can be valued using Equation (9.1), the general dividend-valuation model. (2) After the third year, dividends show a constant growth rate of 6% and this pattern can be valued using Equation (9.5), the constant-growth dividend-valuation model. Thus, our valuation model is:

$$P_0 = \text{PV(Mixed dividend growth)} + \text{PV(Constant dividend growth)}$$

Combining these present values yields the following result:

$$P_0 = \underbrace{\frac{D_1}{1+R} + \frac{D_2}{(1+R)^2} + \frac{D_3}{(1+R)^3}}_{\substack{\text{PV of mixed-growth} \\ \text{dividend payments}}} + \underbrace{\frac{P_3}{(1+R)^3}}_{\substack{\text{Value of constant-growth} \\ \text{dividend payments}}}$$

The value of the constant-growth dividend stream is P_3, which is the value, or price, at time $t = 3$. More specifically, P_3 is the value of the future cash dividends discounted to time period $t = 3$. With a required rate of return of 15%, the value of these dividends is calculated as follows:

$$D_4 = D_3 \times (1+g) = €3.00 \times 1.06 = €3.18$$
$$P_3 = \frac{D_4}{R-g} = \frac{€3.18}{0.15 - 0.06}$$
$$= €35.33$$

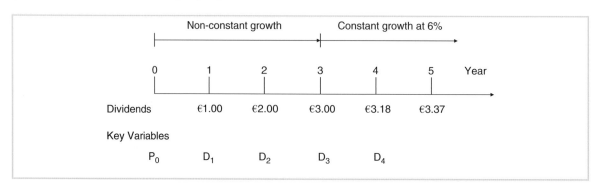

Exhibit 9.5: **Time Line for Non-Constant Dividend Pattern** The exhibit shows a time line for a non-constant growth dividend pattern. The time line makes it easy to see that we have two different dividend patterns. For three years, the dividends are expected to grow at a non-constant rate; after that, they are expected to grow at a constant rate of 6%.

We find the value of P_3 using Equation (9.5), which allows us to compute share prices in the future for shares with constant dividend growth. Note that the equation gives us the value, as of year 3, of a constant-growth perpetuity that begins in year 4. This formula always gives us the value as of one period before the first cash flow.

Now, since P_3 is at time period $t = 3$, we must discount it back to the present ($t = 0$). This is accomplished by dividing P_3 by the appropriate discount factor: $(1 + R)^3$.

Plugging the values for the dividends, P_3 and R into the above mixed-growth equation results in the following:

$$P_0 = \frac{€1.00}{1.15} + \frac{€2.00}{(1.15)^2} + \frac{€3.00}{(1.15)^3} + \frac{€35.33}{(1.15)^3}$$
$$= €0.87 + €1.51 + €1.97 + €23.23$$
$$= €27.58$$

Let us look at another example, this time using Equation (9.6). Suppose that Dimarin plc is a high-tech medical device firm located in County Cork, Ireland. The company is three years old and has experienced spectacular growth since its inception. You are a financial analyst for a stockbroker and have just returned from a two-day visit to the company. You learned that Dimarin plans to pay no dividends for the next five years. In year 6, management plans to pay a large, special cash dividend, which you estimate to be €25 per share. Then, beginning in year 7, management plans to pay a constant annual dividend of €6 per share for the foreseeable future. The appropriate discount rate for the share is 12% and the current market price is €25 per share. Your boss thinks the shares are not worth the price. You think that they are a bargain and that you should recommend them to the firm's clients. Who is right?

Our first step in answering this question is to lay out on a time line the expected dividend payments:

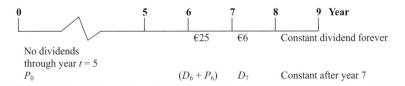

Thus, the value of the shares is €27.58.

We can write a general equation for the supernormal growth situation, where dividends grow first at a non-constant rate until period t and then at a constant rate, as follows:

$$P_0 = \frac{D_1}{1 + R} + \frac{D_2}{(1 + R)^2} + \cdots + \frac{D_t}{(1 + R)^t} + \frac{P_t}{(1 + R)^t} \quad (9.6)$$

If the supernormal growth period ends and dividends grow at a constant rate, g, then P_t is calculated from Equation (9.5) as follows:

$$P_t = \frac{D_{t+1}}{R - g}$$

The two preceding equations can also be applied when dividends are constant over time, since we know that $g = 0$ is just a special case of the constant-growth dividend model ($g > 0$).

This situation is a direct application of Equation (9.6), which is the mixed dividend model. That is, there are two different dividend cash streams: (1) the mixed dividends that in this case comprise a single dividend paid in year 6 [Equation (9.1)] and (2) the constant dividend stream ($g = 0$) of €6 per year forever [Equation (9.5)]. The value of the ordinary share can be computed as follows:

$$P_0 = \text{PV(Mixed dividend growth)} + \text{PV(Constant dividends with no growth)}$$

Applying Equation (9.6) to the cash flows presented in the problem yields:

$$P_0 = \frac{D_1}{1 + R} + \frac{D_2}{(1 + R)^2} + \cdots + \frac{D_t}{(1 + R)^t} + \frac{P_t}{(1 + R)^t}$$
$$= \frac{D_6}{(1 + R)^6} + \frac{P_6}{(1 + R)^6}$$
$$= \frac{D_6 + P_6}{(1 + R)^6}$$

Note that the first term in the second line computes the present value of the large €25 dividend paid in year 6. In the second term, P_6 is the discounted value of the constant €6 dividend payments made in perpetuity, valued to period $t = 6$. To compute the present value of P_6, we divide it by the appropriate discount factor, which is $(1 + R)^6$.

Next, we plug the data given earlier into the above equation:

$$P_0 = \frac{€25 + P_6}{(1.12)^6}$$

We can see that we still need to compute the value of P_6 using Equation (9.5):

$$P_t = \frac{D_{t+1}}{R - g}$$

Equation (9.5) is easy to apply since the dividend payments remain constant over time. Thus, $D_{t+1} = €6$ and $g = 0$. P_6 is calculated as follows:

$$P_6 = \frac{D_7}{R - g} = \frac{€6.00}{0.12 - 0} = \frac{€6.00}{0.12}$$
$$= €50$$

The calculation for P_0 is, therefore:

$$P_0 = \frac{€25.00 + €50.00}{(1.12)^6}$$
$$= \frac{€75.00}{1.9738}$$
$$= €38.00$$

The share's current market price is €25 and, if your estimates of dividend payments are correct, the share's value is €38 per share. This suggests that the share is a bargain and that your boss is incorrect.

Before You Go On

1. What three different models are used to value shares based on different dividend patterns?
2. Explain why the growth rate g must always be less than the rate of return R.

VALUING PREFERENCE SHARES

Learning Objective 6

Explain how valuing preference shares with a stated maturity differs from valuing preference shares with no maturity date and be able to calculate the price of both types of preference share.

As mentioned earlier in the chapter, preference shares are hybrid securities, falling somewhere between bonds and ordinary shares. For example, preference shares have a higher-priority claim on the firm's assets than ordinary shares but a lower-priority claim than the firm's creditors in the event of default. In computing the value of preference shares, however, the critical issue is whether the preference shares have an effective 'maturity'. If the preference shares contract has a sinking fund that calls for the mandatory retirement of the shares over a scheduled period of time, financial analysts will tend to treat the preference shares as if they were a bond with a fixed maturity.

The most significant difference between preference shares with a fixed maturity and a bond is the risk of default. Bond coupon payments are a legal obligation of the firm and failure to pay them results in default, whereas preference share dividends are declared by the board of directors and failure to pay dividends does not result in default. Even though it is not a legal default, the failure to pay a preference share dividend as promised is not a trivial event. It is a serious financial breach that can signal to the market that the firm is in serious financial difficulty. As a result, managers make every effort to pay preference share dividends as promised.

WEB

Monevator offers a good discussion of preference shares at: http://monevator.com/2010/05/18/preference-shares/.

Preference Shares with a Fixed Maturity

Because preference shares with an effective maturity are considered similar to a bond, we can use the bond valuation model developed in Chapter 8 to determine their price, or value. Applying Equation (8.2) requires only that we recognise that the coupon payments (C) are now dividend payments (D) and the preference share dividends are paid semi-annually. Thus, Equation (8.2) can be restated as the price of a preference share (PS_0):

$$\text{Preference share price} = \text{PV(Dividend payments)} + \text{PV(Par value)}$$

$$(9.7)$$

$$PS_0 = \frac{D/m}{1+i/m} + \frac{D/m}{(1+i/m)^2} + \frac{D/m}{(1+i/m)^3} + \cdots$$
$$+ \frac{D/m + P_{mn}}{(1+i/m)^{mn}}$$

where:

$D =$ the annual preference share dividend payment

$P =$ the stated (par) value of the preference share

$i =$ the yield to maturity of the preference share

$m =$ the number of times dividend payments are made each year

$n =$ the number of years to maturity

For preference shares with semi-annual dividend payments, m equals 2.

Consider an example of how this equation is used. Suppose that a utility company's preference shares have an annual dividend payment of €10 (paid semi-annually), a stated (par) value of €100 and an effective maturity of 20 years owing to a sinking fund requirement. If similar preference share issues have market yields of 8%, what is the value of the utility company's preference shares?

First, we convert the data to semi-annual compounding as follows: (1) the market yield is 4% half yearly (8% per year/2), (2) the dividend payment is €5 every six months (€10 per year/2) and (3) the total number of dividend payments is 40 (2 per year × 20 years). Plugging the data into Equation (8.1), we find that the value of the preference share is:

$$PS_0 = \frac{€5}{1.04} + \frac{€5}{(1.04)^2} + \cdots + \frac{€105}{(1.04)^{40}}$$
$$= €119.79$$

WEB

Riskglossary.com offers a good discussion of preference shares (called preferred stock in the United States), including its valuation. Go to www.riskglossary.com/link/preferred_stock.htm.

Learning by Doing Application 9.5

Computing the Yield on Preference Shares

Problem: Electricité de France, the French utility company, has a preference share issue outstanding that has a stated value of €100 that will be retired by the company in 15 years and that pays a €3 dividend every six months. If the preference shares are currently selling for €95, what is the preference shares' yield to maturity?

Approach: We compute the yield to maturity on these preference shares in exactly the same way we compute the yield to maturity on a bond. We already know that the semi-annual dividend rate is €3 but we must convert the number of periods to allow for semi-annual compounding. The total number of compounding periods is 30 (2 per year × 15 years). Using Equation (8.2), we can enter the data and find i, the preference shares' yield to maturity through trial and error. In doing this, we can treat the dividend payments as an annuity with 30 payments and the principal as a one-off payment at maturity discounted at the appropriate interest rate.

Solution: Applying Equation (8.2) and using trial and error:

$$PS_0 = \frac{€3}{1+i} + \frac{€3}{(1+i)^2} + \cdots + \frac{€103}{(1+i)^{30}}$$

$$= €3 \times \left[\frac{1 - \frac{1}{(1+i)^n}}{i} \right] + \frac{€100}{(1+i)^n}$$

Since the preference share is trading at below par, it will have a yield to maturity of more than 6% per annum. We will try 7%:

$$PS_0 = \frac{€3}{1+0.035} + \frac{€3}{(1+0.035)^2} + \cdots$$
$$+ \frac{€103}{(1+0.035)^{30}}$$

$$= €3 \times \left[\frac{1 - \frac{1}{(1+0.035)^n}}{0.035} \right] + \frac{€100}{(1+0.035)^n}$$

$$= €3 \times 21.3551 + €100 \times 0.2526$$

$$= €64.07 + €25.26$$

$$= €89.33$$

This is too low. We know that a yield to maturity of 6% per annum will give us a value of €100. We can therefore apply interpolation to derive the yield on the preference shares:

$$i_{unknown} = i_{low} + \frac{(Value_{low\ i} - Value_{unknown\ i})}{(Value_{low\ i} - Value_{high\ i})}$$
$$\times (i_{high} - i_{low})$$

$$= 3\% + \frac{€100 - €95}{€100 - €89.33} \times (3.5\% - 3\%)$$

$$= 3\% + \frac{€5}{€10.67} \times 0.5\%$$

$$= 3\% + 0.4686 \times 0.5\%$$

$$= 3\% + 0.2343\% = 3.23\%$$

The preference shares' yield is 3.23% per half year and the annual yield is 6.46% (3.23% × 2).

Perpetual Preference Shares

Some preference share issues have no maturity. These securities have dividends that are constant over time ($g = 0$) and the fixed dividend payments go on forever. Thus, these preference shares can be valued as perpetuities, using Equation (9.2):

$$P_0 = \frac{D}{R}$$

where D is a constant cash dividend and R is the interest rate, or required rate of return.

We will work an example. Suppose that Iberia Lineas Aereas de Espana SA has a perpetual preference share issue that pays a dividend of €5 per year. Investors require an 18% return on such an investment. What should be the value of the preference shares? Applying Equation (9.2), we find that the value is:

$$P_0 = \frac{D}{R} = \frac{€5.00}{0.18} = €27.78$$

Before You Go On

1. Why can skipping payment of a preference share dividend be a bad signal?
2. How is a preference share with a fixed maturity valued?

SUMMARY OF LEARNING OBJECTIVES

1. **List and describe the four types of secondary markets.**

   The four types of secondary markets are: (1) direct search, (2) broker, (3) dealer and (4) auction. In direct search markets, buyers and sellers seek each other out directly. In broker markets, brokers bring buyers and sellers together for a fee. Trades in dealer markets go through dealers who buy securities at one price and sell at a higher price. The dealers face the risk that prices could decline while they own the securities. Auction markets have a fixed location where buyers and sellers confront each other directly and bargain over the transaction price.

2. **Explain why many financial analysts treat preference shares as a special type of bond rather than as an equity security.**

   Preference shares represent ownership in a company and entitle the owner to a dividend, which must be paid before dividends are paid to ordinary shareholders. Similar to bonds, preference share issues have credit ratings, are sometimes convertible to ordinary shares and are often callable. Unlike owners of ordinary shares, owners of non-convertible preference shares do not have voting rights and do not participate in the firm's profits beyond the fixed dividends they receive. Because of their strong similarity to bonds, many financial analysts treat preference shares that are not true perpetuities as a form of debt rather than equity.

3. **Describe how the general dividend-valuation model values a share.**

   The general dividend-valuation model values a share as the present value of all future cash dividend payments, where the dividend payments are discounted using the rate of return required by investors for a particular risk class.

4. **Discuss the assumptions that are necessary to make the general dividend-valuation model easier to use and be able to use the model to compute the value of a firm's shares.**

   The problems with the general dividend-valuation model are that the exact discount rate that should be used is unknown, dividends are often uncertain and some companies do not pay dividends at all. To make the model easier to apply, we make assumptions about the dividend payment patterns of firms. These simplifying assumptions allow the development of more manageable models and they also conform to the actual dividend policies of many firms. Dividend patterns include the following: (1) dividends are constant (zero growth), as computed in Learning by Doing Application 9.1; (2) dividends have a constant-growth pattern (they grow forever at a constant rate g), as computed in Learning by Doing Application 9.2; and (3) dividends grow first at a non-constant rate then at a constant rate, as computed in the Dimarin example.

5. **Explain why g must be less than R in the constant-growth dividend model.**

   The constant-growth dividend model assumes that dividends will grow at a constant rate forever. With the constant-growth model, if $g = R$, the value of the denominator is zero and the value of the share is infinite, which of course, is nonsense. If $g > R$, the value of the denominator is negative, as is the value of the share, which also does not make economic sense. Thus, g must always be less than R $(g < R)$.

6. **Explain how valuing preference shares with a stated maturity differs from valuing preference shares with no maturity date, and be able to calculate the price of both types of preference share.**

   When preference shares have a maturity date, financial analysts value them as they value any other fixed obligation – that is, like a bond. To value such preference shares, we can use the bond valuation model from Chapter 8. Before using the model, we need to recognise that we will be using dividends in the place of coupon payments and that the par value of the preference share will replace the par value of the bond. In addition, while bond coupons are often paid annually, preference share dividends are usually paid semi-annually. When a preference share has no stated maturity, it becomes a perpetuity, with the dividend becoming the constant payment that goes on forever. We use the perpetual valuation model represented by Equation (9.2) to price such shares. The calculations appear in Learning by Doing Application 9.5 and the Iberia example.

SUMMARY OF KEY EQUATIONS

Equation	Description	Formula
(9.1)	The general dividend-valuation model	$P_0 = \dfrac{D_1}{1+R} + \dfrac{D_2}{(1+R)^2} + \dfrac{D_3}{(1+R)^3} + \dfrac{D_4}{(1+R)^4}$ $+ \dfrac{D_5}{(1+R)^5} + \cdots + \dfrac{D_\infty}{(1+R)^\infty} = \displaystyle\sum_{t=1}^{\infty} \dfrac{D_t}{(1+R)^t}$
(9.2)	Zero-growth dividend model	$P_0 = \dfrac{D}{R}$
(9.3)	Value of a dividend at time t in a constant-growth scenario	$D_t = D_0 \times (1+g)^t$
(9.4)	Constant-growth dividend model	$P_0 = \dfrac{D_1}{R-g}$
(9.5)	Value of a share at time t when dividends grow at a constant rate	$P_t = \dfrac{D_{t+1}}{R-g}$
(9.6)	Supernormal growth share-valuation model	$P_0 = \dfrac{D_1}{1+R} + \dfrac{D_2}{(1+R)^2} + \cdots + \dfrac{D_t}{(1+R)^t} + \dfrac{P_t}{(1+R)^t}$
(9.7)	Value of preference shares with a fixed maturity	$PS_0 = \dfrac{D/m}{1+i/m} + \dfrac{D/m}{(1+i/m)^2} + \dfrac{D/m}{(1+i/m)^3}$ $+ \cdots + \dfrac{D/m + P_{mn}}{(1+i/m)^{mn}}$

SELF-STUDY PROBLEMS

9.1. Eduardo Cavallas has just bought the ordinary shares of Regietto SA. The company expects to grow at the following rates for the next three years: 30%, 25% and 15%. Last year the company paid a dividend of €2.50. Assume a required rate of return of 10%. Compute the expected dividends for the next three years and also the present value of these dividends.

9.2. Meubles de Montreux SA has been growing at a rate of 6% for the past two years and the company's CEO expects the company to continue to grow at this rate for the next several years. The company paid a dividend of SFr 1.20 last year. If your required rate of return was 14%, what is the maximum price that you would be willing to pay for this company's shares?

9.3. Clarion Electrical has been selling electrical supplies for the past 20 years. The company's product line has seen very little change in the past five years and the company does not expect to add any new items for the foreseeable future. Last year, the company paid a dividend of A$4.45 to its ordinary shareholders. The company is not expected to grow its revenues for the next several years. If your required rate of return for such firms is 13%, what is the current value of this company's shares?

9.4. Brandenburg Infotech AG is a fast-growing communications company. The company did not pay a dividend last year and is not expected to do so for the next two years. Last year the company's growth accelerated and they expect to grow at a rate of 35% for the next five years before slowing down to a more stable growth rate of 7% for the next several years. In the third year, the company has forecasted a dividend payment of €1.10. Calculate the price of the company's shares at the end of its rapid growth period (i.e., at the end of five years). Your required rate of return for such shares is 17%. What is the current price of the shares?

9.5. You are interested in buying the preference shares of a bank that pays a dividend of €1.80 every quarter. If you discount such cash flows at 8%, what is the price of the preference shares?

SOLUTIONS TO SELF-STUDY PROBLEMS

9.1. Expected dividends for Regietto SA and their present value:

0	1	2	3	Year
$D_0 = €2.50$	D_1	D_2	D_3	
$g_1 = 30\%$		$g_2 = 25\%$	$g_3 = 15\%$	

$D_1 = D_0 \times (1 + g_1) = €2.50 \times (1 + 0.30) = €3.25$
$D_2 = D_1 \times (1 + g_2) = €3.25 \times (1 + 0.25) = €4.06$
$D_3 = D_2 \times (1 + g_3) = €4.06 \times (1 + 0.15) = €4.67$
Present value of the dividends $= PV(D_1) + PV(D_2) + PV(D_3)$
$= €2.96 + €3.36 + €3.51$
$= €9.83$

9.2. Present value of the Meubles de Montreux shares:

0	1	2	3	Y
	14%			
$D_0 = $ SFr 2.50	D_1	D_2	D_3	

$g = 6\%$
$D_1 = D_0(1 + g)$
$\quad = $ SFr $1.20 \times (1 + 0.06)$
$\quad = $ SFr 1.27

$P_0 = \dfrac{D_1}{R - g}$
$\quad = \dfrac{\text{SFr } 1.27}{0.14 - 0.06}$
$\quad = $ SFr 15.88

The maximum price you should be willing to pay for the shares is SFr 15.88.

9.3. Present value of Clarion Electrical shares:

0	1	2	3	Year
	13%			
$D_0 = $ A$4.45	D_1	D_2	D_3	

$g = 0\%$

Since the company's dividends are not expected to grow:

$$D_0 = D_1 = D_2 = \cdots = A\$4.45 = D$$

$$P_0 = \frac{D}{R}$$

$$= A\$4.45/0.13$$

$$= A\$34.23$$

9.4. Present value of Brandenburg Infotech AG shares:

$$g_1 \text{ to } g_5 = 35\% \quad g_6 = 7\%$$

$$D_0 = D_1 = D_2 = 0$$

$$D_3 = €1.10$$

$$D_4 = D_3 \times (1 + g_4) = €1.10 \times (1 + 0.35) = €1.485$$

$$D_5 = D_4 \times (1 + g_5) = €1.485 \times (1 + 0.35) = €2.005$$

$$D_6 = D_5 \times (1 + g_6) = €2.005 \times (1 + 0.07) = €2.145$$

Price of the shares at $t = 5$:

$$P_5 = \frac{D_6}{R - g}$$

$$= \frac{€2.145}{0.17 - 0.07}$$

$$= €21.45$$

Present value of the dividends

$$= PV(D_1) + PV(D_2) + PV(D_3) + PV(D_4) + PV(D_5)$$

$$= €0 + €0 + €0.69 + €0.79 + €0.91$$

$$= €2.39$$

Present value of the shares:

$$P_0 = €2.39 + \frac{€21.45}{(1.17)^5}$$

$$= €2.39 + €9.78$$

$$= €12.17$$

9.5. Present value of the bank preference shares:
Quarterly dividend on preference shares $= D = €1.80$
Required rate of return $= 8\%$
Current price of preference shares

$$P_0 = \frac{D}{R}$$

$$= \frac{€1.80 \times 4}{0.08}$$

$$= €90.00$$

CRITICAL THINKING QUESTIONS

9.1. Why can the market price of a security differ from its true value?

9.2. Why are investors and managers concerned about market efficiency?

9.3. Why are ordinary shareholders considered to be more at risk than the holders of other types of securities?

9.4. How can individual shareholders avoid the double taxation of dividends?

9.5. What does it mean when a company has a very high *P/E* ratio? Give examples of

industries in which you believe high *P/E* ratios are justified.

9.6. Preference shares are considered to be non-participating because:

a. Investors do not participate in the election of the firm's directors.

b. Investors do not participate in the determination of the dividend payout policy.

c. Investors do not participate in the firm's earnings growth.

d. None of the above.

9.7. Explain why preference shares are considered to be a hybrid of equity and debt securities.

9.8. Why is share valuation more difficult than bond valuation?

9.9. You are currently thinking about investing in a share valued at €25.00. The shares recently paid a dividend of €2.25 and are expected to grow at a rate of 5% for the foreseeable future. You normally require a return of 14% on shares of similar risk. Are the shares over-priced, underpriced or correctly priced?

9.10. Shares A and B are both priced at €50. Share A has a *P/E* ratio of 17, while share B has a *P/E* ratio of 24. Which is the more attractive investment, considering everything else to be the same, and why?

QUESTIONS AND PROBLEMS

Basic

9.1. **Present value of dividends:** Frescatti S.p.A. is a fast-growing company. The company expects to grow at a rate of 30% over the next two years and then slow down to a growth rate of 18% for the following three years. If the last dividend paid by the company was €2.15, estimate the dividends for the next five years. Compute the present value of these dividends if the required rate of return was 14%.

9.2. **Zero growth:** Nyberg A/S paid a dividend of DKr 4.18 last year. The company does not expect to increase its dividend for the next several years. If the required rate of return is 18.5%, what is the current price of the shares?

9.3. **Zero growth:** Wasser Logistik AG has seen no growth for the past several years and expects the trend to continue. The firm last paid a dividend of €3.56. If you require a rate of return of 13%, what is the current price of the shares?

9.4. **Zero growth:** Romero Santana is interested in buying the shares of Banca Primavera. While the bank expects no growth in the near future, Romero is attracted by the dividend income. Last year the bank paid a dividend of €5.65. If Romero requires a return of 14% on such shares, what is the maximum price he should be willing to pay?

9.5. **Zero growth:** The current share price for L'Argent SA is €44.72. If the required rate of return is 19%, what is the dividend paid by this firm, which is not expected to grow in the near future?

9.6. **Constant growth:** Moribandi SA just declared a dividend of €2.15 yesterday. The company is expected to grow at a steady rate of 5% for the next several years. If shares such as these require a rate of return of 15%, what should be the market value of the shares?

9.7. **Constant growth:** Nyeil Systems AG is a consumer electronics firm growing at a constant rate of 6.5%. The firm's last dividend was €3.36. If the required rate of return was 18%, what is the market value of the shares?

9.8. **Constant growth:** Road Recovery plc is expected to pay a dividend of £2.25 next year. The forecast for the share price a year from now is £37.50. If the required rate of return is 14%, what is the current share price? Assume constant growth.

9.9. **Constant growth:** Proxicam AB is expected to grow at a constant rate of 7%. If the company's next dividend is SKr 1.15 and its current price is SKr 22.35, what is the required rate of return on the shares?

9.10. Preference share valuation: X-Centric Energie AG has issued perpetual preference shares with a par value of €100 and a dividend of 4.5% per annum. If the required rate of return is 8.25%, what is the preference shares' current market price?

9.11. Preference share valuation: The Chelsea Bank has issued perpetual preference shares with a £100 par value. The bank pays a quarterly dividend of £1.65 on the preference shares. What is the current price of the preference shares given a required rate of return of 11.6%?

9.12. Preference shares: The preference shares of Axim A.S. are selling currently at Kč 47.13. If the required rate of return is 12.2%, what is the dividend paid by the shares?

9.13. Preference shares: Every six months, Système Sirkota SA pays a dividend on its perpetual preference shares. Today the shares are selling at €63.37. If the required rate of return for such shares is 15.5%, what is the semi-annual dividend paid by this firm?

Intermediate

9.14. Constant growth: Katrina Williams is interested in purchasing the ordinary shares of Reckers AG, which are currently priced at €37.45. The company expects to pay a dividend of €2.58 next year and expects to grow at a constant rate of 7%.
   a. What should be the market value of the shares, if the required rate of return is 14%?
   b. Is this a good buy? Why or why not?

9.15. Constant growth: The required rate of return is 23%. Jouex Neufs SA has just paid a dividend of €3.12 and expects to grow at a constant rate of 5%. What is the expected price of the shares three years from now?

9.16. Constant growth: Jenny Banks is interested in buying the shares of Breakdancer Productions plc, which are growing at a constant rate of 6%. Last year the firm paid a dividend of €2.65. The required rate of return is 16%. What is the current price for the shares? What is the price of the shares expected to be in year 5?

9.17. Non-constant growth: Applications Technologie Espace SA is a fast-growing technology company. The firm projects a rapid growth of 30% for the next two years, then a growth rate of 17% for the following two years. After that, the firm expects a constant growth rate of 8%. The firm expects to pay its first dividend of €2.45 a year from now. If the required rate of return on such shares is 22%, what is the current price of the shares?

9.18. Non-constant growth: ProCor A/S, a biotechnology firm, forecasted the following growth rates for the next three years: 35%, 28% and 22%. The company then expects to grow at a constant rate of 9% for the next several years. The company paid a dividend of DKr 1.75 last week. If the required rate of return is 20%, what is the market value of the shares?

9.19. Non-constant growth: Poraver AG is a fast-growth share and expects to grow at a rate of 23% for the next four years. It then will settle to a constant growth rate of 6%. The first dividend will be paid in year 3 and be equal to €4.25. If the required rate of return is 17%, what is the current price of the shares?

9.20. Non-constant growth: Quansi plc expects to pay no dividends for the next six years. It has projected a growth rate of 25% for the next seven years. After seven years, the firm will grow at a constant rate of 5%. Its first dividend to be paid in year 7 will be worth £3.25. If your required rate of return is 24%, what are the shares worth today?

9.21. Non-constant growth: Thessaloniki Electricity A.E. will pay dividends of €5.00, €6.25, €4.75 and €3.00 for the next four years. Thereafter, the company expects its growth rate to be at a constant rate of 6%. If the required rate of return is 18.5%, what is the current market price of the shares?

9.22. Non-constant growth: Diaz Cosmetics is growing rapidly at a rate of 35% for the next seven years. The first dividend, to be paid three years from now, will be worth €5. After seven years, the company will settle to a constant growth rate of 8.5%. What is the market value for the shares given a required rate of return of 14%?

9.23. Non-constant growth: Publications Animé Tintin SA is growing rapidly. Dividends are expected to grow at rates of 30%, 35%, 25% and 18% over the next four years. Thereafter the company expects to grow at a constant rate of 7%. The shares are currently selling at €47.85, and the required rate of return is 16%. Compute the dividend for the current year (D_0).

Advanced

9.24. Rijn Departmental Stores NV has forecasted a high growth rate of 40% for the next two years, followed by growth rates of 25% and 20% for the following two years. It then expects to stabilise its growth to a constant rate of 7.5% for the next several years. The firm paid a dividend of €3.50 recently. If the required rate of return is 18%, what is the current market price of the shares?

9.25. Groupe Bancaire du Sud issued perpetual preference shares a few years ago. The bank pays an annual dividend of €4.27 and your required rate of return is 12.2%.
   a. What is the value of the preference shares given your required rate of return?
   b. Should you buy these shares if their current market price is €34.41? Explain.

9.26. Rhea Kirby owns shares in the Ireland-based Runneymede Group. Currently, the market price of the shares is €36.34. The company expects to grow at a constant rate of 6% for the foreseeable future. Its last dividend was worth €3.25. Rhea's required rate of return for such shares is 16%. She wants to find out whether she should sell her shares or add to her holdings.

   a. What is the value of the shares?
   b. Based on your answer to part a, should Rhea buy additional shares in the Runneymede Group? Why or why not?

9.27. Source Perrier SA declared a dividend of €2.50 yesterday. You are interested in investing in this company, which has forecasted a constant growth rate of 7% for the next several years. The required rate of return is 18%.
   a. Compute the expected dividends D_1, D_2, D_3 and D_4.
   b. Find the present value of these four dividends.
   c. What is the price of the shares four years from now (P_4)?
   d. Calculate the present value of P_4. Add the answer you got in part b. What is the price of the shares today?
   e. Use the equation for constant growth [Equation (9.4)] to compute the price of the shares today.

9.28. [EXCEL®] Zweite Pharma is a fast-growing drug company. The company forecasts that in the next three years, its growth rates will be 30%, 28% and 24%, respectively. Last week it declared a dividend of €1.67. After three years, the company expects a more stable growth rate of 8% for the next several years. The required rate of return is 14%.
   a. Compute the dividends for the next three years and find their present value.
   b. Calculate the price of the shares at the end of year 3 when the firm settles to a constant growth rate.
   c. What is the current price of the shares?

9.29. [EXCEL®] Triton NV expects to grow at a rate of 22% for the next five years and then settle to a constant growth rate of 6%. The company's most recent dividend was €2.35. The required rate of return is 15%.
   a. Find the present value of the dividends during the rapid-growth period.
   b. What is the price of the shares at the end of year 5?
   c. What is the price of the shares today?

9.30. EXCEL® Cerebra Construction is expanding very fast and expects to grow at a rate of 25% for the next four years. The company recently declared a dividend of €3.60 but does not expect to pay any dividends for the next three years. In year 4, it intends to pay a €5 dividend and thereafter grow at a constant growth rate of 6%. The required rate of return on such shares is 20%.

a. Calculate the present value of the dividends during the fast-growth period.
b. What is the price of the shares at the end of the fast-growth period (P_4)?
c. What is the share price today?
d. Would today's share price be driven by the length of time you intend to hold the shares?

SAMPLE TEST PROBLEMS

9.1. Maison Dominque is a manufacturer of consumer staples and has experienced no growth for the past five years while paying out a dividend of €3.50 every year. The CFO of the firm expects the firm to have no growth for the foreseeable future. If the required rate of return is 10%, what is the price of the firm's shares today?

9.2. Bicknell plc recently paid a dividend of £2.10. The firm forecasts a growth of 6% for the next several years. What is the price of the shares today with a discount rate of 13%?

9.3. Voyages Brutus NV is growing at a constant rate of 7.2% every year. Last week the company paid a dividend of €1.85. If the required rate of return is 15%, what will be the share price four years from now?

9.4. Wichita Technologies is expected to grow at a rate of 35% for the next three years and then settle to a constant growth rate of 7%. The company will pay no dividend for the first two years and pay a dividend of $1.25 in year 3. What will be the company's price when the company's supernormal growth ends? What is the price of the shares today? The firm's required rate of return is 12%.

9.5. Gruppo Banca Unita has issued preference shares with no maturity date. They have a par value of €100 and pay a quarterly dividend of €2.25. If the required rate of return is 8%, what is the price of the preference shares today?

ENDNOTES

1. Ordinary shares are known as 'common stock' in the United States and both terms may be used in the English versions of the annual reports of European companies. Hence, like the practitioners working in the international financial markets, you need to be aware of the different words used to describe the

same securities. The same applies to preference shares, which are called 'preferred stock' in the United States!

2. Tesco is a remarkable company. There are few other companies that can boast such a rate of growth over such a long period. Furthermore, the company has managed this without experiencing any major commercial setbacks. As you might expect, investors place a high value on the shares but it is arguable whether the company can continue to grow at its past rate. It has expanded internationally, where opportunities are better than in the UK; but it will be a challenge.

PART 4

CAPITAL BUDGETING DECISIONS

CHAPTER

10

The Fundamentals of Capital Budgeting

In this Chapter:

An Introduction to Capital Budgeting
Net Present Value
The Payback Period
The Accounting Rate of Return
Internal Rate of Return
Capital Budgeting in Practice

LEARNING OBJECTIVES

1. Discuss why capital budgeting decisions are the most important investment decisions made by a firm's management.
2. Explain the benefits of using the net present value (NPV) method to analyse capital expenditure decisions and be able to calculate the NPV for a capital project.
3. Describe the strengths and weaknesses of the payback period as a capital expenditure decision-making tool and be able to compute the payback period for a capital project.
4. Explain why the accounting rate of return (ARR) is not recommended for use as a capital expenditure decision-making tool.
5. Be able to compute the internal rate of return (IRR) for a capital project and discuss the conditions under which the IRR technique and the NPV technique produce different results.
6. Explain the benefits of a post-audit review of a capital project.

In 1996, Airbus formed its Large Aircraft Division to design and build a super-large passenger aircraft, an idea it had been working on from 1988 and discussing with major international carriers since 1991. In December 2000, Airbus revealed the A380, the world's first twin-deck, twin-aisle 555 seat passenger superjumbo airliner. The manufacture of the various components (engines, fuselage and wings) began in 2002 and the first delivery to

Singapore Airlines took place in October 2007, with further deliveries taking place thereafter as Airbus geared up to produce the 200 plus aircraft for which it had firm orders. It needs about twice that number to break even on the project.

The superjumbo project has not been without its problems. The first was finance – the need for the company to invest heavily in development and start-up costs. Airbus invested about €13 billion to develop the airliner that has a list price of $300 million apiece.[1] To put the project into perspective, in 2008 Airbus delivered 483 aircraft of all types – but only 13 A380s – and had total revenues of €27.5 billion and EBIT of €1.8 billion. During the development of the new airliner, the company also had to compete with its arch rival Boeing, the Seattle-based airline manufacturer, which was also considering a similar aircraft. In the end, Boeing opted to develop a smaller aircraft, the Dreamliner, based on its analysis of the way air travel is likely to evolve.

The development of the A380 illustrates not only the large amount of cash involved in a major capital project, but also the strategic importance such an investment can have. If Airbus is successful, it will be the only producer of superjumbo airliners and will have the market to itself. The A380 project involves considerable downside risk for Airbus and its parent company EADS. For example, if the demand for superjumbos proves to be less than expected, the project could be a significant drain on future earnings. In addition, there are technical risks with the design, and forecasting passenger demand and the demands of airlines in the future is fraught with uncertainties. In 2009, as a result of the global credit crunch and a downturn in airline travel, some airlines which had ordered A380s were seeking to delay deliveries and hence payment. If these problems persist, the financial consequences for Airbus could be severe.

It is clear that investment decisions of this magnitude must be carefully scrutinised and their costs and benefits carefully weighed. How do firms make capital budgeting decisions that involve large amounts of money? In this chapter, we examine the decision-making process and introduce some of the financial models that aid in the process.

CHAPTER PREVIEW

This chapter is about capital budgeting, a topic we first visited in Chapter 1. Capital budgeting – or investment appraisal – is the process of deciding which capital investments the firm should make.

We begin the chapter with a discussion of the types of capital projects that firms undertake and how the capital budgeting process is managed within the firm. When making capital investment decisions, management's goal is to select projects that will increase the value of the firm.

Next we examine some of the techniques used to evaluate capital budgeting decisions. We first discuss the net present value (NPV) method, which is the capital budgeting approach recommended in this book. The NPV method takes into account the time value of money and provides a direct measure of how much a capital project will increase the value of the firm.

We then examine the payback method and the accounting rate of return. As methods of selecting capital projects, both have some serious deficiencies. Finally, we discuss the internal rate of return (IRR), which is the expected rate of return for a capital project. Like the NPV, the IRR involves discounting a project's future cash flows. It is a popular and important alternative to the NPV technique. However, in certain circumstances, the IRR can lead to incorrect decisions. We close by discussing evidence on techniques financial managers actually use when making capital budgeting decisions.

AN INTRODUCTION TO CAPITAL BUDGETING

Learning Objective 1

Discuss why capital budgeting decisions are the most important investment decisions made by a firm's management.

We begin with an overview of capital budgeting, followed by a discussion of some important concepts you will need to understand in this and later chapters.

The Importance of Capital Budgeting

Capital budgeting decisions are the most important investment decisions made by management. The objective of these decisions is to select investments in real assets that will increase the value of the firm. These investments *create value* when they are worth more than they cost. Capital investments are important because they can involve substantial cash outlays and, once made, are not easily reversed. They also define what the company is all about – the firm's lines of business and its inherent business risk. For better or worse, capital investments produce most of a typical firm's revenues for years to come.

Capital budgeting

the process of choosing the real assets in which the firm will invest

Capital budgeting *techniques* help management systematically analyse potential business opportunities in order to decide which are worth undertaking. As you will see, not all capital budgeting techniques are equal. The best techniques are those that determine the value of a capital project by discounting all of the cash flows generated by the project, and thus account for the time value of money. We focus on these techniques in this chapter.

In the final analysis, capital budgeting is really about management's search for the best capital projects – those that add the greatest value to the firm. Over the long term, the most successful firms are those whose managements consistently search for and find capital investment opportunities that increase firm value.

WEB

You can read about real-world examples of how capital budgeting techniques are used at: http://www.acq.osd.mil/dpap/cpf/docs/contract_pricing_finance_guide/vol2_ch9.pdf and
http://www.hmrc.gov.uk/ebu/npv-and-example.pdf.

The Capital Budgeting Process

The capital budgeting process starts with a firm's strategic plan, which spells out its strategy for the next three to five years. Division managers then convert the firm's strategic objectives into business plans. These plans have a one-year to two-year time horizon, provide a detailed description of what each division should accomplish during the period covered by the plan and have quantifiable targets that each division is expected to achieve. Behind each division's business plan is a capital budget that details the resources management believes it needs to get the job done.

The capital budget is generally prepared jointly by the CFO's staff and financial staff at the divisional and lower levels and reflects, in large part, the activities outlined in the divisional business plans. Many of these proposed expenditures are routine in nature, such as the repair or purchase of new equipment at existing facilities. Less frequently, firms face broader strategic decisions, such as whether to launch a new product, build a new plant, enter a new market or buy a business. Exhibit 10.1 identifies some reasons that firms initiate capital projects.

Capital budgeting decisions are the most important investment decisions made by management. Many of these decisions are routine in nature but, from time to time, managers face broader strategic decisions that call for significant capital investments.

Sources of Information

Where does a firm get all of the information it needs to make capital budgeting decisions? Most of the information is generated within the firm and, for expansion decisions, it often starts with sales representatives and marketing managers who are in the marketplace talking to potential and current customers on a day-to-day basis. For example, a sales manager with a new product idea might present the idea to management and the marketing research group. If the product looks promising, the marketing research group will estimate the size of the market and a market price. If the product requires new technology, the firm's research and development group must decide whether to develop the technology or to buy it. Next, cost accountants and production engineers determine the cost of producing the product and any capital expenditures necessary to manufacture it. Finally, the CFO's staff take the data and estimate the cost of the project and the cash flows it will generate over time. The project is a viable candidate for the capital budget if the present value of the cash benefits exceeds the project's cost.

EXHIBIT 10.1
KEY REASONS FOR MAKING CAPITAL EXPENDITURES

Reason	Description
Renewal:	Over time, equipment must be repaired, overhauled, rebuilt or retrofitted with new technology to keep the firm's manufacturing or service operations going. For example, a company that has a fleet of delivery trucks may decide to overhaul the trucks and their engines rather than purchase new trucks. Renewal decisions typically do not require an elaborate analysis and are made on a routine basis.
Replacement:	At some point, an asset will have to be replaced rather than repaired or overhauled. This typically happens when the asset is worn out or damaged. The major decision is whether to replace the asset with a similar piece of equipment or purchase equipment that would require a change in the production process. Sometimes, replacement decisions involve equipment that is operating satisfactorily but has become obsolete. The new or retrofitted equipment may provide cost savings with respect to labour or material usage and/or may improve product quality. These decisions typically originate at the plant level.
Expansion:	Strategically, the most important motive for capital expenditures is to expand the level of operating output. One type of expansion decision involves increasing the output of existing products. This may mean new equipment to produce more products or expansion of the firm's distribution system. These types of decisions typically require a more complex analysis than a renewal or replacement decision. Another type of expansion decision involves producing a new product or entering a new market. This type of expansion often involves large sums of money and significant business risk, and requires the approval of the firm's board of directors.
Regulatory:	Some capital expenditures are required by government regulations. These mandatory expenditures usually involve meeting workplace safety standards and environmental standards.
Other:	This category includes items such as parking facilities, office buildings and executive aircraft. Many of these capital expenditures are hard to analyse because it is difficult to estimate their cash inflows. Ultimately, the decisions can be more subjective than analytical.

Classification of Investment Projects

Potential capital budgeting projects can be classified into three types: (1) **independent projects**, (2) **mutually exclusive projects** and (3) **contingent projects**.

Independent projects

projects whose cash flows are unrelated

Mutually exclusive projects

projects for which acceptance of one precludes acceptance of the other

Contingent projects

projects whose acceptance depends on the acceptance of another project

Independent Projects

Projects are independent when their cash flows are unrelated. With independent projects, accepting or rejecting one project does not eliminate the other projects from consideration (assuming the firm has unlimited funds to invest). For example, suppose a firm has unlimited funding and management wants to: (1) build a new parking ramp at its headquarters; (2) acquire a small competitor; and (3) add manufacturing capacity to one of its plants. Since the cash flows for each project are unrelated, accepting or rejecting one of the projects will have no effect on the others.

Mutually Exclusive Projects

When projects are mutually exclusive, acceptance of one project precludes acceptance of the others. Typically, mutually exclusive projects perform the same function and, thus, only one project needs to be accepted. For example, when BMW decided to manufacture automobiles in the United States, it considered three possible manufacturing sites (or capital projects). Once BMW management had selected the Spartanburg, South Carolina, site, the other two possible locations were out of the running.

Contingent Projects

With contingent projects, the acceptance of one project is contingent on the acceptance of another. There are two types of contingency situations. In the first type of situation, the contingent product is *mandatory*. For example, when a public utility company (such as your local electric company) builds a power plant, it must also invest in suitable pollution control equipment to meet environmental standards. The pollution control investment is a mandatory contingent project. When faced with mandatory contingent projects, it is best to treat all of the projects as a single investment for the purpose of evaluation. This provides management with the best measure of the value created by these projects.

In the second type of situation, the contingent project is *optional*. For example, in the Airbus situation above, consider the adaptation of the A380 to carry cargo. The cargo version of the superjumbo is a contingent project and is optional. In these situations, the optional contingent project should be evaluated *independently* and should be accepted or rejected on its own merits.

Basic Capital Budgeting Terms

In this section we briefly introduce two terms that you will need to be familiar with – *cost of capital* and *capital rationing*.

Cost of Capital

The **cost of capital** is the rate of return that a capital project must earn to be accepted by management. The cost of capital can be thought of as an opportunity cost. Recall from Chapter 8 that an *opportunity cost* is the value of the most valuable alternative given up if a particular investment is made.

> ### Cost of capital
> the required rate of return for a capital investment

> ### Opportunity cost of capital
> the return an investor gives up when his or her money is invested in one asset rather than the best alternative asset

Let us consider the opportunity cost concept in the context of capital budgeting decisions. When investors buy shares in a company or loan money to a company, they are giving management money to invest on their behalf. Thus, when a firm's management makes capital investments, they are really investing shareholders' and creditors' money in *real assets* – plant and equipment. Since shareholders and creditors

BUILDING INTUITION

Investment Decisions have Opportunity Costs

When any investment is made, the opportunity to earn a return from an alternative investment is lost. The lost return can be viewed as a cost that arises from a lost opportunity. For this reason, it is called an *opportunity cost*. The opportunity cost of capital is the return an investor gives up when his or her money is invested in one asset rather than the best alternative asset. For example, suppose that a firm invests in a piece of equipment rather than returning money to shareholders. If shareholders could have earned an annual return of 12% on shares with cash flows that are as risky as the cash flows the equipment will produce, then this is the opportunity cost of capital associated with the investment in the piece of equipment.

could have invested their money in *financial assets*, the minimum rate of return they are willing to accept on an investment in a real asset is the rate they could have earned investing in financial assets that have similar risk. The rate of return that investors can earn on financial assets with similar risk is an *opportunity cost* because investors lose the opportunity to earn that rate if the money is invested in a real asset instead. It is therefore the rate of return that investors will require for an investment in a capital project. In other words, this rate is the cost of capital. It is also known as the **opportunity cost of capital**. Chapter 13 discusses how we estimate the opportunity cost of capital in practice.

Capital Rationing

When a firm has all the money it needs to invest in all the capital projects that meet its capital selection criteria, the firm is said to be operating without a *funding constraint* or *resource constraint*. Firms are rarely in this position, especially growth firms. Typically, a firm has a fixed amount of money available for capital expenditures and the number of qualified projects that need funding exceeds the funds that are available. Therefore, the firm must allocate its funds to the subset of projects that will provide the largest overall increase in shareholder value. The process of limiting, or rationing, capital expenditures in this way is called **capital rationing**.

Capital rationing and its implications for capital budgeting are discussed in Chapter 12.

> ### Capital rationing
>
> a situation where a firm does not have enough capital to invest in all attractive projects and must therefore ration capital

Before You Go On

1. Why are capital investments the most important decisions made by a firm's management?
2. What are the differences between capital projects that are independent, mutually exclusive and contingent?

NET PRESENT VALUE

Learning Objective 2

Explain the benefits of using the net present value (NPV) method to analyse capital expenditure decisions and be able to calculate the NPV for a capital project.

In this section we discuss a capital budgeting method that is consistent with this goal of financial management – to maximise the wealth of the firm's owners. It is called the **net present value (NPV) method**, and is one of the most basic concepts underlying corporate finance. The NPV method tells us the amount by which the benefits from a capital expenditure exceed its costs. It is the capital budgeting technique recommended in this book.

Net present value (NPV) method

a method of evaluating a capital investment project which measures the difference between its cost and the present value of its expected cash flows

---

WEB

CCH Business Owner's toolkit is a valuable Web source for information about running a business, including capital budget analysis. Go to www.toolkit.cch.com/text/p06_6500 .asp.

Valuation of Real Assets

Throughout this book, we have emphasised that the value of any asset is the present value of its future cash flows. In Chapters 8 and 9, we developed valuation models for financial assets, such as bonds, preference and ordinary shares. We now extend our discussion of valuation models from financial to real assets. The steps used in valuing an asset are the same whether the asset is real or financial:

1. Estimate the future cash flows.
2. Determine the required rate of return, or discount rate, which depends on the riskiness of the future cash flows.
3. Compute the present value of the future cash flows to determine what the asset is worth.

The valuation of real assets, however, is less straightforward than the valuation of financial assets, for several reasons.

First, in many cases, cash flows for financial assets are well documented in a legal contract. If they are not, we are at least able to make some reasonable assumptions about what they are. For real assets, much less information exists. Specialists within the firm, usually from the finance, marketing and production groups, often prepare estimates of future cash flows for capital projects with only limited information.

Second, many financial securities are traded in public markets and these markets are reasonably efficient. Thus, market data on rates of return are accessible. For real assets, no such markets exist. As a result, we must estimate required rates of return on real assets (opportunity costs) from market data on financial assets: this can be difficult to do.

NPV – The Basic Concept

The NPV of a project is the difference between the present value of the project's future cash flows and the present value of its cost. The NPV can be expressed as follows:

$$NPV = PV(\text{Project's future cash flows}) \\ - PV(\text{Cost of the project})$$

If a capital project has a positive NPV, the value of the cash flows the project is expected to generate exceeds the project's cost. Thus, a positive NPV project increases the value of the firm and, hence, shareholders' wealth. If a capital project has a negative NPV, the value of the cash flows from the project is less than its cost. If accepted, a negative NPV project will reduce the value of the firm and shareholders' wealth.

To illustrate these important points, consider an example. Suppose a firm is considering building a new marina for pleasure boats. The firm has a genie that can tell the future with perfect certainty. The finance staff estimate that the marina will cost €3.50 million. The genie volunteers that the market value of the marina is €4.25 million.

Assuming this information is correct, the NPV for the marina project is a positive €750 000 (€4.25 million – €3.50 million). Management should accept the project because the excess of market value over cost increases the value of the firm by €750 000. Why is a positive NPV a *direct* measure of how much a capital project will increase the value of the firm? If management wanted to, the firm could sell the marina for €4.25 million, pay the €3.50 million in expenses and deposit €750 000 in the bank. The value of the firm would increase by the €750 000 deposited in the bank. In sum, the NPV method tells us which capital projects to select and how much value they add to the firm.

NPV and Value Creation

We have just said that any project with a positive NPV should be accepted because it will increase the value of the firm. Let us take a moment to think about this proposition. What makes a capital asset worth more than it costs? In other words, how does management create value with capital investments?

How Value is Created

Suppose that when you were at university, you worked part time at a successful pizza restaurant near your campus. During this time, you learned a lot about the pizza business. After graduation, you purchased a pizza restaurant for €100 000 that was in a good location but had been forced to close because of a lack of profits. The owners had let the restaurant and the quality of the pizzas deteriorate and the staff had been rude, especially to students. Once you purchased the restaurant, you immediately invested €40 000 to fix it up: you painted the building, spruced up the interior, replaced some of the dining room furniture and added an eye-catching, 1950s-style neon sign to attract attention. You also spent €15 000 for a one-time advertising campaign to quickly build a customer base. More important, you improved the quality of the pizzas you sold and you built a profitable takeout business. Finally, you were careful who you hired as staff and trained them to be customer friendly.

Almost immediately the restaurant was earning a substantial profit and generating substantial cash flows. The really good news was that several owners of local pizzerias wanted to buy your restaurant. After intense negotiations with several of the potential buyers, you accepted a cash offer of €475 000 for the business shortly after you purchased it.

What is the NPV for the pizza restaurant? For this investment, the NPV is easy to calculate. We do not need to estimate future cash flows and discount them because we already have an estimate of the present value of the cash flows the pizza restaurant is expected to produce – €475 000. Someone is willing to pay you €475 000 because they believe the future cash flows are worth that amount. The cost of your investment includes the purchase price of the restaurant, the cost to fix it up and the cost of the initial advertising campaign, which totals €155 000 (€100 000 + €40 000 + €15 000). Thus, the NPV for the pizza restaurant is:

$$
\begin{aligned}
\text{NPV} &= \text{PV(Project's future cash flows)} \\
&\quad - \text{PV(Cost of the project)} \\
&= €475\,000 - €155\,000 \\
&= €320\,000
\end{aligned}
$$

The €475 000 price paid for the pizza restaurant exceeds the cost (€155 000) by €320 000. You have created €320 000 in value. How did you do this? You did it by improving the food, customer service and dining ambiance while keeping prices competitive. Your management skills and knowledge of the pizza business resulted in significant growth in the current year's cash flows and the prospect of even larger cash flows in the future.

Where did the €320 000 in value you created go? The NPV of your investment is the amount that your personal net worth increased because of the investment. For an ongoing business, the result would have been a €320 000 increase in the value of the firm.

How about the original owners? Why would they sell a business worth €475 000 to you for €100 000? The answer is simple: if they could have transformed the business as you did, they would have done so. Instead, when they ran the business, it lost money! They sold it to you because you offered them a price reflecting its value to them.

Market Data versus Discounted Cash Flows

Our pizza restaurant example is greatly simplified by the fact that we can observe the price that someone is willing to pay for the asset. In most capital project analyses, we have to estimate the market value of the asset by *forecasting* its future cash flows and discounting them by the cost of capital. The discounted value of a project's future cash flows is an estimate of its value or the market price for which it can be sold.

Framework for Calculating NPV

We now describe a framework for analysing capital budgeting decisions using the NPV method. As you will see, the NPV technique uses the discounted cash flow technique developed in Chapters 5 and 6 and applied in Chapters 8 and 9. The good news, then, is that the NPV method requires only the application of what you already know.

The five-step framework discussed in this section and the accompanying cash flow worksheet (Exhibit 10.2) can help you systematically organise a project's cash flow data and compute its NPV. Most mistakes people make when working capital budgeting problems result from problems with cash flows: not identifying a cash flow, getting a cash flow in the wrong time period or assigning the wrong sign to a cash flow. What can make cash flow analysis difficult in capital budgeting is this: there are often multiple cash flows in a single time period, and some are cash inflows and others are cash outflows.

As always, we recommend that you prepare a time line when doing capital budgeting problems. A sample time line is shown in Exhibit 10.2, along with an identification of the cash flows for each period. Our goal is to compute the net cash flow (NCF) for each time period t, where $NCF_t =$ (Cash inflows $-$ Cash outflows) for the period t. For a capital project, the time periods (t) are usually in years and t varies from the current period $(t = 0)$ to some finite time period that is the estimated life of the project $(t = n)$. Recall that getting the correct sign on each cash flow is critical to getting the correct answer to a problem. As you have seen in earlier chapters, the convention in finance problem solving is that cash inflows carry a positive sign and cash outflows carry a negative sign. Finally, note that all cash flows in this chapter are on an after-tax basis. We will make adjustments for tax consequences on specific transactions such as the calculation of a project's salvage value.

	0	1	2	3	4	5 Year
Time line						
Cash Flows:						
Initial cost	$-CF_0$					
Inflows (CIF)		CIF_1	CIF_2	CIF_3	CIF_4	CIF_5
Outflows (COF)		$-COF_1$	$-COF_2$	$-COF_3$	$-COF_4$	$-COF_5$
Salvage value						SV
Net cash flow	$-NCF_0$	NCF_1	NCF_2	NCF_3	NCF_4	NCF_5

$$NPV = -NCF_0 + \sum_{t=1}^{5} \frac{NCF_t}{(1+k)^t}$$

Exhibit 10.2: Sample Worksheet for Net Present Value Analysis In addition to following the five-step framework for solving NPV analysis problems, we recommend that you use a worksheet with a time line like the one shown here to help you determine the proper cash flows for each period.

Our five-step framework for analysis is as follows:

1. **Determine the cost of the project.** We first need to identify and add up all of the expense items related to the cost of the project. In most cases, the cost of a project is incurred during the first year; hence, this cash outflow is already in current money. However, some projects have negative cash flows for several years because it takes two or three years to get the projects up and running. If the cash payments for the project extend beyond one year, the money paid in the second year and beyond must be discounted for the appropriate time period. Negative cash flows can also occur when a project sustains an operating loss during the start-up years. Turning to Exhibit 10.2, we have incurred a single negative cash flow $(-CF_0)$ for the total cost of the project, where $NCF_0 = -CF_0$; thus, NCF_0 has a negative value.

2. **Estimate the project's future cash flows over its expected life.** Capital projects typically generate some cash inflows from revenues (CIF_t) for each period, along with some cash outflows (COF_t) that represent expenses incurred to generate the revenues. In most cases revenues exceed expenses and, thus, NCF_t is positive where $t \geq 1$. However, this may not always be the case. For example, if the project is the purchase of a piece of equipment, it is possible for NCF_3 to have a negative value $(CIF_3 < COF_3)$ if the equipment is projected to need a major overhaul or must be replaced during the third year. Finally, you also need to pay attention to a project's final cash flow, which is $t = 5$ in Exhibit 10.2. There may be a salvage value (SV) at the end of the project, which is a cash inflow. In that case $NCF = (CIF_5 - COF_5 + SV)$. The important point is that for each time period, we must identify all the cash flows that take place, assign each cash flow its proper sign and algebraically add up all the cash flows; the total is the NCF for that time period with the correct sign.

3. **Determine the riskiness of the project and the appropriate cost of capital.** The third step is to identify for each project its risk-adjusted cost of capital, which takes into account the riskiness of the project's cash flows. The riskier the project, the higher the project's cost of capital. The cost of capital is the discount rate used in determining the present value of the future expected cash flows. In this chapter, the cost of capital and any risk adjustments will be supplied and no calculations will be required for this step.

4. **Compute the project's NPV.** The NPV, as you know, is the present value of the net cash flows the project is expected to generate minus the cost of the project.

5. **Make a decision.** If the NPV is positive, the project should be accepted because all projects with a positive NPV will increase the value of the firm. If the NPV is negative, the project should be rejected; projects with negative NPVs will decrease the value of the firm.

You might be wondering about how to handle a capital project with an NPV of 0. Technically, management should be indifferent to accepting or rejecting projects such as this because they neither increase nor decrease the value of the firm. At a practical level, projects rarely have an NPV equal to 0 and most firms have more good capital projects (with NPV > 0) than they can fund. Thus, this is not an issue that generates much interest among practitioners.

Net Present Value Techniques

The NPV of a capital project can be stated in equation form as the present value of all net cash flows (inflows − outflows) connected with the project, whether in the current period or in the future. The NPV equation can be written as follows:

$$NPV = NCF_0 + \frac{NCF_1}{1+k} + \frac{NCF_2}{(1+k)^2} + \cdots + \frac{NCF_n}{(1+k)^n}$$

$$(10.1)$$

where:

NCF_t = net cash flow (cash inflows − cash outflows) in period t, where $t = 1, 2, 3, \ldots, n$
k = the cost of capital
n = the project's estimated life

Next, we will work an example to see how the NPV is calculated for a capital project. Suppose you are the president of a small regional firm located in Brescia that manufactures frozen pizzas, which are sold to grocery stores and to firms in the hospitality and food service industry. Your market research group has developed an idea for a 'pocket' pizza that can be used as an entrée with a meal or as an 'on the go' snack. The sales manager believes that, with an aggressive advertising campaign, sales of the product will be about €300 000 per year. The cost to modify the existing production line will also be €300 000, according to the plant manager. The marketing and plant managers estimate that the cost to produce the pocket pizzas, to market and advertise them and to deliver them to customers will be about €220 000 per year. The product's life is estimated to be five years and the specialised equipment necessary for the project has an estimated salvage value of €30 000. The appropriate cost of capital is 15%.

When analysing capital budgeting problems, we typically have a lot of data to sort through. The worksheet approach introduced earlier is helpful in keeping track of the data in an organised format. Exhibit 10.3 shows the time line and relevant cash flows for the pocket pizza project. The steps in analysing the project's cash flows and determining its NPV are as follows:

1. *Determine the cost of the capital project.* The cost of the project is the cost to modify the existing production line, which is €300 000. This is a cash outflow (negative sign).

2. *Estimate the capital project's future cash flows over its expected life.* The project's future cash inflows come from sales of the new product. Sales are estimated at €300 000 per year (inflow, therefore this has a positive sign). The cash outflows are the costs to manufacture and distribute the new product, which are €220 000 per year (negative sign). The life of the project is five years. The project has a salvage value of €30 000, which is a cash inflow (positive sign). The net cash flow (NCF) per time period is just the sum of the cash inflows and cash outflows for that period. For example, the NCF for period $t = 0$ is −€300 000, the NCF for period $t = 1$ is €80 000 and so on, as you can see in Exhibit 10.3.

3. *Determine the riskiness of the project and the appropriate cost of capital.* The discount rate is the cost of capital, which is 15%.

4. *Compute the project's NPV.* To compute the project's NPV, we apply Equation (10.1) by plugging in the NCF values for each time period and using the cost of capital, 15%, as the

	0	1	2	3	4	5 Year
Time line						
Cash Flows:						
Initial cost	−€300					
Inflows		€300	€300	€300	€300	€300
Outflows		−€220	−€220	−€220	−€220	−€220
Salvage						30
Net cash flow	−€300	€80	€80	€80	€80	€110

Exhibit 10.3: **Pocket Pizza Project Time Line and Cash Flows (€ thousands)**   The worksheet introduced in Exhibit 10.2 is helpful in organising the data given for the pocket pizza project.

discount rate. The equation looks like this (the figures are in thousands of euros):

$$\text{NPV} = \sum_{t=0}^{n} \frac{\text{NCF}_t}{(1+k)^t}$$

$$= -\text{€}300 + \frac{\text{€}80}{1.15} + \frac{\text{€}80}{(1.15)^2} + \cdots + \frac{\text{€}80}{(1.15)^4}$$

$$+ \frac{(\text{€}80 + \text{€}30)}{(1.15)^5}$$

$$= -\text{€}300 + \text{€}69.57 + \text{€}60.49 + \text{€}52.60$$

$$+ \text{€}45.74 + \text{€}54.69$$

$$= -\text{€}300 + \text{€}283.09 = -\text{€}16.91$$

The NPV for the pocket pizza project is therefore −€16 910.

5. *Make a decision.* The pocket pizza project has a negative NPV, which indicates that the project is not a good investment and should be rejected. If management undertook this project, the value of the firm would be reduced by €16 910 and, if the firm had 100 000 shares outstanding, we can estimate that the project would reduce the value of each share by about 17 cents (€16 910/ 100 000 shares).

Learning by Doing Application 10.1

The Dough is Up: The Self-Rising Pizza Project

Problem: Let us continue our frozen pizza example. Suppose the head of the research and development (R&D) group announces that R&D engineers have developed a breakthrough technology – self-rising frozen pizza dough that, when baked, rises and tastes exactly like fresh-baked dough.

The cost is €300 000 to modify the production line. Sales of the new product are estimated at €200 000 for the first year, €300 000 for the next two years and €500 000 for the final two years. It is estimated that production, sales and advertising costs will be €250 000 for the first year and will then decline to a constant €200 000 per year. There is no salvage value at the end of the product's life and the appropriate cost of capital is 15%. Is the project, as proposed, economically viable?

Approach: To solve the problem, work through the steps for NPV analysis given in the text.

Solution: Exhibit 10.4 shows the project's cash flows.

1. The cost to modify the production line is €300 000, which is a cash outflow and the cost of the project.
2. The future cash flows over the expected life of the project are laid out on the time line in Exhibit 10.4. The project's life is five years. The NCFs for the capital project are negative at the beginning of the project and in the first year (−€300 000 and −€50 000) and thereafter are positive.
3. The appropriate cost of capital is 15%.
4. The values are substituted into Equation (10.1) to calculate the NPV:

$$\text{NPV} = \text{NCF}_0 + \frac{\text{NCF}_1}{1+k} + \frac{\text{NCF}_2}{(1+k)^2} + \cdots$$

$$+ \frac{\text{NCF}_n}{(1+k)^n}$$

$$= -\text{€}300\,000 + \frac{\text{€}50\,000}{1.15} + \frac{\text{€}100\,000}{(1.15)^2}$$

$$+ \frac{\text{€}100\,000}{(1.15)^3} + \frac{\text{€}300\,000}{(1.15)^4} + \frac{\text{€}300\,000}{(1.15)^5}$$

$$= -\text{€}300\,000 + \text{€}47\,478 + \text{€}75\,614$$

$$+ \text{€}65\,752 + \text{€}171\,526 + \text{€}149\,153$$

$$= \text{€}118\,567$$

Time line	0	1	2	3	4	5 Year
Cash Flows:						
Initial cost	−€300					
Inflows		€200	€300	€300	€500	€500
Outflows		−€250	−€200	−€200	−€200	−€200
Salvage						
Net cash flow	−€300	−€50	€100	€100	€300	€300

Exhibit 10.4: Self-Rising Pizza Dough Project Time Line and Cash Flows (€ thousands) The worksheet shows the time line and cash flows for the self-rising pizza dough project in Learning by Doing Application 10.1. As always, it is important to assign each cash flow to the appropriate year and to give it the proper sign. Once you have computed the net cash flow for each time period, solving for the NPV is just a matter of plugging the data into the NPV formula.

The decision is based on the NPV. The NPV for the self-rising pizza dough project is €118 567. Because the NPV is positive, management should accept the project. The project is estimated to increase the value of the firm by €118 567.

USING EXCEL

Net Present Value

Net present value problems are most commonly solved using a spreadsheet program. The program's design is good for keeping track of all the cash flows and the periods in which they occur. The following spreadsheet setup for Learning by Doing Application 10.1 shows how to calculate the NPV for the self-rising pizza dough machine:

Notice that the NPV formula does not take into account the cash flow in year 0. Therefore, you only enter into the NPV formula the cash flows in years 1–5, along with the discount rate. You then add the cash flow in year 0 to the total from the NPV formula calculation to get the NPV for the investment.

	A	B	C	D	E
1					
2		Net Present Value Calculations			
3					
4		Year		Cash Flow	
5		0		−€ 300,000	
6		1		−50,000	
7		2		100,000	
8		3		100,000	
9		4		300,000	
10		5		300,000	
11					
12		Cost of capital		0.15	
13					
14		NPV		€ 118,567	
15		Formula used		=NPV(E12,E6:E10)+E5	
16					

Decision-Making Example 10.1

The IS Department's Capital Projects

Situation: Suppose you are the manager of the information systems (IS) department of the frozen pizza manufacturer we have been discussing. Your department has identified four possible capital projects with the following NPVs: (1) €4500, (2) €3000, (3) €0.0 and (4) −€1000. What should you decide about each project if the proj-

ects are independent? What should you decide if the projects are mutually exclusive?

Decision: If the projects are independent, you should accept projects 1 and 2, both of which have a positive NPV, and reject project 4. Project 3, with an NPV of zero, could be either accepted or rejected. If the projects are mutually exclusive and you can accept only one of them, it should be project 1, which has the largest NPV.

Concluding Comments on NPV

Some concluding comments about the NPV method are in order. First, as you may have noticed, the NPV computations are rather mechanical once we have the cash flows and have determined the cost of capital. The real difficulty is estimating or forecasting the future cash flows. Although this may seem to be a daunting task, firms with experience in producing and selling a particular type of product can usually generate fairly accurate estimates of sales volumes, prices and production costs. However, problems can arise with the cash flow estimates when a project team becomes 'enamoured' with a project. Wanting a project to succeed, a project team can be too optimistic about the cash flow projections.

Second, we must recognise that the calculated values for NPV are estimates based on management's informed judgement; they are not real market data. Like any estimate, they can be too high or too low. The only way to determine a project's 'true' NPV is to put the asset up for sale and see what price market participants are willing to pay for it. An example of this approach was the sale of our pizza restaurant; however, situations such as this are the exception, not the rule.

Finally, there is nothing wrong with using estimates to make business decisions as long as they are based on informed judgements and not

guesses. Most business managers are routinely required to make decisions that involve expectations about future events. In fact, that is what business is really all about – dealing with uncertainty and making decisions that involve risk.

In conclusion, the NPV approach is the method we recommend for making capital investment decisions. The accompanying table summarises NPV decision rules and the method's key advantages and disadvantages.

Summary of Net Present Value (NPV) Method

| **Decision Rule:** | NPV $> 0 \Rightarrow$ Accept the project. |
| | NPV $< 0 \Rightarrow$ Reject the project. |

Key Advantages	Key Disadvantages
1. Uses the discounted cash flow valuation technique to adjust for the time value of money.	Can be difficult to understand without an accounting and finance background.
2. Provides a direct (monetary) measure of how much a capital project will increase the value of the firm.	
3. Consistent with the goal of maximising shareholder value.	

Before You Go On

1. What is the NPV of a project?
2. If a firm accepts a project with a €10 000 NPV, what is the effect on the value of the firm?
3. What are the five steps used in NPV analysis?

THE PAYBACK PERIOD

The payback period is one of the most widely used tools for evaluating capital projects. The **payback period** is defined as the number of years it takes for the cash flows from a project to recover the project's initial investment. With the payback method for evaluating projects, a project is accepted if its payback period is below some specified threshold. Although it has serious weaknesses, this method does provide some insight into a project's risk; the more quickly you recover the cash, the less risky is the project.

> **Payback period**
>
> the length of time required to recover a project's initial cost

Computing the Payback Period

> **Learning Objective 3**
>
> Describe the strengths and weaknesses of the payback period as a capital expenditure decision-making tool and be able to compute the payback period for a capital project.

To compute the payback period, we need to know the project's cost and estimate its future net cash flows. The net cash flows and the project cost are the same values that we used to compute the NPV calculations. The payback (PB) equation can be expressed as follows:

$$PB = \text{Years before cost recovery} + \frac{\text{Remaining cost to recover}}{\text{Cash flow during the year}} \quad (10.2)$$

Exhibit 10.5 shows the net cash flows (row 1) and cumulative net cash flows (row 2) for a proposed capital project with an initial cost of €70 000. The payback period calculation for our example is:

$$
\begin{aligned}
PB &= \text{Years before cost recovery} \\
&\quad + \frac{\text{Remaining cost to recover}}{\text{Cash flow during the year}} \\
&= 2 \text{ years} + \frac{€70\,000 - €60\,000}{€20\,000} \\
&= 2 \text{ years} + 0.5 \\
&= 2.5 \text{ years}
\end{aligned}
$$

We will now look at this calculation in more detail. Note in Exhibit 10.5 that the firm recovers cash flows of €30 000 in the first year and €30 000 in the second year, for a total of €60 000 over the two years. During the third year, the firm needs to recover only €10 000 (€70 000 − €60 000) to pay back the full cost of the project. The third-year cash flow is €20 000, so we will have to wait 0.5 year (€10 000/€20 000) to recover the final amount. Thus, the payback period for this project is 2.5 years (2 + 0.5).

The idea behind the payback period method is simple: the shorter the payback period, the faster the firm gets its money back and the more desirable the project. However, there is no economic rationale that links the payback method to shareholder value maximisation. Firms that use the payback method accept all projects having a

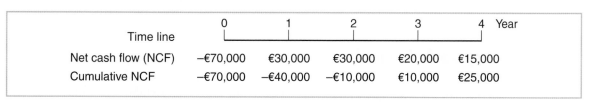

Time line	0	1	2	3	4 Year
Net cash flow (NCF)	−€70,000	€30,000	€30,000	€20,000	€15,000
Cumulative NCF	−€70,000	−€40,000	−€10,000	€10,000	€25,000

Exhibit 10.5: Payback Period Cash Flows and Calculations The exhibit shows the net and cumulative net cash flows for a proposed capital project with an initial cost of €70 000. The cash flow data are used to compute the payback period, which is 2.5 years.

payback period under some threshold and reject those with a payback period over this threshold. If a firm has a number of projects that are mutually exclusive, the projects are selected in order of their payback rank – projects with the shortest payback period are selected first.

Learning by Doing Application 10.2

A Payback Calculation

Problem: A firm has two capital projects, A and B, which are under review for funding. Both projects cost €500 and the projects have the following cash flows:

Year	Project A	Project B
0	−€500	−€500
1	100	400
2	200	300
3	200	200
4	400	100

What is the payback period for each project? If the projects are independent, which project should management select? If the projects are mutually exclusive, which project should management accept? The firm's payback cut-off point is two years.

Approach: Use Equation (10.2) to calculate the number of years it takes for the cash flows from each project to recover the project's initial investment. If the two projects are independent, you should accept the projects that have a payback period that is less than or equal to two years. If the projects are mutually exclusive, you should accept the project with the shortest payback period if that payback period is also less than or equal to two years.

Solution: The payback for project A requires only that we calculate the first term in Equation (10.2) – years before recovery: the first year recovers €100, the second year €200 and the third year €200, for a total of €500 (€100 + 200 + €200). Thus, in three years, the €500 investment is fully recovered, so $PB_A = 3.00$.

For project B, the first year recovers €400 and the second year €300. Since we need only part of the second-year cash flow to recover the initial cost, we calculate both terms in Equation (10.2) to obtain the payback time.

$$PB = \text{Years before cost recovery}$$
$$\quad + \frac{\text{Remaining cost to recover}}{\text{Cash flow during the year}}$$

$$PB_A = 3 \text{ years}$$

$$PB_B = 1 \text{ year} + \frac{€500 - €400}{€300}$$
$$= 1 \text{ year} + \frac{€100}{€300}$$
$$= 1.33 \text{ years}$$

Whether the projects are independent or mutually exclusive, management should accept only project B since project A's payback period exceeds the two-year cut-off point.

How the Payback Period Performs

We have worked through some simple examples of how the payback period is computed. Now we will consider several more complex situations to see how well the payback period performs as a capital budgeting criterion. Exhibit 10.6 illustrates five different capital budgeting projects. The projects

EXHIBIT 10.6

PAYBACK PERIOD WITH VARIOUS CASH FLOW PATTERNS

Year	A	B	C	D	E
0	−€500	−€500	−€500	−€500	−€500
1	200	300	250	500	200
2	300	100	250	0	200
3	400	50	−250	0	200
4	500	0	250	−5000	5000
Payback (years)	2.0	∞	2.0/4.0	1.0/∞	2.5
NPV	€450	−€131	−€115	−€2924	€2815

Cost of capital = 15%

Each of the five capital budgeting projects shown in the exhibit calls for an initial investment of €500 but all have different cash flow patterns. The bottom part of the exhibit shows each project's payback period, along with its net present value for comparison.

all have an initial investment of €500 but each one has a different cash flow pattern. The bottom part of the exhibit shows each project's payback period, along with its net present value for comparison. We will assume that management has set a payback period of two years as the cut-off point for an acceptable project.

Project A: The cash flows for project A are €200 in the first year and €300 in the second, for a total of €500; thus, the project's payback period is two years. Under our acceptance criterion, management should accept this project. Project A also has a positive NPV of €450, so the two capital budgeting decision rules agree.

Project B: Project B never generates enough cash flows to pay off the original investment of €500: €300 + €100 + €50 = €450. Thus, the project payback period is infinite. With an infinite payback period, the project should be rejected. Also, as you would expect, project B's NPV is negative. So far, the payback period and NPV methods have agreed on which projects to accept.

Project C: Project C has a payback period of two years: €250 + €250 = €500. Thus, according to the payback criteria, it should be accepted.

However, the project's NPV is a negative €115, which indicates that the project should be rejected. Why the conflict? Look at the cash flows after the payback period of two years. In year 3 the project requires an additional investment of €250 (a cash outflow) and now is in a deficit position; that is, the cash balance is now only €250 (€250 − €250 + €250). Then, in the final year, the project earns an additional €250, recovering the cost of the original investment. The project's payback is really four years. The payback period analysis can lead to erroneous decisions because the rule does not consider cash flows after the payback period.

Projects D and E: Projects D and E dramatically illustrate the problem when a capital budgeting evaluation tool fails to consider cash flows after the payback period. Project D has a payback period of one year, suggesting that it should be accepted, and project E has a payback period of 2.5 years, suggesting that it should be rejected. However, a simple look at the future cash flows suggests otherwise. It is clear that project D, with a negative €5000 cash flow in year 4, is a disaster and should be rejected, while project E, with a positive €5000 'windfall' in year 4, should be accepted.

Indeed, the NPV analysis confirms these conclusions: project D has a negative NPV of €2924 and project E has a positive NPV of €2815. In both instances, the payback rule led to the wrong economic decision. These examples illustrate that a rapid payback does not necessarily mean a good investment.

Discounted Payback Period

One of the weaknesses of the ordinary payback period is that it does not take into account the time value of money. All the monies received before the cut-off period are given equal weight. To address this problem, some financial managers use a variant of the payback period called the **discounted payback period**. This payback calculation is similar to the ordinary payback calculation except that the future cash flows are discounted by the cost of capital.

> **Discounted payback period**
>
> the length of time required to recover a project's initial cost, accounting for the time value of money

The major advantage of the discounted payback is that it tells management how long it takes a project to reach an NPV of zero. Thus, any capital project that meets a firm's decision rule must also have a positive NPV. This is an improvement over the standard payback calculation, which can accept projects with negative NPVs. Regardless of the improvement, the discounted payback method is not widely used by businesses and it still ignores all cash flows after the arbitrary cut-off period, which is a major flaw.

To see how the discounted payback period is calculated, turn to Exhibit 10.7. The exhibit shows the net cash flows for a proposed capital project along with both the cumulative and discounted cumulative cash flows; thus, we can compute both the ordinary and the discounted payback periods for the project and then compare them. The cost of capital is 10%.

The first two rows show the non-discounted cash flows and we can see by inspection that the ordinary payback period is two years. We do not need to make any additional calculations because the cumulative cash flows equal zero at precisely two years. Now let us turn our attention to the lower two rows, which show

		0	1	2	3 Year
Time line					
Net cash flow (NCF)		−€40,000	€20,000	€20,000	€20,000
Cumulative NCF		−€40,000	−€20,000	€0	€20,000
Discounted NCF (at 10%)		−€40,000	€18,182	€16,529	€15,026
Cumulative discounted NCF		−€40,000	−€21,818	−€5,289	€9,737

Payback period = 2 years + 0/€20,000 = 2 years
Discounted payback period = 2 years + €5,289/€15,026 = 2.35 years
NPV = €49,737 − €40,000 = 9,737
Cost of capital = 10%

Exhibit 10.7: Discounted Payback Period Cash Flows and Calculations The exhibit shows the net and cumulative net cash flows for a proposed capital project with an initial cost of €40 000. The cash flow data are used to compare the discounted payback period for a 10% cost of capital, which is 2.35 years.

the project's discounted and cumulative discounted cash flows. Note that the first year's cash flow is €20 000 and its discounted value is €18 182 (€20 000 × 0.9091); the second year's cash flow is also €20 000 and its discounted value is €16 529 (€20 000 × 0.8264). Now, looking at the cumulative discounted cash flows row, notice that it turns positive between two and three years. This means that the discounted payback period is two years plus some fraction of the third year's discounted cash flow. The exact discounted payback period computed value is 2 + (€5289/€15 026) = 2 + 0.35 = 2.35.

As expected, the discounted payback period is longer than the ordinary payback period (2 < 2.35), and in 2.35 years the project will reach NPV = 0. The project NPV is positive (€9737); therefore, we should accept the project. But notice that the payback decision criteria are ambiguous. If we use 2.0 years as the payback criterion, we reject the project and if we use 2.5 or 3.0 years as criterion, the project is accepted. The lack of a definitive decision rule remains a major problem with the payback period as a capital budgeting tool.

Evaluating the Payback Rule

In spite of its lack of sophistication, the standard payback period is widely used in business in part because it provides an intuitive and simple measure of a project's liquidity risk. This makes sense because projects that pay for themselves quickly are less risky than projects whose paybacks occur further in the future. There is a strong feeling in business that 'getting your money back quickly' is an important standard when making capital investments. Probably the greatest advantage of the payback period is its simplicity; it is easy to calculate and easy to understand, making it especially attractive to business executives with little training in accounting and finance.

When compared with the NPV method, however, the payback method has some serious shortcomings. First, the standard payback method does not use discounting; hence, it ignores the time value of money. Second, it does not adjust or account for differences in the riskiness of projects. Another problem is that there is no economic rationale for establishing cut-off criteria. Who is to say that a particular cut-off, such as two years, is optimal with regard to maximising shareholder value?

Finally, perhaps the greatest shortcoming of the payback method is its failure to consider cash flows after the payback period, as illustrated by projects D and E in Exhibit 10.6. This is true whether or not the cash flows are discounted. As a result of this feature, the payback method is biased towards shorter-term projects, which tend to free up cash more quickly. Consequently, projects for which cash inflows tend to occur further in the future, such as research and development investments, new product launches and entry into new lines of business, are at a disadvantage when the payback method is used. The accompanying table summarises major features of the payback period.

Summary of Payback Method

Decision Rule: Payback period ≤ Payback cut off point ⇨ Accept the project.
Payback period > Payback cut off point ⇨ Reject the project.

Key Advantages	Key Disadvantages
1. Easy to calculate and understand for people without a strong finance background.	Most common version does not account for time value of money.
2. A simple measure of a project's liquidity.	Does not consider cash flows past the payback period.
3.	Bias against long-term projects such as research and development and new product launches.
4.	Arbitrary cut-off point.

THE ACCOUNTING RATE OF RETURN

Learning Objective 4

Explain why the accounting rate of return (ARR) is not recommended for use as a capital expenditure decision-making tool.

We turn next to a capital budgeting technique based on the **accounting rate of return (ARR)**, sometimes called the *book value rate of return*. This method computes the return on a capital project using accounting numbers – the project's net income (NI) and book value (BV) – rather than cash flow data. The ARR can be calculated in a number of ways, but the most common definition is:

$$\text{ARR} = \frac{\text{Average net income}}{\text{Average book value}} \qquad (10.3)$$

where:

Average net income $= (\text{NI}_1 + \text{NI}_2 + \cdots + \text{NI}_n)/n$

Average book value $= (\text{BV}_1 + \text{BV}_2 + \cdots + \text{BV}_n)/n$

$n =$ the project's estimated life

Accounting rate of return (ARR)

a rate of return on a capital project based on average net income divided by average assets over the project's life; also called the *book value rate of return*

Although ARR is fairly easy to understand and calculate, as you probably guessed, it has a number of major flaws as a tool for evaluating capital expenditure decisions. Besides the fact that AAR is based on accounting numbers rather than cash flows, it is not really even an accounting-based rate of return. Instead of discounting a project's cash flows over time, it simply gives us a number based on average figures from the income statement and balance sheet. Thus, the ARR ignores the time value of money. Also, as with the payback method, there is no economic rationale that links a particular acceptance criterion to the goal of maximising shareholder value.

Because of these major shortcomings, the ARR technique should not be used to evaluate the viability of capital projects under any circumstances. You may wonder why we even included the ARR technique in the book if it is a poor criterion for evaluating projects. The reason is simply that we want to be sure that if you run across the ARR method at work, you will recognise it and be aware of its shortcomings.

INTERNAL RATE OF RETURN

Learning Objective 5

Be able to compute the internal rate of return (IRR) for a capital project and discuss the conditions under which the IRR technique and the NPV technique produce different results.

The **internal rate of return**, known in practice as the **IRR**, is an important and legitimate alternative to the NPV method. The NPV and IRR techniques are closely related in that both involve discounting the cash flows from a project; thus, both account for the time value of money. When we use the NPV method to evaluate a capital project, the discount rate is the rate of return required by investors for investments with similar risk, which is the project's opportunity cost of capital. When we use the IRR, we are looking for the rate of return associated with a project so that we can determine whether this rate is higher or lower than the project's opportunity cost of capital.

> ### Internal rate of return (IRR)
>
> the discount rate at which the present value of a project's expected cash inflows equals the present value of the project's outflows

We can define the IRR as the discount rate that equates the present value of a project's expected cash inflows to the present value of the project's outflows:

$$PV(\text{Project's future cash flows}) = PV(\text{Cost of the project})$$

This means that we can also describe the IRR as the discount rate that causes the NPV to equal zero. This relation can be written in a general form as follows:

$$NPV = NCF_0 + \frac{NCF_1}{1 + IRR} + \frac{NCF_2}{(1 + IRR)^2} + \cdots$$
$$+ \frac{NCF_n}{(1 + IRR)^n} = \sum_{t=0}^{n} \frac{NCF_t}{(1 + IRR)^t} = 0$$

(10.4)

Because of their close relation, it may seem that the IRR and the NPV are interchangeable – that is, either should accept or reject the same capital projects. After all, both methods are based on whether the project's return exceeds the cost of capital and, hence, whether the project will add value to the firm. In many circumstances, the IRR

and NPV methods do give us the same answer. As you will see later, however, some of the mathematical properties of the IRR equation can lead to incorrect decisions concerning whether to accept or reject a particular capital project.

Calculating the IRR

The IRR is an expected rate of return like the yield to maturity we calculated for bonds in Chapter 8. Thus, in calculating the IRR, we need to apply the same trial-and-error method we used in Chapter 8. We will be doing IRR calculations by trial and error and interpolation so that you understand the process, but in practice it is helpful to use a spreadsheet or a financial calculator.

Trial-and-Error Method

Suppose that Volkswagen has an investment opportunity with cash flows as shown in Exhibit 10.8 and that the cost of capital is 12%. We want to find the IRR for this project. Using Equation (10.4), we will substitute various values for IRR into the equation to compute the project's IRR by trial and error. We continue this process until we find the IRR value that makes Equation (10.4) equal zero.

A good starting point is to use the cost of capital as the discount rate. Note that when we discount the NCFs by the cost of capital, we are calculating the project's NPV:

$$NPV = NCF_0 + \frac{NCF_1}{1 + IRR} + \frac{NCF_2}{(1 + IRR)^2} + \cdots$$
$$+ \frac{NCF_n}{(1 + IRR)^n}$$

$$NPV_{12\%} = -€560 + \frac{€240}{1.12} + \frac{€240}{(1.12)^2} + \frac{€240}{(1.12)^3}$$

$$= €16.44$$

Recall that the result we are looking for is zero. Because our result is €16.44, the discount rate of 12% is too low and we must try a higher rate. We will try 13%:

$$NPV_{13\%} = -€560 + \frac{€240}{1.13} + \frac{€240}{(1.13)^2} + \frac{€240}{(1.13)^3}$$

$$= €6.68$$

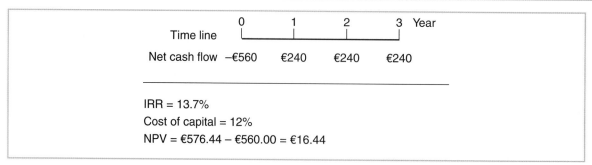

Exhibit 10.8: Time Line and Expected Net Cash Flows for the Volkswagen Project (€ thousands) The cash flow data in the exhibit are used to compute the project's IRR, which is 13.7%. Since the IRR is higher than Volkswagen's cost of capital, the IRR criterion indicates the project should be accepted. The project's NPV is also a positive €16 440, which indicates that Volkswagen should accept the project. Thus, the IRR and NPV methods have reached the same conclusion.

We are very close. We will try 14%:

$$NPV_{14\%} = -€560 + \frac{€240}{1.14} + \frac{€240}{(1.14)^2} + \frac{€240}{(1.14)^3}$$

$$= -€2.81$$

Because our result is now a negative number, we know the correct rate is between 13% and 14%, and looking at the magnitude of the numbers, we know that the answer is closer to 14%. Using interpolation, we find that the IRR is 13.7%:

$$i_{unknown} = i_{low} + \frac{(Value_{low\ i} - Value_{unknown\ i})}{(Value_{low\ i} - Value_{high\ i})}$$
$$\times (i_{high} - i_{low})$$

$$IRR = 13\% + \frac{€6.68 - €0}{€6.68 + €2.81} \times (14\% - 13\%)$$

$$= 13\% + \frac{€6.68}{€9.49} \times 1\%$$

$$= 13\% + 0.7039 \times 1\% = 13.7\%$$

This means that the NPV of Volkswagen's capital project is zero at a discount rate of 13.7%. Volkswagen's required rate of return is the cost of capital, which is 12.0%. Since the project's IRR of 13.7% exceeds Volkswagen's cost of capital, the IRR criterion indicates that the project should be accepted.

The project's NPV is a positive €16 440, which also indicates that Volkswagen should go ahead with the project. Thus, both the IRR and NPV have reached the same conclusion.

Learning by Doing Application 10.3

Calculating the IRR at Giuseppe's Gelateria

Problem: Giuseppe's Gelateria, based in Rome, is famous for its gourmet ice cream.

However, some customers have asked for a low-calorie, soft yoghurt ice cream. The machine that makes this confection costs €5000 plus €1750 for installation. Giuseppe estimates that the machine will generate a net cash flow of €2000 a year (the shop closes during November–March of each year). Giuseppe also estimates the machine's life to be 10 years and that it

Solution: The total cost of the machine is €6750 (€5000 + €1750), and the final cash flow at year 10 is €2400 (€2000 + €400).

$$NPV = NCF_0 + \frac{NCF_1}{1 + IRR} + \frac{NCF_2}{(1 + IRR)^2} + \cdots + \frac{NCF_n}{(1 + IRR)^n} = 0$$

$$NPV_{15\%} = -€6750 + \frac{€2000}{1.15} + \frac{€2000}{(1.15)^2} + \cdots + \frac{€2400}{(1.15)^3} = €3386.41$$

$$NPV_{27.08\%} = -€6750 + \frac{€2000}{1.2708} + \frac{€2000}{(1.2708)^2} + \cdots + \frac{€2400}{(1.2708)^3} = €0$$

will have a €400 salvage value. His cost of capital is 15%. Giuseppe thinks the machine is overpriced and as a result he will lose money on his investment. Is he right?

Approach: The IRR for an investment is the discount rate at which the NPV is zero. Thus, we can use Equation (10.4) to solve for the IRR and then compare this value with Giuseppe's cost of capital. If the IRR is greater than the cost of capital, the project has a positive NPV and should be accepted.

The hand trial-and-error calculations are shown in these equations. The first calculation uses 15%, the cost of capital, our recommended starting point, and the answer is €3386.41 (which is also the project's NPV). Because the value is a positive number, we need to use a larger discount rate than 15%. Our guess based on interpolating 25% and 30% is 27.08%. At that value, NPV = 0; thus, the IRR for the yoghurt machine is 27.08%.

Because the project's IRR exceeds Giuseppe's cost of capital of 15%, the project should be accepted. Giuseppe is wrong.

When the IRR and NPV Methods Agree

In the Volkswagen example, the IRR and NPV methods agree. The two methods will *always* agree when you are evaluating *independent* projects and the projects' cash flows are *conventional*. As discussed earlier, an independent project is one that can be selected with no effect on any other project, assuming the firm faces no resource constraints. A project with **conventional cash flows** is one with an initial cash outflow followed by one or more future cash inflows. Put another way, after the initial investment is made (cash outflow), all the cash flows in each future year are positive (inflows). For example, the purchase of a bond involves a conventional cash flow. You purchase the bond for a price (cash outflow), and in the future you receive coupon payments and a principal payment at maturity (cash inflows).

Conventional cash flow

a cash flow pattern made up of an initial cash outflow that is followed by one or more cash inflows

Let us look more closely at the kinds of situations in which the NPV and the IRR methods agree. A good way to visualise the relation between the

USING EXCEL

Internal Rate of Return

You know that calculating the IRR by hand can be tedious. The trial-and-error method with interpolation can take a long time and can lead to mistakes being made. Knowing all the cash flows and an approximate discount rate will allow you to use a spreadsheet formula to get the answer instantly.

The accompanying spreadsheet shows the layout and formula for calculating the IRR for the low-calorie yoghurt machine at Giuseppe's Gelateria that is described in Learning by Doing Application 10.3.

Here are a couple of important points to note about IRR calculations using spreadsheet programs:

	A	B	C	D	E
1					
2		IRR Calculations			
3					
4		Year		Cash Flow	
5		0		-€ 6,750	
6		1		€ 2,000	
7		2		€ 2,000	
8		3		€ 2,000	
9		4		€ 2,000	
10		5		€ 2,000	
11		6		€ 2,000	
12		7		€ 2,000	
13		8		€ 2,000	
14		9		€ 2,000	
15		10		€ 2,400	
16					
17		Cost of capital		0.15	
18					
19		IRR		27.08%	
20		Formula used		IRR(E5:E15, E17)	
21					
22	Remember to keep track of signs – cash outflows are				
23	negative and cash inflows are positive				
24					

1. Unlike the NPV formula, the IRR formula accounts for all cash flows, including the initial investment in year 0, so there is no need to add this cash flow later.

2. In order to calculate the IRR, you will need to provide a 'guess' value, or a number you estimate is close to the IRR. A good value to start with is the cost of capital. To learn more about why this value is needed, you should go to your spreadsheet's help menu and search for 'IRR'.

IRR and NPV methods is to graph NPV as a function of the discount rate. The graph, called an **NPV profile**, shows the NPV of the project at various costs of capital.

on the horizontal axis, or *x*-axis. We used the calculations from our earlier example and made some additional NPV calculations at various discount rates, as follows:

> **NPV profile**
>
> a graph showing NPV as a function of the discount rate

Discount Rate	NPV (€ thousands)
0%	€160
5	94
10	37
15	−12
20	−54
25	−92
30	−124

Exhibit 10.9 shows the NPV profile for the Volkswagen project. We have placed the NPVs on the vertical axis, or *y*-axis, and the discount rates

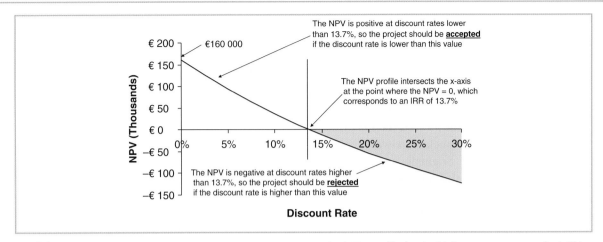

Exhibit 10.9: NPV Profile for the Volkswagen Project In the NPV profile for the Volkswagen project, the NPV value is on the vertical (*y*)-axis and the discount rate is on the horizontal (*x*)-axis. You can see that as the discount rate increases, the NPV profile curve declines smoothly and intersects the *x*-axis at precisely the point where the NPV is 0 and the IRR is 13.7% – the point at which the NPV changes from a positive to a negative value. Thus, the NPV and IRR methods lead to identical accept or reject decisions for the Volkswagen project.

As you can see, a discount rate of 0% corresponds to an NPV of €160 000; a discount rate of 5% to an NPV of €94 000; and so forth. As the discount rate increases, the NPV curve declines smoothly. Not surprisingly, the curve intersects the *x*-axis at precisely the point where the NPV is 0 and the IRR is 13.7%.

The NPV profile in Exhibit 10.9 illustrates why the NPV and IRR methods lead to identical accept/reject decisions for the Volkswagen project. The IRR of 13.7% precisely marks the point at which the NPV changes from a positive to a negative value. Whenever a project is independent and has conventional cash flows, the result will be as shown in the exhibit. The NPV will decline as the discount rate increases and the IRR and the NPV methods will result in the same capital expenditure decision.

When the NPV and IRR Methods Disagree

We have seen that the IRR and NPV methods lead to identical investment decisions for capital projects that are independent and that have conventional cash flows. However, if either of these conditions is not met, the IRR and NPV methods can produce different accept/reject decisions.

Unconventional Cash Flows

Unconventional cash flows can cause a conflict between the NPV and IRR decision rules. In some instances the cash flows for an unconventional project are just the reverse of those of a conventional project: the initial cash flow is positive and all subsequent cash flows are negative. For example, consider a life insurance company that sells a lifetime annuity to a retired person. The company receives a single cash payment, which is the price of the annuity (cash inflow), and then makes monthly payments to the retiree for the rest of his or her life (cash outflows). In this case, we need only reverse the IRR decision rule and accept the project if the IRR is *less* than the cost of capital to make the IRR and NPV methods agree. The intuition in this example is that the life insurance company is effectively borrowing money from the retiree and the IRR is a measure of the cost of that money. The cost of capital is the rate at which the life insurance company can borrow elsewhere. An IRR less than the cost of capital means that the lifetime annuity provides the insurance company with money at a lower cost than alternative sources.

When a project's future cash flows include both positive and negative cash flows, the situation is more complicated. An example of such a project is an assembly line that will require one or more major renovations over its lifetime. Another common business situation is a project that has conventional cash flows except for the final cash flow, which is negative. The final cash flow might be negative because extensive environmental cleanup is required at the end of the project, such as the cost for decommissioning a nuclear power plant, or because the equipment originally purchased has little or no salvage value and is expensive to remove.

Consider an example. Suppose a firm invests in a gold-mining operation that costs €55 million and has an expected life of two years. In the first year, the project generates a cash inflow of €150 million. In the second year, extensive environmental and site restoration is required, so the expected cash flow is a negative €100 million. The time line for these cash flows follows:

0	1	2 Year
−€55 million	€150 million	−€100 million

Once again, the best way to understand the effect of these cash flows is to look at an NPV profile. Shown here are NPV calculations we made at various discount rates to generate the data necessary to plot the NPV profile shown in Exhibit 10.10:

Discount Rate	NPV (€ millions)
0%	−€5.00
10	−1.28
20	0.56
30	1.21
40	1.12
50	0.56
60	−0.31
70	−1.37

Looking at the data in the table, you can probably spot a problem. The NPV is initially negative (−€5.00); then, at a discount rate of 20%, switches to positive (€0.56); and then, at a discount rate of 60%, switches back to negative (−€0.31).

The NPV profile in Exhibit 10.10 shows the results of this pattern: we have two IRRs, one at 16.05% and the other at 55.65%. Which is the correct IRR, or are both correct? Actually, there is no correct answer; the results are meaningless and you should not try to interpret them. Thus, in this situation, the IRR technique provides information that is suspect and should not be used for decision making.

How many IRR solutions can there be for a given cash flow? The maximum number of IRR solutions is equal to the number of sign reversals in the cash flow stream. For a project with a conventional cash flow, there is only one cash flow sign reversal; thus, there is only one IRR solution. In our mining example, there are two cash flow sign reversals; thus, there are two IRR solutions.

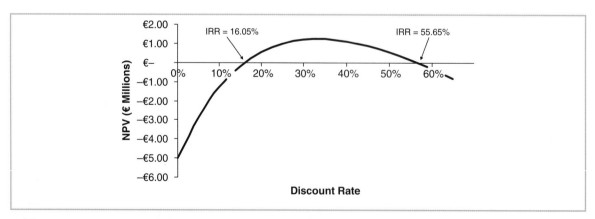

Exhibit 10.10: NPV for Gold Mining Operation Showing Multiple IRR Solutions The gold mining operation has unconventional cash flows. Because there are two cash flow sign reversals, we end up with two IRRs – 16.05% and 55.65% – neither of them correct. In situations like this, the IRR provides a solution that is suspect and therefore, the results should not be used for capital budgeting decisions.

Finally, for some cash flow patterns, it is impossible to compute an IRR. These situations can occur when the initial cash flow ($t = 0$) is either a cash inflow or outflow and is followed by cash flows with two or more sign reversals. An example of such a cash flow pattern is $NCF_0 = €15$, $NCF_1 = -€25$ and $NCF_2 = €20$. This type of cash flow pattern might occur on a building project where the contractor is given a prepayment, usually the cost of materials and supplies (€15); then does the construction and pays the labour cost (−€25); and finally, upon completion of the work, receives the final payment (€20). Note that when it is not possible to compute an IRR, the project either has a positive NPV or a negative NPV for all possible discount rates. In this example, the NPV is always positive.

Mutually Exclusive Projects

The other situation in which the IRR can lead to incorrect decisions is when capital projects are mutually exclusive – that is, when accepting one project means rejecting the other. For example, suppose you own a small store in the business district of Frankfurt that is currently vacant. You are looking at two business opportunities: opening an upscale coffee house or opening a copy centre. Clearly, you cannot pursue both projects at the same location; these two projects are mutually exclusive.

When you have mutually exclusive projects, how do you select the best alternative? If you are using the NPV method, the answer is easy. You select the project that has the highest NPV because it will increase the value of the firm by the largest amount. If you are using the IRR method, it would seem logical to select the project with the highest IRR. In this case, though, the logic is wrong! You cannot tell which mutually exclusive project to select just by looking at the projects' IRRs.

We will consider another example to illustrate the problem. The cash flows for two projects, A and B, are as follows:

Year	Project A	Project B
0	−€100	−€100
1	50	20
2	40	30
3	30	50
4	30	65

The IRR is 20.7% for project A and 19.0% for project B. Because the two projects are mutually exclusive, only one project can be accepted. If you were following the IRR decision rule, you would accept project A. However, as you will see, it turns out that project B might be the better choice.

The following table shows the NPVs for the two projects at several discount rates:

Discount Rate	NPV of Project A	NPV of Project B
0%	€50.0	€65.0
5%	34.5	42.9
10%	21.5	24.9
13%	14.8	15.7
15%	10.6	10.1
20%	1.3	−2.2
25%	−6.8	−12.6
30%	−13.7	−21.3
IRR	20.7%	19.0%

Notice that the project with the higher NPV depends on what rate of return is used to discount the cash flows. Our example shows a conflict in ranking order between the IRR and NPV methods at discount rates between 0% and 13%. In this range, project B has the lower IRR but it has the higher NPV and should be the project selected. If the discount rate is above 15%, however, project A has the higher NPV as well as the higher IRR. In this range there is no conflict between the two evaluation methods.

Now take a look at Exhibit 10.11, which shows the NPV profiles for projects A and B. As you can see, there is a point, called the **crossover point**, at which the NPV profiles for projects A and B intersect. The crossover point here is at a discount rate of 14.3%. For any cost of capital above 14.3%, the NPV for project A is higher than that for project B; thus, project A should be selected if its NPV is positive. For any cost of capital below the crossover point, project B should be selected.

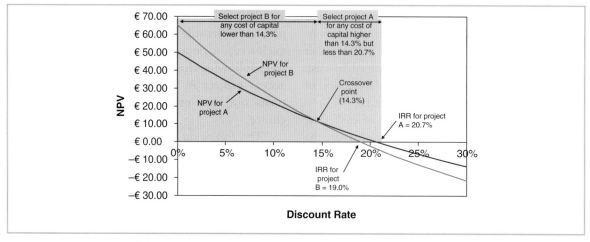

Exhibit 10.11: NPV Profiles for Two Mutually Exclusive Projects
The NPV profiles for two projects often cross over each other. When evaluating mutually exclusive projects, it is helpful to know where this crossover point is. For projects A and B in the exhibit, the crossover point is 14.3%. For any cost of capital above 14.3% but below 20.7%, the NPV for project A is higher than that for project B and is positive; thus, project A should be selected. For any cost of capital below the crossover point, the NPV of project B is higher and project B should be selected.

> **Crossover point**
>
> the discount rate at which the NPV profiles of two projects cross and, thus, at which the NPVs of the projects are equal

Another conflict involving mutually exclusive projects concerns comparisons of projects that have significantly different costs. The IRR does not adjust for these differences in size. What the IRR gives us is a rate of return on each unit of currency invested. In contrast, the NPV method computes the total monetary value created by the project. The difference in results can be significant, as can be seen in Decision-Making Example 10.2.

Decision-Making Example 10.2

The Lemonade Stand versus the Mini Market Store

Situation: Suppose you work for an entrepreneur who owns a number of small businesses in Barcelona, Spain, as well as a small piece of property near Barcelona University, which he believes would be an ideal site for a student-oriented mini market store. His 12-year-old son, who happens to be in the office after school, says he has a better idea: his father should open a lemonade stand. Your boss tells you to find the

NPV and IRR for both projects, assuming a 10% discount rate. After collecting data, you present the following analysis:

Year	Lemonade Stand	Mini Market Store
0	−€1 000	−€1 000 000
1	850	372 000
2	850	372 000
3	850	372 000
4	850	372 000
IRR	76.2%	18.0%
NPV	€1 694	€179 190

Assuming the projects are mutually exclusive, which should be selected?

Decision: Your boss, who favours the IRR method, looks at the analysis and declares his son a genius. The IRR decision rule suggests that the lemonade stand, with its 76.2% rate of return, is the project to choose! You point out that the goal of capital budgeting is to select projects or combinations of projects that maximise the value of the firm, his business. The mini market store adds by far the greater value: €179 190 compared with only €1694 for the lemonade stand. Although the lemonade stand has a high rate of return, its small size precludes it from being competitive against the larger project.[2]

Modified Internal Rate of Return (MIRR)

A major weakness of the IRR method compared with the NPV method concerns the rate at which the cash flows generated by a capital project are reinvested. The NPV method assumes that cash flows from a project are reinvested at the cost of capital, whereas the IRR technique assumes they are reinvested at the IRR. Determining which is the better assumption depends on which rate better represents the rate that firms can actually earn when they reinvest a project's cash flows over time. It is generally believed that the cost of capital, which is often lower than the IRR, better reflects the rate that firms are likely to earn. Using the IRR may thus involve overly optimistic assumptions regarding reinvestment rates.

To eliminate the reinvestment rate assumption of the IRR, some practitioners prefer to calculate the **modified internal rate of return (MIRR)**. In this approach, each operating cash flow is converted to a future value at the end of the project's life, compounded at the cost of capital. These values are then summed up to get the project's *terminal value (TV)*. The MIRR is the interest rate that equates the project's cost (PV_{cost}), or cash outflows, with the future value of the project's cash inflows at the end of the project (PV_{TV}).[3] Because each future value is computed using the cost of capital as the interest rate, the reinvestment rate problem is eliminated.

> **Modified internal rate of return (MIRR)**
>
> an internal rate of return (IRR) measure which assumes that cash inflows are reinvested at the opportunity cost of capital until the end of the project

We can set up the equation for the MIRR in the same way we set up Equation (10.4) for the IRR:

$$PV(\text{Cost of the project}) = PV(\text{Cash inflows})$$
$$PV_{cost} = PV_{TV}$$
$$PV_{cost} = \frac{TV}{(1 + MIRR)^n}$$

$$(10.5)$$

To compute the MIRR, we have to make two preliminary calculations. First, we need to calculate the value of PV_{cost}, which is the present value of the cash outflows that make up the investment cost of the project. Since for most capital projects, the investment cost cash flows are incurred at the beginning of the project, $t = 0$, there is often no need to calculate a present value. If investment costs are incurred over time ($t > 0$), then the cash flows must be discounted at the cost of capital for the appropriate time period.

Second, we need to compute the terminal value (TV). To do this, we find the future value of each operating cash flow at the end of the project's life, compounded at the cost of capital. We then sum up these future values to get the project's TV. Mathematically, the TV can be expressed as:

$$TV = CF_1 \times (1+k)^{n-1} + CF_2 \times (1+k)^{n-2} + \cdots$$
$$+ CF_n \times (1+k)^{n-n}$$
$$= \sum_{t=1}^{n} CF_t \times (1+k)^{n-t}$$

where:

TV = the project's terminal value
CF_t = cash flow from operations in period t
k = the cost of capital
n = the project life

Once we have computed the values of PV_{cost} and TV, we use Equation (10.5) to compute the MIRR.

To illustrate, let us return to the Volkswagen example shown in Exhibit 10.8. Recall that the cost of the project is €560, incurred at $t = 0$ and that the discount rate is 12%. To determine the MIRR for the project, we start by calculating the terminal value of the cash flows, as shown on the following time line:

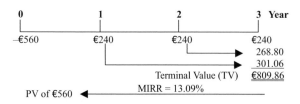

The terminal value of €809.86 equals the sum of the €240 in year 1 compounded at 12% for two years plus the €240 in year 2 compounded at 12% for 1 year plus the €240 in year 3. Mathematically, this calculation is:

$$TV = CF_1 \times (1+k)^{n-1} + CF_2 \times (1+k)^{n-2} + \cdots$$
$$+ CF_n \times (1+k)^{n-n}$$
$$= €240 \times (1.12)^2 + €240 \times (1.12) + €240$$
$$= €809.86$$

With the information that the cost of the project is €560 and the TV is €809.86, we can

calculate the MIRR using Equation (10.5):

$$PV_{cost} = \frac{TV}{(1+MIRR)^n}$$
$$€560 = \frac{€809.86}{(1+MIRR)^3}$$
$$(1+MIRR)^3 = \frac{€809.86}{€560} = 1.4462$$
$$(1+MIRR) = \sqrt[3]{(1.4462)} = 1.1309$$
$$MIRR = 1.1309 - 1 = 0.1309 = 13.09\%$$

At 13.09%, the MIRR is higher than Volkswagen's cost of capital of 12%, so the project should be accepted.

IRR versus NPV: A Final Comment

The IRR method, as noted, is an important alternative to the NPV method. As we have seen, it accounts for the time value of money, which is not true of methods such as the payback period and accounting rate of return. Furthermore, the IRR technique has great intuitive appeal. Many business practitioners are in the habit of thinking in terms of rates of return, whether the rates relate to their equity portfolios or their firms' capital expenditures. To these practitioners, the IRR method just seems to make sense. Indeed, we suspect that the IRR's popularity with business managers results more from its simple intuitive appeal than from its merit.

> **WEB**
>
> To read an article that warns finance managers using the IRR about the method's pitfalls, visit: www.cfo.com/printable/article.cfm/3304945?f=options.

On the downside, we have seen that the IRR method has several flaws. One of these can be eliminated by using the MIRR. Nevertheless, we believe that the NPV should be the primary method used to make capital budgeting decisions. Decisions made by the NPV method are consistent with the goal of maximising the value of the firm's shares, and the NPV tells management the amount by which each project is expected to increase the value of the firm.

Review of Internal Rate of Return (IRR)

Decision Rule:

IRR > Cost of capital ⇨ Accept the project.
IRR < Cost of capital ⇨ Reject the project.

Key Advantages	Key Disadvantages
1. Intuitively easy to understand.	With non-conventional cash flows, IRR approach can yield no usable answer or multiple answers.
2. Based on discounted cash flow technique.	A lower IRR can be better if a cash inflow is followed by cash outflows.
3.	With mutually exclusive projects, IRR can lead to incorrect investment decisions.

Before You Go On

1. What is the IRR method?
2. In capital budgeting, what is a conventional cash flow pattern?
3. Why should the NPV method be the primary decision tool used in making capital investment decisions?

CAPITAL BUDGETING IN PRACTICE

Learning Objective 6
Explain the benefits of a post-audit review of a capital project.

Capital expenditures are major investments for firms and for economies as a whole. For the second quarter of 2009, the gross fixed capital formation for the 16 countries of the Eurozone was €448.6 billion and for the year 2008, it was €20 020.8 billion.

Capital investments also represent large expenditures for individual firms, though the amount spent can vary widely from year to year. For example, over the last several years, the European Aeronautic Defence and Space Company NV (EADS), the parent company of Airbus described in the opening vignette, has been spending billions of euros in capital expenditure as the following table shows:

	Y2004	Y2005	Y2006	Y2007	Y2008
Capital expenditure (€ millions)	€3673	€2858	€2855	€2058	€1837
Capital expenditure as a percentage of Sales	11.56	8.36	7.24	5.26	4.25
Capital expenditure as a percentage of Total Assets	18.80	13.17	12.08	8.27	7.67

The large expenditures between 2004 and 2007 relate to the investments required to launch the A380 Airbus, although EADS has invested heavily in other projects, such as the A400M military transport. Given the large sums and the strategic importance of capital expenditures, it should come as no surprise that corporate managers spend considerable time and energy analysing them.

EXHIBIT 10.12

CAPITAL BUDGETING TECHNIQUES USED BY BUSINESS FIRMS

Capital Budgeting Tool	US*	UK	Netherlands	Germany	France
Payback period	56.7	69.2	64.7	50.0	50.9
Accounting rate of return (ARR)	20.3	38.1	25.0	32.2	16.1
Internal rate of return (IRR)	75.6	53.1	56.0	42.2	44.1
Net present value (NPV)	74.9	47.0	70.0	47.6	35.1

*Data for the USA relates to 1999; data for European firms was collected in 2002.

Source: D. Brounen, A. de Jong and K. Koedij, 'Corporate finance in Europe: confronting theory with practice', *Financial Management*, Winter 2004. Reproduced by permission of Wiley-Blackwell.

The exhibit summarises evidence that examined the use of capital budgeting techniques by European and United States businesses using the same method of investigation. While NPV was the most used technique in the USA, it was only the most popular technique in the Netherlands. In the other countries surveyed the payback period was the dominant technique. Surprisingly, the accounting rate of return method was used by over a quarter of respondents in Europe.

Practitioners' Methods of Choice

Given the importance of capital budgeting, over the years a number of surveys have asked financial managers what techniques they actually use in making capital investment decisions. Exhibit 10.12, which summarises the results from a large-scale survey of European CFOs, shows the percentage of firms that use the different techniques.

Exhibit 10.12 shows that, rather surprisingly, the payback period is the most frequently used capital budgeting tool. In comparison, for the USA, it is only the third most popular tool after IRR and NPV, which are used regularly by three-quarters of the firms surveyed. Amongst European firms the use of discounting techniques is much less common. Only the Netherlands shows a marked preference for NPV, with 70% of firms using this method regularly, although payback is the second most popular method. In the other countries surveyed, the choice of NPV versus IRR differs depending on the country, with the UK and France showing a slight preference for IRR over NPV and Germany the opposite. However, the use of the techniques is not as advanced in these countries, with the highest utilisation rate being for IRR in the UK at just over half of firms and the lowest in Germany where only four in ten firms use the technique. The results also indicate that financial managers use multiple capital budgeting tools for analysing capital projects.

Ongoing and Post-Audit Reviews

Management should systematically review the status of all ongoing capital projects and perform post-audit reviews on all completed capital projects. In a **post-audit review**, management compares the actual performance of a project with what was projected in the capital budgeting proposal. For example, suppose a new passenger aircraft variant was expected to earn a 20% IRR but the product's actual IRR turned out to be 9%. A post-audit examination would determine why the project failed to achieve its expected financial goals. Project reviews keep all people involved in the capital budgeting process honest because they know that the project and their performance will be reviewed and that they will be held accountable for the results.

> ### Post-audit review
>
> an audit to compare actual project results with the results projected in the capital budgeting proposal

Managers should also conduct *ongoing reviews* of capital projects in progress. Such a review should challenge the business plan, including the cash flow projections and the operating cost assumptions. For example, Airbus undoubtedly has periodically reviewed the viability of its A380 project and made adjustments to reflect changing market conditions for wide-bodied aircraft. Business plans are management's best estimates of future events at the time they are prepared but as new information becomes available, the decision to undertake a capital project and the nature of that project must be reassessed.

Management must also evaluate people responsible for implementing a capital project. They should monitor whether the project's revenues and expenses are meeting projections. If the project is not at plan, the difficult task for management is to determine whether the problem is a flawed plan or poor execution by the implementation team. Good plans can fail if they are poorly executed at the operating level.

Before You Go On

1. What do you think accounts for the prevalence of the payback period as the dominant capital budgeting tool used by European companies?

SUMMARY OF LEARNING OBJECTIVES

1. **Discuss why capital budgeting decisions are the most important investment decisions made by a firm's management.**

   Capital budgeting is the process by which management decides which productive assets the firm should invest in. Because capital expenditures involve large amounts of money, are critical to achieving the firm's strategic plan, define the firm's line of business over the long term and determine the firm's profitability for years to come, they are considered the most important investment decisions made by management.

2. **Explain the benefits of using the net present value (NPV) method to analyse capital expenditure decisions and be able to calculate the NPV for a capital project.**

   The net present value (NPV) method leads to better investment decisions than other techniques because the NPV method does the following: (1) it uses the discounted cash flow valuation approach, which accounts for the time value of money, and (2) provides a direct measure of how much a capital project is expected to increase the value of the firm. Thus, NPV is consistent with the top management goal of maximising shareholder value. NPV calculations are described, see also Learning by Doing Application 10.1.

3. **Describe the strengths and weaknesses of the payback period as a capital expenditure decision-making tool and be able to compute the payback period for a capital project.**

   The payback period is the length of time it will take for the cash flows from a project to recover the cost of the project. The payback period is widely used, mainly because it is simple to apply and easy to understand. It also provides a simple measure of liquidity risk because it tells management how quickly the firm will get its money back. The payback period has a number of shortcomings, however. For one thing, the payback period, as most commonly computed, ignores the time value of money. We can overcome this objection by using discounted cash flows to calculate the payback period. Regardless of how the payback period is calculated, however, it fails to take account of cash flows recovered after the payback period. Thus, the payback period is biased in favour of short-lived projects. Also, the hurdle rate used to identify what payback period is acceptable is arbitrarily determined. Payback period calculations are described, see also Learning by Doing Application 10.2.

4. **Explain why the accounting rate of return (ARR) is not recommended as a capital expenditure decision-making tool.**

The ARR is based on accounting numbers, such as book value and net income, rather than cash flow data. As such, it is not a true rate of return. Instead of discounting a project's cash flows over time, it simply gives us a number based on average figures from the income statement and balance sheet. Furthermore, as with the payback method, there is no economic rationale for establishing the hurdle rate. Finally, the ARR does not account for the size of the projects when a choice between two projects of different sizes must be made.

5. **Be able to compute the internal rate of return (IRR) for a capital project, and discuss the conditions under which the IRR technique and the NPV technique produce different results.**

The IRR is the expected rate of return for an investment project; it is calculated as the discount rate that equates the present value of a project's expected cash inflows to the present value of the project's outflows – in other words, as the discount rate at which the NPV is equal to zero. Calculations are shown, see also Learning by Doing Application 10.3. If a project's IRR is greater than the required rate of return, the cost of capital, the project is accepted. The IRR rule often gives the same investment decision for a project as the NPV rule. However, the IRR method does have operational pitfalls that can lead to incorrect decisions. Specifically, when a project's cash flows are unconventional, the IRR calculation may yield no solution or more than one IRR. In addition, the IRR technique cannot be used to rank projects that are mutually exclusive because the project with the highest IRR may not be the project that would add the greatest value to the firm if accepted – that is, the project with the highest NPV.

6. **Explain the benefits of a post-audit review of a capital project.**

Post-audit reviews of capital projects allow management to determine whether the project's goals were met and to quantify the benefits or costs of the project. By conducting these reviews, managers can avoid similar mistakes and possibly better recognise opportunities.

SUMMARY OF KEY EQUATIONS

Equation	Description	Formula
(10.1)	Net present value	$NPV = NCF_0 + \dfrac{NCF_1}{1+k} + \dfrac{NCF_2}{(1+k)^2} + \cdots + \dfrac{NCF_n}{(1+k)^n}$ $= \sum_{t=0}^{n} \dfrac{NCF_t}{(1+k)^t}$
(10.2)	Payback period	$PB = \text{Years before cost recovery} + \dfrac{\text{Remaining cost to recover}}{\text{Cash flow during year}}$

(10.3)	Accounting rate of return	$\text{ARR} = \dfrac{\text{Average net income}}{\text{Average book value}}$
(10.4)	Internal rate of return	$\text{NPV} = \displaystyle\sum_{t=0}^{n} \dfrac{\text{NCF}_t}{(1 + \text{IRR})^t} = 0$
(10.5)	Modified internal rate of return	$\text{PV}_{\text{cost}} = \dfrac{\text{TV}}{(1 + \text{MIRR})^n}$

SELF-STUDY PROBLEMS

10.1. GreenTech Manufacturing plc is evaluating two forklift systems to use in its plant that produces the towers for a windmill power farm. The costs and the cash flows from these systems are shown here. If the company uses a 12% discount rate for all projects, determine which forklift system should be purchased using the net present value (NPV) approach.

	Year 0	Year 1	Year 2	Year 3
Caterpillar Forklifts	−€3 123 450	€979 225	€1 358 886	€2 111 497
Hyster Forklifts	−€4 137 410	€875 236	€1 765 225	€2 865 110

10.2. Markameer Baggaren NV has invested €100 000 in a project that will produce cash flows of €45 000, €37 500 and €42 950 over the next three years. Find the payback period for the project.

10.3. Les Artisanats de Limoges SA is evaluating two independent capital projects that will each cost the company €250 000. The two projects will provide the following cash flows:

Year	Project A	Project B
1	€80 750	€32 450
2	93 450	76 125
3	40 235	153 250
4	145 655	96 110

Which project will be chosen if the company's payback criterion is three years? What if the company accepts all projects as long as the payback period is less than five years?

10.4. Terrell Towels plc is looking into purchasing a machine for its business that will cost £117 250 and will be depreciated on a straight-line basis over a five-year period.

The sales and expenses (excluding depreciation) for the next five years are shown in the following table. The company's tax rate is 34%.

	Year 1	Year 2	Year 3	Year 4	Year 5
Sales	£123 450	£176 875	£242 455	£255 440	£267 125
Expenses	£137 410	£126 488	£141 289	£143 112	£133 556

The company will accept all projects that provide an accounting rate of return (ARR) of at least 45%. Should the company accept this project?

10.5. Refer to Problem 10.1. Compute the IRR for each of the two systems. Is the choice different from the one determined by NPV?

SOLUTIONS TO SELF-STUDY PROBLEMS

10.1. NPVs for two forklift systems.
NPV for Caterpillar Forklifts:

$$\text{NPV} = \sum_{t=0}^{n} \frac{\text{NCF}_t}{(1+k)^t}$$

$$= -€3\,123\,450 + \frac{€970\,225}{1 + 0.12}$$

$$+ \frac{€1\,358\,886}{(1.12)^2} + \frac{€2\,111\,497}{(1.12)^3}$$

$$= -€3\,123\,450 + €874\,308$$

$$+ €1\,083\,296 + €1\,502\,922$$

$$= €337\,076$$

NPV for Hyster Forklifts:

$$\text{NPV} = \sum_{t=0}^{n} \frac{\text{NCF}_t}{(1+k)^t}$$

$$= -€4\,137\,410 + \frac{€875\,236}{1 + 0.12}$$

$$+ \frac{€1\,765\,225}{(1.12)^2} + \frac{€2\,865\,110}{(1.12)^3}$$

$$= -€4\,137\,410 + €781\,461$$

$$+ €1\,407\,227 + €2\,039\,329$$

$$= €90\,607$$

GreenTech should purchase the Caterpillar forklift since it has a larger NPV.

10.2. Payback period for the Markameer Baggaren project:

Year	CF	Cumulative Cash Flow
0	(€100 000)	(€100 000)
1	45 000	(55 000)
2	37 500	(17 500)
3	42 950	25 450

Payback period = Years before cost recovery

$$+ \frac{\text{Remaining cost to recover}}{\text{Cash flow during the year}}$$

$$= 2 + \frac{€17\,500}{€42\,950} = 2.41 \text{ years}$$

10.3. Payback periods for Les Artisanats de Limoges projects A and B:

Project A

Year	Cash Flow	Cumulative Cash Flows
0	(€250 000)	(€250 000)
1	80 750	(169 250)
2	93 450	(75 800)
3	40 235	(35 565)
4	145 655	110 090

Project B

Year	Cash Flow	Cumulative Cash Flows
0	(€250 000)	(€250 000)
1	32 450	(217 550)
2	76 125	(141 425)
3	153 250	11 825
4	96 110	107 935

Payback period for project A:

Payback period = Years before cost recovery

$$+ \frac{\text{Remaining cost to recover}}{\text{Cash flow during the year}}$$

$$= 3 + \frac{€35\,565}{€145\,655}$$

$$= 3.24 \text{ years}$$

Payback period for project B:

Payback period = Years before cost recovery

$$+ \frac{\text{Remaining cost to recover}}{\text{Cash flow during the year}}$$

$$= 2 + \frac{€141\,425}{€153\,250}$$

$$= 2.92 \text{ years}$$

If the payback period is three years, project B will be chosen. If the payback period is five years, both A and B will be chosen.

10.4. Evaluation of Terrell Towels project:

	Year 1	Year 2	Year 3	Year 4	Year 5
Sales	£123 450	£176 875	£242 455	£255 440	£267 125
Expenses	137 410	126 488	141 289	143 112	133 556
Depreciation	23 450	23 450	23 450	23 450	23 450
EBIT	(£37 410)	£26 937	£77 716	£88 878	£110 119
Taxes (34%)	12 719	9 159	26 423	30 219	37,440
Net Income	(£24 691)	£17 778	£51 293	£58 659	£72 679
Beginning Book Value	117 250	93 800	70 350	46 900	23 450
Less: Depreciation	(23 450)	(23 450)	(23 450)	(23 450)	(23 450)
Ending Book Value	£93 800	£70 350	£46 900	£23 450	£0

$$\text{Average net income} = (-€24\,691 + €17\,778 + €51\,293 + €58\,659 + €72\,679)/5 = €35\,143.60$$
$$\text{Average book value} = (€93\,800 + €70\,350 + €46\,900 + €23\,450 + €0)/5 = €46\,900.00$$
$$\text{Accounting rate of return} = €35\,143.60/€46\,900.00 = 74.93\%$$

The company should accept the project.

10.5. IRRs for the two forklift systems.
Caterpillar Forklifts:
First compute the IRR by the trial-and-error approach.

NPV(Caterpillar) = €337 075 > 0
Use a higher discount rate to get NPV = 0!
At $k = 15\%$:

$$= -€3\,123\,450 + \frac{€970\,225}{1 + 0.15} + \frac{€1\,358\,886}{(1.15)^2}$$
$$+ \frac{€2\,111\,497}{(1.15)^3}$$
$$= -€3\,123\,450 + €851\,500$$
$$+ €1\,027\,513 + €1\,388\,344$$
$$= €143\,907$$

Try a higher rate. At $k = 17\%$:

$$= -€3123\,450 + \frac{€970\,225}{1 + 0.17} + \frac{€1\,358\,886}{(1.17)^2}$$
$$+ \frac{€2\,111\,497}{(1.17)^3}$$
$$= -€3\,123\,450 + €836\,944 + €992\,685$$
$$+ €1\,318\,357 = €24\,536$$

Try a higher rate. At $k = 17.5\%$:

$$= -€3\,123\,450 + \frac{€970\,225}{1 + 0.175} + \frac{€1\,358\,886}{(1.175)^2}$$
$$+ \frac{€2\,111\,497}{(1.175)^3}$$

$$= -€3\,123\,450 + €833\,383 + €984\,254$$
$$+ €1\,301\,598 = -€4215$$

Thus, the IRR for Caterpillar is less than 17.5%. Using interpolation, we find that the exact rate is 17.43%:

$$i_{unknown} = i_{low} + \frac{(\text{Value}_{low\,i} - \text{Value}_{unknown\,i})}{(\text{Value}_{low\,i} - \text{Value}_{high\,i})}$$
$$\times (i_{high} - i_{low})$$

$$\text{IRR} = 17\% + \frac{€24\,536 - 0}{€24\,536 - -€4215}$$
$$(17.5\% - 17\%)$$
$$= 17\% + 0.8534 \times 0.5\%$$
$$= 17\% + 0.43\% = 17.43\%$$

Hyster Forklifts:
First compute the IRR using the trial-and-error approach.

NPV(Hyster) = €90 606 > 0

Use a higher discount rate to get NPV = 0!

At $k = 15\%$:

$$= -€4\,137\,410 + \frac{€875\,236}{1 + 0.15} + \frac{€1\,765\,225}{(1.15)^2}$$

$$+ \frac{€2\,865\,110}{(1.15)^3}$$

$$= -€4\,137\,410 + €761\,075 + €1\,334\,764$$
$$+ €1\,883\,856 = -€157\,715$$

Applying interpolation, we get:

$$i_{\text{unknown}} = i_{\text{low}} + \frac{(\text{Value}_{\text{low } i} - \text{Value}_{\text{unknown } i})}{(\text{Value}_{\text{low } i} - \text{Value}_{\text{high } i})}$$

$$\times (i_{\text{high}} - i_{\text{low}})$$

$$\text{IRR} = 12\% + \frac{€90\,607 - €0}{€90\,607 - -€157\,715}$$

$$(15\% - 12\%)$$

$$= 12\% + 0.3649 \times 3\% = 12\%$$

$$+ 1.095\% = 13.1\%$$

Thus, the IRR for Hyster is 13.1%. The exact rate is 13.06%. Based on the IRR, we would still pick the Caterpillar over the Hyster forklift systems.

CRITICAL THINKING QUESTIONS

10.1. Explain why the cost of capital is referred to as the 'hurdle' rate in capital budgeting.

10.2. **a.** A company is building a new plant on the outskirts of a small town. The town has offered to donate the land and, as part of the agreement, the company will have to build an access road from the main highway to the plant. How will the project of building the road be classified in capital budgeting analysis?

b. Systèmes Informatique SA is considering two projects: a plant expansion and a new computer system for the firm's production department. Classify each of these projects as independent, mutually exclusive or contingent projects and explain your reasoning.

c. Your firm is currently considering the upgrading of the operating systems of all the firm's computers. The firm can choose the Linux operating system that a local computer services firm has offered to install and maintain. Microsoft has

also put in a bid to install the new Windows 7 operating system for businesses. What type of project is this?

10.3. In the context of capital budgeting, what is 'capital rationing'?

10.4. Explain why we use discounted cash flows instead of actual market price data.

10.5. **a.** A firm takes on a project that would earn a return of 12%. If the appropriate cost of capital is also 12%, did the firm make the right decision? Explain.

b. What is the impact on the firm if it accepts a project with a negative NPV?

10.6. Identify the weaknesses of the payback period method.

10.7. What are the strengths and weaknesses of the accounting rate of return approach?

10.8. Under what circumstances might the IRR and NPV approaches have conflicting results?

10.9. A company estimates that an average-risk project has a cost of capital of 8%, a below-average-risk project has a cost of capital of 6% and an above-average-risk project has a cost of capital of 10%. Which of the following independent projects should the company accept? Project A has below-average risk and a return of 6.5%. Project B has above-average risk and a return of 9%. Project C has average risk and a return of 7%.

10.10. Oporto Construção SA has an overall (composite) cost of capital of 12%. This cost of capital reflects the cost of capital for an Oporto Construção project with average risk. However, the firm takes on projects of various risk levels. The company experience suggests that low-risk projects have a cost of capital of 10% and high-risk

projects have a cost of capital of 15%. Which of the following projects should the company select to maximise shareholder wealth?

Project	Expected Return	Risk
1. Single-family homes	13%	Low
2. Multi-family residential	12	Average
3. Commercial	18	High
4. Single-family homes	9	Low
5. Commercial	13	High

QUESTIONS AND PROBLEMS

Basic

10.1. **Net present value:** Riggs plc is planning to spend £650 000 on a new marketing campaign. It believes that this action will result in additional cash flows of £325 000 over the next three years. If the discount rate is 17.5%, what is the NPV on this project?

10.2. **Net present value:** Kluwer AG is looking to add a new machine at a cost of €4 133 250. The company expects this equipment will lead to cash flows of €814 322, €863 275, €937 250, €1 017 112, €1 212 960 and €1 225 000 over the next six years. If the appropriate discount rate is 15%, what is the NPV of this investment?

10.3. **Net present value:** Croissant D'Or SA is planning to replace some existing machinery in its plant. The cost of the new equipment and the resulting cash flows are shown in the accompanying table. If the firm uses an 18% discount rate for projects like this, should the firm go ahead with the project?

Year	Cash Flow
0	−€3 300 000
1	875 123
2	966 222
3	1 145 000
4	1 250 399
5	1 504 445

10.4. **Net present value:** Confettiere Agostina, a bonbon producer, is looking to purchase a new jellybean-making machine at a cost of €312 500. The company projects that the cash flows from this investment will be €121 450 for the next seven years. If the appropriate discount rate is 14%, what is the NPV for the project?

10.5. **Payback:** Broderie de Bretagne SA is purchasing machinery at a cost of €3 768 966. The company expects, as a result, cash flows of €979 225, €1 158 886 and €1 881 497 over the next three years. What is the payback period?

10.6. **Payback:** Norge Spesialiteter ASA just purchased inventory-management computer software at a cost of NKr 1 645 276. Cost savings from the investment over the next six years will be reflected in the following cash flow stream: NKr 212 455, NKr 292 333, NKr 387 479, NKr 516 345, NKr 645 766 and NKr 618 325. What is the payback period on this investment?

10.7. Payback: Nakamichi Bank has made an investment in banking software at a cost of ¥1 875 000 000. The institution expects productivity gains and cost savings over the next several years. If the firm is expected to generate cash flows of ¥586 212 000, ¥713 277 000, ¥431 199 000 and ¥318 697 000 over the next four years, what is the investment's payback period?

10.8. Average accounting rate of return (ARR): Klariol AG is expecting to generate after-tax income of €63 435 over each of the next three years. The average book value of their equipment over that period will be €212 500. If the firm's acceptance decision on any project is based on an ARR of 37.5%, should this project be accepted?

10.9. Internal rate of return: Refer to Problem 10.4. What is the IRR that Confettiere Agostina can expect on this project?

10.10. Internal rate of return: Holberg Reisen Hotels AG, a resort company, is refurbishing one of its hotels at a cost of €7.8 million. The firm expects that this will lead to additional cash flows of €1.8 million for the next six years. What is the IRR of this project? If the appropriate cost of capital is 12%, should it go ahead with this project?

Intermediate

10.11. Net present value: Copenhagen Info-systems A/S is investigating two computer systems. The Alpha 8300 costs DKr 31 223 000 and will generate annual cost savings of DKr 13 455 000 over the next five years. The Beta 2100 system costs DKr 37 500 000 and will produce cost savings of DKr 11 250 000 in the first three years and then DKr 20 million for the next two years. If the company's discount rate for similar projects is 14%, what is the NPV for the two systems? Which one should be chosen based on the NPV?

10.12. Net present value: Briarcrest Condiments plc of Galway, Ireland, is a spice-making firm. Recently, it developed a new process for producing spices. This calls for acquiring machinery that would cost €1 968 450. The machine will have a life of five years and will produce cash flows as shown in the table. What is the NPV if the discount rate is 15.9%?

Year	Cash Flow
1	€512 496
2	−242 637
3	814 558
4	887 225
5	712 642

10.13. Net present value: Picard Submersibles SA is expanding its product line and its production capacity. The costs and expected cash flows of the two independent projects are given in the following table. The firm uses a discount rate of 16.4% for such projects.

a. Are these projects independent or mutually exclusive?

b. What are the NPVs of the two projects?

c. Should both projects be accepted, or either, or neither? Explain your reasoning.

Year	Product Line Expansion	Production Capacity Expansion
0	−€2 575 000	−€8 137 250
1	600 000	2 500 000
2	875 000	2 500 000
3	875 000	2 500 000
4	875 000	2 500 000
5	875 000	2 500 000

10.14. Net present value: Thanet Mills plc is evaluating two heating systems. Costs and projected energy savings are given in the following table. The firm uses 11.5% to discount such project cash flows. Which system should be chosen?

Year	System 100	System 200
0	−£1 750 000	−£1 735 000
1	275 223	750 000
2	512 445	612 500
3	648 997	550 112
4	875 000	384 226

10.15. Payback: Creative Solutions, Inc., has invested $4 615 300 in equipment. The firm uses payback period criteria of not accepting any project that takes more than four years to recover costs. The company anticipates cash flows of $644 386, $812 178, $943 279, $1 364 997, $2 616 300 and $2 225 375 over the next six years. Does this investment meet the firm's payback criteria?

10.16. Discounted payback: Tempus Fabricerend NV is evaluating two projects. The company uses payback criteria of three years or less. Project A has a cost of €912 855 and project B's cost will be €1 175 000. Cash flows from both projects are given in the following table. What are their discounted payback periods and which will be accepted with a discount rate of 8%?

Year	Project A	Project B
1	€86 212	€586 212
2	313 562	413 277
3	427 594	231 199
4	285 552	

10.17. Payback: Vestidos Regente SA is evaluating three competing pieces of equipment. Costs and cash flow projections for all three are given in the following table. Which would be the best choice based on payback period?

Year	Type 1	Type 2	Type 3
0	−€1 311 450	−€1 415 888	−€1 612 856
1	212 566	586 212	786 212
2	269 825	413 277	175 000
3	455 112	331 199	175 000
4	285 552	141 442	175 000
5	121 396		175 000
6			175 000

10.18. Discounted payback: Deutsche Telecom AG is investing €9 365 000 in new technologies. The company expects significant benefits in the first three years after installation (as can be seen by the cash flows) and a constant amount for four more years. What is the discounted payback period for the project assuming a discount rate of 10%?

Years	1	2	3	4–7
Cash Flows	€2 265 433	€4 558 721	€3 378 911	€1 250 000

10.19. Modified internal rate of return (MIRR): Morningside Bakeries of Edinburgh, Scotland, has recently purchased equipment at a cost of £650 000. The firm expects to generate cash flows of £275 000 in each of the next four years. The cost of capital is 14%. What is the MIRR for this project?

10.20. Modified internal rate of return (MIRR): Norges Vindu is looking to acquire a new machine that can create customised windows. The equipment will cost NKr.263 400 and will generate cash flows of NKr.85 000 over each of the next six years. If the cost of capital is 12%, what is the MIRR on this project?

10.21. Internal rate of return: Great Flights, Inc., an aviation firm, is exploring the purchase of three aircraft at a total cost of $161 million. Cash flows from leasing these aircraft are expected to build slowly as shown in the following table. What is the IRR on this project? The required rate of return is 15%.

Years	Cash Flow
1–4	$23 500 000
5–7	72 000 000
8–10	80 000 000

10.22. Internal rate of return: Compute the IRR on the following cash flow streams:
   a. An initial investment of €25 000 followed by a single cash flow of €37 450 in year 6.
   b. An initial investment of €1 million followed by a single cash flow of €1 650 000 in year 4.
   c. An initial investment of €2 million followed by cash flows of €1 650 000 and €1 250 000 in years 2 and 4, respectively

10.23. Internal rate of return: Compute the IRR for the following project cash flows.
   a. An initial outlay of €3 125 000 followed by annual cash flows of €565 325 for the next eight years.
   b. An initial investment of €33 750 followed by annual cash flows of €9430 for the next five years.
   c. An initial outlay of €10 000 followed by annual cash flows of €2500 for the next seven years.

Advanced

10.24. Kupio Sahatavara Käsittely Oy is evaluating two independent projects. The company uses a 13.8% discount rate for such projects. Cost and cash flows are shown in the table. What are the NPVs of the two projects?

Year	Project 1	Project 2
0	–€8 425 375	–€11 368 000
1	3 225 997	2 112 589
2	1 775 882	3 787 552
3	1 375 112	3 125 650
4	1 176 558	4 115 899
5	1 212 645	4 556 424
6	1 582 156	
7	1 365 882	

10.25. Refer to Problem 10.24.
   a. What are the IRRs for both projects?
   b. Does the IRR decision criterion differ from the earlier decisions?
   c. Explain how you would expect the management of Kupio Sahatavara Käsittely to decide.

10.26. Košice Dravid A.S. is currently evaluating three projects that are independent. The cost of funds can be either 13.6% or 14.8% depending on their financing plan. All three projects cost the same at €500 000. Expected cash flow streams are shown in the following table. Which projects would be accepted at a discount rate of 14.8%? What if the discount rate was 13.6%?

Year	Project 1	Project 2	Project 3
1	€0	€0	€245 125
2	125 000	0	212 336
3	150 000	500 000	112 500
4	375 000	500 000	74 000

10.27. Trabajo Impávido SA is looking to invest in two or three independent projects. The costs and the cash flows are given in the following table. The appropriate cost of capital is 14.5%. Compute the IRRs and identify the projects that will be accepted.

Year	Project 1	Project 2	Project 3
0	–€275 000	–€312 500	–€500 000
1	63 000	153 250	212 000
2	85 000	167 500	212 000
3	85 000	112 000	212 000
4	100 000		212 000

10.28. Hansel und Gretel AG is evaluating two mutually exclusive projects. Their cost of capital is 15%. Costs and cash flows are given in the following table. Which project should be accepted?

Year	Project 1	Project 2
0	−€1 250 000	−€1 250 000
1	250 000	350 000
2	350 000	350 000
3	450 000	350 000
4	500 000	350 000
5	750 000	350 000

10.29. Masai Automotive, a manufacturer of auto parts, is planning to invest in two projects. The company typically compares project returns to a cost of funds of 17%. Compute the IRRs based on the given cash flows, and state which projects will be accepted.

Year	Project 1	Project 2
0	−R 475 000	−R 500 000
1	300 000	117 500
2	110 000	181 300
3	125 000	244 112
4	140 000	278 955

10.30. EXCEL® Compute the IRR for each of the following cash flow streams:

Year	Project 1	Project 2	Project 3
0	−€10 000	−€10 000	−€10 000
1	4 750	1 650	800
2	3 300	3 890	1 200
3	3 600	5 100	2 875
4	2 100	2 750	3 400
5		800	6 600

10.31. EXCEL® Primus Lagerung Überführen AG is planning to convert an existing warehouse into a new plant that will increase its production capacity by 45%. The cost of this project will be €7 125 000. It will result in additional cash flows of €1 875 000 for the next eight years. The discount rate is 12%.
  a. What is the payback period?
  b. What is the NPV for this project?
  c. What is the IRR?

10.32. EXCEL® Quasar Tech Co. is investing $6 million in new machinery that will produce the next-generation routers. Sales to its customers will amount to $1 750 000 for the next three years and then increase to $2.4 million for three more years. The project is expected to last six years and cost the firm annually $898 620 (excluding depreciation). The machinery will be depreciated to zero by year 6 using the straight-line method. The company's tax rate is 30% and the cost of capital is 16%.
  a. What is the payback period?
  b. What is the average accounting return (ARR)?
  c. Calculate the project NPV.
  d. What is the IRR for the project?

10.33. EXCEL® Approvisionnement en Vol SA, an airline caterer, is purchasing refrigerated trucks at a total cost of €3.25 million. After-tax net income from this investment is expected to be €750 000 for the next five years. Annual depreciation expense was €650 000. The cost of capital is 17%.
  a. What is the discounted payback period?
  b. Compute the ARR.
  c. What is the NPV on this investment?
  d. Calculate the IRR.

10.34. EXCEL® Dreizack AG is evaluating two independent projects. The costs and expected cash flows are given in the following table. The cost of capital is 10%.

Year	A	B
0	−€312 500	−€395 000
1	121 450	153 552
2	121 450	158 711
3	121 450	166 220
4	121 450	132 000
5	121 450	122 000

  a. Calculate the project's NPV.
  b. Calculate the project's IRR.
  c. What is the decision based on NPV? What is the decision based on IRR? Is there a conflict?

d. If you are the decision maker for the firm, which project or projects will be accepted? Explain your reasoning.

Year	0	1	2	3	4	5
Cash Flow	−€50 000	€15 000	€15 000	€20 000	€10 000	€5000

10.35. EXCEL® Colocador de Telhas SA is looking to move to a new technology for its production. The cost of equipment will be €4 million. The discount rate is 12%. Cash flows that the firm expects to generate are as follows.

Years	CF
0	−€4 000 000
1–2	0
3–5	845 000
6–9	1 450 000

a. Compute the payback and discounted payback period for the project.

b. What is the NPV for the project? Should the firm go ahead with the project?

c. What is the IRR, and what would be the decision under the IRR?

CFA Problems

10.36. Given the following cash flows for a capital project, calculate the NPV and IRR. The required rate of return is 8%.

Year	0	1	2	3	4	5
Cash Flow	−€50 000	€15 000	€15 000	€20 000	€10 000	€5000

The NPV and IRR are:

	NPV	IRR
a.	€1905	10.9%
b.	€1905	26.0%
c.	€3379	10.9%
d.	€3379	26.0%

10.37. Given the following cash flows for a capital project, calculate its payback period and discounted payback period. The required rate of return is 8%.

The discounted payback period is:

a. 0.16 year longer than the payback period.

b. 0.80 year longer than the payback period.

c. 1.01 years longer than the payback period.

d. 1.85 years longer than the payback period.

10.38. An investment of €100 generates after-tax cash flows of €40 in year 1, €80 in year 2 and €120 in year 3. The required rate of return is 20%. The net present value is closest to

a. €42.22

b. €58.33

c. €68.52

d. €98.95

10.39. An investment of €150 000 is expected to generate an after-tax cash flow of €100 000 in one year and another €120 000 in two years. The cost of capital is 10%. What is the internal rate of return?

a. 28.19%

b. 28.39%

c. 28.59%

d. 28.79%

10.40. An investment has an outlay of 100 and after-tax cash flows of 40 annually for four years. A project enhancement increases the outlay by 15 and the annual after-tax cash flows by 5. As a result, the vertical intercept of the NPV profile of the enhanced project shifts

a. up and the horizontal intercept shifts left;

b. up and the horizontal intercept shifts right;

c. down and the horizontal intercept shifts left;

d. down and the horizontal intercept shifts right.

SAMPLE TEST PROBLEMS

10.1. Net present value: Techno Systèmes SA is considering developing new computer software. The cost of development will be €675 000 and the company expects the revenue from the sale of the software to be €195 000 for each of the next six years. If the discount rate is 14%, what is the net present value of this project?

10.2. Payback method: Parker Office Supplies is looking to replace its outdated inventory-management software. The cost of the new software will be $168 000. Cost savings is expected to be $43 500 for each of the first three years and then to drop off to $36 875 for the next two years. What is the payback period for this project?

10.3. Accounting rate of return: Frescati S.p.A. is expecting to generate after-tax income of €156 435 over each of the next three years.

The average book value of its equipment over that period will be €322 500. If the firm's acceptance decision on any project is based on an ARR of 40%, should this project be accepted?

10.4. Internal rate of return: Refer to Problem 10.1. What is the IRR on this project?

10.5. Net present value: Port de Brest needs a new overhead crane and two alternatives are available. Crane T costs €1.35 million and will produce cost savings of €765 000 for the next three years. Crane R will cost €1.675 million and will lead to annual cost savings of €815 000 for the next three years. The required rate of return is 15%. Which of the two options should Port de Brest choose based on NPV calculations, and why?

ENDNOTES

1. Although Airbus is a European company and reports its financial statements in euros, the market for commercial airliners is US dollar-denominated and prices are quoted in US dollars.
2. The solution ignores the opportunity cost of the land. As we will discuss in Chapter 11, if your boss could sell the land or use it in some other way that has value, then there is an opportunity cost associated with using it for the convenience store.
3. As we pointed out in Chapter 5, financial decision-making problems can be solved either by discounting cash flows to the beginning of the project or by using compounding to find the future value of cash flows at the end of a project's life.

CHAPTER

11

Cash Flows and Capital Budgeting

In this Chapter:

Calculating Project Cash Flows

Estimating Cash Flows in Practice

Forecasting Free Cash Flows

Special Cases (Optional)

LEARNING OBJECTIVES

1. Explain why incremental after-tax free cash flows are relevant in evaluating a project and be able to calculate them for a project.
2. Discuss the five general rules for incremental after-tax free cash flow calculations and explain why cash flows stated in nominal (real) money should be discounted using a nominal (real) discount rate.
3. Describe how distinguishing between variable and fixed costs can be useful in forecasting operating expenses.
4. Explain the concept of equivalent annual cost and be able to use it to compare projects with unequal lives, decide when to replace an existing asset and calculate the opportunity cost of using an existing asset.
5. Determine the appropriate time to disinvest an asset.

In early September 2009, Kraft Inc., the US food group, made approaches to Cadbury's, the confectionery company best known for its Dairy Milk chocolate and Trident and Dentine chewing gum, with a view to acquiring the UK-listed company at a price of about £10.2 billion ($16.8 billion). Following the announcement, Cadbury's share price rose 33% and that for Kraft fell 6% on the day when, at the same time, the US stock market rose by 1.3%. The decline in Kraft's share price represented a drop of $2.4 billion in the total value of Kraft's shares. This drop, combined with the increase in the US market, suggests that investors thought the acquisition of Cadbury's had a very large negative net present value (NPV).

When the managers at Kraft announced their interest in acquiring Cadbury's they were really announcing a £10.2 billion investment. Notwithstanding its size, this investment was viewed by stock market investors from the same perspective as any capital project that a firm might pursue. Investors tried to estimate whether the NPV of the cash flows from the proposed Cadbury's acquisition was positive or negative. The financial model that they used to evaluate this investment is the same one that you saw in Chapter 10. The decrease in the value of Kraft's shares on the day of the announcement reflected the market's estimate of the NPV from this investment proposal.[1]

In Chapter 10, we stressed understanding the NPV concept and the mechanics of discounting cash flows. This chapter focuses on *which* cash flows are discounted and *how* they are calculated and used in practice. The topics covered in this chapter are central to the goal of value creation. It is necessary to understand them in order to determine which projects have positive NPVs and which projects have negative NPVs. Only if you can do this will you be able to choose the projects that create value.

CHAPTER PREVIEW

In Chapter 10 we saw that capital budgeting involves comparing the benefits and costs associated with a project to determine whether the project creates value for shareholders. These benefits and costs are reflected in the cash flows that the project is expected to produce. The NPV is a monetary measure of the amount by which the present value of the benefits exceeds the present value of the costs. Chapters 11–13 discuss how analysts actually apply the concepts introduced in Chapter 10 in capital budgeting. This chapter and Chapter 12 focus on cash flows, while Chapter 13 covers concepts related to the discount rate.

The major focus of this chapter is on the cash flows from a project. We begin with a discussion of how to calculate the cash flows used to compute the NPV of a project and how these cash flows differ from accounting earnings. We then present five rules to follow when you calculate free cash flows. We also address some concepts that will help you better understand cash flow calculations.

Next, we discuss how analysts actually forecast a project's cash flows. Since the cash flows generated by a project will almost certainly differ from the forecasts, it is important to have a framework that helps minimise errors and ensures that forecasts are internally consistent. We discuss such a framework in this part of the chapter.

In the last section, we examine some special cases that arise in capital budgeting problems. For example, we describe how to choose between two projects that have different lives, how to determine when an existing piece of equipment should be replaced, how to determine the cost of using excess capacity for a project and when to dispose of (sell or disinvest) an asset.

CALCULATING PROJECT CASH FLOWS

We begin our discussion of cash flows in capital budgeting by describing the mechanics of cash flow calculations and the rules for estimating the cash flows for individual projects. You will see that the approach we use to calculate cash flows is similar to that used to prepare the accounting statement of cash flows discussed in Chapter 3. However, there are three very important differences.

1. Most important, the cash flows used in capital budgeting calculations are based on forecasts of *future* cash revenues, expenses and investment outlays. In contrast, the accounting statement of cash flows is a record of *past* cash flows that might not reflect what can be expected in the future.

2. The accounting statement of cash flows reports a measure of the cash flows for the firm as a whole. In capital budgeting we generally forecast cash flows associated with an individual project.

3. The capital budgeting cash flow calculation is designed to estimate total cash flows, while the accounting statement of cash flows is intended to reconcile changes in the balance sheet cash accounts (for example, bank account balances). If there are any cash outflows or inflows to or from creditors or shareholders, total cash flows will differ from the changes in the cash balances because the total cash flow calculation does not include these inflows or outflows.

BUILDING INTUITION

Capital Budgeting is Forward Looking

In capital budgeting, we estimate the NPV of the cash flows that a project is *expected to produce in the future*. In other words, all of the cash flow estimates are forward looking. This is very different from the accounting statement of cash flows, which provides a record of historical cash flows.

Incremental After-Tax Free Cash Flows

The cash flows we discount in an NPV analysis are the **incremental after-tax free cash flows** that are expected from the project. The term *incremental* refers to the fact that these cash flows reflect how much the firm's total after-tax free cash flows will change if the project is adopted. Thus, we define the incremental after-tax free cash flows (FCF) for a project as the total after-tax free cash flows the firm would produce with the project less the total after-tax free cash flows the firm would produce without the project:

$$FCF_{Project} = FCF_{Firm\ with\ project} - FCF_{Firm\ without\ project} \quad (11.1)$$

In other words, $FCF_{Project}$ equals the net effect the project will have on the firm's cash revenues, costs, taxes and investment outlays. This is what shareholders care about.

> ## Incremental after-tax free cash flows
>
> the difference between the total after-tax free cash flows at a firm with a project and the total after-tax free cash flows at the same firm without that project; a measure of a project's total impact on the free cash flows at a firm

Throughout the rest of this chapter, we will refer to the total incremental after-tax free cash flows associated with a project simply as the FCF from the project. For convenience, we will drop the 'Project' subscript from the FCF in Equation (11.1).

The FCF for a project is what we generically referred to as NCF in Chapter 10. The term *free cash flows*, which is commonly used in practice, refers to the fact that the firm is free to distribute these cash flows to creditors and shareholders because these are the cash flows that are left over after a firm has made the necessary investments in working capital and long-term assets. The cash flows associated with financing a project (cash outflows or inflows to or from creditors or shareholders) are not included in the FCF calculation because, as we will discuss in Chapter 13, these are accounted for in the discount rate that is used in an NPV analysis. All of these points will become clearer as we discuss the FCF calculation next.

The FCF Calculation

The FCF calculation is illustrated in Exhibit 11.1. We will start with an overall review of how the calculation is done. After that, we will look more closely at details of the calculation.

When we calculate the FCFs for a project, we first compute the **incremental cash flow from operations (CF Opns)** for each year during the project's life. This is the cash flow that the project is expected to generate after all operating expenses and taxes have been paid. To obtain the FCF, we then subtract the **incremental capital expenditures (Cap Exp)** and the **incremental additions to working capital (Add WC)** required for the project. Cap Exp and Add WC represent the investments in long-term assets, such as property, plant and equipment, and in working capital items, such as accounts receivable, inventory and accounts payable, which must be made if the project is pursued.

> ## Incremental cash flow from operations (CF Opns)
>
> the cash flow that a project generates after all operating expenses and taxes have been paid but before any cash outflows for investments

EXHIBIT 11.1
THE FREE CASH FLOW CALCULATION

Explanation	Calculation	Formula
The change in the firm's cash income, excluding interest expense, resulting from the project.	Revenue	Revenue
	−Cash operating expenses	−Op Ex
	Earnings before interest, taxes, depreciation and amortisation	EBITDA
	−Depreciation and amortisation	−D&A
	Operating profit	EBIT
	×(1 − Firm's marginal tax rate)	×(1 − t)
	Net operating profit after tax	NOPAT
Adjustments for the impact of depreciation and amortisation and investments on FCF.	+ Depreciation and amortisation	+D&A
	Cash flow from operations	CF Opns
	−Capital expenditures	−Cap Exp
	−Additions to working capital	−Add WC
	Free cash flow	FCF

This exhibit shows how the incremental after-tax free cash flow (FCF) for a project is calculated. The FCF equals the change in the firm's cash income, excluding interest expense, that the project is responsible for, plus depreciation and amortisation for the project, minus all required capital expenditures and investments in working capital. FCF also equals the incremental after-tax cash flow from operations minus the capital expenditures and investments in working capital required for the project.

Incremental capital expenditures (Cap Exp)

the investments in property, plant and equipment and other long-term assets that must be made if a project is pursued

Incremental additions to working capital (Add WC)

the investments in working capital items, such as accounts receivable, inventories and accounts payable, that must be made if the project is pursued

Since the FCF calculation gives us the after-tax cash flows from operations over and above what is necessary to make any required investments, the FCFs for a project are the cash flows that the security holders can expect to receive from the project. This is why we discount the FCFs when we compute the NPV.

The formula for the FCF calculation can also be written as:

$$FCF = [(\text{Revenue} - \text{Op Ex} - \text{D\&A}) \times (1 - t)] + \text{D\&A} - \text{Cap Exp} - \text{Add WC}$$

(11.2)

where Revenue is the incremental revenue (net sales) associated with the project, D&A is the **incremental depreciation and amortisation** associated with the project and t is the **firm's marginal tax rate**.

BUILDING INTUITION

Incremental After-Tax Free Cash Flows are what Shareholders Care About

When evaluating a project, managers focus on the FCF that the project is expected to produce because that is what shareholders care about. The FCFs reflect the impact of the project on the firm's overall cash flows. They also represent the additional cash flows that can be distributed to security holders if the project is accepted. Only after-tax cash flows matter because these are the cash flows that are actually available for distribution after taxes are paid to the government.

Incremental depreciation and amortisation (D&A)

the depreciation and amortisation charges that are associated with a project

Firm's marginal tax rate (*t*)

the tax rate that is applied to each additional monetary unit of earnings at a firm

To see how it works, we will use Equation (11.2) to work through an example. Suppose you are considering purchasing a new truck for your plumbing business. This truck will increase revenues by €50 000 and operating expenses by €30 000 in the next year. Depreciation and amortisation charges for the truck will equal €10 000 next year and your firm's marginal tax rate will be 35%. Capital expenditures of €3000 will be required to offset wear and tear on the truck but no additions to working capital will be required. To calculate the FCF for the project in the next year, you can simply substitute the appropriate values into Equation (11.2):

$$
\begin{aligned}
FCF &= [(\text{Revenue} - \text{Op Ex} - \text{D\&A}) \times (1 - t)] \\
&\quad + \text{D\&A} - \text{Cap Exp} - \text{Add WC} \\
&= [€50\ 000 - €30\ 000 - €10\ 000) \\
&\quad \times (1 - 0.35)] + €10\ 000 - €3000 - €0 \\
&= €13\ 500
\end{aligned}
$$

The FCF calculated with Equation (11.2) equals the total cash flow the firm will produce with the project less the total cash flow the firm will produce without the project. Even so, it is important to note that it is not necessary to actually estimate the firm's total cash flows in an NPV analysis. We need only estimate the cash outflows and inflows that arise as a direct result of the project in order to value it. The idea that we can evaluate the cash flows from a project independently of the cash flows for the firm is known as the **stand-alone principle**. The stand-alone principle says that we can treat the project as if it were a stand-alone firm that has its own revenue, expenses and investment requirements. NPV analysis compares the present value of the FCF from this stand-alone firm with the cost of the project.

Stand-alone principle

the principle that allows us to treat each project as a stand-alone firm when we perform an NPV analysis

To fully understand the stand-alone principle, it is helpful to consider an example. Suppose that you own shares in Nokia OY and that Nokia's shares are currently selling for €29.35. Now suppose that Nokia's management announces it will immediately invest €2.3 billion in a new production and distribution centre that is expected to produce after-tax cash flows of €0.6 billion per year forever. Since Nokia has 3.7 billion shares outstanding and uses very little debt, this means that the investment will equal about 62 cents per share (€2.3/3.7) and that the annual increase in the cash flows is expected to be 16 cents per share (€0.6/3.7). How should this announcement affect the value of Nokia shares?

If the appropriate cost of capital for the project is 10%, then from Equation (9.2) and the discussion in Chapter 10, we know that the value of a Nokia share should increase by D/R = €0.16/0.10 = €1.60 less the 62 cents invested, or €1.60 – €0.62 = €0.98, making each Nokia share worth €29.35 + €0.98 = €30.33 after the announcement. This example illustrates how the stand-alone principle allows us to simply add the value of a project's cash flows to the value of the firm's other cash flows to obtain the total value of the firm with the project.

Cash Flows from Operations

Let us examine Exhibit 11.1 in more detail to better understand why FCF is calculated as it is. First, note that the incremental cash flow from operations, CF Opns, equals the **incremental net operating profits after tax (NOPAT)** plus D&A.

> ### Incremental net operating profits after tax (NOPAT)
>
> a measure of the impact of a project on the firm's cash net income, excluding the effects of any interest expenses associated with financing the project

If you refer back to the discussion of the income statement in Chapter 3, you will notice that NOPAT is essentially a cash measure of the incremental net income from the project without interest expenses. In other words, it is the impact of the project on the firm's cash net income, excluding the effects of any interest expenses associated with financing the project. We exclude interest expenses

when calculating NOPAT because, as we mentioned earlier, the cost of financing a project is reflected in the discount rate.

We use the firm's marginal tax rate, t, to calculate NOPAT because the profits from a project are assumed to be incremental to the firm. Since the firm already pays taxes, the appropriate tax rate for FCF calculations is the tax rate that the firm will pay on any *additional* profits that are earned because the project is adopted. You may recall from Chapter 3 that this rate is the marginal tax rate. We will discuss taxes in more detail later in this chapter.

We add incremental depreciation and amortisation, D&A, to NOPAT when calculating CF Opns because, as in the accounting statement of cash flows, D&A represents a non-cash charge that reduces the firm's tax obligation. Note that we subtract D&A before computing the taxes that the firm would pay on the incremental earnings for the project. This accounts for the ability of the firm to deduct D&A when working out taxes. However, since D&A is a non-cash charge, we have to add it back to NOPAT in order to get the cash flow from operations right.

The net effect of subtracting D&A, computing the taxes and then adding D&A back is to reduce the taxes attributable to earnings from the project. For example, suppose that EBITDA for a project is €100.00, D&A is €50.00 and t is 35%. If we did not subtract D&A before computing taxes and add it back to compute CF Opns, the taxes owed for the project would be €100.00 × 0.35 = €35.00 and CF Opns would be €100.00 – €35.00 = €65.00. This would understate CF Opns from this project by €17.50 since deducting D&A reduces the firm's tax obligation by this amount. With this deduction, the correct tax obligation is (€100.00 – €50.00) × 0.35 = €17.50 and the correct CF Opns is €100.00 – €17.50 = €82.50. We get exactly this value when we compute CF Opns as shown in Exhibit 11.1 and Equation (11.2):

$$\text{CF Opns} = [(\text{Revenue} - \text{Op Ex} - \text{D\&A}) \times (1 - t)] + \text{D\&A}$$

Since Revenue − Op Ex = EBITDA, as shown in Exhibit 11.1, we can write:

$$CF\ Opns = [(EBITDA - D\&A) \times (1 - t)] + D\&A$$
$$= [(€100.00 - €50.00) \times (1 - 0.35)]$$
$$\qquad + €50.00$$
$$= €82.50$$

Note also that the definition of CF Opns differs from that in the accounting statement of cash flows in that it ignores changes in working capital accounts and other accounting adjustments. In financial calculations, investments in working capital are treated separately and there is no need for special accounting adjustments because CF Opns is based on cash flow estimates, not accounting numbers.

Cash Flows Associated with Investments

Once we have estimated CF Opns, we simply subtract cash flows associated with the required investments to obtain the FCF for a project in a particular period. Investments can be required to purchase long-term **tangible assets**, such as property, plant and equipment, to purchase **intangible assets**, such as a patent, or to fund **current assets**, such as accounts receivables and inventories. Recall from Chapter 3 that net investments in property, plant and equipment, and working capital items, are also deducted in the accounting statement of cash flows. You can see this in the long-term investing and operating activities sections of that statement.

> ### Tangible assets
> physical assets such as property, plant and equipment

> ### Intangible assets
> non-physical assets such as patents, mailing lists or brand names

> ### Current assets
> assets, such as accounts receivable and inventories, that are expected to be liquidated (collected or sold) within one year

It is important to recognise that all investments that are incremental to a project must be accounted for. The most obvious investments are those in the land, buildings and machinery and equipment that are acquired for the project. However, investments in intangible assets can also be required. For example, a manufacturing firm may purchase the right to use a particular production technology. Incremental investments in long-term tangible assets and intangible assets are collectively referred to as incremental capital expenditures (Cap Exp).

In addition to tangible and intangible assets, such as those described earlier, it is also necessary to account for incremental additions to working capital (Add WC). For example, if the product being produced is going to be sold on credit, thereby generating additional accounts receivable, the cost of providing that credit must be accounted for. Similarly, if it will be necessary to hold product in inventory, the cost of financing that inventory must be considered.

The FCF Calculation: An Example

We will work through a more comprehensive example to see how FCF is calculated in practice. Suppose that you work at an outdoor performing arts centre and are evaluating a project to increase the number of seats by building four new box seating areas and adding 5000 seats for the general public. Each box seating area is expected to generate €400 000 in incremental annual revenue, while each of the new seats for the general public will generate €2500 in incremental annual revenue. The incremental expenses associated with the new boxes and seating will amount to 60% of the revenues. These expenses include hiring additional personnel to handle concessions, ushering and security. The new construction will cost €10 million and will be fully depreciated (to a value of zero) on a straight-line basis over the 10-year life of the project. The centre will have to invest €1 million in additional working capital immediately, but the project will not require any other working capital investments during its life. This working capital will be recovered in the last year of the project. The centre's marginal tax rate is 30%. What are the incremental cash flows from this project?

When evaluating a project, it is generally helpful to first organise your calculations by setting up a worksheet such as the one illustrated in Exhibit 11.2. A worksheet like this helps ensure that the calculations are completed correctly. The left-hand column in Exhibit 11.2 shows the actual calculations that will be performed. Other columns are included for each of the years during the life of the project, from year 0 (today) to the last year in the life of the project (year 10). In this example the cash flows will be exactly the same for years 1–9; therefore, for illustration purposes, we will only include a single column to represent these years. If you were using a spreadsheet program, you would normally include one column for each year.

Unless there is information to the contrary, we can assume that the investment outlay for this project will be made today (year 0). We do this because in a typical project, no revenue will be generated and no expenses will be incurred until after the investment has been made. Consequently, the only cash flows in year 0 are those for new construction (Cap Exp = €10 000 000) and additional working capital (Add WC = €1 000 000). The FCF in year 0 will therefore equal −€11 000 000.

In years 1–9, the incremental revenue (Revenue) will equal:

Box seating (€400 000 × 4)	€ 1 600 000
Public seating (€2500 × 5000)	€12 500 000
Total incremental net revenue	€14 100 000

EXHIBIT 11.2
FCF CALCULATION WORKSHEET FOR THE PERFORMING ARTS CENTRE PROJECT

	Year 0	Years 1 to 9	Year 10
Revenue			
−Op Ex			
EBITDA			
−D&A			
EBIT			
×(1 − t)			
NOPAT			
+D&A			
CF Opns			
−Cap Exp			
−Add WC			
FCF			

A free cash flow (FCF) calculation table is useful in evaluating a project. It helps organise the calculations and ensure that they are completed correctly.

Incremental Op Ex will equal $0.60 \times €14\,100\,000 = €8\,460\,000$. Finally, depreciation (there is no amortisation in this example) is computed as:

$$D\&A = (Cap\ Exp - Salvage\ value\ of\ Cap\ Exp)/\\ Depreciable\ life\ of\ the\ investment\\ = (€10\,000\,000 - €0)/10\\ = €1\,000\,000$$

Note that only Cap Exp is depreciated and that these capital expenditures will be completely depreciated or written off over the 10-year life of the project because no salvage value is anticipated. Working capital is not depreciated because it is an investment that will be recovered at the end of the project.

The cash flows in year 10 will be the same as those in years 1–9 except that the €1 million invested in additional working capital will be recovered in the last year. The €1 million is added back to (or a negative number is subtracted from)

the incremental cash flows from operations in the calculation of the year 10 cash flows.

The completed cash flow calculation worksheet for this example is presented in Exhibit 11.3. We could have completed the calculations without the worksheet. However, as mentioned, a cash flow calculation worksheet is a useful tool because it helps us make sure we do not forget anything. Once we have set the worksheet up, calculating the incremental cash flows is simply a matter of filling in the blanks. As you will see in the following discussion, correctly filling in some blanks can be difficult at times, but the worksheet keeps us organised by reminding us which blanks have yet to be filled in.

Notice that with a discount rate of 10%, the NPV of the cash flows in Exhibit 11.3 is €15 487 664. As in Chapter 10, the NPV is obtained by calculating the present values of all the cash flows and adding them up. You might confirm this by doing the calculation yourself.

EXHIBIT 11.3

COMPLETED FCF CALCULATION WORKSHEET FOR THE PERFORMING ARTS CENTRE PROJECT

	Year 0	Years 1 to 9	Year 10
Revenue		€14 100 000	€14 100 000
−Op Ex	_____	8 460 000	8 460 000
EBITDA		€ 5 640 000	€5 640 000
−D&A	_____	1 000 000	1 000 000
EBIT		€ 4 640 000	€4 640 000
×(1 − t)	_____	0.70	0.70
NOPAT		€3 248 000	€3 248 000
+D&A	_____	1 000 000	1 000 000
CF Opns		€4 248 000	€4 248 000
−Cap Exp	€10 000 000		
−Add WC	1 000 000		−1 000 000
FCF	−€11 000 000	€4 248 000	€5 248 000
NPV @ 10%	€15 487 664		

The completed calculation table shows how the incremental after-tax free cash flows (FCF) for the performing arts centre project are computed, along with the NPV for that project when the cost of capital is 10%.

USING EXCEL

Performing Arts Centre Project

Cash flow calculations for capital budgeting problems are best set up and solved using a spreadsheet application. Here is the setup for the performing arts centre project:

	A	B	C	D	E	F	G	H	I	J	K	L	M	N	O	P	Q	R	S	T	U	V
1	Key Assumptions																					
2	Life of the project (years)	10																				
3	Number of new boxes	4																				
4	Annual incremental revenue per box	€ 400,000																				
5	Number of new seats	5000																				
6	Annual incremental revenue per new seat	€ 2,500																				
7	Incremental expenses (% of revenue)	60%																				
8	Construction cost (Cap Exp)*	€ 10,000																				
9	Depreciation (per year)*	€ 1,000																				
10	Additional investment in Year 0 (Add WC)*	€ 1,000																				
11	WC to be recovered in Year 10*	-€ 1,000																				
12	Tax rate	30%																				
13	Cost of capital	10%																				
14	Note * denotes figures in millions of euros																					
15																						
16	Cash Flow Calculations for Performing Arts Centre (€ millions)																					
17											Year											
18		0		1		2		3		4		5		6		7		8		9		10
19	Revenue			€ 14,100		€ 14,100		€ 14,100		€ 14,100		€ 14,100		€ 14,100		€ 14,100		€ 14,100		€ 14,100		€ 14,100
20	Operating expenses			8,460		8,460		8,460		8,460		8,460		8,460		8,460		8,460		8,460		8,460
21	EBITDA			€ 5,640		€ 5,640		€ 5,640		€ 5,640		€ 5,640		€ 5,640		€ 5,640		€ 5,640		€ 5,640		€ 5,640
22	Less Depreciation and Amortisation			1,000		1,000		1,000		1,000		1,000		1,000		1,000		1,000		1,000		1,000
23	EBIT			€ 4,640		€ 4,640		€ 4,640		€ 4,640		€ 4,640		€ 4,640		€ 4,640		€ 4,640		€ 4,640		€ 4,640
24	Less Taxes			1,392		1,392		1,392		1,392		1,392		1,392		1,392		1,392		1,392		1,392
25	NOPAT			€ 3,248		€ 3,248		€ 3,248		€ 3,248		€ 3,248		€ 3,248		€ 3,248		€ 3,248		€ 3,248		€ 3,248
26																						
27	Plus Depreciation and Amortisation			1,000		1,000		1,000		1,000		1,000		1,000		1,000		1,000		1,000		1,000
28	Cash Flows from Operations			€ 4,248		€ 4,248		€ 4,248		€ 4,248		€ 4,248		€ 4,248		€ 4,248		€ 4,248		€ 4,248		€ 4,248
29	Less Capital Expenditures	€ 10,000																				
30	Less Changes in Working Capital	€ 1,000																				-€ 1,000
31																						
32	Free Cash Flow	€ 11,000		€ 4,248		€ 4,248		€ 4,248		€ 4,248		€ 4,248		€ 4,248		€ 4,248		€ 4,248		€ 4,248		€ 5,248
33																						
34	NPV	€ 15,488																				
35																						
36																						
37																						
38																						
39				0.909		0.826		0.751		0.683		0.621		0.564		0.513		0.467		0.424		0.386
40		€ 26,488		€ 3,862		€ 3,511		€ 3,192		€ 2,901		€ 2,638		€ 2,398		€ 2,180		€ 1,982		€ 1,802		€ 2,023

The following is the formula setup for the performing arts centre project. As in Exhibit 11.3, we have combined years 1–9 in a single column to save space. As mentioned in previous chapters, notice that none of the values in the actual worksheet are hard coded but instead use references from the key assumptions list, or specific formulas. This allows for an easy analysis of the impact of changes in the assumption.

	A	B	C	D	E	V
1	Key Assumptions					
2	Life of the project (years)	10				
3	Number of new boxes	4				
4	Annual incremental revenue per box	400000				
5	Number of new seats	5000				
6	Annual incremental revenue per new seat	2500				
7	Incremental expenses (% of revenue)	0.6				
8	Construction cost (Cap Exp)*	10000				
9	Depreciation (per year)*	1000				
10	Additional investment in Year 0 (Add WC)*	1000				
11	WC to be recovered in Year 10*	-1000				
12	Tax rate	0.3				
13	Cost of capital	0.1				
14	Note * denotes figures in millions of euros					
15						
16	Cash Flow Calculations for Performing Arts Centre (€ millions)					
17				Year		
18		0		1-9		10
19	Revenue			=($B$3*$B$4+$B$5*$B*$6)/1000		=($B$3*$B$4+$B$5*$B*$6)/1000
20	Operating expenses			=$B$7*D19		=$B$7*V19
21	EBITDA			=D19-D20		=V19-V20
22	Less Depreciation and Amortisation			=$B$9		=$B$9
23	EBIT			=D21-D22		=V21-V22
24	Less Taxes			=D23*$B$12		=V23*$B$12
25	NOPAT			=D23-D24		=V23-V24
26						
27	Plus Depreciation and Amortisation			=$B$9		=$B$9
28	Cash Flows from Operations			=D25+D27		=V25+V27
29	Less Capital Expenditures			0		0
30	Less Changes in Working Capital			0		=B11
31						
32	Free Cash Flow	=B28-B29-B30		=D28-D29-D30		=V28-V29-V30
33						
34	NPV	=NPV(B13,D32:V32)+B32				
35						

FCF versus Accounting Earnings

It is worth stressing again that the FCF we have been discussing in this section is what matters to investors. The impact of a project on a firm's overall value or on its share price does not depend on how the project affects the company's accounting earnings. It depends only on how the project affects the company's FCF.

Recall that accounting earnings can differ from cash flows for a number of reasons, making accounting earnings an unreliable measure of the costs and benefits of a project. For example, as soon as a firm sells a good or provides a service, its income statement will reflect the associated revenue and expenses, regardless of whether the customer has made any actual payments.

Accounting earnings also reflect non-cash charges, such as depreciation and amortisation, which are intended to account for the costs associated with deterioration of the assets in a business as those assets are used. Depreciation and amortisation rules can cause substantial differences between cash flows and reported income because the assets acquired for a project are generally depreciated over several years, even though the actual cash outflow for their acquisition typically takes place at the beginning of the project.

Decision-Making Example 11.1

Free Cash Flows

Situation: You have saved €6000 and plan to use €5500 to buy a motorcycle. However, just before you go to visit the motorcycle dealer, a friend of yours asks you to invest your €6000 in a local pizza delivery business he is starting. Assuming he can raise the money, your friend has two alternatives regarding how to market the business. As illustrated below, both of these alternatives have an NPV of €2614 with an opportunity cost of capital of 12%. You will receive all free cash flows from the business until you have recovered your €6000 plus 12% interest. After that, you and your friend will split any additional cash proceeds. Which alternative would you prefer that your friend choose?

	Alternative 1			Alternative 2		
	Year 0	Year 1	Year 2	Year 0	Year 1	Year 2
Revenue		€12 000	€12 000		€16 000	€8 000
−Op Ex		4 000	6 000		8 000	4 240
EBITDA		€8 000	€6 000		€8 000	€3 760
−D&A		2 500	2 500		2 500	2 500
EBIT		€5 500	€3 500		€5 500	€1 260
×(1 −t)		0.75	0.75		0.75	0.75
NOPAT		€4 125	€2 625		€4 125	€945
+D&A		2 500	2 500		2 500	2 500
CF Opns		€6 625	€5 125		€6 625	€3 445
−Cap Exp	€5 000	2 000	500	€5 000	500	500
−Add WC	1 000		(1 000)	1 000		(1 000)
FCF	−€6 000	€4 625	€5 625	−€6 000	€6 125	€3 945
NPV at 12%	€2 614			€2 614		

Decision: If you expect no cash from other sources during the next year, you should insist that your friend choose alternative 2. This is the only alternative that will produce enough FCF next year to purchase the motorcycle. Alternative 1 will produce €6625 in CF Opns but will require €2000 in capital expenditures. You will not be able to take more than €4625 from the business in year 1 under alternative 1 without leaving the business short of cash.

Before You Go On

1. Why do we care about incremental cash flows at the firm level when we evaluate a project?
2. Why is D&A first subtracted and then added back in FCF calculations?
3. What types of investments should be included in FCF calculations?

ESTIMATING CASH FLOWS IN PRACTICE

Learning Objective 2

Discuss the five general rules for incremental after-tax free cash flow calculations and explain why cash flows stated in nominal (real) money should be discounted using a nominal (real) discount rate.

Now that we have discussed what FCFs are and how they are calculated, we are ready to focus on some important issues that arise when we estimate FCFs in practice. The first of these issues is determining which cash flows are incremental to the project and which are not. In this section we begin with a discussion of five general rules that help us do this. We then discuss why it is important to distinguish between nominal and real cash flows and to use one or the other consistently in our calculations. Next, we discuss some concepts

regarding tax rates and depreciation that are crucial to the calculation of FCF in practice. Finally, we describe and illustrate special factors that must be considered when calculating FCF for the final year of a project.

Five General Rules for Incremental After-Tax Free Cash Flow Calculations

As discussed earlier, we must determine how a project would change the after-tax free cash flows of the firm in order to calculate its NPV. This is not always simple to do, especially in a large firm that has a complex accounting system and many other projects that are not independent of the project being considered. Fortunately, there are five rules that can help us isolate the FCFs specific to an individual project even under the most complicated circumstances.

Rule 1: Include cash flows and only cash flows in your calculations. Do not include allocated costs unless they reflect cash flows. Examples of allocated costs are charges that accountants allocate to individual businesses to reflect their share of the corporate overhead (the costs associated with the senior managers of the firm, centralised accounting and finance functions, and so forth).

To see how allocated costs can differ from actual costs (and cash flows), consider a firm with €3 million of annual corporate overhead expenses and two identical manufacturing plants. Each of these plants would typically be allocated one-half, or €1.5 million, of the corporate overhead when their accounting profitability is estimated.

Suppose now that the firm is considering building a third plant that would be identical to the other two. If this plant is built, it will have no impact on the annual corporate overhead cash expense. Someone in accounting might argue that the new plant should be able to support its 'fair share' of the €3 million overhead, or €1 million, and that this overhead should be included in the cash flow calculation. Of course, this person would be wrong. Since total corporate overhead costs will not change if the third plant is built, no overhead should be included when calculating the incremental FCFs for this plant.

Rule 2: Include the impact of the project on cash flows from other product lines. If the product associated with a project is expected to affect sales of one or more other products at the firm, you must include the expected impact of the new project on the cash flows from the other products when computing the FCFs. For example, consider the analysis that analysts at Apple Computer would have done before giving the go-ahead for the development of the iPhone. Since, like the iPod, the iPhone can store music, these analysts might have expected that the introduction of the iPhone would reduce annual iPod sales. If so, they would have had to account for the reduction in cash flows from lost iPod sales when they forecast the FCFs for the iPhone. Similarly, if a new product is expected to boost sales of another, complementary, product, then the increase in cash flows associated with the new sales from that complementary product line should also be reflected in the FCFs. For example, suppose that the introduction of the iPhone will increase the total number of music-playing devices (iPhones plus iPods) that Apple sells by 1 million units per year and that the average purchaser of a music-playing device buys and downloads 100 digital songs from Apple. The digital music that Apple sells is a complementary product and the cash flows from the sale of 100 million (1 million music-playing devices × 100 songs) additional songs each year should be included in the analysis of the iPhone project. If Apple did not introduce the iPhone, it would not have those sales.

Rule 3: Include all opportunity costs. By opportunity costs, we mean the cost of giving up another opportunity.[2] Opportunity costs can arise in many different ways. For example, a project may require the use of a building or a piece of equipment that could otherwise be sold or leased to someone else. To the extent that selling or leasing the building or piece of equipment would generate additional cash flow for the firm and the opportunity to realise that cash flow must be forgone if the project is adopted, it represents an opportunity cost.

To see why this is so, suppose that a project will require the use of a piece of equipment that the firm already has and that can be sold for €50 000 on the used-equipment market. If the project is accepted, the firm will lose the opportunity to sell the piece of equipment for €50 000. This is a €50 000 cost that must be included in the project analysis. Accepting the project reduces the amount of money that the firm can realise from selling excess equipment by this amount.

Rule 4: Forget sunk costs. Sunk costs are costs that have already been incurred. All that matters when you evaluate a project at a particular point in time is how much you have to invest in the future and what you can expect to receive in return for that investment. Past investments are irrelevant.

To see this, consider the situation in which your company has invested €10 million in a project that has not yet generated any cash inflows. Also assume that circumstances have changed so the project, which was originally expected to generate cash inflows with a present value of €20 million, is now expected to generate cash inflows with a value of only €2 million. To receive this €2 million, however, you will have to invest another €1 million. Should you do it? Of course you should!

If you stop investing now, you will have lost €10 million. If you make the investment, your total loss will be €9 million. Although neither is an attractive alternative, it should be clear that it is better to lose €9 million than it is to lose €10 million. The conclusion is the same if you ignore the previous investment and recognise that the choice is between never receiving anything and receiving an NPV of €1 million (€1 million investment and €2 million return). The point here is that, while it is often painful to do, you should ignore sunk costs when computing FCF.

Rule 5: Include only after-tax cash flows in the cash flow calculations. The incremental pre-tax earnings of a project matter only to the extent that they affect the after-tax cash flows that the firm's investors receive. For an individual project, as mentioned earlier, we compute the after-tax cash flows using the firm's marginal tax rate because this is the rate that will be applied against the incremental cash flows generated by the project.

Let us use the performing arts centre project to illustrate how these rules are applied in practice. Suppose the following requirements and costs are associated with this project:

1. The chief financial officer requires that each project be assessed 5% of the initial investment to account for costs associated with the accounting, marketing and information technology departments.
2. It is very likely that increasing the number of seats will reduce revenues next door at the cinema that your employer also owns. Attendance at the cinema is expected to be lower only when the performing arts centre is staging a big event. The total impact is expected to be a reduction of €500 000 each year, before taxes, in the operating profits (EBIT) of the cinema. The depreciation of the cinema's assets will not be affected.
3. If the project is adopted, the new seating will be built in an area where exhibits have been placed in the past when the centre has hosted guest

lectures by well-known painters or sculptors. The performing arts centre will no longer be able to host such events and revenue will be reduced by €600 000 each year as a result.
4. The centre has already spent €400 000 researching demand for new seating.
5. You have just discovered that a new salesperson will be hired if the centre goes ahead with the expansion. This person will be responsible for sales and service of the four new luxury boxes and will be paid €75 000 per year, including salary and benefits. The €75 000 is not included in the 60% figure for operating expenses that was previously mentioned.

What impact will these requirements and costs have on the FCFs for the project?

1. The 5% assessment sounds like an allocated overhead cost. To the extent that this assessment does not reflect an actual increase in cash costs, it should not be included. It is not relevant to the project. The analysis should include only cash flows.
2. The impact of the expansion on the operating profits of the cinema is an example of how a project can erode or cannibalise business in another part of a firm. The €500 000 reduction in EBIT is relevant and should be included in the analysis.
3. The loss of the ability to use the exhibits area represents a €600 000 opportunity cost. The centre is giving up revenue from guest lecturers that require exhibit space in order to build the additional seating. This opportunity cost will be partially offset by elimination of the operating expenses associated with the guest lectures.
4. The €400 000 for research has already been spent. The decision on whether to accept or reject the project will not alter the amount spent for this research. This is a sunk cost that should not be included in the analysis.
5. The €75 000 annual salary for the new salesperson is an incremental cost that should be included in the analysis. Even though the marketing department is a corporate overhead department, in this case the salesperson must be hired specifically because of the new project.

EXHIBIT 11.4

ADJUSTED FCF CALCULATIONS AND NPV FOR THE PERFORMING ARTS CENTRE PROJECT

	Year 0	Years 1 to 9	Year 10
Revenue		€13 500 000	€13 500 000
−Op Ex		8 100 000	8 100 000
−New salesperson's salary		75 000	75 000
−Lost cinema EBIT		500 000	500 000
EBITDA		€4 825 000	€4 825 000
−D&A		1 000 000	1 000 000
EBIT		€3 825 000	€3 825 000
×(1 −*t*)		0.70	0.70
NOPAT		€2 677 500	€2 677 500
+D&A		1 000 000	1 000 000
CF Opns		€3 677 500	€3 677 500
−Cap Exp	€10 000 000	0	0
−Add WC	1 000 000	0	21,000,000
FCF	−€11 000 000	€3 677 500	€4 677 500
NPV @ 10%	€11 982 189		

The adjustments described in the text result in changes in the FCF calculations and a different NPV for the performing arts centre project.

Exhibit 11.4 shows the impact of the changes described earlier on the cash flows outlined in Exhibit 11.3. Note that Revenue and Op Ex after year 0 have been reduced from €14 100 000 and €8 460 000, respectively, in Exhibit 11.3 to €13 500 000 and €8 100 000, respectively, in Exhibit 11.4. These changes reflect the €600 000 loss of revenues and the reduction in costs (60% of revenue) associated with the loss of the ability to host guest lectures. The €75 000 expense for the new salesperson's salary and the €500 000 reduction in the EBIT of the cinema are then subtracted from Revenue, along with Op Ex. These changes result in EBITDA of €4 825 000 in Exhibit 11.4, compared with EBITDA of €5 640 000 in Exhibit 11.3. The net result is a reduction in the project NPV from €15 487 664 (in Exhibit 11.3) to €11 982 189 (in Exhibit 11.4).

Learning by Doing Application 11.1

Using the General Rules for FCF Calculations

Problem: You have owned and operated a pizza restaurant for several years. The space that you lease for your pizza restaurant is considerably larger than the space you need. To more efficiently utilise this space, you are considering subdividing it and opening a hamburger outlet. You know that your analysis should consider the overall impact of the hamburger project on the total cash flows of your business, but beyond estimating revenues and costs from hamburger-related sales and the investment required to get the hamburger business started, you are unsure what else you should consider. Based on the five general rules for incremental after-tax cash flow calculations, what other factors should you consider?

Approach: Careful consideration of each of the five rules provides insights concerning the other factors that should be considered.

Solution: Rule 1 suggests that you should consider the impact of the hamburger outlet on actual overhead expenses, such as the cost of additional accounting support. Rule 2 indicates that you should consider the potential for the hamburger business to take sales away from (or cannibalise) the pizza business. Rule 3 suggests that you should carefully consider the opportunity cost associated with the excess space or any excess equipment that might be used for the hamburger business. If you could lease the extra space to someone else, for example, then the amount that you could receive by doing so is an opportunity cost and should be included in the analysis. Similarly, the price for which any excess equipment could be sold represents an opportunity cost. Rule 4 simply reminds you to consider cash flows from this point forward only. Forget sunk costs. Finally, Rule 5 tells you not to forget to account for the impact of taxes in your cash flow calculations.

WEB

You can learn more about incremental free cash flows at Investopedia.com: www.investopedia.com.

Nominal versus Real Cash Flows

In addition to following the five rules for incremental after-tax cash flow calculations, it is very important to make sure that all cash flows are stated in either nominal values or real values – not a mixture of the two. The concepts of nominal and real values are directly related to the discussion in Chapter 2 that distinguishes between (1) the nominal rate of interest and (2) the real rate of interest. **Nominal values** are the money that we typically think of. They represent the actual monetary amounts that we expect a project to generate in the future, without any adjustments. To the extent that there is inflation, the purchasing power of each nominal unit of currency will decline over time. When prices are going up, a given nominal amount will buy less and less over time. **Real values** represent monetary values stated in terms of constant purchasing power. When we forecast in real terms, the purchasing power of the money in one period is equal to the purchasing power of money in any other period.

Nominal value

money amounts that are not adjusted for inflation. The purchasing power of a nominal unit of currency amount depends on when that amount is received

Real value

inflation-adjusted money amounts; the actual purchasing power of money stated in 'real' terms is the same regardless of when the money is received

To illustrate the difference between nominal and real value, let us consider an example. Suppose that the rate of inflation is expected to be 5% next year and that you just lent €100 to a friend for one year. If your friend is not paying any interest, the nominal amount you expect to receive in one year is €100. At that time, though, the purchasing power, in today's terms, of this

€100 is expected to be only €95.24: €100/(1 + ΔP_e) = €100/1.05 = €95.24, where ΔP_e is the expected rate of inflation, as discussed in Chapter 2. In other words, if inflation is as expected, when your friend repays the €100, it will buy only what €95.24 would buy today. You will have earned a real return of (€95.24 − €100)/€100 = −0.0476, or −4.76%, on this loan. Another way of thinking about this loan is that your friend is expected to repay you with money having a real value of €95.24.

To understand the importance of making sure that all cash flows are stated in either nominal values or real values, it is useful to write the cost of capital (k) from Chapter 10 as:

$$1 + k = (1 + \Delta P_e) \times (1 + r) \qquad (11.3)$$

In Equation (11.3), k is the nominal cost of capital that is normally used to discount cash flows and r is the real cost of capital.[3] This equation tells us that the nominal cost of capital equals the real cost of capital, adjusted for the expected rate of inflation.

a year in years 1–4. With a 15% nominal cost of capital, the NPV for this project is:

$$NPV = FCF_0 + \frac{FCF_1}{1 + k} + \frac{FCF_2}{(1+k)^2} + \frac{FCF_3}{(1+k)^3} + \frac{FCF_4}{(1+k)^4}$$

$$= -€50\,000 + \frac{€20\,000}{1.15} + \frac{€20\,000}{(1.15)^2} + \frac{€20\,000}{(1.15)^3} + \frac{€20\,000}{(1.15)^4}$$

$$= -€50\,000 + €17\,391 + €15\,123 + €13\,150 + €11\,435$$

$$= €7099$$

Equation (11.3) can be used to calculate the real cost of capital if we recognise that it can be rearranged algebraically as:

$$r = \frac{1 + k}{1 + \Delta P_e} - 1$$

With a 5% expected rate of inflation, the real cost of capital is therefore:

$$r = \frac{1 + k}{1 + \Delta P_e} - 1 = \frac{1.15}{1.05} - 1$$

$$= 0.09524, \text{ or } 9.524\%$$

Discounting the nominal cash flows by the rate of inflation tells us that the real cash flows are:

Year 0	Year 1	Year 2	Year 3	Year 4
−€50 000	$\dfrac{€20\,000}{1 + 0.05}$	$\dfrac{€20\,000}{(1 + 0.05)^2}$	$\dfrac{€20\,000}{(1 + 0.05)^3}$	$\dfrac{€20\,000}{(1 + 0.05)^4}$
= −€50 000	= €19 047.6	= €18 140.6	= €17 276.8	= €16 454.0

This means that whenever we discount a cash flow using the nominal cost of capital, the discount rate we are using reflects both the expected rate of inflation (ΔP_e) and a real return (r). If, on the one hand, we discounted a *real cash flow* using the *nominal cost of capital*, we would be overcompensating for expected inflation in the discounting process. On the other hand, if we discounted a *nominal cash flow* using the *real cost of capital* (r), we would be undercompensating for expected inflation.

In capital budgeting, we normally forecast cash flows in nominal values and discount them using the nominal cost of capital.[4] As an alternative, we can state the cash flows in real terms and discount them using the real cost of capital. This alternative calculation will give us exactly the same NPV. To see this, consider a project that will require an investment of €50 000 in year 0 and will produce FCFs of €20 000

Therefore, when we discount the real cash flows using the real cost of capital, we see that the NPV is:

$$NPV = -€50\,000 + \frac{€19\,047.6}{1.09524} + \frac{€18\,140.6}{(1.09524)^2} + \frac{€17\,276.8}{(1.09524)^3}$$

$$+ \frac{€16\,454.0}{(1.09524)^4}$$

$$= -€50\,000 + €17\,391 + €15\,123 + €13\,150$$

$$+ €11\,435$$

$$= €7099$$

Notice that the present value of each of the annual cash flows is exactly the same when we use nominal cash flows and when we use real cash flows. This has to be the case because when we stated the NPV calculation in real values we first divided the discount rate by 1.05. We then reduced the value of the future cash flows by discounting them by 5%. This is equivalent to reducing the numerator and the denominator in each present value calculation by the same fraction, which must result in the same answer.

The Investment Decision and Nominal versus Real Values

Problem: You are trying to decide how to invest €25 000, which you just inherited from a distant relative. You do not want to take any risks with this money because you want to use it as a down payment on a home when you graduate in three years' time. Therefore, you have decided to invest the money in securities that are guaranteed by the government. You are considering two alternatives: a three-year government bond and an inflation-indexed government security. If you invest in the three-year bond, you will be paid 3% per year in interest and will get your €25 000 back at the end of three years. If you invest in the inflation-indexed security, you will be paid 1% per year plus an amount that reflects actual inflation in each of the next three years. For example, if inflation equals 2% per year for each of the next three years, you will receive 3% each year in total interest. This interest on the inflation-indexed security will compound, and you will receive a single payment at the end of three years. If you expect inflation to average 2.5% per year over the next three years,

should you invest in the three-year government bond or in the inflation-indexed security?

Approach: Compare the 3% return on the three-year government bond, which is a nominal rate of return, with the nominal rate of return that you can expect to receive from the inflation-indexed security and invest in the security with the highest rate. The nominal rate on the inflation-indexed security in each year equals the real rate of 1% plus the rate of inflation.

Solution: Without doing any detailed calculations, it is apparent that you should invest in the inflation-indexed security. The reason is that if the rate of inflation turns out to be 2.5%, the inflation-indexed security will yield 3.5% (1% plus the 2.5% inflation adjustment) per year. With this investment, the real purchasing power of your money will increase by 1% per year. This will be true regardless of what inflation turns out to be during the three-year period. Assuming that you can reinvest the annual interest payments from the three-year government bond at 3%, if you buy this security, the real purchasing power of your money will increase by only 0.5% (3% interest rate less 2.5% inflation) per year.

You can calculate the impact of inflation on purchasing power using the inflation calculator at www.westegg.com/inflation. This calculator tells you how much it would cost you, in nominal money, to buy the same goods in any two years, beginning in the year 1800

Tax Rates and Depreciation

Most countries have a complicated corporate tax system. Companies can pay taxes at the national, regional and local levels. Some governmental jurisdictions tax income, while others tax property or some other measure of value. Furthermore, a wide variety of deductions and adjustments are made to income or other measures of value when computing the actual taxes that a firm owes. A detailed discussion of the different taxes that companies pay and how they are calculated is beyond the scope of this textbook. At this point, it is important that you understand how a progressive tax system works and how this affects the amount of taxes a firm pays overall versus the amount of taxes that will be due if a new project is undertaken. In addition, since depreciation works to offset taxes, it is important to understand the methods used when calculating corporate tax obligations. Familiarity with these concepts is especially important in capital budgeting.

Marginal and Average Tax Rates

A **progressive tax system**, which is fairly typical of most European countries, is one in which taxpayers pay a progressively larger share of their income in taxes as their income rises. This happens in a progressive tax system because the marginal tax rate at low levels of income is lower than the marginal tax rate at high levels of income. Recall from Chapter 3 that the marginal tax rate is the rate paid on the last unit of profit earned. The tax system is progressive for individuals and also is likely to be so for companies. In a progressive system, the tax rate increases as taxable income increases. In other words, the marginal tax rate, as well as the average tax rate,

increases as an individual moves from one tax bracket to the next.

> ### Progressive tax system
>
> a tax system in which the marginal tax rate at low levels of income is lower than the marginal tax rate at high levels of income

Exhibit 11.5 shows the 2008 tax rate schedule faced by a typical Belgian company (you may recall that a variation of this tax rate schedule is also presented in Exhibit 3.6). Notice that this schedule is progressive. The Belgian corporate tax system in 2008 was structured so that the marginal rate exactly equalled the average tax rate for all levels of income above €322 500. If the company's taxable income is below €322 500, the marginal tax rate will not necessarily be the same as the average tax rate. These rates differ in the tax brackets below €322 500 and indicate a progressive rate depending on the level of reported income. Remember that since we use marginal tax rates in capital budgeting, you cannot simply divide the amount of taxes paid by the taxable income for a company to estimate the tax rate. This calculation gives you the average, not the marginal, tax rate.

EXHIBIT 11.5

BELGIAN CORPORATE TAX SCHEDULE IN 2008

Taxable Income			Tax Owed
More Than	**But Not More Than**		**Tax Owed**
€0	€25 000		24.25% of amount beyond €0
€25 001	€90 000	€6 063	+31.00% of amount beyond €25 000
€90 001	€322 500	€26 212	+34.50% of amount beyond €90 000
€322 501	—	€80 212	+36.00% of amount beyond €322 500

The Belgian tax system for companies is progressive, with marginal tax rates ranging from 24.25% up to 36.00%.

Calculating Marginal and Average Tax Rates

Problem: Assume that you are operating the pizza restaurant and hamburger outlet described in Learning by Doing Application 11.1. Because the business has become complicated, you have incorporated as a limited liability company. From now on, earnings are subject to the corporate tax rates presented in Exhibit 11.5. If your company's total taxable income is €200 000 in 2009, how much does it owe in taxes? What are the company's marginal and average tax rates? If you were considering buying a new oven, which tax rate would you use when computing the free cash flows?

Approach: Use the rates presented in Exhibit 11.5 to calculate the total amount that you owe.

The marginal tax rate is the rate in the 'Tax Owed' column in Exhibit 11.5 that corresponds to the row in which the total taxable income earned by your restaurant is found. The ratio of the total amount that you owe divided by your total taxable income equals the average tax rate. You would use the tax rate that would be applied to the incremental after-tax free cash flows associated with the new oven.

Solution: From Exhibit 11.5, you can see that with a taxable income of €200 000, your company will owe taxes of €26 212 + ((€200 000 − €90 000) × 0.345 = €37 950) = €64 162. The marginal tax rate is 34.5%, and the average tax rate is €64 162/€200 000 = 0.321, or 32.1%. You will use the marginal rate of 34.5% when computing the free cash flows for the new oven.

Tax Depreciation

Companies keep two sets of books. One set is kept for preparing financial statements in accordance with generally accepted accounting principles (GAAP). These are the financial statements that appear in the annual report and other documents filed with the appropriate regulatory agencies. The other set is kept for computing the taxes that the company actually pays. Companies must keep two sets of books because the GAAP rules for computing income are different from the rules that the tax authority uses.

One especially important difference from a capital budgeting perspective is that the depreciation methods allowed by GAAP differ from those allowed by the tax authorities. The straight-line depreciation method illustrated earlier in this chapter in the performing arts centre example is allowed by GAAP and is often used for financial reporting.

In contrast, **tax depreciation** may take several forms. We will explore three ways it is carried out. In the United Kingdom, tax depreciation is called tax allowance and is usually set as a declining balance of the asset – currently 20%. However, there are exceptions for items such as buildings, research and development, and some investment categories where the allowance may be as high as 100% in the first year. The standard schedule and the amount of tax for equipment costing £100 000 is given in Exhibit 11.6.

Tax depreciation

the amount of depreciation on an asset allowed against profit in a particular reporting period

EXHIBIT 11.6

EXAMPLE OF TAX DEPRECIATION CAPITAL ALLOWANCE FOR THE UNITED KINGDOM

Year	Book Value of Asset for Tax Purposes at Start of Year	Tax Depreciation in Year	Book Value of Asset for Tax Purposes at Start of Year	Tax Saving at 30% Corporate Tax Rate
0	£100 000	£20 000	£80 000	£6 000
1	80 000	16 000	64 000	4 800
2	64 000	12 800	51 200	3 840
3	51 200	10 240	40 960	3 072
4	40 960	8 192	32 768	2 458
5	32 768	6 554	26 214	1 966
	etc.			

The capital allowance rate is 20% of the book value of the asset for tax purposes at the start of the tax year. The depreciation continues until such time as the asset is sold or written off, at which point there is either a corresponding tax liability, if the asset is sold at a price higher than the depreciated value for tax purposes, or a tax credit, if less. Note that some assets are subject to special capital allowance criteria, for instance property, which has a lower capital allowance rate of 4% and research and development, where the enhanced deduction rate for qualifying expenditures varies between 175% for small businesses and 130% for large companies. Other business assets, such as motor vehicles, are also subject to a different schedule. There is also a special Annual Investment Allowance that gives business 100% depreciation on the first £50 000 of any acquisition of eligible assets. A company that qualified for this allowance could write off £70 000 of the investment in its first year. This is not used to calculate the values in the exhibit.

When a company buys equipment, it can deduct the tax depreciation from its taxable profit before paying tax. In the case of the example in Exhibit 11.6, in the first year of operation, the company can charge £20 000 (£100 000 × 20%) against its taxable profit. If it pays tax at 30%, this translates to a tax saving of £6000. That is, it will pay £6000 less tax as a result, as can be shown below:

	Without Investment	With Investment	Tax saving
Profit before Tax	£100 000	£100 000	
Tax Depreciation	0	20 000	
Taxable Income	£100 000	£80 000	
Tax at 30%	30 000	24 000	£6 000
Net Profit	£70 000	£56 000	

Without the investment the company pays tax on £100 000, which at the tax rate of 30% is

£30 000; with the investment, the tax allowance or depreciation is £20 000 and the taxable income is now £80 000 (£100 000 – £20 000). The tax is therefore 30% of £80 000, that is, £24 000. By investing in the new asset, the company has saved £6000 in tax (£30 000 – £24 000). Note that we could have simply multiplied the tax depreciation by the tax rate to arrive at this figure (£20 000 × 0.30 = £6000).

Contrast the way the United Kingdom tax authority allows depreciation with that for Belgium. In this case, the straight-line depreciation method is the normal approach, which is the same method we used in the performing arts centre project. However, in some cases the Belgian tax authority allows the use of the double declining balance method, which is more akin to the UK's capital allowance approach.[5] The depreciation rate, or equally the amount that can be written off, depends on the nature of the asset. Some examples from the Belgian tax code are given below:

Type of Asset	Permitted Depreciation Rate in Tax Year
Small office purchases	100%
Computers, software, videos and mobile phones	33
Vehicles	20–33
Office buildings	3
Industrial buildings	5
Chemical plants	8–10
Office equipment	10–20
Machinery and equipment	20
Goodwill	10–20
Energy saving investments & research and development	33.3
Ships	8-year depreciation with maximum rate of 20% in year 1

Note that the depreciation ultimately adds up to 100%. This is because the tax law allows firms to depreciate 100% of the cost of an asset regardless of the expected salvage value of that asset. Consequently, when we use a tax depreciation method to determine the tax depreciation, we do not have to worry about the expected salvage value for the asset. However, a firm selling an asset above its depreciated value for tax purposes will incur a clawback charge on the difference. So in the case of the asset in Exhibit 11.6, if at the end of year 4, the company sold the asset for £41 500, it would have to pay tax on the difference of £8732 (£40 500 – £32 768).

The type of specificity in tax depreciation that is found in the Belgian tax code is also a feature of the US tax code, where an 'accelerated' method of depreciation, called the Modified Accelerated Cost Recovery System (MACRS), is in use. MACRS is an accelerated system in the sense that depreciation charges for all assets other than non-farm real property (for example, buildings) are higher in the early years of an asset's life than with the straight-line method. MACRS, like the United Kingdom's capital allowances and some aspects of the Belgium system, enables a firm to deduct depreciation charges sooner, thereby realising the tax savings sooner and increasing the present value of the tax savings.

Exhibit 11.7 lists the percentage of the cost of an asset that can be depreciated in each year for assets with 3-, 5-, 7-, 10-, 15- and 20-year allowable recovery periods using MACRS. The recovery periods for specific types of assets are specified in the tax law. For instance, in 2007, the allowable recovery period was 5 years for computers and automobiles, 7 years for office furniture, 10 years for water transportation equipment such as barges, 15 years for telephone distribution facilities, 20 years for farm buildings, 27.5 years for residential rental property and 39.5 years for non-residential real property (such as manufacturing buildings). Residential rental and non-residential real property are depreciated using the straight-line method. Depreciation charges are intended to represent the cost of wear and tear on assets in the course of business. However, since they are set through a political process, they may be greater than or less than the actual cost of this wear and tear.

When evaluating a project, we want to estimate the actual incremental cash flows from a project in capital budgeting – we use the depreciation method allowed by the tax authority in our calculations. This is the method that determines how much of a tax deduction a company actually receives for an investment. It is important to know which assets in the project are subject to which set of depreciation rules for tax purposes as this will affect the after-tax cash flows.

Let us consider an example to show how the United States' MACRS is applied. Suppose you are evaluating a project that will require the purchase of an automobile for $25 000. Since an automobile is a 5-year asset under MACRS, you can use the percentages for a 5-year asset in Exhibit 11.7 to calculate the annual depreciation deductions:

Year 1:	$25 000 × 0.2000 =	$5 000
Year 2:	$25 000 × 0.3200 =	$8 000
Year 3:	$25 000 × 0.1920 =	$4 800
Year 4:	$25 000 × 0.1152 =	$2 880
Year 5:	$25 000 × 0.1152 =	$2 880
Year 6:	$25 000 × 0.0576 =	$1 440
Total		$25 000

Notice that even though the automobile is a 5-year asset, there is a depreciation charge in the sixth year. This is because MACRS assumes that the

EXHIBIT 11.7

MACRS DEPRECIATION SCHEDULES BY ALLOWABLE RECOVERY PERIOD

Year	3-Year	5-Year	7-Year	10-Year	15-Year	20-Year
1	33.33%	20.00%	14.29%	10.00%	5.00%	3.75%
2	44.45	32.00	24.49	18.00	9.50	7.22
3	14.81	19.20	17.49	14.40	8.55	6.68
4	7.41	11.52	12.49	11.52	7.70	6.18
5		11.52	8.93	9.22	6.93	5.71
6		5.76	8.92	7.37	6.23	5.29
7			8.93	6.55	5.90	4.89
8			4.46	6.55	5.90	4.52
9				6.56	5.91	4.46
10				6.55	5.90	4.46
11				3.28	5.91	4.46
12					5.90	4.46
13					5.91	4.46
14					5.90	4.46
15					5.91	4.46
16					2.95	4.46
17						4.46
18						4.46
19						4.46
20						4.46
21						2.24
Total	100.00%	100.00%	100.00%	100.00%	100.00%	100.00%

The MACRS schedule lists the tax depreciation rates that firms use for assets placed into service after the Tax Reform Act of 1986 went into effect. The table indicates the percentage of the cost of the asset that can be depreciated in each year during the period that it is being used. Year 1 is the year in which the asset is first placed into service.

asset is placed in service in the middle of the first year. As a result, the firm is allowed a deduction for half a year in year 1, a full year in years 2–5, and half a year in year 6.

Recall that the FCF calculation, Equation (11.1), included incremental depreciation along with incremental amortisation (D&A). We put depreciation and amortisation together in the calculation because amortisation is a non-cash charge (deduction) like depreciation. It is beyond the scope of this book to discuss amortisation in detail because the rules that govern it are complex. However, you should know that amortisation, like depreciation, is a deduction that is allowed under the tax law to compensate for the decline in value of certain, mainly intangible, assets used by a business.

Computing the Terminal-Year FCF

The FCF in the last, or terminal, year of a project's life often includes cash flows that are not typically included in the calculations for other years. For instance, in the final year of a project, the assets acquired during the life of the project may be sold and the working capital that has been invested may be recovered. The cash flows that result from the sale of assets and recovery of working capital must be included in the calculation of the terminal-year FCF.

In the performing arts centre example discussed earlier, the cash flows in year 0 are different from the cash flows in the other years (see Exhibit 11.3). The year 0 cash flows include only cash flows associated with incremental capital expenditures (Cap Exp) and additions to working capital (Add WC). They do not include incremental cash flows from operations (CF Opns). The principle behind including only these cash flows in year 0 is that the investments must be made before any cash flows from operations are realised. In some cases, such as large construction projects, up-front investments may be required over several years, but these investments are typically also made before the project begins to generate revenue.

The year-10, or terminal-year, cash flows in the performing arts centre example are also different from those in the other years. They include both CF Opns and investment cash flows that reflect recovery of net working capital investments. Net incremental additions to working capital (Add WC) that are due to the project are calculated as follows:

$$
\begin{aligned}
\text{Add WC} = {} & \text{Change in cash and cash equivalents} \\
& + \text{Change in accounts receivable} \\
& + \text{Change in inventories} \\
& - \text{Change in accounts payable}
\end{aligned}
$$

$$(11.4)$$

where the changes in cash and cash equivalents, accounts receivable, inventories and accounts payable represent changes in the values of these accounts that result from the adoption of the project.

Looking at the components of Add WC, we can see that cash and cash equivalents, accounts receivable and inventories require the investment of capital, while accounts payable represent capital provided by suppliers. When a project ends, the cash and cash equivalents are no longer needed, the accounts receivable are collected, the inventories are sold and the accounts payable are paid. In other words, the firm recovers the net working capital that has been invested in the project. To reflect this in the FCF calculation, the cash flow in the last year of the project typically includes a *negative investment in working capital* that equals the cumulative investment in working capital over the life of the project. It is very important to make sure that the recovery of working capital is reflected in the cash flows in the last year of a project. In some businesses, working capital can account for 20% or more of revenue and excluding working capital recovery from the calculations can cause you to substantially understate the NPV of a project.

In some projects, there will also be incremental capital expenditures (Cap Exp) in the terminal year. This is because the assets acquired for the project are being sold or there are disposal costs associated with them. In the performing arts centre example, Cap Exp is €0 in year 10. This is because we were assuming that, other than the working capital, the investments at the beginning of the project would have no salvage value, there would be no disposal costs associated with the assets and there would be no clean-up costs associated with the project in year 10. When an asset is expected to have a salvage value, we must include the salvage value realised from the sale of the asset and the impact of the sale on the firm's taxes in the terminal-year FCF calculations. Any costs that must be incurred to dispose of assets should also be included. Finally, clean-up costs, such as those associated with restoring the environment after a strip-mining project, must also be included in the terminal-year FCF.

The salvage value realised from the sale of the assets used in a project includes both the cash that is actually realised when they are sold and, if the salvage value of any asset differs from its depreciated value, the tax implications from the sale. To better understand how taxes affect the terminal-year cash flows for a project, let us make the performing arts centre example more realistic. Recall that the initial Cap Exp in the performing arts centre example was €10 million, that we used straight-line depreciation, and that we assumed the salvage value would be €0 in year 10. Now that we know about the different

EXHIBIT 11.8

DOUBLE DECLINING DEPRECIATION FOR THE PERFORMING ARTS CENTRE PROJECT (€ THOUSANDS)

	Year 1	Year 2	Year 3	Year 4	Year 5	Year 6	Year 7	Year 8	Year 9	Year 10
Depreciation calculations										
Beginning book value	€10 000	€8 000	€6 400	€5 120	€4 096	€3 277	€2 621	€2 097	€1 678	€1 342
Double declining balance percentage	20%	20%	20%	20%	20%	20%	20%	20%	20%	20%
Depreciation	€2 000	€1 600	€1 280	€1 024	€819	€655	€524	€419	€336	€268
Ending book value	€8 000	€6 400	€5 120	€4 096	€3 277	€2 621	€2 097	€1 678	€1 342	€1 074

Using the double declining balance of 20%, rather than the straight-line approach, we calculate the amount of tax depreciation for each year of the life of the performing arts centre project.

tax depreciation systems, let us more realistically assume that the project is situated in Belgium and can benefit from the double declining balance method for this investment as it fits in with the country's social and economic objectives.

Exhibit 11.8 presents the depreciation calculations for this investment under the double declining balance method. Note that since the amount of depreciation now changes over time, we can no longer present years 1–9 together as we did in Exhibit 11.3.

If we still assume a salvage value of €0 for this investment, the fact that the book value is positive means that the firm will have a tax loss when it writes off the remaining value of the investment at the end of the project. In other words, when the project ends, the firm will take a deduction when computing its taxes that equals the remaining €1 074 000 book value of the asset. With a 30% tax rate, this will result in a tax saving of €1 074 000 × 0.30 = €322 200. This tax saving must be reflected in the cash flow calculations in year 10. Exhibit 11.9 illustrates the cash flow and NPV calculations for the performing arts centre example with these changes. The €322 200 tax saving is included as a negative capital expenditure in year 10 (as €322 since we are rounding to thousands).[6] Notice that the NPV has increased

from €15 487 664 in Exhibit 11.3 to €15 685 692. The €198 028 difference reflects the present value of the tax savings from using double declining balance depreciation instead of straight-line depreciation plus the tax savings from the disposal of the asset. This is because the use of double declining balance depreciation has accelerated the tax depreciation and reduced the taxable profit in the early years of the project.

If the salvage value is greater than €0 but less than the book value of €1 074 000, the tax savings will be smaller than €322 123 and, if the salvage value exceeds the book value, the firm will actually have a gain on the sale of the asset that will increase its tax liability. In either of these cases, you must include the proceeds from the sale of the assets and the tax effects in your cash flow calculations.

The general formula for calculating the tax on the salvage value for an asset is:

Tax on sale of an asset = (Selling price of asset − Book value of asset) × t

where t is the firm's marginal tax rate.

To make sure we know how we use this equation, suppose that the salvage value (selling price) in year 10 of the €10 000 000 investment in the performing arts

EXHIBIT 11.9

FCF PERFORMING ARTS CENTRE WITH DOUBLE DECLINING DEPRECIATION (€ THOUSANDS)

	Year 0	Year 1	Year 2	Year 3	Year 4	Year 5	Year 6	Year 7	Year 8	Year 9	Year 10
Revenue		€14 100	€14 100	€14 100	€14 100	€14 100	€14 100	€14 100	€14 100	€14 100	€14 100
−Op Ex		8 460	8 460	8 460	8 460	8 460	8 460	8 460	8 460	8 460	8 460
EBIDA		€ 5 640	€ 5 640	€ 5 640	€ 5 640	€ 5 640	€ 5 640	€ 5 640	€ 5 640	€ 5 640	€ 5 640
−D&A		2 000	1 600	1 280	1 024	819	655	524	419	336	268
EBIT		€ 3 640	€ 4 040	€ 4 360	€ 4 616	€ 4 821	€ 4 985	€ 5 116	€ 5 221	€ 5 304	€ 5 372
×(1 − *t*)		0.70	0.70	0.70	0.70	0.70	0.70	0.70	0.70	0.70	0.70
NOPAT		€ 2 548	€ 2 828	€ 3 052	€ 3 231	€ 3 375	€ 3 489	€ 3 581	€ 3 654	€ 3 713	€ 3 760
+D&A		2 000	1 600	1 280	1 024	819	655	524	419	336	268
CF Opns		€ 4 548	€ 4 428	€ 4 332	€ 4 255	€ 4 194	€ 4 145	€ 4 105	€ 4 074	€ 4 049	€ 4 029
Cap Ex	€ 10 000	0	0	0	0	0	0	0	0	0	−322
Add WC	1 000	0	0	0	0	0	0	0	0	0	−1 000
FCF	€ 11 000	€ 4 548	€ 4 428	€ 4 332	€ 4 255	€ 4 194	€ 4 145	€ 4 105	€ 4 074	€ 4 049	€ 5 351
NPV @ 10%	€15 685.7										

This exhibit shows the FCF calculations and the NPV for the performing arts centre when double declining depreciation is used to compute the tax depreciation. These calculations correspond to those in Exhibit 11.3, which reflect straight-line depreciation. Notice that the NPV is greater with double declining depreciation because the tax shields from the depreciation are realised sooner.

centre project is expected to be €2 000 000 and that the book value remains €1 074 000. In this case the firm will pay additional taxes of (€2 000 000 − €1 074 000) × 0.30 = €277 800 on the sale of the asset. Deducting this amount from the €2 000 000 that the firm receives from the sale of the assets yields after-tax proceeds of €1 722 123 and the cash flows illustrated in Exhibit 11.10.

EXHIBIT 11.10

FCF CALCULATIONS AND NPV FOR THE PERFORMING ARTS CENTRE WITH A €2 MILLION SALVAGE VALUE IN YEAR 10 (€ THOUSANDS)

	Year 0	Year 1	Year 2	Year 3	Year 4	Year 5	Year 6	Year 7	Year 8	Year 9	Year 10
CF Opns		€4 548	€4 428	€4 332	€4 255	€4 194	€4 145	€4 105	€4 074	€4 049	€4 029
Cap Ex	€ 10 000										−1 722
Add WC	1 000										−1 000
FCF	−€ 11 000	€4 548	€4 428	€4 332	€4 255	€4 194	€4 145	€4 105	€4 074	€4 049	€6 751
NPV @ 10%	€16 225.5										

This exhibit shows the FCF calculations and the NPV for the performing arts centre project assuming that the salvage value of the €10 million capital investment is €2 million in year 10. All other assumptions are the same as in Exhibit 11.9.

Accounting for Taxes when Assets are Sold

Problem: You have decided to replace an oven in your pizza restaurant. The old oven originally cost €20 000. Depreciation charges of €15 000 have been taken since you acquired it, resulting in a current book value of €5000. The owner of a restaurant down the street has offered you €3000 for the old oven. If you accept this offer, how will the sale affect the cash flows from your business? Assume the marginal tax rate for your business is 39%.

Approach: First use the general formula presented above to calculate the tax on the salvage value. Then subtract (add) any tax obligation (savings) from (to) the amount that you will receive for the oven to obtain the total impact of the sale on the cash flows to your business.

Solution: If you sell the old oven, you will receive a cash inflow of €3000 from the purchaser in return for an asset with a book value of €5000. With a 39% marginal tax rate, this will result in a tax of:

$$\text{Tax on sale of an asset} = (\text{Selling price of asset} - \text{Book value of asset}) \times t$$
$$= €3000 - €5000) \times 0.39$$
$$= -€780$$

Since you are selling the oven for less than its book value, you will realise a tax saving of €780. Therefore, the total impact of the sale on the cash flows from your business will be €3000 + €780 = €3780. Of course, the purchase price of the new oven will probably more than offset this amount.

Note that if the sale price exceeded the book value of the oven by €2000, you would have a taxable gain and would have to pay €780. In this case, the cash flows received from the purchaser would be reduced, rather than increased, by €780.

Expected Cash Flows

It is very important to realise that in an NPV analysis we use the *expected* FCF for each year of the life of the project. Similar to the expected values calculated in Chapter 7, the expected FCF for a particular year equals the sum of the products of the possible outcomes (FCFs) and the probabilities that those outcomes will be realised.

To better illustrate this point, suppose that you have just invented a new board game and are trying to decide whether you should produce and sell it. If you decide to go ahead with this project, you estimate that it will cost you €100 000 for the equipment necessary to produce and distribute the game. Also suppose you think there are three possible outcomes if you make this investment – the game is very successful, game sales are acceptable but not exceptional and game sales are poor – and that the probabilities associated with these outcomes are 25%, 50% and 25%, respectively. If the FCFs under each of these three outcomes are as illustrated in Exhibit 11.11, then the expected values that you would discount in your NPV analysis are –€100.00, €48.75, €53.75 and €35.00 for years 0, 1, 2 and 3, respectively.[7] You should confirm that each of these values is correct to make sure that you understand how to calculate an expected FCF.

With these FCF estimates, we can now calculate the NPV of the board game project. For

EXHIBIT 11.11

EXPECTED FCFs FOR NEW BOARD GAME (€ THOUSANDS)

Outcome	Probability	0	1	2	3
			Year		
Game is very successful	0.25	−€100	€70	€90	€60
Game sales are acceptable	0.50	−100	50	55	40
Game sales are poor	0.25	−100	25	15	0
Expected FCF		−€100.00	€48.75	€53.75	€35.00

The expected FCF for each year during the life of the board game project equals the weighted average of the possible FCFs in that year.

instance, if your cost of capital is 10%, the NPV is:

$$NPV = FCF_0 + \frac{FCF_1}{1+k} + \frac{FCF_2}{(1+k)^2} + \frac{FCF_3}{(1+k)^3}$$

$$= -€100 + \frac{€48.75}{1.10} + \frac{€53.75}{(1.10)^2} + \frac{€35.00}{(1.10)^3}$$

$$= -€100 + €44.32 + €44.42 + €26.30$$

$$= €15.04$$

Since the project has a positive NPV, you should accept it.

We use *expected* FCFs in an NPV analysis because uncertainties regarding project cash flows that are unique to the project should be reflected in the cash flow forecasts. In Chapter 13, we will discuss why analysts who try to account for such uncertainties by adjusting the discount rate rather than the cash flows are wrong.

Before You Go On

1. What are the five general rules for calculating FCF?
2. What is the difference between nominal and real values? Why is it important not to mix them in an NPV analysis?
3. What is a progressive tax system? What is the difference between a firm's marginal and average tax rates?
4. How can FCF in the terminal year of a project's life differ from FCF in the other years?
5. Why is it important to understand that cash flow forecasts in an NPV analysis are expected values?

BUILDING INTUITION

We Discount *Expected* Cash Flows in an NPV Analysis

Not only are the FCFs that we discount forward looking, but they also reflect expected FCFs. Each FCF is a weighted average of the cash flows from each possible future outcome, where the cash flow from each outcome is weighted by the estimated probability that the outcome will be realised. The expected FCF represents the single best estimate of what the actual FCF will be.

FORECASTING FREE CASH FLOWS

Learning Objective 3

Describe how distinguishing between variable and fixed costs can be useful in forecasting operating expenses.

Earlier, we discussed how to calculate the incremental free cash flows (FCFs) for a project. Of course, when we evaluate a project, we do not know exactly what the cash flows will be and so we must forecast them. As the performing arts centre example suggests, analysts do this for each line item in the FCF calculation for each year during the life of a project. We are now ready to discuss how these forecasts are prepared.

Cash Flows from Operations

To forecast the incremental cash flows from operations (CF Opns) for a project, we must forecast the incremental net revenue (Revenue), operating expenses (Op Ex) and depreciation and amortisation (D&A) associated with the project, as well as the firm's marginal tax rate. To forecast Revenue, analysts typically estimate the number of units that will be sold and the per-unit sales price for each year during the life of the project. The product of the number of units sold and the per-unit sales price equals the Revenue (assuming that the project does not affect other product lines). Separating the Revenue forecast into incremental unit sales and price forces the analyst to think clearly about how well the project has to perform in terms of actual unit sales in order to achieve the forecasted Revenue.

When forecasting Op Ex, analysts often distinguish between **variable costs**, which vary directly with unit sales and **fixed costs**, which do not. To illustrate the difference, consider a situation in which the managers of a firm plan to introduce a video game player that uses virtual reality technology. An overseas design and manufacturing company will produce the components and ship them to

the company, which will assemble, package and ship the finished product. The main variable costs will be those associated with purchasing the components; the labour required for assembling the players; packaging materials; shipping and perhaps sales and marketing. These variable costs will rise in direct proportion to the number of units produced. If the number of units doubles, for example, we would expect these costs to approximately double. Fixed costs, such as the costs associated with assembly space (assuming output can be increased by adding shifts rather than obtaining additional space) and administrative expenses, will not increase directly with the number of units sold.[8]

Variable costs

costs that vary directly with the number of units sold

Fixed costs

costs that do not vary directly with the number of units sold

WEB

You can find a number of free Excel spreadsheets that can be used to forecast free cash flows and use these cash flows to value projects and entire firms at Matt Evans's website: www.exinfm.com/free_spreadsheets.html. Follow the links to the websites of the individual contributors and you will find even more free cash flow models and related information

Distinguishing between variable and fixed costs simplifies the forecasting problem. If company analysts estimate Revenue for a project from unit sales and price forecasts, as described earlier, then the analysts can forecast variable costs by multiplying the variable cost per unit by the number of units expected to be sold each year. Fixed cost forecasts, in contrast, will not typically vary as closely with unit sales. They tend to be based on explicit estimations of the cost of manufacturing (assembly) space, salaries and number of people required for administration of the project, and other establishment costs created by the project.

Since D&A is determined by the amounts invested in depreciable assets and the lives over which these assets can be depreciated, this line item in the CF Opns calculation is computed based on the incremental capital expenditures (Cap Exp) associated with the project, the allowable recovery period and the depreciation method used. Consequently, it is very important to carefully think through the size and timing of the Cap Exp and the nature of those assets to properly estimate the D&A element.

As discussed earlier, the tax rate that should be used when forecasting CF Opns is the marginal rate the firm expects to pay on the incremental cash flows generated by the project *in the future*. Past tax rates are relevant only to the extent that they tell us something about future tax rates. National, state and local officials can change tax rates in the future and, to the extent that such changes can be predicted, they should be reflected in the cash flow forecasts. Unfortunately, such changes are difficult to predict. As a result, analysts normally use the firm's current marginal tax rate.

Investment Cash Flows

As discussed earlier, we must consider two general classes of investments when calculating FCF: incremental capital expenditures (Cap Exp) and incremental additions to working capital (Add WC). Each presents its own special challenges in the preparation of forecasts. In this section, we consider several issues related to forecasting Cap Exp and Add WC.

Capital Expenditures

Cap Exp forecasts in an NPV analysis reflect the expected level of investment during each year of the project's life, including any inflows from salvage values and any tax costs or benefits associated with asset sales. As illustrated in the performing arts

centre example, capital expenditures are typically required at the beginning of a project. Many projects require an initial investment for the assets necessary to produce a product and then little or no investment until the end of the project, when the assets are sold for their salvage value.

Some projects, however, require substantial periodic investments to replace or refurbish assets or to shut down operations (clean-up costs) at the end of the project's life. For example, a chemical plant project might require a substantial investment every few years to refurbish worn equipment. In addition, environmental regulations are likely to require that the property on which a chemical plant is built be restored to its previous condition when it is dismantled. These are like the clean-up costs for the strip mine that we mentioned earlier. Investments such as these should be included in cash flow forecasts wherever appropriate.

Working Capital

As shown in Equation (11.4), cash flow forecasts in an NPV analysis include four working capital items: (1) cash and cash equivalents, (2) accounts receivable, (3) inventories and (4) accounts payable.

Requirements for cash and cash equivalents and accounts receivable are typically forecast as constant percentages of revenue. The cash and cash-equivalent requirements represent the amount of cash needed to make timely payments to suppliers and employees, as well as for other ongoing expenses. This amount tends to vary with the nature of the project, but analysts can gain insights into the required level of cash, as a percentage of revenue, by examining the cash-to-revenue ratios for companies that operate comparable businesses. For example, if you are forecasting cash flows for a hotel project, you might look at the ratio of cash to revenue at public companies that operate hotels for an indication of how much cash is required per unit of revenue.

Forecasting accounts receivable is relatively straightforward. If customers will be given 30 days to pay for purchases and, on average, are expected to take 30 days to pay, the average accounts receivable balance will equal 30 days' worth of revenue or 30 days/365 days per year $= 0.0822$, or 8.22% of annual revenue. This represents the amount of money that must be set aside to finance purchases by customers. For example, a company with €100 million in annual revenue can expect to have €8.22 million invested in accounts receivable at any point in time if its customers take an average of 30 days to pay for their purchases.

Inventories and accounts payables are generally forecast as a percentage of the cost of goods sold. Inventories are forecast this way because the cost of goods sold represents a measure of the amount of money actually invested in inventories. Accounts payable are forecast this way because the cost of goods sold is a measure of the amount of money actually owed to suppliers.

Before You Go On

1. What is the difference between variable and fixed costs and what are examples of each?
2. How are working capital items forecast? Why are accounts receivable typically forecast as a percentage of revenue and accounts payable and inventories as percentages of the cost of goods sold?

SPECIAL CASES (OPTIONAL)

Learning Objective 4

Explain the concept of equivalent annual cost and be able to use it to compare projects with unequal lives, decide when to replace an existing asset and calculate the opportunity cost of using an existing asset.

Now that we have discussed the fundamental concepts underlying NPV analysis (in Chapter 10) and how cash flows are calculated (in this chapter), we can turn our attention to some special cases that arise in capital budgeting. As you will see, dealing with these special cases generally involves the application of concepts that we have already discussed, along with a dose of common sense.

Projects with Different Lives

One problem that arises quite often in capital budgeting involves choosing between two mutually exclusive investments. Recall from Chapter 10 that if investments are mutually exclusive, the manager can choose one investment or the other but not both. This choice is simple if the expected lives of the two investments are the same. We choose the investment with the larger NPV. This type of problem was illustrated in Chapter 10.

The analysis becomes more complicated, however, if the investments have different lives. For example, suppose that you run a lawn-mowing service and have to replace one of your mowers. Furthermore, suppose that you have two options: mower A, which costs €250 and is expected to last two years, and mower B, which costs €360 and is expected to last three years.

If the mowers are identical in every other way and you expect to be in the mowing business for a long time (in other words, you are going to continue to replace mowers as they wear out for the foreseeable future), then you cannot decide which mower to buy simply by comparing the €250 cost of mower A with the €360 cost of mower B. Mower A will provide two years of service, while mower B will provide three years of service.[9]

You might be tempted to choose the mower with the lowest initial investment per year of service. For example, you might choose mower B because the initial investment is €120 per year of service (€360 for three years) while mower A requires an initial investment of €125 per year of service (€250 for two years). As you will see, however, this reasoning can get you into trouble.

In this situation, we can effectively make the lives of the mowers the same by assuming repeated investments over some identical period and comparing the NPVs of their costs. In the mower example, we can do this by considering a six-year investment period. We determine the six-year period by multiplying the life of mower A by the life of mower B ($2 \times 3 = 6$). In six years you would buy mower A three times – in years 0, 2 and 4 – or mower B twice – in years 0 and 3. If we assume that the cost of each mower will remain the same over the next six years and, if we use a 10% opportunity cost of capital, the NPVs of the *costs* of the two alternatives are:

$$NPV = FCF_0 + \frac{FCF_1}{1+k} + \frac{FCF_2}{(1+k)^2} + \cdots + \frac{FCF_n}{(1+k)^n}$$

$$NPV_A = -€250 + \frac{-€0}{1.10} + \frac{-€250}{(1.10)^2} + \frac{-€0}{(1.10)^3}$$

$$+ \frac{-€250}{(1.10)^4} + \frac{-€0}{(1.10)^5} + \frac{-€0}{(1.10)^6}$$

$$= -€627.36$$

$$NPV_B = -€360 + \frac{-€0}{1.10} + \frac{-€0}{(1.10)^2} + \frac{-€360}{(1.10)^3}$$

$$+ \frac{-€0}{(1.10)^4} + \frac{-€0}{(1.10)^5} + \frac{-€0}{(1.10)^6}$$

$$= -€630.47$$

Notice that mower A is actually cheaper over a six-year investment cycle. Over this period, it costs €627.36/6 = €104.56 per year in today's money, while mower B costs €630.47/6 = €105.08 per year.

Often, a much more efficient way of solving a problem of this nature is to compute the **equivalent annual cash flow (EAC)**. The EAC can be calculated as follows:

$$EAC_i = kNPV_i \left[\frac{(1+k)^t}{(1+k)^t - 1} \right] \quad (11.5)$$

where k is the opportunity cost of capital, NPV_i is normal NPV of the investment i and t is the life of the investment.

Equivalent annual cash flow (EAC)

the annual monetary amount of an annuity that has a life equal to that of a project and that also has a present value equal to the present value of the cash flows from the project; the term comes from the fact that

the EAC calculation is often used to calculate a constant annual cost associated with projects in order to make comparisons

Using Equation (11.5), we find that the EACs for mowers A and B are:

$$EAC_A = (0.1)(-€250) \left[\frac{(1+0.1)^2}{(1+0.1)^2 - 1} \right]$$

$$= -€144.05$$

and

$$EAC_B = (0.1)(-€360) \left[\frac{(1+0.1)^3}{(1+0.1)^3 - 1} \right]$$

$$= -€144.76$$

We can see that the EAC gives us the same answer as equating the lives of the investments and calculating the NPVs over a six-year investment cycle. This is to be expected, since the EAC simply reflects the annuity that has the same present value as the cost of an investment over the investment period we are considering. For instance, the NPV of the EAC for mower A over a six-year period is:

$$NPV_A = \frac{-€144.05}{1.1} + \frac{-€144.05}{(1.1)^2} + \frac{-€144.05}{(1.1)^3}$$

$$+ \frac{-€144.05}{(1.1)^4} + \frac{-€144.05}{(1.1)^5} + \frac{-€144.05}{(1.1)^6}$$

$$= -€627.38$$

This is the same NPV we obtained earlier (allowing for rounding differences).

The problem is similar but a bit more complicated if the revenues or operating costs associated with the two mowers differ. For simplicity, we will continue to assume that the mowers will generate the same revenue per year, but we will also assume that mower A will cost €50 per year to maintain and mower B will cost €55 per year to maintain. The NPVs of the two mowers in this case are:

$$NPV_A = -€250 + \frac{-€50}{1.10} + \frac{-€50}{(1.10)^2} = -€336.78$$

$$NPV_B = -€360 + \frac{-€55}{1.10} + \frac{-€55}{(1.10)^2} + \frac{-€55}{(1.10)^3}$$

$$= -€496.78$$

The EACs are

$$EAC_A = (0.1)(-€336.78)\left[\frac{(1+0.1)^2}{(1+0.1)^2 - 1}\right]$$

$$= -€194.05$$

and

$$EAC_B = (0.1)(-€496.78)\left[\frac{(1+0.1)^3}{(1+0.1)^3 - 1}\right]$$

$$= -€199.76$$

Of course, we still want to choose mower A in this case since all that has really happened is that the EAC of mower A has gone up by €50 and the EAC of mower B has gone up by €55. In contrast, if the annual cost of maintaining mower A is €50 and the annual cost of maintaining mower B is €49, we would choose mower B. As confirmation, you should try the calculations for this example.

One other point should be made about the EAC concept. In spite of its name, it does not apply only to costs. If we included revenues in the above analysis and both mowers had positive NPVs, we could still use the EAC formula to compare the two alternatives. The only difference in this case is that the decision criteria would be to choose the most positive EAC instead of the least negative.

Learning By Doing Application 11.5

Using EAC to Compare Projects

Problem: You are looking at new ovens for your pizza restaurant, and you see two models that would work equally well. Model A would cost €40 000 and last 10 years. Model B would cost €50 000 but would last 12 years and would require €500 less electricity per year than model A. Which model is less expensive? Assume a 10% opportunity cost of capital.

Approach: Use the EAC formula in Equation (11.5) to calculate the EAC of the initial investment for each model of oven. Add the annual electricity savings to the EAC of the initial investment for model B. Choose the model with the smallest total EAC.

Solution: The EACs for the initial investments in the two ovens are as follows:

$$EAC_A = (0.1)(-€40\,000)\left[\frac{(1+0.1)^{10}}{(1+0.1)^{10} - 1}\right]$$

$$= -€6509.82$$

$$EAC_B = (0.1)(-€50\,000)\left[\frac{(1+0.1)^{12}}{(1+0.1)^{12} - 1}\right]$$

$$= -€7338.17$$

Now since the electricity savings would be €500 per year in nominal terms, we can simply add this amount to the EAC calculated for model B above to get the true $EAC_B = -€7338.16 + €500 = -€6838.16$.[10] Since the EAC for model B is still more negative than that for model A, we would conclude that model A would be less expensive over its expected useful life.

When to Disinvest from an Asset

Learning Objective 5

Determine the appropriate time to disinvest an asset.

Another problem that arises from time to time involves deciding when to disinvest. A classic example occurs in the timber industry, where a decision must be made about when to fell the timber. The longer the logging is delayed, the greater the amount of saleable timber that can be obtained (since trees grow) and, assuming the price of timber is constant, the greater the value of the wood. If the amount of timber that will be realised when logging and the price per cubic metre of timber at any point in time is known, making the right decision involves a relatively straightforward application of concepts that we have already discussed.

For example, suppose that you own some land on which you planted pine trees 10 years ago. The trees can be harvested and sold to a pulp mill at any time now, but you want to make sure that you choose the point in time that maximises the NPV of your investment in the trees. You have estimated the NPV (which equals the after-tax cash flow *at the time of the harvest*) of harvesting the trees today (year 10) and for each of the next four years to be as follows:

$$NPV_{10} = €35\,000$$
$$NPV_{11} = €40\,250$$
$$NPV_{12} = €45\,483$$
$$NPV_{13} = €49\,576$$
$$NPV_{14} = €52\,550$$

If each of these NPVs is stated in money as of the time when the harvest would take place, we cannot compare them directly. They must first be restated in money adjusted to the same point in time. If the opportunity cost of capital is 10%, we can make this adjustment simply by discounting each of the NPV values to year 10. The discounted values are as follows:

$$NPV_{10} = €35\,000$$
$$NPV_{10,11} = €40\,250/1.1 = €36\,591$$
$$NPV_{10,12} = €45\,483/(1.1)^2 = €37\,589$$
$$NPV_{10,13} = €49\,576/(1.1)^3 = €37\,247$$
$$NPV_{10,14} = €52\,550/(1.1)^4 = €35\,892$$

where $NPV_{x,y}$ refers to the NPV in year x money if the trees are felled in year y. From these numbers, we can see that logging at the end of year 12 will produce the largest NPV in today's money.

If you calculate the percentage increase in the nominal NPV values above, you can see that they increase by 15% from year 10 to 11, by 13% from year 11 to 12, by 9% from year 12 to 13 and by 6% from year 13 to 14. The optimal time to log the trees is at the end of the year before the first year in which the rate of increase is no longer greater than or equal to the cost of capital. At this time it becomes optimal to log the trees and invest the proceeds in alternative investments that yield the opportunity cost of capital because you can earn more from the alternative investments. An alternative way of thinking about this is that you do not want to cut down the trees as long as the asset is earning a return that is greater than or equal to the opportunity cost of capital. This general principle applies to all problems of this kind.

In our example, we are ignoring the fact that the sooner we log the trees, the sooner we can plant the next crop. In this sense the solution is somewhat simplistic – we should really be considering the NPVs for a series of crops – but it illustrates the key points that (1) you must state all NPV values as of the same point in time and (2) the optimal time to disinvest an asset is when it is no longer earning at least the opportunity cost of capital.

Outside the timber industry, these ideas are widely used to decide when to exit investments. For example, leveraged-buyout specialists, who buy companies with the intention of improving and then selling them within a few years, perform a very similar type of analysis when choosing the appropriate time to sell a company.

When to Replace an Existing Asset

Occasionally, financial managers are asked to determine the appropriate time to replace an existing piece of equipment that is still operating. In these situations, they must answer two fundamental questions: do the benefits of replacing the existing machine exceed the costs and, if they do not now, when will they?

Let us examine how these questions can be answered for a situation that commonly arises in the lawn-mowing business. Suppose you have an old mower that is working perfectly well, but you are considering upgrading to a faster model. The old mower will run for another three years before it has to be replaced and will generate cash inflows, net of costs, of €6500 for each of the next three years. The new mower costs €2000 and would bring in net cash flows of €7000 for four years. When should you replace the old mower?

Solving this problem is simply a matter of computing the EAC for the new mower and comparing it with the annual cash inflows from the old mower. With a 10% opportunity cost of capital, the NPV of the new mower is:

$$\text{NPV}_{\text{New mower}} = -€2000 + \frac{€7000}{1.1} + \frac{€7000}{(1.1)^2}$$
$$+ \frac{€7000}{(1.1)^3} + \frac{€7000}{(1.1)^4}$$

$$= -€2000 + €6364 + €5785$$
$$+ €5259 + €4781$$
$$= €20\,189$$

Therefore, the EAC is:

$$\text{EAC}_{\text{New mower}} = (0.1)(€20\,189)\left[\frac{(1+0.1)^4}{(1+0.1)^4 - 1}\right]$$

$$= €6369$$

In this example, the old mower should not be replaced until it wears out because it will generate net cash inflows of €6500 for each of the next three years, while the EAC for the new mower is only €6369.

Now suppose that, instead of remaining constant at €6500, cash inflows from the old mower will decline from €6500 in year 1, to €6000 in year 2 and to €5500 in year 3 as maintenance expenditures and downtime increase near the end of the old mower's useful life. If the EAC for the new mower is €6369, the old machine should be replaced after the first year.

Decision-Making Example 11.2

Deciding When to Replace an Asset

Situation: You are trying to decide when to replace your car. It is already five years old, and maintenance costs keep increasing each year as more and more parts wear out and need to be replaced. You do not really care whether or not your car is new. You just want a car that gets you around at the lowest cost. You expect maintenance costs for your car over the next five years to increase by €500 per year from €500 this past year. Your car will be worthless in five years. As an alternative, you can buy a new car with a five-year warranty that will cover all maintenance costs. The new car will cost €15 000, and you expect to be able to sell it for €10 000 in five years. The fuel consumption for both cars is the same. Remembering what you learned in corporate finance, you calculate the

EAC for each option using a 10% opportunity cost of capital. The NPV for your old car is:

$$NPV_{Old\ car} = \frac{-€1000}{1.1} + \frac{-€1500}{(1.1)^2} + \frac{-€2000}{(1.1)^3}$$
$$+ \frac{-€2500}{(1.1)^4} + \frac{-€3000}{(1.1)^5}$$
$$= -€7221.69$$

and the EAC is –€1905.06. The NPV for the new car is:

$$NPV_{New\ car} = -€15\,000 + \frac{€10\,000}{(1.1)^5}$$
$$= -€8790.79$$

and the EAC is –€2318.99. When should you replace your old car?

Decision: The EAC for the new car is more negative than the EAC for your old car, suggesting that you should not replace your old car. However, if you compare the EAC for the new car with the annual maintenance costs you expect for your old car, you will see that the annual maintenance costs rise above the EAC of the new car in year 4. Assuming that the economics of the new car remain the same, you should replace your car after year 3.

The Cost of Using an Existing Asset

We have already discussed five general rules for calculating the incremental after-tax free cash flows associated with a project. The third rule is *to include all opportunity costs*. Unfortunately, opportunity costs are not always directly observable. Sometimes they have to be calculated. This is particularly true when the opportunity cost relates to the use of excess capacity associated with an existing asset.

To see how we can evaluate opportunity costs of this kind, consider an example. Suppose you run a plant that mixes, bags and ships potting soil – the soil often used for potted plants kept in people's homes. The bagging machine at your plant has sufficient excess capacity to handle forecasted increases in sales for the next five years if you stick to the potting-soil business. However, one of your managers has proposed that your plant diversify into the mulch business. If you began using the existing bagging machine to bag mulch, you would have to purchase a second bagging machine in three years instead of in five years. The cost of a second, identical machine would be €100 000 and this machine would have a five-year life. If the appropriate opportunity cost of capital is 10%, how should you account for the opportunity cost of using the bagging machine when computing the NPV of the mulch project?

The first step is to compute the EAC for the second bagging machine. It is:

$$EAC_{Bagging\ machine} = (0.1)(-€100\,000)\left[\frac{(1+0.1)^5}{(1+0.1)^5 - 1}\right]$$
$$= -€26\,380$$

This tells us that the bagging machine costs €26 380 per year. If you decide to get into the mulch business, this cost, which would not otherwise be incurred until year 5, will also be incurred in years 3 and 4. Therefore, the opportunity cost of using the excess bagging capacity equals the present value of the additional cost incurred in years 3 and 4:

$$NPV_{Bagging\ machine\ opportunity\ cost}$$
$$= \frac{-€26\,380}{(1.1)^3} + \frac{-€26\,380}{(1.1)^4} = -€37\,838$$

This cost should be included in the incremental cash flows for the mulch business. If the mulch project has a negative NPV with this cost, you might consider examining whether it has a positive NPV if you run the mulch business for only the next three years, while there is no constraint on the bagging capacity. A positive NPV in this latter analysis would indicate that the project should be pursued for three years and then abandoned.

Before You Go On

1. When can we *not* simply compare the NPVs of two mutually exclusive projects?
2. How do we decide when to harvest an asset?
3. Under what circumstance would you replace an old machine that is still operating with a new one?

SUMMARY OF LEARNING OBJECTIVES

1. **Explain why incremental after-tax free cash flows are relevant in evaluating a project and be able to calculate them for a project.**

    The incremental after-tax free cash flows, FCFs, for a project equal the expected change in the total after-tax cash flows of the firm if the project is adopted. The impact of a project on the firm's total cash flows is the appropriate measure of cash flows because these are the cash flows that reflect all of the costs and benefits from the project and only the costs and benefits from the project. The incremental after-tax free cash flows are calculated using Equation (11.2). This calculation is also illustrated in Exhibit 11.1.

2. **Discuss the five general rules for incremental after-tax free cash flow calculations and explain why cash flows stated in nominal (real) values should be discounted using a nominal (real) discount rate.**

    The five general rules are as follows.

    Rule 1: *Include cash flows and only cash flows in your calculations.* Shareholders care about only the impact of a project on the firm's cash flows.

    Rule 2: *Include the impact of the project on cash flows from other product lines.* If a project affects the cash flows from other projects, we must take this fact into account in NPV analysis in order to fully capture the impact of the project on the firm's total cash flows.

    Rule 3: *Include all opportunity costs.* If an asset is used for a project, the relevant cost for that asset is the value that could be realised from its most valuable alternative use. By including this cost in the NPV analysis, we capture the change in the firm's cash flows that is attributable to the use of this asset for the project.

    Rule 4: *Forget sunk costs.* The only costs that matter are those to be incurred from this point on.

    Rule 5: *Include only after-tax cash flows in the cash flow calculations.* Since shareholders receive cash flows after taxes have been paid, they are concerned only about after-tax cash flows.

    Since a nominal discount rate reflects both the expected rate of inflation and a real return, we would be over-adjusting for inflation if we discounted a real cash flow with a nominal rate. Similarly, if we discounted a nominal cash flow using a real discount rate, we would be undercompensating for expected inflation in the discounting process. This is why we discount nominal cash flows using only a nominal discount rate and we discount real cash flows using only a real discount rate.

3. **Describe how distinguishing between variable and fixed costs can be useful in forecasting operating expenses.**

Variable costs vary directly with the number of units sold, while fixed costs do not. When forecasting operating expenses, it is often useful to treat variable and fixed costs separately. We can forecast variable costs by multiplying unit variable costs by the number of units sold. Fixed costs are more accurately based on the specific characteristics of those costs, rather than as a function of sales. Separating fixed costs from the variable also makes it easier to identify the factors that will cause them to change over time and therefore easier to forecast them.

4. **Explain the concept of equivalent annual cost and be able to use it to compare projects with unequal lives, decide when to replace an existing asset and calculate the opportunity cost of using an existing asset.**

The equivalent annual cost (EAC) is the annualised cost of an investment that is stated in nominal values. In other words, it is the annual payment from an annuity that has the same NPV and the same life as the project. Since it is a measure of the annual cost or cash inflow from a project, the EAC for one project can be compared directly with the EAC from another project, regardless of the lives of those two projects. Applications of the EAC concept are presented.

5. **Determine the appropriate time to disinvest an asset.**

The appropriate time to disinvest an asset is that point in time where disinvesting the asset yields the largest present value, in today's money, of the project NPV.

SUMMARY OF KEY EQUATIONS

Equation	Description	Formula
(11.1)	Incremental free cash flow description	$FCF_{Project} = FCF_{Firm\ with\ project} - FCF_{Firm\ without\ project}$
(11.2)	Incremental free cash flow calculation	$FCF = [(Revenue - Op\ Ex - D\&A) \times (1 - t)] + D\&A - Cap\ Ex - Add\ WC$
(11.3)	Inflation and real cost of capital	$1 + k = (1 + \Delta P_e) \times (1 + r)$
(11.4)	Incremental additions to working capital	Add WC = Change in cash and cash equivalents + Change in accounts receivable + Change in inventories – Change in accounts payable
(11.5)	Equivalent annual cost	$EAC_i = kNPV_i \left[\dfrac{(1 + k)^t}{(1 + k)^t - 1} \right]$

SELF-STUDY PROBLEMS

11.1. Explain why the announcement of a new investment is usually accompanied by a change in the firm's share price.

11.2. In calculating the NPV of a project, should we use all of the cash flows associated with the project or incremental free cash flows from the project? Why?

11.3. You are considering opening another restaurant in the TexasBurgers chain. The new restaurant will have annual revenue of €300 000 and operating expenses of €150 000. The annual depreciation and amortisation for the assets used in the restaurant will equal €50 000. An annual capital expenditure of €10 000 will be required to offset wear and tear on the assets used in the restaurant but no additions to working capital will be required. The marginal tax rate will be 40%. Calculate the incremental annual free cash flow for the project.

11.4. Le Soleil Enchanté SA is launching a new boutique in a shopping mall in Nice. The annual revenue of the boutique depends on the weather conditions in the summer in Nice. The annual revenue will be €240 000 in a sizzling summer with a probability of 0.3, €80 000 in a cool summer with a probability of 0.2 and €150 000 in a normal summer with a probability of 0.5. What is the expected annual revenue for the boutique?

11.5. Costruzione Della Nave de Trieste S.p.A. needs to purchase a new central air-conditioning system for a plant. There are two choices. The first system costs €50 000 and is expected to last 10 years and the second system costs €72 000 and is expected to last 15 years. Assume that the opportunity cost of capital is 10%. Which air-conditioning system should Costruzione Della Nave de Trieste purchase?

SOLUTIONS TO SELF-STUDY PROBLEMS

11.1. A firm's investments cause changes in its future after-tax cash flows and shareholders are the residual claimants (owners) of those cash flows. Therefore, the share price should rise when shareholders expect an investment to have a positive NPV and fall when it is expected to have a negative NPV.

11.2. We should use incremental free cash flows from the project. Incremental cash flows reflect the amount by which the firm's total cash flows will change if the project is adopted. In other words, incremental cash flows represent the net difference in cash revenues, costs and investment outlays at the firm level with and without the project, which is precisely what shareholders care about.

11.3. The incremental annual free cash flow is calculated as follows:

$$
\begin{aligned}
\text{FCF} &= [(\text{€}300\ 000 - \text{€}150\ 000 - \text{€}50\ 000) \\
&\quad \times (1 - 0.4)] + \text{€}50\ 000 - 10\ 000 \\
&= \text{€}100\ 000
\end{aligned}
$$

11.4. The expected annual revenue is:

$$
(0.3 \times \text{€}240\ 000) + (0.2 \times \text{€}80\ 000) \\
+ (0.5 \times \text{€}150\ 000) = \text{€}163\ 000
$$

11.5. The equivalent annual cost for each system is as follows:

$$
\text{EAC}_1 = (0.1)(\text{€}50\ 000)\left[\frac{(1.1)^{10}}{(1.1)^{10} - 1}\right]
$$

$$
= \text{€}8137.27
$$

$$
\text{EAC}_2 = (0.1)(\text{€}72\ 000)\left[\frac{(1.1)^{12}}{(1.1)^{12} - 1}\right]
$$

$$
= \text{€}9466.11
$$

Therefore, Costruzione Della Nave de Trieste should purchase the first one.

CRITICAL THINKING QUESTIONS

11.1. Do you agree or disagree with the following statement given the techniques discussed in this chapter? We can calculate future cash flows precisely and obtain an exact value for the NPV of an investment.

11.2. What are the differences between forecasted cash flows used in capital budgeting calculations and past accounting earnings?

11.3. Suppose that FRA GmbH already has divisions in both Düsseldorf and Hamburg. FRA is now considering setting up a third division in Munich. This expansion will require that one senior manager from Düsseldorf and one from Hamburg relocate to Munich. Ignore relocation expenses. Is their annual compensation relevant to the decision to expand?

11.4. MusicHeaven Ltd is a producer of MP3 players, which currently have either 20 gigabytes or 30 gigabytes of storage. Now the company is considering launching a new production line making mini MP3 players with 5 gigabytes of storage. Analysts forecast that MusicHeaven will be able to sell 1 million such mini MP3 players if the investment is taken. In making the investment decision, discuss what the company should consider other than the sales of the mini MP3 players.

11.5. Quality Living Trust is a property company that builds and remodels apartment buildings in the West of England. It is currently considering remodelling a few idle buildings that it owns into luxury apartment buildings in Bristol. The company bought those buildings eight months ago. How should the market value of the buildings be treated in evaluating this project?

11.6. Haut Mode bought a production line for making ankle-length skirts last year at a cost of €500 000. This year, however, miniskirts are all the fashion in the market and ankle-length skirts are completely out of fashion. Haut Mode has the option to rebuild the production line and use it to produce miniskirts with a cost of €300 000 and expected revenue of €700 000. How should the company treat the cost of €500 000 of the old production line in evaluating the rebuilding plan?

11.7. How does the declining balance capital allowance tax depreciation method used in the UK differ from that under GAAP rules? What iss the implication on incremental after-tax cash flows from firms' investments?

11.8. Explain the difference between marginal and average tax rates and identify which of these rates is used in capital budgeting and why.

11.9. When two mutually exclusive projects have different lives, how can an analyst determine which is better? What is the underlying assumption in this method?

11.10. What is the opportunity cost of using an existing asset? Give an example of the opportunity cost of using the excess capacity of a machine.

11.11. You are providing financial advice to a shrimp farmer who will be harvesting his last crop of farm-raised shrimp. His current shrimp crop is very young and, therefore, will grow and become more valuable as their weight increases. Describe how you would determine the appropriate time to harvest the entire crop of shrimp.

QUESTIONS AND PROBLEMS

Basic

11.1. Calculating project cash flows: Why do we use forecasted free cash flows instead of forecasted accounting earnings in estimating the NPV of a project?

11.2. The FCF calculation: How do we calculate incremental after-tax free cash flows from forecasted earnings of a project? What are the common adjustment items?

11.3. The FCF calculation: How do we adjust for depreciation when we calculate incremental after-tax free cash flow from EBITDA? What is the intuition for the adjustment?

11.4. Nominal versus real cash flows: What is the difference between nominal and real cash flows? Which rate of return should we use to discount each type of cash flow?

11.5. Taxes and depreciation: What is the difference between the average tax rate and the marginal tax rate? Which one should we use in calculating incremental after-tax cash flows?

11.6. Computing terminal-year FCF: Zum Wohl AG, a pharmaceutical company, bought a machine that produces pain-reliever medicine at a cost of €2 million five years ago. The machine has been depreciated over the past five years and the current book value is €800 000. The company decides to sell the machine now at its market price of €1 million. The marginal tax rate is 30%. What are the relevant cash flows? How do they change if the market price of the machine is €600 000 instead?

11.7. Cash flows from operations: What are variable costs and fixed costs? What are some examples of each? How are these costs estimated in forecasting operating expenses?

11.8. Investment cash flows: Jederzeit Offen Shop AG is considering opening up a new convenience store in downtown Frankfurt. The expected annual revenue is €800 000. To estimate the increase in working capital, analysts estimate the ratio of cash and cash-equivalents to revenue to be 0.03 and the ratios of receivables, inventories and payables to revenue to be 0.05, 0.10 and 0.04, respectively, in the same industry. What is the incremental cash flow related to working capital when the store is opened?

11.9. Investment cash flows: The Keswick Supply Company wants to set up a division that provides copy and fax services to businesses. Customers will be given 20 days to pay for such services. The annual revenue of the division is estimated to be £25 000. Assuming that the customers take the full 20 days to pay, what is the incremental cash flow associated with accounts receivable?

11.10. Expected cash flows: Define *expected cash flows* and explain why this concept is important in evaluating projects.

11.11. Projects with different lives: Explain the concept of equivalent annual cost and how it is used to compare projects with different lives.

11.12. Replace an existing asset: Explain how we decide the optimal time to replace an existing asset with a new one.

Intermediate

11.13. Nominal versus real cash flows: You are buying a sofa. You will pay €200 today and make three consecutive annual payments of €300 in the future. The real rate of return is 10% and the expected inflation rate is 4%. What is the actual price of the sofa today?

11.14. Nominal versus real cash flows: You are graduating in two years. You want to invest your current savings of €5000 in bonds and use the proceeds to purchase a new car when you graduate and start work. You can invest the money in either bond A, a two-year bond with a 3% annual interest rate, or bond B, an inflation-indexed two-year bond paying 1% real interest above the inflation rate (assume this bond makes annual interest payments). The inflation rate over the next two years is expected to be 1.5%. Assume that both bonds are default-free and have the same market price. Which bond should you invest in?

11.15. Marginal and average tax rates: Given the Belgian Corporate Tax Rate Schedule in Exhibit 11.6, what is the marginal tax rate and average tax rate of a company that generates a taxable income of €350 000?

11.16. EXCEL® **Investment cash flows:** Zum Wohl AG is considering investing in a new production line for eye drops. Other than investing in the equipment, the company needs to increase its cash and cash equivalents by €10 000, increase the level of inventories by €30 000, increase accounts receivable by €25 000 and increase accounts payable by €5000 at the beginning of the project. Zum Wohl will recover these changes in working capital at the end of the project 10 years later. Assume the appropriate discount rate is 12%. What are the present values of the relevant cash flows?

11.17. EXCEL® **Cash flows from operations:** Given the soaring price of fuel, Fiat is considering introducing a new production line of gas/electric hybrid cars. The expected annual unit sales of the hybrid cars is 30 000; the price is €22 000 per car. Variable costs of production are €10 000 per car. The fixed overhead including salary of top executives is €80 million per year. However, the introduction of the hybrid sedan will decrease Fiat's sales of regular cars by 10 000 cars per year; the regular cars have a unit price of €20 000, a unit variable cost of €12 000 and fixed costs of €250 000 per year. Depreciation costs of the production plant are €50 000 per year. The marginal tax rate is 40%. What is the incremental annual cash flow from operations?

11.18. EXCEL® **FCF and NPV for a project:** Cava Tempranillo SA is considering buying a new vineyard that it plans to operate for 10 years. The farm will require an initial investment of €12 million. This investment will consist of €2 million for land and €10 million for tractors and other equipment. The land, all tractors and all other equipment is expected to be sold at the end of 10 years for a price of €5 million, €2 million above book value. The vineyard is expected to produce revenue of €2 million each year and annual cash flow from operations equals €1.8 million. The marginal tax rate is 35% and the appropriate discount rate is 10%. Calculate the NPV of this investment.

11.19. EXCEL® **Projects with different lives:** You are starting a family pizza restaurant and need to buy a motorcycle for delivery orders. You have two models in mind. Model A costs €9000 and is expected to run for six years; model B is more expensive, with a price of €14 000 and has an expected life of 10 years. The annual maintenance costs are €800 for model A and €700 for model B. Assume that the opportunity cost of capital is 10%. Which one should you buy?

11.20. EXCEL® **When to disinvest an asset:** Predator LLC, a leveraged-buyout specialist, recently bought a company and wants to determine the optimal time to sell it. The partner in charge of this investment has estimated the after-tax cash flows at different times as follows: $700 000 if sold one year later; $1 000 000 if sold two years later; $1 200 000 if sold three years later; and $1 300 000 if sold four years later. The opportunity cost of capital is 12%. When should Predator sell the company? Why?

11.21. EXCEL® **Replace an existing asset:** Viticultores del Gorner SA is considering updating its current manual accounting system with a high-end electronic system. While the new accounting system would save the company money, the cost of the system continues to decline. Viticultores del Gorner's opportunity cost of capital is 10% and the costs and values of investments made at different times in the future are as follows:

Year	Cost	Value of Future Savings (at time of purchase)
0	€5000	€7000
1	4500	7000
2	4000	7000
3	3600	7000
4	3300	7000
5	3100	7000

When should Viticultores del Gorner buy the new accounting system?

11.22. EXCEL® **Replace an existing asset:** You have a 1993 Nissan that is expected to run for another three years but you are considering buying a new Hyundai before the Nissan wears out. You will donate the Nissan to a green recycling group when you buy the new car. The annual maintenance cost is €1500 per year for the Nissan and €200 for the Hyundai. The price of your favourite Hyundai model is €18 000 and it is expected to run for 15 years. Your opportunity cost of capital is 3%. Ignore taxes. When should you buy the new Hyundai?

11.23. **Replace an existing asset:** Assume that you are considering replacing your old Nissan with a new Hyundai, as in the previous problem. However, the annual maintenance cost of the old Nissan increases as time goes by. It is €1200 in the first year, €1500 in the second year and €1800 in the third year. When should you replace the Nissan with the new Hyundai in this case?

11.24. **When to disinvest an existing asset:** Anaconda Manufacturing Company currently owns a mine that is known to contain a certain amount of gold. Since Anaconda does not have any gold-mining expertise, the company plans to sell the entire mine and base the selling price on a fixed multiple of the spot price for gold at the time of the sale. Analysts at Anaconda have forecast the spot price for gold and have determined that the price will increase by 14%, 12%, 9% and 6% during the next one, two, three and four years, respectively. If Anaconda's opportunity cost of capital is 10%, what is the optimal time for Anaconda to sell the mine?

11.25. **Replace an existing asset:** You are thinking about delivering pizzas in your spare time. Since you must use your own car to deliver the pizzas, you will wear out your current car one year earlier, which is one year from today, than if you did not take on the delivery job. You estimate that when you purchase a new car, regardless of when that occurs, you will pay €20 000 for the car and it will last you five years. If your opportunity cost of capital is 7%, what is the opportunity cost of using your car to deliver pizzas?

Advanced

11.26. EXCEL® You are the CFO of SlimBody, Inc., a retailer of the exercise machine Slimbody6® and related accessories. Your firm is considering opening up a new store in Los Angeles. The store will have a life of 20 years. It will generate annual sales of 5000 exercise machines and the price of each machine is $2500. The annual sales of accessories will be $600 000, and the operating expenses of running the store, including labour and rent, will amount to 50% of the revenues from the exercise machines. The initial investment in the store will equal $30 million and will be fully depreciated on a straight-line basis over the 20-year life of the store. Your firm will need to invest $2 million in additional working capital immediately and recover it at the end of the investment. Your firm's marginal tax rate is 30%. The opportunity cost of opening up the store is 10%. What are the incremental free cash flows from this project at the beginning of the project as well as in years 1–19 and 20? Should you approve it?

11.27. EXCEL® Madrier de Sierre SA is considering purchasing a new wood saw that costs SFr 50 000. The saw will generate revenues of SFr 100 000 per year for five years. The cost of materials and labour needed to generate these revenues will total SFr 60 000 per year and other cash expenses will be SFr 10 000 per year. The machine is expected to sell for SFr 1000 at the end of its five-year life and will be depreciated on a straight-line basis over five years to zero. Madrier de Sierre's tax rate is 34% and its opportunity cost of capital is 10%. Should the company purchase the saw? Explain why, or why not.

11.28. EXCEL® A beauty product company is developing a new fragrance named Eternité. There is a probability of 0.5 that consumers will love Eternité and, in this case, annual sales will be 1 million bottles; a probability of 0.4 that consumers will find the smell acceptable and annual sales will be 200 000 bottles; and a probability of 0.1 that consumers will find the smell weird and annual sales will be only 50 000 bottles. The selling price is €38 and the variable cost is €8 per bottle. Fixed production costs will be €1 million per year and depreciation will be €1.2 million. Assume that the marginal tax rate is 40%. What are the expected annual incremental cash flows from the new fragrance?

11.29. EXCEL® La Forme Idéal SA is a company that makes clothing. The company has a product line that produces women's tops of regular sizes. The same machine could be used to produce petite sizes as well. However, the remaining life of the machines will be reduced from four years to two years if the petite size production is added. The cost of identical machines with a life of eight

years is €2 million. Assume the opportunity cost of capital is 8%. What is the opportunity cost of adding petite sizes?

11.30. Biotech Partners LLC has been farming a new strain of radioactive-material-eating bacteria that the electrical utility industry can use to help dispose of its nuclear waste. Two opposing factors affect Biotech's decision on when to harvest the bacteria. The bacteria are currently growing at a 22% annual rate, but due to known competition from other top firms, Biotech analysts estimate that the price for the bacteria will decline according to the schedule below. If the opportunity cost of capital is 10%, when should Biotech harvest the entire bacteria colony at one time?

Year	Change in Price Due to Competition (%)
1	5%
2	−2
3	−8
4	−10
5	−15
6	−25

11.31. EXCEL® ACME Manufacturing is considering replacing an existing production line with a new line that has a greater output capacity and operates with less labour than the existing line. The new line would cost $1 million, have a five-year life and be depreciated using MACRS over three years. At the end of five years, the new line could be sold as scrap for $200 000 (in year-5 dollars). Because the new line is more automated, it would require fewer operators, resulting in savings of €40 000 per year before tax and unadjusted for inflation (in today's dollars). Additional sales with the new machine are expected to result in additional net cash inflows, before tax, of $60 000 per year (in today's dollars). If ACME invests in the new line, a one-time investment of $10 000 in additional working capital will be required. The tax rate is 35%, the opportunity cost of capital is 10% and the annual rate of inflation is 3%. What is the NPV of the new production line?

11.32. [EXCEL®] The alternative to investing in the new production line in Problem 11.31 is to overhaul the existing line, which currently has both a book value and a salvage value of $0. It would cost $300 000 to overhaul the existing line but this expenditure would extend its useful life to five years. The line would have a $0 salvage value at the end of five years. The overhaul outlay would be capitalised and depreciated using MACRS over three years. Should ACME replace or renovate the existing line?

CFA Problems

11.33. ZITAB is considering the purchase of new equipment. The equipment costs €350 000 and an additional €110 000 is needed to install it. The equipment will be depreciated straight-line to zero over a five-year life. The equipment will generate additional annual revenues of €265 000, and it will have annual cash operating expenses of €83 000. The equipment will be sold for €85 000 after five years. An inventory investment of €73 000 is required during the life of the investment. ZITAB is in the

40% tax bracket and its cost of capital is 10%. What is the project NPV?

a. €47 818
b. €63 658
c. €80 189
d. €97 449

11.34. After estimating a project's NPV, the analyst is advised that the fixed capital outlay will be revised upwards by €100 000. The fixed capital outlay is depreciated straight-line over an eight-year life. The tax rate is 40% and the required rate of return is 10%. No changes in cash operating revenues, cash operating expenses or salvage value are expected. What is the effect on the project NPV?

a. €100 000 decrease
b. €73 325 decrease
c. €59 988 decrease
d. No change

11.35. When assembling the cash flows to calculate an NPV or IRR, the project's after-tax interest expenses should be subtracted from the cash flows for:

a. The NPV calculation, but not the IRR calculation.
b. The IRR calculation, but not the NPV calculation.
c. Both the NPV calculation and the IRR calculation.
d. Neither the NPV calculation nor the IRR calculation.

SAMPLE TEST PROBLEMS

11.1. You purchased 100 shares in an oil company, Texas Energy, Inc., at $50 per share. The company has 1 million shares outstanding. Ten days later, Texas Energy announced an investment in an oil field in east Texas. The

probability that the investment will be successful and generate an NPV of $10 million is 0.2; the probability that the investment will be a failure and generate an NPV of negative $1 million is 0.8. How would you expect the share price to change upon the company's announcement of the investment?

11.2. A chemical company is considering buying a magic fan for its plant. The magic fan is expected to work forever and help cool the machines in the plant and, hence, reduce their maintenance costs by €4000 per year. The cost of the fan is €30 000. The appropriate discount rate is 10% and the marginal tax rate is 40%. Should the company buy the magic fan?

11.3. Del Rey Zásobování (DRZ) is considering switching from its old food maker to a new machine. Both food makers will remain useful for the next 10 years but the new food maker will generate a depreciation expense of €5000 per year, while the old food maker will generate a depreciation expense of €4000 per year. What is the after-tax cash flow effect from depreciation of switching to the new food maker for DRZ if the firm's marginal tax rate is 40% and the discount rate is 12%?

11.4. The Long-Term Financing Company has identified an alternative project that is similar to a project currently under consideration in all respects except one. That is, the new project will reduce the need for working capital by £10 000 during the 30-year life of the project. The cost of capital is 18% and the marginal corporate tax rate for the firm is 34%. What is the after-tax present value of this new alternative project?

11.5. Keuze Meester BV must choose between two projects of unequal lives. Project 1 has an NPV of €50 000 and will be viable for five years. The discount rate for project 1 and project 2 is 10%. Project 2 will be viable for seven years. In order for Keuze Meester to be indifferent between the two projects, what must the NPV of project 2 be?

ENDNOTES

1. The argument put forward for the benefits of merging the two companies was that by integrating and rationalising the two companies' distribution networks and capitalising on Cadbury's strong brand position in chocolate and chewing gum, together with other initiatives that were possible with the merged group, the proposed acquisition made sound economic sense. Note too that analysts at the time of the announcement estimated that Kraft would have to pay in excess of £11 billion ($18.1 billion) for Cadbury's.

2. The concept of opportunity cost here is similar to that discussed in Chapter 10 in the context of the opportunity cost of capital.

3. As discussed in Chapter 2, if we multiply the two terms on the right-hand side of Equation (11.3), we get $1 + k = 1 + \Delta P_e + r + \Delta P_e r$. Since the last term in this equation, $\Delta P_e r$, is the product of two fractions, it is a very small number and is often ignored in practice. Without this term, Equation (11.3) becomes $1 + k = 1 + \Delta P_e + r$ or $k = \Delta P_e + r$.

4. Note that when we use the term *cost of capital* without distinguishing between the nominal or real cost of capital, we are referring to the *nominal* cost of capital. This is the convention that is used in practice. In this example, we use the terms *nominal* or *real* whenever we refer to the cost of capital for clarity. In the rest of this book, however, we follow convention by simply using the term *cost of capital* to refer to the nominal cost of capital.

5. The double declining balance method is a variant of the straight-line method. If we assume an asset has a 5-year life then the straight-line depreciation is 20% per annum; 100%/5 = 20%. The double declining balance sets the first year's depreciation at twice the straight-line rate, or 40%, and the same in year 2, year 3 and subsequent years. This accelerates the amount of depreciation against the asset in its early life and hence is similar to the way the UK's capital allowances work. The total amount of depreciation is capped at 40% in Belgium if this method is used.

6. Under GAAP accounting rules, if the salvage value can be estimated with reasonable certainty, it should be used in computing depreciation. However, in practice the expected salvage value of new assets is so uncertain that it is typically assumed to equal zero even for financial reporting purposes.

7. For simplicity, the monetary values in Exhibit 11.11 and the associated calculations on this page are reported in thousands.

8. In some instances, costs are 'fixed' in the short run but variable in the long run. For example, if a firm leases manufacturing space under a long-term contract, it may not be possible to reduce the lease expense immediately if demand for the firm's products falls. However, it will be possible to do so at the expiration of the lease.

9. If you do not expect to replace the machines as they wear out (for instance, if you plan to quit the mowing business in one year), then you can calculate the NPV of each mower, including the salvage values that you expect to realise for each at the end of the year, and choose the mower with the larger NPV.

10. We could also have calculated the NPV for model B by discounting the €500 annual electricity savings by 10% and adding the present value of that savings stream to the €50 000 initial cost. Using this NPV in the EAC formula would also yield −€6838.16.

CHAPTER

12

Evaluating Project Economics and Capital Rationing

In this Chapter:

Variable Costs, Fixed Costs and Project Risk

Calculating Operating Leverage

Break-Even Analysis

Risk Analysis

Investment Decisions with Capital Rationing

LEARNING OBJECTIVES

1. Explain and be able to demonstrate how variable costs and fixed costs affect the volatility of pre-tax operating cash flows and accounting operating profits.
2. Calculate and distinguish between the degree of pre-tax cash flow operating leverage and the degree of accounting operating leverage.
3. Define and calculate the pre-tax operating cash flow and accounting operating profit break-even points and the crossover levels of unit sales for a project.
4. Define sensitivity analysis, scenario analysis and simulation analysis, and describe how they are used to evaluate the risks associated with a project.
5. Explain how the profitability index can be used to rank projects when a firm faces capital rationing and describe the limitations that apply to the profitability index.

In September 2009, EBI Food Safety B.V., the Netherlands-based privately held life sciences company that develops and produces natural bacteriophage products for the food industry, was nominated for Deloitte's prestigious Fast 50 Rising Star Benelux Award.[1] The nomination cited the company's commercialisation and development of its biotechnology in food safety and the original and leading nature of its research. Two years earlier, it had won the Food Industry Europe (FIE) Gold Award, which is considered the 'Oscar' of the food industry, for its innovative approach to food safety. EBI's products protect foodstuffs by acting against dangerous bacteria in food. The presence of bacteria such as listeria strains in the production of meat, cheese, fish, vegetables, fruit and other food products can be a problem. The advantage of EBI's Listex™ processing aid, its first commercially approved product, is that it has no effect on the properties of the treated foods and does not affect other bacteria, such as desired bacteria in starter cultures, and due to its rapid inactivation it

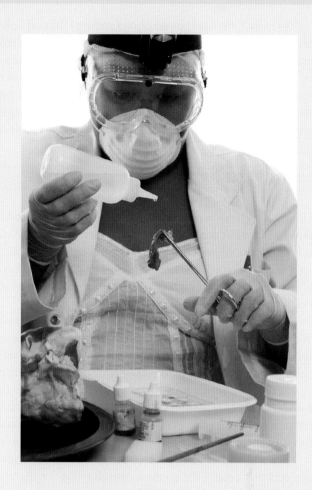

has no effect on the final food product – both highly desirable characteristics. Listex™ was categorised by the Food and Drug Administration and the Department of Agriculture as 'generally recognized as safe' (GRAS) for use in 2007, and this opened the way for the sale of EBI's Listex™ in the United States – the first such licence for a bacteriophage product.

The company's scientific network includes collaborations with universities and research centres around the world.

As with any other capital investment, starting a business involves a great deal of uncertainty. If you put yourself in the shoes of Mark Offerhaus, CEO of EBI, you can imagine the concerns he had when he founded the company. Would the technology work? How large would the market be for their products in the future? How big a share of the market could his firm get before other competitors started offering similar products? The size of the market would depend on many things that were out of his control, such as the demand for food safety, the willingness of the food industry to adopt new technologies and whether regulators would authorise the use of the product. EBI Food Safety's share of the market and, ultimately, its profitability would depend on the firm's ability to meet users' expectations and provide solutions that were more appealing to food companies than those of competing companies.

As Mark Offerhaus contemplated starting EBI Food Safety, he was no doubt asking himself a number of questions: What level of unit sales would be required to cover costs? What would happen if the business did not earn enough to cover its costs? What if the business was initially successful but competitors reacted by developing similar products and slashing the prices of existing ones? What were the odds that the business would be successful? If it was not successful, how bad were things likely to get? If it was successful, how good would the upside be? Answering questions such as these is part of any thorough project analysis. This chapter discusses some of the tools and methods used to obtain the answers.

CHAPTER PREVIEW

Financial analysts who forecast the free cash flows used in an NPV analysis realise that actual cash flows will almost certainly differ from their forecasts. No one can predict the future! For this reason, it is important to understand the economic characteristics of a project and the implications of being wrong. This chapter discusses key tools and methods that analysts use to develop this understanding. It also discusses how managers choose from among available positive NPV projects when they do not have enough money to invest in all of them.

We first discuss how a project's cost structure affects its risk and how analysts measure this effect. We then describe break-even analysis, which is used to determine how many units must be sold in order for a project to break even. These concepts help analysts better understand the economic characteristics of projects and provide insights into how projects can be structured to maximise their value.

We next describe how financial analysts evaluate the uncertainties associated with cash flow forecasts. These techniques allow analysts to determine which characteristics of a project have the greatest impact on the level of the cash flows, how market or economic conditions affect the cash flows of the business, and the probability that certain levels of cash flows will be realised.

We end with a discussion of the tools and methods that help managers choose the bundle of projects that creates the greatest overall value for shareholders when there is not enough capital to invest in all of the positive NPV projects that managers have identified.

VARIABLE COSTS, FIXED COSTS AND PROJECT RISK

Learning Objective 1

Explain and be able to demonstrate how variable costs and fixed costs affect the volatility of pre-tax operating cash flows and accounting operating profits.

Two questions are always on the mind of a financial analyst evaluating a project: 'How wrong can my free cash flow forecasts be?' and 'What are the implications if my forecasts are wrong?' It is natural to ask these questions, since the actual free cash flows (FCF) for a project will almost certainly differ from the forecasted FCF. This and the following sections discuss some important tools that help provide answers.

To fully understand how to evaluate project risk, you must first understand how variable costs and fixed costs affect the risk of a business. Recall from Chapter 11 that variable costs are costs that vary directly with the number of units sold. An example of a variable cost is the cost of the ingredients that a pizza restaurant uses to make its pizzas. The total cost of these ingredients increases or decreases as the number of pizzas sold increases or decreases. Fixed costs, in contrast, do not vary with unit sales – at least in the short run. An example of a fixed cost in a pizza restaurant is the salary of the manager. As pizza sales go up and down from month to month, the cost of the manager's salary remains constant.

The cash flows and accounting profits for a project are sensitive to the proportion of its costs that are variable and the proportion that are fixed. A project with a higher proportion of fixed costs will have cash flows and accounting profits that are more sensitive to changes in revenues than an otherwise identical project with a lower proportion of fixed costs. This is because the costs of a project with a higher proportion of fixed costs will not change as much when revenue changes.

To illustrate this point, we can represent the incremental cash operating expenses, Op Ex, from Equation (11.2) as:

$$\text{Op Ex} = \text{VC} + \text{FC} \qquad (12.1)$$

where VC are the incremental variable costs associated with a project and FC are the incremental fixed costs. Equation (12.1) simply says that all cash operating expenses are either variable costs or fixed costs.

Let us carry this equation a bit further. We know from Exhibit 11.1 that

$$\text{EBITDA} = \text{Revenue} - \text{Op Ex}$$

Thus, Equation (12.1) suggests that we can write EBITDA as:

$$\text{EBITDA} = \text{Revenue} - \text{VC} - \text{FC}$$

You might recall from Chapter 11 that EBITDA is the incremental earnings before interest, taxes, depreciation and amortisation and Revenue is the incremental revenue from a project. EBITDA is often called pre-tax operating cash flow because

it equals the incremental pre-tax *cash* operating profits from a project. Strictly speaking, EBITDA is not a complete measure of operating cash flow because it does not include the effects of working capital requirements on cash flows. Nevertheless, it is a very commonly used measure.

> **Pre-tax operating cash flow**
>
> earnings before interest, taxes, depreciation and amortisation, or EBITDA

Cost Structure and Sensitivity of EBITDA to Revenue Changes

To see how writing the calculation of EBITDA in terms of fixed and variable costs can be helpful, consider this situation: you have been trying to decide whether to buy a hammock-manufacturing business in which hammocks are currently made by hand.[2] Now you have become aware of the existence of an automated hammock-manufacturing system. This means that, in addition to deciding whether to go into the hammock business, you must choose between two manufacturing alternatives: (1) investing in manufacturing equipment that will largely automate the production process and (2) relying on the current manufacturing method in which hammocks are produced by hand. Assume that the per-unit variable costs (Unit VC) and the total FC and depreciation and amortisation (D&A) for the two alternatives are as presented in Exhibit 12.1. How would you evaluate the relative advantages and disadvantages of the automated and the manual production alternatives?

One thing you might do is compare the sensitivity of EBITDA to changes in revenue for the two alternatives. This can help you better understand the risks and returns for the alternatives. To see why, assume that the sensitivity of EBITDA to changes in revenue is higher for one alternative than for the other. This means that EBITDA for the more sensitive alternative will decline more when revenue is lower than expected. A larger decline in EBITDA can cause problems not only because it

EXHIBIT 12.1

UNIT AND ANNUAL COSTS FOR HAMMOCK PROJECT

	Automated Production	Manual Production
Unit VC:		
Labour	€1	€5
Rope	5	5
Spacer bars	2	2
Hardware	2	2
Packaging	2	2
Shipping and other	4	4
Total	€16	€20
FC	€35 000	€4 000
D&A	€10 000	€1 000

To evaluate the automated and manual production alternatives in our hammock-manufacturing example, we start with information about the variable costs per unit (Unit VC), fixed costs (FC) and depreciation and amortisation (D&A).

EXHIBIT 12.2

EBITDA UNDER ALTERNATIVE PRODUCTION TECHNOLOGIES

	Automated Production	Manual Production
Units sold	10 000	10 000
Unit price	€25	€25
Unit VC	€16	€20
Revenue	€250 000	€250 000
– VC	160 000	200 000
– FC	35 000	4 000
EBITDA	€ 55 000	€ 46 000

Here we calculate EBITDA for the automated and manual production alternatives in the hammock-manufacturing example. The calculations use the information provided in Exhibit 12.1 and assume that 10 000 units are sold at a price of €25 per unit.

reduces the value of the project more but also because it has a greater impact on the amount of cash that the firm has available to fund other positive NPV projects. In an extreme case, a drop in EBITDA can unexpectedly force the firm to invest additional money into the project. On the positive side, EBITDA will increase more when revenue is greater than expected if the level of sensitivity is higher. Whether this potential benefit justifies the risks is a decision that you would have to make when choosing between the two alternatives. Comparing the sensitivity of EBITDA to changes in revenue for the two alternatives will at least help you better understand the trade-offs.

Distinguishing between fixed and variable costs enables us to calculate the sensitivity of EBITDA to changes in revenue. For example, suppose you expect to sell 10 000 hammocks next year at an average price of €25 each. Based on the costs in Exhibit 12.1, you would forecast EBITDA to be €55 000 under the automated production alternative and €46 000 under the manual production alternative.[3] These calculations are presented in Exhibit 12.2.

Although selling 10 000 units represents your best estimate of what you can expect, you might also envision a situation in which demand would be poor and sales would equal only 8000 units – 20% less than your best estimate of 10 000 units. Distinguishing between fixed and variable costs makes it relatively straightforward to determine how EBITDA would be affected if only 8000 units were sold. This 'Poor Demand' scenario is illustrated in columns 2 and 4 of Exhibit 12.3 for the automated production and manual production alternatives (assuming that Unit VC does not change with unit sales). Columns 1 and 3 are identical to the two columns in Exhibit 12.2.

Exhibit 12.3 shows that EBITDA is much more sensitive to changes in revenue with the automated production process than with the manual process. A 20% decline in revenue results in a 32.7% decline in EBITDA with the automated production process but only a 21.7% decline in EBITDA with the manual production process – an 11 percentage point difference. The reason for the difference is

EXHIBIT 12.3

CHANGES IN EBITDA UNDER ALTERNATIVE PRODUCTION TECHNOLOGIES

	Automated Production		Manual Production	
	Expected Demand (1)	Poor Demand (2)	Expected Demand (3)	Poor Demand (4)
Units sold	10 000	8 000	10 000	8 000
Unit price	€25	€25	€25	€25
Unit VC	€16	€16	€20	€20
Revenue	€250 000	€200 000	€250 000	€200 000
−VC	160 000	128 000	200 000	160 000
−FC	35 000	35 000	4 000	4 000
EBITDA	€ 55 000	€ 37 000	€ 46 000	€ 36 000
Per cent change in revenue[a]		−20.0%		−20.0%
Per cent change in EBITDA		−32.7%		−21.7%

[a]The per cent change in revenue is calculated as:

Per cent change $= (\text{Revenue}_{Poor} - \text{Revenue}_{Expected})/\text{Revenue}_{Expected}$

$\qquad = (€200\,000 - €250\,000)/€250\,000 = -0.20,\ \text{or}\ -20\%$

All other per cent changes are calculated this way in the exhibits.

EBITDA for the automated and manual production alternatives in the hammock-manufacturing example decline by different amounts when the number of units sold declines by 20% and the unit price remains the same.

that more of the total costs are fixed with the automated process, making it more difficult to adjust costs when revenue changes. Because of this difference, the difference in EBITDA under the two production alternatives shrinks from €9000 (€55 000 − €46 000) to only €1000 (€37 000 − €36 000) when unit sales are 8000 instead of 10 000.

You can see how the difference in EBITDA shrinks as the number of units sold decreases in Exhibit 12.4, which shows how EBITDA changes as the number of units sold changes for both the manual and the automated production process. Notice that the relation between EBITDA and the number of units sold is steeper with the automated production process, where there are more fixed costs. A steeper line indicates that EBITDA

for the automated production process is more sensitive to changes in the number of units sold.

Note also that the effect of changes in the number of units sold is symmetrical because the relation between EBITDA and the number of units sold is linear. This means that the automated production process will produce larger declines in EBITDA when unit sales are lower than expected as well as larger increases in EBITDA when unit sales are higher than expected. This is exactly what we were referring to earlier when we said that when pre-tax operating cash flows are more sensitive to changes in revenue, they will decline more when revenue is lower than expected and increase more when revenue is greater than expected.

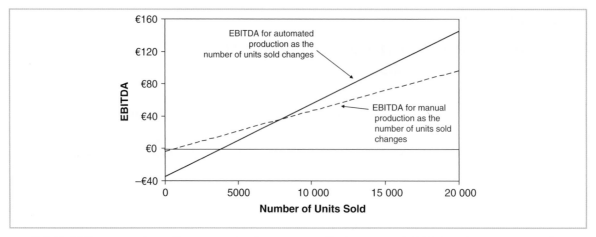

Exhibit 12.4: EBITDA for Different Levels of Unit Sales   The sensitivity of EBITDA to changes in unit sales differs for the automated and manual production alternatives in the hammock-manufacturing example. The steeper line for the automated production alternative means that EBITDA for this alternative is more sensitive to changes in the number of units sold.

Cost Structure and Sensitivity of EBIT to Revenue Changes

Exhibit 12.5 expands the analysis in Exhibit 12.3 to illustrate how the sensitivity of accounting operating profits (EBIT) to changes in revenue differs under the two manufacturing alternatives. The sensitivity of EBIT to changes in revenue is of concern to managers because EBIT is a performance measure that is of interest to investors.

In Exhibit 12.5 you can see that the 20% decline in revenue results in a 40% decline in EBIT with the automated production process but only a 22.2% decline in EBIT with the manual production process. The difference in the decline in EBIT is 17.8 percentage points! This difference is larger than the 11 percentage point difference for EBITDA because the EBITDA calculation does not include D&A. Depreciation and amortisation acts just like a fixed cost when we include it in the calculation because it is based on the amount that was invested in the project, rather than on unit sales. Therefore, when we include D&A in the EBIT calculation, we effectively increase the proportion of costs that are fixed. Since D&A is larger for the automated production alternative, in turn, this makes EBIT more sensitive to changes in revenue.

If we recreated Exhibit 12.4 for EBIT, the lines would also be linear and the slope would be steeper for the automated production process than for the manual production process. As was the case with EBITDA, the linear relation between changes in revenue and EBIT indicates that there are benefits and costs associated with using the automated production process. When deciding whether to use the automated process, you must weigh the prospect of higher accounting operating profits if unit sales exceed expected levels against concerns about lower accounting operating profits if unit sales are below expectations. In other words, you must decide whether the potential for earning a higher return with the automated manufacturing process justifies the risks. In Chapter 16 we will discuss how greater volatility in operating profits increases the chances that a firm will be forced into bankruptcy.

EXHIBIT 12.5

CHANGES IN EBITDA AND EBIT UNDER ALTERNATIVE PRODUCTION TECHNOLOGIES

	Automated Production		Manual Production	
	Expected Demand (1)	Poor Demand (2)	Expected Demand (3)	Poor Demand (4)
Units sold	10 000	8 000	10 000	8 000
Unit price	€25	€25	€25	€25
Unit VC	€16	€16	€20	€20
Revenue	€250 000	€200 000	€250 000	€200 000
– VC	160 000	128 000	200 000	160 000
– FC	35 000	35 000	4 000	4 000
EBITDA	€ 55 000	€ 37 000	€ 46 000	€36 000
– D&A	10 000	10 000	1 000	1 000
EBIT	€ 45 000	€ 27 000	€ 45 000	€35 000
Per cent change in revenue		−20.0%		−20.0%
Per cent change in EBITDA		−32.7%		−21.7%
Per cent change in EBIT		−40.0%		−22.2%

The EBIT values for the automated and manual production alternatives in the hammock-manufacturing example decline more than the EBITDA values when the number of units sold declines by 20% and the unit price remains the same. This occurs because the fixed nature of depreciation and amortisation (D&A) charges has the same effect as other fixed costs. When D&A is greater than zero, the percentage change in EBIT is greater than the percentage change in EBITDA.

BUILDING INTUITION

High Fixed Costs Mean Larger Fluctuations in Cash Flows and Profits

The higher the proportion of fixed costs to variable costs in a project, the more pre-tax operating cash flows (EBITDA) and accounting operating profits (EBIT) will vary as revenue varies. This is true because it is more difficult to change fixed costs than to change variable costs when unit sales change. If unit sales decline, EBITDA and EBIT will drop more in a business where fixed costs represent a larger proportion of total costs. Conversely, if unit sales increase, EBITDA and EBIT will increase more in a business with higher fixed costs.

Forecasting EBIT

Problem: You have decided to start a business that provides in-home technical computer support to people in the community near your university. You have seen national advertisements for a company that provides these services in other communities. You would run this business out of your university accommodation and you know plenty of students who have the necessary technical skills and would welcome the opportunity to earn more than the university pays under its work/study programmes. To get up and running quickly, you would have to invest in a computer system, an advertising campaign, three vehicles and tools. You would also want to have enough cash to keep the business going until it began to generate positive cash flows. All of this would require about €100 000, which is about all that you think you can borrow on your credit cards, against your car and from friends and family.

You are now working on the financial forecasts for the business. You plan to charge €45 for house calls lasting up to 30 minutes and €25 for each additional 30 minutes. Since you expect that the typical house call will require 60 minutes, you expect it to result in revenue of €70. You also estimate that monthly fixed operating costs (FC), which include an advertising contract with a local radio station and a small salary for you, will total €3000. Unit VC, including the technicians' pay, petrol for the car and other incidental expenses, will total €20 for the typical house call. Monthly depreciation and amortisation charges (D&A) will be €1000. Finally, you expect that after six months the business will average 120 house calls per month. Given this information, what do you expect the monthly EBIT to be in six months?

Approach: Since EBIT = Revenue – VC – FC – D&A (see, for example, Exhibit 12.5), you can forecast the expected monthly EBIT in six months by using this equation and the values for Revenue, VC, FC and D&A that you expect in six months.

Solution: The calculation is as follows:

Revenue	€70 per house call × 120 calls	€8400
– VC	€20 per house call × 120 calls	2400
– FC		3000
– D&A		1000
EBIT		€2000

Fixed Costs and Fluctuations in EBIT

Problem: As you prepare the financial forecast for your computer-support business, you worry about the impact of fluctuations in the number of house calls on EBIT. You decide to examine how converting some fixed costs to variable costs will affect the sensitivity of EBIT to changes in the number of house calls. In a conversation with the manager at the radio station where you would be advertising, you discover that instead of paying €1500 per month under a long-term advertising contract, you can get the same level of advertising for €1600, where €1000 of the total cost is fixed and €600 is variable. That is, in a given month, if you used the full level of advertising, you would pay €1600 but you would also have the ability to reduce advertising costs to €1000 by cutting back on the number of advertisements. You wonder how this contract would affect the sensitivity of EBIT to a decrease in the monthly number of house calls – say, from 120 to 90.

Approach: To determine how the sensitivity of EBIT differs between the €1500 per month long-term contract and the contract that has only €1000 of fixed costs, you must calculate EBIT under each alternative contract for 120 house calls and for 90 house calls. Using these EBIT values, you must next calculate the percentage decrease in EBIT if the number of monthly house calls declines from 120 to 90 for each alternative. You can then compare the percentage decreases to see the difference in the sensitivity of EBIT to the decrease in the number of house calls.

Solution: For the €1500 monthly fixed contract, as we determined in Learning by Doing Application 12.1, EBIT is €2000 with 120 house calls per month. With 90 house calls per month instead of 120, revenue would be €6300 (€70 per house call × 90) per month instead of €8400 (€70 per house call × 120) and EBIT would decline to €500:

$$EBIT = Revenue - VC - FC - D\&A$$
$$= €6300 - (€20 \times 90) - €3000$$
$$- €1000$$
$$= €500$$

This represents a 75% decrease in EBIT ([€500 – €2000]/€2000 = −0.75, or −75%).

For the €1600 monthly contract with €1000 fixed, switching to the alternative advertising arrangement would increase unit variable costs by €5 (€600/120 calls) but would decrease fixed costs by €500 (from €3000 to €2500). EBIT with 120 house calls per month would equal €1900:

$$EBIT = Revenue - VC - FC - D\&A$$
$$= €8400 - (€25 \times 120) - €2500$$
$$- €1000$$
$$= €1900$$

With 90 house calls, EBIT would decline to €550:

$$EBIT = €6300 - (€25 \times 90) - €2500$$
$$- €1000$$
$$= €550$$

This represents a 71% decrease in EBIT ([€550 – €1900]/€1900 = −0.71, or −71%).

If the business averaged 120 house calls per month, EBIT under the alternative advertising arrangement would be €100 lower than EBIT under the original advertising arrangement. However, it would actually be €50 higher if the business averaged only 90 house calls per month because you would be able to cut back on advertising expenses under the alternative agreement if demand was poor.[4]

USING EXCEL

Examining the Impact of Changes in Your Assumptions

One of the main advantages of using a spreadsheet program for financial analysis is that it enables us to perform a sensitivity analysis in a matter of seconds. Once the spreadsheet is carefully set up with all the relevant key assumptions and calculations, we can change any one of the assumptions and immediately see the effect on the bottom line.

Following is a setup for Learning by Doing Applications 12.1 and 12.2 that analyses the impact of the alternative advertising schemes on the EBIT of the in-home technical computer-support business.

	A	B	C	D	E	F	G	H	I	J
1										
2	Key Assumptions	Fixed Advertising Contract with More House Calls		Alternative Advertising Contract with Few House Calls						
3	House call up to 30 minutes	€45		€45						
4	Each additional 30 minutes	€25		€25						
5	Revenue from typical call - unit (60 min.)	€70		€70						
6	FC	€3,000		€2,500						
7	VC/unit (technician's pay, petrol, etc.)	€20		€20						
8	Alternative advertising option			€500						
9	VC/unit of alternative advertising option			€5	=D8/B11					
10	Monthly D&A	€1,000		€1,000						
11	Volume of calls per month	120		90						
12										
13										
14	Fixed Advertising Contract:						Alternative Advertising Contract:			
15	Revenue	€8,400	=B11*B5				Revenue	€6,300	=D11*D5	
16	Less Variable cost (VC)	€2,400	=B11*B7				Less Variable cost (VC)	€2,250	=D11*D7+D11*D9	
17	Less Fixed cost (FC)	€3,000	=B6				Less Fixed cost (FC)	€2,500	=D6	
18	Less Depreciation and Amortisation	€1,000	=B10				Less Depreciation and Amortisation	€1,000	=D10	
19	EBIT	€2,000	=B15-B16-B17-B18				EBIT	€550	=H15-H16-H17-H18	
20										

Once again, notice that the actual EBIT calculation is entirely derived from formulas utilising inputs from the key assumptions. To see how you can use the model for sensitivity analysis, change the volume number in the alternative advertising scenario back to 120. When you do this, EBIT will equal €1900, just as it does in the text.

Before You Go On

1. Why do analysts care about how sensitive EBITDA and EBIT are to changes in revenue?
2. How is the proportion of fixed costs in a project's cost structure related to the sensitivity of EBITDA and EBIT to changes in revenue?

The examples so far illustrate the impact of **operating leverage** (also called *operational gearing*) on pre-tax operating cash flows and on accounting operating profits when revenue changes. Operating leverage is a measure of the relative amounts of fixed and variable costs in a project's cost structure. It is the major factor that determines the sensitivity of EBITDA or EBIT to changes in revenue. The higher a project's operating leverage, the greater these sensitivities. Two measures of operating leverage often used by analysts are the degree of pre-tax cash flow operating leverage and the degree of accounting operating leverage.

CALCULATING OPERATING LEVERAGE

Learning Objective 2

Calculate and distinguish between the degree of pre-tax cash flow operating leverage and the degree of accounting operating leverage.

Operating leverage (gearing)

a measure of the relative amounts of fixed and variable costs in a project's cost structure; operating leverage is higher with more fixed costs

> **Degree of pre-tax cash flow operating leverage (Cash Flow DOL)**
>
> a measure of the sensitivity of cash flows from operations (EBITDA) to changes in revenue

Degree of Pre-tax Cash Flow Operating Leverage

The **degree of pre-tax cash flow operating leverage** (Cash Flow DOL) provides us with a measure of how sensitive pre-tax operating cash flows are to changes in revenue. It is calculated using the following formula:

$$\text{Cash Flow DOL} = 1 + \frac{\text{Fixed costs}}{\text{Pre-tax operating cash flows}} \quad (12.2)$$

$$= 1 + \frac{\text{FC}}{\text{EBITDA}}$$

Using the FC and EBITDA values in Exhibit 12.2, we can calculate Cash Flow DOL for the

EXHIBIT 12.6

EBITDA WITH UNIT SALES OF 10 000 AND 20 000 FOR THE AUTOMATED PRODUCTION ALTERNATIVE

Units sold	10 000	20 000
Unit price	€25	€25
Unit VC	€16	€16
Revenue	€250 000	€500 000
– VC	160 000	320 000
– FC	35 000	35 000
EBITDA	€ 55 000	€145 000

For the automated production alternative in the hammock-manufacturing example, EBITDA increases from €55 000 to €145 000 when unit sales increase from 10 000 to 20 000 units.

automated production alternative in the hammock-manufacturing example as follows:

$$\text{Cash Flow DOL}_{\text{Automated}}$$
$$= 1 + \frac{\text{FC}}{\text{EBITDA}} = 1 + \frac{€35\,000}{€55\,000} = 1.64$$

This indicates that a 1% change in revenue will change pre-tax operating cash flow, EBITDA, by 1.64%. A measure such as this provides analysts with a convenient way of summarising how much pre-tax operating cash flow will differ from forecasts if revenue is below or above the expected level.

You should be aware of one limitation to this measure: Cash Flow DOL changes with the level of revenue. In other words, the sensitivity is not the same for all levels of revenue. As a result, a particular Cash Flow DOL measure is only useful for modest changes in revenue. To understand why this limitation exists, notice that the numerator in the fraction in Equation (12.2), FC, does not vary with revenue. In contrast, the denominator, EBITDA, varies directly with revenue if the pre-tax operating cash flow margin is positive. If revenue is larger, the denominator in Equation (12.2) will be larger for any project that has a positive pre-tax operating cash flow margin. This, in turn, will cause Cash Flow DOL to become smaller as revenue increases. In contrast, if revenue is lower, the denominator in the fraction will be smaller, and Cash Flow DOL will be larger.

Consider, for example, how Cash Flow DOL changes for the automated production alternative if unit sales are 20 000 instead of 10 000. Exhibit 12.6 shows us that EBITDA will equal €145 000 with unit sales of 20 000. Therefore, Cash Flow DOL under the automated production alternative would be only 1.24:

$$\text{Cash Flow DOL}_{\text{Automated}} = 1 + \frac{€35\,000}{€145\,000} = 1.24$$

Degree of Accounting Operating Leverage

While Cash Flow DOL is a measure of the sensitivity of pre-tax operating cash flows to changes in revenue, the **degree of accounting operating leverage** (Accounting DOL) is a measure of how sensitive accounting operating profits (EBIT) are to changes in revenue. The formula for Accounting DOL is as follows:

$$\begin{aligned} \text{Accounting DOL} &= 1 + \frac{\text{Fixed charges}}{\text{Accounting operating profits}} \\ &= 1 + \frac{\text{FC} + \text{D\&A}}{\text{EBITDA} - \text{D\&A}} \\ &= \frac{\text{FC} + \text{D\&A}}{\text{EBIT}} \end{aligned}$$

(12.3)

In this formula, D&A is treated as a fixed cost and is added to FC to obtain the total of the cash and non-cash fixed costs that would be reflected in the income statement if the project were adopted. This total is then divided by total accounting operating profits (EBIT).[5]

> **Degree of accounting operating leverage (Accounting DOL)**
>
> a measure of the sensitivity of accounting operating profits (EBIT) to changes in revenue

The only difference between Accounting DOL and Cash Flow DOL is that Accounting DOL focuses on EBIT whereas Cash Flow DOL focuses on EBITDA. This means that the calculations differ only in the way that D&A is treated, since EBIT = EBITDA − D&A. Note that Accounting DOL will always be larger than Cash Flow DOL if D&A is greater than zero. This is because, compared with the calculation in Equation (12.2), the calculation in Equation (12.3) will have a larger numerator and a smaller denominator when D&A is greater than zero.

Let us apply the Accounting DOL formula to the automated production alternative in the hammock example. Using the values of FC, D&A and EBIT from column 1 in Exhibit 12.5, we get:

$$\begin{aligned} \text{Accounting DOL}_{\text{Automated}} &= 1 + \frac{\text{FC} + \text{D\&A}}{\text{EBIT}} \\ &= 1 + \frac{\text{\euro}35\,000 + \text{\euro}10\,000}{\text{\euro}45\,000} \\ &= 2.00 \end{aligned}$$

This tells us that a 1% change in revenue will result in a 2% change in EBIT. In other words, EBIT will change by twice as much, in percentage terms, as revenue with the automated production alternative!

In comparison, the Accounting DOL for the manual production alternative (column 3 in Exhibit 12.5) is only 1.11:

$$\begin{aligned} \text{Accounting DOL}_{\text{Manual}} &= 1 + \frac{\text{\euro}4000 + \text{\euro}1000}{\text{\euro}45\,000} \\ &= 1.11 \end{aligned}$$

A 1% change in revenue will result in only a 1.11% change in EBIT with the manual production alternative.

Learning by Doing Application 12.3

Calculating Cash Flow and Accounting DOL

Problem: You have decided to calculate the operating leverage for the in-home computer-support business you are thinking about starting.

What will Cash Flow DOL and Accounting DOL be in six months if EBIT is €2000, FC is €3000 and D&A is €1000?

Approach: Use Equations (12.2) and (12.3) to calculate Cash Flow DOL and Accounting DOL, respectively.

Solution: From Equation (12.2), Cash Flow DOL is:

$$\text{Cash Flow DOL} = 1 + \frac{FC}{EBIT + D\&A}$$

$$= 1 + \frac{€3000}{€2000 + €1000}$$

$$= 2.00$$

From Equation (12.3), Accounting DOL is:

$$\text{Accounting DOL} = 1 + \frac{FC + D\&A}{EBIT}$$

$$= 1 + \frac{€3000 + €1000}{€2000}$$

$$= 3.00$$

One important insight that you should take away from this discussion is that the volatility of pre-tax operating cash flows (EBITDA) and accounting operating profits (EBIT) is strongly influenced by two factors: (1) volatility in revenue and (2) operating leverage. If there is no uncertainty regarding costs, these are the only two factors that determine volatility in EBITDA and EBIT. It is always a good idea to pay special attention to these two factors when you are evaluating the uncertainty associated with the cash flows or the accounting profits from a project.

Before You Go On

1. How does operating leverage change when there is an increase in the proportion of a project's costs that are fixed?
2. What do the degree of pre-tax cash flow operating leverage (Cash Flow DOL) and the degree of accounting operating leverage (Accounting DOL) tell us?

BREAK-EVEN ANALYSIS

Learning Objective 3

Define and calculate the pre-tax operating cash flow and accounting operating profit break-even points and the crossover levels of unit sales for a project.

A question that naturally comes to mind when we consider operating leverage is this: What level of unit sales or revenue is necessary for a project to break even? This is an important question because it helps us better understand how successful the project will have to be in order to succeed. In this section, we discuss **break-even analysis**, which tells us how many units must be sold in order for a project to break even on a cash flow or accounting profit basis. Break-even analysis also helps us understand how sensitive cash flows and accounting profits are to changes in the number of units that will be sold.

BUILDING INTUITION

Revenue Changes Drive Profit Volatility through Operating Leverage

If there is no uncertainty about costs, volatility in pre-tax operating cash flows (EBITDA) and accounting operating profits (EBIT) will be driven entirely by changes in revenue and operating leverage. If a project has any fixed costs associated with it, operating leverage will magnify changes in revenue. The degree of operating leverage is a direct measure of how much more volatile EBITDA and EBIT will be than revenue.

Break-even analysis

an analysis that tells us how many units must be sold in order for a project to break even on a cash flow or accounting profit basis

WEB

See what the US Small Business Administration has to say about break-even analysis at: www.sba.gov/starting_business/financing/breakeven.html.

Pre-tax operating cash flow (EBITDA) break-even point

the number of units that must be sold for pre-tax operating cash flow to equal zero

Pre-Tax Operating Cash Flow Break-Even

When evaluating a project, we might want to know what level of unit sales is necessary for the project to break even on operations from a pre-tax operating cash flow perspective. In other words, how many units must be sold for pre-tax operating cash flow to equal zero? This is a very important question: if the project fails to break even from a pre-tax operating cash flow perspective, the firm will have to put more cash into the project to keep it going. The pre-tax operating cash flow (EBITDA) break-even point is calculated as follows:

$$\text{EBITDA Break} - \text{even} = \frac{\text{FC}}{\text{Price} - \text{Unit VC}} \tag{12.4}$$

For our hammock-manufacturing example, we can calculate the EBITDA break-even points for the

automated and manual production alternatives as follows:

$$\text{EBITDA Break-even}_{\text{Automated}} = \frac{€35\,000}{€25 - €16}$$
$$= 3889 \text{ units}$$

$$\text{EBITDA Break-even}_{\text{Manual}} = \frac{€4000}{€25 - €20}$$
$$= 800 \text{ units}$$

In each of these calculations, we are simply dividing the fixed costs, FC, by the **per-unit contribution** (Price − Unit VC). The per-unit contribution is how much is left from the sale of a single unit after all the variable costs associated with that unit have been paid. This is the amount that is available to help cover FC for the project.

Per-unit contribution

the amount that is left over from the sale of a single unit after all the variable costs associated with that unit have been paid; this is the amount that is available to help cover FC for the project

WEB

Learn more about fixed and variable costs and how they relate to break-even analysis from the CCH Business Owner's Toolkit at: www.toolkit.cch.com/text/P06_7510.asp.

Crossover level of unit sales (CO)

the level of unit sales at which cash flows or profitability for one project alternative switches from being lower than that of another alternative to being higher

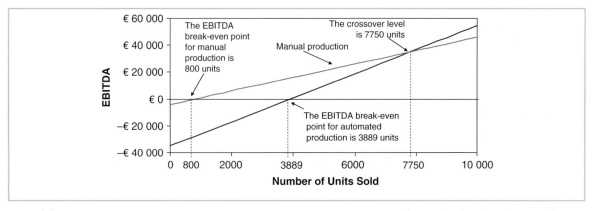

Exhibit 12.7: EBITDA Break-even Points and Crossover Level of Sales The EBITDA break-even points for the automated and manual production alternatives in the hammock-manufacturing example tell us the unit sales at which pre-tax operating cash flows equal zero. The crossover level of unit sales for EBITDA (CO$_{EBITDA}$) tells us the number of units at which the pre-tax operating cash flows become higher for the automated process than for the manual process.

In the hammock-manufacturing example, we see that if the automated production alternative is selected instead of the manual production alternative, almost five times as many units (3889 versus 800) will have to be sold before the project breaks even on a pre-tax operating cash flow basis in a particular year. This is because the automated production alternative has much higher fixed costs (€35 000 versus €4000) than the manual production alternative but its per-unit contribution is not proportionately higher (only €9 versus €5).

Because the pre-tax operating cash flow break-even points are the unit sales levels at

for simplicity, it plots EBITDA only from 0 to 10 000 units.

In addition to illustrating the operating cash flow break-even points, Exhibit 12.7 shows that the automated production alternative has a larger EBITDA than the manual production alternative if sales exceed 7750 units. This is because the larger per-unit contribution of the automated production alternative more than makes up for the higher fixed charges at this level of unit sales. We can compute the EBITDA **crossover level of unit sales (CO)** – the level above which the automated production alternative has higher pre-tax operating cash flows – as follows:

$$CO_{EBITDA} = \frac{FC_{Alternative\ 1} - FC_{Alternative\ 2}}{Unit\ contribution_{Alternative\ 1} - Unit\ contribution_{Alternative\ 2}} \qquad (12.5)$$

where Unit contribution stands for the per-unit contribution. The calculation for our example is as follows:

$$CO_{EBITDA} = \frac{FC_{Automated} - FC_{Manual}}{Unit\ contribution_{Automated} - Unit\ contribution_{Manual}} = \frac{€35\ 000 - €4000}{€9 - €5} = 7750\ units$$

which EBITDA equals €0, they are the unit sales levels at which the lines in Exhibit 12.4 cross the €0 point. You can see this in Exhibit 12.7, which is the same as Exhibit 12.4 except that,

Equation (12.5) can be used to calculate the crossover level of unit sales for any two alternatives that differ in the amount of operating leverage they employ.

Calculating the EBITDA Break-Even Point

Problem: Calculate the expected pre-tax operating cash flow (EBITDA) break-even number of house calls for the in-home computer-support business after six months.

Approach: Use Equation (12.4) to calculate EBITDA break-even for a project.

Solution: From Learning by Doing Application 12.1, we know that the monthly fixed costs are €3000, the average revenue per house call (Price) is €70 and the variable cost per house call (Unit VC) is €20. Therefore, using Equation (12.4), we can calculate the EBITDA break-even as follows:

$$\text{EBIT Break-even} = \frac{FC}{\text{Price} - \text{Unit VC}}$$
$$= \frac{€3000}{€70 - €20}$$
$$= 60 \text{ house calls}$$

Accounting Break-Even

We might also be interested in determining what level of unit sales is necessary for the project to break even on operations from an accounting operating profit perspective. This is called the accounting operating profit (EBIT) break-even point. It is calculated using:

$$\text{EBIT Break-even} = \frac{FC + D\&A}{\text{Price} - \text{Unit VC}} \quad (12.6)$$

When we calculate the accounting operating profit break-even point, we are calculating how many units must be sold to avoid an accounting operating loss. This is important to know because an accounting operating loss indicates that the project might not be able to cover its cash expenses and the wear and tear on physical assets as reflected in D&A.

> **Accounting operating profit (EBIT) break-even point**
>
> the number of units that must be sold for accounting operating profit to equal 0

For the automated production alternative in the hammock-manufacturing business, the break-even point is calculated as follows:

$$\text{EBIT Break-even}_{\text{Automated}}$$
$$= \frac{FC_{\text{Automated}} + D\&A_{\text{Automated}}}{\text{Price} - \text{Unit VC}_{\text{Automated}}}$$
$$= \frac{€35\,000 - €10\,000}{€25 - €16}$$
$$= 5000 \text{ units}$$

Similarly, for the manual production alternative:

$$\text{EBIT Break-even}_{\text{Manual}} = \frac{€4000 - €1000}{€25 - €20}$$
$$= 1000 \text{ units}$$

The accounting operating profit break-even points for the automated and manual production alternatives are 5000 and 1000 units, respectively.

The accounting operating profit break-even points are larger than the corresponding pre-tax operating cash flow break-even points because in Equation (12.6) we are including the non-cash D&A charges in the numerator in the calculation. Since the denominator of the fraction is the same in Equations (12.4) and (12.6), the accounting operating profit break-even points will always be larger when D&A is positive.

In addition to the accounting operating profit break-even points, we can also calculate the cross-over level of unit sales for EBIT. The equation that we use to do this is:

$$CO_{EBIT} = \frac{(FC + D\&A)_{Alternative\ 1} - (FC + D\&A)_{Alternative\ 2}}{Unit\ contribution_{Alternative\ 1} - Unit\ contribution_{Alternative\ 2}} \quad (12.7)$$

Notice that the only difference between Equations (12.5) and (12.7) is that D&A is included in the numerator in Equation (12.7).

The calculation for our hammock-manufacturing example is as follows:

$$CO_{EBIT} =$$

$$\frac{(FC + D\&A)_{Automated} - (FC + D\&A)_{Manual}}{Unit\ contribution_{Automated} - Unit\ contribution_{Manual}}$$

$$= \frac{(€35\ 000 + €10\ 000) - (€4000 - €1000)}{€9 - €5}$$

$$= 10\ 000\ units$$

Learning by Doing Application 12.5

Calculating the EBIT Break-Even Point

Problem: Calculate the expected accounting operating profit break-even number of house calls for the in-home computer-support business after six months of operation.

Approach: Use Equation (12.6) to calculate EBIT break-even for the business.

Solution: From Learning by Doing Application 12.1, we know that the monthly fixed cost is €3000, the monthly D&A is €1000, the average revenue per house call (Price) is €70 and the variable cost per house call (Unit VC) is €20. Therefore, using Equation (12.6), we find that the accounting operating profit break-even point after six months is:

$$EBIT\ Break\text{-}even = \frac{FC + D\&A}{Price - Unit\ VC}$$

$$= \frac{€3000 + €1000}{€70 - €20}$$

$$= 80\ house\ calls$$

Your company must make 80 house calls to break even on an accounting operating profit basis.

By comparing this calculation and the calculation in Learning by Doing Application 12.4, you can see that the accounting operating profit break-even point (80 house calls) is higher than the pre-tax operating cash flow break-even point (60 house calls). As we explained in the text, this is so because D&A is included in the accounting operating profit break-even calculation.

Decision-Making Example 12.1

Using Break-Even Numbers

Situation: You have just finished calculating the pre-tax operating cash flow and accounting operating profit break-even numbers for the in-home computer-support business. These numbers are as follows:

- Pre-tax operating cash flow break-even point: 720 house calls per year (60 per month).
- Accounting operating profit break-even point: 960 house calls per year (80 per month).

You have also just heard that the national company that provides these services is going to move to the town in which you are located. This has caused you to reduce your estimate of the annual number of house calls you can expect for your business in half, from 1440 (120 per month) to 720. How will this affect your decision to enter this business?

Decision: With annual unit sales of 720, EBIT will be negative and EBITDA will equal €0. With EBITDA of €0, the business will not generate any cash flows that can be used to make necessary investments, let alone enable you to earn the opportunity cost of capital on the money you invest in this business. You can see this by referring back to the FCF calculation in Equation (11.2) or Exhibit 11.1. This is a case where you do not even need to calculate the NPV to know that it is negative.

The cash flow and accounting break-even calculations are useful in helping us understand how many units must be sold to break even in a particular period of time, such as a month or a year. Although these are valuable calculations, it is important to recognise that they do not tell us what it takes for a project to break even in an economic sense – in other words, how many units must be sold over the life of a project to achieve an NPV of zero. This sort of *economic* break-even analysis is typically performed in the context of an NPV analysis.

Before You Go On

1. How is the per-unit contribution related to the accounting operating profit break-even point?
2. What is the difference between the pre-tax operating cash flow break-even point and the accounting operating profit break-even point?

RISK ANALYSIS

Learning Objective 4

Define sensitivity analysis, scenario analysis and simulation analysis, and describe how they are used to evaluate the risks associated with a project.

In the preceding sections, we noted that two key factors – (1) volatility of revenue and (2) operating leverage – determine the volatility of pre-tax operating cash flows (EBITDA) and operating profits (EBIT) when there is no uncertainty regarding costs. We also discussed how changes in unit sales influence the volatility of EBITDA and EBIT.

Unit sales is only one of many factors that an analyst must predict when forecasting the cash flows associated with a project. As with forecasts of unit sales, forecasting the values of these other factors involves a high degree of uncertainty. For example, the price of a product depends on the supply and demand for the product, which is often difficult to predict. Similarly, future values of operating expenses, capital expenditures and additions to working capital can be very uncertain. Financial analysts often resort to sensitivity analysis, scenario analysis and simulation analysis to obtain a better understanding of how errors in forecasting these factors affect the attractiveness of a project. In other words, these analyses help answer the questions 'How wrong can I be?' and 'What are the implications of being wrong?'

In this section we illustrate the application of sensitivity, scenario and simulation analysis using the automated production alternative from our hammock-manufacturing example. With expected unit sales of 10 000 per year and the other indicated assumptions, the yearly free cash flows and NPV for this alternative are calculated in Exhibit 12.8.

EXHIBIT 12.8

INCREMENTAL FREE CASH FLOWS AND NPV FOR THE AUTOMATED HAMMOCK PRODUCTION ALTERNATIVE

Assumptions:

Opportunity cost of capital	10%	Initial investment	€40 000
Unit sales	10 000	D&A	€10 000
Unit price	€25	Annual Cap Exp	€8 000
Unit VC	€16	Add WC	€2 000
FC	€35 000	Tax Rate	35%

		Year			
	0	1	2	3	4
Revenue		€250 000	€250 000	€250 000	€250 000
– VC		160 000	160 000	160 000	160 000
– FC		35 000	35 000	35 000	35 000
EBITDA		€ 55 000	€ 55 000	€ 55 000	€ 55 000
– D&A		10 000	10 000	10 000	10 000
EBIT		€ 45 000	€ 45 000	€ 45 000	€ 45 000
– Taxes		15 750	15 750	15 750	15 750
NOPAT		€ 29 250	€ 29 250	€ 29 250	€ 29 250
+ D&A		10 000	10 000	10 000	10 000
CF Opns		€ 39 250	€ 39 250	€ 39 250	€ 39 250
– Cap Exp	€40 000	8 000	8 000	8 000	8 000
– Add WC		2 000	2 000	2 000	2 000
FCF	(€40 000)	€ 29 250	€ 29 250	€ 29 250	€ 29 250
NPV	€52 719				

This exhibit shows the calculation of the yearly incremental pre-tax free cash flows (FCF) and the NPV of the automated production alternative in the hammock-manufacturing example assuming the project has a four-year life. The FCF calculation is illustrated in Exhibit 11.1.

Sensitivity Analysis

Sensitivity analysis involves examining the sensitivity of the output from an analysis, such as the NPV estimate in Exhibit 12.8, to changes in *individual* assumptions. In a sensitivity analysis, an analyst might examine how a project's NPV changes if there is a decrease in the value of individual cash inflow assumptions or an increase in the value of individual cash outflow assumptions. For example, if unit sales are 10% lower than expected, if FC is 10% higher than expected or if annual Cap Exp is 10% higher than expected, then an analyst could calculate that the NPV of the automated production alternative in Exhibit 12.8 declines by 35.2%, 13.7% and 4.8%, respectively, when these values are changed one at a time. These numbers would tell the analyst that the NPV for the automated alternative is much more sensitive to the unit sales assumption than to the assumptions regarding FC or Cap Exp.

This information is very useful because it helps the analyst identify the critical assumptions. These are the assumptions the analyst should pay special attention to when evaluating the project. It does not make sense to allocate substantial analytical resources to investigating assumptions that are of little importance. In our example, the numbers suggest that the analyst should be especially careful when developing the unit sales forecasts.

Scenario Analysis

As we have just seen, sensitivity analysis is a form of 'what if' analysis that is very useful in identifying key assumptions. However, the individual assumptions in a financial analysis are often related to each other; their values do not tend to change one at a time. As a result, sensitivity analysis is not very useful in examining how the attractiveness of a project might vary under different economic scenarios. An analyst who wants to examine how the results from a financial analysis will change under alternative scenarios will thus perform a **scenario analysis**.

Suppose, for example, that the forecasted cash flows in Exhibit 12.8 represent the performance of the automated hammock-manufacturing alternative under expected future economic conditions. Let us consider how these cash flows might change if economic conditions turn out to be weaker or stronger than expected. In a scenario in which economic conditions are weaker than in the most likely case, we would expect unit sales to be less than 10 000 because overall demand for hammocks will be lower. The price at which the firm sells its hammocks is also likely to be lower because the firm will probably reduce prices in an effort to boost sales. On the bright side, unit variable costs might also be lower because the demand for rope, spacer bars, hardware and so forth will decline in a weak market and producers of those products may reduce the prices they charge the firm. In contrast to the weak economic scenario, stronger economic conditions might result in higher-than-expected unit sales, prices and unit variable costs. Exhibit 12.9 illustrates how these assumptions and the resulting project NPV might vary under the alternative scenarios.

EXHIBIT 12.9

NPV VALUES FOR THE AUTOMATED HAMMOCK PRODUCTION ALTERNATIVE FOR THREE SCENARIOS

Economic Conditions	Unit Sales	Unit Price	Unit Variable Costs	NPV
Strong	12 000	€28	€17	€139 256
Expected	10 000	€25	€16	€52 719
Weak	8 000	€22	€15	(€17 335)

Different economic scenarios result in different NPV values for the automated production alternative in the hammock-manufacturing example. The expected unit sales, unit prices and unit variable costs vary depending on economic conditions.

In Exhibit 12.9 we can see that the project will have a negative NPV if economic conditions are weak. Furthermore, the decline in NPV if economic conditions are weaker than expected (€70 054, the difference between €52 719 and negative €17 335) is less than the increase in NPV if economic conditions are stronger than expected (€86 537, the difference between €139 256 and €52 719). The range of NPV values under the three scenarios is €156 591 (the range between negative €17 335 and €139 256).

Although this analysis can help us better understand how much uncertainty is associated with an NPV estimate, it is important to remember that *there is only one NPV value for a project* and that the FCF values we use in an NPV analysis represent the expected incremental free cash flows. For instance, in our example, suppose there is a 50% chance that the most likely economic conditions will occur, a 25% chance that economic conditions will be weak and a 25% chance that economic conditions will be strong. The NPV calculation would be based on the expected values for unit sales, the unit price and unit variable costs.

Recall that an expected value represents the sum of the products of the possible outcomes and the probabilities that those outcomes will be realised. Therefore, the expected values for unit sales, the unit price and unit variable costs in this example are calculated as follows:

$$\text{Expected unit sales} = (0.25 \times 12\,000)$$
$$+ (0.50 \times 10\,000)$$
$$+ (0.25 \times 8000)$$
$$= 10\,000 \text{ units}$$

$$\text{Expected unit price} = (0.25 \times €28) + (0.50 \times €25)$$
$$+ (0.25 \times €22)$$
$$= €25$$

$$\text{Expected unit variable costs} = (0.25 \times €17)$$
$$+ (0.50 \times €16)$$
$$+ (0.25 \times €15)$$
$$= €16$$

Therefore, the NPV of the project would equal €52 719, as illustrated in Exhibit 12.8.

Simulation Analysis

Simulation analysis is like scenario analysis except that in simulation analysis an analyst uses a computer to examine a large number of scenarios in a short period of time. Rather than selecting individual values for each of the assumptions – such as unit sales, unit price and unit variable costs – the analyst assumes that those assumptions can be represented by statistical distributions. For instance, unit sales might be assumed to have a normal distribution with a mean value of 10 000 units and a standard deviation of 1500 units, while prices might be assumed to follow a related normal distribution with a mean of €25 and a standard deviation of €5. A computer program then calculates the free cash flows associated with a large number of scenarios by repeatedly drawing numbers for the distributions for various assumptions, plugging them into the free cash flow model and computing the yearly free cash flows. It is not uncommon to compute 10 000 alternative sets of free cash flows. The average of the annual free cash flows generated in this way is then computed to obtain the expected free cash flows for each year during the life of the project. These expected free cash flows can then be discounted using the opportunity cost of capital to obtain the NPV for the project.

Simulation analysis

an analytical method that uses a computer to quickly examine a large number of scenarios and obtain probability estimates for various values in a financial analysis

WEB

You can download trial versions of Excel add-in programs for sensitivity analysis and simulation analysis from Treeplan.com at: www.treeplan.com.

In addition to providing an estimate of the expected free cash flows, simulation analysis provides information on the distribution of the free cash flows that the project is likely to produce in each year. For example, if simulation analysis is used to compute 10 000 alternative sets of free cash flows, there will be 10 000 cash flow estimates for each year. From these estimates, an analyst can estimate the probability that the free cash flows in a given year will be greater than zero, greater than €1000 or greater than any other number. By summing up the free cash flows over time within each alternative set of cash flows, the analyst can also estimate the probability of recovering the initial investment in the project by any particular point in the project's life.

A discussion of the actual techniques used in simulation analysis is beyond the scope of this book. However, you should be aware that sophisticated financial analysts commonly use simulation analysis to evaluate the riskiness of projects. You are likely to see it in practice if you are ever involved with project analysis.

INVESTMENT DECISIONS WITH CAPITAL RATIONING

Our discussion of capital budgeting so far has focused on tools that help us determine whether an individual project creates value for shareholders, as well as helping us better understand other economic characteristics of projects. Although these analyses are critical parts of the capital budgeting process, they get us only part way to where we want to be. They do not tell us what to do when, as is often the case, a firm does not have enough money to invest in all available positive NPV projects. In other words, they do not tell us how to identify the *bundle* or combination of positive NPV projects that creates the greatest total value for shareholders when there are capital constraints or, as we called it in Chapter 10, *capital rationing*.

In an ideal world, of course, we could accept all positive NPV projects because we would be able to finance them. If managers and investors agreed on which projects had positive NPVs, investors would provide capital to those projects because returns from them would be greater than the returns the investors could earn elsewhere in the capital markets. However, the world is not ideal and, as noted in Chapter 10, firms often cannot invest in all of the available projects with positive NPVs. It can be difficult for outside investors to accurately assess the risks and returns associated with the firm's projects. Consequently, investors may require returns for their capital that are too high and the firm may face capital constraints. Managers might be forced to reject positive NPV projects because investors are not providing enough capital to fund those projects at reasonable rates.

Capital Rationing in a Single Period

The basic principle that we follow in choosing the set of projects that creates the greatest value in a given period is to select the projects that yield the largest value *per unit of money invested*. We can do this by computing the profitability index (PI) for each project and choosing the projects with the largest profitability indexes until we run out of money. The profitability index is computed as follows:

$$PI = \frac{\text{Benefits}}{\text{Costs}}$$

$$= \frac{\text{Present value of future free cash flows}}{\text{Initial investment}}$$

$$= 1 + \frac{\text{NPV}}{\text{Initial investment}}$$

(12.8)

where Initial investment is the up-front investment required to fund the project.

> ### Profitability index (PI)
>
> a measure of the value a project generates for each unit of money invested in that project

To illustrate, we will return to the example from Chapter 11 in which we were considering when to replace a lawn mower. Recall that the new mower would cost €2000 and would bring in net cash flows of €7000 for four years. With a discount rate of 10%, we saw that the NPV of this mower is €20 189. The PI for this investment is calculated as follows:

$$PI = €20\ 189/€2000$$
$$= 10.09 \text{ or } 1 + (€20\ 189 - €2000)/€2000$$

This means that an investment in the new mower is expected to generate €10.09 of value for every euro invested. A value above 1 indicates that the investment has a positive NPV and a value below 1 indicates it has a negative NPV. An example would illustrate this further. A project costs €400, has net cash flows of €200 per year for three years and the appropriate discount rate is 7%. The present value of the cash flows is €338.64. Using the present value of the cash flows, we calculate the PI as 0.85 (€338.64/€400). The NPV will be −€61.36 (€338.64 − €400) and the profitability index calculated this way (−€61.36/€400 + 1) will also be 0.85.

Now consider the case in which we have several projects to choose from in a given year but do not have enough money to invest in all of them. For example, suppose that we have identified the four positive NPV projects listed in Exhibit 12.10 and have only €10 000 to invest. How do we choose from among the four projects when we cannot afford to invest in all of them?

Our objective in a case such as this is to identify the bundle or combination of positive NPV projects that creates the greatest total value for shareholders. The PI is helpful in such a situation because it helps us choose the projects that create the most value per unit of money invested. We use the PI to do this by following a four-step procedure:

EXHIBIT 12.10
POSITIVE NPV INVESTMENTS THIS YEAR

Project	Year 0	Year 1	Year 2	NPV @ 10%	PI
A	−€5000	€5500	€6050	€5000	2.000
B	−€3000	€2000	€3850	€2000	1.667
C	−€3000	€4400	€0	€1000	1.333
D	−€2000	€1500	€1375	€500	1.250

With only €10 000 to invest, how do we choose among these four positive NPV projects? The exhibit shows the yearly free cash flows, NPV and profitability index (PI) for the projects. The PI values indicate the value of the expected future free cash flows per euro invested in each project.

1. Calculate the PI for each project.
2. Rank the projects from highest PI to lowest PI.
3. Starting at the top of the list (the project with the highest PI) and working your way down (to the project with the lowest PI), select the projects that the firm can afford.
4. Repeat the third step by starting with the second project on the list, the third project on the list and so on to make sure that a more valuable bundle cannot be identified.

Applying this process to the projects in Exhibit 12.10, we would choose to accept projects A, B and D. We would begin by choosing projects A and B because they have the largest PIs and we have enough money to invest in both. Since choosing projects A and B means we would no longer have enough money to invest in project C, we would skip C and choose D, for which we do have enough money. Projects A, B and D would generate a total of €7500 in total value for shareholders. Following the fourth step reveals that no other combination of projects has a larger total NPV than projects A, B and D, so we would select these projects.

> ### Learning by Doing Application 12.6
>
> ## Ranking Projects Using the PI
>
> **Problem:** You have identified the following seven positive NPV investments for your in-home computer-support business. If you have €50 000 to invest this year, which projects should you accept?
>
> **Approach:** Use the four-step procedure presented in the text to determine which projects you should accept.
>
> | Project | Investment | NPV @ 10% |
> |---|---|---|
> | Buy new notebook computer | €3 000 | €500 |
> | Buy employee training programme | 8 000 | 4 000 |
> | Buy new tool set | 500 | 1 000 |
> | Buy office building | 40 000 | 5 000 |
> | Buy used car | 12 000 | 4 000 |
> | Paint existing cars | 4 000 | 2 000 |
> | Buy new test equipment | 10 000 | 2 000 |
>
> **Solution:** Calculating the PI and ranking the projects from highest to lowest PI gives the following:
>
> | Project | Investment | NPV @ 10% | PI |
> |---|---|---|---|
> | Buy new tool set | €500 | €1 000 | €1500/€500 = 3.000 |
> | Buy employee training programme | 8 000 | 4 000 | €12 000/€8000 = 1.500 |
> | Paint existing cars | 4 000 | 2 000 | €6000/€4000 = 1.500 |
> | Buy used car | 12 000 | 4 000 | €16 000/€12 000 = 1.333 |
> | Buy new test equipment | 10 000 | 2 000 | €12 000/€10 000 = 1.200 |
> | Buy new notebook computer | 3 000 | 500 | €3500/€3000 = 1.167 |
> | Buy office condo | 40 000 | 5 000 | €45 000/€40 000 = 1.125 |

With €50 000 to invest, you should invest in all projects except the office building. This strategy will require €37 500 and is expected to result in a total NPV of €13 500. The €12 500 that you have left over can be held in the business until an appropriate use for the money is identified or it can be distributed to the shareholder (you).

Decision-Making Example 12.2

Ranking Investment Alternatives

Situation: The profitability index concept does not apply only to a firm's investments in projects. It can also apply to your personal investments. For example, suppose that you have just inherited €50 000 and want to invest it in ways that create as much value as possible. After researching investment alternatives, you have identified five investments that you believe will have positive NPVs. You estimate that the NPVs and PIs for these investments are as follows:

Project	Investment	NPV	PI
Buy a new car for your business	€20 000	€10 000	1.500
Buy an apartment near the university	50 000	22 500	1.450
Start a small moving business	25 000	10 000	1.400
Invest in your roommate's Internet business	15 000	5 000	1.333
Buy a collection of old comic books	5 000	1 000	1.200

Which investment(s) should you choose?

Decision: You should invest in the apartment. If you begin the selection process by choosing the new car because it has the largest PI and then work your way down the list until you reach a total investment of €50 000, you will see that you can invest in the car, the moving business and the comic books. These three investments have a total NPV of €21 000. However, the investment in the apartment alone has an NPV of €22 500. Investing in the apartment will create more total value.

This problem illustrates why the procedure for using PI to choose projects has four steps. Without the fourth step, which tells us to repeat the third step beginning with the second project, the third project and so on, we would not have identified the apartment as the best alternative.

Capital Rationing Across Multiple Periods

The PI concept is relatively straightforward and easy to apply if you are choosing among projects in a single period. However, if you are faced with capital rationing over several years, the investments you choose this year can affect your ability to make investments in future years. This can happen if you plan on reinvesting some or all of the cash flows generated by the projects you invest in this year. In such a situation, you cannot rely solely on the PI to identify the projects you should invest in this year. You must maximise the total NPV across all of the years in which you will be investing.

Let us look more closely at how multi-period concerns can cause you to deviate from PI-based

EXHIBIT 12.11

POSITIVE NPV INVESTMENTS FOR TWO YEARS

Project	Year 0	Year 1	Year 2	Year 3	Year 0 NPV @ 10%	PI
A	−€5 000	€5 500	€6 050	€0	€5 000	2.000
B	−€3 000	€2 000	€3 850	€0	€2 000	1.667
C	−€3 000	€4 400	€0	€0	€1 000	1.333
D	−€2 000	€1 500	€1 375	€0	€500	1.250
F		−€10 000	€12 000	€11 000	€9 091	1.909
G		−€10 000	€8 000	€11 770	€6 364	1.636
H		−€5 000	€4 000	€2 255	€455	1.091

Investment decision-making with capital rationing becomes more complex when multiple periods are involved. This exhibit shows the yearly free cash flows, NPV and profitability index (PI) for the four positive NPV projects in Exhibit 12.10 and for three other positive NPV projects that are expected to become available in year 1.

investment choices in a given year. Suppose you operate a business that will generate €10 000 per year for new investments. Furthermore, suppose that today (year 0) you are choosing among projects A, B, C and D in Exhibit 12.11 and that, based on the PIs of the individual projects, you choose to invest in projects A, B and D. The total NPV from these projects will be €7500 and the total year 1 cash flow from them will be €9000 (€5500 + €2000 + €1500).

WEB

If you have a strong mathematical background and are interested, you can learn more about linear programming from a site maintained by Northwestern University and Argonne National Laboratory: www-unix.mcs.anl.gov/otc/Guide/faq/linear-programming-faq.html.

Now suppose that you expect projects F, G and H to be available next year (year 1). If other operations yield €10 000 for investments next year, you will have a total of €19 000 to invest in year 1. With this amount of money, you can invest in projects F and H, which require a total investment of €15 000 and have a combined NPV

of €9546 (€9091 + €455). Therefore, in year 0 money, the total value created from investing activities over the two years will be €17 046 (€7500 + €9546).

While €17 046 is a lot of value for a total investment of €25 000 (€10 000 today and €15 000 in year 1), you could do better. Notice that if, instead of projects A, B and D, you invest in projects A, C and D today, you will have enough cash in year 1 to invest in projects F and G. This strategy would yield a total NPV of €21 955 (€5000 + €1000 + €500 + €9091 + €6364)! Ranking and selecting the projects today based on the PI would have yielded a bundle of projects over two years with a lower NPV. This illustrates an important limitation of the profitability index. It does not tell us enough to make informed decisions over multiple periods. Solving a multiple-period problem requires the application of more advanced analytical techniques, such as linear programming, that are beyond the scope of this book.

Before You Go On

1. What decision criteria should managers use in selecting projects when there is

not enough money to invest in all available positive NPV projects?

2. What might cause a firm to face capital constraints?

3. How can the PI help in choosing projects when a firm faces capital constraints? What are its limitations?

SUMMARY OF LEARNING OBJECTIVES

1. **Explain and be able to demonstrate how variable costs and fixed costs affect the volatility of pre-tax operating cash flows and accounting operating profits.**

   Because the fixed costs associated with a project do not change as revenue changes, fluctuations in revenue are magnified so that pre-tax operating cash flows and accounting operating profits fluctuate more than revenue in percentage terms. The greater the proportion of total costs that are fixed, the more the fluctuations in revenue will be magnified. To demonstrate this, you can perform calculations like those in the hammock-manufacturing example and in Learning by Doing Applications 12.1 and 12.2.

2. **Calculate and distinguish between the degree of pre-tax cash flow operating leverage and the degree of accounting operating leverage.**

   The degree of pre-tax cash flow operating leverage is a measure of how much pre-tax operating cash flow will change in relation to a change in revenue. Similarly, the degree of accounting operating leverage is a measure of how much accounting operating profits will change in relation to a change in revenue. The only difference between cash flow operating leverage and accounting operating leverage is that the accounting measure treats incremental depreciation and amortisation charges as a fixed cost in the calculation. These charges are excluded from the cash flow operating leverage measure because they do not reflect actual cash expenses and, therefore, do not affect pre-tax cash flows. Equations (12.2) and (12.3) are used to calculate these two measures.

3. **Define and calculate the pre-tax operating cash flow and accounting operating profit break-even points and the crossover levels of unit sales for a project.**

   The pre-tax operating cash flow break-even point is the number of units that must be sold in a particular year to break even on a pre-tax operating cash flow basis. It is calculated using Equation (12.4).

   The accounting operating profit break-even point is the number of units that must be sold in a particular year to break even on an accounting operating profit basis. A project breaks even on an accounting operating profit basis when it produces exactly zero in incremental operating profits (EBIT). It is calculated using Equation (12.6).

   The crossover level of unit sales is the level of unit sales at which the pre-tax operating cash flows or accounting operating profits for one project alternative switch from being lower than those of another alternative to being higher. The EBITDA and EBIT crossover levels of unit sales are calculated using Equations (12.5) and (12.7), respectively.

4. **Define sensitivity analysis, scenario analysis and simulation analysis and describe how they are used to evaluate the risks associated with a project.**

   Sensitivity analysis is concerned with how sensitive the output from a financial analysis, such as the NPV, is to changes in an individual assumption. It helps identify which assumptions have the greatest impact on the output and, therefore, on the value of a project. Knowing this helps an analyst identify which assumptions are especially important to that analysis. Scenario analysis is used to examine how the output from a financial analysis changes under alternative scenarios. This type of analysis recognises that changing economic and market conditions affect more than one variable at a time and tries to account for how each of the different variables will change under alternative scenarios. Simulation analysis is like scenario analysis except that in simulation analysis a computer is used to examine a large number of scenarios in a short period of time.

5. **Explain how the profitability index can be used to rank projects when a firm faces capital rationing and describe the limitations that apply to the profitability index.**

The profitability index (PI) aids in the process of choosing the most valuable bundle of projects that the firm can afford because it is a measure of value received per unit of currency invested that can be used to rank projects in a given period. The major limitation of the PI is that, while it can be used to rank projects in a given period, it can lead to misleading project choices in a multi-period context.

SUMMARY OF KEY EQUATIONS

Equation	Description	Formula
(12.1)	Op Ex in terms of incremental variable and fixed costs	$Op\,Ex = VC + FC$
(12.2)	Degree of pre-tax cash flow operating leverage	$Cash\,flow\,DOL = 1 + \dfrac{FC}{EBITDA}$
(12.3)	Degree of accounting operating leverage	$Accounting\,DOL = 1 + \dfrac{FC + D\&A}{EBIT}$
(12.4)	Pre-tax operating cash flow break-even point	$EBITDA\,Break\text{-}even = \dfrac{FC}{Price - Unit\,VC}$
(12.5)	Crossover level of unit sales for EBITDA	$CO_{EBITDA} = \dfrac{FC_{Alternative\,1} - FC_{Alternative\,2}}{Unit\,contribution_{Alternative\,1} - Unit\,contribution_{Alternative\,2}}$
(12.6)	Accounting operating profit break-even point	$EBIT\,Break\text{-}even = \dfrac{FC + D\&A}{Price - Unit\,VC}$
(12.7)	Crossover level of unit sales for EBIT	$CO_{EBIT} = \dfrac{(FC + D\&A)_{Alternative\,1} - (FC + D\&A)_{Alternative\,2}}{Unit\,contribution_{Alternative\,1} - Unit\,contribution_{Alternative\,2}}$
(12.8)	Profitability index	$PI = \dfrac{NPV + Initial\,investment}{Initial\,investment}$

SELF-STUDY PROBLEMS

12.1. Gelb Regal AG sells all of its shelves for €100 per shelf and incurs €50 in variable costs to produce each. If the fixed costs for the firm are €2 000 000 per year, then what will be the EBIT for the firm if it produces and sells 45 000 shelves next year? Assume that depreciation and amortisation is included in the fixed costs.

12.2. Hydrogen Batteries sells its specialty automobile batteries for £85 each, while its current variable cost per unit is £65. Total fixed costs (including depreciation and amortisation expense) are £150 000 per year. The firm expects to sell 10 000 batteries next year but is concerned that its variable cost will increase next year due to material cost increases. What is the maximum variable cost per unit increase that will keep the EBIT from becoming negative?

12.3. Les Disques Vinyliques SA is going to take on a project that will increase its EBIT by €90 000 next year. The firm's fixed cost cash expenditures are expected to increase by €100 000 and depreciation and amortisation will increase by €80 000 next year. If the project yields an additional 10% in revenue, what percentage increase in the project's EBIT will result from the additional revenue?

12.4. You are considering investing in a business that has monthly fixed costs of €5500 and sells a single product that costs €35 per unit to make. This product sells for €90 per unit. What is the annual pre-tax operating cash flow break-even point for this business?

12.5. You are considering a project that has an initial outlay of €1 million. The profitability index of the project is 2.24. What is the NPV of the project?

SOLUTIONS TO SELF-STUDY PROBLEMS

12.1. The calculations for Gelb Regal AG are as follows:

Revenue	€100 × 45 000 =	€4 500 000
VC	€50 × 45 000 =	2 250 000
FC+D&A		2 000 000
EBIT		€250 000

12.2. The forecasted EBIT for Hydrogen Batteries is:

Revenue	£85 × 10 000 =	£850 000
VC	£65 × 10 000 =	650 000
FC + D&A		150 000
EBIT		£50 000

Therefore, total variable cost may increase by £50 000, which means that if the firm produces and sells 10 000 batteries, then the variable cost per unit may increase by £5 (£50 000/10 000 units).

12.3. Accounting DOL $= 1 + \dfrac{FC + D\&A}{EBIT}$

$$= 1 + \frac{€100\,000 + €80\,000}{€90\,000}$$

$$= 3$$

Therefore, a 10% additional increase in revenue should result in approximately a 30% increase in EBIT.

12.4. You can solve for the *monthly* pre-tax oper-ating cash flow break-even point using Equation (12.4):

$$\text{EBITDA Break-even} = \frac{FC}{\text{Price} - \text{Unit VC}}$$

$$= \frac{€5500}{€90 - €35} = 100 \text{ units}$$

Therefore, the annual EBITDA break-even point is $100 \times 12 = 1200$ units.

12.5. You can use Equation (12.8) to solve for the NPV:

$$PI = \frac{\text{NPV} + \text{Initial investment}}{\text{Initial investment}}$$

$$= \frac{\text{NPV} + €1\,000\,000}{€1\,000\,000}$$

Therefore:

$$\text{NPV} = €1\,240\,000$$

CRITICAL THINKING QUESTIONS

12.1. You are involved in the planning process for a firm that is expected to have a large increase in sales for the next year. Which type of firm would benefit the most from that sales increase: a firm with low fixed costs and high variable costs or a firm with high fixed costs and low variable costs?

12.2. You own a firm with a single new product that is about to be introduced to the public for the first time. Your marketing analysis suggests that the demand for this product could be anywhere between 500 000 units and 5 000 000 units. Given such a wide range, discuss the safest cost structure alternative for your firm.

12.3. Define *capital rationing* and explain why it can occur in the real world.

12.4. Discuss the interpretation of the degree of accounting operating leverage and degree of pre-tax cash flow operating leverage.

12.5. Explain how EBITDA differs from free cash flows (FCF) and discuss the types of businesses for which this difference would be especially small or large.

12.6. Describe how the pre-tax operating cash flow break-even point discussed in this chapter is related to a break-even point that makes the NPV of a project equal to zero.

12.7. Is it possible to have a crossover point where the accounting break-even point is the same for two alternatives – that is, above the break-even point for a low-fixed-cost alternative but below the break-even point for a high-fixed-cost alternative? Explain.

12.8. In calculus we are able to determine the effect on an entire multivariable equation of a change to a single variable. We call that effect the *partial derivative*. Which is analogous to the partial derivative: sensitivity analysis, scenario analysis or simulation analysis?

12.9. The High Tech Monopoly Company has plenty of cash to fund any conceivable posi-tive NPV project. Can you describe a situation in which capital rationing could still occur?

12.10. The profitability index is a scaleless attri-bute for measuring a project's benefits rel-ative to the costs. How might this help to eliminate bias in project selection?

QUESTIONS AND PROBLEMS

Basic

12.1. Fixed and variable costs: Define *variable costs* and *fixed costs* and give an example of each.

12.2. EBIT: Describe the role that the mix of variable versus fixed costs has in the variation of earnings before interest and taxes (EBIT) for the firm.

12.3. [EXCEL®] **EBIT:** Le Lexique Enchanté SA sells all of its books for €100 per book and it currently costs €50 in variable costs to produce each text. The fixed costs, which include depreciation and amortisation for the firm, are currently €2 million per year. The firm is considering changing its production technology, which will increase the fixed costs for the firm by 50% but decrease the variable costs per unit by 50%. If the firm expects to sell 45 000 books next year, should the firm switch technologies?

12.4. [EXCEL®] **EBIT:** WalkAbout Kangaroo Shoe Stores forecasts that it will sell 9500 pairs of shoes next year. The firm buys its shoes for A$50 per pair from the wholesaler and sells them for A$75 per pair. If the firm will incur fixed costs plus depreciation and amortisation of A$100 000, then what is the percentage increase in EBIT if the actual sales next year equal 11 500 pairs of shoes?

12.5. [EXCEL®] **Cash Flow DOL:** Videra de Lisboa SA has monthly fixed costs of €100 000, EBIT of €250 000 and depreciation charges on its office furniture and computers of €5000. Calculate the Cash Flow DOL for this firm.

12.6. Accounting DOL: Explain how the value of accounting operating leverage can be used.

12.7. Break-even analysis: Why is the per-unit contribution important in a break-even analysis?

12.8. Simulation analysis: What is simulation analysis and how is it used?

12.9. Profitability index: What is the profitability index and why is it helpful in the capital rationing process?

Intermediate

12.10. EBIT: If a manufacturing firm and a service firm have identical cash fixed costs but the manufacturing firm has much higher depreciation and amortisation, then which firm is more likely to have a large discrepancy between its FCF and its EBIT?

12.11. [EXCEL®] **EBIT:** Pallone Internazionale S.p.A. expects to sell 15 000 footballs this year. The balls sell for €110 each and have a variable cost per unit of €80. Fixed costs, including depreciation and amortisation, are currently €220 000 per year. How much can either the fixed costs or the variable cost per unit increase in order to keep the company from having a negative EBIT.

12.12. [EXCEL®] **EBIT:** Spezialität Glühbirnen GmbH anticipates selling 3000 light bulbs this year at a price of €15 per bulb. It costs Spezialität €10 in variable costs to produce each light bulb and the fixed costs for the firm are €10 000. Spezialität has an opportunity to sell an additional 1000 bulbs next year at the same price and variable cost, but by doing so the firm will incur an additional fixed cost of €4000 if it chooses to sell the additional bulbs. Should Spezialität produce and sell the additional bulbs?

12.13. Cash Flow DOL: For Le Lexique Enchanté SA in Self-study Problem 12.3, what percentage increase in pre-tax operating cash flow will be driven by the additional revenue?

Use the following information for Problems 12.14, 12.15 and 12.16:
Velas de los Fieles SA will be producing a new line of candles that do not drip wax in the coming

years and has the choice of producing the candles in a large factory with a small number of workers or a small factory with a large number of workers. Each candle will be sold for €10. If the large factory is chosen, the cost per unit to produce each candle will be €2.50, while the cost per unit will be €7.50 for the small factory. The large factory would have fixed cash costs of €2 million and a depreciation expense of €300 000 per year, while those expenses would be €500 000 and €100 000 in the small factory.

12.14. [EXCEL®] **Accounting operating profit break-even:** Calculate the accounting operating profit break-even point for both factory choices for Velas de los Fieles.

12.15. [EXCEL®] **Crossover level of unit sales:** Calculate the number of candles for Velas de los Fieles for which the accounting operating profit is the same regardless of the factory choice.

12.16. [EXCEL®] **Pre-tax operating cash flow break-even:** Calculate the pre-tax operating cash flow break-even point for both factory choices for Velas de los Fieles.

12.17. **Accounting and cash flow break-even:** Your analysis tells you that at a projected level of sales, your firm will be below accounting break-even but above cash flow break-even. Explain why this might still be a viable project or firm.

12.18. **Sensitivity and scenario analyses:** Sensitivity analysis and scenario analysis are somewhat similar. Describe which is a more realistic method of analysing different scenario impacts on a project.

12.19. **Sensitivity analysis:** Describe the circumstances under which sensitivity analysis might be a reasonable basis for determining changes to a firm's EBIT or FCF.

12.20. [EXCEL®] **Scenario analysis:** Ballina Fuisce plc forecasts that if it sells each bottle of its Freuddwyd Whiskey for €20, then the demand for the product will be 15 000 bottles per year, whereas sales will be 90% as high if the price is raised 10%. Ballina

Fuisce's variable cost per bottle is €10 and the total fixed cash cost for the year is €100 000. Depreciation and amortisation charges are €20 000 and the firm is in the 30% marginal tax rate. The firm anticipates an increased working capital need of €3000 for the year. What will be the effect of the price increase on the firm's FCF for the year?

12.21. **Sensitivity, scenario and simulation analysis:** If you were interested in calculating the probability that your project would have positive FCF, what type of risk analysis tool would you most likely use?

12.22. **Profitability index:** Suppose that you faced the following projects but had only €30 000 to invest. How would you make your decision and which projects would you invest in?

Project	Cost	NPV
A	€8 000	€4 000
B	11 000	7 000
C	9 000	5 000
D	7 000	4 000

12.23. **Profitability index:** Suppose that you face the same projects as in the previous problem but have only €25 000 to invest. Which projects would you choose?

Advanced

12.24. Bodegas St Miguel SA is starting to develop a new product for which the fixed cash expenditures are expected to be €80 000. The projected EBIT is €100 000 and the Accounting DOL will be 2.0. What is the Cash Flow DOL for the firm?

12.25. If a firm has any reasonable fixed asset base, meaning that its depreciation and amortisation for any year is positive, discuss the relationship between a firm's Accounting DOL and its Cash Flow DOL.

12.26. [EXCEL®] Zilver Veelhoek B.V. has determined that if its revenues were to increase by 10%, then EBIT would increase by 25% to €100 000. The fixed costs (cash only) for the firm are €100 000. Given the same

10% increase in revenues, what would be the corresponding change in EBITDA?

12.27. If a firm's costs are absolutely known (variable as well as fixed), then what are the only two sources of volatility for the firm's operating profits or its operating cash flows?

12.28. In most circumstances, given the choice between a higher fixed cost structure and a lower fixed cost structure, which of the two would generate a larger contribution margin?

12.29. Using the same logic as with the accounting break-even calculation in Problem 12.15, adapt the formula for the crossover level of unit sales to find the number of units sold where the pre-tax operating cash flow is the same whether the firm chooses the large or small factory.

12.30. EXCEL® You are analysing two proposed capital investments with the following cash flows:

Year	Project X	Project Y
0	–€20 000	–€20 000
1	13 000	7 000
2	6 000	7 000
3	6 000	7 000
4	2 000	7 000

The cost of capital for both projects is 10%. Calculate the profitability index (PI) for each project. Which project, or projects, should be accepted if you have unlimited funds to invest? Which project should be accepted if they are mutually exclusive?

CFA Problems

12.31. An investment of €20 000 will create a perpetual after-tax cash flow of €2000. The required rate of return is 8%. What is the investment's profitability index?
  a. 1.00
  b. 1.08
  c. 1.16
  d. 1.25

12.32. Fabrikations-Hermann AG is considering an investment of €375 million with expected after-tax cash inflows of €115 million per year for seven years and an additional after-tax salvage value of €50 million in Year 7. The required rate of return is 10%. What is the investment's PI?
  a. 1.19
  b. 1.33
  c. 1.56
  d. 1.75

12.33. Operating leverage is a measure of the
  a. sensitivity of net earnings to changes in operating earnings;
  b. sensitivity of net earnings to changes in sales;
  c. sensitivity of fixed operating costs to changes in variable costs;
  d. sensitivity of earnings before interest and taxes to changes in the number of units produced and sold.

12.34. The Fulcrum Company produces decorative swivel platforms for home televisions. If Fulcrum produces 40 million units, it estimates that it can sell them for £100 each. The variable production costs are £65 per unit, whereas the fixed production costs are £1.05 billion. Which of the following statements is true?
  a. The Fulcrum Company produces a positive operating income if it produces and sells more than 25 million swivel platforms.
  b. The Fulcrum Company's degree of operating leverage is 1.333.
  c. If the Fulcrum Company increases production and sales by 5%, its operating earnings are expected to increase by 20%.
  d. Increasing the fixed production costs by 10% will result in a lower sensitivity of operating earnings to changes in units produced and sold.

SAMPLE TEST PROBLEMS

12.1. Sven Hattar AS forecasts that it will sell 25 000 baseball caps next year. The firm buys its caps for SKr 3 from the wholesaler and sells them for SKr 15 each. If the firm will incur fixed costs plus depreciation and amortisation of SKr 80 000, then what is the percentage increase in EBIT if the actual sales next year equal 27 000 caps?

12.2. Alan's Fine Furniture will be creating custom bed frames. The fixed cash expenditures are expected to be $120 000, the projected EBIT for the project is $130 000 and the Accounting DOL will be 2.5. What is the depreciation and amortisation for the firm, as well as the Cash Flow DOL?

12.3. Les Feux d'Artifice Royale is considering whether to build a large or small factory to produce fireworks. Regardless of the production method, each bundle of firecrackers sells for €4.00. If the large factory is chosen, then the variable cost per bundle of firecrackers will be €0.50, while the fixed costs will be €300 000 and the annual depreciation and amortisation amount will be €100 000. If the small factory is chosen, then the variable cost per bundle of firecrackers will be €1.75, while the fixed costs will be €100 000 and the annual depreciation and amortisation amount will be €10 000. Calculate the number of firecracker bundles for which the accounting operating profit is the same regardless of the factory choice.

12.4. You are the chairperson of the investment committee at your firm. Five projects have been submitted to your committee for approval this month. The investment required and the project profitability index for each of these projects are presented in the following table:

Project	Investment	PI
A	€20 000	2.500
B	50 000	2.000
C	70 000	1.750
D	10 000	1.000
E	80 000	0.800

If you have €500 000 available for investments, which of these projects would you approve? Assume that you do not have to worry about having enough resources for future investments when making this decision.

12.5. Ibrahim's Habanero Sauces forecasts that if it sells each bottle of NitroStrength for €10, then the demand for the product will be 85 000 bottles per year. The company expects that if it sells NitroStrength for a price that is 10% higher, then it will sell 75% as many bottles of the sauce. Ibrahim's variable cost per bottle is €4 and the total fixed cash cost for the year is €20 000. Depreciation and amortisation charges are €3000 and the firm is in the 40% marginal tax rate. The firm anticipates an increased working capital need of €2000 for the year. What effect would the price increase have on the firm's FCF for the year?

ENDNOTES

1. A bacteriophage is a virus that infects bacteria. EBI stands for Exponential Biotherapies.
2. A hammock is a hanging bed that is often made of rope and hung between two trees.
3. VC equals Unit VC (or cost per unit) times the number of units sold. If we know Unit VC, we can therefore calculate VC for different levels of unit sales.

4. We are assuming here that you will cut back on advertising expenditures if revenue declines and that a modest decrease in advertising will not adversely affect demand for your services. Of course, under certain circumstances, you might actually increase advertising expenditures if demand for your service declines.
5. The term *accounting operating profits* is used here to refer to EBIT, even though EBIT is not actually computed using accounting numbers when we forecast cash flows for a financial analysis. The term is used to refer to the fact that non-cash charges, D&A, are subtracted when computing this measure of earnings, just as is done in the calculation of accounting operating profits.

CHAPTER

13

The Cost of Capital

In this Chapter:

LEARNING OBJECTIVES

1. Explain what the weighted average cost of capital for a firm is and why it is often used as a discount rate to evaluate projects.

2. Calculate the cost of debt for a firm.

3. Calculate the cost of ordinary shares and the cost of preference shares for a firm.

4. Calculate the weighted average cost of capital for a firm, explain the limitations of using a firm's weighted average cost of capital as the discount rate when evaluating a project and discuss the alternatives that are available.

In April 2008, Accor SA, the French international hotels and services group, opened its new luxury hotel in Luxembourg – 'Le Grand Ducal' – one of five new additions to the group's Sofitel brand.[1] The hotel has 128 rooms, 13 junior suits and two luxury suites as well as a restaurant on the top floor with panoramic views of the city of Luxembourg, a bar that provides live entertainment and an Asian tearoom with a library. To cater for business needs, the hotel features an executive boardroom that can comfortably seat up to 14 people.

The new hotel is part of Accor's long-term plans to add 200 000 new rooms between 2006 and 2011. In 2008 alone, the group increased its capacity by 28 000 rooms worldwide. As you can imagine, the cost of financing a project like this is quite substantial. Building a hotel business is costly even if – in many instances – hotels can be leased rather than owned outright. Accor spent over €1 billion on expansion in the financial year 2008, down slightly on the €1.2 billion in 2007.

Accor is a highly sophisticated and successful hotel and services chain. Before the company decided on Le Grand Ducal, you can be sure that the managers at Accor carefully evaluated the financial aspects of the project. They evaluated the required investment, what revenues the new hotel was likely to generate and how much it would cost to operate and maintain. They also estimated what it would cost to finance the project – how much they would pay for the debt and the returns equity investors would require for an investment with this level of risk. This 'cost of capital' would be incorporated into their NPV analysis through the discounting process.

Doing a good job of estimating the cost of capital is especially important for capital-intensive projects such as hotels. The cost of financing a hotel can easily claim €90 or €100 from every room rental. In other words, if an average room rents for €200, the cost of financing the project can amount to 45–50% of the revenue the hotel receives from renting a room!

From this example, you can see how important it is to get the cost of capital right. If Accor's managers had estimated the cost of capital to be 7% when it was really 8%, they might have ended up investing in a project with a large negative NPV. How did Accor approach this important task? In this chapter, we discuss how businesses estimate the cost of capital they use to evaluate projects.

CHAPTER PREVIEW

Chapter 7 discussed the general concept of risk and described what financial analysts mean when they talk about the risk associated with a project's cash flows. It also explained how this risk is related to expected returns. With this background, we are ready to discuss the methods that financial managers use to estimate discount rates, the reasons they use these methods and the shortcomings of each method.

We start this chapter by introducing the weighted average cost of capital and explaining how this concept is related to the discount rates that many financial managers use to evaluate projects. Then we describe various methods that are used to estimate the three broad types of financing that firms use to acquire assets – debt, ordinary shares and preference shares – as well as the overall weighted average cost of capital for the firm.

We next discuss the circumstances under which it is appropriate to use the weighted average cost of capital for a firm as the discount rate for a project, and outline the types of problems that can arise when the weighted average cost of capital is used inappropriately. Finally, we examine alternatives to using the weighted average cost of capital as a discount rate.

THE FIRM'S OVERALL COST OF CAPITAL

Learning Objective 1

Explain what the weighted average cost of capital for a firm is and why it is often used as a discount rate to evaluate projects.

Up to this point, our discussions of investment analysis have focused on evaluating individual projects. We have assumed that the rate used to discount the cash flows for a project reflects the risks associated with the incremental cash flows from that project. In Chapter 7, we saw that since *unique risk* can be eliminated by holding a diversified portfolio, *systematic risk* is the only risk that investors require compensation for bearing. With this insight, we concluded that we could use Equation (7.9) to estimate the expected rate of return for a particular investment:

$$E(R_i) = R_{rf} + \beta_i[E(R_m) - R_{rf}]$$

where $E(R_i)$ is the expected return on project i, R_{rf} is the risk-free rate of return, β_i is the beta for project i and $E(R_m)$ is the expected return on the market.

Recall that the difference between the expected return on the market and the risk-free rate $[E(R_m) - R_{rf}]$ is known as the *market risk premium*.

Although these ideas help us better understand the discount rate on a conceptual level, they can be difficult to implement in practice. Firms do not issue publicly traded shares for individual projects. This means that analysts do not have the share returns necessary to use a regression analysis like that illustrated in Exhibit 7.1 to estimate the beta (β) for an individual project. As a result, they have no way to directly estimate the discount rate that reflects the systematic risk of the incremental cash flows from a particular project.

In many firms, senior financial managers deal with this problem by estimating the cost of capital for the firm as a whole and then requiring analysts within the firm to use this cost of capital to discount the cash flows for all projects.[2] A problem with this approach is that it ignores the fact that a firm is really a collection of projects with varying levels of risk. A firm's overall cost of capital is actually a weighted average of the costs of capital for these projects, where the weights reflect the relative values of the projects.

To see why a firm is a collection of projects, consider EADS NV. EADS manufactures a number of different models of civilian and military fixed-wing aircraft and helicopters as well as spacecraft and defence equipment. The commercial aircraft differ in terms of characteristics ranging from the superjumbo A380 down to the turboprop ATR regional airliner. In addition, EADS manufactures several versions of each type to meet the needs of its customers. These versions have different ranges, seat configurations, numbers of seats and other distinguishing factors. Some versions are designed to carry freight. Every version of every model of aircraft at EADS was, at some point in time, a new project. The assets owned by EADS today, and its expected cash flows, are just the sum of the assets and cash flows from all these individual projects plus the other projects at the firm, such as those involving military aircraft.[3] This means that the overall systematic risk associated with EADS' cash flows and the company's cost of capital are weighted averages of the systematic risks and the costs of capital for its individual projects.

If the risk of an individual project differs from the average risk of the firm, the firm's overall cost of capital is not the ideal discount rate to use when evaluating that project. Nevertheless, since this is the discount rate that is commonly used, we begin by discussing how a firm's overall cost of capital is estimated. We then discuss alternatives to using the firm's cost of capital as the discount rate in evaluating a project.

The Market Value Balance Sheet

To understand how financial analysts estimate their firms' costs of capital, you must be familiar with a concept that we call the **market value balance sheet**. The finance balance sheet is like the accounting balance sheet from Chapter 3. The main difference is that it is based on market values rather than book values. Recall that the total book value of the assets reported on an accounting balance sheet does not necessarily reflect the total market value of those assets. This is because the book value is largely based on historical costs, while the total market value of the assets equals

the present value of the total cash flows that those assets are expected to generate in the future. The market value can be greater than or less than the book value but is rarely the same.

> **Market value balance sheet**
>
> a balance sheet that is based on market values of expected cash flows

While the left-hand side of the accounting balance sheet reports the book values of a firm's assets, the right-hand side reports how those assets were financed. Firms finance the purchase of their assets using debt and equity.[4] Since the cost of the assets must equal the total value of the debt and equity that was used to purchase them, the book value of the assets must equal the book value of the liabilities plus the book value of the equity on the accounting balance sheet. In Chapter 3 we called this equality the *balance sheet identity*.

Just as the total book value of the assets at a firm does not generally equal the total market value of those assets, the book value of total liabilities plus shareholders' equity does not usually equal the market value of these claims. In fact, the total market value of the debt and equity claims differ from their book values by exactly the same amount that the market values of a firm's assets differ from their book values. This is because the total market value of the debt and the equity at a firm equals the present value of the cash flows that the debt holders and the shareholders have the right to receive. These cash flows are the cash flows that the assets in the firm are expected to generate. In other words, the people who have lent money to a firm and the people who have purchased the firm's shares have the right to receive all of the cash flows that the firm is expected to generate in the future. The value of the claims they hold must equal the value of the cash flows that they have a right to receive.

The fact that the market value of the assets must equal the value of the cash flows that these assets are expected to generate, combined with the fact that the value of the expected cash flows also

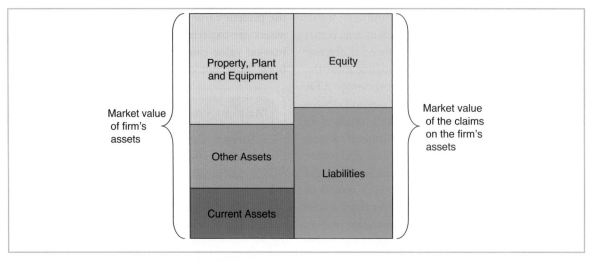

Exhibit 13.1: The Market Value Balance Sheet The market value of a firm's assets, which equals the present value of the cash flows those assets are expected to generate in the future, must equal the market value of the claims on those cash flows – the firm's liabilities and equity.

equals the total market value of the firm's total liabilities and equity, means that we can write the market value (MV) of assets as follows:

$$\text{MV of assets} = \text{MV of liabilities} + \text{MV of equity} \tag{13.1}$$

Equation (13.1) is just like the accounting balance sheet identity. The only difference is that Equation (13.1) is based on market values. This relation is illustrated in Exhibit 13.1.

To see why the market value of the assets must equal the total market value of the liabilities and equity, consider a firm whose only business is to own and manage an apartment building that was purchased 20 years ago for €1 000 000. Suppose that there is currently a mortgage on the building that is worth €300 000, the firm has no other debt

and the current market value of the building, based on the expected cash flows from future rents, is €4 000 000. What is the value of all the equity (shares) in this firm? The answer is €4 000 000 − €300 000 = €3 700 000. If the cash flows that the apartment building is expected to produce are worth €4 000 000, then investors would be willing to pay €3 700 000 for the equity in the firm. This is the value of the cash flows that they would expect to receive after making the interest and principal payments on the mortgage. Furthermore, since, by definition, the mortgage is worth €300 000, the value of the debt plus the value of the equity is €300 000 + €3 700 000 = €4 000 000 – which is exactly equal to the market value of the firm's assets.

If the concept of a balance sheet based on market values seems familiar to you, it is because

BUILDING INTUITION

The Market Value of a Firm's Assets Equals the Market Value of the Claims on Those Assets

The market value of the debt and equity claims against the cash flows of a firm must equal the present value of the cash flows that the firm's assets are expected to generate. This is because, between them, the debt holders and the shareholders have the legal right to receive all of those cash flows.

the idea of preparing an actual balance sheet based on market values was discussed in Chapter 3. In that chapter we pointed out that such a balance sheet would be more useful to financial decision makers than the ordinary accounting balance sheet. Financial managers are much more concerned about the future than the past when they make decisions. You might revisit the discussion of sunk costs in Chapter 11 to remind yourself of why this is true.

How Firms Estimate their Cost of Capital

Now that you understand the basic idea of the finance balance sheet, consider the challenge that financial analysts face when they want to estimate the cost of capital for a firm. If analysts at a firm could estimate the betas for each of the firm's individual projects, they could estimate the beta for the entire firm as a weighted average of the betas for the individual projects. They could do this because, as we discussed earlier, the firm is simply a collection (portfolio) of projects. This calculation would just be an application of Equation (7.10):

$$\beta_{n \text{ Asset portfolio}} = \sum_{i=1}^{n} x_i \beta_i = x_1 \beta_1 + x_2 \beta_2 \\ + x_3 \beta_3 + \cdots + x_n \beta_n$$

where β_i is the beta for project i and x_i is the fraction of the total firm value represented by project i.

The analysts could then use the beta for the firm in Equation (7.9):

$$E(R_i) = R_{\text{rf}} + \beta_i[E(R_{\text{m}}) - R_{\text{rf}}]$$

to estimate the expected return on the firm's assets, which is also the firm's cost of capital. Unfortunately, because analysts are not typically able to estimate betas for individual projects, they generally cannot use this approach.

Instead, analysts must use their knowledge of the finance balance sheet, along with the concept of market efficiency, to estimate the cost of capital for the firm. Rather than using Equations (7.10) and (7.9) to perform the calculations for the *individual projects* represented on the left-hand side of the finance balance sheet, analysts perform a similar

set of calculations for the *different types of financing* (debt and equity) on the right-hand side of the finance balance sheet. They can do this because, as we said earlier, the people who finance the firm have the right to receive all of the cash flows on the left-hand side. This means that the systematic risk associated with the total assets on the left-hand side is the same as the systematic risk associated with the total financing on the right-hand side. In other words, the weighted average of the betas for the different claims on the assets must equal a weighted average of the betas for the individual assets (projects).

Analysts do not need to estimate betas for each type of financing that the firm has. As long as they can estimate the cost of each type of financing – either directly, by observing that cost in the capital markets, or by using Equation (7.9) – they can compute the cost of capital for the firm using the following equation:

$$k_{\text{Firm}} = \sum_{i=1}^{n} x_i k_i = x_1 k_1 + x_2 k_2 + x_3 k_3 + \cdots \\ + x_n k_n \tag{13.2}$$

In Equation (13.2), k_{Firm} is the cost of capital for the firm, k_i is the cost of financing type i and x_i is the fraction of the total market value of the financing (or of the assets) of the firm represented by financing type i. This formula simply says that the overall cost of capital for the firm is a weighted average of the cost of each different type of financing used by the firm. Note that since we are specifically talking about the cost of capital, we use the symbol k_i to represent this cost, rather than the more general notation $E(R_i)$ that we used in Chapter 7.

> **WEB**
>
> Yahoo finance provides estimates for company betas at: http://www.finance.yahoo.com.

The similarity between Equations (13.2) and (7.10) is not an accident. Both are applications of the basic idea that the systematic risk of a portfolio of assets is a weighted average of the systematic risks of the individual assets. Because R_{rf} and $E(R_m)$ in Equation (7.9) are the same for all assets, when we substitute Equation (7.9) into Equation (13.2) – remember that $E(R_i)$ in Equation (7.9) is the same as k_i in Equation (13.2) – and cancel out R_{rf} and $E(R_m)$, we get Equation (7.10). We will not prove this here but you might do so to convince yourself that what we are saying is true.

To see how Equation (13.2) is applied, we will return to the example of the firm whose only business is to manage an apartment building. Recall that the total value of this firm is €4 000 000 and that it has €300 000 in debt. If the firm has only one loan and one type of share, then the fractions of the total value represented by those two types of financing are as follows:

$$x_{Debt} = €300\,000/€4\,000\,000 = 0.075, \text{ or } 7.5\%$$
$$x_{Equity} = €3\,700\,000/€4\,000\,000 = 0.925, \text{ or } 92.5\%$$
$$\text{where } x_{Debt} + x_{Equity} = 0.075 + 0.925 = 1.000$$

This tells us that the value of the debt claims equals 7.5% of the value of the firm and that the value of the equity claims equals the remaining 92.5% of the value of the firm. If the cost of the debt for this business is 6% and the cost of the

equity is 10%, the cost of capital for the firm can be calculated as a weighted average of the costs of the debt and equity:[5]

$$
\begin{aligned}
k_{Firm} &= x_{Debt}k_{Debt} + x_{Equity}k_{Equity} \\
&= (0.075)(0.06) + (0.925)(0.10) \\
&= 0.097, \text{ or } 9.7\%
\end{aligned}
$$

Notice that we have used Equation (13.2) to calculate a **weighted average cost of capital (WACC)** for the firm in this example. In fact, this is what people typically call the firm's cost of capital, k_{Firm}. From this point on, we will use the abbreviation WACC to represent the firm's overall cost of capital.

> **Weighted average cost of capital (WACC)**
>
> the weighted average of the costs of the different types of capital (debt and equity) that have been used to finance a firm; the cost of each type of capital is weighted by the proportion of the total capital that it represents

---

Learning by Doing Application 13.1

Calculating the Cost of Capital for a Firm

Problem: You are a property investor who is considering investing in a new office building that will cost €2 000 000. You plan to finance the building with a €1 500 000 first mortgage at a 6.5% interest rate, a €300 000 second mortgage at an 8% interest rate and €200 000 of your own money. You will own all of the equity (shares) in this investment. You estimate that the opportunity cost of your €200 000

investment – that is, what you could earn on an investment of similar risk in the capital market – is 12% with that much debt. What is the cost of capital for this investment?

Approach: You can think of the office building as a separate firm and use Equation (13.2) to calculate the WACC for this 'firm'. Since you are planning to finance the building with capital from three different sources – two mortgages and your own equity investment – the right-hand side of Equation (13.2) will have three terms.

Solution: We begin by calculating the weights for the different types of financing:

$$x_{\text{1st mortgage}} = €1\,500\,000/€2\,000\,00 = 0.75$$
$$x_{\text{2nd mortgage}} = €300\,000/€2\,000\,00 = 0.15$$
$$x_{\text{Equity}} = €200\,000/€2\,000\,00 = 0.10$$

where $x_{\text{1st mortgage}} + x_{\text{2nd mortgage}} + x_{\text{Equity}}$
$$= 0.75 + 0.15 + 0.10 = 1.00$$

We can then calculate the WACC using Equation (13.2):

$$\text{WACC} = k_{\text{Firm}} = x_{\text{1st mortgage}} k_{\text{1st mortgage}}$$
$$+ x_{\text{2nd mortgage}} k_{\text{2nd mortgage}} + x_{\text{Equity}} k_{\text{Equity}}$$

$$= (0.75)(0.065) + (0.15)(0.08)$$
$$+ (0.10)(0.12)$$
$$= 0.073, \text{ or } 7.3\%$$

On average, you would be paying 7.3% per year on every euro you invested in the office building. This is the opportunity cost of capital for the office building project. It is the rate that you would use to discount the cash flows associated with the office building in an NPV analysis.

BUILDING INTUITION

Firm's Cost of Capital is a Weighted Average of All its Financing Costs

The cost of capital for a firm is a weighted average of the costs of the different types of financing used by a firm. The weights are the proportions of the total firm value represented by the different types of financing. By weighting the costs of the individual financing types in this way, we obtain the overall average opportunity cost of each unit of currency invested in the firm.

Before You Go On

1. Why does the market value of the claims on the assets of a firm equal the market value of the assets?
2. How is the WACC for a firm calculated?
3. What does the WACC for a firm tell us?

THE COST OF DEBT

Learning Objective 2
Calculate the cost of debt for a firm.

In our discussion of how the WACC for a firm is calculated, we assumed that the costs of the

different types of financing were known. This assumption allowed us to simply plug those costs into Equation (13.2) once we had calculated the weight for each. Unfortunately, life is not that simple. In the real world, analysts have to estimate each of the individual costs. In other words, the discussion in the preceding section glossed over a number of concepts and issues that you should be familiar with. This and the following section discuss those concepts and issues and show how the costs of the different types of financing can be estimated.

Before we move on to the specifics of how to estimate the costs of different types of financing, we must stress an important point: All of these calculations depend in some part on financial markets being efficient.[6] We suggested this in the last section, when we mentioned that analysts have to rely on the concept of market efficiency to estimate the WACC. The reason is that analysts often cannot directly observe the rate of return that investors require for a particular type of financing. Instead, analysts must rely on the security prices they can observe in the financial markets to estimate the required rate.

It makes sense to rely on security prices only if you believe that the financial markets are reasonably efficient at incorporating new information into these prices. If the markets were not efficient, estimates of expected returns that were based on market security prices would be unreliable. Of course, if the returns that are plugged into Equation (13.2) are bad, the resulting estimate for WACC will also be bad. With this caveat, we can now discuss how to estimate the costs of the various types of financing.

Key Concepts for Estimating the Cost of Debt

Virtually all firms use some form of debt financing. The financial managers at firms typically arrange for revolving lines of credit to finance working capital items, such as inventories or accounts receivable. These lines of credit are very much like the lines of credit that come with your credit cards. Firms also obtain private fixed-term loans, such as bank loans, or sell bonds to the public to finance ongoing operations or the purchase of long-term assets – just as you would finance your living expenses while you are at university with a student loan or a car with a car loan. For example, an electric utility firm, such as E.On Energy, will sell bonds or borrow to finance a new power plant and a rapidly growing retailer, such as Carrefour, will also use debt to finance new stores and distribution centres. As mentioned earlier, we will discuss how firms finance themselves in more detail in Chapters 15 and 16, but for now it is sufficient to recognise that firms use these three general types of debt financing: lines of credit, private fixed-term loans and bonds.

There is a cost associated with each type of debt that a firm uses. However, when we estimate the cost of capital for a firm, we are particularly interested in the cost of the firm's long-term debt. Firms generally use long-term debt to finance their long-term assets and it is the long-term assets that concern us when we think about the value of a firm's assets. By long-term debt, we usually mean the debt that, when it was borrowed, was set to mature in more than one year. This typically includes fixed-term bank loans used to finance ongoing operations or long-term assets, as well as the bonds that a firm sells in the public debt markets.

Although one year is not an especially long time, debt with a maturity of more than one year is typically viewed as permanent debt. This is because firms often borrow the money to pay off this debt when it matures.

We do not normally worry about revolving lines of credit when calculating the cost of debt because these lines tend to be temporary. Banks typically require that the outstanding balances be periodically paid down to zero (just as we are sure you pay your entire credit card balance from time to time).

When analysts estimate the cost of a firm's long-term debt, they are estimating the cost on a particular date – the date on which they are doing the analysis. This is a very important point to keep in mind because the interest rate that the firm is paying on its outstanding debt does not necessarily reflect its current cost of debt. Interest rates change over time and so does the cost of debt for a firm. The rate a firm was charged three years ago for a five-year loan is unlikely to be the same rate that it would be charged today for a new five-year loan. For example, suppose that E.On Energy issued bonds five years ago for 7%. Since then, interest rates have fallen, so the same bonds could be sold at par value today for 6%. The cost of debt today is 6%, not 7%, and 6% is the cost of debt that management will use in WACC calculations. If you looked in the firm's financial statements, you would see that the firm is paying an interest rate of 7%. This is what the financial managers of the firm agreed to pay five years ago, not what it would cost to sell the same bonds today. The accounting statements reflect the cost

BUILDING INTUITION

The Current Cost of Long-Term Debt is What Matters When Calculating WACC

The current cost of long-term debt is the appropriate cost of debt for WACC calculations. This is the relevant cost because the WACC is the opportunity cost of capital for the firm's investors as of today. Historical costs do not belong in WACC calculations.

of debt that was sold at some time in the past. The same applies to loans from a bank. The appropriate interest rate is the rate at which a bank will make a new loan, not the interest rate on any existing loans as these may not reflect current rates that apply to new loans.

Estimating the Current Cost of a Bond or an Outstanding Loan

We have seen that we should not use historical costs of debt in WACC calculations. We will now discuss how we can estimate the current costs of bonds and other fixed-term loans by using market information.

The Current Cost of a Bond

You may not realise it, but we have already discussed how to estimate the current cost of debt for a publicly traded bond. This cost is estimated using the yield to maturity calculation. Recall that in Chapter 8 we defined the yield to maturity as the discount rate that makes the present value of the coupon and principal payments equal to the price of the bond.

For example, consider a 10-year €1000 bond that was issued five years ago. This bond has five years remaining before it matures. If the bond has an annual coupon rate of 7%, pays coupon interest semi-annually and is currently selling for €1042.65, we can calculate its yield to maturity by using Equation (8.1) and solving for i. Let us use Equation (8.1) for this example.

To do this, as was discussed in the section on semi-annual compounding in Chapter 8, we first

convert the bond data to reflect semi-annual compounding: (1) the total number of coupon payments is 10 (2 per year × 5 years) and (2) the semi-annual coupon payment is €35 [(€1000 × 7%)/2 = €70/2]. We can now use Equation (8.1) and solve for i to find the yield to maturity:

$$P_B = \frac{C_1}{1+i} + \frac{C_2}{(1+i)^2} + \cdots + \frac{C_n + F_n}{(1+i)^n}$$

$$€1042.65 = \frac{€35}{1+i} + \frac{€35}{(1+i)^2} + \frac{€35}{(1+i)^3} + \cdots$$
$$+ \frac{€35}{(1+i)^9} + \frac{€1035}{(1+i)^{10}}$$

Now, by trial and error or with a financial calculator, we solve for i and find:

$$i = k_{\text{Bond}} = 0.030, \text{ or } 3.0\%$$

This semi-annual rate would be quoted as an annual rate of 6% ($2 \times 0.03 = 0.06$, or 6%) in the bond market. However, as explained in Chapter 8, this annual rate fails to account for the effects of compounding. We must therefore use Equation (6.7) to calculate the effective annual interest rate (EAR) in order to obtain the actual current annual cost of this debt:

$$\text{EAR} = \left(1 + \frac{\text{Quoted interest rate}}{m}\right)^m - 1$$
$$= \left(1 + \frac{0.06}{2}\right)^2 - 1$$
$$= (1.03)^2 - 1 = 0.061, \text{ or } 6.1\%$$

If this bond was sold at par, it paid 7% when it was issued five years ago. Someone who buys it today will expect to earn only 6.1% per year. This is the annual rate of return required by the market on this bond, and which is known in the bond market as the effective annual yield.

Notice that the above calculation takes into account the interest payments, the face value of the debt (the amount that will be repaid in five years) and the current price at which the bond is selling. It is necessary to account for all these characteristics of the bond. The return received by someone who buys the bond today will be determined by both the interest income and the capital appreciation (or capital depreciation in this case, since the price is higher than the face value).

We must account for one other factor when we calculate the current cost of bond financing to a company – the cost of issuing the bond. In the above example, we calculated the return that someone who buys the bond can expect to receive. Since a company must pay fees to investment bankers, lawyers and accountants, along with various other costs, to actually issue a bond, the cost to the company is higher than 6.1%.[7] Therefore, in order to obtain an accurate estimate of the cost of a bond, analysis must incorporate *issuance costs* into their calculations. Issuance costs are an example of *direct out-of-pocket costs*, the actual out-of-pocket costs that a firm incurs when it raises capital.

The way in which issuance costs are incorporated into the calculation of the cost of a bond is quite simple. Analysts use the *net proceeds* that the company receives from the bond, rather than the price that is paid by the investor, on the left-hand side of Equation (8.1). Suppose the company in our example sold five-year bonds with a 7% coupon today and paid issuance costs equal to 2% of the total value of the bonds. After paying the issuance costs, the company would receive only 98% of the price paid by the investors. Therefore, the company would actually receive only €1042.65 × (1 − 0.02) = €1021.80 for each bond it sold and the semi-annual cost to the

company would be:

$$P_B = \frac{C_1}{1+i} + \frac{C_2}{(1+i)^2} + \cdots + \frac{C_n + F_n}{(1+i)^n}$$

$$€1021.80 = \frac{€35}{1+i} + \frac{€35}{(1+i)^2} + \frac{€35}{(1+i)^3} + \cdots$$

$$+ \frac{€35}{(1+i)^9} + \frac{€1035}{(1+i)^{10}}$$

$$i = k_{Bond} = 0.0324, \text{ or } 3.24\%$$

Converting the adjusted semi-annual rate to an EAR, we see that the actual annual cost of this debt financing is:

$$EAR = (1.0324)^2 − 1 = 0.066, \text{ or } 6.6\%$$

In this example, the issuance costs increase the effective cost of the bonds from 6.1% to 6.6% per year.

The Current Cost of an Outstanding Loan

Conceptually, calculating the current cost of long-term bank or other private debt is not as straight-forward as estimating the current cost of a public bond because financial analysts cannot observe the market price of private debt. Fortunately, analysts do not typically have to do this. Instead, they can simply call their banker and ask what rate the bank would charge if they decided to refinance the debt today. A rate quote from a banker provides a good estimate of the current cost of a private loan. Loan pricing is discussed in more detail in Chapter 15 when we discuss how firms raise capital.

Taxes and the Cost of Debt

It is very important that you understand one additional concept concerning the cost of debt: in most countries, *firms can deduct interest payments for tax purposes*. In other words, every unit of currency a firm pays in interest reduces the firm's taxable income by the same amount. Thus, if the firm's marginal tax rate is 35%, the firm's total tax bill will be reduced by 0.35. For example, a euro of interest would actually cost this firm only 65 cents because the firm would save 35 cents on its taxes.

More generally, the after-tax cost of interest payments equals the pre-tax cost times 1 minus the tax rate. This means that the after-tax cost of debt is:

$$k_{\text{Debt after tax}} = k_{\text{Debt pre-tax}} \times (1 - t) \quad (13.3)$$

This after-tax cost of debt is the cost that firms actually use to calculate the WACC. The reason is simply that investors care only about the after-tax cost of capital – just as they care only about after-tax cash flows. Investors are concerned about what they actually have to pay for capital, and the actual cost is reduced if the government subsidises debt by providing tax relief on interest.

Taxes affect the cost of debt in the following way. Assume a company borrows €200 000 at a rate of interest of 6% to buy an asset on January 1 and the interest payments total €12 000 in the first year. As the interest is tax deductible, the company can deduct this €12 000 from its taxable income when it calculates its taxes for the year.

Suppose that the company's taxable income before the interest deduction is €75 000 and, for simplicity, that both the average and marginal tax rates are 20%. Without the interest deduction, the company would pay taxes of €15 000 (€75 000 × 0.20). However, because the interest payments reduce the firm's taxable income, the taxes with the interest deduction will be only €12 600 [(€75 000 − €12 000) × 0.20]. The ability to deduct the interest payments has saved the company €2400 (€15 000 − €12 600)! This saving is exactly equal to the interest payment the company makes on the loan times the company's marginal tax rate: €12 000 × 0.20 = €2400. Since the company is saving €2400, the after-tax cost of your interest payments is €9600 (€12 000 − €2400), which means that the after-tax cost of this debt is 4.8% (€9600/€200 000). This is exactly what Equation (13.3) tells us. With $k_{\text{Debt pre-tax}}$ at 6% and t at 20%, Equation (13.3) gives us:

$$
\begin{aligned}
k_{\text{Debt after tax}} &= k_{\text{Debt pre-tax}} \times (1 - t) \\
&= 0.06 \times (1 - 0.20) \\
&= 0.048, \text{ or } 4.8\%
\end{aligned}
$$

Estimating the Cost of Debt for a Firm

Most firms have several different debt issues outstanding at any particular point in time. Just as you might have both a car loan and a student loan, a firm might have several bank loans and bond issues outstanding. To estimate the firm's overall cost of debt when it has several debt issues outstanding, we must first estimate the costs of the individual debt issues and then calculate a weighted average of these costs.

To see how this is done, we will consider an example. Suppose that your pizza restaurant business has grown dramatically in the past three years from a single restaurant to 30 restaurants. To finance this growth, two years ago you sold €25 million of five-year bonds. These bonds pay interest annually and have a coupon rate of 8%. They are currently selling for €1026.24 per €1000 bond. Just today, you also borrowed €5 million from your local bank at an interest rate of 6%. Assume that this is all the long-term debt that you have and that there are no issuance costs. What is the overall average after-tax cost of your debt if your business's marginal tax rate is 35%?

The pre-tax cost of the bonds as of today is the effective annual yield on those bonds. Since the bonds were sold two years ago, they will mature three years from now. Using Equation (8.1), we find that the effective annual yield (which equals the yield to maturity in this example since coupon interest is paid annually) for these bonds is:

$$P_B = \frac{C_1}{1+i} + \frac{C_2}{(1+i)^2} + \cdots + \frac{C_n + F_n}{(1+i)^n}$$

$$€1026.24 = \frac{€80}{1+i} + \frac{€80}{(1+i)^2} + \frac{€1080}{(1+i)^3}$$

$$i = k_{\text{Bond pre-tax}} = 0.07, \text{ or } 7\%$$

The pre-tax cost of the bank loan that you took out today is simply the 6% rate that the bank is charging you, assuming that the bank is charging you the market rate.

Now that we know the pre-tax costs of the two types of debt that your business has outstanding, we can calculate the overall average cost of your debt by calculating the weighted average of their two costs. The weights for the two types of debt are as follows:

$$x_{Bonds} = €25\,000\,000/(€25\,000\,000 + €5\,000\,000)$$

$$= 0.833$$

$$x_{Bank\,debt} = €5\,000\,000/(€25\,000\,000 + €5\,000\,000)$$

$$= 0.167$$

where $x_{Bonds} + x_{Bank\,debt} = 0.833 + 0.167 = 1.000$

The weighted average pre-tax cost of debt is:

$$k_{Debt\,pre\text{-}tax} = x_{Bonds}k_{Bonds\,pre\text{-}tax}$$
$$+ x_{Bank\,debt}k_{Bank\,debt\,pre\text{-}tax}$$
$$= (0.833)(0.07) + (0.167)(0.06)$$
$$= 0.0683, \text{ or } 6.83\%$$

The after-tax cost of debt is therefore:

$$k_{Debt\,after\text{-}tax} = k_{Debt\,pre\text{-}tax} \times (1 - t)$$
$$= 6.83\% \times (1 - 0.35) = 4.44\%$$

**Learning by Doing
Application
13.2**

Calculating the Cost of Debt for a Firm

Problem: You have just successfully completed a leveraged buyout of the firm that you have been working for. To finance this €35 million transaction, you and three partners put up a total of €10 million in equity capital and you borrowed €25 million from banks and other investors. The bank debt consists of €10 million of secured debt borrowed at a rate of 6% from Banco Santander and €7 million of senior unsecured debt borrowed at a rate of 7% from BNP-Paribas. The remaining €8 million was borrowed from an investment group managed by a private equity firm. The rate on this subordinated (junior) unsecured debt is 9.5%. What is the overall after-tax cost of the debt financing used to buy the firm if you expect the firm's average and marginal tax rates both to be 25%?

Approach: The overall after-tax cost of debt can be calculated using the following three-step process: (1) calculate the fraction of the total debt (weight) for each individual debt issue; (2) using these weights, calculate the weighted average pre-tax cost of debt; (3) use Equation (13.3) to calculate the after-tax average cost of debt.

Solution: (1) The weights for the three types of debt are as follows:

$$x_{Secured\,debt} = €10\,000\,000/€25\,000\,000$$
$$= 0.40$$
$$x_{Senior\,unsecured\,debt} = €7\,000\,000/€25\,000\,000$$
$$= 0.28$$
$$x_{Subordinated\,unsecured\,debt} = €10\,000\,000/€25\,000\,000$$
$$= 0.32$$

where $x_{Secured\,debt} + x_{Senior\,unsecured\,debt}$
$$+ x_{Subordinated\,unsecured\,debt}$$
$$= 0.40 + 0.28 + 0.32 = 1.00$$

(2) The weighted average pre-tax cost of debt is:

$$k_{Debt\,pre\text{-}tax} = x_{Secured\,debt}k_{Secured\,debt\,pre\text{-}tax}$$
$$+ x_{Senior\,unsecured\,debt}k_{Senior\,unsecured\,debt\,pre\text{-}tax}$$
$$+ x_{Subordinated\,unsecured\,debt}$$
$$\times k_{Subordinated\,unsecured\,debt\,pre\text{-}tax}$$
$$= (0.40)(0.06) + (0.28)(0.07)$$
$$+ (0.32)(0.095)$$
$$= 0.074, \text{ or } 7.4\%$$

(3) The after-tax cost of debt is therefore:

$$k_{Debt\,after\text{-}tax} = k_{Debt\,pre\text{-}tax} \times (1 - t)$$
$$= 7.4\% \times (1 - 0.25) = 5.55\%$$

Decision-Making Example 13.1

Using the Cost of Debt in Decision Making

Situation: Your pizza restaurant business has developed such a strong reputation that you have decided to take advantage of the restaurant's name recognition by selling frozen pizzas through grocery stores. In order to do this, you will have to build a manufacturing facility. You estimate that this will cost you €10 million. Since your business currently has only €2 million in the bank, you will have to borrow the remaining €8 million. You have spoken with two bankers about possible loan packages. The banker from Easy Money Financial Services offered you a loan for €6 million with a 6% rate and €2 million with a 7.5% rate. You calculate the pre-tax

cost of debt for this package to be:

$$
\begin{aligned}
K_{\text{Loans pre-tax}} &= (\text{€}6\,000\,000/\text{€}8\,000\,000)(0.06) \\
&\quad + (\text{€}2\,000\,000/\text{€}8\,000\,000)(0.075) \\
&= 6.375\%
\end{aligned}
$$

Your local banker offered you a single €8 million loan for 6.350%. Which financing should you choose if all terms on all of the loans, other than the interest rates, are the same?

Decision: This is an easy decision. You should choose the least expensive alternative – the loan from your local bank. In this example, you can directly compare the pre-tax costs of the two alternatives. You do not need to calculate the after-tax costs because multiplying each pre-tax cost by the same number, $1 - t$, will not change your decision.

Before You Go On

1. Why do analysts care about the *current* cost of long-term debt when estimating a firm's cost of capital?
2. How do you estimate the cost of debt for a firm with more than one type of debt?
3. How do taxes affect the cost of debt?

THE COST OF EQUITY

Learning Objective 3

Calculate the cost of ordinary shares and the cost of preference shares for a firm.

The cost of equity for a firm is a weighted average of the costs of the different types of shares that the firm has outstanding at a particular point in time.

We saw in Chapter 9 that some firms have both preference shares and ordinary shares outstanding. In order to calculate the cost of equity for these firms, we have to know how to calculate the cost of both ordinary shares and preference shares. In this section, we discuss how financial analysts can estimate the costs associated with these two different types of shares.

Ordinary Shares

Just as information about market rates of return is used to estimate the cost of debt, market information is also used to estimate the cost of equity. There are several ways to do this. The particular approach a financial analyst chooses will depend on what information is available and how reliable the analyst believes it is. Next we discuss three alternative methods for estimating the cost of ordinary shares. It is important to remember throughout this discussion that the 'cost' we are referring to is the rate of return that investors require for investing in the shares at a particular point in time, given their systematic risk.

Method 1: Using the Capital Asset Pricing Model (CAPM)

The first method for estimating the cost of ordinary shares is one that we discussed in Chapter 7. This method uses Equation (7.9):

$$E(R_i) = R_{rf} + \beta_i[E(R_m) - R_{rf}]$$

In this equation, the expected return on an asset is a linear function of the systematic risk associated with that asset.

If we recognise that $E(R_i)$ in Equation (7.9) is the cost of the ordinary share capital used by the firm (k_{os}) when we are calculating the cost of equity and that $[E(R_m) - R_{rf}]$ is the market risk premium, we can rewrite Equation (7.9) as follows:

$$k_{os} = R_{rf} + (\beta_{os} \times \text{Market risk premium}) \quad (13.4)$$

Equation (13.4) is just another way of writing Equation (7.9). It tells us that the cost of ordinary shares equals the risk-free rate of return plus compensation for the systematic risk associated with the ordinary shares. You already saw some examples of how to use this equation to calculate the cost of equity in the discussion of the Capital Asset Pricing Model (CAPM) in Chapter 7. In those examples, you were given the current risk-free rate, the beta for the shares and the market risk premium and were asked to calculate k_{os} using the equation. Now we turn our attention to some practical considerations that you must be concerned with when choosing the appropriate risk-free rate, beta and market risk premium for this calculation.

The Risk-Free Rate First, let us consider the risk-free rate. The current effective annual yield on a risk-free asset should always be used in Equation (13.4). This is because the risk-free rate at a particular point in time reflects the rate of inflation that the market expects in the future. Since the expected rate of inflation changes over time, an old risk-free rate might not reflect current inflation expectations.

When analysts select a risk-free rate, they must choose between using a short-term rate, such as that for treasury bills, or a longer-term rate, such as those for government bonds. Which of these choices is most appropriate? This question has been hotly debated by finance professionals for many years. We recommend that you use the risk-free rate on a long-term government security (bond) when you estimate the cost of equity capital because the equity claim is a long-term claim on the firm's cash flows. As you saw in Chapter 9, the shareholders have a claim on the cash flows of the firm in perpetuity. By using a long-term government security, you are matching a long-term risk-free rate with a long-term claim. A long-term risk-free rate better reflects long-term inflation expectations and the cost of getting investors to part with their money for a long period than a short-term rate.

WEB

You can find current yields on treasury bills and bonds for the European Union at the website of the European Central Bank, at: http://www.ecb.int/stats/money/long/html/index.en.html.
For the United States, the Federal Reserve Bank provides similar information: www.federalreserve.gov/releases/H15/update.

The Beta If the ordinary shares of a company are publicly traded, then you can estimate the beta for the shares using a regression analysis similar to that illustrated in Exhibit 7.10. However, identifying the appropriate beta is much more complicated if the ordinary shares are not publicly traded. Since most companies are privately owned and do not have publicly traded shares, this is a problem that arises quite often when someone wants to estimate the cost of ordinary shares for a firm.

Financial analysts often overcome this problem by identifying a 'comparable' company with publicly traded shares that is in the same business and that has a similar amount of debt. For example, suppose you are trying to estimate the beta for your pizza business. The company has now grown to include more than 2000 restaurants throughout the world. The frozen-foods business, however, was never successful and had to be shut down. You know that Domino's Pizza, Inc., one of your major competitors, has publicly traded equity and that the proportion of debt to equity for Domino's is similar to the proportion for your firm. Since Domino's overall business is similar to yours, in that it is only in the pizza business and competes in similar geographic areas, it would be reasonable to consider Domino's a comparable company.

> **WEB**
>
> Companies with publicly traded equity usually provide a lot of information about their businesses and financial performance on their websites. The Domino's Pizza website is a good example. Go to: http://phx .corporate-ir.net/phoenix.zhtml?c=135383& p=irol-irhome.

The systematic risk associated with the shares of a comparable company is likely to be similar to the systematic risk for the private firm because systematic risk is determined by the nature of the firm's business and the amount of debt that it uses. If you are able to identify a good comparable company, such as Domino's Pizza, you can use its beta in Equation (13.4) to estimate the cost of equity capital for your firm. Even when a good comparable company cannot be identified, it is sometimes possible to use an average of the betas for the public firms in the same industry.

The Market Risk Premium It is not possible to directly observe the market risk premium. We just do not know what rate of return investors expect for the market portfolio – $E(R_m)$ – at a particular point in time. Therefore, we cannot simply calculate the market risk premium as the difference between the expected return on the market and the risk-free rate – $[E(R_m) - R_{rf}]$. For this reason, financial analysts generally use a measure of the average risk premium investors have actually earned in the past as an indication of the risk premium they might require today.

The annualised equity premium, relative to treasury bills from 1900 to 2009, was 5.4% for the United States, 4.2% for the world excluding the USA and 4.7% for the world including the USA. The annualised premium relative to bonds was 4.3% for the USA and 3.9% for the world.[8]

> **WEB**
>
> Credit Suisse provide a Global Investment Returns Yearbook that summarises stock market performance in major countries and is available at: http://emagazine.credit-suisse.com.

If, on average, investors earned the risk premium that they expected, the figures reflect the average market risk premiums over the period from 1900 to 2009. If a financial analyst believes that the market risk premium in the past is a reasonable estimate of the risk premium today, then he or she might use 3.9% as the market risk premium in Equation (13.4).

With this background, let us work an example to illustrate how Equation (13.4) is used in practice to estimate the cost of ordinary shares for a firm. Suppose that it is 6 October 2010 and we want to estimate the cost of the ordinary shares for Royal Dutch Shell, the Anglo-Netherlands oil company. Using yields reported in the *Wall Street Journal Online* on that day (http://online.wsj.com/mdc/public/page/marketsdata_europe.html), we determine that 30-day treasury bills have an effective annual yield of 0.35% and that 10-year government bonds have an effective annual yield of 3.35%. From the MSN Money website (http://moneycentral.msn.com), we find that the beta for Royal Dutch Shell shares is 0.93. We know that the market risk premium averaged 3.9% from 1900 to 2009. What is the expected rate of return on Royal Dutch Shell shares?

Since we are estimating the expected rate of return on ordinary shares and ordinary shares are a long-term asset, we use the long-term government bond yield of 3.35% in the calculation. Notice that the treasury bill and government bond rates differed by 3.00% ($3.35 - 0.35 = 3.00$) on 6 October 2010. They often differ by this amount or more, so the choice of which rate to use can make quite a difference in the estimated cost of equity.

Once we have selected the appropriate risk-free rate, we can plug it, along with the beta and market risk premium values, into Equation (13.4) to calculate the cost of common equity for Royal

Dutch Shell:

$$k_{os} = R_{rf} + (\beta_{os} \times \text{Market risk premium})$$
$$= 0.0335 + (0.93 \times 0.039) = 0.0698, \text{ or } 6.98\%$$

This example illustrates how Equation (13.4) is used to estimate the cost of ordinary shares for a company. How would the analysis differ for a private company? The only difference is that we would not be able to estimate the beta directly. We would have to estimate the beta from betas for similar public companies.

Learning by Doing Application 13.3

Calculating the Cost of Equity Using a Share's Beta

Problem: You have decided to estimate the cost of the ordinary shares in your pizza business on 6 October 2010. As noted earlier, the risk-free rate and the market risk premium on that day were 3.35% and 3.90%, respectively. Since you have already decided that Domino's Pizza is a reasonably comparable company, you obtain Domino's beta from the Yahoo! finance website (http://finance.yahoo.com). This beta is 1.06.

What do you estimate the cost of ordinary shares in your pizza business to be?

Approach: Method 1 for calculating the cost of equity is to use the Capital Asset Pricing Model (CAPM). Therefore, in this example we will use Equation (13.4).

Solution:

$$k_{os} = R_{rf} + (\beta_{os} \times \text{Market risk premium})$$
$$= 0.0335 + (1.06 \times 0.039)$$
$$= 0.0748, \text{ or } 7.48\%$$

Method 2: Using the Constant-Growth Dividend Model

In Chapter 9 we noted that if the dividends received by the owner of ordinary shares are expected to grow at a constant rate in perpetuity, then the value of the shares today can be calculated using Equation (9.5):

$$P_0 = \frac{D_1}{R - g}$$

where D_1 is the dividend expected to be paid one period from today, R is the required rate of return

and g is the annual rate at which the dividends are expected to grow in perpetuity.

We can replace the R in Equation (9.5) with k_{os}, since we are specifically estimating the expected rate of return for investing in ordinary shares (also the cost of equity). We can then rearrange this equation to solve for k_{os}:

$$k_{os} = \frac{D_1}{P_0} + g \qquad (13.5)$$

While Equation (13.5) is just a variation of Equation (9.5), it is important enough to identify as a separate equation because it provides a direct way of estimating the cost of equity under certain circumstances. If we can estimate the dividend that shareholders will receive next period, D_1, and we can estimate the rate at which the market expects dividends to grow over the long run, g, then we can use today's market price, P_0, in Equation (13.5) to tell us what rate of return investors in the firm's ordinary shares are expecting to earn.

Consider an example. Suppose that the current price for the ordinary shares of Henkel AG & Co. KGaA, the Düsseldorf-based cosmetics and home-care company, is €30, that the firm is expected to pay a dividend of €2.01 per share to its shareholders next year and that the dividend is expected to grow at a rate of 3% in perpetuity after next year. Equation (13.5) tells us that the required rate of return for Henkel's shares is:

$$k_{os} = \frac{D_1}{P_0} + g = \frac{€2.01}{€30} + 0.03 = 0.097, \text{ or } 9.7\%$$

This approach can be useful for a firm that pays dividends when it is reasonable to assume dividends will grow at a constant rate and when the analyst has a good idea what that growth rate will be. An electric utility firm is an example of this type of firm. Some electric utility firms pay relatively high and predictable dividends that increase at a consistent rate. In contrast, this approach would not be appropriate for use by a high technology firm that pays no dividends or that pays a small dividend which is likely to increase at a high rate in the short run. Equation (13.5), like any other equation, should be used only if it is appropriate for the particular share.

You might be asking yourself at this point where you would get P_0, D_1 and g in order to use Equation (13.5) for a particular share. You can get the current price of a share as well as the dividend that a firm is expected to pay next year quite easily from many different websites on the Internet – for example, Reuters and Yahoo! Finance, which were both mentioned earlier. The financial information includes the monetary value of dividends paid in the past year and the dividend that the firm is expected to pay in the next year.

WEB

You can obtain recent stock prices and financial information for a large number of firms from Yahoo! Finance at: http://finance.yahoo.com/ or Reuters at: http://uk.reuters.com/business/markets/europe.

Estimating the long-term rate of growth in dividends is more difficult, but there are some guidelines that can help. As we discussed in Chapter 9, the first rule is that dividends cannot grow faster than the long-term growth rate of the economy in a perpetuity model such as Equation (9.5) or (13.5). Assuming dividends will grow faster than the economy is the same as assuming that dividends will eventually become larger than the economy itself! We know this is impossible.

What is the long-term growth rate of the economy? Well, historically it has been the rate of inflation plus about 3%. This means that if inflation is expected to be 4% in the long run, then a reasonable estimate for the long-term growth rate in the economy is 7% (4% inflation plus 3% real growth). This tells us that g in Equation (13.5) will not be greater than 7%. What exactly it will be depends on the nature of the business and the industry in which it operates. If it is a declining industry, then g might be negative. If the industry is expected to grow with the economy and the particular firm you are evaluating is expected to retain its market share, then a reasonable estimate for g might be 6% or 7%.

Method 3: Using a Multistage-Growth Dividend Model

Using a **multistage-growth dividend model** to estimate the cost of equity for a firm is very similar to using a constant-growth dividend model. The difference is that a multistage-growth dividend model allows for faster dividend growth rates in the near term, followed by a constant long-term growth rate. If this concept sounds familiar, that is because it is the idea behind the *mixed (supernormal) growth dividend model* discussed in Chapter 9. In Equation (9.6) this model was written as:

$$P_0 = \frac{D_1}{1+R} + \frac{D_2}{(1+R)^2} + \cdots + \frac{D_t}{(1+R)^t} + \frac{P_t}{(1+R)^t}$$

where D_i is the dividend in period i, P_t is the value of constant-growth dividend payments in period t and R is the required rate of return.

> ### Multistage-growth dividend model
>
> a model that allows for varying dividend growth rates in the near term, followed by a constant long-term growth rate; another term used to describe the mixed (super-normal) dividend growth model discussed in Chapter 9

To refresh your memory of how this model works, let us consider a three-stage example. Suppose that a firm will pay a dividend one year from today (D_1) and that this dividend will increase at a rate of g_1 the following year, g_2 the year after that and g_3 per year thereafter. The value of the shares today thus equals:

$$P_0 = \frac{D_1}{1+k_{os}} + \frac{D_1(1+g_1)}{(1+k_{os})^2} + \frac{D_1(1+g_1)(1+g_2)}{(1+k_{os})^3} + \left[\frac{D_1(1+g_1)(1+g_2)(1+g_3)}{k_{os} - g_3}\right]\left[\frac{1}{(1+k_{os})^3}\right]$$

In this equation, we have replaced the R in Equation (9.6) with k_{os} since we are specifically estimating the expected rate of return for the ordinary shares. We have also written all of the dividends in terms of D_1 to illustrate how the different growth rates will affect the dividends in each year. Finally, we have written P_t in terms of the constant-growth model. If we substitute D_1, D_2, D_3 and D_4 where appropriate, you can see that this is really just Equation (9.6), where we have

replaced R with k_{os} and written P_t in terms of the constant-growth model:

$$P_0 = \frac{D_1}{1+k_{os}} + \frac{D_2}{(1+k_{os})^2} + \frac{D_3}{(1+k_{os})^3} + \left[\frac{D_4}{k_{os} - g_3}\right]\left[\frac{1}{(1+k_{os})^3}\right]$$

All this equation does is add the present values of the dividends that are expected in each of the next three years and the present value of a growing perpetuity that begins in the fourth year. Exhibit 13.2 illustrates how cash flows relate to the four terms in the equation.

Note that the fourth term in Exhibit 13.2 is discounted only three years because, as we saw in Chapters 6 and 9, the constant-growth model gives you the present value of a growing perpetuity as of the year before the first cash flow. In this case, since the first cash flow is D_4, the model gives you the value of the growing perpetuity as of year 3.

A multistage-growth dividend model is much more flexible than the constant-growth dividend model because we do not have to assume that dividends grow at the same rate forever. We can use a model such as this to estimate the cost of ordinary shares, k_{os}, by plugging P_0, D_1 and the appropriate growth rates into the model and solving for k_{os} using trial and error – just as we solved for the yield to maturity of bonds in Chapter 8 and earlier in this chapter. The major issues we have to be concerned about when we use a growth dividend model are (1) that we have chosen the right model, meaning that we have included enough stages or growth rates, and (2) that our estimates of the growth rates are reasonable.

We will work an example to illustrate how this model is used to calculate the cost of ordinary shares. Suppose that we want to estimate the cost of ordinary shares for a firm that is expected to pay a dividend of €1.50 per share next year. This dividend is expected to increase 15% the following year, 10% the year after that, 7% the year after that and 5% annually thereafter. If the firm's ordinary shares are currently selling

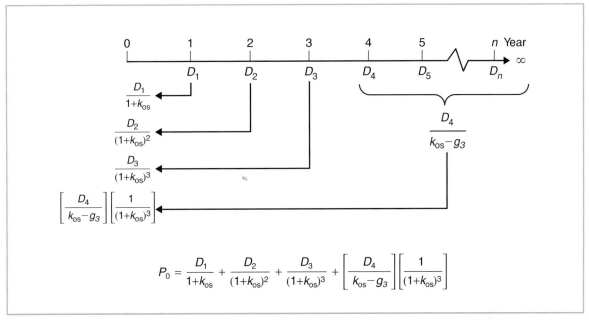

Exhibit 13.2: The Three-Stage Dividend Growth Model In the three-stage dividend growth model shown here, the price of a share equals the present values of dividends expected to be received at the end of years 1, 2 and 3 plus the present value of a growing perpetuity that begins in year 4 and whose dividends are assumed to grow at a constant rate g_3 for ever.

for €24 per share, what is the rate of return that investors require for investing in the shares?

Because there are four different growth rates in this example, we have to solve a formula with five terms:

$$P_0 = \frac{D_1}{1+k_{os}} + \frac{D_2}{(1+k_{os})^2} + \frac{D_3}{(1+k_{os})^3}$$
$$+ \frac{D_4}{(1+k_{os})^4} + \left[\frac{D_5}{k_{os}-g_4}\right]\left[\frac{1}{(1+k_{os})^4}\right]$$

From the information given in the problem statement, we know the following:

$D_1 = €1.50$

$D_2 = D_1 \times (1+g_1) = €1.500 \times 1.15 = €1.725$

$D_3 = D_2 \times (1+g_2) = €1.725 \times 1.10 = €1.898$

$D_4 = D_3 \times (1+g_3) = €1.898 \times 1.07 = €2.031$

$D_5 = D_4 \times (1+g_4) = €2.031 \times 1.05 = €2.133$

Substituting these values into the above equation gives us the following, which we solve

for k_{os}:

$$€24 = \frac{€1.500}{1+k_{os}} + \frac{€1.725}{(1+k_{os})^2} + \frac{€1.898}{(1+k_{os})^3}$$
$$+ \frac{€2.031}{(1+k_{os})^4} + \left[\frac{€2.133}{k_{os}-g_4}\right]\left[\frac{1}{(1+k_{os})^4}\right]$$

As mentioned earlier, we can solve this equation for k_{os} using trial and error. When we do this, we find that k_{os} is 12.2%. This is the rate of return at which the present value of the cash flows equals €24. Therefore, it is the rate that investors currently require for investing in the shares.

Which Method Should We Use?

We have now discussed three methods of estimating the cost of ordinary shares for a firm. You might be asking yourself how you are supposed to know which method to use. The short answer is that, in practice, most people use the CAPM (Method 1) to estimate the cost of ordinary shares if the result is going to be used in the discount rate for evaluating a project. One reason is that, assuming the theory is

USING EXCEL

Solving for k_{os} Using a Multistage-Growth Dividend Model

Because trial-and-error calculations can be somewhat tedious when you perform them by hand, you may find it helpful to use a spreadsheet program. If you would like to use a spreadsheet program to solve the preceding problem yourself, the output from the spreadsheet below shows you how to do it using trial and error.

	A	B	C	D
1				Comment
2	k_{os} =	0.12205		Change this number until P_0 equals €24.00
3	g_1 =	0.15		Growth rate in year 1
4	g_2 =	0.10		Growth rate in year 2
5	g_3 =	0.07		Growth rate in year 3
6	g_4 =	0.05		Growth rate for perpetuity
7				
8	P_0 =	€ 24.00		Formula: =NPV(B2, B11:B14) - This formula calculates the present value of the future dividends
9				in cells B11 to B14 using the discount rate in cell B2.
10	Year			
11	1	€ 1.500		D_1
12	2	€ 1.725		D_2 = B11*(1+B3)
13	3	€ 1.898		D_3 = B12*(1+B4)
14	4	€ 31.619		D_4 = [B13*(1+B5)]+[B13*(1+B5)*(1+B6)]/(B2-B6) - This formula calculates the value of D_4 plus
15				the value of all cash flows after year 4 in year 4 euros.
16				

Once you input the indicated numbers and formulas into cells B3–B14, you can then vary the number in cell B2 until the number in cell B8 equals €24. Once you have built the model, you can also use the 'goal seek' or 'solver' functions in Excel to avoid having to manually solve the problem by trial and error. See the 'Help' feature in Excel for information on how to use these functions.

valid, CAPM tells managers what rate of return investors should require for equity having the same level of systematic risk that the firm's equity has. This is the appropriate opportunity cost of equity capital for an NPV analysis if the project has the same risk as the firm and will have similar leverage. Furthermore, CAPM does not require financial analysts to make assumptions about future growth rates in dividends, as Methods 2 and 3 do.

Used properly, Methods 2 and 3 provide an estimate of the rate of return that is implied by the current price of a firm's shares at a particular point in time. If the stock markets are efficient, then this should be the same as the number that we would estimate using CAPM. However, to the extent that the firm's shares are mis-priced – for example, because investors are not informed or have misinterpreted the future prospects for the firm – deriving the

cost of equity from the price at one point in time can yield a bad estimate of the true cost of equity.

Preference Shares

As we discussed in Chapter 9, preference shares are a form of equity that has a stated value and specified dividend rate. For example, a share of preference shares might have a stated value of €100 and a 5% dividend rate. The owner of such a share would be entitled to receive a dividend of €5 (€100 × 0.05) each year. Another key feature of preference shares is that they do not have a maturity date. In other words, preference shares continue to pay the specified dividend in perpetuity, unless the firm repurchases them or goes out of business.

These characteristics of preference shares allow us to use the perpetuity model, Equation (6.3), to estimate the cost of preferred equity. For example, suppose that investors would pay €85 for the preference shares mentioned above. We can rewrite Equation (6.3):

$$PVA_\infty = \frac{CF}{i}$$

as:

$$P_{ps} = \frac{D_{ps}}{k_{ps}}$$

where P_{ps} is the present value of the expected dividends (the current preference shares price), D_{ps} is the annual preference share dividend and k_{ps} is the cost of the preference shares. Rearranging the formula to solve for k_{ps} yields:

$$k_{ps} = \frac{D_{ps}}{P_{ps}} \qquad (13.6)$$

Plugging the information from our example into Equation (13.6), we see that k_{ps} for the preference shares in our example is:

$$k_{ps} = \frac{D_{ps}}{P_{ps}} = \frac{€5}{€85} = 0.059, \text{ or } 5.9\%$$

This is the rate of return at which the present value of the annual €5 cash flows equals the market price of €85. Therefore, 5.9% is the rate that investors currently require for investing in the preference shares.

It is easy to incorporate issuance costs into the above calculation to obtain the cost of the preference shares to the firm that issues it. As in the earlier bond calculations, we use the net proceeds from the sale rather than the price that is paid by the investor in the calculation. For example, suppose that in order for a firm to sell the above preference shares, it must pay an investment banker 5% of the amount of money raised. If there are no other issuance costs, the company would receive €85 × (1 − 0.05) = €80.75 for each share sold and the total cost of this financing to the firm would be:

$$k_{ps} = \frac{D_{ps}}{P_{ps}} = \frac{€5}{€80.75} = 0.062, \text{ or } 6.2\%$$

You may recall from the discussion in Chapter 9 that certain characteristics of preference shares look a lot like those of debt. The equation $P_{ps} = D_{ps}/k_{ps}$ shows that the value of preference shares also varies with market rates of return in the same way as debt. Because k_{ps} is in the denominator of the fraction on the right-hand side of the equation, whenever k_{ps} increases, P_{ps} decreases and whenever k_{ps} decreases, P_{ps} increases. That is, the value of preference shares is negatively related to market rates.

It is also important to recognise that the CAPM can be used to estimate the cost of preference shares, just as it can be used to estimate the cost of ordinary shares. A financial analyst can simply substitute k_{ps} for k_{os} and b_{ps} for b_{os} in Equation (13.4) and use it to estimate the cost of preference shares. Remember from Chapter 7 that the CAPM does not apply only to ordinary shares; rather, it applies to any asset. Therefore, we can use it to calculate the rate of return on any asset if we can estimate the beta for that asset.

Learning by Doing Application 13.4

Estimating the Cost of Preference Shares

Problem: You work in the Treasury Department at Deutsche Bank and your manager has asked you to estimate the cost of each of the different types of shares that Deutsche Bank has outstanding. One of these issues is the 6–3/8% non-cumulative trust preferred securities, a type of preference share, issued to US investors that has a stated value of $25 and is currently selling for

$21.25. Although this preference share is publicly traded, it is not a liquid security. This means that you cannot use the CAPM to estimate k_{ps} because you cannot get a good estimate of the beta using regression analysis. How else can you estimate the cost of this preference share and what is this cost?

Approach: You can also use Equation (13.6) to estimate the cost of the preference shares.

Solution: First, you must find the annual dividend that someone who owns the trust preferred shares will receive. The dividend rate for the shares is quoted in eighths, or units of 0.125 of a per cent. Therefore, in decimal terms, this preference shares issue pays an annual dividend (for simplicity we are assuming one dividend payment per year) that equals 6% + 0.375 (3/8)% = 6.375%. The annual dividend equals this percentage times the $25 stated value, or 6.375% of $25 = $25 × 0.06375 = $1.5938. Substituting the annual dividend and the market price into Equation (13.6) yields:

$$k_{ps} = \frac{D_{ps}}{P_{ps}} = \frac{\$1.5938}{\$21.25} = 0.075, \text{ or } 7.5\%$$

Before You Go On

1. What information is needed to use the CAPM to estimate k_{os} or k_{ps}?
2. Under what circumstances can you use the constant-growth dividend formula to estimate k_{os}?
3. What is the advantage of using a multi-stage-growth dividend model, rather than the constant-growth dividend model, to estimate k_{os}?

USING THE WACC IN PRACTICE

Learning Objective 4

Calculate the weighted average cost of capital for a firm, explain the limitations of using a firm's weighted average cost of capital as the discount rate when evaluating a project and discuss the alternatives that are available.

We have now covered the basic concepts and computational tools that are used to estimate the WACC. At this point, we are ready to talk about some of the practical issues that arise when financial analysts calculate the WACC for their firms.

When financial analysts think about calculating the WACC, they usually think of it as a weighted average of the firm's after-tax cost of debt, cost of preference shares and cost of ordinary shares. Equation (13.2) is usually written as:

$$\text{WACC} = x_{\text{Debt}}k_{\text{Debt pre-tax}}(1 - t) + x_{ps}k_{ps} + x_{os}k_{os}$$

$$(13.7)$$

where $x_{\text{Debt}} + x_{ps} + x_{os} = 1$. If the firm has more than one type of debt outstanding or more than one type of preference shares or ordinary shares, analysts will calculate a weighted average for each of those types of securities and then plug those averages into Equation (13.7). Financial analysts will also use the *market values*, rather than the accounting book values, of the debt, preference shares and ordinary shares to calculate the weights (the *x*'s) in Equation (13.7). This is because, as we have already seen, the theory underlying the discounting process requires that the costs of the different types of financing be weighted by their relative market values. Accounting book values have no place in these calculations unless they just happen to equal the market values.

Calculating WACC: An Example

An example provides a useful way of illustrating how the theories and tools that we have discussed are used in practice. Assume that you are a financial analyst at a manufacturing company that has used three types of debt, preference shares and ordinary shares to finance its investments.

- **Debt.** The debt includes a €4 million bank loan that is secured by machinery and equipment. This loan has an interest rate of 6% and your firm could expect to pay the same rate if the loan were refinanced today. Your firm also has a second bank loan (a €3 million mortgage on your manufacturing plant) with an interest rate of 5.5%. Again, the rate would be the same today. The third type of debt is a bond issue that the firm sold two years ago for €11 million. The market value of these bonds today is €10 million. Using the approach we discussed earlier, you have estimated that the effective annual yield on the bonds is 7%.
- **Preference Shares.** The preference shares pay an annual dividend of 4.5% on a stated value of €100. The preference shares are currently selling for €60 and there are 100 000 shares outstanding.
- **Ordinary Shares.** There are 1 million ordinary shares outstanding, and they are currently selling for €21 each. Using a regression analysis, you have estimated that the beta of these shares is 0.95.

The 10-year government bond rate is currently 4.66% and you have estimated the market risk premium to be 3.90% using the returns on shares and bonds for the period 1900 to 2009. Your firm's marginal tax rate is 35%. What is the WACC for your firm?

The first step in computing the WACC is to calculate the pre-tax cost of debt. Since the market value of the firm's debt is €17 million (€4 + €3 + €10), we can calculate the pre-tax cost of

debt as follows:

$$
\begin{aligned}
k_{\text{Debt pre-tax}} &= x_{\text{Bank loan 1}} k_{\text{Bank loan 1 pre-tax}} \\
&\quad + x_{\text{Bank loan 2}} k_{\text{Bank loan 2 pre-tax}} \\
&\quad + x_{\text{Bonds}} k_{\text{Bonds pre-tax}} \\
&= (€4/€17)(0.06) + (€3/€17)(0.055) \\
&\quad + (€10/€17)(0.07) \\
&= 0.065, \text{ or } 6.5\%
\end{aligned}
$$

Note that because the €4 million and €3 million loans have rates that equal what it would cost to refinance them today, their market values equal the amount that is owed. Since the €10 million market value of the bond issue is below the €11 million face value, the rate that firm is actually paying must be lower than the 7% rate you estimated to reflect the current cost of this debt. Recall that as interest rates increase, the market value of a bond decreases. This is the negative relation that we referred to earlier in this chapter.

We next calculate the cost of the preference shares using Equation (13.6), as follows:

$$
\begin{aligned}
k_{\text{ps}} &= \frac{D_{\text{ps}}}{P_{\text{ps}}} = \frac{0.045 \times €100}{€60} \\
&= \frac{€4.5}{€60} = 0.075, \text{ or } 7.5\%
\end{aligned}
$$

From Equation (13.4), we calculate the cost of the ordinary shares to be:

$$
\begin{aligned}
k_{\text{os}} &= R_{\text{rf}} + (\beta_{\text{os}} \times \text{Market risk premium}) \\
&= 0.0466 + (0.95 \times 0.0390) \\
&= 0.0837, \text{ or } 8.4\%
\end{aligned}
$$

We are now ready to use Equation (13.7) to calculate the firm's WACC. Since the firm has €17 million of debt, €6 million of preference shares (€60 × 100 000 shares) and €21 million of ordinary shares (€21 × 1 000 000 shares), the total market value of its capital is €44 million (€17 + €6 + €21). The firm's WACC is therefore:

$$
\begin{aligned}
\text{WACC} &= x_{\text{Debt}} k_{\text{Debt pre-tax}}(1 - t) + x_{\text{ps}} k_{\text{ps}} + x_{\text{os}} k_{\text{os}} \\
&= (€17/€44)(0.065)(1 - 0.35) \\
&\quad + (€6/€44)(0.075) + (€21/€44)(0.084) \\
&= 0.0666, \text{ or } 6.66\%
\end{aligned}
$$

Calculating the WACC with Equation (13.7)

Problem: After calculating the cost of the ordinary shares in your pizza business to be 7.45% (see Learning by Doing Application 13.3), you have decided to estimate the WACC. You recently hired a business appraiser to estimate the value of your shares, which includes all of the outstanding ordinary shares. His report indicates that it is worth €500 million.

In order to finance the 2000 restaurants that are now part of your company, you have sold three different bond issues. Based on the current prices of the bonds from these issues and the issue characteristics (face values and coupon rates), you have estimated the market values and effective annual yields to be:

Bond Issue	Value (€ millions)	Effective Annual Yield
1	€100	6.5%
2	187	6.9
3	154	7.3
Total	€441	

Your company has no other long-term debt or any preference shares outstanding. Both the marginal and average tax rates for your company are 20%. What is the WACC for your pizza business?

Approach: You can use Equation (13.7) to solve for the WACC for your pizza business. To do so, you must first calculate the weighted average cost of debt. You can then plug the weights and costs for the debt and ordinary shares into Equation (13.7). Since your business has no preference shares, the value for this term in Equation (13.7) will equal zero.

Solution: The weighted average cost of the debt is:

$$k_{Debt\ pre\text{-}tax} = x_1 k_{1\ Debt\ pre\text{-}tax} + x_2 k_{2\ Debt\ pre\text{-}tax}$$
$$+ x_3 k_{3\ Debt\ pre\text{-}tax}$$
$$= (€100/€441)(0.065)$$
$$+ (€187/€441)(0.069)$$
$$+ (€154/€441)(0.073)$$
$$= 0.070,\ or\ 7.0\%$$

and the WACC is:

$$WACC = x_{Debt} k_{Debt\ pre\text{-}tax}(1 - t) + x_{ps} k_{ps} + x_{os} k_{os}$$
$$= (€441/[€441 + €500])(0.07)(1 - 0.20)$$
$$+ 0 + (€500/[€441 + €500])(0.0748)$$
$$= 0.066,\ or\ 6.60\%$$

WEB

You can see real-world applications of the WACC calculation at the New Zealand website for PricewaterhouseCoopers, the international accounting and consulting firm, at: www.pwcglobal.com/Extweb/pwcpublications .nsf/docid/748F5814D61CC2618525693A007 EC870.

Decision-Making Example 13.2

Interpreting the WACC

Situation: You are a financial analyst for the company for which we just calculated the WACC of 6.66% in the main text. One day, your manager walks in to your office and tells you that she is thinking about selling €23 million of ordinary shares and using the proceeds from the sale to pay back both of the firm's loans and to repurchase all of the outstanding bonds and preference shares. She tells you that this is a smart move because if she does this, the beta of the firm's ordinary shares will decline to 0.70 and the overall k_{os} will decline from 8.37% to 7.39%:

$$k_{os} = R_{rf} + (\beta_{os} \times \text{Market risk premium})$$
$$= 0.0466 + (0.70 \times 0.039)$$
$$= 0.0739, \text{ or } 7.39\%$$

What do you tell your manager?

Decision: You should politely point out that she is making the wrong comparison. Since the refinancing will result in the firm being financed entirely with equity, k_{os} will equal the firm's WACC. Therefore, the 7.39% should really be compared with the 6.66% WACC. If your manager goes through with the refinancing, she will be making a bad decision. The average after-tax cost of the capital that your firm uses will *increase* from 6.66% to 7.39%.

Limitations of WACC as a Discount Rate for Evaluating Projects

At the beginning of this chapter, we told you that financial managers often require analysts within the firm to use the firm's current cost of capital to discount the cash flows for individual projects. They do so because it is very difficult to directly estimate the discount rate for individual projects. You should recognise by now that the WACC is the discount rate that analysts are often required to use. Using the WACC to discount the cash flows for a project can make sense under certain circumstances. However, in other circumstances, it can be very dangerous. The rest of this section discusses when it makes sense to use the WACC as a discount rate and the problems that can occur when the WACC is used incorrectly.

Chapter 11 discussed how an analyst forecasting the cash flows for a project is forecasting the incremental after-tax free cash flows at the firm level. These cash flows represent the difference between the cash flows that the firm will generate if the project is adopted and the cash flows that the firm will generate if the project is not adopted.

Financial theory tells us that the rate that should be used to discount these incremental cash flows is the rate that reflects their systematic risk. This means that the WACC is going to be the appropriate discount rate for evaluating a project only when the project has cash flows with systematic risks that are exactly the same as those for the firm as a whole. Unfortunately, this is not true for most projects. The firm itself is a portfolio of projects with varying degrees of risk.

When a single rate, such as the WACC, is used to discount cash flows for projects with varying levels of risk, the discount rate will be too low in some cases and too high in others. When the discount rate is too low, the firm runs the risk of accepting a negative NPV project. To see how this might happen, assume that you work at a company that manufactures soft drinks and that the managers at your company are concerned about all the

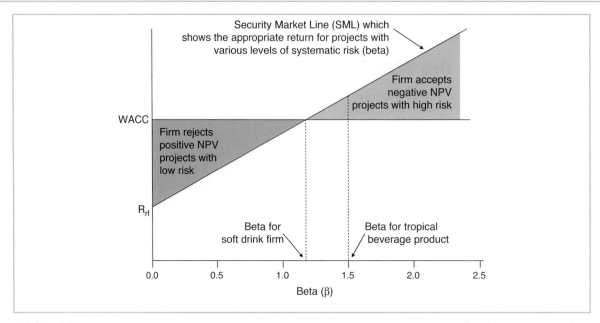

Exhibit 13.3: Potential Errors When Using the WACC to Evaluate Projects Two types of problem can arise when the WACC for a firm is used to evaluate individual projects: a positive NPV project may be rejected or a negative NPV project may be accepted. For the tropical beverage example, if the projected return on that project was below the level indicated by the SML but above the firm's WACC, the project might be accepted even though it would have a negative NPV.

competition in the core soft drink business. They are thinking about expanding into the manufacture and sale of exotic tropical beverages. The managers believe that entering this market would allow the firm to better differentiate its products and earn higher profits. Suppose also that the appropriate beta for soft drink projects is 1.2 while the appropriate beta for tropical beverage projects is 1.5. Since your firm is only in the soft drink business right now, the beta for its overall cash flows is 1.2. Exhibit 13.3 illustrates the problem that could arise if your firm's WACC is used to evaluate a tropical beverage project.

In the exhibit, you can see that since the beta of the tropical beverage project is larger than the beta of the firm as a whole, the expected return (or discount rate) for the tropical beverage project should be higher than the firm's WACC. The Security Market Line indicates what this expected return should be. Now, if the firm's WACC is used to discount the expected cash flows for this project and the expected return on the project is above the firm's WACC, then the estimated NPV will be

positive. So far, so good. However, as illustrated in the exhibit for the tropical beverage example, some projects may have an expected return that is above the WACC but below the SML. For projects such as those, using the WACC as the discount rate may actually cause the firm to accept a negative NPV project! The estimated NPV will be positive even though the true NPV is negative. The negative NPV projects that would be accepted in those situations have returns that fall in the red shaded area below the SML, above the WACC line, and to the right of the firm's beta.

In Exhibit 13.3 you can also see that using the WACC to discount expected cash flows for low-risk projects can result in managers at the firm rejecting projects that have positive NPVs. This problem is, in some sense, the mirror image of the case where the WACC is lower than the correct discount rate. Financial managers run the risk of turning down positive NPV projects whenever the WACC is higher than the correct discount rate. The positive NPV projects that would be rejected are those that fall into the green shaded area that is below the WACC but above the SML and to the left of the firm's beta.

To see how these types of problem arise, consider a project that requires an initial investment of €100 and that is expected to produce cash inflows of €40 per year for three years. If the correct discount rate for this project is 8%, its NPV will be:

$$NPV = FCF_0 + \frac{FCF_1}{1+k} + \frac{FCF_2}{(1+k)^2} + \frac{FCF_3}{(1+k)^3}$$

$$= -€100 + \frac{€40}{1+0.08} + \frac{€40}{(1+0.08)^2}$$

$$+ \frac{€40}{(1+0.08)^3}$$

$$= €3.08$$

This is an attractive project because it returns more than the investors' opportunity cost of capital.

Suppose, however, that the financial managers of the firm considering this project require that all projects be evaluated using the firm's WACC of 11%. When the cash flows are discounted using a rate of 11%, the NPV is:

$$= -€100 + \frac{€40}{1+0.11} + \frac{€40}{(1+0.11)^2} + \frac{€40}{(1+0.11)^3}$$

$$= -€2.25$$

As you can see, when the WACC is used to discount the cash flows, the firm will end up rejecting a positive NPV project. The firm will be passing up an opportunity to create value for its shareholders. (As an exercise, you might try constructing a numerical example in which a firm accepts a negative NPV project.)

It is also important to recognise that when a firm uses a single rate to evaluate all of its projects, there will be a bias towards accepting more risky projects. The average risk of the firm's assets will tend to increase over time. Furthermore, because some positive NPV projects are likely to be rejected and some negative NPV projects are likely to be accepted, new projects on the whole will probably create less value for shareholders than if the appropriate discount rate had been used to evaluate all

projects. This, in turn, can put the firm at a disadvantage when compared with its competitors and adversely affect the value of its existing projects.

The key point to take away from this discussion is that it is only correct to use a firm's WACC to discount the cash flows for a project if the expected cash flows from that project have the same systematic risk as the expected cash flows from the firm as a whole. You might be wondering how you can tell when this condition exists. The answer is that we never know for sure. Nevertheless, there are some guidelines that you can use when assessing whether the systematic risk for a particular project is similar to that for the firm as a whole.

The systematic risk of the cash flows from a project depends on the nature of the business. Revenues and expenses in some businesses are affected more by changes in general economic conditions than revenues and expenses in other businesses. For example, consider the differences between a company that makes bread and a company that makes recreational vehicles. The demand for bread will be relatively constant in good economic conditions and in bad. The demand for recreational vehicles will be more volatile. People buy fewer recreational vehicles during recessions than when the economy is doing well. Furthermore, as we discussed in Chapter 12, operating leverage magnifies volatility in revenue. Therefore, if the recreational vehicle manufacturing process has more fixed costs than the bread manufacturing business, the difference in the volatilities of the pre-tax operating cash flows will be even greater than the difference in the volatilities of the revenues.

While total volatility is not the same as systematic volatility, we find that businesses with more total volatility (uncertainty or risk) typically have more systematic volatility. Since beta is a measure of systematic risk and systematic risk is a key factor in determining a firm's WACC, this suggests that the firm's WACC should be used only for projects with business risks similar to those for the firm as a whole. Since financial managers usually think of systematic risk when they think of underlying business risks, we can restate this condition as follows:

Condition 1. A firm's WACC should be used to evaluate the cash flows for a new project only if the level of systematic risk for the project is the same as that for the portfolio of projects that currently comprise the firm.

You have to consider one other factor when you decide whether it is appropriate to use a firm's WACC to discount the cash flows for a project. That is the way in which the project will be financed and how this financing compares with the way the firm's assets are financed. To better understand why this is important, consider Equation (13.7):

$$\text{WACC} = x_{\text{Debt}}k_{\text{Debt pre-tax}}(1 - t) + x_{\text{ps}}k_{\text{ps}} + x_{\text{os}}k_{\text{os}}$$

This equation provides a measure of the firm's cost of capital that reflects both how the firm has financed its assets – that is, the mix of debt and preference shares and ordinary shares it has used – and the current cost of each type of financing. In other words, the WACC reflects both the x's and the k's associated with the firm's financing. Why is this important? Because the costs of the different types of capital depend on the fraction of the total firm financing that each represents. If the firm uses more or less debt, the cost of debt will be higher or lower. In turn, the cost of both preference shares and ordinary shares will be affected. This means that even if the underlying business risk of the project is the same as that for the firm as a whole, if the project

is financed differently than the firm, the appropriate discount rate for the project analysis will be different from that for the firm as a whole.

Condition 2. A firm's WACC should be used to evaluate a project only if that project uses the same financing mix – the same proportions of debt, preference shares and ordinary shares – used to finance the firm as a whole.

In summary, WACC is a measure of the current cost of the capital that the firm has used to finance its projects. It is an appropriate discount rate for evaluating projects only if (1) the project's systematic risk is the same as that of the firm's current portfolio of projects and (2) the project will be financed with the same mix of debt and equity as the firm's current portfolio of projects. If either of these two conditions does not hold, then managers should be careful in using the firm's current WACC to evaluate a project.

Alternatives to Using WACC for Evaluating Projects

Financial managers understand the limitations of using a firm's WACC to evaluate projects; but they also know that there are no perfect alternatives. As we noted earlier in this chapter, there are no publicly traded ordinary shares for most individual projects within a firm. It is, therefore, not possible to directly estimate the beta for the ordinary shares used to finance an individual project.[9] Although it might be possible to obtain an estimate of the cost

BUILDING INTUITION

Why WACC Only Works for the Current Mix of Liabilities

The weighted average cost of capital of a firm depends on the weight of the debt and equity as well as the cost of these elements and hence will change if debt or equity is added or redeemed. So the firm's WACC will change if the proportion of debt and equity changes. As a result, in using WACC, the analyst is assuming that the firm's capital structure will remain constant over the life of the project.

of debt from the firm's bankers, without an estimate of the ordinary shares, beta – and, therefore, the cost of ordinary shares – it is not possible to obtain a direct estimate of the appropriate discount rate for a project using Equation (13.7).

If the discount rate for a project cannot be estimated directly, a financial analyst might try to find a public firm that is in a business that is similar to that of the project. For example, in our exotic tropical beverage example, an analyst at the soft drink company might look for a company that produces only exotic tropical beverages and that also has publicly traded shares. This public company would be what financial analysts call a pure-play comparable because it is exactly like the project. The returns on the pure-play company's shares could be used to estimate the expected return on the equity that is used to finance the project. Unfortunately, this approach is generally not feasible due to the difficulty of finding a public firm that is only in the business represented by the project. If the public firm is in other businesses as well, then we run into the same sorts of problem that we face when we use the firm's WACC.

> ### Pure-play comparable
>
> a comparable company that is in exactly the same business as the project or business being analysed

From a practical standpoint, financial managers, such as company treasurers and chief financial officers, do not like letting analysts estimate the discount rates for their projects. Different analysts tend to make different assumptions or use different approaches, which can lead to inconsistencies that make it difficult to compare projects. In addition, analysts may be tempted to manipulate discount rates in order to make pet projects look more attractive.

In an effort to use discount rates that reflect project risks better than the firm's WACC, while retaining control of the process through which

discount rates are set, financial managers sometimes classify projects into categories based on their systematic risks. They then specify a discount rate that is to be used to discount the cash flows for all projects within each category. The idea is that each category of projects has a different level of systematic risk and therefore a different discount rate should be used for each. Exhibit 13.4 illustrates such a classification scheme.

The scheme illustrated in Exhibit 13.4 includes four project categories:

1. *Efficiency projects*, such as the implementation of a new production technology that reduces manufacturing costs for an existing product.
2. *Product extension projects*, such as those in which EADS created variations of its aircraft, such as the Airbus A320 family, to help meet customer needs.
3. *Market extension projects*, in which existing products are sold in new markets, such as when Texas Instruments considers selling a new version of a computer chip that has been used in digital phones to digital camera manufacturers.
4. *New product projects*, in which entirely new products are being considered.

When using the scheme illustrated in Exhibit 13.4, the financial manager would assign a discount rate for each category that reflects the beta in the middle of the indicated range of betas. Such an approach is attractive because it is not generally difficult for analysts to figure out in which of the four categories particular projects belong, and it limits their discretion in choosing discount rates. Most important, it can reduce the possibility of accepting negative NPV projects or rejecting positive NPV projects. We can see the latter benefit by comparing the shaded areas in the figures in Exhibits 13.3 and 13.4. The total size of the shaded areas, which represents the possibility of making an error, is much smaller in Exhibit 13.4.

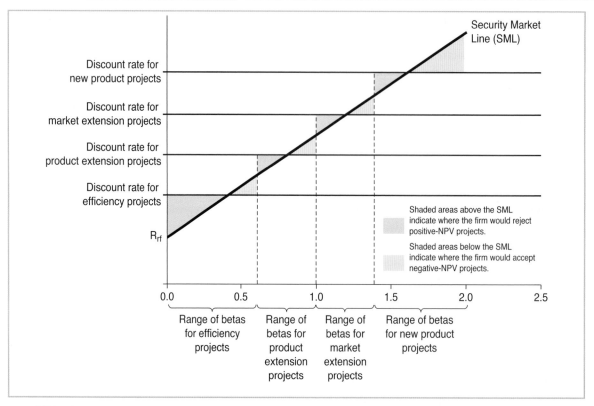

Exhibit 13.4: Potential Errors When Using Multiple Discount Rates to Evaluate Projects The potential for errors – either rejecting a positive NPV project or accepting a negative NPV project – is smaller when discount rates better reflect the risk of the projects that they are used to evaluate. You can see this by noting that the total size of the shaded areas in this figure is smaller than the size of the shaded areas in Exhibit 13.3. In an ideal situation, where the correct discount rate is used for each project, there would be no shaded area at all in a figure like this.

Before You Go On

1. Do analysts use book values or market values to calculate the weights when they use Equation (13.7)? Why?

2. What kinds of error can be made when the WACC for a firm is used as the discount rate for evaluating all projects in the firm?
3. Under what conditions is the WACC the appropriate discount rate for a project?

SUMMARY OF LEARNING OBJECTIVES

1. **Explain what the weighted average cost of capital for a firm is and why it is often used as a discount rate to evaluate projects.**

   The weighted average cost of capital (WACC) for a firm is a weighted average of the current costs of the different types of financing that a firm has used to finance the purchase of its assets.

When the WACC is calculated, the cost of each type of financing is given a weight according to the fraction of the total firm value represented by that type of financing. The WACC is often used as a discount rate in evaluating projects because it is not possible to directly estimate the appropriate discount rate for many projects. As we also discuss later, having a single discount rate reduces inconsistencies that can arise when different analysts in the firm use different methods to estimate the discount rate and can limit the ability of analysts to manipulate discount rates to favour pet projects.

2. **Calculate the cost of debt for a firm.**

The cost of debt can be calculated by solving for the yield to maturity of the debt using the bond pricing model [Equation (8.1)], computing the effective annual yield and adjusting for taxes using Equation (13.3).

3. **Calculate the cost of ordinary shares and the cost of preference shares for a firm.**

The cost of ordinary shares can be estimated using the CAPM, the constant-growth dividend formula and a multistage-growth dividend formula. The cost of preference shares can be calculated using the perpetuity model for the present value of cash flows.

4. **Calculate the weighted average cost of capital for a firm, explain the limitations of using a firm's weighted average cost of capital as the discount rate when evaluating a project and discuss the alternatives that are available.**

The weighted average cost of capital is estimated using either Equation (13.2) or Equation (13.7), with the cost of each individual type of financing estimated using the appropriate method.

When a firm uses a single rate to discount the cash flows for all of its projects, some project cash flows will be discounted using a rate that is too high and other project cash flows will be discounted using a rate that is too low. This can result in the firm rejecting some positive NPV projects and accepting some negative NPV projects. It will bias the firm towards accepting more risky projects and can cause the firm to create less value for shareholders than it would have if the appropriate discount rates had been used.

One approach to using the WACC is to identify a firm that engages in business activities that are similar to those associated with the project under consideration and that have publicly traded shares. The returns from this pure-play firm's shares can then be used to estimate the ordinary shares beta for the project. In instances where pure-play firms are not available, financial managers can classify projects according to their systematic risks and can use a different discount rate for each classification. This is the type of classification scheme illustrated in Exhibit 13.4.

SUMMARY OF KEY EQUATIONS

Equation	Description	Formula
(13.1)	Finance balance sheet identity	MV of assets = MV of liabilities + MV of equity
(13.2)	General formula for weighted average cost of capital (WACC) for a firm	$k_{Firm} = \sum_{i=1}^{n} x_i k_i = x_1 k_1 + x_2 k_2 + x_3 k_3 + \cdots + x_n k_n$
(13.3)	After-tax cost of debt	$k_{Debt\ after\text{-}tax} = k_{Debt\ pre\text{-}tax} \times (1 - t)$

(13.4)	CAPM formula for the cost of ordinary shares	$k_{os} = R_{rf} + (\beta_{os} \times \text{Market risk premium})$
(13.5)	Constant-growth dividend formula for the cost of ordinary shares	$k_{os} = \dfrac{D_1}{P_0} + g$
(13.6)	Perpetuity formula for the cost of preference shares	$k_{ps} = \dfrac{D_{ps}}{P_{ps}}$
(13.7)	Traditional WACC formula	$\text{WACC} = x_{Debt} k_{Debt\ pre\text{-}tax}(1 - t) + x_{ps} k_{ps} + x_{os} k_{os}$

SELF-STUDY PROBLEMS

13.1. The market value of a firm's assets is €3 billion. If the market value of the firm's liabilities is €2 billion, what is the market value of the shareholders' investment and why?

13.2. La Maison Casterman SA has borrowed €100 million and is required to pay investors €8 million in interest this year. If La Maison Casterman is in the 35% marginal tax bracket, what is the after-tax cost of debt (in euros as well as in annual interest) for La Maison Casterman?

13.3. Explain why the after-tax cost of equity (ordinary or preference shares) does not have to be adjusted by the marginal income tax rate for the firm.

13.4. Camisetas de Javier has debt claims of €400 (market value) and equity claims of €600 (market value). If the cost of debt financing (after tax) is 11% and the cost of equity is 17%, then what is Javier's weighted average cost of capital?

13.5. You are analysing a firm that is financed with 60% debt and 40% equity. The current cost of debt financing is 10% but, due to a recent downgrade by the rating agencies, the firm's cost of debt is expected to increase to 12% immediately. How will this change the firm's weighted average cost of capital if you ignore taxes?

SOLUTIONS TO SELF-STUDY PROBLEMS

13.1. Since the accounting identity Assets = Liabilities + Equity holds for market values as well as book values, then we know that the market value of the firm's equity is €3 billion – €2 billion, or €1 billion.

13.2. Since La Maison Casterman enjoys a tax deduction for its interest charges, the after-tax interest expense for La Maison

Casterman is €8 million × (1 – 0.35) = €5.2 million, which translates into an annual after-tax interest expense of €5.2/€100 = 0.052, or 5.2%.

13.3. Tax authorities allow a deduction for interest expense incurred on borrowing. Preference and ordinary shares are not considered debt and, thus, do not benefit from an interest deduction. As a result, there is no distinction between the before-tax and after-tax cost of equity capital.

13.4. Camisetas de Javier's total firm value = €400 + €600 = €1000. Therefore,

Debt = 40% of financing

Equity = 60% of financing

$$WACC = x_{Debt}k_{Debt}(1 - t) + x_{ps}k_{ps} + x_{os}k_{os}$$

$$WACC = (0.4 \times 0.11) + (0.6 \times 0.17) =$$

0.146, or 14.6%

13.5. The pre-tax debt contribution to the cost of capital is $x_{Debt} \times k_{Debt}$, and since the firm's pre-tax cost of debt is expected to increase by 2%, we know that the effect on WACC (pre-tax) will be $0.6 \times 0.02 = 0.012$, or 1.2%. Incidentally, if we assume that the firm is subject to the 40% marginal tax rate, then the after-tax increase in the cost of capital for the firm would be $0.012 \times (1 - 0.4) = 0.0072$, or 0.72%.

CRITICAL THINKING QUESTIONS

13.1. Explain why the required rate of return on a firm's assets must be equal to the weighted average cost of capital associated with its liabilities and equity.

13.2. Which is easier to calculate directly, the expected rate of return on the assets of a firm or the expected rate of return on the firm's debt and equity? Assume that you are an outsider to the firm.

13.3. With respect to the level of risk and the required return for a firm's portfolio of projects, discuss how the market and a firm's management can have inconsistent information and expectations.

13.4. Your friend has recently told you that governments effectively subsidise the cost of debt (compared to equity use) for companies. Do you agree with that statement? Explain.

13.5. Your firm will have a fixed interest expense for the next 10 years. You recently found out that the marginal income tax rate for the firm will change from 30% to 40% next year. Describe how the change will affect the cash flow available to investors.

13.6. Describe why it is not usually appropriate to use the coupon rate on a firm's bonds to estimate the pre-tax cost of debt for the firm.

13.7. Rimini Falcone S.p.A. has not checked its weighted average cost of capital for four years. Firm management claims that since Rimini Falcone has not had to raise capital for new projects since that time, they should not have to worry about their current weighted average cost of capital since they have essentially locked in their cost of capital. Critique that statement.

13.8. Ten years ago, Electricité de France issued preference shares with a price equal to the par amount of €100. If the dividend yield on that issue was 12%, explain why the firm's current cost of preference shares is not likely to be equal to 12%.

13.9. Discuss under what circumstances you might be able to use a model that assumes constant growth in dividends to calculate the current cost of equity capital for a firm.

13.10. Your manager just finished computing your firm's weighted average cost of capital. He is relieved because he says that he can now use that cost of capital to evaluate all projects that the firm is considering for the next four years. Evaluate that statement.

QUESTIONS AND PROBLEMS

Basic

13.1. Market-value balance sheet: Mark bis Knie-Mann AG has total debt obligations with a book and market value equal to €30 million and €28 million, respectively. It also has total equity with a book and market value equal to €20 million and €70 million, respectively. If you were going to buy all the assets of Mark bis Knie-Mann today, how much should you be willing to pay?

13.2. WACC: What is the weighted average cost of capital?

13.3. [EXCEL®] Current cost of a bond: You are analysing the cost of debt for a firm. You know that the firm's 14-year maturity, 8.5% coupon bonds are selling at a price of £823.48. The bonds pay interest semi-annually. If these bonds are the only debt outstanding for the firm, what is the after-tax cost of debt for this firm if the firm is in the 30% marginal tax rate?

13.4. Taxes and the cost of debt: How are taxes accounted for when we calculate the cost of debt?

13.5. Taxes and the cost of debt: BioPro SA has earnings before interest and taxes equal to €500. If the firm incurred interest expense of €200 and pays taxes at the 35% marginal tax rate, what amount of cash is available for BioPro's investors?

13.6. Cost of ordinary shares: List and describe each of the three methods used to calculate the cost of ordinary shares.

13.7. [EXCEL®] Cost of ordinary shares: Pinturas de Pared Blanca SA just paid a €1.60 dividend on its ordinary shares. If Pinturas de Pared Blanca is expected to increase its annual dividend by 2% per year into the foreseeable future and the current price of Pinturas de Pared Blanca's ordinary shares is €11.66, what is the cost of ordinary shares for Pinturas de Pared Blanca?

13.8. [EXCEL®] Cost of ordinary shares: Cacerolas de Toledo SA is expected to pay a dividend of €1.10 one year from today on its ordinary shares. That dividend is expected to increase by 5% every year thereafter. If the price of Cacerolas de Toledo is €13.75, what is Cacerolas de Toledo's cost of ordinary shares?

13.9. [EXCEL®] Cost of ordinary shares: Voyages Jules Verne's ordinary shares are expected to pay an annual dividend equal to €1.25 and it is commonly known that the firm expects dividends paid to increase by 8% for the next two years and by 2% thereafter. If the current price of Voyages Jules Verne's ordinary shares is €17.80, what is the cost of ordinary shares for the firm?

13.10. Cost of preference shares: Fjord Luxury Liners has preference shares outstanding that pay an annual dividend equal to NKr 15 per year. If the current price of Fjord preference shares is NKr 107.14, what is the after-tax cost of preferred shares for Fjord?

13.11. Cost of preference shares: Kresler Autos has preference shares outstanding that pay annual dividends of €12 and the current price of the shares is €80. What is the after-tax cost of new preference shares for Kresler if the flotation (issuance) costs for a new issue of preferred are 5%?

13.12. WACC: Describe the alternatives to using a firm's WACC as a discount rate when evaluating a project.

13.13. WACC for a firm: Bilancio Patrimoniale S. p.A. has a capital structure that is financed, based on current market values, with 50% debt, 10% preference shares and 40% ordinary shares. If the return offered to the investors for each of those sources is 8%, 10% and 15% for debt, preference shares and ordinary shares, respectively, what is Bilancio Patrimoniale's after-tax

WACC? Assume that the firm's marginal tax rate is 40%.

13.14. WACC: What are direct out-of-pocket costs?

Intermediate

13.15. Market-value balance sheet: Describe why the total value of all the securities financing the firm must be equal to the value of the firm.

13.16. Market-value balance sheet: Describe why the cost of capital for the firm is equal to the expected rate of return to the investors of the firm.

13.17. Current cost of a bond: You know that the after-tax cost of debt capital for Bubbles Champagne is 7%. If the firm has only one issue of five-year maturity bonds outstanding, what is the current price of the bonds if the coupon rate on those bonds is 10%? Assume the bonds make semi-annual coupon payments and the marginal tax rate is 30%.

13.18. Current cost of a bond: Perpetual Ltd has issued bonds that never require the principal amount to be repaid to investors. Correspondingly, Perpetual must make interest payments into the infinite future. If the bondholders receive annual payments of £75 and the current price of the bonds is £882.35, what is the after-tax cost of this borrowing for Perpetual if the firm is in the 40% marginal tax rate?

13.19. Taxes and the cost of debt: Holding all other things constant but assuming that the marginal tax rate for a firm decreases, does that provide incentive for the firm to increase its use of debt or decrease that use?

13.20. EXCEL® **Cost of debt for a firm:** You are analysing the after-tax cost of debt for a firm. You know that the firm's 12-year maturity, 9.5% coupon bonds are selling at a price of €1200. If these bonds are the only debt outstanding for the firm, what is the after-tax cost of debt for this firm if the marginal tax rate for the firm is 34%? What if the bonds are selling at par?

13.21. EXCEL® **Cost of ordinary shares:** Investigar SA's ordinary shares currently sell for €36. The firm believes that its shares should really sell for €54. If the firm just paid an annual dividend of €2 per share and the firm expects those dividends to increase by 8% per year forever (and this is common knowledge to the market), what is the current cost of ordinary shares for the firm and what does the firm believe is a more appropriate cost of ordinary shares for the firm?

13.22. Cost of ordinary shares: Write out the general equation for the price of ordinary shares that will grow dividends very rapidly for four years after our next predicted dividend and thereafter at a constant, but lower, rate for the foreseeable future. Discuss the problems in estimating the cost of equity capital for such shares.

13.23. Cost of ordinary shares: You have calculated the cost of ordinary shares using all three methods described in the chapter. Unfortunately, all three methods have yielded different answers. Describe which answer (if any) is most appropriate.

13.24. WACC for a firm: A firm financed totally with ordinary shares is evaluating two distinct projects. The first project has a large amount of non-systematic risk and a small amount of systematic risk. The second project has a small amount of non-systematic risk and a large amount of systematic risk. Which project, if taken, will have a tendency to increase the firm's cost of capital?

13.25. EXCEL® **WACC for a firm:** La Lampe Magique SA currently has €300 million of market value debt outstanding. The 9% coupon bonds (semi-annual pay) have a maturity of 15 years and are currently priced at €1440.03 per bond. The firm also has an issue of 2 million preference shares outstanding with a market price of €12.00. The preference shares offer an annual dividend of €1.20. La Lampe Magique also has 14 million ordinary shares outstanding with a price of €20.00. The firm is expected to pay a €2.20 ordinary share dividend one year from today and that dividend is expected to increase by 5% per year forever. If La Lampe Magique is subject to a 40% marginal tax rate, then what is the firm's weighted average cost of capital?

13.26. **Choosing a discount rate:** For La Lampe Magique firm in Problem 13.25, calculate the appropriate cost of capital for a new project that is financed with the same proportion of debt, preference shares and ordinary shares as the firm's current capital structure. Also assume that the project has the same degree of systematic risk as the average project that the firm is currently undertaking (the project is also in the same general industry as the firm's current line of business).

13.27. **Choosing a discount rate:** If a firm anticipates financing a project with a capital mix different from the firm's current capital structure, describe in realistic terms how the firm is subjecting itself to a calculation error if it chooses to use its historical WACC to evaluate the project.

Advanced

13.28. You are analysing the cost of capital for Schnelle Bewegungen AG, which develops software operating systems for computers. The firm's dividend growth rate has been a very constant 3% per year for the past 15 years. Competition for the firm's current products is expected to develop in the next year and Schnelle Bewegungen is currently expanding its revenue stream into the multimedia industry. Evaluate using a 3% growth rate in dividends for Schnelle Bewegungen in your cost of capital model.

13.29. You are an external financial analyst evaluating the merits of a particular share. Since you are using a dividend discount model approach to calculating a cost of equity capital, you need to estimate the dividend growth rate for the firm in the future. Describe how you might go about that process.

13.30. You know that the return of Attività Dinamica Congiunturale (ADC) ordinary shares reacts to macroeconomic information 1.6 more times than the return of the market. If the risk-free rate of return is 4% and the market risk premium is 6%, what is ADC's cost of ordinary shares?

13.31. In your analysis of the cost of capital for a firm's ordinary shares, you calculate a cost of capital using a dividend discount model that is much lower than the calculation for the cost of capital using the CAPM model. Explain a possible source for the discrepancy.

13.32. EXCEL® Mudanzas Internacionales SA has a preference shares issue outstanding that pays an annual dividend of €1.30 per year. The current cost of preference shares for Mudanzas Internacionales is 9%. If Mudanzas Internacionales issues additional preference shares that pay exactly the same dividend and the investment banker retains 8% of the sale price, what is the cost of new preference shares for Mudanzas Internacionales?

13.33. The Enigma Company's management believes that the firm's cost of capital (WACC) is too high because the firm has been too secretive with the market concerning its operations. Evaluate that statement.

13.34. Discuss what valuable information would be lost if you decided to use book values in order to calculate the cost of each of the capital components within a firm's capital structure.

CFA Problems

13.35. The cost of equity is equal to the:
   a. expected market return;
   b. rate of return required by shareholders;

c. cost of retained earnings plus dividends;

d. risk the company incurs when financing.

13.36. E-Business plc has determined that it could issue £1000 face value bonds with an 8% coupon paid semi-annually and a five-year maturity at £900 per bond. If E-Business's marginal tax rate is 38%, its after-tax cost of debt is closest to:

a. 6.2%

b. 6.4%

c. 6.6%

d. 6.8%.

13.37. Morgan Insurance Ltd issued fixed-rate perpetual preference shares three years ago and placed the issue privately with institutional investors. The shares were issued at £25.00 per share with a £1.75 dividend. If the company were to issue preference shares, the yield would be 6.5%. The privately placed preference shares current value is:

a. £25.00

b. £26.92

c. £37.31

d. £40.18.

13.38. Leveraggio Istantaneo S.p.A. has an after-tax cost of debt capital of 4%, a cost of preference shares of 8%, a cost of equity capital of 10% and a weighted average cost of capital of 7%. Leveraggio Istantaneo intends to maintain its current capital structure as it raises additional capital. In making its capital-budgeting decisions for the average-risk project, the relevant cost of capital is:

a. 4%

b. 7%

c. 8%

d. 10%.

13.39. Suppose the cost of capital of the Gadget Company is 10%. If Gadget has a capital structure that is 50% debt and 50% equity, its before-tax cost of debt is 5% and its marginal tax rate is 20%, then its cost of equity capital is closest to:

a. 10%

b. 12%

c. 14%

d. 16%.

SAMPLE TEST PROBLEMS

13.1. Équilibre Libre SA has three different product lines of business. Its least risky product line has a beta of 1.7, while its middle-risk product line has a beta of 1.8 and its most risky product line has a beta of 2.1. The market value of the assets invested in each product line is €1 billion for the least risky line, €3 billion for the middle-risk line and €7 billion for the riskiest product line. What is the beta of Équilibre Libre SA?

13.2. Ellwood plc has a five-year bond issue outstanding with a coupon rate of 10% and a price of £1039.56. If the bonds pay coupons semi-annually, what is the pre-tax cost of the debt and what is the after-tax cost of the debt? Assume the marginal tax rate for the firm is 40%.

13.3. Deutsche Kessel AG expects the growth in the dividends of its ordinary shares to be a very steady 1.5% per year for the indefinite future. The firm's shares are currently selling for €18.45 and the firm has just paid a dividend of €3.00 yesterday. What is the cost of ordinary shares for this firm?

13.4. Tiempo de Miqueas Portales SA has a preference shares issue outstanding that pays an annual dividend of €2.50 per year and is currently selling for €27.78 a share. What is the cost of preference shares for this firm?

13.5. Les Époques Anciennes SA has a portfolio of projects with a beta of 1.25. The firm is currently evaluating a new project that involves a new product in a new competitive market. Briefly discuss what adjustment Les Époques Ancienne might make to its 1.25 beta in order to evaluate this new project.

ENDNOTES

1. The other hotels were in Argentina, China, Macau and the United Kingdom, emphasising the international reach of the group. The Accor group may be more familiar to you via its portfolio of hotel brands, which include Sofitel, Pullman, Novotel, Mercure, ibis, Etap, HotelF1 and others.

2. Surveys of capital budgeting practices at major public firms in the United States indicate that a large percentage (possibly as high as 80%) of firms use the cost of capital for a firm or a division in capital budgeting calculations. For a discussion of this evidence, see the article entitled 'Best Practices in Estimating the Cost of Capital: Survey and Synthesis' by R.F. Bruner, K.M. Eades, R.S. Harris and R. C. Higgins, which was published in the Spring/Summer 1998 issue of *Financial Practice and Education*.

3. The total expected cash flows at EADS also include cash flows from projects that the firm is expected to undertake in the future, or what are often referred to as *growth opportunities*. This idea is discussed in detail in later chapters. For our immediate purposes, we will assume that these cash flows are expected to equal zero.

4. We will discuss how firms finance their assets in more detail in Chapters 15 and 16. For the time being, we will simply assume that a firm uses some combination of debt and equity. Here we use the term 'debt' in the broadest sense to refer to all liabilities, including liabilities on which the firm does not pay interest, such as accounts payable. As is common practice, we focus only on long-term interest-bearing debt, such as bank loans and bonds, in the cost of capital calculations. The reason for this is discussed in the next section.

5. We are ignoring the effect of taxes on the cost of debt financing for the time being. This effect is discussed in detail and explicitly integrated into subsequent calculations.

6. Recall that we discussed the concept of financial market efficiency in Chapter 8.

7. These types of cost are incurred by firms whenever they raise capital. We only show how to include them in the cost of bond financing and, later, in estimating the cost of preference shares, but they should also be included in calculations of the costs of capital from other sources, such as bank loans and ordinary shares.

8. *Source*: London Business School estimates. They suggest that after adjusting for non-repeatable factors such as the two world wars and the effects of the great depression in the 1930s, investors in ordinary shares should expect an annualised equity risk premium (relative to treasury bills) of around 3–4%.

9. Some firms issue a type of share that has an equity claim on only part of their business, known as a 'tracking share (stock)'. If a project is similar to the part of the business for which a tracking share exists, the returns on the tracking share can be used to estimate the beta for the ordinary shares used to finance a project.

PART 5

WORKING CAPITAL MANAGEMENT AND FINANCING DECISIONS

CHAPTER
14

Working Capital Management

In this Chapter:

Working Capital Basics

The Operating and Cash Conversion Cycles

Working Capital Investment Strategies

Accounts Receivable

Inventory Management

Cash Management and Budgeting

Financing Working Capital

LEARNING OBJECTIVES

1. Define net working capital, discuss the importance of working capital management and be able to compute a firm's net working capital.
2. Define the operating and cash conversion cycles, explain how they are used and be able to compute their values for a firm.
3. Discuss the relative advantages and disadvantages of pursuing (1) flexible and (2) restrictive current asset investment strategies.
4. Explain how accounts receivable are created and managed and be able to compute the cost of trade credit.
5. Explain the trade-off between carrying costs and reorder costs and be able to compute the economic order quantity for a firm's inventory orders.
6. Define cash collection time, discuss how a firm can minimise this time and be able to compute the cash collection costs and benefits of a cash collection account.
7. Identify three current asset-financing strategies and discuss the main sources of short-term financing.

On 13 October 2009, a despondent Gunter Hager found himself in the local district court in Bielefeld to declare the bankruptcy of the small high-performance machine-making company, Hager Werkzeugmaschinen GmbH, he had founded and built up over the past 32 years. In the wake of the crisis of 2008, demand for the type of capital equipment his firm produced had collapsed and for the first six months of 2009, the company had seen no new orders. For the 37-strong workforce, there was less and less to do as existing orders were shipped. Even these existing orders were not without their problems. Hager had to negotiate with cash-strapped buyers who were threatening to cancel orders about payment dates and, in many cases, he

had to agree extended payment terms. Particularly difficult negotiations took place with large public companies that, in the wake of the economic downturn and keen to conserve cash, made demands for deferred payment periods for as long as six months. So even without the need to finance new work in progress, Hager had no option but to ask his bankers to extend existing working capital facilities, let alone provide new finance for new orders.

However, Hager thought he had seen the worst of the economic recession when two months prior to the bankruptcy proceedings, he received a major order worth €1.5 million – enough to keep the company busy for the next 12 months. Nevertheless, several days later, the company's bank announced it was reviewing the company's working capital finance and Hager lamented that, 'The bank even put existing credit lines into question'. With time fast running out, Hager had no success in securing alternative lines of working capital as new lenders took their time to review his business. The poor cash flow situation faced by the company did nothing to help. The inevitable happened and Hager's efforts to save his business came to nothing. He could only look on as the bankruptcy rapidly unravelled what he had toiled to build up.

All companies need to manage their working capital needs and to have sound financing in place. The credit crunch has tested the cash management practices at firms and, in a number of cases, shown how vulnerable the company was to an interruption in cash flow as the firm became insolvent and went out of business. Small and medium-sized companies are the most vulnerable as they mostly lack access to the capital markets and often depend heavily on bank financing. Germany's often small and family-owned Mittelstand companies, like Hager Werkzeugmaschinen, suffered badly since they are heavily reliant on bank credit.

Working capital management, the focus of this chapter, deals with the management of current assets – cash, accounts receivable and inventories – and their financing. Hager's problems are not untypical of a firm that focuses exclusively on technical excellence at the expense of sound financial management. Paying attention to how working capital is being used in the business can help improve the returns on the capital that is invested in a business.

CHAPTER PREVIEW

The previous chapters dealt with long-term investment decisions and their impact on firm value. These capital investment decisions typically commit a firm to a course of action for a number of years and are difficult to reverse. In contrast, this chapter focuses on short-term activities that involve cash inflows and outflows that will occur within a year or less. Examples include purchasing and paying for raw materials, selling finished inventories and collecting cash for sales made on credit. These types of activities are concerned with what is known as *working capital management*.

The term *working capital* refers to the short-term assets necessary to run a business on a day-to-day basis. Typical short-term assets are cash, accounts receivable and inventories, which are often largely funded by short-term liabilities such as accounts payable. Because of the short-term nature of current assets and liabilities, decisions involving them are more flexible and easily reversed than capital investment decisions. The greater flexibility associated with working capital management does not mean that these activities are not important, however. Firms that do not manage their day-to-day operations diligently can suffer severe financial consequences, including bankruptcy.

We begin the chapter by reviewing some basic definitions and concepts. Next, we examine the individual working capital accounts and discuss how to determine and analyse the operating and cash conversion cycles. Then we explain how to manage the different working capital accounts: the cash account, accounts receivable and inventories. We finish by considering the alternative means of financing short-term assets and the risks associated with each.

WORKING CAPITAL BASICS

Learning Objective 1

Define net working capital, discuss the importance of working capital management and be able to compute a firm's net working capital.

Working capital management involves two fundamental questions: (1) What is the appropriate amount and mix of current assets for the firm to hold? (2) How should these current assets be financed? Firms must carry a certain amount of current assets to be able to operate smoothly. For example, without sufficient cash on hand, a company facing an unexpected expense might not be able to pay its bills on time. Without an inventory of raw materials, production might be subject to costly interruptions or shutdowns. Without an inventory of finished goods, sales might be lost because a product is out of stock.

WEB

A detailed discussion of the importance of working capital management can be found at: http://www.mediamergers.com/index.cfm?fuseaction=viewArticle&id=49.14.1 Working Capital Basics.

To provide a background for the discussion of working capital management, we first briefly review some important terminology and ideas. Throughout the chapter, we use financial statements and supporting data from Nokia Corporation to illustrate our discussions. Exhibit 14.1 presents Nokia's balance sheet and income statement for the year ending 2008.

Working Capital Terms and Concepts

In earlier chapters, we discussed the basic terms associated with working capital management. Here, we provide a brief review.

1. *Current assets* are cash and other assets that the firm expects to convert into cash in a year or less. These assets are usually listed on the balance sheet in order of their liquidity. Typical current assets include cash, marketable securities (sometimes also called short-term investments), accounts receivable, inventories and others, such as prepaid expenses. At the end of its 2008 year, Nokia's total current assets were €24.47 billion.
2. *Current liabilities* (or short-term liabilities) are obligations that the firm expects to repay in a year or less. They may be interest bearing, such as short-term borrowings and current maturities of long-term debt or non-interest bearing, such as accounts payable, accrued expenses or accrued taxes and wages. In December 2008, Nokia's total current liabilities were €20.355 billion.
3. *Working capital* (also called *gross working capital*) includes the funds invested in a company's cash and marketable security accounts, accounts receivable, inventories and other current assets. All firms require a certain amount of current assets to operate smoothly and to carry out day-to-day operations. Note that working capital is defined in terms of current assets, so the two terms are one and the same. Thus, it is no surprise that Nokia's working capital was €24.47 billion in December 2008.
4. *Net working capital (NWC)* refers to the difference between current assets and current liabilities:

   NWC = Current assets − Current liabilities

   NWC is important because it is a measure of a firm's liquidity. It is a measure of liquidity because it is the amount of working capital a firm would have left over after it paid off all of its short-term liabilities. The larger the firm's net working capital the greater its liquidity. Almost all firms have more current assets than current liabilities, so net working capital is positive for most companies.[1] Nokia's net working capital in 2008 was €4.11 billion (€24.47 − €20.36).
5. *Working capital management* involves management of current assets and their financing. The financial manager's responsibilities include determining the optimum balance for each of the current asset accounts and deciding what mix of short-term debt, long-term debt and equity to use in financing working capital. Working capital management decisions are usually fast paced as they reflect the pace of the firm's day-to-day operations.
6. *Working capital efficiency* is a term that refers to how efficiently working capital is used. It is most commonly measured by a firm's cash conversion cycle, which reflects the time between the point at which raw materials are paid for and the point at which finished goods made from those materials are converted into cash. The shorter a firm's cash conversion cycle, the more efficient is its use of working capital.
7. *Liquidity* is the ability of a company to convert assets – real or financial – into cash quickly without suffering a financial loss.

Working Capital Accounts and Trade-Offs

Short-term cash inflows and outflows do not always match in their timing or magnitude, creating a need to manage the working capital accounts. The objective of the managers of these accounts is to enable the company to operate with the smallest possible net

EXHIBIT 14.1

NOKIA CORPORATION FINANCIAL STATEMENTS, FISCAL YEAR ENDED 31 DECEMBER 2008 (€ MILLIONS)

Balance Sheet (as at 31 December 2008)

Assets	€m	Liabilities and equity	€m
Non-current assets		**Capital and reserves**	
Intangible assets		Share capital	246
Goodwill	6 257	Share issue premium	442
Other intangible assets	4 157	Treasury shares at cost	(1 881)
Total intangible assets	10 414	Reserves and other items	3 709
		Retained earnings	11 692
Tangible assets			14 208
Plant, property and equipment	2 090	Minority interests	2 302
Investments	608	**Total equity**	16 510
Other non-current assets	2 000	**Non-current liabilities**	
Total tangible assets	4 698	Long-term borrowings	861
		Deferred tax & other long-term liabilities	1 856
Total non-current assets	15 112	**Total non-current liabilities**	2 717
Current assets		**Current liabilities**	
Inventories	2 533	Borrowings	3 591
Accounts receivable	9 444	Other financial liabilities	924
Prepaid expenses and accrued income	4 639	Accounts payable	5 225
Other financial assets	1 034	Accrued expenses and provisions	10 615
Available for sale investments	1 272	**Total current liabilities**	20 355
Cash and cash equivalents	5 548	**Total liabilities**	23 072
Total current assets	24 470		
Total assets	€39 582	**Total shareholders' equity and liabilities**	€39 582

Profit and Loss Account

	€m
Net sales	50 710
Cost of sales	(33 337)
Gross profit	17 373
Operating expenses	
R&D	(5 968)
Sales, general and administration	(5 664)
Other expenses (net)	(775)
	(12 407)
Operating profit	€4 966
Share of results of associated companies	6
Net financial income and expenses	(2)
Profit before tax	€4 970
Tax	(1 081)
Profit before minority interests	3 889
Minority interests	99
Profit attributable to equity holders	€3 988

The exhibit shows the balance sheet and profit and loss account for Nokia Corporation for the financial year ending 31 December 2008. We use this information to illustrate various elements of working capital management.

investment in working capital. To do this, however, managers must make cost/benefit trade-offs. The trade-offs arise because it is easier to run a business with a generous amount of net working capital but it is also more costly to do so. We will briefly look at each working capital account to see what the basic trade-offs are. Keep in mind as you read the discussion that the more working capital assets a firm holds, the greater the cost to the firm. The working capital accounts that are the focus of most working capital management activities are as follows:

1. *Cash (including marketable securities)*. The more cash a firm has on hand, the more likely it will be able to meet its financial obligations if an unexpected expense occurs. If cash balances become too small, the firm runs the risk that it will be unable to pay its bills; and if this condition becomes chronic, creditors could force the firm into bankruptcy. The downside of holding too much cash is that the returns on cash are low even when it is invested in an interest-paying bank account or highly liquid short-term money market instrument, such as government securities.

2. *Receivables*. The accounts receivable at a firm represent the total unpaid credit that the firm has extended to its customers. Accounts receivable can include **trade credit** (credit extended to another business) or **consumer credit** (credit extended to a consumer), or both. Businesses provide trade and consumer credit because doing so increases sales and because it is often a competitive necessity to match the credit terms offered by competitors. The downside to granting such credit is that it is expensive to evaluate customers' credit applications to ensure that they are creditworthy and then to monitor their ongoing credit performance. Firms that are not diligent in managing their credit operations can suffer large losses from bad debts, especially during a recession, when customers may have trouble paying their bills.

> **Trade credit**
>
> credit extended by one business to another

> **Consumer credit**
>
> credit extended by a business to consumers

3. *Inventories*. Customers like firms to maintain large finished goods inventory because, when they go to make a purchase, the item they want will likely be in stock; thus, they do not have to wait. Similarly, large raw material inventories reduce the chance that the firm will not have access to raw materials when they are needed, which can cause costly interruptions in the manufacturing process. At the same time, large inventories are expensive to finance, can require warehouses that are expensive to build and maintain, must be protected against breakage and theft and run a greater risk of obsolescence.

4. *Payables*. Accounts payable are trade credits provided to firms by their suppliers. Because suppliers typically grant a grace period before payables become due to be paid and firms do not have to pay interest during this period, trade credit is an attractive source of financing. For this reason, financial managers do not hurry to pay their suppliers when bills arrive. Of course, suppliers recognise that they provide attractive financing to their customers and that trade credit is expensive for them. Consequently, suppliers tend to provide strong incentives for firms to pay on time (either by providing discounts for paying on time or charging penalties for late payment). As you might expect, firms typically wait until near the end of the grace period to pay for goods and services bought on trade credit. The financial manager at a firm that is having serious financial problems may have no choice but to delay paying its suppliers. However, besides incurring monetary penalties, a manager who is consistently late paying trade credit runs the risk that the supplier will no longer sell to his or her firm.[2]

When the financial manager makes a decision to increase working capital, good things are likely to happen to the firm – sales should increase, relationships with vendors and suppliers should improve, and work or manufacturing stoppages should be less likely. Unfortunately, the extra working capital costs money and there is no simple algorithm or formula that determines the 'optimal' level of working capital the firm should hold. The choice depends on management's strategic preferences, its willingness to bear risk and the firm's line of business.

Before You Go On

1. How do you calculate net working capital and why is it important?
2. What are some of the trade-offs required in the management of working capital accounts?

THE OPERATING AND CASH CONVERSION CYCLES

Learning Objective 2

Define the operating and cash conversion cycles, explain how they are used and be able to compute their values for a firm.

A very important concept in working capital management is known as the **cash conversion cycle**. This is the length of time from the point at which a company actually pays for raw materials until the point at which it receives cash from the sale of finished goods made from those materials. This is an important concept because the length of the cash conversion cycle is directly related to the amount of capital that a firm needs to finance its working capital.

Cash conversion cycle

the length of time from the point at which a company pays for raw materials until the point at which it receives cash from the sale of finished goods made from those materials

The sequence of events that occurs from the point in time that a firm actually pays for its raw materials to the point that it receives cash from the sale of finished goods is as follows: (1) the firm uses cash to pay for raw materials and the cost of converting them into finished goods (conversion costs); (2) finished goods are held in finished goods inventories until they are sold; (3) finished goods are sold on credit to the firm's customers and, finally; (4) customers repay the credit the firm has extended them and the firm receives the cash. The cash is then reinvested in raw materials and conversion costs and the cycle is repeated. If a firm is profitable, the cash inflows increase over time. Exhibit 14.2 shows a schematic diagram of the cash conversion cycle.

Clearly, financial managers want to achieve several goals in managing this cycle:

- Delay paying accounts payable as long as possible without suffering any penalties.
- Maintain the minimum level of raw material inventories necessary to support production without causing manufacturing delays.
- Use as little labour and other inputs to the production process as possible while maintaining product quality.
- Maintain the level of finished goods inventories that represents the best trade-off between minimising the amount of capital invested in finished goods inventories and the desire to avoid lost sales.
- Offer customers terms on trade credit that are sufficiently attractive to support sales and yet minimise the cost of this credit, both the financing cost and the risk of non-payment.
- Collect cash payments on accounts receivable as quickly as possible to close the loop.

All of these goals have implications for the firm's efficiency and liquidity. It is the financial manager's responsibility to ensure that he or she makes decisions that maximise the value of the firm. Managing the length of the cash conversion cycle is one aspect of managing working capital to maximise the value of the firm.[3] Next, we discuss two simple tools to

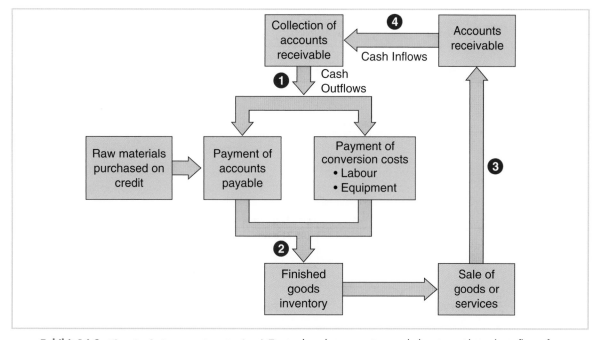

Exhibit 14.2: The Cash Conversion Cycle A Typical cash conversion cycle begins with cash outflows for raw materials and conversion costs and goes through several stages before these resources are turned back into cash. The cash conversion cycle reflects the average time from the point that cash is used to pay for raw materials until cash is collected on the accounts receivable associated with the product produced with those raw materials. One of the main goals of a financial manager is to optimise the time between the cash outflows and the cash inflows.

measure working capital efficiency. As you read the discussion, refer to Exhibit 14.3.

Operating Cycle

The **operating cycle** starts with the receipt of raw materials and ends with the collection of cash from customers for the sale of finished goods made from those materials. The operating cycle can be described in terms of two components: days' sales in inventory and days' sales outstanding. The formulas for these efficiency ratios were developed in Chapter 4. Nokia's ratios and the average industry standard ratios are shown in Exhibit 14.4.

> ### Operating cycle
>
> the average time between receipt of raw materials and receipt of cash for the sale of finished goods made from those materials

Days' sales in inventory (DSI) shows, on average, how long a firm holds inventory before selling it. Recall from Chapter 4 that it is calculated by dividing 365 days by the firm's inventory turnover and that inventory turnover equals cost of goods sold (COGS) divided by inventories. Equation (4.4) and the formula for DSI, along with a calculation for Nokia in 2008, are as follows:

$$
\begin{aligned}
\text{Days' sales in inventories} &= \text{DSI} \\
&= \frac{365 \text{ days}}{\text{Inventories turnover}} \\
&= \frac{365 \text{ days}}{\text{COGS/Inventories}} \\
&= \frac{365}{\text{€33 337/€2533}} \\
&= 27.73 \text{ days}
\end{aligned}
$$

As shown in Exhibit 14.4, the diversified electrical industry average for days' sales in inventories is 60.32, while for Nokia it is 27.73 days.

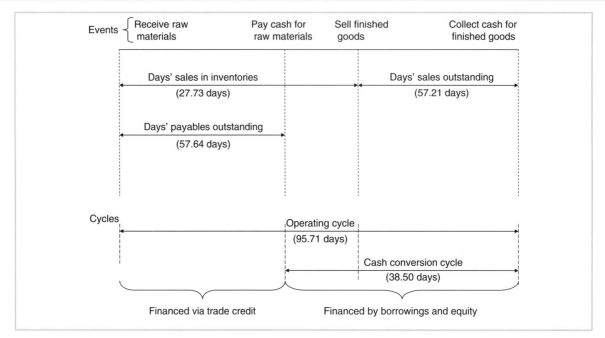

Exhibit 14.3: The exhibit shows the cash inflows and outflows and other key events in a firm's operating cycle and cash conversion cycle, along with the computed values for Nokia Corporation. Both of these cycles are used to measure working capital efficiency.

According to the DSI ratio, it takes Nokia about a month to complete this process, whereas the average competitor requires two months to complete the same task.

Days' sales outstanding (DSO) indicates how long it takes, on average, for the firm to collect its outstanding accounts receivable. Recall from Chapter 4 that DSO is calculated by dividing

EXHIBIT 14.4

SELECTED FINANCIAL RATIOS FOR NOKIA CORPORATION AND THE DIVERSIFIED ELECTRONICS INDUSTRY IN 2008

Financial Ratio	Nokia	Diversified Electronics
Days' sales in inventories	27.73	60.32
Days' sales outstanding	67.98	62.04
Days' payables outstanding	57.21	49.71
Operating cycle	95.71	122.36
Cash conversion cycle	38.50	72.65

When we compare working capital ratios for Nokia Corporation with average ratios for the diversified electronics industry, we can see how well Nokia is performing relative to its peers on the metrics. Nokia holds fewer inventories and has a shorter operating cycle and cash conversion cycle than the industry. The company has a greater number of days' payables outstanding than the industry but conversely has a higher days' sales outstanding. The reason its cash conversion cycle is better than the industry average is due to lower inventories and the offsetting effect of a higher days' payables outstanding.

365 days by accounts receivable turnover and that accounts receivable turnover equals net sales divided by accounts receivable.[4] Sometimes this ratio is called the average collection period. An efficient firm with good working capital management should have a low average collection period compared with that of its industry. Equation (14.6), the DSO formula and the calculation for Nokia are as follows:

$$\begin{aligned} DSO &= \frac{365 \text{ days}}{\text{Accounts receivable turnover}} \\ &= \frac{365 \text{ days}}{\text{Net sales/Accounts receivable}} \\ &= \frac{365}{\text{€50\,710/€9444}} \\ &= 67.98 \text{ days} \end{aligned}$$

Again, referring to Exhibit 14.4 we see that the average firm in the diversified electronics industry has 62.04 days of sales outstanding, while Nokia's figure is 67.98 days. In 2008, Nokia lagged behind the industry average in collecting the cash it was owed by its customers. This ratio goes some way to explain why Nokia has more money invested in current assets than some of its competitors.

We can now calculate the operating cycle simply by summing the days' sales outstanding and the days' sales in inventories:

$$\text{Operating cycle} = DSO + DSI \qquad (14.1)$$

Nokia's operating cycle for 2008 is 95.71 days $(67.98 + 27.73 = 95.71)$, and the industry average is 122.36 days. Nokia manages to complete its operating cycle in about 80% of the time that the average diversified electronics firm takes, which means that Nokia has far less invested in working capital.

Cash Conversion Cycle

The cash conversion cycle is related to the operating cycle but the cash conversion cycle does not begin until the firm actually pays for its inventories. In other words, the cash conversion cycle is the length of time between the actual cash outflow for materials and the actual cash inflow from sales. To calculate this cycle, we need all of the information used to calculate the operating cycle plus one additional measure: days' payables outstanding.

Days' payables outstanding (DPO) tells us how long, on average, a firm takes to pay its suppliers. Recall that it is calculated by dividing 365 days by accounts payable turnover and that accounts payable turnover equals COGS divided by accounts payable. The DPO formula and the calculation for Nokia are:

$$\begin{aligned} DPO &= \frac{365 \text{ days}}{\text{Accounts payable turnover}} \\ &= \frac{365 \text{ days}}{\text{COGS/Accounts payable}} \\ &= \frac{365}{\text{€33\,337/€5225}} \\ &= 57.21 \text{ days} \end{aligned}$$

The industry average DPO is 49.71 days and the DPO for Nokia is 57.21 days. Nokia takes an average of 7.5 days longer than its competitors to make payments to its suppliers.

We can now calculate the cash conversion cycle by summing the days' sales outstanding and the days' sales in inventories and subtracting the days' payables outstanding:

$$\begin{aligned} \text{Cash conversion cycle} &= DSO + DSI - DPO \\ &= 67.98 \text{ days} + 27.73 \text{ days} \\ &\quad - 57.21 \text{ days} \\ &= 38.50 \text{ days} \end{aligned}$$

$$(14.2)$$

Nokia's cash conversion cycle is 38.50 days. Another way to calculate the cash conversion cycle is to notice that it is simply the operating cycle minus the days' payables outstanding, as can be seen in Exhibit 14.3:

$$\text{Cash conversion cycle} = \text{Operating cycle} - DPO$$

$$(14.3)$$

Thus, Nokia's cash conversion cycle for 2008 can be calculated as $95.71 - 57.21 = 38.50$ days.

A positive cash conversion cycle of 38.50 days means that Nokia has to provide working capital for its sales an average of about 39 days after it pays its suppliers. In other words, Nokia has to invest capital in inventories and receivables. An examination of Nokia's accounts receivable and inventory balances with the accounts payable balance in Exhibit 14.1 reveals that the financing provided by Nokia is just over twice the amount the firm has borrowed through accounts payable (€9444 + €2533 in inventories and accounts receivable respectively versus €5225 provided by accounts payable).

While Nokia has to invest in working capital, the industry comparisons show that it is clearly better at managing its operating cycle than its peers. The diversified electronics industry as a whole has a longer cash conversion cycle than Nokia. The industry average is 72.65 days and Nokia's is 38.50 days, or just under half the industry's average.

Measuring Danone's Working Capital Efficiency

Problem: Danone SA is a manufacturing firm in the diversified food industry. The board of directors would like to know how efficiently the firm's working capital is being managed. They are particularly interested in the length of time it takes Danone to collect cash that is paid for raw materials. Exhibit 14.5 shows the financial statements for Danone, as well as some data from the diversified food industry for comparison.

Approach: Calculating the cash conversion cycle will answer the directors' question. This will require first calculating the days' sales outstanding (DSO), days' sales in inventories (DSI) and days' payables outstanding (DPO).

Solution:

$$DSO = \frac{365 \text{ days}}{15\,220/1548} = 37.12 \text{ days}$$

It takes Danone just over 37 days to collect cash from its customers and the industry average is 37.25. Danone is about average in the collection time of its accounts receivable.

$$DSI = \frac{365 \text{ days}}{€7172/861} = 43.82 \text{ days}$$

It takes Danone just under 44 days to transform the raw material into finished goods and sell them, which is lower than the industry average of 90.78 days.

$$DPO = \frac{365 \text{ days}}{€7172/€2306} = 117.36 \text{ days}$$

Danone does not pay cash to its suppliers for more than 117 days. The industry average is 62.40, so Danone is taking nearly twice as long as the industry to pay suppliers.

Danone's cash conversion cycle for 2008 is $37.12 + 43.82 - 117.36 = -36.42$ days. The industry average is 65.63 days.

The diversified food industry as a whole has a much longer cash conversion cycle than Danone. The industry average is 62.40 days while Danone's is −36.42 days. Danone receives financing from its negative cash cycle, as can be seen by the fact that accounts receivable total €1548 million and accounts payable are €2306 million.[5] The information suggests that Danone is being very successful at managing its working capital.

EXHIBIT 14.5

DANONE SA FINANCIAL STATEMENTS, FINANCIAL YEAR ENDED 31 DECEMBER 2008 (€ MILLIONS)

Assets	€m	€m	Liabilities and equity	€m	€m		€m	€m
Non-current assets			**Capital and reserves**			**Net sales**		15 220
Intangible assets			Share capital	128		Cost of sales		(7 172)
Brands	3 961		Share issue premium	255		Gross profit		8 048
Goodwill	12 869		Treasury shares at cost	(1 270)				
Other intangible assets	401		Reserves and other items	311		**Operating expenses**		
Total intangible assets	17 231		Retained earnings	9 594		R&D		(198)
Tangible assets				9 018		Sales, general and administration		(5 494)
Plant, property and equipment	3 035		Minority interests	82		Other expenses (net)		(86)
Investments	1 263		**Total equity**		9 100			(5 778)
Other non-current assets	1 653		**Non-current liabilities**			**Operating profit**		2 270
Total tangible assets	5 951		Non-current financial liabilities	9 855		Share of results of associated companies		(83)
			Deferred tax & other long-term liabilities	1 808		Net financial income and expenses		(584)
Total non-current assets		23 182	**Total non-current liabilities**		11 663	**Profit before tax**		1 603
						Tax		(443)
Current assets			**Current liabilities**			Profit before minority interests		1 160
Inventories	861		Borrowings	2 447		Minority interests		62
Accounts receivable	1 548		Liabilities held for sale	13		**Profit attributable to equity holders**		€1 222
Prepaid expenses and accrued income	793		Accounts payable	2 306				
Other financial assets	493		Accrued expenses and provisions	2 047				
Assets held for sale	151		**Total current liabilities**		6 813			
Cash and cash equivalents	548							
Total current assets		4 394	**Total liabilities**		18 476			
Total assets		€27 576	**Total shareholders' equity and liabilities**		€27 576			

Selected diversified food industry ratios: Days' sales in inventories = 90.78; Days' sales outstanding = 37.25; Days' payables outstanding = 62.40; Cash conversion cycle = 65.63 days.

The exhibit shows the balance sheet and income statement for Danone for the fiscal year ended 31 December 2008, as well as some ratios from the diversified food industry. Use the data to work through and support your analysis in Learning by Doing Application 14.1.

Before You Go On

1. What is the operating cycle and how is it related to the cash conversion cycle?

WORKING CAPITAL INVESTMENT STRATEGIES

Learning Objective 3

Discuss the relative advantages and disadvantages of pursuing (1) flexible and (2) restrictive current asset investment strategies.

One of the financial manager's key decisions with regard to working capital is to determine how much money should be invested in current assets for a given level of sales. To the extent that managers have only limited control over their ability to increase days' payables outstanding without the risk of incurring high costs (losing discounts or having to pay penalties), choosing the level of current assets that the firm holds is essentially the same as choosing the amount of net working capital. Since more net working capital provides a firm with greater financial flexibility, but at a higher cost than a more restrictive (less flexible) strategy of holding less net working capital, choosing the appropriate amount of net working capital involves making trade-offs.

Flexible Current Asset Investment Strategy

A firm that follows a **flexible current asset investment strategy** might hold large balances of cash, marketable securities and inventories. It might also offer liberal credit terms to customers, which results in high levels of accounts receivable. A flexible strategy is generally perceived to be a low-risk and low-return course of action. A principal benefit of such a strategy is that large working capital balances improve the firm's ability to survive unforeseen threats. This reduces the size of the firm's exposure to fluctuations in business conditions.

Flexible current asset investment strategy

current asset investment strategy that involves keeping high balances of current assets on hand

The downsides of such a strategy can include low returns on current assets, potentially high **inventory carrying costs** and the cost of financing liberal credit terms. As discussed earlier, returns on cash and marketable securities can be low. Other current assets also usually earn lower returns than long-term assets. For example, inventories sitting on the shelf earn no interest income. Thus, by investing in current assets, management forgoes the higher rate of return it could have earned by investing in long-term assets. This is an opportunity cost. Furthermore, large investments in some types of inventory can require significant storage, tax and insurance costs.

Inventory carrying costs

expenses associated with maintaining inventory, including interest forgone on money invested in inventories, storage costs, taxes and insurance

Although a flexible current asset investment strategy is a low-return strategy on average, it can yield large payoffs under certain circumstances. For example, having enough cash to weather a severe credit crunch that puts a firm's major competitors out of business can yield very large long-run returns. Similarly, having sufficient cash to take advantage of an unforeseen acquisition opportunity can be very valuable.

Restrictive Current Asset Investment Strategy

A firm that follows a **restrictive current asset investment strategy** keeps levels of current assets at a minimum. The firm invests the minimum possible in cash, marketable securities and inventories, and has strict terms of sale intended to limit credit sales and accounts receivable. A restrictive strategy is a high-return, high-risk alternative to a flexible strategy. A restrictive strategy enables the firm to invest a larger fraction of its money in higher-yielding assets. The high risk comes in the form of exposure to **shortage costs**, which can be either financial or operating costs.

Restrictive current asset investment strategy

current asset investment strategy that involves keeping the level of current assets at a minimum

---

Shortage costs

costs incurred because of lost production and sales or illiquidity

---

Financial shortage costs arise mainly from illiquidity. Firms become illiquid when unforeseen circumstances cause them to run out of cash and marketable securities. If bills come due, the firm can be forced to use expensive external emergency borrowing. Worse yet, if outside funding cannot be secured, the firm may default on some current liability and run the risk of being forced into bankruptcy by creditors.

Operating shortage costs result from lost production and sales. If the firm does not hold enough raw materials, precious hours may be wasted by a halt in production. If the firm runs out of finished goods, sales may also be lost and customer satisfaction may be damaged. Having restrictive credit policies, such as allowing no credit sales, will also result in lost sales. Overall, operating shortage costs can be substantial, especially if the product markets are competitive.

The Working Capital Trade-Off

To determine the optimal investment strategy for current assets, the financial manager must balance shortage costs against carrying costs. This is the *working capital trade-off*. If the costs of running short of working capital (shortage costs) dominate the cost of carrying extra working capital (carrying costs), a firm will move towards a more flexible policy. Alternatively, if carrying costs are greater than shortage costs, then the firm will maximise value by adopting a more restrictive strategy. Overall, management will try to find the level of current

BUILDING INTUITION

Consideration of the Working Capital Trade-offs

There is no formula for determining whether the company should adopt a flexible or restrictive working capital investment strategy. However, some pointers should govern policy in this area. First, are the opportunity costs involved. A company that produces a product that is hard to replace may upset customers if it is subject to frequent stock-outs. Such customers may defect to rivals that are more reliable. After all, these firms will be actively managing their working capital. Second, are the strategic issues. For instance, if the firm's strategy is based on cost advantage then restricting the amount of money tied up in working capital makes sense. On the other hand, if the company is pursuing a differentiated strategy based around product quality and service, then the operating shortage costs (both direct and indirect) may be very high. Deciding on the appropriate strategy involves a clear understanding of the company's long-term goals.

assets that minimises the sum of the carrying costs and shortage costs.

Before You Go On

1. What are the two general current asset investment strategies discussed in this section and how do they differ?
2. What are the types of costs associated with each of these strategies?

ACCOUNTS RECEIVABLE

Learning Objective 4

Explain how accounts receivable are created and managed and be able to compute the cost of trade credit.

We will now consider the components of the operating cycle, starting with accounts receivable, which are at the end of the cash conversion cycle (see Exhibit 14.2). Companies frequently make sales to customers on credit by delivering the goods in exchange for the promise of a future payment. The promise is an account receivable from the firm's point of view. The amount of credit offered to various customers and the terms of the credit are important decisions for the financial manager. Offering credit to customers can help a firm attract customers by differentiating the firm and its products from its competitors, or it might be necessary to offer credit simply to match similar offers by competitors.

Terms of Sale

Whenever a firm sells a product, the seller spells out the terms and conditions of the sale in a document called the *terms of sale*. The simplest alternative is cash on delivery (COD) – that is, no credit is offered. Most firms would prefer to get cash from all sales immediately on delivery but, as

mentioned before, being competitive often requires offering credit.

When credit is part of the sale, the terms of sale spell out the credit agreement between the buyer and seller. The agreement specifies when the cash payment is due and the amount of any discount if early payment is made. Trade credit, which is short-term financing, is typically made with a discount for early payment rather than an explicit interest charge. For example, suppose a firm offers terms of sale of '3/10, net 40'. This firm will grant a 3% discount if the buyer pays the full amount of the purchase in cash within 10 days of the invoice date. Otherwise, the buyer has 40 days to pay the balance in full from the date of delivery.

In this case, the seller is offering to lend the buyer money for an additional 30 days. How expensive is it to the buyer to take advantage of this financing? To calculate the cost, we need to determine the interest rate the buyer is paying. In this case, the buyer pays 97% of the purchase price if it pays within 10 days. Otherwise, the buyer pays the full price within 40 days. The increase in the payment (and therefore the interest implicit in the loan) is $3/97 = 3.09\%$. This is the interest for 30 days $(40 - 10)$. To find the annual interest rate, we need to compute the effective annual interest rate (EAR), which was introduced in Chapter 6. As you recall, the EAR conversion formula accounts for the number of compounding periods and thereby annualises the interest rate.

The formula for calculating the EAR for a problem like this is shown in Equation (14.4), together with the calculation for our example. Notice that to annualise the interest rate, we compound the per-period rate by the number of periods in a year, which is 12.1667 (365 days divided by 30 days in a period):

$$
\begin{aligned}
\text{Effective} \\
\text{annual rate} &= \left(1 + \frac{\text{Discount}}{\text{Discounted price}}\right)^{365/\text{days credit}} - 1 \\
&= (1 + 3/97)^{365/30} - 1 \\
&= 1.4486 - 1 \\
&= 0.4486, \text{ or } 44.86\%
\end{aligned}
$$

By not paying on day 10, but instead waiting until day 40, the firm is paying an effective annual interest rate of 44.86% for the use of the money provided by the seller. The rate seems high, but these terms are not unusual rates for trade credit. Generally speaking, firms do not want to be in the short-term lending business and would prefer to be paid promptly. The terms of sale reflect this preference. If customers need short-term credit, most sellers would prefer that the customers go to firms that specialise in business lending, such as a commercial bank or commercial finance company. An important point to notice in the above example is that trade credit is a loan from the supplier and, as you can see, it can be a very costly form of credit.

Another common credit term is end-of-month payment (EOM). If a firm makes several deliveries to the same customer over the course of a month, it often makes sense to send a single bill at the end of the month for the full amount. Of course, this can be combined with a discount for quick payment. For example, if the terms are '4/10 EOM, net 30', the buyer receives a 4% discount for paying within 10 days of the end of the month in which the delivery was made. Otherwise, the customer has an additional 20 days in which to make the payment. We can calculate the cost of credit in this situation using Equation (14.4), just as we did in the earlier example.

Learning by Doing Application 14.2

Cost of Trade Credit

Problem: Suppose that a firm sells its goods with terms of 4/10 EOM, net 30. What is the implicit cost of the trade credit?

Approach: The terms of sale say that the buyer will receive a 4% discount if the full amount is paid in cash within 10 days of the end of the month. Otherwise, the buyer must pay the full amount in 20 days. Once we have determined the cost of credit for 20 days, we can use Equation (14.4) to find the annualised rate.

Solution: The cost of the credit for 20 days is $4/96 = 4.17\%$.

$$\text{Effective annual rate} = \left(1 + \frac{\text{Discount}}{\text{Discounted price}}\right)^{365/\text{days credit}} - 1$$

$$= (1 + 4/96)^{365/20} - 1$$

$$= (1.0417)^{18.2500} - 1$$

$$= 2.1064 - 1$$

$$= 1.1064, \text{ or } 110.64\%$$

That is expensive credit when annualised!

How do firms determine their terms of sale? One factor is the industry in which the firm operates. For example, purchases of some consumer products, such as cars and consumer durables, are much larger than others. Sales of relatively expensive products can be very sensitive to the availability of credit. The manufacturers of these types of products are therefore usually liberal with their terms of sale and frequently are in the business of offering short- to medium-term

financing. Volkswagen Financial Services, Volkswagen's wholly owned finance division, exists for exactly this purpose. In contrast, companies selling lower-cost perishable products, such as food companies, might ask for payment in full in less than 10 days.

The terms of sale are also affected by the customer's creditworthiness. If the firm is confident that it will be paid, it is far more likely to extend credit than if it has some doubt about payment. If the customer is a particularly wealthy individual or a large firm, or if there is a likelihood of repeat business, then extending credit may be part of the marketing effect to secure the order.

Aging Accounts Receivable

It would be nice if all customers paid their bills when they came due but we all know that is not what happens. As a result, firms that offer sales on credit need tools to identify and monitor slow payers so that they can be prompted to pay. In credit circles, it is well documented that creditors that identify slow payers early and establish contact with them are more likely to be paid in full than those who do not monitor their receivables carefully. A tool that credit managers commonly use for this purpose is an *aging schedule*, which organises the firm's accounts receivable by their age. Its purpose is to identify and track delinquent accounts and to see that they are paid. Aging schedules are also an important financial tool for analysing the quality of a company's receivables. The aging schedule reveals patterns of delinquency and shows where collection efforts should be concentrated. Exhibit 14.6 shows aging schedules for three different firms.

WEB

Some steps a firm can take to monitor and collect on its accounts receivable are discussed at: http://www.moneyinstructor .com/art/accountsreceivable.asp.

The first schedule belongs to Elritze AG, which is extremely effective in collecting its accounts receivable. 60% of Elritze's total accounts receivable are no more than 10 days old and the remaining 40% are between 11 and 30 days old. Elritze does not have any open accounts receivable older than 30 days. Elritze's *effective DSO* can be calculated as follows:

$$\text{Effective DSO} = \sum \Big(\text{Age of account category in days}$$
$$\times \text{Percent of total accounts receivable}$$
$$\text{outstanding for the account category}\Big)$$
$$= (10 \text{ days} \times 0.6) + (30 \text{ days} \times 0.4)$$
$$= 6 \text{ days} + 12 \text{ days}$$
$$= 18 \text{ days}$$

The effective DSO is simply a weighted-average measure of DSO where the weights equal the

EXHIBIT 14.6

AGING SCHEDULE OF ACCOUNTS RECEIVABLE

Age of Account (days)	Elritze AG Value of Account	Elritze AG % of Total Value	Rooney plc Value of Account	Rooney plc % of Total Value	Fabrikations-Eisen GmbH Value of Account	Fabrikations-Eisen GmbH % of Total Value
0–10	€436 043	60%	€363 370	50%	€319 765	44%
11–30	290 696	40	218 022	30	181 685	25
31–45	0	0	109 011	15	116 278	16
46–60	0	0	36 336	5	72 674	10
Over 60	0	0	0	0	36 337	5
Total	€726 739	100%	€726 739	100%	€726 739	100%

An aging schedule shows the breakdown of a firm's accounts receivable by their date of sale; it tells managers how long the accounts have gone unpaid. This exhibit shows the aging schedules for three different firms: Elritze, which is extremely effective in collecting on its accounts receivable, and Rooney and Fabrikations-Eisen, which are not performing as well.

percentage of total accounts receivable outstanding in each account category.

Rooney plc and Fabrikations-Eisen are identical to Elritze in that they sell the same amount of goods for the same price and have the same terms of sale. However, neither company is able to collect all of its accounts receivable on time, which makes their aging schedules different from Elritze's.

Rooney collects only 50% of its receivables in 10 days or less and 30% in 30 days or less. Of the remaining 20%, it collects 15% in 45 days or less and 5% in 60 days or less. Rooney's effective DSO is 23.75 days = (10 days × 0.50) + (30 days × 0.30) + (45 days × 0.15) + (60 days × 0.05), compared with Elritze's 18 days.

Things look even worse for Fabrikations-Eisen. It collects 44% of its receivables in 10 days or less, 25% in 30 days or less, 16% in 45 days or less and 10% in 60 days or less. As for the remaining 5%, they may never be collected. All we know is that these accounts receivable are over 60 days old. The worst-case scenario would be for Fabrikations-Eisen to write these off as bad debt. We will assume that Fabrikations-Eisen can collect the remaining 5% in a year. In that case, Fabrikations-Eisen's effective DSO becomes 43.35 days = (10 days × 0.44) + (30 days × 0.25) + (45 days × 0.16) + (60 days × 0.10) + (365 days × 0.05). It takes Fabrikations-Eisen more than twice as many days as Elritze to collect its accounts receivable.

Financial managers keep close track of both the aging schedule and the effective DSO. If either or both show consistent deterioration, it may be time to reconsider the firm's credit policy or the characteristics of its customers. Note that in some industries, sales vary by season. Managers must be aware of seasonal patterns and make the necessary adjustments before drawing conclusions about a firm's accounts receivable.

Before You Go On

1. What does '4/15, net 30' mean?
2. What is an aging schedule and what is its purpose?

INVENTORY MANAGEMENT

Learning Objective 5

Explain the trade-off between carrying costs and reorder costs and be able to compute the economic order quantity for a firm's inventory orders.

We have discussed the management of accounts receivable, which represents one end of the operating cycle. We now turn to a discussion of inventory management, which starts with the purchase of raw materials and extends through the sale of finished goods inventories. Inventory management is largely a function of operations management, not financial management. For that reason, we touch briefly on a few major points related to operations.

Economic Order Quantity

Manufacturing companies generally carry three types of inventories: raw materials, work in process and finished goods. We have already discussed some of the trade-offs a firm must consider in deciding how much inventory to hold. On the one hand, as explained earlier, a firm that carries too much inventory may incur high inventory carrying costs. On the other hand, a firm that does not carry sufficient inventories may incur high shortage costs.

Closely related to the decision of how much inventory to hold is the decision of how much inventory to order. The more of a particular type of inventory a firm orders, the larger the firm's inventory will be immediately after the order is received. A larger inventory means that the time before inventory must be ordered again will be greater and so fewer orders will be required over the course of a year.

The **economic order quantity** (EOQ) model helps managers choose the appropriate quantity of a particular type of inventory to order. This model mathematically determines the order quantity that minimises the total costs incurred to order and hold inventory. This model accounts for both inventory *reorder costs* and inventory *carrying costs*. Reorder costs are the fixed costs associated with ordering inventory. The trick in determining the optimal amount of inventory to order is to find the trade-off between these two costs. This trade-off exists because as a firm increases the size of its orders, the number of orders declines and thus total reorder costs decline. However, larger order sizes increase the average inventory size and, therefore, the carrying cost of inventory increases. The optimal order size strikes the balance between these two costs.

Economic order quantity (EOQ)

order quantity that minimises the total costs incurred to order and hold inventories

---

The EOQ model makes the following assumptions: (1) that a firm's sales are made at a constant rate over a period; (2) that the cost of reordering inventory is a fixed cost, regardless of the number of units ordered; and (3) that inventory has carrying costs, which includes items such as the cost of space, taxes, insurance and losses due to spoilage and theft. Under these assumptions, the formula for the economic order quantity is:

$$EOQ = \sqrt{\frac{2 \times \text{Reorder costs} \times \text{Sales per period}}{\text{Carrying costs}}}$$

(14.5)

Let us look at an example. Suppose that The Discount House sells Hewlett-Packard colour printers at the rate of 2200 units per year. The total cost of placing an order is £750 and it costs £120 per year to carry a printer in inventory. Using the EOQ formula, what is the optimal order size? Substituting the values into Equation (14.5) yields this result:

$$EOQ = \sqrt{\frac{2 \times £750 \times 2200}{£120}}$$
$$= 165.83, \text{ or } 166 \text{ printers per order}$$

Given The Discount House's cost structure, it should order 166 printers per order. This means that The Discount House should place about 13 orders per year (2200/166 = 13.25). The EOQ formula also assumes that the firm uses up its entire inventory before the next inventory order is placed. Thus, over time, the average inventory is about 83 printers [(166 − 0)/2], with the inventory varying from a minimum of zero to a maximum of 166 printers.

WEB

For a more detailed example of an EOQ challenge, go to: http://www.inventory managementreview.org/2005/11/advanced_econom.html.

The assumption of reordering inventory when it declines to zero is not very realistic. Most firms maintain a buffer or safety stock. The size of the safety stock depends on factors such as the carrying cost of inventory, seasonal sales variations, the reliability of suppliers and the accuracy of the firm's sales projections. In our example, suppose that The Discount House's financial analysts determine that because of future demand uncertainty, the buffer stock should be 15 printers. In that case, the average inventory would be 98 printers (83 + 15).

Learning by Doing Application 14.3

Economic Order Quantity

Problem: Le Chantier Naval de Toulouse, one of the largest boat dealers in the South of France, sells about 1500 dinghies a year. The cost of placing an order with its supplier is €500, the inventory carrying costs are €100 for each dinghy and the safety stock is 20 dinghies. As you would expect, dinghy sales are very seasonal; thus, all of Le Chantier Naval de Toulouse's sales are made during a four-month period (late spring to summer). What should the average inventory be in the boating season? How many orders should the firm place this year?

Approach: The key to this problem is to recognise that it is an application of the EOQ formula and that the sales period is four months and not one year. Recognising these facts, we can apply Equation (14.5) to solve for EOQ.

Solution:

$$EOQ = \sqrt{\frac{2 \times €500 \times 1500}{€100}} = 122.47 \text{ or } 123 \text{ dinghies per order}$$

Le Chantier Naval de Toulouse should order 123 dinghies per order and, over the four-month boating season, the firm should place 12 orders $(1500/122.47 = 12.25)$. The average inventory will then be about 81 dinghies $(122.47 - 0)/2 + 20 = 81.24)$ during the boating season.

Just-in-Time Inventory Management

An important development in the management of raw material inventories is *just-in-time inventory management*, pioneered by Japanese firms such as the Toyota Motor Company, and adopted by a number of large companies around the world. Today, much of the auto industry and many other manufacturing companies have moved to just-in-time or nearly just-in-time supply delivery. In this system, based on the manufacturer's day-by-day or even hour-by-hour needs, suppliers deliver raw materials 'just in time' for them to be used on the production line. A firm using a just-in-time system has essentially no raw material inventory costs and no risk of obsolescence or loss to theft. On the downside, the firm is heavily dependent on its suppliers. If a supplier fails to make the needed deliveries, then production shuts down. Where such systems work, they can reduce the working capital requirements dramatically.

Before You Go On

1. What is the economic order quantity model?
2. Why can investments in inventories be costly?

CASH MANAGEMENT AND BUDGETING

Learning Objective 6

Define cash collection time, discuss how a firm can minimise this time and be able to compute the cash collection costs and benefits of a cash collection account.

Next, we turn to the cash component of working capital. Although cash (and many demand deposits) produce no interest, firms still hold positive cash balances for a variety of reasons. We discuss those reasons next and then cover the issue of cash collection.

Reasons for Holding Cash

There are two main reasons for holding cash. The first is to facilitate transactions. Operational activities usually require cash. Cash collections from customers generate cash inflows, whereas payments for raw materials and payments to employees and to the government generate cash outflows. Because these cash inflows and outflows often do not occur simultaneously, firms hold positive cash balances to facilitate transactions. If a firm runs out of cash, it might have to sell some of its other investments or borrow, either of which will result in the firm incurring transaction costs.

The second reason for holding cash is that banks often require firms to hold minimum cash balances as partial compensation for the loans or other services the banks provide. These are known as **compensating balances**. That is, the bank is, in part, *compensated* for the loans or services it provides by getting the use of the deposits interest free.

> ## Compensating balances
>
> bank balances that firms must maintain to at least partially compensate banks for loans or services rendered

In deciding how much cash to keep on hand, managers concentrate on the transaction motive. Once an appropriate amount is determined, the manager checks to see if the amount also satisfies any compensating balance requirements set by the bank. If it does, then all is well. If not, then the firm must hold the minimum compensating balance. The compensating balance thus forms a lower boundary on the amount of cash a firm will hold.

Cash Collection

The way in which a firm collects payments affects its cash needs. **Collection time**, or **float**, is the time between the point in time when a customer makes a payment and when the cash becomes available to the firm. Collection time can be broken down into three components. First is delivery or mailing time. When a customer mails a payment, it may take several days before that payment arrives at the firm. Second is processing delay. Once the payment is received, it must be opened, examined, accounted for and deposited at the firm's bank. Finally, there is a delay between the time of the deposit and the time the cash is available for withdrawal. For example, if the customer writes

a cheque on a foreign bank, the delay may be several days while the availability of the funds is confirmed.[6]

> ## Collection time (float)
>
> the time between when a customer makes a payment and when the cash becomes available to the firm

Different forms of payment have different cash collection cycles. Cash or debit card payments made at the point of sale are the simplest, with a cash collection time of zero. If a firm takes cheques or credit cards at the point of sale, then mailing time is eliminated but processing and availability delays will still exist. Anything the firm can do to reduce the total collection time will reduce its total cash requirements, so firms spend time evaluating their cash collection procedures. A firm can reduce its total cash collection time in several ways but, as always, the firm's ability to implement them will vary according to its industry and its customers' expectations. For instance, a few restaurants manage to accept only cash, but most find that such a policy hurts their sales.

One way a firm can reduce its collection time is through the use of concentration accounts or lock boxes. A *lock box* system allows geographically dispersed customers to send their payments to a post office box address close to them. For example, customers in Finland would send payments to a Helsinki post office box and Swedish customers to a Stockholm post office box. The firm's bank then empties the box daily (or even several times a day) and processes the payments. A *concentration account* system replaces the post office box with a local branch of the company. The local branch receives the payments by post, processes them and makes the deposits. With either system, the time in the post is reduced because the mail has less distance to travel and the availability delay is often reduced because the cheques are more often drawn on local banks.

Another popular means of reducing cash collection time is through the use of electronic funds transfers. Electronic payments reduce cash collection time in every phase. First, time in the post is eliminated. Second, processing time is reduced or eliminated, since no data entry is necessary.

Finally, there is little or no delay in funds availability. From the firm's point of view, electronic funds transfer offers a perfect solution. For that reason, many firms encourage (and increasingly require) their customers pay in this way.

How much is it worth to reduce cash collection time? If a firm that has daily sales of €1 million can reduce its total collection time by even one day, then at 5% interest per year, the savings amount to about €50 000 per year. This is not a huge amount to a firm with annual sales of €365 million, but it is certainly worth consideration.

Learning by Doing Application 14.4

When is a Lock Box Worth Keeping?

Problem: Siegel Elektronik GmbH is evaluating whether a lock box it is currently using is worth keeping. Management acknowledges that the lock box reduces the mail float by 1.5 days and processing time by half a day. The remittances average €100 000 a day for Siegel Elektronik, with the average cheque being €1000. The bank charges €0.30 per processed cheque. Assume that there are 270 business days in a year and that it costs Siegel Elektronik 5% to finance accounts receivable. Should Siegel Elektronik keep the lock box?

Approach: To solve this problem, we first calculate how much Siegel Elektronik is paying the bank per year to manage the lock box. Then we can calculate the savings the lock box provides to Siegel Elektronik by reducing the processing and mail floats.

Solution: The average number of cheques processed per day is:

Average daily remittance/Average cheque size
$$= \frac{€100\,000}{€1000} = 100$$

Thus, the cost of a lock box is:

100 cheques × €0.30 per cheque × 270 days
= €8100

Next we calculate the savings the lock box provides:

€100 000/day × (1.5 day + 0.5 day) × 0.05
= €10 000

The annual savings are therefore €10 000, which is more than the €8100 cost of the lock box. Siegel Elektronik should keep the lock box.

Before You Go On

1. What is float?
2. Explain how a cash collection account (lock box) is used.

FINANCING WORKING CAPITAL

Learning Objective 7

Identify three current asset-financing strategies and discuss the main sources of short-term financing.

So far, we have been discussing the investment side of working capital management. As with other assets, working capital must be funded in some way. Financial managers can finance working capital with short-term debt, long-term debt, equity or a mixture of all three. We next explore the main strategies used by financial managers to finance working capital, along with their benefits and costs.

Strategies for Financing Working Capital

In order to understand fully the strategies that might be used to finance working capital, it is important to recognise that some working capital needs are short term in nature and others are long term, or permanent, in nature. As suggested earlier, the amount of working capital at a firm tends to fluctuate over time as its sales rise and fall with the business season. For example, a toy company might build up finished goods inventories in the spring and summer as it prepares to ship its products to retailers in the early autumn in time for Christmas. Working capital will remain high through the autumn as finished goods inventories are sold and converted into accounts receivable but will then decline in January as receivables are collected – at which point the seasonal pattern begins again. These fluctuations reflect *seasonal working capital needs*.

Even during the slowest part of the year, the typical firm will hold some inventory, have some outstanding accounts receivable and have some cash and prepaid expenses. This minimum level of working capital can be viewed as **permanent working capital** in the sense that it reflects a level of working capital that will always be on the firm's books.

Permanent working capital

the minimum level of working capital that a firm will always have on its books

Exhibit 14.7 shows three basic strategies that a firm can follow to finance its working capital and fixed assets. The wavy line in each figure indicates the total financing needed for (1) seasonal working capital needs and (2) permanent working capital and fixed assets. The wavy line is upward sloping because we are assuming that the business represented in the figures is a going concern that is growing over time. As businesses grow, they need more working capital as well as more long-term productive assets. We next discuss each of the three strategies illustrated in the exhibit.

The **maturity matching strategy** is shown in Figure A of Exhibit 14.7. Here, all seasonal working capital needs are funded with short-term borrowings. As the level of sales varies seasonally, short-term borrowings fluctuate with the level of seasonal working capital. Furthermore, all permanent working capital and fixed assets are funded with long-term financing. The principle underlying this strategy is very intuitive: the maturity of a liability should match the maturity of the asset that it funds. The 'matching of maturities' is one of the most basic techniques used by financial managers to reduce risk when financing assets.

Maturity matching strategy

financing strategy that matches the maturities of liabilities and assets

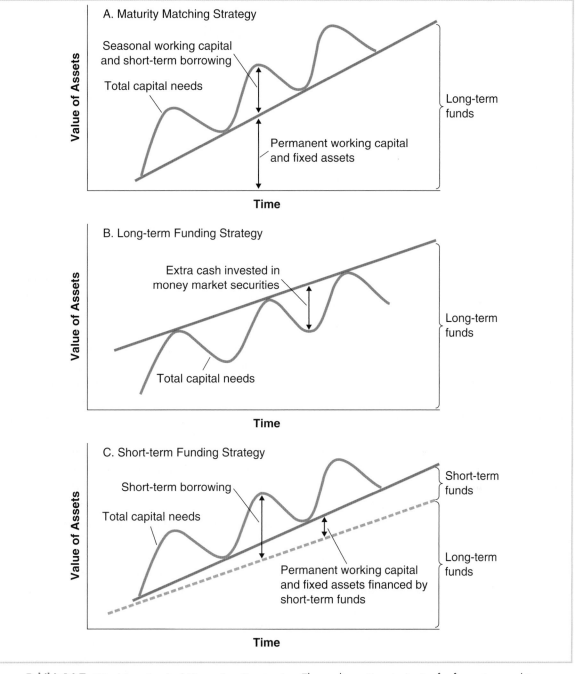

Exhibit 14.7: Working Capital Financing Strategies Three alternative strategies for financing working capital and fixed assets are (1) a maturity matching strategy, which matches the maturities of assets and the sources of funding; (2) a long-term funding strategy, which relies on long-term debt to finance both working capital and fixed assets; and (3) the short-term funding strategy, which uses short-term debt to finance all seasonal working capital needs and a portion of permanent working capital and fixed assets.

The **long-term funding strategy** is shown in Figure B of the exhibit. This strategy relies on long-term debt and equity to finance fixed assets, permanent working capital and seasonal working capital. As shown, when the need for working capital is at its peak, it is funded entirely by long-term funds. As the need for working capital diminishes over the seasonal cycle and cash becomes available, the excess cash is invested in short-term money market instruments to earn interest until the funds are needed again. This strategy reduces the risk of funding current assets; there is less need to worry about refinancing assets, since all funding is long term.

> ### Long-term funding strategy
>
> financing strategy that relies on long-term debt and equity to finance both fixed assets and working capital

Figure C shows a **short-term funding strategy**, whereby all seasonal working capital and a portion of the permanent working capital and fixed assets are funded with short-term debt. The benefit of using this strategy is that it can take advantage of an upward-sloping yield curve and lower a firm's overall cost of funding. Recall from Chapter 8 that yield curves are typically upward sloping, which means that short-term borrowing costs are lower than long-term rates. The downside to this strategy is that a portion of a firm's long-term assets must be periodically refinanced over their working lives, which can pose a significant refunding risk.[7] Also, as discussed in Chapter 8, the yield curve can become inverted, making short-term funds more expensive than long-term funds.

> ### Short-term funding strategy
>
> financing strategy that relies on short-term debt to finance all seasonal working capital and a portion of permanent working capital and fixed assets

Financing Working Capital in Practice

Each working capital funding strategy has its costs and benefits. A financial manager will typically use some variation of one of the strategies discussed here to achieve his or her risk and return objectives.

Matching Maturities

Many financial managers try to match the maturities of assets and liabilities when funding the firm. That is, short-term assets are funded with short-term financing and long-term assets are funded with long-term financing. As suggested in the discussion of the three financing strategies, managers have very sound reasons for matching assets and liabilities.

Suppose a firm buys a manufacturing plant with an estimated economic life of 15 years. If short-term rates are lower than long-term rates, short-term financing can look like a good deal. However, if the firm finances the project with short-term funds and interest rates increase substantially, the firm could find a significant rise in its borrowing costs when it refinances short-term debt at the new market interest rate. If the firm cannot pay the rising interest costs, it could face bankruptcy. Even without the firm becoming insolvent, the project NPV could turn negative. Managers therefore like to finance capital assets and other long-term assets with long-term debt or equity to lock in the cost of funds for the life of the project and to eliminate the risk associated with periodically refinancing assets.

When they finance seasonal working capital requirements for inventories and receivables, most financial managers also prefer to match maturities of assets and liabilities by financing these investments with short-term debt. As a firm's sales rise and fall seasonally, a financial manager can expand or contract working capital by borrowing short term when more assets are needed and, as cash becomes available, using it to pay off the short-term obligations as they mature.

Permanent Working Capital

Many financial managers prefer to fund permanent working capital with long-term funds, as shown in

Figure A of Exhibit 14.7. They prefer to do this in order to limit the risks associated with a short-term financing strategy. To the extent that permanent working capital is financed with long-term funds, the ability of the firm to finance this minimum level of working capital is not subject to short-term credit market conditions.

As illustrated in Figure C of Exhibit 14.7, other managers use short-term debt to finance at least some permanent working capital requirements. These managers subject their firms to more risk in the hope that they will realise higher returns.

Sources of Short-Term Financing

Now that we have discussed working capital financing strategies, we will turn our attention to the most important types of short-term financing instruments used in practice: accounts payable, bank loans and commercial paper.

Accounts Payable (Trade Credit)

Accounts payable (trade credit) deserves special attention because it comprises a large portion of the current liabilities of many businesses. For example, accounts payable constitute about 35% of total current liabilities at publicly traded manufacturing firms. Accounts payable arise, of course, when managers do not pay for purchases with cash on delivery but instead carry the amount owed as an account payable. If a firm orders €1000 of a certain raw material daily and the supplier extends a 30-day credit policy, the firm will be receiving €30 000 of financing from this supplier in the form of trade credit.

We already discussed the cost of extending credit and offering discounts from the seller's point of view. We also discussed from a buyer's point of view that, if a discount is offered, the buyer needs to figure out whether it makes financial sense to pay early and take advantage of the discount or to wait and pay in full when the account is due. Taking advantage of a discount reduces cost of goods sold but it also increases the amount of financing that must be raised from other sources.

Short-Term Bank Loans

Short-term bank loans are also relatively important financing tools. They account for about 20% of total current liabilities for publicly traded manufacturing firms. When securing a loan, the firm and the bank negotiate the amount, the maturity and the interest rate, as well as any binding covenants that might be included. After an agreement is reached, both parties sign the debt contract, which is sometimes referred to as a *promissory note*.

The firm may also have additional borrowing capacity with a bank through a line of credit. Lines of credit are advantageous because they provide easy access to additional financing without requiring a commitment to borrow unnecessary amounts. Lines of credit can be informal or formal.

An **uncommitted line of credit** is a *non-binding agreement* between the firm and the bank, allowing the firm to borrow up to an agreed-upon limit. For example, an uncommitted line of credit for €1 million for three years allows the firm to borrow up to €1 million within the three-year period. If it borrows €600 000 the first year, it will still have a limit of €400 000 for the remaining two years. The interest rate on an uncommitted credit line depends on the borrower's credit standing and the willingness of the bank to make the advance when requested. In exchange for providing the line of credit, a bank may require that the firm hold a compensating balance.

> **Uncommitted line of credit**
>
> a non-binding agreement between a bank and a firm under which the firm can borrow an amount of money up to an agreed-on limit

We mentioned compensating balances earlier as a possible reason for firms to hold cash. In exchange for providing a line of credit (or other loan or service), a bank may require a firm to maintain a compensating balance. When required for a loan, a compensating balance represents an implicit cost that must be included in an analysis for the cost of the loan. If a bank requires a compensating balance as a condition for making a loan, the firm must keep a predetermined percentage of the loan amount in a money market account, which can pay negligible interest. If the rate of return is low, the firm is subject to opportunity costs, which make the effective borrowing rate higher than the percentage stated in the promissory note. For example, suppose the Banque Confédère du Luxembourg (BCL) requires borrowers to hold a 10% compensating balance in an account that pays no interest. If Zortac SA borrows €120 000 from BCL at a 9% stated rate, it will have to maintain a compensating balance of 0.1 × €120 000 = €12 000. Because Zortac cannot use this money, the effective amount borrowed is equal to only €120 000 − €12 000 = €108 000. However, since Zortac must still pay interest on the entire loan amount, the firm's interest expense is 0.09 × €120 000 = €10 800 and the effective rate on the loan is €10 800/€108 000 = 0.1, or 10%, rather than 9%.

A **committed line of credit** is also known as *revolving credit*. Under this type of agreement, the bank has a *contractual obligation* to lend funds to the firm up to a preset limit. In exchange, the firm pays a commitment fee, in addition to the interest expense on the amount borrowed. The commitment fee is usually a percentage of the unused portion of the entire credit line.

Committed line of credit

a contractual agreement between a bank and a firm under which the bank has a legal obligation to lend funds to the firm up to a preset limit

We can illustrate the mechanics of a committed credit line with an example. Higgins Ltd has a formal credit line of £20 million for five years with Barclays Bank. The interest rate on the loan is 6%. Under the agreement, Higgins has to pay 75 basis points (0.75%) on the unused amount as the yearly fee. If Higgins does not borrow at all, it will still have to pay Barclays 0.0075 × £20 000 000 =

£150 000 for each year of the agreement. Suppose Higgins borrows £4 million the first day of the agreement. Then the fee drops to 0.0075 × (£20 000 000 − £4 000 000) = £120 000. Of course, Higgins will also have to pay an annual interest expense of 0.06 × £4 000 000 = £240 000. The effective interest rate on the loan for the first year is (£240 000 + £120 000)/£4 000 000 = 0.09, or 9%.

Another important loan characteristic is whether the loan is secured or unsecured. If the firm backs the loan with an asset, called *collateral*, the loan is *secured*; otherwise, the loan is *unsecured*. Firms often use current assets such as inventories or accounts receivable as collateral when borrowing short term. These types of working capital tend to be highly liquid and therefore are attractive as collateral to lenders. Secured loans allow the borrower to borrow at a lower interest rate, all else being equal. The reason is, of course, that if the borrower defaults, the lender can liquidate the collateral and use the cash generated from their sale to pay off at least part of the loan. The more valuable and liquid the asset pledged as security, the lower the interest rate on the loan.

Commercial Paper

Commercial paper is short-term debt in the form of promissory notes issued by large, financially secure firms with high credit ratings. The number of firms able to make use of the commercial paper market varies depending on the state of the economy. When market conditions and the economy are weak, firms of lesser credit quality are unable to borrow in the commercial paper market.

Commercial paper

short-term debt in the form of promissory notes issued by large, financially secure firms with high credit ratings

Most large companies sell commercial paper on a regular basis. Some large firms, such as Royal Dutch Shell, transact in the market on a daily basis – they issue commercial paper as a source of funds. A firm's demand for commercial paper financing depends on the commercial paper interest rate relative to other borrowing rates and the firm's need for short-term funds at the time.

In Europe, the market for commercial paper is fragmented between domestic financial markets and a cross-border market for Euro Commercial Paper. The buyers of commercial paper are businesses such as banks, insurance companies, mutual funds and other companies. The maturity of commercial paper ranges from one day to a year, with most issues having a maturity of between three and six months. Commercial paper does not have an active secondary market, as nearly all investors hold commercial paper to maturity.

Commercial paper is not secured, which means that the lender does not have a claim on any specific assets of the issuer in the event of default. However, most commercial paper is backed by a credit line from a commercial bank. If the company does not have the money to pay off the paper at maturity, the bank will pay it. Therefore, the default rate on commercial paper is very low, usually resulting in an interest rate that is lower than the rate a bank would charge on a direct loan.

Accounts Receivable Financing

For small and medium-sized businesses, accounts receivable financing is an important source of funds. Accounts receivable can be financed in two ways. First, a company can secure a bank loan by pledging (assigning) the firm's accounts receivable as security. Then, if the firm fails to pay the bank loan, the bank can collect the cash shortfall from the receivables as they come due. If for some reason the assigned receivables fail to yield enough cash to pay off the bank loan, the firm is still legally liable to pay the remaining bank loan. During the pledging process, the company retains ownership of the accounts receivable.

Second, a company can *sell* the receivables to a **factor** at a discount. A factor is an individual or a financial institution, such as a bank or a business finance company, that buys accounts receivable

without recourse. 'Without recourse' means that once the receivables are sold, the factor bears all of the risk of collecting the money due from the receivables. The firm that sells the receivables has no further legal obligation to the factor. The advantage of selling receivables to a factor is that the firm gets money from the receivables immediately rather than waiting for them to be paid as they come due. Factoring is just a specialised type of financing. The 'discount' is the factor's compensation (in the trade, it is called a 'haircut'), which typically ranges from 2% to 5% of the face value of the receivable sold.

> ### Factor
>
> an individual or a financial institution, such as a bank or a business finance company, that buys accounts receivable without recourse

In computing the cost of financing from a factor, it is helpful to analyse the transaction on a per-unit of currency basis. For example, suppose that a firm sells its accounts receivable to a factor for a 2% discount and that the average collection period is one month. This means that for every euro of receivables sold to the factor today, the firm receives 98 cents today; one month later, the factor collects the one-euro receivable. The cost to the firm of receiving the euro one month earlier is 2 cents (€1 − €0.98). The monthly cost in percentage terms is €2/€98 = 0.0204, or 2.04%. This translates to a simple annual rate of 24.48% (12 × 2.04) and, from Equation (6.7), an effective annual rate (EAR) of:

$$
\begin{aligned}
\text{EAR} &= \left(1 + \frac{\text{Quoted interest rate}}{m}\right)^m - 1 \\
&= (1 + 0.0204)^{12} - 1 \\
&= (1.0204)^{12} - 1 = 0.2742, \text{ or } 27.42\%
\end{aligned}
$$

This is the loan-equivalent cost of obtaining financing from the factor.[8]

Effective Annual Interest Rate for Financing from a Factor

Problem: The Kirby Dairy Products Company based in County Cork, Ireland, sells €100 000 of its accounts receivable to a factor at a 5% discount. The firm's average collection period is one month. What is the simple annual cost of the financing provided by the factor and what is the effective annual loan-equivalent cost?

Approach: We must first compute the cost on a per-euro basis, which will enable us to compute the monthly cost in percentage terms. The key to solving the problem, however, is to realise that we must then calculate the EAR by using Equation (6.7), in order to account for the effect of compounding and therefore the true economic cost.

Solution: The discount is 5%, and the average collection period is one month. Therefore, in one month, the factor should be able to collect one euro for every 95 cents paid today. The euro cost to the company of receiving cash one month earlier is 5 cents (€1 × 0.05), and the amount received is 95 cents (€1 × 0.95). Thus, the monthly cost is $5/95 = 0.0526$, or 5.26%. Plugging the appropriate values into Equation (6.7) and solving for the EAR yields:

$$EAR = \left(1 + \frac{\text{Quoted interest rate}}{m}\right)^m - 1$$
$$= (1 + 0.0526)^{12} - 1 = (1.0526)^{12} - 1$$
$$= 0.850, \text{ or } 85.0\%$$

The annualised cost of the financing from the factor is 85.06%.

Before You Go On

1. List and briefly describe the three main short-term financing strategies.
2. What are the advantages and disadvantages of short-term financing?
3. Give some examples of sources of short-term financing.

SUMMARY OF LEARNING OBJECTIVES

1. **Define net working capital, discuss the importance of working capital management and be able to compute a firm's net working capital.**

   Net working capital is the difference between current assets and current liabilities. Working capital management refers to the decisions made regarding the use of current assets and how they are financed. The goal of working capital management is to ensure that the firm can continue its day-to-day operations and pay its short-term debt obligations. The computation of net working capital is illustrated.

2. **Define the operating and cash conversion cycles, explain how they are used and be able to compute their values for a firm.**

   The operating cycle is the period starting with the receipt of raw materials and ending with the receipt of cash for finished goods made from those raw materials. It can be divided into two components: (1) days' sales in inventories, which shows how long a firm keeps its inventories before selling them; and (2) days' sales outstanding, which indicates how long it takes on average for the firm to collect its outstanding accounts receivable. Related to the operating cycle is the cash conversion cycle, which is the length of time between the cash outflow for materials and the cash inflow from sales. An additional measure, days' payables outstanding, is required to calculate the cash conversion cycle. Financial managers compute these cycles to help them monitor the efficiency with which working capital is being managed. The computations are illustrated.

3. **Discuss the relative advantages and disadvantages of pursuing (1) flexible and (2) restrictive current asset investment strategies.**

   A flexible strategy involves maintaining relatively high levels of cash, marketable securities and inventories, while a restrictive strategy keeps the levels of current assets relatively low. In general, a flexible strategy is thought to be low risk and low return; its downsides include low returns on current assets, potentially high inventory carrying costs, and the cost of the money necessary to provide liberal credit terms. The restrictive strategy involves higher risk and return, with higher potential financial and operating shortage costs as its major drawbacks.

4. **Explain how accounts receivable are created and managed and be able to compute the cost of trade credit.**

   Accounts receivable are promises of future payment from customers that buy goods or services on credit. The details of trade credit agreements are defined in the terms of sale, which include the due date, the interest rate charged and any discounts for early payment. The terms of sale are affected by the practice in the industry and the creditworthiness of the customer. To manage accounts receivable, a financial manager keeps close track of both days' sales outstanding and the aging schedule, and takes necessary actions to ensure that neither goes outside the range that is acceptable to senior management.

5. **Explain the trade-off between carrying costs and reorder costs and be able to compute the economic order quantity for a firm's inventory orders.**

   The trade-off between carrying costs and reorder costs exists because as the size of a firm's orders for materials increases, the number of orders and total reorder costs decline. At the same time, larger order sizes increase the average inventory size and, therefore, average inventory carrying costs. The economic order quantity (EOQ) is a tool for mathematically finding the combination of the two costs that minimises the firm's total inventories cost. Learning by Doing Application 14.3 offers practice in computing a firm's EOQ.

6. **Define cash collection time, discuss how a firm can minimise this time and be able to compute the economic costs or benefits of a cash collection account.**

   The cash collection time is the time between when a customer makes a payment and when the cash becomes available to the firm. It has three components: (1) delivery or time in the post, (2) processing delay and (3) delay between deposit time and availability. A firm can minimise this time through lock boxes, concentration accounts, electronic funds transfers and other methods. Learning by Doing Application 14.4 concerns the computations necessary to decide whether a cash collection account is worth keeping.

7. **Identify three current asset-financing strategies and discuss the main sources of short-term financing.**

   Three current asset-financing strategies are: (1) the maturity matching strategy, which matches the maturities of assets with the maturities of liabilities; (2) the long-term funding strategy, which finances both seasonal working capital needs and long-term assets with long-term funds; and (3) the short-term funding strategy, which uses short-term debt for both seasonal working capital needs and some permanent working capital and long-term assets. Sources of short-term financing include accounts payable, short-term bank loans, lines of credit and commercial paper.

SUMMARY OF KEY EQUATIONS

Equation	Description	Formula
(14.1)	Operating cycle	Operating cycle $= $ DSO $+$ DSI
(14.2)	Cash conversion cycle	Cash conversion cycle $=$ DSO $+$ DSI $-$ DPO
(14.3)	Cash conversion cycle	Cash conversion cycle $=$ Operating cycle $-$ DSO
(14.4)	Effective annual rate (EAR)	$EAR = \left(1 + \dfrac{\text{Discount}}{\text{Discounted price}}\right)^{365/\text{days credit}} - 1$
(14.5)	Economic order quantity (EOQ)	$EOQ = \sqrt{\dfrac{2 \times \text{Reorder cost} \times \text{Sales per period}}{\text{Carrying costs}}}$

SELF-STUDY PROBLEMS

14.1. You are provided with the following working capital information for La Corniche Bleu SA:

Account	Beginning Balance	Ending Balance
Inventories	€ 2 600	€2 890
Accounts receivable	€ 3 222	€2 800
Accounts payable	€ 2 500	€2 670
Net sales	€24 589	
Cost of goods sold	€19 630	

If all sales are made on credit, what are the firm's operating and cash conversion cycles?

14.2. Productos Cosméticos de Leon calculates that its operating cycle for last year was 76 days. The company had €230 000 in its accounts receivable account and sales of €1.92 million. Approximately how many days does it take from the time raw materials are received at Productos Cosméticos until the finished products they are used to produce are sold?

14.3. Below is a partial aging of accounts receivable for Bitar Tagdækning Tjenester. Fill in the rest of the information and determine its days' sales outstanding. How does it compare to the industry average of 40 days?

Age of Account (days)	Value of Account	% of Total Account
0–10	DKr 211 000	
11–30	120 360	
31–45	103 220	
46–60	72 800	
Over 60	23 740	
Total	DKr 531 120	

14.4. By obtaining a lock box, Industriale Nizam S. p.A. was able to reduce its total cash collection time by two days. The firm has annual sales of €570 000 and can earn 4.75% annual interest. Assuming that the lock box costs €50 per year, calculate the savings that can be attributed to the lock box.

14.5. Fabricación Particular de San Rafael SA is looking to borrow €250 000 from its bank at an APR of 8.5%. The bank requires its customers to maintain a 10% compensating balance. What is the effective interest rate on this bank loan?

SOLUTIONS TO SELF-STUDY PROBLEMS

14.1. We calculate the operating and cash conversion cycles for La Corniche Bleu as follows:

Inventories = €2890
Accounts receivable = €2800
Accounts payable = €2670
Net sales = €24 589
Cost of goods sold = €19 630

$$DSO = \frac{Accounts\ receivables}{Cost\ of\ sales/365} = \frac{€2800}{€24\,589/365}$$
$$= 41.6\ days$$

$$DSI = \frac{Inventories}{COGS/365} = \frac{€2890}{€19\,630/365} = 53.7\ days$$

$$DPO = \frac{Accounts\ payable}{COGS/365} = \frac{€2670}{€19\,630/365}$$
$$= 49.6\ days$$

Operating cycle = DSO + DSI
$$= 41.6 + 53.7$$
$$= 95.3\ days$$

Cash conversion cycle = DSO + DSI − DPO
$$= 41.6 + 53.7 − 49.6$$
$$= 45.7\ days$$

14.2. The following information describes Productos Cosméticos de Leon's inventory management:

Operating cycle = 76 days
Accounts receivable = €230 000
Net sales = €1 920 000

$$DSO = \frac{Accounts\ receivable}{Credit\ sales/365} = \frac{€230\,000}{€1\,920\,000/365}$$
$$= 43.7\ days$$

Operating cycle = DSO + DSI
$$76 = 43.7 + DSI$$
$$DSI = 32.3\ days$$

Productos Cosméticos de Leon takes 32.3 days to move inventories through as finished products.

14.3. The missing information for Bitar Tagdækning Tjenester is as follows:

Bitar Tagdækning Tjenester

Age of Account (days)	Value of Account	% of Total Account
0–10	DKr 211 000	39.7%
11–30	120 360	22.7
31–45	103 220	19.4
46–60	72 800	13.7
Over 60	23 740	4.5
Total	DKr 531 120	100.0%

Effective DSO = (0.397 × 10) + (0.227 × 30)
$$+ (0.194 × 45) + (0.137 × 60)$$
$$+ (0.045 × 365)$$
$$= 3.97 + 6.81 + 8.73 + 8.22 + 16.43$$
$$= 44.2\ days$$

Bitar takes about 4 days more than the industry average of 40 to collect on its receivables. The firm should focus collection efforts on all credit sales that take 60 days or more to collect.

14.4. The following information applies to Industriale Nizam's lock box:
Annual sales = €570 000
Annual interest rate = 4.75%
Collection time saved = 2 days

$$Average\ daily\ sales = \frac{€570\,000}{365} = €1561.36$$

Savings = (€1561.64 × 0.0475 × 2) − €50
$$= €98.36$$

The firm saves €98.36 each year by using the lock box.

14.5. Fabricación Particular de San Rafael's loan information is as follows:

Amount to be borrowed = €250 000
Stated annual interest rate = 8.5%
Compensating balance = 10%
Amount deposited as compensating balance
= €250 000 × 0.10 = €25 000
Effective borrowing amount equal to
€250 000 − €25 000 = €225 000

Interest expense = €250 000 × 0.085 =
€21 250

$$\text{Effective interest rate} = \frac{€21\,250}{€225\,000} = 9.44\%$$

By setting aside a compensating balance
of 10% or €25 000 on the loan, the firm
increases its interest rate effectively to 9.44%.

CRITICAL THINKING QUESTIONS

14.1. What factors must a financial manager consider when making decisions about accounts receivable?

14.2. List some of the working capital management characteristics you would expect to see in a diversified food company following just-in-time inventory practices, such as Danone.

14.3. What costs would a firm following a flexible current asset investment strategy worry about, and why?

14.4. How are customers and suppliers affected by a firm's working capital management decisions?

14.5. A beverage bottling company in Uppsala has days' sales outstanding of 23.7 days. Is this good? Explain.

14.6. How do the following circumstances affect the cash conversion cycle: (a) favourable credit terms allow the firm to pay its accounts payable more slowly, (b) inventory turnover increases, (c) accounts receivable turnover decreases?

14.7. What are some industries in which the use of lock boxes would especially benefit companies? Explain.

14.8. Suppose you are a financial manager at a big firm and you expect the interest rates to decline in the near future. What current asset investment strategy would you recommend that the company pursue?

14.9. Why is commercial paper available only to the most creditworthy companies?

14.10. Explain what a negative cash conversion cycle means.

QUESTIONS AND PROBLEMS

Basic

14.1. **Cash conversion cycle:** Wolfgang's Masonry estimates that it takes the company 27 days on average to pay off its suppliers. It also knows that it has days' sales in inventory of 64 days and days' sales outstanding of 32 days. How does Wolfgang's cash conversion cycle compare with the industry average of 75 days?

14.2. **Cash conversion cycle:** Nord Fabrikat AS found that during the last year, it took 47 days to pay off its suppliers, while it took 63 days to collect its receivables. The company's days' sales in inventory was 49 days. What is Nord Fabrikat's cash conversion cycle?

14.3. **Cash conversion cycle:** Devon Automotive estimates that it takes the company about 62 days to collect cash from customers on finished goods from the day it receives raw materials and it takes about 65 days to pay its suppliers. What is the company's cash conversion cycle? Interpret your answer.

14.4. Operating cycle: Le Boulanger Souriant distributes its products to more than 75 restaurants and delis. The company's collection period is 27 days and it keeps its inventories for four days. What is Le Boulanger Souriant's operating cycle?

14.5. Operating cycle: Technik NetSpeed GmbH is a telecoms component manufacturer. The firm typically has a collection period of 44 days and days' sales in inventory of 29 days. What is Technik NetSpeed's operating cycle?

14.6. Cost of trade credit: Sybex S.p.A. sells its goods with terms of 2/10 EOM, net 30. What is the implicit cost of the trade credit?

14.7. Cost of trade credit: Juggs SA sells its goods with terms of 4/10 EOM, net 60. What is the implicit cost of the trade credit?

14.8. Lock box: Rosenthal Design has daily sales of €59 000. The financial management team determined that a lock box would reduce the collection time by 1.6 days. Assuming the company can earn 5.2% interest per year, what are the savings from the lock box?

14.9. Lock box: Pacific Traders has annual sales of A$1 895 000. The firm's financial manager has determined that using a lock box will reduce collection time by 2.3 days. If the firm's opportunity cost on savings is 5.25%, what are the savings from using the lock box?

14.10. Effective interest rate: La Banque du Midi requires borrowers to keep an 8% compensating balance. Bijoux Gorman borrows €340 000 at a 7% stated APR. What is the effective interest rate on the loan?

14.11. Effective interest rate: Construcción Goya SA borrowed €1.75 million at an APR of 10.2%. The loan called for a compensating balance of 12%. What is the effective interest rate on the loan?

14.12. Unconditional line of credit: Cosmetici Donato S.p.A. is setting up a line of credit at its bank for €5 million for up to two years. The loan rate is 5.875% and calls for an annual fee of 40 basis points on any unused balance for the year. If the firm borrows €2 million on the day the loan agreement was signed, what is the firm's effective rate?

Intermediate

14.13. Cash conversion cycle: Your boss asks you to compute the company's cash conversion cycle. Looking at the financial statements, you see that the average for the inventories for the year was €26 300, accounts receivable were €17 900 and accounts payable were €15 100. You also see that the company had sales of €154 000 and that cost of goods sold was €122 000. Interpret your firm's cash conversion cycle.

14.14. Cash conversion cycle: Blackwell Automotive plc reported the following information for the last fiscal year.

Blackwell Automotive plc

Assets	As of 3/31/2008	Liabilities and Equity	
Inventories	€212 444		
Accounts receivable	141 258	Borrowings	€21 115
Cash and financial assets available for sale	23 015	Accounts payable and accruals	163 257
Other current assets	11 223		
Total current assets	€387 940	Total current liabilities	€184 372
Net sales	€912 332		
Cost of goods sold	547 400		

Calculate the firm's cash conversion cycle and operating cycle.

14.15. Cash conversion cycle: Hydro-Technologie Noordzee BV has net sales of €13 million and 75% of these are credit sales. Its cost of goods sold is 65% of annual sales. The firm's cash conversion cycle is 41.3 days. The inventories balance at the firm is €1 817 344, while its accounts payable balance is €2 171 690. What is the firm's accounts receivable balance?

14.16. Cash conversion cycle: Karolin Handwerk GmbH has net sales of €4.23 million with 50% being credit sales. Its cost of goods sold is €2.54 million. The firm's cash conversion cycle is 47.9 days and its operating cycle is 86.3 days. What is the firm's accounts payable?

14.17. Operating cycle: Aviva Tech's operating cycle is 81 days. Its inventories level was at €134 000 last year and the company had a €1.1 million cost of goods sold. How long does it take Aviva to collect on its receivables?

14.18. Operating cycle: FRÄMST AS has sales of SKr 812 344 and its cost of goods sold is 70% of sales. Assume all sales are credit sales. If the firm's accounts receivable total SKr 113 902 and its operating cycle is 81.6 days, how much inventory does the firm have?

14.19. Economic order quantity: Outback Trucks is one of the largest auto dealers in Alice Springs and sells about 2800 recreational vehicles a year. The cost of placing an order with Outback's supplier is A$800 and the inventory carrying costs are A$150 for each RV. The company likes to maintain safety stock of 12 RVs. Most of its sales are made in either the spring or the autumn. How many orders will the firm need to place this year?

14.20. Effective interest rate: Moda Bella Italia S.p.A. is looking for a loan of €750 000. The bank will provide the loan at an APR of 6.875%. Since the loan calls for a compensating balance, the effective interest

rate on the loan increased to 9.25%. What is the compensating balance on this loan?

14.21. Effective interest rate: Fensterbrett Reparaturen GmbH is borrowing €1.5 million. The loan requires a 10% compensating balance and the effective interest rate on the loan is 9.75%. What is the stated APR on this loan?

14.22. Unconditional line of credit: Gruppa S.p. A. has just set up a formal line of credit of €10 million with Banco Liguria. The line of credit is good for up to five years. The bank will be charging Gruppa an interest rate of 6.25% on the loan and in addition the firm will pay an annual fee of 60 basis points on the unused balance. The firm borrowed €7.5 million on the first day the credit line became available. What is the firm's effective interest rate on this line of credit?

14.23. Unconditional line of credit: Lansdowne Electronics has a formal line of credit of £1 million for up to three years with HND Bank. The interest rate on the loan is 5.3% and, under the agreement, Lansdowne has to pay 50 basis points on the unused amount as the annual fee. Suppose the firm borrows £675 000 the first day of the agreement. What is the fee the company must pay? What is the effective interest rate?

14.24. Lock box: Jennifer Electrical is evaluating whether a lock box it is currently using is worth keeping. Management estimates that the lock box reduces the mail float by 1.8 days and the processing by half a day. The remittances average £50 000 a day for Jennifer Electrical, with the average cheque being for £500. The bank charges £0.34 per processed cheque. Assume that there are 270 business days in a year and that the firm's opportunity cost for these funds is 6%. What will the firm's savings be from using the lock box?

14.25. Lock box: Gouda Tuinproducten BV has just signed up for a lock box. Management expects the lock box to reduce the mail float by 2.1 days. Gouda Tuinproducten's remittances average €37 000 a day and the average cheque is €125. The bank charges €0.37 per processed cheque. Assume that there are 270 business days in a year. What will the firm's savings be from using the lock box if the opportunity cost for these funds is 12%?

14.26. EXCEL® Aging schedule: The Ginseng Company collects 50% of its receivables in 10 days or fewer, 31% in 11 to 30 days, 7% in 31 to 45 days, 7% in 46 to 60 days and 5% in more than 60 days. The company has HK$1 213 000 in accounts receivable. Prepare an aging schedule for The Ginseng Company.

14.27. EXCEL® Aging schedule: A partial aging of accounts receivable for Les Horloges de Limoges is given in the accompanying table. What percentage of receivables are in the 45-day range? Determine the firm's effective days' sales outstanding. How does it compare with the industry average of 35 days?

Age of Account (days)	Value of Account	% of Total Account
10	€ 271 000	
30	€ 145 220	
45		
60	€ 53 980	
75	€ 31 245	
	€589 218	100.0%

14.28. EXCEL® Aging schedule: The Keswick Fencing Company collects 45% of its receivables in 10 days or fewer, 34% in 10 to 30 days, 12% in 31 to 45 days, 5% in 46 to 60 days and 4% in more than 60 days. The company has €937 000 in its accounts receivable account. Prepare an aging schedule for Keswick Fencing.

14.29. Factoring: Zenex GmbH sells €250 000 of its accounts receivable to factors at a 3% discount. The firm's average collection period is 90 days. What is the monetary cost of the factoring service? What is the simple annual interest cost of the factors loan?

14.30. Factoring: A firm sells €100 000 of its accounts receivable to factors at a 2% discount. The firm's average collection period is one month. What is the monetary cost of the factoring service?

Advanced

14.31. What impact would the following actions have on the operating and cash conversion cycles? Would the cycles increase, decrease or remain unchanged?

a. More raw materials than usual are purchased.
b. The company enters into an off-season and inventories build up.
c. Better terms of payment are negotiated with suppliers.
d. The cash discounts offered to customers are decreased.
e. All else remaining the same, an improvement in manufacturing technique decreases the cost of goods sold.

14.32. What impact would the following actions have on the operating and cash conversion cycles? Would the cycles increase, decrease or remain unchanged?

a. Less raw material than usual is purchased.
b. The company encounters unseasonable demand, and inventories decline rapidly.
c. Tighter terms of payment are demanded by suppliers.
d. The cash discounts offered to customers are increased.
e. All else remaining the same, due to labour turnover and poor efficiency, the cost of goods sold increases.

14.33. EXCEL® The Morgan Sports Equipment Company just reported the following figures:

Morgan Sports Equipment Company

Assets		Liabilities and Equity	
Inventories	€1 312 478	Notes payable	2 113 345
Accounts receivable	1 845 113	Accounts payable	€1 721 669
Cash	677 423		
Total current assets	€3 835 014	Total current liabilities	€3 835 014
Net sales	€9 912 332		
Cost of goods sold	€5 947 399		

a. Calculate the firm's days' sales outstanding.

b. What is the firm's days' sales in inventories?

c. What is the firm's days' payables outstanding?

d. What is the firm's operating cycle? How does it compare with the industry average of 72 days?

e. What is the firm's cash conversion cycle? How does it compare with the industry average of 42 days?

14.34. Dynamo du Midi, one of the largest generator dealers in the South of France, sells about 2000 generators a year. The cost of placing an order with its supplier is €750, and the inventory carrying costs are €170 for each generator. Dynamo du Midi likes to maintain safety stock of 15 at all times.

a. What is the firm's EOQ?

b. How many orders will the firm need to place this year?

c. What is the average inventory for the season?

14.35. Tanzaniqe SA sells €200 000 of its accounts receivable to factors at a 5% discount. The firm's average collection period is 90 days.

a. What is the monetary cost of the factoring service?

b. What is the simple annual interest cost of the loan?

c. What is the effective annual interest cost of the loan?

CFA Problems

14.36. A company increasing its credit terms for customers from 1/10, net 30 to 1/10, net 60 will likely experience:

a. an increase in cash on hand;

b. an increase in the average collection period;

c. higher net income;

d. a higher level of uncollectible accounts.

14.37. Suppose a company uses trade credit with the terms of 2/10, net 50. If the company pays their account on the 50th day, the effective borrowing cost of skipping the discount on day 10 is closest to

a. 14.6%

b. 14.9%

c. 15.0%

d. 20.2%.

The following information relates to Problems 14.38–14.40.

Maria Gonzales is evaluating companies in the office supply industry and has compiled the following information:

	20X1		20X2	
Company	Credit Sales	Average Receivables Balance	Credit Sales	Average Receivables Balance
A	€ 5.0 million	€1.0 million	€ 6.0 million	€1.2 million
B	€ 3.0 million	€1.2 million	€ 4.0 million	€1.5 million
C	€ 2.5 million	€0.8 million	€ 3.0 million	€1.0 million
D	€ 0.5 million	€0.1 million	€ 0.6 million	€0.2 million
Industry	€25.0 million	€5.0 million	€28.0 million	€5.4 million

14.38. Which of the companies has the lowest accounts receivable turnover in the year 20X2?
    a. Company A
    b. Company B
    c. Company C
    d. Company D

14.39. The industry average receivables collection period:
    a. increased from 20X1 to 20X2;
    b. decreased from 20X1 to 20X2;
    c. did not change from 20X1 to 20X2;
    d. increased along with the increase in the industry accounts receivable turnover.

14.40. Which of the companies reduced the average time it took to collect on accounts receivable from 20X1 to 20X2?
    a. Company A
    b. Company B
    c. Company C
    d. Company D

SAMPLE TEST PROBLEMS

14.1. If your firm's DSO is 47.3 days and the days' sales in inventories are 39.6 days, what is the firm's operating cycle?

14.2. If Chalet de Megève SA has an operating cycle of 93.4 days and days' payables outstanding of 48.2 days, what is the firm's cash conversion cycle?

14.3. The Irish Ranger Cleaning Company has borrowed €90 000 at a stated APR of 8.5%. The loan calls for a compensating balance of 8%. What is the effective interest rate for this company?

14.4. Rosetta SA has daily sales of €139 000. The financial manager has determined that a lock box would reduce collection time by 2.2 days. Assuming the company can earn 5.5% interest per year, what are the savings from the lock box?

14.5. Exportations Choi SA is setting up a line of credit at its bank for €7.5 million for up to three years. The loan rate is 7.875% and also calls for an annual fee of 50 basis points on any unused balance for the year. If the firm borrows €5 million on the day the loan agreement is signed, what is the firm's effective rate?

ENDNOTES

1. Notice that the *incremental additions to working capital* (Add WC) in Equations (11.2) and (11.4) is a measure of the additional NWC that will be required to fund a project. Equation (11.4) does not include prepaid or accrued expenses because analysts do not typically forecast these items when they estimate Add WC. Prepaid and accrued expenses tend to be difficult to forecast and, to the extent that they do not cancel each other out in the calculation, are often quite small. All interest-bearing debt is also excluded from the calculation in Equation (11.4) because these sources of financing are either assumed to be temporary (for short-term notes) or, for current maturities of long-term debt, are assumed to be refinanced with new long-term debt and are therefore accounted for in the WACC calculation discussed in Chapter 13.

2. There are a variety of possible sanctions that companies can use against late payers. For instance, firms that are consistently late in making payments under trade credit arrangements may end up having to buy goods for cash.

3. It is not usually in the best interest of the firm's shareholders for managers to simply minimise the cash conversion cycle. If it were, firms would stretch out repayment of their payables and not give credit to customers. Of course, this would upset suppliers, lead the firm to incur late-payment penalties and result in lost sales.

4. For simplicity, we will assume all sales are credit sales, unless otherwise stated.

5. In fact, Danone has a current ratio of less than one since current assets are less than current liabilities. The ratio is 0.65 (€4394/€6813).

6. Cross-border payments within the European area are facilitated by the Trans-European Automated Real-time Gross Settlement Express Transfer System (TARGET). This is an interbank payment system for the real-time processing of cross-border transfers throughout the European Union. It is a layered system that includes national real-time gross settlement systems for payments within a country, a cross-border component as well as the European Central Bank's payment mechanism.

7. For some small and medium-sized enterprises, this last strategy may be the only alternative since longer-term financing may be either prohibitively expensive or simply not available. The mismatching of asset maturities to liabilities creates refunding risk and the possibility that the firm can become insolvent. This was a major problem during the 2008–9 credit crunch, where companies that had used short-term funding to finance longer-term assets had their lines of credit withdrawn.

8. Factoring has certain advantages for small and medium-sized businesses since the factor may also act as the collecting agent and therefore the burden of accounts receivable management is transferred to an organisation that can benefit from scale economies. Also, when the financing is without recourse, the factor will absorb any delinquencies. So while the rate may appear high, a comparison needs to be made to the full economic cost of managing trade credit. A disadvantage is that customers may be aware of the factoring arrangement and see this as a sign of financial weakness in the company.

CHAPTER

15

How Firms Raise Capital

In this Chapter:

Bootstrapping

Venture Capital

Initial Public Offering

IPO Pricing and Cost

Seasoned Offerings by a Public Company

Private Markets and Bank Loans

LEARNING OBJECTIVES

1. Explain what is meant by bootstrapping when raising seed finance and why it is important.
2. Explain the role of venture capitalists in the economy and discuss how they reduce their risk when investing in start-up businesses.
3. Discuss the advantages and disadvantages of going public and be able to compute the proceeds from an IPO.
4. Explain why, when underwriting new security offerings, investment bankers prefer that the securities be underpriced and compute the total cost of an IPO.
5. Discuss the difficulties and costs of bringing a rights issue to market and be able to compute the total cost of issuing a rights issue.
6. Explain why a firm that has access to the public markets might elect to raise money through a private placement.
7. Review some advantages of borrowing from a commercial bank rather than selling securities in financial markets, and discuss bank term loans.

When David Wilkes and Paul Chester, two IT experts, founded Occam Systems Limited in February 1998, they had a vision for their company. However, turning their vision of an effortless way for students to arrange their accommodation at university into a profitable business presented a real challenge. First and foremost, they had to persuade universities to buy their student accommodation management software. Then there was the challenge of having

enough finance to build the business. Having invested their own and friends' money in developing the concept and secured their first customers, it was not until 2004 that they obtained venture capital backing. But by the end of 2008, the company had a range of products, such as Room Service 2000 and PAMS, and 55 customers across the UK. The company began to explore the possibilities of going international.

A different problem faced TGE Marine AG, a privately owned company based in Munich, Germany. The company is a leading provider of engineering services for the design and construction of gas carriers and offshore units. The company became independent as the result of a management buyout in 2006 from a much larger parent and, as a result, had a number of private equity investors. Following the buyout, TGE experienced a rapid increase in business – turnover rose

from €48.5 million for the year to end June 2007 to €82.4 million the following year. The company needed new equity to sustain itself and develop the opportunities it had in the expanding market for LPG systems. At the same time, the original backers wanted to realise some of their investment. Consequently, in 2008, the company chose to go public by listing its shares on London's AIM – a special section of the London Stock Exchange designed to facilitate the raising of capital by smaller businesses. In doing so, TGE raised over £23 million of new money by offering shares to the public. At the time of the initial public offering, a number of existing shareholders – including venture capital investors – sold existing shares in the company to outside investors and were thus able to exit their investment at a profit.

While the line of business of Occam Systems is very different from that of TGE Marine, they both had a similar need – namely to obtain capital to develop the business – and they both had recourse to financing from outside sources. This chapter discusses how firms raise capital to finance their business activities.

In the earlier part of this book and in Chapters 10 and 14, in particular, we discussed how firms go about deciding on which investments to make. We now discuss important issues about how firms raise the capital to finance these investments, either through equity or the various forms of debt. You will see that the financing needs and sources of finance for firms will be different depending on their history, size and line of business.

CHAPTER PREVIEW

This chapter is about how firms raise capital so that they can acquire the productive assets needed to grow and remain profitable. To raise money, a firm can borrow, sell equity – or do both. How a firm actually raises capital depends on factors such as where the firm is in its life cycle, its expected cash flows and its risk characteristics. Management's goal is to raise the amount of money necessary to finance the business at the lowest possible cost.

We start the chapter by examining how many new businesses acquire their first equity funding through 'bootstrapping' and the role venture capitalists play in providing equity to help firms get started. Once a firm is successfully launched, the venture capitalists' job is done and they exit the scene. At this juncture, management has a number of other funding options, and we discuss those options in the remainder of the chapter.

We explain how firms sell their first issue of ordinary shares in the public markets and the role of investment banks in completing these sales. First-time equity sales are known as initial public offerings, or IPOs. We then discuss the role that private markets play in funding business firms and describe factors that managers consider when deciding between a public and a private market sale. We close the chapter with a discussion of the importance of commercial banks in providing short-term and intermediate-term financing.

BOOTSTRAPPING

Learning Objective 1

Explain what is meant by bootstrapping when raising seed finance and why it is important.

New business start-ups are an important factor in determining and sustaining long-term economic growth in a state or regional economy. This fact explains why central and local governments have invested heavily in industrial parks, new business incubators and technology and entrepreneurial programmes at universities and colleges. Although governments can do a lot to foster new business development, they generally only take a minor role in providing the equity capital and the initial support that new businesses need during their embryonic start-up phase.

How New Businesses Get Started

Most businesses are started by an entrepreneur who has a vision for a new business or product and a passionate belief in the concept's viability. New businesses are seldom started in large companies. In fact, entrepreneurs regularly leave large companies to start businesses, often using technology developed by these firms. Large companies are efficient at producing goods and services and bringing them to market but they generally do not excel at incubating new businesses.

The entrepreneur often develops his or her ideas and makes them operational through informal discussions with people whom the entrepreneur respects and trusts, such as friends and early investors. These discussions may involve issues related to technology, manufacturing, personnel, marketing and finance. The discussions are far from glamorous. They are usually low-budget affairs that take place around a kitchen table with lots of coffee. The founder and his or her advisers often have a common bond that has drawn them together. They may have graduated from the same university, have worked for the same company or have family ties.

Initial Funding of the Firm

All new firms face the same issue when they start up: finding the money to enable them to test their product or service and build up the business. The process by which many entrepreneurs raise 'seed' money and obtain other resources necessary to start their businesses is often called bootstrapping. The term *bootstrapping* comes from the old expression 'pull yourself up by your bootstraps', which means to accomplish something on your own.

The ways in which entrepreneurs bootstrap their businesses vary greatly. The initial 'seed' money usually comes from the entrepreneur or other founders. Until the business gets started, entrepreneurs often work regular full-time jobs. The job provides some of the cash flow needed to launch the business and to support the entrepreneur's family (although not always in that order of priority). Other cash may come from personal savings, the sale of assets such as cars and boats, borrowing against the family home, loans from family members and friends and loans secured from credit cards. At this stage of the business development, venture capitalists or banks are not normally willing to fund the business.

Where does the seed money go? In most cases, it is spent on developing a prototype of the product or service and a business plan. The deliverables at this stage are whatever it takes to satisfy investors that the new business concept can become a viable business and deserves their financial support.

Business Incubators

Starting a new business is fraught with uncertainty, financial risks and resource issues and the complexities are multiplied with innovative and entrepreneurial businesses due to the complexity of the products and services being offered and the time it takes to fully develop the product. To support and nurture the creation of new businesses many local governments, business agencies and universities provide **business incubators**. For instance as of 2009, there were 300 incubators in the UK supporting over 12 000 enterprises. Most incubators offer premises on a flexible basis with easy entry and easy exit tenancy terms and some common facilities and services. Business incubators – and even pre-incubators – aim to provide a suitable environment and support for the development of a start-up business. By helping with many of the problems that beset new ventures, business incubators help to reduce the risks involved and improve the chances of the business surviving and prospering.

> **Business incubator**
>
> programme designed to accelerate the successful development of entrepreneurial companies by providing a range of business support resources and services

A key element of incubators is the way they offer access to specialised business support and development services. For instance, where the entrepreneur has developed a new product or technology, the business incubator will have access to intellectual property specialists, specialists in the field who can help to market the product or service, overseas partners with access to international markets and even links with major companies who have the resources to develop or licence the innovation.

Some business incubators – such as those attached to universities – may provide finance to prove use of concept or the money needed to adapt the technology for commercial use.[1] Hence, they may be able to contribute to the seed money to get the business off the ground.

Before You Go On

1. Explain bootstrapping, and list the most common sources of seed money.
2. What is the role of a business incubator?

VENTURE CAPITAL

Learning Objective 2

Explain the role of venture capitalists in the economy and discuss how they reduce their risk when investing in start-up businesses.

The bootstrapping period usually lasts no more than one or two years. At some point, the founders will have developed a prototype of the product and a business plan, which they can 'take on the road' to seek venture capital funding to grow the business.[2] For most entrepreneurs, this is a critical time that determines whether they have a viable business concept that will be funded or will disband because of the lack of investor interest.

Venture capitalists are individuals or firms that help new businesses get started and provide much of their early-stage financing. Individual venture capitalists, so-called **business angels** (or **angel investors**), are typically wealthy individuals who

invest their own money in emerging businesses at the very early stages in small deals. In contrast, venture capital firms typically pool money from various sources to invest it in new businesses. Exhibit 15.1 shows the sources of funds for venture capital and private equity firms in Europe. The predominant source came from institutional investors who provided 59.5% in 2009, while endowments and private sources contributed 9.2%. Corporate investors only contributed 6.3% while government agencies provided 11.8%.[3]

Venture capitalists

individuals or firms that invest by purchasing equity in new businesses and often provide the entrepreneurs with business advice

Business angels (angel investors)

wealthy individuals who invest their own money in new ventures

The Venture Capital Industry

Venture capitalists have always operated in Europe in one form or another. The venture capital industry as we know it today emerged in the late 1960s in the United States with the formation of the first venture capital limited partnerships. Following the success of venture capital funds in the United States, the industry has developed along parallel lines in Europe, although the number and size of venture capital firms versus business angels varies a lot between countries. The United Kingdom has the most evolved venture capital industry, but the rest of Europe is fast catching up. The industry is made up of many different firms that tend to specialise in specific business areas or geographical locations, such as information technology, food manufacturing or medical devices. A significant number of venture capital firms focus on high-technology

EXHIBIT 15.1

SOURCES OF VENTURE CAPITAL FUNDING IN EUROPE 2007–2009

	Percent of Total Funding		
	2007	**2008**	**2009**
Capital markets	7.3	1.6	1.9
Corporate investors	2.4	2.9	6.3
Endowments and foundations	1.6	4.5	2.9
Family offices and private individuals	6.1	9.1	7.7
Government agencies	5.3	4.9	11.8
Pension funds and insurance companies	25.6	31.7	23.7
Other asset managers and funds of funds	15.5	20.8	17.4
Banks	11.5	6.7	18.4
Academic institutions	0.3	0.2	0.2
Undisclosed sources	24.4	17.6	9.7
	100.0	100.0	100.0
Amount invested (€ billion)	€82.9	€81.4	€16.1

Source: European Private Equity and Venture Capital Association. Reproduced with permission.

The most important sources of private equity and venture capital funds are institutional investors (pension funds, insurance companies, asset managers, funds of funds and banks), which for 2009 contributed 59.5% of the total. The next most important source is government agencies, which contributed 11.8%. The remaining 28.7% was either undisclosed or provided by the capital markets, corporate investors, endowments and foundations, family offices, private individuals and academic institutions. The amount invested in venture capital and private equity funds in Europe over the three years averaged over €60 billion per year.

investments since these provide high growth opportunities.

WEB

Visit the website of the European Private Equity and Venture Capital Association at: http://www.evca.eu/ for information on venture capital funding.

Why Venture Capital Funding is Different

Venture capital is important because entrepreneurs have only limited access to traditional sources of funding. It is unlikely that a new business will be able to raise loans from banks or other commercial lenders. Even in cases where start-up finance is available, banks normally require security from the borrowers, which may include a personal guarantee or a second mortgage on the individual's property. This tends to limit the amount of funding available to the entrepreneur. In general, there are three reasons why traditional sources of funding do not work for new or emerging businesses:

1. *The high degree of risk involved.* Starting a new business is a risky proposition. The fact is that a large number of new businesses fail, and it is difficult to identify which firms will be successful. Most suppliers of capital, such as banks, pension funds and insurance companies, are averse to undertaking high-risk investments, and much of their risk-averse behaviour is mandated in regulations that restrict their conduct.

2. *Types of productive assets.* Most commercial loans are made to firms that have tangible assets, such as machinery, equipment and physical inventories. Lenders understand the operations of these 'traditional' firms and their inherent risks; thus, they are comfortable making loans to them. New firms whose primary assets are often intangibles, such as patents, new processes or trade secrets, find it difficult to secure financing from traditional lending sources.

3. *Informational asymmetry problems.* Recall from Chapter 1 that information asymmetry arises when one party to a transaction has knowledge that the other party does not. An entrepreneur knows more about his or her company's prospects than a lender does. When dealing with highly specialised technologies or companies emerging in new business areas, most investors do not have the expertise to distinguish between competent and incompetent entrepreneurs. As a result, they are reluctant to invest in these firms.

For these reasons, many investors – such as pension funds, financial and insurance firms, endowment funds and university foundations – find it difficult to participate *directly* in the venture capital market. Instead, they invest in venture capital funds that specialise in identifying attractive investments in new businesses, managing those investments and selling (exiting) them at the appropriate time.

The Venture Capital Funding Cycle

In order to illustrate how venture capitalists help launch new business firms, we next examine the venture capital funding cycle, which is summarised in Exhibit 15.2. You may want to refer to the exhibit from time to time as we discuss the funding cycle.

Starting a New Business – The Tuscan Pizzeria

Suppose you have been in the pizza business for several years and have developed a concept for a high-end pizzeria that you believe has the potential to grow into a pan-European chain. The shops will have an Italian ambiance: a Tuscan façade with a traditional Italian interior. They will feature pizzas with all-natural ingredients that will be baked in wood-burning ovens. The interior will be designed so that customers can watch their pizzas being prepared and baked. The dough is slow rising and, after baking, is good enough to eat without any adornment. In addition, the pizzerias will feature *panzanella* salads of diced raw vegetables and Italian cold cuts, modestly priced wines and sandwiches made from crackly loaves of bread baked in the wood-burning oven. You are planning to name your firm 'The Tuscan Pizzeria'.

The Business Plan

You have spent nearly six months developing a business plan during the evenings and weekends. You received help from a lawyer and consultants at a local business incubator. In addition, several people who have started successful restaurants have read and commented on your plan. As a result of your efforts, your business plan is well thought out and well executed. The business plan describes what you want the business to become, why consumers will find your pizzerias attractive (the *value proposition*), how you are going to accomplish your objectives and the resources you will need. You approached a venture capital firm that

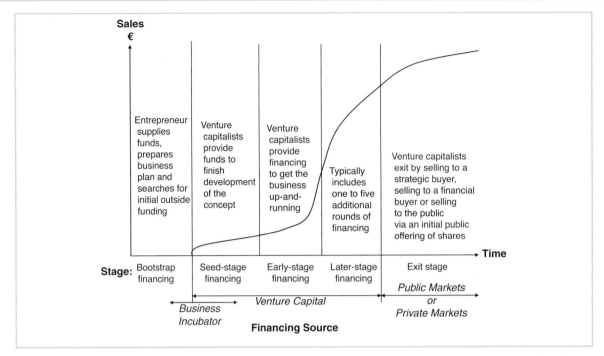

Exhibit 15.2: The Venture Capital Funding Cycle The typical venture capital funding cycle begins when the entrepreneur runs low on bootstrap financing. Venture capitalists then provide equity financing. They will later exit through a private or public sale of their equity stake. The length of time of the cycle is typically five to seven years and only a small percentage of new ventures make it all the way to the public markets.

specialises in the food industry and one of the partners has expressed an interest in taking the proposal forward. This is a positive response because venture capital firms examine many business propositions and follow up on only a few.

First-Stage Financing

After a number of meetings with you and your management team, the venture capital firm agrees to fund the project – but only in stages and for less than the full amount you requested. At this time, the firm is willing to fund €1.6 million of the €6 million you estimate is necessary to build a successful business. In addition, you will have to come up with €400 000 on your own. You plan to do this by using €200 000 of your own money and obtaining the remaining €200 000 from your family and key employees. Financially, you will be stretched to the limit.

How Venture Capitalists Reduce Their Risk

Venture capitalists know that only a handful of new companies will survive to become successful firms. To reduce their risk, they use a number of tactics when they invest in new ventures, including funding the ventures in stages, requiring entrepreneurs to make personal investments, syndicating investments and maintaining in-depth knowledge about the industry in which they specialise.

Staged Funding The key idea behind staged funding is that each funding stage gives the venture capitalist an opportunity to reassess the management team and the firm's financial performance. If the performance does not meet expectations, the venture capitalists can bail out and cut their losses, or, if they still have confidence in the project, they can help management make some changes to the business plan so that the project can proceed. Companies typically go through three to seven funding stages and each stage passed is a vote of confidence for that project. (As you can see in Exhibit 15.2, the latter stages of financing are sometimes called mezzanine financing because these investors did not get in on the ground floor – that is, at the start.)

In our example, the €2 million (€1.6 + €0.4 million) with which you are starting your business makes up the first, or seed-stage, financing. It will be enough to build the prototype pizzeria, make it operational and test the concept's viability in the marketplace. Based on the prototype's success, additional financing (for example, the other €4 million you are seeking) may be allocated to build two additional pizzerias and develop the operating and financial systems needed to operate a chain of Tuscan pizzerias. Later stages of financing will fund further new restaurants.

The venture capitalists' investments give them an equity interest in the company. Typically, this is in the form of preference shares that are convertible into ordinary shares at the discretion of the venture capitalist. Preference shares ensure that the venture capitalists have the most senior claim among the shareholders if the firm fails, and the conversion feature enables the venture capitalists to share in the gains if the business is successful.

Personal Investment Venture capitalists often require an entrepreneur to make a substantial personal investment in the business. In our example, your personal investment of €400 000 confirms that you are confident in the business and highly motivated to make it succeed. Note that it is also unlikely that the venture capitalists will allow you to pay yourself a large salary as manager of the business. They want your financial rewards to come from building a successful business, not from your salary.

Syndication It is a common practice to syndicate seed and early-stage venture capital investments. Syndication occurs when the originating venture capitalist sells a percentage of a deal to other venture capitalists. Syndication reduces risk in

two ways. First, it increases the diversification of the originating venture capitalist's investment portfolio, since other venture capitalists now own a portion of the deal and the originating venture capitalist has less money invested. Second, the willingness of other venture capitalists to share in the investment provides independent corroboration that the investment is a reasonable decision.

In-depth Knowledge Another factor that reduces risk is the venture capitalist's in-depth knowledge of the industry and technology. As we mentioned before, a high degree of specialisation gives the venture capitalist a comparative advantage over other investors or lenders that are generalists.

The Exit Strategy

Venture capitalists are not long-term investors in the companies they back. Typically, they stay with a new firm until it is a successful going concern, which usually takes three to seven years; then they exit by selling their equity in the company.[4] Every venture capital agreement includes provisions identifying who has the authority to make critical decisions concerning the exit process. Those provisions usually include the following: (1) timing (when to exit), (2) the method of exit and (3) what price is acceptable. Exit strategies can be controversial because the venture capitalist and the other owners may not agree on these important details.

There are three principal ways in which venture capital firms exit venture-backed companies: selling to a strategic buyer, selling to a financial buyer and offering shares to the public via an initial public offering.

Strategic Buyer A common way for venture capitalists to exit is to sell the firm's equity to a strategic buyer in the private market. An example of a strategic buyer for the Tuscan Pizzeria would be a restaurant firm such as Groupe Le Duff. Le Duff might view the purchase as a strategic acquisition because one of the company's goals is to expand in the fast-food sector with new brands to complement its existing range of branded outlets. The strategic buyer is looking to create value through synergies between the acquisition and the firm's existing productive assets.

Financial Buyer Sales to financial buyers are one way for venture capitalists to exit a firm. This type of sale occurs when a financial group – often a private equity (leveraged buyout) firm – buys the new firm with the intention of holding it for a period of time, usually three to five years, and then selling it for a higher price. (Private equity firms are discussed in more detail later in this chapter.) The difference between a strategic and a financial buyout is that a financial buyer does not expect to gain from operating or marketing synergies. In a financial buyout, the firm operates independently and the buyer focuses on creating value by improving operations as much as possible. If the firm is performing poorly, the buyer will likely bring in a new management team.

Initial Public Offering A venture capitalist may also exit an investment by taking the company public through an initial public offering (IPO). (We discuss the mechanics of IPOs in the next section.) After an IPO, the venture capitalist will be able to sell their shares over time. Exhibit 15.3 shows the number of IPOs in Europe and the United States between 2004 and 2009. Comparable data for other areas of the world for 2007 to 2009 is also given.

EXHIBIT 15.3
INITIAL PUBLIC OFFERINGS 2004–2009

Europe	2004	2005	2006	2007	2008	2009
Number of initial public offerings[a]	433	573	641	653	247	108
Offering value (€ million)	27 679	51 549	65 715	64 353	9 925	6 233
United States						
Number of initial public offerings[a]	236	205	213	244	43	60
Offering value ($ million)	37 543	27 484	35 910	39 649	16 462	15 477

	Volume[b]			Offering value (€ million)		
	2007	2008	2009	2007	2008	2009
Europe	819	295	126	80 473	13 853	7 112
United States	296	57	69	47 378	19 092	17 294
China (including Hong Kong and Taiwan)	240	157	208	76 333	16 041	42 828
Japan	121	49	19	3 094	897	440
Middle East	34	25	10	9 057	7 955	1 400

Notes: Data for Europe and the United States from 2006 to 2009 excludes investment companies. The data includes divestitures, relistings and privatisations of state-owned businesses.
[a]Excludes investment companies.
[b]Includes investment companies.
Source: PricewaterhouseCoopers IPO Watch Europe, 2010, used with permission.

The table gives data on the number of initial public offerings in Europe for the period 2004–2009 for Europe with comparable data for the United States. For 2009, the average amount raised in an issue in Europe was €58 million versus €258 million in the United States.

Venture Capitalists Provide More Than Financing

A common misconception about venture capitalists is that their sole function is to provide financing for new firms. In actuality, one of their most important roles is to provide advice to entrepreneurs. Because of their industry knowledge and their general knowledge about what it takes for a business to succeed, they are able to provide guidance to entrepreneurs when a business is being started and during the early period of the business's operation. At these points in the development of a business, the people managing it (including the entrepreneur) are often long on technical skills but short on the skills necessary to successfully manage its growth.

The extent of the venture capitalists' involvement in management of the firm depends on the experience and depth of the management team. Venture capital investors may want a seat on the board of directors. At a minimum, they will want an agreement that gives them unrestricted access to information about the firm's operations and financial performance and the right to attend and observe any board meeting. Finally, venture capitalists will insist on a mechanism giving them the authority to assume control of the firm if the firm's performance is poor, as well as the authority to install a new management team, if necessary.

The Cost of Venture Capital Funding

The cost of venture capital funding is very high, but the high rates of return earned by venture capitalists are not unreasonable. First, venture capitalists are bearing a substantial amount of risk when they fund a new business. On average, for every ten businesses backed by venture capitalists, only one or two will prove successful. Thus, the winners have to cover the losses on businesses that fail. Second, venture capitalists spend a considerable amount of their time monitoring the progress of businesses they fund and intervening when a business's management team needs help. If a venture capital-financed new business is successful, more than likely, the venture capitalists will have made a

substantial contribution to creating value for the other owners.

Just what returns do venture capitalists earn on their investments in new businesses? As you might expect, the annual rate of return varies substantially from year to year, and the returns earned by different venture capitalists can differ considerably. It is difficult to generalise; however, a typical venture capital fund may generate annual returns of 15–25% on the money that it invests, compared with an average annual return for the Dow Jones Euro Stoxx 50 index of leading European companies of about 8%. The bottom line is that venture capital investing involves very high risks and rewards.

> ### Before You Go On
>
> 1. Who are venture capitalists and what do they do?
> 2. How do venture capitalists reduce the risk of their investments?
> 3. Explain the venture capital funding cycle.

INITIAL PUBLIC OFFERING

> ### Learning Objective 3
> Discuss the advantages and disadvantages of going public and be able to compute the proceeds from an IPO.

If a business is very successful, at some point it will outgrow the ability of the private sources of equity we have discussed – such as family, friends and venture capitalists – to fund its growth. More money will be needed for investments in plant and equipment, working capital and research and development (R&D) than these sources of capital will provide. One way to raise larger sums of cash or to facilitate the exit of a venture capitalist is through an initial public offering of the company's ordinary shares. Note that undertaking an IPO is variously called going public, listing or floating the company.

As the name implies, an IPO is a company's first sale of ordinary shares in the public market. First-time share issues are given a special name because the marketing and pricing of these issues are distinctly different from those of seasoned offerings. A **seasoned public offering** is a sale of securities (either shares or bonds) by a firm that already has similar publicly traded securities outstanding. The term *public offering* means that the securities being sold can legally be sold to the public at large. Only securities that meet certain requirements can be sold to the public. (Alternatively, securities can be sold directly to institutional investors in the private market, which we discuss later.)

> ### Seasoned public offering
>
> the sale of securities to the public by a firm that already has publicly traded securities outstanding

> ### WEB
>
> For information on IPOs, see www.ipore-sources.org and www.iporesources.org//ipopage.html.

Advantages and Disadvantages of Going Public

When large sums of capital are necessary to fund a business or when the entrepreneur or venture capitalists are ready to sell some or all of their investment in a business, the entrepreneur and the venture capitalists may decide that an IPO, rather than the sale of the business to a strategic or financial buyer, is the appropriate way to achieve their goals. A firm's decision to go public depends on an assessment of whether the advantages outweigh the disadvantages.

Advantages of Going Public

Going public has a number of potential advantages. First, the amount of equity capital that can be raised in the public equity markets is typically larger than the amount that can be raised through private sources. There are millions of investors in public stock markets, and it is easier for firms to reach these investors through public markets. Second, after a firm has completed an IPO, additional equity capital can usually be raised through follow-on seasoned public offerings at a low cost. This is because the public markets are highly liquid and investors are willing to pay higher prices for more liquid shares of public firms than for the relatively illiquid shares of otherwise similar private firms. Third, going public can enable an entrepreneur to fund a growing business without giving up control. The entrepreneur does not have to sell the entire business but only what is needed to raise the necessary funds. Fourth, once a company has gone public, there is an active secondary market in which shareholders can buy and sell the company's shares. This enables the entrepreneur and other managers to more easily diversify their personal portfolios or to just sell shares in order to enjoy some of the rewards of having built a successful business. Of course, it also provides a way for financial backers and venture capitalists to sell their shares and exit the investment.

Another potential advantage of having an active market for a firm's shares is that it can make it easier for the firm to attract top management talent and to better motivate current managers. This is true because senior managers generally own equity in the firm, and some part of their compensation is tied to the performance of the firm's shares. Recall that this aligns management's behaviour with maximising shareholder value. For publicly traded companies, it is easy to offer incentives tied to share performance because market information about the value of their shares is readily available. For privately held companies, market transactions are infrequent and thus the market value of a firm's equity must be estimated.

Disadvantages of Going Public

One disadvantage of going public is the high cost of the IPO. This cost is partly due to the fact that the shares are not seasoned. Seasoned shares, which are traded in a public secondary market, have an established record. Investors can observe how many shares trade on a regular basis (a measure of the liquidity of the shares) and the prices at which the trades take place. In contrast, the likely liquidity for shares that are sold in an IPO is less well known and the value is more uncertain. For this reason, investors are less comfortable buying shares in an IPO and thus will not pay as high a price for them as for similar seasoned shares. In addition, out-of-pocket costs, such as legal fees, accounting expenses, printing costs, travel expenses, listing fees, consultant fees and taxes, can add substantially to the cost of an IPO.

The costs of complying with ongoing disclosure requirements also represent a disadvantage of going public. Once a firm goes public, it must meet a myriad of filing and other requirements imposed by the exchange. For larger firms, these regulatory costs are not terribly important because they represent a relatively small fraction of the total equity value. However, regulatory costs can be significant for small firms.

In addition to the out-of-pocket costs of complying with listing requirements, the transparency that results from this compliance can be costly for some firms. The requirement that firms provide the public with detailed financial statements, detailed information on executive compensation, information about the firm's strategic initiatives and elements related to corporate governance and corporate disclosure can put the firm at a competitive disadvantage relative to private firms that are not required to disclose such information.

Finally, some investors argue that some aspects of listing requirements, such as the need to provide earnings forecasts and interim financial statements, encourages managers to focus on short-term profits rather than long-term value maximisation. Managers who fail to meet their earnings projections often see their firm's share price drop significantly.

To facilitate smaller companies going public, the major exchanges in Europe allow companies that normally would not meet the requirements of the exchange to list on a specialised section of the exchange. Exhibit 15.4 shows the main listing requirements for the London Stock Exchange's Main Market and AIM – the Alternative Investment Market designed to facilitate capital raising by smaller entrepreneurial companies.[5] Note the very difference size of companies on the main market, where the average market capitalisation in October 2009 was £1572 million as against the average AIM company of £42 million.

Investment Banking Services

To complete an IPO, a firm will need the services of investment bankers, who are experts in bringing new securities to market.[6] From Chapter 2, recall that investment bankers provide three basic services when bringing securities to market: (1) *origination*, which includes giving the firm financial advice and getting the issue ready to sell; (2) *underwriting*, which is the risk-bearing part of investment banking; and (3) *distribution*, which involves reselling the securities to the public.

Smaller firms such as Tuscan Pizzeria will probably use the full range of services provided by the investment banker because they have little or no experience in issuing new securities. In contrast, larger firms that go to the seasoned public markets on a regular basis have experienced financial staff and may provide some or all of the origination services themselves.

Identifying the investment bank that will manage the IPO process is an important task for the management of a firm because not all investment banks are equal. Top investment banking firms do

BUILDING INTUITION

Investors View Seasoned Securities as Less Risky than Unseasoned Securities

Investors will pay higher prices (or accept lower yields) for seasoned shares than for otherwise similar shares from an IPO. This is true because the liquidity and value of seasoned shares are better known. The same is true for other types of securities, such as bonds.

EXHIBIT 15.4

DIFFERENCES BETWEEN THE ADMISSION CRITERIA FOR THE LONDON STOCK EXCHANGE'S MAIN MARKET AND AIM

| | London Stock Exchange | |
	Main Market	AIM
Minimum percentage of shares in public hands	25%	No minimum
Trading record prior to listing	3 years	No minimum
for a minimum of company's business entities	75%	
Prior shareholder approval required for substantial transactions	Yes	No[a]
Sponsors needed for certain transactions	Yes	N/A
Minimum market capitalisation	£700 000	No minimum
Pre-vetting by UK Listing Authority[b]	Yes	No
Appointment of sponsor	Yes	—
Appointment of nominated advisor (NOMAD)	—	Yes
Distribution of a prospectus	Yes	No
Working capital available for	12 months	12 months
Comply with Listing Principles	Yes	—
Maintain adequate Financial Reporting Procedures	Yes	Yes
Company has control of majority of assets	Yes	Not stipulated
Average market capitalisation of company listed on exchange (October 2009) (£ millions)	£1 572	£42

[a]Not applicable to reverse takeovers or disposals resulting in a fundamental change in the business.
[b]The UKLA will only vet an AIM admission document when it is a prospectus under the European Union's Prospectus Directive.
Source: London Stock Exchange (www.londonstockexchange.com). http://217.154.230.218/NR/ rdonlyres/0C0CC6CF-8485-47A3-A58C-8218DDF4EE3A/0/BC_RS_costcapital_0606_FR.pdf. Reproduced with permission of one City of London.

The London Stock Exchange's Main Market is the market for larger, more established companies and lists some of the world's largest and most well-known companies. AIM is the exchange's international market for smaller-growth companies and includes a wide range of businesses including early stage, venture capital-backed, as well as more established companies seeking access to growth capital. In October 2009, the average market capitalisation of Main Market companies was £1572 million while that for AIM companies was £42 million.

not want to tarnish their reputation by bringing 'bad deals' to market. Their willingness to underwrite a firm's IPO is an implicit 'seal of approval'. Thus, securing the services of an investment bank with a reputation for quality and honesty will improve the market's receptivity and help ensure a successful IPO. We will walk through the steps that a business takes in bringing a new issue of shares to market via an IPO. Note that the steps are nearly the same for debt issues.

Origination

During the origination phase, the investment banker helps the firm determine whether it is ready for an

IPO. That requires determining whether the management team, the firm's historical financial performance and the firm's expected future performance are strong enough to merit serious consideration by sophisticated investors. If the answer to any of these questions is no, the investment banker might help the firm find private capital to see it through until all of the answers are yes. Other issues that must be decided are how much money the firm needs to raise and how many shares must be sold.

Once the decision to sell shares is made, the firm's management must obtain a number of approvals. The firm's board of directors must approve all security sales and shareholder approval is required if the number of shares is to be increased.

Securities sold to the public must meet listing requirements as laid down by MiFID, the European Union's directive on markets in financial instruments. A two-level system operates in Europe. Larger companies need to comply with the European Union's Prospectus Directive but smaller issues, like those listed on AIM, are subject to national standards, as determined by the home competent authority. Whichever route is chosen, the first step in this process is to file an admission document. As part of this process, companies may file a **preliminary prospectus**.[7] This contains detailed information about the type of business activities in which the firm is engaged, its financial condition, a description of the management team and their experience, a competitive analysis of the industry, a range within which the issuer expects the initial offering price for the shares to fall, the number of shares that the firm plans to sell, an explanation of how the proceeds from the IPO will be used and a detailed discussion of the risks associated with the investment opportunity. While the competent authority is reviewing the admission document and preliminary prospectus, the firm may distribute copies of it to potential customers, but at this point in time no sales can be made from this document. In the case of a small company listing on AIM, the prospectus requirement is relaxed and firms and their advisors prepare a set of listing particulars. These will include much of the same background information on the company that would be in the prospectus.

> ### Preliminary prospectus
>
> the initial admission document filed with the competent authority by a company preparing to issue securities in the public market; it contains detailed information about the issuer and the proposed issue

The information in a prospectus is designed to allow investors to make intelligent decisions about investing in a security issue and the risks associated with it. Approval by the competent regulating authority is not an endorsement of the wisdom or desirability of making a particular investment. Approval means only that the firm has followed various rules and regulations required to issue securities and that the information is complete and accurate.

Underwriting

Once the origination work is complete, the security issue can be sold to investors. The securities can be underwritten in two ways: (1) on a firm-commitment basis or (2) on a best-effort basis.

Firm-Commitment Underwriting

In the typical underwriting arrangement, called a **firm-commitment underwriting**, the investment banker guarantees the issuer a fixed amount of money from the sale of the shares. The investment banker actually buys the shares from the firm at a fixed price and then resells them to the public. The underwriter bears the risk that the resale price might be lower than the price the underwriter pays – this is called *price risk*. The resale price can be lower if the underwriter overestimates the value of the shares when determining how much to pay the firm or if the value of the shares declines before they are resold to the public.

> ### Firm-commitment underwriting
>
> underwriting agreement in which the underwriter purchases securities for a specified price and resells them

The investment banker's compensation is called the *underwriter's spread*. In a firm-commitment offering, the spread is the difference between the investment banker's purchase price and the offer price. The spread covers the investment banker's expenses, compensation for bearing risk and profit. For example, suppose an investment banker buys a firm's shares for €50.00 and the offer price is €53.50. The gross underwriter's spread is €3.50 per share (€53.50 – €50.00), or 7% of the offer price. If the underwriter's total expenses for the offering are €1.50 per share, the underwriter's net profit is €2.00 per share (€3.50 − €1.50). The underwriter's spread is negotiated with the company. Typically, it will be higher for smaller issues, which have a higher level of fixed expenses and have more risk. The spread for TGE Marine AG described in the opening vignette was 10% of the proceeds. The gross amount raised was £23 703 030 and the company received £21 303 030 net of fees, or 90% of the issue price. Existing investors who sold at the time of the IPO raised a further £42.11 million, net of expenses. Therefore, the total amount raised from new investors via the IPO was £65.82 million and the investment bank would have netted £6.58 million, or 10% of the gross proceeds, for their services.

Best-Effort Underwriting

With a **best-effort underwriting**, the investment banking firm makes no guarantee to sell the securities at a particular price. It promises only to make its 'best effort' to sell as much of the issue as possible at a certain price. In best-effort offerings, the investment banker does not bear the price risk associated with underwriting the issue and compensation is based on the number of shares sold. Not surprisingly, most companies issuing shares prefer firm-commitment arrangements to best-effort contracts. Best-effort offerings usually arise when underwriters do not want to accept the risk of guaranteeing the offering price.

> ### Best-effort underwriting
>
> underwriting agreement in which the underwriter does not agree to purchase the securities at a particular price but promises only to make its 'best effort' to sell as much of the issue as possible above a certain price

Underwriting Syndicates

To spread the underwriting risk and to sell a new security issue more efficiently, underwriters may combine to form a group called an **underwriting syndicate**. Each member of the syndicate is responsible for a proportional allocation of the securities being issued. Participating in the syndicate entitles each underwriter to receive a part of the underwriting fee as well as an allocation of the securities to sell to its own customers.

> ### Underwriting syndicate
>
> a group of underwriters that joins forces to reduce underwriting risk

To broaden the search for potential investors, underwriting syndicates may enlist other investment banking firms in a syndicate known as a *selling group*, which assists in the sale of the securities. These firms receive a commission for each security they sell and bear none of the risk of underwriting the issue.

Determining the Offer Price

One of the investment banker's most difficult tasks is to determine the highest price at which the bankers will be able to rapidly sell all of the shares being offered and that will result in a stable secondary market for the shares. One step in determining this price is to consider the value of the firm's expected future cash flows; the analysis and formulas used are like those presented in Chapter 9. In addition, the investment bankers will consider the share price implied by multiples of total firm value to EBITDA or share price to earnings per share for similar firms that are already public. Finally, the investment banker will conduct a *road show* in which management makes presentations about the firm and its prospects to potential investors. The road show is the key marketing and information-gathering event for an IPO. It generates interest in the offering and helps the investment banker determine the number of shares that investors are likely to purchase at different prices.

Due Diligence Meeting

Before the shares are sold, representatives from the underwriting syndicate hold a due diligence meeting with representatives of the issuer. The purpose of the meeting is to list, gather and authenticate matters such as articles of incorporation, by-laws, patents, important contracts and corporate minutes. In addition, the investment bankers have a final opportunity to ask management questions about the firm's financial integrity, intended use of the proceeds and any other issues deemed relevant to the pending security sale.

Investment bankers hold due diligence meetings to protect their reputations and to reduce the risk of investors' lawsuits in the event the investment goes sour later on. Although the due diligence meetings have a perfunctory nature, the meetings are serious in that they ensure that all material issues about the firm and the offering are discovered and, subsequently, fully disclosed to investors.

Distribution

Once the due diligence process is complete, the underwriters and the issuer determine the final offer price in a *pricing call*. The pricing call typically takes place after the market has closed for the day. During this call, the lead underwriter (also known as the book runner because this underwriter assembles the book of orders for the offering) makes its recommendation concerning the appropriate price and the firm's management decides whether that price is acceptable. By either accepting or rejecting the investment banker's recommendation, management ultimately makes the pricing decision. If management finds the price acceptable, the issuer files an amendment to the admission document with the competent authority, which contains the terms of the offering and the final prospectus. Once this is done, the securities can be sold to investors.

The First Day of Trading

The underwriter then typically sells the shares to investors when the market opens on the next day. The syndicate's primary concern is to sell the securities as quickly as possible at the offer price. Speed of sale is important because the offer price reflects market conditions at the end of the previous day and these conditions can change quickly.

In successful offerings, most of the securities will have been pre-placed with investors prior to delivery and, if the issue is not entirely pre-placed, it will be sold out within a few hours. If the securities are not sold within a few days, the underwriting syndicate disbands and members sell the securities at whatever price they can get.

The Closing

At the *closing* of a firm-commitment offering, the issuing firm delivers the security certificates to the underwriter and the underwriter delivers the payment for the securities, net of the underwriting fee, to the issuer. The closing usually takes place on the third business day after trading has started.

The Proceeds

We now arrive at the bottom line: How much money does the firm and the underwriter make from the sale of the new shares? We will look at an example to see how to answer this question. Suppose a small manufacturing firm is doing an IPO of its shares with an investment bank on a firm-commitment basis. The firm plans to issue 2 million shares and the gross underwriting spread is 7%. Following the road show, the CFO accepts a €20 per-share offering price that has been proposed by the underwriter. Based on this information, consider the following questions:

1. What are the total expected proceeds from the sale of ordinary shares?
2. How much money does the issuer expect to get from the offering?
3. What is the investment bank's expected compensation from the offering?

The best approach to calculating these amounts is to first work through the funding allocations on a per-share basis and then compute the total amounts. We know that the IPO's offer price is €20 per share and the underwriter's spread is 7%; thus, the issuer's expected net proceeds are €18.60 per share (€20 per share − (€20.00 × 0.07) or €1.40 per share). The total proceeds from the sale of the shares are expected to equal €40 million (€20 per share ×

2 million shares). The total proceeds will be shared by (1) the firm, with €37.2 million (€18.60 per share × 2 million shares) and (2) the underwriter, with €2.8 million (€1.40 per share × 2 million shares). If the syndicate sells the shares at the offering price of €20, the sale will be deemed 'successful' and both the underwriter and the issuer will receive their expected proceeds.

Learning by Doing Application 15.1

An Unsuccessful IPO

Problem: We will continue with our IPO example from the text. Suppose that the share sale is not successful and the underwriter is able to sell the shares, on average, for only €19 per share. If the underwriter buys the shares from the issuer for €18.60, what will be the proceeds for each party from the sale?

Approach: Because the underwriting is a firm-commitment offering, the underwriter guarantees that the issuer will receive the full-expected amount, as calculated in the text. The underwriter will have to absorb the entire loss.

Solution: On a per-share basis, the total proceeds from the sale are €19 per share. Since the issuer still receives €18.60 per share because of the firm-commitment offering, the underwriter receives only €0.40 per share. Thus, the underwriter's total proceeds from the sale are €0.8 million (€0.40 × 2 million shares) rather than the expected €2.8 million. The total proceeds for the IPO sale are €38 million (€37.2 million + €0.8 million).

Learning by Doing Application 15.2

A Best-Effort IPO

Problem: Now let us assume that the shares in our IPO are sold on a best-effort basis rather than a firm-commitment basis and that the underwriter agrees to a spread of 7% of the selling price. The average selling price remains at €19 per share. What are the net proceeds for the issuer and the underwriter in a best-effort offering?

Approach: The key to working this problem is to recognise that in a best-effort IPO, the underwriter bears no risk. The risk of an unsuccessful sale is borne entirely by the issuing firm. Thus, the underwriter is paid first and the residual goes to the issuer.

Solution: Since the underwriter agreed to a spread of 7% of the price at which each share is sold, the distribution of the proceeds can be calculated as follows. The underwriter's spread for each share sold is €1.33 per share (€19.00 per share × 0.07). The firm's total net proceeds are €35.34 million [(€19.00 × 0.93) × 2 million] and the underwriter's total proceeds are €2.66 million (€1.33 × 2 million). The total proceeds from the IPO sale are still €38 million but are distributed differently.

Before You Go On

1. What is a seasoned offering and why are seasoned securities valued more highly than securities sold in an IPO?
2. Explain the two ways in which a security issue can be underwritten.
3. List the steps in the IPO process.

IPO PRICING AND COST

Learning Objective 4

Explain why, when underwriting new security offerings, investment bankers prefer that the securities be underpriced and compute the total cost of an IPO.

In the preceding section, we mentioned that pricing an IPO is one of the underwriter's most difficult tasks. In this section, we discuss an important pricing issue, underpricing, and then turn once again to the costs of issuing an IPO.

The Underpricing Debate

As you might expect, tension arises between the issuer and the underwriters when the final offer price for the shares is being determined. Clearly, the issuer prefers the share price to be as high as realistically possible. In contrast, the underwriters prefer some degree of underpricing. **Underpricing** is defined as offering new securities for sale at a price below their true value. The lower the offering price, the more likely the securities will sell out quickly – and the less likely the underwriters will end up with unsold securities. Furthermore, investment bankers will argue that some underpricing helps attract long-term institutional investors who help provide stability for the share price once the secondary market for the shares is established. These investors will not sell, or *flip* the shares as quickly, and thereby contribute to price volatility.

Underpricing

offering new securities for sale at a price below their true value

Although the issuer and the underwriters may disagree on pricing, in reality, both face potential costs if the share price is too high or too low. On the one hand, if the shares are priced too high, the entire issue will not sell at the proposed offer price. In an IPO, the underwriters are selling a relatively large number of shares, which may require setting a price below that at which the shares would trade in small numbers. Furthermore, there can be considerable uncertainty about the true value of the shares since they have not yet traded in the public market. This uncertainty also contributes to the pressure to set a lower price. In a firm-commitment offering, the underwriters will suffer a financial loss if the offer price is set too high; under a best-effort agreement, the issuing firm will lose.

On the other hand, if the shares are priced below their true value, the firm's existing shareholders will experience an opportunity loss; that is, the firm will receive less money for the shares than they are worth. In addition, if the underpricing is significant, the investment bank will suffer a loss of reputation for failing to price the new issue correctly and raising less money for its client than it could have. In practice, most market participants agree that some underpricing is good for both the issuer and the underwriter. However, the question of *how much* underpricing is appropriate is open for debate.

IPOs are Consistently Underpriced

Data from the marketplace shows that the shares sold in an IPO are typically priced between 10% and 15% below the price at which they close at the end of the first day of trading. This implies that underwriters tend to sell shares in IPOs to investors for between 90% and 85% of their true market value and hence leave 'money on the table'.

Sometimes the underpricing can be much greater. For example, Zetar plc, an Irish confectionery and snack foods group, listed on AIM in January 2005 at an offer price of 100 pence. The company sold 750 000 shares and raised gross proceeds of £750 000 but netted £674 998 after expenses (a cost of 10% of the money raised). The price closed at the end of the first day at 120 pence and by the end of the month (17 trading days later) at 235 pence. This means that Zetar shares were underpriced by 20 pence based on the first day's trading – or a massive 135 pence based on the end-of-month share price! Zetar shares might have sold for a total of £150 000 (£0.20 per share × 750 000) more based on the end-of-day performance. Who received this value? It went into the pockets of the investors who bought the shares in the IPO.

Exhibit 15.5 shows data on the number of IPOs per year and the capitalisation-weighted average first-day return to investors for the UK for the years 1917–2007 by decade. The average first-day return is a measure of the amount of underpricing that exists – or money left on the table. The results show the long-term persistence of underpricing. The period 1917–1945 averaged underpricing of 8.97%, with £301.3 million left on the table. That is, companies selling shares over this period did not receive this amount, which was a gain to investors who bought the shares when offered. For the period 1946–1986, the average underpricing rose somewhat to 10.50% and £1.84 billion was left on the table. The 1987–2007 period, which in terms of numbers of issues – but not their size – was comparable to the 1946–1986 period, had greater underpricing at 12.49%, but raised nearly six times the amount compared with the previous period for companies going public. The increase in underpricing can be explained by the fact that the more recent period includes younger and riskier companies listing on the AIM market and hence, possibly, subject to greater amounts of information asymmetry. It was also a period of

EXHIBIT 15.5

INITIAL PUBLIC OFFERINGS IN THE UNITED KINGDOM, 1917–2007

Period	Number of IPOs	Capitalisation-Weighted First-Day Returns (%)	Median First-Day Returns (%)	Real Gross Proceeds[a] (£ million)	Underpricing[a] (£ million)
1917–29	357	9.68	1.89	3 377.1	192.4
1930–39	239	7.07	0.63	1 863.3	91.8
1940–49	269	4.64	2.94	2 044.5	96.8
1950–59	348	9.23	8.70	3 131.3	185.5
1960–69	548	12.23	8.82	3 717.0	434.6
1970–79	267	8.87	5.33	3 812.5	321.4
1980–89	762	13.34	9.61	11 867.0	1 593.2
1990–99	641	11.32	7.76	45 059.4	5 839.9
2000–07	1 109	13.05	8.50	57 073.2	7 117.8
1917–45	610	8.97	1.26	5 303.9	301.3
1946–86	1 943	10.50	7.69	19 229.5	1 843.0
1987–2007	1 987	12.49	8.70	107 411.9	13 729.2

Source: David Chambers and Elroy Dimson, 2009. IPO underpricing over the very long run, Journal of Finance 64(3): 1407–1446. Reproduced by permission of Wiley-Blackwell.

[a]Data on proceeds and underpricing is adjusted to 2007 prices for comparison purposes.

We can see variation in the amount of underpricing in this exhibit, which shows the numbers of IPOs per decade from 1917 to 2007, the average capitalisation-weighted return and the median return to investors. The first-day return represents the amount of underpricing. The monetary value of the underpricing (adjusted to 2007 values) indicates the amount of money 'left on the table' for new investors by the IPO process.

EXHIBIT 15.6

INITIAL PUBLIC OFFERINGS, PROCEEDS AND RETURNS, 1995–2004

Country	Number of IPOs	Average First-Day Return (%)	Gross Proceeds (€ million)	Underpricing (€ million)
Austria	23	6.96	12 034	783
Belgium*	58	12.21	7 163	779
Finland	44	27.76	1 885	410
France*	363	5.36	11 663	593
Germany	415	38.93	61 247	17 162
Greece	183	46.68	6 426	2 045
Italy	135	10.26	24 444	2 275
Netherlands*	47	22.92	28 792	5 369
Poland	95	19.55	3 501	573
Portugal*	16	21.30	460	81
Spain	36	10.73	156 959	15 210
Sweden	95	15.93	22 483	3 089
Switzerland	61	18.08	51 279	7 852
Turkey	79	4.62	5 437	240
UK	454	21.27	83 186	14 590
All	2104	22.06	476 959	86 201

*Data for amount of new issues to end year 2000 only.

Source: Jean-Francois Gajewski and Carole Gresse, 2006. A survey of the European IPO market, ECMI Working Paper No. 2. Reproduced with permission of the City of London.

We can see that underpricing of IPOs is a feature of Europe's new issues market, although there are wide variations in the average first-day return across countries.

significant privatisation of state-owned enterprises and the evidence for these very large IPOs suggests that many of these were significantly underpriced in order to facilitate selling large numbers of shares to the general public. What the data does show is that underpricing has been and remains a consistent phenomenon of the new issues market.

There is evidence for IPO underpricing in other countries, although unlike the United Kingdom and the United States, the data is for a shorter period. Exhibit 15.6 shows data for European IPOs for the period 1995–2004. The average underpricing across all markets is 22.06%, although this masks a range from 4.62% for Turkey to 38.93% for Germany. These differences may be attributable to different institutional factors between countries and the number and types of companies coming to market.

Decision-Making Example 15.1

Pricing an IPO

Situation: You are the CFO of a small firm that is planning an IPO. You are meeting with your investment banker to determine the offer price for your first public issue of ordinary shares. The investment banker tells you that an IPO pricing model indicates that the current value of your shares is €20 per share. Furthermore, a firm with similar risk characteristics completed an IPO two months ago and its share price suggests a current market price of €21 per share. The investment banker suggests that the offer price be set at €15 per share. What decision should you make with regard to the investment bank's offer price?

Decision: Given the available information, you should be cautious about the proposed offer price of €15 per share. The investment bank's IPO pricing model estimates that your shares' current market value is €20 per share. This estimate is validated by the fact that it is very close to the price of the similar firm's shares. If you sold the shares for €15 and the closing price at the end of the first day was €20, the first-day return would be 33.3% [(€20 – €15)/€15], which is on the upper end of the first-day returns in Exhibit 15.6. Unless your IPO is unusual in some way, for example, you are issuing a large number of shares or the share price is highly uncertain, a more reasonable price might be €18 per share. With a price of €18 you would expect a first-day return of 11.1% [(€20 – €18)/€18].

EXHIBIT 15.7
DIRECT COSTS OF AN IPO

London Stock Exchange (Based on new funds of £20 million)	Percentage of Gross Proceeds
Underwriting fees	3–5%
Financial advisor costs[a]	1–2%
Legal expenses	1–2%
Accounting and audit fees	0.5–1.5%
Listing fees	<0.1%
Printing, public relations and other costs	<0.5%
Total direct costs as a percentage	5.5–11%
Total direct costs in money terms	£1.1–£2.2 million

Underwriting Fees for Selected Exchanges (%)	Domestic Issuer	Foreign Issuer[b]
UK – Main Market	3.3	3.5
UK – AIM	3.5	4.9
USA – New York Stock Exchange	6.5	5.6
USA – Nasdaq	7.0	7.0
Euronext	1.8	—
Deutsche Börse	3.0	—

[a]These fees may be included in the fees paid to the investment bank underwriting the transaction, possibly leading to lower costs overall.
[b]No data is given for foreign issues for Euronext and the Deutsche Börse.

Source: London Stock Exchange, *The Cost of Capital: An International Comparison*, London, June 2006. Available to download at: http://www.londonstockexchange.com/companies-and-advisors/main-market/documents/brochures/cost-of-capital-aninternational-comparison.pdf. Reproduced with permission of the City of London.

The direct costs of an IPO are principally made up of underwriting fees and advisor, legal and accounting fees. The other costs for listing, printing of the prospectus and other documents, public relations and other costs are less than 1% of the total. To raise £20 million in the London market, a firm will face costs ranging from 5.5% to 11%. Note that costs for smaller issues as a percentage tend to be higher than for larger issues.

Depending on the market used for the IPO, the underwriting fee can vary from a low of 1.8% for Euronext to 7.0% for Nasdaq, the smaller companies market in the USA.

The Cost of an IPO

As we have already mentioned, the cost of going public is high. Bringing our previous discussions together, we can identify three basic costs associated with issuing shares in an IPO:

1. *Underwriting spread.* The underwriting spread is the difference between the proceeds the issuer receives and the total amount raised in the offering.
2. *Out-of-pocket expenses.* Out-of-pocket expenses include other investment banking fees, legal fees, accounting expenses, printing costs, travel expenses, admission to listing fees, consultant fees and taxes.
3. *Underpricing.* Underpricing is typically defined as the difference between the offering price and the closing price at the end of the first day of the

IPO. It is the opportunity loss that the issuer's shareholders incur from selling the securities below their true market value.

Exhibit 15.7 presents some market data on the cost of issuing an IPO in the UK market and some comparable statistics for other major exchanges in Europe and the United States. The first part of the table provides a breakdown in the costs of listing on the London Stock Exchange. For a typical IPO raising £20 million, these direct costs vary between 5.5% and 11% of the amount raised. The major element of those costs comes from underwriting fees and financial advisor and legal fees. The underwriting fee can vary significantly. The pan-European Euronext exchange has the lowest underwriting fee of 1.8%, and the highest is for listing on Nasdaq in the United States.[8]

Learning by Doing Application 15.3

The Cost of an IPO

Problem: Suppose that Técnica Madrid SA, a Spanish company, sells €70 million of shares at €50 per share in an IPO. The underwriter's spread is 3.5%, and the firm's legal fees, listing fees and other out-of-pocket costs are €200 000. The firm's share price increases 15% on the first day. In money terms, what is the firm's total cost of issuing the shares?

Approach: To calculate the firm's total cost of issuing the shares, we must consider all three major costs associated with bringing it to market: underwriting spread, out-of-pocket expenses and underpricing.

Solution:

1. *Underwriting spread.* The underwriter's spread is €1.75 per share (€50.00 × 0.035). The number of shares sold is 1.4 million (€70 million/€50.00 per share). Thus, the underwriting cost is €2.45 million (€1.75 per share × 1.4 million shares).
2. *Out-of-pocket expenses.* The out-of-pocket expenses are €200 000.
3. *Underpricing.* The amount of underpricing is computed as follows. The firm's shares were offered at €50.00 and increased to €57.50 per share (€50.00 per share × 1.15) during the first day of trading; thus, the first-day underpricing is €7.50 per share (€57.50 − €50.00). The total underpricing is €10.5 million (€7.50 per share × 1.4 million shares).

The total cost to the firm of the IPO is €13.15 million, which consists of the following: (1) €2.45 million in underwriting fees, (2) €0.2 million out-of-pocket expenses and (3) €10.5 million market underpricing.

SEASONED OFFERINGS BY A PUBLIC COMPANY

Learning Objective 5
Discuss the difficulties and costs of bringing a rights issue to market and be able to compute the total cost of issuing a rights issue.

The need for funding does not end when a company goes public. Most companies continually make new investments in real assets and working capital. If they do not generate enough cash from operations to fund these investments, their managers must raise capital from outside the firm.

Every business wants to fund itself at the lowest possible cost. If a public firm has a high credit rating, the lowest-cost source of external funds is often by issuing securities on the public market. In raising further capital, firms have two choices: equity or debt. They also may be able to choose whether they make an offer to all their current shareholders and investors or go for a placing with new investors. In the case of debt issues, they can choose between a public offer and a private placement. (We discuss bank loans and private placements in the next section.)

The procedures involved in an issue are summarised here. You will see that there are some similarities between these procedures and those involved in an IPO.

1. *Type of security and amount to be raised.* Management decides how much money the firm needs to raise and what type of security to issue, such as debt, ordinary shares or preference shares.

2. *Approvals.* Approval is obtained from the board of directors to issue securities. If the size of a share issue exceeds the previously authorised number of ordinary or preference shares, approval from shareholders is required as well.

3. *Issue particulars.* The issuer files a prospectus or listing particulars and satisfies all of the securities laws. For a debt issue, the documentation must include a bond indenture that gives the terms and conditions of the bonds.

4. *Offer price.* After assessing demand, the underwriter and the issuer agree on an offer price.

5. *Closing.* At the closing of a firm-commitment offering, the issuer delivers the securities to the underwriter and the underwriter pays for them, net of its fees. The securities are then sold to investors.

The issuer has flexibility in the method of sale and the way the securities are registered. Both of these factors can affect the issuer's funding cost. Next we consider methods of sale and discuss the costs of offers.

Raising Seasoned Equity

If equity is to be raised, this is normally done via a **rights issue** to existing shareholders. Corporate law in most European countries mandates that existing shareholders have pre-emption rights when new shares are issued. This allows existing shareholders to subscribe for more shares in proportion to their existing holding.[9] By buying the new shares on offer, existing shareholders maintain their proportion of the share capital and control rights in the company. This may be important for controlling shareholders who would not like to see their holding diluted by the issuance of new shares. It can be a problem for some shareholders who may not wish to buy the new shares – but they can normally sell on the right to buy the shares to other investors who would like to buy the new shares on offer. The investment bank will often arrange for the sale of the unpaid rights on behalf of those investors who do not wish to subscribe.

Rights issue

offer to existing shareholders where they can buy new shares in the company in proportion to their existing holding. Also called a 'privileged subscription'

In a rights issue, a company will indicate the number of new shares to be issued relative to the number of existing shares. For instance, a company might set a 5 for 1 rights issue. This means that shareholders are asked to buy one new share for every five held. For example if, at the start, the company had 10 million shares outstanding, the rights issue

where $S_{\text{After rights issue}}$ is the price of the shares immediately after the rights issue takes place, $N_{\text{Original shares}}$ is the number of shares outstanding before the rights issue takes place, $S_{\text{Before rights issue}}$ is the price in the market immediately before the rights issue, $M_{\text{New shares}}$ is the number of shares being sold via the rights issue and $S_{\text{Rights offer price}}$ is the price at which the new shares are being offered.

We will continue our earlier example. The company undertaking the 5 for 1 rights issue has 10 million shares outstanding and the current share price is €50. It announces the rights issue and the price is set at €38 per share for the rights. The price of the shares after the rights issue will be:

$$S_{\text{After rights issue}} = \frac{N_{\text{Original shares}} \times S_{\text{Before rights issue}} + M_{\text{New shares}}S_{\text{Rights offer price}}}{N_{\text{Original shares}} + M_{\text{New shares}}} = \frac{10 \times €50 + 2 \times €38}{10 + 2}$$

$$= \frac{€500 + €76}{12} = €48$$

would raise the number to 12 million (= 10 million original shares + 2 million from the rights issue).

We can calculate the effect on the share price from a rights issue. Since more shares will be issued, we can expect the value of the outstanding shares to fall. It will greatly depend on the reasons that the company is raising further equity whether the market views the issue in a positive or negative light. Therefore, it is a matter of some judgement and a major concern for the investment bank underwriting the issue as to how the rights issue should be priced. As a rule, because there will be a delay between the announcement and the payment date, which is the point at which existing shareholders are expected to purchase the new shares, it is customary to offer the new shares at a discount to the current market price to try and anticipate any adverse changes in market conditions between the offer announcement and the payment date. When the rights issue is announced, the price at which the shares will settle is a function of (1) the existing price of the shares and (2) the number of new shares being offered, namely:

It is clear in the above example that if the share price falls below €38 post-announcement, it makes more sense for existing shareholders and other investors not to subscribe to the rights, and to buy the shares in the secondary market instead. To ensure that the company gets the money it needs, it is normal practice for the rights issue to be underwritten, which adds to the cost. Since there is normally a period of at least 10 days between the date shareholders receive their allotment letters and the payment date, these rights represent a future purchase of shares in the company at a fixed price. Holders of the unpaid rights effectively have an option on the company's shares for the period.[10] Consequently, these unpaid rights have a value. It is normal practice that existing shareholders can sell their rights to the new shares rather than subscribe for the new shares on offer. To facilitate this, there is usually a market in these 'nil-paid' rights.

$$S_{\text{After rights issue}} = \frac{N_{\text{Original shares}} \times S_{\text{Before rights issue}} + M_{\text{New shares}}S_{\text{Rights offer price}}}{N_{\text{Original shares}} + M_{\text{New shares}}} \quad (15.1)$$

Learning by Doing Application 15.4

Getting a Rights Issue Right

Problem: It is some years since Técnica Madrid SA, the company that featured in Learning by Doing Application 15.3, went public. It now has a need to raise further equity, as it needs gross proceeds of €30 million to fund further expansion. Since the IPO, Técnica's share price has done well and the shares are currently trading at €75 in the market. The investment bank advising on the transaction has suggested that an appropriate discount on the market price is 20%, to take account of possible

by Doing Application 15.3, we know that the company already has 1.4 million shares outstanding. So post rights issue, it will have issued 1.9 million shares. The company needs to ask existing shareholders for one new share for every 2.8 they already own (1.4/0.5 = 2.8). If the company wants a different ratio for the rights issue, it will need either to agree a different rights price for the new shares, scale up or back down on the amount it raises.

Under the existing terms, the price of the company's shares will be:

$$S_{\text{After rights issue}} = \frac{N_{\text{Original shares}} \times S_{\text{Before rights issue}} + M_{\text{New shares}} S_{\text{Rights offer price}}}{N_{\text{Original shares}} + M_{\text{New shares}}} = \frac{1.4 \times €75 + 0.5 \times €60}{1.9}$$

$$= \frac{€105 + €30}{1.9} = €71.05$$

changes in market conditions. What will be the terms of the rights issue and what is the price we would expect Técnica's shares to be at afterwards? What adjustments would need to be considered to get a ratio of whole old shares to new shares for the rights issue? What are the trade-offs?

Approach: To find the terms of the rights issue, we use Equation (15.1) since we want to work out the ex rights price.

To get a round number of shares held to new shares of, say, 3 for 1 for the rights issue, it can either scale back to €28 million (1.4 × 1/3 = 0.4666 × €60 = €28 million) or offer the shares at €64.3 (€30/0.4666 = €46.3) – a discount of 14.3% on the current share price.

It can get an 8 for 3 rights issue by asking for €31.5 million. In this case Técnica issues slightly more new shares – 525 000 versus 500 000 – and the new share price post rights issue will be:

$$S_{\text{After rights issue}} = \frac{N_{\text{Original shares}} \times S_{\text{Before rights issue}} + M_{\text{New shares}} S_{\text{Rights offer price}}}{N_{\text{Original shares}} + M_{\text{New shares}}} = \frac{1.4 \times €75 + 0.525 \times €60}{1.925}$$

$$= \frac{€105 + €31.5}{1.925} = €70.91$$

Solution: To raise gross proceeds of €30 million the company needs to sell €30 000 000/€60 shares, or 500 000 new shares. From Learning

Which is a slightly lower price, reflecting the additional shares this alternative requires and the fact that the share price will be a bit closer to the rights issue price. This increases the risk somewhat that the rights issue fails to get subscribed if the market experiences adverse conditions. The underwriters might therefore require a higher fee if this alternative is chosen. This is because the company is raising more money and the risks of failure are higher.

What value will these nil-paid rights have? We can calculate the lowest value for these from knowing that existing shareholders will not be worse off as a result. A shareholder with one share who has sold the rights must be in the same position as an investor who has bought five rights and one new share. So the following holds:

Pre-announcement price − 1 Pre-emptive right = Subscription price + 5 Pre-emptive rights

The pre-announcement price was €50 and the subscription price was €38, so we have:

€50 − 1 pre-emptive right = €38
+5 pre-emptive rights
€50 − €38 = 6 pre-emptive rights
€12 = 6 pre-emptive rights
€2 = value of pre-emptive right

The post-announcement share price should therefore be equal to €50 − €2 = €48, which is what we calculated earlier.

We can rearrange Equation (15.1) to solve for the value of the nil-paid subscription right as:

$$P_{\text{Nil-paid rights}} = \left(S_{\text{Before rights issue}} - S_{\text{Rights offer price}}\right) \times \frac{M_{\text{New Shares}}}{N_{\text{Original shares}} + M_{\text{New Shares}}}$$

(15.2)

Shareholders who do not wish to subscribe for the rights are guaranteed at least €2 for each right they own. In practice, as mentioned earlier, the nil-paid rights provide an option on the shares for the duration of the subscription period.

Learning by Doing Application 15.5

The Value of Nil-Paid Rights

Problem: Continuing the example of the rights issue by Técnica Madrid SA used in Learning by Doing Application 15.4, we want to calculate the value of the nil-paid rights at the time of the rights issue. On the advice of its investment bank, the company has decided to ask shareholders to subscribe for an 8 for 3 rights issue at €60 for the new shares. The original number of shares outstanding is 1.4 million and the transaction will increase the number by 525 000. Recall that the shares traded at €75 in the market prior to the announcement. What will be the value of the nil-paid rights?

Approach: We apply Equation (15.2) to find the value of the nil-paid rights.

Solution:

$$P_{\text{Nil-paid rights}}\left(S_{\text{Before rights issue}} - S_{\text{Rights offer price}}\right) \times \frac{M_{\text{New shares}}}{N_{\text{Original shares}} + M_{\text{New shares}}} = (€75 - €60) \times \frac{525}{1400 + 525}$$

$$= €15 \times 0.273 = €4.09$$

The rights are worth €4.09.

We can get the same result if we simply take the solution from Learning by Doing 15.4, which calculated the post-announcement price as €70.91. This is a reduction in the share price of €4.09, which is equivalent to the value of the nil-paid rights.

Problems with Rights Issues

There are a number of problems with rights issues. The first is that, in order to allow time for shareholders to decide, the issue remains open for at least 10 days – if not longer. Most rights issues are underwritten for the same reasons that IPOs are, since companies want to be sure they will get the proceeds from the new shares. Underwriters are unwilling to guarantee a price close to the pre-announcement price since there is a very real risk that the price might drop over the extended offer period. To take account of possible adverse movements in the share price, the new shares are generally offered at a discount of 15–30% to the pre-announcement market price. Note that existing shareholders in a rights issue are not disadvantaged by this discount and – in principle – should not care about the price at which new shares are offered. Even when existing shareholders do not participate in the rights issue, they do not suffer financially since they can sell their rights to the new shares in the market.

A second problem, and a major disadvantage of a rights issue, is that it is a costly way of raising new seasoned equity since all existing shareholders have to be offered the shares first. If they are unwilling to buy the new shares, they may be able to sell their rights to these to other investors during the offering period, who will then take up the rights. However, if the rights remain unexercised, the company will have to find outside investors for any shares that are unsold. As with an IPO, companies seek to reduce the risk of not getting the money they need by having an investment bank underwrite the rights issue. This adds significantly to the cost of raising new equity via this mechanism.

Alternatives to Rights Issues

Since rights issues are expensive, companies that may need to raise equity on a frequent basis are often given some flexibility by their shareholders to bypass their pre-emptive rights and go directly to new investors for new equity. This allows companies to raise small amounts of new equity either via an **open offer** to existing shareholders or through a **placing** of shares with a specific group of investors. The difference between an open offer and a rights issue is that, in a rights issue, shareholders have the opportunity to sell their right to buy new shares to other investors. This is not possible with an open offer since the agreement to buy the new shares on offer is not transferable.

Open offer

offer to existing shareholders, where they can buy new shares in proportion to their existing holding but cannot trade the entitlement. Also known as 'non-renounceable rights'

Placing

issue of new shares which are sold directly to new shareholders

Rights issues are the most time-consuming and costly. Open offers also tend to be expensive, since this is a general offer of sale to existing shareholders. Placings are the quickest and least expensive alternative, since the investment bank will target its customers and arrange for them to be sold new shares in the company. Through its contacts, the investment bank can seek out those investors who would be willing to purchase any new shares that a company might offer. It can then determine whether there is sufficient demand for the placement and the amount that can be sold using this method. Apart from the cost element, this is efficient in that many of the complications of a rights issue or open offer can be avoided.

Companies will seek to minimise the cost of raising seasoned equity by choosing the least-cost mechanism, subject to shareholder approval. This is the position in the UK, where many companies can issue new shares for, say, up to 5% of the existing issued share capital, via open offers or placings, or combinations of the two mechanisms.[11] Therefore, these companies have up to five alternatives to raise new seasoned equity: (1) rights issue, (2) rights issue combined with a placing, (3) open offer, (4) open offer with a placing and (5) placing. Note that there may not be as much flexibility to use alternative mechanisms in other countries where pre-emptive rights remain in force.

The situation is different again in the United States, where rights issues have largely disappeared and companies make general cash offers that are open invitations for all investors to purchase the new shares.

The Costs of a Seasoned Equity Issue

Even though a rights issue or an open offer is a wholesale market transaction, the cost of raising money via these methods is not trivial. Exhibit 15.8 shows the costs involved for a sample of UK and US seasoned equity offerings as a percentage of the funds raised.

For the UK sample, this includes the underwriting spread as a percentage and non-underwriting costs, such as out-of-pocket expenses, brokers, advisors, accounting and legal fees, and other expenses for issues of various size. Data on the total costs of seasoned equity offerings for the US market is given for comparison. In the USA, shareholders do not exercise pre-emptive rights and shares are sold via a general cash offer to all investors, including existing shareholders. Note that this exhibit does not include data on underpricing; total cost includes only underwriting spread and out-of-pocket expenses.

As you can see from comparing the all-in costs as a percentage of funds raised from Exhibit 15.8 with the costs for IPOs in the UK market given in Exhibit 15.7, the cost of a seasoned equity issue is lower. For a comparable amount, the IPO has a range of costs between 5.5% and 11% as against 4.42% for a seasoned equity offer. This reflects the greater risk involved in underwriting an IPO and the higher cost of distributing the IPO. Exhibit 15.8 also reveals significant economies of scale in raising capital. For very small issues with amounts below £6.25 million of gross proceeds, the total cost is 11.38%. For large issues above £125 million, the cost is only 2.41%.

Issuing Bonds

Large, well-established companies can offer bonds to investors in the same way as companies offer shares to investors via an IPO or a seasoned equity offer. Companies can either raise money via their domestic bond markets or, increasingly, via the **Eurobond** market. Domestic bonds are sold to investors in the issuer's home country. The Eurobond market is an international market where the main issuance and trading is based in Europe but which includes investors from all parts of the world. As a result of the introduction of the euro, for large parts of Europe, there is a growing single market for corporate bonds denominated in the euro issued by large companies.

Eurobond

a bond that is marketed internationally

Unlike equity issues, only large, well-established companies can issue public bonds. The reason is that bond investors are very credit risk conscious. Recall from Chapter 8, bond investors are subject to default risk. As a result, there is less demand for

EXHIBIT 15.8

DIRECT COSTS OF SEASONED EQUITY OFFERS IN THE UNITED KINGDOM AND UNITED STATES

United Kingdom				United States	
Gross Proceeds (£ million)	Non-underwriting Costs (%)	Underwriting (%)	Total Costs (%)	Gross Proceeds ($ million)	Total Costs (%)
125+	0.80	1.61	2.41	500+	3.15
50–124.9	1.34	1.86	3.19	100–499.9	3.85
25–49.9	1.61	1.77	3.38	60–99.9	4.96
6.25–24.9	2.88	1.54	4.42	20–59.9	6.40
0.1–6.24	10.19	1.19	11.38	2–9.9	8.72
Total	4.18	1.53	5.78		7.11

Source: Seth Armitage, 2000. The direct cost of UK rights issues and open offers, *European Financial Management* 6(1): 57–68. Reproduced with permission of Wiley-Blackwell.

Data for the UK is based on rights issues and open offers and does not include placings. For the US market, the data is for general cash offers. For the UK, the average cost is 5.78% of the gross amount raised, which compares favourably with the USA, where the average is 7.11%. You can see that the cost of seasoned equity declines as the size increases, as there are considerable fixed costs involved. For very small issues, non-underwriting costs predominate while these costs decline dramatically as a percentage as the amount raised increases. So for a large seasoned equity offer of over £125 million, the total costs are only 2.41% of the amount raised, compared with costs of 11.38% for issue sizes up to £6.25 million. The average underwriting fee for the UK market for seasoned equity offers is much lower than that for IPOs, reflecting the fact that the company's shares are already traded in the public market.

corporate bonds by poorly rated companies and the market is generally limited to the best-quality companies.

The cost of bond issuance is very low compared with that for raising equity. The London Stock Exchange study that provides the data for Exhibit 15.7 also estimated the cost of issuing debt. The study found that the average underwriting fee was 0.33%. Issuers would also have other issue costs, such as the preparation of a prospectus, listing fees, advisor fees and so forth. These typically add another 0.10% to the overall cost. In addition, the issuer will have to pay a spread over the risk-free interest rate (usually taken as the yield on government bonds). If a company issuing a 5-year Eurobond (which pays interest annually) is required to offer a 2% spread and the government yield is 4%, the required coupon is 6%. The company's all-in cost for the bond issue – including issuing costs – will mean it will receive €99.57 (€100 – €100 × 0.0043) for every €100 of debt issued. Using the approach developed in Chapter 8, we can derive the all-in yield to maturity on the bond as:

$$€99.57 = \frac{€6.00}{1+R} + \frac{€6.00}{(1+R)^2} + \frac{€6.00}{(1+R)^3}$$
$$+ \frac{€6.00}{(1+R)^4} + \frac{€106.00}{(1+R)^5}$$

Solving for R, we find that the all-in yield is 6.10%.

Before You Go On

1. Explain why firms generally sell their equity through rights issues.
2. What are the attractions of making a placing of shares rather than having a rights issue?
3. For most companies, what limits the availability of debt finance through the public bond markets?

PRIVATE MARKETS AND BANK LOANS

Learning Objective 6

Explain why a firm that has access to the public markets might elect to raise money through a private placement.

As we have noted, the public markets for debt and equity are wholesale markets where firms can often sell securities at the lowest possible cost. For various reasons, however, firms may sometimes need – or prefer – to sell their securities in private markets. In this section, we first consider various aspects of the private securities markets and then briefly discuss private placements of equity and debt.

Private versus Public Markets

As mentioned above, firms that sell securities in the public markets are typically large, well-known firms with high credit quality and sustainable profits. Of course, not every firm reaches these levels of achievement. As a result, many small and medium-sized enterprises (SMEs) and firms of lower credit standing have limited access, or no access, to the public markets. Their cheapest source of external funding is often the private markets.

Market conditions also affect whether a firm can sell its securities in the public markets. When market conditions are unstable, some smaller firms that were previously able to sell securities in the public markets can no longer do so at a reasonable price. The reason for this is that during periods of market instability, investors seek and want to hold high-quality securities, and they are reluctant to purchase or hold high-risk securities in their portfolios. This phenomenon is called *flight to quality* and refers to moving capital to the safest possible investments to protect oneself during unsettled periods in the market.

A number of sizable companies of high credit quality prefer to sell their securities in the private markets even though they can access public markets. Entrepreneurs, families or family foundations own many of these private companies. Two examples of large 'family' businesses that avoid public markets and fund themselves privately are Bosch, the German automotive supplier, and IKEA, the Swedish-based international home products retailer. Such firms elect to avoid the public markets for different reasons. Some wish to avoid the regulatory costs and transparency requirements that come with public sales of securities, as discussed earlier. Others believe that their firms have intricate business structures or complex legal or financial structures that can best be explained to a small group of sophisticated investors rather than to the public at large.

We should mention that bootstrapping and venture capital financing are part of the private market as well. We discussed these two processes at the beginning of the chapter because they are primary sources of funding for new businesses.

Private Placements

As you may recall from Chapter 2, a *private placement* occurs when a firm sells unlisted securities directly to investors such as insurance companies, commercial banks or wealthy individuals. Most private placements involve the sale of debt issues but equity issues can also be placed privately. About half of all corporate debt is sold through the private placement market.

Investment banks and commercial banks often assist firms with private placements. They help the issuer locate potential buyers for their securities, put the transaction together and assist in the documentation and other elements of the placement.

They may also help negotiate the terms and price of the sale but they do not underwrite the issue. In a traditional private placement, the issuer sells the securities *directly* to investors.

For certain issuers, private placements have a number of advantages, relative to public offerings. The cost of funds, net of transaction costs, may be lower, especially for smaller firms and those with low credit ratings. In addition, private lenders, because of their intimate knowledge of the firm and its management, are more willing to negotiate changes to a bond contract, if changes are needed. Furthermore, if a firm suffers financial distress, the problems are more likely to be resolved without going into bankruptcy proceedings. Other advantages include the speed at which private placements can be completed and flexibility in issue size. If the issuer and the investor already have a relationship, a sale can be completed in a few days and placements of sums as small as €10 million are possible.

The biggest drawback of private placements involves the ability of the purchaser to resell the securities. As their name indicates, private placement securities have limited marketability and are illiquid securities unless the firm subsequently lists the issue on an exchange. This limits the sale of private placements to investors who are willing to hold the securities to maturity and who are not obliged to hold listed securities for regulatory reasons. To address their concern about the lack of marketability, investors in private placements require a higher yield relative to a comparable public offering, or that the firm agrees to list the securities shortly after the transaction is complete. While illiquidity is a problem, in many countries, rules exist which allow large financial institutions to trade unlisted securities among themselves.

Competitive or Negotiated Sale

In an offer of new securities, management must decide whether to place the securities on a competitive or a negotiated basis. In a *competitive placement*, the firm specifies the type and number of securities it wants to sell and hires an investment bank to do the origination work; once the origination is complete, the firm invites underwriters to bid *competitively* to buy the issue.[12] The investment banking firm that pays the highest price for the securities wins the bid. The winning underwriter then pays for the securities and makes them available to individual investors at the offer price.

In a *negotiated sale*, the issuer selects the underwriter at the beginning of the origination process. At that time, the scope of the work is defined and the issuer negotiates the origination and underwriter's fees to be charged. The issuer and underwriter then work closely to design the issue and determine the most favourable time to take the securities to market. Following an assessment of demand, the offer price is set and the underwriter pays the issuer for the securities and sells them to individual investors.

Lowest-Cost Method of Sale

Which method of sale – competitive or negotiated – results in the lowest possible funding cost for the issuing firm? This question has been hotly debated and the results from empirical studies are mixed.

The argument for competitive bidding is straightforward: competition keeps everyone honest. That is, the greater the number of bidders, the greater the competition for the security issue and the lower the cost to the issuer. Negotiated sales lack competition and therefore should be the more costly method of sale.

Not everyone agrees with this argument, however. Proponents of negotiated sales argue that in a negotiated sale the investment banker works closely with the issuer and thus has intimate knowledge of the firm and its problems. As a result, the investment banker is in a better position to reduce uncertainty surrounding the issue and tell the firm's 'story' to potential investors, resulting in a lower issue cost. Proponents also argue that negotiated sales involve *potential competition*. The potential competitors are the other investment banks that were not chosen to underwrite the current issue but would like to underwrite the firm's next issue. These investment bankers will not hesitate to drop by and tell the issuer's CFO how much better they could have done than the underwriter that was chosen. Thus, the threat of potential competition provides many of the same benefits as direct competition.

Selecting the Best Method

In the end, the best method of sale depends on the complexity of the sale and the market conditions at the time of sale. It also depends on the type of securities being offered.

For debt issues, most experts believe that competitive sales are the least costly method of selling so-called *vanilla bonds* when market conditions are stable. Recall that vanilla bonds are bonds with no unusual features. Their terms and conditions are standardised and well known to market participants, and they lack complex features. These securities are like commodities because market participants understand the risks of investing in them and are comfortable buying them. In contrast, when there are complex circumstances to explain or when market conditions are unstable, negotiated sales provide the least costly method of sale for debt issues. In these situations, a negotiated sale allows the underwriter to better manage uncertainty and explain the firm's situation, which results in the lowest funding cost.

For equity securities, negotiated sales generally provide the lowest-cost method of sale. Equity issues by their very nature tend to be complex and, for the reasons just mentioned, complexities are better handled when sales are negotiated. Thus, it is no surprise that virtually all equity issues, including IPOs, involve negotiated sales.

Private Equity Firms

Like venture capitalists, private equity firms pool money from pension funds, insurance companies, foundations and endowments and other sources to make investments. Unlike venture capitalists, private equity firms invest in more mature companies and they often purchase 100% of a business. They are particularly active in **management buyouts**, where a large company disposes of a business unit and this is purchased by the existing managers and

the private equity firm. Private equity firm managers look to increase the value of the firms they acquire by closely monitoring their performance and providing better management. Once value is increased, they sell the firms for a profit. Private equity firms generally hold investments for three to five years.

> ### Management buyout
>
> purchase of a company by the existing management team

While private equity firms often purchase 100% of a business, they also represent a potential source of capital for large public firms that have businesses – such as divisions or individual plants – which they are interested in selling. Large public firms often sell businesses when they no longer fit the firms' strategies or when they are offered a price they cannot refuse. Selling such businesses via a management buyout is an alternative to selling equity or debt as a means of raising new capital.[13]

Private equity firms establish *private equity funds* to make investments. These funds are often organised as *limited partnerships* (or, more recently, limited liability companies), which consist of (1) *general partners* who manage the firm's investments – the acquired firms – and (2) *limited partners* who invest money in the firm but have limited liability and are not involved in the day-to-day activities of the firm.[14] As owners, the limited partners share in the income, capital gains and tax benefits from the private equity funds. The general partners, who also invest in the funds, receive income, capital gains and tax benefits that are proportionate to their investments. In addition, as compensation for managing the funds, general partners collect management fees and receive a percentage of the income and capital gains that are earned with the limited partners' money.

Private equity funds have historically focused on investments in small and medium-sized firms that have stable cash flows and where there is the potential to improve those cash flows substantially. In recent years, however, private equity firms have been able to raise so much capital that they have started doing large deals that involve taking public companies private. For instance, VNU NV, the Netherlands-based global information and media company, went private in 2006 in an €8.7 billion transaction. Other notable deals are the French companies Pages Jaunes (€3.4 billion), Europcar (€3.3 billion) and the German Kion Group (€4.0 billion).

Private equity investors focus on firms that have stable cash flows because they use a lot of debt to finance their acquisitions. A firm must have stable positive cash flows in order to make the interest and principal payments. A private equity firm may borrow as much as €3 or €4 for every euro it invests. By adding more debt, the private equity firm frees up its own cash, allowing it to make additional investments and increasing its return on its equity investments. When a large amount of leverage is used to take over a company, the transaction is called a *leveraged buyout*.[15]

How do private equity firms improve the performance of firms in which they invest? First, they make sure that the firms have the best possible management teams. Since a private equity firm typically owns 100% of the equity in a firm it invests in, its general partners have the ability to replace the management team when necessary. Second, private equity investors closely monitor each firm's performance and provide advice and direction to the firm's management team. General partners have in-depth knowledge of the industries in which they invest and some have been CEOs of similar firms. Third, private equity investors often facilitate mergers and acquisitions that help improve the competitive positions of the companies in which they invest.

Agency problems tend to be smaller in firms owned by private equity investors than in public firms. In public firms, shareholders are the owners. However, we know that it is not practical for dispersed shareholders to be actively engaged in managing the firm. Day-to-day decision-making responsibilities are delegated to the firm's managers. Managers are shareholders' agents and are supposed to act in the best interest of shareholders. Yet, as we discussed in Chapter 1, managers tend to pursue their own self-interest instead of the interests

of shareholders. The misalignment between the owners' best interests and the manager's self-interest results in agency costs. Private equity funds have much lower agency costs than the average publicly held firm. Since the general partners in a private equity fund are owners and benefit greatly from the value they create, they have every incentive to act in a manner consistent with maximising the value of limited partners' investments.

Finally, we should note that private equity firms carry a much smaller regulatory burden and fewer financial reporting requirements than do public firms. Specifically, private equity firms are able to avoid many of the listing and compliance costs and other regulatory burdens, such as compliance with corporate governance principles.

Commercial Bank Lending

> ### Learning Objective 7
> Review some advantages of borrowing from a commercial bank rather than selling securities in financial markets, and discuss bank term loans.

The previous sections have discussed long-term debt and equity funding that is obtained in private and public financial markets. A major source of funds for businesses comes from commercial banks. Almost every company has a working relationship with at least one bank, and smaller companies depend on them for funding and for financial advice. Next, we review some of the most common types of bank loans used by business firms. Most small and medium-sized firms borrow from commercial banks on a regular basis. A survey by the OECD indicates that for small and medium-sized enterprises (SMEs), over 80% of them rely on bank loans as their primary source of funds.

Floating Rate Loans

The most common type of business loan is a *floating rate loan* or *overdraft*. The borrowing rate is based on the bank's *base rate* or *prime rate of interest*, which is historically the loan rate that banks charge their most creditworthy customers. In practice, many customers are able to borrow at a spread to the *interbank rate*, which is the interest rate at which banks lend to each other and which is lower than the prime rate.[16] These loans are often used to finance working capital needs, such as the purchase of inventory or to finance accounts receivable. To ensure these short-term loans are not used as long-term financing, banks may require that the loan balance be brought to zero for a short time each year.

The prime rate charged by a bank might be higher than other market borrowing rates as represented by the interbank rate. This is because banks provide a range of services with these loans, much as venture capitalists provide services to start-up businesses. For example, small and medium-sized firms often rely on the bank's lending officer to serve as the firm's financial adviser and keep the CFO abreast of current developments and trends in financing. Thus, the cost of a prime-rate loan can include the cost of the advisory services as well as the cost of the financing.

Bank Term Loans

Term loans are defined as business loans with maturities greater than one year. Term loans are the most common form of intermediate-term financing provided by commercial banks and there is wide diversity in how these loans are structured. In general, they have maturities between 1 and 15 years, but most are in the 1–5-year range. Bank term loans may be secured or unsecured and the funds can be used to buy inventory or to finance plant and equipment. As in all bank commercial lending, banks maintain close relationships with borrowers and bank officers closely monitor borrower performance. These loans may carry a fixed or floating rate of interest and may include the possibility of drawing down and repaying the loan over its life. In this case, it is known as a *revolving term loan*.

> **Term loan**
>
> a business loan with a maturity greater than one year

The Loan Pricing Model

We have mentioned that the prime rate is the rate banks historically charge their most creditworthy customers. The prime rate is not a market-determined interest rate, since bank management sets it. However, the prime rate is subject to market forces that affect the bank's cost of funds and the rate the bank's customers are willing to accept. Thus, as the general level of interest rates in the economy increases or decreases, bank management raises or lowers the prime rate to adjust for the bank's cost of funds and to respond to competitive conditions.

In determining the interest rate to charge on a loan, the bank takes the prime rate plus two other factors into account. The calculation, called the bank loan pricing model, is as follows:

$$k_l = PR + DRP + MAT \qquad (15.3)$$

where:

k_l = the loan rate (%)
PR = the prime rate (%)
DRP = the adjustment for default risk above the prime rate (%)
MAT = the adjustment for the yield curve for term loans (%)

Before making a loan, the bank conducts a credit analysis of the customer. The first step is to determine the customer's credit category. Banks usually have seven to ten credit risk categories, which look very much like bond ratings. If the customer is of the highest credit standing, it is classified as a prime-rate customer and, thus, borrows at the prime rate (or the interbank rate if it does not require substantial services). For all other customers, there is some mark-up above the prime rate to take account of the differential in credit risk (DRP). For example, if a bank customer is 'prime + 2', the customer borrows at the prevailing prime rate plus 2%.

The second step, if the customer wants a term loan, is to adjust for the term to maturity (MAT). MAT is defined as the difference between the yield on a government security with the same maturity as the term loan and the yield on a three-month treasury bill. Mathematically, that can be expressed as follows:

$$MAT = y_n - y_{3\text{-mo}}$$

where y_n is the yield on a government security with n years to maturity and $y_{3\text{-mo}}$ is the yield on a three-month treasury security. (As a practical matter, most financial analysts treat the prime rate as a three-month interest rate.) Suppose, for example, that a customer wants a two-year term loan. If the yield on a two-year government security is 4.00% and the yield on a three-month treasury bill is 1.25%, then the appropriate MAT is 2.75% (4.00 − 1.25).

We will consider an example of credit analysis for a short-term loan, which requires consideration of only the prime rate and the DRP. Suppose a bank has two customers that are medium-sized business firms. Firm A has the bank's highest credit standing and firm B's credit standing is prime + 3. The bank prime rate is 1.75%. What is the appropriate loan rate for each customer, assuming the loan is not a term loan?

Firm A, with its high credit standing, is clearly a prime customer, so its borrowing rate is the prime rate, 1.75%. Firm B's credit rating is prime + 3, or prime plus 3%, so its borrowing cost is 4.75% (1.75 + 3.00). Note that the prime rate is a floating rate. Thus, if the bank raises its prime rate by 25 basis points, both firms' borrowing costs increase by 25 basis points, firm A's to 2.0% and firm B's to 5.0%.

Learning by Doing Application 15.6

Pricing a Term Loan

Problem: In our text example, firm B's borrowing cost for a short-term loan is 4.75%. Suppose, however, that firm B's CFO would like to lock in the borrowing cost for five years and asks for a quote on a five-year term loan. The lending officer has access to the following information: a three-month treasury bill yields 1.00% and a five-year government security yields 2.80%. What loan rate should the bank quote?

Approach: We first need to find the appropriate MAT, which in this case is the difference between the five-year and the three-month government borrowing rates. Then, by applying Equation (15.3), we can calculate the five-year term loan rate.

Solution: First, we find the MAT:

MAT = 5-year government security −
  3-month treasury bill rate
 = 2.80% − 1.80%
 = 1.80%

We can now apply Equation (15.3):

k_l = PR + DRP + MAT
 = 1.75% + 3.00% + 1.80%
 = 6.55%

Lease Finance

Leasing is a way for firms to finance tangible assets. In a **lease**, the leasing company, which is usually a bank or finance company, purchases the asset and then provides it to the firm which makes periodic payments in exchange, just like it would if it had borrowed the money. Typically the leasing agreement, which will run for a good part of the economic life of the asset, has several features that make it attractive to firms: (1) the contract allows the firm to acquire the asset at a pre-agreed price at the end of the leasing period, (2) the present value of the payments the firm makes are about the same as the asset price at the start of the agreement and (3) the leased asset can be very specific to the needs of the firm. There may also be break clauses giving the company the option to terminate the lease in the future. Given these features, one can see that leasing is another way for firms to borrow to finance their investment in fixed assets. From the leasing company's perspective, offering leases is attractive as the asset remains its property until all the conditions of the contract are fulfilled.

Lease

finance arrangement where the lender retains ownership of the asset but the firm makes periodic payments for the use of the asset for the term of the lease

Firms, especially small and medium-sized enterprises, find leasing attractive since they may not have the borrowing capacity to purchase the assets and the interest rate in the lease offered by leasing companies is very competitive.

How to evaluate a lease? As we have mentioned before, managers are concerned with raising finance at the least possible cost. The decision to borrow and buy or lease is made the same way as a capital budgeting analysis for two mutually exclusive investments. As always, firms are interested in the *after-tax* cost and it is therefore necessary to take into account what the cash flows are if the company borrows and buys the asset as against leasing the asset.

Let us consider an example. Rotterdam Kanaal Baggeren NV wants to purchase a dredger that will cost €1 million. The company can lease the dredger for its economic life, which is 5 years, at a cost per year of €210 000, starting with an immediate payment, so there are six payments in all. For simplicity, we will assume there is no salvage value for the barge at the end of year 5. We also need to know the company tax rate – which is 40% for Kanaal Baggeren – and that it can borrow for five years at 10% per year.

First we must lay out the cash flows from the decision to lease. By leasing, the company 'gives up' on the tax depreciation that it would otherwise get from owning the asset. Straight-line depreciation is applied to this asset, so the company can set off against profits €200 000 per year (€1 million/5 years). If it leases, it does not own the asset so it gives up the tax benefit of owning, which is the tax depreciation benefit or tax shield. This is simply the depreciation times the tax rate, which is €80 000 per year (€200 000 × 0.40). The lease payments are an allowable expense for tax purposes, so there is a tax saving from these payments. This will be €84 000 per year (€210 000 × 0.40). We now have all the information we need to lay out the cash flows for comparing the two alternatives and they are presented below:

In thousands of euros (€000s)	Year 0	Year 1	Year 2	Year 3	Year 4	Year 5
Cost of the dredger	€1000					
Loss of depreciation tax shield	—	−80	−80	−80	−80	−80
Lease payment	−210	−210	−210	−210	−210	−210
Lease payment tax shield	84	84	84	84	84	84
Lease cash flows	€ 874	−€206	−€206	−€206	−€206	−€206

To find out whether this lease is Kanaal Baggeren's least-cost alternative, we have to work out the net present value of the transaction. The company can borrow at 10%. The after-tax cost of debt, which is appropriate here since we are comparing two debt alternatives, is 6% ($0.10 \times (1 - 0.40)$). We now need to discount the lease cash flows at this after-tax cost of debt, namely:

$$\begin{aligned} NPV &= €874 + \frac{-€206}{1.06} + \frac{-€206}{(1.06)^2} + \frac{-€206}{(1.06)^3} \\ &\quad + \frac{-€206}{(1.06)^4} + \frac{-€206}{(1.06)^5} \\ &= €874 - €194.2 - €183.2 - €172.9 \\ &\quad - €163.1 - €153.8 \\ &= €7 \end{aligned}$$

The analysis shows a positive net present value of €7000. This shows that leasing the barge is cheaper than buying it directly and borrowing the money at 10% to do so.

Note the issues involved. The attractiveness of leasing as against borrowing depends on the company's tax rate, how assets are depreciated for tax purposes, whether the company can use the tax shields from acquiring the asset and the rate at which the leasing company offers finance. Changes in each of these variables will alter the decision between leasing and borrowing.

Of course, for many firms there is not much of a choice. For instance, Kanaal Baggeren's balance sheet may not have supported a further €1 million borrowing due to the firm already having excessive leverage. In this case, leasing companies may be more prepared to provide finance, since they retain ownership of the assets, than banks, which may well only have a general charge against the assets of the business, some of which may have little value if the business goes bankrupt. Consequently, we find that many highly leveraged, asset-intensive businesses which have a ready market in their assets (airlines are an example) often make extensive use of leasing. Banks are reluctant to lend directly to such businesses but are quite prepared to lease them the assets they need for their operations.

Learning by Doing Application 15.7

Evaluating a Lease Decision

Problem: Alexis Business Airways (ABA) provides executive travel services. It needs to acquire a second-hand Phenom 100, an executive jet made by Embraer. The jet will cost €800 000 and is expected to last for five years, after which it will have no value. ABA pays company tax at 30% and can borrow from a bank at a fixed rate of 13% per year for five years. If the company buys the Phenom, it will depreciate it for tax purposes using straight-line depreciation. A leasing company has said it will lease the aircraft to ABA for five years with the company making six payments of €184 000, with the first payment being made immediately and thereafter at the end of each year.

Approach: To decide whether leasing or buying the Phenom is the more attractive, we first need to work out the differences in the cash flows between the two alternatives, taking into account the loss in tax depreciation from not purchasing, the gain in the tax shield from the lease payment expenses and not having to borrow to purchase the aircraft. These differences must then be present-valued at ABA's after-tax borrowing rate.

Solution: First, we calculate the loss of tax shield from depreciating the Phenom that is given up if the lease alternative is chosen. The plane costs €800 000, the depreciation will be €160 000 and hence the tax shield given up will be €48 000 (€160 000 × 0.30). The company will offset the leasing expense against taxes and the tax shield will be €63 000 (€211 000 × 0.30). The payments in thousand of euros will therefore be:

$$NPV = €652 + \frac{-€177}{1.091} + \frac{-€177}{(1.091)^2} + \frac{-€177}{(1.091)^3}$$
$$+ \frac{-€177}{(1.091)^4} + \frac{-€177}{(1.091)^5}$$
$$= €652 - €161.9 - €148.4 - €136.0$$
$$- €124.6 - €114.2$$
$$= -€14$$

	Year					
	0	1	2	3	4	5
Cost of Phenom 100	€800					
Loss of depreciation tax shield		−48	−48	−48	−48	−48
Lease payment	−184	−184	−184	−184	−184	−184
Lease payment tax shield	55	55	55	55	55	55
Lease cash flows	€671	−€177	−€177	−€177	−€177	−€177

The final step is to present-value the lease cash flows at the after-tax cost of debt. The pre-tax cost of debt is 13% and the after-tax cost will be 9.1% (0.13 × (1 − 0.30)). The calculation is:

The lease finance alternative has a negative net present value of −€14 000 compared with the borrowing alternative. Alexis Business Airways should borrow the money and buy the Phenom 100 as it will cost less than leasing it.

Concluding Comments on Funding the Firm

This chapter has focused on how firms raise capital to fund their current operations and growth. How a firm actually raises capital depends on the firm's stage in its life cycle, its expected cash flows and its risk characteristics. For new businesses, funding comes from friends, family, credit cards and venture capitalists. More mature firms rely heavily on (1) public markets, (2) private markets and (3) bank loans. Each market has particular characteristics and firms select the method of financing that provides the best combination of low-cost borrowing and favourable terms and conditions. It should be emphasised that there are no simple rules or formulas on how to fund the enterprise. In Chapter 16, we tackle a number of important questions regarding the choice of debt or equity and how this affects a firm's capital structure and the use of financial leverage.

Before You Go On

1. What are the disadvantages of a private placement sale compared with a public sale?
2. Why can some companies borrow at an interest rate below the bank's prime rate of interest?

SUMMARY OF LEARNING OBJECTIVES

1. **Explain what is meant by bootstrapping when raising seed financing and why it is important.**

   Bootstrapping is the process by which many entrepreneurs raise 'seed' money and obtain other resources necessary to start new businesses. Seed money often comes from the entrepreneur's savings and credit cards and from family and friends. Bootstrapping is important because business start-ups are a significant factor in determining and sustaining long-term economic growth in a region or national economy. Indeed, some state and local governments have invested heavily in business incubators, hoping to foster new business formation.

2. **Explain the role of venture capitalists in the economy and discuss how they reduce their risk when investing in *start-up businesses*.**

   Venture capitalists specialise in helping business firms get started by advising management and providing early-stage financing. Because of the high risk of investing in start-up businesses, venture capitalists finance projects in stages and often require the owners to make a significant personal investment in the firm. The owners' equity stake signals their belief in the viability of the project and ensures that management actions are focused on building a successful business. Risk is also reduced through syndication and because of the venture capitalist's in-depth knowledge of the industry and technology.

3. **Discuss the advantages and disadvantages of going public and be able to compute the net proceeds from an IPO.**

   The major advantages of entering public markets are that they provide firms with access to large quantities of money at relatively low cost, enable firms to attract and motivate good managers and provide liquidity for existing shareholders, such as entrepreneurs, other managers and venture capitalists. Disadvantages include the high cost of the IPO, the cost of ongoing disclosure requirements, the need to disclose sensitive information and possible incentives focus on short-term profits rather than on long-term value maximisation. The main text and Learning by Doing Application 15.1 provide practice in computing IPO proceeds.

4. **Explain why, when underwriting new security offerings, investment bankers prefer that the securities be underpriced and compute the total cost of an IPO.**

   When underwriting new securities, investment bankers prefer that the issue be underpriced because it increases the likelihood of a successful offering. The lower the offering price, the more likely that the issue will sell out quickly – and the less likely that the underwriters will end up with unsold securities. Furthermore, many investment bankers will argue that some underpricing helps attract long-term institutional investors who help provide stability for the share price.

   The total cost of issuing an IPO includes three elements: (1) the underwriter's spread; (2) out-of-pocket expenses, which include legal fees, listing fees and other expenses; and (3) the cost of underpricing. For calculations of these costs, see the main text including Learning by Doing Application 15.3. Exhibit 15.6 gives the average costs for IPOs in recent years.

5. **Discuss the difficulties and costs of bringing a rights issue to market and be able to compute the total cost of issuing a rights issue.**

   Companies with existing listed shares often raise additional equity capital by rights issues. Existing shareholders have pre-emptive rights that mean they get preference in any seasoned offer of new shares. Rights issues are offered at a discount to the existing share price since there is a period between the offer and the time shareholders need to take up their rights. Once the issue is announced, the share price will fall and Learning by Doing Application 15.4 shows how the new price can be calculated based on the number of new shares on offer and the current shares outstanding. The nil-paid rights which shareholders can sell to other investors also have a value.

Because rights issues are relatively costly but lower than the cost of issuing an IPO, various alternative mechanisms have been developed that are used to raise small amounts of new equity. Some average costs are listed in Exhibit 15.7.

6. **Explain why a firm that has access to the public markets might elect to raise money through a private placement.**

    There are a number of advantages to private placements, even for companies with access to the public markets. A private placement may be more cost effective and can be accomplished much more rapidly. In addition, some larger companies, especially those owned by entrepreneurs or families, may not wish to be exposed to the public scrutiny that comes with public sales of securities.

7. **Review some of the advantages of borrowing from a commercial bank rather than selling securities in financial markets and discuss bank term loans.**

    Most small and medium-sized firms borrow from commercial banks on a regular basis. Small and medium-sized firms are likely to have limited access to the financial markets. For these firms, banks provide not only funds but a full range of services, including financial advice. Furthermore, if a firm's financial circumstances change over time, it is much easier for the firm to borrow or renegotiate the debt contract with a bank than with other lenders. For many companies, bank borrowing may be the lowest-cost source of funds.

    Bank term loans are business loans with maturities greater than one year. Most bank term loans have maturities from one to five years, though the maturity may be as long as 15 years. The cost of the loans depends on three factors: the prime rate, an adjustment for default risk and an adjustment for the term to maturity.

SUMMARY OF KEY EQUATIONS

Equation	Description	Formula
(15.1)	Ex-rights issue announcement price	$S_{\text{After rights issue}} = \dfrac{N_{\text{Original shares}} \times S_{\text{Before rights issue}} + M_{\text{New shares}} S_{\text{Rights offer price}}}{N_{\text{Original shares}} + M_{\text{New shares}}}$
(15.2)	Price of nil-paid rights	$P_{\text{Nil-paid rights}} = \left(S_{\text{Before rights issue}} - S_{\text{Rights offer price}} \right) \times \dfrac{M_{\text{New shares}}}{N_{\text{Original shares}} + M_{\text{New shares}}}$
(15.3)	Bank loan pricing model	$k_l = PR + DRP + MAT$

SELF-STUDY PROBLEMS

15.1. Vigneto di Lombardi S.p.A. is planning to raise €1 million in new equity through a private placement. If the sale price is €18 per share, how many shares does the company have to issue?

15.2. Suppose a firm does an IPO and the investment bank offers to buy the securities for €34 per share with an offering price of €42. What is the underwriter's spread? Assume that the underwriter's cost of bringing the security to the market is €5 per share. What is the net profit?

15.3. Le Coureur SA, designer and marketer of athletic clothing, is planning an expansion into foreign markets and needs to raise €10 million to finance this move. The company plans a rights issue offering for €13 a share. The company's underwriters charge a 5% spread. How many shares does the company need to sell to achieve its goal?

15.4. Freizeitbooten GmbH needs to borrow €23 million for a factory equipment upgrade. Management decides to borrow the money from the bank. As part of the analysis, the CFO of the company determines that the 3-month treasury bill yields 4.32%, the firm's credit rating is AA and the yield on 10-year government bonds is 1.06% higher than that for 3-month bills. Double A bonds are selling for 1.35% above the 10-year government bond rate. What is the borrowing cost for this transaction?

15.5. You are considering starting a new online dating service, but you lack the initial capital. What are your options for financing?

SOLUTIONS TO SELF-STUDY PROBLEMS

15.1. To raise €1 million, Vigneto di Lombardi has to issue 55 556 shares (€1 000 000/ €18 = 55 556).

15.2. The underwriter's spread: €42 – €34 = €8, or 23.5% (€8/€34)
Net profit: €8 – €5 = €3 per share

15.3. The underwriter's spread = 5%
Price per share for the firm = [€13.00 × (1 – 0.05)] = €12.35
To raise €10 million, the company needs to issue 809 717 new shares (€10 000 000/ €12.35 = 809 717).

15.4. The borrowing cost for Freizeitbooten can be calculated as follows:

$$K_1 = 4.32\% + 1.35\% + 1.06\%$$
$$= 6.73\%$$

15.5. Possible sources of capital include your own savings, friends and family, wealthy individuals (business angels), venture capital firms and financial institutions.

CRITICAL THINKING QUESTIONS

15.1. Assume you work for a venture capital firm and are approached by a couple of recent college graduates with a request to fund their new business. If you are interested in the idea, what process will you follow?

15.2. Identify the three basic services an investment banker provides to help firms bring new security issues to the market. During which stage of the IPO does the investment banker take on the risk of the offering? Is there an alternative in which the risk remains with the company going public?

15.3. Define *underpricing*, and discuss why the majority of IPOs are underpriced. What role do investment banks play in this process?

15.4. Explain why a company might choose to remain private.

15.5. Identify the three cost components that make up the total cost for a company to issue securities. Briefly explain each.

15.6. What are the characteristics of a public bond? (Think in terms of comparing it to private placement and bank term loans.)

15.7. Discuss the advantages of a placing. Under what conditions would shareholders be most likely to accept surrendering their pre-emptive rights by allowing a company to complete a placing of its shares?

15.8. Identify whether each of the following factors implies a lower or higher price for a bond.
  a. Low marketability of the security
  b. Short term to maturity
  c. Low credit rating of the issuer
  d. No call provision

15.9. Explain why time might play a significant role during periods of low interest in a decision whether to do a private placement deal or a public sale.

15.10. Managers at a large firm are looking for a medium-sized loan with a long term to maturity and low liquidity. Which of the following types of debt would be the most appropriate?
  a. Public bond
  b. Private placement
  c. Bank term loan

QUESTIONS AND PROBLEMS

Basic

15.1. **Venture capital:** What items in a business plan does a venture capitalist look for in deciding whether to provide initial financing?

15.2. **Venture capital:** You finally decide to act on your brilliant idea and start an online textbook rental company. You develop a detailed business plan and calculate that you will need about €350 000 of initial funding to get the business going. Luckily for you, you have lined up two venture capital firms offering to supply the funding. What criteria should guide your decision to select one firm over the other?

15.3. **Venture capital:** What are some viable exit strategies for a start-up company?

15.4. **IPO:** Briefly describe the IPO process.

15.5. **IPO:** Based on your knowledge from previous chapters, what are some methods an investment banker uses to determine an IPO price? What factors will play a significant role in the calculation?

15.6. **Cost of debt versus equity:** What are some of the possible reasons raising debt financing is cheaper than equity financing?

15.7. **IPO pricing:** Trajax AG, a high-technology firm in Dortmund, issues a €91 million IPO priced at €27 per share and the offering price to the public is €33 per share. The firm's legal fees, listing fees and other administrative costs are €450 000. The firm's share price increases 17% on the first day. What is the firm's total cost of issuing the securities?

15.8. IPO pricing: Milan Biotech S.p.A. plans a €114 million IPO pricing its shares at €43 and the offering price to the public for the shares is €51. The firm's legal fees, listing fees and other administrative costs total €525 000. The firm's share price increases 14% on the first day. What is the firm's total cost of issuing the securities?

15.9. Rights issues: Are the following statements true or false?

a. Rights issues disadvantage existing shareholders at the expense of new shareholders.

b. An existing shareholder will lose out if they do not take up their nil paid preemptive rights and subscribe for the new shares on offer.

c. Deeply discounted rights issues mean that existing shareholders lose out from the dilution of their investment.

d. With a rights issue, the time gap between the announcement and payment dates works against existing shareholders' interests.

e. Rights issues provide legal protection to existing shareholders against dilution of their interest in the company.

15.10. Rights issue: What are the steps in a rights issue? Explain each step.

15.11. Rights issue: Collegial de Lisboa SA needs to raise €25 million. It currently has 5 million shares outstanding and the current price for the shares is €32. Their investment bank suggests that a discount of 20% is required for the rights issue. What ratio of new to old shares does the company need for the rights issue so that it gets all the money it needs and there is a whole number of shares in the offer?

15.12. Issuing securities: Explain what is meant by economies of scale in issuing securities.

15.13. Bank term lending: Explain how term to maturity affects the price of a bank loan.

15.14. Prime-rate lending: Suppose two firms want to borrow money from a bank for a period of one year. Firm A has excellent credit, whereas firm B's credit standing is prime +2. The current prime rate is 6.75%, the 30-year government bond yield is 4.35%, the three-month treasury bill yield is 3.54% and the 10-year government bond yield is 4.22%. What are the appropriate loan rates for each customer?

15.15. Prime-rate lending: Now suppose that firm B from Problem 15.14 decides to get a term loan for 10 years. How does this affect the company's borrowing cost?

Intermediate

15.16. Venture capital: You work for a venture capital firm and are approached to finance a new high-tech start-up. While you believe in the business idea, you feel it is very risky. What strategies can help to mitigate the risk to your firm? Explain how these measures would work.

15.17. IPO: Brokerin Manderin is a broker that brings new issues of small firms to the market. Their most recent deal for Dextra AG had the following characteristics:

Number of shares: 1 000 000
Price of shares to the public: €15
Proceeds to Dextra: €13 500 000

Legal fees were €150 000, printing costs were €56 000 and all other expenses were €72 000. What is the profit or loss for Brokerin Manderin?

15.18. IPO: When Abbigliamento Pascale S.p.A. went public in September 2008, the offer price for the shares was €22.00 and the closing price at the end of the first day was €23.90. The firm issued 4.9 million shares. What was the loss to the company due to underpricing?

15.19. IPO: Bellex Technik AG issues an IPO sold on a best-effort basis. The company's investment bank demands a spread of 17% of the offer price for the shares, which is set at €30.

Three million shares are issued. However, the bank was overly optimistic and eventually is only able to sell the shares for €28. What are the proceeds for the issuer and the underwriter?

15.20. IPO: Suppose a biotech company in Nice, France, issues an €85 million IPO priced at €72 per share. The offering price to the public is €75 per share. The out-of-pocket expenses are €340 000. The shares' closing price at the end of the first day is €84. What is the firm's total cost of issuing the securities?

15.21. IPO: An online medical advice company just completed an IPO with an investment bank on a firm-commitment basis. The firm issued 5 million ordinary shares and the underwriting fees were €4.20 per share. The offering price was €26 per share.
  a. What were the total proceeds from the sale of the ordinary shares?
  b. How much money did the company actually make from the transaction?
  c. How much money did the investment bank make?

15.22. IPO underpricing: Suppose that a biotech firm in Valencia raises €120 million in an IPO. The firm receives €23 for the shares and these are sold to the public for €25. The firm's legal fees, listing fees and other administrative costs are €270 000. The firm's share price increases 17.5% on the first day. What is the firm's total cost of issuing the securities?

15.23. Rights issue: Haarlem Technologie NV has 4 million shares outstanding and the shares are currently trading at €45 in the market. The company has been informed that a rights issue discount of 20% is appropriate. The company wants to raise

€36 million before expenses. What will be the share price after the announcement of the rights issue?

15.24. Rights issue: Seagram Exploitation Associates plc has announced a rights issue at a price of €24 per share. Before the announcement, the shares were trading at €30 in the market. The company has 4 million shares outstanding and the company is raising €6 million before expenses. What is the value of the nil-paid rights per share?

15.25. Long-term corporate debt: The 20-year government rate is 4.67% and the firm's credit rating is BB. Suppose the firm decides to raise €20 million by selling 20-year bonds. Management determines that since it has plenty of experience, it will not need an investment banker. At present, 20-year BB bonds are selling for 185 basis points above the 20-year government rate and it is forecast that interest rates will not stay this low for long. What is the cost of borrowing? What role does timing play in this case?

15.26. Lease finance: The Mason's Reclamation Company (MRC) wants to buy a second-hand reconditioned architrave extractor. The extractor will cost €120 000 and last for five years, at which point it will have no scrap value. A leasing company has offered to finance the purchase and MRC would need to make six yearly payments, the first starting immediately, of €27 550. MRC can borrow for five years at a rate of 9% per year and has a company tax rate of 32%. If the company buys the extractor, it would be subject to straight-line depreciation over its life for tax purposes. Should MRC borrow and buy the extractor or lease it?

SAMPLE TEST PROBLEMS

15.1. L'Étoile Filante SA, a solar cell maker, is planning an expansion and needs to raise €22 million to finance this. The company plans to raise the money through a rights issue priced at €18.50 per share. L'Étoile Filante's underwriters charge a 6.50% spread. How many shares does the company have to sell to raise the €22 million it needs?

15.2. HALVMÅNE AB is planning an IPO, and the investment bank offers to buy the securities for SKr 21.50 per share and offer them to the public at SKr 23.00. What is the gross underwriter's spread? Assume that the underwriter's cost of bringing the security to the market is SKr 1.00 per share. What is the net profit?

15.3. Selkirk Electronics plc issues an IPO sold on a best-effort basis. The company's investment bank demands a spread of 7% of the offer price, which is set at £2.40 per share. Two million shares are issued. However, the bank was overly optimistic and eventually is able to sell the shares for an average price of £2.36 per share. What are the proceeds for the issuer and the underwriter?

15.4. Piastrelle in Ceramica di Padua S.p.A. needs to borrow €17 million for a factory equipment upgrade. Management decides to sell 10-year bonds. They determine that the 3-month treasury bill rate is 3.84%, the firm's credit rating is Baa and the yield on 10-year government bonds is 1.36% higher than that for 3-month treasury bills. Bonds with a Baa rating are selling for 75 basis points above the 10-year government bond rate. What is the borrowing cost to do this transaction?

15.5. When Swiss Pharma went public in July 2010, the offer price was SFr 68.50 per share and the closing price at the end of the first day was SFr 85. The firm issued 3.6 million shares. What was the loss to the company due to underpricing?

ENDNOTES

1. An example of such a scheme is the Edinburgh Pre-Incubator Scheme (EPIS) operated by the University of Edinburgh, Scottish Enterprise (an agency of the Scottish Government) and the European Regional Development Fund (a fund established by the European Union to address regional inequalities in economic performance). See: http://www.epis.org.uk/.

2. A business plan is like a road map for a business. It presents the results from a strategic planning process that focuses on how the business will be developed over time. Business plans and their uses are discussed in detail in Chapter 18.

3. The data probably underestimates the contribution by the corporate sector since the data relates to funds contributed to private equity and venture capital funds and therefore excludes any funds provided by the corporate sector directly to businesses.

4. This is to be expected since the venture capitalist firm is a specialised investor, which seeks to maximise the returns on its investment by backing early-stage businesses. To do so, it provides hands-on management to these businesses. It has less to contribute to an established business. Returns are

likely to be lower for such businesses once they reach a certain size. As a result, the venture capitalist will wish to disinvest to either repay the providers of funds or to start the cycle again by investing in other early-stage businesses.

5. The London Stock Exchange also offers a third alternative called the Professional Securities Market that, as its name suggests, only allows securities to be traded by sophisticated professional investors and where securities are not directly available to the general public. Note that other exchanges in Europe, such as the Paris Bourse with its Second Marché and Nouveau Marché, have similar arrangements to cater for smaller less well-established companies.

6. We use the term investment banker here for a variety of different types of financial specialist firm that advise and facilitate the listing of new companies. For instance, in some countries, a key advisor for smaller firms seeking to go public might be a stockbroker or an accountancy firm that also offers corporate finance services. In the case of London's AIM it is likely that the nominated advisor (NOMAD) would be a stockbroking firm.

7. A prospectus is sometimes called an offering circular.

8. This does not mean that an IPO on Euronext is the cheapest since the underwriting fee is only part of the overall costs involved and may be offset by higher costs elsewhere, for instance by higher financial advisor fees. Firms issuing in the more expensive markets may also benefit in other ways, for instance, from a higher issue price and lower underpricing.

9. This applies with IPOs as well but in this case, the small number of shareholders makes it relatively easy for them to waive their pre-emption rights prior to the issue. Note that in the United States and Japan rights issues are quite rare and companies normally make general cash offers open to all investors, rather than being restricted to existing shareholders.

10. Options are discussed in Chapter 20.

11. In most European countries shareholders must give the board of directors the right to bypass their pre-emptive rights. When this is granted, it typically allows an addition to the existing issued share capital of between 5% and 15% to be raised without resorting to a rights issue.

12. The investment banking firm that does the origination work is excluded from bidding on the issue because its intimate knowledge of the deal would be considered an unfair advantage by other bidders and thus would discourage them from bidding.

13. Less common is the case where a private equity firm will team up with a group of managers to purchase the business from the selling company in what is known as a management buy-in.

14. Limited liability companies are discussed in Chapter 18. The same forms of organisation are used by venture capital funds.

15. In a leveraged buyout, a private equity firm takes over a company by using a high proportion of borrowed funds. The target company's assets provide security for the loans taken out by the acquiring firm.

16. The interbank rate is normally prefixed by the location of the interbank lending. A major reference rate for all sorts of loans is the London interbank offered rate (LIBOR), which is the rate at which London banks lend to each other. That is, the interest rates at which short-term deposits are offered by the bank to other banks. The Euro interbank offered rate (EURIBOR) provides a similar benchmark interest rate for the European Monetary Union area.

CHAPTER

16

Capital Structure Policy

In this Chapter:

Capital Structure and Firm Value

The Benefits and Costs of Using Debt

Two Theories of Capital Structure

Practical Considerations in Choosing a Capital Structure

LEARNING OBJECTIVES

1. Describe the two Modigliani and Miller propositions, the key assumptions underlying them and their relevance to capital structure decisions.

2. Discuss the benefits and costs of using debt financing.

3. Describe the trade-off and pecking order theories of capital structure choice and explain what the empirical evidence tells us about these theories.

4. Discuss some of the practical considerations that managers are concerned with when they choose a firm's capital structure.

n the three-month period January–March 2009, companies listed on the London Stock Exchange raised a total of £29.5 billion from 97 rights issues and other issues of shares. This contrasts with the same period in 2008 when just £1.9 billion in new equity was raised. A prime reason given by companies in the rush to raise new equity was to rebuild their balance sheets that had been ravaged by the credit crunch and the recession that followed it. One of the top ten companies for the amounts raised, Premier Foods plc, asked shareholders for £404 million of new equity. At the time of the announcement, its chief executive, Robert Schofield, said that the deal would 'put in place an appropriate capital structure' and leave the company on a 'solid platform for Premier's future development'.

In a survey of capital structure policies in Europe, Professors Brounen, de Jong and Koedijk found that two-thirds of the companies they sampled aimed for a target debt ratio.[1] The capital structure companies chose reflected the trade-offs between the benefits and the costs of debt. For example, because interest payments are deductible when companies calculate their taxable income, higher debt levels mean they would pay less income tax. Nevertheless, the survey also found that with less debt companies had more flexibility in reacting to changing industry, economic and technological conditions in their markets.

What was apparent was that the appropriate capital structure for a firm depends on the firm's characteristics. When it comes to capital structure policy, one size does not fit all. The appropriate mix of debt and equity financing differs across firms and, even within the same firm, it can change over time. In this chapter, we discuss the factors that influence a firm's capital structure policy.

CHAPTER PREVIEW

In Chapter 15, we discussed how firms raise capital to finance their investments. That discussion focused on individual sources of capital. In this chapter, we focus on the choice between the various types of financing. In particular, we examine how a firm's value is affected by the mix of debt and equity used to finance its investments and the factors that managers consider when choosing this mix. Managers use the concepts and tools discussed in this chapter to make financing decisions that create value for their shareholders.

We begin with a discussion of two propositions that provide valuable insights into how the choice between debt and equity financing can affect the value of a firm and its cost of equity. These insights provide a framework that we then use to examine the benefits and costs associated with using debt financing. We next describe and evaluate two theories of how managers choose the appropriate mix of debt and equity financing. Finally, we discuss some of the practical considerations that managers say influence their choices.

CAPITAL STRUCTURE AND FIRM VALUE

Learning Objective 1

Describe the two Modigliani and Miller propositions, the key assumptions underlying them and their relevance to capital structure decisions.

As you know, a firm's capital structure is the mix of debt and equity used to finance its activities. This mix will always include ordinary shares and will often include debt and preference shares. In addition, the same firm can have different types of ordinary shares, debt and preference shares. For example, the firm may have several classes of ordinary shares with different voting rights and, possibly, a different claim on the cash flows available to shareholders. The debt at a firm can be long term or short term, secured or unsecured, convertible or not convertible into ordinary shares, and so on. Preference shares can be cumulative or non-cumulative and convertible or not convertible into ordinary shares.

The fraction of the total financing that is represented by debt is a measure of the *financial leverage* in the firm's capital structure. A higher fraction of debt indicates a higher degree of financial leverage. The amount of financial leverage in a firm's capital structure is important because, as we discuss next, it affects the value of the firm.

The Optimal Capital Structure

When managers at a firm choose a capital structure, their challenge is to identify the mix of securities that minimises the cost of financing the firm's activities. We refer to this mix as the **optimal capital structure** because the capital structure that minimises the cost of financing the firm's projects is also the capital structure that maximises the total value of those projects and, therefore, the overall value of the firm.

Optimal capital structure

the capital structure that minimises the cost of financing a firm's activities

You can see why the optimal capital structure maximises the value of the firm if you think back to our discussions of NPV analysis for a single project. Recall that the incremental after-tax free cash flows we discount in an NPV analysis are not affected by the way a project is financed. There is no interest or principal payment in Equation (11.2):

$$FCF = [(\text{Revenue} - \text{Op Ex} - \text{D\&A}) \times (1 - t)] + \text{D\&A} - \text{Cap Ex} - \text{Add WC}$$

Recall also that the discount rate or weighted average cost of capital (WACC) for a project accounts for the way that it is financed. The lower the cost of financing a project, the lower the discount rate and, therefore, the larger the present value of the cash flows. This same idea applies for the total portfolio of projects in a firm. If the overall cost of financing those projects is lower, the present value of the total cash flows they produce is larger.

The Modigliani and Miller Propositions

To understand what determines the optimal capital structure for a particular firm, it is necessary to be

BUILDING INTUITION

The Optimal Capital Structure Minimises the Cost of Financing a Firm's Activities

The optimal capital structure for a firm is the capital structure that minimises the overall cost of financing the firm's portfolio of projects. Minimising the overall cost of financing the firm's projects maximises the value of the firm's cash flows.

familiar with the mechanisms through which financing decisions affect financing costs. The Modigliani and Miller (M&M) propositions provide essential insights into these mechanisms. These propositions, originally proposed by Franco Modigliani and Merton Miller 50 years ago, are still very relevant today.[2] We discuss them in this section and explore their implications throughout much of this chapter.

M&M Proposition 1

Modigliani and Miller's Proposition 1, which we will denote M&M Proposition 1, states that the capital structure decisions a firm makes will have no effect on the value of the firm if (1) there are no taxes, (2) there is no information or transaction cost and (3) the real investment policy of the firm is not affected by its capital structure decisions. The **real investment policy** of the firm includes the criteria it uses to decide in which real assets (projects) to invest. A policy to invest in all positive NPV projects is an example of a real investment policy. We will discuss each of the three conditions above in detail later, but let us first discuss the intuition behind M&M Proposition 1.

> **WEB**
>
> You can see what the Nobel Prize selection committee said about Professors Modigliani and Miller if you visit the economics page on the Nobel Prize website at: http://nobelprize .org.

> **Real investment policy**
>
> the policy relating to the criteria the firm uses in deciding which real assets (projects) to invest in

Assume that a firm pays no taxes and that the present value of the free cash flows produced by the assets of the firm can be represented as a pie that is divided between the shareholders and the debt holders, as illustrated in Exhibit 16.1. The slice of the pie labelled V_{Equity} represents the value of the cash flows to be received by the shareholders and the slice labelled V_{Debt} represents the value to be received by the debt holders.

From the discussion of the finance market value balance sheet in Chapter 13, we know that the market value of the debt plus the market value of the equity must equal the market value of the cash flows produced by the firm's assets (V_{Assets}). In practice, we also refer to V_{Assets} as the **firm value** or the firm's **enterprise value** (V_{Firm}), which means that we can write Equation (13.1) as:

$$V_{Firm} = V_{Assets} = V_{Debt} + V_{Equity} \qquad (16.1)$$

M&M Proposition 1 says that if the size of the pie (representing the present value of free cash flows the firm's assets are expected to produce in the future) is fixed, and no one other than the shareholders and the debt holders gets a slice of the pie, then the combined value of the equity and debt claims does not change when you change the capital structure. You can see this in Exhibit 16.1, where each of the three pies represents a different capital structure. No matter how you slice the pie, the total value of the debt plus the equity remains the same. If the three conditions specified by M&M hold, the capital structure of the firm specifies how that pie is to be sliced but it does not change the overall size of the pie or the combined size of the debt and equity slices.

> **Firm value, or enterprise value**
>
> the total value of the firm's assets; it equals the value of the equity financing plus the value of the debt financing used by the firm

Understanding M&M Proposition 1 To help you better understand M&M Proposition 1, we will consider its implications in the context of an example. Assume that the three conditions identified by M&M apply and consider a company, Millennium Motors, which is financed entirely with equity. Millennium Motors produces annual cash flows of €100, which are expected to continue forever. If the appropriate discount rate for Millennium's

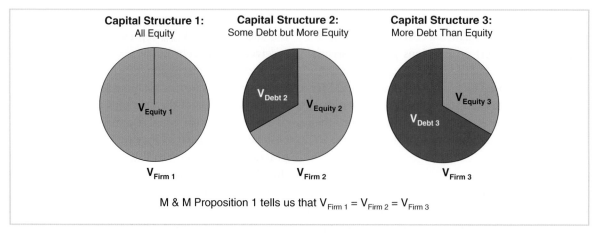

Exhibit 16.1: Capital Structure and Firm Value under M&M Proposition 1 The size of the pie represents the present value of the cash flows that the assets of a firm are expected to produce in the future (V_{Firm}). The sizes of the slices reflect the value of the total cash flows that the debt holders (V_{Debt}) or shareholders (V_{Equity}) are entitled to receive for three different capital structures. Under the three conditions identified by M&M, the total value of the cash flows to the firm does not change, regardless of which capital structure the firm uses.

cash flows is 10%, we can use the perpetuity model, Equation (6.3), to calculate the value of the firm:

$$V_{Firm} = PVA_\infty = \frac{CF}{i} = \frac{€100}{0.1} = €1000$$

Since the firm is financed entirely with equity, the equity is also worth €1000. Suppose that the management of Millennium Motors is considering changing its capital structure from €1000 (100%) equity to €800 (80%) equity and €200 (20%) debt. The company would accomplish this change by selling €200 worth of perpetual bonds and paying the €200 to shareholders through a one-time special dividend.

The change that Millennium is contemplating is an example of a **financial restructuring**. A financial restructuring is a combination of financial transactions that change the capital structure of the firm without affecting its real assets. These transactions might involve issuing debt and using the proceeds to repurchase shares or to pay a dividend, or selling shares and using the proceeds to repay debt. No new money is actually being invested in the firm.

Financial restructuring

a combination of financial transactions that changes the capital structure of the firm without affecting its real assets

BUILDING INTUITION

Capital Structure Does Not Affect Firm Value If It Does Not Affect Total Cash Flows to Security Holders

Capital structure choices will not affect a firm's value if all the following three conditions exist: (1) there are no taxes, (2) there are no information or transaction costs, (3) the way in which the firm is financed does not affect its real investment policy. This is M&M Proposition 1.

Now suppose that you are currently the only investor in Millennium – you own 100% of the outstanding shares – and that the firm would have to pay 5% interest on the debt after the restructuring. If the restructuring took place, you would immediately receive a €200 special dividend. After that, each year you would be entitled to the €90 that is left over after the €10 interest payment on the bonds.[3]

M&M showed that if you, as an investor, decided that you did not like the effect the restructuring would have on your cash flows, management could go ahead with the restructuring and you could undo its effect on the cash flows you received by making offsetting trades for your own account. To undo the effects of the proposed financial restructuring, you would simply use the entire €200 special dividend to buy all of the perpetual bonds the firm issues. From that point forward, you would receive the first €10 that the firm earns each year as an interest payment on your bonds. In addition, you would receive any remaining cash flows because you would still own 100% of the shares. Just as before the restructuring, you would be receiving all of the cash flows generated by the firm. Only now, instead of receiving all of those cash flows as dividends, you would receive some cash in the form of interest payments.

What if Millennium Motors had more than one shareholder? It does not matter – the result would be the same. For instance, if you owned only 10% of the firm's equity before the restructuring, you could still undo the change by using your special dividend to purchase 10% of the bonds. You would receive the same cash flows after the restructuring that you did before.

Furthermore, M&M Proposition 1 suggests that transactions such as those we have described need not be used to undo a financial restructuring that the firm undertakes – investors can also use them to create their own restructuring. For example, as before, suppose you own 100% of the shares in Millennium Motors. This time, however, let us assume that management has no intention of adding debt to the firm's capital structure but that you wish they would. You would like management to alter the capital structure so that it would include 80% equity and 20% debt and pay you a €200 special dividend.

You could easily produce the same effect by making trades in your investment account that would alter your cash flows. You could borrow €200 at a 5% interest rate and pay the interest on the debt out of the annual cash flows you receive from the company. Of course, in order for this transaction to exactly duplicate a similar restructuring by the firm, you would have to be able to borrow at the same interest rate as the firm.[4] If you borrowed at the same rate, your cash flows would be exactly the same as if Millennium Motors had borrowed the money and paid you the special dividend. You would receive €200 from the loan today and you would have €90 left over each year after you paid interest on that loan.

Undoing the Effects of a Financial Restructuring on Your Own

Problem: You own 5% of the shares in a company that is financed with 80% equity and 20% debt. Like Millennium Motors, the company generates cash flows of €100 per year before any interest payments and has a total value of €1000. Management has announced plans to increase the proportion of debt in the firm's capital structure from 20% to 30% by borrowing

€100 and paying a special dividend equal to that amount. Assume that the interest rate on debt is 5% regardless of how much debt the company has. How can you undo the effect of the financial restructuring on the cash flows that you receive in your personal account? Show that when you do this, your cash flows after the restructuring are the same as they were before.

Approach: As illustrated in the example in the text, you can undo the effect of this restructuring by using all of the money you receive from the special dividend to purchase some of the firm's debt. To show that the cash flows you are entitled to receive remain unchanged, you must calculate the dividends and interest you are entitled to receive before the financial restructuring and afterwards.

Solution: Since the company currently has €200 of debt (20% × €1000), it pays €10 in interest annually (5% interest rate × €200).

Therefore, the shareholders receive €90 in dividends each year, and you receive an annual dividend of 0.05 × €90.00 = €4.50 for your 5% of the total shares.

When the restructuring takes place, you will receive a special dividend equal to 5% of the €100 total dividend, or €5. Since the company will then have to pay interest of €15 each year (5% interest rate × €300), the total dividend after the restructuring will be €85. Your portion of the total dividend will be 0.05 × €85.00 = €4.25. Therefore, you will receive €5 up-front and a dividend of €4.25 per year thereafter.

If you use the €5 that you receive from the special dividend to buy €5 of the new debt issue, you will receive €4.25 per year in dividends and 0.05 × €5.00 = €0.25 in interest, for a total of €4.50. This is exactly what you were receiving before the company restructured.

Conclusion from M&M Proposition 1   As our examples illustrate, in perfect financial markets – markets in which the three conditions specified in M&M Proposition 1 hold – investors can make changes in their own investment accounts that will replicate the cash flows for any capital structure that the firm's management might choose or that investors might want. Since investors can do this on their own, they are not willing to pay more for the shares of a firm that does it for them. Therefore, the value of the firm will be the same regardless of its capital structure. This is true because changes in capital structure will not change the total value of the claims that debt holders and shareholders have on the cash flows – which is the point of M&M Proposition 1 and is illustrated in Exhibit 16.1.

M&M Proposition 2

Under the three conditions outlined in M&M Proposition 1, a firm's capital structure does not affect the value of the firm's real assets. That is because the capital structure decisions do not affect the level, timing or risk of the cash flows produced by those assets. Although the risk of the cash flows produced by the assets does not change with the firm's capital structure, the risk of the equity claims on those cash flows – and therefore the required return on equity – does change. M&M's Proposition 2 states that the cost of (required return on) a firm's ordinary shares is directly related to the debt-to-equity ratio.[5] To see why, let us return to the WACC formula, Equation (13.7):

$$\text{WACC} = x_{\text{Debt}}k_{\text{Debt pre-tax}}(1-t) + x_{\text{ps}}k_{\text{ps}} + x_{\text{os}}k_{\text{os}}$$

If there are no taxes, as M&M Proposition 1 assumes, then $t = 0$ and Equation (13.7) is:

$$\text{WACC} = x_{\text{Debt}}k_{\text{Debt pre-tax}} + x_{\text{ps}}k_{\text{ps}} + x_{\text{os}}k_{\text{os}}$$

Furthermore, if we assume (for simplicity) that the firm has only one type of equity, ordinary shares, then this equation can be simplified further, since

BUILDING INTUITION

The Cost of Equity Increases with Financial Leverage

The required rate of return on the firm's equity (cost of equity) increases as the firm's debt-to-equity ratio increases. This is M&M Proposition 2.

there are no preference shares:

$$\text{WACC} = x_{\text{Debt}}k_{\text{Debt pre-tax}} + x_{\text{os}}k_{\text{os}} \quad (16.2)$$

where $x_{\text{Debt}} + x_{\text{os}} = 1$.

Since, under the M&M Proposition 1 conditions, capital structure choices do not affect the risk of the cash flows produced by a firm's assets, the WACC must not change with the firm's capital structure. The reason is that, as a weighted average of the cost of debt and the cost of equity, the WACC reflects the riskiness of the cash flows generated by the firm's assets (k_{Assets}). Now if we recognise that the proportions of debt and equity in the firm's capital structure are calculated as:

$$x_{\text{Debt}} = \frac{V_{\text{Debt}}}{V_{\text{Debt}} + V_{\text{os}}}$$

and

$$x_{\text{os}} = \frac{V_{\text{os}}}{V_{\text{Debt}} + V_{\text{os}}}$$

where V_{Debt} is the value of the debt and V_{os} is the value of the ordinary shares, we can write Equation (16.2) as follows:

$$\begin{aligned}\text{WACC} &= k_{\text{Assets}} \\ &= \frac{V_{\text{Debt}}}{V_{\text{Debt}} + V_{\text{os}}}k_{\text{Debt pre-tax}} \\ &+ \frac{V_{\text{os}}}{V_{\text{Debt}} + V_{\text{os}}}k_{\text{os}}\end{aligned}$$

Finally, using basic algebra, we can rearrange this equation to solve for k_{os} in terms of k_{Assets} and k_{Debt}. We find that:

$$k_{\text{os}} = k_{\text{Assets}} + \left(\frac{V_{\text{Debt}}}{V_{\text{os}}}\right)(k_{\text{Assets}} - k_{\text{Debt}}) \quad (16.3)$$

Equation (16.3) is M&M's Proposition 2, which shows that the cost of (required return on) a firm's ordinary shares is directly related to the debt-to-equity ratio. You can see this in the equation by noting that as the ratio $V_{\text{Debt}}/V_{\text{os}}$ increases on the right-hand side, k_{os} will increase on the left-hand side. We have demonstrated this relation assuming that a firm has only ordinary shares outstanding. However, you can rest assured that it also holds if the firm also has preference shares outstanding.[6]

Understanding M&M Proposition 2 We can think of the two terms on the right-hand side of Equation (16.3) as reflecting two sources of risk in the cash flows to which shareholders have a claim. The first source of risk is the underlying risk of the assets. This risk is reflected in the required return on the firm's assets (k_{Assets}) and is known as the **business risk** of the firm. It is the risk associated with the characteristics of the firm's business activities.

> ### Business risk
> the risk in the cash flows to shareholders that is associated with uncertainty due to the characteristics of the business itself

The second source of risk, which is reflected in the second term, is the capital structure of the firm. The capital structure determines the **financial risk**, which reflects the effect that the firm's financing decisions have on the riskiness of the cash flows that the shareholders will receive. The more debt financing a firm uses, the greater the financial risk. As you know from our earlier discussions, debt holders have the first claim on the cash flows produced by the assets. Interest and principal payments must be made before any cash can be distributed to the shareholders. Therefore, the larger the proportion of debt in a firm's capital structure, the larger the interest and principal payments and the greater the uncertainty associated with the cash flows to which the shareholders have a claim.

Financial risk

the risk in the cash flows to shareholders that is due to the way in which the firm has financed its activities

If we assume that a firm's net income is a reasonable measure of the cash flows to which shareholders have a claim, then we can use the simple income statement in Exhibit 16.2 to illustrate the distinction between business and financial risk.[7] The exhibit shows that business risk is associated with the operations of the business. If you think of business risk as the systematic risk associated with operating profits, and you recall the discussion of operating leverage in Chapter 12, you can see that a firm's business risk reflects the systematic variation in (1) unit sales, (2) unit prices, (3) the costs of producing and selling the firm's products and (4) the degree of operating leverage in the production process.[8]   Financial risk, in contrast, is associated with required payments to a firm's lenders. The total risk of the cash flows that the shareholders have a claim to depends on both the business risk and the financial risk.

The numerical example in Exhibit 16.3 illustrates the distinction between business risk and financial risk and shows how they combine to determine total equity risk. Consider a firm that sells recreational vehicles and that has the income statement illustrated in column 1. The firm has €100 in revenue, costs of goods sold of €60 and selling, general and administrative expenses of €15. If we assume

EXHIBIT 16.2

RELATIONS BETWEEN BUSINESS RISK, FINANCIAL RISK AND TOTAL EQUITY RISK

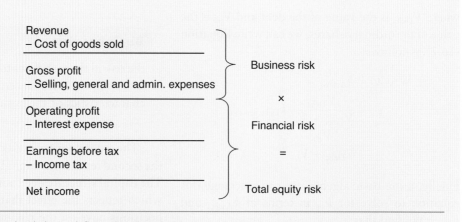

The total risk associated with the cash flows that shareholders are entitled to receive reflects the risk related to the firm's assets (business risk) and the risk related to the way those assets are financed (financial risk). (We assume here that net income (net profit or net earnings) is a reasonable measure of these cash flows.)

EXHIBIT 16.3

ILLUSTRATION OF RELATIONS BETWEEN BUSINESS RISK, FINANCIAL RISK AND TOTAL RISK

	No Financial Risk				Financial Risk			
	Low Operating Leverage		High Operating Leverage		Low Operating Leverage		High Operating Leverage	
Column	1	2	3	4	5	6	7	8
Variable costs as % of total costs	80%		40%		80%		40%	
Interest expense	€0.00		€0.00		€15.00		€15.00	
	Before	After	Before	After	Before	After	Before	After
Revenue	€100.00	€80.00	€100.00	€80.00	€100.00	€80.00	€100.00	€80.00
− Cost of goods sold (VC)	60.00	48.00	30.00	24.00	60.00	48.00	30.00	24.00
Gross profit	40.00	32.00	70.00	56.00	40.00	32.00	70.00	56.00
− Selling, general & admin. (FC)	15.00	15.00	45.00	45.00	15.00	15.00	45.00	45.00
Operating profits	25.00	17.00	25.00	11.00	25.00	17.00	25.00	11.00
− Interest expense	0.00	0.00	0.00	0.00	15.00	15.00	15.00	15.00
Earnings before tax	25.00	17.00	25.00	1.00	10.00	2.00	10.00	−4.00
− Income taxes (35%)	8.75	5.95	8.75	3.85	3.50	0.70	3.50	−1.40
Net income	€16.25	€11.05	€16.25	€7.15	€6.50	€1.30	€6.50	−€2.60
Percentage change in net income		−32.0%		−56.0%		−80.0%		−140.0%

The exhibit shows how a decrease in revenue affects net income (total equity risk) for four different combinations of debt (financial risk) and operating leverage (business risk). In columns 1 and 2, we see the effect on a firm with no debt and low operating leverage; in columns 3 and 4, no debt and high operating leverage; in columns 5 and 6, debt and low operating leverage; and in columns 7 and 8, debt and high operating leverage. As you can see, total equity risk, represented by the percentage drop in net income, is greater when operating leverage is higher (for example, compare columns 1 and 2 with columns 3 and 4) and when a firm has financial risk (for example, compare columns 1 and 2 with columns 5 and 6). Furthermore, financial risk magnifies operating risk (for example, compare columns 3 and 4 with columns 7 and 8).

that costs of goods sold are all variable costs (VC) and that selling, general and administrative expenses are all fixed costs (FC), 80% [€60/(€60 + €15)] of the total costs at this firm are variable costs and 20% [€15/(€60 + €15)] are fixed. This cost structure, combined with variation in unit sales, the unit pricing and the costs of producing and selling the firm's products, determines the business risk of the firm. Looking farther down the income statement in

column 1, we can see that the firm has no interest expense, which means that it has no debt. In other words, this firm has no leverage and therefore no financial risk.

Now suppose that the price of fuel increases significantly, causing a drop in the demand for recreational vehicles and a 20% decline in revenue from €100 to €80. Column 2 in Exhibit 16.3 shows that net income would decline to €11.05

(you should verify this calculation), which is a 32% decrease [(€11.05 − €16.25)/€16.25] from the net income in column 1. Since the firm has no debt, and we are assuming that the only change in costs is the reduction in variable costs that occurs when fewer units are sold, this change reflects only the decrease in revenue and the operating leverage of the firm.

If the firm had greater operating leverage, the decline in net income would be even larger. For example, in columns 3 and 4, we show the income statements for a company that has variable costs representing only 40% [€30/(€30 + €45)] of total costs and that has no debt. In this case, a 20% decline in net revenue results in a 56% [(€7.15 − €16.25)/€16.25] decline in net income, illustrating how greater operating leverage magnifies changes in revenue even more.

Next, consider a firm with the income statement presented in column 5. This firm is exactly like the one in column 1 except that it uses some debt financing. You can see that it has an annual interest expense of €15. If revenue drops by 20%, the net income of the firm in column 5 will drop by 80% [(€1.30 − €6.50)/€6.50]. 32% of the decline is due to the nature of the business (remember that it is just like the business in columns 1 and 2), and the remaining 48% is due to the use of debt financing. The financial risk magnifies the effect of the operating leverage on net income.

> **WEB**
>
> An Excel model called 'Leverage' will help you calculate the impact of leverage on a company's earnings. Find this model on Matt Evans's website at: www.exinfm.com/free_spreadsheets.html.

Columns 7 and 8 show that if a firm with the same cost structure as the firm in column 3 had to make a €15 interest payment, the decline in net income would increase from 56% to 140% − a

difference of 84%! The examples in columns 5–8 illustrate why the proportion of debt in a firm's capital structure is called financial leverage.[9] Just as fixed operating costs create operating leverage, fixed interest costs create financial leverage, which magnifies the effect of changes in revenue on the bottom line of the income statement. This is why the risk and, as M&M told us in their Proposition 2, the cost of ordinary shares increases with financial leverage.

Using M&M Proposition 2 to Calculate the Return on Equity   M&M Proposition 2 can be used to calculate the cost of ordinary shares following a financial restructuring. To see how this is done, we will return to the Millennium Motors example.

Before the restructuring, the return on equity for Millennium Motors was the same as the return on assets: 10%. We know this because the firm used 100% equity financing, which means that the shareholders received all of the cash flows produced by the assets.

After the proposed restructuring, however, the firm would be financed with 20% debt and 80% ordinary shares. The return on assets would still be 10%, and as noted earlier, the return on the debt would be 5%. From Equation (16.3), we learn that the cost of equity will be:

$$k_{os} = k_{Assets} + \left(\frac{V_{Debt}}{V_{os}} \right) (k_{Assets} - k_{Debt})$$

$$= 0.10 + \left(\frac{0.2}{0.8} \right) (0.10 - 0.05)$$

$$= 0.1125, \text{ or } 11.25\%$$

The financial restructuring would increase the cost of equity from 10% to 11.25%.

Note, too, that if you (as the only investor in Millennium Motors) had offset the effect of the restructuring by using the €200 special dividend to purchase all of the bonds, then the expected return on your combined portfolio would be $(0.2 \times 0.05) + (0.8 \times 0.1125) = 0.10$, or 10%, just as it was before the restructuring. Again, the restructuring would not change the riskiness of the firm's real assets or the value of those assets.

Learning by Doing Application 16.2

Using M&M Proposition 2 to Calculate k_{os}

Problem: The required rate of return on the assets of a firm is 12%, the firm has a debt-to-ordinary shares ratio of 30% and the cost of debt is 6%. If the firm has no preference shares and the three conditions specified by M&M hold, what is the expected rate of return on the firm's ordinary shares?

Approach: The expected return on the firm's ordinary shares can be calculated using Equation (16.3).

Solution:

$$k_{os} = k_{Assets} + \left(\frac{V_{Debt}}{V_{os}}\right)(k_{Assets} - k_{Debt})$$

$$= 0.12 + (0.3)(0.12 - 0.06)$$

$$= 0.138, \text{ or } 13.8\%$$

How the Costs of Assets, Debt and Equity Change with Leverage Exhibit 16.4 illustrates M&M Proposition 2 by plotting the cost of ordinary shares (k_{os}) against the debt-to-equity ratio. Recall from Equation (16.3) that k_{os} equals k_{Assets} if the firm uses no debt financing ($V_{Debt}/V_{os} = 0$) and has no preference shares. In Part A of the exhibit, you can see that these costs both equal 10% if the firm has no leverage in this example. Equation 16.3 also tells us that as the debt-to-equity ratio increases from zero, the cost of equity will increase by (V_{Debt}/V_{os})($k_{Assets} - k_{Debt}$). This increase is illustrated by the blue upward-sloping line.

Part A in Exhibit 16.4 assumes that the cost of debt will remain 5% regardless of the amount of debt financing that the firm uses. Part B shows a more realistic plot of how the costs of assets, debt and equity change with the debt-to-equity ratio. The key things to understand about the plot in Part B are that (1) *both* the cost of debt and the cost of equity increase as the debt-to-equity ratio increases and (2) the cost of debt increases at an increasing rate. We explain why the cost of debt increases as it does in the next section.

What the M&M Propositions Tell Us

M&M provided elegant analyses of how capital structure choices are related to firm value and how financial leverage affects the cost of equity. However, they recognised that the three conditions underlying their analyses are unrealistic. Firms do pay taxes, there are information and transaction costs and, as you will soon see, financing decisions do affect the real investment policies of firms. The value of the M&M analysis is that it tells us exactly where we should look if we want to understand how capital structure affects firm value and the cost of equity. If financial policy matters, it must be because (1) taxes matter, (2) information or transaction costs matter, or (3) capital structure choices affect a firm's real investment policy. We discuss each of these possibilities in the next section.

Before You Go On

1. What is the optimal capital structure for a firm?
2. What is M&M Proposition 1? M&M Proposition 2?
3. What is the difference between business risk and financial risk?
4. How can the three conditions specified by M&M help us understand how the capital structure of a firm affects its value?

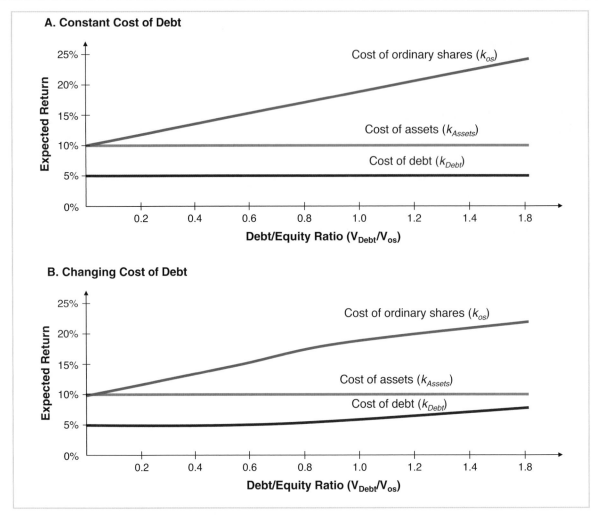

Exhibit 16.4: Illustration of M&M Proposition 2 The exhibit shows the cost (required return) of assets, ordinary shares and debt for different debt-to-equity ratios. Panel A assumes that the cost of debt remains constant and Panel B assumes that the cost of debt increases with leverage. The cost of assets, which is the return investors require to compensate them for the business risk, does not change with leverage. As M&M Proposition 2 tells us, the cost of ordinary shares increases with leverage.

THE BENEFITS AND COSTS OF USING DEBT

Learning Objective 2

Discuss the benefits and costs of using debt financing.

The use of debt in a firm's capital structure involves both benefits and costs. Studies suggest that for

very low levels of debt, the benefits outweigh the costs and the use of more debt reduces the firm's WACC. However, as the amount of debt in the firm's capital structure increases, the costs become relatively greater and eventually begin to outweigh the benefits. The point at which the costs just equal the benefits is the point at which the WACC is minimised. Understanding the location of this point requires an understanding of the costs and benefits and how they change with the amount of debt used by a firm. In this section, we use the framework provided by the three M&M conditions to discuss the benefits and costs of debt.

The Benefits of Debt

We have noted that including debt in the capital structure has advantages for a firm. We now discuss these benefits in detail.

Interest Tax Shield Benefit

The most important benefit from including debt in a firm's capital structure stems from the fact that, as we discussed in Chapter 13, firms can deduct interest payments for tax purposes but cannot deduct dividend payments.[10] This makes it less costly to distribute cash to securityholders through interest payments than through dividends.

To understand the implications of the tax deductibility of interest payments for firm value, let us return to the pie analogy in Exhibit 16.1. If we relax the M&M assumption that firms pay no taxes, while assuming that the other two M&M conditions still apply, the pie is now cut into three slices instead of two. In addition to the slices for

debt holders and shareholders, there is now a tax slice for the government.

Exhibit 16.5 illustrates the new situation. As shown in the pie on the left, if the firm is financed entirely with equity, there is no interest expense, the firm pays taxes on all of the income from operations and the value of the firm equals the present value of the after-tax cash flows that the shareholders have a right to receive. Now if the firm uses debt, some of the income from operations will be tax deductible, and the tax slice – the present value of the taxes the firm must pay – will be smaller than in the first pie. This is illustrated for one level of debt in the second pie and for an even greater level of debt in the third pie. Note that the value of the firm, which equals the combined values of the debt and equity slices, increases as the tax slice gets smaller.

Just how large is the value of the interest tax shield? Suppose a firm has fixed perpetual debt equal to the amount D, on which it pays an annual interest rate of k_{Debt}. The total amount of interest paid each year – and, therefore, the amount that will be deducted from the firm's taxable income – is

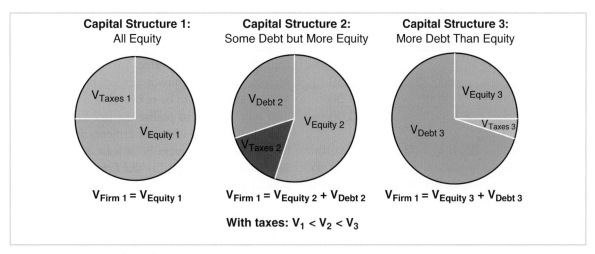

Exhibit 16.5: Capital Structure and Firm Value with Taxes Leverage can increase the value of the firm when interest payments are tax deductible but dividend payments are not. The pie on the left represents a firm financed 100% via equity. The slice labelled $V_{Taxes\ 1}$ reflects the proportion of the cash flows from operations that this firm pays in taxes. The two pies to the right illustrate how the value of the cash flows paid in taxes decreases as leverage is increased. By reducing the fraction paid in taxes, leverage increases the value of the firm in these examples.

$D \times k_{\text{Debt}}$. This will result in a reduction in taxes paid of $D \times k_{\text{Debt}} \times t$, where t is the firm's marginal tax rate that applies to the interest expense deduction.

To put this tax reduction in perspective, consider a firm that has no debt and annual earnings before interest and taxes, EBIT, of €100, which is expected to remain constant in perpetuity. Because the firm has no debt, it currently pays taxes equal to 35% of EBIT. Management is considering borrowing €1000 at an interest rate of 5%. If the firm borrows the money, it will thus pay interest of €50 each year.

The after-tax earnings for the firm without the debt equal €65 [€100 × (1 – 0.35) = €65] and the taxes paid by the firm equal €35 (€100 × 0.35 = €35). If the firm borrows the €1000, its after-tax earnings will be €32.50 [(€100 – €50) × (1 – 0.35) = €32.50] and it will pay taxes of €17.50 [(€100 – €50) × 0.35 = €17.50]. The new debt will reduce the taxes that the firm pays each year by €17.50 ($D \times k_{\text{Debt}} \times t$ = €1000 × 0.05 × 0.35 = €17.50). The total cash flows to the government, the shareholders and the debt holders in each situation are as follows:

	No Debt	After €1000 Loan
Government (taxes)	€ 35.00	€ 17.50
Shareholders	65.00	32.50
Debt holders	0.00	50.00
Total	€100.00	€100.00

How much is the reduction in taxes worth? Since we know the annual money value of the tax reduction and we know that this reduction will continue in perpetuity, we can use Equation (6.3), the perpetuity model, to calculate the present value of the tax savings from debt:

$$V_{\text{Tax-saving debt}} = \text{PVA}_{\infty} = \frac{\text{CF}}{i} = \frac{D \times k_{\text{Debt}} \times t}{i}$$

All we need now is the appropriate discount rate. In this case, it is reasonable to assume that the appropriate discount rate equals the 5% cost of

debt. This is a reasonable assumption because we know that the discount rate should reflect the risk of the cash flow stream that is being discounted. Since the firm will benefit from the interest tax shield only if it is able to make the required interest payments, the cash savings associated with the tax shield are about as risky as the cash flow stream associated with the interest payments. This implies that the value of the future tax savings is:

$$V_{\text{Tax-saving debt}} = \frac{D \times k_{\text{Debt}} \times t}{i} = \frac{€17.5}{0.05} = €350$$

If you look closely at this calculation, you will see that €350 is exactly equal to the product of the €1000 that the firm would borrow and its 35% tax rate ($D \times t$). In other words:

$$V_{\text{Tax-saving debt}} = D \times t \qquad (16.4)$$

This is because k_{Debt} is in both the numerator and the denominator in the formula and cancels out.

You can see in the above example that the value of the interest tax shield increases with the amount of debt that a firm has outstanding and with the corporate tax rate. More debt or a higher tax rate implies a larger benefit.

It is important to recognise that the income tax benefit we calculated using the perpetuity model is an upper limit for this value. This is true for several reasons. The perpetuity model assumes that (1) the firm will continue to be in business forever, (2) the firm will be able to realise the tax savings in the years in which the interest payments are made (the firm's EBIT will always be at least as great as the interest expense) and (3) the firm's tax rate will remain at 35%.

In the real world, each of these conditions is likely to be violated. While a company has an indefinite life, the fact is that companies go out of business. Of course, at that point the tax benefit ends. Even firms that do not go out of business are unlikely to realise the full benefit of the tax shield. Virtually all firms sometimes have poor operating performance. This can make it impossible to realise the benefit of the interest deduction in the year when

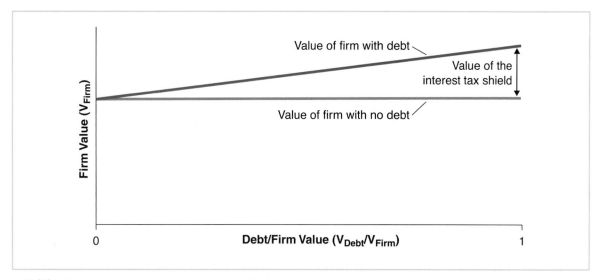

Exhibit 16.6: How Firm Value Changes with Leverage when Interest Payments are Tax Deductible and Dividends are Not The value of a firm increases with leverage when interest payments are tax-deductible and dividends are not and when the second and third M&M conditions apply; namely, there are no transaction costs and the real investment policy of the firm is not affected by its capital structure decisions.

the payment is made. In such cases, firms often must carry the tax loss forward and apply it to earnings in a future year. Carrying a tax deduction forward reduces its value by pushing it further into the future. Finally, even if the firm is profitable, the effective tax rate can fall below 35% because earnings are lower than expected or the firm has other deductions that reduce the value of the interest tax shield.

You might be asking yourself, too, whether it is reasonable to assume that a firm will borrow money forever. The *consols*, discussed in Chapter 6, are the only perpetual fixed-rate bonds that we know of which have been issued. Nevertheless, it is reasonable to assume that the long-term borrowings by firms will be in place as long as the firm is in business. While the specific debt instruments used by firms are not perpetuities, firms do tend to roll over their maturing debt by borrowing new money to make required principal payments. As long as a firm does not shrink, prompting it to pay down some of its debt, and as long as the firm does not currently have too much debt, long-term debt can be considered permanent.

The value of the interest tax shield adds to the total value of a firm. In other words, the value of a

firm with debt equals the value of that firm without debt plus the present value of the interest tax shield. If only the tax condition, from among the three conditions identified by M&M, is violated, the more debt a firm has, the more it will be worth. This is illustrated in Exhibit 16.6, where we plot the value of a firm with debt, a financially leveraged firm, against the proportion of the firm's total capital represented by debt.

A very thorough analysis by John Graham of Duke University estimated that the tax benefit of debt realised by the average firm in the USA equalled 9.7% of *firm* value.[11] When we look at the actual capital structure of US companies, we find that the typical firm has debt that is worth about 25% of firm value at the time of the Graham analysis. If we consider a firm with a total value of $100, this implies that tax benefits from debt represent $9.70 of this $100 and that the firm's outstanding debt is worth $25.0. Using Equation (16.4) to solve for t implies a tax rate of:

$$V_{\text{Tax-savings debt}} = D \times t$$

$$t = \frac{V_{\text{Tax-savings debt}}}{D} = \frac{\$9.7}{\$25.0} = 0.388, \text{ or } 38.8\%$$

This tax rate agrees with US corporate tax rates when we consider both federal and state taxes. It suggests that Equation (16.4) provides a reasonable estimate for the value of the interest tax shield.

Using the data from the Brounen, de Jong and Koedijk study for Europe discussed at the start of this chapter, and taking the average amount of debt for the companies in their study and using Equation (16.4), we find that the value of the future tax saving varies between 7.39% for the UK and 11.20% for the Netherlands:

	Debt as a Percentage	Corporate Tax Rate in 2004 (%)	Value of Future Tax Savings (%)
France	22.4	34.3%	7.67%
Germany	27.7	38.5	10.65
Netherlands	32.5	34.5	11.20
United Kingdom	24.6	30.0	7.39
Europe	29.4	34.0	10.09
USA	29.6	40.0	11.85

These values probably overestimate the future value of tax savings since they do not incorporate the corrections that Graham includes in his analysis. Certainly the value for the US companies above is that computed by Graham, who estimated the value at 9.7% versus our estimate of 11.85%. The data does suggest that for companies in Europe which have modest amounts of debt and corporate income tax rates between 30% and 40%, the value of future tax savings is less than 10% of the firm's total value.

To illustrate how taxes affect firm value, we will return to the initial Millennium Motors example. This time, we will assume that the company must pay corporate taxes equal to 35% of its taxable income. As before, the firm is financed entirely with ordinary shares and management is considering changing its capital structure by selling a €200 perpetual bond with an interest rate of 5% and paying a one-time special dividend of €200. The firm produces annual cash flows of €100 and the appropriate discount rate for these cash flows is 10%. What is the value of the firm without any debt, and what will the value be if the restructuring is completed?

We begin by calculating the value of Millennium Motors without any debt. If the entire €100 in pre-tax cash flows that the firm generates is taxable, Millennium's after-tax cash flows will equal €65 per year [€100 × (1 − t)]. Using the perpetuity formula, we find that the value of the all-equity firm is €650 (€65/0.10 = €650) with a 10% discount rate.

We next calculate the value of the interest tax shield that would accompany the new debt. This value is €70 ($D \times t$ = €200 × 0.35 = €70). The total value of the firm after the restructuring is equal to the value of the all-equity firm plus the value of the tax shield. In this case, that is €720 (€650 + €70 = €720).

We can also calculate the WACC for Millennium Motors after the financial restructuring using Equation (13.7). To do so, we must first calculate the value of the equity (V_{Equity}). In this case, since we know from Equation (16.1) that $V_{Firm} = V_{Equity} + V_{Debt}$, we can calculate the value of the equity to be €520 ($V_{Equity} = V_{Firm} − V_{Debt}$ = €720 − €200 = €520). Since we also know that the cash flows available to shareholders after the restructuring will equal €58.50 [(€100 − €10) × (1 − 0.35) = €58.50], we can calculate the required return on equity to be 11.25% (€58.50/€520 = 0.1125). This is the same number we got when we used Equation (16.3). With these values, we are now ready to calculate the WACC:

$$\text{WACC} = x_{Debt}k_{Debt\ pre-tax}(1 - t) + x_{ps}k_{ps} + x_{os}k_{os}$$

$$= \left(\frac{€200}{€730}\right)(0.05)(1 - 0.35) + 0$$

$$+ \left(\frac{€520}{€720}\right)(0.1125) = 0.0903, \text{ or } 9.03\%$$

As Exhibit 16.4 illustrates, the cost of ordinary shares increases with the amount of debt in the firm's capital structure. In this example, it goes from 10% to 11.25%. However, with the interest tax deduction, the WACC actually decreases from 10% (recall that the cost of equity equals the WACC for a firm with no debt) to 9.03%.

When we perform the same calculations for other potential debt levels at Millennium, we see how the value of the firm increases and the WACC decreases with the amount of debt in the capital structure. This is illustrated in Exhibit 16.7 for levels of debt ranging from €0 to €800.

You should note several other points concerning Exhibit 16.7. First, we do not show the calculations for a firm with 100% debt because all firms must have some equity. Second, the payments to securityholders and firm value increase as the amount of debt financing increases. This is because the size of the government's slice of the pie gets smaller. Third, for simplicity, we assume that the cost of debt remains constant. However, even though the cost of equity increases, the WACC decreases. This decrease is entirely due to the interest tax shield. Finally, while the value of the firm under each scenario is calculated as we have illustrated, you can confirm the answer by noting that the firm value for each capital structure equals the payments to securityholders for the unleveraged firm, €65, divided by the WACC. The payments to securityholders for the unleveraged firm are used in this calculation, regardless of the firm's capital structure, because, as was the case for project analysis in Chapter 10, the effects of capital structure choices are reflected in the discount rate rather than the cash flows.

EXHIBIT 16.7

THE EFFECT OF TAXES ON THE FIRM VALUE AND WACC OF MILLENNIUM MOTORS

Total debt	€ 0	€ 200	€ 400	€ 600	€ 800
Cost of debt	5.00%	5.00%	5.00%	5.00%	5.00%
EBIT	€100.00	€100.00	€100.00	€100.00	€100.00
Interest expense	—	10.00	20.00	30.00	40.00
Earnings before taxes	€100.00	€ 90.00	€ 80.00	€ 70.00	€ 60.00
Taxes (35%)	35.00	31.50	28.00	24.50	21.00
Net income	€ 65.00	€ 58.50	€ 52.00	€ 45.50	€ 39.00
Dividends	€ 65.00	€ 58.50	€ 52.00	€ 45.50	€ 39.00
Interest payments	—	10.00	20.00	30.00	40.00
Payments to securityholders	€ 65.00	€ 68.50	€ 72.00	€ 75.00	€ 79.00
Value of equity	€650.00	€520.00	€390.00	€260.00	€130.00
Cost of equity	10.00%	11.25%	13.33%	17.50%	30.00%
Firm value	€650.00	€720.00	€790.00	€860.00	€930.00
WACC	10.00%	9.03%	8.23%	7.56%	6.99%

The value of Millennium Motors increases and its WACC decreases with the amount of debt in the capital structure. The calculations assume that the cost of debt remains constant regardless of the amount of leverage and that the second and third M&M conditions apply.

Calculating the Effect of Debt on Firm Value and WACC

Problem: Up to this point, you have financed your pizza restaurant chain entirely with equity. You have heard about the tax benefit associated with using debt financing and are considering borrowing €1 million at an interest rate of 6% to take advantage of the interest tax shield. You do not need the extra money, so you will distribute it to yourself through a special dividend. You are the only shareholder.

Your pizza business generates taxable (pre-tax) cash flows of €300 000 each year and pays taxes at a rate of 25%; the cost of assets, k_{Assets} (which equals k_{os} for your unleveraged firm), is 10%. What is the value of your firm without debt and how much would debt increase its value if you assume that all cash flows are perpetuities and that the second and third M&M conditions hold (that is, there are no information or transaction costs and the real investment policy of the firm is not affected by its capital structure decisions)? In addition, what would the WACC for your business be before and after the proposed financial restructuring?

Approach: The value of your restaurant chain equals the present value of the after-tax cash flows that the shareholders and debt holders expect to receive in the future. Without debt, this value equals the present value of the dividends that you can expect to receive as the only shareholder. The value with debt equals the value without debt plus the value of the interest tax shield.

The WACC before the financial restructuring equals k_{os}, since your firm currently has no

preference shares or debt. Equation (13.7) can be used to calculate the WACC with debt.

Solution: The value of your business without debt can be calculated using the perpetuity model as follows:

$$V_{Firm} = [€300\,000 \times (1 - 0.25)]/0.10$$
$$= €2\,250\,000$$

The value of the tax shield is:

$$D \times t = €1\,000\,000 \times 0.25 = €250\,000$$

Therefore, after the restructuring, the value of the firm would be €2.5 million (€2 250 000 + €250 000 = €2 500 000).

The WACC before the financial restructuring equals:

$$WACC = k_{os} = 10\%$$

To calculate the WACC after the restructuring, we must first calculate the cost of the ordinary shares. Since the values of the firm and debt will be €2.5 million and €1 million, respectively, the value of the equity must equal €1.5 million. The after-tax cash flows to shareholders will equal €180 000 {[€300 000 − (€1 000 000 × 0.06)] × [1 − 0.25] = €180 000}. Therefore, k_{os} equals 12% (€180 000/€1 500 000 = 0.12). We can now calculate the WACC using Equation (13.7) as follows:

$$WACC = x_{Debt}k_{Debt\,pre\text{-}tax}(1 - t) + x_{ps}k_{ps}$$
$$+ x_{os}k_{os}$$
$$= \left(\frac{€1\,000\,000}{€2\,500\,000}\right)(0.06)(1 - 0.25)$$
$$+ 0 + \left(\frac{€1\,500\,000}{€2\,500\,000}\right)(0.12)$$
$$= 0.09, \text{ or } 9.0\%$$

Other Benefits

Any firm that must pay taxes can benefit from the interest tax shield. Not surprisingly, most financial managers cite it as a major benefit from using debt in a firm's capital structure.

Although the tax benefit is important, you should be aware of other benefits. For example, it is less expensive to issue debt than to issue shares. Underwriting spreads and out-of-pocket costs are more than three times as large for share sales as they are for bond sales. For example, you saw in Chapter 15 (Exhibit 15.6) that a firm raising £20 million will typically pay between 5.5% and 11% of the amount raised to sell stock but only 0.43% of the amount raised to sell bonds – a substantial difference. This benefit is related to the second of the three conditions identified by M&M. Issuance costs are a form of transaction costs. If there were no transaction costs, then debt issues would not have this cost advantage.

Another benefit associated with using debt financing is that debt provides managers with incentives to focus on maximising the firm's cash flows. Unlike dividends, which are discretionary, interest and principal payments must be made when they are due. Because managers must make these payments or face the prospect of bankruptcy, the use of debt puts more pressure on managers to focus on the efficiency of the business. Because being involved in a bankruptcy can destroy a manager's career, managers will work very hard to avoid letting this happen. Providing managers with these incentives can increase the overall value of the firm.

Finally, debt can be used to limit the ability of bad managers to waste the shareholders' money on things such as fancy jet aircraft, plush offices and other negative NPV projects that personally benefit the managers. It does this by forcing managers to distribute excess cash to the securityholders. In some very famous cases, such as Daewoo, Vivendi, Enron and WorldCom in the 1990s, managers wasted very large amounts of corporate assets on negative NPV projects. Clearly, the managers at these firms had a great deal of discretion over the use of the large sums of cash generated by their businesses. If the firms had been more highly leveraged, the managers would have had less discretion.

The benefits arising from providing managers with incentives to focus on the cash flows generated by their firms and limiting their ability to make poor investments are related to the second and third conditions identified by M&M. These benefits are related to information and transaction costs because if investors had enough information to know whether managers were doing the right thing, or if it were reasonably inexpensive to provide the managers with pay packages that gave them incentives to do the right thing on their own, there would be no such benefits from debt. The benefits also relate directly to the M&M condition that capital structure decisions do not affect the real investment policies of the firm. The whole point of using debt to limit the investments managers can make is to change firms' real investment policies so that managers focus on investing in only positive NPV projects.

The Costs of Debt

We have discussed several benefits associated with using debt. If this were the whole story, choosing the optimal capital structure would be straightforward. More debt would imply a higher firm value, and financial managers would use as much debt as possible. In other words, a plot of a firm's value against the proportion of debt in its capital structure would look like the upward-sloping line in Exhibit 16.6. Managers would try to move their firms' capital structures as far to the right as possible and we would expect to see firms using as close to 100% debt financing as possible.

Recall, however, that the debt of a typical public firm represents only about 25% of the value of the firm. The fact that this number is so much lower than 100% raises a question: Is it simply that financial managers do not understand the benefits of debt or is something else going on? As you might suspect, the answer to this question is that financial managers are smart and are limiting the amount of debt in their firms' capital structures for some very

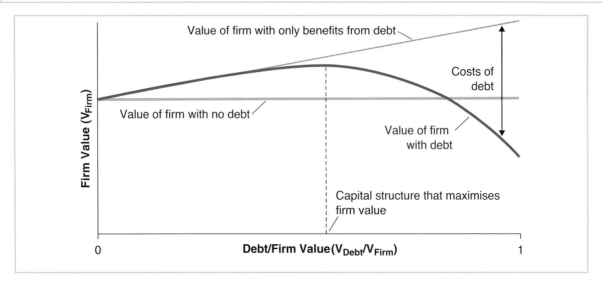

Exhibit 16.8: Trade-Off Theory of Capital Structure The benefits and costs of debt combine to affect firm value. For low levels of debt, adding more debt to a firm's capital structure increases firm value because the additional (marginal) benefits are greater than the additional (marginal) costs. However, at some point, which is the point at which the value of the firm is maximised, the costs of adding more debt begin to outweigh the benefits and the value of the firm decreases as more debt is added. The difference between the upward-sloping line and the curved line reflects the costs associated with debt.

good reasons. Offsetting the benefits of debt are costs and these costs can be quite substantial at high levels of debt.

Exhibit 16.8 illustrates how the costs of using debt combine with the benefits to result in an optimal capital structure that includes less than 100% debt. At low levels of debt, the benefits are greater than the costs and adding more debt increases the overall value of the firm. However, at some point, the costs begin to exceed the benefits and adding more debt financing destroys firm value. Financial managers want to add debt just to the point at which the value of the firm is maximised.

The costs of using debt fall into two general categories: bankruptcy costs and agency costs.

Bankruptcy Costs

Bankruptcy costs, also referred to as the **costs of financial distress**, are costs associated with financial difficulties that a firm might get into because it uses debt financing. The term *bankruptcy costs* is used rather loosely in capital structure discussions to refer to costs incurred when a firm gets into

financial distress. Financial distress occurs when a firm is not able to make all of the interest and principal payments that it owes its lenders. A financially distressed firm might subsequently enter into a formal legal bankruptcy process but not all financially distressed firms will do this.[12] Consequently, as you will see shortly, firms can incur the bankruptcy costs discussed in this section even if they never actually file for bankruptcy.

> ### Bankruptcy costs or costs of financial distress
>
> costs associated with financial difficulties a firm might experience because it uses debt financing

> ### Direct bankruptcy costs
>
> out-of-pocket costs that a firm incurs when it gets into financial distress

Direct Bankruptcy Costs   **Direct bankruptcy costs** are out-of-pocket costs that a firm incurs as a result of financial distress. These costs include fees paid to lawyers, accountants and consultants. One of the first actions a firm's management takes when the firm gets into financial distress is to initiate negotiations with its lenders to defer its interest and principal payments. This deferment can give management more time to correct whatever went wrong with the firm's operations that made it difficult to make interest and principal payments in the first place. Lawyers are experienced in assisting in these negotiations and in writing the necessary legal documents. Additional accounting support often becomes necessary to satisfy demands for information from lenders and to help management figure out what went wrong. Consultants might be hired to help identify and implement changes to improve the firm's performance. The costs of hiring all of these people are included in direct bankruptcy costs. Since the probability of financial distress increases with the amount of debt that a firm uses, the expected size of these costs increases with leverage, driving up the interest rate that investors charge the firm for its debt. Investors charge a higher interest rate when the expected value of direct bankruptcy costs increases because the payment of these costs is likely to come out of the cash flows that they would otherwise receive.

You might be asking yourself why the lenders to a firm would defer interest and principal payments. After all, pushing these payments further into the future reduces the present value of the payments that the lenders are promised. The reason is simple: it can cost lenders even more if they refuse to work with management and the firm is forced to file for bankruptcy. Once a firm files for bankruptcy, legal fees increase, because the firm must also hire lawyers to help with the bankruptcy process, and accounting fees increase, because the bankruptcy process will require the firm to generate even more information. In addition, the firm must reimburse the court for the costs that it incurs. By negotiating with management up-front, the lenders might be able to help the firm avoid incurring the costs associated with the formal bankruptcy process. This leaves more value in the firm, which can be used to satisfy the lender's claims.

Direct bankruptcy costs are a form of transaction costs that must be incurred to facilitate negotiations with lenders and to navigate the bankruptcy process. The second condition identified by M&M – that there are no transaction and information costs – assumes that these transaction costs do not exist. Because the costs do exist, they tend to offset, at least to some extent, the benefits associated with debt. In fact, researchers have estimated that direct bankruptcy costs can amount to as much as 3–5% of firm value. Although these costs are substantial, they are not large enough to offset the benefits of debt that we have discussed. Direct bankruptcy costs alone are not large enough to cause the firm value curve to turn downwards in the manner illustrated in Exhibit 16.8.

Indirect Bankruptcy Costs   **Indirect bankruptcy costs** are costs associated with changes in the behaviour of people who deal with a firm when it becomes financially distressed. The interests of many people who deal with a firm are normally similar to those of the shareholders – they all want to maximise the firm's value. However, when a firm gets into financial distress, the interests of these people begin to differ and the actions they take to protect their interests often reduce firm value.

> ### Indirect bankruptcy costs
>
> costs associated with changes in the behaviour of people who deal with a firm when the firm gets into financial distress

For example, suppose a firm's products come with warranties or require after-sales service or parts (automobiles, for example) and it becomes known that the firm is having financial difficulties. Some of this firm's potential customers will decide to purchase a competitor's products because of concerns that the firm will not be able to honour its warranties or that parts or service will not be available in the future. Other customers will demand a lower price to compensate them for these risks. In either case, the firm's revenues will decline below what they would otherwise have been.

When suppliers learn that a firm is in financial distress, they worry about not being paid. They can do little about goods they have already shipped, but to protect against losses for future shipments, they often begin to require cash on delivery. In other words, they will deliver supplies only if the firm pays cash for them. This requirement can be devastating for a financially distressed firm because such a firm typically does not have much cash. For example, if a retailer, like a department store, cannot pay cash for its merchandise, the amount of merchandise on the shelves in its stores will decline over time. Customers will not be able to find what they want and they will respond by shopping at competitors' stores. This will cause revenues to decline even faster than they might otherwise have done. In the worst case, suppliers' demands for cash payments can force a firm to stop operating altogether.

Employees at a distressed firm worry that their jobs or benefits are in danger and some start looking for new jobs. The loss of highly skilled employees can reduce the value of the firm, especially if they take jobs with direct competitors. Even when employees do not leave, their productivity will often decline because the firm's problems lead to lower morale and distractions.

Like direct bankruptcy costs, indirect bankruptcy costs are transaction costs that would not exist under the second condition identified by M&M. They are transaction costs because they represent costs incurred in the course of contracting with the people who deal with the firm.

If the firm enters into the formal bankruptcy process, it incurs another indirect bankruptcy cost. This cost stems from the fact that the bankruptcy judge must approve all of the firm's major investments. Bankruptcy judges are responsible for representing the interests of the creditors and tend to be more conservative than the shareholders would like. This results in a change in the firm's real investment policy and a violation of the third M&M condition.

The nature of indirect bankruptcy costs differs from company to company. For example, loss of skilled workers is more damaging to a technology firm than to a retailer. Potential customers of an automobile manufacturer worry a lot more about the implications of financial distress than potential customers of a company that makes T-shirts, whereas suppliers are concerned in both of these cases. In spite of these differences, indirect bankruptcy costs are often very substantial and are reflected in the interest rates that firms must pay. Researchers have estimated that indirect bankruptcy costs range from 10% to 23% of firm value, suggesting that they can be large enough to offset the interest tax shield benefit by themselves.

It is worth stressing that indirect bankruptcy costs occur at absolutely the worst time for a firm. The point at which a firm gets into financial distress is the point at which it can benefit most from the support of people who deal with it. However, this is exactly when it is often in the best interests of those people to provide less support and, in many cases, to abandon the firm. The associated changes in behaviour can accelerate the firm's deterioration and push it into formal bankruptcy.

BUILDING INTUITION

People Behave Differently towards a Firm in Financial Distress and this Increases Bankruptcy Costs

When a firm gets into financial distress, the people who deal with the company take actions to protect their interests. These actions often contribute to the firm's problems because when the firm is financially distressed, the interests of people such as customers, suppliers and employees differ from those of shareholders.

Agency Costs

The managers and shareholders of a firm also often behave in ways that reduce a firm's value when the firm becomes financially distressed. The resulting costs are a type of *agency cost*. You may recall from Chapter 1 that agency costs result from conflicts of interest between principals and agents. In agency relationships, one party, known as the *principal*, delegates decision-making authority to another party, known as the *agent*. The agent is expected to act in the interests of the principal. However, agents' interests sometimes conflict with those of the principal.

To better understand agency costs, consider the following example. Suppose that you have a newspaper route and you want to go out of town for a week. You offer a friend €100 to deliver your papers while you are gone. If your friend agrees to the arrangement, you will have entered into a principal–agent relationship. Now assume that you deliver the *Wall Street Journal Europe* and that all papers are supposed to be on your customers' doorsteps by 6:00 A.M., before they leave home for work. You tell this to your friend before you leave town but he likes to sleep late in the morning, so he does not get all the papers delivered until 9:00 A.M. Because the papers are late for five days in a row, a few customers complain and some do not give you a tip at the end of the year as they have in the past. Any problems that arise because of the complaints and the lost tips are examples of agency costs. These costs arose because you delegated decision-making authority to your friend and he acted in his best interests rather than yours.

Shareholder–Manager Agency Costs Shareholders hire managers to manage the firm on their behalf. In this relationship, managers receive considerable decision-making authority. While the board of directors approves major decisions and monitors the performance of the managers on behalf of the shareholders, managers still make many decisions that the board never observes. To the extent that the managers' incentives are not identical to those of the shareholders, managers will make some decisions that benefit themselves at the expense of shareholders.

As we saw in our discussion of the benefits of debt, a firm's use of debt financing can help align the interests of managers with those of shareholders. Using debt financing provides managers with incentives to focus on maximising the firm's cash flows and limits the ability of bad managers to waste the shareholders' money on negative NPV projects. These benefits amount to reductions in the agency costs associated with the principal–agent relationship between shareholders and managers.

Although the use of debt financing can reduce agency costs, it can also increase these costs by altering the behaviour of managers. Managers often have a high proportion of their wealth riding on the success of the firm, through their shareholdings, future income and reputations. Consequently, they tend to prefer less risk than shareholders who hold more diversified portfolios. As you know, the use of debt increases the volatility of a firm's earnings and the probability that the firm will get into financial difficulty. This increased risk causes managers to make decisions that are more conservative. For example, managers of firms with more financial leverage will have greater incentives to turn down positive NPV projects with high risk compared with managers at firms with less leverage. Similarly, managers at highly financially leveraged firms will prefer to distribute fewer profits to shareholders because retained earnings provide a buffer against possible bankruptcy. These types of actions reduce the overall value of the firm and are examples of agency costs associated with the use of debt financing.

Recall that the third M&M condition is that the use of debt financing does not affect the firm's real investment policy. However, in the extent to which using debt financing causes managers to turn down high-risk positive NPV projects and distribute fewer earnings, financing decisions do affect real investment policies. Leverage provides managers with incentives to invest in lower-risk positive NPV projects rather than in all positive NPV projects. It also provides them with incentives to retain excess earnings. They might even have incentives to invest some of the excess retained earnings in low-risk negative NPV projects. The fact that managers may act in this way is another reason that debt financing affects the value of the firm.

Shareholder–Lender Agency Costs   A principal–agent relationship also exists between lenders and shareholders. When investors lend money to a firm, they delegate authority to the shareholders to decide how that money will be used. The lenders expect that the shareholders, through the managers they appoint, will invest the money in a way that enables the firm to make all of the interest and principal payments that have been promised. However, shareholders may have incentives to use the money in ways that are not in the best interests of the lenders.

For example, shareholders might decide that instead of investing the money to grow the firm they will distribute it to themselves as a dividend. The liability of shareholders is limited to the amount of money they have invested in the firm. Since loans that are made to a company are contracts between the lenders and the company, not the shareholders, paying such a dividend reduces the resources in the firm that are available to repay the lenders and therefore the value of the lender's claims. Unless the dividend violates the loan agreement or otherwise violates the law, the lenders have no way to get that money back. This is an example of what we call a *wealth transfer* from the lenders to the shareholders. Wealth has been transferred because the shareholders have made themselves better off at the expense of the lenders.

Lenders know that shareholders have incentives to distribute some or all of the funds that they borrow as dividends. To protect themselves against this sort of behaviour, lenders often include provisions in loan agreements that limit the ability of shareholders to pay dividends. However, these provisions are not foolproof. Shareholders can be very innovative in transferring wealth from lenders to themselves.

For example, in October 1992 Marriott Corporation had a substantial amount of debt that had been borrowed to build new hotels. The economy was in a recession and there was growing concern about the ability of Marriott to make all of its promised interest and principal payments. If the company defaulted, the shareholders stood to lose a good deal of the value of their shares.

In response to this situation, Marriott management announced a *spin-off* in which the company would be split into two separate companies. After the spin-off, shareholders would own one share in each of the two new companies for every share that they had owned in the original company. While spin-offs are quite common, this one was unique in that the company was spinning off its most profitable businesses into one company and leaving much of its debt, some property and a small operating business in the other. The spin-off effectively reduced the value of the assets that the lenders would have to rely on to receive their interest and principal payments while reducing the assets that the shareholders could lose if there was a default. When the spin-off was announced, the market value of Marriott's public bonds decreased 16.51%, or $333.3 million, while the market value of Marriott's outstanding shares increased by $236.3 million.[13] The increase in the value of the shares represented a wealth transfer from the lenders to the shareholders. In addition, the fact that the value of the debt went down more than the value of the equity increased suggests that the capital markets did not like this transaction: the total value of the firm (debt plus equity) went down.

Notice that when we talk about shareholder–lender agency costs, we assume that managers do exactly what the shareholders would like them to do. However, in the discussion of shareholder–manager agency costs we saw that managers are not always so cooperative. This results in some conflicting possibilities with respect to how financial leverage affects the managers' decisions. For example, in a firm that uses debt financing, managers prefer to invest in low-risk projects, whereas diversified shareholders prefer high-risk projects. Shareholders will pressure managers to invest in riskier projects but whether shareholders get what they want will depend on how strong the corporate governance system is in the firm.

To better understand the nature of the conflict between shareholders and lenders, consider the following example. Suppose a firm has €50 million invested in 10% risk-free bonds that will pay €55 million in one year. The firm also has one-year debt on which €50 million of interest and principal will be due when it matures in a year. In other words, this firm is solvent and will be able to repay its debt but the equity will be worth only €5 million, since this is all that will be left over after the lenders are paid.

Now suppose that the shareholders decide to sell the risk-free bonds and invest in a project that has a 50% chance of returning €95 million in one year and a 50% chance of returning only €15 million. Instead of receiving €50 million with no risk, the lenders will now face a 50% chance of receiving the €50 million they are owed and a 50% chance of receiving only €15 million. The value that the lenders expect to receive is €32.5 million:

$$E(V_{Bonds}) = (0.50 \times €50) + (0.50 \times €15)$$
$$= €32.5 \, \text{million}$$

This amount is €17.5 million less than the €50 million that the lenders expected to receive when the firm held the risk-free bonds. On the other hand, the value that the shareholders expect to receive has increased by €17.5 million, from €5 million to €22.5 million:

$$E(V_{Shares}) = [0.50 \times (€95 - €50)] + (0.50 \times €0)$$
$$= €22.5 \, \text{million}$$

The change to riskier assets has resulted in a €17.5 million wealth transfer. This is known as the **asset substitution problem**. Once a loan has been made to a firm, the shareholders have an incentive to substitute more risky assets for less risky assets.

> **Asset substitution problem**
>
> the incentive that shareholders in a financially leveraged firm have to substitute more risky assets for less risky assets

Under certain circumstances, shareholders will actually have incentives to invest in risky *negative* NPV projects. To see how this can happen, assume that the shareholders in our example sell the €50 million of risk-free bonds and invest the proceeds in a project that has a 50% chance of returning €70 million and a 50% chance of returning €10 million. The expected return on the €50 million investment is €40 million [(0.50 × €70) + (0.50 × €10) = €40 million]. This is a negative NPV project. However, the value that the shareholders can expect to receive is €10 million – twice as much as the €5 million they could expect to receive when the firm owned the risk-free bonds:

$$E(V_{Stock}) = [0.50 \times (€70 - €50)] + (0.50 \times €0)$$
$$= €10 \, \text{million}$$

The lenders bear the €15 million loss in firm value (€55 million – €40 million) and they pay for the €5 million gain to the shareholders. The lenders now expect to receive €20 million less than the €50 million they would have received if the risk-free bonds had not been sold:

$$E(V_{Bonds}) = (0.50 \times €50) + (0.50 \times €10)$$
$$= €30 \, \text{million}$$

Shareholders of financially distressed firms can also have incentives to turn down positive NPV projects. This situation is known as the **underinvestment problem**. It occurs in a financially distressed firm when the value that is created by investing in a positive NPV project is likely to go to the lenders instead of the shareholders.

> **Underinvestment problem**
>
> the incentive that shareholders in a financially leveraged firm have to turn down positive NPV projects when the firm is in financial distress

To see how this can happen, suppose that a company has debt with a face value of €50 million outstanding and that the value of the company's assets is €32.5 million. If this financially distressed firm were sold today, the lenders would receive €32.5 million and the shareholders would receive nothing. Now suppose that the managers of the firm identify a project that requires a €5 million investment and will return €17.5 million tomorrow with no risk. Since the firm is distressed, management will have to sell shares to raise the €5 million required for this investment. Does it make sense for the shareholders to make the investment?

The answer is no, because if the shareholders invest the €5 million, they can expect to get nothing back if the firm is subsequently sold. Both the €5 million that the shareholders invest and the €12.5 million NPV from the project will go to the lenders. Instead of receiving €32.5 million, the lenders will receive €50 million and the shareholders will be out by €5 million.

This example illustrates why, in the real world, financially distressed businesses have a very difficult time selling equity. Just when they need the support of their shareholders, the shareholders abandon them.

It is important to note that without financial leverage, there would be no asset substitution or underinvestment problems. Shareholders would always want to invest in positive NPV projects and reject negative NPV projects regardless of their risk.

Lenders know that debt provides shareholders with incentives to alter their firms' investment policies to engage in asset substitution and to turn down positive NPV projects. However, it is difficult to write contracts that protect lenders against this sort of behaviour. Therefore, as with any other risk that they cannot eliminate, lenders compensate by increasing the interest rate that they charge. This increases the cost of adding more debt to a firm's capital structure.

The fact that there are a number of different benefits and costs associated with the use of debt financing suggests that managers will balance, or trade off, the benefits against the costs when they choose a firm's capital structure. We discuss this idea, along with an alternative theory for how managers choose their firms' capital structures, in the next section.

Before You Go On

1. What are some benefits of using debt financing?
2. What are bankruptcy costs, and what are the two types of bankruptcy costs?
3. What are agency costs, and how are they related to the use of debt financing?

TWO THEORIES OF CAPITAL STRUCTURE

Learning Objective 3

Describe the trade-off and pecking order theories of capital structure choice and explain what the empirical evidence tells us about these theories.

How do managers choose the capital structures for their firms? Next, we consider two theories that attempt to explain how this choice is made: the trade-off theory and the pecking-order theory.

The Trade-Off Theory

The **trade-off theory** of capital structure states that managers choose a specific target capital structure based on the trade-offs between the benefits and the costs of debt. This target capital structure is the capital structure that maximises the value of the firm, as illustrated in Exhibit 16.8.

Trade-off theory

the theory that managers trade off the benefits against the costs of using debt to identify the optimal capital structure for a firm

Underlying the trade-off theory is the idea that when a firm uses a small amount of debt financing, it receives the interest tax shield and possibly some of the other benefits we discussed. Since leverage is low and the chances that the firm will get into financial difficulties are also low, the costs of debt are small relative to the benefits and firm value increases. However, as more and more debt is added to the firm's capital structure, the costs of debt increase and eventually reach the point where the cost associated with the next euro that is borrowed equals the benefit. Beyond this point, the costs of adding additional debt exceed the benefits and any additional debt reduces firm value. The trade-off theory of capital structure says that managers will increase debt to the point at which the costs and benefits of adding another dollar of debt are exactly equal because this is the capital structure that maximises firm value.

The Pecking-Order Theory

The trade-off theory makes intuitive sense, but there is another popular theory of how the capital structures of firms are determined. This is known as the **pecking-order theory**. The pecking-order theory recognises that different types of capital have different costs and that this leads to a pecking order in the financing choices that managers make. Managers choose the least expensive capital first then move to increasingly costly capital when the lower-cost sources of capital are no longer available.

> **Pecking-order theory**
>
> the theory that in financing projects, managers first use retained earnings, which they view as the least expensive form of capital, then debt, and finally externally raised equity, which they view as the most expensive

Under the pecking-order theory, managers view internally generated funds, or cash on hand, as the cheapest source of capital.[14] Debt is more costly to obtain than internally generated funds but is still relatively inexpensive. In contrast, raising money by selling shares can be very expensive. As we saw in Exhibit 15.6, the out-of-pocket costs of selling equity are much higher than the comparable costs for bonds. In addition, the disclosure requirements by regulators are greater and the stock market tends to react negatively to announcements that firms are selling new shares. When firms announce that they will sell shares, their share price often declines because such sales are often interpreted as evidence that the firms are not profitable enough to fund their investments internally. Of course, a lower share price reduces the value of everyone's shares and makes future share issues even more costly since more shares will have to be sold to raise the same amount.

The pecking-order theory says that firms use internally generated funds as long as they are available. Following that, they tend to borrow money to finance additional projects until they are no longer able to do so because of restrictions in loan agreements or until high interest rates make debt unattractive. Only then will managers choose to sell equity. Notice that the pecking-order theory does not assume that managers have a target capital structure. Rather, it implies that the capital structure of a firm is, in some sense, a by-product of the firm's financing history.

The Empirical Evidence

At this point, you might be asking yourself what we actually know about how capital structures are determined in the real world. A great deal of research has been done in this area, and the evidence supports both of the theories we have just described. When researchers compare the capital structures in different industries, they find evidence that supports the trade-off theory. Industries with a great many tangible assets, such as the air transportation, automobile and gas, electric and sanitary services industries, typically use relatively large amounts of debt. In contrast, industries with more intangible assets and numerous growth opportunities, such as the computer and drug

EXHIBIT 16.9

AVERAGE CAPITAL STRUCTURES FOR SELECTED INDUSTRIES IN EUROPE AT THE END OF 2006

Industry Group	Number of Firms	Debt/Firm Value
Automobiles: cars/light trucks	10	66.4%
Water	20	54.3%
Airlines	14	49.1%
Automotive parts and equipment	22	36.4%
Brewing	39	34.4%
Food retail	24	32.4%
Hotels and motels	27	31.2%
Building: heavy construction	42	29.7%
General machinery	47	26.9%
Beverages: wine and spirits	26	24.9%
Restaurants	20	24.4%
Diversified manufacturing	34	24.0%
Diversified chemicals	21	21.7%
Consulting services	27	20.0%
Telecom services	36	15.7%
Computer services	66	14.5%
Electronics: semiconductors	24	10.7%
Computer software	13	5.1%
Medical drugs	52	3.5%
Web portals/ISP	15	1.2%

This table shows average capital structures for different industries in Europe as of the end of 2005. The industries are arranged in order of declining debt-to-firm value ratios. Industries with a great many tangible assets, such as airlines, automobile and water industries, tend to have larger debt-to-firm value ratios.

industries, use relatively little debt. What accounts for this difference? At least in part, the difference exists because indirect bankruptcy costs and agency costs tend to be lower in industries with more tangible assets. The assets in these industries have higher liquidation values and it is more difficult for shareholders to engage in asset substitution. Exhibit 16.9 shows the extent of the variation in capital structures across industries.

Some researchers argue that, on average, debt levels appear to be lower than the trade-off theory suggests they should be. Firms pay large amounts of taxes that could be reduced through greater debt financing, even though their current capital structures are such that they face little possibility of financial distress. For example, in 2009, the cash and short-term securities at Sanofi-Aventis, the French pharmaceutical company, were about €5 billion, or 63% of the amount of short-term and long-term debt.

The evidence also indicates that the more profitable a firm is, the less debt it tends to have. This is exactly opposite to what we should see under the trade-off theory. Under the trade-off theory, more profitable firms pay more taxes so they should use more debt to take advantage of the interest tax shield. Instead, this evidence is consistent with the pecking-order theory. Highly profitable firms have plenty of cash on hand that can be used to finance their projects, and over time, using this cash will drive down their debt ratios.

The pecking-order theory is also supported by the fact that, in an average year, public firms actually issue very few new shares. Internally generated funds represent the largest source of financing for new investments and debt represents the largest source of external financing.

Both the trade-off theory and the pecking-order theory offer some insights into how managers choose the capital structures for their firms. However, neither of them is able to explain all of the capital structure choices that we observe. For instance, there is some evidence for market timing by managers. That is, they seek to issue equity when they think the stock market overvalues shares or will be receptive to new shares.

The truth is that capital structure decisions are very complex and it is difficult to characterise them with a single general theory. In the next section, we briefly discuss some of the practical issues that managers say they consider when they make capital structure decisions.

Before You Go On

1. What is the trade-off theory of capital structure?
2. What is the pecking-order theory of capital structure?
3. What does the empirical evidence tell us about the two theories?

PRACTICAL CONSIDERATIONS IN CHOOSING A CAPITAL STRUCTURE

Learning Objective 4

Discuss some of the practical considerations that managers are concerned with when they choose a firm's capital structure.

When managers talk about their capital structure choices, their comments are sprinkled with terms such as *financial flexibility, risk* and *earnings impact*. Managers do not think only in terms of a trade-off or a pecking order. Rather, they are concerned with how their financing decisions will influence the practical issues that they must deal with when managing a business.

For example, *financial flexibility* is an important consideration in many capital structure decisions. Managers must ensure that they retain sufficient financial resources in the firm to take advantage of unexpected opportunities and to overcome unforeseen problems.[15] In theory, if a positive NPV investment becomes available, managers should be able to obtain financing for it. Unfortunately, financing might not be available at a reasonable price for all positive NPV projects at all times. For example, it might be difficult to convince investors that a project is as good as management thinks it is. As a result, investors may require too high a return, making the project's NPV negative and causing the firm to pass up a good opportunity. Similarly, if the firm does not have enough financial flexibility, an unforeseen problem might end up being more costly than it should be. For instance, suppose that a firm's major manufacturing facility was destroyed by the L'Aquila earthquake in central Italy in April 2009. Insurance would eventually cover much of the loss but by the time the insurance settlement was received, the company might be out of business. In such cases, cash is needed immediately to help employees so that key skills are not lost and to relocate or start rebuilding as quickly as possible.

Managers are also concerned about the impact of financial leverage on the volatility of the firm's earnings. Most businesses experience fluctuations in their operating profits over time and we know that fixed-interest payments magnify fluctuations in operating profits, thereby causing even greater variation in net income. Managers do not like volatility in reported earnings because it causes problems in their relationships with outside investors, who do not like unpredictable earnings.

Furthermore, as we have seen, if a firm is too highly leveraged, it runs a greater risk of defaulting on its debt, which can lead to all sorts of bankruptcy costs and agency costs. Managers use the term *risk* to describe the possibility that normal fluctuations in operating profits will lead to financial distress. They try to manage their firms' capital structures in a way that limits the risk to a reasonable level – one that allows them to sleep at night.

A third factor that managers think about when they choose a capital structure is the impact of financial leverage on the firm's earnings. The interest expense associated with debt financing reduces the reported *value of net income*. However, depending on the market value of the firm's shares, using debt instead of equity to finance a project can increase the reported value of earnings per share. Many managers are very concerned about the earnings per share that their firms report because they believe that it affects the share price. Financial theory states that managers should not be so concerned about accounting earnings because cash flows are what really matters. Whether they are right or wrong, if managers believe that accounting earnings matter, their capital structure decisions will reflect this belief.

WEB

You can read more about the agencies that rate corporate bonds and find links to their websites on the Wikipedia website at: http://en.wikipedia.org/wiki/Credit_rating_agency.

Another factor that managers consider when making capital structure decisions is the *control implications* of their decisions. The choice between equity and debt financing affects the control of the firm. For example, suppose that a firm is controlled by the founding family, which owns 55% of the ordinary shares, and

that the firm must raise capital to fund a large project. The project has a zero NPV and will result in a 20% increase in the size of the firm. On the one hand, using equity financing will drop the founding family's ownership (voting rights) below 50% if the family does not buy some of the new shares. In fact, they will end up with 45.8% of the shares [55/(100 − 20) = 0.458]. On the other hand, their ownership will remain at 55% and they will retain absolute control of the firm if the project is financed entirely with debt. In such a situation, the founding family is likely to prefer debt financing. Of course, although debt can help a controlling shareholder retain control of a firm, too much debt can cause that shareholder to lose control. This can happen if the firm uses so much debt that fluctuations in business conditions put the firm in financial distress. When this happens, the ability of the creditors to control what happens to the firm can overwhelm the ability of the controlling shareholder to do so.

These are just some examples of practical considerations that managers must deal with when choosing the appropriate capital structure for a firm. There is no set formula that they can follow in making financing decisions because many of these considerations are difficult to quantify and their relative importance is unique to each firm. Nevertheless, it is safe to say that the ultimate objective of a firm's shareholders – and of managers who have the shareholders' interests in mind – is to choose the capital structure that maximises the value of the firm.

Before You Go On

1. Why is financial flexibility important in the choice of a capital structure?
2. How can capital structure decisions affect the risk associated with net income?
3. How can capital structure decisions affect the control of a firm?

SUMMARY OF LEARNING OBJECTIVES

1. **Describe the two Modigliani and Miller propositions, the key assumptions underlying them and their relevance to capital structure decisions.**

   M&M Proposition 1 states that the value of a firm is unaffected by its capital structure if the following three conditions hold: (1) there are no taxes, (2) there are no information or transaction costs and (3) capital structure decisions do not affect the real investment policies of the firm. This proposition tells us the three reasons that capital structure choices affect firm value.

2. **Discuss the benefits and costs of using debt financing.**

   Using debt financing provides several benefits. A major benefit is the deductibility of interest payments. Since interest payments are tax deductible and dividend payments are not, distributing cash to securityholders through interest payments can increase the value of a firm. Debt is also less expensive to issue than equity. Finally, debt can benefit shareholders in certain situations by providing managers with incentives to maximise the cash flows produced by the firm and by reducing their ability to invest in negative NPV projects.

   The costs of debt include bankruptcy and agency costs. Bankruptcy costs arise because financial leverage increases the probability that a firm will get into financial distress. Direct bankruptcy costs are the out-of-pocket costs that a firm incurs when it gets into financial distress, while indirect bankruptcy costs are associated with actions the people who deal with the firm take to protect their own interests when the firm is in financial distress. Agency costs are costs associated with actions taken by managers and shareholders who are acting in their own interests rather than in the best interests of the firm. When a firm uses financial leverage, managers have incentives to take actions that benefit themselves at the expense of shareholders and shareholders have incentives to take actions that benefit themselves at the expense of lenders. To the extent that these actions reduce the value of lenders' claims, the expected losses will be reflected in the interest rates that lenders require.

3. **Describe the trade-off and pecking-order theories of capital structure choice and explain what the empirical evidence tells us about these theories.**

   The trade-off theory says that managers balance, or trade off, the benefits of debt against the costs of debt when choosing a firm's capital structure in an effort to maximise the value of the firm. The pecking-order theory says that managers raise capital as they need it in the least expensive way available, starting with internally generated funds, then moving to debt, then to the sale of equity. In contrast to the trade-off theory, the pecking-order theory does not imply that managers have a particular target capital structure. There is empirical evidence that supports both theories, suggesting that each helps explain the capital structure choices made by managers.

4. **Discuss some of the practical considerations that managers are concerned with when they choose a firm's capital structure.**

   Practical considerations that concern managers when they choose a firm's capital structure include the impact of the capital structure on financial flexibility, risk, net income and the control of the firm. Financial flexibility involves having the necessary financial resources to take advantage of unforeseen opportunities and to overcome unforeseen problems. Risk refers to the possibility that normal fluctuations in operating profits will lead to financial distress. Managers are also concerned with the impact of financial leverage on their reported net income, especially on a per-share basis. Finally, the impact of capital structure decisions on who controls the firm also affects capital structure decisions.

SUMMARY OF KEY EQUATIONS

Equation	Description	Formula
(16.1)	Value of the firm as the sum of the debt and equity values	$V_{Firm} = V_{Assets} = V_{Debt} + V_{Equity}$
(16.2)	Formula for weighted average cost of capital (WACC) for firm with only ordinary shares and no taxes	$WACC = x_{Debt}k_{Debt} + x_{os}k_{os}$
(16.3)	Cost of ordinary shares in terms of the required return on assets and the required return on debt	$k_{os} = k_{Assets} + \left(\dfrac{V_{Debt}}{V_{os}}\right)(k_{Assets} - k_{Debt})$
(16.4)	Value of tax savings of debt (upper bound)	$V_{Tax\text{-}savings\ debt} = D \times t$

SELF-STUDY PROBLEMS

16.1. If any of the three assumptions in Modigliani and Miller Proposition 1 are relaxed, which has the most predictably quantifiable impact on the value of the firm?

16.2. If we assume that the cash flows for a firm with financial leverage are equal to the cash flows for the same firm without financial leverage, what can we say about the value of this firm if its cost of capital does not vary with the degree of leverage utilised either?

16.3. Are taxes necessary for the cost of debt financing to be less than the cost of equity financing?

16.4. You are offered jobs with identical responsibilities by two different firms in the same industry. One has no debt in its capital structure and the other has 99% debt in its capital structure. Will you require a higher level of compensation from one firm than from the other? If so, which firm will have to pay you more?

16.5. You are valuing two firms in the same industry. One firm has a corporate jet for every executive at the vice president level and above, while the other does not have a single corporate jet. More than likely, which firm has the greatest shareholder–manager agency costs?

SOLUTIONS TO SELF-STUDY PROBLEMS

16.1. The assumption with the most measurable impact is that involving taxes. We can directly measure the present value of the tax shield generated by the interest costs of borrowing. The impacts of the other two assumptions, though real, are more difficult to predict.

16.2. If the cash flows produced by the firm and the cost of capital for the firm are the same, regardless of the amount of leverage utilised, we can then say that the value of the firm is also unchanged by the amount of financial leverage.

16.3. The deduction for interest expense does make debt borrowing more attractive than it would otherwise be. However, even without the interest deduction benefit, the cost of debt is less than the cost of equity because equity is a riskier investment than debt. This means that the pre-tax cost to the firm for debt is still lower than the cost of equity.

16.4. The firm with the large amount of debt financing (the 99% debt firm) has a higher probability of entering bankruptcy.

Therefore, you should require greater compensation from that firm.

16.5. If we can assume that the jets are used largely for the convenience of management, then it appears that the multi-jet firm has higher shareholder–manager agency costs than the no-jet firm. Perhaps the no-jet firm uses more of its cash for positive NPV projects than the multi-jet firm.

CRITICAL THINKING QUESTIONS

16.1. List and briefly describe the three key assumptions in Modigliani and Miller's Proposition 1 that are required for total firm value to be independent of capital structure.

16.2. Evaluate the statement that the weighted average cost of capital (WACC) for a firm (assuming that all three assumptions of Modigliani and Miller's propositions hold) is always less than or equal to the cost of equity for the firm.

16.3. If the value of the firm remains constant as a function of its capital structure and the three Modigliani and Miller assumptions apply, how might the overall cost of capital change or not change as capital structure changes.

16.4. Consider the WACC for a firm that pays taxes. Explain what a firm's best course of action would be to minimise its WACC and thereby maximise the firm value. Use the WACC formula for your explanation.

16.5. The Modigliani and Miller propositions, when the no-tax assumption is relaxed, suggest that the firm should finance itself with as much debt as possible. If we take that suggestion to the fullest extent, does that mean it would be practical to finance the firm with 100% debt and no equity?

16.6. Crossler Automobiles sells cars in a market where the standard car comes with a 10-year/100 000-kilometre warranty on all parts and labour. Describe how an increased probability of bankruptcy could affect sales of cars at Crossler.

16.7. The principal–agent problem occurs due to the divergent interests of the non-owner managers and shareholders of a firm. Propose a capital structure change that might help align a portion of these divergent interests.

16.8. If a firm increases its debt to a very high level, then the positive effect of debt in aligning the interests of management with those of shareholders tends to become negative. Explain why this occurs.

16.9. Using the Modigliani and Miller framework but excluding the assumptions that there are no taxes and no information or transaction costs, describe the value of the firm as a function of the proportion of debt in its capital structure.

16.10. When we observe the capital structure of many firms, we find that they tend to utilise lower levels of debt than that predicted by the trade-off theory. Offer an explanation for this effect.

QUESTIONS AND PROBLEMS

Basic

16.1. M&M Proposition 1: The Modigliani and Miller theory suggests that the value of the firm's assets is equal to the value of the claims on those assets and is not dependent on how the asset claims are divided. The common analogy to the theorem is that the total amount of pie available to be eaten (the firm) does not depend on the size of each slice of pie. If we continue with that analogy, then what if we cut up the pie with a very dull knife such that the total amount of pie available to be eaten is less after it is cut than before it was cut. Which of the three Modigliani and Miller assumptions, if relaxed, is analogous to the dull knife? *Hint:* Think about the process by which investors could undo the effects of a firm's capital structure decisions.

16.2. M&M Proposition 1: Describe what exactly is meant when someone is describing the value of the firm versus the value of the equity of the firm.

16.3. M&M Proposition 1: Under Modigliani and Miller's Proposition 1, where all three of the assumptions remain in effect, explain how the value of the firm changes due to changes in the proportion of debt and equity utilised by the firm.

16.4. M&M Proposition 1: Cerberus Security produces a cash flow of €200 and is expected to continue doing so in the infinite future. The cost of equity capital for Cerberus is 20% and the firm is financed totally with equity. The firm would like to repurchase €100 of its shares by borrowing €100 at a 10% rate (assume that the debt will also be outstanding into the infinite future). Using Modigliani and Miller's Proposition 1, what is the value of the firm today and what will be the value of the claims on the firm's assets after the share

repurchase? What will be the rate of return on ordinary shares required by investors after the share repurchase?

16.5. M&M Proposition 1: A firm financed completely with equity currently has a cost of capital equal to 15%. If Modigliani and Miller's Proposition 1 holds and the firm is thinking about changing its capital structure to 50% debt and 50% equity, then what will be the cost of equity after the change if the cost of debt is 10%?

16.6. M&M Proposition 1: Swan Specialty Cycles is currently financed with 50% debt and 50% equity. The firm pays €125 each year to its debt investors (at a 10% cost of debt) and the debt has no maturity date. What will be the value of the equity if the firm repurchases all of its debt and raises the funds by issuing equity? Assume that all of the assumptions in Modigliani and Miller's Proposition 1 hold.

16.7. M&M Proposition 1: The weighted average cost of capital for a firm, assuming all three Modigliani and Miller assumptions hold, is 10%. What is the current cost of equity capital for the firm if the cost of debt for the firm is 8%, given that the firm is financed by 80% debt?

16.8. Interest tax shield benefit: Legitron AG has €350 million of debt outstanding at an interest rate of 9%. What is the amount of the tax shield on that debt, just for this year, if Legitron is subject to a 35% marginal tax rate?

16.9. Interest tax shield benefit: FAJ S.p.A. has €500 million of debt outstanding at an interest rate of 9%. What is the present value of the tax shield on that debt if it has no maturity and if FAJ is subject to a 30% marginal tax rate?

16.10. Interest tax shield benefit: Springer AG has €250 million of debt outstanding at an interest rate of 11%. What is the present value of the debt tax shield if the debt has no maturity and if Springer is subject to a 40% marginal tax rate?

16.11. Interest tax shield benefit: Constructions Specialisés SA currently has an equity cost of capital equal to 15%. If the Modigliani and Miller assumptions hold, with the exception of the assumption that there are no taxes and the firm's capital structure is made up of 50% debt and 50% equity, then what is the weighted average cost of capital for the firm if the cost of debt is 10% and the firm is subject to a 40% marginal tax rate?

16.12. Practical considerations in capital structure choice: List and describe three practical considerations that concern managers when they make capital structure decisions.

Intermediate

16.13. M&M Proposition 1: Keyboard Chiropractic Clinics produces €300 000 of cash flow each year. The firm has no debt outstanding and its cost of equity capital is 25%. The firm would like to repurchase €600 000 of its equity by borrowing a similar amount at a rate of 8% per year. If we assume that the debt will be perpetual, find the cost of equity capital for Keyboard after it changes its capital structure. Assume that Modigliani and Miller's Proposition 1 holds.

16.14. M&M Proposition 1: Les Grandes Galleries SA has a current WACC of 21%. If the cost of debt capital for the firm is 12% and the firm is currently financed with 25% debt, then what is the current cost of equity capital for the firm? Assume that the assumptions in Modigliani and Miller's Proposition 1 hold.

16.15. M&M Proposition 1: Evaluate the effect on Modigliani and Miller's Proposition 1 of relaxing the assumption that there are no information or transaction costs.

16.16. M&M Proposition 1: The weighted average cost of capital for a firm (assuming all three Modigliani and Miller assumptions) is 15%. What is the current cost of equity capital for the firm if its cost of debt is 10% and the proportion of debt to total firm value for the firm is 0.5?

16.17. M&M Proposition 2: Mikos Processed Foods is currently valued at €500 million. Mikos will be repurchasing €100 million of its equity by issuing a perpetual debt issue at a 10% annual interest rate. Mikos is subject to a 30% marginal tax rate. Given all of the Modigliani and Miller assumptions, except the assumption that there are no taxes, what will be the value of Mikos after the recapitalisation?

16.18. M&M Proposition 2: Painture Freche SA has a WACC of 12.6%, and it is subject to a 40% marginal tax rate. It has €250 million of debt outstanding at an interest rate of 9% and €750 million of equity (market value) outstanding. What is the expected return of the equity given this capital structure?

16.19. The costs of debt: Briefly discuss the costs of financial distress to a firm that may arise when employees believe it is highly likely that the firm will declare bankruptcy.

16.20. The costs of debt: Milan Fashions S.p.A. is a retailer that has just begun having financial difficulties. Milan Fashions' suppliers are aware of the increased possibility of bankruptcy. What might Milan Fashions' suppliers do based on this information?

16.21. Shareholder–manager agency costs: Deficit SA has determined that it will come up short by €50 million on its debt obligations at the end of this year. Deficit has identified a positive NPV project that will require a great deal of effort on the part of management. However, this project is expected to generate only €40 million at the end of the year. Assume that all the members of

Deficit's management team will lose their jobs if the firm goes into bankruptcy at the end of the year. Will Deficit take the positive NPV project? If it declines the project, what kind of cost will Deficit incur?

16.22. **Two theories of capital structure:** Use the following table to make a suggestion for the recommended proportion of debt that the firm should utilise for its capital structure.

Benefit or (cost)	No debt	25% debt	50% debt	75% debt
Tax shield	€0	€10	€20	€30
Agency cost	−€10	−€5	−€5	−€20
Financial distress cost	−€1	−€3	−€10	−€10

16.23. **Two theories of capital structure:** Problem 16.22 has reintroduced taxes and information and transaction costs to the simplified Modigliani and Miller model. If the marginal tax rate for the firm were to suddenly increase by a material amount, would the capital structure that maximises the firm include less or more debt?

16.24. **Two theories of capital structure:** Describe the order of financial sources for managers who subscribe to the pecking-order theory of financing. Evaluate that order by observing the costs of each source relative to the costs of other sources.

16.25. **Two theories of capital structure:** The pecking-order theory suggests that managers prefer to first use internally generated equity to finance new projects. Does this preference mean that these funds represent an even cheaper source of funds than debt? Justify your answer.

16.26. **The costs of debt:** Discuss how the legal costs of financial distress may increase with the probability that a firm will fall into bankruptcy even if the firm has not reached the point of bankruptcy.

Advanced

16.27. Operating a firm without debt is generally considered to be a conservative measure. Discuss how such a conservative approach to a firm's capital structure is good or bad for the value of the firm in the absence of information or transaction costs and any effect of debt on the real investment policy of the firm.

16.28. Infinitum SA has €250 million of debt outstanding at an interest rate of 11%. What is the present value of the debt tax shield if the debt will mature in five years (and no new debt will replace the old debt), assuming that Infinitum is subject to a 40% marginal tax rate?

16.29. Le Grand Bâillement SA is currently valued at €900 million but management wants to completely pay off its perpetual debt of €300 million. Le Grand Bâillement is subject to a 30% marginal tax rate. If Le Grand Bâillement pays off its debt, what will be the total value of its equity?

16.30. If we drop the assumption that there are no information or transaction costs, in addition to dropping the no-tax assumption, then will the Modigliani and Miller model still suggest that the firm should take on greater proportions of debt in its capital structure? Explain.

16.31. Pollyanna plc has an abundant cash flow. It is so high that the managers take Fridays off for a weekly luncheon in Cork using the corporate jet. Describe how altering the capital structure of the firm might make the management of this firm stay in the office on Fridays in order to work on new positive NPV projects.

CFA Problems

16.32. Consider two companies that operate in the same line of business and have the same degree of operating leverage: De Base SA and Grundlegend AG. De Base has no debt in its capital structure but Grundlegend has a capital structure that consists of 50%

debt. Which of the following statements is true?

a. Grundlegend has a degree of total leverage that exceeds that of De Base by 50%.
b. Grundlegend has the same sensitivity of net earnings to changes in earnings before interest and taxes as De Base.
c. Grundlegend has the same sensitivity of earnings before interest and taxes to changes in sales as De Base.
d. Grundlegend has the same sensitivity of net earnings to changes in sales as De Base.

16.33. Which of the following applies? According to the pecking-order theory:

a. new debt is preferable to new equity;
b. new equity is preferable to internally generated funds;
c. new debt is preferable to internally generated funds;
d. new equity is always preferable to other sources of capital.

16.34. Which of the following applies? According to the static trade-off theory:

a. the amount of debt a company has is irrelevant;
b. debt should be used only as a last resort;
c. debt will not be used if a company's tax rate is high;
d. companies have an optimal level of debt.

SAMPLE TEST PROBLEMS

16.1. The Valentino Acting School produces annual cash flows of €5000 and is expected to continue doing so in the infinite future. The cost of equity capital for Valentino's is 16% and the firm is financed completely with equity. The firm would like to repurchase as much equity as possible but will not pay more than €500 in interest expense to service the debt on the borrowing to finance the repurchase. Valentino can borrow at a 10% rate (assume that the debt will also be outstanding into the infinite future). Using Modigliani and Miller's Proposition 1 and all of its assumptions, what will be the value of each of the claims on the firm's assets after the share repurchase?

16.2. Attica und Gara is considering issuing €25 million of debt to repurchase shares of the firm. If Attica und Gara follow through on the capital restructuring, what is the present value of the tax shield on that debt if it has no maturity and Attica und Gara is subject to a 34% marginal tax rate?

16.3. GreenBack Landscapers produces an enormous amount of cash each year. The shareholders of the firm believe that this level of cash flow has left the managers without much motivation for finding new projects. The shareholders have hired a financial consultant to give them estimates concerning the value of the tax shield, agency costs and financial distress costs of the firm, given four alternative capital structure scenarios. Use the following table to make a suggestion for the recommended proportion of debt that GreenBack should utilise for its capital structure.

Benefit or (Cost)	No debt	25% debt	50% debt	75% debt
Tax shield	€ 0	€3	€6	€ 9
Agency cost	−€10	−€1	€0	−€ 5
Financial distress cost	−€ 0	−€2	−€4	−€20

16.4. It may be difficult to provide incentives for managers to work hard when the firm is not experiencing any financial distress. One solution that capital structure theory provides for that problem is to increase the proportion of debt in the capital structure of the firm. If a firm is currently financed with 90% debt, will additional debt help to further reduce the agency costs between shareholders and managers?

16.5. Mayan Imports has recently found a number of new positive NPV projects that it will need to finance. Mayan has €100 million of cash on hand. It also has plenty of financial room to increase its debt as a proportion of its capital structure. If Mayan follows the pecking-order theory, what source would you expect it to use for its projects, which require €60 million in assets?

ENDNOTES

1. Dirk Brounen, Abe de Jong and Kees Koedijk, 2006. 'Capital Structure Policies in Europe: Survey Evidence', *Journal of Banking and Finance* **30**: 1409–1442. The survey covered companies in the UK, Netherlands, Germany, France and the United States for comparison purposes.

2. The Nobel Prize Committee cited the M&M propositions when it awarded Nobel Prizes in Economics to Professor Modigliani in 1985 and to Professor Miller in 1990.

3. Since we are assuming that there are no taxes, the after-tax cost of the interest is €10.

4. In order for this transaction to have precisely the same effect as if Millennium's capital structure had been altered by management, you would also have to use the firm's shares as the only collateral for this borrowing. That way, if you failed to pay the interest, you would forfeit the equity to the lender and have no further obligation. The assumption that you can borrow at the same rate as the firm and use the shares as collateral is implied by the M&M condition that there are no information or transaction costs. If you paid a higher interest rate than the firm, then some of the value you are entitled to receive from the firm would be transferred from you to the lender.

5. In finance, we use the terms *cost* of debt or equity interchangeably with *required return* on debt or equity because, by definition, the *pre-tax* cost of a particular type of capital to a firm equals the rate of return that investors require. Note that since firms can deduct interest payments, the *after-tax* cost of debt to the firm will be lower than the rate of return required by its creditors.

6. M&M assumed that the cost of debt was constant and equal to the risk-free rate when they derived their Proposition 2. Of course, we know that the rate of return required by investors increases with risk and that the riskiness of the interest and principal payments on debt increases with leverage. Therefore, the cost of debt must also increase with leverage. If you look carefully at Equation (16.3), you will notice that $(k_{Assets} - k_{Debt})$ gets smaller as leverage increases because, while k_{Debt} gets larger, k_{Assets} does not change. Although this suggests that k_{os} can get smaller as leverage increases (specifically, the decrease in $k_{Assets} - k_{Debt}$ might more than offset the increase in V_{Debt}/V_{cs}), this never happens in practice. The cost of ordinary shares always increases with leverage.

7. In earlier chapters, we discussed a number of reasons that net income might differ from the cash flows to which shareholders have a claim. For example, accounting accruals may cause net income to differ from cash flows or depreciation charges might not equal actual cash expenditures on capital

equipment or working capital in a particular year. For the time being, we will ignore these potential complications.

8. Recall from Chapter 12 that operating leverage is a measure of the relative amounts of fixed and variable costs in a project's cost structure. It is the major factor that determines the sensitivity of operating profit (EBIT) to changes in revenue. The higher a project's operating leverage, the greater this sensitivity.

9. In Exhibit 16.3, the percentage decrease in net income is 1.75 times as large in the firm with financial leverage as it is in the firm without financial leverage, regardless of whether the firm has low or high operating leverage ($-56.00\%/-32.00\% = 1.75$ and $-140.00\%/-80.00\% = 1.75$). This is because the fixed-interest expense in this example is the same percentage of revenue in both businesses.

10. This effect may be offset somewhat in some countries by the fact that dividends and capital gains may be taxed at a lower rate than interest income. However, this effect is secondary to the corporate income tax effect because it is smaller in magnitude and because many investors, such as pension funds, endowments, charities and foundations, pay no taxes at all.

11. John Graham, 2000. 'How Big are the Tax Benefits of Debt?' *Journal of Finance* 55(5): 1901–1941. His estimate for the USA is 9.7% of firm value, which is lower than the 11.85% given in the table. This is because the value in the table is based on official tax rates (which tend to overstate the actual amount of tax paid by firms) and excludes the modifiers identified by Graham as reducing the tax benefits of debt. What the evidence suggests is that, at moderate levels of leverage, the tax benefit of debt is not huge.

12. You can find a discussion of different countries' bankruptcy processes on WileyPlus if you would like to read about what happens when a firm enters into bankruptcy.

13. The 2008 credit crunch provides a clear example of the problems firms faced when they did not have sufficient funds. The debt market and banks were closed to most companies and this created liquidity problems for a number of them. For example, in October 2008, Swissmed, a hospital group listed on the Warsaw Stock Exchange, was forced to issue a public statement denying it was suffering from liquidity problems.

14. R. Parrino, 'Spin-offs and Wealth Transfers: The Marriott Case', *Journal of Financial Economics* 43 (1997) 241–274.

15. Since internally generated funds are reinvested on behalf of the shareholders, the true cost of these funds equals the cost of equity. However, using internally generated funds enables the firm to avoid the costs associated with borrowing or selling shares, which, in turn, can make internal funds most attractive.

CHAPTER
17

Dividends and Dividend Policy

In this Chapter:

Dividends

Share Repurchases

Dividend Policy and Firm Value

Share Dividends and Share Splits

Setting a Dividend Policy

LEARNING OBJECTIVES

1. Explain what a dividend is and describe the different types of dividends and the dividend payment process.
2. Explain what shares repurchase is and how companies repurchase their shares.
3. Discuss the benefits and costs associated with dividend payments and compare the relative advantages and disadvantages of dividends and share repurchases.
4. Define share dividends and share splits and explain how they differ from other types of dividends and from share repurchases.
5. Describe factors that managers consider when setting the dividend policies for their firms.

On 18 February 2010, Thales SA, the European aerospace, space, defence, security and transportation group, announced a major reduction in the dividend following the announcement of a net loss of €128 million for its 2009 financial year. It had made a profit of €650 million in 2008. Following the announcement, the share price fell over 10%. In the period following, the share price continued to underperform as the following figure indicates.

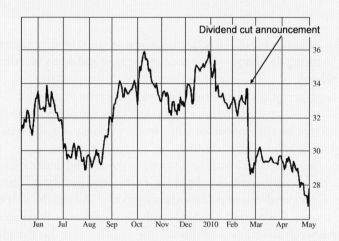

Dividend cut announcement

The operating performance of the group helps to explain the decision to cut the dividend. While revenues had risen by 2% between the two years, the operating cash flow had fallen from €1135 million in 2008 to €485 million in 2009, although the free operating cash flow had risen to €800 million (2008: €377 million) as the company had made significant reductions in its working capital requirement. However, further reductions in working capital were unlikely to be sustainable in future years. Consequently, the underlying trend in cash generation was not particularly favourable and the company faced difficulties in its business areas, with the air transport sector singled out as particularly problematic.

In 2008, the company had paid out a dividend of €1.05 per share, which amounted to €195 million in dividends in 2008. The reduction in the 2009 dividend still meant the group paid out €205 million in dividend payments, which represented a quarter of its free operating cash flow or over half the operating cash flow. Prior to this, the group had been increasing the dividend on a regular basis – the details are given below:

Year	2005	2006	2007	2008	2009
Dividend per share paid to shareholders	€0.83	€0.87	€1.00	€1.05	€0.50
Percentage change	–	+8.8%	+14.9%	+5%	−52%

The reasoning behind the decision to cut the dividend was to preserve cash in the face of continuing severe business conditions and the need to restructure the group. In announcing the decision, Luc

Vigneron, the new group chief executive, said: 'Our environment remains difficult [and] what has affected the group in certain activities is not superficial'. He cited the economic crisis and the sharp downturn in commercial aerospace driving volumes down. As further justification, he cited delays in the commercial launch of several aircraft models, combined with the appreciation of the euro against the US dollar, as well as internal problems with some major programmes leading to cost overruns.

CHAPTER PREVIEW

In Chapter 16, we discussed factors that influence capital structure decisions of firms. In this chapter, we look at some different but related financing decisions – those concerning how and when to return value (cash or other assets) to shareholders.

We begin by describing the various types of dividends and the dividend payment process. We then introduce an alternative to dividends – share repurchases. Although they are not technically dividends, share repurchases are a potential component of any dividend policy because, like dividends, they are a means of distributing value to shareholders.

We next discuss the benefits and costs associated with making dividend payments and describe how share prices react when a company makes an announcement about future dividend payments. These discussions provide insights into the ways in which dividend policies affect firm value. We end this part of the chapter by directly comparing the benefits and costs of dividends with those of share repurchases.

We then describe share splits and scrip dividends and discuss the reasons managers might want to split their company's shares or pay a dividend in shares. Finally, we conclude the chapter with a discussion of factors that managers and their boards of directors consider when they set dividend policies.

DIVIDENDS

Learning Objective 1

Explain what a dividend is and describe the different types of dividends and the dividend payment process.

Decisions concerning whether to distribute value to shareholders, how much to distribute and how best to distribute it are very important financing decisions that have implications for a firm's future investment and capital structure policies. Any time value is distributed to a firm's shareholders, the amount of equity capital invested in the firm is reduced. Unless the firm raises additional equity by selling new shares, distributions to shareholders reduce the availability of capital for new investments and increase the firm's financial leverage.

The term **dividend policy** refers to a firm's overall policy regarding distributions of value to

BUILDING INTUITION

Dividends Reduce the Shareholders' Investment in a Firm

A dividend reduces the shareholders' investment in a firm by returning some of that investment to them. The value that shareholders receive through a dividend was already theirs. A dividend simply takes this value out of the firm and returns it to them.

shareholders. In this section, we discuss the use of dividends to distribute this value. A **dividend** is something of value that is distributed to a firm's shareholders on a pro-rata basis – that is, *in proportion to the percentage of the firm's shares that they own*. A dividend can involve the distribution of cash, assets or something else, such as discounts on the firm's products that are available only to shareholders.

> ### Dividend policy
>
> the overall policy concerning the distribution of value from a firm to its shareholders

> ### Dividend
>
> something of value distributed to a firm's shareholders on a pro-rata basis – that is, in proportion to the percentage of the firm's shares that they own

When a firm distributes value through a dividend, it reduces the value of the shareholders' claims against the firm. To see this, consider a firm that has €1000 in cash plus other assets that have a market value of €9000. If the firm has no debt and there are 10 000 shares outstanding, what is the value of each share? Each share of this firm is worth €1, since the total value of the cash and the other assets is €10 000 and the shareholders own it all.

Now, suppose management distributes the €1000 of cash as a dividend. Each shareholder receives 10 cents (€1 000/10 000 shares = €0.10)

for each share that he or she owns and the value of each share declines to 90 cents. This is true because the firm is now worth €9000 and there are still 10 000 shares. Note that each shareholder still has €1 of value for each share owned but now the share represents only 90 cents of the total. The other 10 cents is in the hands of the shareholder, who can spend or reinvest it.[1]

Types of Dividends

As we mentioned, dividends can take various forms. The most common form is the **regular cash dividend**, which is a cash dividend that is paid on a regular basis. These dividends are generally paid semi-annually and sometimes quarterly and are a common means by which firms return some of their profits to shareholders. The dividend payments made by the vast majority of firms are part of regular cash dividend payment programmes.

> ### Regular cash dividend
>
> a cash dividend that is paid on a regular basis, typically half-yearly or quarterly

In the chapter opener, you saw that, in 2010, Thales more than halved its regular cash dividend from €1.05 per share per year to €0.50 per share per year, having in previous years increased the dividend. The size of a firm's regular cash dividend is typically set at a level that management expects the company to be able to maintain in the long run. This is because, barring some major change in the fortunes of the company, management does not want to have to reduce the dividend. As we discuss later, investors in a company's shares often take a negative view of a reduction in the dividend.

Management can afford to err on the side of setting the regular cash dividend too low because it always has the option of paying an **extra dividend** if earnings are higher than expected. Extra dividends are sometimes paid at the same time as regular cash dividends, and a few companies use them to ensure that a minimum portion of earnings is distributed to shareholders each year. For example, suppose that the management of a company wants to distribute 40% of the company's net income to shareholders each year. If the company earns €2 per share in a particular year and the regular cash dividend is 60 cents per share, management can pay an extra 20 cent dividend at the end of the year to ensure that the company hits its 40% payout target [(€0.60 + €0.20)/€2.00 = 0.40, or 40%].

Extra dividend

a dividend that is generally paid at the same time as a regular cash dividend to distribute additional value

---

Special dividend

a one-time payment to shareholders that is normally used to distribute a large amount of value

---

A **special dividend**, like an extra dividend, is a one-time payment to shareholders. However, special dividends tend to be considerably larger than extra dividends. They are normally used to distribute unusually large amounts of cash. A company might use a special dividend to distribute excess cash from operations. For instance, in October 2000, BASF AG, the German speciality chemicals company, announced it would pay out all its earnings as a special dividend worth 35 cents per share on top of the regular dividend of 65 cents per share. At the

time of the announcement, BASF's share price was €22.10 so the distribution amounted to a return to shareholders of 4.5% (€1/€22.10). The effect of this special dividend was to reduce BASF's retained earnings from €9002 million in 1999 to €8851 million at the end of 2000. A special dividend might also be used to distribute the proceeds from the sale of a major asset or business or as a means of altering a company's capital structure. In 2008, Schiphol Nederland BV – the Amsterdam airport operator – announced a special dividend of €500 million and up to the same amount again in 2009. As a result, the net book value of share capital and reserves fell from €2938 million in 2007 to €2868 million in 2008.

It can also feature in the terms and conditions of a major reorganisation or merger. For instance, when Suez SA merged with Gaz de France SA, the former company paid shareholders a special dividend of 80 cents per share as part of the terms of the acquisition.

A **liquidating dividend** is a dividend that is paid to shareholders when a firm is liquidated. When we say that a firm is liquidated, we mean that its assets are sold, the proceeds from the sale of the assets are distributed to creditors, shareholders and others who have a claim on the firm's assets, and the firm ceases to exist. When a company is wound up, the proceeds from the sale of a company's assets are first used to repay all of the company's obligations to suppliers, lenders, the various taxing authorities and any other party that has a claim on those assets. Only after all these obligations are satisfied can the company pay a liquidating dividend to the shareholders. These priorities highlight the fact that the shareholders are truly the residual claimants to a firm's assets.

Liquidating dividend

the final dividend that is paid to shareholders when a firm is liquidated

---

Distributions of value to shareholders can also take the form of discounts on the company's products, free samples and the like. Often, these non-cash distributions are not thought of as dividends, in part because the value received by shareholders is not in the form of cash and in part because the value received by individual shareholders does not often reflect their proportional ownership in the firm.

For example, BT plc, the British telecommunications company, offers its shareholders a range of discounts including a special credit card and a reduction on installing a broadband connection. The value of these offers is the same whatever the number of shares owned. Obviously, for larger shareholders the value of these offers is small compared to the value of the cash dividend.

The discounts offered to BT shareholders are true distributions of non-cash value. Because the company could charge the full installation price or interest rate on the credit card, there is a very real opportunity cost associated with these non-cash offers.

The Dividend Payment Process

A relatively standard sequence of events takes place before a dividend is paid. This process is more easily defined for companies with publicly traded shares than for private companies. For this reason, we first focus on the process for public companies and then discuss how it differs for private companies. The time line for the sequence of events in the dividend payment process at a public company is illustrated in Exhibit 17.1.

The Board Vote

The process begins with a vote by a company's board of directors to pay a dividend. As shareholder representatives, the board must approve any distribution of value to shareholders.

The Public Announcement

After the board vote, the company announces to the public that it will pay the dividend. The date on which this announcement is made is known as the **declaration date**, or announcement date, of the dividend. The announcement typically includes the amount of value that shareholders will receive for each share that they own, as well as the other dates associated with the dividend payment process.

> **Declaration date**
>
> the date on which a dividend is publicly announced

The price of a firm's shares often changes when a dividend is announced. This happens because the public announcement sends a signal to the market about what management thinks the future performance of the firm will be. If the signal differs from what investors expected, they will adjust the prices at which they are willing to buy or sell the company's shares accordingly. For example, the announcement that a company will pay an unexpectedly large

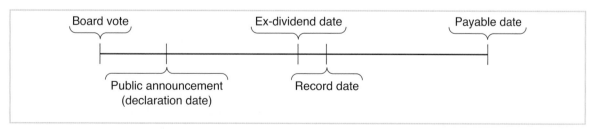

Exhibit 17.1: The Dividend Payment Process Timeline for a Public Company   The dividend process begins when the board votes to pay a dividend. Shortly afterwards, the firm publicly announces its intention to pay a dividend, along with, at a minimum, the amount of the dividend and the holder of record date. The ex-dividend date, which is set by the stock exchange, normally precedes the record date by two days. The payable date is the date on which the firm actually pays the dividend.

BUILDING INTUITION

Dividend Announcements Send Signals to Investors

A dividend announcement reveals information about management's view of a company's prospects. Investors use this information to refine their expectations concerning future cash flows from the company. A change in investor expectations will cause the company's share price to change at the time of the public announcement.

dividend can indicate that management is optimistic about future profits – suggesting that future cash flows are higher than expected. This, in turn, can result in an increase in the company's share price. In contrast, the decision to cut or eliminate a dividend can send a signal that management is pessimistic and can cause the shares price to go down. We have more to say about how share prices react to dividend announcements later in this chapter. For now, it is important to remember that a dividend decision sends information to investors and that information is incorporated into share prices at the time of the public announcement.

The Ex-Dividend Date

An important date included in the public announcement is the **ex-dividend date** – the first date on which the shares will trade without rights to the dividend. An investor who buys shares before the ex-dividend date will receive the dividend, while an investor who buys the shares on or after the ex-dividend date will not. Before the ex-dividend date, a share is said to be trading *cum dividend*, or with dividend. On or after the ex-dividend date, the share is said to trade *ex dividend*.

> ### Ex-dividend date
> the first day on which a share trades without the rights to a dividend

It is important for investors to know the ex-dividend date because it can have significant implications for the taxes and transaction costs they pay. If an investor purchases the company's shares before the ex-dividend date, the investor knows that he or she will soon receive a dividend on which taxes may have to be paid. (Dividends received by investors may already have been subject to withholding tax but may be subject to further tax, depending on the tax status of the recipient.) In addition, a dividend can create difficulties for a shareholder who wants to have a specific amount of money invested in the firm. By returning value to the shareholder, a firm that pays a dividend may reduce the shareholder's investment below the level preferred by the shareholder, thereby making it necessary for the shareholder to purchase additional shares and incur the associated brokerage fees and possibly other transaction costs.

As you might suspect, the price of the firm's shares changes on the ex-dividend date even if there is no new information about the firm. This drop simply reflects the difference in the value of the cash flows that the shareholders are entitled to receive before and after the ex-dividend date. To see how this works, consider a company that recently announced a €1 per share dividend. The company's shares are currently trading for €10 per share and the ex-dividend date is tomorrow. In this example, the €10 price includes the value of the dividend because an investor who purchases this company's shares before the ex-dividend day will receive the dividend. You can think of the €10 as consisting of a €1 dividend plus the value of the shares on the ex-dividend date. Since an investor who buys the shares tomorrow will receive only the shares and not the dividend, the price of the shares will certainly be below €10 tomorrow.

Does it follow that the shares price will drop by €1 tomorrow? No. Research has shown that shares prices drop on the ex-dividend date but that this drop is smaller than the full amount of the dividend. In our example, this means that the drop will be less than €1. Why would the price not drop by the full €1? Because the dividend will be taxed. If you knew that you would have to pay a 40% tax on a dividend that you received, would you pay 100% of the value of that dividend? We hope not. By this point in the book, you should realise that a €1 dividend has an after-tax value of only €0.60 if you have to pay a 40% tax on it [€1.00 × (1 − 0.40) = €0.60]. If investors pay a 40% tax on dividends, the €10 price of the shares in our example should include €0.60 for the dividend and €9.60 (€10.00 − €0.40) for other cash flows, so the shares price should drop to €9.60 on the ex-dividend date.

Learning by Doing Application 17.1

Shares Prices and Dividend Payments

Problem: It is 9 December 2010 and Jarlberg AG shares are trading at €23.50. Jarlberg just announced that the ex-dividend date for its next regular cash dividend would be 15 January 2011 and that the dividend payment would be €0.40 per share. If all investors pay taxes of 30% on dividends, what would you expect to happen to Jarlberg's share price between the time the market closes on 12 January 2011 and the time it opens on 13 January 2011?

Approach: The share price should decline by an amount that equals the after-tax value of the dividend; you can therefore answer this question by calculating this after-tax value.

Solution: You would expect the price of Jarlberg shares to decrease by €0.40 × (1 − 0.30) = €0.28. You cannot say what the actual shares price will be after this decrease because you do not know what the price will be beforehand. The €23.50 price is for 9 December 2010, not for 12 January 2011, the day immediately before the ex-dividend date.

The Record Date

The **record date** typically follows the ex-dividend date by two business days. The record date is the date on which an investor must be a *shareholder of record* (that is, officially listed as a shareholder or *holder-of-record*) in order to receive the dividend. The board specifies the record date when it votes to make the dividend payment. Once the company informs the exchange on which its shares is traded what the record date is, the exchange sets the ex-dividend date. The ex-dividend date precedes the record date because it takes time to update the shareholder list when someone purchases shares. If you buy the shares before the ex-dividend date, the exchange will ensure that you are listed as a shareholder of record for that company as of the record date.

> **Record date**
>
> the date by which an investor must be a shareholder of record in order to receive a dividend

> **Payable date**
>
> the date on which a company pays a dividend

The Payable Date

The final date in the dividend payment process is the **payable date,** when the shareholders of record actually receive the dividend. The payable date is typically a couple of weeks after the record date.

An Example of the Dividend Payment Process

We can use Royal Dutch Shell, the Anglo-Dutch oil company, to illustrate the dividend payment process. The company announces in advance the timing of its dividends. Following the release of its annual report for 2009 on 29 January 2010, the company's quarterly cash dividend of €0.42 per share (€0.3125) was announced on 4 February 2010.[2]

Shell also specified the other key dates. The cash dividend would be paid to investors of record as of 12 February 2010. This was the record date. The ex-dividend date was 10 February 2010 – two days earlier – and the payable date was 17 March 2010. Exhibit 17.2 summarises the sequence of events for Shell's dividend.

The Dividend Payment Process in Private Companies

The dividend payment process is not as well defined for private companies as it is for public companies, because in private companies shares are bought and sold less frequently, there are fewer shareholders and no stock exchange is involved in the dividend payment process. The

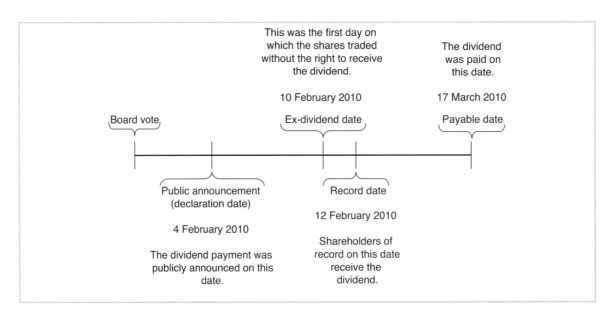

Exhibit 17.2: Key Dates for Royal Dutch Shell's 2009 Fourth-Quarter Dividend This exhibit summarises the key dates and time line for the regular cash dividend that Royal Dutch Shell paid on 17 March 2010.

board members know the identities of the shareholders when they vote to authorise a dividend – generally, the list of shareholders is relatively short and the largest shareholders are on the board. As a result, it is easy to inform all shareholders of the decision to pay a dividend and it is easy to actually pay it. There is no public announcement and there is no need for an ex-dividend date. Consequently, the record date and payable date can be any day on or after the day that the board approves the dividend.

Before You Go On

1. How does a dividend affect the size of a shareholder's investment in a firm?
2. List and define four types of dividends.
3. What are the key events and dates in the dividend payment process?

SHARE REPURCHASES

Learning Objective 2
Explain what shares repurchase is and how companies repurchase their shares.

Share repurchases are another popular method of distributing value to shareholders. With a **share repurchase**, or *share buyback* (and known as a stock repurchase in the United States), a company buys some of its shares from shareholders.

Share repurchase

the purchase of shares by a company from its shareholders; an alternative way for the company to distribute value to shareholders

---

How Share Buybacks Differ from Dividends

Share repurchases differ from dividends in a number of important ways. First, they do not represent a pro-rata distribution of value to the shareholders because not all shareholders participate. Individual shareholders decide whether they want to participate in a share repurchase. Some shareholders participate, while others do not. In contrast, in a dividend distribution, all shareholders receive the dividend whether or not they want it.

Second, when a company repurchases its own shares, it removes them from circulation. This reduces the number of shares held by investors. Removing a large number of shares from circulation can change the ownership of the firm. It can increase or decrease the fraction of shares owned by the major shareholders and thereby diminish their ability to control the company. Also, if a company with a relatively small number of shares in the public market distributes a lot of cash to investors through a share repurchase, there will be less liquidity for the remaining shares. An extreme example of this occurs when a public company repurchases most of its outstanding shares and 'goes private'. Since a dividend does not affect who owns the shares or the number of shares outstanding, it does not have these effects on ownership and liquidity.

Third, share repurchases are taxed differently from dividends. As we saw in the discussion of the ex-dividend date, the total value of dividends is normally taxed.[3] In contrast, when a shareholder sells shares back to the company, the shareholder is taxed only on the profit from the sale. For example, suppose a shareholder purchased 100 shares for €150 and then sold them to the company for €200 a year later. In this example, the €50 profit (€200 – €150) that the shareholder earned on the sale would be treated as a capital gain and would be taxed at the capital gains rate, which is often lower than the personal income tax rate. The following table compares the personal income tax rate (based on the highest level of income tax that an individual can pay) and the capital gains tax rate for a selection of countries in Europe in 2009:

Country	Personal Income Tax Rate	Capital Gains Tax Rate
France	40%	18%
Germany	45%	25%
Italy	43%	43%
Netherlands	52%	30%
Spain	43%	18%
United Kingdom	40%	18%

There are clear differences between income and capital gains rates. Only in Italy would income in the form of dividends and capital gains be taxed equally. In the other countries, the headline rates indicate that, on the whole, capital gains are taxed at rates that are somewhat below the highest rates on income.

Using Germany as an example, the maximum total tax on the sale of the shares would be €12.50 (€50 × 0.25). In contrast, if the company had distributed the €200 as a dividend, the tax would

have been €90 (€200 × 0.45) – over seven times as much! Of course, this difference is even more significant when you remember that shareholders who receive dividends have no choice as to when they must pay the tax because a dividend is not optional. In contrast, since shareholders choose whether to participate in a repurchase plan, they are able to choose when they pay taxes on the profits from selling their shares.

Finally, dividends and share repurchases are accounted for differently on the balance sheet. For example, when a company pays a cash dividend, the cash account on the assets side of the balance sheet and the retained earnings account on the liabilities and shareholders' equity side of the balance sheet are reduced. In contrast, when a company uses cash to repurchase shares, the cash account on the assets side of the balance sheet is reduced, while the treasury shares account on the liabilities and shareholders' equity side of the balance sheet is increased (becomes more negative).

Learning by Doing Application 17.2

Share Repurchases and Taxes

Problem: Your pizza restaurant business has been doing very well and, as a result, you have more cash than you can productively reinvest in the business. You have decided to distribute this cash to yourself, the only shareholder, through a share repurchase. When you started the business, you invested €300 000 and received 10 000 shares. In other words, each share cost you €30. There are no other shares outstanding and your business valuation adviser tells you that the shares are worth €800 000 today. If you want to distribute €80 000 through a share repurchase, how many shares will the company have to repurchase? If you pay taxes

of 15% on capital gains, how much money will you have left over after paying taxes on the proceeds from the sale of your shares?

Approach: First, calculate the current share price. Next, divide the amount of cash that you want to distribute by the share price to obtain the number of shares the company will have to repurchase. To calculate the amount of money you would have left over after paying taxes, first compute the capital gain (profit) per share on the shares and multiply this amount by the tax rate and the number of shares the company will have to purchase to obtain the total tax. Then, subtract the total tax from €80 000 to obtain the answer.

Solution: Each share is worth €80 (€800 000/ 10 000) today. This means that the company would have to repurchase 1000 shares (€80 000/€80) in order to distribute €80 000. The capital gain per share from the sale would be €50 (€80 – €30). With a 15% tax rate, you would pay taxes of €7500 (€50 × 0.15 × 1000 shares) on the capital gain, leaving you with gross proceeds from the sale of €72 500 (€80 000 – €7500).

How Shares are Repurchased

Companies repurchase shares in three general ways. First, they can simply purchase shares in the market, much as an individual would. These kinds of purchases are known as **open-market repurchases** and are a very convenient way of repurchasing shares on an ongoing basis. For example, a company might use such repurchases to distribute some of its profits instead of paying a regular cash dividend.

> ### Open-market repurchase
>
> the repurchase of shares by a company in the open market

When a company has a large amount of cash to distribute, open-market repurchases can be cumbersome because there may be limits on the number of shares that a company can repurchase over a given period. These limits, which are intended to restrict the ability of firms to influence their share price through trading activity, mean that it could take months for a company to distribute a large amount of cash using open-market repurchases.

When the management of a company wants to distribute a large amount of cash at one time and does not want to use a special dividend, it can repurchase shares using a **tender offer**. A tender offer is an open offer by a company to purchase shares.[4] There are two types of tender offers: *fixed price* and *Dutch auction*. With a fixed-price tender offer, management announces the price that will be paid for the shares and the maximum number of shares that will be repurchased. Interested shareholders then tender their shares by letting management know how many shares they are willing to sell. If the number of shares tendered exceeds the announced maximum, then the maximum number

of shares is repurchased and each shareholder who tendered shares participates in the repurchase in proportion to the fraction of the total shares that he or she tendered.

> ### Tender offer
>
> an open offer by a company to purchase shares

With a Dutch auction tender offer, the firm announces the number of shares that it would like to repurchase and asks the shareholders how many shares they would sell at a series of prices, ranging from just above the price at which the shares are currently trading to some higher price. The alternative prices are set higher than the market price to make the offer attractive to shareholders. Shareholders then tell the company how many of their shares they would sell at the various offered prices. Once these offers to sell have been collected, management determines the price that would allow them to repurchase the number of shares that they want. All of the tendering shareholders who indicate a willingness to sell at or below this price will then receive this price for their shares.

The third general way in which shares are repurchased is through direct negotiation with a specific shareholder. These **targeted share repurchases** are typically used to buy blocks of shares from large shareholders.[5] Such repurchases can benefit shareholders who are not selling because managers may be able to negotiate a per-share price that is below the current market price. This is possible because the shareholder who owns a large block of shares might have to offer the shares for a below-market price in order to sell them all in the open market. Therefore, managers can often negotiate a discounted price that is higher than the price that would have to be offered in the open market. Of course, targeted share repurchases can also be attractive to managers for other reasons – notably, if the company repurchases the block of shares, there is less chance that the shares will fall into the hands of an unfriendly investor.

> ## Targeted shares repurchase
>
> a shares repurchase that targets a specific shareholder

Before You Go On

1. What is a share repurchase?
2. How do share repurchases differ from dividends?
3. In what ways can a company repurchase its shares?

DIVIDEND POLICY AND FIRM VALUE

Learning Objective 3

Discuss the benefits and costs associated with dividend payments and compare the relative advantages and disadvantages of dividends and share repurchases.

One reason that we devote an entire chapter in this book to dividend policy is that it can affect the value of a firm. In this section, we explain why. The best way to begin is by recalling, from Chapter 16, the general conditions under which capital structure policy does *not* affect firm value:

1. There are no taxes.
2. There are no information or transaction costs.
3. The real investment policy of the firm is fixed.

These are the three conditions identified by Modigliani and Miller (M&M). Since a dividend payment has implications for a firm's capital structure, the factors that cause dividend policies to affect firm values are very closely related to the conditions identified by M&M. In fact, if the above conditions hold, then a firm's dividend policy will not affect its value.

Dividend policy does not matter under these conditions because a shareholder can 'manufacture' any dividends he or she wants at no cost and the total cash flows a firm produces from its real assets are not affected by its dividend policy. To see how a shareholder can manufacture dividends, consider a retired shareholder who owns 50 000 shares of a company and needs to receive a €1 per-share dividend each year on this investment to cover his or her living expenses. If the company pays such a dividend, there is no problem. But what if the company does not pay such a dividend? Well, under the above conditions, the shareholder could 'manufacture' his or her own dividend by selling €50 000 worth of shares each year. This would reduce the total value of this investor's shares by €50 000, just as a €50 000 dividend would. Remember that we are assuming that no taxes must be paid, so the decline in the value of the shares would exactly equal the value of the dividend if one were paid.

A shareholder could also undo a company's dividend policy by simply reinvesting the dividends that the company pays in new shares. For instance, if a company paid a €50 000 dividend, thereby reducing the value of a shareholder's shares, that shareholder could increase his or her ownership in the company's shares to its previous level by purchasing €50 000 worth of shares.

Just as with changes in capital structure policy, if investors could replicate a company's dividend policy on their own at no cost and the dividend policy does not affect the total cash flows the firm produces, investors would not care whether or not the company paid a dividend. In other words, they would not be willing to pay more or less for the shares of a firm that pays a dividend than for the shares of a firm that does not pay a dividend.

Benefits and Costs of Dividends

Of course, we know that the M&M assumptions do not apply in the real world. But that is good news in the sense that the imperfect world we live in provides companies with the opportunity to create value through their dividend policies. Doing so involves balancing benefits and costs, just as we do in choosing a capital structure. We now turn our attention to a discussion of the benefits and costs associated with paying dividends.

Benefits of Dividends

One benefit of paying dividends is that it attracts investors who prefer to invest in shares that pay dividends. For example, consider the retired shareholder we discussed earlier. While he or she could simply sell some shares each month to cover expenses, in the real world it may be less costly – and it is certainly less trouble – to simply receive regular cash dividend payments instead. Recall that under the M&M conditions, there are no transaction costs. In the real world, though, the retiree will have to pay brokerage commissions each time he or she sells shares. The dividend, in contrast, simply arrives each quarter. Of course, the retiree will have to consider the impact of taxes on the value of dividends versus the value of proceeds from the sale of shares; but it is quite possible that receiving dividends might, on balance, be more appealing.

Another type of investor that might prefer income-paying shares is an institutional investor, such as an endowment or a foundation. Because of their investment guidelines, some institutional investors are only allowed to spend proceeds that are received as income from their investments. These institutions face limitations on their ability to sell shares to replicate a dividend.

Unfortunately, the ability to appeal to certain investors is not a very compelling reason for paying dividends. While retirees and some institutional investors might prefer dividends, investors with no current need for income from their investment portfolios might prefer not to receive dividends. Those investors might actually choose to avoid shares that pay high dividends since they might have to pay taxes on the dividends and would face transaction costs when they reinvest the dividends they receive.

Furthermore, the fact that some investors prefer to receive dividends does not necessarily mean that an individual company can increase the value of its shares by paying dividends. After all, a wide range of dividend-paying shares are already available on the market. The addition of one more such share is unlikely to markedly increase the options available for investors looking for dividends. Therefore, these investors will not be willing to pay a higher price for these shares.

Some people have argued that a large regular dividend indicates that a company is financially strong. This 'signal' of strength, they say, can result in a higher share price. This argument is based on the assumption that a company that is able to pay a large dividend, rather than holding on to cash for future investments, is a company that is doing so well that it has more money than it needs to fund its available investments. The problem with this line of reasoning is that such a company might have more than enough money for all its future investment opportunities because it does not have many future investment opportunities. In this situation, the fact that the company does not need the cash would be a bad signal, not a good one.

Another benefit of paying dividends is suggested by the fact that many companies pay regular cash dividends on the one hand while routinely selling new shares on the other. One possible explanation is that management is just trying to appeal to investors who prefer dividends, as we discussed earlier. But another explanation is that this practice helps to align the incentives of managers and shareholders.

We will look more closely at this second explanation. Consider a company that is so profitable that it never has to go to the debt or equity markets to raise external capital. This company can pay for all of its needs with earnings from operations. The managers in charge of the company might have incentives to operate the business less efficiently than the shareholders would like them to. For example, they might invest in negative NPV assets – such as corporate jets, plush offices or a company chalet in Davos, Switzerland – that benefit them but do not create value for shareholders. These managers might also spend more time than they should away from the office, perhaps serving on the boards of other companies or golfing, letting the operating performance of the company fall below the level that could be achieved if they focused on running the business. Shareholders understand that managers at highly profitable firms have these incentives. Thus, they are likely to reduce the price that they are willing to pay for this company's shares to reflect the loss of value associated with the managers' unproductive behaviours.

Now suppose that the company's board of directors votes to pay dividends that amount to more than the excess cash that the company is producing from its operations. Since the money to pay the dividends will have to come from somewhere, the board is effectively forcing management to sell equity periodically in the public markets. The need to raise equity in the capital markets will help align the incentives of managers with those of shareholders. Why? Because it increases the cost to managers of operating the business inefficiently. In order to raise equity at a reasonable cost, the managers must be careful how efficiently they are operating the business. The process of raising new equity involves a special audit that is more detailed than an annual audit and invites the close attention of lawyers, investment bankers and outside experts. These outside parties provide a certification function that increases the amount of public information about the firm's activities. Voluntarily submitting to such outside certification – by paying a dividend and issuing equity rather than just keeping cash inside the firm – can ultimately lead to better company performance and the willingness of investors to pay a higher price for the company's shares.

One last potential benefit of paying dividends is that dividends can be useful in managing the capital structure of a company. The trade-off theory of capital structure, which we discussed in Chapter 16, tells us that there is an optimal mix of debt and equity that maximises the value of a firm. To the extent that a company is internally generating more equity than it can profitably invest, the fraction of debt in its capital structure will always be decreasing over time unless the company borrows more money (which it does not need) or distributes cash to shareholders. Paying dividends can help keep the firm's capital structure near its optimal mix.

Costs of Dividends

In addition to benefits, there are costs associated with dividends. Taxes are among the most important of these costs. As we discussed earlier, dividends are taxable and the shareholders of firms that pay dividends have no choice but to receive the dividends and pay the associated taxes if they want to own the shares. In most countries, dividends are taxed as part of income.[6] Shareholders can always sell some of their shares to 'manufacture' their own dividends, as we discussed earlier. If they do this, they pay taxes only on the profit of the sale. Unless the shareholder received the shares for free, this profit is a smaller amount than the amount the dividend would be. Furthermore, most countries' tax systems typically treat capital gains differently from dividends. In Germany, for instance, income tax can be as high as 47.5%, whereas it is only 25% on capital gains. This means German investors who pay income tax would prefer to take part in share buybacks rather than receive dividends.

In addition to paying taxes on dividends, owners of shares that pay dividends often have to pay brokerage fees if they want to reinvest the proceeds. To eliminate this cost, some companies offer **dividend reinvestment programmes (DRIPs)**. Through a DRIP, a company sells new shares, commission free, to dividend recipients who elect to automatically reinvest their dividends in the company's shares. While DRIPs eliminate transaction costs, they do not affect the taxes that must be paid on the dividends. Also, since it is costly to administer a DRIP, these programmes effectively transfer the cost from the shareholder who wants to reinvest to the firm (which means all shareholders).

> **Dividend reinvestment programme (DRIP)**
>
> a programme in which a company sells new shares, commission free, to dividend recipients who elect to automatically reinvest their dividends in the company's shares

It is worth remembering that the total value of the assets in a company goes down when a dividend is paid. To the extent that a company uses a lot of debt financing, paying dividends can increase the cost of debt. This will happen if the payment of dividends reduces the value of the assets underlying debt holder claims on the cash flows from the firm. With less valuable assets, the debt holders face greater risk of default. To compensate for this greater risk, they will charge the company a higher rate on its debt.

Share Price Reactions to Dividend Announcements

In the earlier discussion of the dividend payment process, we stated that the price of a company's shares often changes when a dividend is announced. We also noted that this happens because the public announcement sends a signal to the market about what management thinks the future performance of the firm will be. Let us consider this issue in more detail.

We can think about the market's reaction to a dividend announcement in the context of what we call the *cash flow identity*, a term which means that, during any period, the *sources* of cash must equal the *uses* of cash in a firm:

Sources	=	**Uses**

$$CF\ Opns_t + Equity_t + Debt_t = Div_t + Interest_t + Principal_t + Inv_t$$

where:

$CF\ Opns_t$ = net cash flow from operations in period t

$Equity_t$ = proceeds from the sale of shares in period t

$Debt_t$ = proceeds from the sale of debt in period t

Div_t = dividends paid in period t

$Interest_t$ = interest payments in period t

$Principal_t$ = principal payments in period t

Inv_t = investments in period t

How can this identity help us to understand how investors use dividend announcements to infer what management thinks the firm's future performance will be? Let us consider an example. Assume that a company has just announced an increase in its dividend payments that investors did not expect. If the company is not selling new equity or debt and its investments in real assets and working capital are not changing, this means that Div_t is going up and that $Equity_t$, $Debt_t$, $Interest_t$, $Principal_t$ and Inv_t are not changing. Since investors know that the cash flow identity must hold, it must be true that CF $Opns_t$, the cash flow from operations, is expected to increase. This situation can be illustrated as follows:

$$CF\ Opns_t + Equity_t + Debt_t = Div_t + Interest_t + Principal_t + Inv_t$$
$$\Uparrow \qquad \Rightarrow \qquad \Rightarrow \qquad \Uparrow \qquad \Rightarrow \qquad \Rightarrow \qquad \Rightarrow$$

An expected increase in the cash flow from operations is a good signal and investors will interpret it as suggesting that cash flows to shareholders will increase in the future. As a result, the share price should go up.

Evidence from studies of share price reactions to dividend announcements is generally consistent with this theory. This evidence indicates that when a company announces that it will begin paying a regular cash dividend, its share price increases by an average of about 3.5%. Similarly, announcements of increases in regular cash dividends are associated with an average share price increase of 1–2%. In contrast, the announcement that a company will reduce its regular cash dividend is associated with a 3.5% decrease in its share price, on average. An announcement that a company will pay a special dividend is associated with an average share price increase of about 2%.

It is important to recognise that we cannot interpret these studies as proof that changes in dividend policies *cause* changes in share prices. Rather, the cash flow identity suggests that managers change dividend policies when something fundamental has changed in the business. It is this fundamental change that causes the share price to change. The dividend announcement is really just the means by which investors find out about the fundamental change. Although there are benefits and costs associated with dividend payments, the sizes of these benefits and costs tend to be relatively small compared with the changes in value associated with the fundamental changes that take place in firms. By the same token, there is no evidence that it is possible to increase firm value by increasing dividends. Again, dividend changes only provide a signal concerning a fundamental change at the firm. In this sense, they are only by-products of the change.

Dividends versus Share Repurchases

As we noted earlier, share repurchases are an alternative to dividends as a way of distributing value. Our discussion has already suggested that share repurchases have some distinct advantages over dividends. They give shareholders the ability to choose when they receive the distribution, which affects the timing of the taxes they must pay as well as the cost of reinvesting funds that are not immediately needed. In addition, shareholders who sell shares back to a company pay taxes only on the gains they realise and historically these capital gains have been taxed at a lower rate than dividends.

From management's perspective, share repurchases provide greater flexibility in distributing value. We have already discussed how share prices react to announcements of changes in dividend payments. We can therefore imagine why managers might find share repurchases relatively more attractive. Even when a company publicly announces an ongoing open-market share repurchase programme, as opposed to a regular cash dividend, investors know that management at any time can always quietly cut back or end the repurchases. In contrast, dividend programmes represent a stronger commitment to distribute value in the future because they cannot

be quietly ended. For this reason, investors know that managers will initiate dividend programmes only when they are quite confident that they will be able to continue them for the long run.

Thus, if future cash flows are not certain, managers are likely to prefer to distribute extra cash today by repurchasing shares through open-market purchases because this enables them to preserve some flexibility. If cash flows decline in the future, management can quietly cut back on the repurchases without a pronounced effect on the company's share price.

Potentially offsetting the advantages of share repurchases are a few notable disadvantages. One of these disadvantages is the flip side of the signalling benefit discussed in the previous paragraph. Since most ongoing share repurchase programmes are not as visible as dividend programmes, they cannot be used as effectively to send a positive signal about the company's prospects to investors.

A more subtle issue concerns the fact that managers can choose when to repurchase shares in a share repurchase programme. Just like other investors, managers prefer purchasing shares when they believe that the shares are undervalued in the market. The problem is that since managers have better information about the company's prospects than do other investors, they can take advantage of this information to the detriment of other investors. If managers are taking advantage of superior information, their repurchases are effectively transferring value from shareholders who choose to sell their shares (perhaps because they simply need money to live on) to shareholders who choose to remain invested in the company. A transfer of wealth from one group of shareholders to another is a problem. Remember that management is supposed to act in the best interests of *all* its shareholders.

Companies have historically distributed more value through dividend payments than through share repurchases. This suggests that managers have, on balance, found dividends more attractive. However, in recent years the popularity of share repurchases has increased as companies have been allowed to undertake such programmes. Many countries, such as the United Kingdom, used to prohibit share buybacks but the rules were changed in 1993 and companies can now repurchase their own shares.

SHARE DIVIDENDS AND SHARE SPLITS

Learning Objective 4

Define share dividends and share splits and explain how they differ from other types of dividends and from share repurchases.

Recall that earlier we defined a dividend as something of value distributed to a firm's shareholders on a pro-rata basis. The term *dividend* is not always used so precisely. In this section, we discuss actions taken by financial managers that are associated with dividends but do not involve a distribution of value and are therefore not really dividends.

Share Dividends

One type of 'dividend' that does not involve the distribution of value is known as a **share dividend**. When a company pays a share dividend, it distributes new shares on a pro-rata basis to existing shareholders. For example, if a company pays a 10% share dividend, it gives each shareholder a number of new shares equal to 10% of the number of shares the shareholder already owns.[7] If an investor owns 100 shares, that investor receives 10 additional shares. An investor who owns 500 shares receives 50 additional shares, and so on. Although share dividends are not as common as regular cash dividends, a number of companies pay regularly scheduled share dividends.

Share dividend

a distribution of new shares to existing shareholders in proportion to the percentage of shares that they own (pro rata); the value of the assets in a company does not change with a share dividend

To understand why no value is distributed when a share dividend is paid, consider again a company that pays a 10% share dividend. Assume that the company has total assets with a market value of €11 000, that it has 10 000 shares outstanding and that it has no debt. Since there is no debt, the shareholders own all of the assets in the firm and each share is worth €1.10 (€11 000/10 000).

When the 10% share dividend is paid, the number of shares outstanding increases by 10% – from 10 000 to 11 000. Notice that this is really just an accounting change, since no assets are going out of the company. As a result, the value of the total assets in the company does not change and the value of each share decreases from €1.10 to €1.00 (€11 000/11 000). All that happens when the share dividend is paid is that the number of shares each shareholder owns increases and their value goes down proportionately. The shareholder is left with exactly the same value as before. In our example, a shareholder who owned 100 shares worth €110 (€1.10 × 100 shares) before the share dividend will own 110 shares worth €110 (€1.00 × 110 shares) afterwards.

Share Splits

A **share split** is quite similar to a share dividend but it involves the distribution of a larger multiple of the outstanding shares.[8] As the name suggests, we can think of a share split as an actual division of each share into more than one share. For example, in a share split, shareholders frequently receive one additional share for each share they already own. This is known as a two-for-one share split. Share splits can also involve even larger ratios. For example, there might be a three-for-one share split in which each shareholder receives two additional shares for each share he or she owns. Besides their size, a key distinction between share dividends and share splits is that share dividends are typically regularly scheduled events, like regular cash dividends, whereas share splits tend to occur infrequently during the life of a company.

> ## Share split
>
> a pro-rata distribution of new shares to existing shareholders that is not associated with any change in the assets held by the firm; share splits involve larger increases in the number of shares than share dividends

An example of a share split is the two-for-one share split that BASF SE, the German chemical company, announced on 23 April 2008. In this share split, each BASF shareholder received one additional share for each share that he or she owned on 29 May 2008.

As with a share dividend, nothing substantial changes when a share split takes place. A shareholder might own twice as many shares after the split but because the split does not change the nature of the company's assets, those shares represent the same proportional ownership in the company as the original shares. In the BASF example, the prices per share at the close of trading on 30 and 29 May were €43.29 and €85.58, respectively. This 50.5% [(€43.29 − €85.58)/€85.58] price decline was almost equal to the 50% decline that you would expect from a two-for-one share split.[9] The number of shares doubled, while the value of the expected cash flows against which shareholders had claims remained largely unchanged.

Reasons for Share Dividends and Splits

At this point, you might be asking why companies pay share dividends or split their shares. The most often-cited reason is known as the *trading range* argument. This argument proposes that successful companies use share dividends or share splits to make their shares more attractive to investors. Why would share dividends or splits have this effect? Suppose the price of the shares of a successful company was allowed to continue to increase over a long period of time. Eventually, few investors would be able to afford to purchase a *round lot* of 100 shares. This, in turn, could affect the company's share price.

To understand this argument, you must know that it has historically been more expensive for investors to purchase *odd lots* of less than 100 shares than round lots of 100 shares. Odd lots are less liquid than round lots because more investors want to buy round lots. Furthermore, it is relatively expensive for companies to service odd-lot owners (consider, for example, the cost per share of sending shareholders annual reports and prospectuses or writing and paying dividends). Because of these disadvantages, investors tend to be less than enthusiastic about purchasing odd lots of less than 100 shares and managers prefer that they do not. According to the trading range argument, when buying a round lot becomes too expensive, investors might avoid buying the shares at all. Share dividends and splits offer ways to bring the price of the shares down to the appropriate 'trading range'.

Although the trading range argument may be appealing to some, researchers have found little support for it. After a share split, the shares' trading volume does not appear to be higher than it was before the split. Also, the transaction costs argument no longer carries much weight, as there is now little difference in the costs of purchasing round lots and odd lots.

In fact, some companies trade at per-share prices that are far above what is typically thought of as a *normal* trading range. For instance in mid-2010, Rio Tinto plc, the Anglo-Australian global mining company, had a share price of around £30 (€34.5). Most companies listed on the London Stock Exchange have a share price about a tenth of this – where a price range of £2–£5 (€2.3–€5.75) would be considered normal.

One real benefit of share splits is that they can send a positive signal to investors about management's outlook for the future. This, in turn, can lead to a higher share price. After all, management is unlikely to want to split the shares of a company two-for-one or three-for-one if it expects the share price to decline. It is only likely to split the shares when it is confident that the shares' current market price is not too high. A number of research studies have reported evidence indicating that investors tend to interpret share splits as good news.[10]

Companies occasionally do *reverse* share splits, in which the number of shares owned by each shareholder is reduced. For example, in a 1-for-10 reverse split, a shareholder receives one share in exchange for each ten shares he or she owned before. If you owned 1000 shares of such a company, you would have only 100 (1000/10) shares after the reverse share split.

Before You Go On

1. What is a share dividend?
2. How does a share dividend differ from a share split?
3. How does a share dividend differ from other types of dividends?

SETTING A DIVIDEND POLICY

Learning Objective 5

Describe factors that managers consider when setting the dividend policies for their firms.

An important question that you may be asking yourself is exactly how managers set the dividend policies for their firms. In this section, we discuss the results from two important surveys. These surveys deal with how managers select their dividend policies and what practical considerations managers must balance when they choose a dividend policy.

What Managers Tell Us

The best known survey of dividend policy was published in 1956, more than 50 years ago, by John Lintner. The survey asked managers at 28 industrial firms how they set their firms' dividend policies.[11] The key conclusions from the Lintner study are as follows:

1. Firms tend to have long-term target payout ratios.
2. Dividend changes follow shifts in long-term sustainable earnings.
3. Managers focus more on dividend changes than on the level (monetary amount) of the dividend.
4. Managers are reluctant to make dividend changes that might have to be reversed.

These results are consistent with the idea that managers tend to use dividends to distribute excess earnings and that they are concerned about unnecessarily surprising investors with bad news.

A more recent study, published in 2005, updates Lintner's findings.[12] The authors conducted a survey of 384 financial executives and personally interviewed 23 other managers. They found that managers continue to be concerned about surprising investors with bad news. Indeed, maintaining level dividend payments is as important to executives as the investment decisions they make. The authors also found, as Lintner did, that the expected stability of future earnings affects dividend decisions. However, the link between earnings and dividends is weaker today than when Lintner conducted his survey.

In response to the increased use of share repurchases, the authors of the 2005 study asked managers about their views on repurchases. They found that rather than setting a target level for repurchases, managers tend to repurchase shares using cash that is left over after investment spending. In addition, many managers prefer repurchases because repurchase programmes are more flexible than dividend programmes and because they can be used to time the market by repurchasing shares when management considers a company's share price to be too low. Finally, the managers who were interviewed appeared to believe that institutional investors do not prefer dividends over repurchases or vice versa. In other words, the choice between these two methods of distributing value has little effect on who owns the company's shares.

Practical Considerations in Setting a Dividend Policy

In this chapter, we have discussed a wide range of factors that enter into managers' decisions regarding the selection of their firms' dividend policies. While the details are important, it is easy to get caught up in them and to lose sight of the big picture. A company's dividend policy is largely a policy about how the excess value in a company is distributed to its shareholders. Central to setting this policy is the question of how much value should be distributed. It is extremely important that managers choose their firms' dividend policies in a way that enables them to continue to make the investments necessary for the firm to compete in its product markets. With this in mind, managers should consider several practical questions when selecting a dividend policy, including the following:

1. Over the long term, how much does the company's level of earnings (cash flow from operations) exceed its investment requirements? How certain is this level?
2. Does the firm have enough financial reserves to maintain dividend payouts in periods when earnings are down or investment requirements are up?
3. Does the firm have sufficient financial flexibility to maintain dividends if unforeseen circumstances wipe out its financial reserves when earnings are down?
4. Can the firm quickly raise equity capital if necessary?
5. If the company chooses to finance dividends by selling equity, will changes in the number of shareholders have implications for control of the company?

Before You Go On

1. How are dividend policies affected by expected earnings?
2. What did the 2005 study conclude about how managers view share repurchases?
3. List three practical considerations managers should take into account when setting a dividend policy.

SUMMARY OF LEARNING OBJECTIVES

1. **Explain what a dividend is and describe the different types of dividends and the dividend payment process.**

   A dividend is something of value that is distributed to a firm's shareholders on a pro-rata basis – that is, in proportion to the percentage of the firm's shares that they own. There are four types of dividends: (1) regular cash dividends, (2) extra dividends, (3) special dividends and (4) liquidating dividends. Regular cash dividends are the cash dividends that firms pay on a regular basis (typically semi-annually or quarterly). Extra dividends are paid, often at the same time as a regular cash dividend, when a firm wants to distribute additional cash to its shareholders. Special dividends are one-time payments that are used to distribute a large amount of cash. A liquidating dividend is the dividend that is paid when a company goes out of business and is liquidated.

The dividend payment process begins with a vote by the board of directors to pay a dividend. This vote is followed by public announcement of the dividend on the declaration date. On the ex-dividend date, the shares begin trading without the right to receive the dividend. The record date, which follows the ex-dividend date by two days, is the date on which an investor must be a shareholder of record in order to receive the dividend. Finally, the payable date is the date on which the dividend is paid.

2. **Explain what a share repurchase is and how companies repurchase their shares.**

A share repurchase is a transaction in which a company purchases some of its own shares from shareholders. Like dividends, share repurchases are used to distribute value to shareholders. The three ways in which shares are repurchased are (1) open-market repurchases, (2) tender offers and (3) targeted share repurchases. With open-market repurchases, the company purchases shares on the open market, just like any investor does. A tender offer is an open offer by a company to purchase shares. Finally, targeted share repurchases are used to purchase shares from specific shareholders.

3. **Discuss the benefits and costs associated with dividend payments and compare the relative advantages and disadvantages of dividends and share repurchases.**

The potential benefits from paying dividends include (1) attracting certain investors who prefer dividends, (2) sending a positive signal to the market concerning the company's prospects, (3) helping to provide managers with incentives to manage the company more efficiently and (4) helping to manage the company's capital structure. One cost of dividends is the fact that a shareholder must take a dividend and pay taxes on the dividend, whether or not he or she wants the dividend. Shareholders who want to reinvest the dividend in the company must, unless there is a dividend reinvestment programme (DRIP), pay brokerage fees to reinvest the money. Finally, paying a dividend can increase a company's leverage and thereby increase its cost of debt.

With a share repurchase programme, investors can choose whether they want to sell their shares back to the company. Share repurchases also receive more favourable tax treatment. From management's point of view, share repurchase programmes offer more flexibility than dividends and can have less of an effect on the company's share price. One disadvantage of share repurchases involves an ethical issue: managers have better information than others about the prospects of their companies and a share repurchase can enable them to take advantage of this information in a way that benefits the remaining shareholders at the expense of the selling shareholders.

4. **Define share dividends and share splits and explain how they differ from other types of dividends and from share repurchases.**

Share dividends involve the pro-rata distribution of additional shares in a company to its shareholders. Share splits are much like share dividends but involve larger distributions of shares than share dividends. Share dividends and share splits differ from other types of dividends because they do not involve the distribution of value to shareholders. The total value of each shareholder's shares is the same after a share dividend or share split as it was before the distribution. Since they do not involve the distribution of value, share dividends are not really dividends at all.

5. **Describe factors that managers consider when setting the dividend policies for their firms.**

A company's dividend policy is largely a policy about how excess value in the company is distributed to its shareholders. Setting the policy depends on several factors: the expected level and certainty of the firm's future profitability, the firm's future investment requirements, the firm's financial reserves and financial flexibility, the firm's ability to raise capital quickly if necessary and the control implications of financing dividends by selling equity.

SELF-STUDY PROBLEMS

17.1. You would like to own shares that have a record date of Friday 19 March 2010. What is the last date that you can purchase the shares and still receive the dividend?

17.2. You believe that the average investor is subject to a 10% tax rate on dividend payments. If a firm is going to pay a €0.30 dividend, by what amount would you expect the share price to drop on the ex-dividend date?

17.3. Veillon AG just announced that instead of a regular dividend this quarter, it will be repurchasing shares using the same amount of cash that would have been paid in the suspended dividend. Should this be a good or bad signal from the firm?

17.4. Bernard Rubbel SA has just declared a three-for-one share split. If you own 12 000 shares before the split, how many shares do you own after the split? What if it were a one-for-three reverse share split?

17.5. Two publicly traded companies in the same industry are similar in all respects except one. Whereas Publick has issued debt in the public markets (bonds), Privick has never borrowed from any public source. In fact, Privick always uses private bank debt for its borrowing. Which firm might be marginally more inclined to have a more aggressive regular dividend payout than the other? Explain.

SOLUTIONS TO SELF-STUDY PROBLEMS

17.1. The ex-dividend date is the first day that the shares will be trading without the rights to the dividend and that occurs two days before the record date, or on Wednesday 17 March 2010. Therefore, the last day that you can purchase the shares and still receive the dividend will be the day before the ex-dividend date, Tuesday 16 March 2010.

17.2. If the tax rate of the average investor is reflected in the share price change, we would expect investors to receive 90% (1.0 – 0.1) of the dividend after paying taxes. This implies a €0.27 (0.9 × €0.30) drop in the share price of the firm on the ex-dividend date.

17.3. Veillon AG has replaced a committed cash flow with one that is stated but does not have to be acted on. Therefore, the firm's actions should be greeted with suspicion. The signal is not a good one.

17.4. You will own three shares of Bernard Rubbel SA for every one share that you currently own. Therefore, you will own 3 × 12 000 = 36 000 shares of the company. In the case of the reverse split, you will own 1/3 × 12 000 = 4000 shares of the company.

17.5. If all other things are the same about the two companies, then Publick could be expected to have a more aggressive dividend payout policy. Since Publick has issued debt in the past, while Privick has not, then we could expect that Publick would have greater access to the capital markets than Privick. Firms with greater access to capital markets can be more aggressive in their dividend payouts to the extent that they can raise capital more easily (cheaply).

CRITICAL THINKING QUESTIONS

17.1. Suppose that you live in a country where it takes 10 days to settle a share purchase. How many days before the record date will be the ex-dividend date?

17.2. The price of a share is €15.00 on 15 February 2011. The record date for a €0.50 dividend is 17 February 2011. If there are no taxes on dividends, what would you expect the price of a share to be on February 14–17? Assume that there is no other information that could change the price of the shares over this period.

17.3. You find that you are the only investor in a particular share which is subject to a 15% tax rate on dividends (all other investors are subject to a 5% tax rate on dividends). Is there greater value to you in holding the shares beyond the ex-dividend date or selling the shares and then repurchasing them on or after the ex-dividend date? Assume that the share is currently selling for €10.00 per share and the dividend will be €0.25 per share.

17.4. Discuss why the dividend payment process is so much simpler for private companies than for public companies.

17.5. You are the CEO of a firm that has been the subject of a hostile takeover. Thibeaux Piques has been accumulating your shares and now holds a substantial percentage of the outstanding shares. You would like to purchase the shares that he owns. What method of share repurchase will you opt for?

17.6. You have accumulated a 20% interest in a firm that does not pay cash dividends. You have read that, according to Modigliani and Miller, you can create a 'homemade' dividend should you require cash. Discuss why this choice may not be very good for your position.

17.7. You have just read a press release in which a firm claims that it will be able to generate a higher level of cash flows for its investors going forward. Explain the choice of dividends that could credibly convey that information to the market.

17.8. Some may argue that a high tax rate on dividends creates incentives for managers to continue about their business without credibly convincing investors that the firm is doing well, even when it is. Discuss how this may be true.

17.9. Exploitation Minière du Sud Puys SA's management does not like to pay cash dividends due to the volatility of the company's cash flows. Exploitation Minière's management has found, however, that when it does not pay dividends, its share price becomes too high for individual investors to afford round lots. What course of action could Exploitation Minière take to get its share price down without dissipating value for shareholders?

17.10. Lintner found that firms are reluctant to make dividend changes that might have to be reversed. Discuss the rationale for that behaviour.

QUESTIONS AND PROBLEMS

Basic

17.1. Dividends: Náutica Mediterráneo SA has paid a €0.25 dividend per quarter for the past three years. Náutica Mediterráneo just lowered its declared dividend to €0.20 for the next dividend payment.

Discuss what this new information might convey concerning Náutica Mediterráneo's management's belief concerning the future of the company.

17.2. Dividends: Consulenti Politici Marx S.p.A. has decided to discontinue all of its business operations. The firm has total debts of €7 million and the liquidation value of its assets is €10 million. If the book value of the firm's equity is €5 million, then what will be the amount of the liquidating dividend when the firm liquidates all of its assets?

17.3. Dividends: Place the following in the proper chronological order and describe the purpose of each: ex-dividend date, record date, payment date and declaration date.

17.4. Dividend policy and firm value: Explain how the repurchase of new securities by a firm can produce useful information about the issuing firm. Why does this information make the shares of the firm more valuable even if this information is a confirmation of existing information about the firm?

17.5. Dividends: Explain why holders of a firm's debt should insist on a covenant that restricts the amount of cash dividends.

17.6. Share splits and share dividends: Explain why firms prefer that their shares trade in a moderate price range instead of a high value per share. How do firms keep the shares trading in a moderate price range?

17.7. Dividends: Scintilla plc is trading for €10.00 per share on the day before the ex-dividend date. If the amount of the dividend is €0.25 and there are no taxes, what should the price of the shares be on the ex-dividend date?

17.8. Dividends: A company announces that it will make a €1.00 dividend payment. Assuming all investors are subject to a 15% tax rate on dividends, how much should the company's share price drop on the ex-dividend date?

Intermediate

17.9. Dividend policy and firm value: Explain how a share repurchase, although it places cash in the hands of shareholders, is different from a dividend payment.

17.10. Dividend policy and firm value: You have just encountered two identical firms with identical investment opportunities, as well as the ability to fund these opportunities. You have found that one of the firms has just announced an introductory dividend policy, while the other has continued with a no-dividend policy. Which of the two firms is worth more? Explain.

17.11. Dividend policy and firm value: Explain what the introduction of transaction costs will do to the Modigliani and Miller assumption that dividends are irrelevant. Start with a firm that pays dividends to a group of its investors that does not want to receive dividend payments. Do not consider taxes.

17.12. Dividend policy and firm value: CashCo has been increasing its cash dividends each quarter for the past eight quarters. While this may signal that the firm is financially very healthy, what else could we conclude from these actions?

17.13. Dividend policy and firm value: Currently, in Hungary, dividends are taxed at 10%. The government is proposing to change this favourable treatment and have dividends taxed as income. What would you expect to happen to the share prices of dividend-paying shares versus those of non-dividend-paying shares if this happens?

17.14. Dividends: Undecided plc has additional cash on hand right now, although management is not sure about the level of cash flows going forward. If the firm would like to put cash in its shareholders' hands, what kind of dividend should it pay and why?

17.15. Dividend policy and firm value: A firm can deliver a negative signal to shareholders by increasing the level of dividends or by reducing the level of dividends. Explain.

17.16. Dividend policy and firm value: You own shares in a firm that has enough cash on hand to distribute to shareholders. You do not want the cash. What course of action would you prefer the firm take?

17.17. Dividend policy and firm value: Share repurchases, once announced, do not actually have to occur in total or in part. From a signalling perspective, why would a special dividend be better than a share repurchase?

17.18. Dividend policy and firm value: Consider a firm that repurchases shares from its shareholders in the open market and explain why this action might be detrimental to the shareholders to whom the firm is attempting to deliver value through its action.

17.19. Dividend policy and firm value: Explain why a firm might raise money to pay a cash dividend by selling equity to new shareholders.

17.20. Share repurchases: Briefly discuss the methods available for a firm to repurchase its shares and explain why you might expect the share price reaction to the announcement of each of these methods to differ.

17.21. Share repurchases: What is the advantage of a Dutch auction over a fixed-price tender offer?

Advanced

17.22. In the early 1990s, the amount of time that elapsed between purchasing shares and actually obtaining the shares was five business days. This period was known as the settlement period. The settlement period for share purchases is now two business days. Describe what should have happened to the number of days between the ex-dividend date and the record date at the time of this change.

17.23. WeAreProfits plc has not issued any new debt securities in 10 years. It will begin paying cash dividends to its shareholders for the first time next year. Explain how a

dividend might help the firm get closer to its optimal capital structure of 50% debt and 50% equity.

17.24. Les Ombres SA had shares outstanding that were valued at €120 before a two-for-one share split. After the share split, the shares were valued at €62 per share. If we accept that the firm's financial manoeuvre did not create any new value, then why might the market be increasing the total value of the firm's equity?

17.25. Saguaro SA currently has 30 000 shares outstanding. Each share has a market value of €20. If the firm pays €5 per share in dividends, what will each share be worth after the dividend payment? Ignore taxes.

17.26. La Cholla S.p.A. currently has 30 000 shares outstanding. Each share has a market value of €20. If the firm repurchases €150 000 worth of shares, then what will be the value of each share after the repurchase? Ignore taxes.

17.27. You purchased 1000 shares of Koogal five years ago at €30. Today, Koogal is repurchasing its shares through a fixed-price tender offer price of €80 per share. What is the amount of after-tax proceeds that you will get to keep if only the capital gain is taxed at a 15% rate?

17.28. You purchased 1000 shares of Zebulon Copper Co. five years ago at €50 per share. Today, Zebulon is trying to decide whether to repurchase shares at €70 per share through a fixed-price tender offer or pay a €70 cash dividend per share. If capital gains are taxed at a 15% rate, then at what rate must dividends be taxed for you to be indifferent between receiving the dividend and selling your shares back to Zebulon?

17.29. The Llama Substitute Wool Company is trying to do some financial planning for the coming year. Llama plans to raise €10 000 in new equity this year and wants to pay a total dividend to shareholders of €30 000. The firm must pay €20 000 interest during the year and will also pay down principal on its debt obligations by €10 000. If the firm continues with its capital budgeting plan, it will require €100 000 for capital expenditures during the year. Given the above information, how much cash must be provided from operations for the firm to meet its plan?

17.30. You are the CFO of a large publicly traded company. You would like to convey positive information about the firm to the market. If you intuitively understand (and agree with) the results from the Lintner study, will you keep paying your currently high dividend or raise that dividend by a small amount?

SAMPLE TEST PROBLEMS

17.1. Is it possible to own a share for a single day and receive the cash dividend paid on the shares although you do not own the shares at the time of payment?

17.2. Is it possible for your voting interest in a firm to increase without your having to purchase additional shares in that firm?

17.3. Since dividends that are not yet declared by the firm are not legal obligations of the firm, can the firm alter its dividend payouts without cost?

17.4. Evaluate the statement that the government does not have an impact on the valuation of shares.

17.5. A recent survey of financial executives found that they favour share repurchases over dividends. How does that finding seem to contradict the idea that firms use distribution decisions to signal future firm prospects to the market?

ENDNOTES

1. Notice that we are assuming the ex-dividend date is tomorrow; thus, we do not have to worry about the time value of money in this example.
2. Note that this announcement does not obligate Royal Dutch Shell to continue paying quarterly dividends at that level. In fact, Royal Dutch Shell has increased its dividend payment on a regular basis but there is no reason that the board could not reduce the quarterly dividend payment at some point in the future.
3. An exception is when the dividend is viewed as a return of the capital that the shareholders have invested in the firm, rather than a distribution of profits. Dividends generally are not a return of capital unless they are very large or when they are liquidating dividends.
4. The term *tender offer* is commonly used to refer to any open offer to purchase any shares, not just the shares of the firm making the announcement. For example, when a company tries to take over another company, it might begin with a tender offer for that other company's shares.
5. In some countries, due to securities regulations, targeted repurchases may not be allowed.
6. For instance, individual tax rates in Belgium, which are not untypical of much of Europe, are progressive and can be as much as 50% of income. Long-term Belgian investors may prefer to receive

income as capital gains since, if shares have been held for a long time, there may be no tax on any capital gains.

7. Fractional shares are generally made up for by a small cash payment.

8. Note that for accounting purposes, a share split and a share dividend are treated differently. From a finance point of view, however, they are similar events.

9. If nothing else happened and the split had none of the effects discussed in the following section, we would expect the share price to drop by exactly 50%. However, changes in market conditions and other circumstances at the firm, as well as possible effects of the split on the attractiveness of BASF shares, apparently combined to cause a price decline of just less than 50%.

10. For an example of such a study, see R.M. Conroy and R.S. Harris, 'Stock Splits and Information: The Role of Stock Price', *Financial Management* **28** (Autumn 1999) 28–40.

11. J. Lintner, 'Distribution of Incomes of Corporations among Dividends, Retained Earnings, and Taxes', *American Economic Review* **46** (1956) 97–113.

12. A. Brav, J.R. Graham, C.R. Harvey and R. Michaely, 'Payout Policy in the 21st Century', *Journal of Financial Economics* **77** (2005) 483–527.

PART 6

BUSINESS FORMATION, VALUATION AND FINANCIAL PLANNING

CHAPTER
18

Business Formation, Growth and Valuation

In this Chapter:

Starting a Business

The Role of the Business Plan

Valuing a Business

Important Issues in Valuation

LEARNING OBJECTIVES

1. Explain why the choice of organisational form is important and describe two financial considerations that are especially important in starting a business.

2. Describe the key components of a business plan and explain what a business plan is used for.

3. Explain the three general approaches to valuation and be able to value a business with commonly used business valuation approaches.

4. Explain how valuations can differ between public and private companies and between young and mature companies, and discuss the importance of control and key person considerations in valuation.

I t takes some effort to spend £125 million (€150 million) in six months, but this is what Boo.com – an Internet start-up – managed to do. The company was set up by Ernst Malmsten, Kajsa Leander and Patrik Hedelin during the dotcom boom of the late 1990s in order to sell branded fashion apparel over the Internet. Following presentations about their business plans, a number of venture capital firms and high net worth individuals contributed the start-up money. Ultimately, the company intended to go public via an initial public offering. However, a number of problems plagued the new venture – including delays in launching the website and fixing problems users experienced subsequently when using it. By the time the company ran out of money, it had achieved sales of about €500 000 in the two weeks prior to going bankrupt in May 2000.

Boo.com's business model was straightforward enough and has since been imitated successfully. The main reason for failure was that the company had an extremely aggressive growth plan that involved simultaneous launches across Europe and a complex and challenging website, which was costly to set up and widely criticised as poorly thought through as it went against the conventions on ease of use. Furthermore, the plan assumed the ready availability of more money from the firm's backers and hence little attention was given to costs. From the beginning, a large number of staff and contractors were employed without considering what they were supposed to achieve and the drain on the company's cash resources.

This chapter discusses some of the financial aspects of forming, growing and financing a new business. It also discusses, in detail, the methods used to value both small and large businesses. Business valuation concepts were certainly on the minds of Boo.com's owners when they were raising capital and negotiating with investors about exactly how much of the company's equity they would have to give up to obtain the funds they needed to grow the business.

CHAPTER PREVIEW

In earlier chapters, we discussed how businesses are organised and how financial managers make long-term investment decisions, manage working capital and finance the investments and activities of their businesses. In this chapter, we re-examine these concepts in the context of a discussion of business formation, growth and valuation. The chapter provides an integrated perspective on how the decisions that financial managers make affect firm value.

We begin by considering the decision by an entrepreneur to start a business and the choice of how the business should be organised. The organisational form of a business affects many important financial decisions through its impact on the availability and cost of capital, the control of the business, the ability to attract and retain high-quality managers, the taxes that must be paid and the agency problems that might arise in the business, among other factors. We then discuss financial considerations that are important to managers of young, rapidly growing firms.

Next we focus on the role that a carefully prepared business plan plays in raising capital for a young, rapidly growing business and in providing a road map of where the business is going for use in managerial decision making. The importance of a business plan cannot be understated. The act of preparing a business plan forces an entrepreneur to think carefully about the aspects of the business that are crucial to its success. This helps him or her to better communicate to others what the prospects for the business are and to manage the business more effectively.

The last two sections of the chapter address business valuation concepts. These sections provide a broad overview of the business valuation approaches used by financial managers and describe how differences in the characteristics of companies affect valuation analyses. The impact of control considerations and key people on business valuations is also considered.

STARTING A BUSINESS

Learning Objective 1

Explain why the choice of organisational form is important and describe two financial considerations that are especially important in starting a business.

People start their own business for a wide variety of reasons. Some have an idea for a new product or service that they think will revolutionise an industry and make them rich. Others live in an area where there are no attractive employment opportunities for them. Others simply want to be their own boss.

Regardless of their motives, all of these people face the decision of whether to start their own business or purchase an already established business. Starting your own business can provide greater potential rewards but is inherently more risky than buying and growing a business that someone else has already built. The founder of a company must start from scratch by choosing the products to sell, the markets to sell them in and the best strategy for selling them. He or she must then raise the money necessary to develop the products, acquire the necessary assets and hire the right people. Of course, as the business is being built, the founder must also manage the day-to-day operations to ensure that his or her overall plan is being implemented as well as possible.

In this section, we discuss factors that entrepreneurs consider when deciding to launch a new business, factors that affect the form of organisation that they choose, and financial considerations associated with starting a business.

Making the Decision to Proceed

Hundreds of thousands of new businesses are started each year, but many do not succeed. The European Commission estimate that for the European Union, about 1.8 million new businesses are established each year, although there is a very high failure rate since at the same time 1.5 million cease activity. Among those that do survive, only a few will provide high returns to their founders.

Businesses fail for many reasons. Some fail because consumers do not accept their products. Others fail because the founders pursue a poorly thought-out strategy or do not have the management skills to properly execute a good strategy. Another common reason for new business failures is that founders underestimate how much money it will take to get their businesses up and running. For example, they underestimate the amount of money that will be needed to cover cash outflows until cash inflows from sales are large enough to do so. These founders fail to ensure that they have enough money to give the business a fighting chance.

The fact that many new businesses fail does not mean that you should not start a business if you believe that you have a good idea. It simply means that you should carefully think through your new business idea before you make the decision to proceed. Not thinking carefully about your idea can lead you to pursue a poor strategy, fail to realise that you might need help in executing your strategy, or underestimate how much money you will need.

It is beyond the scope of this book to tell you how to properly evaluate a business idea, a strategy for pursuing it, or your management abilities. Fortunately, a lot has been written on these topics by others.

The only advice that we can give you in these areas is to be careful and realistic in assessing your opportunities. On the one hand, do not jump into a business without careful thought. On the other hand, do not over-analyse opportunities to the point where you are just convincing yourself not to proceed. Taking calculated risks is part of business. The important thing to remember is that the risks you take should be 'calculated'. Also, do not think that failure will ruin your chances of ultimately achieving business success. Many successful entrepreneurs and executives have failed more than once in their careers. Successful people learn from both their failures and their successes.

Choosing the Right Organisational Form

Once you have made the decision to start a business, you must decide what form of organisation will work best. Chapter 1 discussed some of the more common basic forms of business organisation – sole proprietorships, partnerships and companies – and some of their advantages and disadvantages. In that discussion, you saw that there are variations in the basic forms of business organisation. For example, Chapter 1 describes general, limited and limited liability partnerships. There are also a number of different types of companies, as well as hybrids between partnerships and companies. The reason that so many different forms of organisation exist is that the needs of businesses vary considerably. The wide range of choices has made the decision of how to organise a business so complex that many people do not even try to make this decision without legal advice.

In this section, we extend the discussion begun in Chapter 1 by focusing, from a financial perspective, on factors that affect the choice of the appropriate organisational form for a new business. We highlight some of the most common forms of organisation and identify important characteristics of these alternatives that should be considered when choosing the form of organisation for a business.

Exhibit 18.1 compares the common forms of business organisation on a number of different dimensions. You will note that there are two forms of organisation in this table that are not discussed in detail in Chapter 1: *limited liability companies (LLCs)* and *private companies*. We first briefly describe LLCs and private companies and we then focus on the differences between the various forms of organisation shown in the exhibit.

LLCs and Private Companies

Since it was first developed in the USA in the 1970s and subsequently adopted in a number of other countries, the LLC form of organisation has benefited founders of many businesses that would otherwise have been organised as limited partnerships. An LLC is a hybrid of a limited partnership and a company. Like a company, an LLC provides limited liability for the people who make the business decisions in the firm, while enabling all investors to retain the tax advantages of a limited partnership. For instance in Germany, a limited

EXHIBIT 18.1

COMPARISON OF BUSINESS ORGANISATION TITLES FOR A SELECTION OF COUNTRIES

Country	Sole Proprietorship	Partnership		Private Limited Company	Public Limited Company
		General	Limited		
Austria, Germany and Switzerland	Einzelunternehmen	Offene Gesellschaft (OG)	Kommanditgesellschaft (KG)/Kommanditgesellschaft auf Aktien (KGA)	Gesellschaft mit beschränkter Haftung (GmbH)	Aktiengesellschaft (AG)
Brazil		Sociedade em Nome Coletivo	Sociedade em Comandita Simples/Sociedade em Comandita por Ações	Limitada (Ltda)	Sociedade Anónima (SA)
Denmark	Enkeltmandsvirksomhed	Interessentskab (I/S)	Kommanditselskab (K/S)	Anpartsselskab (ApS)	Aktieselskab (A/S)
Egypt		Sharikat Tadamun	Sharikat Tawssiyah Bassita	Limited Liabilities Company (LLC)	Sharikat al-Mossahamah (SAE)
European Union				Societas Privata Europaea (SPE)	Societas Europaea (SE)
Finland	Yhden omistajan	avoin yhtiö (AY)	kommandiittiyhtiö (KY)	osakeyhtiö (OY)	julkinen osakeyhtiö (OYJ)
France, Luxembourg and Switzerland	Entreprise individuelle	Société en nom collectif (SNC)	Société en commandite simple (SCS)/Société en commandite par actions (SCA)	Société à responsabilité limitée (SARL)	Société anonyme (SA)
Italy and Switzerland	Ditta individuale	Società semplice (Ss)/Società in nome collettivo (Snc)	Società in accomandita semplice (Sns)	Società a responsabilità limitata (Srl)	Società per Azioni (SpA)
Netherlands	Eenmanszaak	Vennootschap Onder Firma (VOF)	Commanditaire Vennootschap (CV)	Besloten Vennootschap (BV)	Naamloze Vennootschap (NV)

	Enkeltpersonforetak	Ansvarlig selskap (ANS)	Kommandittselskap (KS)	Aksjeselskap (AS)	Allmennaksjeselskap (ASA)
Norway	Enkeltpersonforetak	Ansvarlig selskap (ANS)	Kommandittselskap (KS)	Aksjeselskap (AS)	Allmennaksjeselskap (ASA)
Poland	jednoosobowa działalność gospodarcza	spółka jawna (Sp.j)	spółka komandytowa (Sp.k)	spółka z ograniczoną odpowiedzialnością (Spzoo)	spółka akcyjna (SA)
Spain	Unipersonal	Sociedad Colectiva (SC)	Sociedad Comanditaria (Scra)	Sociedad Limitada (SL)	Sociedad Anónima (SA)
Sweden	Enskild firma	Handelsbolag (HB)	Kommanditbolag (KB)	Aktiebolag (AB)	Publikt aktiebolag (AB (publ))
United Kingdom	Sole trader/sole proprietorship	General partnership	Limited liability partnership (LLP)	Limited (Ltd)	public limited company (plc)
United States	Sole proprietorship	General partnership	Limited liability partnership (LLP)/Limited liability partnership company (LLPC)	Corporation (Corp.), Incorporated (Inc.)	

The exhibit shows the names used for the different organisational forms for a selection of countries. Most countries have similar legal forms; namely, a sole proprietorship, general and limited partnerships, private and public companies. Company laws in the different countries differentiate between the various types of organisations. For a few of the countries in the list, the limited liability partnership includes the names for limited liability partnerships by shares. For example, France offers both a partnership form of limited liability called a 'société en commandite simple' (SCS) and a similar structure using shares called a 'société en commandite par actions' (SCA). The only difference is that in the SCA the partners' interest in the firm is evidenced by the issue of shares (called 'actions' in French) to the partners.

partnership, called a 'Kommanditgesellschaft' (KG), can be set up in the normal manner or can be established using shares, called 'Aktien' in German, where the resulting partnership is called a 'Kommanditgesellschaft auf Aktien' (KGA).

A private or closely held company is simply a restricted form of a limited liability company that places restrictions on the number of shareholders and the transferability of the company's shares and will not have a listing on a stock exchange. For instance, exiting shareholders may be required to offer their shareholdings to the other shareholders prior to being able to sell them to a third party. In addition, the minimum amount of capital that is required may be less than that for a public company. In many countries there is a name difference. For instance in France, a public limited company (abbreviated as plc in the UK) is called a 'société anonyme' (SA), whereas a private limited company (abbreviated as Ltd) is called a 'société à responsabilité limitée' (SARL). Other countries have similar distinctions. Exhibit 18.1 shows the names of these different organisational forms for a selection of countries.

Choosing an Organisational Form

As you can see in Exhibit 18.2, a sole proprietorship is the least expensive type of business to start. To start a sole proprietorship, all you have to do is obtain the business licences required by your local and state governments. Limited partnerships are more costly to form because the partners must hire a lawyer to draw up and maintain the *partnership agreement*, which specifies the nature of the relationship between the partners. Forming a company also requires hiring a company lawyer to draft a document that spells out things such as how many shares can be issued, what voting rights the shareholders will have and who the board members are. Over the life of a successful business, these out-of-pocket costs are not very important. However, to a cash-strapped entrepreneur, they can seem substantial.

Because the life of a sole proprietorship is limited to the life of the proprietor, it ceases to exist when the proprietor gets out of the business. In contrast, the lives of all other forms of organisation can be made independent of the life of the founder. Partnership agreements, including the related agreement in an LLC, can be amended to allow for the business to continue when the founder leaves. Companies, which are legal persons under company law, automatically have an indefinite life. You will notice that Exhibit 18.2 indicates that the lives of partnerships and LLCs are flexible. This is because, while partnership and LLC agreements can be written so that their lives are indefinite, they can also be written with a fixed life in mind. For example, private equity and venture capital limited partnerships and LLCs are typically structured so that they last only 10 years.

The ability to make the life of a business independent of that of the founder increases the liquidity of the ownership interests, making it easier for the business to raise capital or for investors to sell their interests at an attractive price. Since a sole proprietorship has no ownership interest that can be sold directly, the proprietor can sell only the assets of the business. There is no way to sell a partial ownership interest.

Even with partnerships and companies, it can be quite expensive to raise capital for the business or for an investor to sell an ownership interest. Common restrictions in partnership and LLC agreements, and the need to amend the partnership and LLC documents to reflect a change in ownership, can make transferring ownership time-consuming and costly. Selling shares in a company can be costly if that company is not publicly traded.[1]

Making sure that a new business has access to enough capital is always an important concern for an entrepreneur. By their nature, sole proprietorships must rely on equity contributions from the proprietor and debt or lease financing. In contrast, partnerships can turn to all of the partners for additional capital and companies can sell shares to outsiders. Limited partnerships and LLCs are less constrained than general partnerships because they can raise money from limited partners or from 'members', as outside investors in LLCs are called, who are not directly involved in running the business. Public companies can have a virtually unlimited number of potential shareholders.

EXHIBIT 18.2

CHARACTERISTICS OF DIFFERENT FORMS OF BUSINESS ORGANISATION

	Sole Proprietorship	Partnership		Limited Liability Company (LLC)	Company	
		General	Limited		Private	Public
Cost to establish	Inexpensive	More costly	More costly	More costly	More costly	More costly
Life of entity	Limited	Flexible	Flexible	Flexible	Indefinite	Indefinite
Access to capital	Very limited	Limited	Less limited	Less limited	Less limited	Excellent
Control by founder	Complete	Shared	Shared	Shared	Depends on ownership	Depends on ownership
Cost to transfer ownership	High	High	High	High	High	Can be low
Specialisation of management and investment	No	No	Yes	Yes	Yes	Yes
Potential owner/ manager conflicts	No	No	Some	Some	Potentially high	Potentially high
Ability to provide incentives to attract and retain high-quality employees	Limited	Good	Good	Good	Good	Good
Liability of owners	Unlimited	Unlimited	Unlimited for general partner	Limited	Limited	Limited
Tax treatment of income	Flow through	Flow through	Flow through	Varies between countries	Company tax/double taxation	Company tax/double taxation
Tax deductibility of owner benefits	Limited	Limited	Limited	Limited	Limited	Less limited

Choosing the appropriate form of business organisation is an important step in starting a business. This exhibit compares key characteristics of the most popular forms of business organisation in Europe. Note that there will be specific country differences from the above table.

The downside of being able to raise equity capital from other people is the need to share control. An entrepreneur who chooses a form of organisation other than a sole proprietorship and who does not retain 100% ownership must give up some control. Of course, the entrepreneur may have little choice in this trade-off if the business requires more capital than he or she can personally provide.

It is important to recognise that certain investors who are especially important sources of capital for young, rapidly growing firms will only invest in companies. For example, since venture capitalists do not typically want to become full operating partners in the businesses in which they invest, and because the cost of transferring ownership interests can be much lower for companies, they will generally invest only in businesses that are organised this way.

Chapter 1 discussed the concept of separation of ownership and control and how it is related to agency problems. This separation has benefits as well as costs. While it is true that agency problems can arise when owners delegate decision-making authority to professional managers, these costs might be smaller than the benefits. Specifically, the ability to separate ownership from management control enables a firm to raise capital from investors who have no interest in being directly involved in the business. This can greatly increase the number of potential investors. Another benefit is that an entrepreneur can turn over day-to-day control of a business to a more capable manager, become less involved in the business and yet continue to benefit from its successes as an investor.

Another key concern of all entrepreneurs is being able to attract and retain high-quality employees. Being able to offer a potential or current employee an ownership interest in the business or the prospect of becoming a partner can help greatly in recruiting and retention. The inability to offer ownership interests is a major disadvantage of sole proprietorships.

Financial liabilities associated with a business are also an important consideration when choosing the form for a business. On this dimension, sole proprietorships, general partnerships and limited partnerships are at a disadvantage. Sole proprietors and general partners face the possibility that their personal assets can be taken from them to satisfy claims on their businesses. In contrast, the liabilities of investors in limited partnerships and companies are limited to the money that they have invested in the business.

The choice of organisational form also affects how the business's operating profits will be taxed. More taxes mean that the owners get less. In each of the organisational forms in Exhibit 18.2, all profits flow through to the owners in proportion to their ownership interests. These owners pay taxes on the business profits when they file their personal tax returns. Profits earned in companies are taxed at the corporate tax rate and the after-tax profits may be taxed a second time when they are distributed to shareholders in the form of dividends. On the bright side, because profits are taxed in the company, certain benefits, such as health insurance, that are paid to shareholders who work

in a company are potentially tax deductible. These benefits may not generally be deductible with the other forms of organisation.

Financial Considerations

The most important financial concern of any entrepreneur is making sure that the business has access to enough money to be successful. Unlike a successful mature company, which can rely on cash flows from sales of other products to fund new product introductions, an entrepreneur must obtain funding from outside the firm. This makes it especially important for the entrepreneur to understand the cash requirements of the business.

The margin for error is small. If the entrepreneur miscalculates how much money is necessary, it may be too late to raise more money by the time this miscalculation is recognised. Raising external capital can be a time-consuming process and becomes increasingly difficult as a firm becomes more and more cash constrained. Outside investors are especially careful about investing in businesses that have run short of cash. The fact that the business has got into such a position can suggest that the business idea might not be viable or that the entrepreneur may not be the right person to build it, or both.

Two tools are particularly useful in understanding the cash requirements of a business and in estimating how much financing a new business will require: (1) the cash flow break-even analysis discussed in Chapter 12 and (2) the cash budget.

Cash Flow Break-Even

Recall that pre-tax operating cash flow (EBITDA) break-even analysis is used to compute the level of unit sales that is necessary to break even on operations from a pre-tax operating cash flow perspective. It is calculated using Equation (12.4):

$$\text{EBITDA Break-even} = \frac{FC}{\text{Price} - \text{Unit VC}}$$

where FC is the fixed costs associated with the business and Price − Unit VC is the per-unit contribution.

It is important for an entrepreneur to understand the concept of EBITDA break-even and how to calculate this point for each product a business produces. This calculation focuses the entrepreneur's attention on the importance of maximising a product's per-unit contribution and minimising overhead costs. It also provides a means of estimating how long it will take for a product to reach the break-even point and, therefore, how much money will be needed to launch a new product or business.

Although it might seem obvious that an entrepreneur should want to maximise the per-unit contribution of each product and minimise total fixed costs, entrepreneurs often lose sight of these objectives. An entrepreneur can get so caught up in developing the best possible product that he or she does not adequately consider how much customers are willing to pay for that product. For example, adding another feature to a word-processing program can be expensive and consumers might not be willing to pay the additional cost if they are unlikely to use that feature. Of course, being too sensitive to the possibility of overinvesting in new product development can harm a business by causing it to lose its competitive advantage. An entrepreneur should always be looking for ways to maximise the per-unit contribution of the firm's products while maintaining the firm's competitive position.

Many entrepreneurs also lose sight of the importance of controlling fixed costs. We can point to many very public examples of this during the dotcom era, when money seemed to flow freely to certain high-tech firms, as it did in the opening case of Boo.com. Many of these companies spent a great deal of money on things like team-building activities in which they took their entire product development staff on week-long trips to vacation resorts. Although expenses such as these might help to increase sales or to encourage more creativity and hard work among the development staff, they also increase the number of units that a business must sell to break even. Unfortunately, many companies during the dotcom era ran out of money before they ever broke even.

Cash Inflows and Outflows

The cash budget is also a very useful planning tool for entrepreneurs. It summarises the cash flows into and out of a firm over a period of time. Cash budgets often present the inflows and outflows on a monthly basis but can be prepared for any period, including daily or weekly. Preparing a cash budget helps an entrepreneur better understand where money is coming from, where it is going, how much external financing is likely to be needed and when the need is likely to arise. Understanding where the money is coming from and where it is going helps an entrepreneur maintain control of the company's finances. Knowing how much external financing is likely to be needed, and when, helps the entrepreneur plan fund-raising efforts before it is too late.

WEB

The *Cash Flow Template*, Excel spreadsheet #60 on the website maintained by Matt H. Evans, is an example of a comprehensive Excel model for forecasting monthly cash flows. See the spreadsheet at: www.exinfm. com/free_spreadsheets.html.18.1.

To better understand how a cash budget can help an entrepreneur, we will consider an example. Suppose that it is 1 March 2011, and you are planning to open a new restaurant called the Pizza Palace. You have saved €25 000, which you intend to invest in the business, and you have obtained a five-year loan for €50 000 at an APR of 8% (8%/ 12 = 0.667% per month). The loan principal will be repaid in five equal instalments of €10 000 at the end of each of the next five years. Exhibit 18.3 presents a monthly cash budget for your restaurant investment.

The initial cash balance in row 1 of the March column of your budget equals the €75 000 that you have raised to finance the project. You estimate that it will take two weeks to actually open the restaurant and, knowing that you will have to build a customer base from scratch, you expect to have

EXHIBIT 18.3

PIZZA PALACE MONTHLY CASH BUDGET FOR THE PERIOD MARCH 2011 TO FEBRUARY 2012ᵃ

Row		Mar.	Apr.	May	June	July	Aug.	Sept.	Oct.	Nov.	Dec.	Jan.	Feb.	Total
1	**Beginning cash balance**	€75 000	€6 097	€5 000	€5 000	€5 000	€5 000	€5 000	€6 497	€7 993	€9 490	€10 987	€12 483	
2	**Cash receipts**													
3	Cash sales	3 000	12 000	15 000	20 000	25 000	30 000	35 000	35 000	35 000	35 000	35 000	35 000	€315 000
4	Collections from credit accounts	—	—	—	—	—	—	—	—	—	—	—	—	—
5	Investments by owner	—	9 457	9 103	6 553	4 004	1 253	—	—	—	—	—	353	30 723
6	**Total cash receipts**	3 000	21 457	24 103	26 553	29 004	31 253	35 000	35 000	35 000	35 000	35 000	35 353	345 723
7	**Total cash available**	78 000	27 554	29 103	31 553	34 004	36 253	40 000	41 497	42 993	44 490	45 987	47 836	
8	**Cash payments**													
	Operations													
9	Food purchases	1 200	4 800	6 000	8 000	10 000	12 000	14 000	14 000	14 000	14 000	14 000	14 000	126 000
10	Gross wages	10 800	10 800	10 800	10 800	10 800	10 800	10 800	10 800	10 800	10 800	10 800	10 800	129 600
11	Payroll expenses	1 620	1 620	1 620	1 620	1 620	1 620	1 620	1 620	1 620	1 620	1 620	1 620	19 440
12	Misc. supplies	500	500	500	500	500	500	500	500	500	500	500	500	6 000
13	Repairs and maintenance	150	600	750	1 000	1 250	1 500	1 750	1 750	1 750	1 750	1 750	1 750	15 750
14	Advertising	1 000	1 000	1 000	1 000	1 000	1 000	1 000	1 000	1 000	1 000	1 000	1 000	12 000
15	Accounting and legal	3 000	200	200	200	200	200	200	200	200	200	200	200	5 200
16	Rent	1 500	1 500	1 500	1 500	1 500	1 500	1 500	1 500	1 500	1 500	1 500	1 500	18 000
17	Telephone and utilities	1 000	1 200	1 400	1 600	1 800	1 800	1 800	1 800	1 800	1 800	1 800	1 800	19 600
18	Other expenses	—	—	—	—	—	—	—	—	—	—	—	—	—
19	**Operations total**	€20 770	€22 220	€23 770	€26 220	€28 670	€30 920	€33 170	€33 170	€33 170	€33 170	€33 170	€33 170	€351 590
	Financing and investments													
20	Interest payments	€333	€333	€333	€333	€333	€333	€333	€333	€333	€333	€333	€333	€4 000
21	Principal payments on loans	—	—	—	—	—	—	—	—	—	—	—	10,000	10,000
22	Capital expenditures	50,000	—	—	—	—	—	—	—	—	—	—	—	50,000
23	Start-up costs	800	—	—	—	—	—	—	—	—	—	—	—	800
24	Withdrawals by owner	—	—	—	—	—	—	—	—	—	—	—	—	
25	**Total cash payments**	€71 903	€22 553	€24 103	€26 553	€29 003	€31 253	€33 503	€33 503	€33 503	€33 503	€33 503	€43 503	€416 390
26	**Ending cash balance**	€6 097	€5 000	€5 000	€5 000	€5 000	€5 000	€6 497	€7 993	€9 490	€10 987	€12 483	€4 333	€4 333

ᵃSome totals do not appear to add up precisely because the actual values computed in the model are rounded to the nearest whole number for presentation in this exhibit. At a minimum, it presents the cash inflows

A monthly cash budget summarises the cash that management expects to flow into and out of a business each month. At a minimum, it presents the cash inflows and outflows for each of the next 12 months and for the entire 12-month period. Monthly cash budgets can extend beyond 12 months.

only €3000 in sales during the first month. You do not anticipate providing any credit to your customers, so all of the proceeds from the sales will be received in cash. As shown in rows 8–25 of Exhibit 18.3, you expect cash operating expenses to total €20 770 and interest expenses, capital expenditures and start-up costs to be €333, €50 000 and €800, respectively, during March. With only €3000 in cash inflows, these expenditures will reduce the cash balance by the end of March to only:

$$\begin{aligned} &€75\,000 + €3000 - €20\,770 - €333 \\ &\quad - €50\,000 - €800 \\ &\quad = €6097 \end{aligned}$$

While the restaurant is expected to have a positive cash balance at the end of March, the cash balance will be negative by the end of April if no additional financing is obtained. You can see this by noting that the beginning cash balance of €6097 plus the cash sales of €12 000 would provide a total of only €18 097 with which to pay €22 220 in operating expenses and €333 of interest. This would result in an ending cash balance of:[2]

$$€6097 + €12\,000 - €22\,220 - €333 = -€4457$$

Since a restaurant cannot operate without at least some cash for the cash register, you will have to invest more than €4457 in the business during the month of April. For example, if you decide that you want to maintain a cash balance of at least €5000, you will have to invest an additional €4457 + €5000 = €9457. This investment is shown in row 5 of the April column in Exhibit 18.3. In this example, the investment is treated as an investment by the owner rather than as additional debt. You can tell this by the fact that there is no change in the interest payments in row 20. However, we could easily have treated this amount as a loan instead.

Notice that the cash budget tells you that if the cash forecasts in your budget are correct, you will have to raise a total of:

$$\begin{aligned} &€9457 + €9103 + €6553 + €4004 + €1253 \\ &\quad = €30\,370 \end{aligned}$$

by the end of August to ensure that your restaurant's cash balance does not fall below €5000. Knowing this at the beginning of March can be very helpful in planning your fund-raising activities for the year.

You might also note that the cash budget indicates that €353 will have to be invested in February 2012. This is because the first principal payment on the debt is due at the end of that month. If you plan to maintain total debt of €50 000 in this business, you could cover this requirement by obtaining a new €10 000 loan, which you would use to make the debt principal payment.

We can also calculate the cash flow break-even for the Pizza Palace restaurant. If, for simplicity, we assume that the average customer spends €10 for pizza and a drink and that the only unit variable costs are those associated with the food, then we can calculate that the unit contribution will be €6 per customer when the business is up and running in September 2011. We know that the unit contribution is €6 because food purchases represent €14 000/€35 000 = 40% of cash sales. This leaves 60% of cash sales, or €6 per customer, to cover fixed costs. Knowing the unit contribution and assuming all costs other than those associated with food purchases are fixed, we can calculate the cash flow break-even as follows:

$$\begin{aligned} \text{EBITDA Break-even} &= \frac{FC}{\text{Price} - \text{Unit VC}} \\ &= \frac{€33\,170 - €14\,000}{€10 - €4} \\ &= 3\,195 \text{ customers} \end{aligned}$$

In other words, your restaurant will have to serve at least 3195 customers per month (approximately 107 per day) in order to break even on a cash flow basis once it is up and running.

We have simplified our example by assuming that the restaurant does not provide credit to customers or hold any material inventories of food, supplies and so forth. However, we could have incorporated these characteristics into our cash budget using the working capital management concepts discussed in Chapter 14.

Decision-Making Example 18.1

Using a Cash Budget

Situation: It is 1 January and you have prepared the following cash budget for the next four months for your new business venture:

If you plan to finance the business entirely with equity, how much money should you invest now to ensure that there is at least €1000 still in the business at the end of April? How much will you have to invest each month after April to

Monthly Cash Budget

	Jan.	Feb.	Mar.	Apr.	Total
Beginning cash balance	€0	(€18 510)	(€25 270)	€28 530)	
Cash receipts					
Cash sales	2 500	5 000	12 000	20 000	€39 500
Investments by owner	–	–	–	–	–
Total cash receipts	€2 500	€5 000	€12 000	€20 000	€39 500
Total cash available	€2 500	(€13 510)	(€13 270)	(€8 530)	
Cash payments					
Operations					
Merchandise purchases	€1 250	€2 500	€6 000	€10 000	€19 750
Gross wages and payroll	5 760	5 760	5 760	5 760	23 040
Advertising	1 000	1 000	1 000	1 000	4 000
Rent	1 500	1 500	1 500	1 500	6 000
Other expenses	1 000	1 000	1 000	1 000	4 000
Operations total	€10 510	€11 760	€15 260	€19 260	€56 790
Financing and investments					
Capital expenditures	€10 000	–	–	–	€10 000
Start-up costs	500	–	–	–	500
Withdrawals by owner	–	–	–	–	–
Total cash payments	€21 010	€11 760	€15 260	€19 260	€67 290
Ending cash balance	(€18 510)	(€25 270)	(€28 530)	(€27 790)	

maintain a €1000 cash balance if the cash inflows and outflows in the following months look like those for April?

Decision: Assuming that your cash forecast is correct, you should invest €28 790 today. This will cover the €27 790 cash shortfall reflected in the ending cash balance for April while leaving

€1000 in the business. The ending cash balance for April reflects the cumulative cash shortfall over the four-month period because the beginning cash balance for January has been set to zero. You will not have to invest any money after April because the cash inflows exceed the cash outflows in April, and this is not expected to change in the following months.

Before You Go On

1. What are three general reasons that new businesses fail?
2. How do financing considerations affect the choice of organisational form?
3. How does a cash budget help an entrepreneur?

THE ROLE OF THE BUSINESS PLAN

Learning Objective 2

Describe the key components of a business plan and explain what a business plan is used for.

In our discussion of the cash budget, we assumed that any cash required by the business would come from the owner or from a loan. Unfortunately, financing a business is not always so simple. An important tool in financing a young, rapidly growing business – as well as in managing it – is the business plan.

Why Business Plans are Important

Recall from Chapter 15 that the equity capital used by entrepreneurs includes their own money, investments from friends and family, investments by venture capitalists, equity raised by selling shares in the stock market, and so on. Debt financing can also come from a wide variety of sources, including the entrepreneur, a bank, a local individual investor, another business and the sale of debt in the public debt markets, among others.

Ensuring that a young, rapidly growing business has enough cash is a simple matter if the money comes from the entrepreneur. The entrepreneur only has to decide to make the investment. Things are more complicated when the money comes from elsewhere. The entrepreneur must convince potential investors that purchasing debt

or equity in the firm will yield attractive returns. In other words, they must be persuaded that they will be adequately compensated for the risks they bear.

Convincing outsiders to invest in a company can be difficult enough if the business has a well-established track record. Raising money from outsiders can be immensely difficult for a young company. The entrepreneur often begins the process with little more than an idea of where the business is headed and some limited operating results in the form of unaudited and often incomplete financial statements. To overcome the scepticism of outside investors, many entrepreneurs prepare a business plan.

A **business plan** is like a road map for a business. It presents the results from a strategic planning process that focuses on how the business will be developed over time. It describes where the company is going and what steps the company will follow to get there. A well-prepared business plan makes it easier for an entrepreneur to communicate to potential investors precisely what he or she expects the business to look like in the future, how he or she expects to get it to that point, and what returns an investor might expect to receive. The fact that an entrepreneur has prepared such a document also demonstrates to investors that the entrepreneur has carefully thought through the business idea. This is especially important when the business is in a very early stage of development and the entrepreneur must convince investors that he or she is capable of building it.

Business plan

a document that describes the details of how a business will be developed over time

WEB

To learn more about business plans and to see sample plans, visit the planware website at: www.planware.org or the bplans website at: www.bplans.com.

In addition to its usefulness in raising capital, a business plan can help an entrepreneur set the goals and objectives for the company, serve as a benchmark for evaluating and controlling the company's performance and communicate the entrepreneur's ideas to managers, outside directors, customers, suppliers and others. A comprehensively thought-out plan can help a business owner avoid problems and better deal with those that arise. In short, business planning is extremely important to the survival of a small and growing company.

The Key Elements of a Business Plan

The depth and scope of business plans vary widely, but most well-developed business plans include the following:

- An *executive summary*, which summarises the key points made in the report.
- A *company overview*, which describes what the company does and what its comparative advantages are.
- A detailed description of the *products and services* the company will sell, their current state of development or market penetration, competitive advantages, product life cycle and any patents or legal protections that might provide a competitive advantage.
- A *market analysis*, which discusses the markets for the firm's products and highlights the important characteristics of these markets as they relate to the company.
- A discussion of the *marketing and sales* activities that will enable the business to achieve the sales and profits reflected in the financial forecasts.
- A discussion of the *operations* of the business – how the product is (will be) produced and distributed, who the suppliers are and any competitive advantages the business has in this area.
- A discussion of the *management team*, which includes the company's organisational structure and describes the talents and skills of the managers. The discussion of the managers should explain why they are especially well qualified to manage and grow this particular business. This is an especially important part of the business plan when it comes to raising capital. Investors in young businesses invest in the key people as much as in the business idea itself.
- A description of the *ownership* structure, including the types of securities the firm has issued and who owns them. Potential investors use this information when they value the securities they are considering purchasing and to help them understand the incentives that managers and other owners have to make the business a success.
- A discussion of *capital requirements and uses*. This section covers the current capital requirements of the business as well as capital requirements over the next five years and provides a detailed account of how the money will be used.
- Historical *financial results*, when they are available, along with *financial forecasts*. If sufficient historical results are available, this section will also include an analysis of those results using the tools discussed in Chapter 4. The forecasts include a month-by-month cash budget for the next two or three years as well as yearly forecasts of operating results. The cash budget helps the reader understand what the cash inflows and outflows will be and their timing. The yearly results provide an indication of what types of returns might be expected from the business.
- *Appendices* that contain detailed supporting information for the above discussions and analyses.

Before You Go On

1. Why is a business plan important in raising capital for a young company?
2. What else can a business plan be used for?
3. Why is it important to discuss the qualifications of the management team in a business plan?

VALUING A BUSINESS

Learning Objective 3
Explain the three general approaches to valuation and be able to value a business with commonly used business valuation approaches.

Successful decision makers in both small and large firms must understand what determines the value of a business. It is not possible to consistently make investment and operating decisions that create value without knowing how to identify positive NPV projects or how operating decisions affect the value of a firm. This knowledge is also crucial when making financing decisions. In Chapters 16 and 17, we also saw how a firm's value is affected by capital structure and dividend policies. Decision makers must understand business valuation concepts in order to be able to identify the optimal capital structure and dividend policy.

In this section, we discuss fundamental business valuation concepts. You will see that financial analysts apply many of the concepts that have already been discussed in this book when they value a business. The reason is that a business is really just a bundle of related projects and the value of the business equals the total value of this bundle. In other words, the value of a business is determined by the magnitude of the cash flows that it is expected to produce, the timing of those cash flows and the likelihood that the cash flows will be realised.

Fundamental Business Valuation Principles

Before we discuss the specific ways in which businesses are valued, you should be aware of two important valuation principles.

First principle: The value of a business changes over time. Changes in general economic and industry conditions, and decisions made by the managers, all affect the value of the cash flows that a business is expected to generate in the future. For example, changes in interest rates affect the firm's

cost of capital and, therefore, the present value of future cash flows. A change in interest rates can also affect the demand for a firm's products if customers typically finance the purchases of those products with loans, as they often do for big-ticket items such as automobiles and houses. Similarly, competitors enter and exit industries, introduce new products, change prices and other such factors that affect business conditions. These actions affect the value of a business. Finally, the value of a business is affected by managers' investment, operating and financing decisions.

Because the value of a business changes over time, it is important to specify a **valuation date** when valuing a business. Normally, this date is the date on which we do the analysis, but it can be an earlier date in some situations. For example, when companies are sued or when shareholders are involved in a dispute with the tax authorities, the value of the business or its shares as of some date in the past must often be estimated. A shareholder may claim that managers sold shares for less than they were worth at some time in the past, or the tax authorities may claim that the value of shares passed to an heir was greater than claimed when the taxes were filed by the estate of a deceased shareholder. By specifying the valuation date, the person who values a business makes it clear to anyone who uses the value estimate precisely what economic, industry and firm conditions are reflected in that estimate.

> **Valuation date**
>
> the date on which a value estimate applies

Second principle: There is no such thing as *the* value for a business. The value of a business can be different for different investors. To understand why, consider two different investors who are interested in purchasing a business that is for sale. Suppose that one investor is a competitor of the business that is for sale and the other is an individual who just wants to invest some money and plans to let the same management continue to operate the business

BUILDING INTUITION

The Value of a Business is Specific to a Point in Time

The value of a business is affected by general economic and industry conditions as well as the decisions made by managers. All of these factors affect the cash flows that a business is expected to produce in the future and the rate at which those cash flows should be discounted. Since all of these factors change over time, so will the value of the business.

independently. The competitor, who is what we call a *strategic investor*, might be willing to pay a higher price for the business than the other investor, who is what we call a *financial investor*, because the strategic investor might be able to combine the business with his or her current business in a way that reduces costs or increases revenues. The financial investor does not have the potential to benefit from these *synergies*.

The key implication of the idea that the value of a business can vary between investors is that the purpose of a valuation affects the way we do the analysis. If a valuation is being performed to determine what price a particular investor would be willing to pay for a business, the analysis must consider how that investor will operate the business. In the business valuation terminology, we would refer to this as an estimate of the **investment value** of the business to that investor.

> ### Investment value
>
> the value of a business to a specific investor

If, instead of estimating the value of a business to a particular investor, an analyst is trying to estimate the price that a typical investor would pay for a business, he or she would be estimating the **fair market value** of the business. The fair market value of a business is the value of that business to a hypothetical person who is knowledgeable about the business. It does not include the value of *synergies* or the effects of any investor-specific management style. For this reason, the fair

market value can differ considerably from the investment value of a business.

> ### Fair market value
>
> the value of a business to a typical investor

Business Valuation Approaches

There are a wide variety of business valuation methods, but most can be classified into one of three general categories: (1) cost approaches, (2) market approaches and (3) income approaches. Cost, market and income valuation approaches can be used to value a wide range of assets. They do not apply only to business valuation.

For example, the house or apartment building you live in has at some point been valued using a cost, market or income approach – possibly even all three. When the building was insured, the insurance company probably used a cost approach to estimate its replacement cost. The appraiser for the local taxing authority is likely to have used a market approach, in which the estimated value was based on recent prices paid for similar properties in the local property market. Finally, if your house or apartment building was ever evaluated as a potential rental property by an investor, the investor probably used an income approach. In this analysis, the investor estimated the present value of the cash flows that the property would produce if it were rented.

While the ways in which the cost, market and income approaches are used to value a business differ

BUILDING INTUITION

The Value of a Business is Not the Same to All Investors

The value of a business is not the same to all investors because different investors will obtain different benefits from owning a business. For example, the benefits to passive investors will differ from the benefits to investors who are active in the management of the business. Benefits will also differ among active investors because they will have different skill levels, operating preferences and abilities to benefit from synergies.

from the ways they are used to value property, the basic principles are the same. We next describe how these approaches are used to value businesses.

WEB

You can learn more about business valuation and find a wide range of Excel templates that can be used to value businesses and their securities on the website maintained by Aswath Damodaran at:
http://pages.stern.nyu.edu/~adamodar.

Cost Approaches

Two cost approaches that are commonly used to value businesses or their individual assets are the replacement cost and adjusted book value approaches.

Replacement Cost The **replacement cost** of a business is the cost of duplicating the business's assets in their present form as of the valuation date. It thus reflects both the nature and condition of the assets. For example, if one of the assets is a 15-year-old electric wood saw that is in relatively good condition, the replacement cost of this saw equals what it would cost to purchase an identical used saw in the same condition.

Replacement cost

the cost of duplicating the assets of a business in their present form on the valuation date

The replacement cost valuation approach is generally used to value individual assets within a business when they are being insured, but it is rarely used to value an entire business. Since investors are concerned with the value of the cash flows that the business can be expected to generate in the future, they use valuation approaches that reflect the value of these cash flows when deciding how much to pay for firms.

Although the replacement cost approach tends to be more useful for insurance purposes, it can be helpful in conducting a buy-versus-build analysis when managers are thinking about making an acquisition. Before purchasing a business, it usually makes sense to ask if you could build the same business in a way that would result in a greater NPV – in other words, whether it is cheaper to build the business yourself or to buy one that already exists. This sort of comparison can serve as a useful sanity check on whether you might be paying too much for the business.

When using the replacement cost approach in a buy-versus-build analysis, you must be sure to include the cost of all tangible assets, such as property, plant and equipment, and all intangible assets, such as brand names and customer lists. You must also include the cost of hiring the people necessary to run the business and the time that it would take to build the business. The time it would take to build the business is important because it can take a long time to build a business and until the business is up and running it will produce smaller cash flows than a business you might acquire.

Adjusted Book Value   The **adjusted book value** approach involves estimating the market values of the individual assets in a business and adding them up. When this approach is used, the fair market value of each asset is estimated separately and the values are summed to arrive at the total value of the business. As with the replacement cost approach, an adjusted book value analysis should include all tangible and intangible assets, whether they are actually included on the balance sheet or not.

> ### Adjusted book value
>
> the sum of the fair market values of the individual assets in a business

The adjusted book value approach is useful in valuing holding companies whose main assets are publicly traded or other investment securities, but it is generally less applicable to operating businesses. The value of an operating business is usually greater than the sum of the values of its individual assets because the present value of the cash flows expected from the company is greater. The difference between the value of the expected cash flows and that of the assets is referred to as the **going-concern value**.

> ### Going-concern value
>
> the difference between the adjusted book value and the value of a business as a going concern (the present value of the expected cash flows)

The going-concern value reflects the value associated with additional cash flows the business is expected to produce because of the way in which the individual assets are managed as a whole. A lot of different factors determine the going-concern value of a business. For example, one business can have a larger going-concern value than another business because it has a stronger management team that is able to invest in and utilise the business's assets more efficiently. The going-concern value might also be larger because the employees of the company are more skilled or work better together or because the government provides some special benefit to a particular business.

To see how going-concern value might be created, suppose that you just obtained the exclusive right to produce and sell a patented type of specialty brick in the United Kingdom that has been very popular among homebuilders in Europe. Also assume that you expect to be able to satisfy demand for this brick with a single manufacturing plant. No matter where you build this plant, its adjusted book value will be the same, assuming that the assets in the plant, such as kilns, forklifts, conveyer belts and other items, are commonly available and used all over the country. However, the actual value of the right that you have just obtained will depend in part on where you decide to build the plant if transportation costs will be an important component of your overall costs (bricks are heavy and cost a lot to transport). If you build the plant in the middle of the country, it will be worth more than if you build it in one corner of the country because transportation costs will be lower.

Although the adjusted book value approach does not capture the going-concern value associated with a business, it is useful under certain circumstances. We might use this approach: (1) when it is especially difficult to forecast a business's likely cash flows; (2) when we suspect that the going-concern value of the business is negative – in other words, the owners of the business would be better off if the business were simply shut down and its assets were sold off; or (3) if we are explicitly considering liquidation. The adjusted book value approach might also be used as a 'sanity check' when using one of the other valuation approaches. If your value estimate is lower than the adjusted book value when you use another approach, it might indicate that there is an error in your analysis. Of course, if you find no errors, this might also be an indication that you would be better off shutting down the business and liquidating it.

When using the adjusted book value approach to estimate the liquidation value of a business, we must make sure to subtract liquidation-related expenses such as sales commissions, legal and accounting fees, and the cost of dismantling and hauling away the assets. To see how the adjusted book value approach might be used to estimate the liquidation value of a business, consider the following situation. Last year you started a business that prints custom logos on T-shirts for business clients. Unfortunately, the economy went into a recession shortly after you started your business and it never got off the ground. You have virtually run out of cash and have decided to shut down the business rather than invest any more money. The current balance sheet of this business is as follows:

Assets:		Liabilities and Equity:	
Cash	€78	Accounts payable	€480
Accounts receivable	2368	Loan balance	2000
T-shirt inventory	1600	Shareholders' equity	2366
Printing press	800		
Total assets	€4846	Total liabilities & equity	€4846

What is the liquidation value of your ownership interest in this business?

The first step in estimating the liquidation value of the business is to estimate how much value will be realised from the individual assets after accounting for liquidation costs. Let us begin with the cash. Since the objective of the liquidation process is to convert all assets into cash, the liquidation value of any cash on the balance sheet, €78 in this example, simply equals its face value. Assuming that your customers are reputable business people, you expect to collect all of the receivables with little effort. However, since you will incur some expenses in the collection process, you estimate that you will actually receive a net amount that equals 95% of the face value of the receivables. A call to your T-shirt supplier reveals that you can return unused inventory to the supplier and receive an 80% refund. You do not believe that anyone else will pay you more for the T-shirts. Finally, a supplier of T-shirt printing equipment has offered to pay you €600, or 75% of the book value, for your printing press.

With this information, you estimate the liquidation value of the assets to be €4208:

Cash	€ 78	×	100%	=	€ 78
Accounts receivable	2368	×	95%	=	2250
T-shirt inventory	1600	×	80%	=	1280
Printing press	800	×	75%	=	600
Total assets	€4846				€4208

Therefore, after paying your accounts payable and the loan, your equity ownership interest has a liquidation value of €4208 − €480 − €2000 = €1728.

Learning by Doing Application 18.1

Using the Adjusted Book Valuation Approach

Problem: You are considering purchasing a company that manufactures specialised components for recreational vehicles. The company sells the components to the companies that manufacture the vehicles. As part of your analysis of this opportunity, you decide to estimate the liquidation value of the company. Management has provided you with the following information on the assets of the company. All values are in thousands of euros.

Cash	€ 444
Accounts receivable	739
Inventories	1 436
Net PP&E	8 463
Total assets	€11 082

Management has also told you that you can reasonably expect to collect 93% of the receivables, that the inventory could be sold to realise 85% of its book value, and that the sale of the property, plant and equipment would yield €6100. What is the liquidation value of this company?

Approach: Calculate the value that will be realised for each of the individual assets and sum those values to obtain the liquidation value of the company.

Solution: The liquidation value is:

Cash	€ 444 × 100% = € 444
Accounts receivable	739 × 93% = 687
Inventories	1 436 × 85% = 1 221
Net PP&E	8 463 6 100
Total assets	€11 082 €8 452

You could expect to realise €8.452 million from the liquidation of this company if there were no liquidation expenses that are not accounted for in these numbers.

Market Approaches

Two market approaches are commonly used in business valuation. The first approach, which is often called **multiples analysis,** uses share price or other value multiples that are observed for similar public companies to estimate the value of a company or its equity. The second approach, often called **transactions analysis,** uses information from transactions involving the purchase of a similar business to estimate the value of a company or its shares.

Market approaches reflect prices that have actually been paid for a company's shares or for the entire company. While it is not always obvious why people pay a particular price, the information on what they pay can yield useful insights into how those people view the prospects for similar businesses. Market approaches can also provide useful benchmarks against which valuations based on other methodologies can be compared.

> **Multiples analysis**
>
> a valuation approach that uses the share price or other value multiples for public companies to estimate the value of another company's shares or its entire business

---

> **Transactions analysis**
>
> a valuation approach that uses transactions data from the sale of businesses to estimate the value of another company's shares or its entire business

---

Multiples Analysis   Multiples analysis is widely used in business valuation. This approach involves: (1) identifying publicly traded companies engaged in business activities that are similar to those of the company being analysed and (2) using the prices at which shares of those *comparables* are trading, along with accounting data, to estimate the value of the company of interest. Multiples analysis can be especially useful in estimating the price at which the shares of a private company can be sold. This approach is often used to help identify the price at which shares can be sold when a company does its initial public offering (IPO), or when some or all of its shares are being sold privately to investors.

Price/earnings (*P/E*) and price/revenue multiples (ratios) are commonly used to estimate directly the value of the shares in a company. These ratios divide a measure of share price by an accounting measure of profits and revenue, respectively. Analysts typically estimate one of these multiples using data from comparable public companies and then they use an average or, if one comparable is clearly better than the others, a multiple from a single comparable company to estimate the value of the company of interest.

Suppose, for example, that we want to estimate the value of the equity of a private department store chain that we are considering purchasing. The chain earned net income of €3.65 million last year. We have identified a publicly traded company that is very similar to the company we are valuing and notice in the *Wall Street Journal Europe* that the *P/E* ratio for its ordinary shares is 17.63. From this information, we can estimate that the market value of the equity (V_E) of the company that we are considering purchasing is:

$$V_E = \left(\frac{P}{E}\right)_{\text{Comparable}} \times \text{Net income}_{\text{Company being valued}}$$
$$= 17.63 \times €3.65 \text{ million}$$
$$= €64.35 \text{ million}$$

It is important to recognise that because the shares of the comparable companies are publicly traded, and shares that are bought and sold in public markets are more liquid than shares that are not publicly traded, we must be careful when using multiples analysis to value a private company. The prices paid for shares that are not publicly traded can be considerably less than the prices paid for public shares. While the size of this *marketability discount* depends on many factors, such as the fraction of the total shares being bought or sold, it can amount to well more than 30% in some instances.[3]

A multiples analysis is conceptually straightforward but can be difficult in a real situation. One complicating factor is that truly comparable public companies are difficult to find. The ideal comparable company would match the company being valued on many dimensions. It would sell the same products, compete in the same markets, be of similar size, have similar revenue growth prospects, have similar profit margins and have similar management quality, among other characteristics. In addition, if an equity ratio (such as price/earnings or price/revenue) is being used, the comparable should have a similar capital structure because, all else being equal, capital structure can have a dramatic impact on those ratios.

The importance of identifying comparable companies that are similar to the company being analysed can be illustrated by considering the characteristics that determine a company's price/earnings multiple. Recall from Chapters 9 and 13 that the constant-growth dividend model, Equation (9.4), can be used to estimate the value of a share. Using the notation from Chapter 13, this model can be written as:

$$P_0 = \frac{D_1}{k_{os} - g}$$

where P_0 is the current share price, D_1 is the dividend that is expected next year, k_{os} is the required return on the ordinary shares and g is the expected growth rate in dividends. If we recognise that dividends equal the fraction of earnings distributed to the shareholders times the earnings of the firm, we can rewrite Equation (9.4) as:

$$P_0 = \frac{E_1 b}{k_{os} - g}$$

where E_1 is the earnings per share expected next year and b is the fraction of the firm's earnings that is paid out as dividends. Finally, we can rearrange this equation to obtain the price/earnings multiple:

$$\frac{P_0}{E_1} = \frac{b}{k_{os} - g} \qquad (18.1)$$

This equation tells us that the *P/E* multiple can be thought of as equal to the payout ratio over k_{os} minus g.[4]

By focusing on the variables that drive the *P/E* multiple in this simple framework, we can see the importance of identifying comparable companies that are as similar to the company of interest as possible. For example, consider what company characteristics determine k_{os}. The Capital Asset Pricing Model (CAPM) tells us that k_{os} depends on beta, which is a measure of the systematic risk associated with a company's share price. Since this systematic risk is closely related to the volatility of the earnings of the company, our discussion of total risk in Chapter 16 (see the discussion of Exhibit 16.3) suggests that the cost of equity depends on both business and financial risk. In other words, it depends on things such as the products the company sells, the markets it sells them in, its profit margins, and its operating and financial leverage. The growth rate of dividends, *g*, is determined by the same factors that affect k_{os}. This means that if we cannot identify a comparable company that is similar to the company of interest in both its business and financial characteristics, the *P/E* multiple we obtain for the comparable company will not be a good measure for our analysis.

Because *P/E* ratios are sensitive to leverage, many analysts use ratios that divide the total value of a company's equity plus its debt by an accounting measure of cash flows available to all providers of capital (debt and equity). These ratios provide a direct measure of the total value of a company's equity plus its debt, which is known as its **enterprise value**.[5] The total value of the firm was written in Equation (16.1) as $V_{Firm} = V_{Debt} + V_{Equity}$. In the interest of brevity, we will write it in this chapter as:

$$V_F = V_D + V_E$$

where V_F is the value of the firm, V_D is the value of the debt and V_E is the value of the equity. Multiples that are based on the total value of the firm are known as enterprise multiples. Examples include enterprise value/revenue and enterprise value/EBITDA.

> ### Enterprise value
>
> the value of a company's equity plus the value of its debt; also the present value of the total cash flows the company's assets are expected to generate in the future

To see how an enterprise multiple can be used to estimate the total value of a firm, let us return to the example in which we were valuing the department store chain. Assume that, in addition to the *P/E* ratio analysis, we want to estimate the enterprise value of the business using an enterprise value/EBITDA ratio. We have estimated that EBITDA last year was €8.67 million for the department store chain we are valuing. In the *Wall Street Journal Europe*, we find that the current price of the comparable company's shares is €31.25 and, from the balance sheet in the annual report, we observe that the comparable company has 3.67 million shares outstanding. We also estimate that the value of the comparable company's outstanding debt is €19.46 million, and we note that EBITDA for this company was €14.35 million last year. Using this information, we can calculate the enterprise value/EBITDA ratio as follows:

$$\text{Enterprise value} = V_D + V_E$$
$$= €19.46 \text{ million}$$
$$+ (€31.25 \times 3.67 \text{ million})$$
$$= €134.15 \text{ million}$$
$$\left(\frac{\text{Enterprise value}}{\text{EBITDA}}\right)_{Comparable} = \frac{€134.15}{€14.35} = 9.35$$

and we can estimate the enterprise value for the company we are valuing as:

$$V_F = \left(\frac{\text{Enterprise value}}{\text{EBITDA}}\right)_{Comparable} \times \text{EBITDA}_{\text{Company being valued}}$$
$$= 9.35 \times €8.67 \text{ million}$$
$$= €81.06 \text{ million}$$

Learning by Doing Application 18.2

Using Multiples Analysis

Problem: In addition to performing the liquidation analysis in Learning by Doing Application 18.1, you have decided to estimate the enterprise value of the company that manufactures specialised components for recreational vehicles. You have collected the following information for a comparable company and for the company you are valuing:

Comparable company	Company you are valuing
Share price = €10.62	Value of debt = €1.25 million
Number of shares outstanding = 9.55 million	EBITDA last year = €2.37 million
Value of outstanding debt = €11.67 million	Net income last year = €0.45 million
EBITDA last year = €10.85 million	
Net income last year = €2.67 million	

Estimate the enterprise value of the company you are valuing using the *P/E* and enterprise value/EBITDA multiples.

Approach: First, calculate the *P/E* and enterprise value/EBITDA multiples for the comparable company. Next, use these multiples to estimate the value of the company you are valuing. Multiply the *P/E* multiple for the comparable company by the net income of the company you are valuing to estimate the equity value. Add this equity value to the value of the outstanding debt to obtain an estimate of the enterprise value. Multiply the enterprise value/EBITDA multiple for

the comparable company by the EBITDA for the company you are valuing to obtain a direct estimate of the enterprise value.

Solution: The *P/E* and enterprise value/EBITDA multiples for the comparable company are:

$$\left(\frac{P}{E}\right)_{Comparable} = \left(\frac{Share\ price}{Earnings\ per\ share}\right)_{Comparable}$$

$$= \frac{€10.62}{€2.67/9.55\ million\ shares} = 38.0$$

$$\frac{Enterprise\ value}{EBITDA_{Comparable}} = \frac{V_D + V_E}{EBITDA_{Comparable}}$$

$$= \frac{€11.67 + (€10.62 \times 9.55\ million\ shares)}{€10.85}$$

$$= 10.42$$

Using the *P/E* multiple, we calculate the value of the equity as:

$$V_E = \left(\frac{P}{E}\right)_{Comparable} \times Net\ income_{Company\ being\ valued}$$

$$= 38.0 \times €0.45\ million$$

$$= €17.1\ million$$

which suggests an enterprise value of:

$$V_F = V_D + V_E = €1.25\ million + €17.1\ million$$
$$= €18.35\ million$$

Using the enterprise/EBITDA multiple, we estimate the enterprise value to be:

$$V_F = \left(\frac{Enterprise\ value}{EBITDA}\right)_{Comparable} \times EBITDA_{Company\ being\ valued}$$

$$= 10.42 \times €2.37\ million$$

$$= €24.70\ million$$

Whenever we use multiples analysis, we must remember that we are estimating the *fair market value* of a company's equity or its enterprise value and that this value is based on transactions involving small ownership interests. The transaction prices that we observe in the stock market are typically based on trades that involve unknown investors buying small numbers of shares that do not give them the ability to control the business. In other words, a multiples analysis does not provide an estimate of *investment value* because the identities of the buyers are not known. This means that value estimates based on multiples analysis do not reflect the synergies that might be realised by combining the company with another business. These estimates also do not include the value associated with being able to *control* a business, an important consideration that we discuss in more detail later.

When performing a multiples analysis, it is also important to make sure that the numerator and the denominator of the ratio we are using are consistent with each other. In other words, if the share price is in the numerator, some measure of cash flow to equity must be in the denominator. If enterprise value is in the numerator, a measure of total cash flows from the entire business must be in the denominator.

The exception to this rule is the price/revenue ratio. This ratio can be useful in valuing the shares of a relatively young company that is not yet generating profits. Shares in very young companies are often bought and sold based on multiples of their revenue. Implicit in those multiples are expectations about future margins, as well as growth in revenue. By using price to revenue, the analyst is effectively assuming that, over time, the company being analysed will have profit margins similar to those that are anticipated by the market in pricing the publicly traded comparables.

Another important point to keep in mind when doing multiples analysis is that the data used to compute the multiple for the comparable company should include the share price as of the valuation date and that accounting data for the two companies should be from the same period. Since any value estimate is specific to a particular date, we must be sure to use multiples for the appropriate point in time. If we use accounting data from the past 12 months to estimate the ratio for a comparable company, for example, we must use accounting data from the same 12-month period to calculate the value of the company of interest.

Transactions Analysis   The information used in a transactions analysis is typically obtained from public companies that have acquired other companies or from services that collect and sell this information. The information is used to compute the same types of multiples that are used in a multiples analysis, and these multiples are used in the same way to value a company. Transaction data reflect the price that a particular investor paid for an entire company. For this reason, it provides an estimate of the *investment value* to that investor.

Like multiples analysis, transactions analysis can be difficult to use in practice, although the reasons for the difficulty are different. One problem is that transactions data are not typically as reliable as the data available for multiples analysis, especially when the transactions involve private companies. For example, the available data on transactions might include revenues of the private company but not data on its profitability. The data might include the net income but not enough information to estimate cash flows. This can make it difficult to compute some of the key ratios.

In addition, unlike stock market transactions, transactions involving the purchase or sale of an entire business occur relatively infrequently. This means that the data available for a transactions analysis often include only transactions that occurred months or even years earlier. Since the value of a business is specific to a particular point in time, the price that was paid for a business becomes less useful as an indicator of what the business is worth as time passes after the sale.

Finally, the terms of the transactions can be difficult to assess. While the *P/E* multiple for a publicly traded company is an indication of the price that might be obtained in a cash transaction, transactions involving the sale of an entire company often involve some combination of cash, debt or equity payments. A whole package of such securities, some of which can be difficult to value, could be included in the reported transaction price and this may not be apparent to the analyst. The value estimates for those securities and claims can also be distorted if the buyer or seller has reason to prefer reporting a higher or lower price.

Income Approaches

At the beginning of this section, we said that the value of a business is determined by the magnitude of the cash flows that it is expected to produce, the timing of those cash flows and the likelihood that the cash flows will be realised. The cost and market approaches are useful for estimating this value in certain situations – such as in doing a buy-versus-build analysis, estimating the liquidation value of a firm or when good comparable firms or transactions are available. The most direct approaches for estimating the value of the cash flows a business is expected to produce, however, are the income approaches. Like NPV analysis, these approaches directly estimate the value of those cash flows.

Before we discuss specific income valuation approaches, we should note that the market and income approaches differ in one very important way. Because the market approaches rely on prices that have been paid for companies or their securities, the value estimates that they yield are estimates of *what people are willing to pay*. In contrast, the income approaches provide estimates of the *intrinsic, or true, value* of a company or its securities.

While the market value can equal the intrinsic value, the two values are not necessarily the same. For example, if you are valuing the company you work for, you might have better information about its prospects than do stock market investors. By using an income approach, you would be able to incorporate your superior information directly into the valuation analysis in a way that you would not be able to do with a market approach.

Using Income Approaches   The life of a business is not usually known when it is valued. Whereas a

project might be expected to last a specific number of years, a business can have an indefinite life. This makes it more difficult to use an income approach to value a business than a project. It is difficult enough to forecast cash flows for a relatively short period, such as three or five years, let alone for the indefinite future.

Another complication in business valuation is that businesses often have cash or other assets that are not necessary for operations. These can include cash that was earned in the past but has not been distributed to shareholders and assets that are left over from old projects. We call these **non-operating assets (NOA)**. When we estimate the value of an individual project, we do not have to worry about NOA because there are none. However, when we value a business, NOA are an additional source of value. NOA can be distributed directly to shareholders or sold and the proceeds distributed to shareholders without affecting the cash flows that the operations of the business are expected to generate.

> **Non-operating assets (NOA)**
>
> cash or other assets that are not required to support the operations of a business

In practice, we account for the indefinite life associated with a business and the possibility that it has NOA by estimating the value of the business as the sum of three numbers. This calculation can be represented as follows:

$$V_F = PV(FCF_T) + PV(TV_T) + NOA \quad (18.2)$$

where V_F is the value of the firm, $PV(FCF_T)$ is the present value of the free cash flows (FCF) that the business is expected to produce over the next T years, $PV(TV_T)$ is the present value of all free cash flows after year T, and NOA is the value of all the non-operating assets in the firm. Note that the present value of all free cash flows after year T is generally known as the **terminal value**. Note also that if we only want to calculate the value of the equity, we can do this by first calculating the value of the firm using Equation (18.2) and then subtracting the value of the debt. This follows from the fact that $V_E = V_F - V_D$.

Terminal value

the value of the expected free cash flows beyond the period over which they are explicitly forecast

---

Free Cash Flow from the Firm Approach When using the **free cash flow from the firm (FCFF) approach,** an analyst values the free cash flows that the assets of the firm are expected to produce in the future. The present value of these free cash flows equals the total value of the firm, or its enterprise value.

Free cash flow from the firm (FCFF) approach

an income approach to valuation in which all free cash flows the assets are expected to generate in the future are discounted to estimate the enterprise value

---

The free cash flows used in a FCFF analysis are almost identical to the free cash flows from the left-hand side of the finance market value balance sheet that was illustrated in Exhibit 13.1. The only difference is that when we value a business, we do not include cash necessary to pay short-term liabilities that do not have interest charges associated with them, such as accounts payable and accrued expenses. The costs associated with these non-interest-bearing current liabilities, which are included in the firm's cost of sales and other operating expenses, are subtracted in the calculation of FCFF. Exhibit 18.3 shows precisely what we are referring to when we refer to the value of FCFF.

The most common FCFF approach involves using the weighted-average cost of capital (WACC), which we discussed in Chapter 13, to discount the FCFF. This is often referred to as the WACC valuation method. In this approach, the

total value of the firm (V_F) is computed as the present value of the FCFF, discounted by the firm's WACC:

$$V_F = \sum_{t=0}^{\infty} \frac{\text{FCFF}_t}{(1 + \text{WACC})^t} \qquad (18.3)$$

In this equation, t equals the period when the cash flow is produced.

We compute the FCFF using the same calculation that we used for the free cash flows for a project in Chapter 11. The only differences are: (1) that since business valuation involves valuing all of the projects in the firm, we compute the total cash flows the firm's assets are expected to produce rather than the incremental cash flows from a project and (2) we use the average tax rate instead of the marginal tax rate. The FCFF calculation is shown in Exhibit 18.4. Notice that this calculation is just like the calculation in Exhibit 11.1.

Analysts typically estimate future FCFF by forecasting each of the individual components and then performing the calculation shown in Exhibit 18.5. Next, the resulting FCFF values are discounted back to the present using the WACC, as already mentioned. Recall that the WACC is calculated using Equation (13.7):

$$\text{WACC} = x_{\text{Debt}} k_{\text{Debt pre-tax}}(1 - t) + x_{\text{ps}} k_{\text{ps}} + x_{\text{os}} k_{\text{os}}$$

where $x_{\text{Debt pre-tax}} + x_{\text{ps}} + x_{\text{os}} = 1$ and where $k_{\text{Debt pre-tax}}$, k_{ps} and k_{os} are the pre-tax cost of debt and the after-tax costs of preference shares and ordinary shares, respectively. Also, t is the tax rate that applies to interest deductions, and $x_{\text{Debt pre-tax}}$, x_{ps} and x_{os} are the proportions of the value of the firm that are represented by debt, preference shares and ordinary shares.

When analysts use the WACC approach to value a business, they must make an assumption about how the firm's operations will be financed in the future. For example, the financing might be 80% equity and 20% debt. Or it might be 30% equity and 70% debt. These are very important assumptions because, as we saw in Chapter 16 (see Exhibit 16.8), the capital structure choice affects the value of the firm. The FCFF calculation is not affected by the firm's capital structure, but from

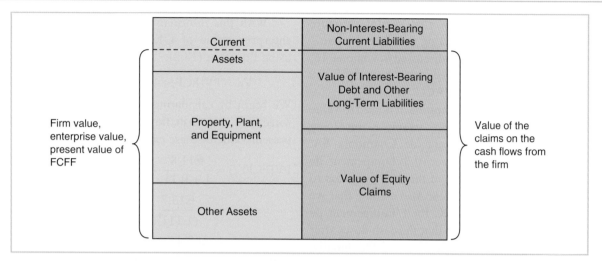

Exhibit 18.4: The Market Balance Sheet and the Value of the Firm The value of a firm (enterprise value) equals the present value of the future free cash flows from the firm (FCFF). Since the owners of the interest-bearing debt and other long-term liabilities and the stockholders, collectively, have the right to receive all of the FCFF, the total value of those claims equals the value of the firm.

EXHIBIT 18.5

THE FCFF CALCULATION

Explanation	Calculation	Formula
The firm's cash income, excluding interest expense	Revenue	Revenue
	−Cash operating expenses	−Op Ex
	Earnings before interest, taxes, depreciation and amortisation	EBITDA
	−Depreciation and amortisation	−D&A
	Operating profit	EBIT
	×(1 − Firm's average tax rate)	×(1 − t)
	Net operating profit after tax	NOPAT
Adjustments for the impact of depreciation and amortisation and investments on FCFF.	+Depreciation and amortisation	+D&A
	Cash flow from operations	CF Opns
	−Capital expenditures	−Cap Exp
	−Additions to working capital	−Add WC
	Free cash flow from the firm	FCF

Free cash flows from the firm (FCFF) are calculated in the same way as the incremental after-tax free cash flows (FCF) that are expected from a project. The only differences between the FCFF calculation and the FCF calculation, which is illustrated in Exhibit 11.1, are that in the FCFF calculation (1) we use *total* cash flows rather than *incremental* cash flows and (2) we use the *average* tax rate instead of the *marginal* tax rate when we are valuing a company that is operating independently of any other company.

Equation (18.3) we know that capital structure affects firm value by affecting the discount rate – the WACC. In fact, as we discussed in Chapter 16, the optimal capital structure for a business is the one that minimises the WACC.

To see how the FCFF approach is used to value a business, consider an example involving L'Équipement de Montagne de Chamonix SA. Assume that we have forecast L'Équipement de Montagne's FCFF in each of the next five years to be as shown in Exhibit 18.6. Also assume that we have estimated the WACC for L'Équipement de Montagne to be 11% and that the cash flows after year 5 will grow at an annual rate of 3%. Finally, we observe that L'Équipement de Montagne has excess cash of €14.68 million but no other NOA.

With this information, we can calculate the enterprise value of L'Équipement de Montagne using Equation (18.2):

$$V_F = PV(FCF_T) + PV(TV_T) + NOA$$

We begin by calculating the present value of the forecasted free cash flows in Exhibit 18.6. The present value of these cash flows is:

$$PV(FCFF_5) = \frac{€11.8}{1+0.11} + \frac{€13.1}{(1.11)^2} + \frac{€13.4}{(1.11)^3}$$
$$+ \frac{€13.7}{(1.11)^4} + \frac{€14.1}{(1.11)^5}$$
$$= €48.45 \text{ million}$$

In this example, we prepared cash flow forecasts for five years. The length of the period for which detailed

EXHIBIT 18.6

FCFF CALCULATION FOR L'ÉQUIPEMENT DE MONTAGNE DE CHAMONIX SA (€ MILLIONS)

	Year				
	1	2	3	4	5
Revenue	€100.0	€106.0	€112.4	€119.1	€126.2
– Cash operating expenses	70.0	74.2	78.7	83.4	88.4
– Depreciation and amortisation	8.0	8.3	8.5	8.8	9.0
Operating profit	€22.0	€23.5	€25.2	€26.9	€28.9
– Taxes	7.7	8.2	8.8	9.4	10.1
Net operating profits after tax	€14.3	€15.3	€16.4	€17.5	€18.8
+ Depreciation and amortisation	8.0	8.3	8.5	8.8	9.0
Cash flow from operations	€22.3	€23.6	€24.9	€26.3	€27.8
– Capital expenditures	10.0	10.0	11.0	12.0	13.0
– Additions to working capital	0.5	0.5	0.5	0.6	0.7
Free cash flow from the firm	€11.8	€13.1	€13.4	€13.7	€14.1

This exhibit presents forecasts of free cash flow from the firm (FCFF) for L'Équipement de Montagne de Chamonix SA for each of the next five years.

projections are produced depends on the level of uncertainty surrounding the future of the business. In general, we want to forecast the cash flows out to a point in time where we expect the business to reach a steady-state growth rate. We can then estimate the cash flows for the remainder of the business's life (the terminal value) by (1) calculating the present value of all cash flows after the final year of the detailed forecast using the formula for a growing perpetuity and (2) discounting this value to the present. For L'Équipement de Montagne, these calculations are as follows:

$$TV_5 = \frac{FCFF_5(1+g)}{WACC - g} = \frac{€14.1 \times (1+0.03)}{0.11 - 0.03}$$

$$= €181.54 \text{ million}$$

and:

$$PV(TV_5) = \frac{TV_5}{(1+WACC)^5} = \frac{€181.54}{(1+0.11)^5}$$

$$= €107.74 \text{ million}$$

Finally, we can use Equation (18.2) to calculate the total value of L'Équipement de Montagne de Chamonix SA:

$$V_F = PV(FCF_T) + PV(TV_T) + NOA$$

$$= €48.45 + €107.74 + €14.68$$

$$= €170.87 \text{ million}$$

Using the FCFF Income Approach

Problem: You have decided to use the FCFF income approach to refine your valuation of the business that manufactures components for recreational vehicles. You expect cash flows to grow very rapidly during the next five years and to level off after that. Based on this, you forecast the cash flows for each of the next five years to be:

			Year		
	1	2	3	4	5
FCFF (€ millions)	−€0.284	€0.108	€0.998	€2.110	€2.857

You expect cash flows to be constant after year 5. There are no NOA in this firm. If the appropriate WACC is 9%, what is the enterprise value of this business? What is the value of the equity if the value of the debt equals €1.25 million?

Approach: First calculate the total present value of the individual FCFF that you have forecast by discounting them to year 0 using the WACC and summing them up. Next, calculate the terminal value, assuming no growth in the cash flows after year 5, and discount this value to year 0. The enterprise value equals the present value of the individual cash flows plus the present value of the terminal value. The value of the equity can then be calculated by subtracting the value of the debt.

Solution: The present value of the cash flows in the first five years is:

$$PV(FCFF_5) = \frac{-€0.284}{1+0.09} + \frac{€0.108}{(1+0.09)^2}$$

$$+ \frac{€0.998}{(1+0.09)^3} + \frac{€2.110}{(1+0.09)^4}$$

$$+ \frac{€2.857}{(1+0.09)^5}$$

$$= €3.95 \text{ million}$$

The present value of the terminal value is:

$$PV(TV_5) = \frac{TV_5}{(1+WACC)^5}$$
$$= \frac{€2.857/(0.09-0)}{(1+0.09)^5}$$
$$= €20.63 \text{ million}$$

Therefore, the total enterprise value is:

$$V_F = PV(FCF_T) + PV(TV_T) + NOA$$
$$= €3.95 + €20.63 + €0 = €24.58 \text{ million}$$

and the value of the equity equals €24.58 million − €1.25 million = €23.33 million.

Free Cash Flow to Equity Approach   The **free cash flow to equity (FCFE) approach** is very similar to the FCFF approach. However, instead of valuing the total cash flows the assets of the business are expected to generate, we value only the portion of the cash flows that are available for distribution to shareholders. To see how the FCFF and FCFE approaches are related, ask yourself the following question: If you wanted to value only the equity claims, how would you adjust the cash flows that are used in the FCFF approach? The answer is that you would simply strip out the cash flows to or from the people who lend money to the firm. Since the value of the firm equals the value of the debt plus the value of the equity, stripping out the cash flows to or from the lenders leaves the cash flows available to shareholders.

> **Free cash flow to equity (FCFE) approach**
>
> an income approach to valuation in which all cash flows that are expected to be available for distribution to shareholders in the future are discounted to estimate the value of the equity

Exhibit 18.7 shows how FCFE is calculated. Notice that this calculation includes three cash flows that are not in the FCFF calculation. One is the interest expense, which is a cash flow to the lenders. The others are the cash flows associated with the repayment of debt principal and the

proceeds from new debt issues. As mentioned, then, this approach takes the total cash flows from the business and removes any cash flows to or from lenders, leaving cash flows available to the shareholders.

Because cash flows available to shareholders are residual cash flows, they are riskier than the total cash flows from the firm (assuming the firm has any debt). Consequently, in using the FCFE valuation approach, the cost of equity (k_E) is used to discount the cash flows:

$$V_E = \sum_{t=0}^{\infty} \frac{FCFE_t}{(1+k_E)^t} \qquad (18.4)$$

Other than the difference in the way that the cash flows are calculated, the procedure for estimating the value of a firm's equity using the FCFE approach is the same as that used to estimate the total value of the firm using the FCFF approach.

Dividend Discount Model Approach   The **dividend discount model (DDM) approach** is very similar to the FCFE approach. In this approach, we estimate the value of equity directly by discounting cash flows to shareholders. However, there is a subtle difference. The DDM approach values the stream of cash flows that shareholders *expect to receive* through dividend payments. In contrast, the FCFE approach values cash flows that are *available for distribution* to shareholders. The firm may or may not be expected to distribute all available cash flows in any particular year.

EXHIBIT 18.7

THE FCFE CALCULATION

Explanation	Calculation	Formula
The firm's cash income	Revenue	Revenue
	−Cash operating expenses	−Op Ex
	Earnings before interest, taxes, depreciation and amortisation	EBITDA
	−Depreciation and amortisation	−D&A
	Operating profit	EBIT
	−Interest	−Int
	Earnings before tax	EBT
		$\times(1-t)$
	Net income (profit) after tax	NI
Adjustments for the impact of depreciation and amortisation and investments on FCFF and debt repayments and new issues	+Depreciation and amortisation	+D&A
	Cash flow from operations	CF Opns
	−Capital expenditures	−Cap Exp
	−Additions to working capital	−Add WC
	−Repayment of debt principal	−Debt Pmt
	+Proceeds from new debt issues	+Debt Proc
	Free cash flow to equity	FCFE

Free cash flow to equity (FCFE) equals free cash flow from the firm (FCFF) less any net cash outflows to debt holders. In the FCFE calculation, we subtract the interest and principal payments to the debt holders and add any proceeds from the sale of new debt.

Dividend discount model (DDM) approach

an income approach to valuation in which all dividends that are expected to be distributed to shareholders in the future are discounted to estimate the value of the equity

The constant-growth dividend model, Equation (9.4), is an example of a DDM:

$$P_0 = \frac{D_1}{k_{os} - g}$$

Notice that in this model the price of a share is computed by discounting future dividends.

Since the constant-growth model assumes that the firm currently pays dividends and that these dividends will increase at a constant rate forever, this approach is really useful for only a limited number of mature firms that pay dividends. More often, use of the DDM approach involves discounting dividends that either will not begin until some point in the future or that are currently growing at a high rate that is not sustainable in the long run. In these cases, an approach such as that illustrated for the FCFF approach above must be used. The expected dividends must be individually discounted for some period, and then a terminal value must be estimated once the growth rate in dividends stabilises at some level that is sustainable over the long run. This is the mixed (supernormal) growth dividend model from Chapter 9.

Decision-Making Example 18.2

Choosing an Appropriate Valuation Approach

Situation: You have decided to make an offer for the recreational vehicle manufacturing business that you have been evaluating in Learning by Doing Applications 18.1, 18.2 and 18.3. Your analysis had yielded the following estimates:

Liquidation value	€ 8.45 million
Value from multiples analysis	
P/E multiple	€18.35 million
Enterprise/EBITDA multiple	€24.70 million
FCFF value	€24.58 million

The seller of the company is asking for €18 million. Is this price reasonable?

Decision: The price appears to be reasonable. It is almost €10 million greater than the liquidation value, but this value does not include the going-concern value associated with the business. The other three estimates, which all reflect the company's going-concern value, suggest that the fair market value of the business is greater than the seller's asking price.

Before You Go On

1. Why is it important to specify a valuation date when you value a business?
2. What is the difference between investment value and fair market value?
3. What are the two market approaches that can be used to value a business and how do they differ?
4. What is a non-operating asset and how are such assets accounted for in business valuation?
5. What are three income approaches used to value a business?
6. What is the difference between FCFE and dividends?

IMPORTANT ISSUES IN VALUATION

Learning Objective 4

Explain how valuations can differ between public and private companies and between young and mature companies, and discuss the importance of control and key person considerations in valuation.

We conclude this chapter by discussing some important issues in valuing businesses. Whether a business is public or private, whether it is young or old, and whether a minority interest or a controlling interest is involved can make a difference in valuation. In addition, we may have to take account of the role of key employees.

Public versus Private Companies

The same valuation approaches are used to value both public and private companies. However, there are some important differences, which we consider next.

Financial Statements

While financial statements of public companies must be audited and filed with the regulator, there is no requirement that the financial statements of private companies be audited. As a result, the completeness and reliability of financial statements for private companies vary considerably. Some private companies have complete, audited financial statements, whereas others have incomplete financial statements that are not prepared in accordance with the generally accepted accounting principles (GAAP) discussed in Chapter 3. Incomplete and unreliable financial statements can complicate the process of valuing a private business, making it more difficult to accurately assess its value.

Financial statements of private companies also differ from those of public companies in some of the expense accounts. Owners of private businesses have incentives to pass some of their personal expenses through the business because this enables them to deduct the expenses on their taxes. Examples might include the owner's car, 'business' trips to Hawaii or South America, the company condominium in Paris, or the box at the local football stadium. While there may be legitimate reasons for a business to incur expenses such as these – for example, entertaining important customers in the box – there are often more such expenses in private companies.

Owners of private companies can also have incentives to pay themselves more than it would cost to hire someone to do their job. If the income from the company is taxed before it is distributed to the owners, this *excess compensation* reduces the taxes that the company must pay. Compensation payments are deductible for the company and are therefore only taxed as income to the owner. If, instead of paying themselves excess compensation, owners distributed the money as dividends, it would be taxed twice – once as income to the company and a second time as income to the owner. In addition to having incentives to pay themselves excess compensation, owners of private companies often employ family members at wages that are above what would ordinarily be paid for the services they provide. When valuing a private company, analysts typically adjust for excess compensation to the owner and family members by estimating what it would cost to hire other people to perform the services and, using this, change the actual expense reported in the income statement accordingly.

Marketability

In the discussion of multiples analysis, we mentioned that the prices paid for shares in a company whose shares are not publicly traded can be considerably less than the prices paid for publicly traded shares of a similar company. One reason is that shareholders of a public firm can generally sell their shares by simply going online or calling a broker and paying a small fee. In contrast, a shareholder in a private firm may have to spend considerable resources (both money and time) to sell his or her shares. Now suppose that an investor is offered the opportunity to buy identical equity claims to the cash flows of a public and a private firm (that is, the cash flows have the same size, timing and risk). The investor is not going to require the same rate of return for both investments. Because of the higher transaction costs associated with the shares of the private firm, the investor will not be willing to pay as much for these shares (and will therefore expect a higher return) as for the publicly traded shares. This must be taken into account in estimating the value of any claim to the cash flows of a firm. As we mentioned earlier, differences in marketability can result in discounts of 30% or more for the shares of private companies. Where analysts are able to estimate the appropriate size of such a discount, they deduct the discount directly from the final value estimate that is obtained using the methods described in the preceding section.

Young (Rapidly Growing) versus Mature Companies

Another important issue that arises in business valuation concerns the fact that young, rapidly growing companies tend to be more difficult to value than mature, stable companies. Both entrepreneurs and investors in new businesses, such as venture capitalists, must deal with these difficulties when young companies seek financing. One factor that makes it more difficult to value a young company is that there is less reliable historical information available. A company may have only two or three years of historical financial records and those records may reflect the company at a different stage in its development.

In addition, the future of a young, rapidly growing company is often less certain than that of a mature company because much of the young company's future growth depends on investment, operating and financing decisions that have not yet been made. This makes it much more complicated to identify appropriate comparable companies for a multiples or transactions analysis and more difficult to estimate expected cash flows for an income analysis.

Furthermore, many young, rapidly growing companies are not yet profitable. With no profits, it is difficult to use earnings multiples to value the business, leaving price/revenue or enterprise value/revenue multiples as the only viable alternatives for a multiples analysis. When analysts use these multiples, they are indirectly assuming that the business they are valuing will become as profitable (specifically, have the same profit margins) as the public companies that were used to estimate the multiples and that the risks of the business will also be similar. These can be very heroic assumptions when the company being valued is only a couple of years old.

Finally, many young companies invest a considerable amount of money in order to grow. This can make it very difficult to use an income valuation approach. The cash flows will be negative until the business becomes profitable and its profits exceed its investment expenditures. Since it can take several years for this to happen, expected cash flows are typically negative for several years. This means that positive cash flows, which represent the value that the business is expected to produce for its owners, are further in the future and are therefore less certain. The bottom line is that this increases the overall level of uncertainty associated with an income-based valuation.

Controlling Interest versus Minority Interest

Another important issue that we must consider when we value a business is whether we are valuing a controlling ownership interest or a minority interest. The number of shares required for an investor to exercise control varies depending on the ownership structure of the company. For example, a shareholder with just 20%, or possibly even less, of the total votes in a public company can effectively control that company if there are no other large shareholders. Even if there are other large shareholders, that investor can control the public company if friendly shareholders provide enough

additional votes. In private companies, which tend to have relatively few shareholders, a shareholder must generally control 50% of the shares, either directly or indirectly through friendly shareholders, to control the firm. A shareholder who has such control can run the business as he or she wants. He or she can select the board of directors, choose the business strategy, hire and fire managers and approve or disapprove any investment, operating or financing decisions.

Whether a controlling ownership interest is being sold has important implications for a valuation analysis. Recall that in the discussion of multiples analysis we noted that a multiples analysis does not reflect the value associated with being able to control a business. Thus, when we are using multiples computed using public stock market prices to estimate the value of a controlling interest, we must make adjustments to reflect the benefits of control. Similarly, when we use an income approach to value a business, the cash flow forecasts and discount rate assumptions we use will differ depending on whether we are valuing a *minority* or a *controlling* ownership interest.

Let us consider an example of how these differences arise when the income approach is used. Suppose we are valuing 100 shares of Nokia. Since owning 100 shares of Nokia will not enable us to exercise any control, the expected cash flows that we should discount simply reflect the cash flows that we can expect Nokia to generate under its current management (assuming we know of no imminent management changes). In contrast, if we are valuing a controlling interest in Nokia shares for a potential buyer, we would discount the cash flows that Nokia would be expected to generate if it were under the control of that buyer.

It is also important to note that the market rates of return that we use to calculate the cost of equity with the Capital Asset Pricing Model (CAPM) discussed in Chapter 7 are based on small share transactions. If having control would enable an investor to better manage the systematic risk associated with a business, a discount rate based on small transactions would be higher than a discount rate estimated from a transaction that involves a controlling position. Therefore, a discount rate based on CAPM might be too high for a valuation that involves a controlling position.

Unfortunately, while the discount rate we estimate using CAPM might be too high when we value a controlling interest, the CAPM theory provides us with no insights concerning how we might adjust that rate. As a result, analysts typically adjust for the effects of an incorrect discount rate (as well as for any possible cash flows that are not reflected in an income-based valuation) by adding a **control premium**. For instance, if the value of a firm's equity is estimated to be €100 million using an income approach, a 20% premium might be added to arrive at a final value of €120 million. Of course, the magnitude of the adjustment depends on the situation.

> ### Control premium
>
> an adjustment that is made to a business value estimate to reflect value associated with control that is not already reflected in the analysis

Key People

If the cash flows that a business is expected to generate depend heavily on the retention of a particular individual or group of individuals, then the analyst must also consider whether it is appropriate to adjust the estimated value of the business for the likelihood that these 'key people' may not remain with the firm as long as expected. An example of a key person might be the CEO of a service firm who has strong personal ties with the major customers. If an analyst believes that those customers might transfer their business to a competitor if the CEO departs, then a **key person discount** may be appropriate. The issue is similar to the one that arises when a firm receives a significant portion of its business from a small number of customers. In either case, it is difficult to forecast the cash flows for the firm.

> ### Key person discount
>
> an adjustment to a business value estimate that is made to reflect the potential loss of value associated with the unexpected departure of a key person

Before You Go On

1. How might financial statements for private companies differ from those for public companies?
2. Why is marketability an important issue in business valuation?
3. What is a key person?

SUMMARY OF LEARNING OBJECTIVES

1. **Explain why the choice of organisational form is important and describe two financial considerations that are especially important in starting a business.**

   The choice of organisational form is important because it affects the returns from a business in a number of ways. For example, it affects the cost of getting started, the life of the business, management's ability to raise capital and grow the business, the control of the business, the ability to attract and retain good managers, the exposure of the investors to liabilities and the taxes that are paid on the earnings of the business.

Two especially important financial considerations are the cash flow break-even point for the business and its overall cash inflows and outflows. The cash flow break-even point represents the level of unit sales that must be achieved in order for the business to break even on a cash flow basis. Entrepreneurs must also understand where money is coming from, where it is going, and how much external financing is likely to be needed and when. The cash budget helps with this understanding.

2. **Describe the key components of a business plan and explain what a business plan is used for.**

The key components of a business plan include the executive summary, a company overview, a description of the company's products and services, a market analysis, a discussion of marketing and sales activities, a discussion of the business's operations, a discussion of the management team, the ownership structure of the firm, capital requirements and uses and financial forecasts.

A business plan helps an entrepreneur set the goals and objectives for a company, serves as a benchmark for evaluating and controlling the company's performance, and helps communicate the entrepreneur's ideas to managers and others (including investors) outside the firm.

3. **Explain the three general approaches to valuation and be able to value a business with commonly used business valuation approaches.**

The three general valuation approaches are (1) cost approaches, (2) market approaches and (3) income approaches. Cost approaches commonly used in business valuation are the replacement cost and adjusted book value approaches. The market approaches are multiples analysis and transactions analysis. Three key income approaches are the free cash flow from the firm, free cash flow to equity and dividend discount approaches. The application of these approaches is discussed.

4. **Explain how valuations can differ between public and private companies and between young and mature companies and discuss the importance of control and key person considerations in valuation.**

Valuations differ between public and private companies for a number of reasons, including (1) the quality of the financial statements and (2) the marketability of the securities being valued. Marketability is important because it affects the price that investors are willing to pay for a security. The less marketable a security, the lower the price investors are willing to pay.

Young, rapidly growing companies are more difficult to value than mature companies because there is less reliable historical information on young companies and their futures tend to be less certain.

Control is an important consideration in business valuation because having control of a business provides an investor with more flexibility in managing the business. Investors value this flexibility and, therefore, will pay more for a controlling interest in a company.

If the cash flows that a business is expected to generate depend heavily on certain employees, those employees are key people. When valuing a business, an analyst must account for the possibility that the key people will unexpectedly leave the company and must consider the associated impact on the company's cash flows.

SUMMARY OF KEY EQUATIONS

Equation	Description	Formula
(18.1)	Price/earnings multiple based on constant-growth model	$\dfrac{P_0}{E_1} = \dfrac{b}{k_{os} - g}$
(18.2)	Implementing the income approach to business valuation	$V_F = PV(FCF_T) + PV(TV_T) + NOA$

(18.3)	FCFF approach	$V_F = \displaystyle\sum_{t=0}^{\infty} \dfrac{FCFF_t}{(1 + WACC)^t}$
(18.4)	FCFE approach	$V_F = \displaystyle\sum_{t=0}^{\infty} \dfrac{FCFE_t}{(1 + k_E)^t}$

SELF-STUDY PROBLEMS

18.1. Your sister wants to open a store that sells antique-style jewellery and accessories. She has €15 000 of savings to invest, but opening the store will require an initial investment of €20 000. Net cash inflows will be −€2000, −€1000 and €0 in the first three months. As the store becomes better known, net cash inflows will become +€500 in the fourth month and grow at a constant rate of 5% in the following months. You want to help your sister by providing the additional money that she needs. How much money do you have to invest each month to start and keep the store operating with a minimum cash balance of €1000?

18.2. You have the following information for a company you are valuing and for a comparable company:

Comparable company	Company you are valuing
Stock price = €23.45	Value of debt = €3.68 million
Number of shares outstanding = 6.23 million	Est. EBITDA next year = €4.4 million
Value of debt = €18.45 million	Est. income next year = €1.5 million
Est. EBITDA next year = €17.0 million	
Est. income next year = €5.3 million	

Estimate the enterprise value of the company you are evaluating using the P/E and enterprise value/EBITDA multiples.

18.3. How do the cash flows that are discounted when the WACC approach is used to value a business differ from those that are discounted when the free cash flow to equity (FCFE) approach is used to value the equity in a business?

18.4. You are valuing a company using the WACC approach and have estimated that the free cash flows from the firm (FCFF) in the next five years will be €36.7, €42.6, €45.1, €46.3 and €46.6 million, respectively. Beginning in year 6, you expect the cash flows to decrease at a rate of 3% per year for the indefinite future. You estimate that the appropriate WACC to use in discounting these cash flows is 10%. What is the value of this company?

18.5. You want to estimate the value of a local advertising firm. The earnings of the firm are expected to be €2 million next year. Based on expected earnings next year, the average price-to-earnings ratio of similar firms in the same industry is 48. Therefore, you estimate the firm's value to be €96 million.

Further investigation shows that a large portion of the firm's business is obtained through connections that Jan Boers, a senior partner of the firm, has with various advertising executives at customer firms. Mr Boers only recently started working with his junior partners to establish similar relationships with these customers.

Mr Boers is approaching 65 years of age and might announce his retirement at the next board meeting. If he does retire, revenues will drop significantly and earnings are estimated to shrink by 30%. You estimate that the probability that Mr Smith will retire this year is 50%. If he does not retire this year, you expect that Mr Boers will have sufficient time to work with his junior partners so his departure will not affect earnings when he departs. How does this information affect your estimate of the value of the firm?

SOLUTIONS TO SELF-STUDY PROBLEMS

18.1. You will have to invest €5000 to open the store (the difference between €20 000 and €15 000). You will then have to invest an additional €3000 during the first month to cover the cash flow of –€2000 and to establish a cash balance of €1000. Another €1000 will be required in the second month to cover the negative cash flow during that month. Since cash flows will be positive beginning in the third month, you will not have to invest any additional funds after the second month.

18.2. The *P/E* and enterprise value/EBITDA multiples for the comparable company are:

$$\left(\frac{P}{E}\right)_{\text{Comparable}} = \left(\frac{\text{Share price}}{\text{Earnings per share}}\right)_{\text{Comparable}}$$
$$= \frac{€23.45}{€5.3/6.23 \text{ shares}}$$
$$= 27.6$$

$$\left(\frac{\text{Enterprise value}}{\text{EBITDA}}\right)_{\text{Comparable}} = \left(\frac{V_D + V_E}{\text{EBITDA}}\right)_{\text{Comparable}}$$
$$= \frac{€18.45 + (€23.45 \times 6.23 \text{ shares})}{€17.0}$$
$$= 9.68$$

Using the *P/E* multiple, we can calculate the value of the equity as:

$$V_E = \left(\frac{P}{E}\right)_{\text{Comparable}} \times \text{Net income}_{\text{Company being valued}}$$
$$= 27.6 \times €1.5 \text{ million}$$
$$= €41.4 \text{ million}$$

Using Equation (18.2), this suggests an enterprise value of:

$$V_F = V_E + V_D = €41.4 \text{ million} + €3.68 \text{ million}$$
$$= €45.08 \text{ million}$$

Using the enterprise/EBITDA multiple, we obtain:

$$V_F = \left(\frac{\text{Enterprise value}}{\text{EBITDA}}\right)_{\text{Comparable}}$$
$$\times \text{EBITDA}_{\text{Company being valued}}$$
$$= 9.68 \times €4.4 \text{ million}$$
$$= €42.59 \text{ million}$$

18.3. The cash flows that are discounted when the WACC approach is used to value a business are calculated in the same way that the cash flows are calculated for a project analysis. These cash flows represent the total cash flows that the business is expected to generate from operations. The cash flows that are discounted when the FCFE approach is used are the total cash flows from the business that are available for distribution to the shareholders. In other words, they equal the total cash flows that the business is expected to generate less the net cash flows to the debt holders. The net cash flows to the debt holders are equal to the interest and principal payments that the firm makes less any proceeds for the sale of new debt.

18.4. The present value of the cash flows expected over the next five years is:

$$PV(FCFF_5) = \frac{€36.7}{1+0.1} + \frac{€42.6}{(1+0.1)^2}$$
$$+ \frac{€45.1}{(1+0.1)^3} + \frac{€46.3}{(1+0.1)^4}$$
$$+ \frac{€46.6}{(1+0.1)^5}$$

The terminal value is:

$$TV_5 = \frac{FCFF_5 \times (1+g)}{WACC - g} = \frac{€46.6 \times (1-0.03)}{0.1+0.03}$$
$$= €347.71 \text{ million}$$

and the present value of the terminal value is:

$$PV(TV_5) = \frac{TV_5}{(1+WACC)^5} = \frac{€347.71}{(1+0.1)^5}$$
$$= €215.90 \text{ million}$$

Therefore, if there are no non-operating assets, the value of the firm is:

$$V_F = €163.01 \text{ million} + €215.90 \text{ million}$$
$$= €378.91 \text{ million}$$

18.5. Mr Boers is a *key person* in this firm. An adjustment should be made to the valuation to account for his potential departure this year.

Taking the possibility that Mr Boers will retire into account, the expected earnings next year will be:

$$(€2\,000\,000 \times 0.5)$$
$$+ [€2\,000\,000 \times (1-30\%) \times 0.5]$$
$$= €1\,700\,000$$

Therefore, the adjusted value for the firm is: €1.7 million × 48 = €81.6 million. We can see that this implies a 15% key person discount from the original estimate of €96 million [(€81.6 − €96.0)/€96.0 = −0.15, or −15%].

CRITICAL THINKING QUESTIONS

18.1. Given that many new businesses fail in the first four years, how should an entrepreneur think about the risk of failure associated with a new business? From what you have learned in this chapter, what can an entrepreneur do to increase the chance of success?

18.2. Explain how the taxation of a company differs from the taxation of the other forms of business organisation discussed in this chapter.

18.3. What is a business plan? Explain how a business plan can help an entrepreneur succeed in building a business.

18.4. You are entering negotiations to purchase a business and are trying to formulate a negotiating strategy. You want to determine the minimum price you should offer and the maximum you should be willing to pay. Explain how the concepts of fair market value and investment value can help you do this.

18.5. You have just received a business valuation report that is dated six months ago. Describe the factors that might have changed during the past six months and, therefore, caused the value of the business today to be different from the value six months ago. Which of these changes affect the expected cash flows and which affect the discount rate that you would use in a discounted cash flow valuation of this company?

18.6. Is the replacement cost of a business generally related to the value of the cash flows that the business is expected to produce in the future? Why or why not? Illustrate your answer with an example.

18.7. You want to estimate the value of a company that has three very different lines of business. It manufactures aircraft, is in the data processing business and manufactures automobiles. How could you use an income approach to value a company such as this – one with three very distinct businesses that will have different revenue growth rates, profit margins, investment requirements, discount rates and so forth?

18.8. Your boss has asked you to estimate the intrinsic value of the equity for Google, which does not currently pay any dividends. You are going to use an income approach and are trying to choose between the free cash flow to equity (FCFE) approach and the dividend discount model (DDM) approach. Which would be more appropriate in this instance? Why? What concerns would you have in applying either of these valuation approaches to a company such as this?

18.9. Explain how the financial statements of a private company might differ from those of a public company. What does this imply for valuing a private company?

18.10. Explain why it is difficult to value a young, rapidly growing company.

QUESTIONS AND PROBLEMS

Basic

18.1. **Organisational form:** List some common forms of business organisation and discuss how access to capital differs across these forms of organisation.

18.2. **Starting a business:** What are some of the things that the founder of a company must do to launch a new business?

18.3. **Organisational form:** Explain how financial liabilities differ among different forms of business organisation.

18.4. **Cash requirements:** List two useful tools to help an entrepreneur to understand the cash requirements of a business and to estimate the financing needs of his or her business.

18.5. **Cash requirements:** You believe you have a great business idea and want to start your own company. However, you do not have enough savings to finance it. Where can you get the additional funds you need?

18.6. **Raising capital:** Why is it especially difficult for an entrepreneur with a new business to raise capital? What tool can help him or her to raise external capital?

18.7. **Replacement cost:** What is the replacement cost of a business?

18.8. **Multiples analysis:** It is 4 April 2007, and your company is considering the possibility of purchasing the Chrysler automobile manufacturing business from the German car manufacturer DaimlerChrysler. DaimlerChrysler has hinted that it might be interested in selling Chrysler. Since Chrysler does not have publicly traded shares of its own, you have decided to use Ford Motor Company as a comparable company to help you determine the market value of Chrysler.

This morning, Ford's shares were trading at $8.15 and the company had 1.89 billion shares outstanding. You estimate that the market value of all the company's other outstanding securities (excluding the ordinary shares but including special shares owned by the Ford family) is $100 billion and that its revenues from auto sales were $143.3 billion last year. Chrysler's revenue in 2006 was $62.2 billion. Based on the enterprise value/revenue ratio, what is the total value of Chrysler that is implied by the Ford market values?

18.9. **Non-operating assets:** Why is excess cash a non-operating asset (NOA)? Why does it make sense to add the value of excess cash to the value of the discounted cash flows when we use the WACC or FCFE approach to value a business?

18.10. **Dividend discount approach:** You want to estimate the total intrinsic value of a large gas and electric utility company. This company has publicly traded shares and has been paying a regular dividend for many years. You decide that, due to the predictability of the dividend that this company pays, you can use the dividend discount valuation approach. The company is expected to pay a dividend of €1.25 per share next year and the dividend is expected to grow at a rate of 3% per year thereafter. You estimate that the appropriate rate for discounting future dividends is 12%. In addition, you know that the company has 46 million shares outstanding and that the market value of its debt is €350 million. What is the total value of the company?

18.11. **Public versus private company valuation:** You are considering investing in a private company that is owned by a friend of yours. You have read through the company's financial statements and believe that they are reliable. Multiples of similar publicly traded companies in the same industry suggest that the value of a share in your friend's

company is €12. Should you be willing to pay €12 per share?

18.12. **Control:** Does the expected rate of return that is calculated using CAPM, with a beta estimated from the return on shares in the public market, reflect a minority or a controlling ownership position? How is it likely to differ between a minority and a controlling position?

Intermediate

18.13. **Organisational form:** Compare an LLC with a partnership and a company.

18.14. **Organisational form:** Discuss the pros and cons of the limited liability partnership form of organisation against those of a company.

18.15. **Break-even:** You have started a business that sells a home gardening system that allows people to grow vegetables on the countertop in their kitchens. You are considering two options for marketing your product. The first is to advertise on local TV. The second is to distribute flyers in the local community. The TV option, which costs €50 000 annually, will promote the product more effectively and create a demand for 1200 units per year. The flyer advertisement costs only €6000 annually but will create a demand for only 250 units per year. The price per unit of the indoor gardening system is €100 and the variable cost is €60 per unit. Assume that the production capacity is not limited and that the marketing cost is the only fixed cost involved in your business. What are the break-even points for both marketing options? Which one should you choose?

18.16. **Going-concern value:** Melhores Carros Preços SA is a chain of used car dealerships that has publicly traded shares. Using the adjusted book value approach, you have estimated the value of Melhores Carros Preços to be €45 646 000. The company has €40.5 million of debt outstanding. Its share price is

€5.5 per share and there are 1 378 000 shares outstanding. What is the going concern value of Melhores Carros Preços?

Use the following information concerning Macchina Utensile S.p.A. in Problems 18.17, 18.18 and 18.19.

Macchina Utensile's income statement from the fiscal year that ended this past December is:

Revenue	€995
Cost of goods sold	652
Gross profit	€343
Selling, general and administrative expenses	135
Operating profit (EBIT)	€208
Interest expense	48
Earnings before taxes	€160
Taxes	64
Net income	€ 96

All values are in millions. Depreciation and amortisation expenses last year were €42 million and the company has €533 million of debt outstanding.

18.17. EXCEL® **Multiples analysis:** You are an analyst at a firm that buys private companies, improves their operating performance and sells them for a profit. Your boss has asked you to estimate the fair market value of the Macchina Utensile S.p.A. Milan Ingeneria S.p.A. is a public company with business operations that are virtually identical to those at Macchina Utensile. The most recent income statement for Milan Ingeneria is as follows:

Revenue	€1 764
Cost of goods sold	1 168
Gross profit	€ 596
Selling, general and administrative expenses	211
Operating profit (EBIT)	€ 385
Interest expense	12
Earnings before taxes	€ 373
Taxes	147
Net income	€ 226

All values are in millions. Milan Ingeneria had depreciation and amortisation expenses of €71 million last year and 200 million shares and €600 million of debt outstanding as of the end of the year. Its shares are currently trading at €12.25.

Using the *P/E* multiple, what is the value of Macchina Utensile's shares? What is the total value of Macchina Utensile S.p.A.?

18.18. EXCEL® **Multiples analysis:** Using the enterprise value/EBITDA multiple, what is the total value of Macchina Utensile S.p.A.? What is the value of Macchina Utensile's shares?

18.19. EXCEL® **Multiples analysis:** Which of the above multiples analyses do you believe is more appropriate?

18.20. EXCEL® **Income approaches:** You are using the FCFF approach to value a business. You have estimated that the FCFF for next year will be €123.65 million and that it will increase at a rate of 8% for each of the following four years. After that point, the FCFF will increase at a rate of 3% forever. If the WACC for this firm is 10%, what is it worth?

18.21. EXCEL® **Valuing a private business:** You want to estimate the value of a privately owned restaurant that is financed entirely with equity. Its most recent income statement is as follows:

Revenue	€3 000 000
Cost of goods sold	600 000
Gross profit	€2 400 000
Salaries and wages	1 400 000
Selling expenses	100 000
Operating profit (EBIT)	€ 900 000
Taxes	315 000
Net income	€ 585 000

You note that the profitability of this restaurant is significantly lower than that of comparable restaurants, primarily due to high salary and wage expenses. Further investigation reveals that the annual salaries for the owner and his wife, the firm's accountant, are €900 000 and €300 000, respectively. These salaries are much higher than the industry median salaries for these two positions of €100 000 and €50 000, respectively. Compensation for other employees (€200 000 in total) appears to be consistent with the market rates. The median *P/E* ratio of comparable restaurants with no debt is 10. What is the total value of this restaurant?

18.22. Valuing a private business: A few years ago, a friend of yours started a small business that develops gaming software. The company is doing well and is valued at €1.5 million based on multiples for comparable public companies after adjustments for their lack of marketability. With 300 000 shares outstanding, each share is estimated to be worth €5. Your friend, who has been serving as CEO and CTO (chief technology officer), has decided that he lacks sufficient managerial skills to continue to build the company. He wants to sell his 160 000 shares and invest the money in an MBA education. You believe you have the appropriate managerial skills to run the company. Would you pay €5 each for these shares? What are some of the factors you should consider in making this decision?

Advanced

18.23. EXCEL® You plan to start a business that sells waterproof sun block with a unique formula that reduces the damage of UVA radiation 30% more effectively than similar products on the market.

You expect to invest €50 000 in plant and equipment to begin the business. The targeted price of the sun block is €15 per bottle. You forecast that unit sales will total 1500 bottles in the first month and will increase by 20% in each of the following months during the first year. You expect the cost of raw materials to be €3 per bottle. In addition, monthly gross wages and payroll are expected to be €13 000, rent is expected to be €3000 and other expenses are expected to total €1000. Advertising costs are estimated to be €35 000 in the first month but to remain constant at €5000 per month during the following 11 months.

You have decided to finance the entire business at one time using your own savings. Is an initial investment of €75 000 adequate to avoid a negative cash balance in any given month? If not, how much more do you need to invest up front? How much do you need to invest up front to keep a minimum cash balance of €5000? What is the break-even point of the business?

18.24. EXCEL® For the previous question, assume that you do not have sufficient savings to cover the entire amount required to start your sun-block business. You are going to have to get external financing. A local banker whom you know has offered you a six-month loan of €20 000 at an APR of 12%. You will pay interest each month and repay the entire principal at the end of six months.

Assume that instead of making a single up-front investment, you are going to finance the business by making monthly investments as cash is needed in the business. Assuming the proceeds from the loan go directly into the business on the first day and are therefore available to pay for some of the capital expenditures, how much money do you need to pull out of your savings account every month to run the business and keep the cash balances positive?

18.25. Your friend is starting a new company. He wants to write a business plan to clarify the company's business outlook and raise venture capital. Knowing that you have taken this course, he has asked you, as a favour, to help him prepare a template for a business plan. Prepare a template that includes the key elements of a business plan.

18.26. A friend of yours is trying to value the equity of a company and, knowing that you have read this book, has asked for your help. So far she has tried to use the FCFE approach. She estimated the cash flows to equity to be as follows:

Sales	€800.0
− CGS	−450.0
− Depreciation	−80.0
− Interest	−24.0
Earnings before taxes (EBT)	€246.0
− Taxes (0.35 × EBT)	−86.1
− Cash flow to equity	€159.9

She also computed the cost of equity using CAPM as follows:

$$k_E = k_F + b_E(\text{Risk premium})$$
$$= 0.06 + (1.25 \times 0.084)$$
$$= 0.165, \text{ or } 16.5\%$$

where the beta is estimated for a comparable publicly traded company.

Using this cost of equity, she estimates the discount rate as:

$$\text{WACC} = x_{\text{Debt}}k_{\text{Debt pre-tax}}(1 - t) + x_{os}k_{os}$$
$$= [0.20 \times 0.06 \times (1 - 0.35)]$$
$$+ (0.80 \times 0.165)$$
$$= 0.14, \text{ or } 14\%$$

Based on this analysis, she concludes that the value of equity is €159.9 million/0.14 = €1142 million.

Assuming that the numbers used in this analysis are all correct, what advice would you give your friend regarding her analysis?

18.27. La Tecnología Siempre los Jóvenes SA is a biochemical company that is two years old. Its main product, an antioxidant drink that is supposed to energise the consumer and delay aging, is still under development. The company's equity consists of €5 million invested by its founders and €5 million from a venture capitalist. The company has spent €3 million in each of the past two years, mostly on lab equipment and R&D costs. The company has had no sales so far. What are the challenges associated with valuing such a young and uncertain company?

18.28. EXCEL® Mad Rock plc is a company that sells MP3 music online. It is expected to generate earnings of €1 per share this year after its website is upgraded and online marketing is stepped up. Given the popularity of iPod and other MP3 players, the share price of Mad Rock has rocketed from €8 to €95 in the past 12 months. The cost of capital for the company is 18%.

Of course, the future of a young Internet company such as Mad Rock is highly uncertain. Nevertheless, using the very limited information provided in this problem, do you think €95 per share could be a fair price for its shares? Support your argument with a simple analysis.

SAMPLE TEST PROBLEMS

18.1. You own a business that specialises in designing and producing roofs for houses in central Spain. Your annual costs include office rent of €14 400, salaries for four designing engineers of €240 000, design software costs of €12 000 and other overhead costs of €3000. An average roof in this region is priced at €3500. It costs €1200 in raw material, €1100 in labour and €100 in other expenses (for example, purchasing building permits). What is the minimum number of roofs you need to sell to earn a profit? What can you do to reduce the break-even level of sales?

18.2. Explain why the replacement cost approach is rarely used to value an entire business.

18.3. Why is the rate used to discount FCFF different from the rate used to discount FCFE?

18.4. You are valuing the equity of a company using the FCFE approach and have estimated that the FCFE in the next five years will be €6.05, €6.76, €7.36, €7.85 and €8.15 million, respectively. Beginning in year 6, you expect the cash flows to increase at a rate of 2% per year for the indefinite future. You estimate that the cost of equity is 12%. What is the value of equity in this company?

18.5. You are interested in investing in a private company. Based on earnings multiples of similar publicly traded firms, you estimate the value of the private company's shares to be €11. You plan to acquire a majority of the shares in the company. The expected control premium is 10%. You estimate the marketability discount for such a firm to be 20%. The discount for the key person, one of the founders who may leave the firm upon your control of the firm, is 15%. What price should you be willing to pay for these shares?

ENDNOTES

1. In Chapter 15 we provided information on the costs for raising debt and equity.
2. The actual result of the calculation shown here is −€4456, rather than −€4457. The €1 difference is due to rounding. The interest expense is actually €333.33 ([0.08/12] × €50 000) and the beginning cash balance is €6096.67, which yields −€4456.66.
3. Marketability discounts are also sometimes called *discounts for lack of marketability* or *liquidity discounts*.
4. This is not strictly true for most firms because it assumes that the share price can be estimated using a constant-growth perpetuity model and most firms either do not pay dividends at all or do not increase dividends at a constant rate. Nevertheless, this model does provide a useful way of thinking about *P/E* multiples.
5. Enterprise value is typically defined as: Market value of ordinary shares + Market value of preference shares + Market value of debt − Excess cash and cash equivalents (marketable securities).

CHAPTER
19

Financial Planning and Forecasting

In this Chapter:

Financial Planning

Financial Planning Models

A Better Financial Planning Model

Beyond the Basic Planning Models

Managing and Financing Growth

LEARNING OBJECTIVES

1. Explain what a financial plan is and why financial planning is so important.
2. Discuss how management uses financial planning models in the planning process and explain the importance of sales forecasts in the construction of financial planning models.
3. Discuss how the relation between projected sales and balance sheet accounts can be determined and be able to analyse a strategic investment decision using a percentage of sales model.
4. Describe the conditions under which fixed assets vary directly with sales and discuss the impact of so-called lumpy assets on this relation.
5. Explain what factors determine a firm's sustainable growth rate, discuss why it is of interest to management and be able to compute the sustainable growth rate for a firm.

There is no mistaking the iconic toy building blocks made by Lego. Now the fifth largest toy manufacturer in the world, the company was founded in Billund, Denmark, in 1932 by Ole Kirk Kristiansen and is still family owned. International success came with the introduction of the plastic building block system introduced in the 1950s. From a simple set of bricks, the company developed a whole range of new products, such as Duplo and Lego Technics, which routinely generated three-quarters of

its sales. Using a well-tested approach, the company could count on increased sales year-on-year, although there was significant seasonality with 60% of sales taking place in the months leading up to the December holidays. It had over 3% of the global toy market and the connectable construction blocks were voted the 'Toy of the 20th Century' by *Fortune* magazine in 2000.

However, all that began to change in the late 1990s as rapid changes in the toy market began to threaten Lego's business. The company lost money in four out of the seven years from 1998 to 2004. Sales fell 30% in 2003 and a further 10% the following year. Drastic action was called for. The company faced a range of challenges about its business plan, its costs and its position in the market. A thorough examination of the business identified that the new products, the engine of growth, were delivering less and less profit as each new product added more complexity and cost. To gain time, the company sold off its theme parks and closed other peripheral activities, reorganised its product development and transformed the way it made and sold its products. Following this radical overhaul, the company returned to profitability – sales grew 12% in 2005 and the company reported its first profit (€61 million) for three years. Further improvements continued in 2006 and thereafter the company's performance stabilised. Today the company is highly profitable.

Lego's story is not unusual. Firms often find their strategies need to adjust to changing market conditions and managers need to understand the intricacies of the business and the financial implications of their decisions. In the 1990s for Lego, planning took second place to a growth strategy that expanded the firm too fast in different directions, increased costs ahead of revenues and led to significant losses that threatened the business. Following the crisis of the early part of the 21st century that threatened to sink the 'Toy of the 20th Century', Lego introduced a more thoughtful approach to planning for the future. This chapter explains how firms plan for the future and manage growth to create value.

CHAPTER PREVIEW

It is often said that a company that fails to plan for the future may have no future. In the short run, a firm may do well being opportunistic – reacting quickly to events as they unfold. To succeed over the long term, however, a firm must be innovative and they must plan and employ a strategy that generates sustainable profits. Top executives spend a lot of time thinking about the types of investment the firm needs to make and how to finance them. The process that executives go through is called financial planning and the result is called a financial plan.

This chapter focuses on long-term financial planning. We begin with a discussion of the firm's strategic plan and its components. We then discuss the preparation of a financial plan. Next, we turn our attention to financial planning models used in the preparation of financial plans. These models generate projected financial statements that estimate the amount of external funding needed and identify other financial consequences of proposed strategic investments. We end the chapter by examining the relation between a firm's growth and its need for external financing. Managing growth is an important topic, because growth without sufficient profits can lead to cash flow shortages and insolvency.

Financial planning

the process by which management decides what types of investment the firm needs to make and how to finance those investments

Financial plan

a plan outlining the investments a firm intends to make and how it will finance them

FINANCIAL PLANNING

Learning Objective 1

Explain what a financial plan is and why financial planning is so important.

Top management engages in long-term financial planning because experience has shown that having a well-articulated financial plan helps them create value for shareholders. Planning is important for established businesses because it forces management to systematically think through the firm's strategies, much like preparing a business plan helps an entrepreneur. Not surprisingly, the lack of planning is a common reason for poor performance and business bankruptcy. The problems at Lego mentioned in the chapter opening can be attributable in part to poor strategies that arose from a weak planning process. While Lego survived its problems, other firms have gone bankrupt as a result.

The Planning Documents

When top management begins to prepare a company's financial plan, it must answer four basic questions. First, where is the company headed? Second, what assets does it need to get there? Third, how is the firm going to pay for these assets? And finally, does the firm have enough cash to pay its day-to-day bills as they come due?

These questions are answered in four important planning documents: (1) the *strategic plan*, which describes where the firm is headed and articulates the strategies that will be used to get it there; (2) the *investment plan*, which identifies the capital assets needed to execute the strategies; (3) the *financing plan*, which explains how the firm will raise the money to buy the assets; and (4) the *cash budget*, which determines whether the firm will have sufficient cash to pay its bills. These four planning documents provide the foundation for the firm's *financial plan*, which consolidates the documents into a single scheme. Thus, the financial plan is a blueprint for the firm's future.

Exhibit 19.1 shows the relations among the various plans and budgets. Notice that information

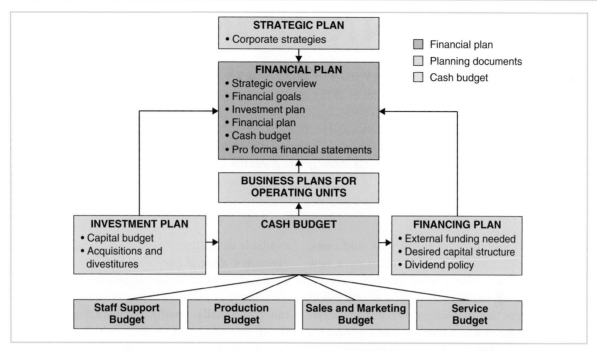

Exhibit 19.1: The Financial Planning Process Various planning and budget documents flow into a financial plan and form its foundation. The completed financial plan articulates the firm's strategic goals and identifies what types of investments the firm should make to achieve its goals, as well as how to finance those investments.

from the strategic plan *flows down* to the financial plan and information from the other plans and cash budgets *flows up* to the financial plan.

Strategic Plan

Strategic planning is the most crucial planning step. The strategic plan sets out the vision for the firm – what management wants the firm to become – and establishes the strategies that management will use to achieve its vision. Overall, the strategic plan provides high-level direction to management for making business decisions and guidance about what the firm will and will not do.

> **Strategic planning**
>
> the process by which management establishes the firm's long-term goals, the strategies that will be used to achieve the goals, and the capabilities that are needed to sustain the firm's competitive position

Preparing the strategic plan is the responsibility of top management, with the financial manager as a key participant and the board of directors as approver of the plan. The strategic plan covers all areas in the firm, such as operations, marketing, finance, information systems and human resource management. The plan determines the lines of business in which the firm will compete and the relative emphasis placed on each business activity. It also identifies major areas for investments in earning assets: capital expenditures, the acquisition of a new firm or the launch of a new line of business. When deemed necessary, the plan also identifies mergers, alliances and divestitures that management may seek to strengthen the firm's business portfolio.

Investment Plan

The investment plan, also known as the capital budget, lays out the firm's proposed spending on capital assets for the year.[1] The capital expenditures support the firm's business strategy. Some capital

BUILDING INTUITION

A Firm's Strategy Drives its Business Decisions

The firm's business strategy drives all of its decisions. It determines the firm's lines of business, the products it will sell, its method of producing them and the geographic markets in which it will compete. Thus, strategy defines a company's competitive position in an industry. To be successful, a firm must formulate the right strategy and have a management team that can implement it. Management is always searching for a strategy that gives the firm a sustainable competitive edge.

expenditures pay for significant new additions, such as a new building, a new plant or a new production line. Other capital expenditures are for more routine items, such as the replacement of old equipment and machinery. Once made, capital expenditures define a firm's line of business for years to come. For example, Volkswagen could not suddenly start making tennis shoes instead of cars because Volkswagen's long-term assets hardly lend themselves to manufacturing shoes and the cost of conversion would be prohibitive. The preparation of the capital budget and the decision criteria for selecting capital projects are discussed in Chapters 10–13.

Financing Plan

Once the capital budget is set, management must decide how to finance the assets. The simplest financing environment is one in which all capital projects are financed from *internally* generated funds. This means that the firm's earnings, less cash dividends, provide the necessary capital. However, only rarely does a firm finance all its projects in this way, as most firms have more capital projects than they can fund internally. Thus, management must seek *external* financing from a variety of sources, such as bank borrowing, selling of long-term debt and issuance of additional equity. Overall, the goal of the financing plan is to determine how much external funding the firm needs.

The financing plan has three components. First, a financing plan states the amount of *external financing needed* and identifies the sources of funds

available to the firm. Second, the plan states management's *desired capital structure* for the firm. This statement is important because it determines the relative amounts of debt and equity funds to be raised externally. Finally, the financing plan states the firm's *dividend policy*, which is relevant because it directly affects the amount of funds available for new investment projects. That is, the more funds the firm pays out as cash dividends, the more external capital the firm must raise. Capital structure policy is discussed in Chapter 16, and dividend policy in Chapter 17.

An important point to note here is that the investment (capital budgeting) and financing decisions *cannot* be made independently – they must be considered together. The reason is that when management makes an investment decision, it must already have identified a source of funds to pay for the investment. This is no different from what you would do in your personal life. For example, you would not walk into a BMW dealership to buy a high-priced new car without having lined up a source of financing. Nor, for that matter, would the dealer sell you the car without having the financing already arranged. The investment decision (buy the car) and the financing decision (get a consumer loan) are made simultaneously and hence are not independent.

Divisional Business Plans

Another component of the financial plan is made up of the *business plans* prepared by the various divisions or operating units within the firm. Each divisional business plan describes what the division will do to achieve the firm's strategic goals. It also identifies the resources the division needs and includes a detailed budget. It is here at the divisional level that much of the firm's budget work is done.

For example, assume that one of Volkswagen's strategic goals is to manufacture and sell jet water skis through its marine division. The division has some idle capacity in one of its manufacturing plants. Thus, as part of the division's business plan, it submits a capital budgeting request to enter the jet ski market. (To be included in Volkswagen's capital budget, the jet ski project must have a positive NPV.)

Cash Budget

The cash budget for the firm is the aggregation (adding up) of the cash budgets from all the operating units plus the cash budget for the corporate offices. The cash budget focuses exclusively on when the firm actually receives and pays out cash. The firm's cash needs may vary weekly, monthly and seasonally, as well as with predictable events such as payroll payments, payment of cash dividends and debt retirements. If a shortfall of cash develops, the cash budget indicates the amount of money the firm needs to borrow and the anticipated borrowing cost.

As Exhibit 19.1 shows, the planning process drills down deep into the firm and gathers cash budget information on the myriad of activities that take place. If cash budgets are not well managed and monitored, serious cash shortages can occur. Tools used in cash management are discussed in Chapter 14 and the preparation of cash budgets is covered in Chapter 18.

Concluding Comments

The principal benefit of financial planning is that it establishes financial and operating goals for the firm and communicates them throughout the organisation. The financial plan also helps to align the actions of managers and their operating units with the firm's strategic goals. Thus, the plan acts as a catalyst to get everyone in the firm moving in the same direction. To build support for the financial plan and energise people's actions, top management should involve managers and other leaders in the firm at all levels in the planning process. An old axiom in management says that people support plans when they have had meaningful involvement in the plans' preparation.

> **Before You Go On**
>
> 1. What are the four planning documents on which the financial plan is based?
> 2. What is the strategic plan?
> 3. How are the investment decision and financing decision related?

FINANCIAL PLANNING MODELS

> **Learning Objective 2**
>
> Discuss how management uses financial planning models in the planning process and explain the importance of sales forecasts in the construction of financial planning models.

Financial planning models are used to analyse how proposed investments and financing alternatives affect a firm's financial statements. The models are usually run on computer spreadsheets, which reduce the drudgery of tracing investment, financing and operating decisions through a company's accounting system. While commercial planning models have an aura of sophistication about them, most are built around the same basic concepts presented in this chapter.

In this section, we build a simple financial planning model to show how such models are constructed, how they work and how their output is generated. Once you understand this model, you can easily step up to more advanced models.

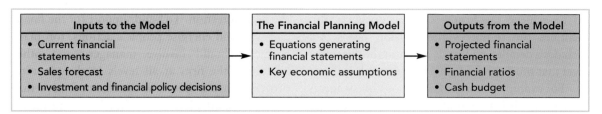

Inputs to the Model	The Financial Planning Model	Outputs from the Model
• Current financial statements • Sales forecast • Investment and financial policy decisions	• Equations generating financial statements • Key economic assumptions	• Projected financial statements • Financial ratios • Cash budget

Exhibit 19.2: The Components of a Financial Planning Model We can categorise the parts of a financial planning model as inputs, the model itself, and outputs. Once constructed, models allow management to generate projected financial statements to see the financial impact of strategic initiatives.

The Sales Forecast

The sales forecast is the most important input for developing a financial planning model. Most firms generate their own sales forecasts. However, forecasting techniques vary widely, ranging from 'seat-of-the-pants' forecasts – wherein the sales manager and key sales staff members talk it over and give their best estimate – to forecasts generated by complex multivariate statistical models. In addition, because the state of the national economy has a direct effect on a company's sales volume, most companies use economic forecasts as part of their sales forecasting process. Large companies often hire consulting firms that specialise in forecasting to help prepare sales forecasts under different scenarios. As you would expect, their services are quite expensive; many banks provide economic forecasts as part of their service to clients.

Building a Financial Planning Model

Learning Objective 3

Discuss how the relation between projected sales and balance sheet accounts can be determined and be able to analyse a strategic investment decision using a percentage of sales model.

A financial planning model is no more than a series of equations that are used to generate projected financial statements for a company, such as an income statement or a balance sheet. The three

basic components of a financial planning model, shown in Exhibit 19.2, are: (1) inputs to the model, (2) the model itself and (3) outputs from the model – the projected financial statements. We will discuss each component in turn.

Inputs to the Model

As shown in the exhibit, important inputs to the financial planning model include current financial statements, sales forecasts, and investment and financial policy decisions.

Current Financial Statements   The starting point for constructing a financial planning model is the firm's current income statement and balance sheet. These statements serve as a baseline.

Sales Forecasts   For most financial planning models, the principal input variable is a forecast of the firm's sales or sales growth rate. The sales forecast is the key driver in financial models because so many items on the income statement and balance sheet vary with changes in the level of sales. For example, if sales increase, it stands to reason that the firm will use more labour and raw materials. Higher sales may also require additional investments in capital assets.

Sales forecasts are given for some time period, such as a quarter or a year, and are often expressed as percentage growth in sales:

$$\%\Delta S = \frac{(S_{t+1} - S_t)}{S_t} \qquad (19.1)$$

where:

$\%\Delta S$ = percentage change in net sales
S_t = level of net sales in period t
S_{t+1} = level of net sales in period $t + 1$

Sales are calculated as the number of units sold times the price at which they are sold. For an example of how Equation (19.1) is used, if the current year's sales (S_t) are €100 million and the forecasted sales for next year (S_{t+1}) are €120 million, applying Equation (19.1) yields the percentage growth in sales over the coming year:

$$\%\Delta S = \frac{(S_{t+1} - S_t)}{S_t} = \frac{(€120 - €100)}{€100}$$
$$= 0.20, \text{ or } 20\%$$

Investment and Financial Policy Decisions Preparing a financial planning model requires top management to make a number of investment and financial policy decisions. These decisions impose constraints on the financial model's outputs that must be recognised during its preparation. Some important investment and financial policy decisions are:

• *Investment policy decisions.* Identify the investment decisions to be evaluated as part of the financial planning process. Typically, these are large capital expenditures such as building a new

manufacturing facility, entering a new line of business or acquiring another firm.
• *Financial policy decisions*
  - *Capital structure decision.* Determines management's targeted capital structure – its willingness to use financial leverage.
  - *Financing decision.* Determines the acceptable type of financing – retained earnings, equity, preference shares and/or long-term debt.
  - *Dividend decision.* Identifies the firm's dividend policy for the sales period.

The Financial Planning Model

A financial planning model is a set of equations that generate projected financial statements. Along with the sales forecast and the investment and financial policy decisions, management must specify key assumptions regarding how the income statement and the balance sheet accounts vary with sales. For example, suppose that, based on historical data, a company finds that cost of goods sold is 80% of sales and inventory and accounts receivable are each 15% of sales. In such a case, it might be reasonable to assume that these relations will hold for the projected income statement and balance sheet. Thus, if sales are projected to be €100 million next year, the projected cost of goods sold will be €80 million (€100 × 0.80) and inventory and accounts receivable will both be €15 million (€100 × 0.15).

Learning by Doing Application 19.1

Financial Statement Items Often Vary with Sales

Problem: You have the following information: (1) sales this year are €50 million; (2) sales are expected to grow by 20% next year; (3) for the current year, accounts receivable are 7% of sales and inventory is 10% of sales. Your boss

has asked you to calculate next year's sales, accounts receivable and inventory.

Approach: You can rearrange Equation (19.1) to find next year's sales level (S_{t+1}). Then, assuming accounts receivable and inventory grow proportionally with sales, you can use the result to calculate the expected levels of accounts receivable and inventory for next year.

Solution:

$$\%\Delta S = \frac{(S_{t+1} - S_t)}{S_t}$$

$$0.2 = \frac{(S_{t+1} - €50\,000\,000)}{€50\,000\,000}$$

$$S_{t+1} = (0.2 \times €50\,000\,000)$$
$$+ €50\,000\,000$$
$$= €60\,000\,000$$

$$\text{Accounts receivable} = €60\,000\,000 \times 0.17$$
$$= €4\,200\,000$$

$$\text{Inventory} = €60\,000\,000 \times 0.10$$
$$= €6\,000\,000$$

Outputs from the Model: Projected Financial Statements

The outputs from the financial planning model are projected financial statements called **pro forma financial statements**. In finance and accounting, the term *pro forma* means forecasted or projected.[2] The statements produced by a financial planning model are forecasted based on the inputs and assumptions entered into the model. In addition to pro forma financial statements, computer-based planning models usually generate a set of financial ratios similar to those discussed in Chapter 4 and include features that enable management to prepare a cash budget.

> **Pro forma financial statements**
>
> projected financial statements that reflect a set of assumptions concerning investment, financing and operating decisions

A Simple Planning Model

Let us work through a simple example to see how a financial planning model generates projected financial statements and is used to analyse a strategic investment.[2] This simple model, along with the other planning models presented in this chapter, is a **percentage of sales model**, in which most of the variables in the model vary directly with the level of sales. Keep in mind that more sophisticated planning models are built around the same basic concepts – there are just more assumptions to deal with. The important point here is to make sure you understand how the model is

built on a set of assumptions and how it generates the pro forma financial statements.

> **WEB**
>
> An overview of basic concepts relating to financial planning can be found at: http://nalu.hpu.edu/mlane/BusinessFinance Online/FF/FinancialForecasting.html.

> **Percentage of sales model**
>
> a type of simple financial planning model that assumes that most income statement and balance sheet accounts vary proportionally with sales

Generating Projected Statements

Pro Forma SE's financial statements for the current year are shown in simplified form in the following table:

Pro Forma SE
Current Financial Statements (€ millions)

Income Statement		Balance Sheet			
Net sales	€1000	Assets	€600	Debt	€400
Costs	700			Equity	200
Net income	€ 300	Total	€600	Total	€600

Pro Forma SE's management expects sales to increase by 15% for the coming year. Assume that the financial statement accounts vary directly with changes in sales and that management has no financing plan at this time. Given this information, we can make the following calculations:

$$\text{Projected sales} = €1000 \text{ million} \times 1.15$$
$$= €1150 \text{ million}$$

$$\text{Projected costs} = €700 \text{ million} \times 1.15$$
$$= €805 \text{ million}$$

We now have the sales and cost figures for the firm's pro forma income statement:

Pro Forma SE
Forecast Income Statement (€ millions)

Net sales	€1150
Costs	805
Net income	€ 345

Thus, the firm's projected net income is €345 million.

Turning to the balance sheet, since we are assuming that all financial statement items vary with the change in sales, the projected values for the balance sheet accounts are:

$$\text{Projected assets} = €600 \text{ million} \times 1.15$$
$$= €690 \text{ million}$$
$$\text{Projected debt} = €400 \text{ million} \times 1.15$$
$$= €460 \text{ million}$$
$$\text{Projected equity} = €200 \text{ million} \times 1.15$$
$$= €230 \text{ million}$$

and the resulting pro forma balance sheet is:

Pro Forma SE
Projected Balance Sheet (€ millions)

Assets	€690	(€90)	Debt	€460	(€60)
			Equity	230	(30)
Total	€690	(€90)	Total	€690	(€90)

The numbers in parentheses are the changes between the current and projected amounts. Notice that all the balance sheet figures have increased by 15% and that the balance sheet balances. This is because both the sources and

use of funds have increased by 15%. The €90 million in new assets is being financed by €30 million from retained earnings (internal financing) and €60 million from new long-term debt (external financing).

The balance sheet balances, but if you look back at the income statement, you may notice that the equity account does not look right. Recall that Pro Forma SE's projected net income was €345 million. Adding this amount to the initial equity account balance of €200 million yields a final equity balance of €545 million (€345 + €200). As you can see, the equity balance in the pro forma balance sheet is €230 million. Why the apparent conflict?

As a general rule, whenever account balances differ or there is some confusion about an account, the easiest way to determine what is going on is to reconcile the account. For the equity account, if the firm did not sell or repurchase shares, there are two basic transactions that could take place during the year: (1) the firm could generate income that is added to retained earnings and (2) management could pay a cash dividend, which is subtracted from retained earnings. Since the pro forma equity balance is lower than the sum of the initial equity account balance plus Pro Forma SE's net income, the firm must have paid a dividend. We can calculate how large this dividend is as follows:

Beginning equity balance	= €200 million
+ Net income	= €345 million
− Dividends	= X
Ending equity balance	= €230 million

Solving for X, we find that:

$$\text{Dividends} = (€200 \text{ million} + €345 \text{ million})$$
$$- €230 \text{ million}$$
$$= €315 \text{ million}$$

The reconciliation makes the dividend transaction transparent. It is clear that with a net income of €345 million and the constraint that the ending equity balance is €230 million, the firm must pay a €315 million cash dividend.

Evaluating an Investment Opportunity

Now let us suppose that Pro Forma SE is considering building a new manufacturing plant. The project is estimated to cost €200 million and is to be financed entirely with debt. As in the prior example, sales are expected to increase by 15% for the year, and the plant will be placed in service the following year. Finally, assume that all financial statement accounts vary directly with changes in sales and that the current dividend policy is to pay a €315 million cash dividend.

To determine whether the project is feasible as planned, management needs to prepare a set of pro forma financial statements that include the cost of the new facility. Pro Forma's income statement will not change because of the building project. Thus, we can use Pro Forma SE's income statement shown earlier. The preliminary pro forma balance sheet for the project, which excludes external financing, is as follows:

Pro Forma's Building Project
Preliminary Projected Balance Sheet (€ millions)

Asset	€690	(€90)	Debt	€400	
New facility	200	(€200)	Equity	230	(€30)
Total	€890		Total	€630	

We can see that total assets are €890 million, composed of the €690 million (€600 × 1.15) we calculated earlier plus €200 million for the new facility. The value of the equity account remains unchanged at €230 million (€200 × 1.15), because it is subject to the 15% growth limit, and management must pay the €315 million cash dividend. Since we do not know the amount of debt needed, we enter debt at the current balance sheet amount of €400 million.

Now, comparing the totals, we see that the balance sheet does not balance: total assets are €890 million, while total debt and equity equals €630 million. The difference between the two numbers is €260 million (€890 – €630). This 'plug value' is the amount of **external funding needed (EFN)** by the firm. EFN is the additional debt or equity a firm needs to issue so that it can meet its total funding requirements. In this analysis, we refer to EFN as the plug value because it is the number we have to plug into the balance sheet to get it to balance. In our example, the firm must issue €260 million of debt because, as you recall, management made a decision to finance the new project entirely with debt.

External funding needed (EFN)

the additional debt or equity a firm must raise from external sources to meet its total funding requirements

---

The final balance sheet, which includes the building project, is shown in the table below. Overall, the firm is financing €290 million of new assets: €200 million for the new facility and €90 million for new assets to support the increase in sales expected next year. The funding is a combination of internal and external funding, which totals €290 million: €260 million in debt (external) and €30 million in additions to retained earnings (internal). The firm is also able to pay the required €315 million of cash dividends. If the firm can borrow the €260 million at a reasonable rate, it will be able to generate sufficient funds to finance the €200 million capital project and pay the required cash dividend of €315 million.

Pro Forma's Building Project
Final Projected Balance Sheet (€ millions)

Asset	€690	(€90)	Debt	€660	(€260)
New facility	200	(200)	Equity	230	(30)
Total	€890	(€290)	Total	€890	(€290)

Decision-Making Example 19.1

Informed Judgement about Risk

Situation: You are given some additional information about Pro Forma SE's use of financial leverage, as shown:

Debt to total assets before capital project
= €400/€600 = 66.7%

Debt to total assets after capital project =
€660/€890 = 74.2%

Industry average debt to total assets = 40.0%

What should management do in light of this information?

Decision: Pro Forma's current leverage ratio of 66.7% is already high compared with the industry average of 40%. If the firm goes ahead with the project, the leverage ratio will increase to 74.2%, which is even higher. The high debt ratio makes the firm more risky and could negatively affect its share price, its borrowing cost and even its ability to borrow money in the marketplace. A more prudent alternative for Pro Forma would be to fund at least part (possibly all) of the €290 million of new assets (€90 + €200) from internally generated funds by reducing its dividend payments, externally by selling new shares, or both.

The important point here is that financial planning models do not think for management. Even though the balance sheet balances and results are consistent with the firm's financing plan, management must apply informed judgement.

Before You Go On

1. Why is the sales forecast the key component of a financial model?
2. What are pro forma financial statements, and why are they an important part of the financial planning process?
3. What is the plug factor in a financial model?

A BETTER FINANCIAL PLANNING MODEL

The preceding section presented a simple financial planning model that assumes *all* income and balance sheet accounts vary directly with sales. Although that assumption is helpful to simplify calculations, it does not reflect what happens in the real world. We now relax our assumptions so that our model is more realistic and generates more accurate forecasts. We assume that all working capital accounts – current assets and liabilities – vary directly with sales. For other accounts in the financial statements, independent forecasts may be required, or values may be set by management based on other criteria. To illustrate the process, we will work through an example.

Travaux Maritime SA

Travaux Maritime SA is a small, privately owned company located in Brest, France. The firm serves the oil and gas exploration industry in Europe and, in particular, the North Sea continental shelf. It sells and does light manufacturing of rigging equipment for oil and gas exploration. The firm's management owns 75% of the ordinary shares, with the balance owned by friends and outside investors. Travaux Maritime's management is projecting a banner year, as sales are expected to increase 30%. The reason for the large increase is an oil and gas shortage caused by political instability in the Middle East. Because of the high-risk nature of their business, management is very conservative with respect to any action that might materially increase the firm's risks. Some of the management team is concerned about the risks associated with increasing sales by 30% in a one-year period.

The financial manager looks at the firm's current and historical financial statements and provides the following information:

- Net sales for the current year are €2 million.
- Historical and current financial data indicate that the total cost of producing the firm's services and products averages about 85% of sales.
- The firm's marginal tax rate is 34% and is not expected to change.
- The firm's dividend policy is to pay one-third of earnings as a cash dividend.

The Income Statement

Exhibit 19.3 shows the firm's current and projected income statements. Let us look at the calculations used to arrive at the projected income statement. Management expects sales to increase by 30% next year, and so projected sales are €2 million × 1.30 = €2.6 million. Since total costs have averaged 85% of sales, projected total costs are €2.6 million × 0.85 = €2.21 million. Projected taxes, which are 34.1% of

taxable income, are $0.341 \times €390\,000 = €132\,990$, which we will round to €133 000 for simplicity. Subtracting taxes from taxable income, we arrive at the firm's projected net income of €257 000.

Travaux Maritime's cash dividend is €86 000 ($0.335 \times €257\,000 = €86\,095$, which we will round to €86 000), and the remaining €171 000 of net income ($0.665 \times €257\,000$) is retained in the firm as an addition to retained earnings.

These amounts relate to two ratios we will use in this chapter: the dividend payout ratio and the retention ratio, or plowback ratio. Their formulas and calculations for Travaux Maritime are as follows:

$$\text{Dividend payout ratio} = \frac{\text{Cash dividends}}{\text{Net income}}$$
$$= \frac{€86\,000}{€257\,000} \quad (19.2)$$
$$= 0.335, \text{ or } 33.5\%$$

$$\text{Retention ratio} = \frac{\text{Retained earnings}}{\text{Net income}}$$
$$= \frac{€171\,000}{€257\,000} \quad (19.3)$$
$$= 0.665, \text{ or } 66.5\%$$

EXHIBIT 19.3

TRAVAUX MARITIME SA: CURRENT AND PROJECTED INCOME STATEMENTS (€ THOUSANDS)

	Current	Projected	Assumptions
Net sales	€2000	€2600	Sales increase: 30%
Costs	1700	2210	Total costs = 85% of sales
Taxable income	€ 300	€ 390	
Taxes (34.1%)	102	133	
Net income	€ 198	€ 257	
Dividends	€ 66	€ 86	Dividend policy: 33.5% of net income
Addition to retained earnings	€ 132	€ 171	

The projected income statement for Travaux Maritime SA assumes that the income statement items vary directly with sales.

The dividend payout ratio tells what percentage of the firm's earnings is paid out as cash dividends to shareholders. Similarly, the retention ratio tells what percentage of the firm's earnings is retained in the firm. Generally speaking, smaller, fast-growing companies plowback all or most of their earnings into the business; whereas more established firms with slower growth rates and larger cash flows distribute more of their profits to shareholders. Notice that the retention ratio plus the payout ratio equals 1.000 (0.335 + 0.665). This must be true, because net income is paid out as a cash dividend and/or retained in the firm.

The Balance Sheet

To generate a projected balance sheet, we start with the current balance sheet, as shown in Exhibit 19.4. For each account that varies directly with sales, the exhibit gives the relation as a percentage of sales for the current year. Notice that these percentages differ among the accounts. How do we determine which accounts vary with sales, and how do we know what the relevant percentages are? Fortunately, the process is straightforward.

Historical Trends

We begin by looking at balance sheet accounts that might vary with sales. To do this we gather four or five years of historical accounting data and express those data as a percentage of sales. A trend may be self-evident, or some simple trend lines can be fitted to the data to identify trends. In either case, this process allows the financial manager to decide which financial accounts can safely be estimated as a percentage of sales and which must be forecast using other information.

The following table shows several years of historical data from Travaux Maritime's balance

EXHIBIT 19.4

TRAVAUX MARITIME SA: CURRENT BALANCE SHEET (€ THOUSANDS)

Assets			Liabilities and Shareholders' Equity		
	Current	Project % of sales		Current	Project % of sales
Net non-current assets	€ 640	32%	Shareholders' equity		
Current assets			Ordinary shares	€10	n/a
Inventories	140	7%	Retained earnings	590	n/a
Accounts receivable	120	6%	Total shareholders' equity	600	n/a
Cash	100	5%	Non-current liabilities		
Total current assets	360		Long-term debt	200	n/a
			Current liabilities		
			Notes payable	140	n/a
			Accounts payable	60	4%
			Total current liabilities	200	
			Total liabilities	400	
Total assets	€1000	50%	Total liabilities and shareholders' equity	€1000	50%

In this balance sheet for Travaux Maritime SA, many accounts vary directly with sales. The projected percentage of sales is shown for each of these accounts. The accounts labelled 'n/a' do not change proportionally with sales.

sheet accounts, and the far right column contains the final forecast values. We now discuss the rationale for assigning a percentage of sales figure to each balance sheet account. We look first at the working capital accounts: cash, accounts receivable, inventory and accounts payable.

| | Percentage of Sales | | | | |
	2008	2009	2010	2011	Forecast 2012
Cash	5%	5%	4%	5%	5%
Accounts receivable	10	9	9	9	6
Inventory	7	8	7	6	7
Accounts payable	4	4	4	3	4
Net fixed assets	30	32	34	32	32

Working Capital Accounts

The key working capital accounts tend to vary directly with sales. Take inventories as an example. As sales increase, the firm needs to increase the level of inventories proportionally to support the higher sales level. The historical data in the table support this view. Inventory levels have been a relatively constant percentage of sales, varying from 6% to 8%. In selecting the appropriate percentage for the planning process, management must consider what the firm's optimal inventory ratio is. On the one hand, as discussed in Chapter 14, management would like to minimise inventory levels, because inventory is expensive to finance. On the other hand, if inventory levels become too low, the firm may lose sales because of stock outs, which occur when an order comes in and there is no product to sell. Let us assume that Travaux Maritime's management determines that 7% of projected sales is the right inventory-to-sales ratio for the firm.

The ratio of accounts receivable to sales has been 9% for the last several years. However, firms with similar credit policies operate with a receivables-to-sales ratio of 6%. As sales have increased, Travaux Maritime has provided proportionally more credit to its customers. To improve the firm's performance to industry standards, management decides to collect receivables more aggressively and

targets the ratio at 6%. The firm has targeted the cash accounts at 5% of sales. Management believes that a 5% cash ratio provides adequate liquidity to fund ongoing operations and for unexpected emergencies, yet does not tie up an excessive amount of cash in low-yielding assets.

On the liability side, the firm's historical data show that accounts payable vary with sales. This seems reasonable, since the greater a firm's sales, the more orders the firm will have to place with its suppliers. Management is satisfied with the firm's vendor relationships and the payment schedule for vendors. Hence, accounts payable are forecast to be 4% of sales.

Fixed Assets

We assume that the company's net fixed assets vary with the level of sales. An examination of historical data shown earlier confirms that this is a reasonable assumption. Travaux Maritime's management decides to use the firm's four-year historical average – 32% – for the projected ratio of fixed assets to sales. Thus, for every €100 in sales, the firm needs €32 of fixed assets to support the sales.

We should note that the relation of fixed assets to sales may not always hold. The reason is that fixed assets may vary directly with sales only when a firm is operating at full capacity and fixed assets can be added in small increments. For example, if a firm has a large amount of unused capacity, its sales could increase by 20% without adding any new fixed assets. We will come back to this issue in more detail later in the chapter. For Travaux Maritime, the data support the proportional fixed assets-to-sales ratio, so we can proceed on that basis.

As a final comment, notice in Exhibit 19.4 – on the asset side of the balance sheet – that the total percentage of sales for asset items adds up to 50%. This means that total assets are 50% of sales. The ratio of total assets to sales is called the *capital intensity ratio* and is calculated for Travaux Maritime as follows:

$$\text{Capital intensity ratio} = \frac{\text{Total assets}}{\text{Net sales}}$$
$$= \frac{\text{€1 million}}{\text{€2 million}} \quad (19.4)$$
$$= 0.50, \text{ or } 50\%$$

The capital intensity ratio tells us something about the amount of assets the firm needs to generate €1 in sales. The higher the ratio, the more capital the firm needs to generate sales – that is, the more *capital intensive* is the firm. Firms that are highly capital intensive tend to be more risky than similar firms that use less fixed assets. As discussed in Chapter 12, if there is a downturn in sales, profits decrease sharply for firms with high fixed costs because fixed costs cannot be reduced in the short term. High capital intensities are generally associated with high fixed assets and high fixed costs. With a 50% capital intensity ratio, Travaux Maritime is not a highly capital-intensive firm. Examples of capital-intensive industries are the airline and automobile industries; for example, both Lufthansa and Renault have capital intensity ratios greater than 150%.

Liabilities and Equity

For most firms, the remaining liability accounts on the balance sheet do not vary with sales. Their values typically change because of management decisions, such as the decision to pay off a loan or issue debt. Thus, each liability and equity account must be evaluated separately.

Turning to individual accounts, notes payable typically represent short-term borrowing. This account value will only change with some decision by Travaux Maritime's management, such as making a payment on a note or borrowing more money from a bank. Thus, the account's value does not vary with sales, as indicated by the 'n/a' (not applicable) in Exhibit 19.4. Similarly, the account value for long-term debt changes only when management decides to issue or retire debt. The same argument holds for the ordinary share account, which changes only when management decides to sell or retire ordinary shares. The last account is retained earnings. Retained earnings may or may not vary directly with sales. The reason for the ambiguity is that the amount of funds in retained earnings depends not only on the firm's earnings, but also on the firm's dividend policy, which is set by management. Thus, for now, both the ordinary share and the retained earnings accounts are entered as n/a in Exhibit 19.4.

The Preliminary Projected Balance Sheet

We are now in a position to construct a preliminary projected balance sheet, as shown in Exhibit 19.5. The preliminary projected balance sheet is a first approximation in deciding how the firm should fund the assets it needs to support an increase in sales of 30%. Once it is constructed, management can begin its detective work to find a suitable financing plan.

To construct the preliminary projected balance sheet, we follow these steps:

1. First, calculate the anticipated values for all the accounts that vary with sales, and enter these values into the preliminary projected balance sheet.
2. Then, compute and enter the future value of any other balance sheet accounts for which an end-of-period value can be forecast or otherwise determined.
3. For all the accounts for which end-of-period values could not be forecast or otherwise determined (the n/a accounts), enter the current year's value.
4. Typically, the balance sheet will not balance at this point. We thus compute the plug value, which balances the balance sheet. The plug value will involve the accounts marked 'n/a' in the initial balance sheet (e.g., Exhibit 19.4). We must analyse these accounts in light of the firm's capital structure and dividend policies. The plug value is usually the amount of external financing needed, because we are usually adding new assets to the balance sheet to support growth; thus, total assets exceed total liabilities plus equity.

We will work through each step using numbers from the Travaux Maritime case.

Step one. We calculate the projected balance sheet values for the accounts that vary with sales as follows (projected sales are €2.6 million):

- Cash is projected to be 5% of sales: €2.6 million × 0.05 = €130 000.
- Accounts receivable is projected to be 6% of sales: €2.6 million × 0.06 = €156 000.

EXHIBIT 19.5

TRAVAUX MARITIME SA: PRELIMINARY PROJECTED BALANCE SHEET (€ THOUSANDS)

Assets			Liabilities and Shareholders' Equity		
	Projected	**Change**		**Projected**	**Change**
Net non-current assets	€ 832	€192	Shareholders' equity		
Current assets			Ordinary shares	€ 10	
Inventory	182	42	Retained earnings	761	€171
Accounts receivable	156	36	Total shareholders' equity	771	
Cash	130	30	Non-current liabilities		
Total current assets	468	108	Long-term debt	200	
			Current liabilities		
			Notes payable	140	
			Accounts payable	104	44
			Total current liabilities	244	
			Total liabilities	444	
Total assets	€1300	€300	Total liabilities and shareholders' equity	€1215	€215
			External financing needed (EFN)	€ 85	€215

This preliminary projected balance sheet for Travaux Maritime is a first approximation in deciding how to fund anticipated growth. At this stage of the analysis, the balance sheet will not balance (A ≠ L + SE) and the difference will be the plug value, which is usually the amount of external financing the firm will need in order to fund investments and operations.

- Inventories are projected to be 7% of sales: €2.6 million × 0.07 = €182 000.
- Net fixed assets are projected to be 32% of sales: €2.6 million × 0.32 = €832 000.
- Accounts payable is projected to be 4% of sales: €2.6 million × 0.04 = €104 000.

These values, along with the differences between the current and forecast amounts, are shown in Exhibit 19.5.

Step two. We now consider the balance sheet accounts that do not vary with sales. We can determine the value of retained earnings, since the firm has a dividend policy of paying out one-third of earnings as dividends. Recall from our earlier discussion that projected net income is €257 000 and the proportion of that amount going to retained earnings is €171 000 (2/3 × €257 000 = €171 000). Thus, the end-of-year account balance is €761 000 (€590 000 + €171 000 = €761 000), where €590 000 is the current retained earnings balance.

Step three. The remaining accounts that do not vary with sales represent sources of financing for the firm: notes payable, long-term debt and ordinary shares. These accounts are entered into the preliminary projected balance sheet at their current values, as shown in Exhibit 19.5.

Step four. As predicted, the preliminary projected balance sheet does not balance at this point: projected assets total €1.3 million, and projected sources of funding (debt and equity) total €1.215 million. The difference between these two values is our plug value. The plug value represents external funding needed, which is €85 000 (€1.3 million − €1.215 million = €85 000). Since we are dealing with a financing situation, all accounts with the n/a designation represent possible financing options. Management must use financial judgement and knowledge of Travaux Maritime to select a financing option for the firm.

What the Findings Mean

What does all the information in Exhibit 19.5 tell management? First, if sales increase as projected, the firm's total assets will expand by €300 000. Of that €300 000 increase, €108 000 will go to increase current assets and €192 000 will go to increase the firm's fixed assets.

Second, the €300 000 in additional assets could be financed as follows: €171 000 from internally generated funds (the addition to retained earnings), €44 000 from expanded trade credit (the increase in accounts payable), and €85 000 of external financing from the sale of debt or equity or both.

Management's Decision

How should Travaux Maritime fund the €300 000 to support the 30% increase in sales? The firm could issue debt, equity or reduce dividends. Alternatively, the firm could also rethink its strategy and scale back the 30% targeted growth figure. Suppose Travaux Maritime's management team meets to discuss the findings from Exhibit 19.5. After much discussion, they reach a consensus on the following points:

1. The firm has a unique opportunity to ride a strong economy and wants to pursue the 30% sales growth targeted.

2. Management is concerned about issuing more debt because of the volatility of the oil and gas exploration business.
3. Management prefers not to issue more ordinary shares for fear of diluting earnings.
4. Management would like to pay an annual dividend but only when justified.

What does management do? In the end, management decides to pay no cash dividend to shareholders for the coming year. Thus, the €300 000 increase in assets is funded entirely from earnings. This decision is made to avoid the risks associated with additional debt and the dilution of earnings that would result from issuing additional common share.

The Final Projected Balance Sheet

Exhibit 19.6 shows the final projected balance sheet reflecting the decision to temporarily suspend dividends and fund the expansion with internal funds (retained earnings). As you will recall, Travaux Maritime's net income is €257 000; and thus, the retained earnings account is increased by €257 000, making the final balance €847 000 (€590 000 + €257 000). Since the proposed dividend of €86 000 now goes entirely into retained earnings (a source of funds), and the firm's additional financing needs are €85 000, there is €1000 (€86 000 − €85 000) available to reduce debt. The most likely course of action is to reduce notes payable by €1000, making notes payable €139 000 rather than €140 000.[3]

Finally, it is important to note that financial models do not make decisions: only the firm's management can do that. Financial models can only generate numbers given the inputs and assumptions made when constructing the model. Once constructed, financial models can help management evaluate strategic alternatives, assess their financial impact on the firm and determine whether they are consistent with the firm's financial policies. In the Travaux Maritime case, management suspended its dividend policy.

EXHIBIT 19.6

TRAVAUX MARITIME SA: FINAL PROJECTED BALANCE SHEET (€ THOUSANDS)

Assets	Current	Change	Liabilities and Shareholders' Equity	Current	Change
Net non-current assets	€832	€192	Owner's equity		
Current assets			Ordinary shares	€10	
Inventory	182	42	Retained earnings	847	€257
Accounts receivable	156	36	Total shareholders' equity	857	
Cash	130	30	Non-current liabilities		
Total current assets	468	108	Long-term debt	200	
			Current liabilities		
			Notes payable	139	−1
			Accounts payable	104	44
			Total current liabilities	243	
			Total liabilities	443	
Total assets	€1300	€300	Total liabilities and shareholders' equity	€1300	€300
			External financing needed (EFN)	€0	€300

The final pro forma balance sheet reflects Travaux Maritime management's decision to temporarily suspend dividends and fund its growth with internal funds (retained earnings). Although financial models can determine the amount of EFN needed, management must make the final decision about how to fund the firm's capital requirements.

Travaux Maritime's Alternative Plan

Problem: Let us continue the Travaux Maritime case. Suppose that Travaux Maritime's management now decides to pay a cash dividend but to reduce the payout to 10% of net income. Reconcile Travaux Maritime's retained earnings account.

Approach: First, we must calculate the new dividend payout and the amount of funds going into retained earnings. Since net income remains unchanged at €257 000, we calculate the dividends and addition to retained earnings by multiplying the net income by the payout and the retention percentages. Second, we must calculate the impact of the new dividend policy on the retained earnings account. An easy way to do this is to reconcile the retained earnings account.

Solution: The calculations for the new dividend payout and the addition to retained earnings are:

(1) Cash dividends = 0.10 × €257 000 = €25 700

(2) Addition to retained earnings = 0.90 × €257 000 = €231 300

The calculations to reconcile the retained earnings account are:

Beginning retained earnings balance	€590 000
+ Net income	257 000
− Dividends	25 700
Ending retained earnings balance	€821 300

Thus, the new retained earnings balance is €821 300.

Before You Go On

1. How are historical financial data used to determine the forecast values of balance sheet accounts?
2. Why might you expect accounts receivable to vary with sales?

BEYOND THE BASIC PLANNING MODELS

Learning Objective 4

Describe the conditions under which fixed assets vary directly with sales and discuss the impact of so-called lumpy assets on this relation.

In this section, we tie up some important loose ends concerning financial planning models. We first consider some shortcomings of the simple models we have been discussing and describe how more sophisticated models address those shortcomings. We then discuss additional benefits of financial planning.

Improving Financial Planning Models

Much of the discussion concerning the planning models developed in this chapter focuses on the underlying process for generating projected statements. We readily admit that our models lack sophistication. However, our goal is to have you understand how planning models work so that when you move to more elegant computer-based models, you will be an informed user capable of understanding the programs' limitations and strengths. We now discuss some of the improvements you should expect to find incorporated in most computer-based models.

Interest Expense

One omission from the models presented in this chapter is that they fail to account for interest expenses in the financial statements. A problem we face in modelling is that interest expenses cannot be estimated accurately until the cost and amount of borrowing have been determined, and the cost of borrowing depends in part on the amount of borrowing. Thus, we cannot accurately estimate one without the other. More sophisticated financial models estimate the interest payments and borrowings simultaneously.

Working Capital Accounts

Another weakness in our percentage of sales model is the assumption that working capital increases proportionally with sales. Seasoned financial managers know that increases in some working capital accounts are not proportional to sales; this is particularly true for cash balances and inventories. Exhibit 19.7, for example, shows the inventory-to-sales ratios for two situations: one where inventory varies directly with sales and one where it does not. The blue line illustrates the assumption that changes in inventory vary in proportion to changes in sales. Notice that inventory gets very small as sales approach zero. When inventory varies in proportion to sales, the inventory-to-sales ratio is 50%, regardless of the level of sales. The red line illustrates a different relationship. Here, at sales of €300, the inventory-to-sales ratio is 70%

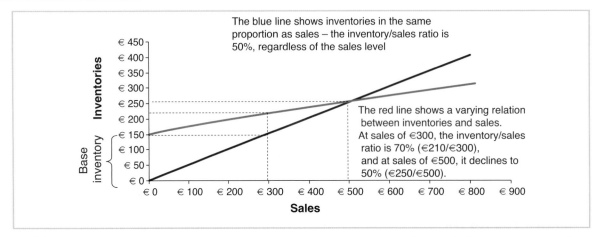

Exhibit 19.7: Relation between Inventory Levels and Changes in Sales   This graph shows inventory-to-sales ratios for two situations: one in which inventories vary directly with sales (blue line) and one in which it does not (red line). Financial managers know from experience that most working capital accounts, such as inventories, do not increase directly with sales. Instead, they increase at a decreasing rate as sales increase.

(€210/€300), and at sales of €500 it declines to 50% (€250/€500). The important point here is not the ratio calculations but the fact that working capital does not increase directly with sales. Instead, it increases at a decreasing rate as sales increase. This is a common relation between inventory and sales.

Fixed Assets

Another weakness is in the way we handle fixed assets. Specifically, we assumed that when sales increase, fixed assets are added in small increments and that production facilities are always operating near or at full capacity. This is not typically the case. In most instances, fixed assets are added as large discrete units and much of a firm's capacity may not be utilised for some period of time. These types of assets are often called **lumpy assets**. Let us look at an example.

> **Lumpy assets**
>
> fixed assets added as large, discrete units; these assets may not be used to full capacity for some time, leaving the company with excess capacity

Suppose you and a group of investors decide to enter the market for frozen Mexican snack foods, which you believe is a growing market. You buy a small food-manufacturing facility that can easily be converted to manufacture Mexican snack foods. Exhibit 19.8 illustrates your initial situation. After you make the purchase, your sales are zero and you have €100 000 in fixed assets, which will support sales of up to €150 000. Thus, the facility has €150 000 in excess capacity.

Over time, sales expand to €75 000. At this level, no additional assets are needed (point A in the exhibit) because the firm still has excess capacity of €75 000 (€150 000 – €75 000). When the firm's sales expand to €150 000 (point B), however, the firm no longer has idle capacity. Your production manager determines that a €200 000 addition to fixed assets is the most economical way to gain additional capacity. If you make this investment, the firm will have €300 000 (€100 000 + €200 000) in fixed assets, which will support sales up to €400 000. Notice that when your firm is at point B, the threshold point, even a small increase in sales results in more than doubling the firm's fixed assets.

In financial planning, management must account for the fact that fixed assets often come in very large increments, or 'lumps'. Furthermore, a significant amount of lead time is often required to bring them on line. Thus, as a firm nears full manufacturing capacity, management should begin planning to acquire additional fixed assets in the future. In

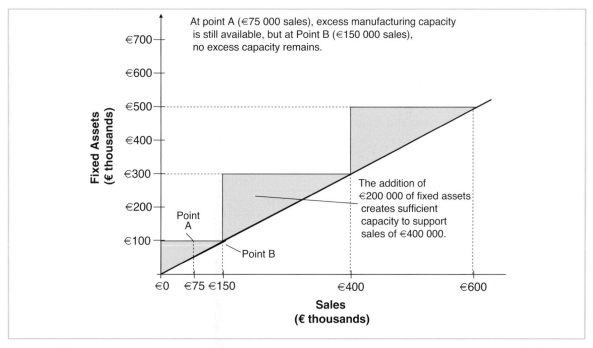

At point A (€75 000 sales), excess manufacturing capacity is still available, but at Point B (€150 000 sales), no excess capacity remains.

The addition of €200 000 of fixed assets creates sufficient capacity to support sales of €400 000.

Exhibit 19.8: Fixed Assets are Usually Acquired in Large, Discrete Units In real-world situations, fixed assets usually do not vary directly with sales, as we assumed in our simplified financial models. Management often adds fixed assets in very large increments in order to add capacity in the most economical way.

contrast, if a firm has considerable excess capacity, sales growth will not require additions to fixed assets.

Before You Go On

1. Why is it that some working capital accounts may not vary proportionally with sales?
2. What are lumpy assets, and how do these assets vary with sales?

MANAGING AND FINANCING GROWTH

Learning Objective 5

Explain what factors determine a firm's sustainable growth rate, discuss why it is of interest to management and be able to compute the sustainable growth rate for a firm.

We close the chapter with a discussion of how a business can grow and the need to manage growth. When companies add assets through acquisition or the capital budgeting process, they grow in size. If the rate of growth is rapid, much of the asset expansion will likely require external financing. Rapid growth is often a goal of management because it helps a company gain market share quickly and strengthens its competitive position in the marketplace. In addition, management in companies with high growth rates often receives accolades and recognition from investors and their peers for their business acumen. Overall, rapid growth is considered a desirable achievement for the management of a firm.

Rapid growth can have a dark side, however. As a firm grows rapidly, management might finance the growth with long-term debt in a way that increases the firm's overall financial leverage. Higher financial leverage increases the probability that a firm will face bankruptcy, if business conditions deteriorate. If management is using a lot of debt financing and sales then unexpectedly plunge, causing cash flows to decline, the firm may not have enough cash to pay long-term debt holders and other creditors.

An example of a firm using too much debt to finance growth is the Brazilian low-cost carrier, GOL Linhas Aéreas Inteligentes. Key financials and selected ratios for the year end from 2005 to 2009 are given below:

figures for 2009 indicate, growth at any price is now a thing of the past and managing the firm's cash flow and profitability are the rule.

How does rapid growth cause businesses to get into trouble? GOL is an example of the classic formula: rapid expansion, a lack of solid long-term planning and an insufficient equity base or, put another way, the use of too much financial leverage.

Financials	Year to 31 December				
Millions of Brazilian Real (R$)	2005	2006	2007	2008	2009
Revenue	R$2669	R$3802	R$4941	R$6406	R$6025
Cost of revenue	1613	2437	4230	5451	4733
SGA and other	434	663	701	1044	879
Operating expense	2048	3101	4931	6495	5612
Net operating profit	R$621	R$701	R$10	−R$89	R$413
Total assets	R$2556	R$4258	R$7486	R$7132	R$8720
Total equity	1822	2205	2392	1072	2610
Total liabilities	734	2053	5094	6060	6110
Ratios					
Sales growth	36.1	42.4	30.0	29.7	−5.9
Operating return on assets	24.3	16.5	0.1	−1.2	4.7
Operating margin	60.4	64.1	85.6	85.1	78.5
Debt/equity ratio	40.3	93.1	212.9	565.5	234.1
Return on equity	28.2	25.8	7.0	−115.7	34.1

The sales growth for the company has been very rapid, with sales increasing by an average of just over 36% per year in the period 2005–2007. At the same time, the total assets increased from R$2556 million in 2005 to R$7132 million in 2007, an increase of 193%. Assets increased faster than revenue growth, and the operating margin deteriorated from around 64% to 85%. As the operating return on assets shows, the company was not earning a decent return on its assets and, to cap it all, the debt-to-equity ratio was exploding. As the financial information shows, GOL has used a lot of debt to finance its growth. It all came to a head in 2007–2008, when the company experienced very tough trading conditions following the global credit crunch. It was only because shareholders and lenders supported the company that it was able to pull through. It was a close thing! As the

External Funding Needed

When a firm expands rapidly, its operations might not be able to generate sufficient cash flows to meet all of its current financial obligations. If this happens, management must look for outside funding – debt or equity. We now explore the factors affecting management's decision to seek external financing. We do so by developing some relationships between a firm's growth rate and the amount of external funding needed (EFN).

Growth and External Funding

The best way to understand the relation between growth and external funding is in the context of a rapidly growing firm and its financial statements. The firm we use is called Vorlauf Immobilien AG, which is a hypothetical property investment company located in Berlin that engages in property

EXHIBIT 19.9

VORLAUF IMMOBILIEN AG: INCOME STATEMENT AND BALANCE SHEET (€ MILLION)

Income Statement

Net sales	€100.0
Costs	90.0
Net income	€ 10.0
Dividends	€ 6
Addition to retained earnings	€ 4

Balance Sheet

Assets		Percentage of Sales	Liabilities and Shareholders' Equity		Percentage of Sales
Assets	€50.0	20%	Equity	€30.0	n/a
			Total debt	20.0	n/a
Total assets	€50.0		Total liabilities and shareholders' equity	€50.0	

The exhibit shows the current income statement and balance sheet for Vorlauf Immobilien AG. Management believes that the firm can increase sales by 20% for the coming year. All costs and assets are assumed to grow at the same rate as sales and 60% of earnings are paid out as dividends.

development and property management. Vorlauf Immobilien is a public company whose share is listed on the Deutsche Börse, the German stock exchange.

Exhibit 19.9 shows the current income statement and balance sheet for Vorlauf Immobilien. Last year Vorlauf Immobilien had total assets of €50 million, book equity of €30 million and generated €10 million of earnings on €100 million in sales. Vorlauf Immobilien's management team believes the firm can increase sales by 20% for the coming year. All costs and assets are assumed to grow at the same rate as sales, 60% of earnings are paid as cash dividends and the board of directors is reluctant to issue additional ordinary shares.

Given this information, we can prepare the projected income statement and balance sheet for Vorlauf Immobilien, which appear in Exhibit 19.10. The income statement shows both sales and

costs increasing by 20% for the year: projected sales are €120 million (€100 million × 1.20), projected costs are €108 million (€90 million × 1.20) and thus, the firm's projected net income is €12 million (€120 million – €108 million).

Turning to the projected balance sheet, we see that the total assets for the firm are €60 million (€50 million × 1.20). For the moment, total debt remains constant at €20 million because this account will be the plug value – the EFN to support the 20% increase in sales. The firm's dividend policy calls for 40% of earnings to be retained in the firm, since 60% will be paid to shareholders as a dividend. Thus, given net income of €12 million, the addition to retained earnings is €4.8 million (0.40 × €12 million). The equity account is increased to €34.8 million (€30.0 million + €4.8 million).

After these changes have been made, the projected balance sheet does not balance. Total assets

EXHIBIT 19.10

VORLAUF IMMOBILIEN AG: PRO FORMA INCOME STATEMENT AND BALANCE SHEET (€ MILLIONS)

Income Statement

Net sales	€120.0
Costs	108.0
Net income	€ 12.0
Dividends	€ 7.2
Addition to retained earnings	€ 4.8

Balance Sheet

Assets			Liabilities and Shareholders' Equity		
		Change			Change
Assets	€60.0	10.0	Equity	€34.8	€4.8
			Total debt	20.0	0.0
Total assets	€60.0	€10.0	Total liabilities and shareholders' equity	€54.8	€4.8
			External financing needed (EFN)	€ 5.2	5.2

The projected balance sheet for Vorlauf Immobilien AG does not balance and the difference is the amount of EFN. Because the company's board does not wish to issue ordinary shares, the funding will have to take the form of long-term debt.

equal €60.0 million and total liabilities and equity equal €54.8 million. The difference, €5.2 million (€60.0 million – €54.8 million), is the EFN. The €10 million (€4.8 million + €5.2 million) investment is being financed from two sources: €4.8 million from the addition to retained earnings and €5.2 million from external funding. The EFN could be either debt or equity, but in Vorlauf Immobilien's case it will be long-term debt, since Vorlauf Immobilien's board is reluctant to issue equity.

So far, we have calculated EFN exactly as we did in the previous sections. However, we are now going to build a mathematical model to calculate EFN. The model will allow us to better understand the relation between a firm's growth ambitions and the amount of EFN.

A Mathematical Model

Looking at the projected balance sheet calculations for Vorlauf Immobilien (Exhibit 19.10), we can see that new investments are determined by the firm's total assets and projected growth in sales:

New investments = Growth rate × Initial assets

For Vorlauf Immobilien, the calculation is €10 million = 0.20 × €50 million. Note that to calculate new investments, we multiply the firm's initial total assets by the expected growth rate in sales forecasted by management. The new investments are the capital expenditure plus the increase in working capital necessary to sustain the increase in sales.

Conceptually, the new investments are funded first by internally generated funds, which come from earnings retained in the firm. Once those funds are exhausted, the remainder of new investments must be financed externally by the sale of debt or equity, or some combination of both. Thus, the amount of EFN can be expressed as:

$$\text{EFN} = \text{New investments} - \text{Addition to retained earnings} \quad (19.5)$$

Substituting Growth rate × Initial assets for New investments in Equation (19.5) yields the following:

$$\text{EFN} = (\text{Growth rate} \times \text{Initial assets}) - \text{Addition to retained earnings} \quad (19.6)$$

Applying Equation (19.6) to our Vorlauf Immobilien situation, we get the following results:

$$\begin{aligned}
\text{EFN} &= (0.20 \times \text{€}50 \text{ million}) - \text{€}4.8 \text{ million} \\
&= \text{€}10 \text{ million} - \text{€}4.8 \text{ million} \\
&= \text{€}5.2 \text{ million}
\end{aligned}$$

The result, €5.2 million, agrees with the financial planning model calculation for Vorlauf Immobilien presented earlier.

Equation (19.6) highlights two important points. First, holding dividend policy constant, the amount of EFN depends on the firm's projected growth rate. The faster management expects the firm to grow, the more the firm needs to invest in new assets and the more capital it has to raise. The potential sources of external capital are the sale of new shares and the sale of long-term debt. Second, the firm's dividend policy also affects EFN. Holding growth rate constant, the higher the firm's payout ratio, the larger the amount of external debt or equity financing needed.

A Graphical View of Growth

Exhibit 19.11 graphically illustrates Equation (19.6) – the connection between growth rate in

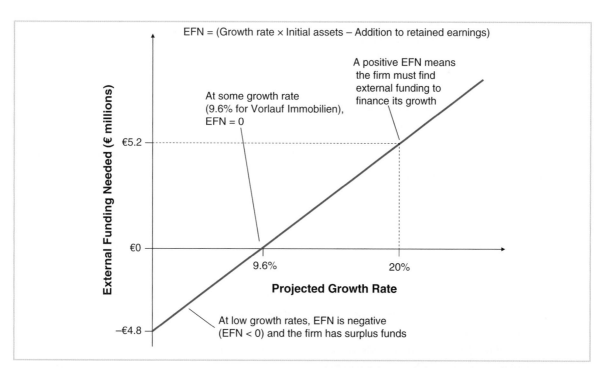

Exhibit 19.11: External Funding Needed (EFN) and Growth for Vorlauf Immobilien AG The exhibit graphically illustrates Equation (19.6), showing the connection between the growth rate in sales and EFN. The horizontal axis plots the firm's projected growth rate and the vertical axis plots EFN. The upward slope of the line illustrates how external financing increases with the growth rate, assuming that the dividend policy is held constant.

sales and EFN – for Vorlauf Immobilien. The horizontal axis plots the firm's projected growth rate and the vertical axis plots EFN. The slope of the line illustrates how external financing increases with the growth rate, assuming that dividend policy is held constant. As you can see, the line is upward sloping. This means that as the growth rate increases, the amount of EFN increases.

As a reference point in the exhibit, we plotted Vorlauf Immobilien's EFN value of €5.2 million when the firm's sales are growing at a 20% rate. If you want to generate the line yourself, all you need to do is make another calculation of EFN at a different growth rate, plot the points and connect them with a straight line. However, the important point here is not the mechanics of generating the graph in Exhibit 19.11 but the interpretation of the line.

Turning to the exhibit, you can see that at low growth rates Vorlauf Immobilien will generate more funds from earnings than it will spend on new investments. In these situations, the calculated value for EFN is negative (EFN < 0) and the firm has a 'surplus' of funds. In other words, the internally generated funds available from earnings exceed the firm's planned investments. With the surplus funds, management may elect to retire some of its debt or buy back some of its outstanding ordinary shares. For example, at a 0% rate of growth, no funds are needed for expansion and all the retained earnings are surplus, as we can see by using Equation (19.6):

$$\text{EFN} = (\text{Growth rate} \times \text{Initial assets})$$
$$- \text{Addition to retained earnings}$$
$$= (0.0 \times \text{€50 million}) - \text{€4.8 million}$$
$$= \text{€4.8 million}$$

With an increased growth rate, the surplus becomes smaller and smaller as more and more funds are used to finance the new investments. At a growth rate of 9.6%, the surplus equals zero, as does the calculated value of EFN. Next we explain how to calculate the growth rate at which the surplus equals zero. The key point here is that the higher the rate at which a firm grows, the more external funding it requires.

The Internal Growth Rate

Management often has an interest in knowing the rate at which the firm can grow using just internally generated funds. This rate is called the **internal growth rate (IGR)**. The IGR is defined as the maximum growth rate that a firm can achieve without external financing. To determine this rate, we set Equation (19.6) equal to zero (EFN = 0) and solve for the growth rate. Thus:

> **Internal growth rate (IGR)**
>
> the maximum growth rate that a firm can achieve without external financing

$$\text{EFN} = (\text{Growth rate} \times \text{Initial assets})$$
$$- \text{Addition to retained earnings}$$
$$= 0$$

Rearranging terms yields the internal growth rate:

$$\text{IGR} = \frac{\text{Additions to retained earnings}}{\text{Initial assets}} \quad (19.7)$$

The managerial implications of the formula are straightforward. Firms that can generate a higher volume of retained earnings and/or use fewer assets can sustain a higher growth rate without raising more capital. For the Vorlauf Immobilien example, the internal growth rate is calculated as:

$$\text{IGR} = \frac{\text{Additions to retained earnings}}{\text{Initial assets}}$$
$$= \frac{\text{€4.8 million}}{\text{€50 million}} = 0.096, \text{ or } 9.6\%$$

To gain more insight into what factors determine a firm's internal growth rate, we can manipulate Equation (19.7) by multiplying both the numerator and the denominator by net income and equity, as follows:

$$\text{IGR} = \frac{\text{Additions to retained earnings}}{\text{Initial assets}}$$
$$\times \frac{\text{Net income}}{\text{Net income}} \times \frac{\text{Equity}}{\text{Equity}}$$

If we then rearrange terms, we arrive at the following expression:

$$IGR = \frac{\text{Additions to retained earnings}}{\text{Net income}} \times \frac{\text{Net income}}{\text{Equity}} \times \frac{\text{Equity}}{\text{Initial assets}}$$

From the discussions in Chapter 4 and in this chapter, we know the following: (1) plowback ratio = addition to retained earnings/net income; (2) return on equity = net income/equity; and (3) equity multiplier = total assets/equity.[4] This means that we can write the above equation as:

$$IGR = \text{Plowback ratio} \times \text{Return on equity} \times \text{Measure of leverage}$$

(19.8)

Equation (19.8) tells us that firms that achieve higher growth rates without seeking external financing tend to have the following characteristics:

• Dividend policies that retain a high proportion of earnings inside the firm – that is, they have a high plowback ratio.
• Ability to generate a high net income with a smaller amount of equity than other firms and hence have a high return on equity (ROE).
• Use low amounts of leverage; thus, their debt-to-equity ratios are low.

The Sustainable Growth Rate

Another growth rate helpful in long-term planning is the **sustainable growth rate (SGR)**, which is the rate of growth that the firm can sustain without selling additional equity while maintaining the same capital structure. You may wonder why management is interested in the sustainable growth rate. The sustainable growth rate is important to managers of firms that are likely to generate excess funds internally and who want to determine the payout ratio that enables them to fund their firms' growth while maintaining their current capital structures.

Sustainable growth rate (SGR)

the rate of growth that a firm can sustain without selling additional equity while maintaining the same capital structure

The sustainable growth rate is the rate at which a firm can grow using only (1) internally generated funds from earnings and (2) external funds from the sale of new debt while maintaining a constant debt-to-equity ratio. As it turns out, SGR is a function of the firm's plowback ratio and the return on equity (ROE). SGR can be expressed as follows:

$$SGR = \text{Plowback ratio} \times ROE$$ (19.9)

For Vorlauf Immobilien, the sustainable growth rate is:

$$SGR = 0.4 \times \frac{€10 \text{ million}}{€30 \text{ million}}$$
$$= 0.4 \times 0.333$$
$$= 0.133, \text{ or } 13.3\%$$

The 13.3% rate is a fairly high SGR that is driven by the company's rather hefty 33.3% return on equity.

An analysis of a company's SGR relative to the company's actual growth rate can provide management with some insights into problems the firm may face in the future. For example, if a firm's actual growth rate consistently exceeds its SGR, management knows that unless they sell new equity, the firm will have a cash shortage problem in the future because of the need to purchase new assets to generate the growth. The SGR model does not, however, tell management how fast the firm should grow. That decision requires informed judgement about the attractiveness of the investment opportunities available to the firm.

Decision-Making Example 19.2

Vorlauf Immobilien's Ambitious Growth Plan

Situation: You are part of the Vorlauf Immobilien finance team. The firm's strategic plan calls for revenues to grow at 20% next year. As mentioned, the board of directors is not interested in using any additional external equity financing. Some members of the team question whether these goals are realistic.

You have just been asked to comment on the proposed growth plan at a meeting. You have a little over an hour to prepare. During the time available, you complete the following calculations using data from the most recent and the projected income statements and balance sheets (Exhibits 19.8 and 19.9):

- EFN = (Growth rate × Initial assets) – Addition to retained earnings = (0.20 × €50 million) – €4.8 million = €5.2 million.
- IGR = Addition to retained earnings/Initial assets = €4.8 million/€50 million = 0.96, or 9.6%.

- SGR = Plowback ratio × ROE = 0.40 × 0.333 = 13.3%.

Given the above information, what can you say about this ambitious growth plan?

Decision: You begin by applauding the visionary nature of the strategic plan. Clearly, you want to keep your job. You point out, however, that the firm is facing some challenges. First, Vorlauf Immobilien's IGR is 9.6%, which is the maximum growth rate the firm can achieve without any kind of external financing. This amount is substantially below the desired growth rate of 20%. Second, you note that Vorlauf Immobilien's EFN is €5.2 million. This means that €5.2 million of external capital will have to be raised by selling equity, debt or some combination of the two. Finally, Vorlauf Immobilien's SGR is 13.3% – also below the 20% growth target. Vorlauf Immobilien cannot grow more than 13.3% without selling equity if management wants to keep the firm's capital structure at its current level.

Learning by Doing Application 19.3

Sustainable Growth and Financial Statements

Problem: Because of your presentation (see Decision-Making Example 19.2), Vorlauf Immobilien's top management team has had second thoughts about their goal of growing the firm 20% during the next year. As a result, they have asked that you prepare projected financial statements at a sales growth rate equal to the firm's SGR of 13.3%.

Approach: For the income statement, all costs grow at the same rate as revenues. Thus, you can multiply the current period's sales and costs by 1.133 to calculate the projected values of sales and costs. To construct the balance sheet, you must first compute the values of accounts that vary with sales. Since you have no information about how much of Vorlauf Immobilien's total debt is long-term debt, you should enter its total debt value of €20 million, along with all the information you have on the balance sheet accounts. Finally, to make the balance sheet balance, you should calculate the amount of EFN.

Solution:

$$\text{Sales} = €100 \text{ million} \times 1.133$$

$$= €113.30 \text{ million}$$

$$\text{Costs} = €90 \text{ million} \times 1.133$$

$$= €101.97 \text{ million}$$

Income statement:

Vorlauf Immobilien AG
Projected Income Statement (€ millions)

Sales	€113.30
Costs	101.97
Net income	€ 11.33

Dividend = Net income × Payout ratio = €11.33 million × 0.60 = €6.80 million
Addition to retained earnings = Net income × Plowback ratio = €11.33 million × 0.4 = €4.53 million

Forecast value of the assets = €50 million × 1.133 = €56.65 million

Value of the equity = €30 million + €4.53 million = €34.53 million, where €30 million is the initial value and €4.53 million is the addition to retained earnings

Value of debt plus equity = €20 million + €34.53 million = €54.53 million

The balance sheet does not balance (€56.65 million > €54.53 million) and the difference (€2.12 million) is the plug number, which is the EFN. Thus, to achieve the 13.3% rate of growth, Vorlauf Immobilien will need to issue €2.12 million in long-term debt, which will bring the debt account to €20 million + €2.12 million = €22.12 million. The resulting balance sheet is as follows:

Vorlauf Immobilien AG
Projected Balance Sheet (€ millions)

Assets		Liabilities and Shareholders' Equity	
Assets	€56.65	Equity	€34.53
		Debt	20.00
Total assets	€56.65	Total liabilities and shareholders' equity	€54.53
		EFN (new debt)	€ 2.12

Growth Rates and Profits

So far, we have focused on a firm's rate of growth. In the final analysis, however, the critical question in business is not how fast the firm can grow, but whether the firm can sustain rapid growth and maintain a satisfactory level of profits. In reality, it is very difficult to achieve and sustain rapid growth in a competitive market and remain profitable. The business arena is littered with growth firms that run into difficulties, like GOL.

To provide a reality check, only a very small number of publicly traded European companies increase both revenues and operating profits by an average of 10% a year. Small high-technology companies can grow fast, but generally make operating losses; mature companies make profits, but grow slowly, if at all. Experts generally agree that growth rates at or above 10% are very difficult to sustain for established companies.

Decision-Making Example 19.3

GOL's Growth

Situation: It is early 2007 and you are advising GOL Linhas Aéreas Inteligentes, the Brazilian low-cost carrier described earlier about its financial strategy going forward. Having read this chapter and understood the issues, what advice would you give the company? The company currently pays no dividends. For ease, the financial and ratio information for 2005 and 2006 is reproduced below:

Millions of Brazilian Real	2005	2006
Revenue	R$2669	R$3802
Cost of revenue	1613	2437
SGA and other	434	663
Operating expense	2048	3101
Net operating profit	R$621	R$701
Net profit for the year	R$513	R$569
Total assets	R$2556	R$4258
Total equity	R$1822	R$2205
Total liabilities	734	2053

Ratios		
Sales growth	36.1	42.4
Operating return on assets	24.3	16.5
Operating margin	60.4	64.1
Debt/equity ratio	40.3	93.1
Return on equity	28.2	25.8

Decision: You know that, as things stand, the company is expanding at a rate that exceeds its sustainable growth rate. As the company pays no dividends, and if it is to maintain the current debt-to-equity ratio, it can only grow at 25.8%, the return on equity (ROE). If it continues to grow at a rate that is higher than this, it will have to do one or more of the following: (1) increase the operating return on assets, as this will lead to a higher ROE; (2) increase the amount of leverage as it has to borrow more; and/or (3) raise further equity from shareholders. If the company does not improve its operating return on assets, or raise further equity, and it continues to grow faster than its sustainable growth rate, it will find the leverage will increase as it will be forced to borrow to finance its rapid growth. You tell them this is unsustainable in the long run as the debt burden will become overwhelming. It is probably not a message the management wants to hear – but without addressing the issue before it becomes a crisis, the airline puts its survival at risk.

Growth as a Planning Goal

The final question we address is whether growth by itself is an acceptable strategic goal. We pose this question because it is common for top management to set growth rates as goals for the firm or operating divisions. In fact, there is nothing a CEO likes to do better at the annual meeting than point out that 'last year, under my leadership, Pro Forma exceeded its goal of 10% growth', followed by a hearty round of applause. Growth rate goals are popular because they are easy to communicate and understand. But are they appropriate goals for financial planning? The short answer is 'no'. We will consider why this is the case.

As we discussed in Chapter 1, an appropriate goal for management is maximising the market value of shareholders' equity. If management invests in productive assets with positive NPVs, finances them at the lowest possible cost and skilfully manages these assets, the company should be profitable and grow in size. This growth results from making sound business decisions and executing strategies that create sustainable competitive advantages over the long term. In other words, asset growth results from managing a profitable business. Thus, growth is an acceptable goal as long as it is anchored by a sound business strategy that will generate an increase in profitability.

> **Before You Go On**
>
> 1. What two factors determine the amount of EFN?
> 2. What is IGR and why is it of interest to management?
> 3. If a firm continually exceeds its SGR, what problems may it face in the future?

SUMMARY OF LEARNING OBJECTIVES

1. **Explain what a financial plan is and why financial planning is so important.**

   A financial plan is a set of actionable goals derived from the firm's strategic plan and other planning documents, such as the investment and financing plans. The financial plan focuses on selecting the best investment opportunities and determining how they will be financed. The financial plan is a blueprint for the firm's future. Financial planning is important to management because the plan communicates the firm's strategic goals throughout the organisation, builds support for the firm's strategies and helps align operating units with the firm's strategic goals.

2. **Discuss how management uses financial planning models in the planning process and explain the importance of sales forecasts in the construction of financial planning models.**

   Financial models are the analytical part of the financial planning process. A planning model is simply a series of equations that model a firm's financial statements, such as the income statement and balance sheet. Once the model is constructed, management can generate projected financial statements to determine the financial impact of proposed strategic initiatives on the firm.

   For most financial planning models, a forecast of the firm's sales is the most important input variable. The sales forecast is the key driver in financial planning models because many items on the income statement and balance sheet vary directly with sales. Thus, once sales are forecasted, it is easy to generate projected financial statements using the historical relationship between a particular account and sales.

3. **Discuss how the relation between projected sales and balance sheet accounts can be determined, and be able to analyse a strategic investment decision using a percentage of sales model.**

   Historical financial data can be examined to determine whether and how a variable changes with sales. One way to do this is to prepare a table that shows four or five years of historical financial statement account data as a percentage of sales. Then fit trend lines to the data to see what type of relation exists between that variable and sales. Most income statement and balance sheet items vary directly with sales, but others may vary in a non-linear manner. The analysis in the Pro Forma SE example illustrates how to analyse a strategic investment decision.

4. **Describe the conditions under which fixed assets vary directly with sales and discuss the impact of so-called lumpy assets on this relation.**

   Fixed assets vary directly with sales only when assets can be added in small increments and production facilities are operating near full capacity. This is typically not the case. In most situations, fixed assets are added in large, discrete units and, as a result, much of the new capacity may go unused for a period of time. These types of assets are often called lumpy assets. After lumpy assets are added, sales can increase for a period of time with no corresponding change in the level of fixed assets.

5. **Explain what factors determine a firm's sustainable growth rate, discuss why it is of interest to management and be able to compute the sustainable growth rate for a firm.**

A firm's sustainable growth rate (SGR) is the maximum rate at which the firm can grow without external equity financing and with leverage held constant. The determinants of a firm's SGR are: (1) profit margins (the greater a firm's profit margin, the greater the firm's SGR); (2) asset utilisation (the more efficiently a firm uses its assets, the higher its SGR); (3) financial leverage (as a firm increases its use of leverage, its SGR increases); (4) dividend policy (as a firm decreases its payout ratio, its SGR increases); and (5) economic conditions (the more favourable the economic environment, the higher the firm's SGR). Management may be interested in knowing the SGR for two reasons. First, the SGR is the rate of growth at which a firm's capital structure (debt to equity) will remain constant without the firm selling or repurchasing shares. Second, if a firm's actual growth rate exceeds its SGR, the firm could face cash shortage problems in the future unless it can sell new equity. Learning by Doing Application 19.3 uses the SGR formula.

SUMMARY OF KEY EQUATIONS

Equation	Description	Formula
(19.1)	Percentage change in sales	$\%\Delta S = \dfrac{(S_{t+1} - S_t)}{S_t}$
(19.2)	Percentage of net income paid out	$\text{Dividend payout ratio} = \dfrac{\text{Cash dividends}}{\text{Net income}}$
(19.3)	Percentage of net income retained	$\text{Retention ratio} = \dfrac{\text{Retained earnings}}{\text{Net income}}$
(19.4)	Level of assets needed to generate €1 of sales	$\text{Capital intensity ratio} = \dfrac{\text{Total assets}}{\text{Net sales}}$
(19.5)	External funding needed to support growth in sales	$\text{EFN} = \text{New investments}$ $+ \text{Addition to retained earnings}$
(19.6)		$= (\text{Growth rate} \times \text{Initial assets})$ $- \text{Addition to retained earnings}$
(19.7)	Internal growth rate (level of growth that can be supported without raising external funds)	$\text{IGR} = \dfrac{\text{Additions to retained earnings}}{\text{Initial assets}}$
(19.8)		$= \text{Plowback ratio} \times \text{Return on equity}$ $\times \text{Measure of leverage}$
(19.9)	Sustainable growth rate (level of growth that can be supported without raising external equity or increasing current leverage)	$\text{SGR} = \text{Plowback ratio} \times \text{ROE}$

SELF-STUDY PROBLEMS

19.1. The financial statements for the year ended 30 June 2011 are given here for Clair de Lune SA. The firm's sales are projected to grow at a rate of 20% next year and all financial statement accounts will vary directly with sales. Based on that projection, develop a projected balance sheet and income statement for the fiscal year ending 30 June 2012.

company pays 45% of its income as dividend every year. In addition, the company plans to expand production capacity by building a new facility that will cost €225 000. The firm has no plans to issue new equity this year. Prepare a projected balance sheet using this information. Any

Clair de Lune SA Balance Sheet and Income Statement for Fiscal Year Ended 30 June 2011

Balance Sheet

Assets		Liabilities and Shareholders' Equity	
Net fixed assets	€325 422	Ordinary shares	€150 000
Other non-current assets	13 125	Retained earnings	97 118
Total non-current assets	€338 547	Total shareholders' equity	€247 118
Current Assets		Non-current liabilities	
Inventories	167 112	Long-term debt	223 125
Accounts receivable	43 758	Current liabilities	
Cash	25 135	Notes payable	36 454
Total current assets	€236 005	Accounts payable	67 855
		Total current liabilities	€104 309
		Total liabilities	€327 434
Total assets	€574 552	Total liabilities and shareholders' equity	€574 552

Income Statement

Revenues	€1 450 000
Costs	812 500
EBITDA	€ 637 500
Depreciation	175 000
EBIT	€ 462 500
Interest	89 575
EBT	€ 372 925
Taxes (35%)	130 524
	€242 401

19.2. Use the financial information for Claire de Lune SA from Problem 19.1. Assume now that equity accounts do not vary directly with sales but change when retained earnings change or new equity is issued. The

funds that need to be raised will be in the form of long-term debt.

19.3. Use the financial statements from Problem 19.1 and the information from Problem 19.2. Calculate the company's retention ratio, external funds needed (EFN), internal growth rate (IGR) and sustainable growth rate (SGR).

19.4. Wienerwald AG has a dividend payout ratio of 60%, return on equity of 14.5%, total assets of €11 500 450 and equity of €4 652 125. Calculate the firm's internal rate of growth (IGR).

19.5. Reprise Pop SA has net income of €1.25 million and a dividend payout ratio of 35%. It currently has equity of €2 875 223. What is the firm's sustainable growth rate?

SOLUTIONS TO SELF-STUDY PROBLEMS

19.1. The projected statements for Claire de Lune are as follows:

Retained earnings from 2011 income statement = €290 882 × (1 − 0.45) = €159 985

Claire de Lune SA Balance Sheet and Income Statement for Fiscal Year Ended 30 June 2012

Balance Sheet

Assets		Liabilities and Shareholders' Equity	
Net fixed assets	€390 506	Ordinary shares	€180 000
Other non-current assets	15 750	Retained earnings	116 542
Total non-current assets	€406 256	Total shareholders' equity	€296 542
Current Assets		Non-current liabilities	
Inventories	200 534	Long-term debt	267 750
Accounts receivable	52 510	Current liabilities	
Cash	30 162	Notes payable	43 745
Total current assets	€283 206	Accounts payable	81 426
		Total current liabilities	€125 171
		Total liabilities	€392 921
Total assets	€689 462	Total liabilities and shareholders' equity	€689 462

Income Statement

Revenues	€1 740 000
Costs	975 000
EBITDA	€ 765 000
Depreciation	210 000
EBIT	€ 555 000
Interest	107 490
EBT	€ 447 510
Taxes (35%)	156 629
Net income	€ 290 882

- This is the amount by which retained earnings will increase in 2012 from €97 118 to €257 103.
- No new equity is added.
- The increase in assets is financed externally by long-term debt.

19.2. The pro forma income statement is the same as that shown in the solution to Problem 19.1. We now have to accommodate payment of dividends. Since the company pays 45% of its net income as dividends, the amount of retained earnings is calculated as follows:

The pro forma balance sheet is as follows:

Balance Sheet

Assets		Liabilities and Shareholders' Equity	
Net fixed assets	€390 506	Ordinary shares	€150 000
Addition to fixed assets	225 000	Retained earnings	257 103
Other non-current assets	15 750	Total shareholders' equity	€407 103
Total non-current assets	€631 256	Non-current liabilities	
Current Assets		Long-term debt	382 188
Inventories	200 534	Current liabilities	
Accounts receivable	52 510	Notes payable	43 745
Cash	30 162	Accounts payable	81,426
Total current assets	€283 206	Total current liabilities	€125 171
		Total liabilities	€507 359
Total assets	€914 462	Total liabilities and shareholders' equity	€914 462

19.3. The retention ratio, external funds needed, internal growth rate and sustainable growth rate are calculated as follows:

$$\text{Retention ratio} = \frac{\text{Retained earnings}}{\text{Net income}}$$

$$= \frac{€159\,985}{€290\,882}$$

$$= 0.55, \text{ or } 55\%$$

EFN = (Growth rate × Initial assets)

      − Addition to retained earnings

$$= (0.20 × €574\,552) = €159\,985$$

$$= -€45\,075$$

Thus, without considering the investment of €225 000 for the new facility, the firm will not need any external financing. However, if you add that in, then:

EFN = Total new investments

      − Addition to retained earnings

$$= (0.20 × €574\,552) + €225\,000$$

$$- €159\,985$$

$$= €179\,925$$

$$\text{IGR} = \frac{\text{Additions to retained earnings}}{\text{Initial total assets}}$$

$$= \frac{€159\,985}{€574\,552}$$

$$= 0.278, \text{ or } 27.8\%$$

SGR = Plowback ratio × ROE

$$= \frac{\text{Addition to retained earnings}}{\text{Net income}}$$

$$× \frac{\text{Net income}}{\text{Total equity}}$$

$$= 0.55 × 0.715$$

$$= 0.933, \text{ or } 39.3\%$$

19.4. We calculate Wienerwald's internal growth rate as follows:

IGR = Plowback ratio × ROE

      × Equity ratio

$$= 0.40 × 0.145 × \frac{€4\,652\,125}{€11\,500\,450}$$

$$= 0.0235, \text{ or } 2.35\%$$

19.5. Reprise Pop's sustainable growth rate is:

SGR = Plowback ratio × ROE

$$= 0.65 × \frac{€1\,250\,000}{€2\,875\,223}$$

$$= 0.283, \text{ or } 28.3\%$$

CRITICAL THINKING QUESTIONS

19.1. What is financial planning? What four types of plans are involved in financial planning?

19.2. Why is the capital budget an important part of a firm's financial planning?

19.3. Why do financing and investment decisions have to be made concurrently?

19.4. Explain how sales can be used to develop projected financial statements.

19.5. Why are sales not always a good measure to forecast fixed assets?

19.6. List all the accounts affected by the 'plug' value. How does this value help managers?

19.7. Explain why the fixed asset account may or may not vary with sales.

19.8. How does the dividend payout ratio affect the amount of funds needed to fund growth?

19.9. Define the internal growth rate (IGR). Identify the characteristics of a high-growth firm with no external funds needed.

19.10. What is the sustainable growth rate? Why is it important?

QUESTIONS AND PROBLEMS

Basic

19.1. Strategic plan: Explain the importance of the strategic plan.

19.2. Capital budget: What are the various steps in preparing a capital budget?

19.3. Financing plan: What are the elements of a financing plan?

19.4. Financial planning: Identify the steps in the financial planning process.

19.5. Financial modelling: List the various elements of financial modelling.

19.6. Payout ratio: Define the retention ratio and the dividend payout ratio.

19.7. Addition to retained earnings: Reprise Pop SA has revenue of €455 316 and costs of €316 487 and pays a tax rate of 31%. If the firm pays out 45% of its earnings as dividends every year, what is the amount of retained earnings and what is the firm's retention ratio?

19.8. Payout and retention ratio: Ripresa Lombardi S.p.A. has revenues of €12 112 659,

costs of €9 080 545, interest payment of €412 375 and a tax rate of 34%. It paid dividends of €1 025 000 to its shareholders. Find the firm's dividend payout ratio and retention ratio.

19.9. Capital intensity ratio: Define the capital intensity ratio and explain its significance.

19.10. Capital intensity ratio: Tantrix International SE has total assets of €3 257 845 and sales of €5 123 951. What is the firm's capital intensity ratio?

19.11. Capital intensity ratio: Metallteile Wotan GmbH has been able to generate sales of €13 445 196 on assets of €9 145 633. What is the firm's capital intensity ratio?

19.12. Capital intensity ratio: For Metallteile Wotan in Problem 19.11, how much must sales grow if the capital intensity ratio has to drop to 60%? Indicate your answer in both percentage of sales and sales increase in euros.

19.13. Internal growth rate: Tapiola SE has net income of €1 212 335 on assets of €12 522 788 and retains 70% of its income every year. What is the company's internal growth rate?

19.14. Sustainable growth rate: If Le Monde Acrobate SA has a ROE of 13.7% and a dividend payout ratio of 32%, what is its sustainable growth rate?

19.15. EFN and growth: Refer to Exhibits 19.10 and 19.11 in the text. The EFNs for several growth rates follow:

Growth Rate (%)	EFN (€)
0	−4.8
5	−2.3
9.6	0.0
10	0.2
15	2.7
20	5.2

As a drill, you may want to check the calculations and plot the line to replicate the graph in Exhibit 19.11.

Intermediate

19.16. Retention ratio: Refer to Problem 19.7. Reprise Pop SA expects to increase its sales by 15% next year, and all costs vary directly with sales. Reprise Pop wants to retain €65 000 as retained earnings next year. Will it have to change its dividend payout ratio? If so, what will be the new dividend payout ratio and retention ratio for the firm?

19.17. Capital intensity: Identify two industries (other than airlines) that are capital intensive. Using online or other data sources, compute the capital intensity ratio for the largest firm in each of the chosen industries.

19.18. Percentage of sales: Tomey Austeilung GmbH's financial statement for the most recent fiscal year is shown in this problem. The company projects that sales will increase by 20% next year. Assume that all costs and assets increase directly with sales. The company has a constant 33% dividend payout ratio and has no plans to issue new equity. Any financing needed will be in the form of long-term debt. Prepare projected financial statements for the coming year based on this information, and determine the EFN.

Tomey Austeilung GmbH
Income Statement and Balance Sheet

Income Statement	Balance Sheet
Revenues	€1 768 121
Costs	1 116 487
EBT	651 634
Taxes (35%)	228 072
Net income	€423 562
Assets:	
Net fixed assets	€713 655
Current assets	280 754
Total assets	€994 409
Liabilities and Equity:	
Ordinary shares	€200,000
Retained earnings	307 627
Long-term debt	319 456
Current liabilities	167 326
Total liabilities and equity	€994 409

19.19. Internal growth rate: Using the projected financial statements for Tomey Austeilung developed in Problem 19.18, find the internal growth rate for Tomey Austeilung GmbH.

19.20. Sustainable growth rate: Use the following pro forma information for Tomey Austeilung for next year: net income = €508 275; addition to retained earnings = €340 544; ordinary shares = €848 171; net sales = €2 121 745. Assume the company does not want its ratio of long-term debt to equity to exceed its current long-term debt-to-equity ratio of 63% and it does not want to issue new equity. What level of sales growth can it sustain? Calculate the new sales level.

19.21. Sustainable growth rate: The Rowan Tree Company has a net profit margin of 8.3%, debt ratio of 45%, total assets of €4 157 550 and sales of €6 852 654. If the company has a dividend payout ratio of 67%, what is the company's sustainable growth rate?

19.22. Sustainable growth rate: Refer to the information for The Rowan Tree Company in Problem 19.21. The firm's management desires a growth rate (SGR) of 10% but does not wish to change its level of debt or its payout ratio. What will the firm's new net profit margin have to be in order to achieve the desired growth rate?

19.23. Sustainable growth rate: Vendite Roccioso S.p.A. has current sales of €1 215 326 and net income of €211 253. It has a debt ratio of 25% and a dividend payout ratio of 75%. The company has total assets of €712 455. What is the company's sustainable growth rate?

19.24. Sustainable growth rate: Ellicott Textile Mills has reported the following financial information for the year ended 30 September 2011. The company generated a net income of €915 366, reflecting a net profit margin of 6.4%. It has a dividend payout ratio of 50%. The company has a capital intensity ratio of 62% and a debt ratio of 45%. What is the company's sustainable growth rate?

19.25. Internal growth rate: Given the information in Problem 19.24, what is the internal growth rate of Ellicott Textile Mills?

19.26. Internal growth rate: La Boutique Imaginaire SA has a return on equity of 17.5%, an equity ratio of 65% and a dividend payout ratio of 75%. What is the company's internal growth rate?

19.27. EFN: London Pub Brewers for the year ended 30 September 2011 generated revenues of £12 125 800 with a 72% capital intensity ratio. Its net income was £873 058.

With the introduction of a half dozen new specialty beers, the brewery expects to grow its sales by 15% next year. Assume that all costs vary directly with sales and that the firm maintains its dividend payout ratio of 70%. What will be the EFN needed by this firm? If the company wants to raise no more than £750 000 externally and is not averse to adjusting its payout policy, what will be the new dividend payout ratio?

19.28. EFN: Ritchie Marmo Azienda S.p.A. has total assets of €12 899 450, sales of €18 174 652 and net income of €4 589 774. The company expects its sales to grow by 25% next year. All assets and costs (including taxes) vary directly with sales and the firm expects to maintain its payout ratio of 65%. Calculate the EFN.

19.29. EFN: Nordsee Consulting NV expects to add €1 213 777 to retained earnings and currently has total assets of €23 159 852. If the company has the ability to borrow up to €1 million, how much growth can the firm support if it is willing to borrow to its maximum capacity?

19.30. Maximum sales growth: Helsinki Design expects to add €271 898 to retained earnings this year. The company has total assets of €3 425 693 and wishes to add no new external funds for the coming year. If assets and costs vary directly with sales, how much sales growth can the company support while retaining an EFN of zero? What is the firm's internal growth rate?

Advanced

19.31. The financial statements for the year ended 30 June 2011 are given for Morgan Byggeri AS. The firm's revenues are projected to grow at a rate of 25% next year and all financial statement accounts will vary directly with sales. Based on that projection, develop a projected balance sheet and an income statement for the 2011–2012 fiscal year.

Morgan Byggeri AS Balance Sheet and Income Statement for Fiscal Year Ended 30 June 2011
Balance Sheet

Assets:		Liabilities and Shareholders' Equity:	
Non-current assets		Shareholders' equity	
Net fixed assets	€43,362,482	Ordinary shares	€19 987 500
Other assets	1 748 906	Retained earnings	12 940 974
	€45 111 388	Total shareholders' equity	€32 928 474
Current assets		Non-current liabilities	
Inventories	22 267 674	Long-term debt	29 731 406
Accounts receivable	5 830 754	Current liabilities	
Cash	3 349 239	Notes payable	4 857 496
	€31 447 667	Accounts payable	9 041 679
		Total current liabilities	€13 899 175
		Total liabilities	€43 630 581
Total assets	€76 559 055	Total liabilities and equity	€76 559 055

Income Statement

Revenues	€193 212 500
Costs	145 265 625
EBITDA	€47 946 875
Depreciation	23 318 750
EBIT	€ 24 628 125
Interest	11 935 869
EBT	€ 12 692 256
Taxes (35%)	4 442 290
Net income	€ 8 249 966

19.32. Use the financial information for Morgan Byggeri AS from Problem 19.31. Assume now that equity accounts do not vary directly with sales but change when retained earnings change or new equity is issued. The company pays 75% of its income as dividends every year. In addition, the company plans to expand production capacity by expanding the current facility and acquiring additional equipment. This will cost the firm €10 million. The firm has no plans to issue new equity this year. Prepare a projected balance sheet using this information. Any funds that need to be raised (in addition to changes in current liabilities) will be in the form of long-term debt. What is the external financing needed in this case?

19.33. Using the information for Morgan Byggeri AS in the preceding problem, calculate the firm's internal growth rate and sustainable growth rate.

19.34. Use the information for Morgan Byggeri AS from Problems 19.31 and 19.32. Assume that equity accounts do not vary directly with sales but change when retained earnings change or new equity is issued. The company's long-term debt-to-equity ratio is approximately 90% and its equity-to-total assets ratio is about 43%. The company wishes to increase its equity-to-total assets ratio to at least 50%. It is willing to reduce its payout ratio but will retain no more than 40% of its retained earnings. The company will raise any additional funds needed, including funds for expansion in new equity. No new long-term debt will be issued. Prepare projected statements to reflect the new scenario.

a. What is the external financing needed to accommodate the expected growth?

b. What is the firm's internal growth rate?

c. What is the firm's sustainable growth rate?

d. How much new equity will the firm have to issue?

e. What is the firm's new equity ratio and debt-to-equity ratio?

19.35. Munson Informationen GmbH has just reported earnings for the year ended 30 June 2011. Given in this problem are the firm's income statement and balance sheet. The company has a 55% dividend payout ratio for the last 10 years and does not plan to change this policy. Based on internal forecasts, the company expects the demand for its products to grow at a rate of 20% for the next year and has projected the sales growth for 2012 to be 20%. Assume that equity accounts and long-term debt do not vary directly with sales but change when retained earnings change or additional capital is issued.

Munson Informationen GmbH Balance Sheet and Income Statement for Fiscal Year Ended 30 June 2011

Balance Sheet

Assets:		Liabilities and Shareholders' Equity:	
Net fixed assets	€22 380 636	Ordinary shares	€10 165 235
Other assets	1 748 906	Retained earnings	9 676 351
Total non-current assets	€24 129 542		€19 841 586
Current assets		Non-current liabilities	
Inventories	11 492 993	Long-term debt	13 345 242
Accounts receivable	3 009 421	Current liabilities	
Cash	1 728 639	Notes payable	2 507 094
Total current assets	€16 231 053	Accounts payable	4 666 673
		Total current liabilities	€ 7 173 767
		Total liabilities	€20 519 009
Total assets	€40 360 595	Total liabilities and equity	€40 360 595

Income Statement

Revenues	€79 722 581
Costs	59 358 499
EBITDA	20 364 082
Depreciation	7 318 750
EBIT	13 045 332
Interest	3 658 477
EBT	9 386 855
Taxes (35%)	3 285 399
Net income	6 101 456

a. What is the firm's internal growth rate (IGR)?

b. What is the firm's sustainable growth rate (SGR)?

c. What is the external financing needed (EFN) to accommodate the expected growth?

d. Construct the firm's 2012 projected financial statements under the assumption that all external financing will be done with long-term debt.

SAMPLE TEST PROBLEMS

19.1. Mercure SA has revenues of €2 512 654, costs of €1 080 227, interest payment of €132 375 and a tax rate of 34%. It paid dividends of €525 000 to its shareholders.

Find the firm's dividend payout ratio and retention ratio.

19.2. Assume that Thor AS is operating at a capital intensity ratio of 63.5% and is able to generate net sales of SKr.3 123 443. What is the firm's level of assets?

19.3. Millennium Biere GmbH currently has sales of €1 415 326 and net income of €411 253. It has a debt ratio of 25% and a dividend payout ratio of 70%. The company has total assets of €1 850 325. What is the company's sustainable growth rate?

19.4. Given the information in Problem 19.3, what is the internal growth rate of Millennium Biere?

19.5. Mirabelle SA has total assets of €3 267 450, sales of €5 174 652 and net income of €1 789 774. The company expects its sales to grow by 20% next year. All assets and costs (including taxes) vary directly with sales and the firm expects to maintain its payout ratio of 75%. Calculate the external financing needed (EFN).

ENDNOTES

1. The investment plan consists of the capital budget plus any acquisitions or divestitures management plans to make. To simplify our discussion in this chapter, we treat the investment plan and capital budget as one and the same because, for most firms, acquisitions and divestitures are not regular events.

2. Note that to simplify the analysis, some of the income statement and balance sheet accounts used in the planning model are aggregated. For example, in our initial planning model, the balance sheet lists only total assets, debt and equity.

3. Alternatively, we could have redone the preliminary pro forma balance sheet and found: total assets = €1.3 million and total liabilities and shareholders' equity = €1301 million (€244 000 + €200 000 + €857 000). Since liabilities and shareholders' equity < total assets, we have more funds than we need. To make the balance sheet balance, we elect to reduce the notes payable by €1000.

4. Note that the measure of leverage in Equation (19.8), equity/total assets, is the inverse of the equity multiplier.

PART 7

CORPORATE RISK MANAGEMENT AND INTERNATIONAL DECISIONS

CHAPTER
20

Corporate Risk Management

In this Chapter:

Why Companies Manage Corporate Risks
Managing Operational, Business and Financial Risks
Forwards and Futures
Swaps
Financial Options
Option Valuation
Real Options
Agency Costs

LEARNING OBJECTIVES

1. Explain the factors that make it desirable for firms to manage their risks.
2. Describe the risks faced by firms and how they are managed.
3. Define forward and futures contracts and be able to determine their prices.
4. Define interest rate and cross-currency swaps and know how they are valued.
5. Define a call option and a put option and describe the payoff function for each of these options.
6. List and describe the factors that affect the value of an option.
7. Name some of the real options that occur in business and explain why traditional NPV analysis does not accurately incorporate their values.
8. Describe how the agency costs of debt and equity are related to options.

Gold conjures up visions of treasure hoards and beautiful works of art. More prosaically, it is used today in dentistry and electronics because of its resistance to corrosion and its excellent characteristics for conducting electricity. While gold has largely lost its functions as a currency and store of wealth, it is nevertheless in demand and a considerable number of mining companies are involved in its extraction – two of the largest are Barrick Gold and AngloGold Ashanti. For gold producers such as Barrick, it is the reason for their huge investment in deep mines with their expensive extraction equipment. They invest in order to sell the gold they mine. Unfortunately, the value of gold fluctuates a lot. The collapse of the Bretton Woods agreement, when gold was worth $35/oz, considerably raised its price such that it peaked at over $850/oz in 1980. In the following years, the gold price drifted downwards with occasional recoveries, until it touched a low of $252.80/oz in 2000. During this period, gold miners faced a dilemma. Mining

gold was expensive and much of the cost had to be paid upfront in drilling the deep shafts to the ore deposits; the cost of extraction was also high. A declining price for their output was bad news.

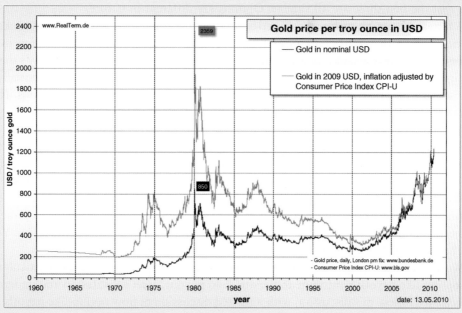

Source: www.RealTerm.de, used by permission.

Because of the falling gold price following the peak in the 1980s, Barrick Gold and AngloGold Ashanti, and other mining companies, faced the prospect of having to meet their large production costs out of a declining revenue stream as the gold price trended downwards. Their solution was to sell forward part or all of their production at a fixed price. This ensured a minimum price for their production, gave them a stable cash flow and allowed them to raise finance, since investors were reassured they would be paid back with a high degree of certainty. By 1999, these forward sales transactions represented more than a year of total output by the entire industry.[1]

CHAPTER PREVIEW

The gold mining industry illustrates a key challenge for companies. What set of risks should companies take and what risks can the company lay off elsewhere? A key factor in determining corporate risk management policies is the nature and extent of these risks. Generally, companies will accept risks in their core business areas where they have a degree of competitive advantage. On the other hand, they will seek to eliminate or minimise other risks that have the capacity to derail the company from its objective of creating value for shareholders. Generally, firms will seek to manage macroeconomic risks, such as interest rate, commodity price, currency and credit risks.

Corporate risk management can take a number of forms, which boil down to either the way the company organises its means of production or the use of financial instruments, principally derivatives, to modify the underlying risks in acceptable ways – or more typically a combination of both processes.

We begin with a discussion of the rationale for corporate risk management before briefly looking at corporate risk management processes. We then examine the way derivatives are valued. Derivatives fall into two broad categories: those where the buyer or seller is locked into the contract and those that allow the buyer to walk away, if they should choose to do so. There are a number of different derivative instruments, variously known as forwards, futures, swaps and options. We will show that the first three are all similar. Options are different in nature.

A forward contract, such as those used by gold mining companies, allows the buyer or seller to set the price at which they will purchase or sell a commodity or financial asset at a given date in the future. Futures contracts do the same thing, but are traded on an exchange, just like a company's shares. Swaps are slightly more complicated in that there are multiple cash flows, but serve essentially the same purpose of setting prices now for a predetermined number of exchanges in future periods. The buyer or seller of a forward, futures or swap has specific obligations that last until the contract is completed and, in particular, both parties must complete the transaction whatever the circumstances in the future. On the other hand, the buyer or owner of an option has the right, but not the obligation, to purchase or sell a commodity or financial asset, such as a share, at a pre-specified price on or before a given date. This means that option buyers only have to complete the transaction if they choose to do so.

We then turn to options on real assets, known as real options. Real options often arise in corporate investment decisions. Managers often have options to delay investing in a project, expand a project, abandon a project, change the technology employed in a project, and so on. You will see that the value of these options is not adequately reflected in an NPV analysis.

We next revisit the agency costs of debt that we discussed in Chapter 16. In particular, we show how option-like payoffs contribute to the dividend payout, asset substitution and underinvestment conflicts. We follow this discussion with a related discussion of how option-like payoffs contribute to conflicts between shareholders and the managers who work for them.

WHY COMPANIES MANAGE CORPORATE RISKS

Learning Objective 1

Explain the factors that make it desirable for firms to manage their risks.

In Chapter 6, we explained the nature of discounted cash flows and valuation. Value depends on the size, timing and riskiness of future cash flows and the rate of return required by investors. This suggests that corporate risk management may add value if it can positively affect expected cash flows and the required rate of return that is appropriate to those cash flows. A simple example will illustrate the point. Let us assume that a gold producer will have an annual cash flow of €500 million over the next 30 years, after which mining operations cease.[2] The appropriate risk-adjusted discount rate for the cash flows is 12%. Recall that the discount rate reflects the riskiness of the underlying cash flows. The present value of the business today is therefore simply €500 million times a 30-year annuity at 12% (8.0552), or €4028 million (€500 × 8.0552). Now the company decides to engage in risk management activity that costs it €50 million per year over the life of the mine. At the same time, the required rate of return, given that the cash flows have less risk, is reduced to 10% (the annuity factor will now be 9.4269). The new value becomes (€500 − €50) × 9.4269 = €4242 million. Using risk management in this situation has raised the value of the firm by €214 million (€4242 − €4028 = €214 million). Consequently, the owners of the business are better off if the gold producer undertakes risk management.

A number of different factors will influence the extent to which firms manage their risks. These include financial reporting, corporate taxation, the costs of bankruptcy and contracting with providers of capital, as well as issues such as agency costs and employee compensation and retention. Furthermore, shareholders benefit when a company manages its risks in ways they cannot reproduce themselves. For instance, tax losses at the company level are not directly transferable to shareholders, so asymmetries in payoffs may lead firms to manage these risks.

If the company does not hedge, there will be variability in the cash flows it generates from its operations as economic conditions change and the prices of its inputs and outputs change. Shortfalls, as a result of adverse movements in output prices or input costs, will either mean the company has to raise money externally or reduce its future investments – and consequently may have to pass up on attractive positive net present value projects. As we have seen in Chapter 15, raising external capital is costly and time-consuming. In addition, the issues discussed in Chapter 16 about the effect of capital structure and the problems of financial distress apply. These affect the ability of firms to raise external finance when distressed. A case in point is the British company BAe, or British Aerospace as it was then. In the 1980s, it had diversified away from aerospace into property and automobiles (by acquiring the Rover Group). In 1991, it suddenly indicated that all was not well in its businesses and announced a £432 million rights issue to repair its balance sheet. Shareholders were angry at the unexpected losses and having to subscribe more capital. For a while, there was a real risk of the company not getting the money it needed. The chairman and other senior managers were forced to resign and a new management team was recruited before shareholders were willing to subscribe for the new shares on offer.[3]

Taxes may also help explain why firms engage in risk management. If the tax system operates in such a way that the tax paid by the company rises with the amount of profit or earnings, it becomes attractive for firms to reduce the uncertainty of future earnings. In this situation, a more volatile earnings stream leads to higher expected taxes than a less volatile earnings stream. The reason is that firms have a number of potential tax offsets, such as tax depreciation and allowances, which act to reduce their taxable income. These are generally fixed in size so that if pre-tax earnings increase, they are likely to pay a higher tax rate overall. As

BUILDING INTUITION

Risk Management Can Help Firms Avoid Having to Raise Capital When it is Difficult to Do So

A key question external providers of finance wish to resolve when firms come asking for new funds is the company's motivation. The added disclosure required when external finance is being sought rapidly determines whether the company is in trouble – or not. If the finance is required to rescue the company, is this the management's fault or just bad luck? It is difficult for outsiders to know whether the financially troubled condition of the company is a result of bad management or simply bad luck. If the managers are at fault, lenders do not wish, as the saying goes, 'to throw good money after bad' by providing more finance to a failing management. Better to wind up or sell the firm. Consequently, from the perspective of a company's managers, seeking external finance when things have gone wrong is to be avoided as much as possible. Undertaking risk management that reduces the likelihood of financial distress and the need for external finance makes sense when providers of finance find it difficult to understand what is happening in the business.

we also saw in Chapter 3, many countries have a low starter rate of company tax. For instance, take the example of a company that has pre-tax earnings of either €50 or €200 with equal probability and will pay an effective rate of tax of 25% if its earnings are low or 35% if it has high earnings. The expected profit before tax will be €125 (€50 × 0.50 + €200 × 0.50). The expected tax will be €40 ([€50 × 0.25] × 0.50 + [€200 × 0.35] × 0.50). The expected after-tax profit will then be €125 − €40 = €85. Now consider the situation where the company can use risk management to eliminate the variability in future pre-tax earnings such that it will have earnings before tax of €125 with complete certainty. The corporate tax rate for this level of income is 27%. The company will pay €34 in tax (€125 × 0.27). The after-tax earnings are now €125 − €34 = €91. The company has saved €6 in taxes and increased after-tax profits from an expected €85 to €91. In this situation, risk management creates value for shareholders.

As the opening vignette indicates, lenders are concerned about repayment. For a given level of debt, risk management can reduce the probability that a company will find itself in the situation where it is finding it hard or is unable to repay the debt. As Chapter 16 indicates, in situations where financial distress is costly, risk management may increase the firm's debt capacity. Higher debt levels may also be desirable in reducing agency problems and where this creates increased risk of financial distress, risk management is likely to be beneficial.

A key rationale for firms to engage in risk management is that they are better able to address problems of managerial motivation, capture the benefits of tax management and reduce the costs of financial distress in ways that shareholders cannot. The ability of firms to manage their risks may also allow them to exploit investment opportunities that they would otherwise have to pass by because it is costly or impossible to raise external finance.

There is less rationale for firms to manage those risks that shareholders and lenders can easily manage for themselves. For instance, it is not clear that unrelated diversification at the company level is beneficial since shareholders are able to create well-diversified portfolios by holding shares in a range of different companies at less cost and with more flexibility.

The Risk Management Process

Companies need a risk management process. At its simplest, it requires them to examine their

BUILDING INTUITION

Risk Management Can Help Firms Address Capital Market Imperfections

Corporate risk management is desirable when capital market imperfections and asymmetries reduce the value of firms and make access to outside finance costly for firms that do not control risks. Unless this rationale is present, risk management should be left to capital providers.

operations in the broadest sense in order to recognise the risks that can affect the firm's future cash flows. This involves identifying the risks, their assessment or evaluation, the selection of the risk management techniques, their implementation and keeping the programme under review. For instance, the pizza restaurant group would want to look at where it sources its inputs and in what way, what could go wrong when preparing, serving and delivering pizzas. At the same time, it would also consider how wider factors outside the company, such as the economy and social trends, might affect the business's future profitability.

The process can be broken down into a number of logical steps. These would typically include:

- *Identification.* This would involve the financial manager in surveying the various business units and determining the profile of the business risks involved. Exposures can be simply classified according to the way they could affect the firm's operations. For instance, the pizza restaurant group may use an integrated accounting system – failure here would have a major effect in that the company may be unable to operate. Hence, the risk that such a critical system could fail would be classified as having a very significant impact.
- *Evaluation.* Wherever possible, the impact of the risk is quantified in monetary terms. This helps in ranking the risks according to the severity of their effect. When combined with estimates of their frequency, this provides a way of scoring the result. For instance, at individual pizza restaurants, it may be that there are often inconsistencies in the till receipts against goods sold. However, their monetary effect is likely to be very small.

Hence, while problems in this area are frequent, their severity is minimal. A decision would need to be reached as to whether this risk needs managing. On the other hand, the IT system failure may be very infrequent – but its impact on the business could be seen as very severe.

- *Management.* The final element is a clear framework for managing the risks once they have been identified and evaluated. Here a key criterion is whether they have the capacity to derail the firm's strategy. The management of the risks is therefore integrated into the company's strategic goals. At the operational level, the company will establish procedures and assign responsibility to oversee the management of these unacceptable risks. Hence, it is often the function of the financial manager to use financial techniques or source instruments to mitigate the risks. For instance, by buying insurance cover against specific risks.
- *Review.* The final step is to repeat the process and keep the risks under review, since conditions change and firms evolve over time.

Before You Go On

1. What two factors affect the value of a business that can be modified when a firm manages its risks?
2. What firm-specific reasons may prompt a business to engage in risk management?
3. What are the adverse consequences to companies from changes in input and output prices?

MANAGING OPERATIONAL, BUSINESS AND FINANCIAL RISKS

Learning Objective 2

Describe the risks faced by firms and how they are managed.

Every transaction a firm undertakes includes multiple risks. For instance, Volkswagen sells its cars in the Chinese market. In doing so, Volkswagen is betting that its cars are competitive in that market. However, it is also betting on the exchange rate between the renminbi and the euro. In the past, the renminbi has been linked to the US dollar and hence has fluctuated against the euro as the US dollar has risen and fallen over time.[4] In order to develop its market presence in China, Volkswagen has to invest in this market by advertising the attractions of its cars and developing a dealer and repair network. These investments would be lost if changes in the market made it unattractive to the company. Volkswagen may be upbeat about the opportunity to sell its cars in China, but be less optimistic on the future of the exchange rate. A fall in the renminbi would leave it selling cars at a loss and hence the currency risk reduces the attractiveness of the fast-growing Chinese market. The solution is to split these risks, and for the company to accept the risks in which it sees itself as having a competitive advantage and removing those which can derail its business strategy. The company would therefore seek to manage the currency risk in such a way as to eliminate the problem.

The risks that a company such as Volkswagen faces are either **operational risks** or **market risks**. Operational risks are either internal to the firm or arise from the nature and extent of its activities. The internal risks are largely under the control of management in that decisions on how the firm sets up and operates its production systems can be organised so as to minimise the risks involved. On the other hand, many of the external risks are the result of changes in macroeconomic conditions and relate to changes in interest rates, commodity prices and exchange rates. These are market risks, and companies seek to reduce the effect of these on the firm's operations and profitability. In addition, transactions with third parties create credit risk, which was discussed in Chapter 14.

Operational risks

any risk arising from the execution of a company's business functions

Market risks

exposure to a change in the value of some market factor, such as interest rates, foreign exchange rates, equity or commodity prices

Operational and Business Risks

Companies such as Volkswagen are involved in complex activities and face a number of internal and external risks. There are risks in its production processes from potential factory fires, breakdown in critical equipment and the development of new technologies that render existing ones redundant or uncompetitive. Some of these **production risks** are insurable. Firms also have input and output risks. The gold mining companies described at the start of this chapter have significant output risk from unexpected changes in the market price of gold over time. These **price risks** affect both the costs of a firm's inputs and its outputs and hence its future profitability. Typically, these risks include commodities, raw materials, finished products, interest rates, energy, currencies and the prices of other market-determined inputs and outputs.

> **Production risk**
>
> all the elements of the production process that can go wrong: for instance, fires and equipment failures

> **Price risks**
>
> changes in the prices of a firm's inputs and outputs over time due to changes in demand and supply

To the extent that a company has changes in input prices (from unanticipated supply effects) and outputs (from unanticipated demand effects), it will experience variability in its cash flows. At a basic level, it will want to ensure that revenues cover all its costs. Since it incurs costs before revenues, this is to some extent a timing problem. However, firms may have trouble in raising prices. In the case of Volkswagen, if the demand for its cars was independent of their price, a fall in the value of the renminbi against the euro would be compensated for by increasing the sales price in China to maintain the value in euros. For most firms, a number of factors may prevent this happening: (1) local competitors will be largely unaffected by the movement in the currency; (2) demand may be significantly conditional on price; and (3) other foreign suppliers may be willing to cut their local currency prices to maintain or increase their market share.

Risk Management Methods

Companies have a range of techniques that they can use to reduce the risks they face. Some of these relate to the way the firm operates. The solution for the company is to anticipate that prices will change and to position itself accordingly. Continuing our Volkswagen example, the company could organise itself so as to site in China that part of its production facilities that supplies the market. Then, costs and revenues would both be in the same currency. When cash flows are matched in this way, it is known as **hedging**.

> **Hedging**
>
> any technique designed to reduce or eliminate risk; for example, taking two positions that will offset each other if prices change

As indicated above, Volkswagen can set up manufacturing facilities in the markets in which it sells its cars. This works to an extent, but can lead to a dispersion of production and higher costs than concentrating facilities in units that can benefit from economies of scale and scope. Typically, firms will organise themselves to be efficient producers and seek to address the remaining risks by using the capital markets to hedge – a process known as **financial risk management**. This involves the company in dealing in financial instruments that are designed to transfer or modify risks. This can involve the firm using **insurance** or **derivatives**. A great advantage of these instruments is that they are low cost and can be added and removed as required as circumstances change. Contrast this to the time and expense involved if the company decides to change the location of its production or switches the markets in which it sells.[5]

> **Financial risk management**
>
> the practice of protecting and creating economic value in a firm by using financial instruments to manage exposure to risks

> **Insurance**
>
> a contract that protects against the financial losses (in whole or in part) of specified unexpected events

> **Derivatives**
>
> financial instruments or securities whose value varies with the value of an underlying asset

BUILDING INTUITION

Financial Risk Management Allows Firms to Exploit their Comparative Advantages

A key reason firms use financial hedging is that they want to optimise the way they go about their business but also only accept those risks in which they have a competitive advantage. By using the financial markets to lay off those risks that the firm is unwilling or unable to accept, it both ensures that these risks do not derail its strategy and allows it to concentrate resources in areas where it has the best prospects of earning good returns.

There are three generic ways in which a firm can manage its various risks that involve hedging, insurance and diversification. The choice of method will depend on a number of factors. When a firm hedges, it reduces its exposure to the possibility of a loss but this also leads to the firm giving up the possibility of a gain. Insurance means paying a premium, the cost of the insurance, to avoid losses. In this case, the company retains the possibility of gain, but eliminates the exposure to potential loss. Note the difference between hedging and insurance: with hedging, the risk of loss is eliminated by giving up the potential for gain; with insurance, you pay a premium to eliminate the risk of loss and retain the potential for gain.

Companies also use diversification to reduce their risks. We know from the way portfolios work that the aggregated portfolio risk will be less than the sum of the individual risks as long as the

components of the portfolio are less than perfectly correlated.[6] As discussed earlier, while Volkswagen will not aim to exactly match its production facilities to its markets, nevertheless it does operate a number of different production facilities spread around the globe. This diversification makes sense in that it does reduce Volkswagen's overall risks. But diversification of this kind is only advisable to the extent that it does not adversely affect the firm's operational efficiency. As mentioned earlier, firms will seek to be efficient producers and use financial instruments to manage the remaining risks.

As we will see later, when we look at how derivatives are valued, the cost of risk management will depend on the future uncertainty. The higher this uncertainty, the greater the costs involved. While risk management is costly, there are real benefits to companies from being able to manage their risks by hedging, through insurance or via

BUILDING INTUITION

Corporate Risk Management Decisions are Based on Cost–Benefit Trade-offs

There are a number of different methods that, taken together, companies use to manage their risks. Companies will weigh the costs of using the method against the benefit of risk reduction. Companies can use diversification, insurance and hedging. These have different costs and benefits. Hence, there is no single solution that is appropriate in all circumstances. The benefits and costs of each approach have to be worked out for each method for all the different risks.

diversification, and to reduce or eliminate the risks that would otherwise lead firms to underinvest in productive projects.

Over time, to cater to the needs of firms, various organisations and contractual arrangements have emerged to expand the scope of diversification and by providing greater specialisation in risk management. For instance, insurance companies cover a wide range of production and other risks while derivatives markets in forward contracts, futures, swaps and options have a prominent place in financial markets.

Before You Go On

1. In what areas does a company face risks from its business?
2. What are the different ways in which a company can manage its risks?
3. What determines the balance between operational hedging and financial hedging?

FORWARDS AND FUTURES

Learning Objective 3
Define forward and futures contracts and be able to determine their prices.

A forward contract involves a delayed sale and purchase by the two parties to the contract. Consider the situation where Airbus is selling one of its commercial jets to a customer. These are usually manufactured to order and delivery may take place several years later. What are the risks for both sides if the terms and conditions are not set at the outset? Exhibit 20.1 shows a payoff diagram that graphically illustrates the way the buyer and seller are exposed to the future uncertain changes in the price of the airliner. First and foremost, both parties have price risk in that –

when the delivery date finally arrives – the price for Airbus jets has changed. Airbus will do well if demand is high and aircraft prices have risen. The buyer will lose out by having to pay more. Equally, if demand is low and jetliner prices have fallen, the buyer wins as they pay less – and Airbus receives less. Given the uncertainties about the future price, both parties stand to lose if future prices are not the same as the current price for the airliner. They both have an incentive to ensure the contract for the aircraft specifies a price for the aircraft today but payable upon delivery. Commercial arrangements where prices and quantities are agreed today for future delivery are **forward contracts**. These contrast to *spot contracts*, where the buyer and seller make an immediate exchange.

Forward contract
agreement between two parties to buy or sell an asset at a specified point of time in the future at a price agreed today

Because forward contracts address the price risk facing buyers and sellers, they are very common in business. In addition to commercial contracts, such as that between Airbus and its client, there are numerous financial forward contracts that can be negotiated in the financial markets and these cover a very wide range of business risks. There are contracts on currencies, commodities, interest rates, stock market indices and individual shares, credit risks, energy and even the weather – to list the most common types.

Valuing a Forward Contract
As the Airbus example illustrates, these contracts work by 'locking-in' the prices at which firms buy and sell in the future. What should determine the price for the forward contract? In Chapter 5, we looked at investment and future values and so we

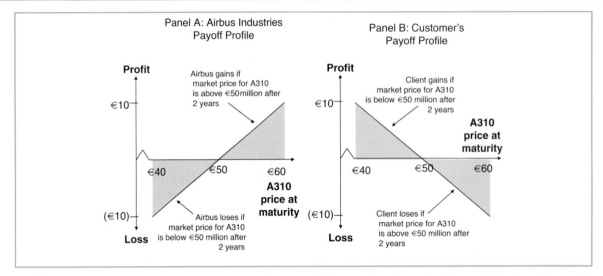

Exhibit 20.1: Payoff Diagrams for the Price Risks Facing the A310 Buyer and Airbus Industries   A payoff diagram shows the profit and loss from the deferred purchase of the A310 jet. If, when the contract is agreed, the contracted price is €50 million and it does not change, neither buyer nor seller gains. If the price rises, the buyer loses and the seller gains, the profit and loss being the difference between the original price and the new price. So if the price rises to €60 million, the seller has a profit of €10 million and the buyer loses €10 million. The gains and losses for both sides are the same and hence the payoffs to both parties are symmetrical.

Panel A shows the payoff profile for Airbus Industries. The company will profit if the market price of the A310 airliner is above €50 million in 2 years' time. It will lose if the market price is below €50 million. How much it will lose will depend on the future price uncertainty for the A310.

Panel B shows the customer's payoff profile. You will notice it has exactly the reverse set of gains and losses. The customer's risk is exactly the opposite of that of Airbus Industries in that it loses if the price rises and gains if the price falls. Both Airbus and the customer have an incentive to manage the risk that the price will change. They will do so by entering into a forward contract that establishes the price now that will be paid upon delivery in 2 years' time.

already know how to value future cash flows. A forward contract works in exactly the same way, except we want to start with the current price of what will be delivered in the future and work out its future value. At its simplest, a forward contract therefore will be determined by Equation (5.1):

$$FV_n = PV \times (1 + i)^n$$

where:

FV_n = future value of investment at the end of period n

PV = original principal or present value

i = rate of interest per period, which is often a year

n = number of periods (typically a year, but it can be a quarter, a month, a day or some other period of time)

$(1 + i)^n$ = future value factor

Let us assume that Airbus is selling the A310 model to the customer as described earlier. These are listed for immediate delivery at a price of €50 million each. However, the agreed delivery date is 2 years away and the annual rate of interest for euros is 4%. The forward price will therefore be €50 × $(1 + 0.04)^2$ = €54.08 million. If there are no other factors that affect the forward price, this is a fair deal to both sides. The client could immediately buy at €50 million. On the other hand, if they do not want the aircraft immediately, they have use of the money for the two intervening years and – if they invest it at the 4% interest rate – they will earn €4.08 million, so will be no better or worse off from buying immediately or waiting. What of Airbus? If they sell the A310 for forward delivery, they receive €54.08 million. The present value of this is €50 million. By agreeing to sell at the higher forward price, they are compensated for the delay in receiving the money. Airbus has to wait two years to get the price of the aircraft and – notionally at least – may have to borrow the money while it waits to deliver the A310 to the customer. It can borrow the present value of the forward price – which is, of course, €50 million. The forward price is such that it is fair to both sides and compensates them for the delayed delivery.

The pricing of forward contracts is known as the **cost of carry** and equates the gains and losses of both sides such that neither wins or loses. As such, it is a zero net present value transaction in that – as shown above – neither the buyer nor the seller loses out from the delay. The cost of carry may take account of more than just interest rates as it includes all those elements that change the value between the present and the future and is the *net cost* to the seller in the transaction. For instance, Airbus may have to store the aircraft for the two years and will incur costs from doing so. This would raise the future price of the aircraft. On the other hand, it is possible that Airbus could lease out the aircraft and earn income over the two years, something the client could also do. Airbus gains from this, but the buyer loses the opportunity to gain the rental income until the time for delivery.[7] This will reduce the forward price.

The difference between the cash market price and the forward price (PV – FV) will be the cost of carry and will include the costs and benefits from the delay. The elements that go into the cost of carry and their effects on the forward price are as follows:

- The *interest rate* (*i*) will work to increase the cost of carry and hence the forward price.
- *Storage costs and wastage* (*u*) will increase the cost of carry and the forward price. Some assets are subject to wastage when stored, such as agricultural commodities which tend to deteriorate over time, and this will mean the amount that can be delivered eventually will be less than the amount stored initially.
- Any *income received prior to delivery* will decrease the cost of carry and the forward price because it is a benefit to the seller. This is often expressed as a yield (*q*). Expressed this way, income on the asset can be viewed as a negative interest rate.
- A quantification of the *benefits of immediate ownership* or availability. This is known as the **convenience yield** (*y*) and can be thought of as negative storage costs! For instance, companies that use commodities which are vital to their business operations – and where there is restricted supply – may stockpile needed supplies and forego income in order to have a guaranteed availability. The convenience yield only applies to consumption assets and will be zero for forwards on financial assets.

The effects of the factors that influence the cost of carry are illustrated in Exhibit 20.2.

Cost of carry

the net cost of 'carrying' or holding an asset for future delivery

Convenience yield

a non-monetary return derived from the physical ownership of an asset or commodity

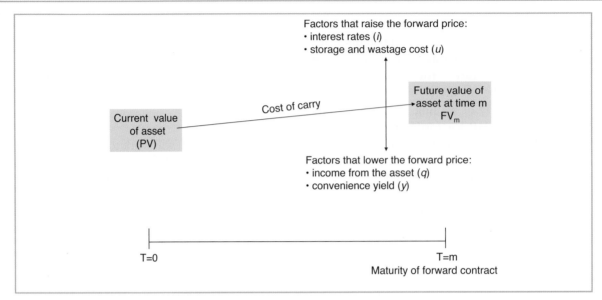

Exhibit 20.2: Factors that Affect the Cost of Carry in a Forward Contract   The price difference between the current market, the present value (PV) and the forward price (FV) will be determined by the interplay of those factors that contribute to the cost of carry: (1) interest rates and (2) storage and wastage costs, which act to increase the forward price; (3) income from the asset and (4) the convenience yield, which reduce the forward price. Note that, because of this interaction, it is quite possible that the forward price is lower than the current market price.

Let us continue the A310 example and see how the factors influence the cost of carry. We have already worked out the case where the only factor is interest rates. In this case, the forward price is €54.08 million. If Airbus has to store the airliner for the two years, it will incur costs. Assume that storage costs are 1% of the aircraft's value per year. This is like adding on 1% to the interest rate, so the future value will be €55.13 million [€50 × $(1 + 0.04 + 0.01)^2$]. On the other hand, if Airbus can lease out the aircraft for two years and earn 3% of the value of the aircraft in lease payments, this will have the effect of reducing the future value. Without leasing, the future value is €54.08 million. The lease payments act like a negative interest rate and reduce the future value, so we need to discount the FV by the leasing rate $(1 + 0.03)^2$, such that €54.08/$(1.03)^2$ = €50.98 million. If there were a convenience yield attached to having physical ownership of the A310, this would also serve to reduce the forward price.

The full cost-of-carry formula is therefore:

$$PV \times \frac{(1 + i + u)^m}{(1 + q + y)^m} = FV_m \qquad (20.1)$$

where:

PV = current price or present value

i = rate of interest per period (which is often a year)

u = storage cost per period, expressed as an interest rate

q = income from the asset per period, expressed as an interest rate

y = convenience yield per period

FV_m = future value at the maturity of the forward contract

m = number of periods to maturity of the forward contract; a period is typically a year, but can be some other period, such as a quarter, month or some other unit of time

Learning by Doing Application 20.1

Problem: You are the purchasing manager at the pizza restaurant chain and are becoming increasingly alarmed by the way the price of wheat is increasing and the effect it is having on the ability to set prices, plan expenditure and its effects on profit margins. Therefore, in order to facilitate planning within the company and to fix the cost of a major ingredient, you decide you would like to hedge and 'lock in' the price of flour for the coming year. You estimate you will need 50 tonnes and decide that a 1-year forward contract is the appropriate hedging instrument. The current price for flour is €175 per tonne, the interest rate is 4% and your contacts in the industry tell you that storage costs are 2% per year. At what price will you be able to execute a forward contract?

Approach: We need to apply Equation (20.1) to determine the future price at which the forward contract will be agreed. To get the correct value, we need to include both the current interest rate and the storage costs in the cost-of-carry formula.

Solution:
Applying Equation (20.1) gives:

$$PV \times \frac{(1 + i + u)^m}{(1 + q + y)^m} = FV_m$$

$$€175 \times \frac{(1 + 0.04 + 0.02)}{(1 + 0 + 0)}$$

$$= €185.50 \text{ per tonne}$$

We should point out that the cost-of-carry model is quite adaptable. For instance, we may not be able to work out the storage cost as an interest rate. Nevertheless, if we know what the storage costs will be in money, we can still use the model. Going back to our Airbus example, let us assume that Airbus contracts with a maintenance company to store the aircraft and the company says it will need to be paid €0.60 million at the end of year 1 and €0.75 million at the end of year 2 to store, maintain and service the aircraft. We can simply apply our understanding of the way the cost-of-carry model works and that these are costs that need to be added to the agreed forward sale price. When only interest rates affect the cost of carry, we have a future value of €54.08 million. We can simply add to this the future value of the storage costs. The timeline for the transaction will be as follows:

We need to work out the value at year 2, which involves the following calculations:

$$PV_{Aircraft} \times (1 + i)^2 = FV_{Aircraft, \text{ Year 2}}$$
$$+ FV_{Storage, \text{ Year 1}} \times (1 + i) = FV_{\text{Year 1 storage, Year 2}}$$
$$+ FV_{Storage, \text{ Year 2}}$$
$$= \text{Forward price}$$

$$€50 \times (1.04)^2 = €54.08$$
$$+ €0.60 \times (1.04) = €0.624$$
$$+ €0.75$$
$$= €55.454 \text{ million}$$

The forward price that Airbus requires so that it is no better or worse off from selling the A310 today is €55.454 million.[8] This price includes the foregone use of the sales proceeds and storage costs.

Learning by Doing Application 20.2

Problem: You are the majority owner of the pizza restaurant group. The company is doing very well at the moment and the shares are currently worth €80. However, you need to have a considerable sum of money in two years' time to provide for your daughter's university education. You are aware that the value of your shares can fall over this period and if so, as a result, you may have to sell more shares than you would like. As your company intends to pay a dividend of €5.20 at the end of the current year and you anticipate a dividend of €5.60 at the end of year two, you want to receive these dividends and not sell the shares until you actually need the money. The current two-year risk-free interest rate is 4% per year. What will be the fair price for the forward sale of your shares?

Approach: We apply the cost-of-carry model and adapt Equation (20.1) to take account of the specific dividends that will be paid on the shares over the life forward contract.

Application: We present-value the future dividend payments and find the price of the shares excluding the two dividend payments and then future-value this ex-dividend share price for two years:

$$\text{Present value of dividends} = \frac{€5.20}{1.04} + \frac{€5.60}{(1.04)^2}$$
$$= €5.00 + €5.18$$
$$= €10.18$$
$$\text{Ex-dividend share price} = €80.00 - €10.18$$
$$= €69.82$$
$$\text{Forward price} = €69.82 \times (1.04)^2$$
$$= €75.517$$

The forward price for the shares is €75.517 each. You can now determine, based on the money you need for your daughter's education, how many shares you need to sell in the forward contract. Note that, as discussed in the text, due to the value leakage from the dividends, the two-year forward price of €75.52 is below the current market price of €80.

The Value of a Forward Contract Prior to Maturity

As Exhibit 20.1 indicates, the payoff for both parties to a forward contract is symmetrical. The buyer and seller's gains and losses are the same, but arise due to changes in the market price of the A310 airliner. Once the terms of the forward contract are agreed (we will take €54.08 million as the contract price), the value of the contract to either party will change as the market price of the asset to be delivered changes. For instance, let us assume that one year has elapsed. Airbus has raised the price of its A310 model to €52 million. At the same

time, interest rates have also changed and are now 5% per year. What is the contract worth? The payoff at maturity for Airbus, the seller, will be the difference between the market price and the agreed price, namely €54.08 − €52 = €2.08 million. They will not receive this for another year, so the present value will be €1.98 million (€2.08/1.05). If Airbus is making a profit from the transaction, then the customer must be losing an equal amount.

Note the effect that greater price changes have on the gains and losses from the contract before maturity. If the A310 price had risen to

€60 million, the payoff from the contract would be €5.92 million (€60 − €54.08). The present value is €5.638 million (€5.92/1.05). What we find is that the greater the changes in price over the life of the forward contract, the greater the value of the forward contract prior to maturity. This shows that the greater the price uncertainty for a firm's inputs and outputs, the greater is the incentive to hedge out these risks and the more valuable the forward contract becomes.

Futures Contracts

You may have realised there is a problem with forward contracts. Think of the situation facing Airbus, if in two years' time the market price of the A310 is now €40 million. The customer has every incentive not to honour the agreement, and buy the same aircraft elsewhere and save €14.08 million by doing so (€54.08 − €40). To ensure it is not left nursing a loss, Airbus will only enter into the forward transaction at the outset if it thinks the customer will honour the forward contract regardless of what happens to the future price at maturity – and, of course, the customer has the same worries. A major problem therefore is that forward contracts are subject to what is called **counterparty credit risk** and this materialises when the other party fails to fulfil its obligations. This will always happen to the party that stands to gain from adhering to the contract. If the price after two years was €60 million, the customer will not renege on the contract even if they do not want the airliner. This is because they can immediately resell it at a profit! Problems with the creditworthiness of counterparties in forward contracts limit the possible parties a company can deal with using forward contracts to those that it knows will pay even if it means they are losing out as a result.

Futures contracts were developed specifically to deal with the counterparty problem. They do this in a number of ways:

- All contracts are made with a clearing house and not directly between buyers and sellers. This means if one of the parties defaults, the contract is still good for the other party since they have a contract with the clearing house.
- To protect the clearing house from losses due to defaults, both buyers and sellers have to post a goodwill deposit when buying or selling a futures contract, known as **margin**, to cover possible losses. The amount that is posted is enough to cover anticipated daily price changes in the contract plus an additional safety margin.
- The values of futures contracts to the buyer and seller are updated daily and the amounts debited and credited to the goodwill deposit. If the amount in the goodwill deposit account (margin account) falls below some predetermined level, further margin is required by the party incurring the losses. If this fails to materialise, the contract is terminated and the margin account used to cover any losses by the clearing house.
- Contracts are standardised to facilitate the market and trading is carried out through an organised exchange.

Futures contract

a standardised, transferable, exchange-traded contract that requires the delivery of a specified asset at a predetermined price on a specified future date

---

Counterparty credit risk

the risk that the other party to a transaction will be unable or unwilling to honour their commitments

---

Margin

collateral that the holder of a futures contract has to deposit to cover the credit risk

These institutional and functional changes made to the way forward contracts work create exchange-traded futures contracts. Because these contracts are standardised and a central counterparty acts as the buyer and seller for market users, there is a liquid market in futures. Buyers can enter the market very rapidly and find sellers through the exchange. Unlike a forward contract that has to be unwound with the other party, when the buyer comes to sell through the exchange they can easily find another market user who wants to take on their position. Furthermore, transaction costs are very low and this adds to the attraction of the instruments for short-term risk management purposes. As a result, there are large volumes of futures contracts being traded on numerous exchanges. The most important ones in Europe are the NYSE/Euronext/Liffe group and EUREX. The largest exchange in the world is the Chicago-based CME Group.

WEB

The major exchanges have information about their contracts and how they can be used. The two major ones in Europe are the NYSE Euronext group http://www.euronext.com and Eurex http://www.eurexchange.com. The largest exchange in the world is the CME Group in Chicago http://www.cmegroup.com.

Typically, a futures contract will be based on a representative asset for the particular asset class or a recognised benchmark asset. For instance, the copper futures contract traded on the London Metal Exchange, a commodities futures exchange, specifies that it must be Grade A copper bars conforming to a defined standard of purity. A number of asset types have no representative asset. An example is corporate bonds, and there is no corporate bond futures contract since there is no such thing as a 'representative company'. In this case, market participants have to use government bonds, for which there are futures contracts. This means that hedging will be less than perfect. For companies, using futures or forwards involves a trade-off between the advantages of having a ready market and low transaction costs and using a standardised contract, in futures; and being able to agree to buy and sell a specific asset and the problems of credit risk and illiquidity, in forward contracts.

Apart from the institutional arrangements and the fact that using futures requires both buyer and seller to post margin, as far as companies are concerned, forwards and futures serve very much the same purpose: both types of contract allow firms to set the prices at which they enter into a specific purchase or sale transaction in the future and to manage the price risk for inputs or outputs.

Before You Go On

1. What are the elements that go to determine the price at which a forward contract is agreed? Which elements will increase the forward price and which elements will reduce the forward price?
2. How does a forward contract create counterparty credit risk?
3. What are the main differences between a forward contract and a futures contract?

SWAPS

Learning Objective 4
Define interest rate and cross-currency swaps and know how they are valued.

Companies often enter into long-term agreements that have predetermined cash flows. For instance, a company may borrow via issuing a fixed-rate bond. Other companies, in particular small ones that do not have access to the bond market, have to borrow at a variable rate from a bank or other financial institution. These fixed or variable-rate loans may create undesirable risks. Managers like to be able to plan ahead and know the costs of the various factors of production. For a company to borrow at a variable rate creates the risk that interest rates increase over the life of the loan. This is likely to happen just when there is also pressure on the firm's profit margins and sales. It is therefore desirable to manage the interest rate risk. It is possible to use forward and futures contracts to do this. However, these have some disadvantages: there may not be suitable contracts for the longer maturities or they are expensive and the prices will change with the maturity of the contracts. Think back to the Airbus example: if the contract had been for three years, the forward price would have been more than the two-year price, given the way the cost-of-carry formula works. Furthermore, forwards and futures only cover a single purchase or sale transaction.

> ### Interest rate swap
>
> exchange agreement where one party exchanges a stream of interest payments for another party's stream of cash flows

would rather make fixed payments on its loan – i.e., just like a bond's payments. What it would like to do is exchange the variable-rate liability for a fixed set of payments. This is precisely what **interest rate swaps** do. They are agreements where one party agrees to make a set of fixed interest payments to another party conditional upon the other party making variable payments in exchange. To determine the payment amounts, the contract specifies a notional amount of principal to calculate what each party is due. The variable rate is determined using an index of interest rates, such as the euro interbank offered rate (Euribor). Take the example of SEBA AG, a German machinery manufacturer that has borrowed €20 million at a floating rate from Commerzbank. The company wants to lock in the interest it will pay on this loan and enters into a five-year interest swap that exactly matches the amount and maturity of the loan. The fixed rate is preset at 5% and hence the fixed side (also called the coupon) on the swap will be €1 million (€20 million × 0.05) and that for the floating side will be €20 million × $Euribor_t$. This is 'reset' at each period, which for simplicity we will assume is 1 year, although in most cases it is more frequent – typically, every six months, to match the interest due on the loan. The swap would therefore have the following cash flows:

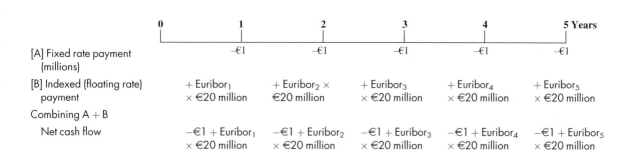

	0	1	2	3	4	5 Years
[A] Fixed rate payment (millions)		−€1	−€1	−€1	−€1	−€1
[B] Indexed (floating rate) payment		+ $Euribor_1$ × €20 million	+ $Euribor_2$ × €20 million	+ $Euribor_3$ × €20 million	+ $Euribor_4$ × €20 million	+ $Euribor_5$ × €20 million
Combining A + B						
Net cash flow		−€1 + $Euribor_1$ × €20 million	−€1 + $Euribor_2$ × €20 million	−€1 + $Euribor_3$ × €20 million	−€1 + $Euribor_4$ × €20 million	−€1 + $Euribor_5$ × €20 million

Swaps get around the problems with forwards and futures by using the same price for all the exchanges in cash flows. Take the situation where a company borrows money at a variable rate, but

In this transaction SEBA has borrowed via a loan, where the interest rate is set by reference to Euribor. By using the interest rate swap, the company has transformed the payment flows such that

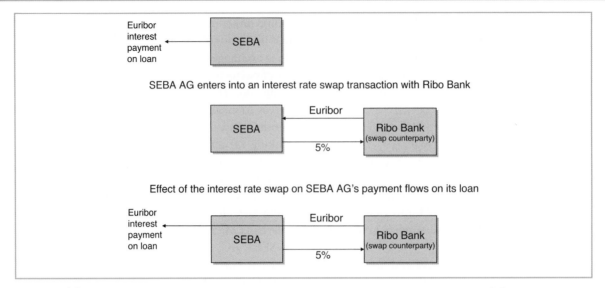

Exhibit 20.3: **How the Interest Rate Swap Transforms SEBA AG's Floating-Rate Liability into a Fixed-Rate Liability**   The interest rate swap transforms SEBA's floating-rate loan payments into fixed-rate payments when SEBA contracts to pay the fixed rate, or coupon, on the swap and receive the floating-rate payments. As a result, the floating rate it receives matches the payments it makes on the loan and its obligation is now to make the fixed payment of 5% on the notional amount of the swap. As the loan and the swap are both for €20 million, the company has a fixed-rate payment each year of €1 million from entering into the swap.

its loan now has a fixed interest payment of 5% per year with a known future interest payment at the end of each year of €1 million. Exhibit 20.3 illustrates the way the loan's variable interest rate is transformed into a fixed rate by adding the interest rate swap.

An interest rate swap allows a company such as SEBA to make either fixed-rate payments or floating-rate payments. Hence, the swap would work equally well if SEBA had borrowed at a fixed rate and wanted to make a floating-rate payment. Because companies and financial institutions often have offsetting needs, a market in swaps brokered via major banks has evolved and a major bank will usually be the counterparty to any corporate swap transaction.

Learning by Doing Application 20.3

Problem: As the financial manager at the pizza restaurant group, you note there is an inverse relationship between the revenues of the restaurants and interest rates. This means that if interest rates rise, the group's cash flow suffers disproportionately since revenues go down just when interest costs go up. The pizza restaurant business has borrowings of €5 million that mature in four years' time. These consist of a loan that has an interest rate indexed to Euribor plus 2%. The four-year interest rate swaps rate is 3.25%. What can you do to reduce the effect of higher interest rates on the group's cash flow? What will be the fixed rate if you use an interest rate swap?

Approach: You need to enter into an interest rate swap to 'lock in' the current swaps rate plus the margin over Euribor – the interest rate index – that the pizza restaurant pays on its loan for the next four years.

Application: The pizza restaurant group agrees to pay on the fixed (coupon) side of the four-year swap, which is 3.25% per year. In exchange, it

will receive Euribor from the swaps counterparty. This will result in the following:

	Loan	Interest Rate Swap	Net
Payments in		– 3.25%	– 3.25%
Payments out	– (Euribor + 2.0%)	+ Euribor	– 2.0%
			– 5.25%

By entering into the swap, the pizza restaurant group can obtain a fixed rate of 5.25% on its borrowings. Even if interest rates rise over the four years, the group's total interest expense is now fixed at €262 500 per year (€5 million × 0.0525).

Valuing Interest Rate Swaps

The value of an interest rate swap will be the difference between the payments that the company makes and those it receives. We can apply our understanding of how cash flows are valued by noting that a swap is created if we borrow at a floating rate and agree to pay the indexed rate and use the proceeds to invest in a fixed-rate par bond. The cash flows from these transactions will look as follows:

lending, we can use our understanding of how to value the fixed side and the floating side to determine the swap's value. The swap's value will simply be:

Value of interest rate swap
= Value of bond with swap coupon rate   (20.2)
  – value of loan with swap floating rate

In Chapter 8, we learned that the way to price bonds is to discount their cash flows using

	0	1	2	3	4	n Years
[A] Borrow amount P at a floating rate (i %)	$+P$	$-P \times i_1\%$	$-P \times i_1\%$	$-P \times i_1\%$	$-P \times i_1\%$	$-P \times i_1\%$ $-P$
[B] Invest proceeds P in a fixed-rate par bond paying $k\%$	$-P$	$+P \times k\%$	$+P \times k\%$	$+P \times k\%$	$+P \times k\%$	$+P \times k\%$ $+P$
Combining A + B						
Net cash flow	—	$-P \times i_1\%$ $+P \times k\%$	$-P \times i_1\%$ $+P \times k\%$	$-P \times i_1\%$ $+P \times k\%$	$-P \times i_1\%$ $+P \times k\%$	$-P \times i_1\%$ $+P \times k\%$

The net payments will be simply the interest differential between the fixed side payment and the then prevailing floating-rate payment. Since the swap is simply the product of a package made up of a floating-rate borrowing and a fixed-rate

Equation (8.1):

$$P_B = \frac{C_1}{1+i} + \frac{C_2}{(1+i)^2} + \cdots + \frac{C_n + F_n}{(1+i)^n}$$

where:

P_B = price of the bond or present value of the stream of cash payments

C_t = coupon payment in period t, where $t = 1$, $2, 3, \ldots, n$

F_n = par value or face value (principal amount) to be paid at maturity

i = market interest rate (discount rate or market yield)

n = number of periods to maturity

This will work well for the fixed side. But what of the floating side? We know what the interest rate is for the first period since we will know the value of the index, but we do not know what the interest rates will be at $t = 2$ and thereafter. This makes it seemingly impossible to value the floating-rate loan. However, this is to ignore the fact that at the start of period 2, the loan's interest rate will be set by the index at the then current prevailing interest rate. This means that the loan value will be its par value or principal amount. This means that the value of the loan will be its principal amount at the reset date.

Let us check this out by assuming that we have perfect foresight and know the interest rates that will prevail on the fixed and floating sides of the following €100 million five-year interest rate swap that has a fixed-rate payment of 4.383%:

$$P_B = \frac{€4.383}{1.04383} + \frac{€4.383}{(1.04383)^2} + \frac{€4.383}{(1.04383)^3}$$
$$+ \frac{€4.383}{(1.04383)^4} + \frac{€4.383}{(1.04383)^5} + \frac{€100}{(1.04383)^5}$$

$$P_B = €100 \text{ million}$$

$$P_L = \frac{€4.0}{1.04383} + \frac{€4.2}{(1.04383)^2} + \frac{€4.4}{(1.04383)^3}$$
$$+ \frac{€4.6}{(1.04383)^4} + \frac{€4.8}{(1.04383)^5} + \frac{€100}{(1.04383)^5}$$

$$P_L = €100 \text{ million}$$

The value of this swap is zero since both sides have equal value ($P_B = P_L$). We would call this an 'at-market' swap since it has a zero net present value. Just as with forwards and futures, the price at which we can enter swaps that are being offered in the market is their fair value. In the above swap, neither side stands to win or lose. Of course, in practice, the payer and receiver of the floating payment do not know in advance what these payments will be. However, since we know that the floating side remains at or very close to the notional principal on the swap, all the value change will occur as the present value of the fixed payments rise and fall with changes in interest rates.[9]

An 'off-market' interest rate swap is valued in the same way as an at-market interest rate swap by

	0	1	2	3	4	5 Years
[A] Fixed-rate payment (millions)		−€4.383	−€4.383	−€4.383	−€4.383	−€4.383
[B] Indexed (floating-rate) payments (millions)		+€4.0	+€4.2	+€4.4	+€4.6	+€4.8
Combining A + B Net cash flow		−€0.383	−€0.183	+€0.017	+€0.217	+€0.417

The five-year interest rate is 4.383% per year. We first present-value the cash flows, treating the fixed-rate side as a bond and the floating-rate side as a loan (where, exceptionally, we know what these floating-rate payments will be):

noting that the floating-rate side is unaffected by changes in interest rates. What will be the value of a five-year swap when the fixed side or coupon payment is not 4.383%, but 3.90% and 4.70%, respectively?

To answer this question, we simply need to recalculate the fixed side of the swap with the new coupon rates:

$$P_{B,3.9\%} = \frac{€3.9}{1.04383} + \frac{€3.9}{(1.04383)^2} + \frac{€3.9}{(1.04383)^3}$$

$$+ \frac{€3.9}{(1.04383)^4} + \frac{€3.9}{(1.04383)^5} + \frac{€100}{(1.04383)^5}$$

$$P_B = €97.874 \text{ million}$$

$$P_{B,4.7\%} = \frac{€4.7}{1.04383} + \frac{€4.7}{(1.04383)^2} + \frac{€4.7}{(1.04383)^3}$$

$$+ \frac{€4.7}{(1.04383)^4} + \frac{€4.7}{(1.04383)^5} + \frac{€100}{(1.04383)^5}$$

$$P_B = €101.397 \text{ million}$$

So in the case where the coupon rate is less than the market interest rate or at-market swaps coupon rate (3.9% < 4.383%), the value of the swap will be +€2.126 million (−€97.874 + €100). In the case where the coupon rate on the swap is greater than the market interest rate (4.7% > 4.383%), the value of the swap will be −€1.397 million. Of course, there are two sides to a swap, just as there

are in forwards and futures, and hence the gains and losses here will depend on whether one is paying or receiving the fixed rate. The situation will therefore be:

	Coupon Rate > At-market Swaps Rate	Coupon Rate < At-market Swaps Rate
Receive the fixed rate (Pay the floating rate)	Swap will have a **negative** value	Swap will have a **positive** value
Pay the fixed rate (Receive the floating rate)	Swap will have a **positive** value	Swap will have a **negative** value

Swaps are direct obligations between the two parties, like forwards, and have the same problem with counterparty credit risk. Credit risk will arise if the present value of the future receipts is greater than the present value of future payments.

Learning by Doing Application 20.4

Problem: The current four-year 'at-market' interest rate swaps rate is 4.00%. You have a swap with exactly four years to maturity with a notional principal amount of €50 million and you are receiving a fixed rate of 3.75% on the swap. What is the swap's value?

Approach: We apply the swap valuation approach where we treat the value of the swap as the difference between a fixed-rate bond (P_B) and a floating-rate loan (P_L) in order to work out the net present value of the swap, taking the floating-side value to be the notional principal amount.

Application: The amount of interest (or the coupon payment) on the fixed side of the swap will be €1 875 000 (€50 000 000 × 0.0375). The present value of the bond element (P_B) will therefore be:

$$P_B = \frac{€1\,875000}{1.04} + \frac{€1\,875000}{(1.04)^2} + \frac{€1\,875000}{(1.04)^3}$$

$$+ \frac{€1\,875000}{(1.04)^4} + \frac{€50\,000\,000}{(1.04)^4}$$

$$= €1\,802\,885 + €1\,733\,543 + €1\,666\,868$$

$$+ €44\,342\,967$$

$$= €49\,546\,263$$

The value of the swap will be $P_B - P_L$, that is $+€49\ 546\ 263 - €50\ 000\ 000$, or $-€453\ 737$. From your perspective, the swap is a liability since the present value of the payments out exceeds the present value of the payments to be received. That is, $3.75\% < 4.00\%$.

Cross-Currency Swaps

A **cross-currency swap** is like an interest rate swap except that instead of being in one currency, it involves the exchange of cash flows between two different currencies. So, for instance, one side of a cross-currency swap may be denominated in US dollars and the other side in euros. In this case, for the swap to work, both parties must exchange both the interest payments. For example, if Airbus enters into a cross-currency swap for €100 million at an agreed exchange rate of US €1.3000 = €1, with fixed interest payments of 3.5% in euros and 4.1% in US dollars for five years – where it pays in US dollars and receives in euros – the cash flows will be as follows:[10]

What we need to understand at this point is that by using a cross-currency swap, Airbus has effectively made a fixed-rate loan in euros against a fixed-rate borrowing in US dollars.

> ### Cross-currency swap
>
> the exchange of principal and interest in one currency for the principal and interest in another currency

There are a good many reasons why Airbus, or any other company, might want to enter into a

	0	1	2	3	4	5 Years
Cash flows in euros (millions)	−€100	+€3.5	+€3.5	+€3.5	+€3.5	+€3.5 +€100
Cash flows in US dollars (millions)	+$130	−$5.33	−$5.33	−$5.33	−$5.33	−$5.33 −$130

To receive the US dollars, Airbus provides €100 million at the start of the transaction. The euro-side interest payments are €3.5 million (€100 × 0.035). On the dollar side, Airbus initially receives €130 million (that is, €100m × 1.3000) based on the agreed exchange rate. The interest is $5.33 million ($130 × 0.041). At the maturity of the swap, both parties re-exchange the principal. A key feature of the cross-currency swap is that the exchange rate is fixed throughout. In the next chapter we discuss how exchange rates work and why managing exchange rate risk is important.

cross-currency swap. In Airbus's case, its costs and borrowings will be largely in euros, but its airliner sales will be largely in US dollars. Therefore, the motivation may be to reduce the effect of currency movements on its costs, which are largely in euros. Other motivations include using the company's borrowing cost advantage in euros to fund US dollar-denominated investments, such as a North American subsidiary. The motivations for corporate risk management discussed at the start of the chapter stimulate the corporate use of cross-currency swaps.

Learning by Doing Application 20.5

Problem: The pizza restaurant group is considering expanding its operations into Sweden. You have been tasked with providing the necessary finance to support this move, which is estimated to need €2 million. You have been in contact with a Swedish bank and they say the company can borrow Swedish krona (SKr) 20 million at a fixed rate of 6.20% per year for five years. In your research, you discover you can do a cross-currency swap between the euro and the Swedish krona for five years at 6.10% per year against a fixed rate in euros of 5.10% per year. The company currently has the ability to raise fixed rate using an interest rate swap as per Learning by Doing 20.3 at 5.25% per year. Which represents the better financing deal?

Approach: We need to compare the two alternatives, which are (1) borrowing directly from the Swedish bank or (2) borrowing in euros and using the cross-currency swap to obtain the Swedish krona for the new venture.

Solution: The two alternatives provide the following cost of borrowing:

(1) Direct borrowing from the Swedish bank is 6.20%.

(2) The swaps rate is euros 5.10% and 6.10% in Swedish krona. The company pays 0.15% on its euro borrowing (5.25% − 5.10%) but pays 0.20% less on its Swedish krona via the swap (6.30% − 6.10%). Netting the two differences means that it is saving a modest 0.05% per year (0.15% − 0.20%) by borrowing in euros and swapping into Swedish krona. Borrowing in euros and swapping to fixed rate in euros gives an all-in cost of 6.15% in Swedish krona.

Valuing Cross-Currency Swaps

The valuation of cross-currency swaps is the same as that for interest rate swaps. We simply present-value the cash flows of the two sides and convert one of the present values into the other currency using the prevailing exchange rate. Let us value the Airbus swap given above and, to do so, we will assume that one year has passed and interest rates and the exchange rate have both changed. The exchange rate has now moved to $1.3500 = €1$, that is, the US dollar has fallen against the euro. The interest rate in US dollars has risen slightly to 4.5%, as has that in euros, which is now 3.75%.

The original market conditions at the initiation of the cross-currency swap and the new market conditions and changes are given below:

$$P_{B,euro} = \frac{€3.5}{1.0375} + \frac{€3.5}{(1.0375)^2} + \frac{€3.5}{(1.0375)^3}$$
$$+ \frac{€103.5}{(1.0375)^4}$$
$$= €99.087 \text{ million}$$

$$P_{B,US\ dollars} = \frac{\$5.33}{1.045} + \frac{\$5.33}{(1.045)^2} + \frac{\$5.33}{(1.045)^3}$$
$$+ \frac{\$135.33}{(1.045)^2} = \$128.134 \text{ million}$$

The last step is to convert one of the currencies into the other at the current exchange rate for the US dollar and the euro ($1.3500/€). The value of the swap in euros is therefore €4.173 million (€99.087 − $128.134/$1.3500). Of course, this value will depend on whether one is receiving

	Original Market Conditions	Market Conditions After One Year	Change From Original Market Conditions
Euro interest rate	3.50%	3.75%	+0.25%
US dollar interest rate	4.10%	4.50%	+0.40%
Foreign exchange rate	$1.300/€	$1.3500/€	+$0.0500
Maturity	5 years	4 years	−1 year

Using the current market conditions, we now *revalue* the swap using the same approach that we used for the interest rate swap. We therefore present-value the remaining cash flows as follows:

the euro cash flows or the US dollar ones. For one side, it is a gain and for the other side, a loss. To better understand where the gains and losses are coming from, we can break the swap into its constituent value change components: (1) change in value of euro component, (2) change in value of US dollar component and (3) changes in the exchange rate. We therefore have:

originally borrowed. To put it another way, to replace the dollar-denominated cash flows, Airbus can provide $128.134 million rather than the original $130 million, thus saving $1.866 million.

(millions)	Original Value	New Value	Value if Paying the Euros and Receiving the US Dollars	Value if Paying the US Dollars and Receiving the Euros
(1) Euro-side value change	€100	€99.087	+€0.913	−€0.913
(2) US dollar-side value change	$130	$128.134	−$1.866 or −€1.382 (−$1.866/$1.3500)	+$1.866 or +€1.382 ($1.866/$1.3500)
(3) Change from movement in the currency	$130	$135	−$5 or −€3.704 (−$5/$1.3500)	+$5 or +€3.704 ($5/$1.3500)
(1 + 2 + 3) Net effect of changes in value			−€4.173	+€4.173

The table shows that the components of value change have led to the cross-currency swap either being an asset (if the party is paying US dollars and receiving euros) or a liability (if receiving US dollars and paying euros).

We will look at the cross-currency swap from Airbus's perspective, but this is simply a mirror image to that of the counterparty on the other side of the swap. From the table we can see that there is a change in value of −€0.913 million (€99.087 − €100) from the increase in the rate of interest on the euro side of the swap. The original interest rate was 3.50% and it has increased to 3.75%. This leads to a reduction in the present value of the cash flows denominated in euros that Airbus will receive. The same has happened for the US dollar side, where interest rates have risen from 4.10% to 4.50% and the value has fallen from $130 million to $128.134 million (−$1.866). Whether this is good or bad news depends on whether one is paying or receiving US dollars on the cross-currency swap. As the dollar side is a liability to Airbus since it is paying, a reduction in value is good news. This is because Airbus can now terminate the swap at the current market conditions and pay back less than

If Airbus had been receiving the US dollar cash flows, it would have lost money from the change in interest rates – as it has done from the increase in the rate of interest in the euro. The same logic applies for the change in the value of exchange rate between the euro and the US dollar. The original swap required $130 million to equate to €100 million; with the fall in value of the US dollar, $135 million is needed. This means an additional $5 million is needed, depending on whether one is due to repay or receive dollars. Since Airbus is due to repay $130 million, it now needs fewer euros to repay the originally contracted amount of $130 million. At the start, €100 million bought $130 million, now €100 million buys $135 million, so Airbus would only need to provide $130/$135 × €100 million (€96.296), saving €3.704 million. Adding all these effects together, and converting the dollars to euros, gives a net change in value of €4.173 million. This is the sum that the euro payer (US dollar receiver) needs to pay to the euro receiver (US dollar payer) to terminate the swap. Since Airbus has contracted to pay US dollars and receive euros, it will receive €4.173 million if the swap is terminated by mutual agreement.[11]

Learning by Doing Application 20.6

Problem: The pizza restaurant decided to use the cross-currency swap discussed in Learning by Doing 20.5 and entered into a 5-year agreement to pay Swedish krona (SKr) and receive euros. The fixed rate on the swap is 6.30% in krona per year and 5.10% in euros. The amount of the swap is €2 million and SKr 19.6 million, respectively.

It is now the pizza restaurant's year end and the auditors want to know what is the swap's current value as, under the IFRS rules, derivative transactions need to be marked-to-market and reported on the company's balance sheet. That is, they need to be revalued to their fair value for financial reporting purposes. Since the swap was initiated, one year has passed and the exchange rate of the euro to the Swedish krona is now at SKr 9.9/€, the Swedish krona interest rate for four-year swaps is 6.25% and that for euros is 5.05%. What is the swap's fair value for reporting purposes?

Approach: We need to apply the valuation approach for cross-currency swaps where we present-value the two sets of remaining cash flows for the four years at the now-prevailing interest rates and convert the two sides to a common currency before determining the net value. The pizza restaurant group is paying Swedish krona (which is the liability side) and receiving euros (the asset side). Since the reporting currency is the euro, it is necessary to convert the value of the cross-currency swap to this currency.

Solution: We first need to calculate the remaining cash flows on the two sides of the swap. The euro side is worth €2 million and the interest rate is 5.10%, so the fixed payments are €102 000 per year (€2 million × 0.051%). On the krona side, the fixed payment is SKr 1 196 000 (SKr 19.6 × 6.10).

$$P_{B,euro} = \frac{€102\,000}{1.0505} + \frac{€102\,000}{(1.0505)^2} + \frac{€102\,000}{(1.0505)^3} + \frac{€2\,102\,000}{(1.0505)^4}$$

$$= €2\,003\,542$$

$$P_{B,SKr} = \frac{SKr\,1\,196\,000}{1.0625} + \frac{SKr\,1\,196\,000}{(1.0625)^2}$$

$$+ \frac{SKr\,1\,196\,000}{(1.0625)^3} + \frac{SKr\,21\,196\,000}{(1.0625)^4} = SKr\,19\,498\,706$$

The final stage is to convert the krona value into euros (we do this since the pizza restaurant reports its results in euros) at the current exchange rate, which gives a value in euros of €1 969 566 (SKr 19 498 706/SKr 9.9/€). The company receives the euros, so this is a cash inflow and pays the krona, so the net value of the swap is €33 976 (€2 003 542 − €1 969 566). This is a positive value, so this is the amount that will be reported as a long-term financial asset on the balance sheet at the year-end.

Before You Go On

1. How can we characterise the cash flows from an interest rate swap and a cross-currency swap?
2. Why does a swap only have credit risk when it has a positive value?
3. In what ways do swaps transform the risk of firms' assets and liabilities?

FINANCIAL OPTIONS

Learning Objective 5

Define a call option and a put option and describe the payoff function for each of these options.

A **financial option** is a derivative in that, like forwards, futures and swaps, its value is derived from the value of another asset. The owner of a financial option has the right, but not the obligation, to buy or sell an asset on or before a specified date for a specified price. The asset that the owner has a right to buy or sell is known as the **underlying asset**. The last date on which an option can be exercised is called the **exercise date,** or *expiration date*, and the price at which the option holder can buy or sell the asset is called the **strike price,** or *exercise price*.

Financial option

the right to buy or sell a financial security, such as a share of stock, on or before a specified date for a specified price

Underlying asset

the asset from which the value of an option is derived

Exercise (expiration) date

the last date on which an option can be exercised

Strike (exercise) price

the price at which the owner of an option has the right to buy or sell the underlying asset

Call Options

Let us consider how the value of an option is derived from the value of an underlying asset. Suppose you own an option to buy one share of Siemens AG, the German engineering company, for €50 and today is the exercise date – if you do not exercise the option today, it will expire and become worthless. If the price of Siemens shares is less than €50, it does not make sense to exercise your option, because if you did, you would be paying €50 for something you could buy for less than €50 in the open market. Similarly, if the share price is €50, there is no benefit to be had from exercising your option. If, however, the price is above €50, then you will benefit from exercising the option. Even if you do not want to own the Siemens share, you can buy it for €50 and immediately turn around and sell it for a profit. The value of the option to you is the difference between the market price of Siemens shares and the strike price of the option. For example, if the Siemens shares are trading for €60 in the market, then the option is worth €10 (€60 share price – €50 strike price) to you. If the shares are trading at €70, then the value of the option is €20 (€70 – €50), and so on.

The relation between the value of an option and the price (value) of the underlying asset – such as the Siemens shares – is known as the **option payoff function**. Part A in Exhibit 20.4 illustrates the payoff function at expiration (actually, the instant before the option expires) for the owner of an option that is like the option on the Siemens shares we just discussed. This option is known as a **call option** because it gives the owner the right to buy, or 'call', the underlying asset.

> **Option payoff function**
>
> the function that shows how the value of an option varies with the value of the underlying asset

> **Call option**
>
> an option to buy the underlying asset

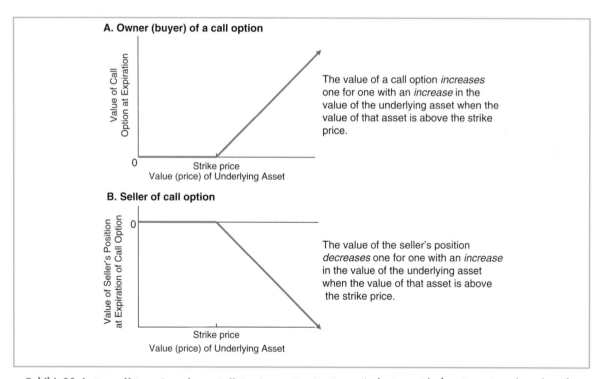

A. Owner (buyer) of a call option

The value of a call option *increases* one for one with an *increase* in the value of the underlying asset when the value of that asset is above the strike price.

B. Seller of call option

The value of the seller's position *decreases* one for one with an *increase* in the value of the underlying asset when the value of that asset is above the strike price.

Exhibit 20.4: Payoff Functions for a Call Option at Expiration At the instant before it expires, the value of a call option to the owner equals either: (1) zero, if the value of the underlying asset is less than or equal to the strike price, or (2) the value of the underlying asset less the value of the strike price, if the value of the underlying asset is greater than the strike price.

The value of the seller's position equals either: (1) zero, if the value of the underlying asset is less than or equal to the strike price, or (2) the strike price less the value of the underlying asset if the value of the underlying asset is greater than the strike price.

With an exercise price of €50, the value of the Siemens call option equals €0 if the price of the underlying shares is €50 or less. As we noted earlier, it would not make sense to exercise the option if the price of the shares is not greater than €50. Since an option is the *right* to buy or sell an underlying asset, rather than an *obligation* to buy or sell, the owner of the option can simply let it expire if it does not make sense to exercise it. This limits the downside for the owner of the option to €0. In this way, options are very different to the forwards, futures and swaps discussed earlier.

If the underlying asset price is above the strike price, the value of the call option at exercise increases unit for unit with the price of the underlying asset. You can see this relation in part A of the exhibit. For every euro that the asset price exceeds the strike price, the value of the call option increases by one euro. In other words, the slope of the payoff function equals one when the underlying asset price is above the exercise price.

Part B of Exhibit 20.4 illustrates the payoff function for a person who sells a call option (also known as *writing the option*). Notice that the payoff function for the seller (or writer) is the mirror image of that for the owner (buyer) of the call option. This makes sense, since any gain for the owner is a loss for the seller. To see why this is true, let us return to the Siemens option example. Recall that if the shares are trading at €60 when the option expires, the call option is worth €10 to the owner, who can purchase the shares for €50 and then immediately sell them on the market for €60. The seller of the call option, though, must sell shares that are worth €60 for €50 – resulting in a €10 loss.

Part B of Exhibit 20.4 shows that the payoff to the seller of the call option is never positive. It is negative when the price of the underlying asset is greater than the strike price, and it equals zero when the price of the underlying asset is equal to or less than the strike price. You may be wondering why anyone would ever sell a call option if the return were never positive. The reason is simply

that the buyer pays the seller a fee to purchase the option. This fee, known as the **call premium**, makes the total return to the seller positive when the price of the underlying asset is near or below the strike price.

> ### Call premium
>
> the price that the buyer of a call option pays the seller for that option

A call premium is just like the premium you pay when you purchase insurance for your car. In return for the insurance premium, the insurance company agrees to pay you if certain events occur, such as if you collide with another car or if a hailstorm damages the car. The seller of a call option is simply selling insurance to the buyer which pays the buyer when the value of the underlying asset is above the strike price.

Put Options

While the owner of a *call option* has the right to *buy* the underlying asset at a pre-specified price on or before the expiration date, the owner of a **put option** has the right to *sell* the underlying asset at a pre-specified price. The payoff function for the owner of a put option is similar to that for a call option but it is the reverse in the sense that the owner of a put option profits if the price of the underlying asset is *below* the strike price. This is illustrated in Exhibit 20.5.

> ### Put option
>
> an option to sell the underlying asset

Part A of the exhibit shows that the owner of a put option will not want to exercise that option if the price of the underlying asset is above the strike price. Obviously, it does not make sense to sell an asset for less than you can get on the open market.

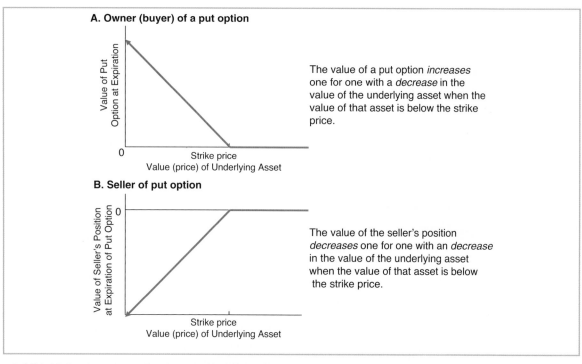

A. Owner (buyer) of a put option

Value of Put
Option at Expiration

0   Strike price
Value (price) of Underlying Asset

The value of a put option *increases*
one for one with a *decrease* in the
value of the underlying asset when the
value of that asset is below the strike
price.

B. Seller of put option

Value of Seller's Position
at Expiration of Put Option

0

Strike price
Value (price) of Underlying Asset

The value of the seller's position
decreases one for one with an *decrease*
in the value of the underlying asset
when the value of that asset is below
the strike price.

Exhibit 20.5: Payoff Functions for Put Option at Expiration   At the instant before it expires, the value of a put option to the owner equals either: (1) zero, if the value of the underlying asset is greater than or equal to the strike price, or (2) the strike price less the value of the underlying asset, if the value of the underlying asset is less than the strike price.

The value to the seller of a put option equals either: (1) zero, if the value of the underlying asset is greater than or equal to the strike price, or (2) the value of the underlying asset less the strike price, if the value of the underlying asset is less than the strike price.

When the value of the underlying asset is below the strike price, however, the owner of the put option will find it profitable to exercise the option. For example, suppose that you own a put option that is expiring today and that entitles you to sell shares in Siemens for €50. If the current price of Siemens shares in the market is €45, the put option is worth €5, because exercising the option will enable you to buy the shares for €45 and then turn around and sell them for €50. Similarly, if the current price of Siemens shares is €30, the put option is worth €20, because you can buy the shares for €30 and sell them for €50.

Part B of Exhibit 20.5 shows that the payoff for the seller of the put option is negative when the price of the underlying asset is below the strike price. This is because the seller of the put option is obliged to purchase the asset at a price that is higher than its market price. For instance, in the Siemens put option example, if the exercise price is €50 and the current market price is €30, the seller of the put option must buy the shares for €50 but can only sell them for €30. This results in a €20 loss.

As with a call option, the payoff for the seller of a put option, which is illustrated in part B of Exhibit 20.5, is never positive. The seller of a put option hopes to profit from the fee, or **put premium**, that he or she receives from the buyer of the put option.

> **Put premium**
>
> the price that the buyer of a put option pays the seller of that option

BUILDING INTUITION

Payoff Functions for Options are Not Linear

Payoff functions for options are not straight lines. This is because the owners of options have the right, rather than the obligation, to buy or sell the underlying assets. If it is not in the owner's best interest to exercise an option, he or she can simply let it expire without exercising it. This limits the owner's potential loss to the value of the premium he or she paid for the option. This makes options from forwards, futures and swaps where the gains and losses are symmetrical.

American, European and Bermudan Options

At the beginning of this section, we said that the owner of a financial option has the right to buy or sell a specific asset *on or before a specified date* for a specified price. In the real world, there are actually several different arrangements concerning when an option can be exercised. Some options can only be exercised on the expiration date. These are known as *European options*. Other options, known as *American options*, can be exercised at any point in time on or before the expiration date. There are also exotic options, such as so-called *Bermudan* options, which can be exercised only on specific dates during the life of the option. Most exchange-traded options are American options.

More on the Shapes of Option Payoff Functions

It is important to note that the payoff functions in Exhibits 20.4 and 20.5 illustrate the values of options to owners and sellers at the instant before they expire. These payoff functions have similar, but somewhat different, shapes at earlier points in time. We discuss why this is the case in the next section.

It is also important to recognise that the payoff functions in Exhibits 20.4 and 20.5 are not straight lines for all possible values of the underlying asset. Each payoff function has a 'kink' at the strike price. This kink exists because the owner of the option has a right, not an obligation, to buy or sell the underlying asset. If it is not in the owner's interest to exercise the option, he or she can simply let it lapse. Later, we will discuss how this feature of options causes agency problems and how it can be useful in managing the risks faced by a firm.

WEB

You can learn more about call options and put options on the Options.Net website at: http://www.theoptions.net/option-trading-strategies/pay-off-diagrams-for-option/.

Decision-Making Example 20.1

When it Makes Sense to Exercise an Option

Situation: You own a call option and a put option on Fiat shares. The strike price for both of these options is €8 and both options expire today. If the current price of Fiat shares is €7, would you exercise either of these options? If so, which one?

Decision: You should exercise the put option. It allows you to sell Fiat shares for €8 that would cost you only €7 to buy. It does not make sense to exercise the call option because the strike price is greater than the market price of Fiat shares.

OPTION VALUATION

Learning Objective 6

List and describe the factors that affect the value of an option.

We saw in the last section that determining the value of a call or a put option at the instant before it expires is relatively simple. For a call option, if the value of the underlying asset is less than or equal to the strike price, the value of the option to the owner is zero. If the value of the underlying asset is greater than the strike price, the value to the owner is simply the value of the underlying asset minus the strike price. For a put option, if the value of the underlying asset is greater than or equal to the strike price, the value of the option is zero to the owner. If the value of the underlying asset is less than the strike price, the value to the owner is the strike price minus the value of the underlying asset.

It is more complicated to determine the value of an option at a point in time before its expiration date. We do not know exactly how the value of the underlying asset will change over time and therefore we do not know what value we will ultimately receive from the option. In this section, we discuss the key variables that affect the value of an option prior to expiration and describe one method that is commonly used to value options. Our objective is not to make you an expert in option valuation but

rather to help you develop some intuition about what makes an option more or less valuable. This intuition will help you better understand how options affect corporate finance decisions.

Limits on Option Values

We will begin by using some common sense to put limits on what the value of a call option can possibly be prior to its expiration date. We focus on call options here because, as you will see, there is a simple relation that enables us to calculate the value of a put option once we know the value of a call option with the same strike price and expiration date.

We already know that the value of a call option can never be less than zero, since the owner of the option can always decide not to exercise it, if doing so is not beneficial. A second limit on the value of a call option is that it can never be greater than the value of the underlying asset. It would not make sense to pay more for the right to buy an asset than you would pay for the asset itself. These two limits suggest that the value of a call option prior to expiration must be in the shaded area in part A of Exhibit 20.6. The shaded area is bounded below by the horizontal axis, because the value of the option must be greater than zero, and it is bounded above by the line that slopes upward at a 45-degree angle, because an option value greater than this would exceed the value of the underlying asset.

There are two other limits on the value of a call option prior to expiration, and these limits are somewhat more subtle. First, the value of a call option prior to the expiration date will never be less than the value of that option if it were exercised immediately. This is true because there is always a possibility that the value of the underlying asset will be greater than it is today at some time before the option expires. Of course, it is possible that the value will be lower but, since the value of the option cannot be less than zero and there is no limit on how high it can go, the expected effect of an increase in the value of the underlying asset on the value of the option is greater than the expected

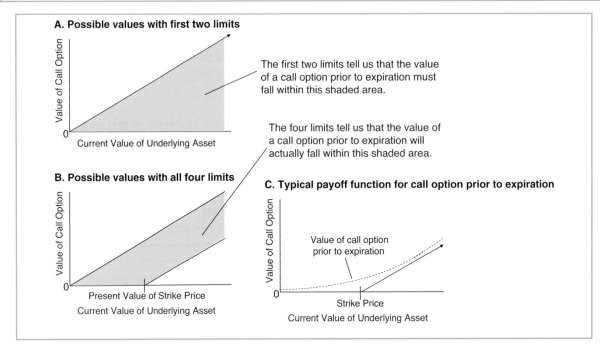

Exhibit 20.6: Possible Values of a Call Option Prior to Expiration   The value of a call option: (1) must be greater or equal to zero (horizontal axis) and (2) cannot be greater than the value of the underlying asset (45-degree line).

In addition to the two limits illustrated in part A, the value of a call option prior to expiration: (3) will never be less than the value of the option if it were exercised immediately where (4) the value of the option is calculated using the present value of the strike price, discounted from the expiration date at the risk-free interest rate. These conditions are both illustrated by the lower 45-degree angle.

Part C shows the typical relation between the value of a call option prior to expiration and its value at expiration. The value of the option prior to expiration is farthest from the value of the option at expiration when the price of the underlying asset is near the strike price.

effect of a decrease. The bottom line is that, prior to expiration, the value of a call option will be greater than the value represented by the solid line in part A of Exhibit 20.4.[12]

The final limit arises because of the time value of money. When we consider the value of a call option at some time prior to expiration, we must compare the current value of the underlying asset with the *present value of the strike price*, discounted at the *risk-free interest rate*. We would be comparing apples and oranges if we did not do this. The present value of the strike price is the amount that an investor would have to invest in risk-free securities at any point prior to the expiration date to ensure that he or she would have enough money to exercise the option when it expired. Thus, when we compare the value of a call option prior to expiration with the value at

expiration, represented by the solid line in part A of Exhibit 20.4, we must use the present value of the strike price to draw the line. The shaded area in part B of Exhibit 20.6 illustrates the possible values for a call option prior to expiration under all four of the limits we have discussed.

In practice, we find that, prior to expiration, call options have a shape that is very similar to the one illustrated by the dotted line in part C of Exhibit 20.6. Notice that this dotted line approaches zero as the value of the underlying asset gets very small relative to the strike price. This makes sense because, with a very low asset value, it becomes highly unlikely that the owner of the option will ever choose to exercise it.

On the right side of the dotted line, you can see that the value of a call option prior to expiration approaches the value of the call option at expiration.

This is because, when the current value of the underlying asset is far to the right of the kink in the payoff function, the probability that this value will fall below the strike price is very small. In other words, the expected effect of an increase in the value of the underlying asset on the value of the option is no longer much greater than the expected effect of a decrease. In this situation, the call option is very much like a forward contract on the underlying asset.

Finally, notice that the dotted line is furthest above the value of the call option at expiration when the price of the underlying asset is near the strike price. At the strike price, the expected effect of an increase in the value of the underlying asset on the value of the option exceeds the expected effect of a decrease by the greatest amount.

Variables that Affect Option Values

Five variables affect the value of a call option prior to expiration. Four of them are related to the following questions:

1. How likely is it that the value of the underlying asset will be higher than the strike price the instant before the option expires?
2. How far above the strike price might it be?

The first two variables are relatively easy to understand. They are the *current value of the underlying asset* and the *strike price*. The higher the current value of the underlying asset, the more likely it is that the value of the asset will be above the strike price when the call option nears expiration. Furthermore, the higher the current value of the asset, the greater the likely difference between the value of the asset and the strike price. This means that, holding the strike price constant, investors will pay more for a call option if the underlying asset value is higher, because the expected value of the option as it nears expiration is higher.[13] For example, suppose that you are considering purchasing a three-month American call option on Siemens shares with a strike price of €50. You should be willing to pay more for

this option if the current price of Siemens shares is €55 than if it is €50.

The opposite relation applies to the strike price. That is, the lower the strike price, the more likely that the value of the underlying asset will be higher than the strike price when the option nears expiration. In addition, the lower the strike price, the greater the likely difference between these two amounts. Thus, the lower the strike price, the more valuable the option is likely to be at expiration. Of course, if the option is expected to be more valuable at expiration, it will also be more valuable at any point prior to expiration. Returning to our Siemens example, we see that a call option with a strike price of €45 is worth more than a call option with a strike price of €50.

We turn next to two variables that affect the value of call options in somewhat more subtle ways. These variables are the *volatility of the value of the underlying asset* and the *time until the expiration of the option*. To understand how these factors affect the value of a call option, recall from part C of Exhibit 20.6 that the payoffs function for a call option prior to expiration is not symmetric. If the value of the underlying asset is well above the strike price, then the value of the option varies in much the same way as the value of the underlying asset. However, if the value of the underlying asset is well below the strike price, then the value of the option approaches zero but changes at a much lower rate than the value of the underlying asset changes. It does not matter if the underlying asset value is just a little bit below the strike price or is worthless – a call option cannot be worth less than zero.

To show how the volatility of the underlying asset value affects the value of an option, we will consider a call option on an underlying asset that has a value exactly equal to the strike price of the option. The value of this option will increase more when the value of the underlying asset goes up than it will decrease when the value of the underlying asset goes down. Let us suppose that the value of the underlying asset is equally likely to go up or down. In this case, the further the value of the asset is likely to move (the greater its volatility), the higher will be the value of a call option on this asset. In other words, the greater the volatility of the underlying asset value, the higher the value of a call option on the asset prior to expiration.

In our Siemens example, suppose the strike price for a call option on Siemens shares is €50, the current price of the shares is €50 and the option expires in one year. Further, suppose that the standard deviation, σ, of the return on the Siemens shares is 30% per year. Recall from the discussion in Chapter 7 that with a standard deviation of 30%, there is a 5% chance that the Siemens share price will change by more than 58.8% (1.96 standard deviations × 30%) by the time the option expires. In other words, there is a 5% chance that the Siemens share price will be less than €20.60 (€50 × [1 − 0.588]) or greater than €79.40 (€50 × [1+0.588]) in a year. If, instead of 30%, the standard deviation of Siemens shares were 40% per year, there would be a 5% chance that the price would be below €10.80 or above €89.20. (You should check these numbers to make sure you know how they are calculated.) As you can see, with the higher standard deviation the share price is more volatile. Investors will pay more for an option on a share that has a more volatile price, because the potential change in the price is greater.

The time until the expiration affects the value of a call option through its effect on the volatility of the value of the underlying asset. The greater the time to maturity, the more the value of the underlying asset is likely to change by the time the option expires. For example, we will return once again to the Siemens example. Suppose that the option expires in two years rather than in one year. People who study statistics have found that the standard deviation of the return on an asset increases over time by the square root of n, where n is the number of periods. Thus, if the standard deviation of the return on Siemens shares is 30% per year, the standard deviation over two years will be:

$$\sigma_{2\ years} = \sigma \times (n)^{1/2} = 30 \times (2)^{1/2} = 30 \times 1.414$$
$$= 42.42\%$$

Clearly, then, a two-year option will be worth more than a one-year option if all the other characteristics of the two options are the same.

We have now discussed four of the five variables that affect the value of an option. The fifth variable is the *risk-free rate of interest*. The value of a call option increases with the risk-free interest rate. Exercising a call option involves paying cash in the future for the underlying asset. The higher the interest rate, the lower the present value of the amount that the owner of a call option will have to pay to exercise it.

WEB

You can read about what affects the values of financial options and how they are traded at the websites for the Chicago Board Options Exchange (CBOE) at: http://www.cboe.com/ and the International Securities Exchange (ISE) at: http://www.iseoptions.com/.

The Binomial Option Pricing Model

In this section, we use a simple model to show how we can calculate the value of a call option at some point in time before the expiration date. This model assumes that the underlying asset will have one of only two possible values when the option expires. The value of the underlying asset will either increase to some value above the strike price or decrease to some value below the strike price.

Arbitrage

buying and selling assets in a way that takes advantage of price discrepancies and yields a profit greater than that which would be expected based solely on the risk of the individual investments

To solve for the value of the call option using this model, we must assume that investors have no arbitrage opportunities with regard to this option. **Arbitrage** is the act of buying and selling assets in a way that yields a return above that suggested by the Security Market Line (SML), which we discussed in Chapter 7. In other words, the absence of arbitrage opportunities means that investors cannot earn a return that is greater than that justified by the systematic risk associated with an investment. As an example of an arbitrage opportunity, suppose that the shares of a particular company are being sold for a lower price in one country than in another country. An investor could simultaneously buy the shares in the country where they are less expensive and sell them in the country where they are more expensive. Assuming that the profit exceeds any transaction costs, the investor would earn an instantaneous risk-free profit. Since it is instantaneous, this profit would be, by definition, above the SML because the SML would predict that the expected return on a risk-free investment is zero if the holding period is zero.

To value the call option in our simple model, we will first create a portfolio that consists of the asset underlying the call option and a risk-free loan. The relative investments in these two assets will be selected so that the combination of the asset and the loan has the same cash flows as the call option, regardless of whether the value of the underlying asset goes up or down. This is called a *replicating portfolio*, since it replicates the cash flows of the option. The replicating portfolio must have the same

value as the option today, since it has the same cash flows as the call option in all possible future outcomes. If the replicating portfolio did not have the same value as the option, an investor could construct an arbitrage portfolio by buying the cheaper of the two and selling the more expensive of the two. Such trading would eventually drive the values of the option and the replicating portfolio together.

To see how a replicating portfolio is constructed, consider an example. Suppose that DRYAD SA shares currently trade for €50 and that its price will be either €70 or €40 in one year. We want to determine the value of a call option to buy DRYAD shares for €55 in one year. First, notice that the value of this option is €15 if the share price goes up to €70 (€70 − €55 = €15) and that it is zero if the share price goes down to €40, since the option will not be exercised. Suppose also that the risk-free rate is 5%.

We can construct a portfolio consisting of x DRYAD SA shares and a risk-free loan with a value of y euros that produces a payoff of either €70 or €40. As you will see, this risk-free loan may involve either borrowing or lending. For each risk-free euro lend, we know that we will receive €1.05 regardless of what happens to the price of the DRYAD shares. In the same way, if we borrow €1, we will owe €1.05 at the end of the year. The value of the shares, the risk-free loan, and the option today and at expiration can be illustrated as follows:

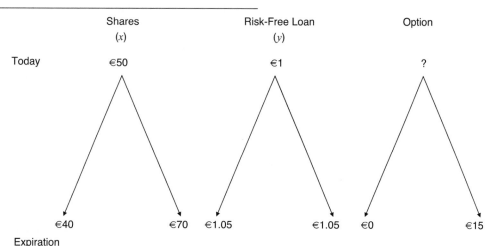

The value of each asset when the share price goes up to €70 is shown on the right arrow and the value when the shares go down to €40 is shown on the left arrow. Notice that we do not know the value of the option today – that is what we are trying to calculate.

We can write two equations that define the replicating portfolio that we want to construct:

$$€15 = (€70 \times x) + (1.05 \times y)$$
$$€0 = (€40 \times x) + (1.05 \times y)$$

The first equation represents the case in which the share price increases to €70 and the second equation represents the case in which the share price goes down to €40. The first equation says that we want the portfolio to be worth €15 when the share price increases to €70 and that the €15 value will consist of x shares worth €70 and a risk-free loan with a face value of y and a value in one year of €1.05 per euro of face value. Similarly, the second equation says that if the share price falls to €40, we want the portfolio to be worth zero (€0). In this case, the portfolio will consist of x shares worth €40 and a risk-free loan with a face value of y and a value in one year of €1.05 per euro of face value.

Since we have two equations and there are two unknowns, x and y, we can solve for the values of the unknowns. Recall from your algebra class that we can solve for x and y by first writing one equation in terms of either x or y and then substituting the result into the second equation. For example, the first equation can be written in terms of x as follows:

$$x = \frac{€15 - (1.05 \times y)}{€70}$$

Now, substituting into the second equation gives us:

$$€0 = \left(€40 \times \frac{€15 - (1.05 \times y)}{€70}\right) + (1.05 \times y)$$

We can now solve this equation for y. For example, we can write this relation as follows:

$$€0 = \left(€40 \times \frac{€15 - (1.05 \times y)}{€70}\right) + (1.05 \times y)$$
$$€0 = €8.5714 - (0.6 \times y) + (1.05 \times y)$$
$$€0 = €8.5714 + 0.45y$$
$$0.45y = -€8.5714$$

Therefore:

$$y = \frac{-€8.5714}{0.45} = -€19.05$$

Finally, substituting this value back into the first equation gives us the value of x:

$$x = \frac{€15 - (1.05 \times -€19.05)}{€70}$$
$$x = \frac{€15 + €20.00}{€70}$$
$$x = 0.5$$

This tells us that the replicating portfolio consists of half a DRYAD SA share ($x = 0.50$) and a €19.05 risk-free loan ($y = -19.05$).[14] The negative value for y tells us that we would borrow, rather than lend, €19.05 at the risk-free interest rate. If we buy half a share and borrow €19.05, then in one year our replicating portfolio will have exactly the same payoff as the call option with a strike price of €55.

If the value of the shares declined to €40, we would own half a share worth €20 and we would owe €19.05 × 1.05 = €20 on the loan. Since the value of the half-share would exactly equal the amount owed on the loan, the portfolio would have a total value of exactly zero. In contrast, if the value of the shares increased to €70, the half a share would be worth €35. Since we would still owe only €20 in this case, the portfolio would have a total value of €15. Since these payoffs are the same as those for the option, this portfolio must have the same value as the option.

At this point, we know what the replicating portfolio is and we know that the replicating portfolio must have the same value as the call option. Now all we have to do to estimate the value of the call option is figure out what is the present value of the replicating portfolio. To do this, we simply determine how much of our own money we would actually have to invest to construct the replicating portfolio. In our example, we could use the €19.05 loan to help purchase the shares, so we would not have to come up with all the money for the shares on our own. In fact, since DRYAD SA shares are currently worth €50, a half share would cost only €25. Therefore, we would have to come up with only €5.95 (€25.00 – €19.05) over and above the amount received from the loan to buy the shares. Since €5.95 is the amount of money that we would actually have to invest to obtain the replicating portfolio, it is the value of this portfolio and therefore the value of the option.

The equation for calculating the value of the replicating portfolio, and therefore the value of the call option, can be expressed as follows:

Value of the call option today

$$= C = (€50 \times y) + (1 \times y)$$
$$= (€50 \times 0.5) + (1 \times -€19.05)$$
$$= €5.95$$

Notice, too, that the strike price, the current price of the underlying shares, the possible future prices of the underlying shares and the risk-free interest rate are all that entered into our calculations. We did not even mention the probabilities that the share price would go up or down at any point. That is because the volatility of the underlying shares value is accounted for by how far apart the two possible future values are. Similarly, the time to expiration is not directly considered. However, the time to expiration affects how high and how low the share price can be when the option expires.[15]

This model may seem surprisingly simple. However, that is largely because we chose to illustrate a simple example. The model can be extended in several ways. For example, we can incorporate possible prices for the underlying asset between now and the expiration date of the option. The underlying asset price might take one of two values one month (or day or hour) from now, and then for each of those values there might be two possible values in the following month (day or hour), and so on. Solving a model such as this requires us to work backwards from the expiration date to find the value of the option at each intermediate date and price until we finally arrive at the value of the option today. Most modern option pricing models are extensions of this type of model.

Learning by Doing Application 20.7

Valuing a Call Option

Problem: You are considering purchasing a call option on Le Terrain Agricole SA shares. Le Terrain Agricole shares currently trade for €35 and you predict that its price will be either €25 or €50 in one year. The call option would enable you to buy Le Terrain Agricole shares in one year for €30. What is this option worth if the risk-free interest rate is 4%?

Approach: The value of the option can be determined by computing the cost of constructing a portfolio that replicates the payoffs from that option.

Solution: The option will be worth €20 if the share price rises to €50 (€50 – €30 strike price) and will be worth €0 if the share price declines to €25. Therefore, the replicating portfolio for this option can be determined from the following two equations:

$$€20 = (€50 \times x) + (1.04 \times y)$$
$$€0 = (€25 \times x) + (1.04 \times y)$$

Solving for x and y, we find that $x = 0.80$ and $y = €19.23$. Therefore, the replicating portfolio consists of 0.8 Le Terrain Agricole shares and a €19.23 loan. Since 0.8 of a share would cost €28 (0.8 × €35) and €19.23 of this amount would be covered by the loan, this replicating portfolio would cost €8.77 (€28.00 − €19.23) to construct. Therefore, the call option is worth €8.77.

Put–Call Parity

> ### Put–call parity
>
> the relation between the value of a call option on an asset and the value of a put option on the same asset that has the same exercise price

To this point, our discussion has focused on call options. As mentioned earlier, this is possible because there is a simple relation that enables us to calculate the value of a put option once we know the value of a call option with the same strike price and expiration date. This relation is called **put–call parity**. The formula for put–call parity is:

$$P = C + Xe^{-rt} - V \qquad (20.3)$$

where P is the value of the put option, C is the value of the call option, X is the strike price, r is the risk-free interest rate, t is the amount of time before the option expires, and V is the current value of the underlying asset. The term e^{-rt} is the exponential function that you can calculate using the 'e^x' key on your calculator; it is simply a discount factor that assumes continuous compounding. It is important to make sure that the r and t are both stated in the same units of time (for example, months or years).

To see how this formula works, we will consider the option on the DRYAD SA shares that we just valued. We know that $C = €5.95$, $X = €55$, $r = 0.05$, $t = 1$ and $V = €50$. Substituting these values into the put–call parity formula and solving for P, we get:

$$\begin{aligned} P &= €5.95 + €55e^{-(0.05)(1)} - €50 \\ &= €5.95 + €52.32 - €50 \\ &= €8.27 \end{aligned}$$

Notice that the variables used in this calculation are the same variables that determine the value of a call option. This means that the same factors that affect the value of a call option also affect the value of a put option. Notice, too, that the value of the put option (€8.27) is greater than the value of the call option (€5.95) in this example. This will not always be true. However, it is true in our example because the current share price of €50 is below the €55 strike price.

Learning by Doing Application 20.8

Valuing a Put Option

Problem: In Learning by Doing Application 20.7, we found that a call option on Le Terrain Agricole SA shares is worth €8.77 when the share price is €35, the strike price is €30, the risk-free interest rate is 4% and the time to maturity is 1 year. What is the value of a put option on the shares if the strike price and all other variables have the same values?

Approach: Use the put–call parity relation, Equation (20.3), to calculate the value of a put option.

Solution: The value of the put option is as follows:

$$P = C + Xe^{-rt} - V$$
$$P = €8.77 + €30e^{-(0.04)(1)} - €35$$
$$= €8.77 + €28.82 - €35$$
$$= €2.59$$

Note that the value of the put option is less than the value of the call option in this example. This is because the current price of the shares is above the strike price.

Options and Risk Management

We have seen how options have kinked payoffs. This makes them very useful for corporate risk management. To see how risks can be managed using options, consider an oil company that is producing and selling oil to refiners. Suppose that the price of crude oil has recently risen above $130 per barrel and the company wants to make sure that, even if prices drop below $125 per barrel, it will receive at least $125 per barrel for each barrel of oil that it sells during the next three months. If the company plans to sell 100 000 barrels of oil in the next three months, the financial manager can hedge the price risk by purchasing put options on 100 000 barrels of oil with a strike price of $125 per barrel plus the cost of the options. The maturity dates on the options must be selected to match the timing of the company's oil output over the next three months. In addition, the actual strike prices on the options must be slightly greater than $125 to account for the premiums that the company pays to purchase the options. This will ensure that the company actually receives $125 per barrel after paying for the options.

One interesting benefit of using options in this way is that they provide downside protection but do not limit the upside to the company if oil prices continue to increase. Put options give the company the right to sell its oil at the strike price if crude oil prices fall but, because there is no obligation to sell, the company can still benefit if oil prices increase. As discussed earlier, this is just like buying insurance. In fact, insurance contracts can be seen as specialised put options.

In addition to using options and other derivative instruments to manage commodity price risks, as in the oil company example, companies can use these instruments to manage risks associated with changing interest rates and exchange rates. Large swings in interest rates can cause a great deal of volatility in the net income of a highly financially leveraged company whose managers rely on floating-rate debt. As interest rates go up and down, the company's interest expense also goes up and down, which can lead to cash flow problems.

Options can also be used to manage risks associated with foreign exchange rates. For example, as we discussed earlier, the revenues that a company reports can be strongly affected by changes in exchange rates if the company manufactures products in Europe and has significant sales in foreign currencies. If the euro strengthens against foreign currencies, the company will have to increase the overseas prices of its products in order to maintain the same euro price per unit. This, in turn, can prompt consumers in overseas markets to purchase fewer of the company's products. By using options and other derivative instruments to protect against exchange rate movements, managers can limit declines in revenues that occur because of such movements.

Finally, options can be used to manage risks associated with equity prices. This is especially important to companies that have traditional defined-benefit pension plans, which provide retirees with guaranteed retirement payments. Companies are required to put money aside to cover the costs of these payments and this money is partially invested in equities. When the stock market declines significantly, these companies must replace any lost value with new contributions, which must come from earnings. As you might expect, companies are very interested in managing the risk that they will have to make such contributions.

Before You Go On

1. What are the limits on the value of a call option prior to its expiration date?
2. What variables affect the value of a call option?
3. Why are the variables that affect the value of a put option the same as those that affect the value of a call option?

REAL OPTIONS

Learning Objective 7

Name some of the real options that occur in business and explain why traditional NPV analysis does not accurately incorporate their values.

Many investments in business involve **real options** – options on real assets. NPV analysis does not adequately reflect the value of these options. While it is not always possible to directly estimate the value of the real options associated with a project, it is important to recognise that they exist when we perform a project analysis. If we do not even consider them, we are ignoring potentially important sources of value. In this section, we provide an overview of the types of real options commonly associated with real investments.

WEB

You can find a list of websites with information about real options at: http://www.real-options.com/resources_links.htm.

Real option

an option for which the underlying asset is a real asset

Options to Defer Investment

Companies often have considerable flexibility as to the timing of their investments. For instance, consider the case of an oil company that owns property expected to contain oil deposits. The oil company can choose to wait to see what happens to oil prices before deciding whether to invest in developing the deposits. This ability to wait and see involves what is known as an *option to defer investment*. The underlying asset in this option is the stream of cash flows that the developed oil field would produce, while the strike price is the amount of money that the company would have to spend to develop it (drill the well and build any necessary infrastructure). Just as the value of shares might go up or down, the value of the cash flows produced by the oil field might increase or decrease with the price of oil.

Property developers often purchase options on land. For example, a developer might pay a landowner €100 000 for a one-year option to purchase a property at a particular price. By accepting the payment, the landowner agrees not to sell the property to anyone else for a year. Such an option provides the developer with time to make a final decision regarding whether or not to actually purchase the land and proceed with a project. Since the developer will still have to buy the land if he or she decides to proceed with the project, the cost of the option reflects a cost of being able to collect more information before making a final decision.

The value of an option to defer investment is not reflected in an NPV analysis. Recall that the NPV rule tells us to accept a project with a positive NPV and to reject one with a negative NPV. NPV analysis does not allow for the possibility of deferring an investment decision. It assumes that we invest either now or never. However, if we have the option of deferring an investment decision, it may make sense to do so. After all, a project that has a negative NPV today might have a positive NPV at some point in the future. The price of the product may increase, production costs may decline or the cost of capital may go down, making the project attractive. We need not assume that an investment that is unattractive today will never be attractive.

Options to Make Follow-On Investments

Another very important type of real option is an *option to make follow-on investments*. Some projects open the door to future business opportunities that would not otherwise be available. For example, at the end of 2008, Électricité de France (EDF) acquired a controlling interest in the UK's sole nuclear energy utility, British Energy plc, for £12.5 billion. At first glance, this did not look like a very good move since an NPV analysis of the purchase carried out by outside analysts indicated that the acquisition would be, at best, only marginally positive. However, the move created options for a wide range of follow-on investments. The NPV analysis did not take account of the fact that the UK electricity market, which traditionally relied largely on fossil fuels, was changing and renewable and nuclear power generation were both seen as the way forward. By acquiring British Energy and agreeing to build two new power stations in the UK, based on its tried and tested designs, EDF would be able to rapidly add to its generating capacity if market demand and the economics of nuclear power made further investments attractive. In fact, the acquisition provided EDF with several different options to make follow-on investments, not just to make additional investments in nuclear capacity. Without these, EDF would probably not have been willing to acquire British Energy – or pay the amount it did. In other words, acquiring British Energy provided EDF with options to enter other areas of the UK's energy market.

Another example of an option to make follow-on investments concerns an investment in a new technology that can be extended to other products. For instance, in the early 1990s, Airbus invested in a computer-aided aircraft design system as part of the development of the A380 series aircraft. This system allowed the company to complete much more of the design work for a new aircraft on a computer before building a prototype, thereby lowering the cost of designing and building a new aircraft. While the cost of the new system and the associated facilities was high, the investment provided benefits that extended well beyond the project. For example, the technologies could be used in the design of other new aircraft, both civilian and military. By reducing the cost of developing new aircraft, the design system had the potential to make projects economically attractive that would not have been attractive otherwise.

Options to make follow-on investments are inherently difficult to value because, at the time we are evaluating the original project, it may not be obvious what the follow-on projects will be. Even if we know what the projects will be, we are unlikely to have enough information to estimate what they are worth. Of course, this makes it impossible to estimate directly the value of any option associated with them. Nevertheless, it is important for managers to consider options to make follow-on investments when evaluating projects. Doing so is a central part of the process of evaluating projects in the context of the overall strategy of the firm. Projects that lead to investment opportunities that are consistent with a company's overall strategy are more valuable than otherwise similar projects that do not.

> **WEB**
>
> Real options are considered by NASA when space systems and other investments are evaluated. See the following page on the NASA website for references to additional readings in this area: http://ceh.nasa.gov/webhelpfiles/Real_Option_Valuation.htm.

Options to Change Operations

In addition to options to defer investment and options to make follow-on investments, which are real options related to the investment decisions themselves, there are also real options that are related to the flexibility managers have once an investment decision has been made. These options, which include the options to change operations and to abandon a project, affect the NPV of a project and must be taken into account at the time the investment decision is made.

In an NPV analysis, we discount the expected cash flows from a project. We often consider several alternative scenarios and use our estimates of the probabilities associated with those scenarios to compute the expected cash flows. While this sort of analysis does consider alternative scenarios, it does not fully account for the fact that once a project has begun, the managers at a company have *options to change operations* as business conditions change. This means that there is a value associated with being able to change operations that is not fully reflected in a scenario analysis.

The changes that managers might make can involve something as simple as reducing output if prices decline or increasing output if prices increase. Businesses do this all the time in response to changing demand for their goods and services. At the extreme, managers might temporarily suspend operations entirely if business conditions are weak. This is quite common in the auto industry, where we often hear of plants being temporarily shut down during periods of slow auto sales. Other changes in operations can involve fundamentally altering the way in which a product is produced, as when a new production technology becomes available, making the old technology uncompetitive.

Having the flexibility to react to changing business conditions can be very valuable. Since we do not know how conditions are likely to change, however, it can be difficult to estimate just how valuable this flexibility will be. Nevertheless, we can see that managers do recognise the importance of flexibility by observing how they structure projects. For example, most modern office buildings do not have permanent internal walls. Not having permanent walls provides flexibility in configuring the offices and workspaces in the building. If more people must be put into a building than originally anticipated, the workspaces can be compressed to fit them. If the company finds that it does not need all of the space, having a flexible interior makes it easier to change things so that the excess space can be leased. Similarly, when

a company plans to build a new manufacturing facility, it often acquires more land than is immediately needed and designs the facility to accommodate the addition of unexpected increases in production capacity.

Building flexibility into a project costs money, but this can be money well spent if things change unexpectedly. The flexibility to expand, scale back or temporarily shut down a project, or to change the methods or technology employed in a project, are all options that managers should consider when evaluating projects. Projects with more flexibility in these dimensions are inherently more valuable.

Options to Abandon Projects

A project can also be terminated if things do not go as well as anticipated.[16] In other words, management often has an *option to abandon a project*. The ability to choose to terminate a project is a bit like a put option. By shutting down the project, management is saving money that would otherwise be lost if the project kept going. The amount saved represents the gain from exercising this option.

As with flexibility, we can see that managers recognise the importance of having an option to abandon a project by observing the way they design projects. Consider, for example, that most industrial buildings are built like big boxes that can easily be reconfigured as manufacturing spaces, warehouses or even retail outlets, depending on which use is most valuable. Suppose a company is building a facility to use as a warehouse. If the building is only able to accommodate a warehouse, it might end up sitting empty for long periods of time – for example, if the area has excess warehouse space at some point in the future. Designing the building so that it can be reconfigured relatively inexpensively for some other use increases the likelihood that the building will remain fully utilised in the future.

Concluding Comments on NPV Analysis and Real Options

We have stated that NPV analysis does not deal well with real options. This is true because the riskiness of a project that has real options associated with it varies with time and the appropriate discount rate varies with the risk. For example, deciding to expand operations may be very risky, but until the decision is actually made, the *option* to expand is relatively risk free. In order to use NPV analysis to value such an option, we would not only have to estimate all the cash flows associated with the expansion, but would also have to estimate the probability that we would actually undertake the expansion and determine the appropriate rate at which to discount the incremental cash flows from the expansion back to the present. The discount rate might even change with the value of the underlying asset.

In some cases, we can incorporate the value of a real option into an investment analysis by valuing the option separately and then adding this value to the NPV estimate. In these cases, we value the real option using valuation methods similar to those used to value financial options.

Decision-Making Example 20.2

The Value of Real Options

Situation: You work for a company that manufactures cardboard packaging for consumer product companies under long-term contracts. For example, your company manufactures the boxes for several popular cereal and pharmaceutical products. You have just won a large five-year contract to produce packaging materials for a company that sells furniture on the Internet. Since this contract will require you to produce much larger boxes than you currently can produce, you must purchase some new equipment. You have narrowed your choices to two alternatives. The first is a capital-intensive process that will cost more up-front but will be less expensive to operate. This process requires very specialised equipment that can be used only for the type of packaging that your furniture client needs. The second alternative is a labour-intensive process that will require a smaller up-front investment but will have higher unit costs. This process involves equipment that can be used to produce a wide range of other packages. If the expected life of both alternatives is 10 years and you estimate the NPV to be the same for both, which should you choose?

Decision: You should choose the labour-intensive alternative. Your contract is only for five years and there is a chance that it will not be renewed before the equipment's useful life is over. If the contract is not renewed, it will be easier to convert the labour-intensive equipment to another use. In other words, the labour-intensive alternative gives you the added value of having the option to abandon producing packaging for furniture.

Before You Go On

1. What is a real option?
2. What are four different types of real options commonly found in business?
3. Is it always possible to estimate the value of a real option? Why or why not?

AGENCY COSTS

Learning Objective 8

Describe how the agency costs of debt and equity are related to options.

Agency conflicts arise between shareholders and debtholders and between shareholders and managers because the interests of shareholders, lenders (creditors) and managers are not perfectly aligned. In fact, their interests can greatly diverge. One reason is that the claims they have against the cash flows produced by the firm have payoff functions that look like different types of options. We now discuss how these payoff functions lead to agency conflicts and their related costs.

Agency Costs of Debt

In Chapter 16, we discussed agency costs that arise in a company that uses debt financing. We noted that these costs occur because the incentives of people who lend to a company differ from those of the shareholders. If you were to carefully reread those discussions now, you might notice that the problems we discussed arise because the payoff functions for shareholders and lenders (creditors) differ like those for the different options we have been discussing.

To understand why this is the case, consider a company that has a single loan outstanding. This loan will mature next year and all of the interest and principal will be due at that time. Now, consider what happens when the debt matures. On the one hand, if the value of the company is less than the amount owed on the debt, the shareholders will simply default and the lenders will take control of the assets of the company. The shareholder claims will be worth zero in this case. If, on the other hand, the value of the company is greater than the amount owed on the loan, the shareholders will pay off the loan and retain control of the assets. In this case, the shareholder claims will be worth the difference between the value of the firm and the amount owed to the lenders.

In other words, the payoff function for the shareholders looks exactly like that for the owner of a call option, where the strike price is the amount owed on the loan and the underlying asset is the firm itself. If the value of the firm exceeds the strike price, the shareholders will choose to exercise their option; and if it does not exceed the strike price, they will let their option expire unexercised. Part A of Exhibit 20.7 illustrates the payoff function for the shareholders in this simple example.

The payoff function for the lenders in our example is illustrated in part B of Exhibit 20.7.

If the value of the firm is less than the amount owed, the lenders receive only the assets of the firm; and if the value of the firm is greater than the amount owed, the lenders receive only the amount owed. One way to think about the payoff function for the lenders is that when they lend money to the firm, they are essentially selling a put option to the shareholders.[17] This option gives the shareholders the right to 'put' the assets to the lenders with a strike price that equals the amount they owe. When the value of the firm is less than the strike price, the shareholders will exercise their option by defaulting. Of course, the shareholders are able to default and walk away only because our bankruptcy laws limit their liability to the amount that they have invested in the company.

The Dividend Payout Problem

Knowing that debt and equity claims are like options in which the underlying asset is the firm, we can use the intuition gained from the discussion of the determinants of option value to better understand the agency costs of debt. The incentives that shareholders of a leveraged firm have to pay themselves dividends arise because of their option to default. If a company faces some realistic risk of going bankrupt, the shareholders might decide that they are better off taking money out of the firm by paying themselves dividends. This situation can arise because the shareholders know that the bankruptcy laws limit their possible losses. If the firm goes bankrupt and the lenders end up receiving, for example, 50% rather than 80% of what they are owed, it will make no difference to the shareholders, who will get nothing from the liquidation of the company's assets in either case.

The Asset Substitution Problem

In Chapter 16, we saw that when bankruptcy is possible, shareholders have an incentive to invest in very risky projects, some of which might even have negative NPVs. Shareholders have this incentive because they receive all of the benefits if things turn out well but do not bear all of the costs if things turn out poorly. Since equity claims are like call options on the assets of the firm, this *asset*

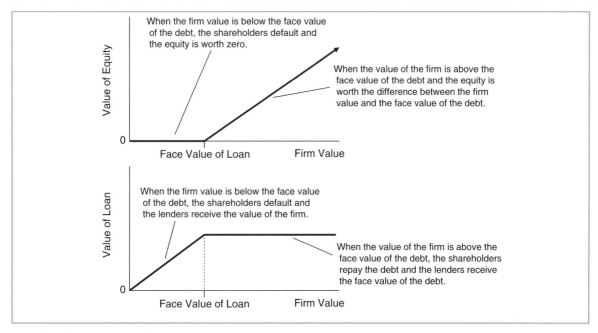

When the firm value is below the face value of the debt, the shareholders default and the equity is worth zero.

When the value of the firm is above the face value of the debt and the equity is worth the difference between the firm value and the face value of the debt.

Value of Equity

0

Face Value of Loan   Firm Value

When the firm value is below the face value of the debt, the shareholders default and the lenders receive the value of the firm.

When the value of the firm is above the face value of the debt, the shareholders repay the debt and the lenders receive the face value of the debt.

Value of Loan

0

Face Value of Loan   Firm Value

Exhibit 20.7: Payoff Functions for Shareholders and Lenders   The equity in a leveraged company is like a call option on the underlying assets of the firm. The shareholders exercise their option by paying off the debt if the firm is worth more than the face value of the debt when the debt matures. If the value of the firm is lower than the face value of the debt, the shareholders can default (let their option expire) without incurring losses beyond their investment in the firm.

The lenders' payoff function is like that for the seller of a put option. They have effectively agreed to purchase the firm for an amount that equals the face value of the firm's debt, at the discretion of the shareholders.

substitution problem should not be surprising. We pointed out earlier in this chapter that the more volatile the value of the underlying asset, the more valuable a call option on that asset will be. Shareholders of leveraged firms know this and therefore have an incentive to invest in risky projects that increase the overall volatility of the value of their companies' assets.

Lenders, in contrast, do not want the firm to invest in high-risk projects. As you can see from their payoff function in Exhibit 20.7, the lenders bear costs as the value of the firm drops below the amount they are owed but do not benefit at all as the value of the firm's assets increases above the amount that they are owed. Lenders to companies that are worth more than they are owed can only expect to lose when a project increases the overall riskiness of a company's assets.

The Underinvestment Problem

Chapter 16 also explained that shareholders have incentives to turn down positive NPV projects when all of the benefits are likely to go to the lenders. You can see how this *underinvestment problem* arises from the differences in the payoff functions in Exhibit 20.7. Suppose that the company will owe €10 million when the loan matures, that the company is currently worth €5 million and that the loan matures next week. This company is financially distressed because its assets are not even worth as much as its outstanding debt – so it is unlikely to have enough money to finance new investments. Now suppose that management identifies a positive NPV project that would require a €3 million investment and that has a positive NPV of €1 million which will be realised before the debt payment must be made. Management would have a hard time convincing the shareholders to invest an additional €3 million in the firm, because even if the investment turns out to be worth €4 million, all of the money will go to the lenders. The shareholders have a strong incentive to turn down this positive NPV project.

Agency Costs of Equity

So far, we have assumed that managers act in the best interests of the shareholders. Since managers are hired to manage the firm on behalf of the shareholders, this might appear to be a reasonable assumption. However, as you already know, managers do not always act in the shareholders' best interests. This is because the payoff function for a manager can be quite different from that for shareholders. In fact, a manager's payoff function can look a lot like a lender's payoff function.

To see how this is possible, consider the connection between managers' personal wealth and the performance of the companies for which they work. The present value of managers' future earnings is a large part of their overall wealth. If a company gets into financial difficulty and a manager is viewed as responsible, that manager could lose his or her job and find it difficult to obtain a similar job at another company. Of course, the most obvious way for a company to get into financial difficulty is to default on its debt. Therefore, as long as a company is able to avoid defaulting on its debt, a manager has a reasonable chance of retaining his or her job. Once the firm defaults, the chances of job loss increase dramatically. In addition, researchers have found that senior managers of financially distressed large public companies who lose their jobs find it difficult to obtain similar jobs afterwards.[18] We might also expect that the worse the company's financial distress, the worse the manager's future employment prospects and the lower the present value of the compensation that he or she can expect to receive in the future. If this is so, when the value of a firm is less than the amount it owes, the payoff function for a manager will look something like that for the lender in part B of Exhibit 20.7 – it will slope downwards as the value of the firm decreases.

On the positive side, we would expect the present value of a manager's future earnings to increase with the value of the firm when this value is above the amount that the company owes to its lenders. Managers will receive larger bonuses and larger pay raises and any shares or options that they receive will be more valuable. However, these increases will not be nearly as large as those for shareholders. The shareholders are not likely to give the managers a large proportion of any increase in firm value. The net result is that the payoff function for managers can look something like the one in Exhibit 20.8.

The fact that the payoff function for a manager resembles that for a lender means that managers, like lenders, have incentives to invest in less risky assets and to distribute less value through dividends and share repurchases than the shareholders would like them to. These tendencies are reinforced by the fact that managers are individuals who do not hold diversified portfolios, since most of their wealth is tied to the performance of their firms. Managers tend to make conservative investment, financing and dividend decisions because the personal cost to them of failure can be very great.

Boards of directors understand how the incentives of managers differ from those of shareholders. Consequently, boards put a great deal of effort into designing compensation plans that make the payoff functions for managers look as much as possible like those of shareholders. Ultimately, this is a key to minimising agency conflicts between shareholders and the managers that represent them.

Before You Go On

1. What do the payoff functions for shareholders and lenders look like?
2. What does the payoff function for a typical manager look like?

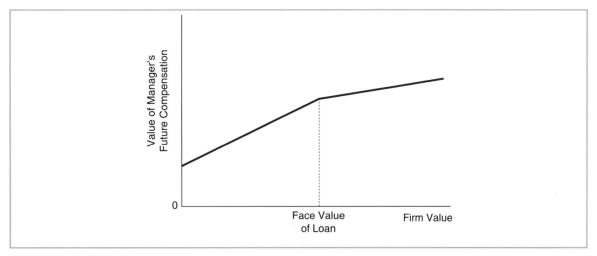

Exhibit 20.8: Representative Payoff Function for a Manager The payoff function for a manager with a typical compensation arrangement is more similar in shape to the payoff function for a lender than for a shareholder. While a shareholder's payoff function is flat to the left of the face value of the loan, the value of the manager's compensation is downward sloping, much like the payoff of a lender. When the value of the firm is greater than the face value of the loan, the value of the manager's compensation does not increase as much as the value of the firm's shares (the line of the payoff function is not as steep). Because managers' payoff functions differ from those for shareholders, managers have incentives to take actions that are not in the best interests of shareholders.

SUMMARY OF LEARNING OBJECTIVES

1. **Explain the factors that make it desirable for firms to manage their risks.**

    Companies have a number of risks from inputs, production and outputs that increase the variability of their cash flows. Factors that will influence the decision to manage these risks include: financial reporting, corporate taxation, bankruptcy costs, the cost of capital, agency costs and employee compensation and retention. Firms start by first identifying the risks they face, evaluating them and managing these in appropriate ways and keeping their risks under review. A key motivation for firms to manage certain risks is that they can add value by so doing and are able to manage some risks that shareholders cannot, such as tax losses.

2. **Describe the risks faced by firms and how they are managed.**

    Risks from a firm's operations and unanticipated changes to market prices or rates lead to undesirable cash flow volatility. Companies can use insurance against production risks. Firms can hedge their risks by taking positions that offset each other if prices change. For market risks, they can adjust their exposures to risks associated with commodity prices, interest rates, foreign exchange rates and equity prices by using financial risk management. Derivatives, such as forward contracts, futures, swaps and options, are frequently used since they are flexible and are low cost. The cost of risk management depends on future uncertainty and this has to be weighed against the benefits of risk reduction.

3. **Define forward and futures contracts and be able to determine their prices.**

    A forward contract is an agreement to buy and sell an asset at a predetermined price at a future date. The key elements for the delayed sale determined in advance are (1) the forward date, (2) the asset and (3) the agreed price. A futures contract is a standardised forward contract that is traded on an organised exchange and is very similar to a forward contract. The pricing of forwards and futures is known as the cost of carry and is based on time value of money principles such that the forward price, when the transaction is agreed, is determined so that neither side is worse off as a result. The risk-free interest rate to the forward date and any costs associated with storing the asset will raise the future price. Income earned by the asset and the demand for physical ownership – known as the convenience yield – will reduce the forward price. The balance between these factors will determine whether the forward price is higher or lower than the current price. Over time, the relationship between the contracted forward price and the current price will change and one party will own an asset and the other will have a liability. This means that forward contracts have credit risk. Futures contracts were developed to address this problem, as well as providing liquidity since futures contracts are made with a centralised clearing house that facilitates buying and selling on the exchange. Futures users are required to post margin that protects the clearing house against default.

4. **Define interest rate and cross-currency swaps and know how they are valued.**

   An interest rate swap is an agreement to exchange a set of fixed future cash flows against a set of cash flows based on an index of interest rates using a notional principal amount that determines the amounts to be paid. A cross-currency swap involves exchanging cash flows in one currency against corresponding payments in another currency. As such, a cross-currency swap can be considered a package of borrowing and lending where a term loan in one currency is financed by lending in another currency. When initially transacted, swap terms are designed so that the present value of the cash flows from both sides is equal. Changes in market conditions mean that, over time, the present values of each side of the swap will diverge and the swap will become either a liability or an asset. A swap will have credit risk if the present value of the cash flows to be received is greater than the present value of the cash flows to be paid out. Companies use swaps for asset-liability risk management purposes and, in the case of cross-currency swaps, to fund or borrow in different currencies without incurring exchange rate risk.

5. **Define a call option and a put option, and describe the payoff function for each of these options.**

   An option is the right, but not the obligation, to buy or sell an asset for a given price on or before a specific date. The price is called the strike or exercise price and the date is called the exercise date or expiration date of the option. The right to buy the asset is known as a call option. The payoff from a call option equals zero if the value of the underlying asset is less than the strike price at expiration. If the value of the underlying asset is higher than the strike price at expiration, then the payoff from a call option is equal to the value of the asset value minus the strike price. The right to sell the asset is called a put option. The payoff from a put option is zero if the value of the underlying asset is greater than the strike price at expiration. If the value is lower than the strike price, then the payoff from a put option equals the strike price minus the value of the underlying asset.

6. **List and describe the factors that affect the value of an option.**

   The value of an option is affected by five factors: (1) the current price of the underlying asset, (2) the strike price of the option, (3) the volatility of the value of the underlying asset, (4) the time left until the expiration of the option and (5) the risk-free rate.

7. **Name some of the real options that occur in business and explain why traditional NPV analysis does not accurately incorporate their values.**

   Real options that are associated with investments include options to defer investment, make follow-on investments, change operations and abandon projects. Traditional NPV analysis is designed to make a decision to accept or reject a project at a particular point in time. It is not designed to include the potential value associated with deferring the investment decision. Incorporating the value of the other options into an NPV framework is technically possible but would be very difficult to do because the rate used to discount the cash flows would change over time with their riskiness. In addition, the information necessary to value real options using the NPV approach is not always available.

8. **Describe how the agency costs of debt and equity are related to options.**

   The chapter discusses two principal classes of agency conflicts. The first is between shareholders and lenders. When there is a risk of bankruptcy, shareholders may have incentives to increase the volatility of the firm's assets, turn down positive NPV projects or pay out assets in the form of dividends. Shareholders have these incentives because their payoff functions look like those for the owner of a call option.

   The other principal class of agency conflicts is between managers and owners. Managers tend to prefer less risk than shareholders do and prefer to distribute fewer assets in the form of dividends because their payoff functions are more like those of lenders than those of shareholders are. These preferences are magnified by the fact that managers are risk-averse individuals whose portfolios are not well diversified.

SUMMARY OF KEY EQUATIONS

Equation	Description	Formula
(20.1)	Cost of carry	$PV \times \dfrac{(1+i+u)^m}{(1+q+y)^m} = FV_m$
(20.2)	Interest rate swap value	Value of interest rate swap = Value of bond with swap coupon rate – value of loan with floating rate
(20.3)	Put–call parity	$P = C + Xe^{-rT} - V$

SELF-STUDY PROBLEMS

20.1. What will determine whether a firm should – or should not – manage particular risks in its business?

20.2. You own property which has a value of €5 million and will pay rental income of €450 000 at the end of the first year and €500 000 at the end of the second year. You have been approached by a property company and they would like you to sell the property to them at the end of the second year but at a price agreed today. The interest rate is 4.3% per year. What would be a fair price for the property, if agreed now?

20.3. Your company is considering opening a new factory in the Middle East to serve the growing demand for your product there. Your home currency is the euro but you need US dollars for the investment that will cost US$25 million and will last for five years. You decide that a cross-currency swap is the best way of financing the investment. The exchange rate between the US dollar and the euro is $1.3475 = €1 and the five-year swap rates for the euro and the US dollar are 3.5% and 4.2% per year, respectively, paid annually. Lay out the cash flows for the swap.

20.4. Deutsche Euroshop AG shares are currently selling for €12. Over the next year, the company is undertaking a new supermarket project. If the project is successful, the com-

pany's shares are expected to rise to €24. If the project fails, the shares are expected to fall to €8. The risk-free interest rate is 6%. Calculate the value today of a one-year call option on one Deutsche Euroshop share with a strike price of €20.

20.5. Fiera Milano S.p.A. is an Italian company that organises trade fairs and is listed on the Milan Stock Exchange. The company's shares are currently trading at €50. Depending on the outlook for the economy and the demand for trade conferences, the company's share price is expected to be either €65 or €30 in six months. The risk-free interest rate is 8% per year. What is the value of a put option on one Fiera Milano share that has a €40 strike price?

SOLUTIONS TO SELF-STUDY PROBLEMS

20.1. The decision will be based on assessing the costs versus the benefits. Firms will manage those risks for which the benefits can only be captured by the firm but not its owners. These include, but are not limited to, corporate taxation, bankruptcy costs, the cost of capital from outside providers, employee compensation and retention and financial reporting.

20.2. We want to apply the cost of carry model to determine the forward price, knowing that we have discrete value distributions at the end of years 1 and 2. We start by present-valuing these at the risk-free interest rate and subtracting them from the value of the property before then future-valuing the property at the risk-free interest rate for two years:

$$PV_{\text{Year 1 income}} = \frac{€450\,000}{1.043} = €431\,448$$

$$PV_{\text{Year 1 income}} = \frac{€500\,000}{(1.043)^2} = €459\,623$$

$$\text{Forward price} = (€5\,000\,000 - €431\,448$$
$$- €459\,623) \times (1.043)^2$$
$$= €4\,469\,895$$

The two-year forward price will be €4 469 895.

20.3. The first step is to determine the amount of euros that are required in exchange for receiving US25 million at the start of the swap. With an exchange rate of $1.3475/€ this requires $25 000 000/$1.3475 = €18 552 876 to be paid at the start. The interest on the euro side will therefore be

€18 552 876 × 0.035 = €649 351 per year. For the US dollar side, it is $25 000 000 × 0.042 = $1 050 000 per year. From the perspective of the company, the cross-currency swap cash flows will look as follows:

Cash Flows for the Cross-Currency Swap

Time (years)	Euros	US dollars
0	−18 552 876	25 000 000
1	649 351	−1 050 000
2	649 351	−1 050 000
3	649 351	−1 050 000
4	649 351	−1 050 000
5a	649 351	−1 050 000
5b	18 552 876	−25 000 000

20.4. First determine the payoffs for the shares, a risk-free loan and the call option under the two possible outcomes. In one year, the share price is expected to be either €8 or €24. The loan will be worth €1.06 regardless of whether the project is successful. If the project fails, the share price will be less than the strike price of the call option. The option will not be exercised and will be worth €0. If the project is successful, the share price will be higher than the strike price of the call option. The option will be exercised and its value will be the difference between the share price and the strike price, €4.

The shares and loan can be used to create a replicating portfolio which has the same payoff as the call option:

$$(€8 \times x) - (1.06 \times y) = €0$$
$$(\$24 \times x) - (1.06 \times y) = €4$$

Solving the two equations yields: $x = 0.25$, $y = -€1.887$

The value of the call option is the same as the current value of this portfolio:

$$(€12 \times 0.25) - (€1 \times -€1.887) = 1.11$$

20.5. Here we solve directly for the value of the put option. First we determine the payoffs for the shares, a risk-free bond and the put option under the two possible outcomes. To determine the payoff of the bond in six months' time, we must calculate the six-month risk-free interest rate given the one-year risk-free rate listed in the problem statement:

Six-month risk-free rate
$$= (1 + 0.08)^{1/2} - 1 = 1.039, \text{ or } 3.9\%$$

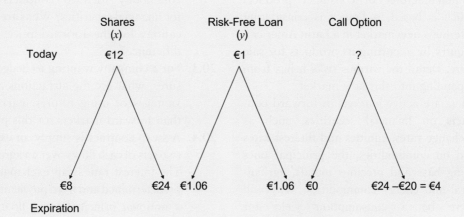

Today

	Shares (x)		Risk-Free Loan (y)		Call Option
	€12		€1		?

Expiration: €8   €24 €1.06   €1.06 €0   €24 −€20 = €4

The payoffs are therefore:

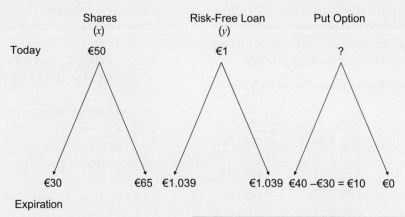

Shares (x)	Risk-Free Loan (y)	Put Option
Today €50	€1	?

€30   €65   €1.039   €1.039 €40 −€30 = €10   €0

Expiration

Now we can use the shares and the bond to create a replicating portfolio, which will give the same payoff as the put option:

$$(€30 \times x) - (1.039 \times y) = €10$$
$$(€65 \times x) - (1.039 \times y) = €0$$

Solving the two equations, we determine $x = -0.286$, $y = €17.87$

The value if the put option is the same as the current value of this portfolio:

$$(€50 \times -0.286) - (€1 \times €17.87)$$
$$= €3.58$$

Alternatively, you could solve this problem by calculating the value of a call option with the same strike price of €40 and then using the put–call parity relation. The value of the call option is €15.09 (you may like to check this by calculating it yourself) and the value of the associated put option calculated using the put–call parity relation is €3.52. The difference (€3.58 vs. €3.52) is due to rounding and the compounding assumption for the discount rate.

CRITICAL THINKING QUESTIONS

20.1. A manufacturer of consumer products which is based in France is considering entering a new market in a Latin American country by exporting its products for sale there. Detail the various risks it has from expanding into this new market.

20.2. There are active markets in forward contracts on financial securities, such as exchange rates, equities and interest rates and on commodities, the principal ones being base and precious metals, agricultural and energy commodities. Why will there be a consumption yield for commodity forward contracts and not for financial securities? What are the implications for the forward price from this difference?

20.3. For a company wanting to hedge its exposures, what are the attractions and disadvantages of using futures markets rather than forward markets for this purpose?

20.4. A swap contract is simply an exchange of two sets of cash flows over an agreed period. The interest rate swap exchanges a set of predetermined and fixed payments based on a notional principal for a floating set of payments based on an interest rate index. What other possible types of swaps can be created given the way such swaps work?

20.5. Which is likely to have more credit risk, an interest rate swap or a cross-currency swap – and why?

20.6. A writer of a call option may or may not actually own the underlying asset. If he or she owns the asset, and therefore will have the asset available to deliver should the option be exercised, he or she is said to be writing a *covered call*. Otherwise, he or she is writing a *naked call* and will have to buy the underlying asset on the open market should the option be exercised. Draw the payoff diagram of a covered call (including the value of the owned underlying asset) and compare it with the payoff of other options.

20.7. What kinds of real options should be considered in the following situations?

a. Fiat S.p.A. is considering two sites for a new car factory. One is just large enough for the planned facility, while the other is three times larger.

b. Hellenistic Cruises is purchasing three new cruise ships to be built sequentially. The first ship will commence construction today and will take one year to build. The second will then be started. Hellenistic Cruises can cancel the order for a given cruise ship at any time before construction begins for a small fee.

20.8. Zukunft Betrieb AG is considering a factory that will include an option to expand operations in three years. If things go well, the anticipated expansion will have a value of €10 million and will cost €2 million to undertake. Otherwise, the anticipated expansion will have a value of only €1 million and will not take place. What information would we need in order to analyse this capital budgeting problem using the traditional NPV approach that we would not need using option valuation techniques?

20.9. Companies frequently include employee share options as part of the compensation for their managers and sometimes for all their employees. These options allow the holder to buy the shares of the company for a preset price like any other option, but they usually have very long maturities, of up to 10 years not being uncommon. The goal of share option plans is to align the incentives of employees and shareholders. What are the implications of these plans for current shareholders?

20.10. You are a bondholder of DRYAD SA. Using option-pricing theory, explain what agency concerns you would have if DRYAD SA were in danger of bankruptcy.

20.11. A bond covenant is part of a bond contract that restricts the behaviour of the firm, barring it from taking certain actions. Using the terminology of options, explain why a bond contract might include a covenant preventing the firm from making large dividend payments to its shareholders.

QUESTIONS AND PROBLEMS

Basic

20.1. **Managing corporate risks:** Why do companies usually seek to hedge out the risks from financial markets?

20.2. **Managing corporate risks:** Renault, the French carmaker, sells its vehicles within Europe and elsewhere. What effect has the introduction of the euro in France, Germany, Spain, Italy and other member countries had on Renault's sales in these countries?

20.3. Forward contracts: What are the three elements that have to be defined in a forward contract?

20.4. Forward contracts: What are the payoff profiles for (a) a long forward and (b) a short forward at maturity?

20.5. Forward contract valuation: What factors raise the price of a forward contract and what factors reduce the value of a forward contract?

20.6. Swaps: There are four possible types of cross-currency swaps based on the nature of the cash flows to the two parties. What are the four possible types?

20.7. Option characteristics: Explain how the payoff functions differ for the owner (buyer) and the seller of a call option. Of a put option.

20.8. Option valuation: What is the value of an option if the share price is zero? What if the share price is extremely high (relative to the strike price)?

20.9. Option valuation: Like owners of shares, owners of options can lose no more than the amount they invested. They are far more likely to lose that full amount but they cannot lose more. Do sellers of options have the same limitation on their losses?

20.10. Option valuation: What is the value at expiration of a call option with a strike price of €65 if the share price is €1? €50? €65? €100? €1000?

20.11. Option valuation: Suppose you have an option to buy NASDAL shares for €100. The option expires tomorrow and the current price of NASDAL shares is €95. How much is your option worth?

20.12. Option valuation: You hold an American option to sell one share of Cimbalom. The option expires tomorrow. The strike price of the option is €50 and the current share price is €49. What is the value of exercising the option today? If you wanted to sell the option instead, about how much would you expect to receive?

20.13. Real options: What is the difference between a financial option and a real option?

20.14. Real options: List and describe four different types of real options that are associated with investment projects.

20.15. Agency costs: How are options related to the agency costs of debt and equity?

Intermediate

20.16. Managing corporate risks: Why do companies prefer to use financial hedging, if available, rather than operational hedging? When might operational hedging be a better choice?

20.17. Risk management methods: When might a company prefer to use insurance rather than hedging to protect itself against a particular risk?

20.18. Forward contract valuation: If the current asset price is €350 and the risk-free interest rate is 3% per year, the asset provides a continuous dividend yield of 5.2% per year, what will be the forward price for the asset in a forward contract if the agreed delivery date is 18 months?

20.19. Forward contracts: What will be the value of the forward contract in 20.18 if the contract now has six months to maturity, the spot asset price is now €355, the risk-free interest rate is 3.6% per year and the dividend yield is now 4.7% per year? If you had taken a long position in the contract in 20.18, is the forward contract now an asset or a liability?

20.20. Interest rate swap valuation: Valencia Fabricación SA has an interest rate swap where it pays a fixed rate of 4.6% per year. The notional amount of the swap is €30 million and the swap has currently exactly 3 years to maturity. The current 3-year swap rate is 3.9%. What is the value of the swap and, from Valencia Fabricación's perspective, is the swap an asset or a liability?

20.21. Option valuation: Shares of Motores Socrates SA are currently trading for €40 and will either rise to €50 or fall to €35 in one month. The risk-free interest rate for one month is 1.5%. What is the value of a one-month call option with a strike price of €40?

20.22. Option valuation: Again assume that the price of Motores Socrates SA shares will either rise to €50 or fall to €35 in one month and that the risk-free interest rate for one month is 1.5%. How much is an option with a strike price of €40 worth if the current share price is €45 instead of €40?

20.23. Option valuation: You are considering a three-month put on Budowlanych Krakow. The company's shares currently trade at Zloty 10.0 and in three months will either rise to Zl. 15.0 or fall to Zl. 7.0. The risk-free interest rate for three months is 2%. What is the appropriate price for a put with a strike price of Zl. 9.0?

20.24. Option valuation: You hold a European put option on Cannello S.p.A. with a strike price of €100. Things have not been going too well for Cannello. The current share price is €2 and you think that it will either rise to €3 or fall to €1.50 at the expiration of your option. The appropriate risk-free interest rate is 5%. What is the value of the option? If this were an American option, would it be worth more?

20.25. Other options: A *golden parachute* is part of a manager's compensation package that makes a large lump-sum payment in the event that the manager is fired (or loses his or her job in a merger, for example). This seems ill-advised to most people when first hearing about it. Explain how a golden parachute can help reduce agency costs between shareholders and managers.

Advanced

20.26. Consider the following two strategies for investing in a company's shares:
  a. buy the shares immediately and hold them for 6 months for €100 before selling these at the end of the six months;

  b. take a long position in a 6-month forward contract for €102 and immediately sell the shares at the maturity of the contract.

The six-month rate of interest is 2%. What will your payoff be in six months' time from both strategies if the share price is €110 and €95? What is the effect on the payoffs if after you have decided, the company subsequently announces and pays a dividend of €5 at the end of month five?

20.27. You want to enter into four sequential forward contracts with maturities of 6, 12, 18 and 24 months, respectively. The risk-free rate of interest for the four periods is 3.0, 3.5, 3.7 and 4.0% per year, respectively. If the spot price is €350 today, what will be the forward prices at which you can transact, if the asset has a dividend yield of 3.6% per year? What do the prices you calculate tell us about the way forward markets work?

20.28. Two years ago, Fabricação Azulejos de Lisboa SA (FALSA) entered into an interest rate swap for €25 million with a maturity of 7 years where the company makes a fixed payment of 4.5% per year against Euribor. Now the company wants to terminate the swap. The five-year swap rate is 4.0%. Will FALSA pay or receive to terminate the swap and how much is involved?

20.29. Dynamo Plastics plc entered into a five-year cross-currency swap for £10 million against the euro when the exchange rate was €1.25/£ and the sterling fixed interest rate was 4.5% per year and that for the euro was 3.7% per year. Dynamo Plastics agreed to pay pounds sterling and receive the euro. Exactly two years have passed and the company wants to terminate the swap. The euro is now trading at €1.10, the sterling 3-year fixed swap rate is 3.2% and the euro 3-year swap rate is 2.8% per year. What is the value change on the swap, will Dynamo Plastics gain or lose from termination, and what are the component value changes from the changes in market conditions?

20.30. Consider the following payoff diagram.

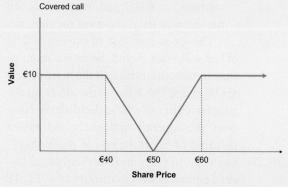

Find a combination of calls, puts, risk-free bonds and shares that has this payoff. (You need not use all of these instruments, and there are many possible solutions.)

20.31. Consider the payoff structures of the following two portfolios:

    a. Buying a call option on one share in one month at a strike price of €50 and saving the present value of €50 (so that at expiration it will have grown to €50 with interest).

    b. Buying a put option on one share in one month at a strike price of €50 and buying one share.

        What conclusion can you draw about the relation between call prices and put prices?

20.32. One way to extend the binomial pricing model is by including multiple time periods. Suppose Splittime, Inc. shares are currently trading at $100. In one month, the price will either increase by $10 (to $110) or decrease by $10 (to $90). The following month will be the same. The price will either increase by $10 or decrease by $10. Notice that in two months, the price could be $120, $100 or $80. The risk-free rate is 1% per month. Find the value today of an option to buy one share of Splittime in two months for a strike price of $105.

(*Hint:* To do this, first find the value of the option at each of the two possible one-month prices. Then use those values as the payoffs at one month and find the value today.)

20.33. Spin The Wheel Company has assets currently worth £10 million in the form of one-year risk-free bonds that will return 10%. The company has debt with a face value of £5.5 million due in one year. (No interest payments will be made.) The shareholders decided to sell £8 million of the risk-free bonds and to invest the money in a very risky venture. This venture consists of Mr William Kid's taking the money now and, in one year, flipping a coin. If it comes up heads, Mr Kid will pay Spin The Wheel £17.6 million. If it is tails, Spin The Wheel gets nothing. (Notice that this is a zero NPV investment.)

    a. What is the value of the debt and equity before the shareholders make this 'investment'?

    b. Using the binomial pricing model, with the payoff to the equity holders representing the option and the assets of the company representing the underlying asset, estimate the value of the equity after the shareholders make the investment.

    c. What is the new value of the debt after the investment?

20.34. The payoff function for the holder of straight debt looks like that for the seller of a put option. Convertible debt is straight debt plus a call option on a firm's shares. How does the addition of a call option to straight debt affect the concern that lenders have about the asset substitution problem, and why?

SAMPLE TEST PROBLEMS

20.1. Draw the payoff diagram representing the payoff for a combination of buying a call with a strike price of €40 and selling a call with a strike price of €50. What would the buyer of such an option hope would happen to the share price?

20.2. Of the five variables identified as affecting the value of an option, which will have the opposite effects on the value of a put and the value of a call? That is, for which variables will a given change increase the value of a call and decrease the value of a put (or vice versa)?

20.3. What kinds of real options are being described?

    a. Fred's Cheap Cars buys the empty field adjacent to its car lot.

    b. Midway through construction, Maxival AG stops construction of an office building that it had planned to use as a corporate headquarters.

    c. Lidl, the German discount retailer, opens its first new store in Morocco.

20.4. If you fail to account for the real options available in a given project, what error might you make in your capital budgeting decision?

20.5. Suppose you are a wheat farmer. Assuming that there is an active market in wheat futures contracts, what trades might you want to use to protect yourself against falling wheat prices? What would be the cost of using them?

ENDNOTES

1. Since 2000, the price has risen spectacularly such that by the spring of 2010, the price was over $1100/oz. Needless to say, gold producers have quickly moved to remove many of the forward contracts that locked them in at lower prices. Notably, Barrick Gold announced in the autumn of 2009 that it would spend $2.9 billion to repurchase forward and other derivative contracts.

2. For simplicity, we will assume there is no salvage or environmental costs at the end of the mining operations.

3. In 1992, BAe made provisions and write-downs of £1 billion, at that time the largest corporate write-down in UK history, to cover staff redundancies and losses in its regional aircraft division.

4. We discuss the foreign exchange market and currency management in the next chapter when looking at international financial management.

5. Economists refer to investment in production facilities as irreversible. The costs involved are largely upfront and will be hard to recover later if the company should change its mind. We will look at this problem from a capital budgeting perspective later in the chapter when we discuss real options.

6. Portfolio theory is discussed in Chapter 7.

7. In this case, there is depreciation in the value to be considered since, if Airbus leases the aircraft, it will no longer be 'new'. The buyer will be receiving a less valuable airplane and would not be willing to pay the full price for a new aircraft. This will reduce the forward price. In financial contracts where depreciation is not an issue, the income received by the seller prior to delivery acts as a negative interest rate and reduces the forward price.

8. We could also have present-valued these costs and then future-valued the total. It will give the same result [€50 + €0.60/(1.04) + €0.75/(1.04)^2] × (1.04)^2 = €55.454 million.

9. Revisit Chapter 8 to review the discussion on how interest rates affect the prices of bonds.

10. The way foreign exchange is quoted and how the currency market works is examined in detail in the next chapter.

11. It can be shown that using this money, Airbus can replace the cross-currency swap with a swap using the current market conditions and be no better or worse off as a result. The sum paid to terminate the swap is used to subsidise the future payments on the new 'at-market' swap such that Airbus has undisturbed cash flows that are exactly the same as those of the original swap.

12. Even if the value of the option ever fell below the line to the right of the exercise price in part A of Exhibit 20.1, it would not stay there. This is because investors would be able to make an instant profit by buying the option, exercising it to get the underlying asset and then selling the underlying asset. Such trading by investors would drive the price of the option back above the line.

13. We are focusing in this discussion on what the value of the underlying asset is likely to be immediately before the option expires because it does not generally make sense to exercise an option before then as long as there is a chance that the value of the underlying asset could increase further. An exception is when the value of the underlying asset is not expected to be higher as the expiration of the option nears because value is being distributed to the owners of the underlying asset (for example, through dividend payments). In a situation like this, it can be appropriate to exercise a call option immediately before such a payment. There are also situations where it is advantageous to exercise a put option early. Such situations can arise if it is very likely that the option will be exercised at expiration. When this happens, the value received from exercising the option today can exceed the present value of the amount that is expected to be received if the option is exercised immediately before expiration.

14. We can also compute the value of x and y by noting that the combined positions in the upper fork and the lower fork are equal if we hold the replicating portfolio and sell the call option (otherwise, the portfolio is not riskless). This means that (€70 × x) + (1.05 × y) − €15 = (€40 × x) + (1.05 × y) − 0. Simplifying, we have (€70 × x) − (€40 × x) = €15. Therefore, as before, x = 0.5. Knowing x, we can now solve for y, since (€40 × 0.5) = (1.05 × y) and therefore, y = €19.05 as before.

15. There are other ways to solve the binomial pricing problem than by actually finding an equivalent portfolio. They differ only in the calculations, however. The underlying concepts are identical. See any advanced investments textbook for details.

16. An exception exists where a contractual agreement prevents the project from being terminated without payment of a penalty that is equivalent to the remaining value of the project.

17. This payoff function is actually like that from the combination of selling a put option and buying a risk-free loan. Lenders receive the face value of the loan from the risk-free bond, but they might have to pay some or all of that value in losses on the put option. Since the risk-free loan payout is unaffected by changes in the value of the firm, it does not affect the discussion above.

18. S. C. Gilson, Management turnover and financial distress, *Journal of Financial Economics* 25 (1989) 241–262.

CHAPTER

21

International Financial Management

In this Chapter:

Introduction to International Finance Management
Foreign Exchange Markets
Country Risk
Cost of Capital for International Projects
International Capital Budgeting
Islamic Finance

LEARNING OBJECTIVES

1. Discuss how the basic principles of finance apply to international financial transactions.
2. Differentiate among the spot rate, the forward rate and the cross rate in the foreign exchange markets, perform foreign exchange and cross-rate calculations, and be able to hedge an asset purchase where payment is made in a foreign currency.
3. Describe the factors that affect country risk and country risk ratings.
4. Explain how the cost of capital is determined for international projects.
5. Identify the major factors that distinguish international from domestic capital budgeting, explain how the capital budgeting process can be adjusted to account for these factors and compute the NPV for a typical international capital project.
6. Discuss how Islamic finance arrangements are different and the implications for financial management in countries that use *Sharī'ah* law.

Mining companies are used to seeking mineral deposits in remote places. Few come as remote as Mongolia, a sparsely populated country where many of the people still live a semi-nomadic life. Ivanhoe Mines, a Canadian mining exploration and development company, discovered the huge copper and gold deposits at Oyu Tolgoi in the south Gobi desert, close to the Chinese border. The reserves are estimated to contain 36 million tonnes of copper and 45 million ounces of gold. After protracted negotiations with the Mongolian government that lasted five years, over the terms of the operating licence for the field, an agreement was signed in the autumn of 2009. To exploit the deposits, Ivanhoe Mines joined with the UK-domiciled multinational mining company Rio Tinto in order to be able to finance the huge investment and massive development that will cost over US$4 billion before the mine begins to produce copper and gold from 2013 onwards.[1] When it reaches full capacity, a process that is expected to

take a decade, the mine is expected to produce 450 000 tonnes of copper and 330 000 ounces of gold per year. It will be one of the largest such mines in the world and comparable in scale with Escondida, the Chilean copper mine in which Rio Tinto also has an interest, which is the world's largest and produces 1.2 million tonnes a year. Other mining operations owned by the company include Kennecott Utah Copper in the USA and interests in the producing copper mines of Grasberg in Indonesia, Northparkes in Australia and Palabora in South Africa. In 2009, the group produced approximately 800 000 tonnes of copper, which placed it among the top five copper producers in the world. Gold and molybdenum are also valuable by-products of the group's copper mining activities.

At the time of the signing of the investment agreement with the Mongolian government, Bret Clayton, head of Rio Tinto's copper division, said that 'Oyu Tolgoi is consistent with Rio Tinto's strategy of investing in large, long life, low cost ore bodies. While the size and grade of the existing Oyu Tolgoi ore reserves and mineral resources are already first class, we are excited by significant exploration upside that still remains. We believe that in time, the surrounding region has the potential to become a world-class mining district. We plan to be a partner with you here in Mongolia for decades to come. Of course, this will take significant investment, and the Investment Agreement represents a very important milestone that will now allow this important work to proceed.' He went on to explain that the partners anticipated that the vast majority of the output would go to China and, as such, would still be an important source of supply for the Chinese market.

As part of the investment, a 290-kilometre rail link would need to be built linking the mine to China. The deposit is about 80 kilometres from the border, while on the Chinese side there is an existing rail network around the coal-producing Chinese province of Inner Mongolia. Extending the rail link further into Mongolia will open up the possibility of exploiting coal reserves that lie to the North of the Oyu Tolgoi deposits.

CHAPTER PREVIEW

So far, we have largely focused on doing business domestically, yet a large proportion of larger companies today engage in international business transactions. This chapter provides an introduction to international financial management. The goal of financial management is the same abroad as it is at home – to maximise the value of the firm. Thus, the financial manager's job is to seek out international business opportunities in which the value of the assets acquired exceeds their cost. If this is done, the firm's international activities will increase the value of the firm.

We start the chapter by providing some background information about the globalisation of the world economy, the rise of multinational corporations and the key factors that distinguish domestic from international business transactions. We emphasise that the basic principles of finance remain valid for international business transactions, even though some of the variables used in financial models change. We also introduce two risks that are not present in domestic business transactions: foreign exchange risk and country risk.

Next, we discuss the markets for foreign exchange and explain how firms protect themselves from fluctuations in exchange rates. We then discuss the problem of country risk in international investments and how companies assess the risks. We first consider how to calculate the cost of capital for foreign investments, a necessary input to correctly using the NPV method. We then revisit capital investment appraisal in an international context and how to compute the NPV for projects where the cash flows are in a foreign currency.

Finally, we end the discussion with an overview of Islamic finance and the way it integrates culture, ethics and religion into business practice and its implications for international financial management.

INTRODUCTION TO INTERNATIONAL FINANCIAL MANAGEMENT

Learning Objective 1

Discuss how the basic principles of finance apply to international financial transactions.

Businesses operate in a far different world today than they did only a generation or two ago. Because of the globalisation of the world economy, management – including financial management – has changed in many respects. Yet, as you will see, the goals and principles of financial management remain essentially the same.

Globalisation of the World Economy

Over the past 30 years, we have witnessed the **globalisation** of business and financial markets. Globalisation refers to the removal of barriers to free trade and the integration of national economies. Today, on average, large companies, whether they are based in Europe, the United States or another country, generate around half of their sales revenue overseas. As you read the business section of any major newspaper, you will see numerous reminders that we live in a globalised world economy.

> ### Globalisation
>
> the removal of barriers to free trade and the integration of national economies

For example, as *consumers*, Europeans routinely purchase clothing and shoes made in China, oil from Saudi Arabia, natural gas from Russia, pasta and high-fashion shoes from Italy, wines from France, coffee from Brazil, TV sets from Korea and textiles from India. Foreigners, in turn, purchase European-made power systems, aircraft, automobiles, medical technology, software, machine tools and numerous other products.

> ### WEB
>
> Look up current issues in international finance management in the International section of *News* at: http://money.cnn.com/news/international/index.html.

The *production* of goods and services has also become highly globalised. As large multinational companies have emerged, the leading economies of the world have become increasingly interdependent. Most multinational companies have integrated sales and production operations in a dozen or more countries. These firms seek to purchase components and locate production where costs are lower to generate higher margins. For example, Volkswagen has 60 different production facilities in 21 countries worldwide including Brazil and China and it sells its vehicles in 153 countries.

Like product markets, the *financial system* has also become highly integrated. Much of the impetus has come from the governments of the major

Asian and Western nations as they began deregulating their foreign exchange markets, money and capital markets and banking systems. For example, in 1985, the Tokyo Stock Exchange began allowing foreign firms to become members. In 1986, the London Stock Exchange also began admitting foreign firms as full members. Similar changes have been taking place in Europe and the United States.

The Rise of Multinational Corporations

A major factor driving globalisation of the world economy is direct investment by multinational corporations. According to a study by the United Nations, there are about 60 000 multinational companies worldwide with over 500 000 foreign affiliates. A **multinational corporation** is a business firm that operates in more than one country. These corporations engage in traditional lines of business such as manufacturing, mining, gas and oil and agriculture, as well as consulting, accounting, law, telecommunications and hospitality. They may purchase raw materials from one country, obtain financing from a capital market in another country, produce finished goods with labour and capital equipment from a third country, and sell finished goods in a number of other countries. Many have easily identifiable brands, such as Volkswagen and L'Oreal, others – such as Rio Tinto, the multinational corporation that features in the opening vignette – are relatively unknown.

> ### Multinational corporation
>
> a business firm that operates in more than one country

> ### Transnational corporation
>
> a multinational firm that has widely dispersed ownership and that is managed from a global perspective

Multinationals are owned by a mixture of domestic and foreign shareholders. In fact, the ownership of some firms is so widely dispersed that they are known as **transnational corporations**. Transnational corporations, regardless of the location of their headquarters, are managed from a global perspective rather than the perspective of a firm residing in a particular country. This fact has made them politically controversial because they are viewed as *stateless corporations* with no allegiance or social responsibility to any nation or region of the world. An example of a transnational firm is the Royal Dutch/Shell group, which has a dual Netherlands–United Kingdom nationality.

Exhibit 21.1 lists the top 40 transnational firms ranked by foreign assets. General Electric of the United States ranks first, followed by the United Kingdom's Vodafone Group, then the Royal Dutch Shell group, then BP and Exxon, another company domiciled in the United States. By country of origin, 26 of the top 40 firms are headquartered in Europe, with the balance in the Far East and the United States. As you can see, many of the firms on the list are household names.

> **WEB**
>
> Visit www.shell.com for an overview of the business scope of a transnational corporation.

Factors Affecting International Financial Management

As we suggested earlier, the basic finance principles discussed in this book apply to international financial management. However, six factors can cause international business transactions to differ from domestic transactions. We look at these factors next.

Currency Differences

Most sovereign nations have their own currencies. Thus, businesses that engage in international transactions are likely to deal in two or more currencies.[2] If

this is the case, financial managers need to know how unexpected fluctuations in exchange rates can affect the firm's cash flows and, hence, the value of the firm. The uncertainty of future exchange rate movements is called **foreign exchange rate risk**, or just **exchange rate risk**, and we discuss it later in the chapter.

> **Foreign exchange rate risk or exchange rate risk**
>
> the uncertainty associated with future exchange rate movements

Differences in Legal Systems and Tax Codes

Differences in legal systems and tax codes can also affect the way firms operate in foreign countries. Some countries, including the United States, Canada and India, operate under legal systems derived from British common law, whereas Western European countries such as France, Germany and Italy have legal systems derived from the French Napoleonic codes. Chinese law and other Asian legal systems evolved over centuries, with an emphasis on moral teaching and legally stipulated punishments.

What emerges from the world's legal systems and tax codes is a patchwork of different systems that can vary substantially from country to country and can affect how foreign business firms are treated within a particular country's borders. Legal systems can vary on simple matters, such as the requirements for opening a business, selecting a site location and hiring employees, as well as more complex matters, such as the taxation of companies and dividends, the rights and legal liabilities of ownership and the resolution of business conflicts. Thus, legal and tax differences can affect financial decisions on what assets to acquire, how to organise the firm and what capital structure to use.

Language Differences

There are two important levels of communication in international business: business communication and social communication. Most multinational negotiations and legal contracts use English.

EXHIBIT 21.1

THE WORLD'S LARGEST NON-FINANCIAL TRANSNATIONAL CORPORATIONS RANKED BY FOREIGN ASSETS (2007)

Rank	TNI[a]	Company	Home economy	Industry	Assets Foreign	Assets Total
1	76	General Electric	United States	Electrical and electronic equipment	420 300	795 337
2	6	Vodafone Group Plc	United Kingdom	Telecommunications	230 600	254 948
3	35	Royal Dutch/Shell Group	Netherlands/United Kingdom	Petroleum exploration, refining and distribution	196 828	269 470
4	23	BP Plc	United Kingdom	Petroleum exploration, refining and distribution	185 323	236 076
5	41	ExxonMobil	United States	Petroleum exploration, refining and distribution	174 726	242 082
6	75	Toyota Motor Corporation	Japan	Motor vehicles	153 406	284 722
7	26	Total	France	Petroleum exploration, refining and distribution	143 814	167 144
8	94	Electricité De France	France	Electricity, gas and water	128 971	274 031
9	78	Ford Motor Company	United States	Motor vehicles	127 854	276 459
10	69	E.ON AG	Germany	Electricity, gas and water	123 443	202 111
11	3	ArcelorMittal	Luxembourg	Metals and metal products	119 491	133 625
12	38	Telefónica SA	Spain	Telecommunications	107 603	155 856
13	59	Volkswagen Group	Germany	Motor vehicles	104 382	213 981
14	90	ConocoPhillips	United States	Petroleum exploration, refining and distribution	103 457	177 757
15	33	Siemens AG	Germany	Electrical and electronic equipment	103 055	134 778
16	63	DaimlerChrysler AG	Germany	Motor vehicles	100 458	198 872
17	56	Chevron Corporation	United States	Petroleum exploration, refining and distribution	97 533	148 786
18	74	France Telecom	France	Telecommunications	97 011	148 952

	TNI	Company	Country	Industry		
19	85	Deutsche Telekom AG	Germany	Telecommunications	96 005	177 630
20	39	Suez	France	Electricity, gas and water	90 735	116 483
21	61	BMW AG	Germany	Motor vehicles	84 362	131 013
22	13	Hutchison Whampoa Limited	Hong Kong, China	Diversified	83 411	102 445
23	16	Honda Motor Co Ltd	Japan	Motor vehicles	83 232	110 663
24	68	Eni Group	Italy	Petroleum exploration, refining and distribution	78 368	149 360
25	29	EADS	Netherlands	Aircraft and parts	75 126	111 079
26	50	Procter & Gamble	United States	Diversified	70 241	143 992
27	89	Deutsche Post AG	Germany	Transport and storage	68 321	346 630
28	7	Nestlé SA	Switzerland	Food, beverages and tobacco	65 676	101 874
29	97	Wal-Mart Stores	United States	Retail	62 961	163 514
30	47	Nissan Motor Co Ltd	Japan	Motor vehicles	61 673	104 732
31	84	General Motors	United States	Motor vehicles	61 507	148 883
32	22	Roche Group	Switzerland	Pharmaceuticals	58 808	69 465
33	55	IBM	United States	Electrical and electronic equipment	57 699	120 431
34	92	RWE Group	Germany	Electricity, gas and water	56 127	123 113
35	87	Endesa	Spain	Electricity, gas and water	55 082	120 244
36	93	Mitsubishi Motors Corporation	Japan	Motor vehicles	54 606	103 109
37	71	Pfizer Inc	United States	Pharmaceuticals	54 360	115 268
38	45	Fiat Spa	Italy	Motor vehicles	54 313	88 526
39	53	Sanofi-aventis	France	Pharmaceuticals	53 817	105 865
40	81	Rio Tinto Plc	Australia/United Kingdom	Mining and quarrying	50 588	101 391

Source: UNCTAD/Erasmus University database.

The TNI is a transnationality index and is calculated as the average of the following three ratios: foreign assets to total assets; foreign sales to total sales; and foreign employment to total employment.

A number of the world's 40 largest transnational corporations are household names; 26 have Europe as their home economy, 4 are from the Far East and 8 the United States.

Industry classification is based on the Standard Industrial Classification (SIC).

English is the language of choice for international business throughout much of the world. Thus, reading and speaking fluent English are necessary skills for anyone planning to be a senior manager in a multinational corporation.

English is not, however, the world's social language – the language spoken when important social relationships that build trust are formed. Local languages are important for social relationships. For example, suppose that you are the CEO of a French food-processing firm and you are negotiating a deal to manufacture food products in Guangzhou, China (about 60 miles from Hong Kong). You are partnering with a Dutch firm that you know well. During the day, business and contract negotiations are conducted in English. Most members of the Chinese management team will probably speak English; indeed, some will have MBAs from European, American or Australian business schools.

At the traditional Chinese business dinner banquets, however, the preferred social language will be Cantonese, a regional Chinese dialect, or French, which is a common second language spoken by educated Chinese in Southeast Asia. It goes without saying that those who speak only English or Dutch in this situation would be at a disadvantage. Historically, most business executives spoke only their native language; however, this is changing rapidly as more managers receive foreign assignments and business students recognise the importance of a second or even a third language.

Cultural Differences

Culture is defined as the socially transmitted behaviour patterns, beliefs and attitudes of a group. Cultural views and attitudes are powerful forces that bind people together and define a particular society. The cultures of different countries and even different regions within the same country can vary considerably.

Cultural views also shape business practices and people's attitudes towards business. For example, in Japan business firms that belong to industrial groupings, known as zaibatsu, are generally expected to buy shares in other member companies, thus creating an interlocking set of cross-holdings between member firms. This is seen as a way of cementing relationships. Other areas of business that differ by culture are willingness to assume risk, management style, tolerance for inflation and attitude towards race, gender and business failure. At the end of the chapter we briefly discuss Islamic finance and the way culture, ethics and religion affect contractual arrangements.

Differences in Economic Systems

An economic system determines how a country mobilises its resources to produce goods and services needed by society, as well as how the production is distributed. In the twentieth century, two basic economic systems competed for government endorsement: (1) centrally planned economies and (2) market economies.

In a centrally planned economy, resources are allocated, produced and distributed under the direction of the central government, as in the former Soviet Union. These economies have no financial markets or banking systems to allocate capital flows. The central government sets interest rates and foreign exchange rates and financial managers need not worry about capital budgeting decisions because capital resources are allocated centrally.

In market economies, resources are allocated, produced and distributed by market forces rather than by government decree. Market economies have proven to be much more efficient in producing goods and services than traditional command economies. This fact is borne out by current trends in what once were the two largest communist countries in the world, the Soviet Union and China. Both China and the nations that formerly made up the Soviet Union are moving towards market-based economies.

Differences in Country Risk

Sovereign nations are usually free to place or remove constraints on businesses. At the extreme, a country's government may even expropriate – that is, take over – a business's assets within its borders. These types of actions clearly can affect a firm's cash flows and, thus, the value of the firm. **Country risk** refers to political uncertainty associated with a particular country. We discuss country risk in more detail later in the chapter.

> ### Country risk
>
> risk that arises from cross-border transactions, including but not limited to legal and political conditions

> ### WEB
>
> To learn about the business environment and other information about a country, you can explore the CIA website at: https://www.cia.gov/library/publications/the-world-factbook/index.html.

Goals of International Financial Management

Throughout the book, we have argued that maximisation of firm value is the proper goal for management to pursue. If this strategy is well executed, it will generate the greatest amount of wealth for the firm's shareholders. Shareholder value maximisation is the accepted goal for firms in market economies. However, it is not as widely embraced in other parts of the world. In parts of Europe, countries such as France and Germany focus on maximising corporate wealth. This means that shareholders are treated no differently from stakeholders, such as management, labour, suppliers, creditors and even the government. The European manager's goal is to create as much wealth as possible while considering the overall welfare of both the shareholders and stakeholders. In Japan, companies form tightly knit, interlocking business groups called *keiretsu*, such as Mitsubishi, Mitsui and Sumitomo, and the goal of the Japanese business manager is to increase the wealth and growth of the keiretsu. As a result, they might focus on maximising market share rather than shareholder value.

In China, which is making a transition from a command economy to a market-based economy, there are sharp differences between state-owned companies and emerging private-sector firms. Although their numbers are declining, the large state-owned companies have an overall goal that can best be described as maintaining full employment in the economy. In contrast, the new private-sector firms fully embrace the Western standard of shareholder value maximisation.

Basic Principles Remain the Same

In today's globalised environment, financial managers must be prepared to handle international transactions and all the complexities that those transactions involve. Fortunately, the basic principles of finance remain the same whether a transaction is domestic or international. The time value of money, for example, is not affected by whether a business transaction is domestic or international. Likewise, we use the same models for valuing capital assets, bonds, shares and entire businesses.

The things that do change are some of the input variables used to make financial calculations. For example, required rates of return often differ between countries and the appropriate rate must be used. Similarly, cash flows may be stated in terms of home or foreign currency. Tax codes and accounting standards also differ across countries. Exhibit 21.2 lists some of the important finance concepts and procedures discussed in the first 20 chapters of this book, and indicates the differences between domestic and international operations.

> ### Before You Go On
>
> 1. What is globalisation?
> 2. What are multinational corporations?
> 3. Explain the differences that can exist between countries on the financial manager's goal of wealth maximisation.

BUILDING INTUITION

The Basic Principles of Finance Apply No Matter Where You Do Business

The principles of finance do not stop at international borders. They apply no matter where the firm is headquartered or where it operates. Although basic finance principles do not change, international financial management does involve complications stemming from factors such as differences in accounting standards and tax codes, differences in interest rates, the presence of foreign exchange rate risk and country risk, and cultural differences.

EXHIBIT 21.2

THE BASIC PRINCIPLES OF FINANCE APPLY IN INTERNATIONAL FINANCE

Finance Concepts and Procedures	Differences Between Domestic and International Operations
Business risk	Foreign exchange and country risk must be taken into account
Form of business organisation	Varies with countries' legal systems
Ethical norms	Differ with countries' cultural norms
Nominal rate of interest	Affected by the rate of inflation in a given country
Accounting standards	Vary by country, although many countries conform to International Financial Reporting Standards
Financial statement analysis	Financial statements must be adjusted for cross-country comparisons
Tax codes	Vary by country
Concept of cash flows	Cash is cash, but monetary units are different
Goal of maximising shareholders' wealth	Proper goal for firms in market economies, but may vary by country
Time value of money	No difference
Bond valuation	Basic valuation concepts are the same, but market conditions differ
Valuation of equity	Basic valuation concepts are the same, but market conditions differ
Net present value	No difference
Operating and financial leverage	No difference
Breakeven analysis	No difference
Expected returns and variance	No difference
Cost of debt and equity	Basic concepts are the same, but market conditions and tax systems differ
Weighted average cost of capital	Basic concepts are the same, but market conditions and tax systems differ
Optimal capital structure	Basic concepts are the same, but market conditions and tax systems differ
Dividend policy	Basic concepts are the same, but tax systems differ
Working capital management	Basic concepts are the same, but market conditions differ
Business valuation	Basic concepts are the same, but market conditions and tax systems differ

Most of the basic finance principles discussed in this book remain unchanged in the international context. Where there are differences, they generally result from differences in accounting standards, tax codes, legal systems, monetary systems and interest rates.

FOREIGN EXCHANGE MARKETS

Learning Objective 2

Differentiate among the spot rate, the forward rate and the cross rate in the foreign exchange markets, perform foreign exchange and cross-rate calculations, and be able to hedge an asset purchase where payment is made in a foreign currency.

The **foreign exchange markets** are international markets where currencies are bought and sold in wholesale amounts. Foreign exchange markets provide three basic economic benefits:

1. A mechanism to transfer purchasing power from individuals who deal in one currency to individuals who deal in a different currency, facilitating the import and export of goods and services.
2. A way for companies to pass the risk associated with foreign exchange price fluctuations to professional risk-takers. This hedging function is particularly important for companies in the present era of floating, or variable, exchange rates.
3. A channel for importers and exporters to acquire credit for international business transactions. The time span between shipment of goods by exporters and their receipt by importers can be considerable.

Foreign exchange market

international markets where currencies are bought and sold in wholesale amounts

While the goods are in transit, they must be financed. Foreign exchange markets provide a mechanism through which financing and currency conversions can be accomplished efficiently and at low cost.

The foreign exchange markets are very large, with a daily volume of more than US$4 trillion in 2007,

according to the survey by the Bank for International Settlements. This is more than the value of all the cars, wheat, oil and other products sold daily in the real economy. In 2007, London was by far the largest foreign exchange trading centre, with an average daily volume of $1148 billion (34.1% of volume). New York City was second with $434 billion (16.6%) and Tokyo was third with $149 billion (6.0%). In this section, we examine how the foreign exchange markets are structured and how they work.

Market Structure and Major Participants

There is no single formal foreign exchange market. Rather, as suggested earlier, there are a group of informal markets closely interlocked through international banking relationships. Participants are linked by telephone, electronic communication networks and the Internet. The market trades any time of day or night and every day of the year. Nearly all countries have some type of active foreign exchange market.

The major participants in the foreign exchange markets are multinational commercial banks, large investment banking firms and small currency boutiques that specialise in foreign exchange transactions. In Europe, the market is dominated by large banks, with London being the prime location of trading activity. The other major participants are countries' central banks, which intervene in the markets primarily to smooth out fluctuations in exchange rates.

Foreign Exchange Rates

When firms buy raw materials or finished goods, they want to get the best possible deal – the quality they need at the lowest price. When suppliers are located in the same country, comparisons of the alternatives are quite easy. Both the supplier and the customer keep their books and pay their bills in the same currency.

When the suppliers are not located in the same country, comparisons are more difficult. Buyers prefer to pay for purchases in their local currency, but the foreign supplier must pay employees and other local expenses with its domestic currency. Hence, one of the two parties in the transaction will be forced to deal in a foreign currency and incur foreign exchange rate risk (recall that this risk arises because of the uncertainty of future exchange rate movements).

Fortunately, we can easily compare prices stated in different currencies by checking the foreign exchange rate quotes in major newspapers. A foreign exchange rate is the price of one monetary unit, such as the British pound, stated in terms of another currency, such as the euro.

The exchange rate quotation relates a variable amount (which changes as the exchange rate changes due to market conditions) of one currency, known as the quoted currency, against a unit of the other currency. For instance, the exchange rate between the US dollar and the euro is expressed in terms of a variable number of US currency (the quoted currency) versus one euro. It would be written as $/€, which means that $(variable) = €1.

As an example, assume you are the CFO of a German firm and you can buy steel from the United States at $190 per tonne and from Britain for £116 per tonne, or locally at €156.25 per tonne. Furthermore, a Japanese company is willing to sell steel for ¥17 000 per tonne. Which supplier should you choose? The exchange rate between the euro and the British pound is £0.72/€, and between the euro and the US dollar is $1.29/€. These exchange rates are quoted so that one euro equals £0.72, or 72 pence

per euro, and one euro equals $1.29. This means the price for the steel in euros for the German firm when buying from the United States is €147.29 (that is, $190/$1.29/€). The steel from the British supplier will cost €161.11 (£116/£0.72/€). Given these prices, the German firm will prefer to buy steel from the American supplier at €147.29 per tonne, as this is the cheapest. If the exchange rate between the yen and the euro is ¥123/€, which means that one euro costs ¥123, the Japanese steel will cost ¥17 000/¥123/€ = €138.21 per tonne. This price is €9.08 per tonne (€147.29 −€138.21), less than the American supplier's price of $190 per tonne. Assuming that the price quotation of ¥17 000 includes all transportation costs and tariffs, or that the sum of those costs is less than €9.08 per tonne, then the German manufacturer will find it cheaper to purchase steel from the Japanese supplier. The first three rows in Exhibit 21.3 show the calculations we used to reach this conclusion.

> **WEB**
>
> For foreign exchange rate data, go to www.x-rates.com.

Now suppose that the exchange rate between the dollar and the euro changes from $1.29/€ to

EXHIBIT 21.3

FOREIGN EXCHANGE RATES AND THE PRICE OF STEEL IN INTERNATIONAL MARKETS

Supplier	Price in Local Currency	Foreign Exchange Rate	Conversion to Price in Euros	Price of Steel in Euros
German	€156.25		—	€156.25
British	£116	£0.72	£116/£0.72/€ =	€161.11
US	$190	$1.29	$190/$1.29/€ =	€147.29
Japanese	¥17 000	¥123	¥17 000/¥123/€ =	€138.21
US	$190	$1.39	$190/$1.39/€ =	€136.69

The exhibit shows the calculations necessary to decide which supplier offers the best price: American, British, German or Japanese. If the exchange rate between the euro and the US dollar is $1.29/€, the euro and the British pound is £0.72/€, and the euro and the Japanese yen is ¥123/€, then it makes economic sense to select the Japanese supplier. The situation changes when the exchange rate between the euro and the US dollar falls to $1.39/€.

$1.39/€. Either this can be seen as a US dollar depreciation (that is, more US dollars are required to buy one euro) or as an appreciation of the euro (one euro buys more US dollars). Because the exchange rates for the world's major currencies float freely, based on market forces, such fluctuations occur continuously. At this point, the steel from the United States can be bought for $190/$1.39/€ = €136.69 (row 4 in Exhibit 21.3). The American firm has become the low-cost supplier, even though it has done nothing itself to lower its price.

Notice that it now takes more US dollars to buy one euro and, conversely, fewer euros to purchase one US dollar. Therefore, it is correct to say that the value of the US dollar has fallen against the euro or that the value of the euro has risen against the US dollar. Both statements indicate that goods and services priced in US dollars are now cheaper to someone holding euros and that purchases priced in euros are now more expensive to someone holding US dollars.

Also notice that, other things remaining equal, the demand for a country's products will be higher when the value of the country's currency declines relative to the value of other currencies. In our example, the change in the exchange rate led to a change in the German company's purchase decisions; at $1.29/€, steel from the United States was more expensive than steel supplied from Japan but when the exchange rate rose to $1.29/€, steel from the United States was the cheapest.

Learning by Doing Application 21.1

Exchange Rates and the Blue Sweater

Problem: While in a clothing store on Saville Row in London, you find the blue cashmere sweater of your dreams. The sweater is on sale at 50% off, priced at £250. 'At 50% off, the sweater must be a bargain', you say to yourself. In your home country, a sweater like that costs about €320. If the current exchange rate is £0.75/€, is the sweater a bargain?

Approach: Of course, the relevant question is, what is the 50% off? The shops on Seville Street in London are very pricey. You will need to use the exchange rate to calculate the price in euros before comparing the price with that of a comparable sweater in your home country.

Solution: The price of the sweater in euros is £250/£0.75/€ = €333.33, which is higher than the €320 price in your home country. It is not such a good deal.

Decision-Making Example 21.1

Exchange Rate Movement: Good or Bad News?

Situation: You are the purchasing agent for the German firm buying steel in the example discussed in the text. Your assistant, Omar, who is a British subject, runs into the office and breathlessly says: 'The pound is stronger against the euro! The new exchange rate is £0.83/€!' Is Omar's report good news or bad news?

Decision: Omar is incorrect in saying that the pound has risen in value against the euro: it has fallen in value. That is bad news for Omar, because the British pounds he owns will now buy fewer German goods. For your firm, it is good news. It now takes fewer euros to purchase one British pound. At the new exchange rate, the British steel costs €139.76 per tonne (£116/£0.83/€).

The Equilibrium Exchange Rate

Exhibit 21.4 shows the supply and demand for British pounds and the equilibrium exchange rate between the euro and the pound. As you can see, the supply of and demand for pounds move in opposite directions as the exchange rate changes. The demand for pounds increases as the euro appreciates in value against the pound. In other words, as pounds become less expensive in relation to euros, British products become less expensive for Europeans to buy. More British goods will be sold to countries using the euro; therefore, there is an increase in the demand for British pounds to pay for those goods. This is illustrated by the *downward-sloping demand curve* in Exhibit 21.4.

At the same time, the supply of pounds decreases as the euro price of pounds declines. From the point of view of a British buyer, the lower the euro price of pounds, the greater the number of pounds that must be given up to obtain euros to buy foreign goods whose prices are denominated in euros. Thus, the lower the price of pounds against the euro, the more likely British residents are to switch from imported to domestic products. When purchases are diverted in this way to domestic goods, British residents will supply fewer pounds to the foreign exchange markets because they no longer want to buy as many imports. This is shown by the *upward-sloping supply curve* in the exhibit.

Exhibit 21.4 also shows the *equilibrium exchange rate* (€/£), which is at the point where the supply and demand curves intersect and the quantity of the currency demanded exactly equals the quantity supplied. At that rate of exchange, participants in the foreign exchange market will neither be accumulating nor divesting a currency.

The key to understanding movements in exchange rates, then, is to identify factors that cause shifts in the supply and demand curves for foreign currency. In general, whatever causes residents whose currency is the euro to buy more or fewer foreign goods shifts the demand curve for the foreign currency. Similarly, whatever causes foreigners to buy more or fewer goods priced in euros shifts the supply curve for the foreign currency.

Foreign Currency Quotations

Exhibit 21.5 shows selected exchange rate quotations. As you can see, there are several types of quotations, which we discuss next.

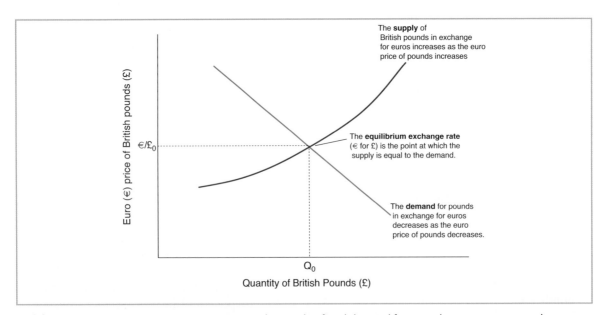

Exhibit 21.4: The Equilibrium Exchange Rate The supply of and demand for pounds move in opposite directions. The equilibrium exchange rate occurs at the intersection of the supply and demand curves. At this point the quantity of the currency demanded equals the quantity supplied.

EXHIBIT 21.5

SPOT FOREIGN EXCHANGE RATES AND CROSS RATES

Panel A: Major world currencies and their cross rates

	EUR	USD	JPY	GBP	CHF	CAD	AUD	HKD
HKD	10.8333	7.7547	0.0941	12.3859	8.0755	7.6723	7.6658	
AUD	1.4132	1.0116	0.0123	1.6157	1.0534	1.0008		0.1304
CAD	1.4120	1.0107	0.0123	1.6144	1.0526		0.9992	0.1303
CHF	1.3415	0.9603	0.0117	1.5338		0.9501	0.9493	0.1238
GBP	0.8747	0.6261	0.0076		0.651994	0.6194	0.6189	0.08074
JPY	115.10	82.39		131.60	85.80	81.52	81.45	10.62
USD	1.3970		0.0121	1.5972	1.041372	0.9894	0.9885	0.1290
EUR		0.7158	0.8688	1.1433	0.7454	0.7082	0.7076	0.0923

Source: XE Corporation (www.xe.com). Reproduced by permission of xe.com Inc.

EUR: euro; USD: US dollar; JPY: Japanese yen; GBP: British pound; CHF: Swiss franc; CAD: Canadian dollar; AUD: Australian dollar; HKD: Hong Kong dollar.

Panel A shows the cross rates between the world's major currencies and shows the two ways a currency can be quoted. Above the diagonal for each column, the currency value is given in units of the currency on the horizontal column. For example, for the euro (EUR) against the British pound (GBP), the value is £0.8747 = €1. For the values below the diagonal, the exchange rate is given in terms of the currency in the vertical column. For British pounds and the euro, the value is €1.1433 = £1.

Panel B: Foreign exchange data for Thursday 7 October 2010

Country/Currency	ISO Currency Code[a]	Currency per EUR Thursday	Currency per EUR Wednesday	EUR Equivalent Thursday	EUR Equivalent Wednesday
Americas					
US dollar	USD	1.3970	1.3856	0.7158	0.7217
Brazilian real	BRL	2.3390	2.3113	0.4275	0.4327
Canadian dollar	CAD	1.4120	1.4018	0.7082	0.7134
Mexican peso	MXN	17.4122	17.2854	0.0574	0.0579
Europe					
British pounds	GBP	0.8747	0.8726	1.1433	1.1460
Croatian kuna	HRK	7.3188	7.3145	0.1366	0.1367
Czech koruna[c]	CZK	24.518	24.530	0.4079	0.4077
Danish krona	DKK	7.4561	7.4547	0.1341	0.1341
Hungarian forint[b]	HUF	273.33	270.33	0.3659	0.3699
Latvian lats	LVL	0.7090	0.7091	1.4104	1.4102
Polish zloty	PLN	3.9655	3.9490	0.2522	0.2532
New Romanian leu	RON	4.2648	4.2720	0.2345	0.2341
Norwegian krona	NOK	8.0830	8.0340	0.1237	0.1245
Swedish krona	SEK	9.3208	9.2993	0.1073	0.1075
Swiss franc	CHF	1.3415	1.3361	0.7454	0.7484
Russian rouble[c]	RUB	41.575	41.360	0.2405	0.2418
Turkish lira	TRY	1.9823	1.965	0.5045	0.5089

(continued)

EXHIBIT 21.5
(*CONTINUED*)

Country/Currency	ISO Currency Code[a]	Currency per EUR Thursday	Currency per EUR Wednesday	EUR Equivalent Thursday	EUR Equivalent Wednesday
Asia-Pacific					
Australian dollar	AUD	1.4132	1.4221	0.7076	0.7032
Chinese yan renminbi	CNY	9.3298	9.2713	0.1072	0.1079
Hong Kong dollar	HKD	10.8333	10.7471	0.0923	0.0930
Indonesian rupiah[d]	IDR	12467.70	12357.62	0.8021	0.8092
Indian rupee[c]	INR	61.768	61.500	0.1619	0.1626
Japanese yen[b]	JPY	115.10	114.98	0.8688	0.8697
South Korean won	KRW	1558.32	1550.99	0.0006	0.0006
New Zealand dollar	NZD	1.8445	1.8423	0.5422	0.5428
Philippine peso[c]	PHP	60.670	60.275	0.1648	0.1659
Singapore dollar	SGD	1.8246	1.8155	0.5481	0.5508
Thai baht[c]	THB	41.714	41.492	0.2397	0.2410
Africa					
South African rand	ZAR	9.6183	9.5445	0.1040	0.1048

Source: European Central Bank (http://www.ecb.int/stats/exchange/eurofxref/html/index.en.html) used with permission.

[a]ISO 4217 currency codes denote a currency by the first two letters of the country (e.g. Canada would be CA) plus an extra character to denote the currency unit, in this case a D.
[b]Represents 100 units of foreign currency per euro.
[c]Represents 10 units of foreign currency per euro.
[d]Represents 10 000 units of foreign currency per euro.

Panel B lists the spot rates: column 1 gives the country and the name given to the currency; column 2 gives the currency identifier used for foreign exchange transactions; columns 3 and 4 show how many units of foreign currency it takes to buy one euro of currency and columns 5 and 6 how many euros it takes to purchase one unit of foreign currency.

WEB

XE Corporation provides foreign exchange quotations for the world's major currencies at: http://www.xe.com.
Reuters has a currency page with a built-in currency converter at: http://www.reuters.com/finance/currencies.

The Spot Rate

Look first at the lower part of the exhibit, Panel B. The quotations here are spot rates. The **spot rate** is the cost of buying a foreign currency today, 'on the spot'. Our example of whether to purchase American, British or Japanese steel used spot rate data.

Spot rate

the exchange rate in the market at any given point in time

In the lower part of the exhibit, the first column shows the name of the country and the name of its currency. Column 2 gives the ISO currency identifier and this is used in foreign exchange contracts since it is unambiguous. A look at the table indicates that a number of countries (United States, Canada, Hong Kong, Taiwan) all use a version of the 'dollar'. It is therefore important to know exactly the currency being transacted in order to avoid mistakes. The ISO identifiers are unique to each currency. Columns 3 and 4 labelled 'Currency per EUR' show how many units of the currency are required to purchase one euro (EUR). Since it is possible to express this the other way round, columns 5 and 6, labelled 'EUR Equivalent', show how many euros (EUR) it takes to buy one unit of the foreign currency. The market will normally quote the currency one particular way. For instance, it is commonly accepted to express the exchange rate between the US dollar and the euro in terms of the US dollar. Because this rate is the price in US dollars for a foreign currency (in this case the euro), it is often called *American terms*. For example, it takes USD 1.3970 to buy one euro.

Columns 5 and 6, labelled 'EUR Equivalent', show how many euros are required to purchase one unit of foreign currency. For example, USD 1 would get you EUR 0.7158. This quote is often called *European terms*, because it is the amount of foreign currency per US dollar (although the foreign currency may not be European). As you may have noted, the second exchange rate is the reciprocal ($1/x$) of the first.

Cross Rates

As a practical matter, most currencies are quoted against the US dollar rather than the euro. Transactions between currencies other than the US dollar, such as between the euro and the Japanese yen, are generally called *cross rates*. This can be confusing, but it arises from the role the US dollar plays in the international monetary system.

People who have to deal with more than one foreign currency often make use of a table of exchange rates called *cross rates*, which are simply exchange rates between two currencies other than the US dollar. The top portion of Exhibit 21.5 shows cross rates for eight of the world's most actively traded currencies. Cross-rate tables can be found in the currency pages of financial news providers and on many financial websites.

It is also possible to calculate cross rates, given enough information. Suppose, for example, that a dealer is interested in finding out the exchange rate between the Hong Kong dollar (HKD) and the euro

(EUR) but only knows the exchange rate between each of these currencies and the US dollar: HKD HK$7.7547/$ and $1.3970/€. The dealer can calculate the desired cross rate as follows:[3]

$$\text{HK\$/US\$} \times \text{US\$/€} = \text{HK\$7.7547} \times \$1.3970$$
$$= \text{HK\$10.8333/€}$$

Turning to Panel A of Exhibit 21.5, you can find the same cross rate for the Hong Kong dollar versus the euro by looking down the column for the euro and matching it with the Hong Kong dollar.

Bid and Ask Rate Quotations

The foreign exchange rate quotes given in Exhibit 21.5 are provided by foreign exchange dealers, most of whom operate in large money centre banks. Like all dealers in financial markets, foreign exchange dealers quote two prices: *bid* and *ask* (or *offer*) quotes. The *bid* quote represents the rate at which the dealer will *buy* foreign currency, while the *ask* (*offer*) quote is the rate at which the dealer will *sell* foreign currency. The prices quoted in Exhibit 21.5 are ask (offer) quotes for wholesale transactions (that is, €1 million or more).

The difference between the bid and ask price is the dealer's spread, which is often calculated in percentage form, as follows:

$$\begin{array}{c}\text{Bid-ask}\\\text{(offer)spread}\end{array} = \frac{\text{Ask(offer)rate} - \text{Bid rate}}{\text{Ask rate}} \quad (21.1)$$

Suppose a dealer is quoting a bid rate for euros (the common currency for members of the European Monetary Union countries) of $1.3405/€ and an ask rate of $1.3415/€. The bid–ask spread is 0.075% [(1.3415 − 1.3405)/1.3415]. Now assume that ABC Corporation Inc., a company domiciled in the United States, decides to buy €1 000 000 to use in a transaction. The dealer sells the euros to the company at the ask rate of $1.3415/€ and the firm pays the dealer a total of US$1 341 500 ($1 000 000 × $1.3415/€). Later in the day, ABC Corporation finds it does not need the euros and decides to sell them back. The dealer buys the euros from the firm at the bid rate of $1.3405/€. The firm receives $1 340 500 (€1 000 000 × $1.3405/€). This represents a loss of $1000, or 0.075% ($1000/$1 341 500). The dealer, though, has made a profit of US$1000, or 0.075%.

Learning by Doing Application 21.2

Cross Exchange Rates

Problem: You are based in Paris and are going on a business trip first to Japan and then, before returning home, you will travel to the United Kingdom. Before you depart, you purchase €10 000 worth of Japanese yen at the prevailing rate of ¥123.96/€. After finishing your business in Japan, you head for London, where you convert the remaining yen to British pounds. You sell ¥512 375 at a rate of ¥137.69/£. You finally return to Paris with £567.35, which you would like to convert to euros. Based only on the rates given, how many euros will you receive if you sell the pounds? What were your total expenses in euros in the two countries?

Approach: In order to solve this problem, you need to know the exchange rate, or cross rate, between the euro and the British pound. Given the other two exchange rates, you can calculate this rate by dividing the ¥/€ rate by the ¥/£ rate.

Solution:

$$\frac{¥137.69/£}{¥123.96/€} = €1.1108/£$$

Starting with €10 000 and converting at the rate against the yen, gives ¥1 239 600 (€10 000 × ¥123.96/€). You have ¥512 375 when leaving Japan, so have spent ¥727 225 (¥1 239 600 − ¥512 375). Converting this at the ¥/€ exchange rate gives €5866.61. The amount you have to spend in London is £3721.22 (¥512 375/¥123.96/£). You have £567.35 left when you leave, so have spent £3153.87. The amount in euros is €3503.20 (£3153.87 × €1.1108/£) and you have €630.19 left over on your return to Paris (£567.35 × €1.1108/£).

Forward Rates

For the major world currencies, such as the US dollar, the British pound and the Japanese yen, the *Wall Street Journal* also lists the forward rates for one month, three months and six months. As discussed above, the spot rate is what you pay to buy money today. The **forward foreign exchange rate**, as we discussed in Chapter 20, is what you agree to pay for delivery in the future – that is, you sign a contract today to buy the money on a date in the future, such as one month, three months or six months from now.

> **Forward foreign exchange rate**
>
> a rate agreed on today for a currency exchange to take place at a specified date in the future

Forward contracts are important because foreign business transactions may extend over long periods. This means that financial managers must anticipate their future needs for foreign currencies. As discussed in Chapter 20, by contracting now to buy or sell foreign currencies at some future date, the businesses can 'lock in' the cost of foreign exchange at the beginning of the transaction and they do not have to worry about the risk of an unfavourable movement in the exchange rate in the future.

Determining the Forward Foreign Exchange Rate

We already know from Chapter 20 how to determine the forward rate. As you might have expected, forward foreign exchange rates, like other forward rates, are determined by the cost of carry. The simplest way of understanding how this works is to use an example. Suppose the spot exchange rate between the euro and the British pound is €1.2500/£ (S_0) and the interest rate in euros is 2% and in British pounds 4%. What will be the one-year forward foreign exchange rate (F_1)?

The forward exchange rate will be:

$$F_{1\text{-year}} = S_0 \times \frac{1 + i_{€}}{1 + i_{£}} = €1.2500/£ \times \frac{1.02}{1.04}$$

$$= €1.2260/£$$

You receive fewer euros or pay less for the British pounds, and we discuss this in the next section.

By applying the cost of carry model, we find that the interest rate in euros (the quoted currency) will raise the forward price whilst the interest rate in British pounds (the base currency) will reduce the price. Why is this happening? This is because we can consider the forward rate to be the product of (1) an immediate purchase of the present value of the amount of foreign currency $PV(F_t)$ we need to deliver at the maturity of the forward contract, (2) the use of this foreign currency (S_0) to earn interest until the maturity of the forward, and (3) a loan for the present value of the base currency we will receive at delivery.

Let us work through the above example with some numbers. An Italian company has a contract with a British customer who will pay £1 million in 1 year's time. The company wants to hedge the exchange rate risk between British pounds and the euro. It therefore borrows the present value of the £1 million it will receive in 12 months' time, which is £961 538.46 (£1 million/1.04). It now immediately exchanges this amount for euros and receives €1 201 923.08 (£961 538.46 × €1.2500/€) and deposits this amount with a bank to earn 2%. At the maturity of the contract the company receives £1 million from the British company and this is used to meet the maturing obligation on the British pounds loan. In the meantime, the deposit in euros has increased to €1 225 961.54. The company has therefore obtained an exchange rate from the above of €1 225 961.54/£1 million = €1.2260/£ (allowing for rounding).

Note that to determine what the forward exchange rate is, we need to work backwards by asking the question: How much do I need to pay at the forward date? As the above shows, we start with the amount of currency that we need to deliver at the maturity of the forward foreign exchange contract. We then present-value this amount and, using the spot exchange rate, determine what this is in the other currency and invest this to the contract's maturity. The ratio of the amount of currency to be delivered at the maturity to the amount of foreign currency held is the forward foreign exchange rate for that date. As discussed in Chapter 20, different dates will have different forward foreign exchange rates – you can see that the forward rates for the British pound against the US dollar for 1, 3 and 6 months in Exhibit 21.5 are all different.

The forward foreign exchange rate represents the interest rate differential between the two currencies. If the interest rates in both British pounds and the euro had been the same, the forward rate would have been the same as the spot rate. We know from Chapter 2 that interest rates are made up of two elements, the real interest rate and the expected inflation rate. The real interest rate is the same in all countries, so the forward foreign exchange rate at any particular time represents the expected difference in inflation between the two currencies. This understanding is useful when we come to consider international projects later in the chapter.

Forward Rate Premiums and Discounts

The forward rate quoted on a particular day is seldom the same as the spot rate on the same day. Whether it is a one-month, three-month or six-month quote, the forward rate is the market's best estimate of what it expects the spot rate to be at that time in the future. The difference between the forward rate and the spot rate is called the *forward premium* or *forward discount*. For example, suppose the spot rate today on the British pound is $1.4903/£, while the three-month forward rate is $1.4895/£. According to the forward quote, the market expects the British pound to cost $1.4895 three months in the future, a value that is less than today's spot rate of $1.4903. Thus, we say that the

**Learning by
Doing
Application
21.4**

Making Your Own Forward

Problem: You are the financial manager at a machine tool company in Germany and have been given an order by a company in Morocco for €900 000. Your usual terms for international sales are payment upon delivery, which will be in six months' time. The Moroccan company has never purchased abroad before and wants to pay in its local currency, the Moroccan dirham (Dh.). Your company policy requires that all transactional currency exposures are hedged. You discover there is an active spot foreign exchange market against the dirham and the current exchange rate is Dh.8.50/€, but there are no forward contracts. You also find out that you can borrow dirham from a local bank at 5.0% per year and you can lend in euros at 1.5% per year. Can you both satisfy your new customer and the company's risk management policies? What is the resultant forward exchange rate you can achieve?

Approach: Recognise from Chapter 20 that a foreign exchange forward contract can be constructed using the cost of carry model, which in this case involves borrowing and lending to determine the forward value. You can construct your own forward price by (1) borrowing Moroccan dirham at 5% for six months, (2) converting the proceeds to euros and (3) investing the proceeds in euros for six months at 1.5%.

Solution: The amount of the contract and hence the amount you need to have at the maturity of the forward contract in euros is €900 000. The present value of this amount discounted at the euro rate of 1.5% for six months is €900 000/$(1.015)0.5$ = €893 325. You convert this to dirham at the spot exchange rate of Dh.8.50/€, that is €893 325 × Dh.8.50/€ = Dh.7 593 262.50. This is the amount you need to borrow from the Moroccan bank for six months.

At the maturity of the loan, the amount will have increased by the interest due, namely: Dh.7 593 262.50 × $(1.05)0.5$ = Dh.7 780 778.70. This is your invoice amount to the customer in their local currency, the Moroccan dirham. The forward exchange rate you are 'locking in' is Dh.7 780 778.70/€900 000 = Dh.8.64531/€, a slightly less favourable rate to your customer than the spot rate, which would have required the customer to pay Dh.7 650 000 (€900 000 × Dh.8.50/€) immediately. The Dh.130 779 difference is the forward premium on the Moroccan dirham for six months.

British pound is at a forward discount against the US dollar or that the dollar is at a forward premium against the British pound.[4]

This forward premium or discount can be measured as a percentage on an annualised basis. Equation (21.2) shows this relationship:

$$\text{Forward premium(discount)}$$
$$= \frac{\text{Forward rate} - \text{Spot rate}}{\text{Spot rate}} \times \frac{360}{n} \times 100$$

$$(21.2)$$

where n is the number of days in the forward agreement. Applying this equation to our example, the forward discount on the pound is equal to:

$$\text{Forward discount} = \frac{\$1.4895 - \$1.4903}{\$1.4903} \times \frac{360}{90}$$
$$\times 100$$
$$= -0.215\%$$

where the negative sign indicates the discount on the British pound against the US dollar.

Hedging a Currency Transaction

We have already discussed the fact that firms want to hedge certain risks. Currency risk is a major problem. In the discussion of forward rates we briefly described how firms can lock in (hedge) the cost of foreign exchange.

Let us take a look at an example of how a firm might hedge a transaction using a forward foreign exchange contract. Suppose an exporter based in Europe sells farm equipment to a British firm for £100 000; the equipment is to be delivered and paid for in 90 days. The English firm will pay for the purchase in pounds. The exporter wants to hedge the transaction. How will this hedging work?

If, at the time of the sale, the spot rate is £1 = €1.20, the farm equipment is worth €120 000 (£100 000 × €1.20/£). However, the actual number of euros to be received for the machinery, which is the relevant price to the firm whose currency is the euro, is not certain. The European firm must wait 90 days to collect the £100 000 and then sell the pounds in the spot market for euros. There is a risk that the euro price of the pound may have declined more than expected. For instance, if in 90 days the pound is worth only €1.10, the exporter will receive only €110 000 (£100 000 × €1.10/£), a loss of €10 000 (€120 000 − €110 000).

To eliminate the foreign exchange rate risk and ensure a certain future price, the European company can hedge by selling the £100 000 forward 90 days. If the forward rate at the time of sale is £1 = €1.1950, the exporter can enter into a forward foreign exchange contract in which it agrees to deliver the £100 000 to the bank in 90 days and receive €119 500 (£100 000 × €1.1950/£) in return. Assume again that the spot rate on the day the exchange is made is £1 = $1.10. In this case, the 'saving' from hedging is €9500, since the firm has received €119 500 instead of the €110 000 it would have received if it had not entered into the forward contract.

Learning by Doing Application 21.5

Forward Premium

Problem: Ian Chappell is planning a trip from Sydney, Australia, to visit his brother, who works in India. He plans to make the trip in six months' time. In preparing his budget for the trip, he finds that the spot rate for Indian rupees is Rs 33.6660 per Australian dollar (A$). He also finds the six-month forward rate to be Rs 31.4532/A$. What is the forward premium or discount on the Indian rupee against the Australian dollar?

Approach: Recognise that the Australian dollar will buy fewer Indian rupees in six months' time. This means that the Indian rupee is at a forward premium against the Australian dollar or that the Australian dollar is at a discount against the rupee. To find out by how much, we use Equation (21.2).

Solution: Using Equation (21.2), we calculate the value as:

$$\text{Forward discount} = \frac{\text{Rs } 31.4532/\text{A\$} - \text{Rs } 33.6660/\text{A\$}}{\text{Rs } 33.6660/\text{A\$}}$$

$$\times \frac{360}{180} \times 100 = -13.15\%$$

Thus, the Australian dollar is at a forward discount of 13.15% against the Indian rupee.

Notice that, even with hedging, the firm has 'lost' €500, because at the time of the sale, when the exchange rate was £1 = €1.20, the machine was worth €120 000. Can this kind of loss be prevented? The answer is that forward contracts cannot protect against *expected* changes in exchange rates, only against *unexpected* changes. At the time of sale, the 90-day forward rate is £1 = €1.1950 and this is the market's best estimate of what the rate will be in 90 days. Of course, in 90 days the spot rate for euros could be £1 = €1.1950, but it probably will have a value that is more or less than the forward rate.

What would happen in our example if the spot rate in 90 days rose to €1.30/£? The unhedged transaction would yield €130 000. However, the forward contract would again provide exactly the number of euros anticipated – €119 500. Although the company may have some regrets because the forward contract prevented it from receiving the benefits of the strengthening pound, most businesses would consider leaving the account receivable exposed (that is, unhedged) to be 'speculation'. As discussed in the previous chapter, firms seek to eliminate risks that detract from their core business objective. Foreign exchange speculation is not a logical or legitimate function of businesses that import or export goods or services.[5]

Before You Go On

1. What is foreign exchange rate risk?
2. How is the equilibrium exchange rate determined?
3. What are the implications of using a forward foreign exchange contract?

COUNTRY RISK

Learning Objective 3

Describe the factors that affect country risk and country risk ratings.

Undertaking cross-border transactions raises a number of new risks. Variously called country risk, or political risk, it results from a combination of additional factors that have to be taken into account when assessing the attractiveness of foreign capital projects.[6] Financial managers must account for country risk when evaluating foreign business activities. Our opening vignette involved foreign firms setting up and making investments in Mongolia. In order to do so successfully, they need to understand the local way of doing business, the political dynamics of the country and the potential for the host country to change the rules of the game in the future. If a firm is located in a country with a relatively unstable political environment, management will require a higher rate of return on capital projects as compensation for the additional risk. At the extreme, a local government could expropriate, or take over, the plant and equipment of the overseas operation without giving the company any compensation. This expropriation of assets is called *nationalisation*. Sometimes, nations may expropriate the assets and offer some form of compensation.

Here are some other ways that a foreign government can affect the risk of a foreign project:

- Change tax laws in a way that adversely affects foreign firms.
- Impose laws related to labour, wages and prices that are more restrictive than those that apply to domestic firms.
- Disallow any remittance of funds from the subsidiary to the parent firm for either a limited period or the duration of the project.
- Require that the subsidiary be headed by a local citizen or have a local firm as a major equity partner.
- Impose tariffs and quotas on any imports.

For foreign firms, changes such as those above will reduce the value of their investments in the country. However, not all countries are the same and the risk is greater for some countries than for others. A firm in France deciding to invest in Germany is reasonably confident that, local laws apart, it will be able to operate very much as it operates at home. On the other hand, some countries, which have attractive opportunities, seem particularly unstable and in order to be able to gauge the likelihood that country risk might turn out to be a problem, it is necessary to evaluate the riskiness of the foreign country where the investment is to be made.

> **WEB**
>
> For country risk information, visit www.prsgroup.com.

Country Risk Analysis

To help firms assess country risk, some private firms, credit rating agencies and government agencies provide assessments of individual countries. These organisations provide ratings, just like those discussed in Chapter 8 for corporate bonds, in order to help investors make decisions regarding investing in, exporting to or importing from a particular country. Exhibit 21.6 shows the ratings for the country risk for a selection of countries by the Compagnie Française d'Assurance pour le Commerce Exterieur (Coface), the French export credit guarantee agency, as of January 2010.

> **WEB**
>
> The US Central Intelligence Agency (CIA) maintains comprehensive coverage of all countries in the world at: https://www.cia .gov/library/publications/the-world-factbook/ index.html.

Country risk ratings reflect a country's economic, financial and political outlook and the risks of doing business in that country. The risk will be different if it involves sales to a business in a particular country. In this case, the risk assessment will need to determine the ability of the country to generate foreign exchange earnings that, in turn,

will allow firms purchasing from abroad to service their foreign currency obligations. There will be a different emphasis if the intention is to set up a permanent operation in the country, such as Rio Tinto's mining operations in Mongolia. In this case, additional factors such as labour regulations, restrictions on the repatriation of profits and/or dividends and the general business environment would have to be considered.[7]

In general, a country's refusal to honour contractual obligations arises from two factors: poor economic policies and political changes (e.g. a change in government and hence policies). In its analysis, Coface analyses a range of factors to determine the rating it assigns to countries based on the macroeconomic and financial environment and the outlook for the country, as well as the business environment. The criteria, which are not unlike the corporate credit criteria discussed in Chapter 8, for Coface's country ratings are given in Exhibit 21.7. In particular, it assesses factors such as:

- the country's social structure and the degree of political stability of political institutions
- the soundness of the economic and financial system
- fiscal policy and budgetary flexibility, with among other things special attention devoted to
  - purposes of public sector borrowing
  - impact of public sector borrowing requirement (the PSBR is the state and state entity borrowings) on the growth of the national debt
  - implications of such activities for the outlook for inflation
- the course of monetary policy and inflationary pressures within the economy
- the public debt burden and debt service track record
- balance of payments flexibility
- external financial position
- the effectiveness of the legal system and commercial code in protecting creditors and enforcing contracts
- the degree of corruption and fraud in the country and, particularly, within the political and legal system and business establishment.

EXHIBIT 21.6

COFACE COUNTRY RISK RATINGS FOR A SELECTION OF COUNTRIES (JANUARY 2010)

Rating	Europe	Americas	Asia	Middle East	Africa
A1	Luxembourg, Sweden, Switzerland				
A2	Austria, Belgium, Cyprus, Czech Republic, Denmark, Finland, France, Germany, Netherlands, Norway	Chile	Australia, Hong Kong, Japan, Malaysia, New Zealand, Singapore, South Korea, Taiwan	Kuwait, Qatar	
A3	Greece, Ireland, Italy, Poland, Portugal, Slovenia, Spain, United Kingdom		China, India, Thailand	Bahrain, Oman, UAE	Mauritius, South Africa
A4	Croatia, Estonia, Lithuania	Brazil, Columbia, Mexico, Panama		Algeria, Israel, Saudi Arabia	Morocco, Tunisia
B	Bulgaria, Latvia, Romania, Turkey	Dominican Republic, El Salvador, Guatemala, Perú, Uruguay	Indonesia, Philippines, Vietnam	Egypt, Jordan	Benin, Gabon, Mozambique, Senegal, Tanzania
C	Macedonia, Serbia, Russia	Argentina, Ecuador, Honduras, Jamaica, Paraguay, Venezuela	Bangladesh, Sri Lanka	Lebanon, Libya, Syria	Angola, Cameroon, Congo, Ethiopia, Ghana, Kenya, Madagascar, Togo, Uganda, Zambia
D	Albania, Belarus, Bosnia, Moldovia, Ukraine	Bolivia, Cuba, Guyana, Haiti, Nicaragua	Afghanistan, Cambodia, Laos, Mongolia, Nepal	Iran, Iraq, Pakistan, Yemen	Burundi, Chad, DR Congo, Ivory Coast, Malawi, Nigeria, Sierra Leone, Sudan, Zimbabwe

Source: Coface (www.coface.fr). Reproduced with permission.

The ratings assigned by Coface reflect the extent to which a country's economic, financial and political outlook influences financial commitments of local companies and are based on the Organisation for Economic Coordination and Development (OECD) consensus country ratings.

EXHIBIT 21.7

COUNTRY RATING SCALE USED BY COFACE (FRANCE)

A1 The **political and economic situation is very good**. A quality business environment has a positive influence on corporate payment behaviour. Corporate default probability is very low on average.

A2 The **political and economic situation is good**. A basically stable and efficient business environment nonetheless leaves room for improvement. Corporate default probability is low on average.

A3 Changes in generally good but **somewhat volatile political and economic environment** can affect corporate payment behaviour. A basically secure business environment can nonetheless give rise to occasional difficulties for companies. Corporate default probability is quite acceptable on average.

A4 A **somewhat shaky political and economic outlook** and a relatively volatile business environment can affect corporate payment behaviour. Corporate default probability is still acceptable on average.

B **Political and economic uncertainties** and an occasionally difficult business environment can affect corporate payment behaviour. Corporate default probability is appreciable.

C A **very uncertain political and economic outlook** and a business environment with many troublesome weaknesses can have a significant impact on corporate payment behaviour. Corporate default probability is high.

D A **high-risk political and economic situation** and an often very difficult business environment can have a very significant impact on corporate payment behaviour. Corporate default probability is very high.

Source: Coface. Reproduced with permission.

The emphasis has been added and is not in the original publication.

The country ratings assigned by Coface reflect the average level of short-term non-payment risk associated with companies in a particular country. It reflects the extent to which a country's economic, financial and political outlook influences financial commitments of local companies.

Under economic, financial and economic prospects, Coface lists risk factors such as:

- growth vulnerability
- sovereign financial vulnerability
- external indebtedness
- foreign exchange liquidity – crisis risk
- bank sector fragilities
- political vulnerabilities.

For the business climate, it indicates factors such as the quality and availability of financial information on local businesses, creditor protection and debt collection and the institutional environment as risk factors.

As with all such assessments, it is possible to look at quantitative variables, for instance the balance of payments and other measures of economic and financial performance of the country in question. However, given the complexities involved it is also normal to use qualitative variables, such as the current political situation and trends in government policy. Consequently, a wide range of indicators are used. Ultimately, the analysis is distilled down to a score or rating that is then assigned to the country. For instance, Exhibit 21.6 indicates that Coface assigns a rating of 'D' to Mongolia. This is the lowest rating in their scale. The mean of the rating is given in Exhibit 21.7 and indicates that the country shows evidence of a high-risk political and economic situation where the business environment is often very difficult and this can have a very significant impact on corporate payment behaviour. In addition, the risk of corporate default is very high.

Before You Go On

1. What are the key factors that determine country risk?
2. What is the major risk facing a company that establishes a business operation in a foreign country?

COST OF CAPITAL FOR INTERNATIONAL PROJECTS

Learning Objective 4

Explain how the cost of capital is determined for international projects.

As part of their assessment of the Oyu Tolgoi investment project and whether to proceed or not, the managers at Rio Tinto would have gauged the country risk. It is clear that international investments carry additional risks compared to domestic projects. We will look at the issues further in the next section, but clearly a key issue will be to incorporate this additional risk in the capital budgeting analysis.

One way to do this is to adjust the project's discount rate for the additional risk. For example, if the cost of capital is 8% and the financial manager's staff estimates that an investment in

South Africa requires an additional 3% expected return to compensate for the extra risk, the appropriate discount rate is 11%. Of course, from Chapters 7 and 13, we know that adjustments like this should only be made to the discount rate to reflect country risk that is systematic. Unsystematic risk should be reflected in the expected cash flows.

How can we incorporate this additional risk in international capital budgeting? Let us work through an example of a five-year mining project that has the following future cash flows (in € millions):

The investment is to be made in South Africa, a country given an 'A3' rating by Coface, and the country risk assessment suggests there is a 2.7% chance that in any year the country will expropriate the mining concession. If it does so, you expect to get no compensation. One should point out that this is somewhat unrealistic since as a foreign investor you would structure the operation to ensure that if expropriation took place, compensation would be paid. However, making this assumption simplifies our analysis.

In year 1, there is a 97.3% chance the operation is allowed to continue without being expropriated (100% − 2.7% = 97.3%). In year 2, the probability remains the same, but the company will only receive revenue from the mine now that it is entering into production if expropriation did not occur in year 1 and the same analysis in the following years. Exhibit 21.8 shows the pattern of the cash flows over the five years of the project. Expropriation will affect the projected cash flows the company receives. If expropriation does not take place, the company receives the estimated cash flows each year. If the country expropriates the mine, the company then receives nothing. Consequently, in each year the expected cash flows will be:

$$\begin{aligned}\text{Expected} \atop \text{cash flow} &= (1 - \text{Probability of expropriation}) \\ &\quad \times \text{Projected cash flows} \\ &\quad + \text{Probability of expropriation} \\ &\quad \times \text{Expropriation cash flow}\end{aligned}$$

(21.3)

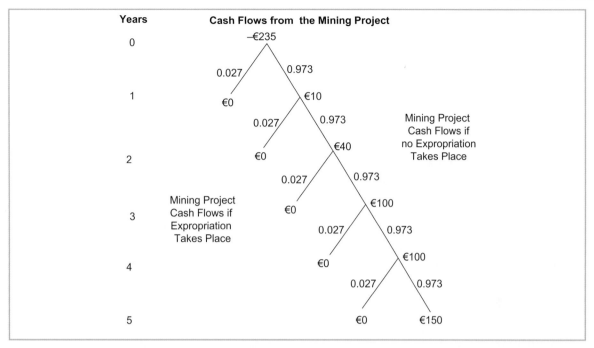

Exhibit 21.8: Expected Cash Flows from the High-Risk Country Mining Project The exhibit shows the possible cash flows for the foreign mining project. There is a 2.7% chance that the mining concession will be expropriated each year. If so, the company gets no compensation. If the mine is not expropriated it receives the estimated cash flows. The expected cash flow in year 1 is $(1 - 0.027) \times$ €10 million $+ 0.027 \times$ €0, or €9.73 million. For year 2, the company will only receive the second-year cash flow if expropriation has not occurred in year 1, so the expected payment will be $(0.973) \times (1 - 0.027) \times$ €40 $+ 0.1 \times$ €0, or €37.87 million. We proceed in the same way to estimate the expected cash flows for the subsequent years.

The expected cash flow in year 1 will be $(1 - 0.027) \times$ €10 million $+ 0.027 \times$ €0, or €9.73 million. For year 2, we only receive the second-year cash flow if there is no expropriation in year 1. The chance of no expropriation is 0.973, so the probability of not being expropriated in years 1 and 2 is 0.973×0.973, so the expected cash flow in year 2 will be $(0.973)^2 \times$ €40 million, that is €37.87 million.[8] The expected cash flows for years 3, 4 and 5 are €92.12, €89.63 and €130.81 million, respectively. We now discount these cash flows at our 8% cost of capital to determine their present value, namely:

The calculation is:

$$PV(\text{Cash flows}) = \frac{€9.73}{1.08} + \frac{€37.87}{(1.08)^2} + \frac{€92.12}{(1.08)^3}$$
$$+ \frac{€89.63}{(1.08)^4} + \frac{€130.81}{(1.08)^5}$$
$$= €9.001 + €32.47 + €73.13$$
$$+ €65.88 + €89.03$$
$$= €269.51$$

The net present value of the mining project is €34.51 million (€269.51 − €235).

Let us now value the capital project using the alternative method of using the add-on risk premium approach to the project discount rate. The company has estimated that the required rate of return for the project requires an additional 3% to

0	1	2	3	4	5	Years
−€235	€9.73	€37.87	€92.12	€89.63	€130.81	

BUILDING INTUITION

It is Best to Adjust the Cash Flows when Modelling Country Risk

Estimating the risk of expropriation or default is complex. In so far as this risk is non-systematic in nature, it is probably best to try and estimate the effect on the future cash flows rather than simply increase the discount rate. By estimating the impact of country risk on the cash flows, there is a real benefit in that it requires the analyst to focus on the risks and leads to better plans to mitigate them.

compensate for the additional country risk. In this case, we now want to discount the project's cash flows without adjusting for the risk of expropriation (that is, ignoring the country risk effect) as this is now captured in the higher discount rate. The calculation is therefore straightforward:

$$PV(\text{Cash flows}) = \frac{€10}{1.11} + \frac{€40}{(1.11)^2} + \frac{€100}{(1.11)^3}$$

$$+ \frac{€100}{(1.11)^4} + \frac{€150}{(1.11)^5}$$

$$= €9.001 + €32.47 + €73.13$$

$$+ €65.88 + €89.03$$

$$= €269.51$$

This leads to the same result as we obtained using the adjusted cash flows.

In practice, it may be very difficult to estimate the expropriation risk in an international capital project as we have done above. If we get it wrong, we are likely to overestimate or underestimate the attractions of the project. In addition, it is unlikely that the risk is the same every year. It is likely to increase with time since there is more uncertainty as we move further into the future. For instance, if in the above example, the risk of expropriation increases with time, starting at 2.7% in year 1, rising to 3.5% in year 2, 4.5% in years 3 and 6, and 7% in years 4 and 5, the net present value of the project would drop to €19.37 million. Hence, the attractions of the project are very dependent on having a good country risk estimate.

Learning by Doing Application 21.6

Estimating the Expected Cash Flows on a Foreign Project

Problem: Travaux Specialisé SA, a specialist construction company based in France, is looking to invest in a project to build a container port in the African state of Ghana. The project will take 3 years and the company will need to invest €50 million to build the port and receive future

cash flows of €20 million at the end of years 1 and 2 and €30 million at the end of year 3 from the port authorities. Ghana is rated 'C' by Coface and hence is seen as having a very uncertain economic and political outlook. Based on its research the company estimates there is a 4% risk of default on the payments the company is expected to receive on the project. If default occurs, the company will recover nothing. What are the expected cash flows and, if the company uses a 10% discount rate to value such projects, should the company go ahead with the investment?

Approach: We need to work out the expected cash flows knowing that the promised cash flows are not the expected cash flows since, if there is a default, the company receives nothing. Once we have the expected cash flows, we can discount these at the project discount rate of 10%.

Solution: Step 1 is to work out the expected cash flows:

Year 1 $E(CF_1) = 0.96 \times €20 + 0.04 \times €0 = €19.2$

Year 2 $E(CF_1) = (0.96)^2 \times €20 = €18.43$

Year 3 $E(CF_1) = (0.96)^3 \times €30 = €26.54$

We now discount these at the 10% required rate of return:

$$PV(CF) = \frac{€19.2}{1.1} + \frac{€18.43}{(1.1)^2} + \frac{€26.54}{(1.1)^3}$$

$$= €17.46 + €15.23 + €19.94$$

$$= €52.63$$

The company has to invest €50 million in the project, so the net present value will be €2.63 million (€52.63 − €50). The project adds value and hence the company can proceed.

Country Risk Premium

The country risk measures, such as the Coface ratings given in the previous section, regrettably do not include the probabilities of expropriation or default. Fortunately, we can use estimates from the securities markets to derive reasonable country risk interest rate adjustment factors. On the other hand, there are a great number of different methods and there is no agreement as to which is the best one. We will use a method developed by Aswath Damodaran that has the virtue of both being relatively simple and intuitive in its approach.[9]

The analysis starts with country ratings and proceeds as follows:

• *Country rating.* Determine the country rating from the various country ratings that are available, such as those provided by, for instance, A.M. Best, Coface, Fitch-IBCA, Institutional Investor, Moody's Investor Services, Political Risk Services or Standard & Poor's.

• *Estimate default spread for the rating.* This is determined by taking the yield on the government bond of the country and subtracting from this the yield on a default-free government bond (for instance, US government or

German government bonds). Market prices include all investors' insights into the underlying country risk and hence provide good estimates of the true likelihoods of default or expropriation.

• *Add default spread to mature market equity risk premium.* The default spread is added to give the country's total risk premium.

• *Adjusted country spread.* This involves adjusting the total risk premium for the relative equity market volatility for the country. This requires us to multiply by the product of the standard deviation of the equity market divided by the standard deviation of the country's bonds. The reason for this is that the bond spread alone underestimates the country risk since it is based on government-issued bonds, which will be given preferential treatment in any financial restructuring. The reason for the adjustment is that investors in corporate assets in foreign countries have more risk than investors in sovereign bonds. Their risk is more like that of an equity investor. Consequently, the spread needs to be adjusted upwards to reflect this fact.

Let us see how the approach works. We will use South Africa, which is an emerging market. As of 2010, the country is variously rated for country risk as follows:

Coface   A3
A.M. Best   CRT-3
Moody's   A3
Standard & Poor's   BBB+

In April 2010, bonds issued by South Africa have a yield of 5.15% compared to the benchmark US treasury bond yield for comparative 3.95%, giving a spread of 1.20% (5.15 − 3.95). The long-run volatility of the equity market in South Africa is 23.4% and for the bond market it is 9.4%.[10] The relative volatility of the equity and bond markets is therefore 2.5 times (23.4/9.4). The adjusted country spread is therefore 3.0% (1.2 × 2.5).

The world equity risk premium is 5.0%. This gives a total risk premium for South Africa of 8% based on the adjusted country spread of 3.0% plus the world equity premium of 5.0%.

We can check how good this estimate is since we have relatively good data for South Africa and the *Credit Suisse Global Investment Returns Yearbook* publishes estimates for the local equity risk premium. The long-run average for the period 1900–2009 for South Africa is 8.2%, when measured against short-term interest rates, and 7.2% measured against long-term interest rates. This is very close to the estimate we calculated.

Returning to our mining example, we now have been able to justify the extra return required on the investment. We first estimate the risk-adjusted rate of return for the capital project and then factor in the country risk to take account of the country-specific risk. Recall that in Chapter 7, we discussed how to estimate the expected return on an asset using Equation (7.9), which states:

$$E(R_i) = R_{rf} + \beta_i[E(R_m) - R_{rf}]$$

where $E(R_i)$ is the required expected return, R_{rf} is the risk-free rate of interest, β_i is asset i's systematic risk or beta and $[E(R_m) - R_{rf}]$ is the market risk premium. Using Equation (7.9) and knowing that

the beta for the project is 0.81, we have a required return of:

$$E(R_i) = R_{rf} + \beta_i[E(R_m) - R_{rf}]$$
$$= 3.95 + 0.81[5.0]$$
$$= 8.0\%$$

However, to account for the country risk and to determine the required return on the capital project, we adapt Equation (7.9) by adding a country risk premium, namely:

$$E(R_i) = R_{rf} + \text{Country risk premium} + \beta_i[E(R_m) - R_{rf}] \qquad (21.4)$$

Given an estimate for the default premium of 3%, as previously calculated, and using Equation (21.4) we can now establish the mining project's required rate of return as:

$$E(R_i) = R_{rf} + \text{Country risk premium} + \beta_i[E(R_m) - R_{rf}]$$
$$= 3.95 + 3.0 + 0.81[5.0]$$
$$= 11.0\%$$

Note that Equation (21.4) treats the country risk as a non-systematic factor. To the extent that country risk is a systematic factor, this will be captured in the beta, which will be higher as a result.

Issues With Country Risk Estimates

The risks of international investments are highest in high-risk countries, which are often seen as synonymous with emerging markets. These risks may include high and variable inflation rates, macroeconomic volatility, controls on the export of capital, political changes, war or civil unrest, changes to regulations, poorly defined or enforced contract and investor rights, lax accounting controls and corruption. Researchers have found that all the above factors do affect the cost of capital and hence the valuation of assets in such countries. Unfortunately, the standard models are often inadequate in dealing with these conditions. Adjusting the future cash flows or the discount rate helps to address this problem. However, there are still issues that can

Learning by
Doing
Application
21.7

Estimating the Required Return on a Foreign Project

Problem: You are assessing whether your company should invest in a capital project to manufacture fertiliser in Indonesia, an emerging market economy. You have the following information on the country. Moody's Investor Services rate it as 'Ba2' and Coface assign a rating of 'B'. Bonds issued by countries with these ratings trade at a 3.50% spread over German government bonds. For emerging markets, the ratio of equity market volatility to bond market volatility is 1.5 times. The world equity risk premium is 5% and the risk-free interest rate is 4%. If the project beta is estimated to be 1.20, what is an appropriate risk-adjusted discount rate to apply to the cash flows of the capital project?

Approach: We use Equation (21.4) to estimate the appropriate discount rate for the project. In order to apply the equation, we must first estimate the country risk premium for Indonesia. We need to work out the additional premium using the spread for Ba2 bonds and adjusting this for the relative volatility.

Solution: The spread is 3.5%. Adjusting this for the relative volatility of emerging market equities to bonds, we obtain 5.25% as the country risk premium (3.5 × 1.5). We can now apply Equation (21.4) to solve for the required return:

$$E(R_i) = R_{rf} + \text{Country risk premium} + \beta_i[E(R_m) - R_{rf}]$$
$$= 4 + 5.25 + 1.2[5.0]$$
$$= 9.25 + 6$$
$$= 15.25\%$$

You would want to discount the project's cash flows at a rate of 15.25% to determine the project's net present value.

greatly complicate the analysis. Some of the issues that affect the ability to obtain good estimates are:

- *Variation in the cost of capital between local firms and global firms.* In emerging markets, global firms in countries that derive a large part of their revenues outside their home market have lower cost of capital than firms in the same industry that operate only domestically. Therefore, for a foreign firm investing in the country, it is not clear whether the local or global cost of capital is appropriate.
- *The cost of capital is context sensitive.* Because of emerging market macroeconomic volatility and a tendency for emerging economies to experience periodic crises, estimates of the cost of

capital can vary significantly, depending on the business cycle and crises. It is therefore unclear whether it is appropriate to use a crisis cost of capital or normal conditions – or a blend of these – in evaluating capital projects. For instance, Moody's Investor Services has undertaken a comparison of default rates that indicates that the average emerging market 10-year cumulative default rate is about 20%, but this masks the fact that for countries that suffer a crisis, the 10-year cumulative rate is much higher at just over 28%. This represents a country risk spread of about 2.35% versus 3.74% in the two cases. Translated into a country risk spread using a 1.5 equity volatility to debt volatility factor gives a country risk premium of either 3.52% or 5.21%, a difference of 1.69%.

- *Lack of suitable data.* The quality of information and the estimation of the model parameters remain a significant issue. Not all emerging market countries have international debt issues and even when these exist, it is not always clear whether they are representative of rates. Domestic interest rates are also suspect in that they may be controlled and reflect the lack of alternative investment opportunities available to local investors. Furthermore, many emerging market countries have small and unrepresentative stock markets. For instance, Ghana, the equatorial African country, has a small stock market that in April 2010 consisted of 37 listed companies. However, one single company – AngloGold Ashanti Limited, the gold mining company – represented 78% of the total stock market capitalisation. Excluding the largest three listed companies, the average size of the remaining listed companies is only GhS 16.8 million (about €9 million). Given this, it is impossible to directly estimate a local cost of capital for firms and projects.

- *Inflation and devaluation.* Inflation rates in emerging markets tend to be both higher than in developed markets and more variable. The DCF approach requires the analyst to input the best estimates of the future expected cash flows and apply the appropriate discount rate. Uncertainty about future inflation creates problems in determining what the expected cash flows are likely to be. As discussed in Chapter 2, inflation affects nominal interest rates but will also affect expected cash flows. Very high levels of inflation, known as hyperinflation, seriously disrupt economic growth and the stability of countries. There is little agreement on how best to incorporate inflation into the project evaluation. Given that emerging market economies are prone to crises, it is no surprise that the currency can evidence sudden and large devaluations against the major world currencies such as the US dollar or the euro.

Before You Go On

1. When analysing a foreign project, what will lead us to adjust the cash flows of a capital project rather than the discount rate?
2. Why is it easier to add a country risk premium to the discount rate rather than estimate a probability of default or expropriation?
3. What are the major complications in deriving country risk estimates for some emerging market countries?

INTERNATIONAL CAPITAL BUDGETING

Learning Objective 5

Identify the major factors that distinguish international from domestic capital budgeting, explain how the capital budgeting process can be adjusted to account for these factors and compute the NPV for a typical international capital project.

Multinational firms have operations outside their home countries that range from simple sales offices to large manufacturing operations. As a legal and practical matter, most multinational firms set up separate foreign subsidiaries for each country in which they operate. When a multinational firm wants to consider overseas capital projects, the financial manager faces the decision of which capital projects should be accepted on a company-wide basis.

Fortunately, the overall decision-making framework and computational methods developed for domestic capital budgeting in Chapters 10–13 apply to international capital projects as well. Thus, the financial manager's goal is to seek out domestic and overseas capital projects whose cash flows yield a positive net present value (NPV). The decision to accept international projects with a positive NPV increases the value of the firm and is consistent with the fundamental goal of financial management, which is to maximise the value of shareholders' equity.

Furthermore, when a firm takes on capital projects overseas, the financial manager must determine the same inputs to compute a project's NPV as for a domestic project: (1) the project's net cash flows and (2) the appropriate discount rate. Although the same basic principles apply to both international and domestic capital budgeting, firms must deal with some differences. We now focus on those differences.

Determining Cash Flows

As we have discussed already, a number of issues complicate the determination of cash flows from overseas capital projects. First, most companies find it more difficult to estimate the incremental cash flows for foreign projects. Some of the problems may stem from the lack of first-hand knowledge by the parent company's financial staff of procedures and systems used at the overseas operations; other problems may arise because of differences in the accounting and legal systems, language and cultural differences.

Second, foreign subsidiaries can remit cash flows to the parent firm in a number of ways, most commonly through: (1) cash dividends; (2) royalty payments or licence agreement payments for use of patents or brand names; and (3) management fees for services the parent provides to a subsidiary. Problems with cash flows can arise when foreign governments restrict the amount of cash that can be repatriated, or returned, to the parent company and therefore out of the country. These **repatriation of earnings restrictions** may arise because foreign governments are politically sensitive to charges that large multinational companies are exploiting their countries and draining vital investment capital from their economies.

> **Repatriation of earnings restrictions**
>
> restrictions placed by a foreign government on the amount of cash that can be repatriated, or returned, to a parent company by a subsidiary doing business in the foreign country

Repatriation of earnings restrictions usually take the form of a ceiling on the amount of cash dividends that a foreign subsidiary can pay to its parent. The ceiling is typically some percentage of the firm's net worth and is intended to force the parent to reinvest in the foreign subsidiary. The repatriation of the project cash flows is a critical issue if there are any significant delays in receiving the funds. From the parent firm's perspective, the relevant cash flow for foreign capital investments is the cash flow that the parent company expects to actually receive from its foreign subsidiary.

Exchange Rate Risk

The next issue that financial managers have to deal with on international capital investments is foreign exchange rate risk. The cash flows from an overseas capital project will most likely be in a foreign currency that must eventually be converted to the parent company's home currency. This is not a simple task because most of the cash flows from capital projects are *future* cash flows. Thus, we cannot use the current spot rate to convert one currency to another. To convert the project's future cash flows into another currency, we need to come up with projected or forecast exchange rates.

Where can firms secure forecasts for exchange rates? Forecasts can be obtained from most banks or from currency specialists. One of the problems with obtaining currency rate forecasts for use in analysis of capital projects is that many capital projects have lives of 20 years, or more. It is difficult to accurately forecast exchange rates that far into the future.

EXHIBIT 21.9

SELECTED OECD COUNTRY RISK RATINGS FROM 1999 TO 2010

The Organisation of Economic Cooperation and Development (OECD) has produced country risk classifications since 1999. There are eight country risk classifications (0–7), where the very best rating is 0 and the worst is 7. The OECD applies (1) a proprietary and undisclosed quantitative assessment called the Country Risk Assessment Model that provides a quantitative assessment of country credit risk and (2) a qualitative assessment of the results of the Model to integrate factors such as political risk and/or other risk factors not taken (fully) into account by the quantitative model.

Country	1999	2004	2006	2008	2010	Difference 1999–2010
Argentina	5	7	7	7	7	−2
Botswana	2	2	2	2	3	−1
Brazil	6	6	4	3	3	3
Croatia	5	4	4	4	5	0
Ghana	6	6	6	6	6	0
Indonesia	6	6	5	5	4	2
Mongolia	7	7	7	6	6	1
Nicaragua	7	7	7	7	7	0
Peru	6	5	4	3	3	3
Slovak Republic	4	3	1	1	0	4
South Africa	3	3	3	3	3	0
Zimbabwe	5	7	7	7	7	−2

Source: Based on data from OECD (2010), Country Risk Classifications of the Participants to the Arrangement on Officially Supported Export Credits, accessed at: http://www.oecd.org/trade/xcred.

The Country Risk Classifications are produced solely for the purpose of setting minimum premium rates for transactions covered by the Export Credit Arrangement. Neither the participants to the arrangement nor the OECD Secretariat take any responsibility if these classifications are used for other purposes.

Country Risk

It is in the nature of many kinds of corporate investments that once the money is committed, they are largely irreversible. As we discussed earlier, when companies invest in foreign projects they enter into a different legal, business and social environment. Consequently, when analysing international investments, country risk assessments and any necessary adjustment to the project's cost of capital are complications that have to be addressed.

An added complication is that country risk does change over time, as Exhibit 21.9 shows. The exhibit uses the country risk classifications produced by the Organisation for Economic Cooperation and Development (OECD) since 1999. While there is obvious stability in the rankings, these have nevertheless changed over time. For the selected countries, Argentina is the worst performer, having fallen two rating categories. On the other hand, the Slovak Republic has risen by four categories. In 1999, the two countries were not dissimilar in their ratings. However, since then the two countries' risk profiles have changed dramatically. This reinforces the need for careful differentiation among countries and business sectors.

For the financial manager, country risk presents an important and complex problem that will be integral to the way the project is structured. Certain risks can be managed through insurance, hedging and other forms of financial planning. The manager should attempt to limit country risks and be aware that country risks can increase over the investment's life.

The SOCAFI Brazil Example

Suppose SOCAFI, a French manufacturing company, is considering the possibility of establishing a manufacturing operation in the São Paulo region of Brazil. SOCAFI wants the overseas capital investment decision to be based on the same criteria as domestic investment decisions. The firm's financial staff forecast the expected incremental after-tax free cash flows for the production plant in millions of Brazilian Real (R$), as shown in the following time line:

	0	1	2	3	4	5	Years
Cash flow	−R$20.0	R$6.00	R$6.00	R$6.00	R$6.00	R$6.00	

There are two ways we can approach the above analysis. The first method is to convert the cash flows into the home currency, the euro. The second is to undertake the analysis in the local currency and then convert the NPV at the current exchange rate. The major difference between the two approaches is when we convert from the foreign currency into the home currency. We will start by showing how SOCAFI would analyse the project using the home currency method and then do the same analysis in the foreign currency method.

Home Currency Method

We need to convert the project's future cash flows into euros. To do so, we need to recognise that the forward value of the exchange rate will follow the model laid out for forward contracts in Chapter 20.[11] The expected exchange rate (EFX) at time t will be:

$$E(S_t) = S_0 \times \frac{(1 + i_D)^t}{(1 + i_F)^t} \quad (21.5)$$

where i_D is the domestic or quoted currency interest rate and i_F is the foreign or base currency interest rate, S_0 is the current spot exchange rate and $E(S_t)$ is the expected exchange rate at time t.

If the exchange rate between the Brazilian Real and the euro is R$2.30/€ and the respective nominal interest rates are 7% in Brazil and 3% in euros, the expected exchange rates for the five years will be:

Year (t)	$(1 + i_D)^t/(1 + i_F)^t$	Expected Exchange Rate (R$/€)
0	1.0000	2.300
1	1.0400	2.389
2	1.0816	2.482
3	1.1249	2.579
4	1.1699	2.679
5	1.2167	2.783

As you can see from the table, the number of Real required to buy one euro increases with time. This is to be expected given that there is a difference in the nominal interest rates between the two currencies.

The next step is to convert the future cash flows at the expected exchange rate into euros, SOCAFI's home currency. This is shown in the following table:

Year (1)	Cash Flow (R$ millions) (2)	EFX Rate (R$/€) (3)	Calculation (4)	Cash Flow (€ millions) (5)
0	−R$17	R$2.300/€	−R$17/R$2.300/€	−€7.39
1	6	2.389	6/2.389	2.51
2	6	2.482	6/2.482	2.42
3	6	2.579	6/2.579	2.33
4	6	2.679	6/2.679	2.24
5	6	2.783	6/2.783	2.16

Column 2 shows the capital project's cash flows in Brazilian Real. Column 3 shows the current spot rate ($t = 0$) and the forecast foreign exchange rates ($t = 1$ to 5). In column 4, the cash flows in Real are divided by the appropriate exchange rate (spot or forecast) to convert to cash flows in euros and the results are shown in column 5. We divide in this case since the base currency for the exchange rate is euros and the quoted currency is the Real, so that there is an exchange rate of R\$2.30 = €1; each Real is worth 0.435 euros. For the investment at $t = 0$, the amount in Real is therefore R\$17.0/2.30 = €7.39 (or, equivalently, R\$17.0 × €0.435).

The required return for the business project in euros is 9% and the financial manager estimates that the project carries a 3% country risk premium. Thus, the appropriate discount rate for the project is 12%.

The NPV for the project is computed by discounting the cash flows by the country-risk-adjusted discount rate of 12%, as follows:

$$NPV = -€7.39 + \frac{€2.51}{1.12} + \frac{€2.42}{(1.12)^2} + \frac{€2.33}{(1.12)^3}$$

$$+ \frac{€2.24}{(1.12)^4} + \frac{€2.16}{(1.12)^5}$$

$$= -€7.39 + €2.24 + €1.93 + €1.66$$

$$+ €1.42 + €1.22$$

$$= €1.08 \text{ million}$$

The project should be accepted because its NPV is positive.

Foreign Currency Method

Using the foreign currency approach, we discount the project's future cash flows in the local currency, namely in Brazilian Real. However, we need to make an adjustment to the discount rate to reflect the higher anticipated inflation that is implied in the differences in interest rates. We would be seriously misguided if we discounted cash flows in Brazilian Real using a discount rate for the euro.[12] We need to make the appropriate

adjustment. The formula is:

$$(1 + \text{foreign required return}) = (1 + \text{local required return})$$
$$\times \frac{(1 + \text{foreign interest rate})}{(1 + \text{local interest rate})}$$

$$(21.6)$$

The appropriate required return when using the foreign currency will be:

$$(1 + \text{foreign required return}) = (1 + 0.12) \times \frac{(1 + 0.07)}{(1 + 0.03)}$$

$$= (1.12) \times 1.03884$$

$$= 1.1635, \text{ or } 16.35\%$$

We now apply this to the local currency cash flows:

$$NPV = -R\$17.0 + \frac{R\$6.0}{1.1635} + \frac{R\$6.0}{(1.1635)^2}$$

$$+ \frac{R\$6.0}{(1.1635)^3} + \frac{R\$6.0}{(1.1635)^4} + \frac{R\$6.0}{(1.1635)^5}$$

$$= -R\$17.0 + R\$5.157 + R\$4.432$$

$$+ R\$3.809 + R\$3.274 + R\$2.814$$

$$= R\$2.487 \text{ million}$$

Converting the amount in Brazilian Real into euros at the spot exchange rate gives €1.08 million (R\$2.487/R\$2.300/€). This is the same value we derived from the home currency method. We get the same value because the two methods are actually the same. With the home currency method, we need to forecast or estimate the future foreign exchange rates. In the foreign currency method, we rely on the implied forecast for the exchange rate reflected in the interest rate differential between the two currencies.

The simplest way is to calculate the NPV of the investment using the foreign currency cash flows and the foreign required return. The alternative method, converting the cash flows into the home currency, requires the company to determine the forward exchange rates that apply to these cash flows and discount these home currency cash flows using the home currency required return.

The home currency approach requires the analyst to forecast the exchange rates over the life of the project. This can lead to valuation errors if not carefully done. For major currencies, publicly quoted forward rates are available for up to a year. But few market-determined forward rates are available beyond that. There are long-term currency forecasts available from a variety of sources, but these often vary widely. They can lead to significant errors in the project values. On the other hand, the use of explicit forecasts can be used for sensitivity analysis to show how shifts in the exchange rate affect the project's NPV. It is also clear how the required return is determined.

It is also important that the cash flows relate to those that the owner can obtain. Often, local rules

mean that some of the cash generated from the foreign project must remain in the country due to restrictions on repatriation. In our example, the cash flows for the project are the cash flows that SOCAFI, France, estimates it will be able to receive from the investment.

Finally, we can see from the analysis that the SOCAFI Brazilian project has a number of different risks. The first is whether the project will return the initial investment. Then there is a second issue relating to the future behaviour of the Brazilian Real against the euro. As discussed in Chapter 20, SOCAFI needs to be clear which commercial bets it wants to take and which it wants to hedge. It may like the business climate in Brazil, but have less confidence in the future of the currency against the euro.

Learning by Doing Application 21.8

International Capital Budgeting

Problem: A German electronics firm is establishing a manufacturing plant in Taiwan to produce components that will be sold by the unit to customers in Taiwan. The cost of the investment is €10 million. The project is expected to last five years and then shut down. The company usually uses a discount rate of 7.5% for domestic projects like this, but for this project, the financial manager adds a 2.5% country risk premium. Shown here are the expected cash flows in millions of Taiwanese dollars (TWD) and the forecasted year-end exchange rates between the euro and the Taiwanese dollar.
What is the NPV of this project?

Approach: Since we know the expected cash flows in the foreign currency and the expected exchange rates, we can calculate the expected cash flows to the parent firm in euros by dividing the TWD cash flows by the appropriate exchange rate. We also must adjust the project discount for the 2.5% country risk premium.

Solution: The following table shows the cash flows the German firm expects to receive from its Taiwanese subsidiary in euros:[13]

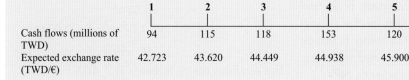

	1	2	3	4	5 Years
Cash flows (millions of TWD)	94	115	118	153	120
Expected exchange rate (TWD/€)	42.723	43.620	44.449	44.938	45.900

Year	Cash Flows (TWD millions)		Exchange Rate		Cash Flows (€ millions)
0					−€10.00
1	94	÷	42.723	=	2.200
2	115	÷	43.620	=	2.636
3	118	÷	44.449	=	2.655
4	153	÷	44.938	=	3.405
5	120	÷	45.900	=	2.614

The appropriate discount rate is 2.5% over the discount rate that the firm normally uses for domestic capital budgeting projects. Thus, the discount rate to be used is 10% (2.5 + 7.5). By

discounting the cash flows at the risk-adjusted discount rate of 10%, we can compute the NPV for this project:

$$NPV = -€10.00 + \frac{€2.200}{1.10} + \frac{€2.636}{(1.10)^2}$$

$$+ \frac{€2.655}{(1.10)^3} + \frac{€3.405}{(1.10)^4} + \frac{€2.614}{(1.10)^5}$$

$$= -€10.00 + €2.000 + €2.179$$

$$+ €1.995 + €2.325 + €1.623$$

$$= €0.12$$

Since the NPV is positive, the project should be accepted.

Learning by Doing Application 21.9

Foreign Currency Required Return for an International Project

Problem: A British company is looking to establish a manufacturing plant in Belgium to service the European market. The company estimates that the beta of the project is 0.90 and the market risk premium is 5%. The risk-free rate is 4% in the United Kingdom and for the eurozone it is 3%. The company has decided to analyse the project based on the future cash flows in euros. It wants to use the correct required return for projects in euros.

Approach: We need to first estimate the project's required return using Equation (7.9) and then convert the required return for the project from British pounds into euros using Equation (21.6). This foreign currency required return can then be used to estimate the project's NPV.

Solution: The first step is to calculate the project's expected return in British pounds using the required return Equation (7.9):

$$E(R_i) = R_{rf} + \beta_i[E(R_m) - R_{rf}]$$

$$= 4 + 0.90[5.0]$$

$$= 8.5\%$$

The next step is to apply Equation (21.6):

$$\left(1 + \begin{array}{c} \text{foreign} \\ \text{required return} \end{array}\right) = \left(1 + \begin{array}{c} \text{local} \\ \text{required return} \end{array}\right)$$

$$\times \frac{(1 + \text{foreign interest rate})}{(1 + \text{local interest rate})}$$

$$= (1 + 0.085) \times \frac{(1 + 0.03)}{(1 + 0.04)}$$

$$= (1 + 0.085) \times 0.9810$$

$$= 1.0746$$

$$= 1.0746 - 1 = 0.0746,$$

or 7.46%

The required return in euros is 7.46%.

Before You Go On

1. What difficulties do firms face in estimating cash flows from an overseas project?
2. Why is the repatriation of cash flows from an overseas project considered critical?
3. When do companies have to consider country or political risk?

ISLAMIC FINANCE

Learning Objective 6
Discuss how Islamic finance arrangements are different and the implications for financial management in countries that use *Sharī'ah* law.

Islamic finance illustrates the possible cultural and institutional differences that exist between countries when doing business – and sometimes within them too. For its followers, Islam governs all aspects of human life (social, economic and political), and consequently affects the way individuals and companies do business. The body of Islamic law that must be adhered to is called *Sharī'ah*, which can be translated as 'the clear path to be followed and observed'.[14] Based on *Sharī'ah*, economic activities are, in a sense, regulated as to whether they are permitted (*halal*) or forbidden (*harram*). This means that, in countries which operate under *Sharī'ah* law, commercial activities are required to conform to these rules.

The key elements of *Sharī'ah* law that influence financial management and are generally referred to as Islamic finance are given in Exhibit 21.10. These relate to social and economic issues, for instance – such as the distribution of wealth, the role of society, fair dealing or transparency in transactions and agreements, and 'asset finance'. A major feature of Islamic finance is that interest on borrowed money or *riba*, which is sometimes translated as usury, is

EXHIBIT 21.10
KEY FEATURES OF ISLAMIC FINANCE

Islamic finance integrates religious, social, ethical and legal concepts in a way that requires companies to work within a religious and ethical framework where there are strong rules as to what constitutes right and wrong actions. Underlying permitted activities (*halal*) and forbidden activities (*harram*) are concepts of how wealth is created and used, risk and profit sharing, as well as a requirement that investments and profit sharing relate to assets. In Islamic finance, money has no value and hence can earn no profit.

1. **Wealth must be equitably distributed** An economy where individuals and organisations can earn interest (*riba*) will lead to wealth being concentrated in the hands of the few at the expense of the many. Lenders will always prefer borrowers with existing assets and collateral, who will use the money to generate further wealth.
2. **The middle path** This means avoiding extremes. From a finance perspective, this means that individuals and organisations are not permitted to disregard society's interest in the pursuit of wealth.
3. **Transparency** Buyers and sellers must be fully informed of the nature of the contract they are entering if it is to be valid. It must have no hidden or unnecessary uncertainties (*gharar*) that would allow one side to benefit at the expense of the other. So a sales contract requires that the quantity and amounts be clearly specified.
4. **Asset finance and the nature of money** Only assets of inherent value can be traded for profit. Consequently, assets without value cannot be traded. Money has no inherent value and hence cannot be traded for profit. Lending money to earn interest (*riba*) is consequently prohibited.

clearly forbidden. There has been some misunderstanding about this concept. *Riba* precludes interest on money, the reason being that money has no intrinsic value; it is simply a measure of value and a means of exchange. Since money has no intrinsic value, there should be no charge (that is, interest) for its use since it is not, of itself, an asset. While interest on money is prohibited, it is permitted to earn a return on economic activities using real assets that provide a return for their use. Consequently, Islamic finance may be considered to be 'asset-based' rather than 'money-based'. That is, an investment is structured around the ownership or exchange of assets, where money is simply the payment mechanism.

There are other differences too. Parties to contracts should not be exposed to *gharar*, which is often translated as preventable ambiguity or uncertainty. This means that both parties should know what they are committing to. For instance, because there is uncertainty in insurance contracts, these are not allowed activities (i.e. they are *harram*). Gharar does not apply to reasonable, unavoidable business risk. Also, activities like gambling (*maisir*) are prohibited. There is a distinction made between the normal risks that arise in business activities and activities designed to produce payoffs linked to chance outcomes. To be acceptable and enforceable, any financial or business arrangement is required to be *Sharī'ah*-compliant.

WEB

You can read about Islamic standards and key interpretations of *Sharī'ah* law at the Islamic Finance Standard Board: http://www.ifsb.org/.

Islamic Finance Instruments

Islamic finance has developed a range of financial instruments or structures that are *Sharī'ah*-compliant. The most common ones are given below.

• *Murabaha.* This is 'cost-plus' pricing. Under this arrangement, commodities are purchased and then resold at a predetermined mark-up price. For example, a German company is engaged to build a power station in a country that requires contracts to conform to *Sharī'ah* law. The contract would be structured as follows. The local utility company would sign a 'promise to purchase' agreement at a predetermined price and payment schedule with the German company. This allows the German company to go ahead and build and deliver the power station. The utility company enters into a *Murabaha* contract to purchase the asset for a fixed price over a fixed period of time. From the perspective of the German company, the cash flows it ultimately receives are the same as those for a normal commercial contract. However, the way the agreement is structured means the contract is *Sharī'ah*-compliant.

• *Ijara.* This is best seen as a lease agreement where the lessee, the party that uses the asset provided under the lease, has an obligation to purchase the asset at the maturity of the lease for a fixed price. To be *Sharī'ah*-compliant, the rental element – that is, the payment for the use of the asset – is treated as separate to payments 'on account' to acquire the asset. The lessor, the party providing the asset and receiving the payments, has a separate contract agreeing to sell the asset to the lessee at the maturity of the *Ijara* contract.

• *Musharaka.* In essence, a partnership contract. It involves a joint venture agreement where the parties contribute either real assets or money to buy real assets, or one party contributes money to buy real assets and the other party provides real assets it already owns. All the essential requirements of Islamic finance are to be found within this *Sharī'ah*-compliant contract: the sharing of risk, the proportionate sharing of profits and losses, the absence of interest and the investment being asset-based. Both parties are, in essence, equity investors, where the profits are shared according to the agreement between the partners while losses are shared pro-rata to the amount each party has invested. There is a variant on *musharaka* called *modaraba*, in which the contribution by the partners is either real assets or expertise rather than simply real assets or money to acquire real assets.

- *Salam* and *Istisna'a* are both forms of forward contract. A *salam* contract involves the immediate payment for assets that are to be delivered at some future date. The agreement is *Sharī'ah*-compliant and is free of *riba* and *gharar* since it is based on the genuine needs of the business and consequently beneficial to both the buyer and seller. The seller gets the money they need in advance in exchange for the obligation to deliver the asset at a later date. The purchaser gets the asset they need at the required time. *Istisna'a* differs from the *salam* contract in that the assets to be delivered do not exist at the time the contract is entered into. As such, it can be considered an order placed with a producer to make the asset for the given delivery date.

If one just looked at the cash flows from the above Islamic instruments and compared these to similar conventional finance arrangements, it would be hard to tell the difference. For a financial manager, as discussed in Chapter 6, the key task is to determine the cash flows and discount them at the appropriate risk-adjusted rate of interest.

Nevertheless, a key issue for a foreign company operating in a country which applies *Sharī'ah* law to commercial arrangements is to comply with the rules and make the corporate structure and contracts *Sharī'ah*-compliant.

Unfortunately, there is no universally recognised interpretation of the law and set of rules, although organisations such as the Islamic Finance Standard Board are seeking to develop agreed instruments. Different countries will have variations based on locally developed interpretation, and it is important to understand how the rules will be interpreted at the country level. For instance, as arrangements above indicate, ownership of assets to be delivered will be held by the foreign company. In some cases, such as building a power station, this could be for a considerable period. It therefore raises legal issues of ownership, for instance, risk to the asset, insurance and maintenance, as well as how these assets and payments will be treated for tax purposes, both in the foreign country and in the company's home country. Finally, contractual arrangements are likely to be complex and require specialist lawyers and advisors, which will raise the cost of doing business in countries where *Sharī'ah* law applies.

Before You Go On

1. Why does Islamic finance prohibit the payment of interest on borrowed money?
2. Why is transparency and openness an important consideration in Islamic finance contracts?

SUMMARY OF LEARNING OBJECTIVES

1. **Discuss how the basic principles of finance apply to international financial transactions.**

   The basic principles of managerial finance remain the same whether a transaction is domestic or international. For example, the time value of money calculations remain the same, as do the models used to calculate asset values. What does change, however, are some of the input variables. These variables may be affected by cultural or procedural differences between countries, such as a country's unique currency, or differences in tax and accounting standards.

2. **Differentiate among the spot rate, the forward rate and the cross rate in the foreign exchange markets, perform foreign exchange and cross rate calculations and be able to hedge an asset purchase where payment is made in a foreign currency.**

   The spot rate is the exchange rate at which one currency can be converted to another immediately, whereas the forward rate is a rate agreed on today for an exchange to take place at a specified point in the future. Forward rates are usually different from spot rates and are the market's best estimate of what a future spot rate will be. The cross rate is simply the exchange rate between two currencies. Learning by Doing Applications 21.1–21.3 are foreign exchange rate problems that you should be able to solve.

3. **Describe the factors that affect country risk and country risk ratings.**

   Engaging in international activities exposes firms to country risk. Financial managers need to take account of country risk in their evaluation. Countries vary in the degree to which unanticipated changes in legal and political conditions will affect a foreign business, including war or public unrest. In the worst case, the local government could expropriate the foreign investment or make business in the country more difficult through changes in tax laws, limiting foreign remittances, or passing laws and regulations concerning the conduct of foreign business activities or ownership. A country risk rating is a summary measure of the risk that companies have in operating in that country and reflects the extent to which a country's economic, political and financial outlook affect contractual commitments.

4. **Explain how the cost of capital is determined for international projects.**

   The cost of capital for international projects needs to include a premium for the additional risk of the foreign country in which the project is to be based. There are two approaches which involve either adjusting the cash flows for the risk or adjusting the required return to include the country risk premium. Learning by Doing Applications 21.6 and 21.7 illustrate the approach to determining the international cost of capital.

5. **Identify the major factors that distinguish international from domestic capital budgeting, explain how the capital budgeting process can be adjusted to account for these factors and compute the NPV for a typical international capital project.**

   One issue that distinguishes international from domestic capital budgeting is the difficulty in estimating the incremental cash flows from an international project. These difficulties can stem from differences in operating, accounting and legal practices, as well as from the variety of ways in which a multinational firm can transfer profits and funds from the subsidiary to the parent corporation. Furthermore, firms engaged in international capital budgeting face two risks that domestic firms do not have to deal with: foreign exchange rate risk and country risk. The SOCAFI Brazil example (see Learning by Doing Application 21.8) illustrates capital budgeting calculations.

6. **Discuss how Islamic finance arrangements are different and the implications for financial management in countries that use *Sharī'ah* law.**

   The way Islamic finance operates reflects the different social and cultural norms of Islam as embodied in *Sharī'ah* law. The way these rules are applied means that finance decisions and structures are not divorced from social issues. There is a requirement for contractual arrangements to consider society at large and to be transparent and fair to both parties. A notable feature of Islamic finance is the prohibition on earning interest (*riba*) on money, which has no intrinsic value. Only assets can earn an economic return. Islamic finance encourages the sharing of risks and the proportionate sharing of profits.

SUMMARY OF KEY EQUATIONS

Equation	Description	Formula
(21.1)	Bid–ask (offer) spread	$\text{Bid–ask(offer)spread} = \dfrac{\text{Ask(offer)rate} - \text{Bid rate}}{\text{Ask rate}}$
(21.2)	Forward premium (discount)	$\text{Forward premium(discount)}$ $= \dfrac{\text{Forward rate} - \text{Spot rate}}{\text{Spot rate}} \times \dfrac{360}{n} \times 100$
(21.3)	Expected cash flow	$= (1 - \text{Probability of expropriation})$ $\times \text{Projected cash flows}$ $+ \text{Probability of expropriation}$ $\times \text{Expropriation cash flow}$
(21.4)	Required return on foreign investment	$E(R_i) = R_{rf} + \text{Country risk premium} + \beta_i[E(R_m) - R_{rf}]$
(21.5)	Expected exchange rate	$E(S_t) = S_0 \times \dfrac{(1 + i_D)^t}{(1 + i_F)^t}$
(21.6)	Foreign currency required return	$(1 + \text{foreign required return})$ $= (1 + \text{local required return})$ $\times \dfrac{(1 + \text{foreign interest rate})}{(1 + \text{local interest rate})}$

SELF-STUDY PROBLEMS

21.1. If a Volkswagen Passat costs $26 350 in the United States and €21 675 in Germany, what is the implied exchange rate between the US dollar and the euro?

21.2. ECN AG, a German electronic systems manufacturer, is planning to purchase flash memory from one of two sources. Kyoto KK, a Japanese company, quotes a price of ¥8900 per gigabyte. The current exchange rate is ¥121.57/€. A South Korean manufacturer offers to supply the same flash memory at a price of KRW118 240 per gigabyte. The spot rate available is KRW11.92/¥. Which is the cheaper source of flash memory for ECN AG?

21.3. Calculate the cost of capital for an international project if the company has estimated that the beta (β) for the project is 1.3, the risk-free interest rate is 4% and the risk premium is 5%. Bonds issued by the country trade at a premium of 2.50% over risk-free government debt and the relative volatility of the stock market to bond market volatilities is 1.5 times.

21.4. Milan International S.p.A., an Italian company engaged in oil and gas construction, has a project in Libya to develop a liquefied gas compression plant. The investment will cost the company €10 million and it will receive the following cash flows:

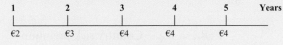

The company estimates the cost of capital for the project at 10%. What is the net present value of the project?

21.5. In 21.4, subsequently, Milan International has been told there is a 5% chance each year that Libya will expropriate the project, in which case, Milan International will receive nothing in compensation. Given this, what is the expected NPV given the risk of expropriation?

SOLUTIONS TO SELF-STUDY PROBLEMS

21.1. Cost of the car in the United States = $26 350

Cost of the car in Germany = €21 675

$$\text{Dollar to euro exchange rate} = \frac{\$26\,350}{€21\,675}$$

$$= \$1.2157/€$$

21.2. Cost from Vendor 1:

Flash memory price quote = ¥8900 per gigabyte

Spot rate for euro = ¥121.57/€

Cost to ECN AG in euro = ¥8900/¥121.57

$$= €73.21$$

Cost from Vendor 2:

Flash memory price quote = KRW118 240 per gigabyte

$$\text{Spot rate for South Korean won} = \text{KRW11.92/¥}$$

To compute the cost in euros, we need to compute the cross rate between the euro and the South Korean won.

¥121.57/€ × KRW11.92/¥ = KRW1449.11/€

Cost to ECN *AG* in euro

= KRW118 240/KRW1449.11/€

= €81.60 per gigabyte

The first vendor has the cheaper quote for ECN AG.

21.3. The cost of capital will be found by solving for:

$$E(R_i) = R_{rf} + \text{Country risk premium} + \beta_i[E(R_m) - R_{rf}]$$

The country risk premium will be 2.5 × 1.5 = 5%.

The cost of capital for the international project will therefore be:

$$E(R_i) = R_{rf} + \text{Country risk premium} + \beta_i[E(R_m) - R_{rf}]$$

$$= 4\% + 5\% + 1.3[5\%]$$

$$= 15.5\%$$

21.4. The net present value for the project is calculated as:

$$NPV = -€10 + \frac{€2}{1.10} + \frac{€3}{(1.10)^2} + \frac{€4}{(1.10)^3}$$

$$+ \frac{€4}{(1.10)^4} + \frac{€4}{(1.10)^5}$$

$$= -€10 + €1.79 + €2.39 + €2.85$$

$$+ €2.54 + €2.27$$

$$= €1.84$$

21.5. When there is a 5% risk of expropriation without compensation, the net present value is:

$$NPV = -€10 + \frac{€2 \times (0.95)}{1.10}$$

$$+ \frac{€3 \times (0.95)^2}{(1.10)^2} + \frac{€4 \times (0.95)^3}{(1.10)^3}$$

$$+ \frac{€4 \times (0.95)^4}{(1.10)^4} + \frac{€4 \times (0.95)^5}{(1.10)^5}$$

$$= -€10 + €1.70 + €2.16 + €2.44$$

$$+ €2.07 + €1.76$$

$$= €0.12$$

CRITICAL THINKING QUESTIONS

21.1. Royal Dutch Shell, an oil company, has headquarters in both the Netherlands and the United Kingdom. What type of firm is it?

21.2. International economic integration and technological changes in the last couple of decades have dramatically increased globalisation across many industries. Explain how a biotech firm or a medical firm (for example, a hospital) takes advantage of these changes.

21.3. In Europe, managers are asked to focus on maximising shareholder value. Is this consistent with the goals of managers in Indonesia and Japan?

21.4. A French farmer's cooperative sold wheat to a grain company in Russia. Under what circumstances will the French farmers be exposed to foreign exchange risk? When will the Russian importer be facing foreign exchange risk?

21.5. What are the main problems with country risk estimates?

21.6. Why is it we treat the 'country risk premium' as separate from the 'market risk premium' when calculating the cost of capital for international projects?

21.7. Madrid Fabrics SA is a Spanish clothes manufacturer with a production plant in Morocco. This morning, the Moroccan government introduced a new law prohibiting the repatriation of any funds from the country for another two years. What type of risk does Madrid Fabrics face?

21.8. When is it appropriate to adjust the cash flows for country risk and when is it appropriate to adjust the required rate of return?

21.9. What is the main difference between using the 'home currency method' as against the 'foreign currency method'?

21.10. Why is it possible to describe Islamic finance as 'asset-based finance'?

QUESTIONS AND PROBLEMS

Basic

21.1. Spot rate: Ryan, on holiday from Ireland, wants to buy a pair of leather shoes at Harrods in London that is priced at £113.60. If the exchange rate that day is €1.1522/£, what is Ryan's cost in euros?

21.2. Spot rate: Crescent Milan S.p.A. made a recent sale to a firm in Mexico that produced revenues of 13 144 800 Mexican pesos (MPs). If Crescent sold the pesos to its bank and was credited with €1 125 579.69, what was the spot rate at which the pesos were converted?

21.3. Spot rate: Given the following direct quotes, calculate the equivalent indirect quotes.
a. €0.0684/Mexican peso
b. £0.6113/€
c. Rs 31.64/C$

21.4. Forward rate: Explain the relationship between each pair of currencies.

	Spot Rate	Forward Rate
a.	$1.8316/£	$1.7874/£
b.	¥110.45/$	¥108.33/$
c.	C$1.3111/$	C$1.2933/$

21.5. Forward rate: Suppose a BMW 745i is priced at $57 750 in New York and €48 387 in Berlin. In which place is the car more expensive if the spot rate is $1.1935/€?

21.6. Forward rate: The spot rate for the Moroccan Dirham (Dh.) against the euro is Dh.9.5/€. If the 1-year interest rate in Morocco is 10% and in the eurozone it is 3.5%, what will be the 1-year forward foreign exchange rate between the two currencies?

21.7. Forward rate: A British company, Brilliant Equipment plc, purchased machinery from a Japanese firm and must make a payment of ¥313.25 million in 45 days. The bank quotes a forward rate of ¥170.75/£ to buy the required yen. What is the cost to Brilliant in British pounds?

21.8. Forward rate: Triumph Automotive AG has contracted with an Indian software firm for design software. The payment of 22 779 750 Indian rupees (Rs) is due in 30 days. What is the cost in euros if the 30-day forward rate is Rs 55.10/€?

21.9. Forward rate: Crane, Inc., sold equipment to an Irish firm and will receive €1 319 405 in 30 days. If the company entered a forward contract to sell at the 30-day forward rate of $1.1912/€, what is the US dollar amount received?

21.10. Bid–ask spread: Nova Scotia Bank offers quotes on the Canadian dollar, as given here. What is the bid–ask spread based on these quotes?

Bid	Ask
C$0.7273/$	C$0.7278/$

21.11. Bid–ask spread: A foreign exchange dealer is willing to buy the Danish krona (DKr) at $0.1556/DKr and will sell it at a rate of $0.1563/DKr. What is the bid–ask spread on the Danish krona against the US dollar?

21.12. Country risk: What happens to country risk spreads if the country risk rating of a particular country is (a) raised and (b) lowered?

21.13. Country risk: What are the two major components of country risk?

21.14. Country risk: What do country risk spreads indicate about country risk?

21.15. Country risk: What are the two main approaches to evaluating country risk?

21.16. International cost of capital: A company has a foreign contract to receive €150 million in two years' time. There is a 2% chance that the foreign buyer will default. If default takes place, the company can expect to recover €80 million from taking out export credit insurance. What is the expected value of the future receipt?

21.17. International cost of capital: Why can we use the spread between a country's bonds as an estimate of country risk?

21.18. International capital budgeting: What is explicit and what is implicit in the analysis when we use the home country method and the foreign currency method for evaluating an international capital investment?

21.19. International capital budgeting: What additional risks is a company taking when it undertakes a foreign project?

21.20. Islamic finance: What do the terms 'halal' and 'harram' mean in the context of a proposed transaction?

Intermediate

21.21. Forward premium: The spot rate on the London market was £0.5514/$, while the 90-day forward rate was £0.5589/$. What is the annualised forward premium or discount on the period?

21.22. Forward premium: Bank of America quoted the 180-day forward rate on the Swiss franc at $0.7902/SFr. The spot rate was quoted at $0.7766/SFr. What is the forward premium or discount on the Swiss franc?

21.23. Forward premium: The foreign exchange department at Tokyo's Daiwa Bank quoted the spot rate on the euro at €0.007269/¥. The 90-day forward rate is quoted at a premium of 5.42% on the euro. What is the 90-day forward rate?

21.24. Bid–ask spread: The foreign exchange department of Bank of India has a bid quote on Indian rupees (Rs) of Rs 43.21/$. If the bank typically tries to earn a bid–ask spread of 0.5% on these foreign exchange transactions, what will the ask rate be?

21.25. International cost of capital: The risk-free interest rate is 4%, the market risk premium is 5% and the beta for the project is 0.95. The spread on the foreign country bonds over risk-free bonds is 1.50%. The volatility of the country stock market is 43% and that

---

Indonesian Rupiahs (millions)

---

for the bond market is 29%. What is the appropriate required return for the project?

21.26. International cost of capital: If a company's local required rate of return is 10%, the local currency risk-free interest rate is 5% and the foreign currency interest rate is 3.5%, what is the company's foreign currency required rate of return?

21.27. EXCEL® **International capital budgeting:** Pejar Construcción SA has been commissioned to build a dam in Iraq. The cost is estimated at US$50 million and future cash flows it will receive from undertaking the project are as follows:

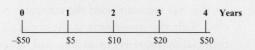

0	1	2	3	4	Years
–$50	$5	$10	$20	$50	

The required return on the project is 16%. What is the NPV (a) based on the cash flows it will receive and (b) given that the company estimates there is a 1% chance of expropriation. If expropriation takes place, the company will receive no compensation.

21.28. International capital budgeting: Which of the three main complications in analysing international projects is also a complication for projects located in a company's home country?

21.29. EXCEL® **International capital budgeting:** DieNeun AG has identified the following project in Indonesia that requires an investment of €20 million. The current exchange rate is Indonesian Rupiah (Rp) 12 048.20/€. The domestic interest rate in Indonesia is 8% and for the eurozone it is 3%. The company uses a 15% required return for evaluating the project in euros. Should the company proceed with the investment?

1	2	3	4	Years
Rp 85 000	Rp 92 000	Rp 108 500	Rp 87 500	

21.30. Islamic finance: What is the major difference between a *Musharaka* and a *Modaraba* agreement?

21.31. Islamic finance: Why is transparency such an important characteristic of Islamic finance contracts?

21.32. Islamic finance: In what way is the following quotation true or untrue of the way Islamic finance works? 'It is permissible to remove uncertainty through forward contracts if there is a real asset that will be delivered at the maturity of the contract.'

Advanced

21.33. Cosmos Sporting Goods plc has imported leather football boots from a Thai firm for a total cost of 3 125 750 bahts. Cosmos plans to purchase the Thai bahts at the time the payment is due in 90 days. Today, the Thai baht has a 90-day forward quote of £0.0201/baht. Now suppose that three months later, Cosmos purchases the bahts at the prevailing spot rate of £0.0196/baht. How much did Cosmos lose by not hedging?

21.34. Covington Industries plc sold equipment to a Mexican firm. Payment of 11 315 000 pesos will be due to Covington in 30 days. Covington has the option of selling the pesos at a 30-day forward rate of pesos 18.69/£. If it waits 30 days to sell the pesos, the expected spot rate is Mexican pesos 18.73/£. In British pounds, how much

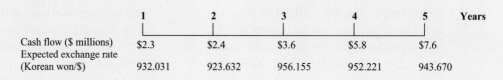

	1	2	3	4	5	Years
Cash flow ($ millions)	$2.3	$2.4	$3.6	$5.8	$7.6	
Expected exchange rate (Korean won/$)	932.031	923.632	956.155	952.221	943.670	

better or worse off is Covington by selling the pesos in the forward market?

21.35. Bayer Garden exports its specialised lawn care products to Canada. It has just made a sale worth C$1 150 000, with the payment due in 90 days. Its banker has given it a forward quote of C$1.3379/€. By using the forward rate, the firm gains an additional €6433.25 over what it would have got if it had sold the Canadian dollars in the spot market 90 days later. What was the spot rate at the time the payment was received?

21.36. Why is the ability of investors undertaking projects in a foreign country to remit funds from the country seen as such an important factor in analysing country risk?

21.37. Rio Tinto Zinc is planning to open a mine in Bolivia. The company estimates that the systematic risk of the project is 1.20, the risk-free rate of interest is 4% and the market risk premium is 5%. The country risk premium on Bolivian bonds is 5.50%. The local stock market has a volatility of 52% and the volatility of Bolivian bonds is 35%. What is the appropriate required return that Rio Tinto Zinc should use on cash flows from the project?

21.38. [EXCEL®] Moon Rhee Auto Supply, a Korean supplier of parts to Kia Motors, is evaluating an opportunity to set up a plant in Alabama, where Kia Motors has an auto assembly plant for its SUVs. The cost of this plant will be $13.5 million. The current spot rate is 946.53 Korean won per US dollar. The firm is expected to use this plant for the next five years and is expecting to generate the following cash flows:

The firm uses a discount rate of 9% for projects in the United States.

What is the NPV of this project? Should Moon Rhee Auto Supply take on this project?

21.39. [EXCEL®] Indesit is considering two mutually exclusive foreign investment opportunities to supply the fast-expanding Pacific-rim area with white goods. The first would be situated in Hawaii (part of the United States) and the second in Australia. The cash flows for the two projects are given below:

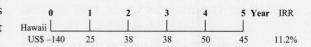

	0	1	2	3	4	5 Year	IRR
Hawaii	US$ –140	25	38	38	50	45	11.2%

An analyst has calculated the internal rate of return (IRR) for the two projects and based on this has recommended the company proceed with the investment in Australia. The financial manager is not so sure and has collected the following additional information:

	Interest rates	Exchange rate
Euro	9.0%	
US dollar	9.7	€0.75/$
Australian dollar	13.0	€0.66/A$

Based on this additional information, which project should the company undertake?

21.40. Slumberger Limited, the global oilfield and information services company, is considering an investment in Saudi Arabia with a local partner firm. Commercial contracts in Saudi Arabia use *Sharī'ah* law. Detail the possible instruments that Slumberger and its local partner might use to create and manage the joint venture.

SAMPLE TEST PROBLEMS

21.1. Traynor Corp. made a sale worth 27.3 million yen (¥) today to a Japanese firm. The spot rate on the Japanese yen today is ¥109.37/$. How much is the sale worth in dollars if the revenue is to be received today? The firm expects to receive payment after 30 days. The one-month forward rate is quoted as ¥110.45/$. How much will the firm receive in one month if the payment is converted at the forward rate?

the cross rate between the Indian rupees and the US dollar?

21.4. Milan Nautical Logistics is considering a contract to build a new container port facility at Mumbai, in India. The firm will need to pay out €40 million immediately in construction costs and expects to generate the following cash flows:

cash flows:	1	2	3	4	Years
Indian rupees (millions)	Rs 650	Rs 820	Rs 1116	Rs 840	
Expected exchange rate (Indian rupees/€)	58.843	59.585	61.268	62.390	

21.2. If the spot rate on the British pound against the euro is €1.1564/£ and the 180-day forward rate is €1.1553/£, what is the forward premium or discount on the British pound against the euro?

21.3. Deutsche Bank has offered the following exchange rate quotes on Indian rupees (Rs): Rs 91.64/£ and the British pound against the US dollar $1.8734/£. What is

The company uses a discount rate of 9% on its projects. What is the NPV of this project? Should Milan Nautical Logistics take on this project?

21.5. Faute de Mieux SA uses a required return for domestic projects of 11%. It is considering an investment in the United States. The interest rate in the eurozone is 3.5% and in the United States it is 4.1%. What is the company's required return for investments in the United States?

ENDNOTES

1. As part of the agreement, Rio Tinto will end up with a 46% ownership of Ivanhoe Mines.
2. An exception is the European Monetary Union (EMU) single currency zone that uses the euro and currently has Austria, Belgium, Cyprus, Finland, France, Germany, Greece, Ireland, Italy,

Kosovo, Luxembourg, Malta, Monaco, Montenegro, Netherlands, Portugal, Slovakia, Slovenia and Spain as members.

3. Whether we multiply or divide depends on the way the two currencies are quoted. If we had wanted the quotation between the Canadian dollar and the euro when the euro against the US dollar is quoted in European terms, we would have divided, that is: $\frac{C\$/US\$}{\text{€}/US\$} = \frac{C\$1.0262/\$}{\text{€}0.7477/\$} = C\$1.3725/\text{€}$.

4. The latter applies if we look at the quotation in European terms. The spot value will be £0.6711/$ and the three-month forward rate will be £0.6714/$.

5. There is a way for companies to avoid large losses and still make large gains without engaging in speculation. This involves the use of foreign currency options.

6. Sovereign nations are nations that have the right of self-rule, which includes the right to regulate commerce within their borders.

7. We have already seen how this is a risk management problem, as discussed in Chapter 20.

8. If there is a value after expropriation then we need to modify this slightly such that we calculate the expected value for the year and then multiply by the probability of no expropriation in the previous year. If, for instance, the company could get €10 million back if expropriation takes place in year 2, the expected value for year 2 cash flow will be $(1 - 0.027) \times \text{€}40 + 0.027 \times \text{€}10 = \text{€}39.19$. We only get this if there is no expropriation in year 1, so the expected value conditional on no expropriation in year 1 is $\text{€}39.19 \times (1 - 0.027) = \text{€}38.13$. Notice how the prospect of recovering some value given expropriation – or default – has raised the expected value. Without any recovery given expropriation, the value is €37.87, a difference of €0.27 million compared to the new value we have estimated.

9. You can access the methodology and country risk estimates at: http://pages.stern.nyu.edu/~adamodar/.

10. This information is based on the long-run data from 1900 to 2009 taken from the Credit Suisse Global Returns Sourcebook, 2010.

11. Economists describe this model for the forward exchange rate as uncovered interest parity and it follows from the theories that explain how currencies evolve over time.

12. The difference in inflation between the two countries means that the nominal interest rate in Brazil will be higher than in the eurozone. In order to correctly value cash flows in Brazil, we need a correspondingly higher nominal interest rate. This is known as the international Fisher effect.

13. You may wonder why there was a currency conversion for the initial cash flow ($t = 0$) in the SOCAFI example and no similar conversion for this problem. The reason is that for the current problem, the initial cash flow of $-\text{€}10$ is already in euros and thus there is no need for a currency conversion. The remaining cash flows ($t = 1$ to 5) are in TWD.

14. *Sharī'ah* law is derived from a number of different sources: the *Qur'ān*, the divine law; the *Sunnah*, the sayings of the Prophet (peace be upon him), where individual sayings are called *Hadith*; the consensus of interpretations known as *Ijma'a* and *Qiyās*, or analogy derived from the above. *Ijtihad*, or the work of scholars who have juristic expertise in *Sharī'ah* law, is important too as they issue edicts on the validity (*halal*) or otherwise of contracts. Other factors that guide interpretation are *Maslhah-e-Mursalah*, or welfare issues as well as prevalent practice, or '*Urf*.

APPENDIX

A

Present Value and Future Value Tables

Table A.1

Future value factors for €1 compounded at i% for N periods

N	1%	2%	3%	4%	5%	6%	7%	8%	9%	10%	11%	12%	13%	14%	15%	20%	25%	30%	35%	40%
1	1.010	1.020	1.030	1.040	1.050	1.060	1.070	1.080	1.090	1.100	1.110	1.120	1.130	1.140	1.150	1.200	1.250	1.300	1.350	1.400
2	1.020	1.040	1.061	1.082	1.103	1.124	1.145	1.166	1.188	1.210	1.232	1.254	1.277	1.300	1.323	1.440	1.563	1.690	1.823	1.960
3	1.030	1.061	1.093	1.125	1.158	1.191	1.225	1.260	1.295	1.331	1.368	1.405	1.443	1.482	1.521	1.728	1.953	2.197	2.460	2.744
4	1.041	1.082	1.126	1.170	1.216	1.262	1.311	1.360	1.412	1.464	1.518	1.574	1.630	1.689	1.749	2.074	2.441	2.856	3.322	3.842
5	1.051	1.104	1.159	1.217	1.276	1.338	1.403	1.469	1.539	1.611	1.685	1.762	1.842	1.925	2.011	2.488	3.052	3.713	4.484	5.378
6	1.062	1.126	1.194	1.265	1.340	1.419	1.501	1.587	1.677	1.772	1.870	1.974	2.082	2.195	2.313	2.986	3.815	4.827	6.053	7.530
7	1.072	1.149	1.230	1.316	1.407	1.504	1.606	1.714	1.828	1.949	2.076	2.211	2.353	2.502	2.660	3.583	4.768	6.275	8.172	10.541
8	1.083	1.172	1.267	1.369	1.477	1.594	1.718	1.851	1.993	2.144	2.305	2.476	2.658	2.853	3.059	4.300	5.960	8.157	11.032	14.758
9	1.094	1.195	1.305	1.423	1.551	1.689	1.838	1.999	2.172	2.358	2.558	2.773	3.004	3.252	3.518	5.160	7.451	10.604	14.894	20.661
10	1.105	1.219	1.344	1.480	1.629	1.791	1.967	2.159	2.367	2.594	2.839	3.106	3.395	3.707	4.046	6.192	9.313	13.786	20.107	28.925
11	1.116	1.243	1.384	1.539	1.710	1.898	2.105	2.332	2.580	2.853	3.152	3.479	3.836	4.226	4.652	7.430	11.642	17.922	27.144	40.496
12	1.127	1.268	1.426	1.601	1.796	2.012	2.252	2.518	2.813	3.138	3.498	3.896	4.335	4.818	5.350	8.916	14.552	23.298	36.644	56.694
13	1.138	1.294	1.469	1.665	1.886	2.133	2.410	2.720	3.066	3.452	3.883	4.363	4.898	5.492	6.153	10.699	18.190	30.288	49.470	79.371
14	1.149	1.319	1.513	1.732	1.980	2.261	2.579	2.937	3.342	3.797	4.310	4.887	5.535	6.261	7.076	12.839	22.737	39.374	66.784	111.120
15	1.161	1.346	1.558	1.801	2.079	2.397	2.759	3.172	3.642	4.177	4.785	5.474	6.254	7.138	8.137	15.407	28.422	51.186	90.158	155.560
16	1.173	1.373	1.605	1.873	2.183	2.540	2.952	3.426	3.970	4.595	5.311	6.130	7.067	8.137	9.358	18.488	35.527	66.542	121.710	217.790
17	1.184	1.400	1.653	1.948	2.292	2.693	3.159	3.700	4.328	5.054	5.895	6.866	7.986	9.276	10.761	22.186	44.409	86.504	164.310	304.910
18	1.196	1.428	1.702	2.026	2.407	2.854	3.380	3.996	4.717	5.560	6.544	7.690	9.024	10.575	12.375	26.623	55.511	112.450	221.820	426.870
19	1.208	1.457	1.754	2.107	2.527	3.026	3.617	4.316	5.142	6.116	7.263	8.613	10.197	12.056	14.232	31.948	69.389	146.190	299.460	597.630
20	1.220	1.486	1.806	2.191	2.653	3.207	3.870	4.661	5.604	6.727	8.062	9.646	11.523	13.743	16.367	38.338	86.736	190.050	404.270	836.680
21	1.232	1.516	1.860	2.279	2.786	3.400	4.141	5.034	6.109	7.400	8.949	10.804	13.021	15.668	18.822	46.005	108.420	247.060	545.760	1171.300
22	1.245	1.546	1.916	2.370	2.925	3.604	4.430	5.437	6.659	8.140	9.934	12.100	14.714	17.861	21.645	55.206	135.520	321.180	716.780	1639.800
23	1.257	1.577	1.974	2.465	3.072	3.820	4.741	5.871	7.258	8.954	11.026	13.552	16.627	20.362	24.891	66.247	169.400	417.530	994.660	2297.800
24	1.270	1.608	2.033	2.563	3.225	4.049	5.072	6.341	7.911	9.850	12.239	15.179	18.788	23.212	28.625	79.497	211.750	542.800	1342.700	3214.200
25	1.282	1.641	2.094	2.666	3.386	4.292	5.427	6.848	8.623	10.835	13.585	17.000	21.231	26.462	32.919	95.396	264.690	705.640	1812.700	4499.800
30	1.348	1.811	2.427	3.243	4.322	5.743	7.612	10.063	13.268	17.449	22.892	29.960	39.116	50.950	66.212	237.370	807.790	2619.900	8128.500	24201.000
35	1.417	2.000	2.814	3.946	5.516	7.686	10.677	14.785	20.414	28.102	38.575	52.800	72.069	98.100	133.170	590.660	2465.100	9727.800	36448.000	130161.000
40	1.489	2.208	3.262	4.801	7.040	10.286	14.974	21.725	31.409	45.259	65.001	93.051	132.782	188.880	267.860	1469.700	7523.100	36118.000	163437.000	700037.000
45	1.565	2.438	3.782	5.841	8.985	13.765	21.002	31.920	48.327	72.890	109.530	163.980	244.641	363.670	538.760	3657.200	22958.000	134106.000	732857.000	
50	1.645	2.692	4.384	7.107	11.467	18.420	29.457	46.902	74.358	117.390	184.560	289.000	450.735	700.230	1083.600	9100.400	70064.000	497929.000		

Table A.2

Present value factors (at i%) for €1 received at the end of N periods

N	1%	2%	3%	4%	5%	6%	7%	8%	9%	10%	11%	12%	13%	14%	15%	20%	25%	30%	35%	40%
1	0.990	0.980	0.971	0.962	0.952	0.943	0.935	0.926	0.917	0.909	0.901	0.893	0.885	0.877	0.870	0.833	0.800	0.769	0.741	0.714
2	0.980	0.961	0.943	0.925	0.907	0.890	0.873	0.857	0.842	0.826	0.812	0.797	0.783	0.769	0.756	0.694	0.640	0.592	0.549	0.510
3	0.971	0.942	0.915	0.889	0.864	0.840	0.816	0.794	0.772	0.751	0.731	0.712	0.693	0.675	0.658	0.579	0.512	0.455	0.406	0.364
4	0.961	0.924	0.888	0.855	0.823	0.792	0.763	0.735	0.708	0.683	0.659	0.636	0.613	0.592	0.572	0.482	0.410	0.350	0.301	0.260
5	0.951	0.906	0.863	0.822	0.784	0.747	0.713	0.681	0.650	0.621	0.593	0.567	0.543	0.519	0.497	0.402	0.328	0.269	0.223	0.186
6	0.942	0.888	0.837	0.790	0.746	0.705	0.666	0.630	0.596	0.564	0.535	0.507	0.480	0.456	0.432	0.335	0.262	0.207	0.165	0.133
7	0.932	0.871	0.813	0.760	0.711	0.665	0.623	0.583	0.547	0.513	0.482	0.452	0.425	0.400	0.376	0.279	0.210	0.159	0.122	0.095
8	0.923	0.853	0.789	0.731	0.677	0.627	0.582	0.540	0.502	0.467	0.434	0.404	0.376	0.351	0.327	0.233	0.168	0.123	0.091	0.068
9	0.914	0.837	0.766	0.703	0.645	0.592	0.544	0.500	0.460	0.424	0.391	0.361	0.333	0.308	0.284	0.194	0.134	0.094	0.067	0.048
10	0.905	0.820	0.744	0.676	0.614	0.558	0.508	0.463	0.422	0.386	0.352	0.322	0.295	0.270	0.247	0.162	0.107	0.073	0.050	0.035
11	0.896	0.804	0.722	0.650	0.585	0.527	0.475	0.429	0.388	0.350	0.317	0.287	0.261	0.237	0.215	0.135	0.086	0.056	0.037	0.025
12	0.887	0.788	0.701	0.625	0.557	0.497	0.444	0.397	0.356	0.319	0.286	0.257	0.231	0.208	0.187	0.112	0.069	0.043	0.027	0.018
13	0.879	0.773	0.681	0.601	0.530	0.469	0.415	0.368	0.326	0.290	0.258	0.229	0.204	0.182	0.163	0.093	0.055	0.033	0.020	0.013
14	0.870	0.758	0.661	0.577	0.505	0.442	0.388	0.340	0.299	0.263	0.232	0.205	0.181	0.160	0.141	0.078	0.044	0.025	0.015	0.009
15	0.861	0.743	0.642	0.555	0.481	0.417	0.362	0.315	0.275	0.239	0.209	0.183	0.160	0.140	0.123	0.065	0.035	0.020	0.011	0.006
16	0.853	0.728	0.623	0.534	0.458	0.394	0.339	0.292	0.252	0.218	0.188	0.163	0.141	0.123	0.107	0.054	0.028	0.015	0.008	0.005
17	0.844	0.714	0.605	0.513	0.436	0.371	0.317	0.270	0.231	0.198	0.170	0.146	0.125	0.108	0.093	0.045	0.023	0.012	0.006	0.003
18	0.836	0.700	0.587	0.494	0.416	0.350	0.296	0.250	0.212	0.180	0.153	0.130	0.111	0.095	0.081	0.038	0.018	0.009	0.005	0.002
19	0.828	0.686	0.570	0.475	0.396	0.331	0.277	0.232	0.194	0.164	0.138	0.116	0.098	0.083	0.070	0.031	0.014	0.007	0.003	0.002
20	0.820	0.673	0.554	0.456	0.377	0.312	0.258	0.215	0.178	0.149	0.124	0.104	0.087	0.073	0.061	0.026	0.012	0.005	0.002	0.002
21	0.811	0.660	0.538	0.439	0.359	0.294	0.242	0.199	0.164	0.135	0.112	0.093	0.077	0.064	0.053	0.022	0.009	0.004	0.002	0.001
22	0.803	0.647	0.522	0.422	0.342	0.278	0.226	0.184	0.150	0.123	0.101	0.083	0.068	0.056	0.046	0.018	0.007	0.003	0.001	0.001
23	0.795	0.634	0.507	0.406	0.326	0.262	0.211	0.170	0.133	0.112	0.091	0.074	0.060	0.049	0.040	0.015	0.006	0.002	0.001	0.001
24	0.788	0.622	0.492	0.390	0.310	0.247	0.197	0.158	0.126	0.102	0.082	0.066	0.053	0.043	0.035	0.013	0.005	0.002	0.001	0.001
25	0.780	0.610	0.478	0.375	0.295	0.233	0.184	0.146	0.116	0.092	0.074	0.059	0.047	0.038	0.030	0.010	0.004	0.001	0.001	
30	0.742	0.552	0.412	0.308	0.231	0.174	0.131	0.099	0.075	0.057	0.044	0.033	0.026	0.020	0.015	0.004	0.001			
35	0.706	0.500	0.355	0.253	0.181	0.130	0.094	0.068	0.049	0.036	0.026	0.019	0.014	0.010	0.008	0.002				
40	0.672	0.453	0.307	0.208	0.142	0.097	0.067	0.046	0.032	0.022	0.015	0.011	0.008	0.005	0.004	0.001				
45	0.639	0.410	0.264	0.171	0.111	0.073	0.048	0.031	0.021	0.014	0.009	0.006	0.004	0.003	0.002					
50	0.608	0.372	0.228	0.141	0.087	0.054	0.034	0.021	0.013	0.009	0.005	0.003	0.002	0.001	0.001					

Table A.3

Future value of annuity factors for €1 compounded at i% for N periods

N	1%	2%	3%	4%	5%	6%	7%	8%	9%	10%	11%	12%	13%	14%	15%	20%	25%	30%	35%	40%
1	1.000	1.000	1.000	1.000	1.000	1.000	1.000	1.000	1.000	1.000	1.000	1.000	1.000	1.000	1.000	1.000	1.000	1.000	1.000	1.000
2	2.010	2.020	2.030	2.040	2.050	2.060	2.070	2.080	2.090	2.100	2.110	2.120	2.130	2.140	2.150	2.200	2.250	2.300	2.350	2.400
3	3.030	3.060	3.091	3.122	3.152	3.184	3.215	3.246	3.278	3.310	3.342	3.374	3.407	3.440	3.472	3.640	3.813	3.990	4.172	4.360
4	4.060	4.122	4.184	4.246	4.310	4.375	4.440	4.506	4.573	4.641	4.710	4.779	4.850	4.921	4.993	5.368	5.766	6.187	6.633	7.104
5	5.101	5.204	5.309	5.416	5.526	5.637	5.751	5.867	5.985	6.105	6.228	6.353	6.480	6.610	6.742	7.442	8.207	9.043	9.954	10.196
6	6.152	6.308	6.468	6.633	6.802	6.975	7.153	7.336	7.523	7.716	7.913	8.115	8.232	8.536	8.754	9.930	11.259	12.756	14.438	16.324
7	7.214	7.434	7.662	7.898	8.142	8.394	8.654	8.923	9.200	9.487	9.783	10.089	10.405	10.730	11.067	12.916	15.073	17.583	20.492	23.853
8	8.286	8.583	8.892	9.214	9.549	9.897	10.260	10.637	11.028	11.436	11.859	12.300	12.757	13.233	13.727	16.499	19.842	23.858	28.664	34.395
9	9.369	9.755	10.159	10.583	11.027	11.491	11.978	12.488	13.021	13.579	14.164	14.776	15.416	16.085	16.786	20.799	25.802	32.015	39.696	49.153
10	10.462	10.950	11.464	12.006	12.578	13.181	13.816	14.487	15.193	15.937	16.722	17.549	18.420	19.337	20.304	25.959	33.253	42.619	54.590	69.814
11	11.567	12.169	12.808	13.486	14.207	14.972	15.784	16.645	17.560	18.531	19.561	20.655	21.814	23.045	24.349	32.150	42.566	56.405	74.697	98.739
12	12.683	13.412	14.192	15.026	15.917	16.870	17.888	18.977	20.141	21.384	22.713	24.133	25.650	27.271	29.002	39.581	54.208	74.327	101.840	139.230
13	13.809	14.680	15.618	16.627	17.713	18.882	20.141	21.495	22.953	24.523	26.212	28.029	29.985	32.089	34.352	48.497	68.760	97.625	138.480	195.920
14	14.947	15.971	17.086	18.292	19.599	21.015	22.550	24.215	26.019	27.975	30.095	32.393	34.883	37.581	40.505	59.196	86.949	127.910	187.950	275.300
15	16.097	17.291	18.599	20.024	21.579	23.276	25.129	27.152	29.361	31.722	34.405	37.280	40.417	43.842	47.580	72.035	109.680	167.280	254.730	386.420
16	17.258	18.639	20.157	21.825	23.657	25.673	27.888	30.324	33.003	35.950	39.190	42.753	46.672	50.980	55.717	87.442	138.100	218.470	344.890	541.980
17	18.430	20.012	21.762	23.698	25.840	28.213	30.840	33.750	36.974	40.545	44.501	48.884	53.739	59.118	65.075	105.930	173.630	285.010	466.610	759.780
18	19.615	21.412	23.414	25.645	28.132	30.906	33.999	37.450	41.301	45.599	50.396	55.750	61.725	68.394	75.836	128.110	218.040	371.510	630.920	1064.600
19	20.811	22.841	25.117	27.671	30.539	33.760	37.379	41.446	46.018	51.159	56.939	63.440	70.749	78.969	88.212	154.740	273.550	483.970	852.740	1491.500
20	22.019	24.297	26.870	29.778	33.066	36.786	40.995	45.762	51.160	57.275	64.203	72.052	80.947	91.025	102.440	186.680	342.940	630.160	1152.200	2089.200
21	23.239	25.783	28.676	31.969	35.719	39.993	44.865	50.423	56.765	64.002	72.265	81.699	92.470	104.760	118.810	225.020	429.680	820.210	1556.400	2925.800
22	24.472	27.299	30.537	34.248	38.505	43.392	49.006	55.457	62.873	71.403	81.214	92.503	105.491	120.430	137.630	271.030	538.100	1067.200	2102.200	4097.200
23	25.716	28.845	32.453	36.618	41.430	46.996	53.436	60.893	69.532	79.543	91.148	104.600	120.205	138.290	159.270	326.230	673.620	1388.400	2839.000	5737.100
24	26.973	30.422	34.426	39.083	44.502	50.816	58.177	66.765	76.790	88.497	102.170	118.150	136.831	158.650	184.160	392.480	843.030	1806.000	3833.700	8032.900
25	28.243	32.030	36.459	41.646	47.727	54.865	63.249	73.106	84.701	98.347	114.410	133.330	155.620	181.870	212.790	471.980	1054.700	2348.800	5176.500	11247.000
30	34.785	40.568	47.575	56.085	66.439	79.058	94.461	113.280	136.300	164.490	199.020	241.330	293.199	356.780	434.740	1181.800	3227.100	8729.900	23221.000	60501.000
35	41.660	49.994	60.462	73.652	90.320	111.430	138.230	172.310	215.710	271.020	341.590	431.660	546.681	693.570	881.170	2948.300	9856.700	32422.000	104136.000	325400.000
40	48.886	60.402	75.401	95.026	120.800	154.760	199.630	259.050	337.880	442.590	581.820	767.090	1013.704	1342.000	1779.000	7343.800	30088.000	120392.000	466960.000	
45	56.481	71.893	92.720	121.020	159.700	212.740	285.740	386.500	525.850	718.900	986.630	1358.200	1874.165	2490.500	3585.100	18281.000	91831.000	447019.000		
50	64.463	84.579	112.790	152.660	209.340	290.330	406.520	573.770	815.080	1163.900	1668.700	2400.000	3459.507	4994.500	7217.700	45497.000	280255.000			

Table A.4

Present value of annuity factors (at % per period for €1 received per period for each of N periods

N	1%	2%	3%	4%	5%	6%	7%	8%	9%	10%	11%	12%	13%	14%	15%	20%	25%	30%	35%	40%
1	0.990	0.980	0.971	0.962	0.952	0.943	0.935	0.926	0.917	0.909	0.901	0.893	0.885	0.877	0.870	0.833	0.800	0.769	0.741	0.714
2	1.970	1.942	1.913	1.886	1.859	1.833	1.808	1.783	1.759	1.736	1.713	1.690	1.668	1.647	1.626	1.528	1.440	1.361	1.289	1.224
3	2.941	2.884	2.829	2.775	2.723	2.673	2.624	2.577	2.531	2.487	2.444	2.402	2.361	2.322	2.283	2.106	1.952	1.816	1.696	1.589
4	3.902	3.808	3.717	3.630	3.546	3.465	3.387	3.312	3.240	3.170	3.102	3.037	2.974	2.914	2.855	2.589	2.362	2.166	1.997	1.849
5	4.853	4.713	4.580	4.452	4.329	4.212	4.100	3.993	3.890	3.791	3.696	3.605	3.517	3.433	3.352	2.991	2.689	2.436	2.220	2.035
6	5.795	5.601	5.417	5.242	5.076	4.917	4.767	4.623	4.486	4.355	4.231	4.111	3.998	3.889	3.784	3.326	2.951	2.643	2.385	2.168
7	6.728	6.472	6.230	6.002	5.786	5.582	5.389	5.206	5.033	4.868	4.712	4.564	4.423	4.288	4.160	3.605	3.161	2.802	2.508	2.263
8	7.652	7.325	7.020	6.733	6.463	6.210	5.971	5.747	5.535	5.335	5.146	4.968	4.799	4.639	4.487	3.837	3.329	2.925	2.598	2.331
9	8.566	8.162	7.786	7.435	7.108	6.802	6.515	6.247	5.995	5.759	5.537	5.328	5.132	4.946	4.772	4.031	3.463	3.019	2.665	2.379
10	9.471	8.983	8.530	8.111	7.722	7.360	7.024	6.710	6.418	6.145	5.889	5.650	5.426	5.216	5.019	4.192	3.571	3.092	2.715	2.414
11	10.368	9.787	9.253	8.760	8.306	7.887	7.499	7.139	6.805	6.495	6.207	5.938	5.687	5.453	5.234	4.327	3.656	3.147	2.752	2.438
12	11.255	10.575	9.954	9.385	8.863	8.384	7.943	7.536	7.161	6.814	6.492	6.194	5.918	5.660	5.421	4.439	3.725	3.190	2.779	2.456
13	12.134	11.348	10.635	9.986	9.394	8.853	8.358	7.904	7.487	7.103	6.750	6.424	6.122	5.842	5.583	4.533	3.780	3.223	2.799	2.469
14	13.004	12.106	11.296	10.563	9.899	9.295	8.745	8.244	7.786	7.367	6.982	6.628	6.302	6.002	5.724	4.611	3.824	3.249	2.814	2.478
15	13.865	12.849	11.938	11.118	10.380	9.712	9.108	8.559	8.061	7.606	7.191	6.811	6.462	6.142	5.847	4.675	3.859	3.268	2.825	2.484
16	14.718	13.578	12.561	11.652	10.838	10.106	9.447	8.851	8.313	7.824	7.379	6.974	6.604	6.265	5.954	4.730	3.887	3.283	2.834	2.489
17	15.562	14.292	13.166	12.166	11.274	10.477	9.763	9.122	8.544	8.022	7.549	7.120	6.729	6.373	6.047	4.775	3.910	3.295	2.840	2.492
18	16.398	14.992	13.754	12.659	11.690	10.828	10.059	9.372	8.756	8.201	7.702	7.250	6.840	6.467	6.128	4.812	3.928	3.304	2.844	2.494
19	17.226	15.678	14.324	13.134	12.085	11.158	10.336	9.604	8.950	8.365	7.839	7.366	6.938	6.550	6.198	4.843	3.942	3.311	2.848	2.496
20	18.046	16.351	14.877	13.590	12.462	11.470	10.594	9.818	9.129	8.514	7.963	7.469	7.025	6.623	6.259	4.870	3.954	3.316	2.850	2.497
21	18.857	17.011	15.415	14.029	12.821	11.764	10.836	10.017	9.292	8.649	8.075	7.562	7.102	6.687	6.312	4.891	3.963	3.320	2.852	2.498
22	19.660	17.658	15.937	14.451	13.163	12.042	11.061	10.201	9.442	8.772	8.176	7.654	7.170	6.743	6.359	4.909	3.970	3.323	2.853	2.498
23	20.456	18.292	16.444	14.857	13.489	12.303	11.272	10.371	9.580	8.883	8.266	7.718	7.230	6.792	6.399	4.925	3.976	3.325	2.854	2.499
24	21.243	18.914	16.936	15.247	13.799	12.550	11.469	10.529	9.707	8.985	8.348	7.784	7.283	6.835	6.434	4.937	3.981	3.327	2.855	2.499
25	22.023	19.523	17.413	15.622	14.094	12.783	11.654	10.675	9.823	9.077	8.422	7.843	7.330	6.873	6.464	4.948	3.985	3.329	2.856	2.499
30	25.808	22.396	19.600	17.292	15.372	13.765	12.409	11.258	10.274	9.427	8.694	8.055	7.496	7.003	6.566	4.979	3.995	3.332	2.857	2.500
35	29.409	24.999	21.487	18.665	16.374	14.498	12.948	11.655	10.567	9.644	8.855	8.176	7.586	7.070	6.617	4.992	3.998	3.333	2.857	2.500
40	32.835	27.355	23.115	19.793	17.159	15.046	13.332	11.925	10.757	9.779	8.951	8.244	7.634	7.105	6.642	4.997	3.999	3.333	2.857	2.500
45	36.095	29.490	24.519	20.720	17.774	15.456	13.606	12.108	10.881	9.863	9.008	8.283	7.661	7.123	6.654	4.999	4.000	3.333	2.857	2.500
50	39.196	31.424	25.730	21.482	18.256	15.762	13.801	12.233	10.962	9.915	9.042	8.304	7.675	7.133	6.661	4.999	4.000	3.333	2.857	2.500

APPENDIX

B

Solutions to Selected Questions and Problems

Chapter 1

1.1 The two basic sources of funds for all businesses are debt and equity.

1.3 A profitable firm is able to generate enough cash flows from productive assets to cover its operating expenses, taxes and payments to creditors. Unprofitable firms fail to do this and therefore they may be forced to declare bankruptcy.

1.5 A firm should undertake a capital project only if the value of its future cash flows exceeds the cost of the project.

1.7 Working capital management is the day-to-day management of a firm's current assets and liabilities. The financial manager has to make decisions regarding the level of inventory to hold, the terms of granting credit (accounts receivable) and the firm's policy on paying accounts payable.

1.9 Advantages: easiest business type to start; least regulated; owners have full control; all income is taxed as personal income. Disadvantages: unlimited liability of proprietor; initial capital limited to proprietor's wealth; difficult to transfer ownership.

1.11 The owners of a company are its shareholders and the evidence of their ownership is represented by ordinary shares.

1.13 The owners of a company are often subject to double taxation – first at the corporate level when the firm's earnings are taxed and then again at a personal level when the dividends they receive are taxed.

1.15 The most important governing body within an organisation is the board of directors. Its primary role is to represent the interests of shareholders. The board also hires (and occasionally fires) the CEO, advises him or her on major decisions and monitors the firm's performance.

1.17 Problems include: difficult to determine what is meant by profits; it does not address the size and timing of cash flows – it does not account for the time value of money; and ignores the uncertainty of risk of cash flows.

1.19 The following factors affect the share price: the firm, the economy, economic shocks, the business environment, expected cash flows and current market conditions.

1.21 If a firm's share price falls sustainably below its maximum potential price, it may attract corporate raiders. These persons look for firms that are fundamentally sound but that are poorly managed, so they can buy the firm, turn it around and sell it for a handsome profit.

1.23 Business dishonesty and lack of transparency lead to corruption and that in turn creates inefficiencies in an economy, inhibits growth of capital markets and slows the rate of economic growth. An example is the Russian economy until it changed its transparency rules in the mid-1990s.

1.25 Insider trading is an example of information asymmetry. The main idea is that investment decisions should be made on an even playing field. Insider trading is considered morally wrong and has been made illegal.

Chapter 2

2.1 The role of the financial system is to gather money from businesses and individuals and channel funds to those who need them. The financial system consists of financial markets and financial institutions.

2.3 Saver-lenders are those who have more money than they need right now. The principal saver-lenders in the economy are households. Borrower-spenders are those who need the money saver-lenders are offering. The main borrower-spenders in the economy are businesses and the federal government.

2.5 Your security seems to be marketable, but not liquid. Liquidity implies that when a security is sold, its value will be preserved, marketability does not.

2.7 Le Vaux SA is more likely to go public because of its larger size. Though the cost of obtaining a listing and compliance is very high, larger firms can offset these costs by the lower funding cost in public markets. Smaller companies find the cost prohibitive for the dollar amount of securities they sell.

2.9 a. secondary; b. secondary; c. primary

2.11 a. €300 000; b. 3.05%; c. €9 850 000

2.13 Financial intermediaries allow smaller companies to access the financial markets. They do this through converting securities with one set of characteristics into securities with another set of characteristics that meet the needs of smaller companies. By repackaging securities, they are able to meet the needs of different clients.

2.15 Money markets are where short-term debt instruments with maturities of less than one year are bought and sold. Capital markets are where equity securities and debt instruments with maturities of more than one year are sold.

2.17 A type of share index where the value of the shares in the index rather than the market capitalisation of the company determines how the index behaves. The value index based on market capitalisation of the shares shows the changes in the total value of the shares in the index. With a price index, higher-priced shares will have more influence on the index's behaviour.

2.19 Treasury bills are short-term government debt. They are the most liquid money market instrument and are considered free of default risk.

2.21 Money markets allow large companies to adjust their liquidity positions by temporarily investing idle cash in money market instruments and then selling them when cash is needed. In addition, some large firms are able to borrow money by selling commercial paper in the money markets when cash is needed.

2.23 Public markets are wholesale markets for securities open to the public to buy securities. To sell securities publicly, issuers must have their securities admitted to a listing. Most companies want access to the public markets because securities can be sold there at the lowest possible funding cost. Private markets are where securities are sold directly to individual investors. Securities sold privately are not admitted to listing and, as a result, securities can be brought to market quickly and at very low transaction cost. However, because the securities are not listed, their sale and secondary market activities are severely restricted.

2.25 The real rate of interest measures the return earned on savings and it represents the cost of borrowing to finance capital goods. The real rate of interest is determined by the interaction between firms that invest in capital projects and the rate of return they expect to earn on those investments, and individuals' time preference for consumption. The rate of interest is determined when the desired level of savings equals the desired level of investments in the economy.

2.27 The Fisher effect is the expected annualised change in commodity prices (ΔP_e).

The so-called inflation premium is used to protect lenders from losses of purchasing power on their loan contracts due to inflation. It is incorporated into a loan contract by adding it to the real interest rate, as can be seen in Equation (2.2).

2.29 Yes. The CD will be worth €1067.50 at the end of the year and the price of the trip will be €1066.

Chapter 3

3.1 SFr 97 118

3.3 FIFO makes sense during times of rising prices because it allows the firm to eliminate the lower-priced inventory first, resulting in a higher profit margin.

3.5 €6 655 610

3.7 €242 401.25

3.9 −€132 085

3.11 Expenses identified on income statement that did not result in cash flows. Depreciation and amortisation are examples.

3.13 Marginal tax rates are appropriate because it is the rate at which the next unit of income is taxed.

3.15 €168 022

3.17 NKr 222 764

3.19 €137 263

3.21 €1 804 545.76

3.23 €621 178

3.25 €218 364.32; 34.5%, 34.5%

3.27 £715 719.75

3.29 €198 152

Chapter 4

4.1 This measure includes only the most liquid of the current assets and hence gives a better measure of liquidity.

4.3 €1 627 579

4.5 2.87 times; 127.1 days

4.7 2.65; 0.623; 29.9%

4.9 Time trend analysis, industry average analysis and peer group analysis.

4.11 €2.55; 21.3 times

4.13 −€767 243

4.15 NKr 843 863

4.17 1.27; 2.27

4.19 51.2%; 19.1%; 12.6%

4.21 0.41; 36%; 18.32%; 25.92%

4.23 34.4 times; 22.04 times

4.25 £6 473 600; 5.7%

4.27 DKr 10 226 559; DKR 88 236 056; 0.82

4.29 Current ratio = 0.77, quick ratio = 0.57, gross margin = 51.2%, profit margin = 19.1%, debt ratio = 0.70, long-term debt to equity = 0.73, interest coverage = 15.6, ROA = 11.4%, ROE = 37.5%.

4.31 Profit margin = 12.61%, total asset turnover = 0.90, equity multiplier = 3.30, ROA = 11.4%, ROE = 37.5%.

4.33 €292 756.63

4.35 Current ratio = 1.81, quick ratio = 1.19, inventory turnover = 3.50, accounts receivable turnover = 5.16, DSO = 70.76, total asset turnover = 1.23, fixed asset turnover = 7.15, total debt ratio = 1.72, debt-to-equity ratio = 1.72, equity multiplier = 2.72, times interest earned = 17.56, cash coverage = 37.30, gross profit margin = 0.36, net profit margin = 0.08, ROA = 0.10, ROE = 0.27.

Chapter 5

5.1 SKr 53 973.12

5.3 €6712.35

5.5 €3289.69

5.7 €154 154.24; €154 637.37; €154 874.91; €154 883.03

5.9 €16 108.92

5.11 €6507.05

5.13 €734.83

5.15 7.42%

5.17 92 016; 101 218

5.19 1045

5.21 10.42%

5.23 11 years

5.25 3.8 years

5.27 a. €2246.57; b. €2073.16; c. €2946.96; d. €2949.88

5.29 13.96%

5.31 Option 1: €26 803.77; Option 2: €23 579.48

5.33 Option C: €7 083 096.26

5.35 13.14%

Chapter 6

6.1 €74 472.48

6.3 €3185.40

6.5 £5747.40

6.7 €5652.06

6.9 €247 609.95

6.11 €1 361 642.36

6.13 €4221.07

6.15 a. €15 000; b. €6000; c. €10 000

6.17 7%

6.19 €5 391 978

6.21 €1 496 377.71

6.23 €1 193 831.54

6.25 NKr 7 000 000

6.27 a. €17 857.14; b. €114 533.97; c. €4250

6.29 b. 8.57%

6.31 €12 847 215.41, €11 374 540.65 and €14 519 339.52

6.33 a. €86 124.36; b. €14 156.64; c. €71 967.72; d. €6 627.21

6.35 €2103.89

Chapter 7

7.1 Total holding period return represents the percentage return to an investor from holding an asset over a given period of time. The expected return is the probability weighted average of the future performance of an investment under all scenarios.

7.3 €78 000

7.5 Share B

7.7 Systematic risk is risk that a security has in common with the market. Because all risky assets in the market have systematic risk, it cannot be eliminated through diversification.

7.9 Since a treasury bill has no risk, its beta should equal 0.

7.11 The CAPM describes the relation between systematic risk and the expected return that investors require for bearing that risk.

7.13 €1250

7.15   0.145; 0.162

7.17   0.125; 0.168

7.19   for $s_{12} = 0.12$, 0.1225; for $s_{12} = -0.12$, 0.0025

7.21   While it has no unsystematic risk, the portfolio will still have an expected return that is higher than that for a risk-free asset if it has systematic risk.

7.23   The statement is false. Even if we could afford such a portfolio and thus completely diversify our portfolio, we would only be eliminating non-systematic risk.

7.25   0.185; 0.165

7.27   0.19

7.29   Diversified investors are willing to pay the highest prices for assets. They drive prices to the point where investments are expected to yield the returns described by CAPM.

7.31   Risk-free asset

7.33   The first security is underpriced and the second is overpriced.

Chapter 8

8.1   £1147.20

8.3   £1008.15

8.5   €975.91

8.7 $359.38

8.9   6.58%; 6.69%

8.11   9.52%

8.13   €1000; the bond's yield equals its coupon rate and so the bond will be at 'par', or its face value.

8.15   A$912.61

8.17   £1079.22

8.19   12.453%

8.21   7.36%

8.23   10.57%

8.25   8.84%

8.27   a. £924.75; b. 4.33%

8.29   a. £904.76; b. £1086.46, £832.53; d. £1063.42, £866.65

Chapter 9

9.1   €14.24

9.3   €27.39

9.5   €8.50

9.7   €31.12

9.9   12.15%

9.11   £56.90

9.13   €2.46

9.15   €21.07

9.17   €23.35

9.19   €32.34

9.21   €25.95

9.23   €2.15

9.25   a. €35.00; b. buy

9.27   b. €7.87; c. €31.88; d. €24.31; e. €24.32

9.29   a. €14.09; b. €74.80; c. €51.28

Chapter 10

10.1   €62 337

10.3   Yes; €134 986

10.5   2.87 years

10.7   3.45 years

10.9   33.8%

10.11   DKr 1 496 910; SKr 1 084 734; alpha 8300

10.13   €27 222; €732 228; both

10.15   No; 4.33 years

10.17   Type 2; 3.6 years

10.19   20.1%

10.21   22.7%

10.23   a. 9%; b. 12.3%; c. 16.3%

10.25   a. 10.7%; 15%; b. No to project I, Yes to project II

10.27   7.6%; 19.2%; 25.1%; 2 & 3 only

10.29   18.8%, 20%; both

10.31   a. 3.8 years; b. €2 189 325; c. 20.3%

10.33   a. 3.21 years; b. 57.7%; c. €1 029 085; d. 32.5%

10.35   a. 6 years, 8.8 years; b. €116 980; c. 12.5%

Chapter 11

11.1   The main reason is that accounting earnings generally differ from cash flows and cash flows are what shareholders care about.

11.3   Subtract depreciation from EBITDA, multiply by (1 − tax rate), and add back depreciation. This enables us to account for the fact that depreciation reduces the taxes that must be paid.

11.5 The average tax rate is the total amount of tax divided by the total amount of money earned, while the marginal tax rate is the rate paid on the last unit of currency earned. Use the marginal tax rate.

11.7 Variable costs are costs that vary directly with the number of units sold. Fixed costs do not vary with the number of units sold.

11.9 £1370

11.11 The Equivalent Annual Cash flow (EAC) is the annual payment from an annuity that has a life equal to that of a project and that has the same NPV as the project.

11.13 €891.84

11.15 Marginal 5 35%; average 5 34.2%

11.17 €168 020 000

11.19 $EAC_A = -€2866.47$; $EAC_B = -€2978.44$; buy Model A

11.21 End of year 3

11.23 End of year 2

11.25 €4558.70

11.27 Yes; the NPV = €38 356

11.29 €532 089.14

11.31 –$363 805

Chapter 12

12.1 Fixed costs are costs which in the short term cannot be changed regardless of how much output the project produces. Variable costs are costs which vary with the number of units of output produced by the project.

12.3 Yes. EBIT is €375 000 with the new technology and €250 000 with the old.

12.5 0.392

12.7 To determine how many units are required to make up for the fixed cost we must know the additional positive cash flow or profits from each additional unit sold.

12.9 PI is the ratio of NPV plus initial investment to initial investment. It is useful in ranking projects by the value created per unit of currency invested.

12.11 Fixed costs could increase by €230 000 and variable cost per unit could increase by €15.33.

12.13 15.9%

12.15 340 000 units

12.17 The accounting break-even is higher because the calculation includes depreciation and amortisation. This is a non-cash charge that might not accurately reflect an incremental cash flow.

12.19 Since sensitivity analysis assumes independence among variables, this analysis will be most useful when this sort of independence exists.

12.21 Simulation analysis.

12.23 Choose projects A, C and D.

12.25 Cash Flow DOL will be less than Accounting DOL.

12.27 Changes in revenue and operating leverage.

12.29 CO = 300 000 units

Chapter 13

13.1 €98 million

13.3 7.7%

13.5 €395

13.7 16%

13.9 10%

13.11 15.8%

13.13 9.4%

13.15 The owners of the securities, collectively, own all of the cash flows that the firm generates. The value of these securities must equal the value of these cash flows and, therefore, the value of the firm.

13.17 €1000

13.19 Decrease

13.21 14%, 12%

13.23 If you can confidently estimate future dividends and you believe the market is efficient, then one of the methods that rely on dividend projections might be appropriate. If not, the CAPM, which does not require dividend forecasts, would probably be the best.

13.25 9.26%

13.27 Since the firm is financing the project with a different capital mix than it has historically used, then we know the weights and rates for debt, preference and ordinary shares in the WACC formula will be different. Therefore, using its historical WACC can result in an error in the NPV estimate for the project.

13.29 Use a combination of historical growth information and available information about future growth prospects.

13.31 Underestimating the dividend growth rate or market inefficiency in the pricing of the shares.

13.33 If the market perceives the risk of the firm to be higher than it actually is due to a lack of information, then the WACC might be too high and the firm might be able to lower it by sharing more information with the market.

Chapter 14

14.1 69 days
14.3 22 days
14.5 73 days
14.7 34.72%
14.9 A$626.91
14.11 11.6%
14.13 75.9 days
14.15 €1 511 918
14.17 36.5 days
14.19 16 orders
14.21 8.775%
14.23 5.54%
14.25 €9324
14.27 28.2 days
14.29 37.1%
14.31 a. Increase, Increase; b. Increase, Increase; c. No change, Decrease; d. Increase, Increase; e. Increase, Unchanged
14.33 a. 67.9 days; b. 80.6 days; c. 105.7 days; d. 148.5 days; e. 42.8 days
14.35 a. €30 000; b. 63.2%; c. 85.1%

Chapter 15

15.1 A description of the business and industry trends, vision and key strategies for the business, principal products or services and any innovative features or patents, the management team and their experience, market analysis and sales forecast, how the products will be marketed and sold, production costs such as materials and labour, facilities needed and estimated costs, capital required and the use of the proceeds, detailed budget with six years of projected financial statements.

15.3 Sell the business at some period, take it public or remain a private company.

15.5 Look at comparable companies and see what they are trading for; do a discounted cash flow analysis.

15.7 €32 465 457

15.9 a. false; b. true; c. true; d. false; e. true

15.11 There are economies of scale in issuing securities, meaning that as the size of the offering increases, the total flotation costs decline.

15.13 Banks require (1) a default premium to reflect the credit risk of the firm and (2) a term premium for longer-maturity loans. Therefore, longer-term-to-maturity loans will have a higher interest cost to the firm.

15.15 9.43%

15.17 €1 220 000

15.19 €68 700 000

15.21 a. €130 million; b. €109 million; c. €21 million

15.23 6.52%

Chapter 16

16.1 The assumption that there are no information or transaction costs.

16.3 The value of the firm is independent of the proportion of debt and equity utilised by the firm under Modigliani and Miller's Proposition 1.

16.5 20%
16.7 18%
16.9 €150 000 000
16.11 10.5%
16.13 42%

16.15 Information or transaction costs would reduce the total value that is available for the debt holders and the shareholders and, therefore, the value of the firm.

16.17 €530 000 000

16.19 Lower productivity due to lower morale and job hunting and higher recruiting costs are among the costs that the firm will incur.

16.21 Managers expect to lose their jobs in one year whether they take on the project and work hard or not. They have no incentive to take on the project. Declining it makes the shortage to the debt holders, as well as the shareholders, greater than it would be if the firm followed the rule of always accepting positive NPV projects.

16.23 Given the information in the question we would expect that an increase in the marginal tax rate will increase the value of the tax shield and increase the amount of debt in the optimal capital structure.

16.25 That internally generated equity is utilised first as a source of financing does not mean that the internally generated funds are cheaper than debt. Internally generated funds belong to shareholders and are therefore really equity financing, which we know to be more expensive than debt.

16.27 Under these conditions, the value of the firm will increase with the amount of debt financing that is used. The conservative approach will not maximise firm value.

16.29 €810 000 000

16.31 If enough debt is used to finance this firm then the challenges of ensuring that the firm produces enough cash to make interest and principal payments would provide managers of the firm with incentives to work on new positive NPV projects rather than spend their Fridays in Cancun.

Chapter 17

17.1 This reduction could indicate that management expects a lower level of profitability in the future (negative signal). It could also indicate that Náutica Mediterráneo requires additional money to invest in positive NPV projects that were not previously available (positive signal).

17.3 (1) Declaration date, (2) Ex-dividend date, (3) Record date, (4) Payment date.

17.5 Any cash paid to shareholders through a dividend reduces the value of the assets that are securing the creditors' claims.

17.7 €9.75

17.9 With a share repurchase, shareholders can decide whether to participate. If they do choose to participate, there are tax advantages for the shareholders, relative to a dividend.

17.11 Relaxing the no-transaction-cost assumption increases the cost of producing a homemade dividend (the cost of undoing unwanted dividends). This makes a firm's dividend policy a relevant factor when valuing its shares.

17.13 The value of dividend-paying shares should decrease relative to the value of non-dividend-paying shares.

17.15 Reducing a dividend may indicate that a firm does not have sufficient cash, which would be a negative signal. On the other hand, when a high-growth firm increases its dividend, the increase may be interpreted as indicating that the firm's growth rate will decline, which is also a negative signal.

17.17 The announcement of a special dividend is a binding commitment.

17.19 This commits a firm to returning to the capital markets periodically to raise capital, which provides managers with incentives to act in the interests of shareholders.

17.21 A Dutch auction enables a firm to repurchase the number of shares that it wants to repurchase at the lowest possible cost.

17.23 Paying a dividend reduces the value of equity and thereby increases the debt-to-total-capital ratio in a levered firm.

17.25 €15

17.27 €72 500
17.29 €150 000

Chapter 18

18.1 The forms of organisation discussed in this chapter include: Sole Proprietorship, Partnership (General Partnership and Limited Partnership), Limited Liability Company (LLC) and Companies.

18.3 With sole proprietors and general partners there is the possibility that personal assets can be taken to satisfy claims on the business. In contrast, the liabilities of investors in LLCs and companies are generally limited to the money that they have invested in the business.

18.5 Equity: friends and family, venture capitalists or other potential investors that you know. Debt: bank loans, cash advances on credit cards or loans from other individual investors or other businesses.

18.7 The cost of duplicating the assets of the business in their present form.

18.9 Excess cash is a non-operating asset because this cash can be distributed to shareholders without affecting the operations of the business and therefore the value of the expected future cash flows. It makes sense to add back the value of excess cash because it represents value over and above that which the business is expected to produce.

18.11 Probably not. The private shares are relatively illiquid and the value would be discounted for this in the market.

18.13 A Limited Liability Company (LLC) is a hybrid of a company and a limited partnership. It has limited liability with the tax advantages of a partnership.

18.15 Break-even for TV option = 1250 units per year. Break-even for flyer option = 150 units per year. Choose the flyer option.

18.17 €1573.64 million

18.19 The enterprise value/EBITDA multiple is more appropriate since the capital structures of Macchina Utensile and Milan Ingeneria differ considerably.

18.21 €12 675 000

18.23 It is not adequate. €9400 or additional capital will be required upfront. €89 400 is needed to maintain a €5000 cash balance. The monthly break-even points for the firm are: 4333.3 bottles in the initial month and 1833.3 bottles in the following months.

18.25 See outline for a business plan in The Role of the Business Plan.

18.27 The company has a short history, high investments, no sales and highly uncertain future cash flows. The cost approach is not valid for such a young biochemical company. It is hard to value the company using multiples because of the lack of sales and negative earnings and because of a lack of comparable public companies. The transaction approach is also likely to be difficult to apply due to the difficulty of finding a comparable transaction.

Chapter 19

19.1 It drives all decision-making within the firm and covers all areas of a firm's operations.

19.3 Identifies EFN, source of funding, target capital structure and dividend policy.

19.5 Sales forecasts, pro forma statements, investment decisions and financing decisions.

19.7 55%

19.9 Measures the amount of assets needed to generate one unit of currency in sales.

19.11 68%

19.13 6.8%

19.17 Electric utilities industry and the aluminium processing industry.

19.19 8%

19.21 8.2%

19.23 9.9%

19.25 5.2%

19.27 35.9%

19.29 9.6%

19.33 3.37%; 6.26%

19.35 **a.** 4.31%; **b.** 13.9%; **c.** €4 777 333

Chapter 20

20.1 Firms normally hedge out the risks from financial markets since these have the capacity to derail the firm's business strategy.

20.3 The delivery date, quantity and price.

20.5 Interest rates and storage and wastage costs will raise the forward price; income on the asset before delivery and the convenience yield will reduce the forward price.

20.7 The payoff function for the owner of a call (put) option will increase linearly with the change in the underlying asset price above (below) the strike price but remain constant below (above) the strike price. The payoff of the seller is the mirror image to that of the owner (holder).

20.9 No. The losses to the seller of a call option are only limited by the extent to which the value of the underlying asset can increase. There is no other limit.

20.11 Your option is worth very slightly more than zero. There is little chance that the share price will move above €100 by tomorrow, but the chance is not zero, so the option still has some value.

20.13 The underlying asset of a financial option is a financial asset, while the underlying asset of a real option is a non-financial asset, such as a project.

20.15 The payoff functions for lenders and shareholders are like those for different types of options. Agency costs arise because these payoff functions are different.

20.17 A company might prefer to use insurance rather than hedging a particular risk when it hoped to benefit from an increase in the value in the future. Hedging eliminates both gains and losses; insurance protects only against losses.

20.19 €13.80

20.21 €7.01

20.23 Zl 1.18

20.25 A golden parachute can help reduce agency problems by reducing the potential cost to a manager of making decisions that shareholders want but that could harm the manager. For example, having a golden parachute can provide a manager with stronger incentives to invest in risky projects or approve a merger that could result in the loss of his or her job.

20.27 $F_{0.5} = $ €348.99; $F = $ €349.66; $F_{1.5} = $ €350.51; $F_2 = $ €352.71. We observe a term structure of forward prices that, due to the higher dividend yield for the early maturities compared to the risk-free rate of interest, initially means the forward prices are lower. When the interest effect outweighs the dividend yield effect, as it does for the later maturities, the forward price is higher than the cash market price.

20.29 €1 416 505.30

Chapter 21

21.1 €130.89

21.3 a. MP 11.8483/$; b. €1.6359/£; c. C$0.0316/Rs

21.5 Same cost in both cities based on the spot rate!

21.7 £1 834 553

21.9 $1 571 675

21.11 0.45%

21.13 The two major components are legal and political risks, but include a range of other factors, such as event risks (e.g. wars and civil unrest).

21.15 The two main approaches are to apply quantitative analysis and qualitative analysis.

21.19 Foreign projects involve country risk and, if the country uses a different currency, exchange rate risk. There may well be additional complications in estimating the project's cash flows.

21.21 5.4% discount

21.23 0.007368/¥

21.25 10.97%

21.27 NPV of promised cash flows = $2.17 million; adjusted for risk of expropriation = −$0.51 million

21.29　No, NPV = −€0.33 million.

21.31　Transparency is important as it allows both parties to know exactly what is involved and to avoid ambiguity (*gharar*) in the contract.

21.33　£3125.75

21.35　C$1.3489/€

21.37　18.2%

21.39　NPV in euros for Hawaii = €4.50 million; for Australia = €4.42 million. It should choose Hawaii.

GLOSSARY

A

accounting operating profit (EBIT) break-even point the number of units that must be sold for accounting operating profit to equal zero

accounting rate of return (ARR) a rate of return on a capital project based on average net income divided by average assets over the project's life; also called the *book rate of return*

adjusted book value the sum of the fair market values of the individual assets in a business

agency conflicts conflicts of interest between a principal and an agent

agency costs the costs arising from conflicts of interest between a principal and an agent; for example, between a firm's owners and its management

amortisation schedule with regard to a loan, a table that shows the loan balance at the beginning and end of each period, the payment made during that period and how much of that payment represents interest and how much represents repayment of principal

amortising loan a loan for which each loan payment contains repayment of some principal and a payment of interest that is based on the remaining principal to be repaid

annual percentage rate (APR) the simple interest rate charged per period multiplied by the number of periods per year

annuity a series of equally spaced and level cash flows extending over a finite number

annuity due an annuity in which payments are made at the beginning of each period

arbitrage buying and selling assets in a way that takes advantage of price discrepancies and yields a profit greater than that which would be expected based solely on the risk of the individual investments

asset substitution problem the incentive that shareholders in a financially leveraged firm have to substitute more risky assets for less risky assets

average tax rate total taxes paid divided by taxable income

B

balance sheet financial statement that shows a firm's financial position at a point in time

bankruptcy legally declared inability of an individual or a company to pay its creditors

bankruptcy costs, or costs of financial distress costs associated with financial difficulties a firm might experience because it uses debt financing

benchmark a standard against which performance is measured

best-effort underwriting underwriting agreement in which the underwriter does not agree to purchase the securities at a particular price but promises only to make its 'best effort' to sell as much of the issue as possible above a certain price

beta (β) a measure of non-diversifiable, systematic or market risk

bid price the price a securities dealer will pay for a given security

book value the net value of an asset or liability recorded on the financial statements that normally reflects historical cost

break-even analysis an analysis that tells us how many units must be sold in order for a project to break even on a cash flow or accounting profit basis

brokers market specialists who bring buyers and sellers together, usually for a commission

business angels (angel investors) wealthy individuals who invest their own money in new ventures

business incubator programme designed to accelerate the successful development of entrepreneurial companies by providing a range of business support resources and services

business plan a document that describes the details of how a business will be developed over time

business risk the risk in the cash flows to shareholders that is associated with uncertainty due to the characteristics of the business itself

C

call option an option to buy the underlying asset

call premium the price that the buyer of a call option pays the seller for that option

callable bond a bond which can be redeemed at the option of the issuer prior to its stated maturity

Capital Asset Pricing Model (CAPM) a model that describes the relation between risk and expected return

capital budgeting the process of choosing the real assets in which the firm will invest

capital markets financial markets where equity and debt instruments with maturities greater than one year are traded

capital rationing a situation where a firm does not have enough capital to invest in all attractive projects and must therefore ration capital

capital structure the mix of debt and equity that is used to finance a firm

cash conversion cycle the length of time from the point at which a company pays for raw materials until the point at which it receives cash from the sale of finished goods made from those materials

chief financial officer (CFO) the most senior financial manager in a company

coefficient of variation (CV) a measure of the risk associated with an investment for each 1% of expected return

collection time (float) the time between when a customer makes a payment and when the cash becomes available to the firm

commercial paper short-term debt in the form of promissory notes issued by large, financially secure firms with high credit ratings

committed line of credit a contractual agreement between a bank and a firm under which the bank has a legal obligation to lend funds to the firm up to a preset limit

common-size financial statement a financial statement in which each number is expressed as a percentage of a base number, such as total assets or total revenues

company a legal entity formed and authorised under law; in a legal sense, a company is a 'person' distinct from its owners

compensating balances bank balances that firms must maintain to at least partially compensate banks for loans or services rendered.

compound annual growth rate (CAGR) the average annual growth rate over a specified period of time

compound interest interest earned both on the original principal amount and on interest previously earned

compounding the process by which interest earned on an investment is reinvested, so in future periods interest is earned on the interest as well as the principal

consumer credit credit extended by a business to consumers

Consumer Credit Directive European Union directive requiring lenders to fully inform borrowers of important information related to non-secured loans, including the annual percentage rate charged

contingent project a project whose acceptance depends on the acceptance of another project

control premium an adjustment that is made to a business value estimate to reflect the value associated with control that is not already reflected in the analysis

convenience yield a non-monetary return derived from the physical ownership of an asset or commodity

conventional cash flow a cash flow pattern made up of an initial cash outflow that is followed by one or more cash inflows

cost of capital the required rate of return for a capital investment

cost of carry the net cost of 'carrying' or holding an asset for future delivery

cost of revenue the cost directly attributable to the production of the product; also known as the cost of goods sold

counterparty credit risk the risk that the other party to a transaction will be unable or unwilling to honour their commitments

country risk the political uncertainty associated with a particular country

coupon payments the interest payments made to bondholders

coupon rate the annual coupon payment of a bond divided by the bond's face value

covariance a measure of how the returns on two assets covary, or move together

cross currency swap the exchange of principal and interest in one currency for the principal and interest in another currency

crossover level of unit sales (CO) the level of unit sales at which cash flows or profitability for one project alternative switches from being lower than that of another alternative to being higher

crossover point the discount rate at which the NPV profiles of two projects cross and, thus, at which the NPVs of the projects are equal

current assets assets, such as accounts receivable and inventories, that are expected to be liquidated (collected or sold) within one year

D

dealers market specialists who 'make markets' for securities by buying and selling from their own inventories

declaration date the date on which a dividend is publicly announced

default risk the risk that a firm will not be able to pay its debt obligations as they come due

degree of accounting operating leverage (Accounting DOL) a measure of the sensitivity of accounting operating profits (EBIT) to changes in revenue

degree of pre-tax cash flow operating leverage (Cash Flow DOL) a measure of the sensitivity of cash flows from operations (EBITDA) to changes in revenue

depreciation allocation of the cost of an asset over its estimated life

derivative security a security that derives its value from the value of another asset; an option is an example of a derivative security

derivatives financial instruments or securities whose value varies with the value of an underlying asset

direct bankruptcy costs out-of-pocket costs that a firm incurs when it gets into financial distress

discount bonds bonds that sell at below par (face) value

discount rate the interest rate used in the discounting process to find the present value of future cash flows

discounted payback period the length of time required to recover a project's initial cost, accounting for the time value of money

discounting the process by which the present value of future cash flows is obtained

diversifiable, unsystematic or unique risk risk that can be eliminated through diversification

diversification a strategy of reducing risk by investing in two or more assets whose values do not always move in the same direction at the same time

dividend something of value distributed to a firm's shareholders on a pro-rata basis; that is, in proportion to the percentage of the firm's shares that they own

dividend discount model (DDM) approach an income approach to valuation in which all dividends that are expected to be distributed to shareholders in the future are discounted to estimate the value of the equity

dividend policy the overall policy concerning the distribution of value from a firm to its shareholders

dividend reinvestment programme (DRIP) a programme in which a company sells new shares, commission-free, to dividend recipients who elect to automatically reinvest their dividends in the company's shares

dividend yield a share's dividend payout divided by its current price

E

earnings per share (EPS) net income divided by the number of ordinary shares outstanding

economic order quantity (EOQ) order quantity that minimises the total costs incurred to order and hold inventory

effective annual interest rate (EAR) the annual interest rate that reflects compounding within a year

effective annual yield (EAY) the annual yield that takes compounding into account; another name for the *effective annual interest rate (EAR)*

efficient capital market market where prices rapidly reflect the knowledge and expectations of all investors

efficient market hypothesis a theory concerning the extent to which information is reflected in security prices and how information is incorporated into security prices

enterprise value the value of a company's equity plus the value of its debt; also the present value of the total cash flows the company's assets are expected to generate in the future

equivalent annual cost (EAC) the annual monetary amount of an annuity that has a life equal to that of a project and that also has a present value equal to the present value of some cash inflows or outflows from the project; the term comes from the fact that the EAC calculation is often used to calculate a constant annual cash flow associated with projects in order to make comparisons

Eurobond a bond that is marketed internationally

ex-dividend date the first day on which a share trades without the rights to a dividend

exercise (expiration) date the last date on which an option can be exercised

expected return an average of the possible returns from an investment, where each return is weighted by the probability that it will occur

external funding needed (EFN) the additional debt or equity a firm must raise from external sources to meet its total funding requirements

extra dividend a dividend that is generally paid at the same time as a regular cash dividend to distribute additional value

F

face value, or par value the amount on which interest is calculated and that is owed to the bondholder when a bond reaches maturity

factor an individual or a financial institution, such as a bank or a business finance company, which buys accounts receivable without recourse

fair market value the value of a business to a typical investor

fair value the amount for which an asset could be exchanged, or a liability settled, between knowledgeable, willing parties in an arm's length transaction

financial intermediation converting of securities with one set of characteristics into securities with another set of characteristics

financial leverage the use of debt in a firm's capital structure; the more debt, the higher the financial leverage

financial option the right to buy or sell a financial security, such as a share, on or before a specified date for a specified price

financial plan a plan outlining the investments a firm intends to make and how it will finance them

financial planning the process by which management decides what types of investments the firm needs to make and how to finance those investments

financial ratio a number from a financial statement that has been scaled by dividing by another financial number

financial restructuring a combination of financial transactions that changes the capital structure of the firm without affecting its real assets

financial risk the risk in the cash flows to shareholders that is due to the way in which the firm has financed its activities

financial risk management the practice of protecting and creating economic value in a firm by using financial instruments to manage exposure to risks

financial statement analysis the use of financial statements to evaluate a company's overall performance and assess its strengths and shortcomings

firm-commitment underwriting underwriting agreement in which the underwriter purchases securities for a specified price and resells them

firm value, or enterprise value the total value of the firm's assets; it equals the value of the equity financing plus the value of the debt financing used by the firm

firm's marginal tax rate (t) the tax rate that is applied to each additional monetary unit of earnings at a firm

fixed costs costs that do not vary directly with the number of units sold

fixed-income securities debt instruments that pay interest in amounts that are fixed for the life of the contract

flexible current asset investment strategy current asset investment strategy that involves keeping high balances of current assets on hand

foreign exchange markets international markets where currencies are bought and sold in wholesale amounts

foreign exchange rate risk, or exchange rate risk the uncertainty associated with future exchange rate movements

formal line of credit a contractual agreement between a bank and a firm under which the bank has a legal obligation to lend funds to the firm up to a preset limit

forward contract agreement between two parties to buy or sell an asset at a specified point of time in the future at a price agreed today

forward foreign exchange rate a rate agreed on today for a currency exchange to take place at a specified date in the future

forward rate a rate agreed on today for an exchange to take place at a specified date in the future

free cash flow from the firm (FCFF) approach an income approach to valuation in which all free cash flows the assets are expected to generate in the future are discounted to estimate the enterprise value

free cash flow to equity (FCFE) approach an income approach to valuation in which all cash flows that are expected to be available for distribution to shareholders in the future are discounted to estimate the value of the equity

future value (FV) the value of an investment after it earns interest for one or more periods

future value of an annuity (FVA) the value of an annuity at some point in the future

futures contract a standardised, transferable, exchange-traded contract that requires the delivery of a specified asset at a predetermined price on a specified future date

G

generally accepted accounting principles (GAAP) a set of rules that defines how companies are to prepare financial statements

globalisation the removal of barriers to free trade and the integration of national economies

going-concern value the difference between adjusted book value and the value of a business as a going concern (the present value of the expected cash flows)

growing annuity an annuity in which the cash flows increase at a constant rate

growing perpetuity a cash flow stream that grows at a constant rate forever

H

hedge a financial transaction intended to reduce risk

hedging any technique designed to reduce or eliminate risk; for example, taking two positions that will offset each other if prices change

I

income statement a financial statement that reports a firm's profits or losses over a period of time, also called the *profit and loss statement* or *account*

incremental additions to working capital (Add WC) the investments in working capital items, such as accounts receivable, inventory and accounts payable, that must be made if the project is pursued

incremental after-tax free cash flows (FCF) the difference between the total after-tax free cash flows at a firm with a project and the total after-tax free cash flows at the same firm without that project; a measure of a project's total impact on the free cash flows at a firm

incremental capital expenditures (Cap Exp) the investments in property, plant and equipment and other long-term assets that must be made if a project is pursued

incremental cash flow from operations (CF Opns) the cash flow that a project generates after all operating expenses and taxes have been paid but before any cash outflows for investments

incremental depreciation and amortisation (D&A) the depreciation and amortisation charges that are associated with a project

incremental net operating profits after tax (NOPAT) a measure of the impact of a project on the firm's cash net income, excluding any interest expenses associated with financing the project

independent projects projects whose cash flows are unrelated

indirect bankruptcy costs costs associated with changes in the behaviour of people who deal with a firm when the firm gets into financial distress

informal line of credit a verbal agreement between a bank and a firm under which the firm can borrow an amount of money up to an agreed-on limit.

information asymmetry the situation in which one party in a business transaction has information that is unavailable to the other parties in the transaction

initial public offering (IPO) the first offering of a company's shares to the public. Also called a *floatation* or *listing* (on the stock exchange)

insolvency the inability to pay debts when they are due

insurance contract that protects against the financial losses (in whole or in part) of specified unexpected events

intangible assets non-physical assets such as patents, mailing lists or brand names

interest on interest interest earned on interest that is earned in previous periods

interest rate risk uncertainty about future bond values that is caused by the unpredictability of interest rates

interest rate swap exchange agreement where one party exchanges a stream of interest payments for another party's stream of cash flows

internal growth rate (IGR) the maximum growth rate that a firm can achieve without external financing

internal rate of return (IRR) the discount rate at which the present value of a project's expected cash inflows equals the present value of the project's outflows

International Standard Industrial Classification (ISIC) System a numerical system developed under the auspices of the United Nations to classify industrial activity by type

inventory carrying costs expenses associated with maintaining inventory, including interest forgone on money invested in inventory, storage costs, taxes and insurance

investment banks firms that underwrite new security issues and provide broker/dealer services

investment value the value of a business to a specific investor

investment-grade bonds bonds with low risk of default that are rated Baa (BBB) or above

K

key person discount an adjustment to a business value estimate that is made to reflect the potential loss of value associated with the unexpected departure of a key person

L

lease finance arrangement where the lender retains ownership of the asset but the firm makes periodic payments for the use of the asset for the term of the lease

limited liability the legal liability of a limited partner or shareholder in a business, which extends only to the capital contributed or the amount invested

limited liability partnerships (LLPs) hybrid business organisations that combine some of the advantages of companies and partnerships; in general, income to the partners is taxed only as personal income, but the partners have limited liability

liquidating dividend the final dividend that is paid to shareholders when a firm is liquidated

liquidity the ability to convert an asset into cash quickly without loss of value

long-term funding strategy financing strategy that relies on long-term debt and equity to finance both fixed assets and working capital

lumpy assets fixed assets added as large discrete units; these assets may not be used to full capacity for some time, leaving the company with excess capacity

M

management buy-out purchase of a company by the existing management team

margin collateral that the holder of a futures contract has to deposit to cover the credit risk

marginal tax rate the tax rate paid on the last unit of income earned

market balance sheet a balance sheet that is based on market values of expected cash flows

market informational efficiency the degree to which current market prices reflect relevant information and, therefore, the true value of the security

market maker dealer in securities at a stock exchange who undertakes to buy or sell at all times accepting the risks involved

market operational efficiency the degree to which the transaction costs of bringing buyers and sellers together are minimised

market portfolio the portfolio of all assets

market price the price at which an item can be sold

market risk a term commonly used to refer to non-diversifiable, or systematic, risk

market risks exposure to a change in the value of some market factor, such as interest rates, foreign exchange rates, equity or commodity prices

market value the price at which an item can be sold

marketability the ease with which a security can be sold and converted into cash

maturity matching strategy financing strategy that matches the maturities of liabilities and assets

modified internal rate of return (MIRR) an internal rate of return (IRR) measure which assumes that cash inflows are reinvested at the opportunity cost of capital until the end of the project

money centre banks large banks that transact in both the national and international money markets, also called *clearing banks*

money markets markets where short-term financial instruments are traded

moral hazard any contract or arrangement that provides incentives for one party to take (or not take) unobservable steps which are prejudicial to another party

multinational corporation a business firm that operates in more than one country

multiples analysis a valuation approach that uses share price or other value multiples for public companies to estimate the value of another company's shares or its entire business

multistage-growth dividend model a model that allows for varying dividend growth rates in the near term, followed by a constant long-term growth rate; another term used to describe the supernormal-growth model discussed in Chapter 9

mutually exclusive projects projects for which acceptance of one precludes acceptance of the other

N

net cash flow a firm's actual cash receipts less cash payments in a given period

net present value (NPV) method a method of evaluating a capital investment project which measures the difference between its cost and the present value of its expected cash flows

net working capital the difference between current assets and current liabilities

nominal rate of interest the rate of interest unadjusted for inflation

nominal value money that is not adjusted for inflation. Nominal value amounts from different time periods cannot be compared directly with each other

non-diversifiable or systematic risk risk that cannot be eliminated through diversification

non-investment-grade bonds bonds rated below Baa (or BBB) by rating agencies; often called *speculative-grade bonds, high-yield bonds* or *junk bonds*

non-operating assets (NOA) cash or other assets that are not required to support the operations of a business

normal distribution a symmetric frequency distribution that is completely described by its mean and standard deviation; also known as a bell curve due to its shape

NPV profile a graph showing NPV as a function of the discount rate

O

offer (ask) price the price at which a securities dealer seeks to sell a given security

open-market repurchase the repurchase of shares by a company in the open market

open offer offer to existing shareholders where they can buy new shares in proportion to their existing holding but cannot trade the entitlement. Also known as *non-renounceable rights*

operating cycle the average time between receipt of raw materials and receipt of cash for the sale of finished goods made from those materials

operating leverage a measure of the relative amounts of fixed and variable costs in a project's cost structure; operating leverage is higher with more fixed costs

operational risks any risk arising from execution of a company's business functions

opportunity cost the return from the best alternative investment with similar risk that an investor gives up when he or she makes a certain investment

opportunity cost of capital the return an investor gives up when his or her money is invested in one asset rather than the best alternative asset

optimal capital structure the capital structure that minimises the cost of financing a firm's activities

option payoff function the function that shows how the value of an option varies with the value of the underlying asset

ordinary annuity an annuity in which payments are made at the ends of the periods

ordinary shares an equity share that represents the basic ownership claim in a company; the most common type of equity security

P

partnership two or more owners joined together legally to manage a business and share in its profits

par-value bonds bonds that sell at par value, or face value; whenever a bond's coupon rate is equal to the market rate of interest on similar bonds, the bond will sell at par

payable date the date on which a dividend is paid by a company

payback period the length of time required to recover a project's initial cost

pecking order theory the theory that in financing projects, managers first use retained earnings, which they view as the least expensive form of capital, then debt and finally externally raised equity, which they view as the most expensive

percentage of sales model a type of simple financial planning model that assumes that most income statement and balance sheet accounts vary proportionally with sales

permanent working capital the minimum level of working capital that a firm will always have on its books

perpetuity a series of level cash flows that continue forever

per-unit contribution the amount that is left over from the sale of a single unit after all the variable costs associated with that unit have been paid; this is the amount that is available to help cover fixed costs for the project

placing issue of new shares which are sold directly to new shareholders

portfolio the collection of assets an investor owns

post-audit review an audit to compare actual project results with the results projected in the capital budgeting proposal

preference shares an equity share in a company that entitles the owner to preferred treatment over owners of ordinary shares with respect to dividend payments and claims against the firm's assets in the event of bankruptcy or liquidation, but that typically have no voting rights

preliminary prospectus the initial admission document filed with the competent authority by a company preparing to issue securities in the public market; it contains detailed information about the issuer and the proposed issue

premium bonds bonds that sell at above par (face) value

present value (PV) the current value of future cash flows discounted at the appropriate discount rate

present value of an annuity (PVA) the present value of the cash flows from an annuity, discounted at the appropriate discount rate

pre-tax operating cash flow earnings before interest, taxes, depreciation and amortisation, or EBITDA

pre-tax operating cash flow (EBITDA) break-even point the number of units that must be sold for pre-tax operating cash flow to equal zero

price-to-earnings (P/E) ratio price per share divided by earnings per share

price risks changes in the prices of a firm's inputs and outputs over time due to changes in demand and supply

primary market a financial market in which new security issues are sold for the first time

principal the amount of money on which interest is paid

private information information that is not available to all investors

private placement the sale of an unregistered security directly to an investor, such as an insurance company

privately held companies companies whose shares are not traded in public markets; also called *closely held companies*

production risk all the elements of the production process that can go wrong: for instance, fires and equipment failures

pro forma financial statements projected financial statements that reflect a set of assumptions concerning investment, financing and operating decisions

productive assets the tangible and intangible assets a firm uses to generate cash flows

profitability index (PI) a measure of the value a project generates for each unit of currency invested in that project

progressive tax system a tax system in which the marginal tax rate at low levels of income is lower than the marginal tax rate at high levels of income

public information information that is available to all investors

public markets financial markets where securities are sold to the general public

pure-play comparable a comparable company that is in exactly the same business as the project or business being analysed

put–call parity the relation between the value of a call option on an asset and the value of a put option on the same asset that has the same strike price

put option an option to sell the underlying asset

put premium the price that the buyer of a put option pays the seller of that option

puttable bond a bond which can be redeemed at the option of the investor (holder) prior to its stated maturity

Q

quoted interest rate a simple annual interest rate, such as the APR

R

real investment policy the policy relating to the criteria the firm uses in deciding which real assets (projects) to invest in

real option an option for which the underlying asset is a real asset

real rate of interest the interest rate that would exist in the absence of inflation

real value inflation-adjusted money; the actual purchasing power of money stated in 'real' terms is the same regardless of when the money is received

realised yield for a bond, the interest rate at which the present value of the actual cash flows generated by a bond equals the bond's price

record date the date by which an investor must be a shareholder of record in order to receive a dividend

regular cash dividend a cash dividend that is paid on a regular basis, typically quarterly

repatriation of earnings restrictions restrictions placed by a foreign government on the amount of cash that can be repatriated, or returned, to a parent company by a subsidiary doing business in the foreign country

replacement cost the cost of duplicating the assets of a business in their present form on the valuation date

residual cash flows the cash remaining after a firm has paid operating expenses and what it owes creditors and in taxes; can be paid to the owners as a cash dividend or reinvested in the business

restrictive current asset investment strategy current asset investment strategy that involves keeping the level of current assets at a minimum

rights issue offer to existing shareholders where they can buy new shares in the company in proportion to their existing holding. Also called a *privileged subscription*

Rule of 72 a rule proposing that the time required to double money invested (TDM) approximately equals $72/i$, where i is expressed as a percentage

S

scenario analysis an analytical method concerned with how the results from a financial analysis will change under alternative scenarios

seasoned public offering the sale of securities to the public by a firm that already has publicly traded securities outstanding

secondary market a financial market in which the owners of outstanding securities can resell them to other investors

Security Market Line (SML) a plot of the relation between expected return and systematic risk

semi-strong form (of the efficient market hypothesis) the theory that security prices reflect all public information but not all private information

sensitivity analysis examination of the sensitivity of the results from a financial analysis to changes in individual assumptions

share dividend a distribution of new shares to existing shareholders in proportion to the percentage of shares that they own (pro rata); the value of the assets in a company does not change with a share dividend

share repurchase the purchase of shares by a company from its shareholders; an alternative way for the company to distribute value to the shareholders

share split a pro-rata distribution of new shares to existing shareholders that is not associated with any change in the assets held by the firm; share splits involve larger increases in the number of shares than share dividends

shortage costs costs incurred because of lost production and sales or illiquidity

short-term funding strategy financing strategy that relies on short-term debt to finance all seasonal working capital and a portion of permanent working capital and fixed assets

simple interest interest earned on the original principal amount only

simulation analysis an analytical method that uses a computer to quickly examine a large number of scenarios and obtain probability estimates for various values in a financial analysis

sole proprietorship or sole trader a business owned by a single individual

special dividend a one-time payment to shareholders that is normally used to distribute a large amount of value

spot rate the exchange rate in the market at any given point in time

stakeholder anyone other than an owner (shareholder) with a claim on the cash flows of a firm, including employees, suppliers, creditors and the government

stand-alone principle the principle that allows us to treat each project as a stand-alone firm when we perform an NPV analysis

standard deviation (σ) the square root of the variance

statement of cash flows a financial statement that shows a firm's cash receipts and cash payments for a period of time

strategic planning the process by which management establishes the firm's long-term goals, the strategies that will be used to achieve the goals, and the capabilities that are needed to sustain the firm's competitive position

strike (exercise) price the price at which the owner of an option has the right to buy or sell the underlying asset

strong form (of the efficient market hypothesis) the theory that security prices reflect all available information

sustainable growth rate (SGR) the rate of growth that a firm can sustain without selling additional equity while maintaining the same capital structure

T

tangible assets physical assets such as property, plant and equipment

targeted shares repurchase a share repurchase that targets a specific shareholder

tax depreciation the amount of depreciation on an asset allowed against profit in a particular reporting period

tender offer an open offer by a company to purchase shares

term loan a business loan with a maturity greater than one year

term structure of interest rates the relation between yield and term to maturity

terminal value the value of the expected free cash flows beyond the period over which they are explicitly forecast

time value of money the difference in value between money in hand today and money promised in the future; money today is worth more than money in the future

total holding period return the total return on an asset over a specific period of time or holding period

trade credit credit extended by one business to another

trade-off theory the theory that managers trade off the benefits against the costs of using debt to identify the optimal capital structure for a firm

transactions analysis a valuation approach that uses transactions data from the sale of businesses to estimate the value of another company's shares or its entire business

transnational corporation a multinational firm that has widely dispersed ownership and that is managed from a global perspective

treasury shares shares that the firm has purchased back from investors

trend analysis analysis of trends in financial data

true (intrinsic) value for a security, the value of the cash flows an investor who owns that security can expect to receive in the future

U

uncommitted line of credit a non-binding agreement between a bank and a firm under which the firm can borrow an amount of money up to an agreed-on limit

underinvestment problem the incentive that shareholders in a financially leveraged firm have to turn down positive NPV projects when the firm is in financial distress

underlying asset the asset from which the value of an option or other derivative is derived

underpricing offering new securities for sale at a price below their true value

underwriting syndicate a group of underwriters that joins forces to reduce underwriting risk

V

valuation date the date on which a value estimate applies

vanilla bonds a debt security whose terms and conditions are standardised and well known to market participants

variable costs costs that vary directly with the number of units sold

variance (σ^2) a measure of the uncertainty surrounding an outcome

venture capitalists individuals or firms that invest by purchasing equity in new businesses and often provide the entrepreneurs with business advice

W

weak form (of the efficient market hypothesis) the theory that security prices reflect all information in past prices but do not reflect all private or all public information

wealth the economic value of the assets someone possesses

weighted average cost of capital (WACC) the weighted average of the costs of the different types of capital (debt and equity) that have been used to finance a firm; the cost of each type of capital is weighted by the proportion of the total capital that it represents

Y

yield curve a graph representing the term structure of interest rates, with the term to maturity on the horizontal axis and the yield on the vertical axis

yield to maturity for a bond, the discount rate that makes the present value of the coupon and principal payments equal to the price of the bond

SUBJECT INDEX

COMPANY INDEX